STANDARD DEDUCTION

Filing Status	1997 Amount
Married individuals filing joint returns and surviving spouses	$6,900
Heads of households	6,050
Unmarried individuals (other than surviving spouses and heads of households)	4,150
Married individuals filing separate return	3,450
Additional standard deductions for the aged and the blind	
Individual who is married and surviving spouses	800*
Individual who is unmarried and not a surviving spouse	1,000*
Taxpayer claimed as dependent on another taxpayer's return	650

*These amounts are $1,600 and $2,000, respectively, for a taxpayer who is both aged and blind.

Personal Exemption: 1997 $2,650 *Reduction in personal and dependency exemptions:* The personal and dependency exemption deductions are reduced or eliminated for certain high-income taxpayers. When a taxpayer's AGI exceeds the "phaseout begins after" amount described below, the deduction is reduced by 2% for each $2,500 (or fraction thereof) by which AGI exceeds such amount. For married persons filing separately, the exemption deduction is reduced by 2% for each $1,250 (or fraction thereof) by which AGI exceeds the "phaseout begins after" amount. The personal exemption deduction amount cannot be reduced below zero. The phaseout ranges are:

Filing Status	Phaseout Begins After	Phaseout Completed After
Married individuals filing joint return and surviving spouses	$181,800	$304,300
Heads of households	151,500	274,000
Unmarried taxpayers (other than surviving spouses and heads of households)	121,200	243,700
Married individuals filing separate returns	90,900	152,150

Itemized Deductions

The itemized deductions that are otherwise deductible for the tax year are reduced by the lesser of (1) 3% of the excess of AGI over a threshold amount, or (2) 80% of the amount of itemized deductions otherwise deductible for the tax year excluding medical expenses, investment interest expense, casualty losses, and wagering losses to the extent of wagering gains. The threshold amount for the 1997 tax year is $121,200 (except for married individuals filing separate returns for which it is $60,600).

PRENTICE HALL'S
FEDERAL TAXATION
1998

Individuals

PRENTICE HALL'S FEDERAL TAXATION

1998

Individuals

EDITORS

THOMAS R. POPE
University of Kentucky

JOHN L. KRAMER
University of Florida

CO-AUTHORS

KENNETH E. ANDERSON
University of Tennessee

D. DALE BANDY
University of Central Florida

N. ALLEN FORD
University of Kansas

ROBERT L. GARDNER
Brigham Young University

ANNOTATIONS

EDMUND D. FENTON
Belmont University

 PRENTICE HALL, Upper Saddle River, NJ 07458

Acquisitions Editor: Diane deCastro
Executive Editor: P.J. Boardman
Editorial Assistant: Jane Avery
Production Editor: Susan Rifkin
Production Coordinator: Cindy Spreder
Managing Editor: Katherine Evancie
Senior Manufacturing Supervisor: Paul Smolenski
Manufacturing Manager: Vincent Scelta
Design Director: Patricia Wosczyk
Interior Design: BB&K Design Inc.
Cover Design: Lorraine Castellano
Composition: Black Dot Graphics
Cover Photo: Marc Muench/Tony Stone Images
Photo Credits: Anita Duncan/Prentice Hall College Archives; courtesy of the Architect of the Capitol

© 1997, 1996, 1995, 1994, 1993 by Prentice-Hall, Inc.
A Simon & Schuster Company
Upper Saddle River, New Jersey 07458

ISBN 0-13-653619-0
ISBN 0-13-659327-5 (IE)
ISBN 0-13-659260-0 (Looseleaf)

Prentice-Hall International (UK) Limited, *London*
Prentice-Hall of Australia Pty. Limited, *Sydney*
Prentice-Hall Canada Inc., *Toronto*
Prentice-Hall Hispanoamericana, S.A., *Mexico*
Prentice-Hall of India Private Limited, *New Delhi*
Prentice-Hall of Japan, Inc., *Tokyo*
Prentice-Hall of Southeast Asia Pte. Ltd., *Singapore*
Editora Prentice-Hall do Brasil, Ltda., *Rio de Janeiro*

Printed in the United States of America
10 9 8 7 6 5 4 3 2 1

OVERVIEW

CONTENTS

CHAPTER 3

▶ GROSS INCOME: INCLUSIONS 3-1

CHAPTER 4

▶ GROSS INCOME: EXCLUSIONS 4-1

CHAPTER 10
▶ DEPRECIATION, COST RECOVERY, DEPLETION, AMORTIZATION, AND INVENTORY COSTS 10-1

ABOUT THE EDITORS

JOHN L. KRAMER   THOMAS R. POPE

John L. Kramer is the Arthur Andersen Professor of Accounting at the Fisher School of Accounting at the University of Florida. He is a recipient of a Teaching Improvement Program award given by the University of Florida in 1994. He holds a Ph.D. in Business Administration, an M.B.A. from the University of Michigan (Ann Arbor), and a B.B.A. from the University of Michigan (Dearborn). He is a past-president of the American Taxation Association and the Florida Association of Accounting Educators, as well as a past editor of *The Journal of the American Taxation Association*.

Kramer has taught for the American Institute of CPAs, American Tax Institute of Europe, and a number of national and regional accounting firms. He is a frequent speaker at academic and professional conferences, as well as having served as an expert witness in a number of court cases. He has published over fifty articles in *The Accounting Review, The Journal of the American Taxation Association, The Tax Adviser, The Journal of Taxation* and other academic and professional journals.

Thomas R. Pope is an Associate Professor of Accounting at the University of Kentucky. He received a B.S. from the University of Louisville and an M.S. and doctorate in business administration from the University of Kentucky where he now serves as Director of Graduate Studies for the Masters of Accountancy program. He teaches partnership and S corporation taxation, tax research and policy, and introductory taxation and has won outstanding teaching awards at the University, College, and School of Accountancy levels. He has published articles in *The Accounting Review, The Tax Adviser, Taxes*, and a number of other journals.

Pope's extensive professional experience includes eight years with Big Six accounting firms. Five of those years were with Ernst & Young, where he earned a position with their National Tax Department in Washington, D.C. He subsequently attained the position of Senior Manager in charge of the Tax Department in Lexington, Kentucky. He has also been a leader and speaker at professional tax conferences all over the United States and is active as a tax consultant.

ABOUT THE AUTHORS

KENNETH E. ANDERSON   D. DALE BANDY   N. ALLEN FORD   ROBERT L. GARDNER

Kenneth E. Anderson is Professor of Accounting at the University of Tennessee. He earned a B.B.A. from the University of Wisconsin-Milwaukee and subsequently attained the level of tax manager with Arthur Young & Company (now part of Ernst & Young). He then earned a Ph.D. from Indiana University. He teaches introductory taxation, corporate taxation, partnership taxation, and tax policy and has twice won the Beta Alpha Psi Outstanding Educator Award (1994 and 1995).

Anderson has published articles in *The Accounting Review*, *The Journal of the American Taxation Association*, *The Journal of Accountancy*, and a number of other journals. In addition, he is an associate editor of *The Journal of the American Taxation Association* and is on the editorial board of *Advances in Taxation*.

D. Dale Bandy is the C.G. Avery Professor of Accounting in the School of Accounting at the University of Central Florida. He received a B.S. from the University of Tulsa, an M.B.A. from the University of Arkansas, and a Ph.D. from the University of Texas at Austin. He helped to establish the Master of Science in Taxation programs at the University of Central Florida and California State University, Fullerton, where he previously taught. In 1985, he was selected by the California Society of Certified Public Accountants as the Accounting Educator of the year.

Bandy has published 8 books and more than 30 articles in accounting and taxation. His articles have appeared in *Journal of Taxation, Journal of Accountancy, Advances in Taxation, Tax Adviser, CPA Journal, Management Accounting* and a number of other journals.

N. Allen Ford is the Larry D. Homer/KPMG Peat Marwick Distinguished Teaching Professor of Professional Accounting at the University of Kansas. He received an undergraduate degree from Centenary College in Shreveport, Louisiana, and both the M.B.A. and Ph.D. in Business from the University of Arkansas. He has published over 30 articles related to taxation, financial accounting, and accounting education in journals such as *The Accounting Review, The Journal of the American Taxation Association*, and *The Journal of Taxation*. He served as president of the American Taxation Association in 1979-80.

Ford has received numerous teaching awards, at the college and university levels. In 1993, he received the Byron T. Shutz Award for Distinguished Teaching in Economics and Business. In 1996 he received the Ray M. Sommerfeld Outstanding Tax Educator Award, which is jointly sponsored by the American Taxation Association and Ernst & Young.

Robert L. Gardner is the Robert J. Smith Professor of Accounting and the Associate Director of the School of Accountancy and Information Systems at Brigham Young University. He received a B.S. and M.B.A. from the University of Utah and a Ph.D. from the University of Texas at Austin. He has authored or coauthored two books and over 25 articles, and has received several teaching awards. Gardner has served on the Board of Trustees for the American Taxation Association and has consulted with several national CPA firms in their continuing education programs.

PREFACE

OBJECTIVES AND USE

This text is designed principally for use in a first course in federal taxation for undergraduate accounting and business students. The text materials have been updated to reflect recent legislative (through January 1, 1997), judicial, and administrative changes in the tax law.

A companion volume, *Prentice Hall's Federal Taxation, 1998: Corporations, Partnerships, Estates, and Trusts*, is published for use in the second course in federal taxation. A combined two-semester volume, *Prentice Hall's Federal Taxation, 1998: Comprehensive*, joins 14 chapters of the *Individuals* volume with 13 chapters of the *Corporations, Partnerships, Estates, and Trusts* volume. Either the *Individuals* text or the *Comprehensive* volume may be used with a one-term survey course for undergraduate or graduate students.

The primary objective has been to provide a readable format with a high level of technical content. We have accomplished this through a process of continuous review, improvement, and clarification of the text, examples, and problem material. If you find what you believe is an error, please provide the item to one of the editors along with your comments. We have been able to maintain this level of content by focusing on primary topics and by relegating minor exceptions to footnotes.

NEW TO THE 1998 EDITION

▶ Expanded coverage of ethics. Seven new and two revised boxes (labeled "What Would You Do in This Situation?") and a reprinting of the AICPA's Statements on Responsibilities in Tax Practice in an appendix expand our coverage of ethics. Based on timely topics, the new boxes include many controversies that are as yet unresolved or currently being considered by the courts. They represent choices that may put the practitioner at odds with the client, and are grounded on ethical parameters discussed in various standards, codes of conduct, or Treasury Department circulars. Students are asked, after analyzing the details of a situation, to indicate what they would do if they found themselves in the same situation as well as the ethical implications of their actions. The ethics boxes and the Statements on Responsibilities enhance the Ethical Point margin notes and the Case Studies already found in the text.

▶ Stop & Think feature. These "speedbumps" ask students to stop and think about a business application of tax, or an extension of the basic material, at various points in the chapter. These are not "boxes," which typically fall outside the running text and can be bypassed. They are part of the text, complete with solutions to show students "how to do it," and identified by the icon you see here in the margin.

▶ Issue identification questions. Part of the process of learning involves sorting out important information from unimportant details. In an area as detail-oriented as taxation, developing the ability to identify key issues is of paramount importance. We include questions at the end of each chapter that call on students to focus on the important questions that a practitioner faces on a daily basis.

▶ Improvements in the Test Bank. Aside from the Solutions Manual, no other supplement is as important to educators as the Test Bank. This year the Test Bank author has placed special emphasis on refining and polishing the test questions.

▶ TaxCut® software. This tax return preparation software was just rated #1 by Money Magazine. We believe that every tax student should be given the opportunity to learn how to prepare and file returns electronically—and at low cost. Block Financial Corporation, which sells TaxCut to Prentice Hall customers for $14.95, has the software in Windows and CD-ROM (for Windows) versions. Students may order their copy of the software by using the order form found in their textbook.

▶ OneDisc CD-ROM. This CD provides all the basic information tools that tax professionals use: Code, regulations, revenue rulings, revenue procedures, IRS technical advice memoranda, letter rulings, court decisions, directories, U.S. tax treaties, and more! Tax Analysts sells the OneDisc to Prentice Hall customers for just $19.99 and has the software available in DOS, Windows, and Macintosh. Students may order their copy of the CD-ROM by using the order form in their textbook.

FEATURES RETAINED FROM PREVIOUS EDITIONS

▶ A careful choice of topics. Since the introduction of this series, users have found favor with the choice of topics and the extent of detail presented throughout the text. Areas where users have been particularly pleased with our balance between exhaustive detail and too little detail include: the history of taxation, tax research, passive activity losses, and alternative minimum tax.

▶ Unique chapter organization. The *Individuals* volume differs from other texts on the market with its early coverage of property transactions, two chapters on the taxation of business entities, and our capstone chapter on tax considerations for investors. A new chapter on tax research has also been added to this edition.

▶ Clear examples. Users regularly praise the clarity and number of examples in this text.

▶ Margin notes. Tax students appreciate learning about more than just tax rules, so we have developed a series of comments in the margins to enrich their learning experience.

Key Points emphasize those areas where students require repetition and reinforcement.

Typical Misconceptions identify those concepts that students are likely to misunderstand, and help them to correct their thinking before they take a wrong approach.

Real World Examples provide facts and anecdotes about actual companies and real-life strategies.

Additional Comments elaborate on the material presented in the text.

Self-Study Questions provide an in-text study guide. Each question is accompanied by a full solution.

Historical Notes offer a more comprehensive understanding of concepts by examining them in their historical context.

Ethical Points focus on ethical questions that confront the tax practitioner, and are designated with an ethics icon.

▶ Topic Reviews. Each chapter contains several topic reviews, presented when a topic has been completed. Topic reviews help students organize their understanding of the material and aid in preparing for exams. Many of these reviews are in tabular form for easy reference.

▶ Tax Planning Considerations. For the forward-looking part of the tax profession, students need to learn how to offer tax-saving advice for their clients. Our Tax Planning Considerations offer this insight once the basics of the rules have been established.

▶ Compliance and Procedural Considerations. Forms, procedures, and timing are addressed in the Compliance and Procedural Consideration sections at the end of each chapter.

▶ Footnotes. An important component of "learning to learn" is knowing where to turn for authoritative information. We have collected important references to the tax authorities in the footnotes for students to use as sources.

▶ A full complement of assignment material. The typical format for each chapter includes: Discussion Questions, Issue Identification Questions, Problems, Comprehensive Problems, Tax Form/Return Preparation Problems, Case Study Problems, and Tax Research Problems. Tax return problems that can be solved using the TaxCut software are also marked with an icon.

▶ Oral and written communications. More emphasis is being placed on oral and written communication skills by the various accounting professional organizations (e.g., the American Institute of CPAs and the Accounting Education Change Commission). The case study problems at the end of each chapter are designed to meet this need, by requiring students to consider a number of alternatives and present a written or oral solution to the problem. None of these case studies require the student to research the tax law.

SUPPLEMENTAL MATERIALS

The text includes a full complement of supplementary and ancillary materials. Adopters are encouraged to use these materials to enhance their teaching effectiveness and the students' learning experience. The following aids are available for instructor and student use:

INSTRUCTION AIDS

▶ Prentice Hall Course Manager, free upon adoption—This three-ring binder of the textbook allows the professor complete flexibility in course customization and is available on demand from Prentice Hall.

▶ Instructor's Guide—This specially crafted Instructor's Guide includes: a sample syllabus for semester- and quarter-length courses, instructor outlines, and solutions to the tax return/tax form problems, case study problems, and tax research problems. Instructor outlines are available in WordPerfect computer files to enable faculty members to make their own modifications to the master outlines prior to using them in class without having to retype the entire outline. Also, there is a cross reference table which cross references problems in the 1997 and the 1998 Editions as well as indicates the nature of the change (if any) to the problems from the 1997 Edition. New to this edition of the Instructor's Guide is a set of chapter-by-chapter transistion notes to help you adapt your lecture notes from West's Federal Taxation to Prentice Hall's Federal Taxation.

▶ Test Bank—Carefully edited, this bank of test questions now includes fully worked-out solutions to many of the more complex problems.

▶ Solutions Manual—Prepared by the authors and thoroughly reviewed by the editors and a pool of graduate tax students, this volume includes solutions to the discussion questions, problems, and comprehensive problems. Solutions to all problems are available in WordPerfect computer files to facilitate the preparation of transparencies. The solutions to the tax form/return preparation problems, case studies, and the tax research problems are included in the *Instructor's Guide*.

▶ Solutions to Prentice Hall's Tax Practice Problems for Individuals, Corporations and Partnerships, 1998 Edition—Contains completed forms to solve the Tax Practice Problems for both volumes.

▶ PowerPoint Transparency—Approximately 300 full color electronic transparencies have been created for each individual chapter to enrich the teaching experience. Instructors can make additions or modifications to the files prior to using them in class.

▶ Prentice Hall Custom Test, DOS and Windows versions—Unmatched by other computerized testing software, Prentice Hall Custom Test is a state-of-the-art classroom management system designed to take the tedium out of creating exams.

▶ Supplemental Tax Law Update—Whenever major tax legislation is passed, we immediately provide an updating supplement. In addition, a mid-year supplement is provided when the inflation-adjusted numbers are available for the new tax year.

▶ Registered Adopter Service—Every year tax instructors have to keep up-to-date on the changes in the tax law. Now Prentice Hall has a service to help. It's our Registered Adopter Service. By returning the registration card provided in the Instructor's Edition of *Prentice Hall's Federal Taxation: Individuals* you can add your name to the list of adopters who receive regular tax law updates, product information on books and supplements, and information on Prentice Hall's Tax seminars for educators. Additionally, we will plant a tree in your schools name through the National Arbor Day Foundation to help reforest an area devastated by a natural disaster once we receive your Registered Adopter card.

STUDENT AIDS

Our foremost goal has been to provide students with a perspective that stresses readability, accuracy, and familiarity with technical aids to tax practice. The following student aids are currently available:

▶ Loose-Leaf Edition—The text is now available for students in a 3-hole punched, shrinkwrapped format, which allows them to carry only the sections of the text they need as well as add in hand-outs from class. Binder is NOT included.

▶ Study Guide—This study guide is designed to give students a better understanding of the laws and concepts presented in the textbook through use of extensive cross-referencing to tables and figures in the textbook.

▶ Prentice Hall's Tax Practice Problems: Individuals, 1997 Edition—This practice set gives the student hands-on experience preparing tax returns either manually or with a computer. The complete package includes three comprehensive tax return problems, IRS forms, and IRS instructions.

ACKNOWLEDGMENTS

Our policy is to provide annual editions and to prepare timely updated supplements when major tax revisions occur. We are most appreciative of the suggestions made by outside reviewers for the 1998 Edition because these extensive review procedures have been valuable to the authors and editors during the revision process.

We wish to acknowledge the following reviewers, whose contributions over the past several years have helped shape the 1998 Edition:

Don Aabel	University of Wisconsin at River Falls
Becky Andrews	Roane State Community College
Alan Attaway	University of Louisville
Robert Barker	California State University—Northridge
Susan Bates	Boise State University
Martin Batross	Franklin University
Cynthia E. Bolt	The Citadel
Faye Bradwick	Indiana University of Pennsylvania
George Britton	Florida Southern College
Sharen Brougham	Metropolitan State College
M. Robert Carver Jr.	Southern Illinois University at Edwardsville
Arthur Cassill	University of North Carolina at Greensboro
Caroline Craig	Illinois State University
Anthony P. Curatola	Drexel University
David Davidson	California State University—Long Beach
M. Peter Dillaway	New Mexico State University
Paul Erickson	Baylor University
Carl Farinacci	Clarion University
Ramon Fernandez	University of St. Thomas (Texas)
Philip R. Fink	University of Toledo
George Frankel	San Francisco State University
Daniel Fulks	University of Kentucky
Edward J. Gac	University of Colorado at Boulder
John Gardner	University of Wisconsin at LaCrosse
Harold Goedde	
Raymond L. Gonzalez	Los Angeles Trade Technical College
W. Michael Gough	DeAnza College
E. Vance Grange	Utah State University
Melvin Greenball	Ohio State University
Merrily Hoffman	San Jacinto College
Michael Holland	Valdosta State University
Jay S. Horton	Greenville Technical College
Evelyn C. Hume	University of South Alabama
Frederick Jacobs	University of Minnesota
Patricia Janes	San Jose State University
Linda Johnson	Northern Illinois University
William Jordan	Florida State University
Kermit Keeling	Loyola College-Maryland
Philip D. Landers	Pennsylvania College of Technology
David Lanning	Tompkins Cortland Community College
Ernest Larkins	Georgia State University
William C. Lathen	Boise State University

Cynthia Bolt Lee	The Citadel
Brian Levinson	SUNY at Binghamton
Roland Lipka	Temple University
Bruce Lubich	Syracuse University
Gary L. Maydew	Iowa State University
A. David Mayer	City University
Thomas McCain	Washington University
Joseph McCauley	Monroe Community College
Edward Milam	Mississippi State University
Kevin Misiewicz	University of Notre Dame
Karen H. Molloy	University of Illinois
Matthew Monippallil	Eastern Illinois University
Michael O'Dell	Arizona State University
Kenneth Orbach	Florida Atlantic University
Edmund Outslay	Michigan State University
Yvonne Phang-Hatami	Borough of Manhattan Community College
Nelson Pion	University of Massachusetts
Steven M. Platau	The University of Tampa
Janis Reeder	University of Delaware
W. Peter Salzarulo	Miami University (Ohio)
Ragnor Seglund	California State University—Sacramento
Kathleen Sinning	Western Michigan University
Jerrold Stern	Indiana University
Paul Streer	University of Georgia
Caroline Strobel	University of South Carolina
Ronald R. Tidd	Syracuse University
Anne Townsend	University of Texas at Dallas
James Trebby	Marquette University
Janet Trewin	University of North Texas
Joanne Turner	Rochester Institute of Technology
Len Weld	Auburn University
Patricia Elliott Williams	Friends University
Robert Wyndelts	Arizona State University
William F. Yancey	Texas Christian University

We are also grateful to the various graduate assistants, doctoral students, and colleagues who have reviewed the text and supplementary materials and checked solutions to maintain a high level of technical accuracy. In particular, we would like to acknowledge the following colleagues who assisted in the preparation of supplemental materials for this text:

Priscilla Kenney (Supplements Coordinator)	University of Florida
Sally Baker	DeVry Institute of Technology
Arthur D. Cassill	University of North Carolina at Greensboro
Edmund Fenton	Belmont University
George Frankel	San Francisco State University
Craig J. Langstraat	University of Memphis
Bobbie Martindale	Dallas Baptist University
Deborah Garvin	University of Florida

In addition, we want to thank Myron S. Scholes and Mark A. Wolfson for allowing us to use the model discussed in their text, Taxes and Business Strategy: A Planning Approach, as the basis for material in Chapter 18.

Thomas R. Pope
John L. Kramer

PRENTICE HALL'S
FEDERAL TAXATION

1998

Individuals

CHAPTER 1

AN INTRODUCTION TO TAXATION

LEARNING OBJECTIVES

After studying this chapter, you should be able to

1 ▸ Discuss the history of taxation in the United States

2 ▸ Differentiate between the three types of tax rate structures

3 ▸ Describe the various types of taxes

4 ▸ Discuss what constitutes a "good" tax structure and the objectives of the federal income tax law

5 ▸ Identify the various tax law sources and understand their implications for tax practice

6 ▸ Describe the legislative process for the enactment of the tax law

7 ▸ Describe the administrative procedures under the tax law

8 ▸ Describe the components of a tax practice and understand the basic tax research process and computer applications

KEY POINT

In many situations, the use of the tax laws to influence human behavior is deliberate. As will be seen later in this chapter, the tax laws are often used to achieve social and economic objectives.

The federal tax system has a substantial effect on investor, business, and personal decisions. Thus, it may alter the allocation of resources within the U.S. economy. The following examples illustrate the impact of the tax law on various segments of our society:

▶ A business decision about whether to invest in a new plant or equipment may depend, in part, on the existence of favorable tax provisions.

▶ An employee may decide to accept a new job because the prospective employer offers favorable tax-free fringe benefits or an attractive deferred compensation plan.

▶ An individual may decide to buy a principal residence rather than rent comparable property because of the availability of tax deductions for mortgage interest and real estate taxes.

▶ The terms of a property settlement agreement pursuant to a divorce decree may be structured to take into account the tax laws governing alimony and property settlements.

The purpose of this text is to provide an introduction to the study of federal income taxation. However, before discussing the specifics of the U.S. federal income tax law, it is helpful to have a broad conceptual understanding of the taxation process. Thus, this chapter provides an overview of the following topics:

▶ Historical developments of the federal tax system

▶ Types of taxes levied and structural considerations

▶ Objectives of the tax law

▶ Tax law sources and the legislative process

▶ Internal Revenue Service (IRS) collection, examination, and appeals processes

▶ The nature of tax practice, including computer applications and tax research

HISTORY OF TAXATION IN THE UNITED STATES

OBJECTIVE 1

Discuss the history of taxation in the United States

HISTORICAL NOTE

The reinstatement of the income tax in 1894 was the subject of heated political controversy. In general, the representatives in Congress from the agricultural South and West favored the income tax in lieu of customs duties. Representatives from the industrial eastern states were against the income tax and favored protective tariff legislation.

EARLY PERIODS

The federal income tax is the dominant form of taxation in the United States. In addition, most states and some cities and counties also impose an income tax. Both corporations and individuals are subject to such taxes.

Before 1913 (the date of enactment of the modern-day federal income tax), the federal government relied predominantly on customs duties and excise taxes to finance its operations. The first federal income tax on individuals was enacted in 1861 to finance the Civil War but was repealed after the war. The federal income tax was reinstated in 1894. However, that tax was challenged in the courts because the U.S. Constitution required that an income tax be apportioned among the states in proportion to their populations. This type of tax system, which would be both impractical and difficult to administer, would mean that different tax rates would apply to individual taxpayers depending on their states of residence.

In 1895, the Supreme Court ruled that the tax was in violation of the U.S. Constitution.[1] Therefore, it was necessary to amend the U.S. Constitution to permit the passage of a federal income tax law. This was accomplished by the Sixteenth Amendment, which was ratified in 1913. The Sixteenth Amendment, while being an extraordinarily important amendment, consists of one sentence.

---

[1] *Pollock v. Farmers' Loan & Trust Co.*, 3 AFTR 2602, (USSC, 1895). Note, however, that a federal income tax on corporations that was enacted in 1901 was held to be constitutional because it was treated as an excise tax. See *Flint v. Stone Tracy Co.*, 3 AFTR 2834, (USSC, 1911).

Sixteenth Amendment to the Constitution of the United States

The Congress shall have power to lay and collect taxes on incomes, from whatever source derived, without apportionment among the several States, and without regard to any census or enumeration.

REVENUE ACTS FROM 1913 TO THE CURRENT PERIOD

HISTORICAL NOTE

The Revenue Act of 1913 contained sixteen pages.

The Revenue Act of 1913 imposed a flat 1% tax (with no exemptions) on a corporation's net income. The rate varied from 1% to 7% for individuals, depending on the individual's income level. However, very few individuals paid federal income taxes because a $3,000 personal exemption ($4,000 for married individuals) was permitted as an offset to taxable income. These amounts were greater than the incomes of most individuals in 1913.

HISTORICAL NOTE

Before 1939, the tax laws were contained in the current revenue act, a reenactment of a prior revenue act plus amendments. In 1939, a permanent tax code was established; it was revised in 1954 and 1986.

Various amendments to the original law were passed between 1913 and 1939. For example, a deduction for dependency exemptions was provided in 1917. In 1939, the separate revenue acts were codified into the Internal Revenue Code of 1939. A similar codification was accomplished in 1954. The 1954 codification, which was known as the Internal Revenue Code of 1954, included the elimination of many "deadwood" provisions, a rearrangement and clarification of numerous code sections, and the addition of major tax law changes. Whenever changes to the Internal Revenue Code (IRC) are made, the old language is deleted and the new language added. Thus, the statutes are organized as a single document, and a tax advisor does not have to read through the applicable parts of all previous tax bills to find the most current law. In 1986, major changes were made to the tax law, and the basic tax law was redesignated as the Internal Revenue Code of 1986.

The federal income tax became a "mass tax" on individuals during the early 1940s. This change was deemed necessary to finance the revenue needs of the federal government during World War II. In 1939, less than 6% of the U.S. population was subject to the federal income tax; by 1945, 74% of the population was taxed.[2] To accommodate the broadened tax base and to avoid significant tax collection problems, Congress enacted pay-as-you-go withholding in 1943.

A major characteristic of the federal income tax since its inception to today is the manner in which the tax law is changed or modified. The federal income tax is changed on an **incremental** basis rather than a complete revision basis. Under so-called incrementalism, when a change in the tax law is deemed necessary by Congress, the entire law is not changed but specific provisions of the tax law are added, changed, or deleted on an incremental basis. Thus, the federal income tax has been referred to as a "quiltwork" of tax laws, referring to the patchwork nature of the law. Without question, one of the principal reasons for the complexity of the federal income tax today is the incremental nature of the tax.

REVENUE SOURCES

As mentioned earlier, the largest source of federal revenues is individual income taxes. Other major revenue sources include social security (FICA) taxes and corporate income taxes (see Table I1-1). Two notable trends from Table I1-1 are 1) the increase in social security taxes from 1965 to 1995, and 2) the decrease in corporate income taxes for the same period. Individual income taxes have remained stable throughout the thirty-year period.

---

[2] Richard Goode, *The Individual Income Tax* (Washington, DC: The Brookings Institution, 1964), pp. 2–4.

▼ TABLE I1-1

Breakdown of Federal Revenues

	1965	1975	1985	1995
Individual income taxes	43%	45%	46%	43%
Social insurance taxes and contribution	20	32	36	36
Corporation income taxes	23	15	8	12
Other	14	8	10	9
Total	100%	100%	100%	100%

Source: Council of Economic Advisors, *Economic Indicators* (Washington, DC: U.S. Government Printing Office, 1967, 1977, 1996), p. 37 (1967), p. 34 (1977), p. 33 (1996).

TYPES OF TAX RATE STRUCTURES

THE STRUCTURE OF INDIVIDUAL INCOME TAX RATES

Virtually all tax structures are comprised of two basic parts: the **tax base** and the **tax rate**. The tax base is the amount to which the tax rate is applied to determine the tax due. For example, an individual's tax base for the federal income tax is her *taxable income*, as defined and determined by the income tax law. Similarly, the tax base for the property tax is generally the fair market value of property subject to the tax. The tax rate is merely the percentage rate applied to the tax base.

Tax rates may be either progressive, proportional, or regressive. A **progressive rate** structure is one where the rate of tax increases as the tax base increases. The most notable tax that incorporates a progressive rate structure is the federal income tax. Thus, as a taxpayer's taxable income increases, a progressively higher rate of tax is applied. Currently, for individuals, the federal income tax rates begin at 15% and increase to 28%, 31%, 36%, and 39.6% as a taxpayer's taxable income increases.[3] Examples I1-1 and I1-2 show how the progressive rate structure of the federal income tax operates.

EXAMPLE I1-1 ▶

Alice, who is single, has $10,000 taxable income and pays $1,500 in federal income taxes because a 15% tax rate is applied to taxable income up to $24,650. (For tax rates, see the inside front cover) Allen, who is also single, has taxable income of $30,000. A 15% rate applies to Allen's taxable income up to $24,650 and a 28% rate applies to taxable income over this amount. Thus, Allen's total tax is $5,196 [(0.15 × $24,650) + (0.28 × $5,350)]. If Allen's taxable income is $70,000, a 31% rate applies to $10,250 of his taxable income ($70,000 − $59,750) because the 31% rate applies to taxable income above $59,750 for a single individual. Thus, the tax rates are progressive because the rate of tax increases as a taxpayer's taxable income increases. ◀

EXAMPLE I1-2 ▶

Assume the same facts as in Example I1-1 except that Alice has taxable income of $125,000. Of Alice's taxable income, $350 ($125,000 − $124,650) is subject to the 36% rate. Also, assume that Allen has taxable income of $280,000. Of Allen's taxable income, $146,400 ($271,050 − $124,650) is subject to the 36% rate and $8,950 ($280,000 − $271,050) is subject to a marginal rate of 39.6%. ◀

---

[3] See the inside front cover for the 1997 tax rates and Chapter I2 for a discussion of the computation procedures. 1996 rate schedules and tax tables are located immediately before Appendix A.

A **proportional tax** rate, sometimes called a **flat tax**, is one where the rate of tax is the same for all taxpayers, regardless of their income levels. This type of tax rate is generally used for real estate taxes, state and local sales taxes, personal property taxes, customs duties, and excise taxes. A flat tax has been the subject of considerable discussion in the last couple of years and promises to be a highly controversial topic as the debate on federal income tax reform continues into the next century.

EXAMPLE I1-3 ▶
ADDITIONAL COMMENT

In the 1950's, the top marginal tax rate for individual taxpayers reached 92%! This astonishingly high rate only applied to taxpayers with very high taxable incomes but is still an extremely confiscatory tax rate.

Assume the same facts as in Example I1-1, except that a 17% tax rate applies to all amounts of taxable income. Based on the assumed flat tax rate structure, Alice's federal income tax is $1,700 on $10,000 of taxable income, and Allen's tax is $5,100 on $30,000 of taxable income and $10,200 on $60,000 of taxable income. The tax rate is proportional because the 17% rate applies to both taxpayers without regard to their income level. ◀

A **regressive tax** rate decreases with an increase in the tax base (e.g., income). Regressive taxes, while not consistent with the fairness of the income tax,[4] are found in the United States. The social security (FICA) tax is regressive because a fixed rate of tax of 7.65% for both the employer and employee is levied up to a ceiling amount of $65,400 (in 1997). The employer and employee's FICA tax rate is only 1.45% for wages earned in excess of the ceiling amount. The sales tax, which is levied by many states, is also regressive when measured against the income base.

THE STRUCTURE OF CORPORATE TAX RATES

The federal corporate income tax reflects a stair-step pattern of progression that tends to benefit small corporations. The corporate rates are as follows:[5]

Taxable Income	Tax
First $50,000	15% of taxable income
Over $50,000 but not over $75,000	$7,500 + 25% of taxable income over $50,000
Over $75,000 but not over $100,000	$13,750 + 34% of taxable income over $75,000
Over $100,000 but not over $335,000	$22,250 + 39% of taxable income over $100,000
Over $335,000	34% of taxable income
Over $10,000,000 but not over $15,000,000	$3,400,000 + 35% of taxable income over $10,000,000
Over $15,000,000 but not over $18,333,333	$5,150,000 + 38% over $15,000,000
Over $18,333,333	35% of taxable income

MARGINAL, AVERAGE, AND EFFECTIVE TAX RATES FOR TAXPAYERS

A taxpayer's **marginal tax rate** is the tax rate applied to an incremental amount of taxable income that is added to the tax base. The marginal tax rate concept is useful for planning because it measures the tax effect of a proposed transaction.

---

[4] See the discussion of equity and fairness later in this chapter.
[5] For corporations with taxable income over $100,000, the lower rates of tax on the first $75,000 of income are gradually phased out by applying a 5-percentage-point surtax on taxable income from $100,000 to $335,000 so that benefits of the favorable rates are eliminated once a corporation's taxable income reaches $335,000. Once taxable income exceeds $335,000

the tax equals 34% of taxable income. A 35% tax rate applies to taxable income in excess of $10 million. For corporations with taxable income in excess of $15 million, a 3 percentage-point-surtax applies to taxable income from $15 million to $18,333,333 to eliminate the lower 34% rate that applies to the first $10 million of taxable income.

EXAMPLE I1-4 ▶ Vania, who is single, is considering the purchase of a personal residence that will provide a $20,000 tax deduction for interest expense and real estate taxes. Vania's taxable income would be reduced from $80,000 to $60,000 if she purchases the residence. Because a 31% tax rate applies to taxable income from $60,000 to $80,000, Vania's marginal tax rate is 31%. Thus, Vania's tax savings from purchasing the personal residence would be $6,200 (0.31 × $20,000). ◀

The **average tax rate** is computed by dividing the total tax liability by the amount of taxable income. This is different from a taxpayer's **effective tax rate**, which is the total tax liability divided by total economic income. **Total economic income** includes exclusions and deductions from the tax base (e.g., tax-exempt bond interest).

EXAMPLE I1-5 ▶ Amelia, who is single, has $30,000 of taxable income and her economic income is $35,000 in 1997. The difference is attributable to $5,000 of tax-exempt bond interest. Based on tax rates applicable to a single taxpayer, Amelia's total tax is $5,196 [(0.15 × $24,650) + (0.28 × $5,350)]. Her average tax rate is 17.32% ($5,196 ÷ $30,000). Amelia's effective tax rate is 14.85% ($5,196 ÷ $35,000). ◀

STOP & THINK

Question: Gwen, a single taxpayer, has seen her income climb to $100,000 in the current year. She wants a tax planner to help her reduce her tax liability. In planning for tax clients, tax professionals almost exclusively use the marginal tax rate in their analysis rather than the average tax rate. Why is the marginal tax rate much more important in the tax planning process than the average tax rate?

Solution: Because tax planning is done at the margin. A single taxpayer who has taxable income of $100,000 has a marginal tax rate of 31% (at 1997 rates), but an average tax rate of 26.003%.

Taxable income		$100,000
Tax on first $59,750 of taxable income		$13,525.50
Remaining taxable income	$40,250	
Times: Marginal tax rate	× 0.31	12,477.50
Total tax liability		$26,003.00

$$\text{Average tax rate} = \frac{\text{Total tax}}{\text{Taxable income}} = \frac{\$26,003}{\$100,000} = 26.003\%$$

If a tax planner could reduce Gwen's taxable income by $10,000, Gwen's tax liability would decrease by $3,100 ($10,000 × 0.31). When the taxpayer wants to know how much she can save through tax planning, the appropriate marginal tax rate yields the answer.

DETERMINATION OF TAXABLE INCOME AND TAX DUE

As will be discussed in later chapters, the federal income taxes imposed on all taxpayers (individuals, corporations, estates, and trusts) are based on the determination of taxable income. In general, taxable income is computed as follows:

ADDITIONAL
COMMENT

In the determination of tax rates, one should consider the incidence of taxation that involves the issue of who really bears the burden of the tax. If a city raises the real property tax but landlords simply raise rents to pass on the higher taxes to their tenants, the tax burden is shifted. The concept has important implications in determining any kind of average or effective tax rate.

Total income (income from whatever source derived)	$xxx
Minus: Exclusions (specifically defined items, such as tax-exempt bond interest)	(xx)
Gross income	$xxx
Minus: Deductions (business expenses and itemized deductions)	(xx)
Exemptions (not applicable for corporations)	(xx)
Taxable income	$xxx
Times: Applicable tax rate	× .xx
Gross income tax liability	$xxx
Minus: Credits and prepayments	(xx)
Net tax payable or refund due	$xxx

Each different type of taxpayer (e.g., individuals, corporations, etc.) computes taxable income in a slightly different manner, but all use the general framework above. Individuals taxpayers (Chapter I2) and corporation taxpayers (Chapter I16) are examined in this book. Corporations (in more detail), estates, and trusts are examined in *Prentice Hall's Federal Taxation: Corporations, Partnerships, Estates, and Trusts.*

TYPES OF TAXES

STATE INCOME AND FRANCHISE TAXES

OBJECTIVE 3

Describe the various types of taxes

Only seven states do not impose an individual income tax.[6] In most instances, state income tax rates are mildly progressive and are based on an individual's federal adjusted gross income (AGI), with minor adjustments.[7] (For example, a typical adjustment to a state income tax return is interest income on federal government obligations, which is generally not subject to state income taxes.) Some states also allow a deduction for federal income taxes in the computation of taxable income for state income tax purposes.

States imposing a state income tax generally require the withholding of state income taxes and have established mandatory estimated tax payment procedures. The due date for filing state income tax returns generally coincides with the due date for the federal income tax returns (e.g., the fifteenth day of the fourth month following the close of the tax year for individuals).

ADDITIONAL
COMMENT

State income tax rates for individuals have increased significantly in the past twenty years. Thirty-three states now have marginal tax rates of 6% or higher.

Most states impose a corporate income tax, although in some instances the tax is called a **franchise tax**. Franchise taxes are usually based on a weighted-average formula consisting of net worth, income, and sales.

WEALTH TRANSFER TAXES

The Tax Reform Act of 1976 created a unified transfer tax system that imposes a single tax on transfers of property taking place during an individual's lifetime (gifts) and at death (estates). (See the inside back cover of the text for the transfer tax rate schedules.) Formerly, the gift and estate tax laws were separate and distinct. The federal estate tax was initially enacted in 1916. The original gift tax law dates back to 1932. The gift tax was originally imposed to prevent widespread avoidance of the estate tax (e.g., taxpayers could make tax-free gifts of property before their death). Both the gift and estate taxes are wealth transfer taxes levied on the transfer of property and are based on the fair market value (FMV) of the transferred property on the date of the transfer. Below are brief descriptions of the gift tax and estate tax.

---

[6] These states are Alaska, Florida, Nevada, South Dakota, Texas, Washington, and Wyoming. New Hampshire has an income tax that is levied only on dividend and interest income and Tennessee's income tax applies only to income from stocks and bonds.

[7] See Chapter I2 for a discussion of the AGI computation.

KEY POINT

The $10,000 annual exclusion is an important tax-planning tool for wealthy parents who want to transfer assets to their children and thereby minimize their gift and estate taxes. A husband and wife who have three children could transfer $60,000 to their children each year without incurring any gift tax.

THE FEDERAL GIFT TAX. The **gift tax** is an excise tax that is imposed on the donor (not the donee) for transfers of property that are considered to be a gift. A gift, generally speaking, is a transfer made gratuitously and with donative intent. However, the gift tax law has expanded the definition to include transfers that are not supported by full and adequate consideration.[8] To arrive at the amount of taxable gifts for the current year, a $10,000 annual exclusion is allowed per donee.[9] In addition, an unlimited marital deduction is allowed for transfers between spouses.[10] The formula for computing the gift tax is as follows:

FMV of all gifts made in the current year			$x,xxx
Minus: Annual donee exclusions ($10,000 per donee)	$xx		
Marital deduction for gifts to spouse	xx		
Charitable contribution deduction	xx	(xxx)	
Plus: Taxable gifts for all prior years		xxx	
Cumulative taxable gifts (tax base)			$x,xxx
Times: Unified transfer tax rates			× .xx
Tentative tax on gift tax base			$ xxx
Minus: Unified transfer taxes paid in prior years			(xx)
Unified credit			(xx)
Unified transfer tax (gift tax) due in the current year			$ xx

Note that the gift tax is cumulative over the taxpayer's lifetime (i.e., the tax calculation for the current year includes the taxable gifts made in prior years). The detailed tax rules relating to the gift tax are covered in both *Prentice Hall's Federal Taxation: Corporations, Partnerships, Estates, and Trusts* and the *Comprehensive* volume. The following general concepts and rules for the federal gift tax are presented as background material for other chapters of this text dealing with individual taxpayers:

ADDITIONAL COMMENT

The gift tax was enacted to make the estate tax more effective. Without a gift tax, estate taxes could be easily avoided by large gifts made before death.

▶ Gifts between spouses are exempted from the gift tax due to the operation of an unlimited marital deduction.

▶ The primary liability for payment of the gift tax is imposed on the **donor**. The donee is contingently liable for payment of the gift tax in the event of nonpayment by the donor.

▶ The donor is permitted a $10,000 annual exclusion for gifts of a present interest to each donee.[11]

▶ Charitable contributions are effectively exempted from the gift tax because an unlimited deduction is allowed.

▶ The tax basis of the property to the donee is generally the donor's cost. It is the lesser of the donor's cost and the property's FMV on the date of the gift if the property is sold by the donee at a loss. (See Chapter I5 for a discussion of the gift tax basis rules.)

▶ A unified tax credit equivalent to a $600,000 deduction is available to offset any gift tax that would otherwise be due on gifts made to someone other than a spouse or a charity that exceed the $10,000 annual exclusion.[12]

---

[8] Sec. 2512(b).
[9] Sec. 2503(b).
[10] Sec. 2523(a).
[11] A gift of a present interest is an interest that is already in existence and the donee is currently entitled to receive the income from the property. A gift of a future interest comes into being at some future date (e.g., property is transferred by gift to a trust in which the donee is not entitled to the income from the property until the donor dies) and is not eligible for the 10,000 annual exclusion.
[12] The $600,000 exemption is in the form of a $192,800 tax credit for 1987 and later years.

EXAMPLE I1-6 ▶ Antonio makes the following gifts in the current year:

- ▶ $25,000 cash gift to his wife
- ▶ $15,000 contribution to the United Way
- ▶ Gift of a personal automobile valued at $25,000 to his adult son
- ▶ Gift of a personal computer valued at $4,000 to a friend

The $25,000 gift to his wife is not taxed because of a $10,000 annual exclusion and a $15,000 tax exemption for transfers to spouses (i.e., the marital deduction). The $15,000 contribution to the United Way is also not taxed because of the $10,000 annual exclusion and the $5,000 deduction for charitable contributions. The $25,000 gift Antonio made to his son is reduced by the $10,000 annual exclusion to each donee, leaving a $15,000 taxable gift.[13] The $4,000 gift to the friend is exempt because of the annual exclusion of up to $10,000 in gifts to a donee in a tax year. Total taxable gifts for the current year that are subject to the unified transfer tax equal $15,000. ◀

STOP & THINK

Question: An important aspect of gift taxes that is frequently overlooked is the interaction of gift taxes and income taxes. In many cases, gifts are made *primarily* for income tax purposes. Why would a gift be made for income tax purposes?

Solution: Gifts are frequently made in order to shift income from one family member to another family member who is in a lower marginal tax bracket. For example, assume Fran and Jan are married, have one 15-year-old son, earn $400,000 per year from their business, and generate $100,000 per year in dividends and interest from a substantial portfolio of stocks and bonds. With such a high level of income, Fran and Jan are in the 39.6% marginal tax bracket. If they make a gift of some of the stocks and bonds to their son, the dividends and interest attributable to the gift are taxed to the son at his marginal tax rate (maybe 15%). If the son's marginal tax rate is lower than 39.6%, the family unit will pay less overall income taxes.

THE FEDERAL ESTATE TAX. The **federal estate tax** is part of the unified transfer tax system that is based on the total property transfers an individual makes during his or her lifetime and at death.

EXAMPLE I1-7 ▶ Amy dies during the current year. The formula for computing the estate tax on Amy's estate is as follows:

TYPICAL MISCONCEPTION

It is sometimes thought that the federal estate tax raises significant amounts of revenue, but it has not been a significant revenue producer since World War II.

Gross estate (FMV of all property owned by the decedent at the date of death)	$xxx,xxx
Minus: Deductions for funeral and administration expenses, debts of the decedent, charitable contributions, and the marital deduction for property transferred to a spouse	(x,xxx)
Taxable estate	$ x,xxx
Plus: Taxable gifts made after 1976	xx
Tax base	$ x,xxx
Times: Unified transfer tax rate(s)	× .xx
Tentative tax on estate tax base	$ xxx
Minus: Tax credits (e.g., the unified tax credit of $192,800)	(xx)
Gift taxes paid after 1976	(xx)
Unified transfer tax (estate tax) due	$ xx

◀

---

[13] This example assumes that the automobile is a gift rather than an obligation of support under state law and also assumes that Antonio's wife does not join with Antonio in electing to treat the gift to the son as having been made by both spouses (a gift-splitting election). In such event, donee exclusions of $20,000 (2 × $10,000) would be available, resulting in a taxable gift of only $5,000.

ADDITIONAL
COMMENT

The unified transfer tax rate schedule contains rates that range from 18% to 55%.

The estate tax rules are discussed in depth in *Prentice Hall's Federal Taxation: Corporations, Partnerships, Estates, and Trusts* and in the *Comprehensive* volume. The following general rules are provided as background material for subsequent chapters of this text dealing with individual taxpayers:

▶ The decedent's property is valued at its FMV on the date of death unless the alternative valuation date (six months after the date of death) is elected. The alternative valuation date may be elected only if the aggregate value of the gross estate decreases during the six-month period following the date of death and the election results in a lower estate tax liability.

▶ The basis of the property received by the estate and by the decedent's heirs is the property's FMV on the date of death (or the alternate valuation date if it is elected).

▶ Property that is transferred to the decedent's spouse is exempt from the estate tax because of the estate tax marital deduction provision.

EXAMPLE I1-8 ▶

Barry died in the current year, leaving a $1,000,000 gross estate. One-half of the property is transferred to his wife, taxable gifts made after 1976 were $150,000, and administrative and funeral expenses and debts of the decedent amount to $200,000. The estate tax due is computed as follows:

Gross estate		$1,000,000
Minus: Marital deduction		(500,000)
Funeral and administrative expenses and decedent's debts		(200,000)
Taxable estate		$ 300,000
Plus: Taxable gifts made after 1976		150,000
Tax base		$ 450,000
Tentative tax on estate tax base		$ 138,800[a]
Minus: Tax credits (unified tax credit)		(192,800)
Unified transfer tax due		$ —0— ◀

[a] $70,800 + (0.34 × $200,000)

Even though the unified tax credit exceeds the gross estate tax amount, the estate is unable to obtain a refund of the excess amount because the estate tax is not a refundable credit.

Because of the generous credit and deduction provisions (e.g., the unified tax credit and the unlimited marital deduction), few estates must pay estate taxes. For example, an individual might leave $1 million of the property in his estate to his wife and $600,000 to his children. No estate tax would be owed because a $1 million marital deduction is allowed and the unified tax credit of $192,800 is equivalent to a $600,000 tax exemption.

OTHER TYPES OF TAXES

ADDITIONAL
COMMENT

Proposals to decrease reliance on the federal income tax have focused on a value added tax and selective energy taxes. A value added tax is a sales tax levied at each stage of production on the "value added."

Although the primary focus of this text is on the federal income tax, some mention should be made of the following other types of taxes levied by federal, state, and local governments.

▶ **Property taxes** are based on the value of a taxpayer's property, which may include both real estate and personal property. Real estate taxes are a major source of revenue for local governments. However, it is not uncommon for state and local governments to levy a personal property tax on intangibles such as securities and tangible personal property (e.g., the value of a personal automobile).

▶ **Federal excise taxes** and **customs duties** on imported goods have declined in relative importance over the years but remain significant sources of revenue. Federal excise taxes are imposed on alcohol, tobacco, gasoline, telephone usage, production of oil and gas, and many other types of goods. Many state and local governments impose similar excise taxes on goods and services.

ADDITIONAL COMMENT

Anheuser-Busch Company ran a television commercial in 1990 during the deliberations on the Revenue Reconciliation Act of 1990 that asked viewers to call a toll-free telephone number to register their criticism of an increase in the excise tax on beer. The commercial asked viewers to "can the beer tax."

▶ **Sales taxes** are a major source of revenue for state and local governments. Sales taxes are imposed on retail sales of tangible personal property (e.g., clothing and automobiles). Some states also impose a sales tax on personal services (e.g., accounting and legal fees). Certain items are often exempt from the sales tax levy (e.g., food items or medicines), and the rates vary widely between individual state and local governments. Sales taxes are not deductible for federal income tax purposes unless incurred to produce income. (See Chapter I7 for a discussion of sales taxes.)

▶ **Employment taxes** include social security (**FICA**) and federal and state unemployment compensation taxes. If an individual is classified as an employee, the FICA tax that is imposed on the employee is comprised of two parts, 6.2% for old-age, survivors, and disability insurance (OASDI) and 1.45% for hospital insurance (HI), for a total of 7.65%. The OASDI portion is imposed on the first $65,400 (1997) of wages, whereas the HI portion has no ceiling. Both of these taxes are imposed on both the employer and employee. If an individual is self-employed, a self-employment tax is imposed at a 15.3% rate (12.4% for OASDI and 2.9% for HI) on the individual's self-employment income, with a ceiling on the OASDI portion of $65,400 (in 1997).[14] Similar to employees, there is no ceiling on the HI portion for self-employed individuals.

▶ Employers are required to pay federal and state unemployment taxes to fund the payment of unemployment benefits to former employees. The federal rate is 6.2% on the first $7,000 of wages for each employee in 1997.[15] However, a credit is granted for up to 5.4% of wages for taxes paid to the state government so that the actual amount paid to the federal government may be as low as 0.8%.[16] The amount of tax paid to the state depends on the employer's prior experience with respect to the frequency and amount of unemployment claims. In Kentucky, for example, the highest rate of unemployment tax imposed by the State is 3% and this rate is subsequently adjusted down if the employer has a small number of unemployment claims.

The types of taxes and structural considerations that were previously discussed are summarized in Topic Review I1-1.

CRITERIA FOR A TAX STRUCTURE

OBJECTIVE 4

Discuss what constitutes a "good" tax structure and the objectives of the federal income tax law

Establishing criteria for a "good" tax structure was first attempted in 1776 by economist Adam Smith.[17] Smith's four "canons of taxation"—equity, certainty, convenience, and economy—are still used today when tax policy issues are discussed.

EQUITY

A rather obvious criteria for a good tax is that the tax be equitable or fair to taxpayers. However, equity or fairness is elusive because of the subjectivity of the concept. What one person may conclude is fair in a particular situation may be considered totally unfair by another person. In other words, fairness is relative in nature and is extremely difficult to measure. For example, the deductibility of mortgage interest on a taxpayer's home certainly seems to be a fair provision for taxpayers. However, for taxpayers who do not own a home but live in a rental apartment, the deductibility of mortgage interest may not be considered as fair because the renter cannot deduct any portion of the rent paid. In

---

[14] Self-employed individuals receive an income tax deduction equal to 50% of taxes paid on their self-employment income and this deduction is also allowed to compute the amount of self-employment income (see Secs. 164(f) and 1402(a)(12) and Chapter I14).

[15] Sec. 3301.

[16] Sec. 3302. State unemployment taxes in some states are levied on tax bases above $7,000. For example, the wage base ceiling in North Carolina is $12,500 in 1997.

[17] Adam Smith, *The Wealth of Nations* (New York: Random House, Modern Library, 1937), pp. 777–779.

Topic Review I1-1

Types of Taxes and Tax Structure

Type of Tax	Tax Structure	Tax Base
Individuals:		
Federal income tax	Progressive	Gross income from all sources unless specifically excluded by law reduced by deductions and exemptions
State income tax	Progressive	Generally based on AGI for federal income tax purposes with adjustments
Federal gift tax	Progressive	FMV of all taxable gifts made during the tax year
Federal estate tax	Progressive	FMV of property owned at death plus taxable gifts made after 1976
Corporations:		
Federal corporate income tax	Progressive	Gross income from all sources unless specifically excluded by law reduced by deductions
State corporate income tax	Proportional or progressive	Federal corporate taxable income with adjustments
State franchise tax	Proportional	Usually based on a weighted-average formula consisting of net worth, income, and sales
Other Types of Taxes:		
Property taxes	Proportional	FMV of personal or real property
Excise taxes	Proportional	Customs and duties on imported and domestic goods from alcohol to telephone usage
Sales taxes	Proportional	Retail sales of tangible personal property or personal services
FICA and self-employment taxes	Regressive	Based on wages or self-employment income
Unemployment taxes	Regressive	Usually first $7,000 of an employee's wages

ADDITIONAL COMMENT

The Revenue Reconciliation Act of 1993 followed through on President Clinton's campaign promise to increase taxes on high-income taxpayers to correct perceived inequities resulting from the lowering of the top tax rates in the Tax Reform Act of 1986.

other types of situations, the federal tax law includes various measures to ensure that taxpayers are treated fairly. For example, a foreign tax credit is available to minimize the double taxation that would otherwise occur when U.S. taxpayers earn income in a foreign country that is taxed by both the United States and the country in which it is earned. (See the glossary at the end of this volume for a definition of tax credits and Chapter I14 for a discussion of the foreign tax credit.) There are two aspects of equity that are commonly discussed in the tax policy literature, **horizontal equity** and **vertical equity**. Horizontal equity refers to the notion that similarly situated taxpayers should be treated equally. Thus, two taxpayers who each have income of $50,000 should both pay the same amount of tax. Vertical equity, on the other hand, implies that taxpayers who are not similarly situated should be treated differently. Thus, if Taxpayer A has income of $50,000 and Taxpayer B has income of $20,000, Taxpayers A and B should not pay the same amount of income tax. Vertical equity provides that the incidence of taxation should be borne by those who have the **ability to pay** the tax, based on income or wealth. The progressive rate structure is founded on the vertical equity premise.

CERTAINTY

A certain tax is one that ensures a stable source of government operating revenues and provides taxpayers with some degree of certainty concerning the amount of their annual tax liability. A tax that is simple to understand and administer provides certainty for taxpayers. For several years, our income tax laws have been criticized as being overly complex and difficult to administer. Consider the following remarks of a noted tax authority at a conference on federal income tax simplification, which was jointly sponsored by the American Bar Association and the American Law Institute:

> Tax advisers—at least some tax advisers—are saying that the income tax system is not working. They are saying that they don't know what the law provides, that the IRS does not know what the law provides, that taxpayers are not abiding by the law they don't know.[18]

This uncertainty in the tax law causes frequent disputes between taxpayers and the IRS and has resulted in extensive litigation.

The federal tax system has made some attempts to provide certainty for taxpayers. For example, the IRS issues advance rulings to taxpayers. This provides some assurance concerning the tax consequences of a proposed transaction for the taxpayer who requests the ruling. The taxpayer may rely on the ruling if the transaction is completed in accordance with the terms of the ruling request. For example, if a merger of two corporations is being considered, the transaction can be structured so that the shareholders and the corporations do not recognize gain or loss. If a favorable ruling is received and the transaction is completed as planned, the IRS cannot later assert that the merger does not qualify for tax-free treatment.

CONVENIENCE

A tax law should be easily assessed, collected, and administered. Taxpayers should not be overly burdened with the maintenance of records and compliance considerations (preparation of their tax returns, payment of their taxes, and so on). One of the reasons that the sales tax is such a popular form of tax for state and local governments is that it is convenient to pay and collect from the vendor. The consumer need not complete a tax return or keep detailed records.

ECONOMY

An efficient tax structure should require only minimal compliance and administrative costs. The IRS collection costs, amounting to less than 0.5% of revenues, are fairly minimal relative to the total collections of revenues from the federal income tax. Estimates of taxpayer compliance costs are less certain. One indicator of total compliance costs for taxpayers is the demand for tax professionals. Tax practice has been and continues to be one of the fastest growing areas in public accounting firms. Most large corporations also maintain sizable tax departments that engage in tax research, compliance, and planning activities. In addition, many commercial tax return preparer services are available to assist taxpayers who have relatively uncomplicated tax returns.

Fortune 500 companies spend over $1 billion annually complying with the tax laws, according to a study commissioned by the IRS.[19] The survey found that about 55% of the

[18] Sidney L. Roberts, "The Viewpoint of the Tax Adviser: An Overview of Simplification," *Tax Adviser*, January 1979, p. 32.
[19] Joel Slemrod and Marsha Blumenthal, "Measuring Taxpayer Burden and Attitudes for Large Corporations: Report to the Coordinated Examination Program of the IRS," *Tax Notes*, December 20, 1993, p. 1422.

cost of compliance goes to pay in-house staff and about 16% goes to outside firms. The federal income tax system accounts for about 70% of this cost. State and local income tax compliance accounts for the remaining 30%. The companies surveyed said that the largest share of their tax compliance costs went to filing tax returns.

A more difficult question is whether the tax structure is economical in terms of taxpayer compliance. The issues of tax avoidance and tax evasion are becoming increasingly more important. Recently, the General Accounting Office (GAO) reported that two-thirds of tax returns are out of compliance, resulting in net income being underreported by 25 percent.[20]

OBJECTIVES OF THE FEDERAL INCOME TAX LAW

The primary objective of the federal income tax law is to raise revenues for government operations. In recent years, the federal government has broadened its use of the tax laws to accomplish various economic and social policy objectives.

ECONOMIC OBJECTIVES

The federal income tax law is used as a fiscal policy tool to stimulate private investment, reduce unemployment, and mitigate the effects of inflation on the economy. Consider the following example: Tax credits for businesses operating in distressed urban and rural areas (empowerment zones) were enacted in 1993 to provide economic revitalization of such areas. This is a clear example of using the federal income tax law to accomplish a desired result.

The tax brackets, personal and dependency exemptions, and standard deduction amounts are adjusted for inflation by an indexation procedure using the consumer price index. These inflation adjustments provide relief for individual taxpayers who would otherwise be subject to increased taxes due to the effects of inflation. (See Chapter I2 for a discussion of the tax computation for individuals.)

ENCOURAGEMENT OF CERTAIN ACTIVITIES AND INDUSTRIES

The federal income tax law also attempts to stimulate and encourage certain activities, specialized industries, and small businesses. One such example is the encouragement of research activities by permitting an immediate write-off of expenses and a special tax credit for increasing research and experimental costs. Special incentives are also provided to the oil and gas industry through percentage depletion allowances and an election to deduct intangible drilling costs.

Certain favorable tax provisions are provided for small businesses, including reduced corporate tax rates of 15% on the first $50,000 of taxable income and 25% for the next $25,000 of taxable income. Favorable ordinary loss (instead of capital loss) deductions are granted to individual investors who sell their small business corporation stock at a loss, provided that certain requirements are met.[21] In addition, noncorporate investors may exclude up to 50% of the gain realized from the disposition of qualified small business stock issued after August 10, 1993 if the stock is held for more than five years.[22]

---

[20] News Report. "Compliance Said to Be Poor Among Sole Proprietorships," *Tax Notes*, December 12, 1994, p. 1328.

[21] Sec. 1244.
[22] Sec. 1202.

Topic Review I1-2

Objectives of the Tax Law

Objective	Example
Stimulate investment and reduce unemployment	Provide a tax credit for the purchase of business equipment
Prevent taxpayers from paying a higher percentage of their income in personal income taxes due to inflation (bracket creep)	Index the tax rates, standard deduction, and personal and dependency exemptions for inflation
Encourage research activities that will in turn strengthen the competitiveness of U.S. companies	Allow research expenditures to be written off in the year incurred and offer a tax credit for increasing research and experimental costs
Encourage venture capital for small businesses	Reduce corporate income tax rates on the first $75,000 of taxable income. Allow businesses to immediately expense $18,000 of certain depreciable business assets acquired each year.
Encourage social objectives	Provide a tax deduction for charitable contributions; provide favorable tax treatment for contributions to qualified pension plans
Stimulate the economy	Provide tax credits for the acquisition of plant and equipment

SOCIAL OBJECTIVES

The tax law attempts to encourage or discourage certain socially desirable or undersirable activities. For example:

▶ Special tax-favored pension and profit-sharing plans have been created for employees and self-employed individuals to supplement the social security retirement system.

▶ Charitable contributions are deductible to encourage individuals to contribute to charitable organizations.

▶ The claiming of a deduction for illegal bribes, fines, and penalties has been prohibited to discourage activities that are contrary to public policy.

EXAMPLE I1-9 ▶ Able Corporation establishes a qualified pension plan for its employees whereby it makes all of the annual contributions to the plan. Able's contributions to the pension trust are currently deductible and not includible in the employee's gross income until the pension payments are distributed during their retirement years. Earnings on the contributed funds are also nontaxable until such amounts are distributed to the employees. ◀

EXAMPLE I1-10 ▶ Anita contributes $10,000 annually to her church, which is a qualified charitable organization. Anita's marginal tax rate is 28%. Her after-tax cost of contributing to the church is only $7,200 [$10,000 − (0.28 × $10,000)]. ◀

EXAMPLE I1-11 ▶ Ace Trucking Company incurs $10,000 in fines imposed by local and state governments for overloading its trucks during the current tax year. None of the fines are deductible because the activity is contrary to public policy. ◀

The tax law objectives previously discussed are highlighted in Topic Review I1-2.

TAX LAW SOURCES

The solution to any tax question may only be resolved by reference to tax law sources (also referred to as tax law authority). Tax law sources are generated from all three branches of the federal government, i.e., legislative, executive, and judicial. The principal sources of tax law are as follows:

Branch	Tax Law Source
Legislative	Internal Revenue Code
	Congressional Committee Reports
Executive (Administrative)	Income Tax Regulations
	Revenue Rulings
	Revenue Procedures
	Letter Rulings
Judicial	Court Decisions

ADDITIONAL COMMENT

Knowledge of tax law sources could be considered the most important topic in this book. It is similar to the old Chinese proverb that states that if you give a person a fish you have fed him for one day, but if you teach a person how to fish you have fed him for the rest of his life. By analogy, if a person has a knowledge of the tax law sources, he or she should be able to locate the answers to tax questions throughout his or her career.

A thorough knowledge of the various sources above as well as the relative weights attached to each source is vital to tax professionals. For example, a decision of the U.S. Supreme Court on a tax matter would certainly carry more weight than a Revenue Ruling issued by the Internal Revenue Service.

Clearly, the most authoritative source of tax law is the Internal Revenue Code, which is the actual tax law passed by Congress. However, Congress is not capable of anticipating every type of transaction that taxpayers might engage, so most of the statutes in the Code contain very general language. Because of the general language contained in the Code, both administrative and judicial interpretations are necessary to apply the tax law to specific situations and transactions. Thus, the regulations and rulings of the IRS and the decisions of the courts are an integral part of the federal income tax law. For a detailed discussion of tax law sources, see Chapter I15. Topic Review I1-3 provides an overview of the tax law sources.

ENACTMENT OF A TAX LAW

Under the U.S. Constitution, the House of Representatives is responsible for initiating new tax legislation. However, tax bills may also originate in the Senate as riders to nontax legislative proposals. Often, major tax proposals are initiated by the President and accompanied by a Treasury Department study or proposal, and then introduced into Congress by one or more representatives from the President's political party.

STEPS IN THE LEGISLATIVE PROCESS

The specific steps in the legislative process are discussed below and are outlined in Table I1-2. These steps typically include:

ADDITIONAL COMMENT

In 1997 the chairman of the House Ways and Means Committee was Rep. William Archer of Texas, and the chairman of the Senate Finance Committee was Sen. William Roth of Delaware.

1. A tax bill is introduced in the House of Representatives and is referred to the House Ways and Means Committee.
2. The proposal is considered by the House Ways and Means Committee, and public hearings are held. Testimony may be given by members of professional groups such as the American Institute of CPAs and the American Bar Association and from various special-interest groups.
3. The tax bill is voted on by the House Ways and Means Committee and, if approved, is forwarded to the House of Representatives for a vote. Amendments to the bill from individual members of the House of Representatives are generally not allowed.

Topic Review I1-3

Tax Law Sources

Source	Key Points	Weight of Authority
LEGISLATIVE		
Internal Revenue Code	Contains provisions governing income, estate and gift, employment, alcohol, tobacco, and excise taxes.	Serves as the highest legislative authority for tax research, planning, and compliance activities.
ADMINISTRATIVE		
Treasury Regulations	Represents the Secretary of the Treasury's interpretation of the tax code. Regulations may be initially issued in proposed, temporary, and final form and are interpretative or legislative.	Legislative regulations have a higher degree of authority than interpretative regulations. Proposed regulations do not have authoritative weight.
IRS Rulings	The IRS issues Revenue Rulings (letter rulings or published rulings), Revenue Procedures, Information Releases, and Technical Advice Memoranda.	These pronouncements reflect the IRS's interpretation of the law and do not have the same level of scope and authority as Treasury Regulations.
JUDICIAL		
Judicial doctrines	Judicial doctrines are concepts that have evolved from Supreme Court cases that are used by the courts to decide tax issues. Examples include substance over form, tax benefit rule, and constructive receipt.	Judicial doctrines that evolve from Supreme Court cases have substantial weight of authority because a finding of the Supreme Court has the force and effect of law.
Judicial interpretations	Tax cases are initially considered by a trial court (i.e., the Tax Court, a Federal district court, or the U.S. Court of Federal Claims). Either the taxpayer or the IRS may appeal to an appeals court. A final appeal is to the U.S. Supreme Court.	A trial court must abide by the precedents set by the court of appeals of the same jurisdiction. An appeals court is not required to follow the decisions of another court of appeals. A Supreme Court decision must be followed by the IRS, taxpayers, and the lower courts.

ADDITIONAL COMMENT

The corridors near Congress's tax-writing rooms are called "Gucci Gulch," so named for the designer clothing worn by many of the lobbyists who congregate there when a tax bill is being considered.

4. If passed by the House, the bill is forwarded to the Senate for consideration by the Senate Finance Committee, and public hearings are held.

5. The tax bill that is approved by the Senate Finance Committee may be substantially different from the House of Representatives' version.

6. The Senate Finance Committee reports the Senate bill to the Senate for consideration. The Senate generally permits amendments (e.g., new provisions) to be offered on the Senate floor.

7. If approved by the Senate, both the Senate and House bills are sent to a Joint Conference Committee consisting of an equal number of members from the Senate and the House of Representatives.

▼ **TABLE I1-2**
Steps in the Legislative Process

1. Treasury studies prepared on needed tax reform
2. President makes proposals to Congress
3. House Ways and Means Committee prepares House bill
4. Approval of House bill by the House of Representatives
5. Senate Finance Committee prepares Senate bill
6. Approval of Senate bill by the Senate
7. Compromise bill approved by a Joint Conference Committee
8. Approval of Joint Conference Committee bill by both the House and Senate
9. Approval or veto of legislation by the President
10. New tax law and amendments incorporated into the Code

HISTORICAL NOTE

The only practicing CPA ever elected to the U.S. Congress is Joe Dio Guardi. He was elected in 1984 from Westchester County, New York.

8. The Senate and House bills are reconciled in the Joint Conference Committee. This process of reconciliation generally involves substantial compromise if the provisions of both bills are differ. A final bill is then resubmitted to the House and Senate for approval.
9. If the Joint Conference Committee bill is approved by the House and Senate, it is sent to the President for approval or veto.
10. A presidential veto may be overturned if a two-thirds majority vote is obtained in both the House and Senate.
11. Committee reports are prepared by the staffs of the House Ways and Means Committee, the Senate Finance Committee, and the Joint Conference Committee as the bill progresses through Congress. These reports help to explain the new law before the Treasury Department drafts regulations on the tax law changes as well as to explain the intent of Congress for passing the new law.

ADMINISTRATION OF THE TAX LAW AND TAX PRACTICE ISSUES

ORGANIZATION OF THE INTERNAL REVENUE SERVICE

OBJECTIVE 7

Describe the administrative procedures under the tax law

The **IRS** is the branch of the Treasury Department that is responsible for administering the federal tax law. It is organized on a national, regional, district, and service center basis. The responsibilities and functions of the various administrative branches include the following:

▶ The Commissioner of Internal Revenue, appointed by the President, is the chief officer of the IRS. This individual is supported by the Chief Counsel's office, which is responsible for preparing the government's case for litigation of tax disputes.

▶ The National Office includes a deputy commissioner, a series of assistants to the commissioner, a chief inspector, and a chief counsel. A significant responsibility of the National Office is to process ruling requests and to prepare revenue procedures that assist taxpayers with compliance matters.

▶ Regional commissioners in the four IRS regions are responsible for the settlement of administrative appeals for disputed tax deficiencies.

▶ District directors supervise the performance of IRS audits and collection of delinquent taxes in thirty-three districts.

ADDITIONAL
COMMENT

In a survey of members of the American Institute of CPAs, it was found that more than half of the 1,036 members who responded had an unfavorable opinion of the IRS, unchanged from a survey of three years ago. However, the accountants gave the IRS good marks for courtesy and a willingness to solve problems.

▶ Ten service centers perform tax return processing work. They also select tax returns for audit.

ENFORCEMENT PROCEDURES

All tax returns are initially checked for mathematical accuracy and items that are clearly erroneous. The Form W-2 amounts (e.g., wages, and so on) and Form 1099 information return amounts (e.g., relating to dividend and interest payments, and so on) are checked against the amounts reported on the tax return. If differences are noted, the IRS Center merely sends the taxpayer a bill for the corrected amount of tax and a statement of the differences. In some instances, the difference is due to a classification error by the IRS, and the additional assessment can be resolved by written correspondence. A refund check may be sent to the taxpayer if an overpayment of tax has been made.

EXAMPLE I1-12 ▶

ADDITIONAL
COMMENT

Individuals may call 800-366-4484 to report misconduct of IRS employees.

Bart is an author of books and properly reports royalties on Schedule C (Profit or Loss from Business). The IRS computer matching of the Form 1099 information returns from the publishing companies incorrectly assumes that the royalties should be reported on Schedule E (Supplemental Income and Loss). If the IRS sends the taxpayer a statement of the difference and an adjusted tax bill, this matter (including the abatement of added tax, interest, and penalties) should be resolved by correspondence with the IRS. ◀

SELECTION OF RETURNS FOR AUDIT

The U.S. tax system is based on self-assessment and voluntary compliance, although a certain amount of enforcement is needed to ensure that taxpayers are in compliance. For example, in past years the IRS conducted a complete (i.e., line-by-line) audit of a small number of taxpayers. The returns used in this audit were selected based on a stratified random sample known as the **Taxpayer Compliance Measurement Program (TCMP)**. This program was intended to determine patterns of taxpayer compliance with the tax law. However, the IRS recently announced (October 23, 1995) that it has decided to postpone the TCMP program indefinitely, citing budget constraints.

ADDITIONAL
COMMENT

A special task force has recommended that the percentage of returns audited be increased to 2.5%. Many individuals feel that the probability of being audited is so low as to be disregarded.

The IRS uses a **Discriminant Function System (DIF)** to select other individual returns for audit. This system is intended to identify tax returns that are most likely to contain errors, which result in the collection of significant amounts of additional tax revenues. In the aggregate, less than 1% of individuals are audited annually. Some examples of situations where individuals are more likely to be audited include the following:

▶ Investments and trade or business expenses that produce significant tax losses

▶ Itemized deductions in excess of an average amount for the person's income level

▶ Filing of a refund claim by a taxpayer who has been previously audited, where substantial tax deficiencies have been assessed

▶ Individuals who are self-employed with substantial business income or income from a profession (e.g., a medical doctor)

ETHICAL POINT

A CPA should not recommend a position to a client that exploits the IRS audit selection process.

AUDIT PROCEDURES. Audits of most individuals are handled through an **office audit procedure** in an office of the IRS. In most cases, an individual is asked to substantiate a particular deduction, credit, or income item (e.g., charitable contributions that appear to be excessive). The office audit procedure does not involve a complete audit of all items on the return.

EXAMPLE I1-13 ▶

Brad obtains a divorce during the current year and reports a $30,000 deduction for alimony. The IRS may conduct an office audit to ascertain whether the amount is properly deductible as alimony and does not represent a disguised property settlement to Brad's ex-wife. Brad may be asked to submit verification (e.g., a property settlement agreement between the spouses that designates the payments as alimony). ◀

KEY POINT

A taxpayer may appear on his or her own behalf before the IRS during an audit. An attorney or CPA in good standing is authorized to practice before the IRS upon the filing of a written statement that he or she is currently so qualified and is authorized to represent the taxpayer.

A **field audit procedure** is often used for corporations and individuals engaged in a trade or business. A field audit is generally broader in scope than the office audit (e.g., several items on the tax return may be reviewed). A field audit is generally conducted at the taxpayer's place of business or the office of his or her tax advisor.

Most large corporations are subject to annual audits. The year under audit may be several years before the current year because the corporation will often waive the statute of limitations pending the resolution of disputed issues.

STATUTE OF LIMITATIONS

Most taxpayers feel a sense of relief after they have prepared their income tax return and have mailed it to the IRS. However, the filing of the tax return is not necessarily the end of the story for that particular taxable year. It is possible, of course, that the IRS may select their tax return for audit after the return has been initially processed or a taxpayer may have filed an amended return to correct an error or omission.

REAL-WORLD EXAMPLE

Based on an IRS audit, the Mustang Ranch, Nevada's most famous legal bordello, was assessed some $13 million in taxes. When the amount owed could not be paid, the IRS sold the property to recoup the taxes.

Both the IRS and taxpayers can make corrections to a return after it has been originally filed. Fortunately, both only have a limited time period in which to make such corrections. This time period is called the **statute of limitations** and prevents either the taxpayer or the IRS from changing a filed tax return after the time period has expired. The general rule for the statute of limitations is three years from the later of the date the tax return was actually filed or its due date.[23] However, a six-year statute of limitations applies if the taxpayer omits items of gross income that in total exceed 25% of the gross income reported on the return.[24] The statute of limitations remains open indefinitely if a fraudulent return is filed or if no return is filed.[25]

EXAMPLE I1-14 ▶

Betty, a calendar-year taxpayer, is audited by the IRS in February 1997 for the year 1994. During the course of the audit, the IRS proposes additional tax for 1994 because Betty failed to substantiate certain travel and entertainment expense deductions. During the course of the audit, it is discovered that Betty failed to file a tax return for 1992, and in 1993 an item of gross income amounting to $26,000 was not reported. Gross income reported on the 1993 return was $72,000. Assuming Betty's 1994 return was filed on or before its due date, the IRS may assess a deficiency for 1994 because the three-year statute of limitations will not expire until April 15, 1998. A deficiency may also be assessed for the 1993 return because a six-year statute of limitations applies because the omission is more than 25% of the gross income reported on the return. A deficiency may also be assessed for 1992 because there is no statute of limitations for fraud. ◀

ADDITIONAL COMMENT

In 1992 the IRS increased the staff that attempts to identify nonfilers to 2,400 from 400.

ADDITIONAL COMMENT

More than 150 penalties can be imposed on taxpayers. In fact, applying the penalties has become so complicated that the IRS is currently considering ways to consolidate and simplify them.

INTEREST

Interest accrues on both assessments of additional tax due and on refunds that the taxpayer receives from the government.[26] No interest is paid on a tax refund if the amount is refunded by the IRS within forty-five days of the day prescribed for filing the

[23] Secs. 6501(a) and (b)(1). Similar rules apply to claims for a refund filed by the taxpayer. Section 6511(a) requires that a refund claim be filed within three years of the date the return was filed or within two years of the date the tax was paid, whichever is later.

[24] Sec. 6501(e). See also *Stephen G. Colestock*, 102 T.C. 380 (1994), where the Tax Court ruled that the extended six-year limitation period applied to a married couple's entire tax liability for the tax year at issue, not just to items that constituted substantial omissions of gross income. Thus, the IRS was able to assert an increased deficiency and additional penalties attributable to a disallowed depreciation deduction.

[25] Sec. 6501(c).

[26] Sec. 6621(a). The rate is adjusted four times a year by the Treasury Department based on the current interest rate for short-term federal obligations. The interest rate individual taxpayers must pay to the IRS on underpayments of tax is the federal short-term rate plus three percentage points. The interest rate paid to taxpayers on overpayments of tax is the federal short-term rate plus two percentage points. The penalty assessed may be very small in some instances even though the taxpayer owes a large tax bill for the year because penalties are imposed on the net tax due.

return (e.g., April 15) determined without regard for extensions.[27] If a return is filed after the filing date, no interest is allowed if the refund is made within forty-five days of the date the return was filed.

EXAMPLE I1-15 ▶ Beverly, a calendar-year taxpayer, files her 1996 tax return on February 1, 1997, and requests a $500 refund. No interest accrues on the refund amount if the IRS sends the refund check to Beverly within 45 days of the due date (i.e., April 15, 1997). ◀

PENALTIES

Various nondeductible penalties are imposed on the net tax due for failure to comply, including

▶ A penalty of 5% per month (or fraction thereof) subject to a maximum of 25% for failure to file a tax return[28]

▶ A penalty of 0.5% per month (or fraction thereof) up to a maximum of 25% for failure to pay the tax that is due[29]

▶ A negligence penalty of 20% of the underpayment attributable to negligence or disregard of rules and regulations[30]

▶ A 75% penalty for fraud[31]

▶ A penalty based on the current interest rate for underpayment of estimated taxes[32]

ADMINISTRATIVE APPEAL PROCEDURES

If an IRS agent issues a deficiency assessment, the taxpayer may make an appeal to the IRS Appeals Division. Some disputes involve a gray area (e.g., a situation where some courts have held for the IRS whereas other courts have held for the taxpayer on facts that are similar to the disputed issue). In such a case, the taxpayer may be able to negotiate a compromise settlement (e.g., a percentage of the disputed tax amount plus interest and penalties) with the Appeals Division based on the "hazards of litigation" (i.e., the probability of winning or losing the case if it is litigated).

COMPONENTS OF A TAX PRACTICE

OBJECTIVE 8

Describe the components of a tax practice and understand the basic tax research process and computer applications

Tax practice is a rapidly growing field that provides substantial opportunities for tax specialists in public accounting, law, and industry. The tasks performed by a tax professional may range from the preparation of a simple Form 1040 for an individual to the conduct of tax research and planning for highly complex business situations. Tax practice consists of the following activities:

▶ Tax compliance and procedure (i.e., tax return preparation and representation of a client in administrative proceedings before the IRS)

▶ Tax research

▶ Tax planning and consulting

▶ Financial planning

ADDITIONAL COMMENT

In addition to the penalties listed on this page, there are also penalties for civil fraud and criminal fraud. Criminal fraud carries a maximum penalty of $100,000, a prison sentence of up to five years, or both.

ADDITIONAL COMMENT

Pete Rose, major league baseball's all-time hit leader, was sent to prison in 1990 for income tax evasion.

---

[27] Sec. 6611(e). This same 45-day rule has been extended to refunds of taxes other than income taxes (i.e., employment, excise, and estate and gift taxes) for returns filed on or after January 1, 1994 and for amended returns, claims for refunds, and IRS-initiated adjustments for returns and refund claims filed on or after January 1, 1995.

[28] Sec. 6651(a)(1). The percentages are increased to 15% per month (or fraction thereof) up to a maximum of 75% if the penalty is for fraudulent failure to file under Sec. 6651(f).

[29] Sec. 6651(a)(2). If both the failure to file penalty (5%) and the failure to pay the tax penalty (0.5%) are both applicable, the failure to file penalty is reduced by the failure to pay penalty per Sec. 6651(c)(1). Further, the penalty is increased to 1% per month after the IRS notifies the taxpayer that it will levy on the taxpayer's assets.

[30] Sec. 6662.

[31] Sec. 6663.

[32] Sec. 6654.

TAX COMPLIANCE AND PROCEDURE

Preparation of tax returns is a significant component of tax practice. Tax practitioners often prepare federal, state, and local tax returns for individuals, corporations, estates, trusts, and so on. In larger corporations, the tax return preparation (i.e., compliance) function is usually performed by a company's internal tax department staff. In such a case, a CPA or other tax practitioner may assist the client with the tax research and planning aspects of their tax practice, and may even review their return before it is filed.

Tax procedure consists of assisting the client in negotiations with the IRS. If a client is audited, the practitioner acts as the client's representative in discussions with the IRS agent. If a tax deficiency is assessed, the practitioner assists the client if an administrative appeal is contemplated with the IRS's Appellate Division. In most instances, an attorney is retained if litigation is being considered.

TAX RESEARCH

Tax research is the search for the best possible defensibly correct solution to a problem involving either a completed transaction (e.g., a sale of property) or a proposed transaction (e.g., a proposed merger of two corporations). Research involves each of the following steps:

▶ Determine the facts.

▶ Identify the problem.

▶ Identify and analyze the tax law sources (i.e., code provisions, Treasury Regulations, administrative rulings, and court cases).

▶ Evaluate nontax (e.g., business) implications.

▶ Solve the problem.

▶ Communicate the findings to the client.

Tax research may be conducted in connection with tax return preparation, tax planning, or procedural activities. A discussion of how to do tax research is presented briefly below and in greater depth in Chapter I15.

TAX PLANNING AND CONSULTING

Tax planning involves the process of structuring one's affairs so as to minimize the amount of taxes *and* maximize the after-tax return. Thus, maximal tax planning is *not* to just pay the least amount of tax but to maximize after-tax cash flows. A noted but out-of-print text on tax research and planning has delineated the following tax planning principles:

▶ Keep sufficient records.

▶ Forecast the effect of future events.

▶ Support the plan with a sound business purpose.

▶ Base the plan on sound legal authorities.

▶ Do not carry a good plan too far.

▶ Make the plan flexible.

▶ Integrate the tax plan with other factors in decision making.

▶ Conduct research to learn whether a similar plan has previously proved unsuccessful (e.g., a court case involving similar facts may have upheld the IRS's position).

▶ Consider the "maximum" risk exposure of the client (e.g., if the plan is subsequently challenged by the IRS and the tax treatment is disallowed, what is the economic impact upon the taxpayer?).

▶ Consider the effect of timing (e.g., whether it is more beneficial to take a deduction in one year versus another).

▶ Shape the plan to the client's needs and desires.[33]

CPAs and attorneys frequently are engaged by their clients to perform consulting services to optimize the client's tax situation. For example, a major corporation client is considering the acquisition of a major international corporation and wants to make sure that the tax implications of such an acquisition are properly managed. The CPA will be engaged to perform a thorough review of the transaction to ensure that the client is fully aware of the tax results of the acquisition, and may possibly request an advance ruling from the IRS.

Because of the importance of planning in tax practice, subsequent chapters in this text include a separate section on tax planning to discuss issues that are related to the topical coverage. These tax planning principles should be kept in mind when attempting to use the tax planning recommendations. Also, a systematic approach to tax planning developed by two noted tax academicians, Myron Scholes and Mark Wolfson, is discussed in Chapter I18.

FINANCIAL PLANNING

A relatively new field for tax professionals is that of financial planning. Since taxes are an integral part of any financial plan and since a tax specialist regularly meets with his or her clients (filing returns and other tax matters), the area of financial planning has become increasingly a part of tax practice. The typical steps in performing a financial planning engagement include the following steps:

▶ Determine the client's financial goals and objectives

▶ Review the client's insurance coverage for adequacy and appropriateness

▶ Recommend an investment strategy, including risk analysis and asset allocation

▶ Review tax returns to ensure that, through proper tax planning, the client is maximizing his or her after-tax cash flow

▶ Review the client's retirement plans to assure compliance with the law and possible new alternatives

▶ Review all documents related to estate and gift planning and work with the client's attorney to minimize all transfer taxes and fulfill the client's objectives.

TAX RESEARCH PROCESS

Tax research is a process involving several steps: determination of the facts, identification of the problem, determination of the best possible solution, and make recommendations to the client. The process includes data gathering, identifying tax issues, and locating and evaluating tax law sources.[34] Figure I1-1 illustrates the steps in the process. Tax research may also be used in the determination of tax policy. For example, policy-oriented research would determine the extent, if any, to which charitable organizations would be affected if contributions were no longer deductible. This type of tax research is usually conducted by economists to assess the effect of actions by the government. Client-oriented tax research involves an investigation of a tax problem that is based on a **closed-fact situation** (i.e., transactions or events that have already occurred) or an **open-fact situation** (i.e., the planning of a future course of action where the facts and events are still controllable). In a closed-fact situation, the research is primarily concerned with applying the law to the facts as they exist to determine how a particular item should be reported

KEY POINT

Information in Figure I1-1 suggests that the first three steps in the tax research process are somewhat circuitous. In other words, after you have determined the issues or located the applicable authorities, you may realize that you have to go back and collect more facts.

---

[33] Fred W. Norwood et al., *Federal Taxation: Research, Planning, and Procedures*, 2nd ed. (Englewood Cliffs, NJ: Prentice Hall, 1979), pp. 215–216.

[34] For a more thorough discussion of tax research procedures, see Chapter I15.

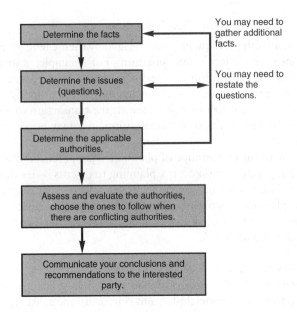

FIGURE I1-1 ▶ STEPS IN THE TAX RESEARCH PROCESS

on a tax return. Unfortunately, in such situations, the tax consequences can be costly because the facts cannot be restructured to obtain more favorable tax results. In an open-fact situation, the principal focus is on tax planning, which usually involves a choice of alternative courses of action.

In a closed-fact situation, the facts are often self-evident. However, if one is researching the tax consequences in an open-fact context, a number of the facts have not yet occurred, and the tax advisor's task is to determine which facts are likely to result in a particular tax outcome. This goal is accomplished by reviewing the authorities, especially court cases, and denoting which facts accompanied a favorable outcome and which produced an unfavorable result. For example, if a client hopes to achieve ordinary loss treatment from the anticipated sale of several plots of land in the same year, the advisor might compare the facts that were present in cases dealing with this type of situation. The advisor should consider cases both won and lost by taxpayers.

Often tax research deals with a gray area, that is, an issue for which no clear-cut, unequivocally correct solution exists. In such a situation, it is best to pursue the issue through a specifically tailored set of detailed questions. For example, in researching whether the taxpayer may deduct a loss as an ordinary loss instead of a capital loss, the tax advisor may need to investigate whether the presence of any investment motive precludes classifying a loss as ordinary.

EXAMPLE I1-16 ▶ Bob tells Bonnie, his tax advisor, that on November 4, 1997, he sold land held as an investment for $500,000 cash. His investment in the land was $50,000. On November 9, 1997, Bob reinvested the sales proceeds in another plot of investment land costing $500,000. This is a closed-fact situation in that Bob merely wants to know what amount of gain (if any) he must recognize. ◀

EXAMPLE I1-17 ▶ Candice seeks advice from Buddy, her tax advisor, about how to minimize her estate taxes. Candice is a widow with three children and five grandchildren and has property valued at $10 million. This is an open-fact situation. Buddy could advise Candice to leave all but a few hundred thousand dollars of her property to a charitable organization so that her estate would owe zero estate taxes. Although this recommendation would minimize Candice's estate taxes, Candice would probably reject it. Candice probably wants her children and grandchildren to receive the majority of her assets. Thus, reducing estate taxes to zero is inconsistent with her other objectives. For a more detailed discussion of the tax research process, see Chapter I15.

◀

COMPUTER APPLICATIONS IN TAX PRACTICE

TAX RETURN PREPARATION

To prepare tax returns, most tax practitioners purchase tax preparation software from companies such as Commerce Clearing House or Intuit. This software allows the preparation of accurate and professional-looking tax returns. A word of caution, however: as with any computer software, the preparation of tax returns using the computer requires as much knowledge and expertise from the preparer as doing the returns by hand. A recent trend in tax return preparation that almost certainly will grow extensively in the near future is the **electronic filing** of tax returns, i.e., a "paperless" tax return. Taxpayers send their returns electronically to the IRS for processing, thereby saving enormous amounts of paper and, hopefully, reducing human error. Computerized tax return software, *Tax Cut,* is available for use with these course materials.

TAX PLANNING APPLICATIONS

For several years many tax practitioners used computer terminal time-sharing systems to make the time-consuming complex tax calculations needed for tax planning. For example, specialized computer programs were available to calculate the income and estate tax effects that would result from a proposed change in the client's tax situation. Many firms are now using software applications on microcomputers to accomplish similar tasks. For example, software applications are used to project depreciation and other tax consequences arising from a proposed acquisition of business assets, to determine whether a corporation has an accumulated earnings tax problem, and to make basis adjustments for real estate partnerships.

TAX RESEARCH APPLICATIONS

Computerized information-retrieval systems are being used in tax research. The oldest of these data bases is LEXIS, which was developed by Mead Data Central. ACCESS, which is offered by Commerce Clearing House, also has widespread use. The database for these computerized systems contains in full text the same tax law sources (e.g., cases, rulings, committee reports, regulations, and commentary and analysis) that are included in a manual tax service, as discussed previously. The system is entered by using a keyword or phrase or by entering a Code section number or case name. Researchers need to be imaginative in thinking of search requests; a computerized system will not locate an authority unless it contains the exact wording the researcher specifies, even though it contains synonymous terms.

EXAMPLE I1-18 ▶

A researcher is interested in whether a certain expenditure for clothing is deductible under Sec. 162 as a uniform expense. The researcher might instruct the computer to retrieve all cases containing the words "uniform" and "Sec. 162" in close proximity to each other. This search will turn up only cases containing those words. Cases using the words "work clothing" will not be retrieved. A more comprehensive search will take place if the researcher instructs the computerized system to look for either "uniform" or "work clothing" within close proximity to "Sec. 162."

◀

Computerized systems can be especially valuable as a backup to the research one has conducted through the tax services. After researchers have located some authorities through the tax services, they can use ACCESS or LEXIS to determine whether there are

ADDITIONAL
COMMENT

Using LEXIS, a tax researcher
even has the ability to find decisions in which a particular
judge concurred or dissented.

additional authorities on point. Both systems are updated for new developments on a very timely basis.

A number of tax services, including CCH's *Federal Tax Service*, RIA's *Federal Tax Coordinator 2d (RIA On Point)*, CCH's *Standard Federal Tax Reporter (CCH Access)* and BNA's *Tax Management Portfolios* are available on CD-ROM (compact disc read-only memory). The materials are organized the same as in the loose-leaf services. The CD-ROMs are generally updated monthly. Information is retrieved from the CD-ROMs by typing key words into the computer. For example, one may locate the index on the disk, consult the index, and then refer to the portion of the disk that discusses the tax consequences of a related issue. The disks, of course, allow pages and pages of information to be stored in practically no space and avoid the need to file new pages. Extensive material is available on the CCH "ACCESS": CD-ROM. For example, the CD-ROM product includes *Standard Federal Tax Reports, State Tax Reports*, letter rulings and IRS positions, Revenue Rulings and Revenue Procedures, IRS publications, tax forms and instructions, and court cases dating back to 1913. Tax-oriented periodicals often provide reviews of computer-based or CD-ROM research products.[35]

Another source of tax materials that is destined to become extremely useful and important are materials on the Internet. The IRS has a home page (WWW.IRS. USTREAS.GOV) that taxpayers can access for forms, publications, and other related materials. All of the major accounting firms have home pages that allow users to access a myriad of tax information.

PROBLEM MATERIALS

DISCUSSION QUESTIONS

I1-1   The Supreme Court in 1895 ruled that the income tax was unconstitutional because the tax needed to be apportioned among the states in proportion to their populations. Why would the requirement of proportionality be so difficult to administer?

I1-2   Why was pay-as-you-go withholding needed in 1943?

I1-3   Congressman Patrick indicates that he is opposed to new tax legislative proposals that call for a flat tax rate that are currently being considered by Congress because the new taxing structure would not be in accord with our traditional practice of taxing those who have the ability to pay the tax. Discuss the position of the congressman, giving consideration to tax rate structures (e.g., progressive, proportional, and regressive) and the concept of equity.

I1-4   The Governor of your state stated in a recent political speech that he has never supported any income tax increases as the tax rates have remained at the same level during his entire term of office. Yet, you believe that you are paying more tax this year than in previous years even though your income has not increased. How can both you and the Governor be correct? In other words, is it possible for the government to raise taxes without raising tax rates?

I1-5   Carmen indicates that her average tax rate is 18% and her marginal tax rate is 28% for the current year. She is considering whether to make a charitable contribution to her church before the end of the tax year. Which tax rate is of greater significance in measuring the tax effect for her decision? Explain.

[35] See Editorial Staff, "CD-ROM Research Products Reviewed by Practitioners," *The Journal of Taxation*, July 1994, pp. 28–38. Also, for a thorough discussion of computerized tax research, see William A. Raabe, Gerald E. Whittenburg, and John C. Bost, *West's Federal Tax Research*, 3rd ed. (Minneapolis/St. Paul, MN: West Publishing Co., 1994), Chapters 13 and 14.

I1-6   Why are the gift and estate taxes both called wealth transfer taxes? What is the tax base for computing each of these taxes?

I1-7   Cathy, who is single, makes two gifts of $15,000 each to her two children.
   a. Is Cathy or her children primarily liable for the gift tax on the two gifts?
   b. If Cathy has never made a taxable gift in prior years, is a gift tax due on the two gifts?

I1-8   Carlos inherits 100 shares of Allied Corporation stock from his father. The stock cost his father $8,000 and had a $10,000 FMV on the date of his father's death. The alternate valuation date was not elected. What is Carlos's tax basis for the Allied stock when it is received from the estate?

I1-9   Most estates are not subject to the federal estate tax.
   a. Why is this the case?
   b. Do you believe most estates should be subject to the federal estate tax?

I1-10   Indicate which of the following taxes are generally progressive, proportional, or regressive:
   a. State income taxes
   b. Federal estate tax
   c. Corporate state franchise tax
   d. Property taxes
   e. State sales taxes

I1-11   Carolyn operates a small business as a sole proprietor (unincorporated). Carolyn is considering operating the business as a corporation because of nontax advantages (e.g., limited liability and ability to raise outside capital). From the standpoint of paying Social Security taxes, would the total Social Security taxes increase or decrease if the business is incorporated? Why?

I1-12   The three different levels of government (federal, state, and local) must impose taxes in order to carry out their functions. For each of the types of taxes below, discuss which level of government primarily uses that type of tax.
   a. Property taxes
   b. Excise taxes
   c. Sales taxes
   d. Income taxes
   e. Employment taxes

I1-13   There are four characteristics of a "good" tax structure.
   a. Briefly discuss the four characteristics.
   b. Using the four characteristics, evaluate the following tax structures:
      1. Federal income tax
      2. State sales tax
      3. Local ad valorem property tax

I1-14   There are two commonly-recognized measures of the fairness of an income tax structure, "horizontal equity" and "vertical equity."
   a. Discuss what is meant by horizontal equity and vertical equity as it pertains to the income tax.
   b. Why is it so difficult to design a "fair" tax structure?

I1-15   How do the carryback and carryover of net operating losses mitigate the effects of our progressive tax rate structure?

I1-16   The primary objective of the federal income tax law is to raise revenue. What are its secondary objectives?

I1-17   If the objectives of the federal tax system are multifaceted and include raising revenues, providing investment incentives, encouraging certain industries, and meeting desired social objectives, is it possible to achieve a simplified tax system? Explain.

I1-18   Why is a thorough knowledge of sources of tax law so important for a professional person who works in the tax area?

I1-19   The Internal Revenue Code is the most authoritative source of income tax law. In trying to resolve an income tax question, however, a tax researcher also consults administrative rulings (Income Tax Regulations, Revenue Rulings, etc.) and court decisions. Why wouldn't the tax researcher just consult the Code since it is the highest authority? Similarly, why is there a need for administrative rulings and court decisions?

I1-20   Congressional committee reports are an important source of information concerning the legislative enactment of tax law.
   a. Name the three Congressional committee re-

ports that are issued in connection with a new tax bill.

b. Of what importance are Congressional committee reports to tax practitioners?

I1-21 What is the primary service function provided by the National Office of the IRS?

I1-22 What types of taxpayers are more likely to be audited by the IRS?

I1-23 Anya is concerned that she will be audited by the IRS.

a. Under what circumstances is it possible that the IRS will review each line item on her tax return?

b. Is it likely that all items on Anya's return will be audited?

I1-24 **a.** What does the term "hazards of litigation" mean in the context of taxation?

b. Why would the IRS or a taxpayer settle or compromise a case based on the "hazards of litigation"?

I1-25 If a taxpayer receives a tax refund from the IRS, does this mean that the IRS feels that the return is correct and will not be subject to audit?

I1-26 State the statute of limitations for transactions involving:

a. Fraud (e.g., failure to file a tax return)

b. Disallowance of tax deduction items

c. The omission of rental income equal to 30% of the taxpayer's gross income

I1-27 In reference to tax research, what is meant by *the best possible defensibly correct solution?*

I1-28 The profession of tax practice involves four principal areas of activity. Discuss these four areas.

I1-29 Many tax professionals have moved into the field of financial planning for their clients.

a. How do taxes impact financial planning for a client?

b. Why do tax professionals have a perfect opportunity to perform financial planning for their clients?

I1-30 Is the principal goal of tax planning to absolutely minimize the amount of taxes that a taxpayer must pay?

I1-31 Explain how a microcomputer can assist a tax practitioner in tax planning activities and making complex tax calculations.

PROBLEMS

I1-32 *Tax Rates.* Latesha, a single taxpayer, had the following income and deductions for the tax year 1997:

INCOME:	Salary	$ 60,000
	Business Income	25,000
	Dividends from stocks	10,000
	Tax-exempt bond interest	5,000
	TOTAL INCOME	100,000
DEDUCTIONS:	Business expenses	$ 10,000
	Itemized deductions	20,000
	Personal exemptions	2,650
	TOTAL DEDUCTIONS	32,650

a. Compute Latesha's taxable income and federal tax liability for 1997.

b. Compute Latesha's marginal, average, and effective tax rates.

c. For tax planning purposes, which of the three rates in b. is the most important?

I1-33 *Marginal Tax Rate.* Jill and George are married and file a joint return. They expect to have $350,000 of taxable income in the next year and are considering whether to purchase a personal residence that would provide additional tax deductions of $80,000 for mortgage interest and real estate taxes.

I1-34   ***Gift Tax.*** Chuck, a married taxpayer, makes the following gifts during the current year: $20,000 to his church, $30,000 to his daughter, and $25,000 to his wife.

a. What is the amount of Chuck's taxable gifts for the current year (assuming that he does not elect to split the gifts with his spouse).

b. How would your answer to Part a change if a gift-splitting election were made?

I1-35   ***Estate Tax.*** Clay dies in the current year and has a gross estate valued at $800,000. Six months after his death, the gross assets are valued at $900,000. The estate incurs funeral and administration expenses of $125,000. It also has debts amounting to $75,000, and Clay bequeaths $350,000 of the property to his wife. During his life Clay made no taxable gifts.

a. What is the amount of Clay's taxable estate?

b. What is the tax base for computing Clay's estate tax?

c. What is the amount of estate tax owed if the tentative estate tax (before credits) is $70,800?

d. Alternatively, if, six months after his death, the gross assets in Clay's estate declined in value to $700,000, can the administrator of Clay's estate elect the alternate valuation date? What are the important factors that the administrator should consider as to whether the alternate valuation date should be elected?

I1-36   ***Interest and Penalties.*** In 1996, Paul, who is single, has a comfortable salary from his job as well as income from his investment portfolio. However, he is habitually late in filing his federal income tax return. He did not file his 1996 income tax return until December 1, 1997 (due date was April 15, 1997) and no extensions of time to file the return were filed. Below are amounts from his 1996 return:

Taxable income	$100,000
Total tax liability on taxable income	26,003
Total federal tax withheld from his salary	18,000

Paul sent a check with his return to the IRS for the balance due of $8,003. He is relieved that he has completed his filing requirement for 1996 *and* has met his financial obligation to the government for 1996.

Has Paul met *all* of his financial obligations to the IRS for 1996? If not, what additional amounts will Paul be liable to pay to the IRS?

I1-37   ***IRS Audits.*** Which of the following individuals is most likely to be audited:

a. Connie has a $20,000 net loss from her unincorporated business (a cattle ranch). She also received a $200,000 salary as an executive of a corporation.

b. Craig has AGI of $20,000 from wages and uses the standard deduction.

c. Dale fails to report $120 of dividends from a stock investment. His taxable income is $40,000 and he has no other unusually large itemized deductions or business expenses. A Form 1099 is reported to the IRS.

I1-38   ***Statute of Limitations.*** In April 1997, Dan is audited by the IRS for the year 1995. During the course of the audit, the agent discovers that Dan's deductions for business travel and entertainment are unsubstantiated and a $600 deficiency assessment is proposed for 1995. The agent also discovers that Dan failed to report $40,000 of gross business income on his 1993 return. Gross income of $60,000 was reported in 1993. The agent also discovers that Dan failed to file a tax return in 1992.

Will the statute of limitations prevent the IRS from issuing a deficiency assessment for 1995, 1993, or 1992? Explain.

CASE STUDY PROBLEM

I1-39 John Gemstone, a wealthy client, has recently been audited by the IRS. The agent has questioned the following deduction items on Mr. Gemstone's tax return for the year under review:

- A $10,000 loss deduction on the rental of his beach cottage.
- A $20,000 charitable contribution deduction for the donation of a painting to a local art museum. The agent has questioned whether the painting is overvalued.
- A $15,000 loss deduction from the operation of a cattle breeding ranch. The agent is concerned that the ranch is not a legitimate business (i.e., is a hobby).

Your supervisor has requested that you represent Mr. Gemstone in his discussions with the IRS.

a. What additional questions should you ask Mr. Gemstone in an attempt to substantiate the deductibility of the above items?

b. What tax research procedures might be applied to build the best possible case for your client?

RESEARCH PROBLEM

I1-40 Read the following two cases and explain why the Supreme Court reached different conclusions for cases involving similar facts and issues:

- *CIR v. Court Holding Co.*, 33 AFTR 593, 45-1 USTC ¶9215 (USSC, 1945)
- *U.S. v. Cumberland Public Service Co.*, 38 AFTR 978, 50-1 USTC ¶9129 (USSC, 1950)

CHAPTER 2

DETERMINATION OF TAX

LEARNING OBJECTIVES

After studying this chapter, you should be able to

1. Use the tax formula to compute an individual's taxable income

2. Determine the amount allowable for the standard deduction

3. Determine the amount and the correct number of personal and dependency exemptions

4. Determine the filing status of individuals

5. Explain the tax formula for corporations

6. Explain the basic concepts of property transactions

Each year, over 100 million individuals and married couples file tax forms on which they compute their federal income tax. The income tax is imposed "on the taxable income of every individual."[1] The amount of tax actually owed by an individual taxpayer is determined by applying a complex set of rules that together make up the income tax law. To understand the income tax, it is necessary to study the basic formula on which the income tax computation is based. Therefore, this chapter introduces the income tax formula and begins the development of its components. Because the income tax formula constitutes the basis of the income tax, most of the remainder of this book is an expansion of the formula. For that reason, it is essential that the reader understand the formula presented here before proceeding to subsequent chapters.

FORMULA FOR INDIVIDUAL INCOME TAX

BASIC FORMULA

OBJECTIVE 1

Use the tax formula to compute an individual's taxable income

Most individuals compute their income tax by using the formula illustrated in Table I2-1. The formula itself appears rather simple. That is because the complexity of the income tax comes from the intricate rules that must be applied in order to arrive at the amounts that enter into the formula rather than from the basic formula.

The tax formula is incorporated into the income tax form. The tax formula illustrated in Table I2-1 can be compared with Form 1040, which is reproduced in Figure I2-1. There are some minor differences between the formula found in the tax law and the tax form itself. For example, taxpayers are generally not required to report exclusions (nontaxable income) on their tax returns. One exception does require taxpayers to disclose tax-exempt interest income. Also, Form 1040 is used to collect other taxes such as the self-employment tax. Hence, a line is provided for that tax on Form 1040. The main reason for differences between the formula and the form is administrative

ADDITIONAL COMMENT

"There is one difference between a tax collector and a taxidermist—the taxidermist leaves the hide." This is a quote from Mortimer Caplan, former Director of the Bureau of Internal Revenue, *Time*, Feb. 1, 1963.

ADDITIONAL COMMENT

The IRS estimates that the average taxpayer will spend 3 hours and 44 minutes to complete Form 1040.

ADDITIONAL COMMENT

Comedian Jay Leno's explanation as to why the IRS calls it Form 1040 was, "For every $50 you earn, you get $10 and they get $40."

▼ **TABLE I2-1**

Tax Formula for Individuals

Income from whatever source derived	$ xxx,xxx
Minus: Exclusions	(xxx)
Gross income	$ xx,xxx
Minus: Deductions for adjusted gross income	(xxx)
Adjusted gross income	$ x,xxx
Minus: Deductions from adjusted gross income:	
Greater of itemized deductions or the standard deduction	(xx)
Personal and dependency exemptions	(xx)
Taxable income	$ x,xxx
Times: Tax rates (from tax table or schedule)	× .xx
Gross tax	$ xx
Minus: Credits and prepayments	(x)
Net tax payable or refund due	$ xx

---

[1] Sec. 1.

ADDITIONAL COMMENT

In the Revenue Reconciliation Act of 1993 there was a provision that increased the amount of the checkoff for the Presidential Election Campaign Fund from $1 to $3. The amount was increased because too few individuals were using the checkoff and a shortfall in the fund was projected for the 1996 election cycle. The checkoff can be found on Form 1040 below the address section.

TYPICAL MISCONCEPTION

It is easy to confuse an exclusion with a deduction. An exclusion is a source of income that can be omitted from the tax base, whereas a deduction is an expense that can be subtracted in arriving at taxable income. Both have the effect of reducing taxable income.

convenience. That is, there is no reason to require taxpayers to disclose income if the income is not subject to tax, and it is convenient to collect other taxes on the same tax form.

Examination of the formula reveals terms such as *gross income, exclusions, adjusted gross income, exemptions, gross tax,* and *credits.* These terms and others that make up the formula are defined below.

DEFINITIONS

INCOME. The term **income** includes both taxable and nontaxable income. Although the term is not specifically defined in the tax law, it does include income from any source.[2] Its meaning is close to that of the term **revenue**. However, it does not include a "return of capital." Thus, in the case of the sale of property, only the gain, not the entire sales proceeds, is viewed as income. This view extends to the sale of inventory, where the gross profit is viewed as income, as opposed to the sale price. Also, where a receipt is offset by a debt, such as in the case of borrowed funds, there is no income.

EXCLUSION. Not all income is taxable. An **exclusion** is any item of income that the tax law says is not taxable. Congress, over the years, has specifically exempted certain types of income from taxation for various social, economic, and political reasons. Chapter I4 discusses specific exclusions and the reasons for their existence. Table I2-2 contains a sample of the items that are excludable from gross income.

▼ **TABLE I2-2**
Major Exclusions

Gifts and inheritances
Life insurance proceeds
Welfare and certain other transfer payments
Certain scholarships and fellowships
Certain payments for injury and sickness
   Personal physical injury settlements
   Worker's compensation
   Medical expense reimbursements
Certain employee fringe benefits
   Health plan premiums
   Group term life insurance premiums
   Meals and lodging
   Employee discounts
   Employee death benefits
   Disability payments
   Dependent care
Certain foreign-earned income
Interest on state and local government bonds
Certain interest of Series EE bonds
Improvements by lessee to lessor's property
Child support payments
Property settlements

---

[2] Sec. 61(a).

▼ TABLE I2-3
Gross Income Items Listed in Sec. 61(a)

Compensation for services, including fees, commissions, and similar items
Gross income derived from business
Gains derived from dealings in property
Interest
Rents
Royalties
Dividends
Alimony and separate maintenance payments
Annuities
Income from life insurance and endowment contracts
Pension
Income from the discharge of indebtedness
Distributive share of partnership income
Income in respect of a decedent
Income from an interest in an estate or trust

GROSS INCOME. **Gross income** is income reduced by exclusions. In other words, it is income from taxable sources. As noted earlier, gross income is the only income that is actually reported on the return (i.e., excluded income need not be disclosed). Section 61(a) contains a partial list of items of gross income. The items listed in Sec. 61(a) are shown in Table I2-3. Note, however, that Sec. 61(a) states that unless otherwise provided, "gross income means all income from whatever source derived, including (but not limited to)" the listed items of income. Thus, the fact that an item is omitted from the list does not necessarily mean that the item is excluded. For example, illegal income, although omitted from the list, is taxable.[3]

DEDUCTIONS FOR ADJUSTED GROSS INCOME. In general, deductions are expenses that are specifically allowed by the tax law. Of course, not all expenses are deductible. On the other hand, there are a few instances where deductions are permitted even if there is no specific corresponding expense. For example, taxpayers are entitled to the standard deduction and a deduction for percentage depletion.

There are two categories of deductions for individual taxpayers: deductions *for* adjusted gross income and deductions *from* adjusted gross income. In general, **deductions for adjusted gross income** are business expenses such as those on an income statement prepared for financial accounting purposes, such as compensation paid to employees, repairs to business property, and depreciation. For the most part, **deductions from adjusted gross income** are personal expenses that Congress has chosen to allow. This classification scheme is not always followed. For example, alimony paid, which would not appear on an income statement, is a deduction *for* adjusted gross income. Table I2-4 contains a partial list of deductions *for* adjusted gross income that is taken from Sec. 62. Deductions for adjusted gross income are discussed further in Chapter I6 of this textbook.

ADJUSTED GROSS INCOME. **Adjusted gross income (AGI)** is a measure of income that falls between gross income and taxable income. It is important because it is the

ADDITIONAL COMMENT

In 1992, 52,019 tax returns were filed that showed AGI of $1,000,000 or more. Of these returns, 0.1% showed no total income tax.

[3] *U.S. v. Manley S. Sullivan*, 6 AFTR 6753, 1 USTC ¶236 (USSC, 1927).

▼ TABLE I2-4

Deductions for Adjusted Gross Income Listed in Sec. 62

Trade and business deductions
Reimbursed employee expenses and certain expenses of performing artists
Losses from the sale or exchange of property
Deductions attributable to rents and royalties
Certain deductions of life tenants and income beneficiaries of property
Contributions to retirement plans (Keoghs and IRAs)
Penalties forfeited because of premature withdrawal of funds from time savings accounts
One-half of self-employment taxes paid
Portion of health insurance costs incurred by a self-employed person
Alimony
Moving expenses
Certain required repayments of supplemental unemployment compensation
Jury duty pay remitted to an individual's employer

measure of income that is used in numerous other tax computations. For example, AGI is used to establish floors for the medical deduction and casualty loss deduction and to establish a ceiling for the charitable contribution deduction.

DEDUCTIONS FROM ADJUSTED GROSS INCOME. Section 62 lists deductions *for* AGI (see Table I2-4). Thus, any deduction not listed in Sec. 62 is a deduction *from* AGI. The two categories of deductions *from* adjusted gross income are itemized or standard deductions and personal and dependency exemptions.[4] Deductions from AGI are discussed further in Chapter I7 of this textbook.

ITEMIZED DEDUCTIONS AND THE STANDARD DEDUCTION. In general, taxpayers cannot deduct personal expenses.[5] Congress, however, has chosen to allow taxpayers to deduct specified personal expenses such as charitable contributions and medical expenses. In addition, taxpayers are allowed to itemize expenses related to the production or collection of income, the management of property held for the production of income, and the determination, collection, or refund of any tax.[6]

Taxpayers generally have a choice of claiming either itemized deductions or the standard deduction. The amount of the standard deduction varies depending on the taxpayer's filing status, age, and vision. As a practical matter, for most taxpayers the standard deduction is greater than the total itemized deductions. Taxpayers with small amounts of deductible expenses do not itemize and, in fact, do not have to keep records of medical expenses and other itemized deductions. The relationship between itemized deductions and the standard deduction is discussed later in this chapter.

PERSONAL AND DEPENDENCY EXEMPTIONS. A **personal exemption** is generally allowed for each taxpayer and his or her spouse and an additional dependency exemption is permitted for each dependent. Both personal and dependency exemptions are deductions equal to $2,550 in 1996 and $2,650 in 1997. The amount of an exemption is adjusted annually for increases in the cost of living.

[4] Sec. 63.
[5] Sec. 262.

[6] Sec. 212.

TAXABLE INCOME. **Taxable income** is adjusted gross income reduced by deductions *from* AGI. It is the amount of income that is taxed.

TAX RATES AND GROSS TAX. Tax rates are the percentage rates, set by Congress, at which income is taxed. There are five individual income tax rates: 15%, 28%, 31%, 36%, and 39.6%. Many taxpayers compute their tax by actually multiplying the percentage rates found in the tax rate schedules times taxable income. Most taxpayers, however, simply look in the tax table to find their gross tax. These two alternatives are discussed in more detail later in this chapter. The **gross tax** is the amount of tax determined by this process.

CREDITS AND PREPAYMENTS. **Tax credits**, which include prepayments, are amounts that can be subtracted from the gross tax to arrive at the net tax due or refund due. Prepayments are amounts paid to the government during the year through means such as withholding from wages. These amounts are often called **refundable tax credits**. Nonrefundable tax credits are allowances, such as the dependent care credit, that have been created by Congress for various social, economic, and political reasons. Nonrefundable tax credits can be subtracted from the tax but will not be paid to the taxpayer in situations where the credits exceed the tax. This is logical because no amount has been paid to the government in advance. A partial list of refundable and nonrefundable tax credits can be found in Table I2-5.

TAX FORMULA ILLUSTRATED

The following example illustrates the tax formula and Form 1040.

▼ **TABLE I2-5**
Partial List of Tax Credits

Refundable

    Withholding from wages and back-up withholding
    Excess Social Security taxes paid
    Nonhighway-use gasoline tax
    Earned income credit
    Regulated investment company credit
    Estimated payments
    Overpayment of prior year's tax
    Payments made with extension request

Nonrefundable

    Credit for the elderly and disabled
    Foreign tax credit
    Child and dependent care credit
    Business energy credit
    Qualified electric vehicle credit
    Research and experimentation credit
    Low-income housing credit
    Building rehabilitation credit

EXAMPLE I2-1 ▶ The following facts relate to Larry S. and Jane V. Lane for 1996.

Salary	$70,000
Interest Income:	
Taxable	1,000
Exempt	500
Individual Retirement Account contribution (IRA)	2,000
Itemized deductions	7,300
Personal and dependency exemptions (3 × $2,550)	7,650
Federal income taxes withheld from salary	11,000 ◀

Their tax is computed as follows:

Income:		
	Salary	$70,000
	Taxable interest	1,000
	Exempt interest	500
	Total	$71,500
Minus:	Exclusion:	
	Exempt interest	(500)
Gross income		$71,000
Minus:	Deductions for AGI:	
	IRA contribution	(2,000)
Adjusted gross income		$69,000
Minus:	Deductions from AGI:	
	Itemized deductions	(7,300)
	Personal and dependency exemptions	(7,650)
Taxable income		$54,050
Gross tax (tax table)		$9,928
Minus:	Credits and prepayments	
	Federal income tax withheld	(11,000)
Tax due (refund)		($1,072) ◀

This tax is also computed on Form 1040 (see Figure I2-1). Note that certain additional information such as the taxpayers' address and Social Security numbers is also included on the return.

DEDUCTIONS FROM ADJUSTED GROSS INCOME

ITEMIZED DEDUCTIONS

Itemized deductions are claimed only if the total of such expenses exceeds the standard deduction. Here, consideration is given to which expenses may be itemized and to the relationship between itemized deductions and the standard deduction.

DEDUCTIBLE ITEMS. Congress has chosen to allow taxpayers to itemize specified personal expenses. These specified expenses include medical expenses,[7] taxes,[8] invest-

---

[7] Sec. 213.
[8] Sec. 164.

Form 1040

Department of the Treasury - Internal Revenue Service

U.S. Individual Income Tax Return 1996 (99)

IRS Use Only - Do not write or staple in this space.

For the year Jan. 1-Dec. 31, 1996, or other tax year beginning _____, 1996, ending _____, 19 ___

OMB No. 1545-0074

Label
(See page 11.)

Use the IRS label. Otherwise, please print or type.

Your first name and initial: **Larry S.** Last name: **Lane**

Your social security number: **123 45 6789**

If a joint return, spouse's first name and initial: **Jane V.** Last name: **Lane**

Spouse's social security number: **987 65 4321**

Home address (number and street). If you have a P.O. box, see page 11. **116 E. Edwards** Apt. no.

For help finding line instructions, see pages 2 and 3 in the booklet.

City, town or post office, state, and ZIP code. If you have a foreign address, see page 11. **Lubbock, Texas 79409**

Presidential Election Campaign (See page 11.)

	Yes	No	**Note:** Checking "Yes" will not change your tax or reduce your refund.
Do you want $3 to go to this fund?		X	
If a joint return, does your spouse want $3 to go to this fund?		X	

Filing Status

Check only one box.

1. ☐ Single
2. ☒ Married filing joint return (even if only one had income)
3. ☐ Married filing separate return. Enter spouse's soc. sec. no. above and full name here. ▶
4. ☐ Head of household (with qualifying person). If the qualifying person is a child but not your dependent, enter this child's name here. ▶
5. ☐ Qualifying widow(er) with dependent child (year spouse died ▶ 19 ___).

Exemptions

6a ☒ **Yourself.** If your parent (or someone else) can claim you as a dependent on his or her tax return, do not check box 6a.

b ☒ **Spouse**

No. of boxes checked on 6a and 6b: **2**

c **Dependents:**

(1) First name Last name	(2) Dependent's social security number if born in Dec. 1996, see inst.	(3) Dependent's relationship to you	(4) No. of months lived in your home in 1996
Betty	725 25 7774	Daughter	12

If more than six dependents, see the instructions for line 6c.

No. of your children on 6c who:
● lived with you: **1**
● didn't live with you due to divorce or separation (see instructions)

Dependents on 6c not entered above

Add numbers entered on lines above ▶ **3**

d Total number of exemptions claimed

Income

Attach Copy B of your Forms W-2, W-2G, and 1099-R here.

If you did not get a W-2, see the instructions for line 7.

Enclose, but do not attach, any payment. Also, please enclose Form 1040-V. (see the instructions for line 62).

7	Wages, salaries, tips, etc. Attach Form(s) W-2	7	70,000
8a	**Taxable** interest. Attach Schedule B if over $400	8a	1,000
b	**Tax-exempt** interest . DO NOT include on line 8a	8b	500	
9	Dividend income. Attach Schedule B if over $400	9	
10	Taxable refunds, credits, or offsets of state and local income taxes	10	
11	Alimony received	11	
12	Business income or (loss). Attach Schedule C or C-EZ	12	
13	Capital gain or (loss). If required, attach Schedule D	13	
14	Other gains or (losses). Attach Form 4797	14	
15a	Total IRA distributions 15a ____ b Taxable amount (see instr.)	15b	
16a	Total pensions and annuities 16a ____ b Taxable amount (see instr.)	16b	
17	Rental real estate, royalties, partnerships, S corporations, trusts, etc. Attach Schedule E	17	
18	Farm income or (loss). Attach Schedule F	18	
19	Unemployment compensation	19	
20a	Social security benefits 20a ____ b Taxable amount (see instr.)	20b	
21	Other income. List type and amount - see instructions _____	21	
22	Add the amounts in the far right column for lines 7 through 21. This is your **total income** ▶	22	71,000

Adjusted Gross Income

If line 31 is under $28,495 (under $9,500 if a child did not live with you), see the instructions for line 54.

23 a	Your IRA deduction (see instructions)	23a	2,000	
b	Spouse's IRA deduction (see instructions)	23b		
24	Moving expenses. Attach Form 3903 or 3903-F	24		
25	One-half of self-employment tax. Attach Schedule SE	25		
26	Self-employed health insurance deduction (see inst.)	26		
27	Keogh & self-employed SEP plans. If SEP, check ▶ ☐	27		
28	Penalty on early withdrawal of savings	28		
29	Alimony paid. Recipient's SSN ▶ _____	29		
30	Add lines 23a through 29.	30	2,000
31	Subtract line 30 from line 22. This is your **adjusted gross income.** ▶	31	69,000

LHA **For Privacy Act and Paperwork Reduction Act Notice, see page 7.**

Form **1040** (1996)

FIGURE I2-1 ▶ FORM 1040

2-8

Tax Computation	32	Amount from line 31 (adjusted gross income)				32	69,000

33a Check if: ☐ **You** were 65 or older, ☐ Blind; ☐ **Spouse** was 65 or older, ☐ Blind.

Add the number of boxes checked above and enter the total here ▶ **33a** ☐

b If you are married filing separately and your spouse itemizes deductions

or you were a dual-status alien, see instructions and check here ▶ **33b** ☐

34 Enter the larger of your:

{ **Itemized deductions** from Schedule A, line 28, **OR**

Standard deduction shown below for your filing status. **But** see the instructions if you checked any box on line 33a or b **or** someone can claim you as a dependent.

● Single - $4,000   ● Married filing jointly or Qualifying widow(er) - $6,700

● Head of household - $5,900   ● Married filing separately - $3,350 }

	34	7,300

	35	Subtract line 34 from line 32	35	61,700

36 If line 32 is $88,475 or less, multiply $2,550 by the total number of exemptions claimed on line 6d. If line 32 is over $88,475, see the worksheet in the inst. for the amount to enter | **36** | 7,650

37 **Taxable income.** Subtract line 36 from line 35. If line 36 is more than line 35, enter -0- | **37** | 54,050

38 **Tax.** See instructions. Check if total includes any tax from **a** ☐ Form(s) 8814

b ☐ Form 4972 ▶ | **38** | 9,928

Credits	39	Credit for child and dependent care expenses. Attach Form 2441	39			
	40	Credit for the elderly or the disabled. Attach Schedule R	40			
	41	Foreign tax credit. Attach Form 1116	41			
	42	Other. Check if from **a** ☐ Form 3800 **b** ☐ Form 8396				
		c ☐ Form 8801 **d** ☐ Form (specify) _____	42			
	43	Add lines 39 through 42			43	
	44	Subtract line 43 from line 38. If line 43 is more than line 38, enter -0- ▶			44	9,928

Other Taxes	45	Self-employment tax. Attach Schedule SE		45	
	46	Alternative minimum tax. Attach Form 6251		46	
	47	Social security and Medicare tax on tip income not reported to employer. Attach Form 4137		47	
	48	Tax on qualified retirement plans, including IRAs. If required, attach Form 5329		48	
	49	Advance earned income credit payments from Form(s) W-2		49	
	50	Household employment taxes. Attach Schedule H		50	
	51	Add lines 44 through 50. This is your **total tax** ▶		51	9,928

Payments	52	Federal income tax withheld from Forms W-2 and 1099	52	11,000		
	53	1996 estimated tax payments and amount applied from 1995 return	53			

Attach Forms W-2, W-2G, and 1099-R on the front.

54 **Earned income credit.** Attach Schedule EIC if you have a qualifying child.

Nontaxable earned income: amount ▶ [_____]

and type ▶ _____ | **54** |

	55	Amount paid with Form 4868 (request for extension)	55			
	56	Excess social security and RRTA tax withheld (see inst.)	56			
	57	Other payments. Check if from **a** ☐ Form 2439 **b** ☐ Form 4136	57			
	58	Add lines 52 through 57. These are your **total payments** ▶		58	11,000

Refund	59	If line 58 is more than line 51, subtract line 51 from line 58. This is the amount you **OVERPAID**	59	1,072
	60a	Amount of line 59 you want **REFUNDED TO YOU** ▶	60a	1,072

Have it sent directly to your bank account! See inst. and fill in 60b, c, and d.

b Routing number _____   **c** Type: ☐ Checking ☐ Savings

d Account number _____

61 Amount of line 59 you want **APPLIED TO YOUR 1997 ESTIMATED TAX** ▶ | 61 |

Amount You Owe	62	If line 51 is more than line 58, subtract line 58 from line 51. This is the **AMOUNT YOU OWE.** For details on how to pay and use **Form 1040-V,** see instructions ▶	62	
	63	Estimated tax penalty. Also include on line 62	63	

Sign Here

Keep a copy of this return for your records.

Under penalties of perjury, I declare that I have examined this return and accompanying schedules and statements, and to the best of my knowledge and belief, they are true, correct, and complete. Declaration of preparer (other than taxpayer) is based on all information of which preparer has any knowledge.

▶ Your signature *Larry S. Lane*   Date 4/15/97   Your occupation *Attorney*

▶ Spouse's signature. If a joint return, BOTH must sign. *Jane V. Lane*   Date 4/15/97   Spouse's occupation *Student*

Paid Preparer's Use Only

Preparer's signature ▶ _____   Date _____   Check if self-employed ☐   Preparer's social security no. _____

Firm's name (or yours if self-employed) and address ▶ _____   EIN _____   ZIP code _____

FIGURE 12-1 ▶ FORM 1040 (CONTINUED)

▼ **TABLE I2-6**
Partial List of Itemized Deductions

Medical expenses (over 7.5% of adjusted gross income)
Certain taxes
  State, local, and foreign income and real property taxes
  State and local personal property taxes
Residential interest and investment interest (limited)
Charitable contributions (limited)
Casualty and theft losses (over 10% of adjusted gross income)
Miscellaneous deductions (over 2% of adjusted gross income)
  Employee expenses (e.g., professional and union dues, professional publications, travel, transportation, education, job hunting, office-in-home, special clothing, and 50% of entertainment expenses)
  Expenses for producing investment income (e.g., accounting and legal fees, safe deposit rental, fees paid to an IRA custodian)
  Tax advice and tax return preparation and related costs
Other miscellaneous deductions
  Federal estate tax attributable to income in respect of a decedent
  Gambling losses to the extent of winnings
  Amortization of bond premium
  Amounts restored under claim of right

ment and residential interest,[9] charitable contributions,[10] casualty and theft losses,[11] and employee expenses.[12] In addition, taxpayers are allowed to itemize expenses related to the production or collection of nonbusiness income, the management of property held for the production of income, and the determination, collection, or refund of any tax.[13] A partial list of itemized deductions is found in Table I2-6.

ADDITIONAL COMMENT

The phase-out of itemized deductions for taxpayers in the 36% tax bracket effectively raises their marginal tax rate by 1.08% which could be considered a hidden tax rate.

ITEMIZED DEDUCTION FLOORS. There are four adjusted gross income floors associated with itemized deductions. Three of the floors apply to specific categories of itemized deductions; the remaining floor applies to total itemized deductions. Only medical expenses over 7.5% of adjusted gross income are deductible. Casualty losses over 10% of AGI and miscellaneous deductions over 2% of AGI are deductible. In 1997, taxpayers must reduce total itemized deductions by the lesser of 3% of AGI over $121,200 ($60,600 for married people filing separate returns) or 80% of the itemized deductions that are otherwise allowable.[14] In 1996, the reduction amount was $117,950 ($58,975 for married individuals filing a separate return).

EXAMPLE I2-2 ▶

In 1997, John and Jane file a joint tax return and report AGI of $150,000. Their itemized deductions include $14,000 of medical expenses and home mortgage interest of $10,000. The AGI floor reduces the medical expense deduction to $2,750 [$14,000 − (0.075 × $150,000)]. The remaining $10,000 of itemized deductions is further reduced to $9,136 [$10,000 − 0.03 × ($150,000 − $121,200)] as a result of the overall floor for itemized deductions. Thus, the total itemized deductions allowed for 1997 would be $11,886 ($2,750 + $9,136). ◀

[9] Sec. 163.
[10] Sec. 170.
[11] Sec. 165(c)(3).
[12] Sec. 67.
[13] Sec. 212.

[14] The reduction in the itemized deductions cannot exceed 80% of the total itemized deductions other than medical expenses, investment interest expenses, casualty losses, and wagering losses. (See Chapter I7 for a discussion of the 80% overall limitation.)

<table>
<tr><td style="width:22%"></td><td>

STANDARD DEDUCTION

Itemized deductions are claimed only if the total amount of such deductions exceeds the standard deduction. The **standard deduction** is a floor set by Congress. It varies depending on the taxpayer's filing status, age, and vision.

</td></tr>
</table>

OBJECTIVE 2

Determine the amount allowable for the standard deduction

KEY POINT

The dollar amount of the standard deduction generally increases each year because it is indexed to the rate of inflation.

Filing Status	Standard Deduction 1996	Standard Deduction 1997
Single individual other than heads of households	$4,000	$4,150
Married couples filing joint returns and surviving spouses	6,700	6,900
Married people filing separate returns	3,350	3,450
Heads of households	5,900	6,050

The differences between the 1996 and 1997 amounts represent adjustments for the increase in the cost of living.

In 1997, a married taxpayer's standard deduction is increased by $800 if he or she is elderly or blind ($1,600 if the taxpayer is elderly and blind) or has a spouse who is elderly or blind (for a maximum possible increase of $3,200). If an unmarried taxpayer is elderly or blind, his or her standard deduction is increased by $1,000 ($2,000 if the taxpayer is elderly and blind). Thus, in 1997, a single taxpayer age 65 is entitled to a $5,150 standard deduction.

▶ The increase in the standard deduction for elderly taxpayers is available if the taxpayer turns 65 during the tax year. It is interesting that a taxpayer is considered to be age 65 on the day before his or her sixty-fifth birthday. The adjustment is allowed on the final return of a deceased taxpayer only if he or she reached age 65 before death.

▶ The IRC defines blindness as corrected vision in the better eye of no better than 20/200 or a field of no greater than 20 degrees. Vision is determined as of the last day of the tax year or, in the case of a deceased taxpayer, as of the date of death.

The purpose of the standard deduction is to simplify the computation. As previously noted, for most taxpayers the standard deduction is greater than total itemized deductions. Those taxpayers do not itemize and, in fact, do not even have to keep records of medical expenses and other itemized deductions.

Who actually itemizes and who does not? Home mortgage interest and property taxes are deductible. Therefore, homeowners who pay home mortgage interest and property taxes often itemize because those expenses alone usually exceed the standard deduction. Also, higher-income taxpayers are more likely to itemize than lower-income taxpayers simply because they incur more expenses that can be itemized. This is true even though the AGI floors (previously discussed) affect higher-income taxpayers more than lower-income taxpayers.

EXAMPLE 12-3 ▶

In 1997, Joan is single, and a homeowner who incurs property taxes on her home of $3,000, state and local taxes of $500, and mortgage interest of $2,000. Joan's adjusted gross income is $30,000. Her taxable income is computed as follows:

Adjusted gross income			$30,000
Minus:	Itemized deductions:		
	State and local taxes	$ 500	
	Property taxes	3,000	
	Mortgage interest	2,000	(5,500)
Minus:	Personal exemption		(2,650)
Taxable income			$21,850

◀

EXAMPLE I2-4 ▶ Assume the same facts as in Example I2-3 except that Joan is not a homeowner. Thus, she has no property taxes or mortgage interest but does pay rent of $600 per month. Her taxable income is computed as follows:

Adjusted gross income	$30,000
Minus: Standard deduction	(4,150)
Minus: Personal exemption	(2,650)
Taxable income	$23,200 ◀

Joan would use the standard deduction because it ($4,150) is greater than her itemized deduction ($500).

LOSS OF THE STANDARD DEDUCTION. Congress has decided that a few taxpayers should not be permitted to use the standard deduction. The standard deduction is unavailable to three categories of taxpayers who would otherwise receive an unintended tax benefit:[15]

▶ An individual filing a return for a period less than twelve months because of a change in accounting period.

▶ A married taxpayer filing a separate return in instances where the other spouse itemizes.

▶ Nonresident aliens.

To illustrate why Congress does not permit certain taxpayers to claim the standard deduction, consider what could happen if a married couple files separate returns but only one spouse itemizes. On a separate return in 1997 when the standard deduction is $3,450, one spouse could claim all itemized deductions while the other uses the standard deduction.

EXAMPLE I2-5 ▶ Clay and Joy, a married couple, have incomes of $15,000 and $14,000, respectively. Their itemized deductions total $4,500. They would claim a $6,900 standard deduction on a joint return. If Clay filed a separate return and claimed all of the deductions, his itemized deductions of $4,500 would be greater than the standard deduction. If Joy could claim the standard deduction on her return, their total deductions would equal $7,950 ($4,500 + $3,450). The law, however, requires that they both itemize or that they both use the standard deduction. ◀

Limitation on the Standard Deduction. A special rule applies to any individual for whom a dependency exemption is allowable to another taxpayer. The standard deduction of the dependent is limited to the greater of 1) the dependent's earned income, or 2) $650. The purpose of this limitation is to prevent parents from shifting unearned income, such as interest and dividends, to their children in order to use their standard deduction.

EXAMPLE I2-6 ▶ Webb and Beth are married, in the 36% marginal tax rate bracket and have one son, Vincent, age 15. Vincent has no income and is claimed as a dependent by his parents. Webb and Beth transfer stocks and bonds to Vincent which earn $3,000 in dividends and interest. Their goal is to shift the $3,000 of income to Vincent to utilize his standard deduction. However, since Vincent is claimed as a dependent by his parents on their return, Vincent's standard deduction is limited to $650, i.e., the *greater* of $650 or his earned income ($0). ◀

EXAMPLE I2-7 ▶ Assume the same facts as in Example I2-6 except Vincent has a part-time job and earns $2,000 in wages. Vincent's standard deduction would be $2,000. Alternatively, if Vincent's wages were $5,000, his standard deduction would be $4,150 (the maximum for a single individual). ◀

---

[15] Sec. 63(c)(6).

OBJECTIVE 3

Determine the amount and the correct number of personal and dependency exemptions

PERSONAL·EXEMPTIONS

In general, taxpayers cannot deduct personal expenses except for certain itemized deductions that are specifically authorized under the tax law. Congress has recognized the need to protect a small amount of income from tax in order to allow the taxpayer to meet personal expenses. Thus, almost every individual taxpayer is allowed a personal exemption of $2,550 in 1996 and $2,650 in 1997. Because there are two taxpayers on a joint return filed by a married couple, there are two personal exemptions. In addition, if a married person files a separate return, the taxpayer can claim a personal exemption for his or her spouse if the spouse has no gross income during the year and the spouse is not the dependent of another taxpayer.[16]

Under current law there is only one exemption for each person. Therefore, if an individual can be claimed as a dependent by another person, that individual is not entitled to a personal exemption on his or her own return. Despite the loss of the personal exemption, most dependents owe little or no tax. Since a person who may be claimed as a dependency exemption typically has a very low amount of income, he or she is usually able to use the standard deduction to offset any income they may have.

DEPENDENCY EXEMPTIONS

ADDITIONAL COMMENT

One should forsake any preconceived notions as to what constitutes a dependent before examining the dependency tests.

KEY POINT

For someone to be claimed as a dependent, *all* five dependency tests must be satisfied.

In addition to claiming one personal exemption, an individual may claim an exemption for each dependent. An individual qualifies as a dependent only if he or she **meets all five** of the following tests:[17]

▶ Support: The taxpayer must provide over 50% of the dependent's support.

▶ Gross income: The dependent's gross income must be less than the amount of the exemption. A taxpayer's children who are either, (1) full-time students and under age 24 or (2) under the age of 19, are exempt from this requirement.

▶ Joint return: In general, a married dependent cannot file a joint return.

▶ Relationship: Dependents must either be related to the taxpayer or reside with the taxpayer.

▶ Citizenship: Dependents must either be U.S. citizens, residents, or nationals or reside in Canada or Mexico.

The full exemption is available for dependents who are born or die during the year. No exemption is available for unborn or stillborn children. All dependents must have social security numbers, and the numbers must be correctly reported on the taxpayer's return.[18]

SUPPORT TEST. The taxpayer normally must provide over one-half of the dependent's financial support during the year. Support includes amounts spent by the taxpayer, the dependent, and other individuals. Welfare[19] and Social Security benefits[20] spent on support count even if they are excluded from gross income.

EXAMPLE I2-8 ▶ Tarer provided $3,000 of support for his mother, Mary. Tarer's sister provided $1,000. Mary spent $4,500 of her savings for her own support. Because Mary provided over half of her own support, she cannot be claimed as a dependent. ◀

EXAMPLE I2-9 ▶ George's father received Social Security benefits of $6,600, of which $1,800 was deposited into a savings account. He spent the remaining $4,800 on food, clothing, and lodging. George

---

[16] Sec. 151(b).
[17] Sec. 152.
[18] Sec. 151(e). The IRS has the authority to disallow dependency exemptions for otherwise qualified dependents without social security numbers and with incorrectly reported social security numbers. A missing or incorrectly

reported social security number may also bar an otherwise eligible individual from claiming head-of-household filing status.
[19] Rev. Rul. 71-468, 1971-2 C.B. 115.
[20] Rev. Ruls. 57-344, 1957-2 C.B. 112, and 58-419, 1958-2 C.B. 57.

spent $5,600 to support his father. George meets the support test because the amount saved is not counted in the support test. ◄

Support includes amounts spent for food, clothing, shelter, medical and dental care, education, and the like.[21] Support is not limited to these items.[22] Support does not include the value of services rendered by the taxpayer to the dependent.[23] A scholarship received by a son or daughter[24] is not counted as support in deciding whether a parent provided over one half of the child's support.[25] Also, the IRS and the courts have excluded various other expenses from support.[26]

Generally, the amount of support is equal to the cost of the item, but in the case of support provided in a noncash form, such as lodging, the amount of support is equal to the fair market value or fair rental value. The cost of an item such as a television or an automobile is included in support if the item actually is support.[27]

EXAMPLE I2-10 ▶

Vicki's mother lives with her. Vicki purchases clothing for her mother costing $800, and provides her with a room that Vicki estimates she could rent for $2,800. Vicki spent $2,500 for groceries she shared with her mother and $1,200 for utilities. In addition, Vicki purchased a television for $750 that she placed in the living room. Vicki and her mother both used the television. Vicki's support for her mother, at a minimum, includes:

Clothing	$ 800
Rental value of room	2,800
Food	1,250
Total	$4,850

Whether a portion of the utilities could be included in support would depend on whether the rental rate for the room included utilities. The fact that the mother used the television set probably would not be sufficient to cause its cost to be viewed as support. On the other hand, if the television set was a gift to the mother, was placed in her room, and was used exclusively by her, the cost would probably qualify as support. ◄

If a taxpayer contributes a lump sum for the support of two or more individuals, the amount is allocated between the individuals on a pro rata basis unless there is proof to the contrary.[28]

EXAMPLE I2-11 ▶

Jaime pays rent of $6,000 for an apartment occupied by his sisters Alice, Beth, and Cindy. Alice spends $3,000 toward her own support, Beth spends $1,000, and Cindy spends $1,000. Jaime is assumed to have provided $2,000 of support for each sister. Thus, assuming the other four tests are met, Jaime can claim exemptions for Beth and Cindy, but not for Alice. ◄

As stated, a taxpayer normally must provide over one-half of a dependent's support. There are two exceptions:

---

[21] Reg. Sec. 1.152-1(a)(2)(i).

[22] Examples of other items that have been held to be support include church contributions (Rev. Rul. 58-67, 1958-1 C.B. 62), telephone (*William K. Price, III,* 1961 PH T.C. Memo ¶61,173, 20 TCM 886), medical insurance premiums (*James Edward Parker,* 1959 PH T.C. Memo ¶52,182, 18 TCM 800), child care (*Marvin D. Tucker,* 1957 PH T.C. Memo ¶57,118, 16 TCM 488), toys (*Loren S. Brumber,* 1952 PH T.C. Memo ¶52,087, 11 TCM 289), and vacations (*George R. Melat,* 1953 PH T.C. Memo ¶53,141, 12 TCM 443).

[23] *Frank Markarian v. CIR.,* 16 AFTR 2d 5785, 65-2 USTC ¶9699 (7th Cir., 1965).

[24] Including adopted children, stepchildren, and foster children (if the foster children live with the taxpayer for the entire year).

[25] Sec. 152(d).

[26] Examples of items that have been excluded are funeral expenses (Rev. Rul. 65-307, 1965-2 C.B. 40), taxes (Rev. Rul. 58-67, 1958-1 C.B. 62), a rifle, lawn mower, and boat insurance (*Harriet C. Flower v. U.S.,* 52 AFTR 1383, 57-1 USTC ¶9655 (D.C. Pa., 1957)), and life insurance premiums (*John F. Miller,* 1959 PH T.C. Memo ¶59,155, 18 TCM 673).

[27] Rev. Rul. 77-282, 1977-2 C.B. 52.

[28] Rev. Rul. 64-222, 1964-2 C.B. 47.

SELF-STUDY QUESTION

A parent provides $4,000 of support for his 17-year-old son. The son earns $5,000 during the year but only spends $3,000 for his own support. Will the parent be considered to have provided over 50% of the son's support?

ANSWER

Yes; only the amount actually spent by the son is taken into account.

▶ A multiple support declaration permits one member of a group of taxpayers who collectively provide over 50% of an individual's support to claim a dependency exemption.

▶ Special rules determine which parent will receive dependency exemptions for children in the case of a divorce.

Often several people contribute to the support of a dependent. Under normal rules, no one would be able to claim a dependency exemption unless one member of the group provided over one-half of the total support. When no member of the group provides over one-half of the support, eligible members of the group may decide to allow one group member to claim the exemption. Each eligible member (other than the taxpayer receiving the exemption) must complete a Multiple Support Declaration (Form 2120) that states he or she will not claim a dependency exemption under these rules. An individual must contribute more than 10% of the dependent's support and meet all requirements for claiming a dependency exemption except the support requirement.[29]

EXAMPLE I2-12 ▶

John T. Abel lives alone. His support comes from the following sources:

John	$ 400
Son	2,800
Daughter	2,000
Friend	2,800
Total	$8,000

Either the son or daughter can claim a dependency exemption if the other completes Form 2120. The friend cannot claim a dependency exemption because the friend is not related and Abel does not live with the friend. For this reason the friend need not complete Form 2120. A completed Form 2120 is illustrated in Figure I2-2. ◀

As noted, special rules determine which parent will receive dependency exemptions for children in the case of a divorce or separation.[30] These rules are intended to avoid disputes over who provided more than one-half of a child's support. Generally, the parent who has custody of a child for the greater part of the year is entitled to the dependency exemption even if he or she did not provide over one-half of the child's support.[31]

The noncustodial parent may claim the dependency exemption only if the custodial parent agrees in writing. The signed statement must be attached to the noncustodial parent's return each year in which the exemption is claimed. Form 8332 may be used for this purpose (see Appendix B). In the case of a divorce or separation, the custodial spouse would probably be reluctant to relinquish the dependency exemption for a child. A noncustodial parent might be able to negotiate the exemption in exchange for increased child support payments.

EXAMPLE I2-13 ▶

In the current year, Hal and Pam obtain a divorce under the terms of which Pam receives custody of their son. Hal is ordered to pay $600 per month of child support. In absence of a written agreement to the contrary, Pam will receive the dependency exemption for the child. ◀

---

[29] Sec. 152(c).

[30] Including adopted children, stepchildren, and foster children (if the foster children live with the taxpayer for the entire year).

[31] This assumes that together the parents provided over one-half of the support, that no multiple support agreement is in effect, that together the parents had custody of the child for over one-half of the year, and that the parents were divorced, separated, or lived apart for the last half of the year (Sec. 152[e]).

Form **2120** (Rev. January 1994) Department of the Treasury Internal Revenue Service	**Multiple Support Declaration** ▶ Attach to Form 1040 or Form 1040A of Person Claiming the Dependent.	OMB No. 1545-0071 Expires 1-31-97 Attachment Sequence No. **50**

Name of person claiming the dependent

Gabe I. Abel

Social security number 123 45 6789

During the calendar year 19 ...96..., I paid over 10% of the support of

John T. Abel

Name of person

I could have claimed this person as a dependent except that I did not pay over 50% of his or her support. I understand that this person named above is being claimed as a dependent on the income tax return of

Gabe I. Abel

Name

111 W. Baker St. Lawrenceville, NJ 08649

Address

I agree not to claim this person as a dependent on my Federal income tax return for any tax year that began in this calendar year.

Mable B. Abel

Your signature

222 11 0001

Your social security number

4/15/96

Date

402 N. Lable Lane

Address (number, street, apt. no.)

Lawrenceville, NJ 08649

City, state, and ZIP code

FIGURE I2-2 ▶ FORM 2120

EXAMPLE I2-14 ▶ Assume the same facts as in Example I2-12 except that Pam negotiates child support payments of $800 per month and agrees in writing to allow Hal to claim the dependency exemption for the child. The written agreement will enable Hal to claim the dependency exemption for the child. ◀

EXAMPLE I2-15

SELF-STUDY QUESTION

A taxpayer provides more than 50% of the support for his elderly father, whose only source of income is $3,000 from the rental of a bedroom in his house and $8,000 from Social Security. There are rental expenses of $1,200. Can the taxpayer claim his father as a dependent?

ANSWER

No, the father has $3,000 of gross income. The rental expenses are deducted in arriving at AGI, not gross income.

Andy and Beth obtain a divorce under the terms of which they share custody of their daughter. Whoever has custody for the greater part of the year receives the dependency exemption for the daughter unless they agree otherwise in writing. ◀

GROSS INCOME TEST. Generally, a dependent's gross income must be less than the amount of the dependency exemption. The statutory definition of gross income is used in applying this limitation. Therefore, nontaxable scholarships, tax-exempt bond interest, and nontaxable Social Security benefits are not considered, but salary, taxable interest, and rent are considered in deciding whether the person meets the limitation.

A very important exception to this requirement exempts from the gross income limitation the taxpayer's children who are either under age 19 or, in the case of full-time students, under age 24.[32] A child is considered to be a student if he or she is in full-time attendance at a qualified educational institution during at least five months of the year. To be full-time, a student must carry the number of hours or courses the educational institution requires a student to take in order to be considered full-time. Note, however, that this is only an exception to the gross income test. Therefore, a self-supporting student cannot be claimed as a dependent by his or her parents. Such a student fails the support test.

EXAMPLE I2-16 ▶ Jim, age 22, is a college student and receives more than half of his support from his parents. Jim earned $6,000 from a summer job. Even though Jim earned more than the dependency exemption amount of $2,650 (1997), his parents may claim him as a dependent because the gross income test is waived and all of the other tests are met. Jim, of course, would not be able

---

[32] Including adopted children, stepchildren, and foster children (if the foster children live with the taxpayer for the entire year).

to claim himself on his own return.

One of the important details of this test is that the dependent must be a *child* of the taxpayer. Thus, if Jim was supported by his aunt and uncle (rather than his parents), the aunt and uncle could not claim Jim because the gross income test is not met. ◀

JOINT RETURN TEST. Generally, a taxpayer loses the dependency exemption if a married dependent files a joint return. However, a taxpayer is entitled to the exemption if the dependent files a joint return solely to claim a refund of tax withheld (i.e., there is no tax on the joint return and there would have been no tax on two separate returns).[33] It is important for married dependents to weigh the taxes that would be saved by the family from an exemption against the taxes that would be saved by filing a joint return. Depending on the circumstances, either alternative may be more beneficial.

TYPICAL MISCONCEPTION

It is sometimes incorrectly believed that in order to claim someone as a dependent, the person must in all cases reside in the home of the taxpayer. They do not always realize that residency is a substitute for the relationship test.

RELATIONSHIP TEST. In order to be claimed as a dependent, a person must be related to the taxpayer or reside with the taxpayer for the entire tax year.[34] Immediate family relationships include those based on blood, adoption, and marriage, and extended family relationships include only those based on blood and adoption.

Immediate family relationships include

▶ Parent (including adoptive parent, stepparent, mother-in-law, and father-in-law)
▶ Sibling (including adoptive sibling, stepbrother, stepsister, brother-in-law, sister-in-law, half brother, and half sister)
▶ Child (including adoptive child, stepchild, son-in-law, daughter-in-law, and foster children who live with the taxpayer for the entire year)

Extended family relationships include

▶ Grandparents and their ancestors
▶ Grandchildren and their descendants
▶ Aunts and uncles
▶ Nephews and nieces

EXAMPLE I2-17 ▶ Jesse supports three people: Tina, an unrelated child who lives with him; his cousin Judy, who lives in another state; and his mother Vicki, who lives in her own home. Jesse can claim two dependency exemptions: one for Tina, who lives with Jesse (a person who lives with the taxpayer need not be related) and one for his mother. Jesse cannot claim a dependency exemption for Judy (cousins do not meet the relationship test). ◀

On a joint return it is necessary only that a dependent be related to one spouse.[35] Once established, an immediate family relationship is not terminated by death or divorce.

EXAMPLE I2-18 ▶ Ken and Lisa support Lisa's mother and claim her as a dependent on a joint return. Following Lisa's death, Ken continues to support Lisa's mother. Lisa's mother continues to be Ken's mother-in-law and can be claimed as a dependent by Ken. On the other hand, if Ken and Lisa had been supporting Lisa's niece, Ken would not be entitled to a dependency exemption.

---

[33] Rev. Ruls. 54-567, 1954-2 C.B. 108, and 65-34, 1965-1 C.B. 86. The theory is that the taxpayer is filing a claim for refund and not actually filing a tax return.
[34] The relationship between the taxpayer and the dependent cannot violate a local law (Sec. 152[b] [5]). The exemption has been disallowed where the relationship constituted "cohabitation" and was illegal in the state (*Cassius L. Peacock, III,*, 1978 PH T.C. Memo ¶78,030, 37 TCM 177).
[35] Reg. Sec. 1.152-2(d).

Although she would continue to be Ken's niece, she is not his niece by blood and cannot be claimed as a dependent unless she resides with Ken. ◄

CITIZENSHIP TEST. A dependent must be either a U.S. citizen,[36] national,[37] or resident,[38] or a resident of Canada or Mexico. The citizenship or residence test need only be met for part of the year.

PHASE-OUT OF PERSONAL AND DEPENDENCY EXEMPTIONS. Both personal and dependency exemptions are phased out for high-income taxpayers. Exemptions are phased out at a rate of 2% for each $2,500 ($1,250 for married people filing separate returns), or fraction thereof, of adjusted gross income above thresholds shown below. Thus, more than $122,500 ($61,250 on separate returns) of adjusted gross income above the threshold results in the phase-out of the entire amount of the taxpayer's personal and dependency exemptions.[39] Below are the phase-out amounts for 1997:

	Phase-Out Begins	*Phase-Out Ends (More Than)*
Single	$121,200	$243,700
Joint return	181,800	304,300
Head of household	151,500	274,000
Married, filing separately	90,900	152,150

EXAMPLE I2-19 ►

In 1997 Lee, a single taxpayer with no dependents, reports AGI of $131,200. The usual amount of the personal exemption of $2,650 is reduced by 8% to $2,438 ($10,000 ÷ $2,500 = 4; 4 × 2% = 8%). ◄

Note that the phase-out begins when the taxpayer's adjusted gross income *exceeds* the threshold. Thus, a single taxpayer with AGI of $121,200 is entitled to the full amount of his or her personal and dependency exemptions, whereas a single taxpayer with AGI of $121,201 is entitled to only 98% of his or her personal and dependency exemptions.

STOP & THINK

Question: Jack and Leslie, who have four dependent children, are in the process of getting a divorce. Leslie is a surgeon and earns a net income of $400,000 per year from her medical practice. Jack is a pilot and earns a salary of $140,000. The only other source of income for either person is $20,000 of income from interest and dividends which will be divided equally. One major stumbling block in structuring the divorce settlement is which person will be allowed to claim the children as dependency exemptions. Either Jack or Leslie will qualify under the income tax rules to claim any or all of the children and both will qualify for head-of-household filing status. The attorneys have come to you for advice. From an income tax standpoint, which parent would benefit the most from being able to claim the children in 1997, or should they each claim two of the children?

---

[36] U.S. citizens living in foreign countries can claim dependency exemptions for adopted children even if the children are not U.S. citizens.

[37] A U.S. national is an individual born in an outlying possession such as American Samoa.

[38] A resident is a person who is not a U.S. citizen and who is legally residing in the United States with intent to stay here permanently (see Sec. 7701(b)).

[39] Sec. 151(d). The thresholds are adjusted for inflation. In 1996, the phase-out began at $117,950 for single taxpayers, $176,950 for a joint return, $147,450 for a head of household, and $88,475 for a married individual filing a separate return.

Topic Review I2-1

Personal and Dependency Exemptions

Exemptions in General

▶ One exemption is available for each taxpayer (except when the taxpayer is the dependent of another) and for each dependent.

▶ The amount of each exemption, which is adjusted annually for inflation, is $2,650 in 1996 and $2,550 in 1995.

▶ Exemptions are phased out for high-income taxpayers. For example, on a joint return the phase-out begins when the couple's adjusted gross income exceeds $181,800 and is completed when AGI exceeds $304,300.

Dependency Exemptions

▶ One exemption is allowed for each dependent. As noted above, the exemptions are phased out for higher-income taxpayers.

▶ Five conditions must be met for each dependency exemption. The dependent must be supported by the taxpayer, must meet a gross income test, generally must not file a joint return, must be related to the taxpayer (or live with the taxpayer), and must meet a citizenship or residence test.

Solution: Since Leslie's income is well above the 1997 phase-out limit for personal and dependency exemptions ($274,000), she would not receive any tax benefit from claiming any or all of the children for income tax purposes. Jack, on the other hand, will get a tax benefit from the dependency exemptions because the phase-out amounts for a taxpayer filing as head of household begin at $151,500 and his AGI is only $150,000 ($140,000 + $10,000). Therefore, for income tax purposes only, Jack should claim the four children since he will receive a tax benefit from the dependency exemptions, whereas Leslie would receive no tax benefit if she claimed the children because her AGI is so high that her deduction for personal and dependency exemptions would be zero.

The rules for deducting personal and dependency exemptions are summarized in Topic Review I2-1.

DETERMINING THE AMOUNT OF TAX

Once taxable income has been computed, the next step is to determine the gross tax. Most individuals determine the amount of gross tax by looking in the tax table (Appendix A). This allows the taxpayer to arrive at the gross tax without the need for multiplication and, therefore, simplifies the computation and reduces the number of errors. Individuals are required to use the tax table unless taxable income exceeds the maximum income in the table (currently $100,000), or if the taxpayer files a short period return on account of a change in the annual accounting period.

Taxpayers who cannot use the tax table instead use the tax rate schedule (located after Chapter 18). Taxpayers using the tax rate schedule must actually compute the tax.

EXAMPLE I2-20 ▶ Liz is single and has taxable income of $48,210 in 1996. Liz's tax is determined by reference to the tax table for single taxpayers. (At the time of this writing, the 1996 tax table was the most recent available.) The tax from the table is $10,383. ◀

EXAMPLE I2-21 ▶ Jack and Pam are married, file a joint tax return, and have taxable income of $105,000 in 1997. They will use the tax rate schedule to compute their tax. The tax is computed as follows:

Tax on $41,200 at 0.15	$ 6,180.00
Tax on next $58,400 at 0.28	16,352.00
Tax on remaining $5,400 at 0.31	1,674.00
Gross tax	$24,206.00

This tax can also be computed by using the rate schedule (Schedule Y) as follows:

$$\$22,532 + [(\$105,000 - \$99,600) \times .31] = \underline{\$24,206}$$ ◀

FILING STATUS

There are five tax brackets applicable to individual taxpayers: 15%, 28%, 31%, 36%, and 39.6%. These rates are progressive in that as a taxpayer's income increases, the taxpayer moves into higher tax brackets. The income level at which higher tax brackets begin depends on the taxpayer's filing status. There are four rate schedules and/or tax tables and five different filing statuses. This is because married couples filing jointly and certain surviving spouses use the same rate schedule or tax table. The five filing statuses are

▶ Joint
▶ Surviving spouse
▶ Head of household
▶ Single
▶ Married filing separately

KEY POINT

Currently the highest tax rates are those for married filing separately, and the lowest are those for married filing jointly.

SELF-STUDY QUESTION

If Congress were to adopt a truly proportional tax system, would it be necessary to have the four different tax rate schedules?

ANSWER

No, in a proportional tax system, there is no need for different rate schedules because all taxable income would be taxed at the same rate.

Before 1948, one rate schedule was used by all taxpayers. If a husband and wife both had income, each filed a return. This was deemed to be unfair because various states allocated income between spouses differently. Some states used a community property law system while other states used a common law system. Today, only a few states continue to use the community property law[40] system.

In general, community property law allocates community income equally between a husband and wife, regardless of which spouse actually earned the income. In other states, income belongs to the spouse who produces the income. With a progressive tax system, placing income on one return instead of two can result in a much greater tax. For this reason, couples residing in noncommunity property states often paid more tax than their counterparts who resided in community property states. In 1948, Congress developed the joint-rate schedule to rectify this problem.[40] Unmarried taxpayers who headed families felt they should also receive tax relief because they

---

[40] Several states had either adopted or had begun to adopt community property laws in order to reduce the federal taxes paid by their residents. After the joint rate schedule was created, states without a tradition of community property law returned to common law.

shared their incomes with their families. So, in 1957, Congress created a rate schedule for heads of households. In 1971, single taxpayers requested and received their own rate schedule. Here we shall consider who is covered by each filing status.

JOINT RETURN

A *joint return* can be filed by a man and woman if they meet certain tests.

▶ They must be legally married as of the last day of the tax year.[41] Whether a couple is married depends on the laws of the state of residence.[42] Couples in the process of a divorce are still considered married before to the date the divorce becomes final. A couple need not be living together in order to file a joint return. A joint return can be filed if one spouse dies during the year as long as the survivor does not remarry before the year-end. The executor of the estate must agree to the filing of a joint return.

▶ They must have the same tax year-end (except in the case of death).[43]

▶ Both the husband and wife must be U.S. citizens or residents.[44] An exception allows a joint return if the nonresident alien spouse agrees to report all of his or her income on the return.[45]

STOP & THINK

Question: Some couples who get married may find their tax liabilities increase even if their combined incomes remain unchanged. Others find that their tax liabilities decrease. Explain why taxes increase for some couples, but decrease for others.

Solution: Couples who marry ordinarily move from two returns where incomes are taxed using the rate schedule for single individuals to one return where the combined incomes are taxed using the joint rate schedule. The less progressive joint rate schedule results in a lower tax if one spouse had most of the income because more of that spouse's income is taxed at lower rates. However, when the husband and wife had approximately equal incomes, their combined incomes are taxed at higher rates on one joint return. Even though the rate schedule for married couples is the least progressive of the individual rate schedules, the combined tax is higher because the second income is added to the first and taxed at higher rates.

SURVIVING SPOUSE

A widow or widower can file a joint return for the year his or her spouse dies if the widow or widower does not remarry. For either of the two years after the year of death, the widow or widower can file as a surviving spouse only if he or she meets specific conditions. The **surviving spouse** (sometimes called a qualifying widow or widower) must[46]

▶ Have not remarried as of the year end in which surviving spouse status is claimed.

▶ Be a U.S. citizen or resident.

▶ Have qualified to file a joint return in the year of death.

---

[41] Sec. 6013.

[42] Thus, common law marriages recognized by the state of residence are covered. On the other hand, an annulled marriage is viewed as never having been valid. Thus, such a couple cannot file a joint return.

[43] Sec. 6013(a)(2).

[44] Sec. 6013(a)(1).

[45] Nonresident aliens are taxed only on income earned in the United States. If a joint return is filed by a U.S. citizen and his or her foreign spouse, they would receive the benefit of the low rate schedule, even though only the U.S. citizen reported income on the return. Thus, to file a joint return, the couple must agree to report both incomes (Sec. 6013(g)).

[46] Sec. 2(a).

▶ Have at least one dependent child[47] living at home during the entire year and the taxpayer must pay over half of the expenses of the home

In the year of death, a joint return can be filed. On the joint return the income of the deceased spouse (earned before death) and the survivor are both reported. Personal exemptions are allowed for both spouses. In the two years following death, surviving spouse status can be claimed only if the conditions outlined above are met. Only the surviving spouse's income is reported and, of course, no personal exemption is available for the deceased spouse. What the two situations have in common is that in both instances, the taxpayer can use the more favorable joint rate schedule.

EXAMPLE I2-22 ▶ Connie's husband dies in 1997. Connie can file a joint return, even though her husband died before the year end. Alternatively, Connie can file as a married individual filing a separate return. In 1998, however, Connie must file as a single taxpayer if she has no dependent who would qualify her as a surviving spouse or a head of household. ◀

HEAD OF HOUSEHOLD

A second rate schedule or tax table is available to a head of household. The head of household rates are significantly higher than those applicable to married taxpayers filing jointly and surviving spouses, but lower than those applicable to other single taxpayers. To claim head-of-household status, a taxpayer must[48]

▶ Be unmarried as of the last day of the tax year. Exceptions apply to individuals married to nonresident aliens[49] and to abandoned spouses.[50] An individual cannot claim head-of-household status in the year his or her spouse died. Such individuals must file a joint return or a separate return.

▶ Not be a surviving spouse.

▶ Be a U.S. citizen or resident.

▶ Pay over half of the costs of maintaining as his or her home a household in which a dependent relative lives for more than half of the tax year. The dependency exemption cannot be based on a multiple support agreement. There are two special rules. First, a taxpayer with a dependent parent qualifies even if the parent does not live with the taxpayer. Second, if an unmarried descendant lives with the taxpayer,[51] that descendant need not be the taxpayer's dependent.

The second exception deserves note as it often comes into play in cases of divorced parents. As noted earlier in the chapter, a written agreement can give the dependency exemption to the noncustodial parent. The rule here may allow the custodial parent to still claim head-of-household status.

EXAMPLE I2-23 ▶ Brad and Ellen divorce. Ellen receives custody of their child and Brad is ordered by the court to pay child support of $6,000 per year. Ellen agrees in writing to allow Brad to claim the dependency exemption for the child. If Ellen maintains the home in which she and her child live, she can claim head-of-household status even though the child is Brad's dependent. ◀

---

[47] Includes an adopted child, a stepchild, or a foster child. Most often, individuals are widowed late in life after their children are grown. As a result, most survivors cannot claim surviving spouse status.

[48] Sec. 2(b).

[49] Specifically, this refers to an individual married to a nonresident alien if he or she meets the remaining head-of-household requirements.

[50] Abandoned spouse rules are discussed under a separate heading later in this chapter.

[51] Includes an adopted child, stepchild, and a descendant of a natural or adopted child.

Topic Review I2-2

Filing Status and Requirements

Filing Status	Must Maintain Household	Must Have Dependent	Marital Status	Must Be Citizen	Tax Rates
Joint	No requirement	No	Married	Yes	Lowest rates, but two incomes are included
Surviving spouse	Yes	Yes, son or daughter	Widowed in prior or second prior year	Yes	Uses same schedule as married couple filing joint return
Head of household	Yes	Generally, yes	Generally, single	Yes	Intermediate tax rates
Single	No requirement	No	Single	No	Highest tax rates for unmarried taxpayers
Separate	No requirement	No	Married	No	Highest tax rates

As noted, the taxpayer must pay over half of the costs of maintaining the household. These expenses include property taxes, mortgage interest, rent, utility charges, upkeep and repairs, property insurance, and food consumed on the premises. Such costs do not include clothing, education, medical treatment, vacations, life insurance, transportation, or the value of services provided by the taxpayer.[52]

ADDITIONAL COMMENT

In 1992 approximately thirty married couples filed joint returns for every married couple that filed separately.

SINGLE TAXPAYER

An unmarried individual who does not qualify as a surviving spouse or a head of household must file as a single taxpayer. The tax rates are higher than those that apply to other unmarried taxpayers.

EXAMPLE I2-24 ▶

KEY POINT

Several disadvantages are associated with the filing of separate returns by married individuals. For example, a taxpayer may lose all or part of the benefits of the deduction for individual retirement accounts, the child care credit, and the earned income credit.

Becky, a single taxpayer with no dependents, files her first tax return. She will file as a single taxpayer. ◀

MARRIED FILING A SEPARATE RETURN

Married individuals who choose to file separate returns use the separate rate schedule. The rates on this schedule are higher than other individual rate schedules. Also, some married couples, such as couples with different tax years, cannot file a joint return and must file separately. The implications of joint returns versus separate returns are discussed later in this chapter.

EXAMPLE I2-25 ▶

On December 31, Rose marries Joe. Because they were married before the year ended, they may elect to file jointly. Alternatively, they may file separate returns with each using the rate schedule applicable to separate returns. ◀

The filing requirements for individuals are summarized in Topic Review I2-2.

---

[52] Reg. Sec. 1.2-2(d).

WHAT WOULD YOU DO IN THIS SITUATION?

CHOICE OF RATE SCHEDULES

Jane Brown married Jim four years ago. Two years ago Jim lost his job. After looking for work for several months, Jim left town to look for work, and Jane has not heard from him. Jim's brother told Jane that he had heard that Jim lived in Texas, but a friend said he heard that Jim had been killed in an automobile accident.

Jane went back to school and completed a program as an medical technician. She returned to work this year, and she earned $35,000. She has asked you to prepare her tax return this year. She has asked you whether she should file as a single taxpayer, married person filing separately, or as a married person filing jointly. Because she has had a low income until recently, she has taken no legal steps to resolve her status. What should she do?

KEY POINT

When one thinks of a person who would qualify as an abandoned spouse, one thinks of a person in dire financial condition. If no relief were granted, this person would be required to use the married filing separately tax rate schedule, which contains the highest rates.

ABANDONED SPOUSE

The particular rate schedule a taxpayer uses can have a great impact on the amount of tax. Without any special rule, an abandoned spouse would be required to file using the rate schedules for a married person filing separately. Congress has provided relief for taxpayers in this situation if they can meet certain conditions. A married individual can claim head-of-household status if [53]

▶ The taxpayer lived apart from his or her spouse for the last six months of the year.

▶ The taxpayer pays over half of the cost of maintaining a household in which the taxpayer and a dependent son or daughter live for over half of the year.[54]

▶ The taxpayer is a U.S. citizen or resident.

The requirement that the taxpayer have a dependent child is met if a taxpayer who is otherwise qualified to claim the child as a dependent signs an agreement that allows the child's noncustodial parent to claim the dependency exemption for the child.[55]

EXAMPLE I2-26 ▶ In October, Bob and Gail decide to separate. Gail supports their children after the separation and pays the costs of maintaining their home. Gail cannot claim abandoned spouse status because Bob lived with her for over one-half of the year. If she had obtained a divorce before the end of the year, she could have filed as a head of household. In the absence of a divorce, Gail must file a separate return, unless both Bob and Gail agree to file a joint return. ◀

EXAMPLE I2-27 ▶ Assume the same facts as in Example I2-26 except that Gail continues to support her children and pay household expenses during the next year. She can file as a head of household even if she has not obtained a divorce. ◀

DEPENDENTS WITH UNEARNED INCOME

In the past, taxpayers in high tax brackets were able to reduce their tax liability by shifting income to children and other dependents. Under prior law, there was no tax due if the income was less than the dependent's personal exemption and standard deduction.

---

[53] Sec. 2(c).
[54] Includes adopted child, stepchild, and foster child.

[55] Sec. 152(e).

Even if the shifted income was greater than these amounts, there was a tax savings if the dependent was in a low tax bracket. Under current law three rules apply that curtail the advantages of shifting income to dependents:

▶ Dependents do not receive a personal exemption on their own returns.

▶ A dependent's standard deduction is reduced to the greater of the dependent's earned income (such as salary) or $650.

▶ The tax on the net unearned income (such as dividends and interest) of a child under age 14 is figured by reference to the parents' tax rate if it is higher than the child's.

The first two rules have been discussed previously in this chapter.

KEY POINT

Children under age 14 will not have their unearned income taxed at their parents' tax rate until their unearned income exceeds $1,300.

EXAMPLE I2-28 ▶ In 1997, Tim is a self-supporting 18-year-old who received $2,000 of dividends and $900 from a part-time summer job. He is entitled to the regular standard deduction and a personal exemption because his parents may not claim him as a dependent (does not meet the support test). Tim owes no tax as these deductions exceed his income. ◀

EXAMPLE I2-29 ▶ Assume the same facts as in Example I2-28 except that Tim is a dependent of his parents, and they are in the 28% tax bracket. Because Tim is a dependent, he is not entitled to a personal exemption. Tim's standard deduction is limited to the greater of $650 or his earned income (but not more than $4,150). Because his earned income is $900, the standard deduction is also $900. Therefore, Tim's taxable income is $2,000 ($2,900 AGI − $900 standard deduction). Because Tim is over age 13, he is not subject to the kiddie tax on his unearned income and his regular tax rate (15%) is used. The tax is $300 (0.15 × $2,000). ◀

Under the third rule, often called the kiddie tax, the first $650 of unearned income can be offset by the standard deduction, the second $650 of unearned income is taxed at the child's own tax rate, but any remaining unearned income is taxed at the parents' marginal tax rate. The tax on a dependent child with unearned income can be computed using a three-step process:

1. Compute the child's taxable income (TI);

2. Compute the child's **net unearned income** (NUI);

3. Compute the child's tax, as follows:

NUI times parents' marginal tax rate	$XXX
Plus: (TI–NUI) times child's tax rate	XXX
Equals: Total tax of child for year	$XXX

Taxable income is computed in the normal fashion for dependents as discussed earlier in this chapter. NUI is computed as follows:

Unearned income

Less: Statutory deduction of $650

Less: Greater of

1. $650 of the standard deduction, or

2. Amount of itemized deductions which are directly connected with the production of the unearned income.

Equals: Net unearned income

Net unearned income represents the portion of the child's taxable income that is *taxed at his or her parents' marginal tax rate.* Unearned income is essentially the child's investment income, including such items as dividends, taxable interest, capital gains, rents, royalties, and any other income that is not earned income.[56]

EXAMPLE I2-30 ▶ Assume the same facts as in Example I2-29 except that Tim is age 13. His standard deduction is still $900 and his taxable income is also $2,000. Since Tim is under age 14, a portion of his unearned income may be subject to tax at his parents' 28% rate. The computation of Tim's tax for 1997 is as follows:

1. Compute Tim's taxable income for 1997

Wages		$ 900
Dividends		2,000
Adjusted gross income		$2,900
Standard deduction	$900	
Personal exemption	0	900
Taxable income		$2,000

2. Compute Tim's Net Unearned Income for 1997

Unearned income: Dividends	$2,000
Statutory deduction	(650)
Portion of standard deduction	(650)
Net unearned income	$ 700

3. Compute Tim's tax for 1997

Tax on NUI: $700 × 28%	$ 196
Tax on TI minus NUI: ($2,000 − $700) × 15%	195
Total income tax for 1997	$ 391 ◀

In figuring the tax where the parents file separate returns, the tax rate of the parent with the greater taxable income is used. If the parents are divorced, the parent with custody is the relevant parent.

Parents of a child under age 14 may elect to include the child's dividend and interest income on their own return.[57] This rule eliminates the need to file a tax return for the child. To be eligible for the election, the child's gross income must come solely from dividends and interest, and such income must not exceed $6,500 in 1996. Furthermore, there can be no withholding or estimated payment using the child's Social Security number.[58]

CORPORATE TAX FORMULA AND RATES

OBJECTIVE 5

Explain the tax formula for corporations

The corporate tax formula and rates are discussed here to provide basic information needed for subsequent chapters. Corporations are divided into two groups. First, **C corporations**, also called **regular corporations**, are treated as separate entities for tax purposes and pay income taxes on the corporation's taxable income. Individuals are taxed on dividends they receive from C corporations but are not taxed on the

---

[56] Sec. 1(g)(4).
[57] Sec. 1(g)(7).
[58] Parents may use Form 8814, Parents' Election to Report Child's Interest and Dividends. If the child's income from dividends and interest is between $650 and $1,300, the child's tax is 15% of the income over $650. If the income is over $1,300, the child's tax is computed by multiplying the parents' tax rate times the child's income over $1,300 and adding $97.50. For example, if the child's dividend income is $2,000 and the parents' tax bracket is 28%, the child's tax is $293.50 [0.28 × ($2,000 − $1,300) + $97.50].

▼ **TABLE I2-7**

Tax Formula for C Corporations

Income from whatever source derived	$xxx,xxx
Minus: Exclusions	(xxx)
Gross income	$ xx,xxx
Minus: Deductions	(xxx)
Taxable income	$ x,xxx
Times: Tax rates	× .xx
Gross tax	$ xx
Minus: Credits and prepayments	(x)
Net tax payable or refund due	$ xx

ADDITIONAL COMMENT

In 1991 there were 3.8 million corporation tax returns filed, of which 1,700,000 returns were from S corporations.

KEY POINT

The tax formula for C corporations differs from the tax formula for individuals in several important respects. The corporate tax formula does not contain an adjusted gross income figure, personal and dependency exemptions, or the standard deduction.

corporation's undistributed income. The second group, **S corporations**, generally are not treated as separate entities for tax purposes but are referred to as flow-through entities. Thus, each S corporation shareholder is required to report a pro rata share of the S corporation's income on his or her tax return even if the income is not distributed. The shareholders must elect to be covered by the S corporation rules. Corporations must also meet a series of conditions, such as having thirty-five or fewer shareholders, before they can elect S corporation status. The detailed rules for C corporations are covered in Chapter I16, S corporations are covered in Chapter I17.

The tax formula for C corporations is presented in Table I2-7. The major difference between the formulas for individual and corporate taxpayers is the fact that there is only one category of deductions for corporations. Personal expenses do not come into consideration. Therefore, there are no itemized deductions, standard deductions, or personal exemptions. The tax rates applicable to C corporations are as follows:[59]

Taxable Income	*Tax*
First $50,000	15% of taxable income
Over $50,000, but not over $75,000	$7,500 + 25% of taxable income over $50,000
Over $75,000, but not over $100,000	$13,750 + 34% of taxable income over $75,000
Over $100,000, but not over $335,000	$22,250 + 39% of taxable income over $100,000
Over $335,000, but not over $10,000,000	$113,900 + 34% of taxable income over $335,000
Over $10,000,000, but not over $15,000,000	$3,400,000 + 35% of taxable income over $10,000,000
Over $15,000,000, but not over $18,333,333	$5,150,000 + 38% of taxable income over $15,000,000
Over $18,333,333	$6,416,667 + 35% of taxable income over $18,333,333

---

[59] Income of certain personal service corporations is taxed at a flat rate of 35%.

Note that the corporate tax rates reflect a stair-step pattern of progression, with the two highest rates of 39% and 38% in the middle of the progression. The benefits of the two lowest tax rates of 15% and 25% are completely eliminated by the application of the 39% tax rate to taxable income between $100,000 and $335,000. Likewise, the benefit of the 34% tax rate on taxable income between $335,000 and $10,000,000 is eliminated by the application of a 38% tax rate on taxable income between $15,000,000 and $18,333,333.

In one sense, there is no formula to compute an S corporation's taxable income because the corporation normally does not pay a tax. S corporations do file returns, but the returns are more informational in nature, much like tax returns of a partnership. A residual income total, known as ordinary income, is computed on the return. Special items, such as capital gains and losses and charitable contributions, are kept separate from the ordinary income amount. This is because every item that would receive special treatment on a shareholder's return is passed through to the shareholder with its status intact. Each shareholder reports his or her share of the ordinary income and his or her share of each special item. Losses pass through and generally can be deducted by shareholders up to their respective bases in the corporation's stock. The deductibility of losses is also subject to other rules, such as the at-risk and passive activity loss rules, and are covered in Chapter I8.

TREATMENT OF CAPITAL GAINS AND LOSSES

OBJECTIVE 6

Explain the basic concepts of property transactions

HISTORICAL NOTE

Net capital gains reported on individual income tax returns dropped from nearly $300 billion in 1986 to about $133 billion in 1987. The latter amount was more in line with 1984 and 1985. The large amount reported in 1986 was due to the fact that a 60% long-term capital gain deduction was available to individuals in 1986, but was repealed as of December 31, 1986. Many taxpayers sold capital assets to take advantage of the lower effective rates that existed in 1986.

Capital gains and losses have been accorded special tax treatment since 1922. Today, however, the primary advantage accorded such gains is that they are not subject to the highest tax rates for individuals (i.e., 31%, 36%, or 39.6%). This preferential treatment is available only to long-term capital gains (discussed below). As a result, individual taxpayers who are in the 31% tax bracket or higher who realize long-term capital gains pay a 28% tax on such gains. Other types of income (e.g., salaries and wages, dividends, interest, and net short-term capital gains) are subject to the regular tax rates. Net long-term capital gains realized by individuals who are in the 15% and 28% tax brackets are taxed at the same rates as their other income.

On the other hand, individuals who suffer net capital losses can deduct only up to $3,000 of the losses from other income. The special rules that apply to property transactions are discussed in detail in Chapters I5, I12, and I13. Nevertheless, a brief introduction to the treatment of gains and losses from the sale or exchange of property is appropriate at this point.

DEFINITION OF *CAPITAL ASSETS*

A purpose of the rules applicable to capital gains and losses is to distinguish capital appreciation from gains attributable to ordinary business transactions and speculation. A **capital gain** or **loss** is the gain or loss from the sale or exchange of a capital asset. Unfortunately, the Code merely defines what does not constitute a capital asset. In other words, **capital assets** are assets other than those listed in Sec. 1221. A detailed discussion of the definition is found in Chapter I5. Here we simply note the major categories of properties included on the list, which are thereby excluded from capital asset status. The major categories are inventory, trade receivables, certain properties created by the efforts of the taxpayer (such as works of art), depreciable business property and business land, and certain government publications. As was noted, a purpose of the rules applicable to capital gains and losses is to distinguish capital appreciation from gains derived from ordinary business operations. Thus, the profit from the sale of inventory and trade receivables is viewed as business profit as opposed to capital appreciation. Similarly, a gain realized by an artist on the sale of one of his or her own works is ordinary income from personal services, whereas a capital gain or loss results if an investor in art sells a painting that was held as an investment.

Depreciable business property and business land are also excluded from capital asset status. These properties are given their own special status and called **Sec. 1231 assets**. The various **Sec. 1231 gains and losses** realized by a taxpayer are netted. If the result is a net gain, that net gain is normally treated as a long-term capital gain. If the result is a net loss, the loss is treated as an ordinary loss. This process is complicated by the fact that other rules can come into play.[60] Under certain circumstances, these rules require taxpayers to report some ordinary income, instead of Sec. 1231 gains.

The major categories of gains are summarized as follows:

Capital gains	Gains attributable to the sale or exchange of appreciated investments (such as stocks and bonds), personal use property (such as a coin collection or personal residence), and certain business property (such as goodwill or a patent).
Sec. 1231 gains	Certain gains attributable to the sale or exchange of depreciable business property and business realty.
Ordinary gains	Gains attributable to the sale or exchange of inventory, trade receivables, certain property created by the taxpayer (such as a painting or musical composition), and certain government publications. May include a portion of the gain attributable to depreciable business property.

NETTING PROCESS

As noted, one purpose of the capital gains rules is to distinguish between gains attributable to capital appreciation and gains attributable to speculation. In an effort to do this, the tax laws divide capital gains and losses into long-term capital gains and losses (LTCG and LTCL) and short-term capital gains and losses (STCG and STCL). **Long-term capital gains** and **losses** are gains and losses attributable to the sale or exchange of a capital asset held for over one year. **Short-term capital gains** and **losses** are gains and losses attributable to the sale or exchange of a capital asset held for one year or less.

TAX TREATMENT OF NET GAINS AND LOSSES

Taxpayers add together LTCGs and LTCLs. STCGs and STCLs are also netted. This leaves two amounts: either a net LTCG or LTCL and a net STCG or STCL. What happens at this point depends on the relative size of the two amounts and whether they are gains or losses. For now, it is essential that you understand the following facts:

▶ Individuals are taxed on the excess of net capital gain over net capital loss. A net STCG (in excess of any net LTCL) is taxed at the same rates as any other income. A net LTCG (in excess of any net STCL) is not subject to the 31%, 36%, or 39.6% tax brackets (i.e., the maximum tax rate for the net capital gain portion of taxable income of individuals is 28%).

---

[60] See, for example, Secs. 1245 and 1250.

▶ Individuals with net capital losses may deduct no more than $3,000 of such losses in any year. A net capital loss in excess of $3,000 can be carried over and offset against future capital gains or, subject to the $3,000 limitation, deducted from other income.

Tax planning considerations

SHIFTING INCOME BETWEEN FAMILY MEMBERS

Because of the progressive tax system, families can often reduce their taxes by **shifting income** to family members who are in lower tax brackets.

EXAMPLE I2-31 ▶ Mary, who is in the 36% tax bracket, shifted $5,000 of income to her 22-year-old son, Steve by making a gift of a 10%, $50,000 corporate bond. Steve had no income as he suffered a business loss. In absence of the shift, 36% of the income would have gone for taxes. There is no tax on Steve's return because the income is offset by his loss. ◀

EXAMPLE I2-32 ▶ Farouk, who is in the 36% tax bracket, shifted $2,000 of income to his 18-year-old daughter, Dana, who is in the 15% tax bracket. The tax savings from the shift is $420 [(0.36 × $2,000) − (0.15 × $2,000)]. ◀

ADDITIONAL COMMENT

All fifty states have enacted laws that simplify the procedures for making gifts to minors. This type of law, which in most states is called the Uniform Gifts to Minors Act, is especially important when making gifts of securities.

As noted earlier in this chapter, the net unearned income of children under the age of 14 is taxed at their parents' tax rate. Hence, a shifting of income to young children is often an ineffective method of minimizing tax.

Shifting income must be distinguished from assigning income. Earned income is taxed to the person who produces it. Income from property is taxed to the person who owns the property. Ordering income to be paid to another is an assignment of income that does not change who is taxed on the income. Normally, in the case of income from property, ownership of the property must be transferred in order to shift the income.

EXAMPLE I2-33 ▶ John owns stock in Valley Corporation. John orders the corporation to pay this year's dividends to his daughter. John will be taxed on the income even though he has assigned it to another. ◀

EXAMPLE I2-34 ▶ Kay owns stock in Valley Corporation. Kay gives the stock to her 17-year-old son. Future dividends on Valley stock will be taxed to the son instead of to Kay. ◀

Individuals are often unwilling to give property away completely. As a result, personal preference may limit the amount of tax planning that is possible.

SPLITTING INCOME

Splitting income consists of creating additional taxable entities, especially corporations, in order to reduce an individual's effective tax rate.

EXAMPLE I2-35 ▶ Tom is a taxpayer in the 36% tax bracket and is involved in a variety of businesses. One business has been producing $20,000 of income per year for several years. Tom incorporates the business. The first $50,000 of a corporation's income is taxed at a 15% rate. Thus, the tax on the income is reduced by $4,200 [(0.36 × $20,000) − (0.15 × $20,000)]. ◀

The creation of a new corporate entity to split income is not always desirable because the corporation's income will be taxed to the shareholder as a dividend if it is distributed. In addition, if income is allowed to accumulate in a corporation indefinitely, it may be subject to the accumulated earnings tax.[61]

MAXIMIZING ITEMIZED DEDUCTIONS

Timing expenditures properly can often increase deductions. In general, cash-basis taxpayers deduct expenses in the year paid. If itemized deductions are less than the standard deduction, the taxpayer will receive no tax benefit from the deductions. A taxpayer in that situation could defer some payments or accelerate others to maximize expenses in one year, thereby creating a sufficient amount of deductions in that year.

EXAMPLE I2-36 ▶

Jean's property taxes are due on January 1 of each year. Jean is a single, cash-basis, calendar-year taxpayer. Itemized deductions other than property taxes total $2,000 in each year. Jean pays the 1997 property taxes of $1,200 on January 1, 1997 and the 1998 property taxes of $1,200 on December 31, 1997. In the absence of doubling up, Jean would not be able to itemize in either year. The itemized deductions of $3,200 ($2,000 + $1,200) would be less than the standard deduction of $4,150. By doubling up, Jean has itemized deductions of $4,400 ($2,000 + $1,200 + $1,200) in 1997. ◀

Medical expenses are deductible only to the extent that they exceed 7.5% of a taxpayer's AGI. In situations where medical expenses are just under 7.5% of AGI, taxpayers may be able to create a deduction by doubling up.

EXAMPLE I2-37 ▶

Troy's AGI is $20,000. So far in 1997, Troy's medical expenses have totaled $1,300. Troy has received a bill from his dentist for $500 that is due January 15, 1998. By paying the bill in 1997, Troy will have a deduction for medical expenses of $300 [$1,300 + $500 − (0.075 × $20,000)]. This assumes that Troy's other itemized deductions exceed the standard deduction.[62] ◀

FILING JOINT OR SEPARATE RETURNS

FACTORS TO BE CONSIDERED. In general, married couples may file either joint or separate returns. As noted earlier, if one spouse has significantly more than half of their combined income, filing separately will increase the couple's total income tax. Because of the potential tax saving from a joint return and because it is simpler to prepare one return than two, most married couples file jointly.

It should be noted that the joint return is not always preferred. Separate returns may result in increased deductions. Because only one spouse's income is reported on a separate return, medical expenses are more likely to exceed the 7.5% of adjusted gross income floor if one spouse incurs most of the medical expenses. Similarly, casualty losses involving personal-use assets, which are allowable only to the extent that they exceed 10% of AGI, may be deductible on separate returns.

Probably the most significant impact of the joint return is the joint income tax liability. Both the husband and wife are liable for taxes owed on a joint return. This could be a major problem if a couple separates or divorces after filing a return.

---

[61] Amounts accumulated in a corporation in excess of $250,000 may be subject to this tax. However, amounts accumulated for business purposes are exempt. This subject is discussed in *Prentice Hall's Federal Taxation: Corporations, Partnerships, Estates and Trusts.*

[62] For a discussion of restrictions on the deductibility of prepaid medical expenses, see Chapter I7.

EXAMPLE I2-38 ▶ Jim and Pat file a joint return. They are both informed as to the relevant information pertaining to the return. The next year they separate, and Jim moves out of town without leaving a forwarding address. The IRS audits their joint return and disallows $400 of charitable contributions deducted on the original return. Pat may be held responsible for the additional taxes owed. The IRS does not have to attempt to locate Jim in order to collect the tax. In this instance, it would make little difference who made the error on the return. ◀

ETHICAL POINT
Because innocent spouse rules are strict, it may sometimes be safer to file a separate return than run the risk of being held responsible for the acts of another.

INNOCENT SPOUSE PROVISION. Generally, each spouse is liable for the entire tax and any penalties imposed when the couple files a joint return.[63] This is true even if all of the income was earned by one spouse. This rule could prove unfair in some instances, especially where one spouse concealed information from the other. For that reason, the Code contains an **innocent spouse** provision. An innocent spouse is relieved of the liability for tax on unreported income if [64]

▶ The amount is attributable to grossly erroneous items of the other spouse.

▶ There is a substantial understatement of tax attributable to the item.

▶ The innocent spouse did not know and had no reason to know that there was such an understatement of tax.

▶ Under the circumstances, it would be inequitable to hold the innocent spouse liable for the understatement.

EXAMPLE I2-39 ▶ Dan and Joy file a joint return. Dan traveled much of the time and Joy had little information as to his whereabouts or income. Joy worked and her own salary was the sole source of her support. Their return was audited by the IRS. The audit disclosed that Dan had not reported income from a job he had held for several months during the year. The salary represented a substantial portion of the combined gross income that should have been reported on the return. In this situation, Joy may be able to use the innocent spouse provision in order to avoid being held liable for the tax on the unreported income. ◀

ELECTING TO CHANGE TO A JOINT RETURN. In general, a husband and wife who file separate returns for a given year may elect to change to a joint return by filing an amended joint return.[65] This change is permitted after the due date but must be within three years of the due date including extensions.[66] Taxpayers may not change from a joint return to separate returns after the due date.[67]

COMPLIANCE AND PROCEDURAL CONSIDERATIONS

ADDITIONAL COMMENT
The IRS is encouraging nonfilers (i.e., individuals and businesses who should have filed previous tax returns but did not) to come forward. The IRS estimates that there were 6 million nonfilers in 1990 alone.

WHO MUST FILE

Whether an individual must file a tax return is based on the amount of the individual's gross income.[68] The fact that the individual owes no tax does not mean that a return need not be filed. The gross income filing levels are as follows:[69]

---

[63] Sec. 6013(d)(3).
[64] Sec. 6013(e).
[65] Sec. 6013(b).
[66] Sec. 6013(b)(2)(B).
[67] Reg. Sec. 1.6013-1(a). However, a couple who filed a joint return whose marriage is later annulled must file amended returns as singles (Rev. Rul. 76-

255, 1976-2 C.B. 40).
[68] *Gross income* has its usual meaning except that the gain excluded from the sale of a personal residence and excluded foreign earned income are included (Sec. 6012(c)).
[69] Sec. 6012(a)(1).

ADDITIONAL
COMMENT

A file-by-telephone system has been tested in some states in the last few years. The filers dial a toll-free telephone number and enter tax return data with a touch-tone telephone. While the taxpayer is still on the line, the IRS calculates any refund or tax due. The taxpayers then mail a signed Form 1040-TEL.

ADDITIONAL
COMMENT

The IRS is required to impound tax refunds to help other agencies collect overdue student loans, child support, etc. However, the IRS found that people whose refunds were offset in 1985 and 1986 were far more likely than others to file no returns in the next two years or to file returns without paying all they owed.

	1997	1996
Single	$ 6,800	$ 6,550
Single (65 or over)	7,800	7,550
Married, filing jointly	12,200	11,800
Married, filing jointly (one spouse 65 or over)	13,000	12,600
Married, filing jointly (both 65 or over)	13,800	13,400
Surviving spouse	9,550	9,250
Surviving spouse (65 or over)	10,550	10,250
Married, filing separately	2,650	2,550
Married, living separately from spouse at year-end	2,650	2,550
Head of household	8,700	8,450
Head of household (65 or over)	9,700	9,450

There are three situations where taxpayers must file even if the gross income is less than the amounts shown above:

▶ Taxpayers who receive advance payments of the earned income credit (see Chapter I14) must file regardless of their income levels.

▶ Taxpayers with net self-employment income of $400 or more must file regardless of their total gross income.

▶ Taxpayers who can be claimed as a dependent by another must file if they have either unearned income over $650 or total gross income over the standard deduction.

In general, taxpayers must file if their gross income equals or exceeds the total of the standard deduction (including the additional standard deduction due to age but not blindness) and personal exemption. The blindness allowance and dependency exemptions are not considered. If the disallowance of the standard deduction rules apply, the standard deduction is ignored in determining whether taxpayers must file.

EXAMPLE I2-40 ▶
KEY POINT

It is possible that a taxpayer may be required to file an income tax return but still have no tax liability.

In 1997, Carol is a single, self-supporting taxpayer with no dependents. Carol must file if her gross income is $6,800 or greater ($4,150 + $2,650). ◀

DUE DATES FOR FILING RETURN

An individual taxpayer must file on or before the fifteenth day of the fourth month following the close of his or her tax year.[70] For calendar-year taxpayers, this is April 15. If the due date falls on a Saturday, Sunday, or a legal holiday, the due date is the next day that is not a Saturday, Sunday, or holiday.[71]

An automatic four-month extension of time to file is given to taxpayers who file Form 4868 by the due date for the return. This is an extension to file the return, not an extension of the time to pay the tax. The taxpayer must estimate the amount of tax due and pay it with Form 4868.[72] Taxpayers who are unable to file their returns within the four-month extension period may request an additional two month extension of time by timely filing Form 2688.

ADDITIONAL
COMMENT

The IRS's electronic filing program is growing rapidly. The IRS is aiming for a 98% paperless operation by the end of the century.

USE OF FORMS 1040, 1040EZ, AND 1040A

The primary individual tax return is Form 1040. Complicated returns often involve many additional forms and schedules. Two shorter forms are available to taxpayers with less-complicated tax returns. Form 1040EZ is available to single taxpayers and married

[70] Sec. 6072(a).
[71] Sec. 7503.

[72] Reg. Sec. 1.6081-4(a)(1)-(5)-(5).

individuals who file a joint return. Such taxpayers must have taxable income of less than $50,000 and claim no dependents. To use Form 1040EZ, the taxpayer's income must consist of salary and wages plus no more than $400 of taxable interest income. No deductions (other than the standard deduction) or credits (other than withholding from salary and wages) can be taken on the return.

Form 1040A is available to taxpayers who have somewhat more involved returns. Form 1040A can be used by taxpayers claiming any number of exemptions or any filing status. Salary, wages, dividends, interest, pension and annuity income, and unemployment compensation can be reported on Form 1040A. Taxpayers may deduct IRA contributions. Taxpayers may also claim credits for withholding, child care, and earned income.

SYSTEM FOR REPORTING INCOME

There is a significant and expanding relationship between computers, tax returns, the taxpayer identification system, and information returns. The IRS keeps records based on taxpayer identification numbers. Individual taxpayers report information based on Social Security numbers, whereas employer identification numbers (EIN) are used by corporations, other taxpayers, and tax-exempt entities. Individuals who employ others have both a Social Security number and an employer identification number.

Employers, banks, stockbrokers, savings and loans, and so on report payments they make to others along with the payee's identification number. Today, the IRS computers match much of the reported information with tax returns, using the taxpayer identification number as the cross-reference. The need for accurate information returns is obvious. Some major information returns are listed below:

Basic Form	Type of Payment	Required if Amount Equals or Exceeds
1099-R	Pensions and annuities	$600
W-2	Salary, wages, etc.	600
1099-DIV	Dividends	10
1099-INT	Interest	600[73]
1099-B	Sale of a security	All
1099-G	Unemployment compensation, tax refunds, etc.	10
1099-MISC	Rent, royalties, etc.	600
1099-R	Total lump-sum distributions from retirement plans	600[74]

This information-reporting system makes it more difficult for taxpayers to avoid IRS detection if they omit income from their returns.

PROBLEM MATERIALS

DISCUSSION QUESTIONS

I2-1 What are the components of the formula for computing an individual taxpayer's taxable income?

I2-2 Explain the distinction between income and gross income.

---

[73] For banks and corporations the amount is $10.

[74] Except that all IRA distributions must be reported.

I2-3 a. Explain the distinction between a deduction and a credit.
      b. Which is worth more, a $10 deduction or a $10 credit?
      c. Explain the difference between refundable and nonrefundable credits.

I2-4 List the five conditions that must be met in order to claim a dependency exemption. Briefly explain each one.

I2-5 a. Briefly explain the concept of support.
      b. If a taxpayer provides 50% or less of another person's support, is it possible for the taxpayer to claim a dependency exemption? Explain.
      c. Does support include the value of an automobile? Explain.

I2-6 Under what circumstances must a taxpayer use a rate schedule instead of a tax table?

I2-7 a. What determines who must file a tax return?
      b. Is an individual required to file a tax return if he or she owes no tax?

I2-8 What conditions must be met by a taxpayer who wishes to claim head-of-household status?

I2-9 What conditions must be met by a taxpayer who wishes to file as a surviving spouse?

I2-10 What is the normal due date for the return of a calendar-year individual taxpayer? What happens to the due date if it falls on a Saturday, Sunday, or holiday?

I2-11 Why are there five filing statuses but only four rate schedules?

I2-12 Can tax-exempt income qualify as support? Explain.

I2-13 Can a scholarship qualify as support?

I2-14 Explain the purpose of the multiple support agreement.

I2-15 Summarize the rules that explain which parent receives the dependency exemption for children in cases of divorce.

I2-16 What conditions must be met by a married couple before they can file a joint return?

I2-17 Explain what is meant by the phrase *maintain a household*.

I2-18 Under what circumstances, if any, can a married person file as a head of household?

I2-19 a. Explain the principal difference in the tax treatment of an S corporation and a C corporation.
       b. Why would a C corporation be used if an S corporation is generally exempt from tax?

I2-20 a. What assets are excluded from capital asset status?
       b. Are capital gains given favorable tax treatment?
       c. What is the significance of an asset being classified as a capital asset?

I2-21 What is Sec. 1231 property?

I2-22 Is there any tax advantage for an individual who has held an appreciated capital asset for eleven months to delay the sale of the asset? Explain.

I2-23 a. Explain the difference between income splitting and income shifting.
       b. Why are taxpayers interested in shifting income from one tax return to another within the same family or economic unit?
       c. Is there a relationship between the tax on unearned income of a minor and taxpayers who attempt to shift income?

I2-24 a. Who is liable for additional taxes on a joint return?
       b. Why is this so important?

I2-25 Can couples change from joint returns to separate returns? Separate to joint?

ISSUE IDENTIFICATION QUESTIONS

I2-26 This year, Yung Tseng, a U.S. citizen, supported his nephew who is attending school in the United States. Yung is a U.S. citizen, but his nephew is a citizen of Hong Kong. The nephew has a student visa, but he hopes to become a permanent U. S. resident. Other family members hope to come to the U.S. What issues must be considered by Yung?

I2-27   Joan's parents were killed in an automobile accident late last year, and she moved in with her sister Joy. Their brother, Ed, provides $300 per month to help with Joan's expenses. Joy provides Joan with a room and she also pays some of Joan's expenses such as clothing and meals. Joan has no source of support other than Joy and Ed. What issues should Joy and Ed consider?

I2-28   Carmen and Carlos, who have filed joint tax returns for several years, separated this year. Carlos works in construction and is often paid in cash. Carlos says he only worked a few weeks this year and made $11,000. In prior years he made approximately $35,000 per year, and Carmen is surprised that his income is so low this year. Carmen received a salary of $38,000 as a medical laboratory technician. They have no dependents and claim the standard deduction. What tax issues should Carmen and Carlos consider?

I2-29   Jane and Bill have lived in a home Bill inherited from his parents. Their son Jim lives with them. Bill and Jane obtain a divorce during the current year. Under the terms of the divorce, Jane receives possession of the home for a period of five years and custody of Jim. Bill is obligated to furnish over one-half of the cost of the maintenance, taxes, and insurance on the home and pay $6,000 of child support per year. Bill lives in an apartment. What tax issues should Jane and Bill consider?

PROBLEMS

I2-30   *Computation of Tax.* The following information relates to two married couples:

	Lanes	Waynes
Salary (earned by one spouse)	$20,000	$108,000
Interest income	1,000	5,000
IRA contribution	2,000	0
Itemized deductions	8,000	7,000
Exemptions	5,300	5,300
Withholding	850	22,000

Compute the 1997 tax due or refund due for each couple. Assume that the itemized deductions have been reduced by the applicable floors.

I2-31   *Dependency Exemptions.* Anna, age 65, who lives with her unmarried son, Mario, received $7,000, which was used for her support during the year. The sources of support were as follows:

Social Security benefits	$1,500
Mario	2,600
Caroline, an unrelated friend	800
Doug, Anna's son	500
Elaine, Anna's sister	1,600
Total	$7,000

a. Who might be able to claim Anna as a dependent?
b. What must be done before Mario can claim the exemption?

c. Can anyone claim head-of-household status based on Anna's dependency exemption? Explain.

d. Can Mario claim an old age allowance for his mother? Explain.

I2-32 ***Computation of Taxable Income.*** The following information for 1997 relates to Tom, a single taxpayer, age 18:

Salary	$1,800
Interest income	1,600
Itemized deductions	600

a. Compute Tom's taxable income assuming he is self-supporting.

b. Compute Tom's taxable income assuming he is a dependent of his parents.

I2-33 ***Joint Versus Separate Returns.*** Carl and Carol have salaries of $14,000 and $22,000, respectively. Their itemized deductions total $5,000. They are married and both are under age 65.

a. Compute their taxable income assuming they file jointly.

b. Compute their taxable income assuming they file separate returns and that Carol claims all of the itemized deductions.

I2-34 ***Joint Versus Separate Returns.*** Hal attended school much of 1997, during which time he was supported by his parents. Hal married Ruth in December 1997. Hal graduated and commenced work in 1998. Ruth worked during 1997 and earned $18,000. Hal's only income was $800 of interest. Hal's parents are in the 28% tax bracket. Thus, claiming Hal as a dependent would save them $742 (0.28 × $2,650) of taxes.

a. Compute Hal and Ruth's gross tax if they file a joint return.

b. Compute Ruth's gross tax if she files a separate return in order to allow Hal's parents to claim him as a dependent.

c. Which alternative would be better for the family? In other words, will filing a joint return save Hal and Ruth more than $742?

I2-35 ***Dependency Exemption: Divorced Parents.*** Joe and Joan divorce during the current year. Joan receives custody of their three children. Joe agrees to pay $1,000 of child support for each child.

a. Assuming there is no written agreement, who will receive the dependency exemption for the children? Explain.

b. Would it make any difference if Joe could prove that he provided over one-half of the support for each child?

I2-36 ***Filing Status and Dependency Exemptions.*** For the following taxpayers, indicate which tax form should be used, the applicable filing status, and the number of personal and dependency exemptions available.

a. Arnie is a single college student who earned $5,000 working part-time. He had $200 of interest income and received $1,000 of support from his parents.

b. Buddy is a single college student who earned $5,000 working part-time. He had $600 of interest income and received $1,000 of support from his parents.

c. Cindy is divorced and received $6,000 of alimony from her former husband and earned $12,000 working as a secretary. She also received $1,800 of child support for her son. According to a written agreement, her former husband is entitled to receive the dependency exemption.

d. Debbie is a widow, age 68, who receives a pension of $8,000, nontaxable social security benefits of $8,000, and interest of $4,000. She has no dependents.

e. Edith is married, but her husband left her two years ago and she has not seen him since. Edith supported herself and her daughter, age 6. She paid all household expenses. Her income of $16,000 consisted of a salary of $15,200 and interest of $800.

I2-37 *Marriage and Taxes.* Bill and Mary plan to marry in December 1997. Bill's salary is $32,000 and he owns his own residence. His itemized deductions total $9,000. Mary's salary is $36,000. Her itemized deductions total only $1,600 as she does not own her own residence. For purposes of this problem, assume 1998 tax rates, exemptions, and standard deductions are the same as 1997.
a. What will their tax be if they marry before year-end and file a joint return?
b. What will their combined taxes be for the year if they delay the marriage until 1998?
c. What factors contribute to the difference in taxes?

I2-38 *Dependency Exemptions.* How many dependency exemptions are the following taxpayers entitled to, assuming the people involved are U.S. citizens?
a. Andrew supports his cousin Mary, who does not live with him. Mary has no income and is single.
b. Bob and his wife are filing a joint return. Bob provided over one-half of his father's support. The father received Social Security benefits of $6,000 and taxable interest income of $800. The father is single and does not live with them.
c. Clay provides 60% of his single daughter's support. She earned $2,600 while attending school during the year as a full-time student. She is 22 years old.
d. Dave provided 30% of his mother's support and she provided 55% of her own support. Dave's brother provided the remainder. The brother agreed to sign a multiple support agreement.

I2-39 *Amount of Personal Exemptions.* Juan and Maria are married and have two young children. Their adjusted gross income in 1997 is $260,000 and have itemized deductions of $38,000. Assuming they can validly claim four personal and dependency exemptions, what is the amount of their personal and dependency exemptions that they will subtract in arriving at taxable income?

I2-40 *Filing Requirement.* Which of the following taxpayers must file a 1997 return?
a. Amy, age 19 and single, has $7,050 of wages, $300 of interest, and $350 of self-employment income.
b. Betty, age 67 and single, has a taxable pension of $4,100 and Social Security benefits of $6,200.
c. Chris, age 15 and single, is a dependent of his parents. Chris has earned income of $1,600 and interest of $400.
d. Dawn, age 15 and single, is a dependent of her parents. She has earned income of $400 and interest of $1,600.
e. Doug, age 25, and his wife are separated. He earned $3,000 while attending school during the year.

I2-41 *Head of Household.* In the following situations, indicate whether the taxpayer qualifies as a head of household.
a. Allen is divorced from his wife. He maintains a household for himself and his dependent mother.

b. Beth is divorced from her husband. She maintains a home for herself and supports an elderly aunt who lives in a retirement home.

c. Cindy was widowed last year. She maintains a household for herself and her dependent daughter, who lived with her during the year.

d. Dick is not divorced, but lived apart from his wife for the entire year. He maintains a household for himself and his dependent daughter. He does not receive any financial support from his wife.

I2-42 *Filing Status.* For the following independent situations, determine the optimum filing status for the years in question.

a. Wayne and Celia had been married for 24 years when Wayne died in an accident in October, 1995. Celia and her son, Wally, age 21 in 1995, continued to live at home in 1995, 1996, 1997, and 1998. Wally worked part-time (earning $5,000 in each of the four years) and attended the University on a part-time basis. Celia provided more than 50% of Wally's support for all four years. What is Celia's filing status for 1995, 1996, 1997, and 1998?

b. Juanita is a single parent who in 1997 maintained a household for her unmarried son Josh, age 19. Josh graduated from high school on 1996 and has not decided whether to attend college. Thus, in 1997, Josh worked full-time and earned $9,000. Juanita provided approximately 40% of Josh's support in 1997 but provided all the expenses of maintaining the household. What is Juanita's filing status for 1997?

c. Gomer and Gertrude are married and have one dependent son in 1997. In April, 1997, Gomer left Gertrude a note informing her that he needed his freedom and he was leaving her. As of December 31, 1997, Gertrude had not seen nor heard a word from Gomer since April. Gertrude fully supported her son and completely maintained the household. What is Gertrude's filing status in 1997 assuming she was still legally married at December 31, 1997?

I2-43 *Computation of Taxable Income.* Jim and Pat are married and file jointly. In 1997, Jim earned a salary of $46,000. Pat is self-employed. Her gross business income was $49,000 and her business expenses totaled $24,000. Each contributed $2,000 to a deductible IRA. Their itemized deductions total $8,000. Compute Parts a, b, and c without regard to self-employment tax.

a. Compute their gross income.

b. Compute their adjusted gross income.

c. Compute their taxable income assuming they have a dependent daughter.

I2-44 *Itemized or Standard Deduction.* Jan, a single taxpayer, has adjusted gross income of $250,000, home mortgage interest of $4,000, and charitable contributions of $3,000. Should she itemize her deductions or claim the standard deduction?

I2-45 *Kiddie Tax.* Debbie is 16 years old and a dependent of her parents. She earns $4,200 working part-time and receives $1,600 interest on savings. She saves both the salary and interest. What is her taxable income? Would her taxable income or tax be different if Debbie were 13 years old?

I2-46 *Personal and Dependency Exemptions.* Determine the number of personal and dependency exemptions in each of the following situations. Assume any condition for a dependency exemption not mentioned is met.

a. Allen supports his older sister, who lives in her own apartment.

b. Bob supports his aunt and her husband, who live in their own apartment.

c. Charles and his two brothers support their mother. They agree to allow Charles to claim the exemption.

d. Dan provides $3,000 of support for his sister, and she spent $2,800 of taxable interest income for her own support.

I2-47 *Computation of Tax, Standard Deduction, and Kiddie Tax.* Anthony and Latrisha are married and have two sons, James, age 16 and Jonas, age 13. Both sons are properly claimed as dependency exemptions. Anthony and Latrisha's taxable income is $130,000 in 1997 and they file a joint return. During 1997, both James and Jonas had part-time jobs as well as some unearned income. Below is a summary of their total income in 1997.

	James	Jonas
Wages	$2,800	$ 400
Dividends from stocks	1,800	2,000

Compute the taxable income and tax liability for James and Jonas for 1997.

I2-48 *Computation of Tax.* Compute the tax on $60,000 of taxable income assuming the taxpayer is the following:
a. A S corporation
b. A C corporation
c. A married couple filing a joint return
d. A single taxpayer

I2-49 *Capital Gains and Losses.* Vicki has a long-term capital gain of $4,000 and a short-term capital loss of $15,000. Vicki has other income of $42,000. How much of the short-term capital loss can she deduct in the current year?

I2-50 *Capital Gains and Losses.*
a. Peter, a single taxpayer, incurred the following capital gains and losses in 1996 and 1997:

	1996	1997
LTCG	$ 4,000	$12,000
LTCL	(14,000)	0
STCG	0	2,000
STCL	0	0

1. If Peter had other taxable income (exclusive of the capital gains and capital losses) in 1996 of $100,000, what will be his taxable income in 1996?
2. If Peter had other taxable income (exclusive of the capital gains and capital losses) in 1997 of $100,000, what amount of additional tax will the capital gains cause in 1997?

b. Discuss how the capital gains and capital losses in a. above would be treated if Peter was a corporation (e.g., Peter Corporation) rather than an individual.

I2-51 *Timing of Deductions.* Virginia is a cash-basis, calendar-year taxpayer. Her salary is $20,000, and she is single. She plans to purchase a residence in 1998. She anticipates her property taxes and interest will total $7,000. Each year, Virginia contributes approximately $1,000 to charity. Her other itemized deductions total approximately $1,000. For purposes of this problem, assume 1998 tax rates, exemptions, and standard deductions are the same as 1997.

    a. What will her gross tax be in 1997 and 1998 if she contributes $1,000 to charity in each year?

    b. What will her gross tax be in 1997 and 1998 if she contributes $2,000 to charity in 1997 but makes no contribution in 1998?

    c. What will her gross tax be in 1997 and 1998 if she makes no contribution in 1997 but contributes $2,000 in 1998?

    d. Alternative c results in a lower tax than either a or b. Why?

I2-52   *Tax Forms and Filing Status.* Which tax form is used by the following individuals?

    a. Anita is single, age 68, and has a salary of $22,000 and interest of $300.

    b. Betty owns an apartment complex that produced rental income of $36,000. Expenses totaled $38,500.

    c. Clay's wife died last year. He qualifies as a surviving spouse. His salary is $24,000.

    d. Donna is a head of household. Her salary is $17,000 and she has $200 of interest income.

I2-53   *Computation of Tax.* Jose is a single taxpayer with a dependent daughter. His salary is $44,000. Jose realized a long-term capital loss on the sale of stock of $45,000. He contributed $2,000 to a deductible IRA. His itemized deductions total $7,000.

    a. Compute Jose's adjusted gross income.

    b. Compute Jose's taxable income.

    c. Compute Jose's gross tax.

I2-54   *Kiddie Tax.* Ralph and Tina (husband and wife) transferred taxable bonds worth $20,000 to Pam, their 12-year-old daughter. Pam received $1,800 of interest on the bonds in the current year. Ralph and Tina have a combined taxable income of $51,000.

    a. Compute Ralph and Tina's gross tax. Assume they do not include Pam's income on their return.

    b. Compute Pam's taxable income and gross tax.

    c. What would be Pam's tax if she were age 16?

I2-55   *Progressive or Proportional Tax.* Assume Gail is a wealthy widow whose husband died last year. Her dependent daughter lives with her for the entire year. Gail has dividend and interest income totaling $370,000 and she pays property taxes and home mortgage interest totaling $20,000.

    a. What filing status applies to Gail?

    b. Compute her taxable income and gross tax.

    c. Assume that Gail does not have a daughter. What is Gail's filing status?

    d. Compute Gail's taxable income and gross tax assuming she does not have a daughter.

TAX FORM/RETURN PREPARATION PROBLEMS

I2-56   Aida Petosa (Soc. Sec. no. 123-45-6789) is the 12-year-old daughter of Alfredo Petosa (Soc. Sec. no. 987-65-4321). Her only income is $2,800 of interest on savings. Alfredo qualifies as a head of household, and his taxable income is $32,000. Compute her tax using Form 8615.

I2-57   James S. (Soc. Sec. no. 123-45-6789) and Lulu B. Watson (Soc. Sec. no. 987-65-4321) reside at 999 E. North Street, Richmond, Virginia 23174. They have one dependent child, Waldo, age 4 (Soc. Sec. no. 123-45-4321) and they are both under 65 years old. They do not wish to take advantage of the presidential election campaign check-off. Other relevant information includes

James's salary as a mechanic	$19,000
Lulu's salary as a teacher	24,000
Interest (First National Bank)	1,100
Withholding	4,500

Complete their Form 1040A.

TAX CUT

I2-58 John R. Lane (Soc. Sec. no. 123-44-6666) lives at 1010 Ipsen Street, Yorba Linda, California 90102. John, a single taxpayer, age 66, provided 100% of his cousin's support. The cousin lives in Arizona. He wants to take advantage of the presidential election campaign check-off. John is an accountant. Other relevant information includes

Salary	$20,000
Taxable pension	30,000
Interest income	300
IRA deduction	2,000
Itemized deductions (from Schedule A)	6,000
Withholding	8,000

Assume that the supplemental Schedule A has already been completed. Complete Form 1040.

CASE STUDY PROBLEMS

I2-59 Bala and Ann purchased as investments three identical parcels of land over a several-year period. Two years ago they gave one parcel to their daughter, Kim, who is now age 12. They have an offer from an investor who is interested in acquiring all three parcels. The buyer is able to purchase only two of the parcels now, but wants to purchase the third parcel two or three years from now, when he expects to have available funds to acquire the property. Because they paid different prices for the parcels, the sales will result in different amounts of gains and losses. The sale of one parcel owned by Bala and Ann will result in a $20,000 gain and the sale of the other parcel will result in a $28,000 loss. The sale of the parcel owned by Kim will result in a $19,000 gain. Kim has no other income and does not expect any significant income for several years. Bala and Ann, however, are in the 31% tax bracket. They do not have any other capital gains this year. Which two properties would you recommend that they sell this year? Why?

I2-60 Larry and Sue separated at the end of the year. Larry has asked Sue to sign a joint income tax return for the year because he feels that the tax will be lower on a joint return. Larry and Sue both work. Sue received a salary of $25,000 and Larry's salary was $20,000. Larry works as a waiter at a local restaurant and received tips. The restaurant asked Larry to indicate the amount of tips he received so that they could report the information to the IRS. Larry reported to the employer that the tips amounted to $3,000, but Sue believes that the amount was probably $6,000 to $10,000. They do not have enough expenses to itemize. Sue has asked you what are the advantages and risks of filing a joint return.

TAX RESEARCH PROBLEMS

I2-61 Ed has supported his stepdaughter, her husband, and their child since his wife's death three years ago. Ed promised his late wife that he would support her daughter from a former marriage and her daughter's husband until they both finished college. They live in another state, and meet gross income filing requirements. Is Ed entitled to dependency exemptions for the three individuals?

A partial list of research sources is

- Sec. 152
- Reg. Sec. 1.152-2
- *Desio Barbetti*, 9 T.C. 1097 (1947)

I2-62 Bob and Sue were expecting a baby in January, but Sue was rushed to the hospital in December. She delivered the baby but it died the first night. Are Bob and Sue entitled to a dependency exemption for the baby?

Research sources include Rev. Rul. 73-156, 1973-1 C.B. 58.

I2-63 Larry has severe vision problems and, in the past, he has claimed the additional standard deduction available to blind taxpayers. This year Larry's doctor prescribed a new type of contact lens that greatly improved his vision. Naturally, Larry was elated, but unfortunately new problems developed. He suffered severe pain, infection, and ulcers from wearing the new lens. The doctor recommended that he remove the lens and after several weeks his eyes healed. The doctor told him that he could wear the contacts again, but only for brief time periods, or the problems would recur. Can Larry claim the additional standard deduction available to blind taxpayers?

Research sources include *Emanuel Hollman*, 38 T.C. 251 (1963).

CHAPTER 3

GROSS INCOME: INCLUSIONS

LEARNING OBJECTIVES

After studying this chapter, you should be able to

1. Explain the difference between the economic, accounting, and tax concepts of income

2. Explain the principles used to determine who is taxed on a particular item of income

3. Determine when a particular item of income is taxable under both the cash and accrual methods of reporting

4. Apply the rules of Sec. 61(a) to determine whether items such as compensation, dividends, alimony, and pensions are taxable

Computation of an individual's income tax liability begins with the determination of income. Although the meaning of the term *income* has long been debated by economists, accountants, tax specialists, and politicians, there is no universally accepted operational definition.

The Sixteenth Amendment to the Constitution gave Congress the power to tax "income from whatever source derived." To ensure the constitutionality of the income tax, this phrase is incorporated in Sec. 61(a), where **gross income** is defined as follows: "Except as otherwise provided . . . gross income means all income from whatever source derived."

This chapter examines the concept of income for the purpose of determining what items of income are taxable. Chapter I4 considers items of income that are not taxable. As noted in Chapter I2, many provisions in the tax law are created by a process of political compromise. Thus, there is no single explanation of why certain items are taxable and others are not. For this reason, determining whether a particular item of income is taxable often proves difficult.

ECONOMIC AND ACCOUNTING CONCEPTS OF INCOME

ECONOMIC CONCEPT

OBJECTIVE **1**

Explain the difference between the economic, accounting, and tax concepts of income

In economics, *income* is defined as the amount an individual could consume during a period and remain as well off at the end of the period as he or she was at the beginning of the period. To the economist, therefore, income includes both the wealth that flows to the individual and changes in the value of the individual's store of wealth.

EXAMPLE I3-1 ▶

Alice earned a salary of $40,000. She consumed $30,000 of food, clothing, housing, medical care, and other goods and services. Assets owned by Alice were worth $100,000 at the beginning of the year. Her assets, including $10,000 of salary that was saved, were worth $115,000 at the end of the year. Her liabilities did not change during the year. Alice's economic income is $45,000 [$30,000 + ($115,000 − $100,000)]. ◀

Under the economist's definition, unrealized gains, as well as gifts and inheritances, are income. Furthermore, the economist adjusts for inflation in measuring income. There is no income to the extent that an increase in the measured value of property is caused by a decrease in the value of the measuring unit. In other words, inflation does not cause an individual to be better off.

ACCOUNTING CONCEPT

In accounting, income is measured by a transaction approach. Accountants usually measure income when it is *realized* in a transaction. Values measured by transactions are relatively objective. Accountants recognize (i.e., report) income, gains, and losses that have been realized as a result of a completed transaction. The accountant believes that the economic concept of income is too subjective to be used as a basis for financial reporting. The accountant has traditionally used historical costs in measuring income instead of using unconfirmed estimates of changes in market value. In accounting, the meaning of the term *realization* is critical to the income measurement process. Realization generally results upon the occurrence of two events, (1) a change in the form or substance of a taxpayer's property (or phrased another way, a severance of the economic interest in the property), and (2) a transaction with a second party. Thus, if a taxpayer sells some property for cash, a realization has clearly occurred, i.e., the property has been changed to cash and the transaction was with a second party. Conversely, the mere increase in value of property owned by a taxpayer will not result in the realization of income because there has no change in the form of the property and no transaction with a second party.

EXAMPLE I3-2 ▶ Assume the same facts as in Example I3-1. The amount consumed by Alice, the increase in the value of the property owned by her, and inflation are all ignored by the accountant in measuring her income. Only when she sells or otherwise disposes of the assets that have increased in value will the accountant recognize the gain. Thus, Alice's accounting income is $40,000. ◀

TAX CONCEPT OF INCOME

The income tax law has essentially adopted the accountant's concept of income rather than the economist's. The reasons for this generally relate to matters of administrative convenience and the wherewithal-to-pay concept.

ADMINISTRATIVE CONVENIENCE

The economic concept of income is considered to be too subjective to be used as a basis for determining income taxes. The need for objectivity in taxation is evident. If taxpayers were required to report increases in value as income, some individuals would feel compelled to understate values in order to reduce their tax liabilities. The IRS and even the most honest taxpayer would often disagree over values and, as a result, the tax system would be practically impossible to administer. The disputes over valuation issues would be constant, and the courts would be burdened with added litigation. This is evidenced by the few situations where valuations are required in the determination of tax. For example, taxpayers who contribute property to charity may generally deduct the value of the property. The courts are continuously having to resolve disputes between taxpayers and the IRS over the value of such contributions. Recently, penalties were added to the law for persons who substantially overvalue contributions. Furthermore, in the case of certain large contributions of property, taxpayers are required to attach to their returns appraisals of the contributed property.

In some instances objectivity is achieved at the price of equity. For example, a taxpayer who owns land that has substantially declined in value generally cannot recognize the decline in value until it is realized through a disposition of the land. Similarly, an increase in value, no matter how large, is not taxed until there is a sale or exchange of the property. A taxpayer with a modest salary may feel that it is unfair that he or she is taxed on the salary while another person is not taxed on unrealized gains amounting to millions of dollars. As noted above, however, it would be practically impossible to fairly and consistently administer an income tax law that was based on values.

WHEREWITHAL TO PAY

The wherewithal-to-pay concept suggests that a tax should be collected when the taxpayer can most easily pay it. A taxpayer who owns property that has increased in value does not necessarily have the cash needed to pay the tax. Taxing the gain when it is realized often means that the tax becomes due at the time the taxpayer collects the sales price. Wherewithal to pay is often at its greatest when income is realized. The wherewithal-to-pay concept is the rationale for certain provisions of the tax law. For example, a taxpayer collects the proceeds from an installment sale transaction after the sale takes place. The tax law allows the taxpayer to report the sale on an installment basis under which the gain is reported as the sales proceeds are collected. Thus, the tax

KEY POINT

Section 446(a) states that taxable income shall be computed under the method of accounting on the basis of which the taxpayer regularly computes his or her income in keeping his or her books. This provision would seem to require that tax accounting rules would conform to financial accounting rules. However, as will be seen later in this and other chapters, there are many differences.

becomes due when the taxpayer has the wherewithal to pay. The installment sale method cannot be used to report losses, as the wherewithal-to-pay concept is not an issue with losses.

The wherewithal-to-pay concept is also used to justify certain differences between tax law and financial accounting principles. In financial accounting, prepaid income is not reported until it is earned, even if collected before it is earned. In contrast, however, prepaid income is taxed as it is collected rather than when it is earned for both cash and accrual-basis taxpayers. At that time, the taxpayer has the cash available to pay the tax. It might prove more difficult to collect the tax if the government waited until the income was earned because the money might have been spent by then.

GROSS INCOME DEFINED

Section 61(a) provides the following general definition and listing of income items:

General Definition.—Except as otherwise provided in this subtitle, gross income means all income from whatever source derived, including (but not limited to) the following items:

1. Compensation for services, including fees, commissions, fringe benefits, and similar items
2. Gross income derived from business
3. Gains derived from dealings in property
4. Interest
5. Rents
6. Royalties
7. Dividends
8. Alimony and separate maintenance payments
9. Annuities
10. Income from life insurance and endowment contracts
11. Pensions
12. Income from discharge of indebtedness
13. Distributive share of partnership gross income
14. Income in respect of a decedent
15. Income from an interest in an estate or trust

This definition is not all-inclusive. It does not indicate whether specific items of income such as insurance settlements, gambling winnings, or illegal income are taxable. One point is apparent: The phrase *except as otherwise provided* means that income is presumed to be taxable unless there is a specific exclusion in the income tax law. The IRS does not have to prove that an item of income is taxable. Rather, the taxpayer must prove that the item of income is excluded. Thus, gambling winnings and illegal income are taxable simply because there are no specific provisions in the tax law excluding such amounts from taxation.

FORM OF RECEIPT. Gross income is not limited to amounts received in the form of cash. According to Reg. Sec. 1.61-1(a), income may be "realized in any form, whether in money, property, or services." The important question is whether the taxpayer receives an economic benefit.

EXAMPLE I3-3 ▶ King Corporation transfers 1,000 shares of its stock to its president. There are no restrictions on the stock, and it is part of the president's compensation. The president must include the value of the stock in gross income. ◀

EXAMPLE I3-4 ▶ Ali, an attorney, performs legal services for Paul, a painter, in exchange for Paul's promise to paint Ali's residence. Each realizes income equal to the value of services received when the services are performed. Thus, Ali must report income in an amount equal to the value of the painting services provided by Paul. Paul must report the value of Ali's legal services. These amounts, assuming an arms-length transaction, should be the same. ◄

EXAMPLE I3-5 ▶ USA Corporation distributes an automobile to Vicki, a shareholder, in lieu of a cash dividend. Vicki must report the value of the automobile as dividend income. ◄

EXAMPLE I3-6 ▶ Len has fallen behind on loan payments due Judy. Judy obtains a court order requiring Len's employer to pay part of Len's wages to her. Len will be taxed on the full wages even though a portion goes directly to Judy. Any interest Judy receives is includible in her gross income but principal payments are not taxable. ◄

EXAMPLE I3-7 ▶ Wayne borrowed $3,000 from his employer. The employer awarded year-end bonuses to other employees but told Wayne that the debt was being forgiven in lieu of a bonus. Wayne must include the $3,000 in income. ◄

STOP & THINK

Question: As noted, income is taxable even if it is paid in a form other than cash. What problem does this produce for the IRS and taxpayers?

Solution: There are two major problems: valuation and enforcement. It is necessary to determine the market value of property and services when income is received in a form other than cash. That can be difficult. Further, enforcement by the IRS is made much more difficult because such income is not documented by canceled checks, credit card receipts, or other records. Thus, as demonstrated in Example I3-4 above, many of these so-called "traded services" are not reported as income. This evasion of income represents billions of lost tax revenues to the government.

INDIRECT ECONOMIC BENEFIT. As indicated earlier, the issue often is whether the taxpayer received an economic benefit. In general, if a taxpayer benefits from an item, it is taxable. Frequently, however, an employer may make an expenditure in which its employees may incidentally or indirectly benefit. For example,

▶ Security guards patrol an employer's plant, protecting both the employer's property and the employees. The employees receive an indirect benefit for the protection provided by the security guards.

▶ An employer requires employees to undergo an annual checkup, the cost of which is paid by the employer.

▶ An employer provides uniforms and protective clothing worn by employees while on the job.

▶ A shipping company provides sleeping accommodations to sailors while ships are at sea.

▶ A company requires certain employees to wear shoes manufactured by the company and provide regular reports on the quality of the shoes.

It is now well-established that taxpayers may exclude such indirect benefits from gross income. This judicially-developed rule holds that an expenditure is excludible if it is made in order to serve the business needs of the employer and any benefit to the employee is secondary and incidental.

This rule has developed over time. In a 1919 ruling, it was held that lodging furnished seamen aboard ship was not taxable.[1] This was followed by a 1925 court decision that

---

[1] O.D. 265, 1 C.B. 71 (1919).

held that an Army officer could exclude the value of quarters provided by the Army.[2] In 1951, the Tax Court concluded that employees need not report income if personal wants and needs of employees are satisfied secondarily and incidentally.[3] In 1961, an appeals court also required that an expenditure must serve a business purpose other than compensating an employee if a benefit is to be excluded from the employee's gross income.[4]

Congress has also established rules dealing with situations where expenditures are made primarily to benefit employees. While expenditures made by employers that primarily benefit employees are generally taxable, there are instances whereby such expenditures are not taxable. These rules, which are discussed in Chapters I4 and I9, permit employees to exclude certain fringe benefits (such as employee discounts) from gross income.

TO WHOM IS INCOME TAXABLE?

OBJECTIVE 2

Explain the principles used to determine who is taxed on a particular item of income

KEY POINT

The law makes a clear distinction between an assignment of income and an assignment of income-producing property. The income is taxable to the assignor in the former case, but where there is a bona fide gift of property the income is taxable to the assignee.

ADDITIONAL COMMENT

The community property states are generally located in the western or southwestern United States. Generally these states were settled by immigrants from France and Spain, and their state laws reflect this fact. The common law is derived from English common law.

Once it is established that income is taxable, it may be necessary to determine to whom it is taxable. Although such determinations are usually easy, there are circumstances where income is not necessarily taxed to the person who receives it. If physical receipt of income was the only test, a family might reduce or eliminate its income tax by having income paid to children and other members who are in low tax brackets or have no tax liability.

ASSIGNMENT OF INCOME

In 1930, the Supreme Court held in a landmark case, *Lucas v. Earl,* that an individual is taxed on the earnings from his or her personal services.[5] Specifically, the Supreme Court held that a husband was taxed on the earnings from his law practice, even though he had signed a legally enforceable agreement with his wife that the earnings would be shared equally. An agreement to assign income does not permit a person to avoid being taxed on the income. The Court used the previously developed analogy that likens income to the fruit and capital to the tree.[6] Accordingly, the fruit (income) could not be attributed to a tree other than the one on which it grew.

In 1940, the Supreme Court, in *Helvering v. Horst,* extended the assignment of income doctrine to income from property.[7] In this case, the taxpayer detached interest coupons from bonds and gave the coupons to his son. The son collected the interest and reported it on his own return. The Supreme Court held that the taxpayer was taxed on the interest income because he owned the bonds. This leads to a basic rule that the income from property is taxed to the owner of the property. To transfer the income from property, the taxpayer must transfer ownership of the property itself.[8]

Although married couples may file joint returns today, this privilege did not become available until 1948. Assignment of income is an issue today when other individuals such as parents and children are involved, and it can still be an issue with married couples if they file separate returns.

---

[2] *Clifford Jones v. U.S.,* 5 AFTR 5297, 1 USTC ¶129 (Ct. Cls., 1925). Section 119, discussed in Chapter I4, now provides specific requirements that must be satisfied before lodging may be excluded.
[3] *Gunnar Van Rosen,* 17 T.C. 834 (1951).
[4] *George D. Patterson v. Thomas,* 7 AFTR 2d 862, 61-1 USTC ¶9310 (5th Cir., 1961).
[5] *Lucas v. Earl,* 8 AFTR 10287, 2 USTC ¶496 (USSC, 1930).
[6] The analogy had been used some ten years earlier in *Eisner v. Myrtle H. Macomber,* 3 AFTR 3020, 1 USTC ¶32 (USSC, 1920). The court originally

used the analogy in efforts to distinguish income from capital.
[7] *Helvering v. Horst,* 24 AFTR 1058, 40-2 USTC ¶9787 (USSC, 1940).
[8] A series of rather specific rules allocates income between the former and current owner when income-producing property is transferred. For example, in the case of bonds transferred by gift, the IRS has ruled that interest must be allocated based on the number of days the bonds were held by each owner during the interest period (Rev. Rul. 72-312, 1972-1 C.B. 22). A similar allocation must be made if bonds are sold (Rev. Rul. 72-224, 1972-1 C.B. 30).

ALLOCATING INCOME
BETWEEN MARRIED PEOPLE

For federal income tax purposes, income is allocated between a husband and wife depending on the state of residence. Forty-two states follow a common law property system, whereas eight states[9] use a community property system. Under common law, income is generally taxed to the individual who earns the income, either through labor or capital. Thus, in the case of a married couple, if the wife owns stock in her separate name and receives dividends from such stock, the income is taxed entirely to the wife. Generally, the only **joint income** in a common law state is income from jointly owned property.[10]

In community property states, income may be either separate or community. **Community income** is considered to belong equally to the spouses. In all community property states, the income from the personal efforts of either spouse is considered to belong equally to the spouses. Furthermore, income from community property is considered to be community income. Thus, if a wife's salary is used to purchase stock, subsequent dividends are community income.

Couples can have separate property even in community property states. **Separate property** consists of all property owned before marriage and gifts and inheritances acquired after marriage. Whether income from separate property is community or separate depends on the state. In Idaho, Louisiana, and Texas, income from separate property is community income. In Arizona, California, Nevada, New Mexico, and Washington, such income is separate income.

EXAMPLE I3-8 ▶ A husband and wife file separate returns. The husband's salary is $40,000 and the wife's salary is $48,000. The wife received $1,000 of dividends on stock she had inherited from her parents. Interest of $1,200 was received on bonds that were purchased from the husband's salary. They received $2,600 in rent from farm land that they purchased jointly. The income would be allocated, depending on the state of residence, as follows:

California (Community Property State)	*Husband*	*Wife*
Salary	$44,000	$44,000
Dividends		1,000
Interest	600	600
Rent	1,300	1,300
Total	$45,900	$46,900
Texas (Community Property State)		
Salary	$44,000	$44,000
Dividends	500	500
Interest	600	600
Rent	1,300	1,300
Total	$46,400	$46,400
Pennsylvania (Common Law State)		
Salary	$40,000	$48,000
Dividends		1,000
Interest	1,200	
Rent	1,300	1,300
Total	$42,500	$50,300 ◀

---

[9] The states are Arizona, California, Idaho, Louisiana, Nevada, New Mexico, Texas, and Washington. Wisconsin's marital property law, though not providing for community property, is basically the same as community property.

[10] Historically, tenancy by the entirety, a form of joint ownership between spouses, allocated all income to the husband. Today, the laws of many states allocate income from property held in tenancy by the entirety equally between the spouses.

These rules are important if couples file separate returns. The community income rules can prove to be a problem if one spouse conceals income from the other. Normally, each spouse is expected to report one-half of all community income. This is inequitable if one spouse is not aware that the community income was earned. Special rules excuse an innocent spouse who fails to report community income on a separate return, provided that the spouse had no knowledge or reason to know of the item and, as a result, the inclusion of the community income would be inequitable.[11] A corresponding provision permits the IRS to include the entire amount in the income of the other spouse.[12]

STOP & THINK

Question: The differences in federal income taxation of income earned in a common law state versus a community property state can be very inconsistent. As noted, the Supreme Court, in *Lucas v. Earl*, decided that a husband was taxed on all his income even though he agreed to share that income with his wife. Nevertheless, community income in a community property state is divided equally between husbands and wives even if one spouse earned all of the income. Why the tax distinction?

Solution: *Lucas v. Earl* dealt with a case in a common law state where the husband was legally entitled to the income, but decided to divide it with his wife. In community property states couples are legally obligated to share their incomes. The federal income tax law respects the different property law systems of the states and taxes the income of persons based on state law. It would be unfairly burdensome to tax individuals on income to which they never had any legal right.

INCOME OF MINOR CHILDREN

As noted earlier, whether a husband or wife is taxed on income is determined by state law. However, earnings of a minor child are taxed to the child regardless of the state's property law system. Therefore, earnings of a child from either personal services (compensation) or from property (dividends, interest, rents, etc.) are taxed to the child, not the child's parents. As noted in Chapter I2, the unearned income of a child under age 14 may be taxed at the parents' tax rate if it is higher than the child's rate. Alternatively, the parents may elect to include the child's unearned income on their return. In the case of spouses, the spouse who has a legal right to such income determines who is taxed on it. In the case of children, however, the individual who earned the income determines who is taxed on it.

WHEN IS INCOME TAXABLE?

OBJECTIVE 3

Determine when a particular item of income is taxable under both the cash and accrual methods of reporting

The year in which income is taxed depends on the taxpayer's accounting method. The three primary overall accounting methods are the **cash receipts and disbursements method**, the **accrual method**, and the **hybrid method**. While taxpayers have the right to choose a method of accounting, the chosen method still must clearly reflect income as determined by the IRS. The IRS has the power to change the accounting method used by a taxpayer if, in the opinion of the IRS, the method being used does not clearly reflect income.[13] Further, the Regulations require taxpayers to use the accrual method for determining purchases and sales when a taxpayer maintains an inventory.[14] In other words, income would not be clearly reflected if beginning and ending inventories were ignored.

---

[11] Sec. 66(b).
[12] Sec. 66(c).

[13] Sec. 446(b).
[14] Reg. Sec. 1.446-1(c)(2)(i).

KEY POINT

Neither the code nor the regulations define the terms *accounting* and *accounting method*.

Section 448 requires C corporations (and partnerships with corporate partners), tax shelters, and certain trusts to use the accrual method of accounting. Farming businesses, qualified personal service corporations, and entities with average gross receipts under $5 million are exempt from the requirement.

Once an accounting method has been adopted, it cannot be changed without permission of the IRS.

CASH METHOD

ADDITIONAL COMMENT

Taxpayers engaged in more than one trade or business may use a different method of accounting for each separate trade or business.

The **cash receipts and disbursements method** of accounting is used by most individual taxpayers and most noncorporate businesses that do not have inventories.[15] (See Chapter I11 for a more complete discussion of who is permitted to use the cash method.) Under this method, income is reported in the year the taxpayer actually or constructively receives the income rather than in the year the income is earned. The income can be received by the taxpayer or the taxpayer's agent and be in the form of cash, other property, or services.[16] In the case of property or services, the amount included in the income is the value of the property or services. An accounts receivable or other unsupported promise to pay is considered to have no value under the cash method and, as a result, no income is recognized until the receivable is collected. Topic Review I3-1 summarizes when various types of income are reported.

ADDITIONAL COMMENT

The use of the cash receipts and disbursements method of accounting gives the taxpayer some control over the timing of the recognition of income and deductions. It also has the advantage of simplicity.

The fact that prepaid income is usually taxed when received, rather than when earned, often results in a mismatching of income and expenses.

EXAMPLE I3-9 ▶

In December of the current year, Troy rents an apartment and collects the first and last months' rent from the tenant. Troy must report two months rent in the current year. The actual expenses associated with the last month's rental are not incurred until the last month. However, Troy must report two months income this year, but may only deduct one month's expenses. ◀

Reporting prepaid income can have harsh results because there are no related deductions. If the income is taxed before the expenses are incurred, the taxpayer may not have enough cash to pay the expenses when they are incurred.[17] This burden is mitigated, in part, by Treasury Regulations and Revenue Procedures discussed in this chapter (e.g., the treatment of prepaid income, page I3-11).

ADDITIONAL COMMENT

There is no recognized doctrine of constructive payment.

REAL-WORLD EXAMPLE

Paul Hornung, a former football player with the Green Bay Packers, was awarded an automobile in 1961 for being the outstanding player in the NFL championship game, but he did not actually receive it until 1962. He attempted to invoke the constructive receipt doctrine and report the income in 1961. The court held that he could not claim constructive receipt because the car was not set aside in the year of the award. *Paul V. Hornung*, 47 T.C. 428 (1967).

CONSTRUCTIVE RECEIPT. As noted, a cash-basis taxpayer must report income in the year in which it is actually or constructively received. Constructive receipt means that the income is made available to the taxpayer so that he may draw upon it at any time. However, income is not constructively received if the taxpayer's control of its receipt is subject to substantial limitations or restrictions. This rule works to prevent taxpayers from deferring income that is otherwise available by merely "turning their backs" on it. A taxpayer cannot defer income recognition by refusing to accept payment.

Examples of constructive receipt where taxpayers are required to report taxable income even though no cash is actually received include

▶ A check received after banking hours[18]

▶ Interest credited to a bank savings account[19]

▶ Bond interest coupons that have matured but have not been redeemed[20]

---

[15] This includes accountants, lawyers, barbers, laundries, and insurance agents.
[16] An agent can be an employee, relative, or other person authorized to receive the income.
[17] This mismatching of income and expenses affects both cash and accrual

basis taxpayers.
[18] *Charles F. Kahler*, 18 T.C. 31 (1952).
[19] Reg. Sec. 1.451-2(b).
[20] Ibid.

Topic Review I3-1

When Income Is Taxable

Item	Cash Basis	Accrual Basis
Compensation	Year actually or constructively received.	Year earned or year received if prepaid.
Interest	Year actually or constructively received.	Year accrued or year received if prepaid.
Discount on Series E or EE Bonds	Choice of reporting interest as it accrues or at maturity.	Year accrued.
Dividends	Year actually or constructively received.	Year actually or constructively received.
Rent	Year actually or constructively received (does not apply to a deposit).	Year accrued or year received if prepaid (year accrued if services are associated, e.g., in a hotel or motel) (does not apply to a deposit).
Services (maintenance contracts, dance lessons, etc.)	Year actually or constructively received.	Year accrued or year received if prepaid except that a taxpayer may report the income as it accrues if all the services are to be performed by the end of the next tax year.
Sale of goods	The cash method cannot be used to report sale of goods if inventories are an income-producing factor.	Year of sale or year cash is received if prepaid except may elect to report in year of sale if goods are not on hand, amount received is less than cost of item, and same accounting method is used for financial accounting.
Subscriptions (newspapers, magazines, etc.)	Year actually or constructively received.	Year earned or year cash is received, if prepaid, except may elect to report income as newspaper, etc., is published.
Memberships (automobile clubs, etc.)	Year actually or constructively received.	Year earned or year received if prepaid (certain nonstock corporations may elect to report prepaid amounts over the membership period, if the period covers three years or less).
Sale of property (other than stock)	Year actually or constructively received.	Year transaction is completed (e.g., the close of escrow in case of sale of real estate).
Sale of stock	Year transaction is executed.	Year transaction is executed.

▶ Salary available to an employee who does not accept payment[21]

An amount is not considered to be constructively received if

▶ It is subject to substantial limitations or restrictions.

▶ The payor does not have the funds necessary to make payment.

▶ The amount is unavailable to the taxpayer.

---

[21] *James J. Cooney*, 18 T.C. 883 (1952).

EXAMPLE I3-10 ▶ Beth owns an ordinary life insurance policy with a cash surrender value. She need not report any income as the cash surrender value increases because the requirement that she cancel the policy in order to collect the cash surrender value constitutes a substantial restriction. ◀

EXAMPLE I3-11 ▶ Cathy has received a paycheck from her employer but has been told to hold the check until the employer has sufficient funds to cover the payroll. Cathy need not report the amount of the check as income until funds are deposited to the employer's account. ◀

EXAMPLE I3-12 ▶ On December 2, 1997, Dan sold land for $100,000 payable on February 2, 1998. During the negotiations, the buyer offered to pay cash. Because the parties did not agree to a cash transaction, there was no constructive receipt in 1997. Under the terms of the sale, funds were not available at the time of sale. Thus, Dan is permitted to defer the recognition of income under the contract since the contract is made before the income is earned. ◀

EXCEPTIONS. There are exceptions to the basic rule that cash-basis taxpayers report income when it is actually or constructively received.

▶ The interest on Series E and Series EE U.S. savings bonds need not be reported until the final maturity date, which varies but may be as long as forty years after the date of issue, and can be deferred even longer if the bonds are exchanged within one year of the final maturity date for Series HH U.S. savings bonds.[22] Many taxpayers purchase bonds with a maturity date that falls after retirement when the taxpayers expect to be in a lower tax bracket.

▶ Special rules also apply to farmers and ranchers. Farmers may report crop insurance proceeds in the year following receipt if the crop would have ordinarily been sold in the following year. Ranchers who sell livestock on account of a drought may delay reporting income one year if the area is designated as eligible for federal drought assistance and the livestock sale would otherwise have taken place in a later tax year. Both rules help taxpayers avoid a bunching of income into one year.

EXAMPLE I3-13 ▶ Tenisha purchased a Series EE U.S. savings bond in the current year for $1,000 that matures in 20 years. The bond will not pay any interest until the bond matures; at maturity, the bond will be worth $2,500. Tenisha is not required to report any interest income for tax purposes until the bond matures. At maturity, when Tenisha receives the $2,500, she will report $1,500 of interest income. If she desires to defer the interest further, she could exchange her Series EE bond for a Series H bond within one year. ◀

REAL-WORLD EXAMPLE

The Ninth Circuit Court of Appeals has held that "markers" customers gave to a gambling casino to evidence their indebtedness to the casino required accrual even though the receivables were legally unenforceable under state law. The court found that there need only be a "reasonable expectancy" that payment would be made. *Flamingo Resort, Inc. v. U.S.*, 50 AFTR 2d 82-502, 82-1 USTC ¶9136 (9th Cir., 1982).

ACCRUAL METHOD

Taxpayers using the accrual method of accounting generally report income in the year it is earned. Income is considered to have been earned when all the events have occurred that fix the right to receive the income and when the amount of income can be determined with reasonable accuracy.[23] In the case of a sale of property, income normally accrues when title passes to the buyer.[24] Income from services accrues as the services are performed.

PREPAID INCOME. A major exception to the normal operation of the accrual method is the rules applicable to the receipt of prepaid income. Prepaid income is generally

---

[22] Series E bonds were issued prior to 1980; Series EE bonds were issued after 1979. The interest on the Series HH bonds is taxable as received.
[23] Reg. Sec. 1.451-1(a).
[24] Regulation Sec. 1.446-1(c)(1)(ii), however, does permit taxpayers the right

to accrue income from the sale of inventory when the goods are shipped, when the product is delivered or accepted, or when title passes, as long as the method is consistently used.

taxable in the year of receipt. For example, if a lender receives January interest in the preceding December, it is taxable in the year received, whether the lender uses the cash or accrual method. This, of course, is unlike financial accounting, where the interest would be reported as it accrues.

Two important exceptions to the general rule are worth noting. Accrual-basis taxpayers may defer recognizing income in the case of certain advance payments for *goods* and in the case of certain advance payments for *services* to be rendered. A taxpayer may generally defer advance payments for goods (inventory) if the taxpayer's method of accounting for the sale is the same for tax and financial accounting purposes.[25]

Under Rev. Proc. 71-21, a taxpayer may defer advance payments for services if the payments are for services to be performed before the end of the tax year following the year of receipt.[26] Such payments may be reported as the services are performed, e.g., the taxpayer may allocate the payment received over the current and succeeding years. The rule is not available if a payment covers a time period that extends beyond the end of the tax year following the year of receipt. The rule can be applied to a variety of services such as dance lessons, maintenance contracts (but not warranties included in the sales price of a product), and rent (if services are associated with the rent, as with a hotel or motel).

EXAMPLE I3-14 ▶

Bear Corporation, an accrual-basis taxpayer that uses the calendar year as its tax year, sells dance lessons under contracts ranging from three months to two years. The contracts which are covered by Rev. Proc. 71-21 varies depending on the month of sale. For example, contracts sold in July for a term of longer than eighteen months are not covered by the rule, and all income must be reported for these contracts in the year of the sale. Assume Bear Corporation sold three contracts in July 1997: one for three months costing $90, one for one year costing $300, and one for two years costing $500. Income would be recognized as follows:

Length of Contract	1997	1998
3 months	$ 90	
12 months	150	$150
24 months	500	

◀

HYBRID METHOD

The **hybrid method** of accounting is a combination of the cash and accrual methods. Under the hybrid method, some items of income or expense are reported under the cash basis and others are reported under the accrual method. The method is most often encountered in small businesses that maintain inventories and are required to use the accrual method of accounting for purchases and sales of goods.[27] Such businesses often prefer to use the cash method of reporting for other items because the cash method is simpler and may provide greater flexibility for tax planning. A taxpayer using the hybrid method of accounting would use the accrual method with respect to purchases and sales of goods but would use the cash method in computing all other items of income and expenses.[28]

---

[25] Reg. Sec. 1.451-5.
[26] 1971-2 C.B. 549.
[27] Reg. Sec. 1.446-1(c)(2)(i).
[28] Reg. Sec. 1.446-1(c)(1)(iv).

ITEMS OF GROSS INCOME: SEC. 61(a)

Section 61(a), quoted earlier in this chapter, states that gross income includes, but is not limited to, fifteen specifically listed types of income. Several of these items are discussed below.

COMPENSATION

Compensation is payment for personal services. It includes salaries, wages, fees, commissions, tips, bonuses, and specialized forms of compensation such as director's fees, jury fees, and marriage fees received by clergymen. What the compensation is called, how it is computed, the form and frequency of payment, and whether the compensation is subject to withholding is of little significance. Similarly, the fact that the services are part-time, one-time, seasonal, or temporary is immaterial.

ADDITIONAL COMMENT

Salaries and wages constituted 77.3% of total income in 1992.

There are exclusions, however, for a variety of employer-provided fringe benefits such as group term life insurance premiums, health and accident insurance premiums, employee discounts, contributions to retirement plans, and free parking. In addition, there is a limited exclusion applicable to foreign-earned income. Both fringe benefits and the foreign-earned income exclusion are discussed in Chapter I4.

BUSINESS INCOME

SELF-STUDY QUESTION

A retailing company had sales of $1,000,000 the following costs: goods sold, $400,000, salaries, $200,000, and rent and other expenses, $100,000. What is the company's gross income?

ANSWER

The gross income is $600,000. The sales figure is reduced by the cost of goods sold.

The term *gross income* usually refers to the total amount received from a particular source. In the case of businesses that provide services (e.g., accounting and law), the gross business income is the total amount received. In the case of manufacturing, merchandising, and mining, however, gross income is total sales less the cost of goods sold.

The cost of goods sold is, in effect, treated as a return of capital. Chapter I4 discusses a well-established tax concept that a return of capital is not income and, therefore, cannot be subject to the income tax. Chapter I10 discusses the methods available for valuing inventory.

GAINS FROM DEALINGS IN PROPERTY

Gains realized from property transactions are included in gross income unless a nonrecognition rule applies. As is true with business inventories, taxpayers may deduct the cost of property in order to arrive at the gain from a property transaction.[29] The tax law contains over thirty nonrecognition rules, which allow taxpayers to postpone the recognition of gains and losses from certain types of property transactions. In a few instances, these rules allow taxpayers to permanently exclude gains from gross income.[30]

Losses are not offset against gains in computing gross income. Rather, most losses are deductions *for* adjusted gross income. Furthermore, net capital losses for individuals are subject to provisions that limit the amount that can be deducted from other income to $3,000 per year. Losses from the sale or disposition of an asset held for personal use are not deductible.

INTEREST

TYPICAL MISCONCEPTION

It is sometimes mistakenly assumed that interest paid on federal obligations such as Treasury bonds, notes, and bills will also qualify for tax exemption.

Interest is compensation for the use of money. Taxable interest includes interest on bank deposits, corporate bonds, mortgages, life insurance policies, tax refunds, U.S. govern-

---

[29] Note that *business income* and *gains from dealings in property* are overlapping terms. The gross profit from the sale of inventory is actually both business income and a gain from a property transaction. Typically, however, the phrase *gains from dealings in property* may be assumed to mean gains from dealings in property other than inventory, so as to avoid

confusion.

[30] For example, Sec. 121 allows taxpayers who are at least 55 years old to permanently exclude a limited amount of gain from a sale of a personal residence.

ment obligations,[31] and foreign government obligations.[32] Nontaxable interest is discussed below.

TAX-EXEMPT INTEREST. Since the inception of the federal income tax in 1913, interest on obligations of states, territories, and U.S. possessions and their political subdivisions has been tax exempt.[33] Bonds issued by school districts, port authorities, toll road commissions, counties, and fire districts have been held to be tax exempt. As noted above, this exclusion does not extend to interest paid on U.S. government obligations or foreign government obligations, nor does the exclusion exempt from taxation gains from the sale of state or local government bonds or interest on tax refunds paid by state and municipal governments.

There has always been some uncertainty as to whether the federal government could tax interest on state and local government obligations. The basic question is whether taxing these obligations would violate the doctrine of intergovernmental immunity in that the tax would reduce the ability of state and local governments to finance their operations because taxable bonds usually pay a higher rate of interest than tax-exempt bonds. The belief that taxing state and local government interest is unconstitutional is no longer widely held. While there have been efforts to tax interest on state and local bonds, the only changes have been to limit the use of bonds for private activities,[34] federally insured loans,[35] and arbitrage.[36]

SERIES EE SAVINGS BOND EXCLUSION. Taxpayers may purchase and eventually redeem Series EE bonds tax-free if they use the proceeds to pay certain college expenses for themselves, a spouse, or dependents.[37]

To qualify for the exclusion:

▶ The bonds must be purchased after 1989 by an individual who is age 24 or older at the time of the purchase.

▶ The bonds must be purchased by the owner and cannot be a gift to the owner.

▶ The receipts from the bond redemption must be used for tuition and fees, which are first reduced by tax-exempt scholarships, veterans benefits, and other similar amounts.[38]

▶ Married couples living together must file a joint return in order to obtain the exclusion.

The full amount of interest is excluded only if the combined amount of principal and interest received during the year does not exceed the net qualified educational expenses (tuition and fees reduced by exempt scholarships, etc.), and the taxpayer's 1997 modified adjusted gross income is not over $50,850 ($76,250 for married individuals filing a joint return). The exclusion is fully phased-out for taxpayers whose 1997 modified AGI is more than $65,850 ($106,250 for married individuals filing a joint return).[39]

---

[31] The interest on many federal obligations issued before March 1, 1942 is tax exempt.

[32] Reg. Sec. 1.61-7.

[33] Sec. 103(a)(1).

[34] Interest from state and local bonds issued for private activities such as the construction of sports facilities, convention centers, and industrial park sites is taxable. A limited amount of tax-exempt bonds can be issued each year by a state for "qualified" private activities such as airport construction, redevelopment, and student loans. The limit is the greater of $150 million or $50 per resident (Sec. 146(d)). Though exempt from regular income tax, interest from these "qualified" private activity bonds is subject to the alternative minimum tax (see Chapter I14). In addition, Sec. 501(c)(3) organizations may issue up to $150 million of tax-exempt bonds. Such

organizations include private universities, hospitals, churches, and similar nonprofit organizations.

[35] Sec. 149(b).

[36] Sec. 148. Interest from state or local government bonds issued for the purpose of using the proceeds to buy higher-yield investments is taxable. Such bonds are called arbitrage bonds.

[37] Sec. 135(c).

[38] The exclusion is not permitted for amounts paid for sports, games, or hobbies unless they are part of a degree program (Sec. 135(c)(2)(B)).

[39] Each of these amounts is adjusted annually for inflation. In 1996, the phase-out started at $49,450 ($74,200 on joint returns) and ended at $64,450 ($104,200 on joint returns).

ANSWER
Yes, the parents' income may increase over the years to such an extent that the interest exclusion will not be available.

If the net qualified education expenses are less than the total principal and interest, a portion of the interest is excluded based on the ratio of the qualified educational expenses to the total principal and interest. The tentative exclusion is equal to

$$\text{Series EE interest} \times \frac{\text{Net qualified educational expenses}}{\text{Series EE interest} + \text{Principal}}$$

EXAMPLE I3-15 ▶

In 1997, Lois redeems Series EE bonds and receives $6,000, consisting of $1,875 of interest and $4,125 of principal. Assume that the net qualifying expenses total $4,800. Lois's educational expenses equal 80% of the total amount received ($4,800 ÷ $6,000). Thus, her exclusion is limited to $1,500 (0.80 × $1,875). ◀

ADDITIONAL COMMENT

A child born today will require about $100,000 for a four-year college education. If interest rates are around 6%, one would have to save about $245 a month until the child entered school to be able to pay this amount.

As noted, the amount of the exclusion is further reduced if modified adjusted gross income exceeds a $50,850 threshold ($76,250 for married individuals filing a joint return). Modified adjusted gross income includes the interest from education savings bonds and certain otherwise excludable foreign income.[40] The reduction is computed as follows:

$$\begin{array}{c}\text{Otherwise}\\\text{excludable}\\\text{amount}\end{array} \times \frac{\text{Excess modified AGI}}{\$15,000\ (\$30,000\ \text{for joint filers})}$$

EXAMPLE I3-16 ▶

Assume the same facts as in Example I3-15. Also assume that Lois is single and has other adjusted gross income of $53,975. Lois's otherwise available exclusion of $1,500 is reduced by $500 to $1,000. This reduction is computed by dividing the excess modified AGI of $5,000 ($53,975 + $1,875 − $50,850) by $15,000 and multiplying the result by $1,500. ◀

RENTS AND ROYALTIES

Amounts received as rents or royalties are included in gross income. As noted earlier, prepaid rent is taxable when received. Security deposits, which are refundable to tenants upon the expiration of a lease are not included in gross income. The deposit is included in gross income only if it is not refunded upon the expiration of the lease.

EXAMPLE I3-17 ▶

In December 1997, Buddy rents an apartment to Gary. Buddy receives the first and last months' rent plus a security deposit of $500. Buddy must include in 1997 gross income both the first and last months' rent. Assume that Gary moves out of the apartment in 1999 and Buddy keeps $300 of the security deposit to cover repairs costing $200 and five days' unpaid rent, which amounts to $100. In 1999, Buddy would include the $300 in gross income and could deduct $200 for repairs. ◀

Royalties from copyrights, patents, and oil, gas, and mineral rights are all taxable as ordinary income. **Royalties** are proceeds paid to an owner by others who do business under some right belonging to the owner. Amounts received by a lessor to cancel, amend, or modify a lease are also taxable.

STOP & THINK

Question: Financial accounting contains extensive rules distinguishing "operating leases" from "capital leases." The IRC has no such rules. While the tax law does require the

---

[40] Specifically, modified adjusted gross income includes amounts that qualify for the foreign earned income exclusion (Sec. 911), the exclusion for possession's income (Sec. 931), and the exclusion for income from Puerto Rico (Sec. 933). The limitation is determined after taking the partial exclusion for Social Security benefits and railroad retirement (Sec. 86), claiming the allowable deduction for retirement contributions (Sec. 219), and applying the passive loss limitation (Sec. 469).

capitalization of leases that are in substance a purchase of the asset, most authority relating to the distinction comes from court cases. Why doesn't the tax law adopt specific rules relating to leased property?

Solution: The financial accounting rules which require businesses to capitalize some leases were established because of concern that long-term lease commitments represented unrecorded liabilities. The unrecorded liabilities distort a company's balance sheet, but may not distort reported income. Since the tax law is concerned with the reporting of income rather than the balance sheet, neither Congress nor the Treasury Department has seen the need to adopt leasing rules like those in financial accounting.

IMPROVEMENTS BY LESSEES. Improvements made by a lessee that increase the value of leased property are included in the lessor's income only if the improvements are made in lieu of paying rent or if rent is reduced because of the improvements. In such situations, the lessor must include the fair market value (FMV) of the improvement in gross income when it is made to the property.[41]

EXAMPLE I3-18 ▶ Rita rents an apartment to Anna. The apartment would normally rent for $500 per month, but Rita agrees to accept $200 per month for the first year if Anna builds a block wall around the property. Rita estimates that she would have to pay someone $3,000 to build the wall. Rita is accepting reduced rent and must report gross income of $3,000 when the wall is added to the property. The $3,000 could be added to Rita's basis in the property and should qualify as a depreciable asset. ◀

Improvements not made in lieu of rent are not income to the lessor. No adjustment is made to the lessor's basis in the property and, therefore, no depreciation is allowable. Gain or loss is recognized only when the property is disposed of.[42] Whether the improvements are in lieu of rent depends on the intent of the parties. This determination is based on the facts of the particular situation. The rental rate, the terms of the rental agreement, and whether the improvements have an estimated useful life exceeding the term of the lease may all be indications of intent.

DIVIDENDS

Distributions to shareholders are taxable as dividends only to the extent they are made from either the corporation's current earnings and profits (a concept similar, although not identical, to current year's net income for financial accounting purposes) or accumulated earnings and profits (a concept similar, although not identical, to beginning of the year retained earnings).[43] Earnings and profits are discussed in greater depth in *Prentice Hall's Federal Taxation: Corporations, Partnerships, Estates & Trusts* text and the *Comprehensive* volume. Distributions in excess of current and accumulated earnings and profits are treated as a nontaxable recovery of capital. Such distributions reduce the shareholder's basis in the stock. Distributions in excess of the basis of the stock are classified as capital gains.

EXAMPLE I3-19 ▶ Liz is the sole shareholder in Atlantic Corporation. The basis of her stock is $250,000. Atlantic distributes $40,000 to Liz in 1997. Accumulated earnings and profits at the beginning of 1997 equal $25,000, and current earnings and profits equal $10,000. Liz will report $35,000 of taxable dividend income and a nontaxable return of capital equal to $5,000. Liz must reduce her basis in the stock by $5,000. ◀

---

[41] Reg. Sec. 1.109-1.
[42] Reg. Sec. 1.1019-1.
[43] Sec. 316(a). The federal income tax became effective on March 1, 1913.

Thus, income accumulated before that date can still be distributed on a tax-exempt basis.

STOCK DIVIDENDS. A **stock dividend** is a distribution by a corporation to its shareholders of the corporation's own stock. In 1920, the Supreme Court held that simple stock dividends could not be taxed because they were not income.[44] More precisely, income had not been realized because there was no real change in the taxpayer's interest or the risks faced by the taxpayer. Over the years, however, the exclusion for stock dividends has been narrowed. If a shareholder has the option of receiving either cash or stock, the shareholder is taxed even if he or she opts to receive stock. The option to receive cash constitutes constructive receipt of the cash. Today, many other features of a stock dividend may cause it to be taxed. For example, a distribution in which preferred stock is distributed to some common shareholders and common stock is distributed to others is taxable.[45] The recipient of a taxable stock dividend includes the value of the stock received in gross income, and that amount becomes the basis of the shares received.

A nontaxable stock dividend has no effect on a shareholder's income in the year received. The basis of the old shares is allocated between the old shares and the new shares. Furthermore, the holding period for the new shares starts on the same date as the holding period of the old.

ADDITIONAL COMMENT

Many mutual funds do not want their shareholders to have a large tax bill on the un-distributed capital gains allocated among the shareholders. Some mutual funds will sell stocks in the portfolio that can be sold at a loss to offset gains incurred earlier in the year.

EXAMPLE I3-20 ▶

In 1997, Carol purchased 100 shares of Mesa Corporation stock for $1,100 (or $11 per share). In 1998, Carol receives 10 shares of Mesa stock as a nontaxable stock dividend. After the dividend, Carol owns 110 shares of stock with a basis of $1,100 (or $10 per share). All of the stock is assumed to have been acquired in 1997. ◀

CAPITAL GAIN DIVIDENDS. A **capital gain dividend** is a distribution by a regulated investment company (commonly called a *mutual fund*) of capital gains realized from the sale of investments in the fund. Such dividends also include any undistributed capital gains allocated to shareholders by such companies.[46] Capital gain dividends are long-term regardless of how long the shareholder has owned the stock of the regulated investment company.

REAL-WORLD EXAMPLE

In the 1989 trial of Leona Helmsley, the billionaire hotel queen, it was disclosed that she had billed her companies for millions of dollars in personal items. The items ranged from a $12.99 girdle to a $1 million limestone-and-marble pool enclosure at her estate. She was sentenced to four years in prison and fined $7.1 million. The amounts paid to her by her companies represented constructive dividends.

CONSTRUCTIVE DIVIDENDS. In many corporations the same individuals are both shareholders and employees. A corporation may not deduct dividends paid to sharehold-ers but is permitted to deduct reasonable compensation. Questions are often raised as to whether amounts identified as compensation are really disguised dividends. If an amount called compensation is unreasonable, it will be disallowed.[47] Often the reasonableness of compensation is determined by comparing the compensation paid to the employee-shareholders with amounts paid to others performing similar services.

EXAMPLE I3-21 ▶

Carmen owns 100% of the stock in Florida Corporation and receives a $400,000 salary for serving as president. The corporation reports no taxable income and pays no dividends. Presidents of similar companies received salaries ranging from $75,000 to $160,000. The IRS would probably disallow a portion of Carmen's salary as unreasonable. The disallowed portion would be treated as a dividend. ◀

Constructive dividends are not limited to shareholder-employee compensation payments but may include situations where the shareholder is also a landlord (e.g., property is rented to the corporation at an amount greater than its fair rental value). A shareholder may also receive a constructive dividend because of a creditor or vendor relationship. It is not necessary that a dividend be formally declared or that distributions

---

[44] *Eisner v. Myrtle H. Macomber*, 3 AFTR 3020, 1 USTC ¶32 (USSC, 1920).
[45] Reg. Sec. 1.305-4.

[46] Sec. 852(b).
[47] Sec. 162(a)(1).

be in proportion to stock holdings. **Constructive dividends** are often distributions that are intended to result in a deduction to the corporation and taxable income (such as compensation) to the shareholder.[48] Other constructive dividends are intended to produce a nonreportable benefit to the shareholder,[49] or even result in a deduction to the corporation without income to the shareholder.[50]

ALIMONY AND SEPARATE MAINTENANCE PAYMENTS

Any payment pursuant to a divorce or legal separation must be classified as one of the following for tax purposes:

(1) Alimony;

(2) Child support; or

(3) Property settlement.

The treatment of a payment depends on its classification. Alimony is deductible by the payor spouse and taxable to the payee spouse. Neither child support payments nor property settlements have any tax ramifications, that is, they are not subject to tax to the payee spouse nor deductible by the payor spouse.

Example I3-22 demonstrates the significant difference in taxation that can occur when a payment is classified as either alimony or a property settlement.

EXAMPLE I3-22 ▶

ADDITIONAL COMMENT

Child-support payments are not treated as alimony and are neither deductible by the payor spouse nor includible in income of the payee spouse.

ADDITIONAL COMMENT

If any amount specified in the divorce instrument will be reduced due to the happening of a contingency relating to a child or reduced at a time that can clearly be associated with such contingency, the amount of the reduction is treated as child support.

Helen earned $500,000 and, as a result of her divorce, she was required to pay William $250,000. If the payment were viewed as a property settlement, Helen could not deduct any of the $250,000 payment and William would not be required to include the payment in his income. However, if the $250,000 were viewed as alimony, Helen could deduct the full amount in computing her adjusted gross income. William would report the $250,000 as alimony income. ◀

The tax law has rather specific rules that distinguish alimony, child support, and property settlements. The rules, which were originally enacted in 1942,[51] were significantly revised in 1984 and 1986. The revised rules apply to agreements reached after 1984 and earlier agreements if the parties so elect in writing.

Under current law, in order to be treated as **alimony**, payments must meet all of the following requirements:

▶ Be made in cash

▶ Be made pursuant to a divorce, separation, or a written agreement between the spouses

▶ Terminate at the death of the payee

▶ Not be designated as being other than alimony (e.g., child support)

▶ Be made between people who are living in separate households

These rules are summarized in Topic Review I3-2. Certain aspects of these rules will be discussed further.

---

[48] Other examples include excessive royalties (*Peterson & Pegau Baking Co.*, 2 B.T.A. 637 (1925)) and rent (*Limericks, Inc. v. CIR*, 36 AFTR 649, 48-1 USTC ¶9146 (5th Cir., 1948)).

[49] Examples include bargain sales of corporate assets to shareholders (*J. E. Timberlake v. CIR*, 30 AFTR 583, 42-2 USTC ¶9822 (4th Cir., 1942)), redemptions of a shareholder's stock (Sec. 302), and loans to shareholders that are actually dividends (*George Blood Enterprises, Inc.*, 1976 PH T.C.

Memo ¶76,102, 35 TCM 436).

[50] Examples include paying an employee's personal expenses (*The Lang Chevrolet Co.*, 1967 PH T.C. Memo ¶67,212, 26 TCM 1054) and purchasing assets for an employee's use (*Joseph Morgenstern*, 1955 PH T.C. Memo ¶55,086, 14 TCM 282).

[51] Before 1942, alimony was not deductible (*Gould v. Gould*, 3 AFTR 2958, 1 USTC ¶13 (USSC, 1917)).

Topic Review I3-2

Tax Rules for Alimony

Treatment of recipient

The recipient of alimony must include the amounts received in gross income. Property settlements and child support payments are not taxable.

Treatment of payor

The payor of alimony may deduct amounts paid *for* adjusted gross income. Property settlements and child support payments are not deductible.

Applicable to

Payments must be pursuant to a divorce, separation, or a written agreement between spouses.

Requirements

Spouses must be living in separate households. Payments must be in the form of cash paid to (or for the benefit of) a spouse or former spouse. Payments must terminate at the death of the payee. Payments may not be designated as being other than alimony (such as child support or a property settlement).

Recapture

If the amount of payments declines in the second or third year, a portion of the early payments may have to be recaptured as income by the payor. The payee may deduct the same recaptured amount.

Dates

Current rules apply to agreements reached after 1984. Current rules also apply to earlier agreements if both parties agree in writing. Different rules apply to other earlier agreements.

ETHICAL POINT

Tax consultants who advise divorcing couples may face an ethical dilemma because advice that benefits one spouse may be detrimental to the other, and because of the need to maintain confidential client relationships.

A **property settlement** is a division of property pursuant to a divorce. In general, each spouse is entitled to the property brought into the marriage and a share of the property accumulated during marriage.[52] A division of property does not result in any income to either spouse, nor does either spouse receive a tax deduction. The basis of property received by either spouse as a result of the divorce or separation remains unchanged.

EXAMPLE I3-23 ▶

As a result of a divorce, Dawn receives stock that she had purchased with her former husband during their marriage. They had purchased the stock for $12,000. At the time of the divorce, the stock was worth $14,000. Neither Dawn nor her former husband reports income from the transfer of the stock because the stock was acquired as a property settlement. If Dawn subsequently sold the stock for $15,000, she would report a $3,000 gain. ◀

One unusual rule found in the current law that relates to alimony is the so-called **recapture provision.** This provision was established to prevent a large property settlement that might take place after a divorce from being treated as alimony so as to

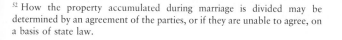

---

[52] How the property accumulated during marriage is divided may be determined by an agreement of the parties, or if they are unable to agree, on a basis of state law.

produce a deduction for the payor. Recapture occurs if payments decrease sharply in either the second or third year. Specifically, the amount of second-year alimony recaptured is equal to the second-year alimony reduced by the total of $15,000 plus the third-year alimony. The amount of first-year alimony recaptured is equal to the first-year alimony reduced by the total of $15,000 plus the average alimony paid in the second year (reduced by the recapture for that year) and the third year. Both first- and second-year amounts are recaptured by requiring the payor to report the excess as income (and allowing the payee to deduct the same amount) in the third year. Recapture is not required if payments cease because of the death of either spouse or remarriage of the recipient.

EXAMPLE I3-24 ▶ As a result of their divorce, Hal is ordered to pay to Rose $100,000 alimony in 1997 and $20,000 per year thereafter until her death or remarriage. Hal must recapture the amount of the decrease in excess of $35,000, or $65,000 ($100,000 − $20,000 − $15,000). The $65,000 of alimony in 1997 must be reported by Hal as income during 1999. Also, Rose may deduct the $65,000 *for* AGI in 1999. ◀

EXAMPLE I3-25 ▶ As a result of their separation, Mary agrees to pay Tom $20,000 per year. The payments are to cease if Tom remarries. In the year after the agreement is reached, Tom remarries and Mary discontinues the payments. No recapture is required because the payments are contingent on the remarriage of the recipient and the payments have been discontinued because of the occurrence of this contingency. ◀

PENSIONS AND ANNUITIES

An **annuity** is a series of regular payments that will continue for a fixed period of time or until the death of the recipient. Taxpayers occasionally purchase annuities from insurance companies to provide a source of funds during retirement years. The insurance company may agree to make payments to the insured for the remainder of the insured's life. The retired individual is assured of a steady flow of funds for life. The price paid for the annuity represents its cost. The insured taxpayer is permitted to recover this cost tax-free.

Individuals receiving an annuity are permitted to exclude their cost, but are taxed on the remaining portion of the annuity. The following steps can be followed to determine the nontaxable portion of the annuity:

▶ Determine the **expected return multiple**. This is the number of years that the annuity is expected to continue. This may be a stated term, say ten years, or it may be for the remainder of the taxpayer's life. In this situation, the expected return multiple (life expectancy) is determined by referring to a table (see Table I3-1) developed by the IRS.

▶ Determine the **expected return**. This is computed by multiplying the amount of the annual payment by the expected return multiple.

▶ Determine the **exclusion ratio**. This is computed by dividing the investment in the contract (its cost) by the expected return (from above).

▶ Determine the **current year's exclusion**. This is computed by multiplying the exclusion ratio (from above) times the amount received during the year.

EXAMPLE I3-26 ▶ David, age 65, purchases an annuity for $30,000. Under the terms of the annuity, David is to receive $300 per month ($3,600 per year) for the rest of his life.

▼ TABLE I3-1
Ordinary Life Annuities (One Life) Expected Return Multiple

Age	Multiple	Age	Multiple	Age	Multiple
5	76.6	42	40.6	79	10.0
6	75.6	43	39.6	80	9.5
7	74.7	44	38.7	81	8.9
8	73.7	45	37.7	82	8.4
9	72.7	46	36.8	83	7.9
10	71.7	47	35.9	84	7.4
11	70.7	48	34.9	85	6.9
12	69.7	49	34.0	86	6.5
13	68.8	50	33.1	87	6.1
14	67.8	51	32.2	88	5.7
15	66.8	52	31.3	89	5.3
16	65.8	53	30.4	90	5.0
17	64.8	54	29.5	91	4.7
18	63.9	55	28.6	92	4.4
19	62.9	56	27.7	93	4.1
20	61.9	57	26.8	94	3.9
21	60.9	58	25.9	95	3.7
22	59.9	59	25.0	96	3.4
23	59.0	60	24.2	97	3.2
24	58.0	61	23.3	98	3.0
25	57.0	62	22.5	99	2.8
26	56.0	63	21.6	100	2.7
27	55.1	64	20.8	101	2.5
28	54.1	65	20.0	102	2.3
29	53.1	66	19.2	103	2.1
30	52.2	67	18.4	104	1.9
31	51.2	68	17.6	105	1.8
32	50.2	69	16.8	106	1.6
33	49.3	70	16.0	107	1.4
34	48.3	71	15.3	108	1.3
35	47.3	72	14.6	109	1.1
36	46.4	73	13.9	110	1.0
37	45.4	74	13.2	111	.9
38	44.4	75	12.5	112	.8
39	43.5	76	11.9	113	.7
40	42.5	77	11.2	114	.6
41	41.5	78	10.6	115	.5

Source: Reg. Sec. 1.72-9 Table V.

Note: This table should be used if any or all investments were made on or after July 1, 1986. If all investments were made before July 1, 1986, use Reg. Sec. 1.72-9 Table I (not shown).

▶ The expected return multiple is 20.0. The multiple is obtained from Table I3-1.

▶ The expected return is $72,000 (20.0 × $3,600).

▶ The exclusion ratio is 0.417 ($30,000 ÷ $72,000).

▶ The exclusion is $1,500 (0.417 × $3,600).

◀

After the entire cost of an annuity has been recovered, the full amount of all future payments is taxable. On the other hand, if an individual dies before recovering the entire cost, the remaining unrecovered cost can be deducted as an itemized deduction on that individual's final return. Insurance companies and businesses with retirement plans compute the taxable portion of annuities and report the amounts to recipients on Form 1099.

SIMPLIFIED METHOD FOR QUALIFIED RETIREMENT PLAN ANNUITIES. Distributions from pensions and other qualified retirement plans are often paid in the form of an annuity. Both the employer and the employee often contribute funds to plans during the years of employment. When an employee retires, the amounts contributed and income accumulated thereon become available to the retired employee. Often the retired employee has the option of receiving a lump-sum payment or an annuity. The employee's cost is limited to amounts contributed (usually through withholding) by the employee that were previously taxed to the employee. The employee may recover this cost tax-free. The employee's cost does not include employer contributions.

A simplified method is used to determine the taxable portion of an annuity paid from a qualified retirement plan (such as a pension) if the annuity start date is after November 18, 1996. Annuities with earlier starting dates are taxed under the same rules shown above. Under the simplified method, the nontaxable portion of each annuity payment is equal to the employee's investment in the annuity divided by the number of anticipated payments as determined from the following table:

Age of Primary Annuitant on the Start Date	Number of Anticipated Payments
55 and under	360
56-60	310
61-65	260
66-70	210
71 and over	160

EXAMPLE I3-27 ▶ Jack, age 62, retires in 1997, and receives a $1,000 per month annuity from his employer's qualified pension plan. Jack contributed $65,000 to the plan prior to his retirement. Under the simplified method, Jack would exclude $250 per month as a return of capital. This is calculated by dividing $65,000 by 260 anticipated payments. ◀

If payments are paid other than monthly, the number of anticipated payments is adjusted accordingly. Thus, if payments are made quarterly, the number from the table is divided by four.

KEY POINT

Under current law, a taxpayer must generally pay tax on a portion of each withdrawal made before the normal starting date of the annuity.

ADVANCE PAYMENTS. Many pensions contain provisions that allow taxpayers to withdraw amounts before the normal starting date. Under current law, an amount withdrawn from a pension before the starting date is considered to be in part a recovery of the employee's contributions and part a recovery of the employer's contributions.[53] After all contributions have been withdrawn, additional withdrawals are fully taxable. In addition to being subject to the regular income tax, any amount withdrawn may also be subject to a 10% nondeductible penalty. The penalty is not applicable to a taxpayer who is age 59½ or older, to a disabled or deceased taxpayer, to a retired employee who is receiving an annuity based on his or her life expectancy, to a taxpayer who has reached age 55 and has taken early retirement, to a taxpayer who uses the distribution to pay medical expenses to the extent deductible under Sec. 213, or to an alternate payee pursuant to a qualified domestic relations order.[54]

---

[53] Sec. 72(e).

[54] Sec. 72(t)(2).

EXAMPLE I3-28 ▶ Dick, age 45 and in good health, withdrew $2,000 from a pension plan during the current year. No exception exempts Dick from the 10% penalty. Dick had contributed $40,000 to the plan, and his employer had contributed $60,000. Dick must include $1,200 (0.60 × $2,000) in income. Because no exception applies, Dick must also pay an additional penalty of $120 (0.10 × $1,200). The penalty is not deductible by Dick. ◀

Nonemployee annuities are subject to different rules, found in Sec. 72(e)(2) and (3). Distributions from nonemployee annuities received before the starting date are taxable to the extent that the cash surrender value of the annuity exceeds the taxpayer's investment in the annuity contract.

INCOME FROM LIFE INSURANCE AND ENDOWMENT CONTRACTS

The face amount of life insurance received because of the death of the insured is not taxable. If the proceeds are left with the insurance company and as a result earn interest, the interest payments are taxable. (See Chapter I4 for a detailed discussion of life insurance and endowment contracts.)

INCOME FROM DISCHARGE OF INDEBTEDNESS

In general, the forgiveness of debt is a taxable event. The person who owed the money must report the amount forgiven as income unless one of several exceptions found in the tax law applies. These exceptions are discussed in Chapter I4.

INCOME PASSED THROUGH TO TAXPAYER

In many instances, income is passed through one entity and is taxed to another. Such entities are referred to as "flow-through entities." Section 61 specifically lists three such instances: the distributive share of a partnership's income, income in respect of a decedent, and income from an interest in an estate or trust. Though not mentioned in Sec. 61, similar treatment is accorded S corporation income. In each case, the income that is produced by the entity merely flows through to the owner or beneficiary of such entity. The rules can be summarized as follows:

KEY POINT

The pass-through of income by a partnership can create a situation known as phantom income. In this situation, a partner is required to report income on his or her individual tax return, but the partner may not have received a cash distribution from the partnership.

▶ Each partner reports his or her share of the partnership's income. Each partner deducts his or her share of the partnership's expenses. The income and deductions are reported by the partners whether or not any amount is actually distributed by the partnership during the year. The income belongs to the partner even if it is not distributed currently.

▶ Income in respect of a decedent is income earned by an individual before death that is paid to another after the death. For example, salary earned by a husband who uses the cash method of accounting before his death in an automobile accident may be paid to his widow after the accident. The recipient, in this case the widow, is taxed on the income if it has not been taxed to the decedent before his death.

▶ Income earned by estates and trusts is subject to taxation.[55] However, distributions to beneficiaries are deductible by estates and trusts and are taxable to the beneficiaries. Thus, if a trust had a net income of $20,000 and distributed $15,000 to the beneficiary of the trust, the trust would be taxed on $5,000 and $15,000 would be taxed to the beneficiary. The income taxation of estates and trusts is covered more

---

[55] Note the distinction between income in respect of a decedent and the income of an estate. Income in respect of a decedent is the income earned before death that was never taxed to the decedent. An example would be interest that was accrued but unpaid at death. Income of an estate is income earned after death that is paid to the estate. An example would be interest that accrues after the decedent's death.

fully in *Prentice Hall's Federal Taxation: Corporations, Partnerships, Estates, and Trusts.*

▶ S corporations are taxed much like partnerships. Each shareholder in the corporation is taxed on his or her proportionate share of the corporation's income whether or not the income is actually distributed.

OTHER ITEMS OF GROSS INCOME

The preceding discussions considered items of gross income specifically listed in Sec. 61(a). The fact that an item of income is listed in Sec. 61(a) does not cause it to be taxable. Rather, the fact that it is not specifically excluded causes an item of income to be taxable. Some items of gross income not mentioned in Sec. 61(a) are discussed below.

PRIZES, AWARDS, GAMBLING WINNINGS, AND TREASURE FINDS

In general, prizes, awards, gambling winnings, and treasure finds are taxable.[56] Winnings in contests, competitions, and quiz shows as well as awards from an employer to an employee in recognition of some achievement in connection with his or her employment are taxable.[57] The value of the goods or services received is included in gross income. Total gambling winnings must be included in gross income.[58] This includes proceeds from lotteries, raffles, sweepstakes, and the like. Gambling losses (up to the amount of the current year's winnings) are allowable as an itemized deduction.[59] The Regulations state that a treasure find constitutes gross income to the extent of its value in the year in which it is reduced to undisputed possession.[60]

EXAMPLE I3-29 ▶ Several years ago, Colleen purchased a used piano at an auction for $15. In the current year, she finds $4,500 of currency hidden in the piano. Colleen must report the $4,500 as income in the current year.[61] ◀

REAL-WORLD EXAMPLE

An accountant collected from a client money that was to be used to pay the client's taxes. Then the accountant appropriated the money for his own use. The accountant was held to have received unreported income. *Richard A. Reeves,* 1977 PH T.C. Memo A 77,114, 36 TCM 500.

ILLEGAL INCOME

Income from illegal activities is taxable.[62] Some people are surprised that this is part of the tax law, but it is this fact that serves as the basis for many criminal convictions. It is reasonable to assume that few criminals report their illegal income. Al Capone was convicted of income tax evasion, not bootlegging or other crimes. It is not necessary to prove that an individual had illegal income, merely that the individual had income.

Individuals have used varied defenses against this rule. One taxpayer was successful in convincing the Supreme Court that he should not be taxed on embezzlement gains because he had an unconditional obligation to repay the amount embezzled,[63] but the Supreme Court reversed this position in a later case.[64] The court concluded that although there is an obligation to repay, there is no "consensual recognition" (intent) to repay. In addition to embezzlement of funds, the courts have held that a kidnapper's ransom was

---

[56] Exclusions for scholarships and fellowships and a limited exclusion for prizes awarded for scientific, charitable, or similar meritorious achievements are discussed in Chapter I4.
[57] Sec. 74 and Reg. Sec. 1.74-1.
[58] *U.S. v. Manley S. Sullivan,* 6 AFTR 6753, 1 USTC ¶236 (USSC, 1927).
[59] Sec. 165(d).
[60] Reg. Sec. 1.61-14(a).

[61] *Ermenegildo Cesarini v. U.S.,* 26 AFTR 2d 5107, 70-2 USTC ¶9509 (6th Cir., 1970).
[62] Reg. 1.61-14(a).
[63] *CIR v. Laird Wilcox,* 34 AFTR 811, 46-1 USTC ¶9188 (USSC, 1946).
[64] *Eugene C. James v. U.S.,* 7 AFTR 2d 1361, 61-1 USTC ¶9449 (USSC, 1961).

taxable,[65] along with profits from bookmaking,[66] card playing,[67] forgery,[68] stealing,[69] bank robbery,[70] sale of narcotics,[71] illegal sale of liquor,[72] and bribes.[73] (See Chapter 16 for a discussion of related deductions.)

UNEMPLOYMENT COMPENSATION

For many years, unemployment compensation was excluded from gross income. In 1978, Congress first taxed unemployment compensation because these benefits are a substitute for taxable wages. Initially, unemployment compensation was taxable if adjusted gross income exceeded certain base amounts. However, beginning in 1987, all unemployment compensation became taxable. This is true for both government-financed programs and employer-financed benefits.

SOCIAL SECURITY BENEFITS

Social Security benefits were excluded from gross income until 1984. Between 1984 and 1993, up to 50% of Social Security benefits were taxable. Beginning in 1994, up to 85% of Social Security benefits may be taxable. Under Sec. 86, the portion of Social Security benefits that are taxable depends on the taxpayer's provisional income and filing status. Provisional income is computed using the following formula:

Adjusted gross income (excluding Social Security benefits)		$xx,xxx
Plus:	Tax-exempt interest	x,xxx
	Excluded foreign income	x,xxx
	50% of Social Security benefits	x,xxx
Provisional income		$xx,xxx

MARRIED FILING SEPARATELY. In the case of a married person filing separately, taxable Social Security benefits are equal to the lesser of

▶ 85% of Social Security benefits, or

▶ 85% of provisional income

MARRIED FILING JOINTLY. For married couples filing jointly, the computation of the taxable portion of Social Security benefits is as follows:

▶ If provisional income is $32,000 or less, no Social Security benefits are taxable.

▶ If provisional income is over $32,000 (but not over $44,000), taxable Social Security benefits equal the lesser of:
> 50% of the Social Security benefits, or
> 50% of the excess of provisional income over $32,000

▶ If provisional income is over $44,000, taxable Social Security benefits are equal to the lesser of:
> 85% of the Social Security benefits, or
> The lesser of (1) $6,000 or (2) 50% of Social Security benefits, plus 85% of provisional income over $44,000.

SINGLE TAXPAYERS. For single taxpayers, the computation of the taxable portion of Social Security benefits is as follows:

ADDITIONAL COMMENT

Welfare payments are not normally required to be included in gross income. However, if the welfare payments are fraudulently received under state or federal assistance programs, they must be included in the recipient's gross income.

REAL-WORLD EXAMPLE

The requirement that tax-exempt income be included in determining the taxable portion of Social Security benefits has been challenged on the basis that such provision is unconstitutional. However, the court held that this provision placed only an indirect burden on the governmental unit that issued the tax-exempt bonds, which was not protected by the intergovernmental immunity doctrine. *H.J. Goldin v. Baker,* 59 AFTR 2d 87-444, 87-1 USTC ¶9128, (2nd Cir., 1987).

[65] *Murray Humphreys v. CIR,* 28 AFTR 1030, 42-1 USTC ¶9237 (7th Cir., 1942).

[66] *James P. McKenna,* 1 B.T.A. 326 (1925).

[67] *L. Weiner,* 10 B.T.A. 905 (1928).

[68] *Cass Sunstein,* 1966 PH T.C. Memo ¶66,043, 25 TCM 247.

[69] *Mathias Schira v. CIR,* 50 AFTR 1404, 57-1 USTC ¶9413 (6th Cir., 1957).

[70] *Gary Ayers,* 1978 PH T.C. Memo ¶78,341, 37 TCM 1415.

[71] *Antonino Farina v. McMahon,* 2 AFTR 2d 5918, 58-2 USTC ¶9938 (D.C. N.Y., 1958).

[72] *U.S. v. Manley S. Sullivan,* 6 AFTR 6753, 1 USTC ¶236 (USSC, 1927).

[73] *U.S. v. Patrick Commerford,* 12 AFTR 364, 1933 CCH ¶9255 (2nd Cir., 1933).

▶ If provisional income is $25,000 or less, no Social Security benefits are taxable.

▶ If provisional income is over $25,000 (but not over $34,000), taxable Social Security benefits are equal to the lesser of

50% of the Social Security benefits, or

50% of the excess of provisional income over $25,000

▶ If provisional income is over $34,000, taxable Social Security benefits are equal to the lesser of:

85% of the Social Security benefits, or

The lesser of (1) $4,500 or (2) 50% of Social Security benefits, plus 85% of provisional income over $34,000

EXAMPLE I3-30 ▶

Holly is a single taxpayer with a taxable pension of $22,000, tax-exempt interest of $10,000, and Social Security benefits of $8,000. Her provisional income is $36,000, determined as follows:

Adjusted gross income		$22,000
Plus:	Tax-exempt interest	10,000
	50% of Social Security benefits	4,000
	Provisional income	$36,000

The taxable Social Security benefits are equal to $5,700, which is the lesser of $6,800 (0.85 × $8,000) or $5,700 (the lesser of $4,500 or $4,000*, plus $1,700**).

*50% of the Social Security benefits.
**($36,000 provisional income − $34,000 threshold) × 0.85. ◀

The result of the computation is to exclude from gross income the Social Security benefits received by lower-income individuals but to tax a portion (up to 85%) of the benefits received by taxpayers with higher incomes.

The term **Social Security benefits** refers to basic monthly retirement and disability benefits paid under Social Security and also to tier-one railroad retirement benefits. It does not include supplementary Medicare benefits that cover the cost of doctors' services and other medical benefits.

ADDITIONAL COMMENT

For a 65-year-old taxpayer who retired in 1994, the maximum monthly individual Social Security benefit was $1,148.

INSURANCE PROCEEDS AND COURT AWARDS

In general, insurance proceeds and court awards are taxable. Two exceptions are accident and health insurance benefits and the face amount of life insurance. (See Chapter I4 for a discussion of these benefits.)

Insurance proceeds or court awards received because of the destruction of property are included in gross income only to the extent that the proceeds exceed the adjusted basis of the property. Involuntary conversion provisions permit taxpayers to avoid being taxed if they reinvest the proceeds in a qualified replacement property.[74] If the proceeds are less than the property's adjusted basis, they reduce the amount of any deductible loss. Proceeds of insurance guarding against loss of profits because of a casualty are taxable.[75] Similarly, if a taxpayer had to sue a customer to collect income owed to the taxpayer, the amount collected is taxable just as it would have been had the taxpayer collected the income without going to court.

---

[74] The involuntary conversion provisions are discussed in Chapter I12.
[75] *Oppenheim's Inc. v. Kavanagh*, 39 AFTR 468, 50-1 USTC ¶9249 (D.C.-Mich., 1950).

EXAMPLE I3-31 ▶ Gulf Corporation's factory was destroyed by fire. Gulf Corporation collected insurance of $400,000, which equaled its basis in the building, and $250,000 for the profits lost during the time the company was rebuilding its factory. The $400,000 is not taxable because it constitutes a recovery of the basis of the factory. The $250,000 is taxable because it represents lost income. Recall that the income would have been taxable had it been earned by the company from regular operations. ◀

Although there are few exclusions designed specifically for insurance proceeds or court awards, such amounts may be covered by other, more general exclusions. For example, Sec. 104(a)(2) excludes "damages (other than punitive damages) received . . . on account of personal physical injuries or sickness." Thus, amounts collected because of physical injury suffered in an automobile accident are excluded (See Chapter I4).

RECOVERY OF PREVIOUSLY DEDUCTED AMOUNTS

On occasion, a taxpayer may deduct an amount in one year but recover the amount in a subsequent year. In general, the amount recovered must be included in the gross income in the year it is recovered. Cash-basis taxpayers encounter this situation more often than accrual-basis taxpayers because their expenses are generally deductible in the year they are paid. If the amount was overpaid, the taxpayer can anticipate a refund.

EXAMPLE I3-32 ▶ During 1997, Cindy's employer withheld $1,000 from her wages for state income taxes. She claimed the $1,000 as an itemized deduction on her 1997 federal income tax return. Her itemized deductions totaled $12,000. Her 1997 state income tax was only $800. As a result, Cindy received a $200 refund from the state in 1998. Because Cindy deducted the full $1,000 in 1997, she must report the $200 refund as income on her 1998 federal income tax return. ◀

Any recovery of a previously deducted amount may lead to income recognition. Recovery, however, is often associated with expenses such as state income taxes or bad debts deducted in one year but recovered in a later year, medical expenses deducted in one year but reimbursed by insurance in a later year, casualty losses deducted in one year but reimbursed by court award or insurance in a later year, and deductions for amounts paid by check where the payee never cashed the check.

Several related rules should be noted:

▶ If the refund or other recovery occurs in the same year, the refund or recovery reduces the deduction and is not reported as income.

▶ Interest on the amount refunded is taxable and is not subject to the tax benefit rule (discussed below).

▶ The character of the income reported in the year of repayment is dependent on the type of deduction previously reported. For instance, if the taxpayer deducted a short-term capital loss in one year, the subsequent recovery would be a short-term capital gain.[76]

TAX BENEFIT RULE. As noted above, a taxpayer who recovers an amount deducted in a previous year must report as gross income the amount recovered. The amount recovered need not be included in income, however, if the taxpayer received no tax benefit. There is a tax benefit only if the deduction reduced the tax for the year.[77]

---

[76] *F. Donald Arrowsmith Exr. v. CIR,* 42 AFTR 649, 52-2 USTC ¶9527 (USSC, 1952).   [77] Sec. 111.

In 1997, Jack's employer withheld $1,200 from his wages for state income tax. Jack claimed the $1,200 as an itemized deduction on his 1997 federal income tax return. Because of a variety of losses incurred by Jack, he reported a negative taxable income of $32,000 during 1997. The state refunded the $1,200 during 1998. Jack will not have to report the $1,200 as gross income on his federal return. He would have owed no federal income tax in 1997 even without the deduction for state income taxes. Therefore, Jack received no tax benefit from the deduction. ◀

REAL-WORLD EXAMPLE

An attorney collected fees from clients of his employer. Because the attorney and his employer were engaged in a dispute over ownership of the money, he deposited the disputed amount in a trust account. The attorney was taxable on the amounts in the year received because he had control over the funds under the claim of right doctrine. *Edward J. Costello, Jr.,* 1985 PH T.C. Memo ¶85,571, 50 TCM 1463.

Tax benefit may be absent in other situations. For example, a taxpayer's total itemized deductions may have been less than the standard deduction, or the expense may have been less than the applicable floor. To illustrate, medical expenses can be deducted only to the extent that they exceed 7.5% of adjusted gross income. If a taxpayer does not deduct medical expenses because they are less than the floor, the taxpayer does not have to report a subsequent reimbursement of the expense as income. If only a portion of an expense produces a tax benefit, only that portion has to be reported as income.

EXAMPLE I3-34 ▶

In 1997, Chris, an unmarried individual, had $1,350 withheld from her wages for state income tax. Her itemized deductions consisted of state income taxes of $1,350 and charitable contributions of $2,950. Her itemized deductions exceed the standard deduction by $150 ($1,350 + $2,950 − $4,150). If Chris received a state income tax refund of $200 in 1998 she must report only $150 as gross income in 1998. She benefited only from $150 of the deduction and so that is all she has to report as income. ◀

CLAIM OF RIGHT

Sometimes taxpayers receive disputed amounts. For example, a contractor may receive payment on a job when the quality of the work is being questioned by the customer, a salesperson may receive commissions when there is a question as to whether the sales are final, or a litigant may receive a court award even though the case is on appeal. Under the claim of right doctrine, the recipient of a disputed amount must include the amount received in gross income as long as the use of the funds is unrestricted.

EXAMPLE I3-35 ▶

Jane wins a court case against a customer requiring the customer to pay her $10,000. The customer is unhappy with the result of the case and indicates that he plans to appeal, but pays the $10,000 to avoid interest on the amount in the event he loses the appeal. Jane must include the $10,000 in gross income even though she will have to repay the amount if she loses the appeal. ◀

EXAMPLE I3-36 ▶

Assume the same facts as in Example I3-35 except that the $10,000 is placed in escrow by the court awaiting the outcome of the appeal. Jane does not have to report the amount as she does not have use of the funds. ◀

Of course, taxpayers may be required to repay the disputed amount in a subsequent year. Such taxpayers may deduct the previously reported amount in the year of repayment. The taxes saved from such a deduction, however, may be considerably less than the original tax. If the repayment is over $3,000, taxpayers have the option of reducing the current tax by the tax paid in the prior year or years on the repaid amount.[78]

EXAMPLE I3-37 ▶

Assume the same facts as in Example I3-35, except that after reporting the disputed $10,000 Jane loses the appeal and must repay the $10,000 to her customer. If Jane was in the 28% tax

---

[78] Sec. 1341.

bracket when she reported the disputed amount, she would have paid a $2,800 (0.28 × $10,000) tax on the disputed amount. If she were in the 15% bracket when she made the repayment, she would recover only $1,500 by deducting the $10,000. Because the amount exceeds $3,000, Jane has the option of determining her current year's tax by deducting from the tax she would otherwise pay the $2,800 tax she paid in the earlier year. This amount is deductible in lieu of receiving a deduction of $1,500 (0.15 × $10,000) by using the current tax rate. ◀

TAX PLANNING CONSIDERATIONS

SHIFTING INCOME

KEY POINT

The advantage of shifting income to children has been increased since the revision of the tax rate schedules in 1993. The highest and lowest marginal tax rates in 1992 were 31% and 15%, respectively. In 1993 and in subsequent years, the highest and lowest marginal rates are 39.6% and 15%, respectively.

A family can reduce its taxes by shifting income from family members who are in high tax brackets (e.g., parents) to family members who are in low tax brackets (e.g., children). Assignment of income rules prevent this from being done by merely redirecting the payment. A father cannot avoid a tax on his salary by ordering his employer to pay the salary to his daughter. Nevertheless, income can be shifted. For example, children may own stock in the family business. Dividends on the stock are taxed to the children. In the case of a child under age 14, the parents' (as opposed to the child's) tax rate, however, is applicable to unearned income in excess of $1,300. Series EE bonds may prove useful because the interest is deferred until the bond is redeemed or matures. The maturity date, of course, may be after the child reaches age 14. A child may work for the family business and be paid a reasonable salary. Such income is taxed at the child's tax rate, even if the child is under 14 years old, and can be offset by the child's own standard deduction.

Shifting of income is constrained by several factors. As noted, the assignment of income doctrine limits transfers. Reasonableness limitations constrain compensation and other payments. Furthermore, outright gifts of property are subject to gift taxes. Also, individuals are reluctant to transfer wealth to children for a variety of personal reasons. However, the tax saving potential of shifting income is often so great as to prompt many well-to-do families to use available shifting techniques.

ALIMONY

Whether payments made in connection with a divorce or separation are classified as alimony is of major tax significance. Such classification results in a deduction for the payor and income to the payee. Alimony is actually one way to shift income.

EXAMPLE I3-38 ▶

Tony, who has a 36% marginal tax rate, makes payments of $40,000 to his former wife. If it is deductible as alimony, Tony will save $14,400 (0.36 × $40,000) a year in federal income taxes. The amount of tax that the former wife must pay depends on how much other income she has and whether she has deductions that reduce the tax. Her tax might be even higher than her former husband's or as little as zero. ◀

Two things are clear. One is that both parties should understand the implication of having amounts treated as alimony. Second, the designation of the payments as alimony may be beneficial to both parties. The payor will, of course, benefit from a tax deduction. The payee may benefit because the fact that the payor can deduct alimony may mean that the payor will agree (and can afford) to make larger payments.

PREPAID INCOME

As explained earlier in this chapter, prepaid income is generally taxable when received. This accelerated recognition of income may be a significant disadvantage to the taxpayer if the related expenses are incurred in a later tax year. Thus, tax planning for prepaid amounts is essential.

EXAMPLE I3-39 ▶ Phil rents units in his apartment complex and requires tenants to pay the first and last months' rent before they move in. ◀

EXAMPLE I3-40 ▶ Rita rents units in her apartment complex and requires tenants to pay the first month's rent and a refundable deposit (which equals one month's rent). ◀

HISTORICAL NOTE

In 1954 Congress passed Sec. 452, allowing deferral of certain prepaid income, but in 1955 Congress retroactively repealed this section.

Although the full amount received by Phil in Example I3-39 is taxable when it is received, only one-half of the amount received by Rita in Example I3-40 is taxable when it is received. Rita is required to refund the deposit, assuming the tenant vacates leaving the property in good condition and having paid all rent. Therefore, the deposit is not taxable.

Taxpayers receiving advance payments in connection with services may be able to meet the requirements of Rev. Proc. 71-21 (discussed earlier in the chapter); taxpayers receiving advance payments associated with the sale of merchandise may be able to meet the requirements of Reg. Sec. 1.451-5 (also discussed in this chapter). As noted, special rules exist for subscription income, membership fees, crop insurance proceeds, and drought sales of livestock, all of which allow taxpayers to defer recognizing income.

TAXABLE, TAX-EXEMPT, OR TAX-DEFERRED BONDS

Which should a taxpayer choose: taxable bonds, tax-exempt bonds, or tax-deferred bonds? The answer depends on the relative interest rates and the taxpayer's current and future tax brackets. **Taxable bonds** yield the highest return, but the interest is taxable, of course. **Tax-exempt bonds** yield a lower return. **Tax-deferred bonds** generally yield a return somewhere close to that of taxable bonds. Interest on U.S. Series EE savings bonds is tax exempt if it is used for educational purposes and if other requirements of Sec. 135 are met (see the discussion earlier in this chapter). If these conditions are not met, the tax is deferred until the bonds are redeemed. The taxpayer may be in a lower bracket when the tax is eventually paid, and in the meantime, the interest that will eventually go to pay taxes is earning additional income.

The decision between taxable and exempt bonds is a rather easy one if the risk of the investments is assumed to be approximately equal. A taxpayer should invest in exempt bonds instead of taxable bonds if the interest on the exempt bonds is greater than the interest on the taxable bonds multiplied by 1 minus the taxpayer's marginal tax bracket (expressed as a decimal). Stated in a formula, this means invest in tax-exempt bonds if

$$\text{Return on the tax-exempt bonds} > \text{Return on the taxable bonds} \times (1 - \text{Marginal tax bracket})$$

EXAMPLE I3-41 ▶ Robert's marginal tax bracket is 28% and he is trying to decide between tax-exempt bonds, which pay 6% interest, and taxable bonds paying 8% interest. Robert should invest in the exempt bonds because 6% is greater than 5.76% [0.08 × (1 − 0.28)]. ◀

Comparison of taxable bonds or exempt bonds to tax-deferred bonds is more complicated. As noted, the advantages of the tax-deferred bonds are twofold. First, the taxpayer may be in a lower tax bracket when the tax is paid (e.g., taxpayers who plan to redeem the bonds after retirement). Second, the amount that will eventually go to pay the tax earns income until the tax must be paid. Although the computation is not covered here, it is noted that taxpayers who anticipate that they will be in lower tax brackets and who plan to leave funds invested for several years may benefit from choosing Series EE U.S. savings bonds over taxable bonds.

REPORTING SAVINGS BOND INTEREST

It may be desirable to purchase Series EE bonds in the name of a child despite the fact that such interest is subject to the kiddie tax (see Chapter I2). This is because there is no income tax as long as the child's annual income is less than $650. However, it is necessary to communicate to the IRS by return an election to report interest annually. This is true even if the taxpayer is not otherwise required to file a return.[79] Taxpayers who have not been reporting savings bond interest annually may change to annual reporting, but are required to report both current and previously accrued interest in the year of the change.[80]

Taxpayers who report savings bond interest annually are allowed to change to the deferral method without IRS approval.[81] This is particularly useful where the decision to report interest currently was made before the imposition of the kiddie tax. Taxpayers who make this election are bound by it for five years.

DEFERRED COMPENSATION ARRANGEMENTS

Deferred compensation plans can be used as a means of avoiding the constructive receipt of income. Although income is normally taxable when the funds become available to the taxpayer, an advance contractual agreement can produce different results. Corporate executives, professional athletes, and others often sign agreements providing for compensation to be paid at future dates. Such agreements can produce tax savings because the recipients expect to be in a lower tax bracket. Because the arrangements are advance contractual agreements, the deferral of income does not constitute taxpayers "turning their backs" on the income.

EXAMPLE I3-42 ▶

Alonzo, a 35-year-old professional basketball player, signs a contract specifying that he will be paid $400,000 per year for ten years even if he does not play. Because of his age, both Alonzo and the team recognize that he will probably play for one or two more years. If the agreement had specified that he was to receive a salary of $1,300,000 per year for two years, most of the income would have been taxed at the highest rates. By spreading the amount over a longer period, Alonzo pays lower tax rates on much of the income. Alonzo is compensated for the delayed payment by receiving a larger total amount [i.e., $4 million ($400,000 × 10 years) versus $2.6 million ($1.3 million × 2 years)]. ◀

COMPLIANCE AND PROCEDURAL CONSIDERATIONS

Form 1040 lists various types of income. Some items of income (wages, tax refunds, alimony, pensions and annuities, unemployment compensation, Social Security benefits, and other income) are listed directly on Form 1040. Most expenses related to these items of income are deducted as miscellaneous itemized deductions on Schedule A.

[79] *Philip Apkin,* 86 T.C. 692 (1986).
[80] Reg. Sec. 1.454-1(a)(4), Ex. (1).

[81] Rev. Proc. 89-46, 1989-2 C.B. 597.

Topic Review I3-3

Reporting of Income

Type of Income	Reported On	Related Deductions Are Claimed On
Wages, salaries, tips, etc.	Form 1040.	Schedule A and various other forms: moving, Form 3903; travel, transportation, etc., Form 2106
Interest	Form 1040 (if less than $400), otherwise Schedule B.	Schedule A (miscellaneous deductions if any, e.g., safe deposit box fees)
Dividends	Form 1040 (if less than $400), otherwise Schedule B.	Schedule A (miscellaneous deductions if any, e.g., safe deposit box fees)
Refund of state or local income taxes	Form 1040 (instructions contain a worksheet).	Schedule A (miscellaneous deductions if any, e.g., fee paid for tax advice)
Alimony	Form 1040.	Schedule A (miscellaneous deduction, if any, e.g., legal fee associated with alimony)
Business income	Schedule C or C-EZ (net income or loss is transferred to Form 1040).	Schedule C or C-EZ (e.g., depreciation, advertising, repairs)
Capital gains	Schedule D (if Schedule D is not needed to report other gains or losses, capital gains dividends [from mutual funds, etc.] can be reported directly on Form 1040 and Schedule B).	Schedule D (capital losses) or Schedule A (investment expenses)
Supplemental gains	Form 4797.	Form 4797 (e.g., ordinary losses)
Pensions and annuities	Form 1040 (instructions contain a worksheet).	Generally no related deductions
Rents, royalties, partnerships, S corporations, estates, trusts, etc.	Schedule E.	Schedule E
Farm income	Schedule F.	Schedule F
Unemployment compensation	Form 1040.	Generally no related deductions
Social Security benefits	Form 1040 (instructions contain a worksheet).	Generally no related deductions
Other income	Form 1040.	Schedule A (miscellaneous deductions, if any)

ADDITIONAL COMMENT

The dollar amount of tax-exempt interest income is recorded on Form 1040, line 8b, but is not included in the tax base. The IRS requires the reporting of this type of income probably because it may affect the taxability of Social Security benefits.

Most other types of income are reported on special schedules (e.g., business income is reported on Schedule C or Schedule C-EZ (for businesses with gross receipts of $25,000 or less or total business expenses of $2,000 or less; capital gains on Schedule D; supplemental gains on Form 4797; rents, royalties, etc. on Schedule E; and farm income on Schedule F). Related deductons are claimed on the same schedules. The net income or loss determined on these forms is transferred to Form 1040.

Dividends and interest income are listed directly on Form 1040 unless the amount of either exceeds $400. In that case, the dividends or interest are reported on Schedule B. The total is then transferred to Form 1040. In either case, related deductions such as a safe deposit box fee paid for storage of investment certificates are miscellaneous itemized deductions. The miscellaneous deductions are allowable only if the total of such deductions exceeds 2% of adjusted gross income. Topic Review I3-3 summarizes the procedures for reporting income.

EXAMPLE I3-43 ▶

KEY POINT

The amount labeled "total income" on line 24 of Form 1040 is not gross income, adjusted gross income, or taxable income.

John J. Alexander has several items of income and related deductions:

Salary	$40,000
Deductible alimony payments	6,000
Taxable interest	300
Dividends: Ford Motor Co.	150
Omaha Mutual Fund ($120 is a return of capital dividend and $50 is a capital gain dividend)	600
Rent income (depreciation, interest, repairs, and other related expenses total $8,000)	11,000

The reporting of these items of income is illustrated on page 1 of Form 1040 (Figure I3-1) and on Schedule B of Form 1040 (Figure I3-2). Salary and interest (because the interest is less than $400) are entered directly on Form 1040. Note that on Schedule B, the capital gain distribution and the nontaxable distribution are subtracted from total dividends. Rental income would be entered on Schedule E (not illustrated), and the net income after deducting related expenses is transferred to Form 1040. Alimony received and alimony payments are reported on page 1 of Form 1040. ◀

PROBLEM MATERIALS

DISCUSSION QUESTIONS

I3-1 What phrase is found in both the Sixteenth Amendment to the Constitution and Sec. 61(a)?

I3-2 Contrast the accounting and economic concepts of income.

I3-3 Why does the tax concept of income more closely resemble the accounting concept of income than the economic concept?

I3-4 Explain the meaning of the term *wherewithal to pay* as it applies to taxation.

I3-5 If a loan is repaid, the lender does not have to include the repayment in gross income. There is no exclusion in the tax law that permits taxpayers to omit such amounts from gross income. How can this be explained?

I3-6 A landlord who receives prepaid rent is required to report that amount as gross income when the payment is received. Why would Congress choose to do this? What problem does this create for the taxpayer?

I3-7 Office space is often rented without carpet, wall covering, or window covering. Furthermore, many rental agreements specify that these improvements cannot be removed by a tenant if removal causes any damage to the property. What issue does this raise?

I3-8 Does the fact that an item of income is paid in a form other than cash mean it is nontaxable? Explain.

I3-9 Explain the significance of *Lucas v. Earl* and *Helvering v. Horst*.

I3-10 Under present-day tax law, community property rules are followed in allocating income between husband and wife. Is this consistent with *Lucas v. Earl*? Explain.

I3-11 Ricardo owns a small unincorporated business. His 15-year-old daughter Jane works in the

Form 1040

Department of the Treasury - Internal Revenue Service

U.S. Individual Income Tax Return

1996 (99)

IRS Use Only - Do not write or staple in this space.

For the year Jan. 1-Dec. 31, 1996, or other tax year beginning , 1996, ending , 19

OMB No. 1545-0074

Label
(See page 11.)

Your first name and initial: **John J.**
Last name: **Alexander**

Your social security number: **123 45 6789**

If a joint return, spouse's first name and initial
Last name

Spouse's social security number

Use the IRS label. Otherwise, please print or type.

Home address (number and street). If you have a P.O. box, see page 11.
41 Oak Street
Apt. no.

For help finding line instructions, see pages 2 and 3 in the booklet.

City, town or post office, state, and ZIP code. If you have a foreign address, see page 11.
Orlando, Florida 32816

Presidential Election Campaign (See page 11.)

Do you want $3 to go to this fund? — No: X

If a joint return, does your spouse want $3 to go to this fund?

Yes | No

Note: Checking "Yes" will not change your tax or reduce your refund.

Filing Status

Check only one box.

1 ☐ Single
2 ☐ Married filing joint return (even if only one had income)
3 ☐ Married filing separate return. Enter spouse's soc. sec. no. above and full name here. ▶
4 ☐ Head of household (with qualifying person). If the qualifying person is a child but not your dependent, enter this child's name here. ▶
5 ☐ Qualifying widow(er) with dependent child (year spouse died ▶ 19).

Exemptions

6a ☒ Yourself. If your parent (or someone else) can claim you as a dependent on his or her tax return, do not check box 6a. ......
b ☐ Spouse

No. of boxes checked on 6a and 6b: **1**

c Dependents:

(1) First name Last name	(2) Dependent's social security number if born in Dec. 1996, see inst.	(3) Dependent's relationship to you	(4) No. of months lived in your home in 1996

No. of your children on 6c who:
● lived with you
● didn't live with you due to divorce or separation (see instructions)

If more than six dependents, see the instructions for line 6c.

Dependents on 6c not entered above

Add numbers entered on lines above ▶ **1**

d Total number of exemptions claimed ....

Income

Attach Copy B of your Forms W-2, W-2G, and 1099-R here.

If you did not get a W-2, see the instructions for line 7.

Enclose, but do not attach, any payment. Also, please enclose Form 1040-V. (see the instructions for line 62).

7 Wages, salaries, tips, etc. Attach Form(s) W-2 .... | 7 | **40,000**
8a Taxable interest. Attach Schedule B if over $400 .... | 8a | **300**
b Tax-exempt interest . DO NOT include on line 8a... | 8b | |
9 Dividend income. Attach Schedule B if over $400 .... | 9 | **580**
10 Taxable refunds, credits, or offsets of state and local income taxes .... | 10 |
11 Alimony received .... | 11 |
12 Business income or (loss). Attach Schedule C or C-EZ .... | 12 |
13 Capital gain or (loss). If required, attach Schedule D .... | 13 | **50**
14 Other gains or (losses). Attach Form 4797 .... | 14 |
15a Total IRA distributions | 15a | b Taxable amount (see instr.) | 15b |
16a Total pensions and annuities | 16a | b Taxable amount (see instr.) | 16b |
17 Rental real estate, royalties, partnerships, S corporations, trusts, etc. Attach Schedule E .... | 17 | **3,000**
18 Farm income or (loss). Attach Schedule F .... | 18 |
19 Unemployment compensation .... | 19 |
20a Social security benefits | 20a | b Taxable amount (see instr.) | 20b |
21 Other income. List type and amount - see instructions | 21 |
22 Add the amounts in the far right column for lines 7 through 21. This is your **total income** .... ▶ | 22 | **43,930**

Adjusted Gross Income

If line 31 is under $28,495 (under $9,500 if a child did not live with you), see the instructions for line 54.

23a Your IRA deduction (see instructions) .... | 23a |
b Spouse's IRA deduction (see instructions) .... | 23b |
24 Moving expenses. Attach Form 3903 or 3903-F .... | 24 |
25 One-half of self-employment tax. Attach Schedule SE .... | 25 |
26 Self-employed health insurance deduction (see inst.) | 26 |
27 Keogh & self-employed SEP plans. If SEP, check ▶ ☐ | 27 |
28 Penalty on early withdrawal of savings .... | 28 |
29 Alimony paid. Recipient's SSN ▶ **987 65 4321** | 29 | **6,000**
30 Add lines 23a through 29. ...... | 30 | **6,000**
31 Subtract line 30 from line 22. This is your **adjusted gross income**. .... ▶ | 31 | **37,930**

LHA   **For Privacy Act and Paperwork Reduction Act Notice, see page 7.**

Form **1040** (1996)

610001
12-13-96

FIGURE 13-1 ▶ FORM 1040 (PAGE 1)

Name(s) shown on Form 1040. Do not enter name and social security number if shown on page 1. | Your social security number

John J. Alexander   *123 45 6789*

Schedule B - Interest and Dividend Income

Attachment Sequence No. **08**

Part I
Interest
Income

Note: *If you had over $400 in taxable interest income, you must also complete Part III.*

1   List name of payer. If any interest is from a seller-financed mortgage and the buyer used the property as a personal residence, see page B-1 and list this interest first. Also show that buyer's social security number and address ▶ _____ | **Amount**

Note: If you received a Form 1099-INT, Form 1099-OID, or substitute statement from a brokerage firm, list the firm's name as the payer and enter the total interest shown on that form.

| | **1** | |

2	Add the amounts on line 1	**2**
3	Excludable interest on series EE U.S. savings bonds issued after 1989 from Form 8815, line 14. You MUST attach Form 8815 to Form 1040	**3**
4	Subtract line 3 from line 2. Enter the result here and on Form 1040, line 8a ▶	**4**

Part II
Dividend
Income

Note: *If you had over $400 in gross dividends and/or other distributions on stock, you must also complete Part III.*

5   List name of payer. Include gross dividends and/or other distributions on stock here. Any capital gain distributions and nontaxable distributions will be deducted on lines 7 and 8 ▶ _____ | **Amount**

Note: If you received a Form 1099-DIV or substitute statement from a brokerage firm, list the firm's name as the payer and enter the total dividends shown on that form.

	Amount
Ford Motor Company	*150*
Omaha Mutual Fund	*600*

6	Add the amounts on line 5	**6**	*750*
7	Capital gain distributions. Enter here and on Schedule D*	**7** *50*	
8	Nontaxable distributions	**8** *120*	
9	Add lines 7 and 8	**9**	*170*
10	Subtract line 9 from line 6. Enter the result here and on Form 1040, line 9 ▶	**10**	*580*

If you do not need Schedule D to report any other gains or losses.

Part III
Foreign
Accounts
and
Trusts

You must complete this part if you **(a)** had over $400 of interest or dividends; **(b)** had a foreign account; or **(c)** received a distribution from, or were a grantor of, or a transferor to, a foreign trust. | **Yes** | **No**

11a At any time during 1996, did you have an interest in or a signature or other authority over a financial account in a foreign country, such as a bank account, securities account, or other financial account? | | X

b If "Yes," enter the name of the foreign country ▶ _____

12 During 1996, did you receive a distribution from, or were you the grantor of, or transferor to, a foreign trust? If "Yes," see page B-2 for other forms you may have to file | | X

LHA   **For Paperwork Reduction Act Notice, see Form 1040 instructions.**   **Schedule B (Form 1040) 1996**

627501
11-05-96

FIGURE 13-2   ▶   FORM 1040 (SCHEDULE B)

business on a part-time basis and was paid wages of $3,000 during the current year. Who is taxed on the child's earnings: Jane or her father? Explain.

I3-12 Define the term *constructive receipt*. Explain its importance.

I3-13 Explain three restrictions on the concept of constructive receipt.

I3-14 When is income considered to be earned by an accrual-basis taxpayer?

I3-15 a. Explain the difference between the treatment of prepaid income under the tax law and under financial accounting.
b. Why are the two treatments so different?
c. What problem does this treatment create for taxpayers?

I3-16 Under what conditions is an accrual-basis taxpayer allowed to defer reporting amounts received in the advance of the delivery of goods?

I3-17 Under what conditions is an accrual-basis taxpayer allowed to defer reporting advance payments received for services?

I3-18 a. Is the interest received from government obligations taxable? Explain.
b. What impact does the fact that some bond interest is tax exempt have on interest rates?
c. Is an investor always better off buying tax-exempt bonds? Explain.

I3-19 Are improvements made by a lessee to a lessor's property included in the income of the lessor?

I3-20 Explain the relationship between dividends and earnings and profits.

I3-21 On what basis did the Supreme Court in *Eisner v. Macomber* decide that stock dividends are nontaxable?

I3-22 What is the significance of a constructive dividend?

I3-23 Explain the importance of the distinction between alimony and a property settlement.

I3-24 a. Are items of income not listed in Sec. 61 taxable? Explain.
b. Because there is no specific exclusion for unrealized income, why is it not taxable?
c. Can income be realized even when a cash-method taxpayer does not receive cash?
d. Does a cash basis taxpayer realize income upon the receipt of a note?

I3-25 a. Briefly explain the tax benefit rule.
b. Is a taxpayer required to report the reimbursement of a medical expense by insurance as income if the reimbursement is received in the year following the year of the expenditure?

I3-26 What opportunities are available for a taxpayer to defer the recognition of certain types of prepaid income? That is, what advice could you give someone who wishes to defer the reporting of prepaid income?

I3-27 Taxpayers who deduct an expense one year but recover it the next year are required to include the recovered amount in gross income. The tax benefit rule provides relief if the original deduction did not result in any tax savings. Does this rule provide relief to taxpayers who are in a higher tax bracket in the year they recover the previously deducted expense?

I3-28 George, a wealthy investor, is uncertain whether he should invest in taxable or tax-exempt bonds. What tax and nontax factors should he consider?

I3-29 Do you agree or disagree with the following statement: A taxpayer should not have to report income when debt is forgiven because the taxpayer receives nothing. Explain.

I3-30 Jack and June are retired and receive $10,000 of social security benefits and taxable pensions totaling $25,000. They have been offered $20,000 for a automobile that they restored after they retired. They did most of the restoration work themselves and the sale will result in a gain of $12,000. What tax issues should Jack and June consider?

ISSUE IDENTIFICATION QUESTIONS

I3-31 State Construction Company is owned equally by Andy, Bill, and Charlie. Andy works in the corporation full-time, and Bill and Charlie work elsewhere. When Andy left his previous job to work for State, he signed a contract specifying that he would receive a salary of $50,000 per year. This year, Andy felt that the company could expand if it purchased more equipment, and he offered to delay receiving $20,000 of his salary so the funds could be used to purchase the equipment. Bill and Charlie agreed, and the equipment was purchased. It is expected that State will have enough cash to pay Andy by April of next year. What tax issues should Andy consider?

I3-32 Lisa and her daughter Jane are equal shareholders is Lisa's Flooring, Inc. Lisa founded the corporation and was the sole owner for over twenty years. The company is very successful and Lisa has accumulated a fairly large estate. When Jane turned age twenty-five last year, Lisa gave her half of the stock of the corporation. The gift was properly reported on Lisa's gift tax return. Both Lisa and Jane now work full-time for the corporation. Lisa received a salary of $55,000 per year before Jane started working for the company. After Jane started working, Lisa reduced her salary to $15,000 and started paying Jane a salary of $50,000. Lisa indicates that she still makes most major decisions in the company, but she hopes that Jane will play a more important role as she becomes more familiar with the company. What tax issues should Lisa and the corporation consider?

I3-33 Larry's Art Gallery sells oil paintings, lithographs, and bronzes to collectors and corporations. Customers often come to Larry looking for special pieces. In order to meet customer needs, Larry often accepts orders and then travels looking for the desired item, which he purchases and delivers to the customer. The pieces are expensive, and Larry requires customers to demonstrate their sincerity by providing deposits. If it turns out that the item costs more than expected, Larry contacts the buyer and asks for additional funds. If the item costs less than expected, Larry refunds the excess amount. Also, Larry sometimes returns amounts he received in advance because he is unable to find what the customer wants. What tax issues should Larry's Art Gallery consider?

PROBLEMS

I3-34 *Noncash Compensation.* For each of the following items indicate whether the individual taxpayer must include any amount in gross income:
a. York Corporation gave 100 shares of stock to each of its employees. York Corporation wanted to retain its cash for expansion, so the company transferred the stock, worth $12 per share, to its employees in lieu of a raise.
b. Yellow Corporation encourages its employees to take flu shots. The company does so to reduce time off due to sickness. The company pays for the shots, which cost $20 each.
c. Zip Corporation paid its directors $1,000 each. One director, who was working in a foreign country for the entire year, received the $1,000 fee, even though he did not attend any directors' meetings.

I3-35 *Constructive Receipt.* Which of the following constitutes constructive receipt?
a. A salary check received at 6:00 p.m. on December 31, after all the banks have closed.

b. A rent check, received on December 30 by the manager of an apartment complex. The manager normally collects the rent for the owner. The owner was out of town.

c. A paycheck received on December 29 that was not honored by the bank because the employer's account did not have sufficient funds.

d. A check received on December 30. The check was postdated January 2 of the following year.

e. A check received on January 2. The check had been mailed on December 30.

I3-36   *Series EE Bond Interest.* In 1993, Harry and Mary purchased Series EE bonds, and in 1997 redeemed the bonds, receiving $500 of interest and $1,500 of principal. Their income from other sources totaled $30,000. They paid $2,200 in tuition and fees for their dependent daughter. Their daughter is a qualified student at State University.

a. How much of the Series EE bond interest is excludable?

b. Assuming that the daughter received a $1,000 scholarship, how much of the interest is excludable?

c. Assuming the daughter received the $1,000 scholarship and that the parents' income from other sources is $81,750, how much of the interest is excludable?

I3-37   *Alimony.* As a result of their divorce, Fred agrees to pay alimony to Tammy of $20,000 per year. The payments are to cease in the event of Fred's or Tammy's death or in the event of Tammy's remarriage. In addition, Tammy is to receive their residence, which cost them $100,000 but is worth $140,000.

a. Does the fact that Tammy receives the residence at the time of the divorce mean that there is a reduction in alimony, which will lead to Fred having to recapture an amount in the subsequent year?

b. How will the $20,000 payments be treated by Fred and Tammy?

c. Would recapture of the payments be necessary if payment ceased because of Tammy's remarriage?

d. What is Tammy's basis in the residence?

I3-38   *Constructive Dividend.* Brad owns a successful corporation that has substantial earnings and profits. During the year, the following payments were made by the corporation:

a. Salary of $250,000 to Brad. Officers in other corporations performing similar services receive between $50,000 and $85,000.

b. Rent of $25,000 to Brad. The rent is paid in connection with an office building owned by Brad and used by the corporation. Similar buildings rent for about the same amount.

c. Salary of $5,000 to Brad's daughter, who worked for the company full-time during the summer and part-time during the rest of the year while she attended high school.

d. Alimony of $40,000 to Brad's former wife. Although Brad was personally obligated to make the payments, he used corporation funds to make the payments.

Discuss the likelihood of these payments being treated as constructive dividends. If a payment is deemed to be a constructive dividend, indicate how such a payment will be treated.

I3-39   *Constructive Dividend.* Which of the following would likely be a constructive dividend?

a. An unreasonable salary paid to a shareholder.

b. An unreasonable salary paid to the daughter of a shareholder.

c. A sale of a corporation's asset to a shareholder at fair market value.

d. A payment by a corporation of a shareholder's debts.

e. A payment by a corporation of a shareholder's personal expenses.

I3-40 *Prepaid Rent.* Stan rented an office building to Clay for $3,000 per month. On December 29, 1996, Stan received a deposit of $4,000 in addition to the first and last months' rent. Occupancy began on January 2, 1997. On July 15, 1997, Clay closed his business and filed for bankruptcy. Stan had collected rent for February, March, and April on the first of each month. Stan had received May rent on May 10, but collected no payments afterwards. Stan withheld $800 from the deposit because of damage to the property and $1,500 for unpaid rent. He refunded the balance of the deposit to Clay. What amount would Stan report as gross income for 1996? for 1997?

I3-41 *Rental Income.* Ed owns Oak Knoll Apartments. During the year, Fred, a tenant, moved to another state. Fred paid Ed $1,000 to cancel the two-year lease he had signed. Ed subsequently rented the unit to Wayne. Wayne paid the first and last months' rents of $800 each and a security deposit of $500. Ed also owns a building that is used as a health club. The club has signed a fifteen-year lease at an annual rental of $17,000. The owner of the club requested that Ed install a swimming pool on the property. Ed declined to do so. The owner of the club finally constructed the pool himself at a cost of $15,000. What amount must Ed include in gross income?

I3-42 *Gross Income.* Joy collected $800 interest on corporate bonds and a salary of $32,000 from her employer. Joy won $100 for having the lowest golf score in her country club's golf tournament. She also won $500 in the state lottery. The ticket cost $5. Joy also stole $50 from her mother's purse when she was not looking. Which amounts are taxable?

I3-43 *Interest Income.* Holly inherited $10,000 of City of Atlanta bonds in February. In March, she received interest of $500, and in April she sold the bonds at a $200 gain. Holly redeemed Series E U.S. savings bonds that she had purchased several years ago. The accumulated interest totaled $800. Holly received $300 of interest on bonds issued by the City of Quebec, Canada. What amount, if any, of gross income must Holly report?

I3-44 *Annuity Income.* Tim retired during the current year at age 58. He purchased an annuity from American National Life Company for $40,000. The annuity pays Tim $500 per month for life.

a. Compute Tim's annual exclusion.

b. How much income will Tim report each year after reaching age 84?

I3-45 *Pension Income.* On July 1, 1997, Beth turned 65 and retired from her position as a garment worker. She immediately began receiving a monthly pension for the remainder of her life of $300. Over the years she worked, Beth made $13,104 of nondeductible contributions to the pension fund through withholding. How much must Beth report as income from the pension during the current year?

I3-46 *Social Security Benefits.* Dan and Diana file a joint return. Dan earned $30,000 during the year before losing his job. He subsequently received unemployment compensation of $1,000. Diana received Social Security benefits of $5,000.

a. Determine the taxable portion of the Social Security benefits.

b. What is the taxable portion of the Social Security benefits if Dan earned $45,000 before losing his job?

I3-47 *Recovery of Previously Deducted Expense.* In 1998, Fred received a $1,000 refund of state income taxes withheld from his salary during 1997. For each of the following cases, indicate whether Fred must include any portion of the refund in his 1998 gross income.

a. Fred did not itemize during 1997.

b. Fred does not itemize during 1998.

c. Fred uses the accrual method for determining his deduction for state income taxes.

d. Fred suffered a net loss during 1997 of $20,000.

e. Fred suffered a net loss during 1998 of $20,000.

f. Fred's itemized deductions during 1997 exceeded the standard deduction by $400.

I3-48   *Social Security Benefits.* Lucia is a 69-year-old single individual who receives a taxable pension of $10,000 per year and Social Security benefits of $7,000. Lucia is considering the possibility of selling stock she has owned for years and using the funds to purchase a summer home. She will realize a gain of $20,000 when she sells the stock, which has been paying $1,000 of dividends each year. Lucia says her brother recommended that she sell half of the stock this year and half next year because selling all of the stock at once would affect the tax treatment of her Social Security benefits.

a. Compute her AGI under the assumption she sells all of the stock now after receiving $1,000 dividends from the stock.

b. Repeat the computation under the assumption she sells only half of the stock this year and also receives $1,000 dividends from the stock.

I3-49   *Recovery of Previously Deducted Expense.* As the result of unexpected surgery, Jan incurred $14,000 of medical expenses in 1997. At the end of 1997, her medical insurance had paid only $5,000. Jan anticipates that the company will eventually pay an additional $7,000 of the bill. Because her AGI is $30,000 and there is a 7.5% floor for medical deductions, Jan can deduct medical expenses over $2,250. Her other itemized deductions exceed the standard deduction.

a. If Jan pays the balance of the $9,000 medical expenses before the end of the year, can she claim a deduction in 1997?

b. If she is reimbursed $7,000 in 1998, how will the reimbursement be treated?

I3-50   *Social Security Benefits.* Gary and Gail file a joint return. Gary's salary is $42,000, and they received taxable interest of $1,000. Gail received $7,000 of Social Security benefits. What amount, if any, of the benefits are taxable?

I3-51   *Adjusted Gross Income.* Amir, who is single, retired from his job this year. He received a salary of $25,000 for the portion of the year that he worked, tax-exempt interest of $3,000, and dividends from domestic corporations of $2,700. On September 1, he began receiving monthly pension payments of $1,000 and Social Security payments of $600. Assume an exclusion ratio of 40% for the pension. Amir owns a duplex that he rents to others. He received rent of $12,000 and incurred $17,000 of expenses related to the duplex. He continued to actively manage the property after he retired from his job. Compute Amir's adjusted gross income.

I3-52   *Court Awards and Insurance Settlements.* What amount, if any, must be included in gross income by the following taxpayers?

a. Allen received $1,000 from his insurance company because his boat, which cost $2,000, was sunk during a storm.

b. Collin owns Collins Construction Company. Len started Colins Construction Company and obtained a number of contracts with people who thought they were dealing with Collins Construction Company. Collin sued and collected $40,000, which was the profit he lost because of the contracts, and punitive damages of $80,000.

c. Dick loaned his brother $2,000. Dick had to sue in order to recover the amount of the loan.

d. Fran, an accountant, had to sue a client in order to collect her audit fee of $8,000. Would Fran's accounting method make any difference?

I3-53 *Claim of Right.* USA Corporation hired Jesse to install a computer system for the company and paid him $8,000 for the work. USA soon realized that there were problems with the system and asked Jesse to refund the payment. At the end of the year the dispute had not been resolved. Jesse is in the 28% tax bracket in the year he did the original work. During the next year, when he is in the 15% tax bracket, Jesse refunds the $8,000 to USA.

a. Is the original payment taxable to Jesse when he receives it?

b. What options are available to Jesse when he repays the $8,000?

c. What option would have been available to Jesse if he had been asked to repay only $2,000?

I3-54 *Tax Planning.* Bart and Kesha are in the 36% tax bracket. They are interested in reducing the taxes they pay each year. They are currently considering several alternatives. For each of the following alternatives, indicate how much tax, if any, they would save.

a. Make a gift of bonds valued at $5,000 that yield $400 per year interest to their 14-year-old daughter, who has no other income.

b. Sell the bonds from Part a rather than give them to their daughter, and buy tax-exempt bonds that pay 6%. Assume the bonds can be sold for $5,000.

c. Give $1,000 cash to a charity. Assume they itemize deductions.

d. Pay their daughter a salary of $10,000 for services rendered in their unincorporated business.

I3-55 *Series EE Bond Interest.* In 1997, Ken and Lynn paid $5,000 to purchase Series EE bonds in the name of their 11-year-old son. The son has no other income, and they are in the 28% tax bracket. The taxable interest during the first year will be $400 if an election is made to accrue the interest on an annual basis.

a. Will the child owe any tax on the bond interest?

b. Does the son need to file a tax return?

c. What are the tax consequences in 1997 and subsequent years if annual gifts are made to their son?

COMPREHENSIVE PROBLEMS

I3-56 Matt and Sandy reside in a community property state. Matt left home in April 1997 because of disputes with his wife, Sandy. Subsequently, Matt earned $15,000. Before leaving home in April, Matt earned $3,000. Sandy was unaware of Matt's whereabouts or his earnings after he left home. The $3,000 earned by Matt before he left home was spent on food, housing, and other items shared by Matt and Sandy. Matt and Sandy have one child, who lived with Sandy after the husband left home.

a. Is any portion of Matt's earnings after he left home taxable to Sandy?

b. What filing status is applicable to Sandy if she filed a return?

c. How much income would Sandy be required to report if she filed?

d. Is Sandy required to file?

I3-57 Gary earned $57,000 as an executive. Gary, who is single, supported his half sister, who lives in a nursing home. Gary received the following interest: $400 on City of Los Angeles bonds, $200 on a money market account, and $2,100 on a loan to his brother.

Gary spent one week serving on a jury and received $50.

Gary received a refund of federal income taxes withheld during the prior year of $1,200 and a state income tax refund of $140. Gary had itemized deductions last year of $8,000.

Gary received dividends on Ace Corporation of $1,000 and on Tray Corporation of $1,400. Gary's itemized deductions equal $9,000, and withholding for federal income taxes is $11,000. Compute Gary's tax due or refund due.

TAX FORM/RETURN PREPARATION PROBLEMS

I3-58 Sally W. Emanual had the following dividends and interest during the current year:

Acorn Corporation bond interest	$ 700
City of Boston bonds interest	1,000
Camp Bank interest	250
Jet Corporation stock dividend	300
North Mutual fund	
Capital gain distribution	100
Ordinary dividend	150
Nontaxable distribution	200
	450
Blue Corporation stock foreign dividend	250

Additional information pertaining to Sally Emanual includes

Salary	$32,000
Rent income	12,000
Expenses related to rent income	14,000
Pension benefits	8,000
Alimony paid to Sally	4,000

The taxable portion of the pension is $7,000. Sally actively participates in the rental activity. Other relevant information includes

Address: 430 Rumsey Place, West Falls, California 92699
Occupation: Credit manager
Social Security number: 123-45-4321
Marital status: Single

Complete Sally's Schedule B and page 1 of her Form 1040. Assume Schedule E has already been prepared.

CASE STUDY PROBLEMS

I3-59 Jim and Linda are your tax clients. They were divorced two years ago and the divorce decree stated that Jim was to make monthly payments to Linda. The court designated $300 per month as alimony and $200 per month as child support, or a total of $6,000 per year. Jim has been unemployed for much of the year and paid Linda $2,000 that he said was for child support. In addition, Jim transferred the title to a three-year-old automobile with a $4,000 FMV and basis of $7,000 in exchange for her promise not to pursue any claim she has against him for the unpaid child support and alimony. Does Linda have to report any alimony and is Jim entitled to an alimony deduction? Draft a memo for the file that discusses the tax consequences for both Jim and Linda.

I3-60 John and Mary (your clients) have two small children and are looking for ways to help fund the children's college education. They have heard that Series EE bonds are a tax-favored way of saving and have requested your opinion on the tax consequences. They have asked your opinion regarding the relative advantages of purchasing Series EE bonds in their names versus the children's names. John and Mary have indicated that they expect to have a high level of income in the future and that their children may receive other income sources from future inheritances. Prepare a client memo making recommendations about the tax consequences of Series EE bond investments for John and Mary.

I3-61 Lee and Jane have been your firm's clients for most of the twenty years they have been married. Recently Lee came to you and said that he and Jane are obtaining a divorce, and he wants you to help him with some of the tax and financial issues that may come up during the divorce. The next day, Jane called asking you for the same assistance. What ethical issues do you see present? What possible conflicts may arise if you represent both Lee and Jane?

TAX RESEARCH PROBLEM

I3-62 William owns a building that is leased to Lester's Machine Shop. Lester requests that William rewire the building for new equipment Lester plans to purchase. The wiring would cost about $4,000, but would not increase the value of the building because its only use is in connection with the specialized equipment. Rather than lose Lester as a lessee, William agrees to forgo one month's rent of $1,000 if Lester will pay for the wiring. Because Lester does not want to move, he agrees. What amount, if any, must William include in gross income?

A partial list of research sources is

- Sec. 109
- Reg. Sec. 1.109-1
- *CIR v. Grace H. Cunningham*, 2 AFTR 2d 5511, 58-2 USTC ¶9771 (9th Cir., 1958)

CHAPTER 4

GROSS INCOME: EXCLUSIONS

LEARNING OBJECTIVES

After studying this chapter, you should be able to

1▸ Explain the conditions that must exist for an item to be excluded from gross income

2▸ Determine whether an item is income

3▸ Decide whether specific exclusions are available

4▸ Understand employment-related fringe benefit exclusion items

KEY POINT

Given the sweeping definition of *income,* it is generally difficult to establish that an item is not income.

EXAMPLE I4-1 ▶

EXAMPLE I4-2 ▶

OBJECTIVE 1

Explain the conditions that must exist for an item to be excluded from gross income

REAL-WORLD EXAMPLE

Grants made to Native Americans by the federal government under the Indian Financing Act of 1974 to expand Native American–owned economic enterprises are excludable from gross income. Rev. Rul. 77-77, 1977-1 C.B. 11.

OBJECTIVE 2

Determine whether an item is income

TYPICAL MISCONCEPTION

It is sometimes erroneously assumed that severance pay, embezzlement proceeds, gambling winnings, hobby income, prizes, rewards, and tips are not taxable.

Chapter I3 discussed specific items that must be included in gross income. This chapter considers items that are excluded from gross income. Under Sec. 61(a), all items of income are taxable unless specifically excluded. Taxpayers who wish to avoid being taxed basically have two alternatives. One approach is to establish that the item is not income. If an item is not income (e.g., if it is a return of capital), it is not subject to the income tax. The second approach is to identify a specific exclusion and establish that the exclusion is applicable to the item of income.

Matt borrowed $10,000 from the bank. Although Matt received $10,000, it is not income because he is obligated to repay the amount borrowed. No specific statutory authority states that borrowed funds are excluded from taxation. Presumably, the fact that borrowed funds are not income is considered to be both fundamental and obvious. ◀

Sheila enrolled in State University. The university awarded her a $1,000 tuition scholarship because of her high admission test scores and grades. Section 117 excludes such scholarships from gross income. As a result, Sheila need not report the scholarship as income. ◀

The major source of exclusions are those specific items contained in the IRC. These exclusions have evolved over the years and were enacted by Congress for a variety of reasons, including social and economic objectives.

The term *administrative exclusion* is occasionally seen. In one sense, there are no administrative exclusions. Exclusions exist because of statute, that is, because of specific provisions in the Internal Revenue Code. The IRS has no authority to create exclusions, yet the IRS must interpret the meaning of the Code. A liberal interpretation of the statute by the IRS may result in a broad definition of what constitutes an exclusion, and such a broad definition may reasonably be termed an administrative exclusion.

For example, Sec. 102 excludes gifts received from gross income. The IRS has followed the practice of excluding certain welfare benefits from gross income, presumably because such benefits may be viewed as gifts.[1] The IRS could take the position that welfare benefits are not gifts. That position would no doubt be challenged in the courts.

The term *judicial exclusions* should be considered in the same vein. Although the courts cannot create exclusions, they can interpret the statute and decide whether a particular item is covered by a statutory exclusion. Such determination may be termed a judicial exclusion.

ITEMS THAT ARE NOT INCOME

As noted above, some items are not income and, therefore, are not subject to the income tax. In addition to amounts obtained by a liability (discussed above), four other items are not considered income:

▶ Unrealized income

▶ Self-help income

▶ Rental value of personal-use property

▶ Gross selling price of property (as opposed to the profit or gain earned on the sale)

UNREALIZED INCOME

In *Eisner v. Macomber,* the Supreme Court held that a stock dividend cannot be taxed because the taxpayer had "received nothing that answers the definition of income within the meaning of the Sixteenth Amendment."[2] An ordinary stock dividend does not alter

---

[1] For example, see Rev. Rul. 57-102, 1957-1 C.B. 26, which excludes public assistance payments to blind persons from gross income.

[2] 3 AFTR 3020, 1 USTC ¶32 (USSC, 1920).

the existing proportionate ownership interest of any stockholder, nor does it increase the value of the individual's holdings. In effect, the court concluded that realization must occur before income is recognized. Although narrowed by subsequent legislation and litigation, ordinary stock dividends continue to be excluded from gross income even today. Perhaps more important, *Eisner v. Macomber* established realization as a criterion for the recognition of income.

SELF-HELP INCOME

Although the concept of self-help income is considered as income by economists, it is not sanctioned by accountants, the IRS, or the courts. Thus, if an individual painted his own residence, even though the value of the residence has increased, he would not be treated as having income. However, if a taxpayer hires someone else, the taxpayer would have to earn income, pay a tax, and use after-tax income to pay the hired painter. In either situation, the taxpayer receives the same economic benefit, but no tax is imposed when the economic benefit is derived from self-help. Of course, taxpayers commonly perform household chores, repair their own automobiles, mow their own lawns, and perform a myriad of other self-help activities.

This should be contrasted with taxable exchanges of services. A mechanic might agree to repair a painter's automobile in exchange for the painter's promise to paint the mechanic's home. In this instance, where the parties exchange services, each party realizes income equal to the value of the services he or she receives. If each did his own work (i.e., the painter fixed his or her own automobile and the mechanic painted his or her own home), neither would have to report any income.

STOP & THINK

Question: The discussion of self-help income refers to an exchange of services between 2 individuals, such as a painter and a mechanic. How can a taxable barter transaction be distinguished from an act of friendship which is repaid?

Solution: When one person helps another without any promise of repayment, the act of kindness does not represent an exchange and is not taxable. Friends help one another from time to time without contractual reciprocity. As a result, such acts are not taxable. The distinction between a taxable barter exchange and acts of friendship is not always easy to make.

RENTAL VALUE OF PERSONAL-USE PROPERTY

Taxpayers are not taxed on the rental value of personally owned property. For example, taxpayers who own their own home receive the economic benefit of occupancy without being taxed on the rental value of the property. It would be very difficult to keep records and value benefits obtained from self-help and the personal use of property. For that reason, no significant effort has ever been made to tax such benefits.[3]

SELLING PRICE OF PROPERTY

If property is sold at a gain, it is the gain and not the entire sales price that is taxable. Because the basic principle is almost universally accepted, the Supreme Court has never had to rule directly on whether the entire sale proceeds could be taxed. The IRS and the courts seemed to accept the basic principle even before the rule became part of the

---

[3] In 1928, the government tried unsuccessfully to tax the value of produce grown and consumed by a farmer (*Homer P. Morris*, 9 B.T.A. 1273 (1928)). The court stated, "To include the value of such products [would be to] in effect include in income something which Congress did not intend should be so regarded." The court did not explain how or why it reached this conclusion. In 1957, the IRS successfully disallowed the deduction of expenses incurred in raising such produce (*Robert L. Nowland v. CIR*, 51 AFTR 423, 57-1 USTC ¶9684 (4th Cir., 1957)).

statute.[4] The primary reason for this principle (often referred to as the "recovery of capital" principle) is that a portion of the selling price represents a return of capital to the seller.

MAJOR STATUTORY EXCLUSIONS

While Congress has created statutory exclusions for a variety of reasons, most exclusions have been enacted for reasons of social policy or reasons of incentive. The concept of social policy, that is, a concept of social generosity or benevolence, has prompted the government to exclude items such as

▶ Payments for personal physical sickness and injury (Sec. 104)

▶ Life insurance proceeds (Sec. 101)

▶ Gifts and inheritances (Sec. 102)

▶ Public assistance payments

▶ Qualified adoption expenses (Sec. 137)

▶ Discharge of indebtedness during bankruptcy or insolvency (Sec. 108)

▶ Gain on sale of personal residence by taxpayers who are age 55 or older (Sec. 121)

▶ Partial exclusions for Social Security benefits (Sec. 86)

Other exclusions may be explained in terms of economic incentive, that is, the government's desire to encourage or reward a particular type of behavior.

▶ Awards for meritorious achievement (Sec. 74(b))

▶ Various employee fringe benefits (Secs. 79, 105, 106, 124, 125, 129, 132)

▶ Partial exclusion for scholarships (Sec. 117)

▶ Foreign-earned income (Sec. 911)

▶ Interest on state and local government obligations (Sec. 103)

Other reasons may exist for some of the exclusions listed above. For example, one reason income from the discharge of indebtedness during bankruptcy is excluded from gross income is the fact that such taxpayers would be unlikely to have the resources needed to pay the tax. (See Chapter I3 for a discussion of tax-exempt interest and Social Security benefits, and Chapter I12 for the treatment of gain on the sale of a personal residence.)

ADDITIONAL COMMENT

Tax expenditure estimates measure the decreases in individual and corporate income tax liabilities that result from provisions in income tax laws and regulations that provide economic incentives or tax relief to particular kinds of taxpayers.

GIFTS AND INHERITANCES

Congress has excluded the value of gifts and inheritances received from gross income since the inception of the income tax in 1913. Section 102 excludes the value of property received during the life of the donor (*inter vivos* **gifts**) and transfers at death (**testamentary gifts**—bequests, devises, and inheritances).[5] The recipient of such property is taxed on the income produced by the property after the transfer.[6] It should be noted that a donor cannot avoid the income tax by making a gift of income. The donor, not the donee, is taxed on the gifted income.

TYPICAL MISCONCEPTION

Because of confusion between the gift tax imposed on donors with the exclusion that applies to donees, it is sometimes mistakenly thought that gifts are taxable above a certain dollar amount.

---

[4] Section 202(a) of the Revenue Act of 1924 is the predecessor of current Sec. 1001(a), which describes that only the gain portion of the sale proceeds is included in gross income. S. Rept. No. 398, 68th Cong., 1st Sess., p. 10 (1924) states that Sec. 202(a) sets forth general rules to be used in the computation of gain or loss. The Senate report further states that the provision "merely embodies in the law the present construction by the Department and the courts of the existing law."

[5] Although excluded from gross income, such transfers may be subject to the gift tax or the estate tax.

[6] Reg. Sec. 1.102-1.

EXAMPLE I4-3 ▶ Stan owns stock in a corporation and orders the corporation to pay dividends on the stock to his daughter. Even though his daughter received the dividends, Stan must include the dividends in his gross income. Stan could avoid being taxed on future dividends by making a gift of the stock to his daughter. ◀

It is often difficult to distinguish gifts, which are not included in the recipient's gross income, from other transfers, which are taxable. Gifts sometimes closely resemble prizes and awards.[7]

EXAMPLE I4-4 ▶ Tina received a free automobile for being the ten millionth paying guest at an amusement park. The automobile is not considered a gift but a prize and is taxable to Tina. ◀

Also, some payments made to employees by employers may resemble gifts.

EXAMPLE I4-5 ▶ At Christmas, Red Corporation paid $500 to each employee who had been with the company for more than five years. These payments are not considered gifts for tax purposes and are taxable to the employees. ◀

REAL-WORLD EXAMPLE
Amounts received by a dealer from players in the operation of a gambling casino were not excludable as gifts even though impulsive generosity or superstition may be the dominant motive. The amounts were similar to tips, which are taxable. *Louis R. Tomburello, 86 T.C. 540 (1986).*

Whether a transfer is a gift depends on the intent of the donor. A donor is expected to be motivated by love, affection, kindness, sympathy, generosity, admiration, or similar emotions. In the two preceding examples, the transfers were probably made for business motives and not necessarily for donative reasons. Thus, the automobile is a taxable prize, and the amounts paid to employees represent taxable awards for services rendered, but see the discussion of Sec. 274 later in this chapter.

Transfers of money or property between family members frequently creates problems of classification. For example, assume a father, who owns his own business, hires his 10-year old son to work in the business. Is the payment to the son a salary (and, therefore, deductible by the business) or is it really just a gift from the father to the son? The answer depends on the true value of the services that are performed by the son. If the son is truly performing services that are commensurate with the salary paid, the payment may properly be classified as a salary. On the other hand, if the son is paid an amount that is greater than the value of the services, the excess amount will be treated as a gift.

LIFE INSURANCE PROCEEDS

Life insurance proceeds paid to a beneficiary because of the insured person's death are not taxable.[8] The exclusion applies whether the proceeds are paid in a lump sum or in installments. Amounts received in excess of the face amount of the policy are usually taxable as interest.

EXAMPLE I4-6 ▶ Buddy is the beneficiary of a $100,000 insurance policy on his mother's life. Upon her death, he elects to receive $13,000 per year for ten years instead of the lump sum. He receives $10,000 per year tax-free ($100,000 ÷ 10), but the remaining $3,000 per year is taxable as interest. ◀

EXAMPLE I4-7 ▶ Assume the same facts as in Example I4-6, except that Buddy elects to receive the full $100,000 face amount upon his mother's death. None of the $100,000 is taxable. ◀

The exclusion exists because life insurance benefits closely resemble inheritances, which are not taxable.

There is one exception that may result in a portion of the face amount of a life

---

[7] Recall that under Sec. 74 (discussed in Chapter I3) most prizes and awards are taxable.

[8] Sec. 101(a).

insurance policy being included in gross income.[9] In general, the life insurance exclusion is not available if the insurance policy is obtained by the beneficiary in exchange for valuable consideration from a person other than the insurance company. For example, an individual may purchase an existing life insurance policy for cash from another individual. In this situation, the exclusion for death benefits is limited to the consideration paid plus the premiums or other sums subsequently paid by the buyer.

EXAMPLE I4-8 ▶

ADDITIONAL COMMENT

The proceeds of a life insurance policy payable to named beneficiaries can be excluded from the federal estate tax when the decedent does not possess any incidents of ownership. This provision and the exclusion from gross income of life insurance proceeds underscore the favored position of life insurance.

Kwame is the owner and beneficiary of a $100,000 policy on the life of his father. Kwame sells the policy to his brother Anwar for $10,000. Anwar subsequently pays premiums of $12,000. Upon his father's death, Anwar must include $78,000 [$100,000 − ($10,000 + $12,000)] in gross income. However, if Kwame gave the policy to his brother, all of the proceeds would be excluded from gross income because the gift of the policy does not constitute valuable consideration. ◀

The proceeds are excludable under the general exclusion for life insurance proceeds if the beneficiary's basis is found by reference to the transferor's basis (as would be true in the case of a gift), or if the policy is transferred to the insured, the insured's partner, a partnership that includes the insured, or a corporation in which the insured is a shareholder or officer.

SURRENDER OR SALE OF POLICY. The exclusion for life insurance is available for amounts payable by reason of the death of the insured. In general, if a life policy is sold or surrendered for a lump sum before the death of the insured, the amount received is taxable to the extent that it exceeds the net premiums paid.[10] On the other hand, no loss is recognized if a life insurance policy is surrendered before maturity and premiums paid exceed the cash surrender value.[11]

SELF-STUDY QUESTION

A corporation acquires a life insurance policy on the president of the corporation, and the corporation is named as the beneficiary of the policy. Are the insurance premiums deductible?

ANSWER

No, the premiums are not deductible because any costs incurred to produce tax-exempt income are nondeductible.

"Accelerated death benefits" received after 1996 may be excluded from gross income. Accelerated death benefits include payments made to a terminally ill person and periodic payments made to a chronically ill person. A person is terminally ill if a physician certifies that he is reasonably likely to die within 24 months. A person is chronically ill if he has a disability requiring long-term care (e.g., nursing home care). In general, the exclusion for periodic payments made to a chronically ill person is limited to the cost of long term care. The exclusion covers amounts received from the insurance provider or from a "viatical settlement provider" (i.e., person in the business of providing accelerated death benefits).

EXAMPLE I4-9 ▶

Harry has been diagnosed with AIDS, and he is expected to live less than a year. Harry is covered by a life insurance policy with a $100,000 face amount. The insurance company offers terminally ill individuals the option of receiving 75% of the policy face amount. If Harry accepts the settlement, the amount he receives is excludable from gross income because he is a terminally ill individual.

EXAMPLE I4-10 ▶

Mary suffered a severe stroke and has been admitted to a nursing home where she is expected to remain for the rest of her life. She is certified by a licensed health care practitioner as being a "chronically ill individual." Her nursing home expenses amount to $30,000 per year. Mary has elected to take $40,000 per year from a $200,000 face amount life insurance policy as accelerated death benefits. Because she is a chronically ill individual, Mary must include $10,000 in her gross income and may exclude $30,000. Chronically ill individuals are only allowed to exclude accelerated death payments to the extent used for long-term care.

---

[9] Sec. 101(a)(2).
[10] Sec. 72(e)(2). In some instances where distributions are made before the recipient reaches age 59½, a 10% penalty applies (see Sec. 72(q)).

[11] *London Shoe Co. v. CIR.*, 16 AFTR 1398, 35-2 USTC ¶9664 (2nd Cir., 1935).

DIVIDENDS ON LIFE INSURANCE AND ENDOWMENT POLICIES. Dividends on life insurance and endowment policies are normally not taxable because they are considered to be a partial return of premiums paid. The dividends are taxable to the extent that the total dividends received exceed the total premiums paid. Also, if dividends are left with the insurance company and earn interest, the interest is taxable.

ADOPTION EXPENSES. Prior to 1997, taxpayers who incurred substantial expenses in connection with the adoption of a child were not provided with any tax benefits. These types of expenses were considered as personal expenses of the taxpayer and therefore, not deductible. For tax years beginning after 1996, Congress provides tax benefits for qualified adoption expenses in the form of tax credits (see Chapter I14) or an exclusion for amounts paid pursuant to an adoption assistance plan created by an employer. An employee is allowed a $5,000 per child exclusion ($6,000 for a child with special needs) from gross income for qualified adoption expenses paid by an employer under an adoption assistance program.[12] The exclusion is phased-out ratably for taxpayers with modified adjusted gross income of $75,000 to $115,000.

Qualified adoption expenses include adoption fees, court costs, attorney fees, and other expenses related to an adoption. An adoption assistance program is a separate written plan of an employer, exclusively for the benefit of its employees, to provide adoption assistance.

EXAMPLE I4-11 ▶ Reggie and Rhonda are married, have AGI of $90,000, and adopted a child in 1997. Rhonda's employer maintains a written adoption assistance program. They spend $8,000 during the year in connection with the adoption, all of which is paid by Rhonda's employer pursuant to the plan. Reggie and Rhonda must include in their gross income for 1997 an amount of $4,875, computed as follows:

Total adoption expenses paid from the plan	$8,000
Maximum exclusion	5,000
Phase-out percentage [$15,000/($115,000 − $75,000)]	37.5%
Reduction in exclusion	1,875
Exclusion amount ($5,000 − $1,875)	3,125
Amount includible in gross income ($8,000 − $3,125)	4,875

AWARDS FOR MERITORIOUS ACHIEVEMENT

As noted in Chapter I3, prizes and awards are generally taxable. An exception is applicable to awards and prizes made for religious, charitable, scientific, educational, artistic, literary, or civic achievement if the recipient

▶ Was selected without action on his or her part to enter the contest or the proceeding,

▶ Does not have to perform substantial future services as a condition to receiving the prize or award, and

▶ designates that the payor is to pay the amount of the award to either a government unit or a charitable organization.[13]

The recipient of such an award normally would owe no tax if he or she collected the proceeds and then contributed the proceeds to a charity. This is because the gift would qualify as a deductible charitable contribution. However, this rule is beneficial only in situations where the taxpayer could not deduct the full amount of the award because of the limitation on the charitable contribution deduction (generally 50% of AGI; see Chapter I7) or in the case of a small award to a taxpayer who does not itemize.

---

[12] Sec. 137.　　　　　　　[13] Sec. 74.

ADDITIONAL COMMENT

Athletic scholarships for fees, books, and supplies awarded by a university to students who are expected, but not required, to participate in a particular sport can be excludable.

KEY POINT

The exclusion for scholarships does not include amounts received for room, board, and laundry.

SCHOLARSHIPS AND FELLOWSHIPS

Subject to certain limitations, scholarships are excluded from gross income.[14] A scholarship is an amount paid or allowed to a student, whether an undergraduate or graduate, to aid degree-seeking individuals.

The exclusion for scholarships is limited to the amount of the scholarship that is used for *qualified tuition and related expenses*. Qualified tuition and related expenses typically include tuition and fees, books, supplies, and equipment required for courses of instruction at an educational organization. The value of services and accommodations supplied such as room, board, and laundry are not excluded. The exclusion for scholarships does not extend to salary paid for services even if all candidates for a particular degree are required to perform the services.[15]

EXAMPLE I4-12 ▶ Becky is awarded a $5,000 per year scholarship by State University. Becky spends $3,000 of the scholarship for tuition, books, and supplies, and $2,000 is for room and board. In addition, Becky works part-time on campus and earns $4,000, which covers the rest of her room and board and other expenses. Becky is taxed on the $2,000 of the scholarship spent for room and board and $4,000 of salary earned from her part-time job. ◀

PAYMENTS FOR INJURY AND SICKNESS

Under prior law, Sec. 104(a) permitted taxpayers to exclude amounts awarded as compensation for "personal injury or sickness." The courts construed the provision to exclude from gross income awards resulting from nonphysical injuries such as damaged reputations[16] and libel.[17] Effective in 1997, Congress limited the exclusion under Sec. 104(a) to the "amount of any damages . . . received . . . on account of personal physical injuries or physical sickness." The result of the change is to tax most insurance and court awards associated with nonphysical injuries. Taxpayers may still exclude amounts that represent reimbursements for related medical care.

EXAMPLE I4-13 ▶ After she was denied a promotion, Jane sued her employer claiming sex discrimination. She was awarded $5,000 to cover the medical bills she incurred because of the related emotional distress, $20,000 to punish her employer for discrimination, and $10,000 to compensate her for lost wages. The $5,000 awarded to cover medical bills is excluded from gross income, but not the amounts awarded as punitive damages or lost wages. ◀

Amounts awarded for physical unjuries or sickness may be excluded from gross income. The exclusion extends to amounts awarded for emotional distress related to physical injuries or sickness and to amounts awarded to other individuals (e.g., the victim's family). On the other hand, punitive damages are taxable even if awarded in connection with physical injuries as the awards are intended to punish the individual who caused the injury rather than compensate the injured individual.

EXAMPLE I4-14 ▶ Mary was injured in an automobile accident caused by another driver. Mary's daughter, Sarah, was in the automobile, but she was not physically injured. The other driver's insurance company paid Mary $10,000 to cover medical bills relating to her injuries and $5,000 to

[14] Sec. 117.

[15] Scholarships may need to be reviewed to determine whether the amount constitutes compensation. A "scholarship" awarded to the winner of a televised beauty pageant by a profit-making corporation was ruled to be compensation for performing subsequent services for the corporation (Rev. Rul. 68-20, 1968-1 C.B. 55). An employer-paid "scholarship" was held to be compensation in a situation where the employee was on leave and was required to return to work after finishing the degree (*Richard E. Johnson v. Bingler*, 23 AFTR 2d 69-1212, 69-1 USTC ¶9348 (USSC, 1969)). However,

in Ltr. Rul. 9526020 (September 10, 1995) the IRS ruled that grants to law students are not taxable even it they are conditioned upon the students agreeing to practice upon graduation in public, nonprofit, or other low paying sectors.

[16] *Dudley G. Seay*, 58 T.C. 32 (1972).

[17] *Wade E. Church*, 80 T.C. 1104 (1983).

compensate her for emotional distress caused by the injuries. Sarah was paid $5,000 to compensate her for distress caused by her witnessing her mother's injuries. None of the amounts are included in gross income as they are all related to Mary's physical injury. If part of the settlement was identified as a punitive award, that amount would be taxable. ◀

Compensatory death benefits (such as those awarded by courts to an accident victim's family to compensate the family for its loss) are also excluded from gross income under Sec. 104. On the other hand, punitive death benefits are taxable except where state law only permits punitive awards.

Furthermore, Sec. 104(a)(3) excludes from gross income amounts collected under an accident and health insurance policy purchased by the taxpayer, even if the benefits are a substitute for lost income. In addition, the law now specifies that benefits received under a qualified long term care insurance contract may be excluded from gross income, but limits the exclusion to the greater of $175 per day (adjusted for inflation beginning in 1998) or the actual cost of such care. Such policies pay for nursing home and other types of long term care. If the benefits exceed the actual cost of such care, but are less than $175 per day, no portion of the benefits are taxable.

EXAMPLE I4-15 ▶ Chuck purchased a disability income policy from an insurance company. Chuck subsequently suffered a heart attack. Under the terms of the policy, Chuck received $1,000 per month for the five months he was unable to work. The amounts received are not taxable, even though the payments are a substitute for the wages lost due to the illness. ◀

This exclusion is not applicable if the accident and health benefits are provided by the taxpayer's employer.[18]

EXAMPLE I4-16 ▶ Assume the same facts as in Example I4-15 except that Chuck's employer paid the premiums on the policy. The amounts received by Chuck are taxable. ◀

If the cost of the coverage is shared by the employer and the taxpayer, a portion of the benefits is taxable. For example, if the employer paid one-half of the premiums, one-half of the benefits would be taxable. The principal reason for the different tax treatment is that employer-paid coverage represents a tax-free employee fringe benefit, whereas employee-paid premiums are from after-tax dollars.

In the case of an award intended to reimburse the taxpayer for medical expenses, it follows that the taxpayer cannot deduct the reimbursed medical expenses.[19] If the award exceeds the actual expense, it is not taxable except in the case of employer-financed accident and health insurance.[20]

State worker's compensation laws establish fixed amounts to be paid to employees suffering specific job-related injuries. Section 104(a)(1) specifically excludes worker's compensation from gross income, even though the payments are intended, in part, to reimburse injured workers for loss of future income and even if the injuries are nonphysical.

EMPLOYEE FRINGE BENEFITS

In general, employee compensation is taxable regardless of the form it takes. Nevertheless, the tax law encourages certain types of fringe benefits by allowing an employer to deduct the cost of the benefit, by permitting the employee to exclude the benefit from

---

[18] A limited credit is available to taxpayers who receive such benefits. See Chapter I14 for a discussion of the credit for the elderly and disabled.
[19] See Chapter I3 for a discussion of the reimbursement of an expense

deducted in a preceding year.
[20] Sec. 105(a).

gross income, or by permitting both the employer deduction and an employee exclusion. Employee fringe benefits subject to special rules include employee insurance, Sec. 132 benefits, meals and lodging, dependent care, and cafeteria plans. These fringe benefits are discussed below.

EMPLOYER-PAID INSURANCE. Employers commonly provide group insurance coverage for employees. In general, employers may deduct the premiums paid for life, health, accident, and disability insurance. Normally an employee does not have to include in gross income premiums paid on his or her behalf for health, accident, and disability insurance. Special rules applicable to life insurance premiums are discussed below.

Benefits received from medical, health, and life insurance coverage are generally excluded from an employee's gross income. Benefits received from a disability policy are normally taxable, but may qualify for the credit for the elderly and disabled (see Chapter I14). The tax treatments of employer-financed and taxpayer-financed insurance coverage are compared in Topic Review I4-1.

In general, premiums paid by an employer on behalf of employees are deductible. However, medical premiums paid by self-employed individuals are subject to special tax treatment. In 1997, a self-employed individual may deduct 40% of the *medical* premiums

Topic Review I4-1

Treatment of Insurance

	Premiums Paid by	
	Employer	*Employee*
Medical and health		
Premiums	Premiums not included in employee's gross income. Premiums deductible by employer.	Premiums deductible as medical expense subject to 7.5% of AGI limitation.
Benefits	Excluded from employee's gross income except when benefits exceed actual expenses.	Excluded from gross income.
Disability		
Premiums	Premiums not included in employee's gross income. Premiums deductible by employer.	Not deductible.
Benefits	Included in employee's gross income. May qualify for credit for elderly and disabled.	Excluded from gross income.
Life insurance		
Premiums	Included in employee's gross income (except for limited exclusion applicable to group term life insurance). Premiums deductible by employer (assuming employer is not the beneficiary).	Not deductible.
Benefits	Excluded from gross income.	Excluded from gross income.

attributable to coverage as a business expense.[21] These business expenses are allowed as a deduction for adjusted gross income (see Chapter I6 for a discussion of classification of deductions for individuals). The self-employed taxpayer may deduct the remaining medical premiums as a medical expense if his total medical expenses exceed 7.5% of the AGI reported on his individual return.

The Sec. 104 rules relating to accident and health insurance are more generous than those for some other types of benefits. Employers can deduct insurance premiums and employees need not report the premiums as income. This is true even if the insurance is offered only to officers and other highly compensated employees.

Some employers provide self-insured accident and health plans to employees. Under such plans the employer pays employee medical expenses directly rather than paying insurance premiums. Such plans are subject to nondiscrimination requirements. *Discrimination* is defined in terms of an eligibility test (whether a sufficient number of non–highly compensated employees are covered) and benefits (whether non–highly compensated employees receive benefits comparable to highly compensated employees). Highly compensated employees include the five highest-paid officers, greater-than-10% shareholders, and highest-paid 25% of all other employees.[22] If a plan discriminates in favor of highly compensated employees, these employees must include in gross income any medical reimbursements they receive that are not available to other employees.

In general, life insurance premiums paid by an employer on an employee's behalf are deductible by the employer and are includable in the employee's gross income.[23] A limited exception is applicable to group term life insurance coverage. Premiums attributable to the first $50,000 of group term life insurance coverage may be excluded from an employee's gross income.[24] To qualify group term life insurance premiums for the exclusion, broad coverage of employees is required. Though somewhat different, the rules may be compared to those associated with self-insurance coverage.[25] The amount of coverage can vary between employees as long as the coverage bears a uniform relationship to each employee's compensation.

EXAMPLE I4-17 ▶

Data Corporation provides group term life insurance coverage for each full-time employee. The coverage is equal to one year's compensation. The arrangement constitutes a qualified group term life insurance plan. ◀

The group term life insurance exclusion is available only for employees, whether active or retired. Thus, proprietors and partners are not employees and, therefore, the premiums paid on their behalf are not deductible.

In the case of coverage that exceeds $50,000, it is necessary to distinguish key employees from other employees. Key employees must include in gross income the greater of actual premiums attributable to the excess coverage or an amount established by the Regulations. (See Table I4-1)

EXAMPLE I4-18 ▶

Joy, age 61, is an officer for USA Corporation. During the year, USA Corporation provides Joy with $150,000 of group term life insurance coverage. USA Corporation pays premiums of $3,000. The premiums exceed the amount provided in the Regulations. Assuming that $1,000 of the premiums is attributable to the first $50,000 of coverage, Joy may exclude $1,000 from

---

[21] Sec. 162(l). The deductible portion of such premiums was 30% in 1996, and is scheduled to be 45% from 1998 through 2002, 50% in 2003, 60% in 2004, 70% in 2005, and 80% in 2006 and thereafter.
[22] Sec. 105(h)(5).
[23] If the employer is the beneficiary of the policy, the employee receives no economic benefit and, as a result, need not include the premiums in gross

income. Such premium payments would not be deductible by the employer. Subsequent benefits would not be included in the employer's gross income.
[24] Sec. 79(a).
[25] For example, the rules refer to "key employees" as opposed to highly compensated employees. The term *key employee* is somewhat narrower in scope.

▼ TABLE I4-1

Uniform One-Month Group Term Premiums for $1,000 of Life Insurance Coverage

Employee's Age	Premiums
Under 30	$0.08
30–34	0.09
35–39	0.11
40–44	0.17
45–49	0.29
50–54	0.48
55–59	0.75
60–64	1.17
65–69	2.10
70 and above	3.76

Source: Reg. Sec. 1.79-3(d)(2).

gross income. Since Joy is a key employee, premiums of $2,000 attributable to the excess coverage must be included in gross income. This $2,000 of actual premiums exceeds the amount from Table I4-1 [($100,000 × $1.17 × 12) ÷ $1,000) = $1,404]. ◀

When group term coverage exceeds $50,000, employees other than key employees must include in gross income an amount established by the Regulations rather than the actual premiums. (See Table I4-1.)

EXAMPLE I4-19 ▶ Irene, age 51, works for USA Corporation and is not a key employee. During the year, USA provides Irene with $150,000 of group term life insurance coverage. Irene must include $576 [($100,000 × $0.48 × 12) ÷ $1,000] in gross income. ◀

STOP & THINK

Question: Does the fact that employers can provide health insurance and group term life insurance to employees on a tax-favored basis mean that such benefits should be provided to all employees? Explain.

Solution: No. Providing such benefits to all employees may be inefficient. Some employees have other health coverage (e.g., coverage through a spouse's employer). Employees with no dependents may not want life insurance coverage. As a result, employers who provide all employees with such benefits may be spending money on coverage that some employees neither want nor need. A cafeteria plan, discussed later in this chapter, is often a more efficient option. Such plans permit employees to choose either cash or from a menu of tax-favored benefits.

HISTORICAL NOTE

A limited exclusion from income for unemployment compensation was repealed in the Tax Reform Act of 1986.

SECTION 132 FRINGE BENEFITS. It has become common for employers to provide employees with such diverse benefits as free parking, membership in professional organizations, and small discounts on products sold by the employer. Section 132 was added to the Code in 1984 to clarify whether certain types of benefits are taxable. Section 132 lists six types of fringe benefits that may be excluded from an employee's gross income (see Topic Review 4-2). Any costs incurred by an employer to provide the specified benefits are deductible under Sec. 162 if they meet the "ordinary and necessary" test of that section.[26] Benefits covered by Sec. 132 include

▶ No-additional-cost benefits (e.g., a hotel employee's use of a vacant hotel room)

▶ Qualified employee discounts (e.g., discounts on merchandise sold by the employer)

▶ Working condition benefits (e.g., membership fees in professional organizations paid by an employer)

▶ De minimis benefits (e.g., coffee provided by the employer)

▶ Qualified transportation and parking fringes (transportation benefits [e.g., transit passes, tokens, and vouchers] limited to $65 per month in 1997 and parking, limited to $170 per month in 1997)

▶ Athletic facilities (e.g., employer-owned tennis courts used by employees)

Discrimination is prohibited with respect to certain benefits. The benefits must be made available to employees in general rather than to highly compensated employees only. (See Topic Review I4-2 for specific rules.)

EMPLOYEE AWARDS. As noted earlier, it is often difficult to distinguish between gifts and awards. The de minimis rule mentioned above permits employers to make small gifts such as a holiday turkey or a watch at retirement without the employee having to include the value of the gift in gross income. The employer is entitled to a deduction for the cost of such gifts.

Section 274 provides a similar rule for **employee achievement awards** and **qualified plan awards**. Such awards must be in the form of tangible personal property other than cash and must be based on safety records or length of service. Employee achievement awards are limited to $400 for any one employee during the year. Furthermore, the awards must be presented as part of a meaningful presentation and awarded under circumstances that do not create a significant likelihood of the payment being disguised compensation. Qualified plan awards must be granted under a written plan and may not discriminate in favor of highly compensated employees. The average cost of qualified plan awards is limited to $400, but individual awards can be as large as $1,600.

▶ An award for length of service cannot qualify under Sec. 274 if it is received during the employee's first five years of employment or if the employee has received a length-of-service award under Sec. 274 during the year or any of the preceding four years.

▶ No more than 10% of an employer's eligible employees may receive an excludable safety achievement award during any year. Eligible employees are employees whose positions involve significant safety concerns.

EXAMPLE I4-20 ▶

Each year USA Corporation presents length-of-service awards to employees who have been with the company five, ten, fifteen, or twenty years. The presentations are made at a luncheon sponsored by the company and include gifts such as desk clocks, briefcases, and watches, none of which cost more than $400. The awards, which qualify as employee achievement awards, are deductible by USA Corporation and are not taxable as income to USA's employees. ◀

---

[26] See Chapter I6 for a discussion of Sec. 162 and its requirements. Section 274 does provide one exception to the general rule. The costs of maintaining recreational facilities (such as swimming pools) are not deductible if the facilities are made available on a discriminatory basis (e.g., only officers may use the facilities).

Topic Review I4-2

Summary of Sec. 132 Fringe Benefits

Section	Benefit	May Be Made Available to	Comments
132(b)	No-additional-cost (e.g., telephone, unused hotel rooms for hotel employees, unused airline seats for airline employees)	Employees, spouses, dependents, and retirees	The services must be of the same types that are sold to customers and in the line of business in which the employee works. Discrimination is prohibited.
132(c)	Qualified employee discounts	Employees, spouses, dependents, and retirees	Discounts on services limited to 20%. Discounts on merchandise are limited to the employer's gross profit percentage. No discount is permitted on real estate, stock, or other investment type property. Discrimination is prohibited.
132(d)	Working condition (e.g., free magazines, out-placement, and memberships)	Employees	Discrimination is permitted. Special rules apply to tuition reductions for employees of educational institutions and to an auto salesperson's demonstrator.
132(e)	De minimis (e.g., free coffee, holiday turkeys, or use of company eating facilities)	Employees	Eating facilities must be made available on a nondiscriminatory basis.
132(f)	Qualified transportation fringes (e.g., transit passes, tokens, and parking)	Employees	Limited in 1997 to $170 per month for parking and $65 per month for other transportation fringes.
132(h)(5)	Recreation and athletic facilities (e.g., gyms, pools, saunas, tennis courts)	Employees, spouses, dependents, and retirees.	If discrimination is present, employer loses deduction.

Gifts to employees that do not qualify as employee achievement awards or qualified plan awards can be excluded by the employee only if the awards can be excluded as de minimis amounts under Sec. 132(e).

MEALS AND LODGING. Section 119 provides a limited exclusion for the value of meals and lodging that are provided to employees at either no cost or a reduced cost.

▶ Meals provided by an employer may be excluded from an employee's gross income if they are furnished on the employer's premises and for the convenience of the employer.

▶ Lodging provided by an employer may be excluded from an employee's gross income if it is furnished on the employer's premises and for the convenience of the employer, and the employee is required to accept the lodging as a condition of employment.

The requirement that meals and lodging be furnished on the premises of the employer refers to the employee's place of employment.[27] In one case, the Tax Court held that the business premises requirement was met in a situation where a hotel manager lived in a residence across the street from the hotel he managed.[28]

The convenience of the employer test considers whether there is a substantial noncompensatory business reason for providing the meals or lodging. Thus, if the owner of an apartment complex furnishes a unit to the manager of the complex because it is necessary to have the manager present on the premises even when he or she is off duty, then the test is met.

The value of lodging cannot be excluded from gross income unless the employee is required to accept the lodging as a condition of employment. This requirement is not met if the employee has a choice of accepting the lodging or receiving a cash allowance. Furthermore, meal allowances do not qualify for the exclusion because the employer does not actually provide the meal.[29] Section 132 (discussed earlier in this chapter) provides a de minimis exception. Some employers provide supper money to employees who must work overtime. If such benefits are occasionally provided to employees, the amount is excludable from the employees' gross income.

EXAMPLE I4-21 ▶ A state highway patrol organization provides its officers with a daily meal allowance to compensate them for meals eaten while they are on duty. Because the officers receive cash instead of meals, the amount provided must be included in the officers' gross income. ◀

EXAMPLE I4-22 ▶ A large corporation requires five of its employees to work overtime two evenings each year when the company takes inventory. The corporation gives each of the employees a small amount to cover the cost of the dinner for the two evenings. The amounts constitute supper money and are excluded from the employees' gross income. ◀

MEALS AND ENTERTAINMENT. One obvious question is whether employees who are reimbursed by their employers when they entertain customers must include the reimbursement in gross income. If they must include the reimbursement in gross income, can they deduct the cost of the entertainment and meals? Assuming conditions for deductibility are met, the tax law clearly allows 50% of the cost of entertaining customers to be deducted (discussed in Chapter I9). Can the employee deduct the meals and entertainment that he personally consumes?

EXAMPLE I4-23 ▶ Joe is a sales representative for Zero Corporation. As a part of his regular duties, Joe buys lunch for Wayne, a Zero Corporation customer. Fifty percent of the cost of Wayne's meal is deductible either by Joe if he pays for the luncheon without being reimbursed by his employer, or by the Zero Corporation if it reimburses Joe for the cost. Can Joe deduct 50% of the cost of his own meal if he pays for it and is not reimbursed? If Zero pays for the meal, must Joe include in his gross income the cost of his own lunch? ◀

In the above question, Joe can apparently deduct the portion of the luncheon that applies to himself. While this issue is not clearcut, the IRS has indicated in Rev. Rul. 63-144 that it will not pursue the issue except where taxpayers claim deductions for substantial amounts of personal expenses.[30] However, in *Richard A. Sutter*[31], a 1953 Tax

---

[27] Reg. Sec. 1.119-1(c)(1).
[28] *Jack B. Lindeman*, 60 T.C. 609 (1973).
[29] *CIR v. Robert J. Kowalski*, 40 AFTR 2d 77-6128, 77-2 USTC ¶9748

(USSC, 1977).
[30] Rev. Rul. 63-144, 1963-2 C.B. 129.
[31] *Richard A. Sutter* 21 T.C. 170 (1953).

WHAT WOULD YOU DO IN THIS SITUATION?

FRINGE BENEFIT

National Boats manufacturers pleasure boats sold to consumers. The boats range in price from $40,000 to $1,500,000. Jake is the president of National Boats. The company provides Jake with one of its more expensive boats. The company pays for fuel, insurance, and other costs, and deducts these expenses along with depreciation on the boat. The company states that Jake is responsible for testing and for demonstrating the boat to possible customers. Jake has had the same boat for two years, and the company plans to provide him with a new boat next month.

You asked Jake how often he uses the boat. He indicated that he uses it once or twice each month on weekends, except during the winter. You asked him who accompanies him, and what types of testing he conducts. He seemed reluctant to answer the question, but acknowledged that his family often accompanies him on the boat, and said that he tests it during ordinary operations to determine how it performs. He added that potential customers who have also accompanied him included neighbors and friends. What tax issues do you see?

Court decision, the Tax Court stated "[T]he cost of meals, entertainment, and similar items for one's self . . . is ordinarily and by its very nature [a nondeductible] personal expenditure." This rule is referred to as the *Sutter* rule. The *Sutter* rule certainly disallows a deduction for the cost of the taxpayer's meal.[32] However, the IRS has not changed its position in Rev. Rul. 63-144 even though the IRS was criticized by the Tax Court in 1978 in *Fenstermaker*[33] for attempting to change an established tax rule. In any case, it is an accepted practice today for taxpayers to deduct the entire cost of a meal (taxpayer and customer) unless the practice is considered abusive.

TYPICAL MISCONCEPTION

It is sometimes mistakenly assumed that amounts such as uncollected salary or unused leave qualify for the $5,000 death benefit exclusion.

EMPLOYEE DEATH BENEFITS. On occasion an employer may make payments to the family or friends of an employee who dies. In some instances, the payments might be viewed as a gift made for reasons such as the financial need of the family, kindness, or charity. Alternatively, the amount might constitute a payment of compensation based on the past services of the deceased employee. Gifts are, of course, excluded from gross income, whereas compensation is taxable. The treatment of payments made to the family or other beneficiaries of the employee's estate is determined by the following rules:

▶ Payments for past services (such as bonuses, accrued wages, and unused vacation pay) are taxable as income to the family and are deductible by the employer. The important issue is whether the employee would have received this amount had he or she lived. If the employer was legally obligated to make the payment at the time of the employee's death, the payments are taxable to the recipient.

▶ Other amounts may be either taxable compensation or excludable gifts depending on the facts and circumstances. If the amount is a gift, it is not deductible by the employer. If the amount is taxable income to the deceased employee's family, it is deductible by the employer.

In determining whether the amount is taxable, the courts have considered such factors as whether the employer derived benefit from the payment, whether the employee had been fully compensated, and whether the payment was made to the family and not to the estate. The Supreme Court stated, "The most critical consideration [in determining whether a transfer is a gift] is the transferor's 'intention.'"[34] Although the

---

[32] The *Sutter* rule has been followed in all of the over fifty cases that have cited it.

[33] *James P. Fenstermaker*, 1978 PH T. C. Memo ¶78,210, 37 TCM 898.

[34] *CIR* v. *Mose Duberstein*, 5 AFTR 2d 1626, 60-2 USTC ¶9515 (USSC, 1960).

case did not deal with death benefits, it did establish the importance of motive in determining whether a payment is a gift. Thus, the transfer should be made for reasons such as kindness, sympathy, generosity, affection, or admiration.

It should be noted that it is more difficult to establish that a payment is a gift in situations where the payments are made to persons owning stock in the corporation making the payment. Such payments may be construed as constructive dividends, which are not deductible by the corporation but are taxable income to the recipients.[35]

ADDITIONAL COMMENT

The $5,000 limit was placed on the exclusion for dependent care assistance programs because it was thought to be inequitable to provide an unlimited dependent care exclusion but a limited child care credit for people who pay their own child care expenses.

DEPENDENT CARE. **Dependent care assistance programs** are employer-financed programs that provide care for an employee's children or other dependents. An employee may exclude up to $5,000 of assistance each year ($2,500 for a married individual filing a separate return).The care must be of a type that, if paid by the employee, would qualify for the dependent care credit. Furthermore, the credit is scaled down if the employee receives benefits under the employer's plan. (See Chapter I14 for a discussion of the child and dependent care rules.) The program cannot discriminate in favor of highly compensated employees or their dependents.[36]

ADDITIONAL COMMENT

The classification of an employee as highly compensated is made on the basis of the facts and circumstances of each case. Any officers and shareholders owning more than 5% of the stock are classified as highly compensated employees.

EDUCATIONAL ASSISTANCE. Under Sec. 127 educational assistance plans, employers pay employee educational costs. Employees may exclude from gross income annual payments of up to $5,250. This rule is scheduled to expire on June 30, 1997, and it is uncertain whether it will be extended.[37]

CAFETERIA PLANS. **Cafeteria plans**, also called flexible spending accounts, are plans that offer employees the option of choosing cash or statutory nontaxable fringe benefits (such as group term life insurance, medical insurance, child care, etc.). If the employee chooses cash, the cash is taxable. However, if the employee chooses a statutory nontaxable fringe benefit, the value of the benefit is excluded from gross income.[38] In other words, the fact that the employee could have chosen cash does not cause the fringe benefit to be taxed. The plan cannot discriminate in favor of highly compensated employees or their dependents or spouses.[39] Employer plans may specify what benefits are offered and may limit the amount of benefits individual employees may receive.

ADDITIONAL COMMENT

About half of the large employers in the United States offer flexible spending accounts.

Some plans supplement wages; others are wage reduction plans. In supplemental wage plans, employer funds are used to pay fringe benefits. In the case of wage reduction plans, employees elect to receive reduced wages in exchange for the fringe benefits. In both cases, employees receive benefits without being taxed on them.

Employers often allow employees to use such funds to pay medical expenses. Typically, the plans supplement medical insurance, and funds are used to pay dental bills and other medical expenses not covered by regular insurance. In general, employees annually elect to set-aside funds to pay medical expenses, and the employer pays the expenses using the set aside funds. One problem with the agreements is that they are binding for one year. As a result, the employee loses the funds if the actual medical expenses are less than the amount set aside. Employers, on the other hand, are obligated to pay expenses up to the agreed amount even if the full amount has not yet been withheld from the employees wages. Thus, the employer may lose money if an employee terminates employment after incurring the designated amount of medical expenses but before the full amount is withheld.

---

[35] *Ernest L. Poyner v. CIR*, 9 AFTR 2d 1151, 62-1 USTC ¶9387 (4th Cir., 1962).
[36] Sec. 129.
[37] The exclusion for costs associated with graduate studies expired on June 30, 1996.

[38] Long-term care insurance (sometimes called nursing home insurance) can be offered to employees on a tax-favored basis, but that benefit cannot be offered as part of a flexible spending account.
[39] Sec. 125.

ADVANTAGE OF FRINGE BENEFITS. The major advantage of taking fringe benefits (such as those descibed above) in lieu of a cash payment is the fact that employees do not have to use after-tax income to obtain the product or service.

EXAMPLE I4-24 ▶

Dan, an employee of Central Corporation, pays the premiums for $40,000 of life insurance coverage out of his salary, which is, of course, subject to the income tax. Kay, an employee for Western Corporation, is covered by a $40,000 group term life insurance policy financed by Western Corporation. Western Corporation pays the premiums on the policy. Kay does not have to report the premiums as income. ◀

STOP & THINK

Question: Employers and employees both pay FICA taxes on salaries. Fringe benefits such as health insurance are exempt from both income taxes and FICA taxes. What is the tax effect of an employee's decision to elect health insurance coverage in exchange for a reduced salary?

Solution: The employee's income and FICA taxes are both lowered. The employer is permitted an income tax deduction for either the salary payment or the payment of the health insurance premium. The employer's FICA tax is reduced because the health insurance benefit is exempt from tax.

INTEREST-FREE LOANS. One benefit that was often used in the past was interest-free loans to employees. The advantage of this type of transaction was diminished by the Tax Reform Act of 1984. Under present law, interest must generally be imputed on interest-free loans. (See Chapter I11 for a detailed discussion of rules applicable to interest-free loans.)

FOREIGN-EARNED INCOME EXCLUSION

In general, the income of U.S. citizens is subject to the U.S. income tax even if the income is derived from sources outside the United States. The foreign income of U.S. citizens may also be taxed by the host country. This can lead to a substantial double tax on the same income. The double tax is mitigated by a **foreign tax credit**. Subject to limitations, U.S. citizens may subtract from their U.S. income tax liability the income taxes they pay to foreign countries. (See Chapter I14 for a discussion of foreign tax credit.)

In the case of foreign-earned income, individuals have available the alternative option of excluding the first $70,000 of foreign income from gross income.[40] The *exclusion* is available in lieu of the foreign tax credit. If both a husband and wife have foreign-earned income, each may claim an exclusion. Community property rules are ignored in determining the amount of the exclusion. Thus, if only one spouse has foreign-earned income, only one exclusion is available. The principal reasons for the exclusion are to encourage U.S. businesses to operate in foreign countries and to hire U.S. citizens and resident aliens to manage the businesses. The hope is that such operations will improve the balance of payments. Taxpayers who elect the exclusion in one year may switch to the foreign tax credit in any subsequent year. Taxpayers who change from the exclusion to the credit may not reelect the exclusion before the sixth tax year after the tax year in which the change was made.[41] The IRS can waive the six-year limitation in special situations (such as an individual employee changing the location of his or her foreign employment).

---

[40] Sec. 911(b)(2)(A).

[41] Sec. 911(e)(2).

TYPICAL
MISCONCEPTION

A taxpayer must be present in
one or more foreign countries
for 330 days during a period of
twelve consecutive months,
rather than 330 days during a
calendar year.

Foreign-earned income includes an individual's earnings from personal services rendered in a foreign country. The place where the services are performed determines whether earned income is foreign or U.S. source income. If an individual is engaged in a trade or business in which both personal services and capital are material income-producing factors, no more than 30% of the net profits from the business may be excluded.[42] Furthermore, pensions, annuities, salary paid by the U.S. government, and deferred compensation do not qualify for the exclusion.[43]

To qualify for the foreign-earned income exclusion, the taxpayer must either be a bona fide resident of one or more foreign countries for an entire taxable year, or be present in one or more foreign countries for 330 days during a period of 12 consecutive months.[44] The exclusion limitation for a year must be prorated if the taxpayer is not present in, or a resident of, a foreign country or countries for the entire year.

EXAMPLE I4-25 ▶ Sondra is given a temporary assignment to work in foreign country T. Although Sondra does not establish a permanent residence in T, she is abroad for 330 days out of a twelve-month period beginning on October 19, 1997. Thus, 73 days fall in 1997 and the rest in 1998. Sondra's exclusion for 1997 is limited to $14,000 [(73 ÷ 365) × $70,000]. She may exclude $14,000 or the income she earns in foreign country T during 1997, whichever is less. ◀

Deductions directly attributable to the excluded foreign-earned income are disallowed. Expenses attributable to foreign-earned income must be allocated if foreign-earned income exceeds the exclusion. The disallowed portion is determined by multiplying the total amount of such expenses by the ratio of excluded earned income over total foreign-earned income.

EXAMPLE I4-26 ▶ Connie earned $120,000 during 1997 while employed in a foreign country. She is entitled to an exclusion of $70,000. Connie incurred $12,000 of travel, transportation, and other deductible expenses attributable to the foreign-earned income. She may deduct only $5,000 of such expenses because $7,000 [($70,000 ÷ $120,000) × $12,000] is allocated to the excluded income. The $5,000 is classified as a miscellaneous itemized deduction and subject to the 2% of AGI floor associated with such deductions. ◀

U.S. citizens working in foreign countries must often pay more for housing than they would pay in the United States. Therefore, an additional exclusion from gross income is available for housing costs incurred in excess of 16% of the salary paid government employees in Step 1 of grade GS-14. This GS-14 grade is used to establish a standard for taxpayers in general.

EXAMPLE I4-27 ▶ Wayne is employed in Tokyo, Japan, and earns a salary of $120,000. His housing costs are $32,000 for the year and are reasonable considering the high cost of living in Tokyo. Assume that 16% of the GS-14 (Step 1) salary is $9,242. Wayne can exclude $92,758 from gross income ($70,000 + $32,000 − $9,242). ◀

INCOME FROM THE DISCHARGE OF A DEBT

If debt of a taxpayer is cancelled or forgiven, the taxpayer may have to include the cancelled amount in gross income. It is important to distinguish a debt cancellation from a gift, a bequest, or a renegotiation of the purchase price.

---

[42] Sec. 911(d)(2)(B).
[43] Sec. 911(b)(1)(B).

[44] Sec. 911(d).

EXAMPLE I4-28 ▶ Farouk loaned his daughter $4,000 to help her purchase an automobile. Several months after she purchased the automobile, but before she repaid the $4,000, Farouk's daughter married. Farouk told his daughter that he was "tearing up" the $4,000 note as a wedding present. In this instance, the amount forgiven would constitute an excludable gift and would not be taxable as income to the daughter. ◀

EXAMPLE I4-29 ▶ Clay purchased a used automobile from a dealer for $6,000. He paid $2,000 down and agreed to pay the balance of $4,000 over three years. After Clay purchased the automobile, he determined that it was defective. Clay tried to return the automobile, but the automobile dealer refused. Clay threatened to sue the dealer. To resolve the problem, the dealer offered to reduce the balance due on the purchase-money debt from $4,000 to $2,500. Clay agreed. The transaction constitutes a reduction in the purchase price of the automobile. Clay will not recognize any income, but must reduce the basis in his automobile from $6,000 to $4,500. ◀

EXAMPLE I4-30 ▶ Blue Corporation issued bonds for $1,000 when interest rates were low. After a few years, interest rates increased and the bond price declined to $850. Blue Corporation purchased the bonds on the open market. Blue will recognize $150 of income from the discharge of indebtedness. ◀

EXAMPLE I4-31 ▶ Indy Coal Company has seen its business decline during the past two years. The Company has a significant amount of bank debt that was incurred over the years to fund its coal operations. In order to maintain its operations, Indy entered into an agreement with the bank whereby the bank agreed to cancel 50% of Indy's debt. Assuming Indy was solvent at the time of the cancellation, Indy must report the discharge of indebtedness as gross income. ◀

ADDITIONAL COMMENT

Also excludable is the income from the cancellation of a student loan pursuant to a provision under which part of the debt is discharged due to working for a period of time in certain professions for a broad class of employers.

REAL-WORLD EXAMPLE

A taxpayer purchased and retired its own bonds. The purchase resulted in a gain because the bonds were payable in British pounds, which had been devalued. The gain was excludable. *Kentucky & Indiana Terminal Railroad Co. v. U.S.*, 13 AFTR 2d 1148, 64-1 USTC ¶9374 (6th Cir., 1964).

STOP & THINK

Question: In Example I4-31, the bank agreed to cancel 50% of Indy Coal Company's debt. Why would a lender agree to unilaterally cancel a borrower's debt?

Solution: A bank might cancel a portion of a borrower's debt in order to protect the remaining portion of the debt. If the debt forced the company into bankruptcy, the bank may be able to collect none or only a small percentage of the debt. If the cancellation would help stabilize Indy, the bank may be able to collect at least 50% of the debt. Further, if Indy becomes a viable company in the years ahead, the bank will have a good customer to earn profits in the future.

The enforceability of a debt under state law may also determine whether the forgiveness results in income. For example, a recent case held that the forgiveness of a gambling debt was not included in gross income where the debt was unenforceable under state law.[45]

Section 61(a)(12) indicates that gross income includes income from the discharge of an indebtedness. Section 108, on the other hand, provides for the following exceptions where the discharge of an indebtedness is not taxable:

▶ The discharge occurs in bankruptcy.

▶ The discharge occurs when the taxpayer is insolvent.

---

[45] *David Zarin v. CIR*, 66 AFTR 2d 90-5679, 90-2 USTC ¶50,530 (3rd Cir., 1990).

These exceptions are intended to allow a "fresh start" for bankrupt and other financially troubled taxpayers. In either case, the taxpayer must reduce tax attributes such as the net operating loss carryover.

KEY POINT

A discharge of debt in bankruptcy does not generate income.

If a debt is reduced during bankruptcy proceedings, the taxpayer recognizes no income even if the reduction in debt exceeds the available tax attributes. In the case of an insolvent taxpayer, no income is recognized as long as the taxpayer is insolvent after the reduction in debt takes place. A taxpayer is insolvent if the debts owed by the taxpayer exceed the FMV of assets owned. Thus, an insolvent taxpayer reduces the tax attributes to the point of solvency. From that point on, any reduction in debt results in the recognition of income even if all tax attributes have not been offset.

EXCLUSION FOR GAIN FROM SMALL BUSINESS STOCK

Noncorporate taxpayers may exclude up to 50% of the gain realized on the disposition of qualified small business stock issued after August 10, 1993, if the stock is held for more than five years.[46] For each issuer of qualified small business stock, there is a limit on the amount of gain a taxpayer may exclude. The amount of gain eligible for the exclusion may not exceed the greater of $10,000,000, reduced by amounts previously excluded for gains on the company's stock, or ten times the taxpayer's aggregate adjusted basis of the stock disposed of during the year.[47] When measuring the taxpayer's aggregate basis for the stock to determine the maximum amount of gain to exclude, the fair market value of the assets contributed to the corporation is used.

EXAMPLE I4-32 ▶

In 1997, Dennis contributed property with a basis of $1,000,000 and an FMV of $4,000,000 to a qualified small business corporation for all of its common stock. If he sells one-half of the stock in year 2003 for $14,000,000, he may exclude $6,750,000 of the $13,500,000 ($14,000,000 − $500,000) realized gain. The maximum gain eligible for the exclusion is the greater of $10,000,000 or $20,000,000 [10 times the $2,000,000 basis ($4,000,000 FMV × 0.50) of the stock sold]. Thus, none of the $13,500,000 realized gain is subject to the limitation. ◀

A corporation may issue qualified small business stock only if the corporation is a C corporation that is not an excluded corporation with an aggregate adjusted basis of not more than $50 million of gross assets, and at least 80% of the value of its assets must be used in the active conduct of one or more qualified trades or businesses.[48]

EXCLUSION FOR SALE OF RESIDENCE

A one-time election permits taxpayers age 55 or older to exclude a gain up to $125,000 on the sale of a personal residence.[49] Another provision permits taxpayers who reinvest the adjusted sales price of a personal residence in a replacement residence within two years to avoid reporting the gain.[50] However, the cost basis of the replacement residence must be reduced by the deferred gain on the original residence. (See Chapter I12 for a detailed discussion of these provisions.)

---

[46] Sec. 1202 (a).
[47] Sec. 1202 (b)(1).
[48] Secs. 1202 (d) and (e). Excluded corporations are those engaged in providing professional services (e.g., law and health), financial services (e.g.,

banking, and insurance), hospitality (e.g., hotels and restaurants), farming, and mining and oil and gas production.
[49] Sec. 121.
[50] Sec. 1034.

TAX PLANNING CONSIDERATIONS

EMPLOYEE FRINGE BENEFITS

The tax law encourages certain forms of fringe benefits by allowing an employer to deduct the cost of the benefit while permitting the employee to exclude the benefit from gross income. This does not represent any tax advantage to the employer because compensation, whether in the form of cash or nontaxable fringe benefits, is deductible if reasonable in amount. It is the employee who benefits from the exclusion of fringe benefits from gross income.

EXAMPLE I4-33 ▶ USA Company has decided to offer $20,000 of group term life insurance coverage for each of its employees at an average annual premium cost of $100 per employee. Tim, an employee of USA Corporation, is in the 15% tax bracket. Because USA is offering a nontaxable fringe benefit, Tim will owe no additional income tax. If Tim had received a salary increase of $100, he would have had to pay an additional income tax of $15 (0.15 × $100). The remaining $85 of after-tax income would probably not have been sufficient to obtain the same amount of life insurance coverage. ◀

Excluding fringe benefits from gross income favors employees who are subject to higher tax rates.

EXAMPLE I4-34 ▶ Assume the same facts as in Example I4-33 except that Tim is in the 36% tax rate. Tim would save $36 (0.36 × $100) of taxes by receiving the group term life insurance coverage instead of the $100 salary increase. ◀

It is not always desirable for employers to offer nontaxable fringe benefits. Some employees are not interested in certain benefits. For example, in the case of married couples where both spouses are employed, it is not necessary for both employers to provide medical insurance coverage for both spouses. Alternatively, single employees may not feel the need for group term life insurance and employees with no children are uninterested in employer-provided child care.

To avoid providing fringe benefits that are unneeded or unwanted, many employers have turned to cafeteria plans. Under cafeteria plans, employees may select from a list of nontaxable fringe benefits. On the other hand, employees who so choose may receive cash in lieu of some or all of the nontaxable benefits. Thus, each employee selects what he or she wants most. One common result is that high-tax-rate employees select the nontaxable fringe benefits, whereas other employees choose to receive cash.

SELF-HELP AND USE OF PERSONALLY OWNED PROPERTY

As noted earlier in this chapter, self-help income and income derived from the use of personal property are not taxable. Thus, self-help and personal ownership of property are favored by the tax system. Taxpayers who rent their personal residences cannot deduct rental payments, but taxpayers who own their residences do not pay rent and may deduct interest and real estate taxes as itemized deductions. Thus, the tax law encourages ownership of personal residences.

Effective tax planning necessitates weighing the tax incentives with other nontax factors. Taxpayers with little accumulated funds may find it difficult to purchase a residence despite the availability of tax incentives. Taxpayers who move frequently may find that transaction costs such as real estate commissions and other closing costs are greater than the tax benefits obtained from home ownership. Other factors such as the personal preference of the taxpayer and anticipated inflation rates must also be considered.

Self-help must be viewed in the same way. Taxpayers who are deciding whether to paint their own residences or hire someone else to do it must consider factors such as personal preference and the amount of income that could be produced if the time were spent working at an activity that produces taxable income.

COMPLIANCE AND PROCEDURAL CONSIDERATIONS

ADDITIONAL COMMENT

Taxpayers filing Form 1040 are asked to report any tax-exempt interest income on line 8b.

Taxpayers are usually not required to disclose excluded income on their tax returns. For example, a taxpayer who receives a tax-exempt scholarship need not disclose that income on his or her tax return. An exception is provided for tax-exempt interest and Social Security benefits, which must be disclosed on the tax return. If a taxpayer's only income is from tax-exempt sources, the taxpayer need not file a tax return. Whether an individual must file a return is based on the amount of the individual's gross income for the year (see Chapter I2).

This chapter considers the taxability of various fringe benefits. The rules regarding the need for an employer to withhold federal income taxes or to report a payment on an employee's Form W-2 (Statement of Income Tax Withheld on Wages) closely parallel the gross income rules. (See Chapter I14 for a discussion of these reporting requirements.) In general, if a fringe benefit is nontaxable, employers do not withhold from the benefit, nor do they report the benefit on the employee's W-2 at year-end. On the other hand, if the benefit is taxable, it is subject to withholding and is reported on the employee's W-2 at year-end. Thus, employers do not withhold for nontaxable meals and lodging provided to employees[51] or a moving expense reimbursement if the expenses are deductible.[52] Similarly, no withholding is required for the following fringe benefits if they are nontaxable: scholarships and fellowships covered by Sec. 117,[53] dependent care covered by Sec. 129,[54] and miscellaneous fringes covered by Sec. 132.[55]

There are exceptions to this basic system. Certain fringe benefits are not subject to withholding even if the benefits are taxable. These include group-term life insurance coverage[56] and medical expense reimbursements.[57]

Employers who are obligated to withhold from employee wages are subject to penalty if they fail to withhold, fail to provide employees with correct W-2s, or fail to correctly report the compensation and withholding information to the IRS.[58] In general, the failure to report wages and withholding to either employees or the IRS is subject to penalty generally equal to $50 per failure. The failure to withhold can result in a penalty equal to 100% of the amount that should have been withheld. The penalty can be imposed on the employer and other people, such as officers or accountants, who are responsible for withholding.

Occasionally, employees do not want employers to withhold taxes from their wages. Officers or others who choose not to withhold from employee wages face an extremely burdensome penalty, particularly if a large number of employees are involved. Therefore, it is important that employers comply with withholding requirements. One closely related issue is whether an individual is an employee subject to withholding or an independent contractor, as only employee wages are subject to withholding (see Chapter I14).

---

[51] Reg. Sec. 31.3401(a)-1(b)(9).
[52] Sec. 3401(a)(15).
[53] Sec. 3401(a)(20).
[54] Sec. 3401(a)(18).

[55] Sec. 3401(a)(20).
[56] Sec. 3401(a)(14).
[57] Sec. 3401(a)(19).
[58] Secs. 6672, 6674, and 6721 respectively.

PROBLEM MATERIALS

DISCUSSION QUESTIONS

I4-1 What is meant by the terms *administrative exclusion* and *judicial exclusion*?

I4-2 There is no specific statutory exclusion for welfare benefits. Nevertheless, the IRS has ruled that such benefits are not taxable. Is this within the authority of the IRS?

I4-3 What was the issue in the tax case *Eisner* v. *Macomber*? Why is the case important?

I4-4 Most exclusions exist for one of two reasons. What are those reasons? Give examples of exclusions that exist for each.

I4-5 a. If a gift of property is made, who is taxed on income produced by the property?
b. How can interfamily gifts reduce a family's total tax liability?

I4-6 a. What role does intent play in determining whether a transfer is a gift and therefore not subject to the income tax?
b. Are tips received by employees from customers excludable from gross income as gifts? Explain.

I4-7 What is the tax significance of the face amount of a life insurance policy?

I4-8 What conditions must be met for an award to qualify for an exclusion under Sec. 74?

I4-9 Which of the requirements for the Sec. 74 awards exclusion most severely limits its use? Does the exclusion benefit taxpayers more if they itemize their deductions or use the standard deduction?

I4-10 a. Define the term *scholarship* as it is used in Sec. 117.
b. If a scholarship covers room and board, is it excludable?
c. If an employer provides a scholarship to an employee who is on leave of absence, is that scholarship taxable?

d. Is the amount paid by a university to students for services excludable from the students' gross income?

I4-11 What special rules are applicable to non–degree candidates who receive scholarships?

I4-12 Is the personal injury exclusion found in Sec. 104 limited to physical injury? Explain.

I4-13 Answer the following questions relative to employer-financed medical and health, disability, and life insurance plans.
a. May employers deduct premiums paid on employee insurance?
b. Do employees have to include such premiums in gross income?
c. Are benefits paid to the employee included in the employee's gross income?

I4-14 Special rules are applicable in situations where group term life insurance coverage exceeds $50,000. How are key employees treated in instances where coverage exceeds $50,000? How are other employees treated?

I4-15 a. What are the six major types of fringe benefits covered by Sec. 132?
b. What tax advantage is offered relative to such benefits?
c. Are such benefits available to employees only or may the benefits also be offered to spouses, dependents, and retirees?
d. Is discrimination prohibited relative to Sec. 132 benefits?
e. What is the tax impact on the employer and employees if an employer's plan is discriminatory?

I4-16 What conditions must be met if an employee is to exclude meals and lodging furnished by an employer?

I4-17 The president and vice president of USA Corporation receive benefits that are unavailable to other employees. These benefits include free parking, payment of monthly expenses in a local club, discounts on products sold by the corporation, and payment of premiums on a whole life insurance policy. Which of the benefits must be included in the gross income of the president and vice president?

I4-18   Are the same fringe benefits that are available to employees also available to self-employed individuals?

I4-19   Explain the *Sutter* rule.

I4-20   Do amounts owed for salary by an employer to a deceased employee qualify for the $5,000 death benefit exclusion? Explain.

I4-21   What types of income qualify for the foreign-earned income exclusion?

I4-22   Are taxpayers who claim the foreign-earned income exclusion entitled to deduct expenses incurred in producing that income? Explain.

I4-23   **a.** Why is it important to distinguish debt cancellation from a gift, bequest, or renegotiation of a purchase price?
         b. What happens to the basis of an asset if the taxpayer renegotiates its purchase price?

I4-24   **a.** Under what conditions is the discharge of indebtedness not taxable?
         b. If a father forgives a daughter's debt to him, is she required to include such amount in her gross income?

I4-25   Bankrupt and insolvent taxpayers do not recognize income if debt is discharged. They must, however, reduce specified tax attributes. List these attributes in the order they must be reduced.

I4-26   Are employee awards in excess of $25 taxable? Explain.

I4-27   Why are cafeteria plans helpful in the design of an employee benefit plan that provides nontaxable fringe benefits?

I4-28   Both high-income and low-income employees are covered by cafeteria plans. Under such plans, all employees may select from a list of nontaxable fringe benefits or they may elect to receive cash in lieu of these benefits.
         a. Which group of employees is more likely to choose nontaxable fringe benefits in lieu of cash? Explain.
         b. Is this result desirable from a social or economic point of view? Explain.

ISSUE IDENTIFICATION QUESTIONS

I4-29   Luke, who retired this year, lives in a four-plex owned by Julie. Luke's income decreased when he retired, and he now has difficulty paying his rent. Julie offered to reduce Luke's rent if he would agree to mow the lawn, wash windows, and provide other maintenance services. Luke accepted, and Julie reduced the monthly rental from $650 to $300. What are the tax issues that should be considered by Luke and Julie?

I4-30   Mildred worked as a maid for twenty-seven years in the home of Larry and Kay. When she retired, they presented her with a check for $25,000, indicating that it was a way of showing their appreciation for her years of loyal service. What tax issues should Mildred and her employer consider?

I4-31   Troy Department Stores offers employees discounts on merchandise carried in the store. Newly hired employees receive a 10% discount. The discount rate increases 1% each year until employees have twenty years of service when the discount rate is capped at 30%. What tax issues should Troy and the employees consider?

I4-32   Jerry works in the human resources department of Ajax Corporation. One of his responsibilities is to interview prospective employees. Two or three days each week, Jerry takes a prospective employee to lunch, and Ajax reimburses him for the cost of the meals. What tax issues should Jerry and Ajax Corporation consider?

PROBLEMS

I4-33 *Self-Help Income.* In which of the following situations would the taxpayer realize taxable income?
a. A mechanic performs work on his own automobile. The mechanic would have charged a customer $400 for doing the same work.
b. A mechanic repairs his neighbor's automobile. In exchange, the neighbor, an accountant, agrees to prepare the mechanic's tax return. The services performed are each worth $200.
c. A mechanic repairs his daughter's automobile without any charge.

I4-34 *Excludable Gifts.* Which of the following would constitute excludable gifts?
a. Alice appeared on a TV quiz show and received a prize of $500.
b. Bart received $500 from his employer because he developed an idea that reduced the employer's production costs.
c. Chuck borrowed $500 from his mother in order to finance his last year in college. Upon his graduation, Chuck's mother told him he did not have to repay the $500. She intended the $500 to be a graduation present.

I4-35 *Life Insurance Proceeds.* Dan is the beneficiary of a $50,000 insurance policy on the life of his mother. Upon her death, Dan has the choice of receiving either the face amount of the policy or five annual installments of $12,000 each.
a. How much income must Dan report if he elects to receive the face value of the policy?
b. How much income must Dan report if he elects to receive the installments?
c. Would it make any difference if the insured had been his wife instead of his mother? Explain.

I4-36 *Transfer of Life Insurance.* Ed is the beneficiary of a $20,000 insurance policy on the life of his mother. Because Ed needs funds, he sells the policy to his sister, Amy, for $6,000. Amy subsequently pays premiums of $8,000.
a. How much income must Amy report if she collects the face value of the policy upon the death of her mother?
b. Would Amy have to report any income if her brother had given her the policy? Assume the only payment she made was $8,000 for the premiums.

I4-37 *Settlement of Life Insurance Policy.* Sue is age 73 and has had a great deal of difficulty living independently as she suffers from severe rheumatoid arthritis. She is covered by a $400,000 life insurance policy, and her children are named as her beneficiaries. Because of her health, Sue decides to live in a nursing home, but she does not have enough income to pay her nursing home bills which are expected to total $42,000 per year. The insurance company offers disabled individuals the option of either a reduced settlement on their policies or an annuity. Given Sue's age and health she has the option of receiving $3,200 per month or a lump sum payment of $225,000. To date, Sue has paid $80,000 in premiums on the policy.
a. How much income must Sue report if she chooses the lump sum settlement?
b. How much income must Sue report if she elects the annuity?
c. How much income would Sue have to report if her nursing home bills amounted to only $36,000 per year?

I4-38   *Insurance Policy Dividends.* Hank carries a $100,000 insurance policy on his life. Premiums paid over the years total $8,000. Dividends on the policy have totaled $6,000. Hank has left the dividends on the policy with the insurance company. During the current year, the insurance company credited $600 of interest on the accumulated dividends to Hank's account.

a. How much income is Hank obligated to report in connection with the policy?

b. Would it make any difference if the accumulated dividends equaled $9,000 instead of $6,000?

I4-39   *Prizes and Awards.* For each of the following, indicate whether the amount awarded is taxable:

a. Irene won $100 playing bingo at her church.

b. Jack was awarded a $100 prize for a painting he entered in a community art show.

c. Kay was selected as coach of the year by the local school board. Kay received a $200 cash award, which was presented at the district's annual awards banquet. Awards were also presented to outstanding teachers, administrators, and students. The board selected the recipients based on its knowledge of each individual and his or her achievements.

I4-40   *Scholarships.* For each of the following, indicate the amount that must be included in the taxpayer's gross income:

a. Larry was given a $1,500 tuition scholarship to attend Eastern Law School. In addition, Eastern paid Larry $4,000 per year to work part-time in the campus bookstore.

b. Marty received a $10,000 football scholarship for attending Northern University. The scholarship covered tuition, room and board, laundry, and books. Four thousand dollars of the scholarship was designated for room and board and laundry. It was understood that Marty would participate in the school's intercollegiate football program, but Marty was not required to do so.

c. Western School of Nursing requires all third-year students to work twenty hours per week at an affiliated hospital. Each student is paid $6 per hour. Nancy, a third-year student, earned $6,000 during the year.

I4-41   *Research Grants.* Otto is a biology professor who teaches at Southern University. The University awarded Otto a $2,000 grant to study the surface of the flatworm. Otto was expected to spend three months during the summer conducting the study. In addition, Otto was awarded $1,500 for supplies and typing, travel, and other incidental costs. The actual expenses totaled $1,500. How much income must Otto report?

I4-42   *Payments for Personal Injury.* Determine which of the following may be excluded as payments for sickness and injury.

a. Pat was injured in an automobile accident. The other driver's insurance company paid him $2,000 to cover medical expenses and a compensatory amount of $4,000 for pain and suffering.

b. A newspaper article stated that Quincy had been convicted of tax evasion. Quincy, in fact, had never been accused of tax evasion. He sued and won a compensatory settlement of $4,000 from the newspaper.

c. Rob, who pays the cost of a commercial disability income policy, fell and injured his back. He was unable to work for six months. The insurance company paid him $1,800 per month during the time he was unable to work.

d. Steve fell and injured his knee. He was unable to work for four months. His employer-financed disability income policy paid Steve $1,600 per month during the time he was unable to work.

e. Ted suffered a stroke. He was unable to work for five months. His employer continued to pay Ted his salary of $1,700 per month during the time he was unable to work.

I4-43 **Employee Benefits.** Ursula is employed by USA Corporation. USA Corporation provides medical and health, disability, and group term life insurance coverage for its employees. Premiums attributable to Ursula were as follows:

Medical and health	$1,800
Disability	300
Group term life (face amount is $40,000)	200

During the year, Ursula suffered a heart attack and subsequently died. Before her death, Ursula collected $14,000 as a reimbursement for medical expenses and $5,000 of disability income. Upon her death, Ursula's husband collected the $40,000 face value of the life insurance policy.

a. What amount can USA Corporation deduct for premiums attibutable to Ursula?

b. How much must Ursula include in income relative to the premiums paid?

c. How much must Ursula include in income relative to the insurance benefits?

d. How much must Ursula's widower include in income?

I4-44 **Group Term Life Insurance.** Data Corporation has four employees and provides group term life insurance coverage for all four employees. Coverage is as follows:

Employee	Age	Key Employee	Coverage	Actual Premiums
Andy	62	yes	$200,000	$4,000
Bob	52	yes	40,000	700
Cindy	33	no	80,000	600
Damitria	33	no	40,000	300

a. How much may Data Corporation deduct for group term life insurance premiums?

b. How much income must be reported by each employee?

I4-45 **Life Insurance Proceeds.** Joe is the beneficiary of a life insurance policy taken out by his father several years ago. Joe's father died this year and Joe has the option of receiving $100,000 cash or electing to receive $14,000 per year for the remainder of his life. Joe is now 65. Joe's father paid $32,000 in premiums over the years.

a. How much must Joe include in gross income this year if he elects to accept the $100,000 face amount?

b. How much must be included in Joe's gross income if he elects to receive installment payments?

I4-46 **Employee Benefits.** Al flies for AAA Airlines. AAA provides its employees with several fringe benefits. Al and his family are allowed to fly on a space-available basis on AAA Airline. Tickets used by Al and his family during the year are worth $2,000. AAA paid for a subscription to two magazines published for pilots. The subscriptions totaled $80. The airline paid for Al's meals and lodging while he was away from home overnight in connection with his job. Such meals and lodging cost AAA $10,000. Although Al could not eat while flying, he was allowed to drink coffee provided by the airline. The coffee was worth about $50. AAA provided Al with free parking, which is valued at $100 per month. The airline treated Al and his family to a one-week all-expenses-paid vacation at a resort near his home. This benefit was awarded because of Al's outstanding safety record. The value of the vacation was $2,300. Which of these benefits are taxable to Al?

I4-47   ***Employee Benefits.*** Jet Corporation is involved in the purchase and rental of several large apartment complexes. Questions have been raised about the treatment of several items pertaining to Jet Corporation and its employees. Jet Corporation employs a manager for each complex. The manager is required to occupy a unit in the complex in order to be available at all hours. The average rental value of the units is $7,800 per year. The corporation's president finds that it is beneficial to the corporation if he entertains bankers and others with whom Jet does business. He does such entertaining about once each month and the corporation pays the cost. Business is discussed at the meals. The cost for the year of such entertaining was $600, and about one-third of the cost was attributable to meals consumed by the president.

Each year as the company closes its books, the controller and certain other members of the accounting staff must work overtime. The company pays each employee supper money totaling $25 during this period.

The corporation's vice president is expected to travel on business-related matters to visit various properties owned by the corporation. Because of the distances involved, the vice president must stay away from home several nights. Total meals and lodging incurred on the trips total $3,000, most of which is attributable to the vice president himself.

Which amounts are deductible by the corporation? Which are taxable to the employee?

I4-48   ***Death Benefits.*** After an illness of several weeks, Phil died. Although there was no legal obligation to make any payment, Phil's former employer made a payment of $15,000 to his widow. The corporation sent the widow a letter with the check indicating that the amount was being awarded in recognition of Phil's many years of loyal service.

a. Is the employer entitled to deduct the amount it paid to Phil's widow?

b. Is any portion of the amount received by Phil's widow taxable? If yes, how much?

I4-49   ***Foreign-Earned Income Exclusion.*** For each of the following cases, indicate the amount of the foreign-earned income exclusion. (Disregard the effect of exemptions for certain allowances under Sec. 912.)

a. Sam, a U.S. citizen, is an assistant to the ambassador to Spain. Sam lives and works in Spain. His salary of $40,000 is paid by the U.S. government.

b. Jim, a U.S. citizen, owns an unincorporated oil drilling company that operates in Argentina, where he resides. The business is heavily dependent on equipment owned by Jim. His profit for the year totaled $100,000.

c. Ken, a U.S. citizen, works for a large Japanese corporation. Ken is employed in the United States, but must travel to Japan several times each year. During the current year he spent sixty days in Japan. This is typical of most years. His salary is $45,000.

I4-50   ***Foreign-Earned Income Exclusion.*** On January 5, Rita left the United States for Germany, where she had accepted an appointment as vice president of foreign operations. Her employer, USA Corporation, told her the assignment would last about two years. Rita decided not to establish a permanent residence in Germany because her assignment was for only two years. Her salary for the year is $210,000. Rita incurred travel, transportation, and other related expenses totaling $6,000, none of which is reimbursed.

a. What is Rita's foreign-earned income exclusion?

b. How much may she deduct for travel and transportation?

I4-51 **Discharge of Debt.** During bankruptcy, USA Corporation debt was reduced from $780,000 to $400,000. USA Corporation's assets are valued at $500,000. USA's NOL carryover was $400,000.

a. Is USA Corporation required to report any income from the discharge of its debts?

b. Which tax attributes are reduced and by how much? Assume USA does not make any special elections when reducing its attributes.

I4-52 **Discharge of Debt.** Old Corporation has suffered losses for several years, and its debts total $500,000; Old's assets are valued at only $380,000. Old's creditors agree to reduce Old's debts by one-half in order to permit the corporation to continue to operate. Old's NOL carryover is $150,000.

a. What impact does the reduction in debt have on Old's NOL?

b. Is Old required to report any income?

I4-53 **Court and Insurance Awards.** Determine whether the following items represent taxable income.

a. As the result of an age discrimination suit, Pat received a cash settlement of $40,000. One-half of the settlement represented wages lost by Pat as a result of the discrimination and the balance represented an award based on personal injury.

b. Matt sued the local newspaper for a story that reported that he was affiliated with organized crime. The court awarded him $50,000 of libel damages.

c. Pam was injured in an automobile accident and received $10,000 from an employer-sponsored disability policy. In addition, her employer-financed medical insurance policy reimbursed her for $15,000 of medical expenses.

I4-54 **Cafeteria Plan.** Jangyoun is a married taxpayer with a dependent 4-year-old daughter. His employer offers a flexible spending account under which he can choose to receive cash or, alternatively, choose from certain fringe benefits. These benefits include health insurance that costs $2,500 and child care that costs $2,600. Assume Jangyoun is in the 28% tax bracket.

a. How much would Jangyoun save in taxes if he chooses to participate in the employer's health insurance plan? Assume that he does not have sufficient medical expenses to itemize his deductions.

b. Would you recommend that Jangyoun participate in the employer's health insurance plan if his wife's employer already provides comparable health insurance coverage for the family?

c. Would you recommend that Jangyoun participate in the employer-provided child care option if he has the alternative option of claiming a child care credit of $480.

I4-55 **Exclusion of Gain from Small Business Stock.** Jose acquired 1,000 shares of Acorn Corporation common stock in January 1997 by transferring property with an adjusted basis of $1,000,000 and fair market value of $4,000,000 for 100% of the stock. Acorn is a qualified small business corporation. In June 2002, Jose sells all of the Acorn Corporation common stock for $16,000,000.

a. What is the amount of gain that may be excluded from Jose's gross income?

b. What would your answer be if the fair market value of the Acorn stock were only $1,000,000 upon its issue in 1997?

c. What would your answer be if the stock were sold in June 1998?

COMPREHENSIVE PROBLEM

I4-56 Pat was divorced from her husband in 1989. During the current year she received alimony of $18,000 and child support of $4,000 for her 11-year old son, who lives with her. Her former husband had asked her to sign an agreement giving him the dependency exemption for the child but she declined to do so. After the divorce she accepted a position as a teacher in the local school district. During the current year she received a salary of $22,000. The school district paid her medical insurance premiums of $1,900 and provided her with group term life insurance coverage of $40,000. The premiums attributable to her coverage equaled $160. During her marriage, Pat's parents loaned her $8,000 to help with the down payment on her home. Her parents told her this year that they understand her financial problems and that they were cancelling the balance on the loan, which was $5,000. They did so because they wanted to help their only daughter.

Pat received dividends from National Motor Company of $4,600 and interest on State of California bonds of $2,850.

Pat sold her personal automobile for $2,800 because she needed a larger car. The automobile had cost $8,000. She purchased a new auto for $11,000. Pat had itemized deductions of $8,600. Assume her withholding and estimated payments total $8,000. Compute her taxable income for the current year.

TAX FORM/RETURN PREPARATION PROBLEMS

I4-57 A. J. Paige, Social Security number 111-22-3333, is the vice president of marketing (Japan) for International Industries, Inc. (III). III is headquartered at 123 Main Street, Los Angeles, California 92601. A. J., who is single, accepted the position and became a resident of Japan on July 8 of last year. Her business address is 86 Sano, Tokyo, Japan. A. J.'s visa permits her to stay in Japan indefinitely. Her only trips to the United States in the current year were for vacations (August 2 to 16 and December 21 to 28). A. J.'s contract specifies that her appointment is to last indefinitely, but states that III is to pay her $4,000 per year to cover the cost of two vacation trips to the United States. Her salary is $140,000, out of which she pays rent on an apartment of $28,000 per year. A. J. has no family or residence in the United States. She paid an income tax in Japan of $23,500. Complete a Form 2555 for the current year.

I4-58 Alice Johnson, Social Security number 222-23-3334, is a single mother of two children, Jack and Jill, ages 15 and 17, respectively, and is employed as a secretary by State University of Florida. She has the following items pertaining to her income tax return for the current year:

- Received a $20,000 salary from her employer, who withheld $4,000 federal income tax.

- Received a gift of 1,000 shares of Ace Corporation stock with a $100,000 FMV from her mother. She also received $4,000 of cash dividends from the Ace Corporation.

- Received $1,000 of interest income on bonds issued by the City of Tampa.

- Received a stock dividend (qualifying under Sec. 305) of 50 shares of Ace Corporation stock with a $5,000 FMV.
- Alice's employer paid $2,000 of medical and health insurance premiums on her behalf.
- Maintains a household for herself and two children and provides more than 50% of their support. In the prior year, however, she entered into an agreement with her ex-husband that provided that he is entitled to the dependency exemptions for the children.
- Received $12,000 alimony and $6,000 child support from her ex-husband (Charlie Johnson).
- State University provided $60,000 of group term life insurance. Alice is 42 years old and is not a key employee.
- Received a $1,000 cash award from her employer for being designated the Secretary of the Year.
- Total itemized deductions are $7,000.

Complete Form 1040 and accompanying schedules for Alice Johnson's federal income tax return for the current year.

CASE STUDY PROBLEMS

I4-59 Able Corporation is a closely held company engaged in the manufacture and retail sales of automotive parts. Able maintains a qualified pension plan for its employees but has not offered nontaxable fringe benefits.

You are a tax consultant for the company who has been asked to prepare suggestions for the adoption of an employee fringe benefit plan. Your discussions with the client's chief financial officer reveal the following:

- Employees currently pay their own premiums for medical and health insurance.
- No group term life insurance is provided.
- The company owns a vacant building that could easily be converted to a parking garage.
- Many of the employees purchase automobile parts from the company's retail outlets and pay retail price.
- The president of the corporation would like to provide a dependent care assistance program under Sec. 129 for its employees.

Required: Prepare a client memo that recommends the adoption of an employee fringe benefit program. Your recommendations should discuss the pros and cons of different types of nontaxable fringe benefits.

I4-60 Jay Corporation owns several automobile dealerships. This year, the corporation initiated a policy of giving the top salesperson at each dealership a free vacation trip to Florida. The president believes that this is an effective sales incentive. The cost of the vacations is deductible by the corporation as compensation paid to employees, and is taxable to the recipients. Nevertheless, the president objects to reporting the value of the vacations as income on the W-2s of the recipients and to withholding taxes from wages for the value of the trips. He feels that this undermines the effectiveness of the incentive. What are the implications of this behavior for the corporation and the president?

TAX RESEARCH PROBLEMS

I4-61 Ann is a graduate economics student at State University. State University awarded her a $1,000 scholarship. In addition, Ann works as a half-time teaching assistant in the Economics Department at State University. For her services she is paid $7,000 per year and her tuition is waived. Her tuition would be $8,000 were it not for the waiver. Ann paid $500 for her books and supplies and she incurred living expenses of $7,400. Determine how much gross income Ann must report.

A partial list of research sources is

- Sec. 117(d)
- Prop. Reg. 1.117-6(d)(5)

I4-62 Kim leased an office building to USA Corporation under a ten-year lease specifying that at the end of the lease USA had to return the building to its original condition if any modifications were made. USA changed the interior of the building, and at the end of the lease USA paid Kim $30,000 instead of making the required repairs. Does Kim have to include the payment in gross income?

A partial list of research sources is

- Sec. 109
- *Boston Fish Market Corp.*, 57 T.C. 884 (1972)
- *Sirbo Holdings Inc. v. CIR*, 31 AFTR 2d 73-1005, 73-1 USTC ¶9312 (2nd Cir., 1973)

I4-63 As a result of a fire damaging their residence, the Taylors must stay in a motel for five weeks while their home is being restored. They pay $2,000 for the room and $500 meals. Their homeowner's policy pays $2,500 to reimburse them for the cost. They estimate that during the five-week period they would normally spend $300 for meals. Is the reimbursement taxable?

A partial list of research sources is

- Sec. 123
- Reg. Sec. 1.123-1

CHAPTER 5

PROPERTY TRANSACTIONS: CAPITAL GAINS AND LOSSES

LEARNING OBJECTIVES

After studying this chapter, you should be able to

1 ▶ Determine the realized gain or loss from the sale or other disposition of property

2 ▶ Determine the amount realized from the sale or other disposition of property

3 ▶ Determine the basis of property

4 ▶ Distinguish between capital assets and other assets

5 ▶ Understand how capital gains and losses affect taxable income

6 ▶ Recognize when a sale or exchange has occurred

7 ▶ Determine the holding period for an asset when a sale or disposition occurs

HISTORICAL NOTE

A preferential tax rate on capital gains was included in the tax law from 1921 to 1987. A modest preferential rate was reintroduced in 1991, with capital gains for noncorporate taxpayers being subject to a maximum 28% tax rate and ordinary income being subject to a maximum tax rate of 31%. The capital gains differential became more significant in 1993 when the highest marginal rate was increased to 39.6%.

Gross income includes "gains derived from dealings in property,"[1] and certain "losses from sale or exchange of property"[2] are allowed as deductions from gross income to determine adjusted gross income. All recognized gains and losses must eventually be classified as either *capital* or *ordinary*. Before 1987, long-term capital gains (LTCGs) generally received more favorable tax treatment than ordinary gains or short-term capital gains (STCGs). The Tax Reform Act of 1986 substantially eliminated the difference in tax treatment for capital gain income and ordinary income.

Although the Tax Reform Act of 1986 eliminated most of the preferential treatment for net capital gain income, Congress retained the distinction between capital assets and other assets in the IRC. By retaining the statutory structure for capital gains, the Conference Committee Report to the 1986 Act indicated that it would be easier to reinstate a capital gains differential if tax rates increased.[3] As tax rates have increased since 1986, Congress has again created preferential treatment for capital gains for certain taxpayers.

For tax years beginning after 1990, the maximum tax rate imposed on net capital gains (the excess of net long-term capital gains over net short-term capital losses) recognized by noncorporate taxpayers is 28%. Because the maximum tax rate is currently 39.6%, noncorporate taxpayers may benefit by having a gain classified as LTCG instead of STCG or ordinary income. In late 1995, Congress sent a bill to the President that would have further increased the preferential treatment for net capital gain, but President Clinton vetoed the Balanced Budget Bill of 1995 on December 6, 1995.

Capital losses must be offset against capital gains, and net capital losses are subjected to restrictions on their deductibility. Thus, most taxpayers prefer to have losses classified as ordinary instead of capital.

Most property transactions have tax consequences to the taxpayer. For example, when a sale, exchange, or abandonment occurs, the taxpayer must determine the realized gain or loss, the portion of the realized gain or loss that must be recognized (if any), and the character of the gain or loss. This chapter focuses on determining the realized gain or loss and the portion of the recognized gain or loss that is classified as capital or ordinary. When classifying a recognized gain or loss, (i.e., the gain or loss actually reported on the taxpayer's tax return) three important questions must be considered:

▶ What type of property has been sold or exchanged?

▶ When has a sale or exchange occurred?

▶ When did the holding period for the property commence?

In this chapter, these three questions are considered as well as difficulties associated with determining the basis of the property sold or exchanged and the amount of realized gains or losses.

DETERMINATION OF GAIN OR LOSS

OBJECTIVE 1

Determine the realized gain or loss from the sale or other disposition of property

REALIZED GAIN OR LOSS

To determine the **realized gain** or **loss**, the amount realized from the sale or other disposition of property is compared with the adjusted basis of that property. A gain is realized when the amount realized is greater than the basis, and a loss is realized when the amount realized is less than the basis of the property.[4]

---

[1] Sec. 61(a)(3).
[2] Sec. 62(a)(3).

[3] H. Rept. No. 99-841, 99th Cong., 2d Sess., p. II-106 (1986).
[4] Sec. 1001(a).

EXAMPLE I5-1 ▶ Jack sells an asset with an adjusted basis of $10,000 to Judy for $14,000. Because the amount realized is greater than the basis, Jack has a realized gain of $4,000 ($14,000 − $10,000). ◀

Despite the fact that most transfers of property involve a sale, gains and losses may also be realized on certain other types of dispositions of property, such as exchanges, condemnations, casualties, thefts, bond retirements, and corporate distributions. However, gains and losses are generally not realized when property is disposed of by gift or bequest.

EXAMPLE I5-2 ▶ Alice owns land that is held for investment and has a basis of $20,000. The land is taken by the city by right of eminent domain, and she receives a payment of $30,000 for the land. This condemnation is treated as a sale or disposition, and Alice's realized gain is $10,000 ($30,000 − $20,000). ◀

EXAMPLE I5-3 ▶ Two years ago, Bob purchased stock of a newly formed corporation for $10,000. During the current year, he receives a $12,000 distribution, constituting a return of capital, from the corporation. This distribution is treated as a sale. Therefore, Bob has a realized gain of $2,000 ($12,000 − $10,000). Bob's basis for the stock is now zero because his basis of $10,000 has been recovered. ◀

For a sale or other disposition to occur, there must be an identifiable event. Mere changes in the value of property are not normally recognized as a disposition for purposes of determining a realized gain or loss.

Many reasons exist for not taxing unrealized gains and losses that arise due to a mere change in value. The Treasury Regulations state that "A loss is not ordinarily sustained prior to the sale or other disposition of the property, for the reason that until such sale or other disposition occurs there remains the possibility that the taxpayer may recover or recoup the adjusted basis of the property."[5] Because of administrative difficulties associated with determining FMV, disputes with the Internal Revenue Service would be greatly increased if unrealized gains were taxed and unrealized losses were allowed as deductions. In addition, payment of tax on income is generally required only when a taxpayer has the wherewithal to pay the tax (e.g., the taxpayer has received cash from the sale or other disposition of property and can therefore pay the tax on the gain).

AMOUNT REALIZED. The **amount realized** from a sale or other disposition of property is the sum of any money received plus the FMV of all other property received.[6]

EXAMPLE I5-4 ▶ Tony sells land to Rita for $15,000 in cash and a machine having a $3,000 FMV. The amount realized by Tony is $18,000 ($15,000 + $3,000). ◀

Determine the amount realized from the sale or other disposition of property

From a practical standpoint, the determination of FMV is a question of fact and often creates considerable controversy between taxpayers and the IRS. **Fair market value (FMV)** is "the price at which property would change hands between a willing buyer and a willing seller, neither being under any compulsion to buy or sell."[7] In some cases, the FMV of the asset given in the exchange may be easier to determine than the FMV of the property received. In those cases, the FMV of the property given may be used to measure the amount realized. If a buyer assumes the seller's liability or takes the property

---

[5] Reg. Sec. 1.1001-1(c)(1).
[6] Sec. 1001(b).

[7] *CIR v. Homer H. Marshman*, 5 AFTR 2d 1528, 60-2 USTC ¶9484 (6th Cir., 1960).

subject to the debt, the courts have included the amount of the liability when determining the amount realized.[8]

EXAMPLE I5-5 ▶ Anna exchanges land subject to a liability of $20,000 for $35,000 of stock owned by Mario. Mario takes the property subject to the liability. The amount realized by Anna is $55,000 ($35,000 + $20,000 liability assumed by Mario). If Anna's adjusted basis for the land exchanged is $42,000, her realized gain is $13,000 ($55,000 amount realized − $42,000 adjusted basis). ◀

In the above example, Anna receives stock with a $35,000 FMV and is relieved of a $20,000 debt. Mario's taking the property subject to the debt is equivalent to providing Anna with cash of $20,000. Thus, the amount realized by Anna is $55,000.

Generally, selling expenses such as sales commissions and advertising incurred in order to sell or dispose of the property reduce the amount realized.

EXAMPLE I5-6 ▶ Doug sells stock of Laser Corporation, which has a cost basis of $10,000, for $17,000. Doug pays a sales commission of $300 to sell the stock. The amount realized by Doug is $16,700 ($17,000 − $300) and he has a realized gain of $6,700 ($16,700 − $10,000). ◀

ADJUSTED BASIS. The initial adjusted basis of property depends on how the property is acquired (e.g., by purchase, gift, or inheritance). Most property is acquired by purchase and therefore its initial basis is the cost of the property. However, if property is acquired from a decedent, its basis to the estate or heir is its FMV either at the date of death or, if the alternate valuation date is elected, six months from the date of death. The rules for determining the adjusted basis are discussed in subsequent sections of this chapter. Once the initial basis is determined, it may be adjusted upward or downward. Capital additions (also called capital expenditures) are expenditures that add to the value or prolong the life of property or adapt the property to a new or different use.[9] Capital additions increase the basis. Capital recoveries, such as the deductions for casualty losses, cost recovery, and depreciation, reduce the basis. A property's adjusted basis can be determined by the following equation:

Initial basis
+ Capital additions (e.g., new porch for a building)
− Capital recoveries (e.g., depreciation deduction)
= Adjusted basis

Capital expenditures are distinguished from expenditures that are deductible as ordinary and necessary business expenses. For example, the cost of repairing a roof may be a deductible expense, whereas the cost of replacing a roof is a capital addition. It is sometimes difficult to determine whether an item is a capital expenditure or a business expense. Because of the preference for an immediate tax deduction, some taxpayers prefer to classify expenditures as expenses rather than as capital expenditures.

EXAMPLE I5-7 ▶ Ellen pays $2,500 for a major overhaul of an automobile used in her trade or business. The $2,500 is capitalized as part of the automobile's cost rather than deducted as a repair expense. ◀

Capital recoveries reduce the adjusted basis. The most common form of capital recovery is the deduction for depreciation or cost recovery. As discussed in Chapter I10, the accelerated cost recovery system (ACRS) provides a deduction for cost recovery and

---

[8] *Beulah B. Crane v. CIR*, 35 AFTR 776, 47-1 USTC ¶9217 (USSC, 1947).   [9] Reg. Sec. 1.263(a)-1(b).

applies to most property placed in service after December 31, 1980, and before 1987. A modified ACRS form of depreciation (MACRS) is mandatory for most tangible depreciable property placed in service after 1986.

EXAMPLE I5-8
ADDITIONAL COMMENT

In addition to depreciation, other capital recoveries that reduce the adjusted basis of property include depletion, amortization, corporate distributions that are a return of basis, compensation or awards for involuntary conversions, deductible casualty losses, insurance reimbursements, and cash rebates received by a purchaser.

Jeremy paid $100,000 for equipment two years ago and has claimed depreciation deductions of $37,000 for the two years. The cost of repairs during the same period was $6,000. At the end of the two-year period, the property's adjusted basis is $63,000 ($100,000 − $37,000). The amount spent for repairs does not affect the basis. ◄

RECOVERY OF BASIS DOCTRINE. The **recovery of basis doctrine** states that taxpayers are allowed to recover the basis of an asset without being taxed because such amounts are a return of capital that the taxpayer has invested in the property. If a taxpayer receives a $12,000 return of capital distribution from a corporation when the taxpayer's basis for its investment in the corporation's stock is $10,000, the first $10,000 received represents a recovery of basis and only the $2,000 excess amount is treated as a gain realized on a sale or exchange of the stock investment. In many cases, basis is recovered in the form of a deduction for depreciation, cost recovery, or a casualty loss. ◄

RECOGNIZED GAIN OR LOSS

TYPICAL MISCONCEPTION

It is sometimes incorrectly believed that all realized gains and losses are recognized for tax purposes. Although most realized gains are recognized, some realized losses are not. For example, losses on the sale or exchange of property held for personal use cannot be recognized.

Realized gain or loss represents the difference between the amount realized and the adjusted basis when a sale or exchange occurs. The amount of gain or loss that is actually reported on the tax return is called the **recognized gain or loss.** In some instances, gain or loss is not recognized due to special provisions in the tax law (e.g., a gain or loss may be deferred or a loss may be disallowed).

Losses are generally deductible if they are incurred in carrying on a trade or business, incurred in an activity engaged in for profit, and casualty and theft losses. Realized losses on the sale or exchange of assets held for personal use are not recognized for tax purposes. Therefore, a taxpayer who incurs a loss on the sale or exchange of a personal-use asset does not fully recover the basis. As explained in Chapter I8, realized losses on personal-use assets may be recognized to some extent if the property is disposed of by casualty or theft.

KEY POINT

The sale of a personal residence or other property held for personal use creates an interesting situation in that gains must be recognized but losses cannot be recognized.

EXAMPLE I5-9 ►

Ralph purchases a personal residence for $60,000. Deductions for depreciation are not allowed because the asset is not used in a trade or business or held for the production of income. If Ralph sells the house for $55,000, the realized loss of $5,000 is not deductible, and he recovers only $55,000 of his original $60,000 basis. ◄

BASIS CONSIDERATIONS

OBJECTIVE 3

Determine the basis of property

COST OF ACQUIRED PROPERTY

In most cases, the basis of property is its cost. **Cost** is the amount paid for the property in cash or the FMV of other property given in the exchange.[10] Any costs of acquiring the property and preparing the property for use are included in the cost of the property.

EXAMPLE I5-10 ►

Penny purchases equipment for $15,000 and pays delivery costs of $300. Installation costs of $250 are also incurred. The cost of the equipment is $15,550 ($15,000 + $300 + $250). ◄

---

[10] Reg. Sec. 1.1012-1(a).

Funds borrowed and used to pay for an asset are included in the cost. Obligations of the seller that are assumed by the buyer increase the asset's cost.

EXAMPLE I5-11 ▶

Peggy purchases an asset by paying cash of $40,000 and signs a note payable to the seller for $60,000. She also assumes a lien against the property in the amount of $2,000. Her basis for the asset is its cost of $102,000 ($40,000 + $60,000 + $2,000). ◀

UNIFORM CAPITALIZATION Rules. Before 1987, taxpayers often had a degree of flexibility with respect to capitalizing or expensing certain costs. The Tax Reform Act of 1986 created one set of capitalization rules applicable to all taxpayers and all types of activities. These uniform capitalization rules, which apply principally to inventory, are provided in Sec. 263A and discussed in Chapter I11.

ADDITIONAL COMMENT

The sales tax is a good example of a tax that would be paid in connection with the acquisition of property.

The uniform capitalization rules also affect property other than inventory if the property is used in a taxpayer's trade or business or in an activity engaged in for profit. Taxes paid or accrued in connection with the acquisition of property are included as part of the cost of the acquired property. Taxes paid or accrued in connection with the disposition of property reduce the amount realized on the disposition.[11]

EXAMPLE I5-12 ▶

The Compact Corporation owns and operates a funeral home. The corporation purchases a hearse for $30,000 and pays sales taxes of $1,500. The cost basis for the hearse is $31,500 ($30,000 + $1,500). ◀

CAPITALIZATION OF INTEREST. Interest on debt paid or incurred during the production period to finance production expenditures incurred to construct, build, install, manufacture, develop, or improve real or tangible personal property must be capitalized.[12] The real or tangible personal property must have "a long useful life, an estimated production period exceeding two years, or an estimated production period exceeding one year and a cost exceeding $1,000,000."[13] Property has a long useful life if it is real property or property with a class life of at least 20 years.[14] The production period starts when "production of the property begins and ends when the property is ready to be placed in service or is ready to be held for sale."[15]

EXAMPLE I5-13 ▶

The Indiana Corporation started construction of a $3 million motel on July 1, 1996, and borrowed an amount equal to the motel's construction costs. The motel is completed and ready for service on October 1, 1997. Interest incurred for the construction loan for the period from July 1, 1996 through October 1, 1997, is included in the motel's cost. The capitalized interest cost is depreciated over the motel's recovery period (see Chapter I10). ◀

ADDITIONAL COMMENT

If a stockholder leaves his or her stock with a broker in street name, the stockholder can specifically identify the shares sold by simply informing the broker which shares he or she wishes to sell. The date basis of the shares sold should appear on the confirmation from the broker.

IDENTIFICATION PROBLEMS. In most cases, the adjusted basis of property is easily identified with the property that is sold. However, problems occur when property is homogenous in nature such as when an investor owns several blocks of common stock of the same corporation that are purchased on different dates at different prices. The Regulations require the taxpayer to adequately identify the particular stock that is sold or exchanged.[16] Many investors allow brokers to hold their stock in street name (i.e., the brokerage firm holds title to the stock certificates) and thus do not make a physical transfer of securities. Such investors need to be careful to provide specific instructions to the broker as to which securities should be sold. If the stock sold or exchanged is not adequately identified, the first-in, first-out (FIFO) method must be used to identify the

---

[11] Sec. 164(a).
[12] Sec. 263A(f).
[13] Sec. 263A(f)(1)(B).

[14] Sec. 263A(f)(4)(A).
[15] Sec. 263A(f)(4)(B).
[16] Reg. Sec. 1.1012-1(c)(1).

stock.[17] With the FIFO method, the stock sold or exchanged is presumed to come from the first lot or lots acquired.

EXAMPLE I5-14 ▶ Tammy purchased 300 shares of the Acme Corporation stock during 1996:

Month Acquired	Size of Block	Basis
January	100 shares	$4,000
May	100	5,000
October	100	6,000

In March 1997 Tammy sells 120 shares of the stock for $5,160. If Tammy specifically identifies the stock sold as being all of the stock purchased in October and 20 shares purchased in May, her realized loss is $1,840 [$5,160 − ($6,000 + $1,000)]. ◀

If Tammy did not specifically identify the stock that is sold, the FIFO method is used, and her realized gain is $160 [$5,160 − ($4,000 + $1,000)].

PROPERTY RECEIVED AS A GIFT: GIFTS AFTER 1921

The basis of property received as a gift is generally the same as the donor's basis.[18] If the FMV of the property at time of the gift is less than the donor's basis, the donee may have to use one basis if the property is subsequently disposed of at a gain and another if the property is disposed of at a loss. As discussed later in this chapter, the basis may be increased by a portion or all of the gift tax paid because of the transfer.

Current rules for determining the donee's basis for property received as a gift are a function of the relationship between the FMV of the property at the time the gift is made and the donor's basis. If the FMV is equal to or greater than the donor's basis, the donee's basis is the same as the donor's basis for all purposes. However, if the FMV is less than the donor's basis, the donee has a dual basis for the property, that is, a basis for loss and a basis for gain. If the donee later transfers the property at a loss, the donee's basis is the property's FMV at the time of the gift (basis for loss). However, if the donee transfers the property at a gain, the donee's basis is the same as the donor's basis (basis for gain).

EXAMPLE I5-15 ▶ Kevin makes a gift of property with a basis of $350 to Janet when it has a $425 FMV. If Janet sells the property for $450, she has a realized gain of $100 ($450 − $350). If Janet sells the property for $330, she has a realized loss of $20 ($330 − $350). Because the FMV of the property at the time of the gift is more than the donor's basis, the donee's basis is $350 for determining both gain and loss. ◀

The following example illustrates the scenario when a taxpayer has a dual basis. The basis for determining a gain is different from the basis for determining a loss.

EXAMPLE I5-16

ADDITIONAL COMMENT

If Chuck in Example I5-16 sells the land for $750, he has a $150 gain. If he sells the land for $400, he has a $100 loss and there is no gain or less if he sells the land for $560.

▶ Chuck makes a gift of property with a basis of $600 to Maggie when the property has a $500 FMV. Maggie's basis for the property is $600 if the property is sold at a gain (i.e., for more than $600), but the basis is $500 if the property is sold at a loss (i.e., for less than $500). If the property is sold for $500 or more but not more than $600, no gain or loss is recognized. ◀

---

[17] For mutual fund investors, the IRS has authorized the use of FIFO, specific identification, or two average cost basis methods if only a portion of the fund shares is redeemed or sold. (See Reg. Sec. 1.1012-1(e) and Chapter I17.)

[18] Sec. 1015(a).

The dual basis rules were designed to prevent tax-avoidance schemes. Taxpayers are prevented from shifting unrealized losses to another taxpayer by making gifts of such "loss" property. For example, a low-income taxpayer who owns property that has depreciated in value might transfer the property by gift to a high-income taxpayer who would receive greater tax benefit from the deduction of the loss upon the subsequent sale of the property. The loss basis rules prevent the donee from recognizing a loss on the sale of the property because the basis for loss is the lesser of the donor's basis or FMV on the date of the gift.

EFFECT OF GIFT TAX ON BASIS: Gifts After 1976. If the donor pays a gift tax on the transfer of property, the donee's basis may be increased. This increase occurs only if the FMV of the property exceeds the donor's basis on the date of the gift. For taxable gifts after 1976,[19] the increase in the donee's basis is equal to a pro rata portion of the gift tax that is attributable to the unrealized appreciation in the property. The amount of the addition to the donee's basis is determined as follows:[20]

$$\text{Gift tax paid} \times \frac{\text{FMV at time of the gift} - \text{Donor's basis}}{\text{Amount of the gift}}$$

The amount of the gift is the FMV of the property less the amount of the annual exclusion.[21]

EXAMPLE I5-17 ▶ During the current year, Cindy makes one gift of property with a $20,000 basis to Jessie when the property has a $60,000 FMV. Cindy pays a gift tax of $20,500. The amount of the gift is $50,000 ($60,000 − $10,000). Jessie's basis for the property for determining both gain and loss is $36,400 [$20,000 + (0.80 × $20,500)]. Thus, 80% [($60,000 − $20,000)/$50,000] of the gift tax is added to Troy's basis. ◀

EXAMPLE I5-18 ▶ During the current year, Sally makes a gift of property with a basis of $50,000 to Troy when the property has a $40,000 FMV. Sally pays a gift tax of $1,000. Troy's basis for the property is not affected by the gift tax paid by Sally because the FMV is less than the donor's basis at the time of the gift. Troy's basis for the property is $50,000 for purposes of determining gain and $40,000 for purposes of determining loss. ◀

STOP & THINK

Question: Pete wants to make a gift of either ABC common stock (basis of $44,000 and FMV of $50,000) or XYZ common stock (basis of $73,000 and FMV of $50,000) to his nephew. Pete and his nephew have the same tax rate. Which stock should he give to his nephew?

Solution: Pete should give his nephew the ABC stock. With ABC stock the nephew's basis for determining a gain or loss is $44,000 plus a portion of any gift tax Pete pays. The nephew's basis for XYZ common stock is $50,000 to determine a loss and $73,000 to determine a gain. If the nephew sells XYZ stock for less than $73,000, no loss is recognized and thus some of the basis is not used. Note that Pete would have a $23,000 loss if he sells the XYZ stock for $50,000. Furthermore, the nephew's basis for the XYZ stock is not increased if Pete has to pay a gift tax on the $40,000 taxable gift.

---

[19] For gifts after September 2, 1958 and before 1977, the entire amount of the gift tax paid is added to the donee's basis. However, the basis may not exceed the property's FMV on the date of the gift.

[20] Sec. 1015(d)(6).
[21] Sec. 1015(d)(2) and Sec. 2503(b).

PROPERTY RECEIVED FROM A DECEDENT

The basis of property received from a decedent is generally the FMV of the property at the date of the decedent's death or an alternate valuation date.[22] This can result in either a step up or step down in basis.

EXAMPLE I5-19 ▶ Patrick inherits property having an $80,000 FMV on the date of the decedent's death. The decedent's basis in the property is $47,000. The executor of the estate does not elect the alternate valuation date. His basis for the property is $80,000. ◀

EXAMPLE I5-20 ▶ Dianna inherits property having a $60,000 FMV at the date of the decedent's death. The decedent's basis in the property is $72,000. The alternate valuation date is not elected. Dianna's basis for the property is $60,000. ◀

REAL-WORLD EXAMPLE

The alternate valuation date was typically used in valuing the estates of individuals owning large portfolios of common stocks who died shortly before the stock market crash in October 1987.

Instead of using the FMV on the date of death to determine the estate tax, the executor of the estate may elect to use the FMV on the alternate valuation date. The alternate valuation date is generally six months after the date of death. If the alternate valuation date is elected, the basis for all of the assets in the estate is their FMV on that date unless the property is distributed by the estate to the heirs or is sold before the alternate valuation date. If the alternate valuation date is used, property distributed or sold after the date of the decedent's death and before the alternate valuation date has a basis equal to its FMV on the date of distribution or the date it is disposed of.[23]

If the estate is small enough that an estate tax return is not required, the value of the property on the alternate valuation date may not be used.[24]

EXAMPLE I5-21 ▶ Marilyn inherits all of the property owned by an individual who dies in April, when the property has a $100,000 FMV. The value of the property six months later is $90,000. Because of the size of the estate, no estate tax is due. The alternate valuation date may not be used, and Marilyn's basis for the property is $100,000. ◀

As noted above, the basis of the property to the estate and the heirs can be affected if the alternate valuation date is used to value the estate's assets. The alternate valuation date may be elected only if the value of the gross estate and the amount of estate tax after credits are reduced as a result of using the alternate valuation date.[25] This means that the aggregate value of the assets determined by using the alternate valuation date may be used only if the total value of the assets has decreased during the six-month period.

EXAMPLE I5-22 ▶ Helmut inherits all of the property owned by an individual who dies in March when the FMV of the property is $900,000. Six months after the date of death, the property has a $950,000 FMV. The property is distributed to Helmut in December. Use of the alternate valuation date is not permitted because the value of the gross estate has increased. Therefore, his basis in the property is $900,000, the FMV on the date of death. ◀

An executor may elect to use the alternate valuation date to reduce the estate taxes owed by the estate. However, the income tax basis of the property included in the estate is also reduced for the heirs who inherit the property.

---

[22] Sec. 1014(a).

[23] Sec. 2032(a).

[24] Rev. Rul. 56-60, 1956-1 C.B. 443. For a decedent dying after 1986, Sec. 6018(a) requires an estate tax return to be filed if the sum of the gross estate and the adjusted taxable gifts made by the decedent after December 31, 1976 exceeds $600,000.

[25] Credits available include the unified transfer tax credit and possibly credits for state death taxes, gift taxes, foreign death taxes, and the credit for taxes on prior transfers.

EXAMPLE I5-23 ▶ Michelle inherits property with a $900,000 FMV at the date of the decedent's death. Because the FMV of the property on the alternate valuation date (six months after the date of the decedent's death) is $850,000, the executor of the estate elects to use $850,000 to value the property for estate tax purposes. Michelle's basis for the property is thus $850,000 instead of $900,000. ◀

COMMUNITY PROPERTY. If the decedent and the decedent's spouse own property under community property laws,[26] one-half of the property is included in the decedent's estate and its basis to the surviving spouse is its FMV.[27] The Code also provides that the surviving spouse's one-half share of the community property is adjusted to the FMV.[28] In effect, the surviving spouse's share of the community property is considered to have passed from the decedent.

EXAMPLE I5-24 ▶ Matt and Jane, a married couple, live in Texas, a community property state, and jointly own land as community property that cost $110,000. The land has an $800,000 FMV when Jane dies, leaving all of her property to Matt. His basis for the entire property is $800,000. ◀

In a common law state, only one-half of the jointly owned property is included in the decedent's estate and is adjusted to its FMV. The survivor's share of the jointly held property is not adjusted.

EXAMPLE I5-25 ▶ Barry and Maria, a married couple, live in Iowa, a common law state, and jointly own land that cost $200,000. The property has a $700,000 FMV when Barry dies, leaving all of his property to Maria. Her basis for the land is $450,000 [$100,000 + (0.50 × $700,000)]. ◀

PROPERTY CONVERTED FROM PERSONAL USE TO BUSINESS USE

Often, taxpayers who own personal-use assets convert these assets to an income-producing use or for use in a trade or business. When this conversion occurs, the property's basis must be determined. The basis for computing depreciation is the lower of the FMV or the adjusted basis of the property at the time the asset is transferred from personal use to an income-producing use or for use in a trade or business.[29] This rule prevents taxpayers from obtaining the benefits of depreciation to the extent that the property has declined in value during the period that it is held for personal use.

EXAMPLE I5-26 ▶ Olga owns a boat that cost $2,000 and is used for personal enjoyment. At a time when the boat has a $1,400 FMV, Olga transfers the boat to her business of operating a marina. The basis for depreciation is $1,400 because the FMV is less than Olga's adjusted basis at the time of conversion to business use. The $600 decline ($2,000 − $1,400) that occurred while Olga used the boat for personal use may not be deducted as depreciation. ◀

If the boat's FMV in Example I5-26 is more than $2,000, the basis for depreciation is $2,000 because the FMV is higher than its adjusted basis at the time the asset is transferred to business use.

If a personal-use asset is transferred to business use when its FMV is less than its adjusted basis, the basis for determining a loss on a subsequent sale or disposition of the property is its FMV on the date of the conversion to business use less any depreciation taken before the disposition.[30]

ADDITIONAL COMMENT

It is important to estimate the FMV of property at the time the property is converted from personal use to business use.

REAL-WORLD EXAMPLE

A taxpayer sold a personal residence to a purchaser, and the purchaser rented the property from the taxpayer until financing could be secured. The rental agreement was executed simultaneously with the sales agreement and was incidental to the sale. The taxpayer was not permitted to recognize any loss on the sale because the property was never converted to rental property. *Henry B. Dawson,* 1972 PH T.C. Memo 31 TCM 5.

---

[26] Community property states are Arizona, California, Idaho, Louisiana, New Mexico, Nevada, Texas, and Washington. Wisconsin has a marital property law that is basically the same as community property.
[27] Sec. 1014(a).
[28] Sec. 1014(b)(6).
[29] Reg. Sec. 1.167(g)-1.
[30] Reg. Sec. 1.165-9(b)(2).

EXAMPLE I5-27 ▶ Susanna purchased a personal residence for $50,000 and subsequently converted the property to rental property. At the time of the conversion, the property had a $46,000 FMV. Assume depreciation of $20,700 has been deducted when the property is sold for $21,000. The basis of the property at the time of the sale is $25,300 ($46,000 − $20,700). Thus, her loss on the sale is $4,300 ($21,000 − $25,300).[31] ◀

The rule for determining the basis, that is, lower of adjusted basis or FMV, applies only to the sale of converted property at a loss. The basis for determining gain is its adjusted basis at the time of conversion less any depreciation taken before the disposition.

EXAMPLE I5-28 ▶ Assume the same facts as in Example I5-27, except that the property is sold for $31,000 instead of $21,000. The basis of the property is $29,300 ($50,000 − $20,700) and her gain is $1,700 ($31,000 − $29,300). ◀

Without the rule for determining basis of personal-use property converted to business property, taxpayers would have an incentive to convert nonbusiness assets that have declined in value to business use before selling the asset to convert nondeductible losses into deductible losses.

EXAMPLE I5-29 ▶ Craig owns a personal-use asset with a basis of $80,000 and a $50,000 FMV. If he sells the asset for its FMV, the $30,000 loss ($50,000 − $80,000) is not deductible because losses on the sale of personal-use assets are not deductible. If Craig converts the asset to business use and then immediately sells the asset for $50,000, no loss is realized because the basis of the asset for purposes of determining loss is $50,000. ◀

REAL-WORLD EXAMPLE

A taxpayer purchased a group of lots and allocated the total cost evenly among the lots. The court, however, held that more cost should be allocated to the waterfront lots than to the interior lots. *Biscayne Bay Islands Co.*, 23 B.T.A. 731 (1931).

ALLOCATION OF BASIS

When property is obtained in one transaction and portions of the property are subsequently disposed of at different times, the basis of the property is allocated to the different portions of the property. Gain or loss is computed at the time of disposal for each portion. If one purchases a 20-acre tract of land and later sells the entire tract, an allocation of basis is not needed. However if the taxpayer divides the property into smaller tracts of land for resale, the cost of the 20-acre tract must be allocated among the smaller tracts of land.

BASKET PURCHASE. If more than one asset is acquired in a single purchase transaction (i.e., a basket purchase), the cost must be apportioned to the various assets acquired.[32] The allocation is based on the relative FMVs of the assets.

EXAMPLE I5-30 ▶ Kelly purchases a duplex for $80,000 to use as a rental property. The land has a $15,000 FMV, and the building has a $65,000 FMV. Kelly's bases for the land and the building are $15,000 and $65,000, respectively. ◀

Because no depreciation deduction is allowed for land, taxpayers tend to favor a liberal allocation of the total purchase price to the building. Appraisals or other measures of FMV may be used to make the allocation.

[31] Reg. Sec. 1.165-9(c), Ex. (1).

[32] Reg. Sec. 1.61-6(a).

COMMON COSTS. As in the case of financial accounting, common costs incurred to obtain or prepare an asset for service must be capitalized and allocated to the basis of the individual assets.

EXAMPLE I5-31 ▶ Priscilla acquires three machines for $60,000, which have FMVs of $30,000, $20,000, and $10,000, respectively. Costs of delivery amount to $2,000, and costs to install the three machines amount to $1,000. The total installation and delivery costs of $3,000 are allocated to each of the three machines based on their FMVs.

The allocation of the $3,000 of common costs occurs as follows:

$$\text{Machine No. 1:} \quad \frac{\$30,000 \text{ FMV}}{\$30,000 + \$20,000 + \$10,000} \times \$3,000 = \$1,500$$

$$\text{Machine No. 2:} \quad \frac{\$20,000 \text{ FMV}}{\$30,000 + \$20,000 + \$10,000} \times \$3,000 = \$1,000$$

$$\text{Machine No. 3:} \quad \frac{\$10,000 \text{ FMV}}{\$30,000 + \$20,000 + \$10,000} \times \$3,000 = \$500$$

The bases for each of the three machines are $31,500, $21,000, and $10,500, respectively. ◀

NONTAXABLE STOCK DIVIDENDS RECEIVED. If a nontaxable stock dividend is received, a portion of the basis of the stock on which the stock dividend is received is allocated to the new shares received from the stock dividend.[33] The cost basis of the previously acquired shares is then reduced by the amount of basis that is allocated to the stock dividend shares. If the stock received as a stock dividend is the same type as the stock owned before the dividend, the total basis of the stock owned before the dividend is allocated equally to all shares now owned.

EXAMPLE I5-32 ▶ Wayne owns 1,000 shares of Bell Corporation common stock with a $44,000 basis. Wayne receives a nontaxable 10% common stock dividend and now owns 1,100 shares of common stock. The basis for each share of common stock is now $40 ($44,000 ÷ 1,100). ◀

If the stock received as a stock dividend is not the same type as the stock owned before the dividend, the allocation is based on relative FMVs.[34]

EXAMPLE I5-33 ▶ Stacey owns 500 shares of Montana Corporation common stock with a $60,000 basis. She receives a nontaxable stock dividend payable in 50 shares of preferred stock. At time of the distribution, the common stock has a $40,000 FMV ($80 × 500 shares), and the preferred stock has a $10,000 FMV ($200 × 50 shares). After the distribution, Stacey owns 50 shares of preferred stock with a basis of $12,000 [($10,000 ÷ $50,000) × $60,000]. Thus, $12,000 of the basis of the common stock is allocated to the preferred stock and the basis of the common stock is reduced from $60,000 to $48,000. ◀

KEY POINT

Corporations issue stock rights to shareholders so that the shareholders will be able to maintain their same proportional ownership in the corporation. This is called the pre-emptive right.

NONTAXABLE STOCK RIGHTS RECEIVED. Stock rights represent rights to acquire shares of a specified corporation's stock at a specific exercise price when certain conditions are met. The exercise price is usually less than the market price when the stock rights are issued. Stock rights may be distributed to employees as compensation,

---

[33] Sec. 307(a).

[34] Reg. Sec. 1.307-1(a).

and they are often issued to shareholders to encourage them to purchase more stock, thereby providing more capital for the corporation.

If the FMV of nontaxable stock rights received is less than 15% of the FMV of the stock, the basis of the stock rights is zero unless the taxpayer elects to allocate the basis between the stock rights and the stock owned before distribution of the stock rights.[35]

EXAMPLE I5-34 ▶ Tina owns 100 shares of Bear Corporation common stock with a $27,000 basis and a $50,000 FMV. She receives 100 nontaxable stock rights with a total FMV of $4,000. Because the FMV of the stock rights is less than 15% of the FMV of the stock (0.15 × $50,000 = $7,500), the basis of the stock rights is zero unless Tina elects to make an allocation. ◀

REAL-WORLD EXAMPLE

In 1993, United States Cellular Corporation issued one right for each common share held. Each whole right entitled the holder to buy one common share for $33.

If in Example I5-34, Tina elects to allocate the basis of $27,000 between the stock rights and the stock, the basis of the rights is $2,000 ([$4,000 ÷ $54,000] × $27,000) and the basis of the stock is $25,000 ([$50,000 ÷ $54,000] × $27,000).

The decision to allocate the basis affects the gain or loss realized on the sale or disposition of the stock rights because the basis of the rights is zero unless an allocation is made. Furthermore, the basis of any stock acquired by exercising the rights is affected by whether or not a portion of the basis is allocated to the rights. The basis of stock acquired by exercising the stock rights is the amount paid plus the basis of the stock rights exercised.

EXAMPLE I5-35 ▶ George receives 10 stock rights as a nontaxable distribution, and no basis is allocated to the stock rights. With each stock right, George may acquire one share of stock for $20. If he exercises all 10 stock rights, the new stock acquired has a basis of $200 ($20 × 10 shares). If George sells all 10 stock rights for $135, he has a realized gain of $135 ($135 − 0). ◀

If the FMV of a nontaxable stock right received is equal to or greater than 15% of the FMV of the stock, the basis of the stock owned before the distribution must be allocated between the stock and the stock rights.

EXAMPLE I5-36 ▶ Helen owns 100 shares of NMO common stock with a $14,000 basis and a $30,000 FMV. She receives 100 stock rights with a total FMV of $5,000. Because the FMV of the stock rights is at least 15% of the FMV of the stock, the $14,000 basis must be allocated between the stock rights and the stock. The basis of the stock rights is $2,000 [($5,000 ÷ $35,000) × $14,000] and the basis of the stock is $12,000 [($30,000 ÷ $35,000) × $14,000]. ◀

A recipient of stock rights generally has three courses of action. The stock rights can be sold or exchanged, in which case the basis allocated to the stock rights, if any, is used to determine the gain or loss. The stock rights may be exercised, and any basis allocated to the rights is added to the purchase price of the acquired stock. The stock rights may be allowed to expire, in which case no loss is recognized, and any basis allocated to the rights is reallocated back to the stock. If the stock rights received in Example I5-36 expire without being exercised, Helen does not recognize a loss and the basis of her 100 shares of common stock is $14,000.

Property basis rules are highlighted in Topic Review I5-1.

---

[35] Sec. 307(b)(1).

Topic Review I5-1

Property Basis Rules

Method Acquired	Basis of the Acquired Property
1. Acquired by direct purchase	1. Basis includes the amount paid for the property, costs of preparing the property for use, obligations of the seller that are assumed by the buyer, and liabilities to which the property is subject.
2. Acquired as a gift. (a) FMV on the date of the gift is equal to or greater than the donor's basis (b) FMV on the date of the gift is less than the donor's basis	2. (a) The donee's basis is the same as the donor's basis plus a pro rata portion of the gift tax attributable to the unrealized appreciation in the property at the time of the gift. (b) The donee's gain basis is the donor's basis and the loss basis is FMV. No increase for any gift tax paid.
3. Received from a decedent (a) Alternative valuation date is not elected (b) Alternative valuation date is elected	3. (a) The basis is its FMV on the date of death. (b) The basis of nondistributed property is its FMV on the alternative valuation date. If the property is distributed or sold before this date, its basis is FMV on the date of sale or distribution.
4. Converted from personal to business use	4. The basis for a loss (as well as for depreciation) is the lesser of its adjusted basis or FMV at the date of conversion. The basis for a gain is its adjusted basis at the date of conversion.
5. Nontaxable stock dividend	5. Basis of the stock dividend shares includes a pro rata portion of the adjusted basis of the underlying shares owned.
6. Nontaxable stock right	6. If the FMV of the rights is less than 15% of the FMV of the stock, the basis of the rights is zero unless an election is made. Basis of the underlying stock is allocated to the rights based on the respective FMV's of the stock and the rights.

DEFINITION OF A CAPITAL ASSET

Instead of defining capital assets, Sec. 1221 provides a list of properties that are **not** capital assets. Thus, a capital asset is any property owned by a taxpayer *other* than the types of property specified in the IRC. Property which is not a capital asset includes the following:

1. Inventory or property held primarily for sale to customers in the ordinary course of a trade or business.
2. Property used in the trade or business and subject to the allowance for depreciation provided in Sec. 167 or real property used in a trade or business. (As explained in Chapter I13, these properties are referred to as *Sec. 1231 assets* if held by the taxpayer more than one year.)
3. Accounts or notes receivable acquired in the ordinary course of a trade or business for services rendered or from the sale of property described in item 1.
4. Other assets including
   a. A letter, memorandum, or similar property held by a taxpayer for whom such property was prepared or produced.
   b. A copyright; a literary, musical, or artistic composition; a letter or memorandum; or similar property held by a taxpayer whose personal efforts created such property or whose basis in the property for determining a gain is determined by reference to the basis of such property in the hands of one who created the property or one for whom such property was prepared or produced.
   c. A U.S. government publication held by a taxpayer who receives the publication by any means other than a purchase at the price the publication is offered for sale to the public.
   d. A U.S. government publication held by a taxpayer whose basis in the property for determining a gain is determined by reference to the basis of such property in the hands of a taxpayer in item 4c (e.g., certain property received by gift).

TYPICAL MISCONCEPTION

It is common in financial accounting classes to include property used in a trade or business in the definition of a capital asset. For example, factory buildings, machinery, trucks, and office buildings would be defined as capital assets. However, such items are excluded from the tax definition of a capital asset.

EXAMPLE I5-37 ▶ Maxine owns a building used in her business. Other business assets include equipment, inventory, and accounts receivable. None of the assets are classified as capital assets. ◀

Chapter I13 provides an in-depth discussion of business assets such as buildings, land, and equipment. Although these items are not capital assets, Sec. 1231 provides in many cases that the gain on the sale or exchange of such an asset is eventually taxed as a long-term capital gain.

EXAMPLE I5-38 ▶ Eric owns an automobile that is held for personal use and also owns a copyright for a book he has written. Because the copyright is held by the taxpayer whose personal efforts created the property, it is not a capital asset. The automobile held for personal use is a capital asset. ◀

SELF-STUDY QUESTION

Doug owns a personal residence, an automobile, 100 shares of Ford Motor Company, and a poem he wrote for his girlfriend. Which of these assets are capital assets?

ANSWER

All of the items are capital assets except the poem, which is a literary composition.

By analyzing Examples I5-37 and I5-38, one can conclude that the classification of an asset is often determined by its use. An automobile used in a trade or business is not a capital asset but is considered a capital asset when it is held for personal use. Examples of assets that qualify as capital assets include a personal residence, land held for personal use, and investments in stocks and bonds.

INFLUENCE OF THE COURTS

In *Corn Products Refining Co.*, the Supreme Court rendered a landmark decision when it determined that the sale of futures contracts related to the purchase of raw materials

ADDITIONAL
COMMENT

If an asset such as an automobile is used in part in a trade or business and in part for personal use, then the business part of the car is not a capital asset, but the other part is a capital asset.

ETHICAL POINT

A CPA should not prepare or sign a tax return for a client unless the position or issue has (1) a realistic possibility of being sustained on its merits, or (2) is not frivolous and is adequately disclosed in the return.

resulted in ordinary rather than capital gains and losses.[36] The Corn Products Company, a manufacturer of products made from grain corn, purchased futures contracts for corn to ensure an adequate supply of raw materials. While delivery of the corn was accepted when needed for manufacturing operations, unneeded contracts were later sold. Corn Products contended that any gains or losses on the sale of the unneeded contracts should be capital gains and losses because futures contracts are customarily viewed as security investments, which qualify as capital assets. The Supreme Court held that these transactions represented an integral part of the business for the purpose of protecting the company's manufacturing operations and that the gains and losses should, therefore, be ordinary in nature.

Although the *Corn Products* doctrine has been interpreted as creating a nonstatutory exception to the definition of a capital asset when the asset is purchased for business purposes, the Supreme Court ruled in the 1988 *Arkansas Best Corporation* case that the motivation for acquiring assets is irrelevant to the question of whether assets are capital assets. Arkansas Best, a bank holding company, sold shares of a bank's stock that had been acquired for the purpose of protecting its business reputation. Relying on the *Corn Products* doctrine, the company deducted the loss as ordinary. The Supreme Court ruled that the loss was a capital loss because the stock is within the broad definition of the term *capital asset* in Sec. 1221 and is outside the classes of property that are excluded from capital-asset status.[37] Although *Arkansas Best* apparently limits the application of *Corn Products* to hedging transactions that are an integral part of a taxpayer's system of acquiring inventory, the U.S. Claims Court ruled in 1991 that a convenience store company whose profits came largely from the sale of gasoline was entitled to an ordinary loss when it sold stock of an oil company.[38]

During the national oil shortages in the 1970s, the Circle K Corporation experienced difficulty in obtaining a sufficient supply of gasoline at competitive prices. To help avoid future shortage problems, the company purchased 12.3% of NuCorp, an oil and gas exploration company, in 1980. In 1983, Circle K sold its interest in NuCorp and realized a loss of more than $27 million.

Before the *Arkansas Best* case in 1988, taxpayers used the *Corn Products* case to sustain an ordinary loss deduction on the sale of corporate stock purchased by a company to obtain access to raw materials. The U.S. Claims Court ruled that *Arkansas Best* did not specifically address the case where stock is purchased to obtain inventory and concluded "that a source of supply stock purchase may qualify as a hedging transaction if it is an integral part of plaintiff's inventory purchase system."[39] Thus, the issue whether a loss is capital or ordinary continues to be litigated.

OTHER IRC PROVISIONS RELEVANT TO CAPITAL GAINS AND LOSSES

A number of IRC sections provide special treatment for certain types of assets and transactions. For example, loss on the sale or exchange of certain small business stock that qualifies as Sec. 1244 stock is treated as an ordinary loss rather than a capital loss to

---

[36] *Corn Products Refining Co. v. CIR*, 47 AFTR 1789, 55-2 USTC ¶9746 (USSC, 1955).
[37] *Arkansas Best Corporation v. CIR*, 61 AFTR 2d 88-655, 88-1 USTC ¶9210 (USSC, 1988).

[38] *The Circle K Corporation v. U.S.*, 67 AFTR 2d 91-1055, 91-1 USTC ¶ 50,260 (Cls. Ct., 1991).
[39] Ibid.

the extent of $50,000 per year ($100,000 if the taxpayer is married and files a joint return).[40]

ADDITIONAL COMMENT

For purposes of Sec. 1236, a security is defined as any share of stock in any corporation, note, bond, debenture, or evidence of indebtedness, or any evidence of an interest in or right to subscribe to or purchase any of the above.

DEALERS IN SECURITIES. Normally, a security dealer's gain on the sale or exchange of securities is ordinary income. Section 1236 provides an exception for dealers in securities if the dealer clearly identifies that the property is held for investment. This act of identification must occur before the close of the day on which the security is acquired, and the security must not be held primarily for sale to customers in the ordinary course of the dealer's trade or business at any time after the close of the day of purchase.[41]

EXAMPLE I5-39 ▶ Allison, a dealer in securities, purchases Austin Corporation stock on April 8, 1997, and identifies the stock as being held for investment on that date. On December 21, 1997, Allison sells the stock. Any gain or loss recognized due to the sale is capital gain or loss. ◀

Once a dealer clearly identifies a security as being held for investment, any loss on the sale or exchange of the security is treated as a capital loss.

EXAMPLE I5-40 ▶ Kris, a dealer in securities, purchases Boston Corporation stock and clearly identifies the stock as being held for investment on the date of purchase. Eight months later, the security is removed from the investment account and held as inventory. If the security is later sold at a gain, the gain is an ordinary gain. However, if the stock is sold at a loss, the loss is a capital loss. ◀

For tax years ending on or after December 31, 1993, securities dealers must use the mark-to-market method for their inventory of securities. Securities must be valued at FMV at the end of each taxable year. Dealers in securities recognize gain or loss each year as if the security is sold on the last day of the tax year. Gains and losses are generally treated as ordinary rather than capital. Gains or losses due to adjustments in subsequent years or resulting from the sale of the security must be adjusted to reflect gains and losses already taken into account when determining taxable income.[42]

EXAMPLE I5-41 ▶ Jim Spikes, a dealer in securities and calendar-year taxpayer, purchases a security for inventory on October 10, 1997 for $10,000 and sells the security for $18,000 on July 1, 1998. The security's FMV on December 31, 1997 is $15,000. Jim recognizes $5,000 of ordinary income in 1997 and $3,000 of ordinary income in 1998. ◀

REAL PROPERTY SUBDIVIDED FOR SALE. A taxpayer who engages in regular sales of real estate is considered to be a dealer, and any gain or loss recognized is ordinary gain or loss rather than capital gain or loss. A special relief provision is provided for nondealer, noncorporate taxpayers who subdivide a tract of real property into lots (two or more pieces of real property are considered to be a tract if they are contiguous).[43] Part or all of the gain on the sale of the lots may be treated as a capital gain if the following provisions of Sec. 1237 are satisfied:

---

[40] Secs. 1244(a) and (b). (See Chapter I8 for additional discussion on small business corporation stock losses.)

[41] For securities acquired before August 14, 1981, Sec. 1236 applies only if the dealer identifies the property as being held for investment within thirty days of the date of acquisition.

[42] Sec. 475. The mark-to-market rule also applies to some securities that are not inventory, but does not apply to any security that is held for investment and certain other transactions (see Sec. 475(b)).

[43] Secs. 1237(a) and (c).

ADDITIONAL COMMENT

The conversion of an apartment building into condominiums does not qualify under Sec. 1237, even if the property has been held for five years and no substantial improvements have been made.

▶ During the year of sale, the noncorporate taxpayer must not hold any other real property primarily for sale in the ordinary course of business.

▶ Unless the property is acquired by inheritance or devise, the lots sold must be held by the taxpayer for a period of at least five years.

▶ No substantial improvement may be made by the taxpayer while holding the lots if the improvement substantially enhances the value of the lot.[44]

▶ The tract or any lot may not have been previously held primarily for sale to customers in the ordinary course of the taxpayer's trade or business unless such tract at that time was covered by Sec. 1237.

The primary advantage of Sec. 1237 is that potential controversy with the IRS is avoided as to whether a taxpayer who subdivides investment property is a dealer. Section 1237 does not apply to losses. Such losses are capital losses if the property is held for investment purposes, or ordinary losses if the taxpayer is a dealer.

If the Sec. 1237 requirements are satisfied, all gain on the sale of the first five lots may be capital gain. Starting in the tax year during which the sixth lot is sold, 5% of the selling price for all lots sold in that year and succeeding years is ordinary income.

EXAMPLE I5-42 ADDITIONAL COMMENT

If a taxpayer sells any lots from a tract and does not sell any others for a period of five years, the remaining property is considered a new tract.

EXAMPLE I5-42 ▶ Jean subdivides a tract of land held as an investment into seven lots, and all requirements of Sec. 1237 are satisfied. The lots have a fair market value of $10,000 each and have a basis of $4,000. Jean incurs no selling expenses and sells four lots in 1996 and three lots in 1997. In 1996, all of the $24,000 [4 lots × ($10,000 − $4,000)] gain is capital gain. In 1997, the year in which the sixth lot is sold, $1,500 of the gain is ordinary income [0.05 × ($10,000 × 3 lots)], and the remaining $16,500 {[3 lots × ($10,000 − $4,000)] − $1,500} gain is capital gain. ◀

EXAMPLE I5-43 ▶ Assume the same facts as in Example I5-42, except that all seven lots are sold in 1996. The amount of ordinary income recognized is $3,500 [0.05 × ($10,000 × 7 lots)], and the remaining $38,500 {[7 lots × ($10,000 − $4,000)] − $3,500} gain is capital gain. ◀

Based on Examples I5-42 and I5-43, the advantage of selling no more than five lots in the first year should be apparent. Expenditures incurred to sell or exchange the lots are also treated favorably because they are first applied against the portion of the gain that is treated as ordinary income.[45] Because selling expenses (e.g., commissions) are often equal to or greater than 5% of the selling price, this offset against ordinary income may result in the elimination of the ordinary income portion of the gain. Selling expenses in excess of the gain taxed as ordinary income reduce the amount realized on the sale or exchange.

NONBUSINESS BAD DEBT. Although the topic of bad debts is discussed in Chapter I8, it is important to note that bad debt losses from nonbusiness debts are deductible only as short-term capital losses (STCLs).[46] This treatment applies regardless of when the debt occurred. A nonbusiness bad debt is deductible only in the year in which the debt becomes totally worthless.

EXAMPLE I5-44 ▶ Two years ago, Alice loaned $2,000 to a friend. During the current year, the friend declares bankruptcy and the debt is entirely worthless. Assuming that Alice has no other gains and losses from the sale or exchange of capital assets during the year, she deducts $2,000 in determining adjusted gross income (AGI). ◀

---

[44] Certain improvements are not treated as substantial under Sec. 1237(b)(3) if the lot is held for at least ten years.

[45] Sec. 1237(b)(2).

[46] Sec. 166(d)(1)(B).

TAX TREATMENT FOR CAPITAL GAINS AND LOSSES OF NONCORPORATE TAXPAYERS

OBJECTIVE 5

Understand how capital gains and losses affect taxable income

To recognize capital gain or loss, it is necessary to have a sale or exchange of a capital asset. Once it is determined that a capital gain or loss has been realized and is to be recognized, it is necessary to classify the gains and losses as either short-term or long-term. To be classified as a long-term capital gain (LTCG) or long-term capital loss (LTCL), the asset must be held for more than a year.[47] If the asset is held for a year or less, the gain or loss is classified as a short-term capital gain (STCG) or a short-term capital loss (STCL).

CAPITAL GAINS

Net capital gain, which may receive favorable tax treatment, is defined as the excess of net long-term capital gains over net short-term capital losses.[48] To compute net capital gain, first determine all short-term capital gains, short-term capital losses, long-term capital gains, and long-term capital losses, and then net gains and losses as described below.

NET SHORT-TERM CAPITAL GAIN. If total STCGs for the tax year exceed total STCLs for that year, the excess is defined as net short-term capital gain (NSTCG). As discussed later, NSTCG may be offset by net long-term capital loss (NLTCL).

EXAMPLE I5-45 ▶

Hal has two transactions involving the sale of capital assets during the year. As a result of those transactions, he has a STCG of $4,000 and a STCL of $3,000. Hal's NSTCG is $1,000 ($4,000 − $3,000), and his AGI increases by $1,000. His gross income increases by $4,000, and he is entitled to a $3,000 deduction for AGI. ◀

NET LONG-TERM CAPITAL GAIN. If the total LTCGs for the tax year exceed the total LTCLs for that year, the excess is defined as net long-term capital gain (NLTCG). As indicated earlier, a net capital gain exists when NLTCG exceeds net short-term capital loss (NSTCL).

EXAMPLE I5-46 ▶

Clay has two transactions involving the sale of capital assets during the year. As a result of the transactions, he has a LTCG of $4,000 and a LTCL of $3,000. Clay has a NLTCG and a net capital gain of $1,000. His AGI increases by $1,000. ◀

EXAMPLE I5-47

SELF-STUDY QUESTION

Mary sells common stock for a gain of $10,000 on December 29, 1997. The settlement date, or date that Mary will receive the proceeds from the stockbroker, is January 2, 1998. Will Mary report the gain on her 1997 or 1998 tax return?

▶

Linda has four transactions involving the sale of capital assets during the year. As a result of the transactions, she has a STCG of $5,000, a STCL of $7,000, a LTCG of $10,000, and a LTCL of $2,000. After the initial netting of short-term and long-term gains and losses, Linda has a NSTCL of $2,000 ($7,000 − $5,000) and a NLTCG of $8,000 ($10,000 − $2,000). Because the NLTCG exceeds the NSTCL by $6,000 ($8,000 − $2,000), her net capital gain is $6,000. ◀

CAPITAL LOSSES

To have a capital loss, one must sell or exchange the capital asset for an amount less than its adjusted basis. As in the case of capital gains, the one-year period is used to determine whether the capital loss is short-term or long-term.

---

[47] Sec. 1222. For assets acquired after June 22, 1984 and before January 1, 1988, the holding period requirement of Sec. 1222 was more than six months.

[48] Sec. 1222(11).

ANSWER

Mary is required to report the gain in the year of the sale (1997). Losses are also recognized in the year of sale.

NET SHORT-TERM CAPITAL LOSS. If total STCLs for the tax year exceed total STCGs for that year, the excess is defined as a net short-term capital loss.[49] As indicated above, the NSTCL is first offset against any NLTCG to determine the net capital gain.

If the NSTCL exceeds the NLTCG, the capital loss may be offset, in part, against other income. The NSTCL may be deducted in full (i.e., on a dollar-for-dollar basis) against a noncorporate taxpayer's ordinary income for amounts up to $3,000 in any one year.[50]

EXAMPLE I5-48 ▶

Bob has gross income of $60,000 before considering capital gains and losses. If Bob has a NSTCG of $10,000 and a NSTCL of $15,000, he has $5,000 of NSTCL in excess of NLTCG and may deduct $3,000 of the losses from gross income. Assuming no other deductions for AGI, Bob's AGI is $57,000 ($60,000 − $3,000). ◀

In Example I5-48, $10,000 of the NSTCL is used to offset the $10,000 of NLTCG, and $3,000 of the NSTCL in excess of the NLTCG is used to reduce ordinary income. However, $2,000 of the loss is not used. This net capital loss is carried forward for an indefinite number of years.[51] The loss retains its original character and will be treated as a STCL occurring in the subsequent year. If a taxpayer dies with an unused capital loss carryover, it expires.

EXAMPLE I5-49
REAL-WORLD
EXAMPLE ▶

In 1975 an amendment was added to a tax bill in the House Ways and Means Committee that would have permitted individuals to take a three-year carryback for capital losses. When *The Wall Street Journal* disclosed that the provision would provide Ross Perot with a $15 million tax break, the amendment was defeated.

Last year, Milt had a NSTCL of $8,000 and a NLTCG of $2,600. The netting of short-term and long-term gains and losses resulted in a $5,400 excess of NSTCL over NLTCG, and $3,000 of this amount was offset against ordinary income. Milt's NSTCL carryforward is $2,400. During the current year he sells a capital asset and generates a STCG of $800. His NSTCL is $1,600 ($2,400 − $800), and the loss is offset against $1,600 of ordinary income. ◀

NET LONG-TERM CAPITAL LOSS. If total LTCLs for the tax year exceed total LTCGs for the year, the excess is defined as net long-term capital loss. If there is both a NSTCG and a NLTCL, the NLTCL is initially offset against the NSTCG on a dollar-for-dollar basis. If the NLTCL exceeds the NSTCG, the excess is offset against ordinary income on a dollar-for-dollar basis up to $3,000 per year.

EXAMPLE I5-50 ▶

In the current year, Gordon has a NLTCL of $9,000 and a NSTCG of $2,000. He must use $2,000 of the NLTCL to offset the $2,000 NSTCG, and then use $3,000 of the $7,000 ($9,000 − $2,000) NLTCL to offset $3,000 of ordinary income. Gordon's carryforward of NLTCL is $4,000 [$9,000 − ($2,000 + $3,000)]. This amount is treated as a LTCL in subsequent years. ◀

If an individual has both NSTCL and NLTCL, the NSTCL is offset against ordinary income first, regardless of when the transactions occur during the year.

EXAMPLE I5-51 ▶

In the current year, Beth has a NSTCL of $2,800 and a NLTCL of $2,000. The entire NSTCL is offset initially against $2,800 of ordinary income on a dollar-for-dollar basis. Because capital losses can be offset against only $3,000 of ordinary income, $200 of NLTCL is used to offset $200 ($3,000 − $2,800) of ordinary income. The NLTCL carryover to the next year is $1,800 ($2,000 − $200). ◀

---

[49] Sec. 1222(6).
[50] Sec. 1211(b). A $1,500 limitation applies to a married individual filing a separate return.

[51] Sec. 1212(b) and Reg. Sec. 1.1212-1(b).

STOP & THINK

Question: Srinija has a salary of $100,000. If she sells a non-personal use asset during the year and has a $40,000 loss, why is it important that the asset not be a capital asset?

Solution: Only $3,000 of a $40,000 capital loss is used as a deduction to reduce her gross income each year. Her AGI is $97,000 if the asset is a capital asset, and she has a $37,000 capital loss carryforward. All of the $40,000 loss is used to reduce her gross income if the asset is not a capital asset and her AGI is $60,000. It is possible that Srinija might not care whether or not the asset is a capital asset if she has capital gains that could be reduced by capital losses. If the asset is a personal-use asset, the loss is not deductible regardless of whether or not it is a capital asset.

KEY POINT

Only taxpayers who have a marginal tax rate of 31% or higher receive any benefit from the 28% maximum rate that applies to net capital gain.

TAX TREATMENT FOR NET CAPITAL GAIN. For tax years after 1990, the maximum tax rate on net capital gains is 28%.[52] Thus, individuals with a 31% or higher marginal tax rate benefit by having a gain classified as LTCG rather than STCG or ordinary income because the lower 28% maximum rate applies to the net capital gain. The increase in the highest tax rate from 31% to 39.6% in 1993 and subsequent years has increased the significance of the preferential treatment that is accorded to net capital gains.

EXAMPLE I5-52 ▶

Rita is single with taxable income of $40,000, including $7,000 of net capital gain in 1997. The fact that $7,000 of taxable income is net capital gain does not result in a tax savings for Rita because her marginal tax rate is 28%. In 1997, the 31% rate for single individuals applies to taxable income over $59,750. If Rita's taxable income is less than $24,650, the net capital gain is taxed at 15%. ◀

EXAMPLE I5-53 ▶
KEY POINT

The reintroduction of a significant differential in effective tax rates between ordinary income and capital gains in 1993 may cause high-income taxpayers to modify their investment ap-

Gary is single with taxable income of $80,000, including $15,000 of net capital gain in 1997. The $15,000 of net capital gain would be taxed at 31% if the maximum tax rate on net capital gain were not limited to 28%. The $15,000 of net capital gain is subject to the 28% maximum capital gain rate because the 31% tax rate otherwise applies to taxable income in excess of $59,750 for single individuals in 1997. Gary's tax liability is $19,353 ($13,525.50 + 0.31 [$65,000 − $59,750] + 0.28 [$15,000]). ◀

EXAMPLE I5-54 ▶

proach to emphasize capital gains rather than dividend and interest income.

Assume the same facts as in Example I5-53 except that Gary has taxable income of $285,000 including $15,000 of net capital gain. The $15,000 of net capital gain would be taxed at 39.6% if the maximum rate on net capital gain were not 28% because a 39.6% rate applies to taxable income in excess of $271,050. The tax savings from applying the preferential 28% capital gain rate is $1,740 [$15,000 × (39.6% − 28%)]. ◀

TAX TREATMENT OF CAPITAL GAINS AND LOSSES: CORPORATE TAXPAYERS

Most topics covered in this chapter concerning capital gains and losses, including the classification of an asset as a capital asset, rules for determining holding periods, and the procedure for offsetting capital losses against capital gains, apply to both corporate and noncorporate taxpayers. However, a major difference is that the 28% maximum tax rate

---

[52] Sec. 1(h). For years prior to 1990, a myriad of rules have applied. Prior to 1987, noncorporate taxpayers received a deduction from gross income equal to 60% of the taxpayer's net capital gain. For years 1987-1990, net capital gains were subject to tax at ordinary income rates.

on net capital gain for noncorporate taxpayers does not apply to corporations. A second significant difference relates to the treatment of capital losses: Unlike the noncorporate taxpayer, who may offset capital losses against ordinary income up to $3,000, corporations may offset capital losses only against capital gains. Corporate taxpayers may carry capital losses back to each of the three preceding tax years (the earliest of the three tax years first and then to the next two years) and forward for five years to offset capital gains in such years. When a corporate taxpayer carries a loss back to a preceding year or forward to a following year, the loss is treated as a STCL.[53]

EXAMPLE I5-55 The Peach Corporation has income from operations of $200,000, a NSTCG of $40,000, and a NLTCL of $56,000 during the current year. The $40,000 NSTCG is offset by $40,000 NLTCL. The remaining $16,000 of NLTCLs may not be offset against the $200,000 of other income but may be carried back three years and then forward five years to offset capital gains arising in these years. ◄

Topic Review I5-2 summarizes the principal differences in the tax treatment of capital gains and losses for corporate and noncorporate taxpayers.

STOP & THINK

Question: Most taxpayers believe that if they have a long-term capital gain, their income taxes will be less on the LTCG than on their other ordinary income. Explain why all taxpayers do not have a tax savings from a net capital gain.

Solution: Noncorporate taxpayers whose marginal tax rate is 28% or less will not have a reduction in taxes even if the gain is a net capital gain. Also, the maximum tax rate of 28% on a net capital gain does not apply to corporate taxpayers.

Sale or exchange

OBJECTIVE 6

Recognize when a sale or exchange has occurred

As previously indicated, capital gains and losses result from the sale or exchange of capital assets. Although Sec. 1222 does not define a sale or an exchange, a **sale** is generally considered to be a transaction where one receives cash or the equivalent of cash, including the assumption of one's debt. An **exchange** is a transaction where one receives a reciprocal transfer of property, as distinguished from a transaction where one receives only cash or a cash equivalent.[54]

EXAMPLE I5-56 Two years ago, Bart acquired 100 shares of Alaska Corporation common stock for $12,000 to hold as an investment. Bart sells 50 shares of the stock to Sandy for $10,000 and transfers the other 50 shares to Gail in exchange for land that has a $10,000 FMV. In each transaction, Bart realizes a $4,000 ($10,000 − $6,000) LTCG due to the sale or exchange of a capital asset. The transfer to Sandy qualifies as a sale, and the transfer to Gail qualifies as an exchange. ◄

TYPICAL MISCONCEPTION

Because the carryover for net operating losses is 15 years, it is sometimes erroneously assumed that the carryover for corporate capital losses is also 15 years instead of five years.

To qualify as a sale or exchange, the transaction must be bona fide. Transactions between related parties such as family members are closely scrutinized. For example, a sale of property on credit to a relative may be a disguised gift if there is no intention of collecting the debt. If this is the case, a subsequent bad debt deduction due to the debt's worthlessness is disallowed. In some instances, the Code specifically states that a particular transaction or event either qualifies or does not qualify for sale or exchange

---

[53] Sec. 1212(a).

[54] Reg. Sec. 1.1002-1(d).

Topic Review I5-2

Comparison of Corporate and Noncorporate Taxpayers: Capital Gains and Losses

	Noncorporate	Corporate
A statutory maximum tax rate applicable to net capital gain	Yes, 28%	No, ordinary corporate tax rates apply
Offset of net capital losses against ordinary income	Yes, up to $3,000	No
Carryback of capital losses	No	Yes, three years as STCLs
Carryforward of capital losses	Yes, indefinitely	Yes, five years as STCLs

treatment. For example, the holder of an option who fails to exercise such an option treats the lapse of the option as a sale or exchange.[55] However, abandonment of property is generally not deemed to be a sale or exchange.[56]

WORTHLESS SECURITIES

ADDITIONAL
COMMENT

The worthlessness of a security is treated as a sale or exchange so that the taxpayer is not forced to arrange for someone to buy the security for a token amount.

If a security that is a capital asset becomes worthless during the year, Sec. 165(g)(1) specifies that any loss is treated as a loss from the sale or exchange of a capital asset on the last day of the tax year. The term includes stock, a stock option, and "a bond, debenture, note or certificate, or other evidence of indebtedness, issued by a corporation or by a government or political division thereof, with interest coupons or in registered form."[57] Whether a security has become worthless during the year is a question of fact, and the taxpayer has the burden of proof to show evidence of worthlessness.[58]

EXAMPLE I5-57 ▶

Charlotte purchased $40,000 of bonds issued by the Jet Corporation in March 1996. In February 1997, Jet is declared bankrupt, and its bonds are worthless. Charlotte has a LTCL of $40,000 because the bonds have become worthless and are deemed to have been sold on the last day of 1997. The more-than-one-year holding period requirement is satisfied by the last day of 1997. ◀

REAL-WORLD
EXAMPLE

A corporation owned 76% of the stock of a Mexican company. The corporation later acquired the remaining 24% of the stock, allegedly for the purpose of avoiding interference by minority shareholders. Later the corporation claimed an ordinary loss on the worthless Mexican stock because it owned at least 80% of the stock. The Court treated the loss as a capital loss because the acquisition of the remaining stock was without a business purpose. *Hunter Mfg. Co.*, 21 T.C. 424 (1953).

SECURITIES IN AFFILIATED CORPORATIONS. If the security that becomes worthless is a security in a domestic affiliated corporation owned by a corporate taxpayer, the worthless security is not considered a capital asset. Thus, a corporate taxpayer's loss due to owning worthless securities in an affiliated corporation is treated as an ordinary loss. Because capital losses are of only limited benefit to corporate taxpayers, the classification of the loss as ordinary is preferable.

To qualify as an affiliated corporation, the parent corporation must own at least 80% of the voting power of all classes of stock and at least 80% of each class of nonvoting stock. The subsidiary corporation must be engaged in the active conduct of an operating business as opposed to being a passive investment company (i.e., more than 90% of its aggregate gross receipts must be from sources other than passive types of income such as royalties, dividends, and interest).[59]

---

[55] Sec. 1234(b) and Reg. Sec. 1.1234-1(b).
[56] Reg. Secs. 1.165-2 and 1.167(a)-8.
[57] Sec. 165(g)(2).

[58] *Minnie K. Young v. CIR*, 28 AFTR 365, 41-2 USTC ¶9744 (2nd Cir., 1941).
[59] Sec. 165(g)(3).

EXAMPLE I5-58 ▶ Ace Corporation owns 80% of all classes of stock issued by the same Jet Corporation described in Example I5-57. Jet Corporation is actively engaged in an operating business and has no income from passive investments before being declared bankrupt. Ace's loss from its worthless stock investment is an ordinary loss instead of a capital loss because Jet is an affiliated corporation; that is, Ace owns at least 80% of all classes of Jet's stock and more than 90% of Jet's gross receipts are from sources other than passive types of income. ◀

RETIREMENT OF DEBT INSTRUMENTS

Generally, the collection of a debt is not a sale or an exchange. However, if a debt instrument is retired, amounts received by the holder are treated as being received in an exchange.[60] Debt instruments include bonds, debentures, notes, certificates, and other evidences of indebtedness.[61]

EXAMPLE I5-59 ▶ In 1992 the Rocket Corporation issued $50,000 of five-year, interest-bearing bonds that were purchased by Elaine as an investment for $49,800. Elaine receives $50,000 at maturity in 1997. Retirement of the debt instrument is an exchange, and the $200 gain is a LTCG.[62] ◀

Although Congress has provided that retirements of debt instruments are treated as exchanges, Congress is not willing to allow taxpayers to convert large amounts of potential ordinary interest income into capital gain by purchasing debt instruments at a substantial discount. As illustrated in Example I5-59, a small amount of bond discount is sometimes converted to capital gain. However, if the discount is large enough to be classified as original issue discount, the discount must be amortized and included in gross income for each day the debt instrument is held.[63] Original issue discount (OID) is defined as "the excess (if any) of the stated redemption price at maturity over the issue price.[64]

EXAMPLE I5-60 ▶ On January 1, 1997, Connie purchases $100,000 of the City Corporation's newly issued bonds for $85,000. The bonds mature in twenty years. In 1997 and in subsequent years Connie must annually recognize as interest income a portion of the $15,000 of OID. ◀

The OID is considered to be zero if the amount of discount "is less than ¼ of 1% of the stated redemption price at maturity, multiplied by the number of complete years to maturity."[65] In Example I5-59, the $200 discount is not OID because it is less than $625 (0.0025 × $50,000 × 5 years). If Connie paid more than $95,000 for the bonds in Example I5-60, the OID would be zero.

ORIGINAL ISSUE DISCOUNT. Instead of spreading the OID ratably over the life of the bond, amortization of the discount is based on an interest amortization method. This method is called the **constant interest rate method**. The total amount of interest income is determined by multiplying the interest yield to maturity by the adjusted issue price.[66] With this method of amortizing the discount, the amount of OID amortized increases for each year the bond is held. In Example I5-60, Connie recognizes a larger amount of interest income in 1998 than in 1997 due to amortization of the OID.

The daily portion of the OID for any accrual period is "determined by allocating to each day in any accrual period its ratable portion to the increase during such accrual period in the adjusted issue price of the debt instrument."[67] The increase in the adjusted issue price for any accrual period is shown below.

[60] Sec. 1271(a).
[61] Sec. 1275(a).
[62] If Rocket Corporation issued the bonds with the intention of calling the bonds before maturity, Sec. 1271(a)(2) treats the gain as ordinary income.
[63] Sec. 1272(a).

[64] Sec. 1273(a)(1).
[65] Sec. 1273(a)(3).
[66] Secs. 1272(a)(1) and (3).
[67] Sec. 1272(a)(3).

$$\text{Increase in the adjusted issue price} = \left[\begin{array}{c} \text{Adjusted issue price at the beginning of the accrual period} \end{array} \times \begin{array}{c} \text{Yield to maturity} \end{array} \right] - \begin{array}{c} \text{Interest payments during the accrual period} \end{array}$$

EXAMPLE I5-61 ▶ On June 30, 1997, Fred purchases a 10%, $10,000 corporate bond for $9,264. The bond is issued on June 30, 1997 and matures in five years. Interest is paid semiannually, and the effective yield to maturity is 12% compounded semiannually. In 1997, Fred recognizes interest income of $556, as illustrated in Table I5-1. The adjusted issue price as of January 1, 1998 is $9,320. This is the sum of the issue price plus any amounts of original issue discount includible in the income of any holder since the date of issue. ◀

If a debt instrument is sold or exchanged before maturity, part of the original issue discount is included in the seller's income. The amount to be included depends on the number of days the debt instrument is owned by the seller within the accrual period.

EXAMPLE I5-62 ▶ Assume the same facts as in Example I5-61, except that Fred sells the corporate bond to Carolyn on February 24, 1999 (the 55th day in the accrual period). Fred must include $20 [(55 days ÷ 181 days in the accrual period) × $67] of accrued interest for the period of January 1, 1999 to February 24, 1999 in income for 1999. Fred's basis for the bond increases by $20. Thus, his basis for determining a gain or loss is $9,462 ($9,442 + $20). ◀

MARKET DISCOUNT BONDS PURCHASED AFTER APRIL 30, 1993. The sale or exchange of a market discount bond may result in part or all of the gain being classified

▼ **TABLE I5-1**

Computation for Interest Income in Examples I5-61 and I5-62

	Interest Received (1)	Amortization of Original Issue Discount (2)	Interest Income (3) = (1) + (2)	Taxpayer's Basis for the Bond
6-30-97				$ 9,264
12-31-97	$ 500	$ 56[a]	$ 556	9,320[b]
6-30-98	500	59	559	9,379
12-31-98	500	63	563	9,442
6-30-99	500	67	567	9,509
12-31-99	500	71	571	9,580
6-30-00	500	75	575	9,655
12-31-00	500	79	579	9,734
6-30-01	500	84	584	9,818
12-31-01	500	89	589	9,907
6-30-02	500	93[c]	593	10,000
	$5,000	$736	$5,736	

[a] 6% × $9,264 − $500 = $56.
[b] $9,264 + $56 = $9,320.
[c] This figure is adjusted for rounding.

as ordinary income. The Revenue Reconciliation Act of 1993 substantially increased the number of bonds subject to the market discount provisions.[68] A market discount bond is a bond that is acquired in the bond market at a discount.[69] Market discount is the excess of the stated redemption price of the bond at maturity over the taxpayer's basis for such bond immediately after it is acquired.

EXAMPLE I5-63 ▶

On January 1, 1997, Stephano purchased $100,000 of 8%, 20-year bonds for $82,000. The bonds were issued at par by the Solar Corporation two years ago on January 1. The bonds are market discount bonds. ◀

Similar to original issue discount, there is a de minimis rule for determining market discount. Market discount is zero if the discount is less than ¼ of 1% of the stated redemption price of the bond at maturity multiplied by the number of complete years to maturity.[70] If Stephano had paid more than $95,500 for the Solar Corporation bonds in Example I5-63, the bonds would not be market discount bonds.[71]

Gain realized on disposition of the market discount bond is ordinary income to the extent of the accrued market discount.[72] The ratable accrual method (straight line method computed on a daily basis) is used to determine the amount of the accrued market discount that is recognized as ordinary income.[73] The market discount is allocated on the basis of the number of days the taxpayer held the bond relative to the number of days between the acquisition date and maturity date.

EXAMPLE I5-64 ▶

Assume the same facts as in Example I5-63 except that Stephano sells the bonds to Kimberly three years later for $86,400. $3,000 (³⁄₁₈ × $18,000) of the $4,400 ($86,400 − $82,000) gain is ordinary income and the remaining gain is LTCG. If Stephano sold the bond for more than $82,000 but less than $85,000, all of the gain is ordinary income. The entire $18,000 gain is ordinary income if the bond is held to maturity. ◀

OPTIONS

The owner of an option to buy property may sell the option, exercise the option, or allow the option to expire. If the option is exercised, the amount paid for the option is added to the purchase price of the property acquired.[74]

EXAMPLE I5-65 ▶

On August 5, 1997, Len pays $600 for an option to acquire 100 shares of Hill Corporation common stock for $80 per share at any time before December 20, 1997. Len exercises the option on November 15, 1997 and pays $8,000 for the stock. Len's basis for the 100 shares of Hill is $8,600 ($8,000 + $600), and the stock's holding period begins on November 15, 1997. ◀

When an option is sold or allowed to expire, a sale or exchange has occurred and gain or loss is therefore recognized.[75] The character of the underlying property determines whether the gain or loss from the sale or expiration of the option is capital or ordinary in nature. If the optioned property is a capital asset, the option is treated as a capital asset and capital gain or loss is recognized on the sale or exchange.

---

[68] Ordinary income treatment for accrued market discount does not apply to owners of taxable market discount bonds issued on or before July 18, 1984 if the bonds were acquired before May 1, 1993. Owners of tax-exempt bonds are not required to accrue market discount if the bonds were acquired before May 1, 1993 (regardless of the issue date).
[69] Sec. 1278(a)(1)(A). This topic is discussed in Chapter I17.
[70] Sec. 1278(a)(2)(C).

[71] $100,000 × .25% × 18 years = $4,500.
[72] Sec. 1276(a)(1).
[73] Sec. 1276(b)(1). A taxpayer may elect to use the constant interest rate method (see Sec. 1276(b)(2)).
[74] Rev. Rul. 58-234, 1958-1 C.B. 279.
[75] Sec. 1234(a).

EXAMPLE I5-66 ▶

On March 2, 1997, Holly pays $270 for an option to acquire 100 shares of Arkansas Corporation stock for $30 per share at any time before December 10, 1997. As a result of an increase in the market value of the Arkansas stock, the market price of the option increases and Holly sells the option for $600 on August 2, 1997. Because the Arkansas stock is a capital asset in the hands of Holly, the option is a capital asset and she must recognize a STCG of $330 ($600 − $270). ◀

EXAMPLE I5-67 ▶

On October 12, 1996, Mary paid $400 for an option to acquire 100 shares of Portland Corporation stock for $50 per share at any time before February 19, 1997. Because the price never exceeds $50 before February 19, 1997, Mary does not exercise the option. Because the option expires, Mary recognizes a STCL of $400 in 1997. ◀

Transactions in which taxpayers purchase or write options to buy (calls) are quite common today. An investor who anticipates that the market value of a stock or security (e.g., common stock) will increase during the next few months may purchase a call option instead of actually buying the stock. As indicated above, the tax treatment for the option depends on whether the call is exercised, sold, or expires. Someone, however, must be willing to write a call on the stock. Typically an owner of the same stock will write a call option. The writer of the call receives a payment for granting the right to purchase the stock at a fixed price within a given period of time.

If the call is exercised, the writer of the call adds the amount received for the call to the sales price to determine the amount realized.[76] If the call is not exercised within the given time period and thus expires, the writer retains the amount received for the option and recognizes a STCG.[77] The gain is short-term even if the option is written and held for more than a year.

EXAMPLE I5-68 ▶

Sam owns 100 shares of Madison Corporation common stock, which he purchased on May 1, 1990, for $4,000. On November 8, 1997, Sam writes a call that gives Joan, an investor, the option to purchase Sam's 100 shares of Madison stock at $60 per share any time before April 19, 1998. The current market price of Madison stock is $56 per share, and Sam receives $520 for writing the call. If the call is exercised, Sam has a LTCG of $2,520 [($6,000 + $520) − $4,000]. If the call is not exercised and expires on April 19, 1998, Sam must recognize a STCG of $520 in 1998. ◀

EXAMPLE I5-69 ▶

Assume the same facts as in Example I5-68, but consider instead the tax treatment for Joan, the holder of the call. If Joan exercises the call, the basis of the stock is $6,520 ($6,000 + $520). If she does not exercise the call, a STCL of $520 is recognized. If Joan sells the call, the amount received is compared with her basis in the call ($520) to compute Joan's gain or loss. ◀

PATENTS

To encourage technological progress and to clarify whether a transfer of rights to a patent is capital gain or ordinary income, Congress created Sec. 1235, which allows the holder of a patent to treat the gain resulting from the transfer of all substantial rights in a patent as LTCG. This tax treatment is more favorable than that accorded to producers of artistic, literary, and musical works, who receive ordinary rather than capital gain from the sale of their works. A taxpayer who recognizes LTCG from the sale of a patent may use the gain to offset capital losses or capital loss carryovers that are otherwise limited by the capital loss limitation rules.

---

[76] Rev. Rul. 58-234, 1958-1 C.B. 279.

[77] Sec. 1234(b) and Reg. Sec. 1.1234-3.

REQUIREMENTS FOR CAPITAL GAIN TREATMENT. Section 1235 provides that the transfer of all substantial rights to a patent by the holder of the patent is treated as a sale or exchange of a capital asset that has been held long-term. Thus, long-term capital gain is recognized on the transfer of a patent regardless of its holding period or the character of the asset. Favorable long-term capital gain treatment applies even if the transferor of the patent receives periodic payments contingent on the productivity, use, or disposition of the property transferred.[78]

EXAMPLE I5-70 ▶ Clay invents a small utensil used to peel shrimp. He has a patent on the utensil and transfers all rights to the patent to a manufacturing company. Clay receives $100,000 plus 40 cents per utensil sold. Because Sec. 1235 applies, the total of the lump-sum payment and the royalty payments received less his cost basis for the patent is recognized as a LTCG. ◀

SUBSTANTIAL RIGHTS. The principal requirement in Sec. 1235 is that the holder must transfer all substantial rights to the patent. The Regulations state that the circumstances of the whole transaction should be considered in determining whether all substantial rights to a patent have been transferred.[79] All substantial rights have not been transferred if the patent rights of the purchaser are limited geographically within the country of issuance or the rights are for a period less than a patent's remaining life.

EXAMPLE I5-71 ▶ Bruce, an inventor, transfers one of his U.S. patents on a manufacturing process to a manufacturer located in Utah. The manufacturer's rights to use the patent are limited to the state of Utah. Because the patent rights are limited to a geographical area, all of the substantial rights have not been transferred, and Sec. 1235 does not apply. Payments received for the use of the patent are royalties and taxed as ordinary income. ◀

DEFINITION OF A HOLDER. Long-term capital gain treatment applies only to a holder of the patent rights. For purposes of Sec. 1235, a holder is an individual whose efforts created the property or an individual who acquires the patent rights from the creator for valuable consideration before the property covered by the patent is placed in service or used. Furthermore, the acquiring individual may not be related to the creator or be the creator's employer.

Section 1235 may not be used by corporate taxpayers because corporations are not permitted to be classified as holders. Although a partnership is not permitted to be a holder, individual partners may qualify as holders to the extent of the partner's interest in the patent owned by the partnership.

EXAMPLE I5-72 ▶ Joy purchases a patent from Martin, whose efforts created the patent. The purchase occurs before the property is placed in service or used. Joy and Martin are unrelated individuals, and Joy is not Martin's employer. For purposes of Sec. 1235, both Joy and Martin qualify as holders. ◀

ADDITIONAL COMMENT

The scope of Sec. 1253 is very broad. A franchise "includes an agreement which gives one of the parties to the agreement the right to distribute, sell, or provide goods, services, or facilities within a specified area."

FRANCHISES, TRADEMARKS, AND TRADE NAMES

Before the enactment of Sec. 1253, significant uncertainty existed as to whether the transfer of a franchise, trademark, or trade name should be treated as a sale or exchange or as a licensing agreement. If the transfer is tantamount to a sale of the property, payments received should be treated by the transferor as a return of capital and capital gain, and the transferee should be required to capitalize and amortize such payments.

---

[78] Sec. 1235(a).

[79] Reg. Sec. 1.1235-2(b).

However, if the transfer represents a licensing agreement, the transferor should recognize ordinary income and the transferee should receive an ordinary deduction for such payments.

Section 1253, which applies to the granting of a franchise, trademark, or trade name, as well as renewals and transfers to third parties, attempts to resolve the uncertainty by stating, "A transfer of a franchise, trademark, or trade name shall not be treated as a sale or exchange of a capital asset if the transferor retains any significant power, right, or continuing interest with respect to the subject matter of the franchise, trademark, or trade name."[80]

The IRC provides examples of some rights that are to be considered a "significant power, right, or continuing interest."[81] These rights include the right to

▶ Disapprove of any assignment.

▶ Terminate the agreement at will.

▶ Prescribe standards of quality for products, product services, and facilities.

▶ Require the exclusive selling or advertising of the transferor's products or services.

▶ Require the transferee to purchase substantially all of its supplies and equipment from the transferor.

If the transferor does not retain any significant power, right, or continuing interest in the property, the transferor treats the transfer as a sale of the franchise and has the benefits of capital gain treatment. However, any amounts received that are contingent on the productivity, use, or disposition of such property must be treated as ordinary income by the transferor.

EXAMPLE I5-73 ▶

Rose, who owns a franchise with a basis of $100,000, transfers the franchise to Ruth and retains no significant power, right, or continuing interest. Rose receives a $250,000 down payment when the agreement is signed and annual payments for five years equal to 10% of all sales in excess of $2,000,000. Rose has a capital gain of $150,000 with respect to the initial payment, but all of the payments received during the next five years will be ordinary income because they are contingent payments. ◀

Under Sec. 1253, the transferee may deduct payments that are contingent on the productivity, use, or disposition of such property as business expenses. Generally, other payments are capitalized and amortized over a period of 15 years.[82] In practice, payments received for the transfer of a franchise are generally treated as ordinary income to the transferor and are deductible by the transferee because in most franchise agreements the transferor desires to maintain significant powers, rights, or continuing interests in the franchise operation. Also, in many instances the payments are, in part, predicated on the success of the franchised business and are, therefore, established as contingent payments.

LEASE CANCELLATION PAYMENTS

A lease arrangement may be terminated before the lease period expires, and a lease cancellation payment may be made as consideration for the other party's agreement to terminate the lease. Either a lessor or a lessee may receive such a payment because the payment is normally made by the person who wants to cancel the lease. The tax treatment may differ significantly depending on which party is the recipient.

---

[80] Sec. 1253(a). Section 1253(e) prevents the basic Sec. 1253 rules from applying to the transfer of a professional sports franchise.

[81] Sec. 1253(b)(2).
[82] Sec. 197(a).

PAYMENTS RECEIVED BY LESSOR. The Supreme Court has ruled that lease cancellation payments received by a lessor are treated as ordinary income on the basis that the payments represent a substitute for rent.[83] Lease cancellation payments are included in the lessor's income in the year received, even if the lessor uses an accrual method.[84]

PAYMENTS RECEIVED BY LESSEE. Payments received by a lessee for canceling a lease are considered amounts received in exchange for the lease.[85] If the lease is a capital asset, any gain or loss is a capital gain or loss.

EXAMPLE I5-74 ▶ Jim has a three-year lease on a house used as his personal residence. The lessor has an opportunity to sell the house and has agreed to pay $1,000 to Jim to cancel the lease. Assuming that Jim has no basis in the lease, the gain of $1,000 is capital gain because the lease is a capital asset. ◀

HOLDING PERIOD

OBJECTIVE 7

Determine the holding period for an asset when a sale or disposition occurs

The length of time an asset is held before it is disposed of (i.e., the *holding period*) is an important factor in determining whether any gain or loss resulting from the disposition of a capital asset is treated as long-term or short-term. To be classified as a long-term capital gain or loss, the capital asset must be held more than one year.[86] To determine the holding period, the day of acquisition is excluded and the disposal date is included.[87]

If the date of disposition is the same date as the date of acquisition, but a year later, the asset is considered to have been held for only one year. If the property is held for an additional day, the holding period is more than one year.

EXAMPLE I5-75

ADDITIONAL COMMENT

When determining the holding period for marketable securities, it is important to use the "trade" dates, not the "settlement" dates.

ADDITIONAL COMMENT

One June 1, 1995, the Securities and Exchange Commission adopted a new set of rules that will require investors who purchase or sell securities to deliver the funds to pay for the securities or deliver the certificates to be sold within three days of when the order is placed. Formerly, investors had five days to deliver funds or certificates.

EXAMPLE I5-76

▶ Arnie purchased a capital asset on April 20, 1996 and sells the asset at a gain on April 21, 1997. The gain is classified as a LTCG. If the asset is sold on or before April 20, 1997, the gain is a STCG. ◀

The fact that all months do not have the same number of days is not a factor in determining the one-year period. Acquisitions made on the last day of any month must be held until the first day of the thirteenth subsequent month in order to have been held for more than one year.

PROPERTY RECEIVED AS A GIFT

If a person receives property as a gift and uses the donor's basis to determine the gain or loss from a sale or exchange, the donor's holding period is added to the donee's holding period.[88] In other words, the donee's holding period includes the donor's holding period. If, however, the donee's basis is the FMV of the property on the date of the gift, the donee's holding period starts on the date of the gift. This situation occurs when the FMV is less than the donor's basis on the date of the gift and the property is subsequently sold at a loss.

▶ Cindy receives a capital asset as a gift from Marc on July 4, 1997, when the asset has a $4,000 FMV. Marc acquired the property on April 12, 1997 for $3,400. If Cindy sells the asset after

---

[83] *Walter M. Hort v. CIR*, 25 AFTR 1207, 41-1 USTC ¶9354 (USSC, 1941).
[84] *Farrelly-Walsh, Inc.*, 13 B.T.A. 923 (1928).
[85] Sec. 1241.
[86] Sec. 1222. A six-month holding period was applied to property acquired after June 27, 1984 and before January 1, 1988.

[87] *H. M. Hooper*, 26 B.T.A. 758 (1932), and Rev. Rul. 70-598, 1970-2 C.B. 168.
[88] Sec. 1223(1) and Reg. Sec. 1.1223-1(b).

April 12, 1998, any gain or loss will be a LTCG or LTCL. Cindy's basis is the donor's cost because the FMV of the property is higher than the donor's basis on the date of the gift. Because Cindy takes Marc's basis, Marc's holding period is tacked on. ◄

EXAMPLE I5-77 ▶ Roy receives a capital asset as a gift from Diane on September 12, 1997, when the asset has a $6,000 FMV. Diane acquired the asset on July 1, 1996, for $6,500. If the asset is sold at a gain (i.e., for more than $6,500), Roy's holding period starts on July 1, 1996, the date when Diane acquired the property, because the donor's basis of $6,500 is used by Roy to compute the gain. If the asset is sold at a loss (i.e., for less than $6,000), Roy's holding period does not start until the date of the gift—September 12, 1997—because Roy's basis is the $6,000 FMV. The FMV is used to compute the loss because it is less than the donor's basis on the date of the gift. ◄

ADDITIONAL COMMENT

The provision permitting the holding period of property received from a decedent to be deemed to be long-term is a rule of convenience. It is not necessary to try to determine when the decedent actually acquired the property.

PROPERTY RECEIVED FROM A DECEDENT

The holding period of property received from a decedent is always deemed to be long-term. The actual time the property is held by the decedent, estate, or heirs is disregarded.[89] Therefore, if the estate or heirs sell or otherwise dispose of property immediately after the decedent's death, the property is deemed to have been held long-term.

EXAMPLE I5-78 ▶ The executor of Paul's estate sells certain securities for $41,000 on September 2, 1997, which are valued in the estate at their FMV of $40,000 on June 5, 1997, the date of Paul's death. The estate has a LTCG of $1,000 because the securities are considered to have been held long-term. ◄

NONTAXABLE EXCHANGES

In a nontaxable exchange, the basis of the property received is determined by taking into account the basis of the property given in the exchange. If the properties are capital assets or Sec. 1231 assets, the holding period of the property received includes the holding period of the surrendered property.[90] In essence, the holding period of the property given up in a tax-free exchange is tacked on to the holding period of the property received in the exchange.

RECEIPT OF NONTAXABLE STOCK DIVIDENDS AND STOCK RIGHTS

If a shareholder receives nontaxable stock dividends or stock rights, the holding period of the stock received as a dividend or the stock rights received includes the holding period for the stock owned by the shareholder.[91] However, if the stock rights are exercised, the holding period for the stock purchased begins with the date of exercise.

EXAMPLE I5-79 ▶ As a result of owning Circle Corporation stock acquired three years ago, Paula receives nontaxable stock rights on June 5, 1997. Any gain or loss on the sale of the rights is long-term, regardless of whether any basis is allocated to the rights, because the holding period of the rights includes the holding period of the stock. ◄

EXAMPLE I5-80 ▶ Assume the same facts as in Example I5-79, except that the stock rights are exercised on August 20, 1997. The holding period for the newly acquired Circle stock begins on the date of exercise. ◄

---

[89] Sec. 1223(11).
[90] Sec. 1223(1).

[91] Sec. 1223(5) and Reg. Sec. 1.1223-1(e).

PREFERENTIAL TREATMENT FOR NET CAPITAL GAINS

HISTORICAL NOTE

In part the preferential treatment of net capital gains was repealed in the Tax Reform Act of 1986 because Congress believed that the reduction of individual tax rates on such forms of capital income as business profits, interest, dividends, and short-term capital gains eliminated the need for a reduced rate for net capital gains.

Preferential treatment for capital gains was first created by the Revenue Act of 1921, which became effective on January 1, 1922. Despite almost continuous controversy concerning the need for preferential treatment, some form of preferential treatment for capital gains has existed since 1922. The range of controversy concerning the need for preferential tax treatment for capital gains is wide. Some maintain that capital gains do not represent income and should not be taxed, whereas others maintain that capital gains are no different from any other type of income and should be taxed accordingly.[92] A few of the most common arguments are discussed below.

MOBILITY OF CAPITAL

Without some form of preferential treatment, taxpayers who own appreciated capital assets may be unwilling to sell or exchange the asset if high tax rates exist, despite the presence of more attractive investment opportunities. In essence, the taxpayer may be "locked in" to holding an appreciated capital asset instead of shifting resources to more profitable investments.

EXAMPLE I5-81 ▶

Carmen owns Missouri Corporation stock with a $4,000 basis and a $20,000 FMV. She anticipates that the future after-tax annual return will be 10% on the Missouri stock and 12% on Kansas Corporation stock that has a similar level of risk. Assume her marginal tax rate is 50% (without consideration of favorable capital gain rates or deductions). Without preferential treatment of capital gains, Carmen will have to pay a tax of $8,000 ($16,000 × 0.50) on the sale of the Missouri stock and will have only $12,000 ($20,000 − $8,000) to invest in the Kansas stock. With a 12% return, she will receive an investment return of only $1,440 ($12,000 × 0.12), as compared with $2,000 ($20,000 × 0.10) if she maintains the investment in the Missouri stock. ◀

ADDITIONAL COMMENT

The American Assembly at Columbia University, in its final report on *Reforming and Simplifying the Federal Tax System* issued in 1985, recommends that capital gains be taxed as ordinary income if they are adjusted for inflation.

The "locked-in" effect is reduced if tax rates are lowered. The justification for eliminating the special 60% deduction for long-term capital gains after 1986 was due to a significant reduction in the top marginal tax rate applicable to ordinary income.

MITIGATION OF THE EFFECTS OF INFLATION AND THE PROGRESSIVE TAX SYSTEM

Because the tax laws do not generally reflect the effect of changes in purchasing power due to inflation, the sale or exchange of a capital asset may produce inequitable results. In fact, taxes may have to be paid even where a transaction results in an inflation-adjusted loss.

EXAMPLE I5-82 ▶

Beverly purchased a capital asset nine years ago for $100,000. If the asset is sold today for $180,000 and the general price level has increased by 100% during the nine-year period, Beverly will have a taxable gain of $80,000, despite suffering an inflation-adjusted loss of $20,000 [$180,000 sale price − ($100,000 × 200%)]. ◀

With a progressive tax system, the failure to adjust for inflation creates an even greater distortion. However, it should be noted that this distortion applies to all assets, not just capital assets.

---

[92] Walter J. Blum, "A Handy Summary of the Capital Gains Argument," *Taxes—The Tax Magazine*, 35 (April 1957), pp. 247–66.

OUTLOOK FOR INCREASED PREFERENTIAL TREATMENT FOR NET CAPITAL GAINS

Proponents for reinstatement of preferential treatment for capital gains cite the need to encourage capital formation to create more jobs and improve our competitive position in the global economy. Furthermore, it is anticipated that a reduction in the tax rate for capital gain income will temporarily increase tax revenue because taxpayers owning appreciated assets will be encouraged to sell. Those opposed to reintroducing preferential treatment for capital gains note the eventual decrease in revenue resulting from the lower rates and see such preferential treatment as benefiting high-income taxpayers.

Although former President George Bush advocated reinstatement of preferential capital gain treatment in the form of a deduction, Congress was unwilling to support his position. When the tax rate on ordinary income was increased by the Revenue Reconciliation Act of 1990 to 31%, Congress also provided for a 28% maximum tax rate on net capital gain recognized by noncorporate taxpayers in tax years beginning after 1990. In the Revenue Reconciliation Act of 1993, Congress did not change the tax rate on net capital gain, but the highest marginal tax rate was increased from 31% to 39.6% thus increasing the preferential treatment for some taxpayers with net capital gain. Congress did make one change that may suggest a goal of the Clinton administration to target preferential tax treatment. A new exclusion up to 50% of the gain realized on the disposition of qualified small business stock issued after August 10, 1993, is available for noncorporate taxpayers who hold qualified stock for more than five years.[93]

Congress has recently indicated support for increasing the preferential treatment for net capital gain. A tax bill that was vetoed in the Spring, 1996 contained a deduction of 50% of net capital gain which is similar to the tax treatment for net capital gain before 1987. Indexing the basis of certain assets acquired after December 31, 2000, for purposes of determining a gain was also included. Furthermore, the tax rate on net capital gains recognized by some corporations was to be reduced.

TAX PLANNING CONSIDERATIONS

SELECTION OF PROPERTY TO TRANSFER BY GIFT

Many tax reasons exist for making gifts of property, although the donor may incur a gift tax liability if the gift is a taxable gift. For example, taxpayers may give income-producing property to a taxpayer subject to a lower tax rate, or property expected to appreciate in the future may be given away to reduce estate taxes. Individuals may annually give property of $10,000 or less to a donee without making a taxable gift.[94]

EXAMPLE I5-83 ▶ Maya, who is single, owns marketable securities with a $6,200 basis and $10,000 FMV. She makes gifts of the marketable securities to Phil and cash of $10,000 to Roy. Because of the $10,000 annual exclusion per donee, Maya's gifts are not taxable gifts. ◀

EXAMPLE I5-84 ▶ Harry, who is single, makes a gift of land with a $240,000 basis and a $930,000 FMV to Rita. Harry's taxable gift is $920,000 ($930,000 − $10,000), and he incurs a gift tax liability. Rita's basis is $240,000 + 75% of the gift tax paid by Harry [(930,000 − 240,000)/920,000 × 75%]. ◀

---

[93] Sec. 1202(a). (See Chapter I4 for a discussion of this topic.)   [94] Sec. 2503(b).

Individuals often reduce future estate taxes by making gifts. By using the annual exclusion, an individual may reduce future estate taxes and avoid the gift tax.

EXAMPLE I5-85 ▶

Christine owns only one asset—cash of $900,000—and has no liabilities. In December of the current year, she gives $10,000 to each of her five grandchildren. Because of the $10,000 annual exclusion per donee, Christine's gifts are not taxable gifts. By making the gifts, she reduces her potential gross estate by $50,000 (5 × $10,000). ◀

ADDITIONAL COMMENT

A husband and wife can each make a $10,000 gift to their daughter, enabling her to receive a total of $20,000 annually without the parents incurring a gift tax.

The selection of which property to give is important if one is attempting to reduce future estate taxes. It is generally preferable to make gifts of properties that are expected to significantly increase in value during the postgift period before the donor's death. Any increases in value after the date of the gift are not included in the donor's gross estate.

EXAMPLE I5-86 ▶

In 1991, Hal owned Sun Corporation stock with a $100,000 FMV and Union Corporation stock with a $100,000 FMV. Hal expected the Sun stock to increase in value at a moderate rate and the Union stock to increase at a substantial rate. In 1991, Hal made a gift of the Union stock to Dana. Hal's taxable gift in 1991 was $90,000 ($100,000 − $10,000). Hal dies in the current year when the FMVs of the Sun and Union stocks are $180,000 and $425,000, respectively. The postgift appreciation of $325,000 ($425,000 − $100,000) is not included in Hal's gross estate. By giving the Union stock instead of the Sun stock in 1991, Hal reduces his gross estate. ◀

Gifts are often made for income tax purposes to shift income to other family members who are in a lower income tax bracket than the donor.

EXAMPLE I5-87 ▶

In 1997, Anne has a marginal tax rate of 28% and owns Atlantic Corporation bonds, which have a $5,000 basis and $8,000 FMV. The bonds pay interest of $700 per year. If Anne gives the bonds to a dependent child, the interest income is shifted to the child. If the child has no other income, the child's taxable income is $50 ($700 − $650 standard deduction), and the child's marginal tax rate is 15%. The gift results in an annual income tax savings to the family unit of $189 [(0.28 × $700) − (0.15 × $50)]. The rate of tax that is imposed may be the parent's rate (see Chapter I2) if the child is less than 14 years old and has net unearned income in excess of $1,300.

In addition to shifting the interest income, Anne has also shifted a potential gain of $3,000. The child's basis for the bonds is $5,000 because the donee takes the donor's basis when the FMV of the property at the time of the gift is greater than the donor's basis. No gain is recognized by Anne when the gift is made, and a future sale of the property by the child may be taxed at a lower income tax rate. ◀

Although gifts of appreciated property may generate desirable income tax benefits, it is not usually advantageous to make a gift of property that has an FMV less than its basis because the donee's basis for determining a loss is the FMV. The excess of the donor's basis over the FMV at the time of the gift may never generate any tax benefit for the donor or the donee. Therefore, the donor should sell the asset and make a gift of the proceeds if the loss on the sale is deductible.

EXAMPLE I5-88 ▶

Bob owns Red Corporation stock with an $8,000 basis and $6,000 FMV, which is held as an investment. Bob wishes to make a graduation gift of the marketable securities to Angela, although he expects her to sell the stock and purchase a car. If Angela sells the stock for $6,000, no gain or loss is recognized because her loss basis for the stock is $6,000. In addition, no loss is recognized by Bob on the gift of the stock to Angela. Instead of giving the stock, Bob should sell it to recognize a $2,000 capital loss and then give the proceeds from the sale to Angela. ◀

The effect of gift taxes paid by the donor on the donee's basis for property received is another reason why it may be more advantageous to give appreciated property rather than property with an FMV less than its basis. A portion of the gift taxes paid as a result of giving appreciated property is added to the property's basis. However, payment of gift taxes due to the gift of property that has an FMV less than its basis does not result in an increase in the donee's basis.

SELECTION OF PROPERTY TO TRANSFER AT TIME OF DEATH

An integral part of estate planning is the selection of property to be transferred to the heirs upon the taxpayer's death. Usually, taxpayers find it advantageous to retain highly appreciated property and transfer the property to the taxpayer's heirs because the basis of the inherited property will be increased to its FMV at the date of death (or six months from the date of death if the alternate valuation date is elected).

Investment and business assets that have declined in value (i.e., the FMV is less than the basis) should normally be sold before death to obtain an income tax deduction for the loss. If the property is not sold or otherwise disposed of before death, the basis of the inherited property is reduced to its FMV.

EXAMPLE 15-89 ▶

Paul owns two farms of similar size and quality. Each farm has a $500,000 FMV. Paul's basis for the first farm is $100,000, and his basis for the second farm is $430,000. Eventually, Paul plans for both farms to be owned by Roberta. However, he would like to transfer ownership of one farm now and retain the other farm until his death. Paul should make a gift of the second farm and transfer the first farm to Roberta upon his death because the second farm has appreciated less in value. When Paul dies and devises the first farm to Roberta, she will have a basis for the property equal to its FMV at the date of death even though Paul's basis is only $100,000. ◀

COMPLIANCE AND PROCEDURAL CONSIDERATIONS

DOCUMENTATION OF BASIS

The importance of being able to determine and document the basis of assets acquired by a taxpayer cannot be overemphasized. Accurate records of asset acquisitions, dispositions, and adjustments to basis are essential. When more than one asset is acquired at the same time, the amount paid must be allocated among the assets acquired based on their relative FMVs. Subsequent adjustments to basis, such as those due to capital improvements and depreciation deductions, must be documented.

Because the basis of property can be determined by reference to another person's basis for that asset (e.g., gifts), taxpayers should be particularly aware of obtaining documentation for that basis at the time of the transfer. In the case of a gift, the taxpayer's basis may be affected by any gift tax paid by the donor. A copy of the donor's gift tax return is useful in documenting the upward adjustment to the donor's basis in determining the donee's basis.

Taxpayers who inherit property may use the decedent's federal Estate Tax Return (Form 706) to determine the FMV at the time of the decedent's death or FMV as of the

SCHEDULE D
(Form 1040)

Department of the Treasury
Internal Revenue Service (99)

Capital Gains and Losses

▶ Attach to Form 1040.   ▶ See Instructions for Schedule D (Form 1040).

OMB No. 1545-0074

1996

Attachment
Sequence No. **12**

Name(s) shown on Form 1040

Virgil Brady

Your social security number

444 44 4444

Part I	Short-Term Capital Gains and Losses - Assets Held One Year or Less					
(a) Description of Property (Example: 100 sh. XYZ Co.)	**(b)** Date acquired / **(c)** Date sold	**(d)** Sales price (See page D-3)	**(e)** Cost or other basis (See page D-3)	**(f)** LOSS If (e) is more than (d), subtract (d) from (e)	**(g)** GAIN If (d) is more than (e), subtract (e) from (d)
1 200 Tennis Corp	10-2-94 / 6-20-95	13,000	8,700		4,300

2 Enter your short-term totals, if any, from line 21 .... **2**

3 **Total short-term sales price amounts.** Add column (d) of lines 1 and 2 ...... **3** | 13,000

4 Short-term gain from Forms 2119 and 6252, and short-term gain or loss from Forms 4684, 6781, and 8824 ...... **4**

5 Net short-term gain or loss from partnerships, S corporations, estates, and trusts from Schedule(s) K-1 ...... **5**

6 Short-term capital loss carryover. Enter the amount, if any, from line 9 of your 1995 Capital Loss Carryover Worksheet ...... **6** | 8,200

7 Add lines 1 through 6, in columns (f) and (g) **7** (8,200)   4,300

8 **Net short-term capital gain or (loss).** Combine columns (f) and (g) of line 7 ...... ▶ **8** (3,900)

Part II	Long-Term Capital Gains and Losses - Assets Held More Than One Year					
9 Piano	4-12-86 / 5-30-95	4,000	2,500		1,500

10 Enter your long-term totals, if any, from line 23 .... **10**

11 **Total long-term sales price amounts.** Add column (d) of lines 9 and 10 ...... **11** | 4,000

12 Gain from Form 4797; long-term gain from Forms 2119, 2439, and 6252; and long-term gain or loss from Forms 4684, 6781, and 8824 ...... **12**

13 Net long-term gain or loss from partnerships, S corporations, estates, and trusts from Schedule(s) K-1 ...... **13**

14 Capital gain distributions **14**

15 Long-term capital loss carryover. Enter the amount, if any, from line 14 of your 1995 Capital Loss Carryover Worksheet **15**

16 Add lines 9 through 15, in columns (f) and (g) ...... **16** ( )   1,500

17 **Net long-term capital gain or (loss).** Combine columns (f) and (g) of line 16 ...... ▶ **17** 1,500

Part III	Summary of Parts I and II

18 Combine lines 8 and 17. If a loss, go to line 19. If a gain, enter the gain on Form 1040, line 13.
Note: If both lines 17 and 18 are gains, see the **Capital Gain Tax Worksheet** on page 23 ...... **18** (2,400)

19 If line 18 is a loss, enter here and as a (loss) on Form 1040, line 13, the **smaller** of these losses:

a The loss on line 18; **or**

b ($3,000) or, if married filing separately, ($1,500) **19** (2,400)

Note: See the **Capital Loss Carryover Worksheet** on page D-3 if the loss on line 18 exceeds the loss on line 19 **or** if Form 1040, line 35, is a loss.

LHA   For Paperwork Reduction Act Notice, see Form 1040 instructions.

Schedule D (Form 1040) 1996

62051 1/12-20-96

FIGURE I5-1   ▶   PARTS I-III OF SCHEDULE D FOR EXAMPLE I5-90

alternate valuation date. However, the appraised value used for estate tax purposes is only presumptively correct for basis purposes. Although the FMVs used to determine the estate tax are typically used to determine basis, neither the taxpayer nor the IRS is barred from using an FMV for basis purposes that differs from the values used for the estate tax return.[95]

REPORTING OF CAPITAL GAINS AND LOSSES ON SCHEDULE D

Capital gains and losses are reported by individuals on Schedule D, which is then attached to Form 1040. Part I is used to report short-term capital gains and losses, and Part II is used to report long-term capital gains and losses. Parts IV and V are used to list individual sales or dispositions of capital gain or loss properties if additional space is needed on Parts I and II on page 1 of Schedule D. If the 28% ceiling rate on net capital gain is applicable, the taxpayer's total tax is computed on a tax worksheet that is included in the Instructions for Schedule D. The total tax is then entered on line 38 of page 2 of Form 1040.

Capital gains due to the sale of a principal residence or due to installment sales are first reported on separate forms before being included on Schedule D. The taxpayer's share of capital gains and losses from partnerships, S corporations, and fiduciaries is reported in Parts I and II. The carryover of capital losses is also included in Parts I and II.

A filled-in copy of Schedule D is shown in Figure I5-1. It includes the computations relating to the information in Example I5-90.

EXAMPLE I5-90 ▶ Virgil Brady uses the following information to prepare his Schedule D for 1996. He sold 200 shares of Tennis Corporation stock for $13,000 on June 20, 1996. The shares were purchased on October 2, 1995 for $8,700. He has an STCL carryforward from 1995 of $8,200. He sold a piano for $4,000 on May 30, 1996. The piano was purchased on April 12, 1987 for $2,500 and used by his two sons.

Virgil has an STCG of $4,300 that is offset by the $8,200 of STCL carryforward on line 6. His NSTCL of $3,900 ($8,200 − $4,300) is shown on line 8. His $1,500 LTCG as a result of the sale of the piano is on line 9. Because this is his only sale of a capital asset held more than one year, his NLTCG on line 17 is 1,500.

On line 18, the NSTCL of $3,900 and NLTCG of $1,500 are combined and shown on line 18 as $2,400. This net capital loss of $2,400 is recorded on line 19 and is deducted on line 13 of Form 1040. ◀

To improve taxpayer compliance with respect to the reporting of sales and exchanges, every person doing business as a broker is required to furnish the government with information pertaining to each customer, including gross proceeds due to any sales or exchanges.[96] The Tax Reform Act of 1986 extended this requirement to real estate brokers and defined the term *real estate broker* as meaning "any of the following persons involved in a real estate transaction in the following order: the person responsible for closing the transaction, the mortgage lender, the seller's broker, or the buyer's broker."[97] The information provided by the broker to the government must be reported to each customer on Form 1099-B. Taxpayers must use Schedule D to reconcile amounts shown on Form 1099-B with the taxpayer's income tax return.

---

[95] Rev. Rul. 54-97, 1954-1 C.B. 113 and *Achille F. Ford v. U.S.*, 5 AFTR 2d 1157, 60-1 USTC ¶9375 (Ct. Cls., 1960).

[96] Sec. 6045(a).

[97] Sec. 6045(c).

PROBLEM MATERIALS

DISCUSSION QUESTIONS

I5-1 What problem may exist in determining the amount realized for an investor who exchanges common stock of a publicly traded corporation for a used building? How is the problem likely to be resolved?

I5-2 In 1987 Ellen purchased a house for $60,000 to use as her personal residence. She paid $12,000 and borrowed $48,000 from the local savings and loan company. In 1989 she paid $10,000 to add a room to the house. In 1991 she paid $625 to have the house painted and $800 for built-in bookshelves. As of January 1 of the current year, she has reduced the $48,000 mortgage to $44,300. What is her basis for the house?

I5-3 Vincent pays $20,000 for equipment to use in his trade or business. He pays sales tax of $800 as a result of the purchase. Must the $800 sales tax be capitalized as part of the purchase price?

I5-4 Sergio owns 200 shares of Palm Corporation common stock, which were purchased during the prior year: 100 shares on July 5, for $9,000; and 100 shares on October 15, for $12,000. When Sergio sells 50 shares for $8,000 on July 18 of the current year, he does not identify the particular shares sold. What are the amount and character of the gain on the sale?

I5-5 On August 5 of the current year, David receives stock of Western Corporation as a gift from his grandfather, who acquired the stock on January 15, 1987. Under what conditions would David's holding period start on
a. August 5 of the current year?
b. January 15, 1987?

I5-6 Jim inherits property from his brother, who dies in March of the current year, when the property has a $980,000 FMV. This property is the only property included in his brother's gross estate and there is a taxable estate. The FMV of the property as of the alternate valuation date is $900,000.
a. Why might the executor of the brother's estate elect to use the alternate valuation date to value the property?
b. Why might Jim prefer the executor to use FMV at time of the death to value the property?
c. If the marginal estate tax rate is 37% and Jim's marginal income tax rate is 28%, which value should the executor use?

I5-7 Martha owns 500 shares of Columbus Corporation common stock at the beginning of the year with a basis of $82,500. During the year, Columbus declares and pays a 10% nontaxable stock dividend. What is her basis for each of the 50 shares received?

I5-8 Mario owns 2,000 shares of Nevada Corporation common stock at the beginning of the year. His basis for the stock is $38,880. During the year, Nevada declares and pays a stock dividend. After the dividend, Mario's basis for each share of stock owned is $18. What is the percentage dividend paid by Nevada?

I5-9 A corporate taxpayer plans to build a $6 million office building during the next eighteen months. How must the corporation treat the interest on debt paid or incurred during the production period?

I5-10 Andy owns an appliance store where he has merchandise such as refrigerators for sale. Roger, a bachelor, owns a refrigerator, which he uses in his apartment for personal use. For which individual is the refrigerator a capital asset?

I5-11 Why did the Supreme Court rule in the *Corn Products* case that a gain due to the sale of futures contracts is ordinary income instead of capital gain?

I5-12 When is the gain on the sale or exchange of securities by a dealer in securities classified as capital gain?

I5-13 In 1982, Florence purchased 30 acres of land. She has not used the land for business purposes or made any substantial improvements to the property. During the current year, she subdivides the land into 15 lots and advertises the lots for sale. She sells four lots at a gain.
a. What is the character of the gain on the sale of the four lots?
b. Explain how the basis of each lot would be determined.

I5-14 Mr. and Mrs. Smith file a joint return for the current year and have $95,000 of taxable income without considering a $10,000 net capital gain. What is their marginal tax rate for the $10,000 net capital gain?

I5-15 Four years ago, Susan loaned $7,000 to her friend Joe. During the current year, the $7,000 loan is considered worthless. Explain how Susan should treat the worthless debt for tax purposes.

I5-16 Why did the Supreme Court rule in *Arkansas Best* that the stock of a corporation purchased by the taxpayer to protect the taxpayer's business reputation was a capital asset?

I5-17 The Top Corporation, a producer of lumber, acquires 25% of the stock of the First Corporation, which operates retail lumber yards. Top's primary reason for making the purchase is to obtain a potential customer. Explain how the *Corn Products* case could be used to argue that the stock of First owned by Top is not a capital asset. Explain how the *Arkansas Best* case could be used to argue that the stock of First owned by Top is a capital asset.

I5-18 Ohio Corporation purchases stock of Buckeye Corporation for investment purposes and to acquire a source of raw materials. If Ohio Corporation later sells the stock at a gain, is the gain taxed as ordinary income or capital gain?

I5-19 Nancy and the Minor Corporation own bonds of the East Corporation. Minor Corporation owns 80% of the stock of East Corporation. East Corporation has declared bankruptcy this year, and bondholders will receive only 26% of the face value of the debt. Explain why the loss is a capital loss for Nancy but an ordinary loss for the Minor Corporation.

I5-20 On January 1 of the current year, the Orange Corporation issues $500,000 of 11%, 20-year bonds for $480,000. Determine the amount of original issue discount, if any.

I5-21 Today, Juanita purchases a 15-year, 7% bond of the Sunflower Corporation that was issued four years ago at par. She purchases the bond as an investment at a discount from the par value. If she sells the bonds two years from now, explain why some or all of the gain may be ordinary income.

I5-22 Judy just obtained a patent on a new product she has developed. Bell Corporation wishes to market the product and will pay 12% of all future sales of the product to Judy. How can she be sure that the payments received will be treated as a long-term capital gain?

I5-23 When is the transferor of a franchise unable to treat the transfer as a sale or an exchange of a capital asset?

I5-24 How does a lessor treat payments received for canceling a lease?

I5-25 What is the first day that an individual could sell a capital asset purchased on March 31, 1997 and have a holding period of more than a year?

I5-26 Phil, a cash-basis taxpayer, sells the following marketable securities, which are capital assets during 1997. Determine whether the gains or losses are long-term or short-term. Also determine the net capital gain for 1997.

Capital Asset	Basis	Date Acquired	Trade Date in 1997	Sales Price
A	$40,000	Feb. 10, 1996	Aug. 12	$52,000
B	20,000	Dec. 5, 1996	May 2	17,000
C	30,000	Apr. 9, 1995	Dec. 10	37,400

I5-27   How might the current treatment of capital losses discourage an individual investor from purchasing stock of a high-risk, start-up company?

I5-28   An individual taxpayer has realized a $40,000 loss on the sale of an asset that had a holding period of eight months. Explain why the taxpayer may be indifferent as to whether the asset is a capital asset.

I5-29   If Pam transfers an asset to Fred and the asset is subject to a liability that is assumed by Fred, how does Fred's assumption of the liability affect the amount realized by Pam? How does Fred's assumption of the liability affect his basis for the property?

I5-30   Calvin, whose tax rate is 40% is considering two alternative investments on January 1, 19Y1. He can purchase $100,000 of 10% bonds due in five years or purchase $100,000 of Hobbes, Inc. common stock. The bonds are issued at par, pay interest annually on December 31, and mature at the end of five years. Interest received can be reinvested at 10%. Assume that he knows with relative certainty that the value of the stock will increase 8% each year (i.e., the value of the Hobbes stock will be $108,000 at the end of 19Y1) and the interest and principal for the bonds will be paid as scheduled. On December 31, 19Y5, he will sell the stock or receive the bond principal plus the last interest payment. Which alternative should Calvin select if he wants to have the greater amount of money as of January 1, 19Y6? Provide supporting information for your answer.

ISSUE IDENTIFICATION QUESTIONS

I5-31   Acorn Corporation, a company that purchases malt barley from farmers and sells it to brewers, is interested in determining whether a new variety of barley will grow successfully in the Pacific Northwest. The corporation has acquired the seed from Europe and will conduct the experiments with the cooperation of farmers in the area. If the experiments prove successful, Acorn will sell the remaining seed to the farmers. What tax issues should Acorn Corporation consider?

I5-32   Lisa and John are in the business of breeding beavers to produce fur for sale. They recently purchased a pair of breeding beavers for $30,000 from XUN, Inc. and agreed to pay interest at 10% each year for five years. After the five-year period, they could pay the debt by delivering seven beavers to XUN, Inc. provided that each beaver was at least nine months old. Identify the tax issues involved in this situation.

I5-33   Mike, a real estate broker in California, recently inherited a farm from his deceased uncle and plans to sell the farm to the first available buyer. His uncle purchased the property twelve years ago for $600,000. The FMV of the farm on the date of the uncle's death was $500,000. Mike sells the farm for $520,000 seven months after his uncle's death. What tax issues should Mike consider?

I5-34   Sylvia, a dentist with a marginal tax rate of 39.6% and excellent skills as a carpenter, started the construction of a house that she planned to give to her son as a surprise when he returned from Saudia Arabia, where he is serving in the military. She began construction on March 23, 1996, and finished the house on July 10, 1997 at a total cost of $70,000. Her son is expected to be home on September 1, 1997.

On July 30, 1997, Roscoe offered Sylvia $145,000 for the house and Sylvia considered the offer to be so attractive that she accepted it. She decided that she could purchase a suitable home for her son for about $100,000. What tax issues should Sylvia consider?

PROBLEMS

I5-35 *Amount Realized.* Tracy owns a nondepreciable capital asset that is held for investment. The asset was purchased for $150,000 six years earlier and is now subject to a $45,000 liability. During the current year, Tracy transfers the asset to Tim in exchange for $74,000 cash and a new automobile with a $40,000 FMV that is to be used by Tracy for personal use; Tim assumes the $45,000 liability. Determine the amount of Tracy's LTCG or LTCL.

I5-36 *Basis of Property Received as a Gift.* Doug receives a duplex as a gift from his uncle. The uncle's basis for the duplex and land is $90,000. At the time of the gift, the land and building have FMVs of $40,000 and $80,000, respectively. No gift tax is paid by Doug's uncle at the time of the gift.
a. To determine gain, what is Doug's basis for the land?
b. To determine gain, what is Doug's basis for the building?
c. Will the basis of the land and building be the same as in Parts a and b for purposes of determining a loss?

I5-37 *Sale of Property Received as a Gift.* During the current year, Stan sells a tract of land for $800,000. The property was received as a gift from Maxine on March 10, 1987, when the property had a $310,000 FMV. The taxable gift was $300,000. Maxine purchased the property on April 12, 1980, for $110,000. At the time of the gift, Maxine paid a gift tax of $12,000. In order to sell the property, Stan paid a sales commission of $16,000.
a. What is Stan's realized gain on the sale?
b. How would your answer to Part a change, if at all, if the FMV of the gift property was $85,000 as of the date of the gift?

I5-38 *Sale of Asset Received as a Gift.* Bud receives 200 shares of Georgia Corporation stock from his uncle on July 20, 1997, when the stock has a $45,000 FMV. The taxable gift is $45,000, since his uncle made another gift to Bud for $10,000 in January. The uncle pays a gift tax of $1,500. The uncle paid $30,000 for the stock on April 12, 1992.
  Without considering the transactions below, Bud has AGI of $25,000 in 1997. No other transactions involving capital assets occur during the year. Analyze each transaction below, independent of the others, and determine Bud's AGI in each case.
a. He sells the stock on October 12, 1998, for $48,000.
b. He sells the stock on October 12, 1998, for $28,000.
c. He sells the stock on December 16, 1997, for $42,000.

I5-39 *Basis of Property Converted from Personal Use.* Irene owns a truck costing $15,000 and used for personal activities. The truck has a $9,600 FMV when it is transferred to her business, which is operated as a sole proprietorship.
a. What is the basis of the truck for determining depreciation?
b. What is Irene's realized gain or loss if the truck is sold for $5,000 after claiming depreciation of $4,000?

I5-40   ***Stock Rights.*** Cathy owns 100 shares of Atlanta Corporation common stock. She purchased the stock on July 25, 1986, for $4,000. On May 2 of the current year, she receives a nontaxable distribution of 100 stock rights. Each stock right has a $10 FMV, and the FMV of the Atlanta common stock is $70 per share. With each stock right, Cathy may acquire one share of Atlanta common for $68 per share. Assuming that Cathy elects to allocate basis to the stock rights, answer the following:

    a. What is the basis allocated to the stock rights?

    b. If she sells the stock rights on June 10 for $1,080, what are the amount and character of the recognized gain?

    c. If she exercises the stock rights on May 14, what is the basis of the 100 shares purchased and when does the holding period start?

    d. If she does not elect to allocate basis to the stock rights, what are the amount and character of the gain if she sells the stock rights on June 10 for $1,080?

I5-41   ***Real Property Subdivided for Sale.*** Beth acquired only one tract of land seven years ago as an investment. In order to sell the land at a higher price, she decides to subdivide it into 20 lots. She pays for improvements such as clearing and leveling, but the improvements are not considered to be substantial. Each lot has a basis of $2,000, and a selling price of $6,000. Selling expenses of $480 were incurred to sell two lots last year. This year, ten lots are sold, and selling expenses amount to $1,900. How much ordinary income and capital gain must be recognized in the prior and current year?

I5-42   ***Computing the Tax.*** Donna files as a head of household in 1997 and has taxable income of $90,000, including the sale of a capital asset at a gain of $20,000. Only one asset was sold during the year and Donna does not have any capital loss carryovers.

    a. What is the amount of Donna's tax liability if the gain is a LTCG?

    b. What is the amount of Donna's tax liability if the gain is a STCG?

I5-43   ***Computing the Tax.*** Wayne is single and has no dependents. Without considering his $11,000 net capital gain, his taxable income in 1997 is as follows:

AGI		$121,200
Interest on acquisition debt	$22,000	
State and local income taxes	8,000	
Charitable contributions	7,000	
Personal exemption	2,650	39,650
Taxable income		$ 81,550

    a. What is Wayne's tax liability without the net capital gain?

    b. What is Wayne's tax liability with the net capital gain?

I5-44   ***Computing the Sales Price.*** An investor in a 28% tax bracket owns a capital asset with a $60,000 basis and a holding period of more than one year. The investor wishes to sell the asset at a price high enough so that he will have $90,000 in cash after paying the taxes. What is the minimum price which the investor could accept?

I5-45   ***Capital Gains and Losses.*** Consider the four independent situations below for an unmarried individual, and analyze the effects of the capital gains and losses on the individual's AGI. For each case, determine AGI after considering the capital gains and losses.

	Situation 1	Situation 2	Situation 3	Situation 4
AGI (excluding property transactions)	$40,000	$50,000	$60,000	$70,000
STCG	6,000	2,000	5,000	6,000
STCL	2,000	5,000	4,000	15,000
LTCG	3,500	15,000	10,000	9,000
LTCL	2,500	4,000	12,000	4,000

I5-46 *Capital Losses.* To better understand the rules for offsetting capital losses and how to treat capital losses carried forward, analyze the following data for an unmarried individual for the period 1994 through 1997. No capital loss carryforwards are included in the figures. For each year, determine AGI and the capital losses to be carried forward to a later tax year.

	1994	1995	1996	1997
AGI (excluding property transactions)	$40,000	$50,000	$60,000	$70,000
STCG	4,000	5,000	7,000	10,000
STCL	9,000	3,000	5,000	12,000
LTCG	6,000	10,000	2,200	6,000
LTCL	5,000	21,000	1,000	9,500
AGI (including property transactions)	———	———	———	———
STCL to be carried forward	———	———	———	———
LTCL to be carried forward	———	———	———	———

I5-47 *Character of Loss.* The Michigan Corporation owns 20% of the Wolverine Corporation. The Wolverine stock was acquired eight years ago to ensure a steady supply of raw materials. Michigan also owns 30% of Spartan Corporation and 85% of Huron Corporation. Stock in both corporations was acquired more than ten years ago for investment purposes. During the current year, Wolverine, Spartan, and Huron are deemed bankrupt, and the stocks are considered worthless. Describe how Michigan should treat its losses.

I5-48 *Original Issue Discount.* On December 31, 1996, Phil purchased $20,000 of newly issued bonds of Texas Corporation for $16,568. The bonds are dated December 31, 1996. The bonds are 9%, 10-year bonds paying interest semiannually on June 30 and December 31. The bonds are priced to yield 12% compounded semiannually.
a. What is the amount of the original issue discount?
b. For the first semiannual period, what is the amount of the original issue discount Phil must recognize as ordinary income?
c. What is the total amount of interest income Phil must recognize in 1997?
d. What is Phil's basis for the bonds as of December 31, 1997?

I5-49 On January 1, 1995, Swen paid $184,000 for $200,000 of the 8%, 20-year bonds of Penn Corporation, issued on January 1, 1991, at par. The bonds are held as an investment.

Determine the gain and the character of the gain if the bonds are sold on January 1, 1997 for

a. $191,000

b. $185,750

c. $183,000

I5-50 *Capital Gains and Losses.* During 1997, Gary receives a $50,000 salary and has no deductions for AGI. In 1996, Gary had a $5,000 STCL and no other capital losses or capital gains. Consider the following sales and determine Gary's AGI for 1997.

- An automobile purchased in 1992 for $10,800 and held for personal use is sold for $7,000.

- On April 10, 1997, stock held for investment is sold for $21,000. The stock was acquired on November 20, 1996, for $9,300.

I5-51 *Call Options.* On February 10, 1997, Gail purchases 20 calls on Red Corporation for $250 per call. Each call represents an option to buy 100 shares of Red stock at $42 per share any time before November 25, 1997. Compute the gain or loss recognized, and determine whether the gain or loss is long-term or short-term for Gail in the following situations:

a. The 20 calls are sold on May 15, 1997, for $310 per call.

b. The calls are not exercised but allowed to expire.

c. The calls are exercised on July 15, 1997 and the 2,000 shares of Red Corporation stock are sold on July 20, 1998, for $50 per share.

I5-52 *Call Writing.* Dan owns 500 shares of Rocket Corporation common stock. The stock was acquired two years ago for $30 per share. On October 2, 1997, Dan writes five calls on the stock, which represent options to buy the 500 shares of Rocket at $75 per share. For each call, Dan receives $210. The calls expire on June 22, 1998. Consider the following transactions and describe the tax treatment for Dan:

a. The five calls are exercised on December 4, 1997.

b. The calls are not exercised and allowed to expire.

I5-53 *Gains and Losses and Basis.* Betty incurs the following transactions during the current year. Without considering the transactions, her 1997 AGI is $40,000. Analyze the transactions and answer the questions below:

- On March 10, 1997, she sells a painting for $2,000. Betty is the artist, and her basis for the painting is $50.

- On June 18, 1997, she receives $28,500 from the sale of stock purchased by her uncle in 1988 for $10,000, which she inherits on February 20, 1997 as a result of her uncle's death. The stock's FMV on that date is $30,000.

- On July 30, 1997, she sells land for $25,000 that was received as a gift from her brother on April 8, 1997, when the land's FMV was $30,000. Her brother purchased the land for $43,000 on October 12, 1989. No gift tax was paid.

a. What is her NSTCL or NSTCG?

b. What is her NLTCL or NLTCG?

c. What is the effect of capital gains and losses on her AGI?

d. What is her capital loss carryforward to 1998?

I5-54   ***Corporate Capital Gains and Losses.*** Determine the taxable income for the Columbia Corporation for the following independent cases:

Case	Income from Operations	STCG (NSTCL)	NLTCG (NLTCL)
A	$110,000	$30,000	$44,000
B	100,000	(50,000)	65,000
C	80,000	(37,000)	30,000
D	90,000	(15,000)	(9,000)

I5-55   ***Original Issue Discount.*** On January 1, 1996, Sean purchased an 8%, $100,000 corporate bond for $92,277. The bond is issued on January 1, 1996 and matures on January 1, 2001. Interest is paid semiannually, and the effective yield to maturity is 10% compounded semiannually. On July 1, 1997, Sean sells the bond for $95,949. A schedule of interest amortization for the bond is shown in Table I5-2 on page 5-44.

a. How much interest income must Sean recognize in 1996?

b. How much interest income must Sean recognize in 1997?

c. How much gain must Sean recognize in 1997 on the sale of the bond?

I5-56   ***Basis and Shifting Income.*** Dale purchased Blue Corporation stock six years ago for $1,000 as an investment. He intends to hold the stock until funds are needed to help pay for his daughter's college education. Today the stock has a $6,500 FMV and Dale decides to sell the stock and give the proceeds, less any taxes paid on the sale, to Tammy, his 18-year-old daughter. Dale's marginal tax rate is 28% and Tammy's marginal tax rate is 15%.

a. After the sale and payment of taxes, how much cash will be given to Tammy?

b. If Dale gives the stock to Tammy and she sells the stock for $6,500, how much cash will Tammy have available for college?

▼ **TABLE I5-2**

Interest Amortization for Problem I5-55

	Interest Received (1)	Amortization of Discount (2)	Interest Income (3) = (1) + (2)
6-30-96	$4,000	$614	$4,614
12-31-96	4,000	645	4,645
6-30-97	4,000	677	4,677
12-31-97	4,000	711	4,711
6-30-98	4,000	747	4,747
12-31-98	4,000	783	4,783
6-30-99	4,000	823	4,823
12-31-99	4,000	864	4,864
6-30-00	4,000	907	4,907
12-31-00	4,000	952	4,952

I5-57   *Capital Gains and Losses.* Martha has $40,000 AGI without considering the following information. During the year, she incurs a LTCL of $10,000 and has a gain of $14,000 due to the sale of a capital asset held for more than a year.

   a. If the $14,000 gain is not properly classified as a LTCG (i.e., is improperly treated as an ordinary gain), determine Martha's AGI.

   b. If the $14,000 gain is properly classified as a LTCG, determine her AGI.

   c. If Martha has a $2,500 STCL carryover from earlier years, how would the answers to Parts a and b be affected?

I5-58   *Corporate Capital Gains and Losses.* In 1992, the City Corporation sold a capital asset and incurred a $40,000 LTCL that was carried forward to subsequent years. That sale was the only sale of a capital asset that City had made until 1997, when City sells a capital asset and recognizes a STCG of $53,000. Without considering the STCG from the sale, City's taxable income is $250,000.

   a. Determine the corporation's NSTCG for 1997.

   b. Determine the corporation's 1997 taxable income.

   c. If the sale of the asset in 1992 had occurred in 1991, determine the corporation's 1997 taxable income.

TAX FORM/RETURN PREPARATION PROBLEMS

TAX CUT

I5-59   Given the following information for Jane Cole, complete Schedule D of Form 1040 through Part III.

- Stock options, which she purchases on February 14 of the current year for $850, expire on October 1.

- On July 1, she sells for $1,500 her personal-use automobile acquired on March 31, 1985 for $8,000.

- On August 16, she sells for $3,100 her stock of York Corporation purchased as an investment on February 16, for $1,600.

- On March 15, she sells for $5,600 an antique brass bed, a gift from her grandmother on January 10, 1988, when its FMV was $1,600. The bed was purchased by her grandmother on April 2, 1979 for $1,800.

- She has a STCL carryover of $250 from last year.

I5-60   Spencer Duck (Soc. Sec. no. 277-31-7264) is single and his eight-year-old son, Mitch, lives with him nine months of the year in a rented condominium at 321 Hickory Drive in Ames, Iowa. Mitch lives with his mother, Spencer's ex-wife, during the summer months. His mother provides more than half of Mitch's support and Spencer has agreed to allow her to claim Mitch as her dependent. Spencer has a salary of $34,000 and itemized deductions of $4,000. Taxes withheld during the year amount to $9,000. On July 14 of the current year, he sold the following assets:

- Land was sold for $35,000. The land was received as a property settlement on January 10, 1989, when the land's FMV amounted to $30,000. His ex-wife's basis for the land, purchased on January 10, 1975, was $18,600.

- A personal-use computer acquired on March 2 last year for $4,000 was sold for $2,480.

- A membership card for a prestigious country club was sold for $8,500. The card was acquired on October 10, 1985 for $6,000.

- Marketable securities held as an investment were sold for $20,000. The securities were inherited from his uncle, who died on March 10 of the current year when FMV of the securities was $21,000. The uncle purchased the securities on May 10, 1985 for $10,700.

In addition to the above sales, Spencer received a $100 refund of state income taxes paid last year. Spencer used the standard deduction last year to compute his tax liability. Prepare Form 1040 and Schedule D for the current year.

CASE STUDY PROBLEMS

I5-61   As a political consultant for an aspiring politician, you have been hired to evaluate the following statements that pertain to capital gains and losses. Evaluate the statement and provide at least a one-paragraph explanation of each statement. As you prepare your answer, consider the fact that the aspiring politician does not have much knowledge about taxation.
   a. The tax on capital gains is considered a voluntary tax.
   b. The tax treatment for capital gains and losses after 1986 and before 1991 made it disadvantageous for individuals to sell or exchange capital assets as opposed to selling or exchanging assets that are not capital assets.
   c. On October 22, 1986, the Tax Reform Act of 1986 was passed, which eliminated the 60% of net capital gain deduction (i.e., an individual taxpayer with $10,000 of net capital gain was entitled to a $6,000 deduction when computing AGI) before January 1, 1987. Many state governments enjoyed a substantial increase in 1986 tax revenue.
   d. High-income taxpayers receive the most benefit from preferential treatment for capital gains.

I5-62   Your client, Apex Corporation, entered into an agreement with an executive to purchase his personal residence at its current FMV in the event that his employment is terminated by the company during a five-year period. The executive was terminated before the end of the five-year period and Apex acquired the house for $500,000. Due to a downturn in the real estate market, a $200,000 loss was incurred by the company upon the resale of the house. The chief financial officer of Apex insists that the loss be characterized as ordinary, based on the *Corn Products* doctrine. Your research into this matter reveals that the weight of authority heavily favors capital loss treatment (i.e., case law based on facts identical to the above issue held that the loss was capital rather than ordinary). You therefore conclude that the client's position does not have a realistic possibility of being sustained administratively or judicially on its merits if challenged by the IRS. What responsibility do you have as a tax practitioner relative to preparing the client's tax return and rendering continuing tax consulting services to the client? (See the Section *Statements on Responsibilities in Tax Practice* in Chapter I1 for a discussion of these issues.)

TAX RESEARCH PROBLEMS

I5-63   Tom Williams is an equal partner in a partnership with the Kansas Corporation. Williams, an inventor, produced a new process while working for the partnership, which has been patented by the partnership. Before making any use of the patent, the partnership entered into a contract granting all rights to use the process for the life of the patent to the Mason Manufacturing Co.

The time between receiving the patent and entering into the contract with Mason amounted to eight months. Mason agreed to pay 0.3% of all sales revenue generated by products produced as a result of the process. If Mason fails to make payments on a timely basis, Mason's right to use the process is forfeited and the agreement between the partnership and Mason is canceled. Will any of the proceeds collected qualify as LTCG under Sec. 1235?

A partial list of research sources is

- Reg. Sec. 1.1235-2
- *George N. Soffron,* 35 T.C. 787 (1961)

I5-64   Lynette, a famous basketball player, is considering the possibility of transferring the sole right to use her name to promote basketball shoes produced and sold by the NIK Corporation. NIK will pay $2 million to obtain the right to use Lynette's name for the next forty years. NIK may use the name on the shoes and as a part of any of the company's advertisements for basketball shoes. If Lynette signs the contract and receives the $2 million payment, will she have to recognize capital gain or ordinary income?

A partial list of research sources is

- Sec. 1221
- Rev. Rul. 65-261, 1965-2 C.B. 281

I5-65   Jack, a tenured university professor, has been a malcontent for many years at Rockport University. The university has recently offered to pay $200,000 to Jack if he will relinquish his tenure position and resign. Jack is of the opinion that tenure is an intangible capital asset and the $200,000 received for release of the tenure should be a long-term capital gain. Explain why you agree or disagree

A partial list of research sources is

- *Harry M. Flower,* 61 T.C. 140 (1973)
- *Estelle Goldman,* 1975 PH T.C. Memo ¶75,138, 34 TCM 639

I5-66   Web Baker was hired three years ago by the Berry Corporation to serve as CEO for the company. As part of his employment contract, the corporation had agreed to purchase his residence at FMV in the event the company decided to fire him. Last year, Berry, unsatisfied with Web's performance, fired him and purchased the residence for $350,000. Berry immediately listed the house with a real estate agency. Soon after the purchase, the real estate market in the area experienced a serious decline, especially in higher-priced homes. Berry sold the house this year for $270,000 and paid selling expenses of $12,000. How should the Berry Corporation treat the $92,000 loss?

A partial list of research sources is

- Sec. 1221
- Rev. Rul. 82-204, 1982-2 C.B. 192
- *Azar Nut Co. v. CIR,* 67 AFTR 2d 91-987, 91-1 USTC ¶50,257 (5th Cir., 1991)

CHAPTER 6

DEDUCTIONS AND LOSSES

LEARNING OBJECTIVES

After studying this chapter, you should be able to

1. ▶ Distinguish between deductions *for* and *from* AGI

2. ▶ Explain when deductions may be taken under both the cash and accrual methods of accounting

3. ▶ Discuss the criteria for deducting business and investment expenses

4. ▶ List the substantiation requirements that must be met to deduct travel and entertainment expenses

5. ▶ Explain the tax consequences of wash sales

6. ▶ Explain the tax consequences of transactions between related parties

7. ▶ Discuss the criteria used to determine whether an activity is a hobby or a trade or business

8. ▶ Determine the tax consequences of vacation homes

The next five I6–I10 chapters, are concerned with *deductions* that a taxpayer may claim in the calculation of taxable income. As you recall from Chapters I3 and I4, the principles governing the reporting of income encompass an "all inclusive" system of taxation, that is, all items of income are includible in gross income unless specifically excluded by statute. In contrast, deductions or losses are not allowed for tax purposes unless the statute specifically provides for the deduction. For example, a taxpayer who pays medical expenses during the year is allowed a deduction for such expenses because the statute specifically allows for the deduction of medical expenses under Sec. 213 of the IRC. The ability of a taxpayer to claim a deduction on his or her tax return is commonly referred to as being permitted as a matter of "legislative grace."

Chapter I6 discusses the general requirements for the deductibility of taxpayer expenditures and losses. Chapter I7 deals with itemized deductions of individual taxpayers, such as medical expenses, taxes, charitable contributions, interest expense and other miscellaneous deductions. Chapter I8 covers two major areas, the deductibility of losses and bad debts. Chapter I9 discusses employee compensation and expenses, and Chapter 10 discusses the subject of tax depreciation, depletion, and amortization, as well as the tax treatment of inventories.

As was mentioned above, deductions are allowed only if specifically allowed by the IRC. However, it would be impossible for the IRC to specify *every* type of deductible expense that a taxpayer might incur. Therefore, the IRC has developed a framework for analyzing the nature of an expenditure, and if the expenditure meets the criteria developed in the framework, the item is deductible. This framework has three general categories of deductions:

(1) Expenses incurred in connection with a **trade or business** (Sec. 162);

(2) Expenses incurred in connection with the **production of income** (Sec. 212);

(3) Other types of expenses that fall within specific provisions of the IRC, such as personal expenditures for such items as medical expenses, taxes, certain types of interest expense, etc.

The first two categories of deductions above, trade or business and production of income expenses, are those incurred in connection with profit-motivated activities. The IRC does not attempt to specify every conceivable type of deductible expense under these two categories (IRC Secs. 162 and 212). Rather, the IRC sets forth general guidelines for deductibility. Any expense incurred in connection with a trade or business or for the production of income is deductible if it falls within these general guidelines. For example, although the IRC does not specifically provide for the deductibility of utilities or maintenance and repairs, these expenditures are deductible if incurred in a profit-motivated activity. These general guidelines are discussed later in this chapter.

A trade or business, as discussed below, is a business activity of the taxpayer. The term production of income includes expenses incurred for the following:

▶ Production or collection of income

▶ Management, conservation, or maintenance of property held for the production of income

▶ Determination, collection, or refund of any tax

ADDITIONAL COMMENT

From a tax forum on America Online someone said, "Taxes: when you care enough to send the very least."

As will be discussed later, the distinction between a trade or business and the production of income is important because it can affect both the amount and type of the deduction. Expenses incurred in both types of activities must meet additional standards of deductibility; that is, they must also be ordinary, necessary, and reasonable in the context of the activity in which they are incurred. Losses incurred in either type of activity are deductible.

IRC Sec. 262 also provides, in general, that no deduction is allowed for any personal, living, or family expenses. However, the tax law does specifically provide for the deductibility of certain personal expenditures or losses. For example, casualty losses (subject to specific limitations) are allowed for personal-use property. Personal expenditures for certain types of interest, taxes, medical expenses, alimony, and retirement savings are also allowed as deductions if they meet strict requirements. These deductions and losses for personal expenditures are discussed in Chapters I7 and I8.

FOR VERSUS FROM ADJUSTED GROSS INCOME (AGI) CLASSIFICATION

ADDITIONAL COMMENT

The classification of deductions between deductions for AGI and deductions from AGI is not used in corporate taxation or in the taxation of estates or trusts.

KEY POINT

Many *for* AGI deductions are either expenses incurred in a trade or business or investment expenses or losses. Most of the deductible personal expenses are deductible *from* AGI.

As demonstrated in Chapter I2, the tax formula for individuals divides all allowable business, investment, and personal deductions into the following two categories:

▶ Deductions subtracted from gross income in order to calculate adjusted gross income (*for* AGI deductions)

▶ Deductions subtracted from AGI to arrive at the amount of taxable income (*from* AGI deductions)

Deductions *for* AGI are specifically identified in IRC Sec. 62. All other deductions for individuals are deductions *from* AGI. The more common *for* AGI deductions include the following, subject to certain limitations:

▶ All allowable expenses incurred in a taxpayer's trade or business, not including business expenses of an employee

▶ Employee business expenses that are reimbursed by the employer

▶ Losses from the sale or exchange of trade, business, or investment property

▶ Expenses attributable to the production of rent or royalty income

▶ Moving expenses

▶ Contributions to certain pension, profit-sharing, or retirement plan arrangements

▶ Penalties paid to a bank or other savings institution because of the early withdrawal of funds from a certificate of deposit or time savings account

▶ Alimony

▶ Self-employed individuals may deduct one-half of the self-employment tax imposed on that individual for the year and 40% (increasing to 45% in 1998) of health insurance costs (see Chapter I14).[1]

For individuals, the distinction between deductions *for* AGI and *from* AGI is critical for two reasons. First, as explained in Chapter I2, the tax formula allows individuals to deduct the greater of the standard deduction or the total of the *from* AGI (itemized) deductions in arriving at taxable income. In cases where the sum of the *from* AGI deductions does not exceed the standard deduction, the benefit of these deductions is lost. Furthermore, certain itemized deductions for taxpayers with adjusted gross income over certain levels are phased out and lost. (See Chapter I7 for

---

[1] Other deductions *for* AGI include deductions for depreciation and depletion for life tenants and income beneficiaries of property, a portion of certain lump-sum distributions from qualified pension plans, reforestation expenses, required repayments of supplemental unemployment compensation benefits, and jury duty pay that is remitted to an employer.

a discussion of these limits.) *For* AGI deductions, on the other hand, reduce AGI (and consequently taxable income), even if the standard deduction is used in computing taxable income. The concept of AGI has no application to corporations, estates, or trusts.

EXAMPLE I6-1 ▶

Brad, a single individual with no dependents, incurs $1,500 of deductible expenses and earns $30,000 in gross income during 1997. If the expenses are all deductions *from* AGI, Brad's taxable income is $23,200 (i.e., Brad receives a $2,650 deduction for his personal exemption and a $4,150 standard deduction). Brad receives no direct tax benefit from the expenses because they do not exceed the standard deduction. However, if the expenses are all deductions *for* AGI, Brad's taxable income is $21,700. In this case, Brad receives a full tax benefit from the expenses.

		Deductions from AGI	Deductions for AGI
Gross income		$30,000	$30,000
Minus:	*For* AGI deductions	0	(1,500)
AGI		$30,000	$28,500
Minus:	Standard deduction	(4,150)	(4,150)
	Personal exemption	(2,650)	(2,650)
Taxable income		$23,200	$21,700 ◀

A second important reason for the proper classification of deductions is that AGI is used as a benchmark in establishing limits on certain deductions *from* AGI, such as medical expenses, casualty losses, charitable contributions, and miscellaneous itemized deductions. For example, an individual may deduct certain miscellaneous itemized deductions only to the extent that the sum of these deductions for the year exceeds 2% of the individual's AGI. These expenses include unreimbursed employee business expenses,[2] expenses incurred to produce investment income,[3] and the cost of tax advice and tax return preparation (see Chapter I7). Medical expenses are deductible only to the extent that their total exceeds 7.5% of the individual's AGI for the year. Casualty losses on personal-use property are first reduced by $100 per casualty event. After this reduction, they are deductible only to the extent that the sum exceeds 10% of the individual's AGI. The deduction for charitable contributions, on the other hand, may not exceed 50% of the taxpayer's AGI. (See Chapter I7 for a discussion of these deductions and their limits.)

STOP & THINK

Question: Jiro, a single individual, has been offered a job with Delaware Corporation. His salary will be $60,000 and Jiro has no other items of income. He estimates that in a typical year his only deductible expenses will be $10,000 of employee business expenses. Exactly how these expenses are to be treated is yet to be resolved with his new employer. Considering only the tax consequences, which arrangement would Jiro prefer: (1) keeping his salary at $60,000 and submitting for a reimbursement of the $10,000 expenses, or (2) increasing his salary to $70,000 and paying for his own expenses without being reimbursed by his employer?

---

[2] These expenses include unreimbursed expenditures for travel and transportation, supplies, special clothing or uniforms, union dues, and subscriptions to trade journals. Reimbursed employee expenses are deductible *for* AGI and thus, are deductible in full. See Chapter I9.

[3] These expenses include rental fees for safe deposit boxes used to hold investment property, subscriptions to investment journals, bank service charges on checking accounts used in an investment activity, and fees paid for consulting advice. Expenses incurred in an investment activity that produces either rental or royalty income are deductions *for* AGI.

Solution: Jiro would prefer keeping his salary at $60,000 and receiving a reimbursement for his expenses because reimbursed employee business expenses are deductions *for* AGI whereas employee business expenses that are not reimbursed are deductions *from* AGI as miscellaneous itemized deductions. A comparison of the two alternatives using the 1997 standard deduction and personal exemption amount is as follows:

Item	Alternative 1	Alternative 2
Salary	$60,000	$70,000
Reimbursement	10,000ª	0
Total Gross Income	$70,000	$70,000
Deduction *for* AGI	(10,000)	0
AGI	$60,000	$70,000
Standard or Itemized Deductionᵇ	(4,150)	(8,600)
Personal Exemption	(2,650)	(2,650)
Taxable Income	$53,200	$58,750

ª As explained in Chapter I9, technically Jiro would not have to report the reimbursement in income and would not take a deduction. By not reporting either, the deduction is effectively a *for* AGI deduction.

ᵇ In Alternative 1, Jiro would take the standard deduction since he does not have any itemized deductions. In Alternative 2, the unreimbursed employee business expenses are deductions *from* AGI and are miscellaneous itemized deductions subject to the 2% of AGI limitation. [$10,000 − ($70,000 × .02) = $8,600]

WHEN AN EXPENSE IS DEDUCTIBLE

OBJECTIVE 2

Explain when deductions may be taken under both the cash and accrual methods of accounting

Because taxable income is generally measured on an annual basis, the question of when a particular expense is deductible is critical. The answer to this question largely depends on which method of accounting is being used.[4] The most common methods include the following:

▶ Cash receipts and disbursements method (cash method)

▶ Accrual method

▶ Hybrid method (a combination of the cash and accrual methods where some items are accounted for on the cash method and other items are accounted for on the accrual method)

Taxpayers normally use the same method for computing taxable income that they use in keeping their regular financial accounting records. However, except for the use of the last-in, first-out (LIFO) method of accounting for inventory, the tax law does not generally require conformity. For example, many companies use the straight-line depreciation method for financial accounting purposes and the modified accelerated cost recovery system (MACRS) for tax purposes.

CASH METHOD

Under the **cash method of accounting**, expenses are deductible when they are actually paid. As long as it is subsequently honored, payment by check is considered a cash payment in the year the check is mailed or delivered, even though it is delivered so late on

ADDITIONAL COMMENT

Section 446(b) provides that in cases where no method of accounting has been regularly used or if the method used does not clearly reflect income, then the computation of taxable income is to be made under a method that, in the opinion of the IRS, does clearly reflect income.

[4] Methods of accounting as they relate to the reporting of income are discussed in Chapter I3. Methods of accounting as they relate to deductibility of expenses and losses are covered in this Chapter. For an overall discussion of accounting methods, see Chapter I11.

the last day of the year that the payee could not have cashed it.[5] Furthermore, the use of a credit card to satisfy an obligation is considered a cash payment at the time of the charge rather than at the time the charge is paid.

A mere promise to pay, or the issuance of a note payable, does not constitute a payment under the cash method. Thus, a charge on an open account with a creditor is not deductible until cash is actually transferred in satisfaction of the charge.

EXAMPLE I6-2 ▶

Peter, a calendar-year taxpayer, is the sole owner of a plumbing repair business. The business uses the cash method of accounting. Under an arrangement with one of his suppliers, Peter and his employees can pick up supplies at any time during the month by merely signing for them. At the end of the month, the supplier sends Peter a bill for the charges. Peter always pays the bill in full during the following month. In December of the current year, Peter charges $1,500 for supplies. During the same month Peter purchases a plumbing fixture for $250 from another supplier. Peter uses his charge card at the time of purchase. Peter must deduct the $250 during the current year. However, the $1,500 charged on the open account is deductible when paid in the following year. ◀

PREPAID EXPENSES. In general, a capital expenditure or the prepayment of expenses by a cash method taxpayer does not result in a current deduction if the expenditure creates an asset having a useful life that extends substantially beyond the close of the tax year.[6] This can occur when a taxpayer makes expenditures for prepaid rent, services, or interest. However, in the case of prepaid rent, a circuit court of appeals decision has held that a current deduction may be taken for the entire amount of an expenditure if the period covered by the prepayment does not exceed one year and the taxpayer is obligated to make the prepayment.[7]

EXAMPLE I6-3 ▶

On November 1 of the current year, Twyla enters into a lease arrangement with Rashad to rent Rashad's office space for the following 36 months. By prepaying the rent for the entire 36-month period, Twyla is able to obtain a favorable monthly lease payment of $800. This prepayment creates an asset (a leasehold) whose useful life extends substantially beyond the end of the taxable year. Thus, only $1,600 ($800 × 2 months) of the total payment is deductible in the current year. The rest must be capitalized and amortized over the life of the lease. However, assume that under the terms of the lease, Twyla is obligated to make three annual payments of $9,600 each November 1 for the subsequent 12 months. On November 1 of the current year, Twyla pays Rashad $9,600 for the first 12-month period. Because Twyla is obligated to make the prepayment and the period covered by the prepayment does not exceed one year, the entire $9,600 is deductible in the current year using the reasoning of the previously cited circuit court decision. ◀

PREPAID INTEREST. The IRC requires that prepaid interest expense be deducted over the period of the loan to which the interest charge is allocated.[8] Receipt of a discounted loan does not represent prepaid interest expense. Instead, the interest is deemed to be paid as the loan is repaid.

EXAMPLE I6-4 ▶

During the current year, Richelle borrows $1,000 from the bank for use in her business. Richelle uses the cash method of accounting in her business. Under the terms of the loan, the bank discounts the loan by $80, paying Richelle $920. When the loan comes due in the

---

[5] *CIR v. Estate of M. A. Bradley*, 10 AFTR 1405, 3 USTC ¶904 (6th Cir., 1932) and *Charles F. Kahler*, 18 T.C. 31 (1952).
[6] Reg. Sec. 1.461-1(a).
[7] *Martin J. Zaninovich v. CIR*, 45 AFTR 2d 80-1442, 80-1 USTC ¶9342 (9th Cir., 1980) and *Bonaire Development Co. v. CIR*, 50 AFTR 2d 82-5167, 82-2 USTC ¶9428 (9th Cir., 1982). See also *Stephen A. Keller v. CIR*, 53 AFTR 2d 84-663, 84-1 USTC ¶9194 (8th Cir., 1984).
[8] Sec. 461(g).

following year, however, Richelle is to repay the full $1,000. The $80 of interest expense is not deductible until Richelle repays the loan in the following year. ◄

Taxpayers often prepay interest in the form of points. A point is one percent of the loan amount. Thus, the payment of two points on a $100,000 loan amounts to $2,000. While points must generally be amortized over the life of the loan, points paid in connection with the purchase or improvement of a principal residence are deductible when paid. According to the IRS, points paid in connection with the purchase (but not the improvement) of a principal residence are automatically deductible in the year paid if the following four requirements are met:

▶ the closing agreement clearly designates the amounts as points

▶ the amount is computed as a percentage of the amount borrowed

▶ the charging of points is an established business practice in the geographic area, and

▶ the points are paid in connection with the purchase of the taxpayer's principal residence which is used to secure the loan.[9]

Although points paid on loans incurred to *improve* the taxpayer's principal residence do not fall under this safe harbor rule, they still are currently deductible if the loan is secured by the residence, the payment of points is an established business practice in the geographic area in which it is incurred, and the amount of the prepayment does not exceed the amount generally charged.

Points paid to refinance a mortgage on a principal residence are not currently deductible because they are not paid in connection with the purchase or improvement of the taxpayer's residence.[10]

EXAMPLE I6-5 ▶

During the current year, Pam purchases a principal residence for $150,000, paying $50,000 down and financing the remainder with a 20-year mortgage secured by the property. Payments on the mortgage are to be made monthly. At the closing, she is required to pay three points as a loan origination fee. Because these points are paid in connection with the purchase of a principal residence, Pam may deduct $3,000 ($100,000 × 0.03) as interest expense during the current year. In addition, Pam may also deduct the interest portion of each monthly payment made during the year. On the other hand, assume that Pam takes out the $100,000 loan in order to refinance her home at a lower interest rate. The $3,000 prepaid interest is not currently deductible. Instead, it is to be deducted ratably over the term of the loan. Thus, Pam may deduct an additional $12.50 ($3,000 ÷ 240 payments) interest expense for each payment that is made during the year. ◄

If a home is sold and the refinanced mortgage is paid off, any unamortized portion of the points is deductible in the year of repayment. Points paid by the seller will be treated as incurred by the purchaser, and therefore are currently deductible by the purchaser if the other requirements are met and they are subtracted from the purchase price of the residence.[11]

Because expenses are generally deductible when paid rather than when they accrue, the cash method of accounting provides some degree of flexibility to taxpayers. Thus,

---

[9] Rev. Proc. 94-27, I.R.B. 94-15, 17. As explained in Chapter I7, acquisition indebtedness incurred to acquire a personal residence is limited to $1,000,000. Hence, points that are allocated to the loan principal in excess of this limit are not deductible either.

[10] Rev. Rul. 87-22, 1987-1 C.B. 146, and Rev. Proc. 87-15, 1987-1 C.B. 624. However, the Eighth Circuit has allowed a current deduction for points paid

upon the refinancing of a mortgage loan because the original loan was merely a "bridge" or temporary loan until permanent financing could be arranged. See *James R. Huntsman v. CIR*, 66 AFTR 2d 90-5020, 90-2 USTC ¶50,340 (8th Cir., 1990).

[11] Rev. Proc. 94-27, I.R.B. 94-15, 17.

subject to the limitations mentioned above with regard to prepaid expenses, taxpayers may to some degree accelerate or defer deductions from one year to another by merely accelerating or deferring payment. However, there are limitations to the use of the cash method. Inventories must be accounted for under the accrual method. Taxpayers who have inventories that are an income producing factor must use either the accrual method or the hybrid method. Furthermore, most C corporations (corporations that have not elected Subchapter S status), partnerships that have a C corporation as a partner, and tax shelters may not use the cash method. However, there are exceptions to this general rule for personal service corporations, small businesses with average annual gross receipts of $5 million or less, and businesses involved in the farming and timber businesses.[12] (See Chapter I11 for a complete discussion of the different accounting methods that may be used for computing taxable income.)

ACCRUAL METHOD

HISTORICAL NOTE

Although Congress began taxing income under the 16th Amendment in 1913, it was not until the Revenue Act of 1916 that the accrual method of accounting was recognized.

An **accrual method** taxpayer deducts expenses in the period in which they accrue. Generally items accrue when both an **all-events test** and an **economic performance test** are met.[13]

ALL-EVENTS TEST. The all-events test is met when both of the following occur:

▶ The existence of a liability is established.

▶ The amount of the liability is determined with reasonable accuracy.

EXAMPLE I6-6 ▶ During the current year, Phil provides services for Louis. Louis uses the accrual method of accounting. Phil claims that Louis owes $10,000 for the services. Louis admits owing Phil $6,000, but contests the remaining $4,000. Because the amount of the liability can be accurately established only with respect to $6,000, Louis can deduct only that amount. If Louis pays the full $10,000, it can be deducted in the year of payment, even though the contested amount ($4,000) is not resolved until a subsequent taxable year.[14] If Phil loses the lawsuit and repays Louis the $4,000, Louis would include that amount in income under the tax benefit rule (see Chapter I11). ◀

Because of the all-events test, reserves for estimated expenses such as warranty expenses may not be deducted until the year in which such work is actually performed.

EXAMPLE I6-7 ▶ Best Corporation uses the accrual method of accounting and is engaged in the business of painting and rustproofing automobiles. A 5-year warranty is provided for new vehicles and a 2-year warranty for used vehicles. The warranty is extended only to the person who owns the car at the time it is painted. Furthermore, in order to keep the warranty in force, the customer is required to present the vehicle to Best Corporation for inspection each year. The warranty is voided if the vehicle is involved in an accident. Even though for financial accounting purposes Best Corporation may provide a reserve for estimated warranty expenses and deduct a reasonable addition to the reserve on an annual basis, no income tax deduction is allowed until the warranty work is actually done. ◀

ECONOMIC PERFORMANCE TEST. To be currently deductible under the accrual method, an expense must also meet an economic performance test. Exactly when economic performance is deemed to have occurred depends on the type of transaction.

---

[12] Sec. 448.
[13] Reg. Sec. 1.461-1(a)(2) and Sec. 461(h).

[14] Reg. Sec. 1.461-2(a)(1).

▼ TABLE I6-1

When Economic Performance Is Deemed to Have Occurred

Event That Gives Rise to Liability	When Economic Performance Is Deemed to Have Occurred
Another person provides the taxpayer with property or services	When the property or services are actually provided[a]
Taxpayer uses property	As the property is used[a]
Taxpayer must provide property or services to another person	As the taxpayer provides property or services to the other person[b]
Taxpayer must make payments to another, including payments for rebates and refunds, awards or prizes, insurance or service contracts, and taxes.	As payments to the other person are made
Taxpayer must make payments to another person because of a tort, breach of contract, violation of law, or injury claim under a worker's compensation act	As payments to the other person are made

[a] Economic performance may be deemed to have occurred at the earlier date of payment if the taxpayer reasonably expects the property or services to be provided within 3½ months after the payment is made. Reg. Sec. 1.461-4(d)(6)(ii).
[b] Economic performance may also occur as the taxpayer incurs costs in connection with the obligation to provide the property or services. Reg. Sec. 1.461-4(d)(4)(i).

Table I6-1 contains a listing of various types of transactions that may arise and identifies when economic performance is deemed to have occurred.[15]

EXAMPLE I6-8 ▶

HISTORICAL NOTE

The economic performance test was added by Congress in the Tax Reform Act of 1984. Congress was concerned that in some situations taxpayers could deduct expenses currently, but the actual cash expenditure might not be made for several years. Taking a current deduction in such situations overstated the real cost because the time value of money was ignored.

ADDITIONAL COMMENT

The economic performance test does not apply to accruals for estimated expenses that are specifically allowed by the IRC.

On December 20 of the current year, Chris, an accrual method taxpayer, enters into a binding contract with Pat to have Pat clean and paint the exterior of Chris's business building. Under the terms of the contract, the work is to be done in March of the following year. The total cost of the job is $4,000. Chris pays 10% down at the time the contract is signed. Because the job is not to be done until the following year, economic performance has not occurred in the current year and Chris may not deduct any portion of the expense in the current year. ◀

An exception to the economic performance test is provided for recurring liabilities. An expense can be treated as accrued and deducted in the current year if all of the following occur:

▶ The all-events test is met during the year.

▶ Economic performance of the item occurs within the shorter of 8½ months after the close of the tax year, or a reasonable period after the close of the tax year.

▶ The expense is recurring and the taxpayer consistently treats the item as incurred in the tax year.

▶ Either the item is not material or the accrual of the item in the tax year results in a more proper matching against income than accruing the item in the tax year in which economic performance occurs.

[15] Sec. 461(h).

This exception for recurring liabilities is available for the first four types of transactions identified in Table I6-1, but may not be used for the last type of transaction in the table.

EXAMPLE I6-9 ▶ Dawn is a calendar-year, accrual method taxpayer. Every year at the end of October, Dawn enters into a contract with Sam to provide snow removal services for the parking lots at Dawn's business. This contract extends for five months through the end of March of the following year. Because the all-events test is met (the liability is fixed), the expense recurs every year, economic performance occurs within the requisite period of time, and the item is not material, Dawn may deduct the entire expense in the year in which the contract is signed. ◀

A special rule under Sec. 461(c) applies to real property taxes. Under this provision, a taxpayer may elect to accrue real property taxes ratably over the period to which the taxes relate. Once made, this election may not be changed without permission from the IRS.

EXAMPLE I6-10 ▶ Under the law of State X, the lien date for real property taxes for calendar year 1997 is January 1, 1997. The tax is payable in full on November 30, 1997. Alpha Corp. is an accrual method taxpayer that has a January 31 fiscal year-end. On January 1, 1997, real property taxes of $100,000 are assessed against a building Alpha Corp. owns. Alpha pays the taxes on November 30, 1997. If Alpha does not make the election to use the ratable accrual method, none of the payment is deductible in Alpha's fiscal year ending January 31, 1997 because the payment date is more than 8½ months after the January 31, 1997 year-end.

On the other hand, if Alpha makes the election, it may deduct $8,333 ($100,000 × $\frac{1}{12}$) in its fiscal year that ends January 31, 1997 and $91,667 ($100,000 × $\frac{11}{12}$) in its fiscal year that ends January 31, 1998.

If the taxes are due and paid on September 30, 1997, Alpha would be better off not making the ratable accrual election. In this case, the recurring item exception applies because the payment is made within 8½ months of Alpha's 1997 fiscal year-end. Thus, if Alpha does not make the election, all of the $100,000 is deductible in the fiscal year ending on January 31, 1997. ◀

The rules for determining when an expense is deductible are presented in Topic Review I6-1.

CRITERIA FOR DEDUCTING BUSINESS AND INVESTMENT EXPENSES

OBJECTIVE 3

Discuss the criteria for deducting business and investment expenses

As mentioned earlier in the chapter, there are general guidelines that determine the deductibility of business or investment expenses. These general guidelines or criteria are set forth below.

For expenditures to be deductible as business or investment expenses, they must be

▶ Related to a profit-motivated activity of the taxpayer (i.e., a business or investment activity rather than a personal expenditure)

▶ Ordinary

▶ Necessary

▶ Reasonable in amount

Topic Review I6-1

When an Expense Is Deductible

Cash Method: Deductible When Paid

Payment Is Made When

▶ Cash or other property is transferred.

▶ A check is delivered or mailed.

▶ An item is charged on a credit card.
   Note: A mere promise to pay or delivery of a note payable is not considered payment.

Prepaid Expenses

▶ Generally are deductible over the period covered.

▶ Deductible when paid if the period covered does not exceed one year.

▶ Generally prepaid interest is deductible ratably over the period covered by the loan.

▶ Points are deductible when paid if:
   —The loan is used to purchase or improve the taxpayer's principal residence.
   —The loan is secured by the residence.
   —Points are established business practice in the geographical area.
   —The points do not exceed the amount generally charged.
   —For points paid to purchase a principal residence, the closing agreement must clearly designate the amounts as points and the amount must be computed as a percentage of the amount borrowed.

Accrual Method: Deductible When Accrued

In General

▶ The accrual method must be used for inventories.

▶ Accrual occurs when both all-events test and economic performance have been met.

All-Events Test

▶ The existence of a liability is established and

▶ The amount of the liability is determined.

Economic Performance

▶ When economic performance is deemed to occur depends on the transaction involved (see Table I6-1).

▶ May be deemed to occur in the year the all-events test is met if all of the following tests are met:
   —Actual economic performance occurs within the shorter of:
      8½ months after taxable year or a reasonable period after the taxable year.
   —The expense is recurring and is treated consistently from year to year.
   —Either:
      The item is immaterial or
      Deducting the expense in the year the all-events test is met results in a more proper matching of income and deductions.

ADDITIONAL COMMENT

A sole proprietor, when asked what his firm did, replied that they filled out tax returns and other government forms and ran a jewelry store on the side.

▶ Properly documented, and

▶ An expense of the taxpayer (not someone else's expense)

Additionally, an expenditure is not deductible if it is

▶ A capital expenditure

▶ Related to tax-exempt income

▶ Illegal or in violation of public policy, or

▶ Specifically disallowed by the tax law

These criteria are discussed below.

BUSINESS OR INVESTMENT REQUIREMENT

As previously explained, except for a few personal expenses, all deductible expenditures or losses must be incurred in a profit-motivated activity. For individuals, most of these expenses are deductible either under Sec. 162 as an expense incurred in a trade or business or under Sec. 212 as an expense incurred for the production of income or for the maintenance and conservation of income-producing property. Thus, this requirement is really two-pronged: (1) a determination whether an expenditure is incurred in an activity engaged in for profit, and (2) a distinction between a trade or business and an investment activity.

REAL WORLD EXAMPLE

A taxpayer attempted to deduct treasure-hunting costs as a business expense, but the court concluded that there was no profit motive. The taxpayer kept no business records, the time spent was negligible and appeared to be recreational in nature, and no income was produced from the activity. *William J. Hezel,* 1985 PH T.C. Memo ¶85,010, 49 TCM 458.

ACTIVITY ENGAGED IN FOR PROFIT. This first part of the test classifies the expense as having been incurred in either a profit-motivated activity or a personal activity.

Categorizing expenses can be quite difficult in some cases. For example, is the activity of coin collecting a hobby that is personal in nature, or a profit-motivated business or investment activity? No single objective test is available. Rather, one must examine all the facts and circumstances surrounding the activity in which the expense is incurred. Reg. Sec. 1.183-2(b) lists several factors that must be considered, including the following:

▶ Whether the taxpayer conducts the activity in a businesslike manner

▶ The expertise of the taxpayer or the taxpayer's advisors

▶ The time and effort expended by the taxpayer in carrying on the activity

▶ Whether the assets used in the activity are expected to appreciate in value

▶ The taxpayer's success in carrying on other similar activities

▶ The taxpayer's history of income or losses with respect to the activity

▶ The amount of occasional profits, if any, that are earned

▶ The taxpayer's financial status

▶ Any elements of personal pleasure or recreation the activity might involve

ADDITIONAL COMMENT

Many of the court cases dealing with profit motive under Sec. 183 are ranch and farm cases. In fact, Sec. 183, now titled "Activities Not Engaged in for Profit" was originally titled "Farm Losses, etc." in the Tax Reform Act of 1969.

No one of these factors is determinative. In fact, other factors not listed may also be taken into consideration. Furthermore, a determination is not made by merely counting the number of factors that are present. Instead, the decision depends on an examination of all the factors together. The IRS can, therefore, make the decision on a more subjective basis than the taxpayer might like. If the IRS asserts that an activity is a personal one (i.e., a hobby) rather than a business or investment, the burden of proof rests on the taxpayer to prove otherwise.

EXAMPLE I6-11 ▶ Paula, a successful attorney with an annual income of $200,000, also enjoys raising and training quarter horses. She generally spends 5 to 6 hours each week training, showing, or racing the horses. Over the last 4 years her winnings from shows and races have amounted to

$16,000. Over that same period, an additional $8,000 of income has been generated from stud fees and the sale of colts. Often the horses are used to take Paula's family or friends riding. In addition, Paula often participates in equestrian clinics and demonstrations for 4-H clubs and other similar groups. A high school student is employed to feed the horses each day and to clean the stalls weekly. A professional horse trainer is hired for 4 hours each week to help Paula train the horses.

In this case, several factors such as the level of earnings, the hiring of professional help, and the amount of time spent in the activity might indicate that Paula is engaged in a business. Other factors, such as the time spent riding with family and friends, the voluntary clinics and demonstrations, and the small amount of revenue generated as compared with Paula's other income, support the position that Paula merely has a hobby of raising horses. ◀

HISTORICAL NOTE

Before the Tax Reform Act of 1986, an activity was presumed to be engaged in for profit if it showed a profit for any 2 years during a consecutive 5-year period.

KEY POINT

Section 183(d) primarily serves to shift the burden of proof from the taxpayer to the IRS.

In cases where a clear profit motive cannot be shown under the factors mentioned above, the Code provides a test whereby an activity may be presumed to be one engaged in for profit. This test is met if the activity shows a profit for any three years during a consecutive five-year period. The five-year period consists of the year in question plus the previous four years.[16] This presumption is rebuttable (i.e., if the taxpayer meets the test, the burden of proof is shifted to the IRS to show that the activity *is not* profit motivated). Otherwise, the taxpayer would be required to prove that the activity *is* profit-motivated.

If the activity is determined to be a business, the taxpayer may deduct all qualified business expenses from the gross income, even if a net loss results.[17] However, if the activity is determined to be a hobby, the expenses are generally deductible as a miscellaneous itemized deduction but only to the extent of the gross income from the activity. A net loss may not be reported from the activity if it is a hobby. Furthermore, the expenses must be deducted in a predetermined order. (See the section titled Special Disallowance Rules in this chapter for a discussion of these hobby loss rules.)

EXAMPLE I6-12 ▶

TYPICAL MISCONCEPTION

When an activity is determined to be a hobby, it is sometimes erroneously concluded that none of the hobby expenses are deductible. Section 183(b) permits the deduction of hobby expenses as miscellaneous itemized deductions up to the amount of income even though the expenses are not actually incurred in connection with a business.

Lorenzo, a stockbroker, enjoys raising and breeding pedigreed poodles. Although this activity is used for recreation and relaxation after work, Lorenzo periodically sells some of his poodles. Lorenzo reports $850 in income and $2,900 in expenses from the activity on his 1997 tax return. Upon auditing Lorenzo's 1997 return, the IRS disallowed the expenses in excess of the income, arguing that the activity is a hobby rather than a business or investment. If he can prove that a profit was realized from the poodle-raising operation for any three years from 1993 through 1997 inclusive, the presumption will be made that the poodles are raised for a profit and not for recreation. The burden of proof is then on the IRS to show that the activity is really a hobby. If Lorenzo cannot show a profit for three years out of the five-year period, he would have to rely on the factors mentioned in the Treasury Regulations to convince the IRS and/or the courts that the activity is a business.

If Lorenzo's poodle-raising activity is determined to be a business, Lorenzo would report a net loss of $2,050 ($2,900 expenses − $850 income), assuming the loss is not incurred in a passive activity (see Chapter I8). If the activity is determined to be a hobby, however, Lorenzo may deduct only $850 of the expenses (up to the amount of the gross income) as an itemized deduction. As explained later, these expenses must be deducted in a certain order. The remaining expenses are not allowed as tax deductions. ◀

---

[16] Sec. 183(d). If the major part of the activity involves breeding, training, showing, or racing horses, the five-year period is extended to a seven-year period, and a profit must be shown in only two, rather than three, of the years covered by that seven-year period.

[17] If the activity is a passive activity, the loss may be suspended. See Chapter I8 for a discussion of the passive loss rules.

TRADE OR BUSINESS VERSUS INVESTMENT CLASSIFICATION. The second part of the general profit-motive test is the determination of whether a particular activity is a trade or business of the taxpayer or is only an investment. This distinction is important for several reasons. First, a loss on the sale of the assets used in the activity may be an ordinary loss if the activity is a trade or business.[18] If it is an investment activity, however, the loss is a capital loss which, as explained in Chapter I5, is given different treatment. Second, this distinction may control whether an expense of the activity is a deduction *for* AGI or a deduction *from* AGI. In general, expenses incurred in a trade or business are deductions *for* AGI. Finally, each year taxpayers may currently deduct up to $18,000 (increasing to $18,500 in 1998) of tangible personal property purchased during the year for use in a trade or business; the same expenditures must be capitalized and depreciated over several years if they are incurred in an investment activity. (See Chapter I10 for a discussion of the Sec. 179 current deduction for capital expenditures.)

EXAMPLE I6-13 ▶

ADDITIONAL COMMENT

Hobby expenses are subject to the 2% of AGI limitation on miscellaneous itemized deductions. However, if the expense is one that is deductible whether or not incurred in an income producing activity, such as real property taxes on a home, it is fully deductible.

Robin is a self-employed financial consultant. She meets daily with a variety of clients to discuss their investments. Because she must keep abreast of the latest market quotes and strategies, Robin subscribes to several trade publications, newsletters, and quote services. She also purchased a $4,000 computer to be used in her consulting business. The expenses incurred for these services are deductions *for* AGI because they are incurred in Robin's consulting business, and she can currently deduct the $4,000 paid for the computer but must depreciate. ◀

On the other hand, most expenses incurred in an investment activity rather than a business are miscellaneous itemized deductions *from* AGI and are deductible only to the extent that they exceed 2% of AGI (see Chapter I7).[19]

EXAMPLE I6-14 ▶

Steve is a wealthy attorney who invests in the stock market and keeps abreast of the latest market quotes and strategies by subscribing to several trade publications and newsletters. He also purchased a computer to use in tracking his investments. Steve generally spends a few hours each day studying this information and analyzing his portfolio. The subscription expenses are deductions *from* AGI because they are incurred in an investment (rather than a business) activity and do not relate to the production of rents and royalties. Furthermore, Steve cannot currently deduct the entire cost of the computer but must depreciate over a period of five years. The deductibility of all of the above items depends on whether Steve's total miscellaneous itemized deductions exceed 2% of his AGI and whether Steve itemizes his deductions instead of using the standard deduction. ◀

ADDITIONAL COMMENT

A trade or business is an activity in which there is a profit motive and where some type of economic activity is involved. An investment activity requires a profit motive but does not require economic activity.

Despite these important differences in treatment, the distinction between an investment activity and a trade or business is not always clear. Neither the IRC nor the Treasury Regulations provide a precise definition of what constitutes a trade or business. Some guidelines may be found in judicial law. In one of the first cases dealing with the issue, the Supreme Court stated that the carrying on of a trade or business involves "holding one's self out to others as engaged in the selling of goods or services."[20] Later, in another case the Supreme Court emphasized that one must examine all the surrounding facts and circumstances in order to determine the underlying nature of an activity. In that case, the taxpayer owned a large portfolio of stocks, bonds, and real estate. The taxpayer's holdings were so large that he rented offices and hired employees to help him manage the properties. The Court, however, regarded these

---

[18] Under Sec. 1231, the exact treatment depends on the total gains and losses from such property for the year. See Chapter I13 for a discussion of Sec. 1231.

[19] However, expenses of an investment activity that produce rents or

royalties are deductions *for* AGI. See Sec. 62(a)(4).

[20] *Deputy v. Pierre S. DuPont*, 23 AFTR 808, 40-1 USTC ¶9161 (USSC, 1940).

activities as investment activities despite the size of the holdings and the amount of work and effort involved because the taxpayer merely kept records and collected interest and dividends from his securities. Other cases, however, indicate that a taxpayer who invests in stocks and bonds may be considered to be in a business if he or she frequently buys and sells securities in order to make a short-term profit on the daily swings in the market.[21]

ORDINARY EXPENSE

To be deductible, a business or investment expense must be **ordinary.** Although the IRC does not provide either a definition or an application of this requirement, the Treasury Regulations under Sec. 212 indicate that for an expense to be ordinary it must be reasonable in amount and it must bear a reasonable and proximate relationship to the income-producing activity or property. This means that there must be more than a remote connection between the expense and the anticipated income. It does not mean that the property must be producing income currently.

KEY POINT

Whether an expense can be considered ordinary is sometimes very subjective. For example, Supreme Court Justice Cardozo in 1933 in *Thomas H. Welch v. Helvering,* 12 AFTR 1456, 3 USTC ¶1164 (USSC, 1933) stated that, ''The standard set up by the statute is not a rule of law; it is a way of life. Life in all its fullness must supply the answer to the riddle.''

EXAMPLE 16-15 ▶
ADDITIONAL COMMENT

A General Accounting Office report finds that tax cheating is widespread among self-employed taxpayers. These workers represent only 13% of all taxpayers, but account for approximately 40% of all underreported individual income. The report identified truckers as one of the least compliant groups.

During the current year, Ahmed purchases a plot of land, on which there is an old vacant warehouse. Ahmed anticipates making a long-run profit from the investment because the value of the land is expected to appreciate eventually due to commercial development in the area. To help cover the costs of holding the property, Ahmed plans to rent storage space in the warehouse. During the current year, the following expenses are incurred, although Ahmed is unable to rent the warehouse:

Expenses	Amount
Property taxes	$1,000
Interest	4,000
Insurance	800
Utilities	200

All of these expenses qualify as ordinary and are deductible under Sec. 212 because they bear a reasonable and proximate relationship to the income Ahmed hopes to obtain, even though no income is generated from the property during the year. However, they might not all be deductible in the current year because of the passive loss limitations explained in Chapter 18. ◀

The Supreme Court has ruled that for an expense to be ordinary it must be customary or usual in the context of a particular industry or business community. Thus, an expenditure may be ordinary in the context of one type of business, but not in the context of another.[22]

EXAMPLE 16-16 ▶

For many years, Hank has been an officer in Green Corporation, which is engaged in the grain business. Green Corporation purchases its grain from various suppliers. Last year, Green Corporation went bankrupt and was relieved from having to pay off its debts to its suppliers. In the current year, Hank enters into a contract to act as a commissioned agent to purchase grain for Green Corporation. To reestablish a relationship with suppliers whom Hank knew previously, Hank decides to pay off as many of Green Corporation's debts as he can. Hank is under no legal obligation to do so. These payments made by Hank are *not* ordinary. Rather, they are extraordinary expenditures made for goodwill to establish Hank in a new trade or business, and they must be capitalized. ◀

---

[21] *Eugene Higgins v. CIR,* 25 AFTR 1160, 41-1 USTC ¶9233 (USSC, 1941). See also *Walter K. Liang,* 23 T.C. 1040 (1955), and *Ralph E. Purvis v. CIR,* 37 AFTR 2d 76-968, 76-1 USTC ¶9270 (9th Cir., 1976); and *Samuel B. Levin v. U.S.,* 43 AFTR 2d 79-612, 79-1 USTC ¶9331 (ct. Cls., 1979).

[22] *Thomas H. Welch v. Helvering,* 12 AFTR 1456, 3 USTC ¶1164 (USSC, 1933) and *Deputy v. Pierre S. DuPont,* 23 AFTR 808, 40-1 USTC ¶9161 (USSC, 1940).

An expense may be ordinary with respect to a particular taxpayer even though that taxpayer encounters it only once.

For several years, Donna has been engaged in the business of making and selling false teeth. Most of the advertisements, orders, and deliveries of the teeth are done through the mail. During the current year, the post office judged that some of the advertisements were false. As a result, a fraud order is issued under which the post office stamps "Fraudulent" on all letters addressed to Donna, and then returns them to the senders. In an unsuccessful suit to prevent the post office from continuing this practice, Donna expends $25,000 in lawyer's fees. These fees are ordinary business expenses because they are incurred in an action that normally or ordinarily would be taken under the circumstances.[23] ◀

The Supreme Court has also indicated that the term *ordinary* as used in this context refers to an expenditure that is currently deductible rather than an expenditure that must be capitalized.[24]

NECESSARY EXPENSE

In addition to being ordinary, a deductible investment or business expense must also be **necessary**. The Supreme Court has indicated that an expense is considered necessary if it is "appropriate and helpful" in the taxpayer's business.[25] To meet this appropriate or helpful standard, an expenditure need not be necessary in the sense that it is indispensable. Rather, the test seems to be whether a reasonable or prudent businessperson would incur the same expenditure under similar circumstances.

REAL WORLD EXAMPLE

Payments made by a corporation to an individual who was a 50% shareholder were necessary in order to prevent him from interfering in the management of the business and damaging the corporation's reputation. *Fairmont Homes, Inc.*, 1983 PH T.C. Memo ¶83,209, 45 TCM 1340.

EXAMPLE I6-18 ▶

The expenditures in Example I6-16 (the payment of debts from a former business) and Example I6-17 (the payment of legal fees) are both necessary because they are appropriate and helpful in each case. However, the expenditure in Example I6-16 is not ordinary and, therefore, is not deductible. The expenditure in Example I6-17 is deductible because it meets both tests. ◀

REASONABLE EXPENSE

Section 162 states that only reasonable amounts paid for salaries are deductible. However, Treasury Regulations under Sec. 212 imply that for any expense to be ordinary and necessary it must be reasonable in amount. Problems with meeting this standard generally arise in the context of salaries being paid to an individual who is both a shareholder and an employee in a closely held business. In a typical situation, a controlling shareholder of a corporation receives a payment, characterized as salary, that the IRS asserts is too large for the services rendered.

REAL WORLD EXAMPLE

Salary paid to a corporate officer, who was the son of the controlling stockholder, was found to be unreasonable in view of his age and lack of qualifications and executive experience. *Transport Manufacturing & Equipment Co. v. CIR*, 26 AFTR2d 70-5556, 70-2 USTC ¶9627 (8th Cir., 1970).

EXAMPLE I6-19 ▶

Brian, the controlling shareholder of Central Corporation, receives an annual salary of $250,000 from the corporation. Based on several factors, such as the size of Central Corporation's total operations and a comparison of salary received by officers of comparably sized corporations, the IRS contends that Brian's salary should be no higher than $150,000. If Central successfully defends the $250,000 salary, the corporation is able to deduct the full amount as salary expense. If the defense is not successful, the excess $100,000 is considered a dividend to the extent of earnings and profits, and no deduction is available to Central Corporation for this amount. In either event, Brian must take the full $250,000 into income. (See the Tax Planning Considerations section in this chapter for a discussion of the use of a payback agreement in these situations.) ◀

---

[23] *CIR* v. *S. B. Heininger*, 31 AFTR 783, 44-1 USTC ¶9109 (USSC, 1943).
[24] Ibid. See also *CIR v. Walter F. Tellier*, 17 AFTR 2d 633, 66-1 USTC ¶9319 (USSC, 1966).

[25] *Thomas H. Welch v. Helvering*, 12 AFTR 1456, 3 USTC ¶1164 (USSC, 1933).

Topic Review I6-2

Tests for Deductibility as a Business or Investment Expense

Test	Application
Ordinary	▶ Based on the facts and circumstances. ▶ Reasonable and proximate relationship to the activity. ▶ Customary or usual in context of the industry. ▶ Need not be encountered by the taxpayer more than once.
Necessary	▶ Based on the facts and circumstances. ▶ Appropriate and helpful. ▶ Need not be indispensable. ▶ Would a reasonable or prudent businessperson incur the same expense?
Reasonable	▶ Based on the facts and circumstances. ▶ Applies to all business and investment expenses. ▶ Compensation paid to an owner-employee of a small corporation is the most commonly contested area. ▶ Compensation in excess of $1 million payable by a publicly held corporation to its key executives may not be deductible.

In an attempt to link executive compensation to productivity and business performance and to discourage a common practice of increasing executive compensation despite declines in business performance, Congress enacted tax legislation that disallows a deduction for certain employee compensation that exceeds a yearly amount of $1 million. These are amounts payable by a publicly held corporation to the corporation's chief executive officer and its four highest compensated officers for the taxable year.[26]

The tests for determining whether an expense is deductible are highlighted in Topic Review I6-2.

CAPITALIZATION VERSUS EXPENSE DEDUCTION

ADDITIONAL COMMENT

The determination of which costs should be considered as capital expenditures is not influenced by the property's use. For example, both the cost of a new addition to a personal residence and the cost of an improvement made to a business machine would have to be capitalized.

GENERAL CAPITALIZATION REQUIREMENTS. Under Sec. 263, current deductions may not be taken for capital expenditures. Generally, expenses that add to the value of, substantially prolong the useful life of, or adapt the property to a new or different use are considered **capital expenditures** and are not currently deductible. Thus, capital expenditures include the cost of acquiring or constructing buildings, machinery, equipment, furniture, and any similar property that has a useful life that extends substantially beyond the end of the tax year. The cost of goodwill purchased in connection with the acquisition of the assets of a going concern is also a capital expenditure.[27] (See Chapter I10 for a discussion of the amortization of goodwill.)

[26] Sec. 162(m). Compensation based on commissions or other performance goals is not subject to this limitation.
[27] Reg. Sec. 1.263(a)-2(h). See also *Indopco, Inc., v. CIR,* 69 AFTR 2d 92-694, 92-1 USTC ¶50,113 (USSC, 1992), where expenses incurred by a corporation that was the target of a "friendly" takeover were held to be nondeductible capital expenditures because they provided long-term benefits to the corporation. In this case, the Supreme Court held that these long-term benefits do not need to be associated with a specific identifiable asset.

Some capital assets, such as buildings, machinery, equipment, furniture and fixtures, purchased goodwill, and customer lists are depreciable or amortizable and may provide deductions that are spread over more than one tax year. Others, such as land, stock, and partnership interests, are neither depreciable nor amortizable. With regard to these assets, the taxpayer must wait until the asset is sold or disposed of to recover the cost. It is sometimes difficult to ascertain whether an asset is subject to depreciation or amortization (e.g., the Tax Court has held that antique violin bows and an antique bass violin are depreciable property, overriding the IRS's arguments that they should not be depreciable because they were actually appreciating in value and it was impossible to determine their useful life).[28]

Maintenance and repair expenditures that only keep an asset in "an ordinarily efficient operating condition" are deductible if they do not increase the value or prolong the useful life of the asset.[29] Distinguishing between a currently deductible expenditure and a capital expenditure can be difficult because expenditures for normal maintenance and repair can cost more than a capital improvement. Normal maintenance and repair may also increase the value of an asset. In one Tax Court case, expenditures incurred in replacing support beams and floor joists to shore up a sagging floor were held to be deductible, whereas the cost of placing a new floor over an old one was held to be a capital expenditure.[30] It is necessary, therefore, to examine all of the facts and circumstances to determine whether the expenditures constitute part of an overall plan of improvement or a change in use of the asset.

ADDITIONAL COMMENT

Some provisions permit taxpayers to depreciate or amortize capital expenditures over a relatively short period of time. For example, there is a rapid write-off available for pollution control facilities under Sec. 169 and for organization costs of corporations under Sec. 248.

ELECTION TO DEDUCT CURRENTLY. A few elections exist that allow a current deduction for certain capital expenditures. Taxpayers often prefer a current deduction over capitalizing and depreciating an asset because of the time value of money. Some expenditures that taxpayers may elect to deduct currently[31] include

▶ Cost of fertilizers incurred by farmers

▶ Cost of soil and water conservation incurred by farmers

▶ Intangible drilling costs incurred in drilling oil and gas wells

▶ Costs for tertiary injectants

▶ Costs for certain mining development projects

▶ Costs incurred to remove architectural and transportation barriers to the handicapped and elderly

▶ Costs for certain qualified research and experimental expenditures

Taxpayers may also elect to deduct certain amounts each year for the purchase of qualified tangible personal property used in a trade or business instead of depreciating the property over its useful life. This deduction is limited to $18,000 in 1997; $18,500 in 1998; $19,000 in 1999; $20,000 in the year 2000; $24,000 in 2001 or 2002; and $25,000 in 2003 and thereafter.[32]

CAPITALIZATION OF DEDUCTION ITEMS. The exceptions mentioned above provide a current deduction for expenditures that are normally capital in nature. Section 266 provides for the capitalization of certain expenses that normally are deductible. Section 266 is elective and applies to the following items:

---

[28] Richard L. Simon, 103 T.C. 247 (1994) and *Brian P. Liddle*, 76 AFTR 2d 95-6255, 95-2 USTC ¶50,488 (3rd Cir., 1959).

[29] Reg. Sec. 1.162-4.

[30] *Standard Fruit Product Co.*, 1949 PH T.C. Memo ¶49,207, 8 TCM 733.

[31] See Secs. 180, 175, 263(c), 193, 616, 190, and 174.

[32] Sec. 179. See Chapter I10 for a further discussion of this topic.

▶ Annual property taxes, interest on a mortgage, and other carrying charges incurred on unimproved and unproductive real estate.

▶ Annual property taxes, interest, employment taxes, and other necessary expenses incurred for the development, improvement, or construction of real property, up to the time the development or construction is completed. For these expenses to be capitalized, the real property may be either improved or unimproved, productive or unproductive.

▶ Interest and employment taxes incurred in transporting and installing personalty (as opposed to realty) up to the time when the property is first put into use by the taxpayer.

A new election to capitalize the expenses on unimproved and unproductive real estate may be made each year.

EXAMPLE 16-20 ▶ During 1997 and 1998, Nancy pays property taxes of $5,000 on a piece of land. During 1997, the land is vacant and unproductive. In 1998, Nancy uses the land as a parking lot, generating $7,000 in income. Nancy can elect to capitalize the taxes in 1997 because the property is both unimproved and unproductive. In 1998, however, the land is productive, and Nancy cannot elect to capitalize the taxes. Because the expenses relate to the production of rental income, they are deductible *for* AGI. If the land remains unproductive during 1998, Nancy can elect to capitalize the taxes paid in 1998. However, the election need not be made for 1998 merely because it is made in 1997. ◀

An election to capitalize the other expenses incurred during the development or construction period remains in effect for that year and for all subsequent years until the end of the construction period. However, the election may be made on each new project separately.

EXAMPLE 16-21 ▶ During the current year, Paul begins construction of an office building and a hotel. Paul incurs $20,000 in property taxes during the construction of the office building and $12,000 for the hotel. The election to capitalize the taxes on the office building does not bind Paul to make the same election with respect to the taxes on the hotel. ◀

If a taxpayer elects to capitalize this type of expense under Sec. 266, it is added to the basis of the property to which it pertains. If the property is depreciable, a deduction is allowed for the expenses as the property is depreciated. Taxpayers are motivated to make this election if they have large net operating loss (NOL) carryovers, or if they expect to be in a significantly higher tax rate in future years and thus feel that the benefit of the deduction is greater in the future.

Section 263A also requires certain taxpayers to capitalize certain costs into inventory instead of taking a current deduction. (See Chapters I10 and I11 for a discussion of inventories.)

LEGAL AND ACCOUNTING FEES

Legal and accounting fees are generally deductible if they are incurred in the regular conduct of a trade or business or for the production of income. Fees incurred for the determination, collection, or refund of any tax are also deductible. As mentioned previously, trade or business expenses and expenses incurred in producing rents and royalties are deductible *for* AGI. Likewise, fees paid for the determination, collection, or refund of any tax are deductible *for* AGI if they are allocable to the taxpayer's trade or business or to the production of rents and royalties. These expenses include fees paid to prepare a taxpayer's Schedule C (Profit or Loss from Business), Part I of Schedule E (Supplemental Income and Loss, which is used to report rental and royalty income), and Schedule F (farm income and expenses).[33] Other tax related fees are deductible *from* AGI as miscellaneous itemized deductions, subject to the 2% of AGI limitation.

Legal fees incurred for personal purposes are not deductible. Likewise, legal fees incurred in the acquisition of property are not deductible; instead, they must be capitalized and added to the cost of the property.

EXAMPLE 16-22 ▶

During the current year, Lia pays legal and accounting fees for the following:

Services rendered with regard to a contract dispute in Lia's business	$ 8,000
Services rendered in resolving a federal tax deficiency relating to Lia's business	2,500
Tax return preparation fees:	
Allocable to preparation of Schedule C	1,600
Allocable to preparation of Schedules A and B and to the remainder of Form 1040	400
Legal fees incident to a divorce	1,200
Total	$13,700

Lia may deduct $12,100 ($8,000 + $2,500 + $1,600) *for* AGI. The legal fees incident to the divorce are personal expenses and generally are not deductible. However, a partial deduction *from* AGI as a miscellaneous itemized deduction subject to the 2% of AGI limitation could be taken to the extent that the legal fees relate to giving tax advice incident to the divorce. The remaining $400 of tax preparation fees is also deductible *from* AGI as a miscellaneous itemized deduction. ◀

In certain cases, legal expenses incurred in defending one's reputation or in defending against criminal charges may be deductible. In these situations, however, the legal action must have a direct relationship to the taxpayer's business or income-producing activity. In criminal proceedings, the Supreme Court has held that as long as the expenses are business expenses, they are deductible, even if the taxpayer is convicted.

EXAMPLE 16-23 ▶

Mario is engaged in the business of underwriting and selling securities to the public. In the current year, Mario is charged and convicted on criminal charges of securities fraud. The conviction is appealed, but the conviction is upheld. Mario incurs $18,000 in attorney's fees in the unsuccessful defense. In this case, the legal expenses are directly related to Mario's business. Additionally, they are ordinary and necessary. Despite Mario's conviction, the $18,000 of attorney's fees is deductible.[34] ◀

EXPENSES RELATED TO EXEMPT INCOME

Under Sec. 265, no deduction is allowed for any expense allocated or related to tax-exempt income. The purpose of this disallowance is to prevent a double tax benefit to the taxpayer.

EXAMPLE 16-24 ▶

Sarah is a self-employed engineering consultant. During the current year, she wins a contract that requires her to work in a foreign country for an extended period of time. Her income attributable to her foreign work is $60,000. During the year she also incurs deductible expenses of $2,500, which are allocable to her foreign income. For the

---

[33] Rev. Rul. 92-29, 1992-1 C.B. 20.

[34] *CIR v. Walter F. Tellier*, 17 AFTR 2d 633, 66-1 USTC ¶9319 (USSC, 1966).

Deductions and Losses ▼ Individuals 6-21

SELF-STUDY QUESTION

Chuck borrows $100,000 at a 10% rate of interest and invests the $100,000 in exempt bonds yielding 8%. Assuming that Chuck is in the 28% tax bracket and that expenses related to exempt income are deductible, calculate Chuck's cash flow on these transactions on an after-tax basis.

ANSWER

Chuck has $8,000 of exempt income and $10,000 of interest expense. However, if the interest expense is deductible, its after-tax cost would be $7,200 ($10,000 − 2,800). Chuck's cash flow is $800 ($8,000 − $7,200) on an unsound economic investment.

year, Sarah is entitled to exclude (subject to the applicable limits) all of her $60,000 foreign-earned income in computing her U.S. taxable income due to the availability of the foreign-earned income exclusion (discussed in Chapter I4). Because her entire $60,000 of foreign-earned income is excluded from income, Sarah may not deduct any of the $2,500 in expenses. ◀

Section 265 specifically disallows interest expense on debt the taxpayer incurs in order to purchase or carry tax-exempt securities. Thus, the disallowance depends on the taxpayer's intended use of the loan proceeds.[35] Intent is generally determined by an examination of all the facts and circumstances surrounding the transaction. Intent to carry the tax-exempt securities can be shown if the tax-exempt securities are used as collateral in securing a loan.[36] If an individual who holds tax-exempt securities later incurs some debt, no disallowance will occur if the debt is incurred to finance personal items (e.g., a mortgage on a personal residence). However, if the debt is incurred to finance an investment, a portion of the interest is generally disallowed. Even though the interest is not incurred to carry tax-exempt securities, it still may not be deductible. For example, if interest is incurred on personal debt, it is not deductible. (See Chapter I7 for a discussion of limitations on the deductibility of personal interest.)

EXAMPLE I6-25 ▶

Sam, an individual, has invested $80,000 in Gold Corporation stock, $120,000 in real estate, and $50,000 in tax-exempt municipal bonds. During the current year, Sam borrows $70,000 for the purpose of investing in a limited partnership. For the year, he pays $6,000 interest on the loan. Under these circumstances, the IRS will presume that Sam has incurred a portion of the debt in order to carry the tax-exempt securities and will disallow a portion of the deduction. Sam may overcome that presumption if he can show that he could not have sold the tax-exempt securities. According to the IRS, however, this presumption cannot be overcome if Sam can show only that the sale of the bonds would have resulted in a loss. If Sam instead borrowed the money to purchase a personal residence, the IRS probably would not attempt to disallow the deduction.[37] (See Chapter I7 for a discussion of restrictions on the deductibility of interest for personal residences.) ◀

EXPENDITURES THAT ARE CONTRARY TO PUBLIC POLICY

Certain expenditures, even though incurred in a profit-motivated activity, may not be deductible if the payment itself is illegal or if the payment is a penalty or fine resulting from an illegal act. These nondeductible expenses generally fall within one of the following categories:

REAL-WORLD EXAMPLE

A subcontractor involved with the construction of a new shopping mall made kickbacks to the supervisor of the primary contractor. The kickbacks were deductible because they were not illegal, and the kickbacks were also ordinary and necessary because the subcontractor would not have been able to continue to work if the kickbacks had not been made. *Raymond Bertolini Trucking Co. v. CIR* 54 AFTR 2d 84-5413, 1984-2 USTC ¶9591 (6th Cir., 1984).

▶ Illegal payments to government officials or employees
▶ Other illegal payments
▶ Kickbacks, rebates, and bribes under Medicare and Medicaid
▶ Payments of fines and penalties
▶ Payment of treble damages under the federal antitrust laws

BRIBES AND KICKBACKS. Under Sec. 162(c)(1), any illegal bribe or kickback made to any official or employee of a government is not deductible. This applies to payments made to

---

[35] Rev. Proc. 72-18, 1972-1 C.B. 740.
[36] *Wisconsin Cheeseman, Inc. v. U.S.*, 21 AFTR 2d 383, 68-1 USTC ¶9145 (7th Cir., 1968).

[37] Rev. Proc. 72-18, supra note 35.

▶ Federal officials and employees

▶ State, local, and foreign government officials and employees

▶ Officials and employees of an agency of a government

EXAMPLE 16-26 ▶ During February of the current year, Road Corporation enters into a contract with the State of Iowa to construct a five-mile stretch of a new highway. Under the terms of the contract, the project is to be completed by October 22 of the current year. If it is not completed and accepted by Iowa on or before that date, Road Corporation will be subject to a fine of $5,000 per day for every day after that date until the project is accepted. By October 20, the project foreman realizes that the company will not make the deadline if it complies with all the requirements imposed by the state inspector assigned to the project. To avoid the fine, the foreman arranges for the inspector to "look the other way" on several of the requirements in exchange for a payment of $8,000. Because this payment constitutes an illegal bribe to a government official, the payment is not deductible. ◀

In the case of illegal payments to officials or employees of a foreign government, no deduction is allowed if the payment is unlawful under the Foreign Corrupt Practices Act of 1977 unless it is found to be a normal way of doing business in that country. In all cases, the burden rests on the government to prove the illegality of the payment.

Illegal bribes, kickbacks, and other illegal payments made to people other than a government official or employee are nondeductible if they are illegal under a federal law that subjects the payor to a criminal penalty or loss of the privilege of doing business. In addition, illegal payments under a state law imposing the same penalties are nondeductible if the state law is generally enforced. Here, the definition of a kickback includes a payment for referring a client, patient, or customer.[38]

EXAMPLE 16-27
ADDITIONAL COMMENT

Illegal price rebates made by the seller directly to the purchaser can be subtracted from gross sales in calculating gross income.

ETHICAL POINT

A CPA discovers that a client included fines and penalties in a miscellaneous expense section of a previously filed tax return. The CPA should recommend the filing of an amended return. However, the CPA is not obligated to inform the IRS, and the CPA may not do so without the client's permission, except where required by law.

▶ Queen Corporation is engaged in the ship repair business. It is Queen's practice to kick back approximately 10% of any repair bill to the captain and chief engineer of a foreign-owned ship. Such payments are illegal under state law and could cause Queen to lose its license. The state law is generally enforced. Queen Corporation may not take any deduction for these payments, regardless of whether Queen Corporation is prosecuted by the state.[39] ◀

The courts and the IRS have made a distinction between an illegal nondeductible kickback and an illegal rebate of the purchase price. If the rebate is made directly to the purchaser by the seller, it is considered an adjustment to the selling price and, as such, is an *exclusion* (rather than a deduction) from gross income.[40] The distinction between the two payments seems to be that the rebate is actually negotiated as part of the selling price.

Section 162(c)(3) specifically disallows a deduction for any kickback, rebate, or bribe under Medicare and Medicaid. These include payments made by physicians or suppliers and providers of goods and services who receive payment under the Social Security Act or a federally funded state plan. Unlike the other two types of payments mentioned above, these payments need not be illegal under federal or state law.

FINES AND PENALTIES. Section 162(f) of the IRC also disallows a deduction for the payment of any fine or penalty paid to a government because of the violation of a law.

---

[38] Sec. 162(c)(2).
[39] Reg. Sec. 1.162-18(b)(5).

[40] Rev. Rul. 82-149, 1982-2 C.B. 56.

EXAMPLE 16-28 ▶ Tim owns a semitrailer truck that is used in Tim's freight-hauling business. To increase the profitability of a particular run, Tim often loads his truck in excess of the allowable weight limit. During the current year, Tim pays $600 in fines to various states because the truck is found to be overweight. Tim may not deduct the $600 in fines because the payments are made because of the violation of state law. ◀

The tax law also disallows a deduction for two-thirds of any payment for damages made as a result of a conviction (or a guilty or no-contest plea) in an action regarding a criminal violation of the federal antitrust laws.[41]

EXAMPLE 16-29 ▶ During the current year, the United States files criminal and civil actions against Allen, the president of Able Corporation, and Betty, the president of Bell Corporation, for conspiring to fix and maintain prices of electrical transformers. Both Allen and Betty enter pleas of no contest, and the appropriate judgments are entered. Subsequent to this action, Circle Corporation sues both Able and Bell Corporations for treble damages of $300,000. In settlement, Able and Bell Corporations each pay Circle Corporation $75,000 in full settlement. The maximum that Able and Bell Corporations may each deduct is $25,000 ($75,000 ÷ 3). ◀

EXPENSES RELATING TO AN ILLEGAL ACTIVITY. Interestingly, although the payment of an illegal bribe or kickback and the payment of a fine or penalty as the result of an illegal act are both nondeductible, expenses incurred in an illegal activity are generally deductible if they are ordinary, necessary, and reasonable and the income from the illegal activity is also reported.[42]

EXAMPLE 16-30 ▶ Fred owns and operates a small financial services business involved in the sale of securities and the lending of money. Fred often sells securities to customers in other states. However, because the business is not registered with the appropriate state or federal authorities, the operation of the business is illegal. During the current year, Fred incurs the following expenses:

TYPICAL MISCONCEPTION

Many people mistakenly believe that ordinary and necessary expenses incurred in carrying on an illegal activity are not deductible.

Interest	$ 20,000
Salaries	140,000
Depreciation	7,000
Printing	5,000
Bribe to employee of state securities commission	12,000
Total	$184,000

If Fred reports the income from this activity, the deductible expenses for the year total $172,000. The illegal payment of $12,000 to the government employee is not deductible. ◀

There is one exception to this general rule. Under Sec. 280E, expenses incurred in an illegal business of trafficking or dealing in drugs are not deductible.

OTHER EXPENDITURES THAT ARE SPECIFICALLY DISALLOWED

The IRC also specifically disallows deductions for certain other expenses, even though they might meet all the requirements mentioned above. These include political contributions and lobbying expenses and, in certain situations, business start-up expenses.

---

[41] Sec. 162(g).
[42] *CIR v. Neil Sullivan, et al.*, 1 AFTR 2d 1158, 58-1 USTC ¶9368 (USSC, 1958).

POLITICAL CONTRIBUTIONS AND LOBBYING EXPENSES. One general category of disallowed expenses is political contributions and lobbying expenses. No deduction is allowed for expenditures made in connection with the following:

▶ Influencing legislation

▶ Participating or intervening in any political campaign of any candidate for public office

▶ Any attempt to influence the general public with respect to elections, legislative matters, or referendums

▶ Any direct communication with the President, Vice President, and certain other federal employees and officials

The law also denies a deduction for contributions to tax-exempt organizations that carry on lobbying activities if a principal purpose of the contribution is to obtain a deduction for what otherwise would have been disallowed.[43] Payments made for advertising in a convention or any other program are also disallowed if any part of the proceeds of the publication will directly or indirectly benefit a specific political party or candidate.[44]

Lobbying expenses incurred to influence legislation on a local level are deductible if the legislation is of direct interest to the taxpayer's business. Local legislation includes actions by a legislative body of any political subdivision of a state (e.g., city or county council), but does not include any state or federal action. These deductible expenditures include expenses of communicating with or dues paid to an organization of which the taxpayer is a member. For administrative convenience, the deduction limit does not apply to any in-house expenditure attributable to such activities as long as the total of such expenditures for the taxable year does not exceed $2,000. In-house expenditures are expenses incurred directly by the taxpayer other than amounts paid to a professional lobbyist or dues that are allocable to lobbying. Additionally, the deduction limit does not apply to taxpayers engaged in the business of lobbying.[45]

EXAMPLE 16-31 ▶ Kate is the senior partner of a large New York law firm. During the year, she flies to Washington, D.C., to testify before a Congressional subcommittee with regard to proposed changes in the Social Security taxes imposed on employers. Such changes directly affect her business because they affect the amount of taxes she must pay on behalf of her employees. Kate's ordinary and necessary expenses incurred with respect to the trip are not deductible because the expenses were incurred to influence federal rather than local legislation. ◀

If the legislation cannot reasonably be expected to directly affect the taxpayer's trade or business, the expenses are not deductible.

EXAMPLE 16-32 ▶ Kate is the owner of several hotels in Chicago. The city of Chicago has proposed legislation to increase the hotel room tax guests pay. Kate spends time researching and traveling to speak to the Chicago City Council regarding this legislation. Kate's lobbying expenses are deductible because they are used to influence legislation on the local level and are of direct interest to her business. ◀

---

[43] Sec. 162(e)(3).
[44] Sec. 276(a). Nondeductible political contributions also include payments for admission to a dinner or program where the proceeds will benefit a party

or candidate, or admission to an inaugural ball, party, or concert if the activity is identified with a political party or candidate.
[45] Sec. 162(e)(2) and (e)(5).

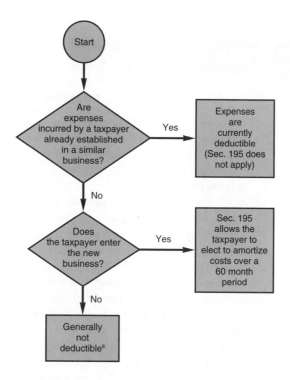

ᵃ Rev. Rul. 57-418, 1957-2 C.B. 143; Morton Frank, 20 T.C. 511 (1953).

FIGURE I6-1 ▶ DEDUCTIBILITY OF BUSINESS INVESTIGATION AND START-UP COSTS

BUSINESS INVESTIGATION AND PREOPENING EXPENSES. Section 195 of the IRC also specifically disallows a current deduction for business start-up expenditures. Instead, these expenses are capitalized and are subject to amortization if an election is made to amortize the start-up costs over a period of not less than 60 months starting with the month in which the new business begins. Start-up expenditures are specifically defined to include three types of expenditures:

▶ *Business investigation expenses.* These expenses are costs a taxpayer incurs in reviewing and analyzing a prospective business before deciding whether to acquire or create it. The key here is that the expenses are incurred before the actual decision. These expenses include such things as analyses and surveys of markets, traffic patterns, products, labor supplies, and distribution facilities.[46]

▶ *Preopening or start-up costs.* Preopening or start-up costs are expenses incurred after the decision to acquire or create the business has been made but before the business activity itself has started. These costs include expenditures for training employees; advertising; securing supplies, distributors, and potential customers; and expenditures for professional services in setting up the business's books and records. These costs must be incurred by a taxpayer who is not engaged in any existing business or is engaged in a business that is unrelated to the business being acquired or created.

ADDITIONAL COMMENT

Costs incurred in connection with the issuance of stock or securities do not qualify as start-up costs. These costs are charged to Paid in Capital.

---

[46] S. Rept. No. 96-1036, 96th Cong., 2d Sess., p. 8 (1980).

Topic Review I6-3

Restrictions on the Deductibility of Expense Items

Item	Restrictions Imposed
1. Capital expenditures	The general rule is that the expenditure is not currently deductible if its life extends beyond the end of the year. Special elections are available to currently deduct certain capital expenditures (e.g., research and experimental costs under Sec. 174; and limited amounts per year for acquisitions of tangible personal property used in a trade or business under Sec. 179).
2. Carrying charges	An election may be made under Sec. 266 to capitalize certain expenses that are normally deductible such as property and employment taxes, interest, and carrying charges on unimproved unproductive real estate.
3. Expenses related to tax exempt income	Expenses such as interest incurred on debt used to purchase or carry tax-exempt securities are disallowed under Sec. 265.
4. Expenditures contrary to public policy	Such expenditures are generally not deductible. Examples include bribes and kickbacks, fines and penalties, and expenses of an illegal activity involved with trafficking or dealing in drugs.
5. Legal and accounting fees	Legal and accounting fees can be either *for* AGI deductible business expenses, nondeductible personal use expenditures, or *from* AGI fees incurred in the determination of any tax (e.g., tax return preparation fees).
6. Political contributions and lobby expenses	The general rule is that such items are not deductible (e.g., costs of influencing public opinion). Certain exceptions are provided (e.g., costs of appearing before local legislative bodies on topics directly related to the taxpayer's business).
7. Business investigation and preopening expenses	The following rules are applied: a. Currently deductible if the taxpayer is already engaged in a similar business. b. Not deductible if the taxpayer is not currently engaged in a similar business and does not enter the new business. c. Amortized over 60 months if the taxpayer enters the new business and makes an election.

▶ *Expenses incurred in connection with an investment activity.* These expenses are costs incurred in connection with an investment activity that the taxpayer anticipates will become an active trade or business.[47]

As defined by Sec. 195, start-up expenditures do not include these same types of expenses when they are incurred by a taxpayer who is already engaged in a business similar to the new one being created or acquired. In such a case, the expenditures may be deducted currently because they are incurred in the taxpayer's existing business.[48] Figure I6-1 summarizes these rules.

STOP & THINK

Question: Shauna works in an automobile manufacturing plant in Detroit, Michigan. In January of the current year, she took a two-week vacation in order to fly to Orlando, Florida. While in Orlando, she spent some time investigating the possibility of opening a store in nearby Coco Beach. In total, she spent $400 on airfare, $1,500 on hotels and food, $300 on equipment rentals, and $300 on a car rental. In addition to spending time on the beach talking to people and checking out the rental equipment, she also spent

---

[47] Sec. 195(c)(1)(A)(iii).

[48] S. Rept. No. 96-1036, 96th Cong., 2d Sess., p. 8 (1980).

some time talking to shop owners and real estate agents. After some analysis, however, Shauna has decided to keep her job in Detroit. What is the proper tax treatment for these expenditures?

Solution: In general, Sec. 162 of the IRC allows a deduction for expenses incurred in a business. Expenses incurred before the business starts are not incurred in a business and thus are not deductible under Sec. 162. However, under Sec. 195 certain expenditures such as business investigation expenses and start-up costs can be capitalized and amortized over a 60-month period, beginning with the month in which the new business begins. Unfortunately for Shauna, she did not open the new business. Thus, none of these expenses may be deducted or amortized.

EXPENSES OF AN ENTERTAINMENT FACILITY

In general, expenses associated with an entertainment facility are not deductible.[49] This disallowance was imposed by Congress in an attempt to prevent taxpayers from deducting expenses incurred with respect to owning or using assets that provide an element of personal recreation for the taxpayer. Thus, no deduction is allowed for maintenance or depreciation of facilities such as hunting lodges and yachts. However, an employer may deduct expenses incurred for recreational, social, or similar activities and facilities that are primarily for the benefit of employees (other than highly compensated employees). The use of these facilities is not gross income to the employees under Sec. 132. (See Chapter I4 for a discussion of fringe benefits that may be excluded from the employee's gross income.) Amounts paid for membership in any club (i.e., club dues) organized for business, pleasure, recreation, or other special purpose are not deductible. These rules are discussed in greater detail in Chapter I9.

Topic Review I6-3 summarizes the restrictions on the deductibility of these items.

PROPER SUBSTANTIATION REQUIREMENT

Generally, the burden of proving the existence of a deduction or loss falls on the taxpayer. Thus, proper substantiation must be made if a taxpayer wants to deduct an expenditure or loss. Items such as receipts, cancelled checks, and paid bills documenting deductible expenditures should be retained in the event the IRS audits a return and requests proof. Occasionally, the courts will allow a deduction that is not properly substantiated by the taxpayer if it is evident that an expenditure has been made. In these cases, the amount of the deduction is estimated based on all the facts and circumstances. This procedure is known as the *Cohan* rule and derives its name from a court case in which the judge allowed a deduction for an estimated amount of certain expenses.[50] The most prudent course of action, of course, is to retain proper documentation rather than to rely upon the *Cohan* rule.

EXAMPLE I6-33 ▶ In April of the current year, Terry took his tax records to a CPA to have his prior year's income tax return prepared. As part of the return, the CPA attached a supplemental schedule listing all

---

[49] Sec. 274(a)(1)(B).
[50] *George M. Cohan v. CIR*, 8 AFTR 10552, 2 USTC ¶489 (2nd Cir., 1930). Interestingly, the *Cohan* case dealt with travel and entertainment expenses.

Because of the subsequent enactment of Sec. 274(d), the *Cohan* rule may not be used in order to deduct these expenses. It is still effective for other types of expenses.

of Terry's items of income and expense. After the return was prepared and filed, Terry's records were stolen. Upon audit two years later, the IRS disallowed Terry's deductions because there were no records to substantiate the expenses. When the case was litigated, the court allowed deductions for an estimated amount of expenses under the *Cohan* rule because of the list that was attached to Terry's return and because the court believed that Terry had testified honestly in his own behalf.[51] ◄

Additionally, the IRC provides specific and more stringent recordkeeping requirements for travel, entertainment, business gifts, computers, and automobiles and other vehicles used for transportation. In these cases no deduction may be taken unless the taxpayer substantiates the expenditure by either an adequate record or sufficient evidence that corroborates the taxpayer's statement.[52] This substantiation may take the form of account books, diaries, logs, receipts and paid bills, trip sheets, expense reports, and statements of witnesses. The information that must be substantiated includes the following:

▶ Amount of the expense

▶ Time and place of the travel or entertainment

▶ Date and a description of the gift

▶ Business purpose of the expenditure

▶ Business relationship to the taxpayer of the person entertained or of the person who received the gift

The *Cohan* rule may not be used for these types of expenses.[53] (See Chapter 19 for a more complete discussion regarding the deductibility of these types of expenses.)

EXPENSES AND LOSSES MUST BE INCURRED BY THE TAXPAYER

Generally, taxpayers may take a deduction only for their own losses and expenses. This requirement prevents taxpayers from engaging in manipulative schemes.

EXAMPLE 16-34 ▶

April and Bruce, the elderly parents of Carol, live in their own home. They have little income and Carol must help to support them. During the current year, the interest and property taxes due on April and Bruce's home total $2,000. April and Bruce file a joint return. They have no other expenses that qualify as itemized deductions. Thus, April and Bruce plan to use the standard deduction, and the benefit of the $2,000 expenditure for interest and taxes will be lost. In an attempt to take advantage of a deduction that otherwise would be lost, Carol pays the interest and taxes. No deduction is allowed to Carol because these expenses are not Carol's own liability. ◄

This general rule applies to all types of expenditures, whether incurred in a trade or business, an investment activity, or a personal activity for which deductions are allowed. There is one exception: Taxpayers may take a deduction for medical expenses paid on behalf of a dependent.[54] Medical expenses also qualify as a deduction if they are paid for a person who would qualify as a dependent except for the fact that the gross income test is not met (see Chapter 12).

---

[51] *Layard M. White,* 1980 PH T.C. Memo ¶80,582, 41 TCM 671.
[52] Secs. 274(d) and 280F(d)(4).

[53] Sec. 274(d) and Temp. Reg. Sec. 1.274-5T(a).
[54] Sec. 213(a).

EXAMPLE I6-35 ▶ During the current year, Dan incurs $3,400 in deductible medical expenses. Dan is not a full-time student and is not under age 19 but is otherwise supported by Tom, his father. Dan's gross income for the year is $15,000. If Tom pays Dan's medical expenses, Tom may deduct the expenses as an itemized deduction even though Tom may not take a dependency exemption for Dan. ◀

SPECIAL DISALLOWANCE RULES

In addition to the general rules of deductibility mentioned above, certain types of transactions are subject to further limitations and disallowances. These include transactions known as wash sales, transactions between related persons, gambling losses, losses associated with an activity determined to be a hobby, expenses of renting a vacation home, and expenses of an office in the taxpayer's home.

WASH SALES

OBJECTIVE 5

Explain the tax consequences of wash sales

Under Sec. 1091, losses incurred on wash sales of stock or securities are disallowed in the year of sale. For purposes of Sec. 1091, a **wash sale** occurs when

▶ A taxpayer realizes a loss on the sale of stock or securities, and

▶ "Substantially identical" stock or securities are acquired by the taxpayer within a 61-day period of time that extends from 30 days before the date of sale to 30 days after the date of sale.[55]

Thus, the purpose of the wash sale rule is to prevent taxpayers from generating artificial tax losses in situations where taxpayers do not intend to reduce their holdings in the stock or securities that are sold.

EXAMPLE I6-36 ▶ Leslie realizes $10,000 in short-term capital gains (STCGs) through dealings in the stock market during the current year. Realizing that STCGs are fully includible in gross income unless they are offset against realized capital losses, Leslie analyzes her portfolio to determine whether she owns any stocks that have declined in value. She finds that the FMV of her Edison Corporation stock is only $8,000, even though she originally purchased it $16,000. Despite this paper loss on the stock, Leslie feels that Edison Corporation is still a good investment and wants to retain the stock. If Leslie attempts to take advantage of the paper loss on the Edison stock by selling the stock she owns and repurchasing a similar number of shares of Edison stock within the 61-day period, the loss is disallowed. ◀

TYPICAL MISCONCEPTION

The wash sale rule applies only to transactions on which there are realized losses, and does not apply to transactions on which there are realized gains.

At times, taxpayers may attempt to circumvent the wash sale provisions through either a sham transaction or an indirect repurchase of the securities. If this is the case, the wash sale provisions still prevent the recognition of the loss. Thus, the Supreme Court has held that losses on sales of stock by a husband were disallowed when the stockbroker was instructed to purchase the same number of shares in the wife's name.[56]

In some instances a taxpayer may be tempted to circumvent the wash sale provisions by merely delaying the repurchase of the substantially identical stock. This tactic should work as long as a written agreement to repurchase the stock does not exist at the time of the sale or at any time within the 61-day period mandated by the Sec. 1091 wash sale

---

[55] Here the term *acquire* includes an acquisition of the stock either by purchase or in a taxable exchange. The term *stock or securities* includes contracts or options to acquire or sell stock or securities (see Sec. 1091(a)).

[56] *John P. McWilliams v. CIR*, 35 AFTR 1184, 47-1 USTC ¶9289 (USSC, 1947).

provisions. If such an agreement is made, however, the courts will disallow the loss, even though the actual purchase does not occur within the 61-day period.[57]

In certain cases, losses on transactions that literally fall within the wash sale requirements may still be recognized. For example, a taxpayer may purchase stock and then sell a portion of those shares within 30 days where the intent is merely to reduce the stock holdings. Taken together, these two transactions meet the tests of Sec. 1091. However, because the purpose of the sale is to reduce the taxpayer's holdings rather than to generate an artificial tax loss, the loss on the sale is not disallowed.[58] Section 1091 also does not apply to losses realized in the ordinary course of business by a dealer in stock or securities.

If fewer shares of stock are acquired within the 61-day period than were disposed of, only a proportionate amount of the total loss is disallowed.

EXAMPLE I6-37 ▶ Henry purchased 100 shares of New Corporation common stock for $2,000 ($20 per share). Several years later, on July 2 of the current year, Henry sells all 100 shares for $1,000. On July 30 of the current year, Henry purchases 75 shares (three-fourths of the original shares) of New Corporation common stock. As a result of the reacquisition, three-fourths of the total loss ($750) is disallowed. The remaining $250 loss is recognized. ◀

SUBSTANTIALLY IDENTICAL STOCK OR SECURITIES. Only the acquisition of substantially identical stock or securities will cause a disallowance of the loss. The IRC and the Treasury Regulations do not define the term *substantially identical*. Judicial and administrative rulings have held that bonds issued by the same corporation generally are not considered substantially identical if they differ in terms (e.g., interest rate and term to maturity). However, bonds of the same corporation that differ only in their maturity dates (e.g., the bonds do not come due for 16 years and mature within a few months of each other) have been held to be substantially identical.[59] The preferred stock of a corporation generally is not considered substantially identical to the common stock of the same corporation.[60]

KEY POINT

The recognition of a loss on a wash sale is only being deferred because the investor can increase the basis of the acquired stock by the disallowed loss.

BASIS OF STOCK. If a loss is disallowed because of the wash sale provisions, the basis of the acquired stock that causes the nonrecognition is increased to reflect the disallowance. This increase means that the disallowed loss is merely postponed and will eventually be recognized either in the form of a reduced gain or an increased loss upon the subsequent sale or disposition of the stock that causes the loss disallowance. Because the amount of the increase in basis is equal to the postponed loss, the taxpayer eventually recovers the cost of the original shares of stock. If there has been more than one purchase of replacement stock and the amount of stock purchased within the 61-day period exceeds the stock that is sold, the stock that is deemed to have caused the disallowance of the loss is accounted for on a chronological basis. Thus, it is the basis of that block of stock that is increased. The holding period of the replacement stock includes the period of time the taxpayer held the stock that was sold.

EXAMPLE I6-38 ▶ Ingrid enters into the following transactions with regard to Pacific Corporation common stock:

[57] Rev. Rul. 72-225, 1972-1 C.B. 59, and *Frank Stein*, 1977 PH T.C. Memo ¶77,241, 36 TCM 992.
[58] Rev. Rul. 56-602, 1956-2 C.B. 527.
[59] *Marie Hanlin, Executrix v. CIR*, 39-2 USTC ¶9783 (3d Cir., 1939).
[60] However, the IRS has held in Rev. Rul. 77-201, 1977-1 C.B. 250, that the convertible preferred stock of a corporation is substantially identical to its common stock if the preferred stock has the same voting rights and is subject to the same dividend restrictions as the common stock, is unrestricted as to its convertibility, and sells at relatively the same price (taking into consideration the conversion ratio).

Date	Transaction	Amount
January 4, 1989	Purchases 600 shares	$30,000
October 2, 1997	Purchases 400 shares	10,000
October 12, 1997	Sells original 600 shares	12,000
October 20, 1997	Purchases 200 shares	5,000
October 25, 1997	Purchases 300 shares	8,400

Because Ingrid purchases more than 600 shares within the 61-day period before and after the date of sale (the purchases made on October 2, 20, and 25), the entire loss of $18,000 ($30,000 − $12,000) is postponed. Four hundred shares (two-thirds of the number of shares sold) are purchased on October 2 and 200 shares (one-third) are purchased on October 20. Thus, the basis of the 400 shares of stock purchased on October 2 is $22,000 [$10,000 purchase price + ($18,000 disallowed loss × 0.667)]. The basis of the 200 shares of stock purchased on October 20 is $11,000 [$5,000 + ($18,000 disallowed loss × 0.333)]. Both of these blocks of stock have a holding period that starts on January 4, 1989.[61] The basis of the 300 shares of stock purchased on October 25 is its purchase price of $8,400. Its holding period begins on October 25. ◀

STOP & THINK

Question: With regard to his investments in the stock market, the current year has been like a roller coaster ride for Doug. He is now wanting to do some year-end tax planning. For the year to date, he has realized a net gain of $12,000 on his stock investments. Although some of his current stock holdings have unrealized losses, he feels that they are excellent investments that will provide excellent returns in the next year or two. His stock broker has suggested that he sell enough of his holdings to realize a $12,000 loss (to offset the $12,000 capital gain) and then simply repurchase some of the stock. What advice would you give Doug as he discusses this strategy with his broker?

Solution: Realizing $12,000 in capital losses this year may enable Doug to offset the capital gains he has already recognized. In order to recognize these losses, however, he must make sure that the wash sale provisions do not apply. Thus, he must either 1) purchase stock of different corporations or 2) delay the repurchase of the same issue of stock for at least 31 days after the date of sale. Since Doug is happy with his current investments, perhaps the second strategy is the best. Of course, other non-tax issues must also be considered. For example, does Doug think that the prices will go up quickly within the next 30 days? If so, he may lose out on some significant gains while he is waiting to repurchase the stock. Additionally, the transaction costs (such as commissions) must also be considered.

TRANSACTIONS BETWEEN RELATED PARTIES

OBJECTIVE 6

Explain the tax consequences of transactions between related parties

Section 267 places transactions between certain related parties under special scrutiny because of the potential for tax abuse. For example, a taxpayer could sell a piece of property at a loss to a wholly owned corporation. Without any restrictions on the deductibility of the loss, the individual could recognize the loss while still retaining effective control of the property. Under Sec. 267, current deductions may not be taken on two specific types of transactions entered into between related taxpayers. These transactions include

---

[61] An asset's holding period is important in determining whether subsequent gain or loss on the asset is long-term or short-term gain or loss. This is explained further in Chapter 15.

ADDITIONAL COMMENT

The word property is not defined in Sec. 267, but it has been given a broad meaning by the IRS and the courts.

▶ Losses on sales of property

▶ Expenses that remain unpaid at the end of the obligor's tax year

RELATED PARTIES DEFINED. Because Sec. 267 applies to transactions between related parties, it is critical to identify who is related for purposes of this provision. Among the relationships defined as related parties under Sec. 267 are the following:

▶ Individuals and their families. *Family* is defined as an individual's spouse, brothers and sisters (including half-brothers and half-sisters), ancestors, and lineal descendants.

▶ An individual and a corporation in which the individual owns more than 50% of the value of the outstanding stock.

▶ Various relationships between grantors, beneficiaries, and fiduciaries of a trust or trusts, or between the fiduciary of a trust and a corporation if certain ownership requirements are met.

▶ A corporation and a partnership if the same persons own more than 50% in value of the stock of the corporation and more than 50% of the partnership.

▶ Two corporations if the same persons own more than 50% in value of the outstanding stock of both corporations and at least one of the corporations is an S corporation.

▶ Other complex relationships involving trusts, corporations and individuals.

Several of these relationships depend on an individual's ownership of a corporation. For example, if a taxpayer does not own more than 50% of a corporation's stock, the individual and the corporation are not considered to be related, and a loss on the sale nonpersonal use of property between the two is deductible. Occasionally individuals might attempt to circumvent the related party rules by dispersing the ownership of a corporation (e.g., among close family members) while retaining economic control. To prevent these tactics, Sec. 267 contains constructive ownership rules whereby a taxpayer is deemed to own stock owned by certain other persons. These constructive ownership rules are as follows:

▶ Stock owned by an individual's family is treated as owned by the individual. Here the definition of *family* is the same as that of *related parties*.

▶ Stock owned by a corporation, partnership, estate, or trust is treated as being owned proportionately by the shareholders, partners, or beneficiaries.

▶ If an individual partner in a partnership owns (or is treated as owning) stock in a corporation, the individual is treated as owning any stock of that corporation owned by any other partner in the partnership. This does not occur, however, if the only stock the individual owns (or is considered to own) is what his or her family owns.[62]

▶ Stock ownership that is attributed to a shareholder or partner from an entity can be reattributed to another taxpayer under any of the constructive ownership rules. However, stock ownership attributed to a taxpayer under the family or partner rules cannot be reattributed.

These rules are illustrated by the following examples:

EXAMPLE 16-39 ▶ Alice and Beth are equal partners in the AB Partnership. Beth owns 60% of First Corporation's stock, and Craig, Alice's husband, owns the other 40%. The ownership of the partnership and the corporation is demonstrated in Figure I6-2. Under the constructive ownership rules, Alice

---

[62] Reg. Sec. 1.267(c)-1(b), Exs. (2) and (3).

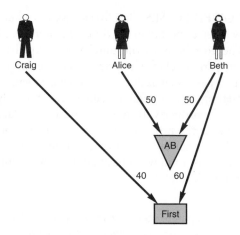

FIGURE 16-2 ▶ ILLUSTRATION FOR EXAMPLE 16-39

is considered to own Craig's 40% of the First Corporation stock. Alice is not considered to own the First Corporation stock owned by her partner, Beth, because the only First Corporation stock Alice owns (or is considered to own) is that owned by her husband. If Alice sells property at a loss to First Corporation, the loss is recognized because Alice does not directly or constructively own more than 50% of the First Corporation stock. ◀

EXAMPLE 16-40 ▶ Assume the same facts as in Example 16-39, except that the First Corporation stock is owned 50% by the AB Partnership and 25% each by Beth and Craig. The ownership of the partnership and the corporation is shown in Figure 16-3. In addition to Craig's 25%, Alice is considered to own 50% of the stock owned by the AB Partnership because of her 50% ownership in AB. The other half of AB's stock ownership is attributed to her partner, Beth. However, Alice is also treated as owning the First Corporation stock Beth owns both actually and constructively (50%). Thus, Alice is treated as owning 100% of the First Corporation stock. In this case, if Alice sells property at a loss to First Corporation, the loss will be disallowed. ◀

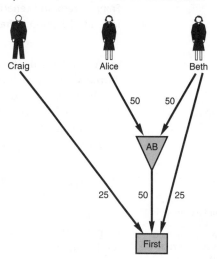

FIGURE 16-3 ▶ ILLUSTRATION FOR EXAMPLE 16-40

ADDITIONAL
COMMENT

A partner is not treated as owning the stock in a corporation owned by his or her partner if the only stock he or she owns is that which is attributed to him or her through the family attribution rules. However, if the partner directly owns as little as one share of the corporation stock, he or she is treated as owning all of the stock owned by his or her partners.

DISALLOWED LOSSES. If a loss is disallowed under Sec. 267, the original seller of the property receives no tax deduction. The disallowed loss has no effect on the purchaser's basis. The cost basis to the purchaser is equal to the amount paid for the property. However, partial relief is provided because on a subsequent sale of the property, the related purchaser may reduce the recognized gain by the amount of the disallowed loss. This offsetting of a subsequent gain is available only to the related person who originally purchased the property. If the disallowed loss is larger than the subsequent gain, or if the purchaser sells the property at a loss, no deduction is allowed for the unused loss. This may result in a partial disallowance of an overall economic loss for the related parties because there is no upward basis adjustment for the previously disallowed loss (as is the case for a wash sale).

EXAMPLE I6-41 ▶

Assume three separate scenarios in which Sam sells a tract of land during the current year. In each case assume that Sam purchased the land from his father, Frank, for $10,000. Frank's basis at the time of the original sale was $15,000 in each case. Thus, Frank's $5,000 loss on each land sale was disallowed.

	Scenario		
	1	2	3
Selling price	$17,000	$12,000	$ 8,000
Minus: Sam's basis	(10,000)	(10,000)	(10,000)
Sam's realized gain (loss)	$ 7,000	$ 2,000	$ (2,000)
Minus: Frank's disallowed loss (up to Sam's gain)	(5,000)	(2,000)	—0—
Sam's recognized gain (loss)	$ 2,000	—0—	($ 2,000)

KEY POINT

The loss disallowance rule for related parties is more severe compared to the loss disallowance rule on wash sales because in a related party transaction, it is possible to lose the tax benefit of all or a portion of the economic loss.

In Scenario 1, Sam and Frank together have incurred an aggregate gain of $2,000 ($17,000 − $15,000). Thus, Frank's full disallowed loss is used to reduce Sam's subsequent gain. In Scenario 2, the aggregate economic loss incurred by Sam and Frank is actually $3,000 ($12,000 − $15,000). However, the actual amount of the tax loss recognized for Sam and Frank is zero. In Scenario 3, the actual tax loss would have been $7,000 ($8,000 − $15,000) instead of $2,000 if Frank had held the land until its eventual sale. ◀

A similar rule found in Sec. 707(b)(1) disallows losses between a partner and a partnership in which the partner owns directly or indirectly over 50% of the partnership and between two partnerships in which the same people own directly or indirectly over 50% in each partnership. The constructive ownership rules of Sec. 267 apply here in determining ownership (see *Prentice Hall's Federal Taxation: Corporations, Partnerships, Estates, and Trusts* text or the *Comprehensive* volume).

KEY POINT

The effect of Sec. 267 with respect to unpaid expenses is to place an accrual method taxpayer on the cash method for amounts owed to a related cash method taxpayer.

UNPAID EXPENSES. Section 267 also causes the obligor of any unpaid expenses to defer the deduction for those expenses until the year in which the related payee recognizes the amount as income. In effect, this rule prevents an accrual-method taxpayer from taking a deduction for an unpaid expense in the earlier year of accrual while the related cash-method taxpayer recognizes the payment as income in the subsequent year.

For purposes of these unpaid expenses, the definition of *related parties* in Sec. 267 is modified to include a personal-service corporation and any employee-owner.[63] A personal-service corporation is one whose principal activity is the performance of personal services that are substantially performed by employee-owners. An employee-

---

[63] Sec. 267(a)(2).

owner is an employee who owns any of the outstanding stock of the personal-service corporation.[64]

EXAMPLE 16-42  Michelle owns 100% of the outstanding stock of Hill Corporation. Michelle is a cash method taxpayer and Hill Corporation is an accrual-method taxpayer. Both taxpayers are calendar-year taxpayers. In a bona fide transaction, Hill borrows some funds from Michelle. By the end of the current year, $8,000 interest had accrued on the loan. However, Hill Corporation does not pay the interest to Michelle until February of the following year. Because Michelle is a cash-method taxpayer, the interest income is reported when she receives it in the following year. Although Hill is an accrual method taxpayer, Hill's deduction for the interest expense is deferred until it is paid in February of the following year. The results are the same if Hill Corporation is a personal-service corporation and Michelle owns only 20% of the Hill stock. ◄

For purposes of these unpaid expenses, the definition of *related parties* is also modified to include various relationships involving partnerships or S corporations and any person who owns (either actually or constructively) any interest in these entities.[65]

OBJECTIVE 7

Discuss the criteria used to determine whether an activity is a hobby or a trade or business

HOBBY LOSSES

Certain activities have both profit-motivated and other attributes. In these cases it is necessary to examine all of the relevant factors to determine the tax status of the activity. The factors the IRS uses to determine whether an activity is profit-motivated were discussed in this chapter under the Criteria for Deducting Business and Investment Expenses section. If an examination of these factors is not determinative, the activity is presumed to be profit-motivated if it generates taxable income in at least three of five consecutive years (at least two of seven years if the activity consists mainly of breeding, training, showing, or racing horses). If this profit test is met, the burden of proof shifts and the IRS must prove that the activity is not profit-motivated. This determination is important because, in general, a deduction is not allowed for losses incurred in an activity that is not profit-motivated. An activity that has no profit motive is likely to be a personal hobby of the taxpayer and is not a trade or business activity.

ADDITIONAL COMMENT

Gross income from an activity not engaged in for profit is defined to include the total gains from the sale, exchange, or other disposition of property, and all other gross receipts derived from such activity. Cost of goods sold can be deducted from gross receipts to calculate gross income.

DEDUCTIBLE EXPENSES. Some hobby activities generate gross income, even though profit is not a primary motive for the activity. In such situations, Sec. 183 allows the taxpayer to deduct the expenses related to the hobby, but only to the extent of the gross income from the hobby. Furthermore, a hobby-related expense is deductible only if it would have been deductible if incurred in a trade or business or an investment activity.

In essence, a taxpayer may deduct all the hobby-related expenses as long as there is enough gross income from the activity to cover the expenses. However, a hobby cannot generate a tax loss that is then used to offset a taxpayer's other types of income.

EXAMPLE 16-43 ▶ Julie, a dentist, enjoys painting in her spare time. During the current year, Julie receives $2,500 from the sale of her paintings. During that same year, she also incurs $1,700 in painting-related expenses. If these expenses were incurred in a trade or business, they would have been deductible. Julie is entitled to deduct the $1,700 in expenses up to the amount of her painting-related income of $2,500. On the other hand, if the expenses related to Julie's

---

[64] Secs. 269A(b) and 441(i)(2). In determining the ownership of an employee-owner, the constructive ownership rules of Sec. 318 as modified by Sec. 441(i)(2) are used. These rules differ substantially from the constructive ownership rules of Sec. 267.

[65] Sec. 267(e). A discussion of these modifications is beyond the scope of this book.

painting activities are $2,900, she may deduct only $2,500 of the expenses (up to the gross income from the activity). ◄

ORDER OF THE DEDUCTIONS. If the hobby expenses exceed the amount of gross income generated by the hobby, the expenses must be deducted against the gross income in the following order:

▶ Tier 1: Expenses that may be deducted even though they are not incurred in a trade or business (e.g., itemized deductions such as taxes, certain interest, and casualty losses)

▶ Tier 2: Other expenses of the hobby that could have been deducted if they had been incurred in a profit-motivated activity, but do not reduce the tax basis of any of the assets used in the hobby (e.g., utilities and maintenance expenses)

▶ Tier 3: The expenses of the hobby that could have been deducted if incurred in a profit-motivated activity and that reduce the basis of the hobby's assets (e.g., depreciation on fixed assets used in the hobby)[66]

KEY POINT

Expenses that cannot be deducted because the activity is a hobby are treated as personal expenditures and are lost forever.

To the extent that the expenses are taken as deductions against the gross income of the activity, they are deductions *from* AGI and are deductible if the taxpayer has itemized deductions in excess of the standard deduction. The tier 1 expenses are reported in their respective sections on Schedule A of Form 1040. The tier 2 and tier 3 expenses allocated to the hobby are treated as miscellaneous itemized deductions and are, therefore, deductible only to the extent that they exceed 2% of AGI (see Chapter I7). Gross income from a hobby is reported as other income on Form 1040. If gross income is not sufficient to cover all of the tier 1 expenses, the excess expenses may also be deducted as itemized deductions on Schedule A of Form 1040 because these expenses are allowed in any event. Any remaining expenses in the other two tiers are disallowed and may not be carried over to a subsequent year.

EXAMPLE I6-44 ▶

As a hobby, Lynn raises various types of plants and flowers in a small greenhouse constructed specifically for that purpose. During the current year, Lynn realizes $1,000 gross income and incurs $1,150 local property taxes on the greenhouse. She also incurs an additional $300 in utilities related to the activity. If the activity were a trade or business, a total of $800 depreciation on the greenhouse could be deducted for the year. For the current year, the $1,000 gross income is included in AGI, and the full $1,150 of taxes are itemized deductions and may be deducted if Lynn has itemized deductions in excess of the standard deduction. No deduction is available for the $300 of utilities expense or the $800 of depreciation. ◄

If depreciation expense is disallowed, it is not necessary to reduce the cost basis of the asset to the extent of the disallowance.[67]

EXAMPLE I6-45 ▶

Assume the same facts as in Example I6-44, except that the gross income is $1,700. In this case, all $1,450 ($1,150 + $300) of taxes and utilities are deductible, because the gross income exceeds that amount. In addition, Lynn can also deduct $250 ($1,700 − $1,450) of the $800 depreciation. The taxes are deductible as taxes on Schedule A of Form 1040, whereas the utilities and the depreciation are miscellaneous itemized deductions and are deductible only to the extent that Lynn's total miscellaneous itemized deductions exceed 2% of AGI. The additional $550 depreciation is not deductible. However, the cost basis of the greenhouse is reduced only by the $250 depreciation that is deducted. ◄

---

[66] Reg. Sec. 1.183-1(b).   [67] Ibid.

VACATION HOME

Because owning a second home or dwelling unit may have both personal and profit-motivated attributes, deductions for expenses related to the rental of a vacation home that is also used as a residence by the taxpayer may be disallowed or limited by Sec. 280A.

RESIDENCE DEFINED. For the restrictive rules of Sec. 280A to apply, the property must be a dwelling unit that qualifies as the taxpayer's residence. As used in this context, the term *dwelling unit* is quite expansive. Items such as boats and mobile homes may be considered dwelling units.[68] The determining factor is whether the property provides shelter and accommodations for eating and sleeping.[69] Thus, a mini-motorhome that contains the appropriate accommodations has been held to be a dwelling unit subject to the rules and limitations of Sec. 280A. The fact that the unit is small and cramped is disregarded.

A dwelling unit is considered to be used by the taxpayer as a residence if the number of days during which the taxpayer uses the property for personal use throughout the year exceeds the greater of the following:

▶ 14 days, or

▶ 10% of the number of days during the year that the property is rented at a fair rental[70]

For purposes of this test, a day of personal use includes any day that the property is used

▶ For personal purposes by the taxpayer or the taxpayer's family. *Family* is defined here as including a taxpayer's spouse, brothers and sisters, ancestors, and lineal descendants.[71]

▶ By any individual under a reciprocal-use arrangement.[72]

▶ By any individual who does not pay a fair rental for the use of the property.[73]

Despite the family-use rule, if a taxpayer rents property at a fair rental to a family member who uses the property as a principal residence, such use does not constitute personal use by the taxpayer.[74]

EXAMPLE 16-46 ▶

During the current year, Peggy purchases a small house as an investment and rents the property to Stan, her married son, who uses the property as his principal residence. Peggy's son pays her a fair rental for the property. Because Stan uses the property as his principal residence and pays Peggy a fair rental for the property, Stan's personal use of the property does not constitute personal use by Peggy. Thus, the rules of Sec. 280A do not apply to limit the expenses that Peggy may deduct. ◀

ALLOCATION OF EXPENSES. To the extent that expenses of the property relate to the taxpayer's personal use, no deduction is allowed for expenses other than qualified

---

[68] Sec. 280A(f)(1).
[69] *Ronald L. Haberkorn*, 75 T.C. 259 (1980), and *John O. Loughlin v. U.S.*, 50 AFTR 2d 82-5827, 82-2 USTC ¶9543 (D.C. Minn., 1982).
[70] Sec. 280A(d)(1). In certain cases, this residence test might be met when a taxpayer uses a property as his or her principal residence for part of the year and rents the property for the rest of the year. This could occur, for example, when a taxpayer moves from his or her home and turns the old residence into a rental unit. In such a case, special rules prevent the home from being classified as a residence under Sec. 280A, thus preventing the application of the limitations.

[71] Under Sec. 280A(d)(2), a day during which the taxpayer spends substantially full time on repairs and maintenance does not count as a personal-use day.
[72] Sec. 280A(d)(2)(B). A reciprocal-use arrangement is one whereby another person uses the taxpayer's property in exchange for the taxpayer's use of the other person's property.
[73] Sec. 280A(d)(2)(C). Exactly what constitutes a fair rental must be determined by an examination of all the associated facts and circumstances.
[74] Sec. 280A(d)(3).

KEY POINT

A second home is going to be classified as either rental property, a residence, or some combination of the two. If it is classified as some combination of rental property and a residence, it is necessary to allocate expenses between the two categories.

interest and taxes, which are deductible on personal residences.[75] However, expenses allocated to the rental use are deductible under Sec. 280A only to the extent of the gross income generated by the property (qualified residential interest and taxes in excess of the rental income may be deducted as itemized deductions). The property may not generate a loss which is used to reduce other income of the taxpayer. Expenses that are not deductible because they exceed the gross income from the property may be carried over to the subsequent year and taken as a deduction, limited to the gross income of that year.[76] Expenses that are allocated to the rental use of the property and deducted against the gross income must be taken in the same order (explained previously) that the expenses under the hobby loss rules of Sec. 183 are deducted. Examples I6-56 and I6-57 illustrate these rules.

Allocation Formula. In allocating expenses between the personal use and the rental use of the property, the following formula is used:[77]

$$\text{Rental use expenses} = \frac{\text{Number of rental days}}{\text{Total number of days used}} \times \frac{\text{Total expenses}}{\text{for the year}}$$

The denominator of the allocation fraction is the sum of the days the property is rented plus the days that the property is used for personal purposes. The days when the property is not used are not included in the formula.

Some courts have ruled that the allocation of qualified residential interest and taxes to the rental use is to be done by taking into account the periods during the year when the property is not used. Thus, the denominator of the allocation formula would be the total number of days in the year.[78] Use of this ratio allocates less interest and taxes to the rental use, allowing more of the other expenses to be deducted against the rental income. Subject to limitations, the interest and taxes not allocated to the rental use are still deductible as itemized deductions. Example I6-47 uses the allocation formula that has been sanctioned by the courts.

EXAMPLE I6-47 ▶ Joan owns a cabin near the local ski resort. During the year, Joan and Joan's family use the cabin a total of 25 days. The cabin is also rented to out-of-state skiers for a total of 50 days during the year, generating rental income of $10,000. Joan also incurs the following expenses:

Expense	Amount
Property taxes	$1,500
Interest on mortgage	3,000
Utilities	2,000
Insurance	1,500
Security and snow removal	2,500

Joan would have been entitled to $12,000 depreciation if the property had been entirely rental property held for investment. However, because the property is also used for personal purposes, the amount of deductions (for AGI) Joan may take with respect to the property during the year is as follows:

[75] No deduction is allowed for interest incurred with respect to a personal residence if the debt on which the interest is paid is not secured by the property or the taxpayer has not chosen the property as a second residence for purposes of deducting the interest as qualified residential interest (see Chapter I7). For purposes of the discussion and examples used here, the assumption is made that the interest qualifies as qualified residential interest.
[76] Sec. 280A(c)(5)(B). The expenses that are carried over to the subsequent year are deductible to the extent of the property's gross income of that year, even though the property is not used by the taxpayer as a residence during that year.
[77] Sec. 280A(e)(1).
[78] *Dorance D. Bolton v. CIR*, 51 AFTR 2d 82-305, 82-2 USTC ¶9699 (9th Cir., 1982). See also *Edith G. McKinney v. CIR*, 52 AFTR 2d 83-6281, 83-2 USTC ¶9655 (10th Cir., 1983).

SELF-STUDY QUESTION

Assume that a taxpayer rents his cabin to an individual who occupies it on a Saturday afternoon. Two weeks later the tenant leaves the cabin on a Saturday morning. Has the cabin been rented for fewer than 15 days?

ANSWER

Yes, although the tenant was on the premises for 15 calendar days, he is treated as having rented the property for only 14 days.

Item	Calculation	Amount
Rental income		$10,000
Interest and taxes	$4,500 \times \dfrac{50}{365}$	(616)[a]
All other expenses except depreciation	$6,000 \times \dfrac{50}{75}$	(4,000)
Depreciation	$12,000 \times \dfrac{50}{75}$	(5,384)[b]
Net income from property		$ 0

[a] Under the approach favored by the IRS, $3,000 ($4,500 × ⁵⁰⁄₇₅) of interest and taxes would be used to offset the gross income and only $3,000 of depreciation would be deductible.
[b] The additional $2,616 ($8,000 − $5,384) can be carried over and deducted in the next year if the gross income of that year is sufficient to cover all the expenses allocable to the rental use. If there had been sufficient gross income, Joan could have taken $8,000 depreciation.

In addition to the deductions above, Joan may also deduct $3,884 ($4,500 − $616) interest and taxes as itemized deductions if her total itemized deductions exceed the standard deduction and the interest is qualified residence interest (see Chapter I7). ◄

NOMINAL NUMBER OF RENTAL DAYS. If a property qualifies as a taxpayer's residence under Sec. 280A but it is rented for less than 15 days during the year, the law takes the approach that the property is completely personal in nature. As such, no rental income is included in gross income and no expenses may be deducted. However, expenses such as qualified residential interest and taxes may still be deducted as itemized deductions. (See Chapter I7 for a discussion of the limitations on interest.)

EXAMPLE I6-48 ▶ Assume the same facts as in Example I6-47, except that during the year Joan's cabin is rented for only 12 days and the amount of rental income is $2,400. The cabin qualifies as Joan's residence because her personal use exceeds 14 days. Because the cabin is rented for less than 15 days during the year, Joan may only take itemized deductions of $4,500 for the qualified residential interest and taxes. The other expenses may not be deducted. In addition, the $2,400 is not included in gross income. ◄

KEY POINT

Assume that a taxpayer owns a beachfront condo. The taxpayer personally uses the condo for only 12 days during the year and rents the property for 35 days. Section 280A does not apply because the taxpayer has not used the property for over 14 days. However, if the taxpayer cannot demonstrate a profit motive, it may still be treated as a hobby. If so, the deductibility of the expenses allocated to the rental use is limited to the gross income generated by the property. Furthermore, the interest allocated to the personal use of the property is not deductible as qualified residential interest (see Chapter I7).

NOMINAL NUMBER OF PERSONAL-USE DAYS. If a taxpayer does not have enough personal-use days during the year to qualify the property as a residence (i.e., the personal use is not more than the greater of 14 days or 10% of the rental days), the Sec. 280A rules and limitations do not apply. Under these circumstances, the property may be considered a hobby if the owner cannot demonstrate a proper profit motive. If this is the case, the hobby loss rules apply. On the other hand, if the owner demonstrates a profit motive, the property is treated as rental property. However, the expenses must still be allocated between the rental use and the personal use. The taxes allocated to the personal use are deductible as itemized deductions. None of the interest allocated to the personal use is deductible because it is not qualified residential interest. (See Chapter I7 for a discussion of the deductibility of personal interest and qualified residential interest.) Tier 2 and 3 expenses allocated to the personal use are not deductible. The income from the property and all of the expenses allocated to the rental use are reported on Schedule E of Form 1040. As such, the expenses are *for* AGI deductions. Any net income or loss from the property is subject to the passive loss rules, which may limit the deductibility of any losses from the property (see Chapter I8). The rules of Sec. 280A regarding the rental of property are summarized in Figure I6-4.

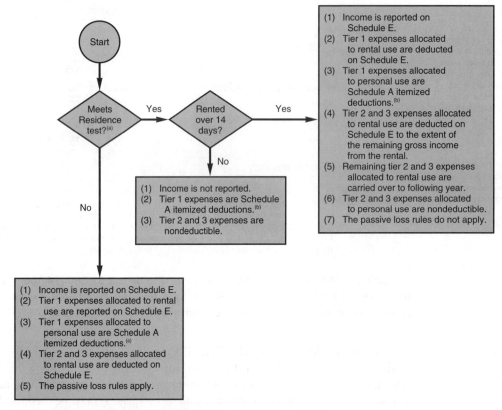

(a) Personal use is more than the larger of (1) 14 days of (2) 10% of rental days.
(b) In order for the interest to be deductible, it must be "qualified residence interest" (See Chapter 7).
(c) In order for the interest to be deductible as qualified residence, the property must not have been rented at all during the year (see Chapter 7).

FIGURE I6-4 ▶ SECTION 280A: LIMITATION OF DEDUCTIONS ON RENTAL OF RESIDENTIAL PROPERTY

EXPENSES OF AN OFFICE IN THE HOME

Unless the taxpayer meets certain strictly imposed requirements, Sec. 280A disallows any deduction for home office expenses. In general, for a taxpayer to deduct office-in-home expenses, the office must have been regularly and exclusively used as either of the following:

▶ The principal place of business for a business of the taxpayer

▶ A place of business where the taxpayer meets or deals with clients in the normal course of business

For employees to take a deduction for home office expenses, the use must also have been for the convenience of the employer. In addition, a separate structure not attached to the taxpayer's house may qualify if regularly and exclusively used in connection with the taxpayer's business. (See Chapter I9 for a comprehensive discussion of these rules.)

TAX PLANNING CONSIDERATIONS

ADDITIONAL COMMENT

Small or "contrived" profits to meet the presumption are generally ignored.

HOBBY LOSSES

Deductions for expenses incurred in a hobby activity are limited to the gross income generated by the hobby for the year. However, if the gross income exceeds the deductions from the activity in at least three out of five consecutive years, the activity is presumed to be a business, and the limits on the deductibility of expenses do not apply. Thus, if possible, taxpayers should use care in timing the realization of items of income and expense. For example, if an activity has shown a profit in only two out of the previous four years, a taxpayer may consider accelerating some of the income into the fifth year or deferring some of the expenses of the activity into the following year. Under the cash method of accounting, this can be done by delaying payment for some of the expenses or accelerating income-generating transactions. Note that meeting the three-out-of-five-year test does not automatically ensure that the activity will be treated as a business. It merely compels the IRS to prove that the activity is *not* a business. Under these circumstances, the IRS may be less inclined to challenge the deductions.

UNREASONABLE COMPENSATION

If the IRS feels that a salary payment to an officer of a corporation is excessive, it will often recharacterize the excess portion as a dividend. If that happens, the corporation is not permitted to deduct the full amount of the salary payment. To prevent a potential future disallowance, a payback or hedge agreement, which provides that the employee must return to the corporation any payment held to be excessive, may be entered into between the parties. A payback agreement must meet the following requirements to be effective:

▶ It must be entered into before the payment is actually made.

▶ It must legally obligate the employee to repay the excess amount.[79]

The IRS may take the position that the existence of the payback agreement itself is evidence that the compensation is excessive.[80] This situation may be avoided if the payback agreement is included in the general corporate bylaws rather than in a specific contract with a particular employee.[81]

TIMING OF DEDUCTIONS

Because of the time value of money, taxpayers generally prefer to deduct an expenditure as a current expense rather than capitalize it. If an expenditure is required to be capitalized, the deductions (e.g., for depreciation or amortization) are spread over several years. In addition, some capital expenditures (e.g., land) are not subject to depreciation or amortization. In some situations, however, it may be preferable for the taxpayer to capitalize rather than expense a particular item. For example, if a taxpayer has net operating losses (NOLs) that are about to expire, a current deduction may prevent the use of these losses.[82]

In some cases it is difficult to determine whether an item should be treated as a capital expenditure or a deduction item (e.g., certain repairs may in the aggregate be treated as a capital expenditure). In addition, certain types of expenditures, such as for research and experimentation, may be either capitalized (subject to amortization) or expensed at the election of the taxpayer. Consideration should be given to the taxpayer's tax situation

ETHICAL POINT

In some cases it is difficult to ascertain whether an activity is a trade or business or a hobby. A CPA should not prepare or sign a tax return unless he or she in good faith believes that the return takes a position that has a realistic possibility of being sustained on its merits.

---

[79] *Vincent E. Oswald*, 49 T.C. 645 (1968); and *J. G. Pahl*, 67 T.C. 286 (1976). See also *Ernest H. Berger*, 37 T.C. 1026 (1962).

[80] *Charles Schneider and Co. v. CIR*, 34 AFTR 2d 74-5422, 74-2 USTC ¶9563 (8th Cir., 1974).

[81] *Plastics Universal Corp.*, 1979 PH T.C. Memo ¶79,355, 39 TCM 32. Additionally, some taxpayers have been successful in defending their current level of compensation where they proved that they had been undercompen-

sated in prior years. See *Acme Construction Co., Inc.*, 1995 RIA T.C. Memo ¶95,600, 69 TCM 1596.

[82] A NOL arises when business expenses exceed business income for a year. This excess can be carried to another year (back three years and forward fifteen years) and is deducted against the income of that year. If the years to which the NOL is carried do not have enough income, the NOL is lost when the carryover period expires. See Chapter 18 for a discussion of NOLs.

WHAT WOULD YOU DO IN THIS SITUATION?

SERIOUS WINE OR HOBBY LOSS?

Mr. Bouteilles Gerbeuses has been your long-time tax client. He has amassed an impressive portfolio of real estate, securities, and joint venture investments. His net worth is substantial.

Despite all his material well-being, Mr. Gerbeuses wants to take on a new challenge—that of producing fine wines. He has not had any formal wine training but he has decided to start his own winery, named *Cuvée de Prestige*. It will be patterned after the great wine houses of Europe.

He already owns several hundred acres of agriculturally zoned land in the wine producing region of the Noir Valley. It happens to adjoin his home in the Wemadeit Country Club and Retirement Resort subdivision. He anticipates a life of semi-retirement by engaging in the art of malolactic fermentation and blending of his *blanc de blancs* and *pinot noir* grapes into his own estate wine. His start-up capital investment is expected to be over $5 million and the first harvest is not expected to take place for at least seven years after the initial planting of grape vines. Any losses are expected to be offset by his other income.

Assuming Mr. Gerbeuses comes to you for tax advice on his new wine venture, what tax and ethical issues should be considered?

when this decision is made. In making this decision, taxpayers should consider NOL carryovers that might be expiring. They should also compare their current marginal tax rate with their anticipated future marginal tax rate.

COMPLIANCE AND PROCEDURAL CONSIDERATIONS

PROPER CLASSIFICATION OF DEDUCTIONS

Individuals report trade or business expenses on Schedule C (Profit or Loss from Business or Profession). It is similar to an income statement for business-related income and expenses. The net income computed on Schedule C is then included in gross income on Form 1040. Because business-related expenses are deducted in arriving at the taxable income from the business, these expenses are deductions *for* AGI. Similar treatment is given to the deductibility of expenses attributable to the production of rental and royalty income because they are reported on Schedule E, which is an income statement. The other deductions *for* AGI have specific lines on Form 1040 itself where they are deducted.[83] All of these deductions appear before line 31 (where AGI appears) of Form 1040.

Deductions *from* AGI are reported on Schedule A, where they are totaled and then transferred to Line 34 of Form 1040.

PROPER SUBSTANTIATION

The burden of proving the deductibility of any expense generally rests on the taxpayer. This has always been the case. However, in recent years Congress and the IRS have become increasingly concerned about the propriety of many deductions. In the case of travel and entertainment expenses, the Code states that no deduction may be taken for an expense that is not properly documented. This information must include the amount of the expense, the time and place of the travel or entertainment activity, the business purpose, and the business relationship of the people entertained.

---

[83] Some of these expenses, such as employee business expenses (Form 2106) and moving expenses (Form 3903), are summarized on separate forms. These separate forms, however, are not net income statements in the same sense that Schedules C and E are.

ADDITIONAL COMMENT

When the election is made to defer the determination of whether a particular activity is engaged in for profit, the statute of limitations is automatically extended for all years in the postponement period. However, the automatic extension applies only to items that might be disallowed under the hobby loss rules.

BUSINESS VERSUS HOBBY

Self-employed individuals who claim a home office deduction on Schedule C must attach Form 8829, which is used to allocate direct and indirect expenses to the appropriate use. Form 8829 need not be filed by employees who claim home office expenses on Form 2106.

When an activity has both profit-making and personal elements associated with it, the burden is normally on the taxpayer to prove that the activity is a business. However, if a taxpayer can show that the activity has generated a profit in at least three out of five consecutive years, the burden of proof shifts to the IRS. Because the statute of limitations generally runs three years after the filing of a return for any particular year (i.e., for audit purposes the year is closed and the IRS cannot assess any tax deficiency for that year), a potential problem exists for taxpayers who want to rely on this presumption during the first year or two of an activity's life. In these cases, the taxpayer may elect to defer the determination of whether the presumption applies until the fifth year of operation. The effect of this election is to keep the year in question open with respect to that activity until sufficient years have passed that the presumptive test may be applied. If the taxpayer subsequently does not meet the presumptive test, the IRS can still assess a deficiency for that activity for the prior year, because the year is still open. This election is made by filing Form 5213 (Election to Postpone Determination as to Whether the Presumption That an Activity Is Engaged In for Profit Applies) and must be filed within three years after the due date for the year in which the taxpayer first engages in the activity. This form includes the following:

▶ Taxpayer's name, address, and identification number

▶ Statement declaring that the taxpayer elects to postpone the hobby versus business determination

▶ Description of the activity for which the election is being made

In addition, the taxpayer must properly consent to an extension of the statute of limitations.[84]

PROBLEM MATERIALS

DISCUSSION QUESTIONS

I6-1 Why is the concept of adjusted gross income (AGI) important for individuals?

I6-2 Why are deductions *for* AGI usually more advantageous than deductions *from* AGI?

I6-3 Sam owns a small house that he rents out to students attending the local university. Are the expenses associated with the rental unit deductions *for* or *from* AGI?

I6-4 During the year, Sara sold a capital asset at a loss of $2,000. She had held the asset as an investment. Is her deduction for this capital loss a deduction *for* or a deduction *from* AGI?

I6-5 Discuss the difference in tax treatment between reimbursed employee business expenses and unreimbursed employee business expenses.

---

[84] Temp. Reg. Sec. 12.9.

I6-6 For the current year, Mario a single individual with no dependents, receives income of $55,000 and incurs deductible expenses of $9,000.
a. What is Mario's taxable income assuming that the expenses are deductions *for* AGI.
b. What is Mario's taxable income assuming that the expenses are miscellaneous itemized deductions *from* AGI.

I6-7 Under what circumstances can prepaid expenses be deducted in the year of payment by a taxpayer using the cash method of accounting?

I6-8 Can a taxpayer use both the cash method and the accrual method of accounting at the same time? Explain.

I6-9 Whether the economic performance test is satisfied depends on the type of transaction and whether the transaction is recurring.
a. When does economic performance occur for a taxpayer who must provide property or services to another person?
b. When does economic performance occur when another person provides the taxpayer with property or services?
c. Explain the exception to the economic performance test for recurring liabilities.

I6-10 a. What are the factors used in determining whether an activity is profit-motivated?
b. Why are these factors so important in making this determination?

I6-11 If an activity does not generate a profit in three out of five consecutive years, is it automatically deemed to be a hobby? Why or why not?

I6-12 Because expenses incurred both in a business and for the production of investment income are deductible, why is it important to determine in which category a particular activity falls?

I6-13 In order for a business expense to be deductible it must be *ordinary*, *necessary*, and *reasonable*. Explain what these terms mean.

I6-14 What criteria must one use in distinguishing between a deductible expense and a capital expenditure?

I6-15 What is the purpose of the disallowance for expenses related to tax-exempt income?

I6-16 Under what circumstances may a taxpayer deduct an illegal bribe or kickback?

I6-17 Michelle pays a CPA $400 for the preparation of her federal income tax return. Michelle's only sources of income are her salary from employment and interest and dividends from her investments.
a. Is this a deductible expense? If so, is it a deduction *for* or *from* AGI?
b. Assume the same facts as in Part a except that in addition to her salary and investment and dividend income, Michelle also owns a small business. Of the $400 fee paid to the CPA, $250 is for the preparation of her Schedule C (Profit or Loss from Business). How much, if any, of the $400 is a deductible expense? Identify as either *for* or *from* AGI.

I6-18 Jennifer flies to her state capital to lobby the legislature to build a proposed highway that is planned to run through the area where her business is located.
a. What part, if any, of her expenses are deductible?
b. Would it make a difference if the proposed road were a city road rather than a state highway, and Jennifer lobbied her local government?
c. Assume the same facts in Part a except that Jennifer's total expenses are $1,500. Are these expenses deductible?

I6-19 During November and December of last year, Tom incurred the following expenses in investigating the feasibility of opening a new restaurant in town:

Expenses to do a market survey	$3,000
Expenses to identify potential supplies of goods	$2,000
Expenses to identify a proper location	$1,000

Explain the proper treatment of these expenses under the following scenarios:
a. Tom already owns another restaurant in town and is wanting to expand. Tom opens the new restaurant in February of the current year.
b. Tom is tiring of his current job as an outside salesperson and wants to go into business for

himself. He opens the restaurant in February of the currect year.

c. Tom is tiring of his current job as an outside salesperson and wants to go into business for himself. However, after getting the results of the investigations back, he decides against opening a restaurant.

I6-20 What documentation is required in order for a travel or entertainment expense to be deductible?

I6-21 Why did Congress enact the wash sale provisions?

I6-22 The wash sale rules disallow a loss in the year of sale when substantially identical stock or securities are acquired by the taxpayer within a 61-day period. What types of stock or securities are considered substantially identical?

I6-23 a. Who is considered a member of a taxpayer's family under the related party transaction rules of Sec. 267?

b. Identify some of the other relationships that are considered related parties for purposes of Sec. 267. Why are these other relationships included in the definition?

I6-24 Under the related party rules of Sec. 267, why has Congress imposed the concept of constructive ownership?

I6-25 If property is sold at a loss to a related taxpayer, under what circumstances can at least partial benefit be derived from the disallowed loss?

I6-26 Assume that Jill is engaged in painting as a hobby. During the year, she earns $1,000 from sales of her paintings and incurs $2,500 expenses for supplies and lessons. Jill's salary for the year is $70,000. What is the tax treatment of the hobby income and expenses?

I6-27 Under Sec. 280A, what constitutes personal use of a vacation home by the taxpayer?

I6-28 Under Sec. 280A, how are expenses allocated to the rental use of a vacation home? In what order must the expenses be deducted against the gross income of the property?

I6-29 Under Sec. 280A, how will a taxpayer report the income and expenses of a vacation home if it is rented out for only 12 days during the year?

ISSUE IDENTIFICATION QUESTIONS

I6-30 David, a CPA for a big-six firm, works 10- to 12-hour days. As a requirement for his position, he must attend social events to recruit new clients. He also has private clients in his unincorporated professional practice. David purchased exercise equipment for $3,000. He works out on the equipment to maintain his stamina and good health that enables him to carry such a heavy workload. What tax issues should David consider?

I6-31 Gus, a football player who was renegotiating his contract with the Denver Broncos, paid his ex-girlfriend $25,000 to drop a sexual assault complaint against him and keep the matter confidential. The Broncos stated that if criminal charges were filed and made public, they would terminate his employment. What tax issues should Gus consider?

I6-32 Kathleen pays $3,000 mortgage interest on the home that she and her husband live in. Kathleen and her husband live with Molly, Kathleen's mother. The title to the home is in Kathleen's name. However, the mortgage is Molly's obligation. Kathleen claims Molly as her dependent on her current tax return. What tax issues should Kathleen consider?

I6-33 While on vacation, Jose, a photography enthusiast, takes scenic photographs for his photo portfolio. The portfolio contains approximately 280 pictures, which he offers for sale to customers. He acquired two cameras with auxiliary equipment for several thousand dollars. Jose displayed, with prices, a sample collection of his photographs at a local doctor's office and at his own place of employment. He sold several photos but reported net losses in the prior two years. During the current year, he reported $1,000 of gross income and incurred $1,500 of expenses. What tax issues should Jose consider?

I6-34 Mark and Carol are avid boaters and water skiers. They also enjoy parasailing. In the current year, they started a parasailing company that sells equipment and gives patrons rides. Mark and Carol are employed full-time in other pursuits, but operate and manage the company during the summer months, on weekends and holidays. Mark has attended classes on boat operation and parasailing instruction. In the prior two years, Mark and Carol had purchased two boats. These boats are used in the company operations and for recreational purposes. Mark and Carol advertise in the yellow pages for the company, maintain a separate bank account, have a sales tax number, and have printed business cards. They keep a journal to record receipts and disbursements. In the current year, the company reported $4,600 of income and $8,900 of expenses. What tax issues should Mark and Carol consider?

PROBLEMS

I6-35 *For or From AGI Deductions.* Jermaine is an attorney employed by a local law firm. During the year, Jermaine incurs the following unreimbursed expenses:

Item	Amount
Bar association fees	$300
Subscriptions to professional journals	150
Travel from the office to the courthouse	200
Photocopying of the firm's law briefs	100
Taking clients to dinner	450

a. Identify which of these expenses are deductible and indicate whether they are deductions *for* or *from* AGI.
b. Would the answer to Part a change if the law firm reimburses Jermaine for these expenses?
c. Assume all of the same facts as in Part a, except that Jermaine is self-employed. Identify which of the expenses are deductible, and indicate whether they are deductions *for* or *from* AGI.

I6-36 *From AGI Deductions.* During the current year, Roger, a single individual, incurred the following deductible expenses (before any limitations are applied):

Medical expenses	$5,000
Real estate taxes	2,000
Interest on a principal residence	3,000
Charitable contributions	1,500
Net personal casualty losses (already reduced by the $100 limit)	2,000
Miscellaneous itemized deductions	1,800

Roger's AGI for the current year is $60,000. What is Roger's taxable income?

I6-37 *For vs. From AGI.* During the current year, Steve, a single taxpayer, reports the following items of income and expense:

Income:	
Salary	$57,000
Dividends from Alta Corporation	600
Interest income from a savings account	1,000
Rental income from a small apartment he owns	7,000
Expenses:	
Medical	3,000
Interest on a principal residence	4,000
Real property taxes on the principal residence	3,000
Charitable contributions	1,500
Casualty loss - personal	6,100
Miscellaneous itemized deductions	800
Loss from the sale of Delta Corporation stock	2,000
Expenses incurred on the rental apartment:	
Maintenance	300
Property taxes	800
Utilities	2,400
Depreciation	1,500
Insurance	600
Alimony payments	8,000

Assuming all of these items are deductible and that the amounts are before any limitations, what is Steve's taxable income for the year?

I6-38 *Prepaid Expenses.* Pamela, an engineering consultant, is self-employed and uses the cash method of accounting. On November 1 of the current year, she entered into a lease to rent some office space for five years. The lease agreement states that the lease payments are $12,000 per year, payable in advance each November 1 for the following 12-month period. Under the terms of the lease Pamela is required to pay a $5,000 deposit, refundable upon the termination of the lease. On December 1 of the current year Pamela also renewed her malpractice insurance, paying $18,000 for the three-year contract. On December 31 of the current year, Pamela mailed out a check for $5,000 for drafting services performed for her by an individual who lives in another city. On December 31 she also picked up $700 worth of stationery and other office supplies. Pamela has an open charge account with the office supply company, which bills Pamela monthly for charges made during the year. Finally, on December 31, Pamela picked up some work that a local printing company had done for her, which amounted to $1,000. She charged the $1,000 with her business credit card.

Compute the amount of Pamela's current year deductions for these transactions.

I6-39 *Prepaid Expenses.* During the current year, John and Sue, a married couple who use the cash method of accounting, purchased a principal residence. They paid $20,000 down and financed $60,000 of the purchase price with a 30-year mortgage. At the closing, they also paid $500 for an appraisal, $500 for a title search, and 1.5 points representing additional interest over the term of the loan. At the end of the year, John and Sue received a statement from the mortgage company indicating that $7,000 of their total monthly payments made during the year represents interest and $1,000 is a reduction of the principal balance.

a. What is the total amount John and Sue may deduct in the current year arising from the purchase and ownership of their home?

b. What is the treatment of the other items that are not deductible?

I6-40

Capitalization Versus Expense. Lavonne incurs the following expenditures on an apartment building she owns:

Item	Amount
Replace the roof	$3,000
Repaint the exterior	1,500
Install new locks	200
Replace broken windows	150
Replace crumbling sidewalks and stairs	2,000

[handwritten annotations: Capital, Expense, Expense, Expense, Capital]

Discuss the proper tax treatment for these expenditures.

I6-41

Political Contributions and Lobbying Expenses. Sam is a sole proprietor who owns several apartment complexes and office buildings. The leasing and managing of these buildings constitutes Sam's only business activity. During the current year Sam incurred the following:

- $900 in airfare and lodging incurred on a trip to Washington, D.C. The purpose of the trip was to protest proposed tax rate increases for individuals and corporations.

- $700 for renting space on billboards along the highway. The billboards express his concern regarding pending legislation that would significantly increase property taxes.

- $500 in airfare and hotel bills incurred on a trip to the state capital. The purpose of the trip was to meet with the legislative subcommittee on property taxation.

- $50 for a subscription to a political newsletter published by a national political party.

- $150 in making a presentation to the county council protesting a proposed increase in the property tax levy.

a. What is the total amount Sam may deduct because of these expenditures?

b. Assume all the same facts as in Part a except that the expenses for the trip to the state capital are only $300 instead of $500. What amount may Sam deduct because of these expenditures?

I6-42

Legal and Accounting Expenses. During the current year, Sam from Problem I6-40 incurs the following expenses. Which of these expenditures are deductible? Are they *for* or *from* AGI deductions?

a. $200 in attorney's fees for title searches on a new property Sam has acquired.

b. $450 in legal fees in an action brought to collect back rents.

c. $500 to his CPA for the preparation of his federal income tax return. $400 is for the preparation of Schedule C (Profit or Loss from Business).

d. $300 in attorney's fees for drafting a will.

e. $250 in attorney's fees in an unsuccessful attempt to prevent the city from rezoning the area of the city where several of his office buildings are located.

I6-43   *Illegal Payments.* Dave is illegally engaged in the business of purchasing and exporting firearms. Following is a list of income and expense items for the year:

Item	Amount
Sales	$500,000
Cost of goods sold	180,000
Salaries	50,000
Freight	15,000
Bribes to customs officials	20,000
Lease payments on warehouses	10,000
Interest expense	8,000

What is Dave's taxable income from the illegal business activity?

I6-44   *Illegal Payments.* Assume the same facts in Problem I6-42, except that Dave's business consists of buying and selling marijuana and cocaine. What is Dave's taxable income from this illegal business activity?

I6-45   *Illegal Payments.* Indicate whether Glenda can deduct the $5,000 payment in each of the following independent situations.

     a. Glenda is a supplier of medical supplies. In order to secure a large sales contract to the regional Veterans Administration Hospital, Glenda makes a gift of $5,000 to the hospital's purchasing agent. The payment is illegal under state law.

     b. Assume the same facts in Part a, except that the payment is made to the purchasing agent of a government-owned hospital in Brazil.

     c. Assume the same facts in Part a, except that the payment is made to the purchasing agent of a privately owned hospital in Idaho.

I6-46   *Business Investigation Expenditures.* During January and February of the current year, Mario incurs $3,000 in travel, feasibility studies, and legal expenses to investigate the feasibility of opening a new entertainment gallery in one of the new suburban malls in town. Mario already owns two other entertainment galleries in other malls in town.

     a. What is the proper tax treatment of these expenses if Mario decides not to open the new gallery?

     b. What is the proper tax treatment of these expenses if Mario decides to open the new gallery?

     c. Assume the same facts except that Mario does not own any other entertainment galleries. Further assume that Mario opens the new entertainment gallery on May 1 of the current year. How much, if any, Mario deduct in the current year?

I6-47   *Business Investigation Expenditures.* Assume the same facts in Problem I6-45, except that Mario does *not* already own the other entertainment galleries.

     a. What is the proper tax treatment of these expenses if Mario does not open the new gallery?

     b. What is the proper tax treatment of these expenses if Mario decides to open the new gallery?

I6-48   *Wash Sales.* Vicki owns 1,000 shares of Western Corporation common stock, which she purchased on March 8, 1992, for $12,000. On October 3, 1997, she purchases an additional 300 shares for $3,000. On October 12, 1997, she sells the original 1,000 shares for $8,500. On November 1, 1997, she purchases an additional 500 shares for $4,000.

a. What is Vicki's recognized gain or loss as a result of the sale on October 12, 1997?

b. What are the basis and the holding period of the stock Vicki continues to hold?

c. How would your answers to Parts a and b change if the stock Vicki purchases during 1997 is Western nonvoting, nonconvertible, preferred stock instead of Western common stock?

I6-49   *Constructive Ownership.* During the current year, Bart sells a small tract of land to Apple Corporation. The selling price is $25,000. Bart purchased the land for $35,000 four years ago. The Apple Corporation stock is owned as follows:

Owner	Percentage Ownership
Bart	10%
Bart's wife	10
Bart's brother	10
Tony (Bart's friend)	25
Bart's uncle	10
Delta Corporation	35

Delta Corporation is owned equally by Bart, Bart's brother, and Bart's uncle.

a. What is Bart's ownership (actual and constructive) of the Apple stock?

b. What is the amount of loss Bart may recognize?

c. How would your answers to Parts a and b change if Bart's brother-in-law owned 10% of Apple corporation's stock instead of Bart's brother?

I6-50   *Related Party Transactions.* Jack is a CPA who computes his taxable income using the cash method of accounting. King Corporation, owned equally by Jack's three children, uses the accrual method of accounting. Jack is a calendar-year taxpayer, whereas King Corporation's fiscal year ends on January 31. During 1997, Jack does some consulting work for King Corporation for a fee of $6,000. The work is completed on December 15. For each of the following assumptions, answer the following questions: During which tax year must Jack report the income? During which tax year must King Corporation deduct the expense?

a. The payment to Jack is made on December 27, 1997.

b. The payment to Jack is made on January 12, 1998.

c. The payment to Jack is made on February 3, 1998.

I6-51   *Related Party Transactions.* During the current year, Delta Corporation sells a tract of land for $80,000. The sale is made to Shirley, Delta Corporation's sole shareholder. Delta Corporation originally purchased the land five years earlier for $95,000.

a. What is the amount of gain or loss that Delta Corporation will recognize on the sale during the current year?

b. Assume that in the following year, Shirley sells the land for $85,000. What is the amount of gain or loss Shirley will recognize? What are the tax consequences to Delta Corporation upon the subsequent sale by Shirley?

c. Assume that in the following year, Shirley sells the land for $70,000. What is the amount of gain or loss Shirley will recognize?

d. Assume that in the following year, Shirley sells the land for $105,000. What is the amount of gain or loss Shirley will recognize?

I6-52 *Related Party Transactions.* During the current year, James sold a mainframe computer to Byte Computer, Inc. for $50,000. James had previously used the computer in his business for two years and its adjusted basis was $90,000 on the date of sale. Byte Computer is owned by ROM Inc. and Card Corporation. ROM owns 4,000 shares of Byte and Card owns the remaining 1,000 outstanding shares. Philip, James' brother, owns 100% of ROM and three of Philip's friends own equal shares of all of the outstanding stock of Card Corporation. Two years after Byte purchases the computer, it sells the machine for $60,000 to an unrelated purchaser. Byte's adjusted basis in the computer on the date of sale is $38,000.

a. What amount of gain or loss is recognized by James?

b. What amount of gain or loss is recognized by Byte on the subsequent sale of the computer?

I6-53 *Hobby Loss Presumptive Rule.* Ira is an attorney who has been engaged in raising and breeding show dogs for the past eight years. During those years Ira has reported the following net income or loss from the activity:

Year	Net Income (Loss)
1990	$(600)
1991	(400)
1992	300
1993	(1,000)
1994	200
1995	(800)
1996	(1,100)
1997	(700)

Ira is audited for the year 1997, and the agent disallows the $700 loss. Can Ira make an election for 1997 to keep the year open in anticipation of meeting the presumptive rule for the year? Why or why not?

I6-54 *Hobby Losses.* Chuck, a dentist, raises prize rabbits for breeding and showing purposes. Assume that the activity is determined to be a hobby. During the year the activity generates the following items of income and expense:

Item	Amount
Sale of rabbits for breeding stock	$800
Prizes and awards	300
Property taxes on rabbit hutches	300
Feed	600
Veterinary fees	500
Depreciation on rabbit hutches	300

a. What is the total amount of deductions Chuck may take during the year with respect to the rabbit raising activities?

b. Identify which expenses may be deducted and indicate whether they are deductions *for* or *from* AGI.

c. By what amount is the cost basis of the rabbit hutches to be reduced for the year?

I6-55   *Hobby Losses.* Assume the same facts as in Problem I6-53, except that the income from the sale of rabbits is $1,200.

a. What is the total amount of deductions Chuck may take during the year with respect to the rabbit raising activities?

b. Identify which expenses may be deducted and indicate whether they are deductions *for* or *from* AGI.

c. By what amount is the cost basis of the rabbit hutches to be reduced for the year?

I6-56   *Rental of Vacation Home.* During the current year, Kim incurs the following expenses with respect to her beachfront condominium in Hawaii:

Item	Amount
Insurance	$ 500
Repairs and maintenance	700
Interest on mortgage	3,000
Property taxes	1,000
Utilities	800

In addition to the expenses listed above, Kim could have deducted a total of $8,000 depreciation if the property had been acquired only for investment purposes. During the year, Kim uses the condominium 20 days for vacation. She also rented it out for a total of 60 days during the year, generating a total gross income of $9,000.

a. What is the total amount of deductions Kim may take during the current year with respect to the condominium?

b. Identify which expenses may be deducted and indicate whether they are deductions *for* or *from* AGI.

c. What is the effect on the basis of the condominium?

I6-57   *Rental of Vacation Home.* Assume all of the same facts in Problem I6-55, except that during the year Kim rents the condominium a total of 14 days. How does Kim report the income and deductions from the property?

COMPREHENSIVE PROBLEM

I6-58   Bryce, a bank official, is married and files a joint return. During the current year he engages in the following activities and transactions:

a. Being an avid fisherman, Bryce develops an expertise in tying flies. At times during the year, he is asked to conduct fly-tying demonstrations, for which he is paid a small fee. He also periodically sells flies that he makes. Income generated from these activities during the year is $2,500. The expenses for the year associated with Bryce's fly-tying activity include $125 personal property taxes on a small trailer that he uses exclusively for this purpose, $2,900 in supplies, $270 in repairs on the trailer, and $200 in gasoline for traveling to the demonstrations.

b. Bryce sells a small building lot to his brother for $30,000. Bryce purchased the lot four years ago for $35,000, hoping to make a profit.

c. Bryce enters into the following stock transactions: (None of the stock qualifies as small business stock).

Date	Transaction
March 22	Purchases 100 shares of Silver Corporation common stock for $2,800
April 5	Sells 200 shares of Gold Corporation common stock for $8,000. The stock was originally purchased two years ago for $5,000.
April 15	Sells 200 shares of Silver Corporation common stock for $5,400. The stock was originally purchased three years ago for $9,400.
May 20	Sells 100 shares of United Corporation common stock for $12,000. The stock was originally purchased five years ago for $10,000.

d. Bryce's salary for the year is $80,000. In addition to the items above, he also incurs $5,000 in other miscellaneous deductible itemized expenses.

Answer the following questions regarding Bryce's activities for the year.

1. How much in total gains and losses from the sale of property should Bryce report for the year?

2. What is the total amount of Bryce's itemized deductions for the year?

3. What is Bryce's basis in the Silver stock he continues to own?

TAX FORM/RETURN PREPARATION PROBLEMS

I6-59 Carolyn Snowflake, a self-employed physician, uses the cash-method of accounting. Carolyn's social security number is 111-33-9999, her employer ID number is 12-1234567, and her business address is Suite 402A, 123 Physicians Way, Anytown, Any State 12345. Dr. Snowflake has been practicing medicine for the past 12 years. During the current year, Carolyn recorded the following items of income:

Revenue from patient visits	$200,000
Interest earned on the office checking balance	150

The following expenses were recorded on the office books:

Property taxes on the office	$3,000
Mortgage interest on the office	8,000
Depreciation on the office	3,000
Malpractice Insurance	25,000
Utilities	2,500
Office staff salaries	34,000
Rent payments on equipment	10,000
Office magazine subscriptions	100
Office supplies	16,000
Medical journals	220

Complete Schedule C of Form 1040 for the current year.

I6-60 Dave and Pam Brighton are married, have no children, and are filing a joint tax return in the current year. They are both managers of local retail stores. Dave and Pam, ages 38 and 37, respectively, have combined salaries of $51,000 from which $9,000 of federal income tax and $2,500 of state income tax are withheld. Dave and Pam own two homes. Their primary residence is located at 11620 N. Mount Ave., Atlanta, Georgia 22222, and their vacation home is located in Vail, Colorado. They often rent their vacation home to skiers to supplement their income. The following items are related to the Brightons' ownership of the two homes:

Item	Atlanta	Vail
Rental income	$ —	$9,000
Qualified residence interest	7,200	5,000
Property taxes	1,400	1,000
Utilities	1,000	1,300
Repairs	200	300
Depreciation	0	3,500
Advertising	0	200
Insurance	1,500	1,500

The Brightons used their Vail home 20 days during the year. They rented the vacation home 60 days during the year. The Brightons have no other income or expense items. Dave and Pam's Social Security numbers are 111-22-3333 and 444-55-6666, respectively.

File the Brightons' income tax return Form 1040, Schedules A and E using the currently available forms and rates.

I6-61 Burton, age 56, and Joyce Winters, age 54, are married and are filing jointly in the current year. Their social security numbers are 123-45-6789 and 987-65-4321, respectively. Burton's salary for the year is $43,000, from which $8,000 of federal income tax and $2,000 of state income tax were withheld. Joyce is the sole owner of Winter's Piano Tuning Company, a proprietorship that supplements the couple's income. Joyce reports the following income and expenses related to her business operation:

Revenues	$4,900
City business license	300
Yellow pages advertisement	40
Depreciation on tools	70
Supplies	300

Joyce subscribes to the following journals:

Piano Tuner's Journal	$40
Wall Street Journal	100
Money Magazine	40
Reader's Digest	50
U.S. News & World Report	40

Burton & Joyce jointly purchase stock in various corporations and make the following transactions in the current year: (None of the stock qualifies as small business stock).

Date	Transaction	Price Paid/Sold
2/15	Bought 50 shares of Lake common stock (own no other Lake stock)	$1,000
5/14	Bought 100 shares of Bass common stock (own no other Bass stock)	3,000
5/24	Sold 25 shares of Lake common stock	500
5/27	Bought 50 shares of Lake common stock	900
	Sold 50 shares of Bass common stock	1,750
7/12	Bought 100 shares of Bass common stock	2,800

During the year, Burton and Joyce receive dividend income of $200 and taxable interest income of $350, make political contributions of $300, and pay $25 for use of a safety deposit box to store certain documents Joyce needs in her business.

Burton and Joyce own only one home at 237 E. 100 N., Kaysville, Ohio 11111. Their deductible mortgage interest for the year is $7,000. Burton and Joyce filed their state income tax return for the prior year in April of this year and paid an additional $400 of state income tax. In April of the current year, they also paid $180 to a CPA for preparing their federal and state income tax returns for the prior year, $100 of which was for the preparation of Joyce's Schedule C.

Burton and Joyce have no other deductions.

Prepare Burton and Joyce's tax return (Form 1040, Schedules A, C, D, and SE) for the current year.

CASE STUDY PROBLEMS

I6-62 John and Kathy Brown have just been audited and the IRS agent disallowed the business loss they claimed in 1995. The agent asserted that the activity was a hobby, not a business.

John and Kathy live in Rochester, New York, near Lake Ontario. Kathy is a CPA and John was formerly employed by an insurance firm. John's firm moved in 1990 and John resolved not to move to the firm's new location. Instead of seeking other employment John felt he could supplement his income by using his fishing expertise. He had been an avid fisherman for 15 years and he owned a large Chris-Craft fly-bridge which he chartered to paying parties.

In 1991 Kathy and John developed a business plan, established a bank account for the charter activities, developed a bookkeeping system, and acquired insurance to cover the boat and the passengers. John fulfilled all the requirements to receive a U.S. Coast Guard operating license, a New York sport trolling license, and a seller's permit. These licenses and permits were necessary to legally operate a charter boat. 1991 was the first year of their activity.

John advertised in local papers and regional sport fishing magazines. He usually had three or four half-day paying parties each week. John spent at least one day maintaining and repairing his boat. Kathy usually accompanied John on charters three or four times each year.

John's charter activity was unprofitable the first two years. In 1993, John and Kathy restructured the activity to improve profitability. The restructuring included increasing advertising, participating in outdoor shows, and negotiating small contracts with local businesses. After the restructuring, the activity provided a small profit in 1993 and 1994.

In 1995 John started working with another insurance company in the area on a full-time basis. Even though he returned to the insurance business, John normally took two paying parties and one nonpaying, promotional party each week throughout the fishing season. John's costs unexpectedly increased and he lost $8,000 in the activity during 1995. John and Kathy deducted the entire loss on Schedule C of their 1995 tax return.

Required: Prepare a memo to the Browns recommending what position they should take and why. Show the logic used in arriving at your recommendation.

I6-63 For several years you have done the tax return for your neighbors, Scott and Cindy Snyder. Scott is a high school teacher and Cindy owns her own business. Over the years, Scott has frequently mentioned to you his love of stock car racing. For years he has spent a great deal of time after work and on weekends out at the track. He also subscribes to several automotive magazines. Unfortunately, up until this year he never has had enough money to buy his own car.

This year, however, things are different. Scott was able to purchase a car that needed a lot of fixing up. After spending a considerable amount of time and money (Scott estimates that he has spent close to $6,500 just on maintenance, repairs, and beefing the car up), the car was finally ready to race. This year Scott has entered only 3 races. In 2 of the races he didn't place. In fact, in the first race he didn't even finish. However, in the third race, he won $200 in prize money. Although Scott is excited about the money, he has boasted to you that the prize money isn't as important as the thrill of racing and winning.

When the Snyders give you their tax information for this year, Scott mentions, "Now that I've won some money from racing, we can finally write off all these expenses against our taxes."

Do you treat Scott's racing activity as a business or as a hobby? You are concerned because you know that Scott will continue in the activity whether or not he generates any more income. (See the *Statements on Responsibilities in Tax Practice* section in Chapter I1 for a discussion of these issues.)

TAX RESEARCH PROBLEM

I6-64 Richard Penn lives in Harrisburg, Pennsylvania. Richard is the president of an architectural firm. Richard has become known throughout the community for excellent work and honesty in his business dealings. Richard believes his reputation is an integral part of the success of the firm.

Oil was found recently in the area around Harrisburg and some geologists believed the reserves were large. A few well-respected businesspeople organized Oil Company to develop a few wells. Although some oil was being extracted, the oil corporation lacked capital to develop the oil fields to their expected potential. After reading the geologists' report, Richard felt that Oil Company was a good investment; therefore, he acquired 25% of the company. A short time after Richard's acquisition, the price of foreign oil decreased sharply. The drop in foreign oil prices caused Oil Company to be unprofitable due to its high production costs. Three months later Oil Company filed bankruptcy.

The bankruptcy proceedings were reported in the local newspaper. Many of Oil Company's creditors were real estate developers that engaged Richard's architectural firm to provide designs. After Oil Company declared bankruptcy the architectural firm's business noticeably decreased.

Richard felt the decline in business was related to the bankruptcy of Oil Company. Richard convinced his partner to use the accumulated earnings of the firm to repay all the creditors of Oil Company.

Richard has asked you whether his firm can deduct the expenses of repaying Oil Company's creditors. After completing your research explain to Richard why the expenses are or are not deductible.

A partial list of research sources is as follows:

- Sec. 162
- *Thomas H. Welch v. Helvering,* 12 AFTR 1456, 3 USTC ¶1164 (USSC, 1933)
- *William A. Thompson, Jr.,* 1983 PH T.C. Memo ¶83,487, 46 TCM 1109

CHAPTER 7

ITEMIZED DEDUCTIONS

LEARNING OBJECTIVES

After studying this chapter, you should be able to

1. Identify qualified medical expenses and compute the medical expense deduction

2. Determine the timing of a medical expense deduction and the effect of a reimbursement

3. Identify taxes that are deductible as itemized deductions

4. Identify different types of interest deductions

5. Compute the amount of investment interest deduction

6. Compute the deduction for qualified residence interest

7. Compute the amount of a charitable contribution deduction and identify limitations

8. Identify certain miscellaneous itemized deductions subject to the 2% of AGI limit

9. Compute total itemized deductions for a taxpayer who is subject to the itemized deduction phase-out.

As explained in Chapter I6, most deductible expenses for individuals can be classified into three general categories:

▶ Expenses incurred in a trade or business

▶ Expenses incurred for the production of income or for the determination of a tax

▶ Certain specified personal expenses

For individuals, all deductible expenses must also be classified as either *for* AGI or *from* AGI deductions, regardless of how the expense is categorized (see list above). *From* AGI deductions are also called **itemized deductions**. This distinction is important because AGI is used as a measuring point in determining the amount of certain deductible expenses such as medical expenses, casualty losses, and miscellaneous itemized deductions. The concept of AGI has no meaning for taxpayers other than individuals. A list of the more common deductions *for* AGI is found in Chapter I6. This chapter deals with the itemized deductions for medical expenses, taxes, interest, and charitable contributions. Unreimbursed employee business expenses are discussed in Chapter I9 and casualty losses are discussed in Chapter I8.

In arriving at taxable income, individuals may subtract from AGI the larger of the standard deduction or the sum of all itemized deductions. However, as explained later in this chapter, certain itemized deductions are reduced if a taxpayer's AGI exceeds certain limits.

MEDICAL EXPENSES

ADDITIONAL COMMENT

In 1993 the deduction for medical expenses represented only 5.4% of the total dollar amount of itemized deductions.

Medical expenses, which comprise one category of deductible personal expenditures, are deductible because Congress felt that excessive medical expenses might ultimately affect a taxpayer's ability to pay his or her federal income tax. However, under Sec. 213 medical expenses are deductible only to the extent that they exceed 7.5% of the taxpayer's AGI. To qualify as a medical expense deduction, the expenditure must have been incurred for the medical care of a qualified individual. No deduction may be taken for medical expenses to the extent that they are reimbursed (i.e., compensated for by insurance or otherwise).

QUALIFIED INDIVIDUALS

HISTORICAL NOTE

The percentage floor on medical expenses was increased from 3% to 5% in 1983 and from 5% to 7.5% in 1987.

Deductible medical expenses must be paid on behalf of either the taxpayer, the taxpayer's spouse, or a dependent of the taxpayer.

TAXPAYER'S DEPENDENT. Medical expenses paid on behalf of a person for whom the taxpayer could take a dependency exemption except for the failure to meet the gross income or joint return tests are included in the taxpayer's medical expenses.[1]

EXAMPLE I7-1 ▶ In March of the current year, Jean's son, Steve, is involved in an automobile accident. Steve is 25 years old at the time of the accident and has worked full-time for part of the year, earning a total of $5,000. Because Steve has no medical insurance and cannot pay the medical bills or support himself as a result of the accident, Jean pays Steve's medical expenses and supports

---

[1] Sec. 152. As explained in Chapter I2, a person qualifies as a taxpayer's dependent if the taxpayer has provided over one-half of that individual's support for the year, there is a proper relationship (generally a member of the taxpayer's family or household) between the taxpayer and the individual, and the individual is a citizen or resident of the United States, Canada, or Mexico. To claim a dependency exemption for an individual, the individual must be the taxpayer's dependent and the following additional requirements must be satisfied: The dependent must have gross income less than the exemption amount (unless he or she is a child of the taxpayer and is either under 19 years of age at the end of the year or a full-time student who has not reached the age of 24 at the close of the year), and the dependent must not have filed a joint return. For 1997 the exemption amount is $2,650.

him for the rest of the year. Because Jean provides over one-half of Steve's support for the year and Steve otherwise qualifies as Jean's dependent, Jean may deduct the medical expenses she pays on his behalf. Jean may not claim a dependency exemption for Steve because the gross income test is not satisfied. ◀

CHILDREN OF DIVORCED PARENTS. As long as one parent is entitled to the dependency exemption under Sec. 152(e), medical expenses paid on behalf of the children of divorced parents are deductible by the parent who pays the expenses. The parent taking the medical expense deduction need not be the parent who is entitled to the dependency exemption. ◀

QUALIFIED MEDICAL EXPENSES

OBJECTIVE 1

Identify qualified medical expenses and compute the medical expense deduction

The **medical expense deduction** is available only for expenditures paid for medical care. Section 213 defines *medical care* as amounts paid for

▶ The diagnosis, cure, mitigation, treatment, or prevention of disease

▶ The purpose of affecting any structure or function of the body

▶ Transportation primarily for and essential to the first two items listed above

▶ Qualified long-term care services

▶ Insurance covering all of the items listed above

DIAGNOSIS, CURE, MITIGATION, TREATMENT, OR PREVENTION OF DISEASE. Although the term *medical expense* is not precisely defined, it is clear that medical expenses are deductible only if they are paid for procedures or treatments that are legal in the locality in which they are performed.[2] The definition of medical care covers preventive measures such as routine physical and dental examinations. However, other expenses should be "confined strictly to expenses incurred primarily for the prevention or alleviation of a physical or mental defect or illness." Thus, unless they are for routine physical or dental examinations, the expenditures must be incurred for the purpose of curing a specific ailment rather than being related to the general health of an individual. This determination is especially critical when the expenditures in question are for items such as vacations, weight loss programs, or programs designed to help the individual stop smoking. Such expenses may or may not be incurred for a specific ailment.

EXAMPLE I7-2 ▶ Helmut is nervous and irritable because of the pressures at work. Furthermore, he begins to suffer angina symptoms. In order to relax and get away from it all, he takes an ocean cruise around the world. Helmut's angina symptoms ease while he is on the cruise. However, the Tax Court held that a cruise is not a proven medical necessity because Helmut's physician did not specifically prescribe it. Although the cruise was beneficial to Helmut's general health, it is not deductible.[3] ◀

EXAMPLE I7-3 ▶ Dave enrolls in a weight reduction program on the advice of two doctors who prescribe the program as a means of relieving his obesity, hypertension, and certain hearing problems. In a private letter ruling, the IRS held that these expenses qualify as deductible medical expenditures because they are incurred for specific medical conditions.[4] ◀

[2] Reg. Sec. 1.213-1(e)(1)(ii). See also Rev. Rul. 78-325, 1978-2 C.B. 124, where amounts paid for laetrile (an illegal drug in the United States) were deductible because its use as a medicine was legal in the area where it was purchased and used.

[3] *Daniel E. Mizl*, 1980 PH T.C. Memo ¶80,227, 40 TCM 552. Even if the taxpayer's physician had prescribed the trip, it still may not have been deductible. See Reg. Sec. 1.213-1(e)(1)(ii).
[4] Ltr. Rul. 8004111 (October 31, 1979).

Although receipt of a doctor's recommendation for incurring the cost appears to lend a great deal of weight to deductibility, it is not always sufficient. For example, the cost of dancing lessons for an emotionally disturbed child was not deductible, even though the lessons proved to be beneficial and were recommended by a physician. Likewise, a taxpayer suffering from arthritis could not deduct the cost of ballroom dance lessons, even though the lessons were recommended by a doctor.[5]

Range of Deductible Medical Services. According to the Treasury Regulations, typical medical expenses include payments for a wide range of medical, dental, and other diagnostic and healing services. Thus, payments to licensed or certified medical professionals such as general practitioners, obstetricians, surgeons, ophthalmologists, opticians, dentists, and orthodontists are all deductible. Furthermore, payment for medical services rendered by individuals such as chiropractors, osteopaths, and psychotherapists who may or may not be required to be licensed or certified is also deductible.[6] Acupuncture treatments are deductible if they are received for a specific medical purpose, as are payments to Christian Science practitioners.[7] Qualified medical expenses also include payment for hospital services, nursing services, laboratory fees, X-rays, artificial teeth or limbs, ambulance hire, eyeglasses, and prescribed medicines and insulin. Expenditures for nonprescription medicines, drugs, vitamins, and other types of health foods that improve the individual's general health are not deductible.

In order to deduct costs incurred for schools and camps, the taxpayer must show that the facility is regularly engaged in providing medical services. Thus, the expense incurred by a taxpayer in sending his mentally handicapped son to a school that had a special curriculum for such children was deductible. The cost of sending a child with psychiatric problems to a school specializing in certain learning disorders was also deductible.[8] However, the cost of sending children with special medical problems to schools or camps that do not have the proper equipment, facilities, or curriculum for such problems is generally not deductible.[9]

MEDICAL PROCEDURES AFFECTING ANY FUNCTION OR STRUCTURE OF THE BODY. Deductible medical expenditures also include payments for services affecting any function or structure of the body, even though no specific illness or disease exists. Thus, expenditures for such items as physical therapy, obstetrical services, eyeglasses, dental examinations and cleaning, and hearing aids all qualify as medical expenses. Under Sec. 213 cosmetic surgery or any other similar procedure does not qualify as a medical expense unless such surgery is necessary to correct a deformity arising from a congenital abnormality, a personal injury resulting from an accident or trauma, or a disfiguring disease. Cosmetic surgery is defined as any procedure undertaken to improve a person's appearance that does not meaningfully promote the proper function of the body or prevent or treat an illness or disease.

TRANSPORTATION ESSENTIAL TO MEDICAL CARE. Transportation primarily for and essential to qualified medical care is deductible. Thus, actual out-of-pocket automobile expenditures, taxis, airfare, ambulance fees, and other forms of transporta-

---

[5] *John J. Thoene,* 33 T.C. 62 (1959) and *Rose C. France v. CIR,* 50 AFTR 2d 81-5504, 1982-1 USTC ¶9225 (6th Cir., 1982).
[6] Reg. Sec. 1.213-1(e)(1) and Rev. Rul. 63-91, 1963-1 C.B. 54. See also Ltr. Rul. 8919009 (February 6, 1989) where a pregnant woman was entitled to a deduction for the cost of childbirth classes to the extent that they prepared her for the childbirth. However, the cost of the classes where she received instructions on the care of the unborn child represented a flat fee that allowed a coach to attend the class with the taxpayer. Thus, one-half of the fee was deemed attributable to the coach and was not allowed as a qualified

medical expense.
[7] Rev. Rul. 72-593, 1972-2 C.B. 180 and IRS Special Ruling, February 2, 1943.
[8] Rev. Rul. 70-285, 1970-1 C.B. 52 and *Lawrence D. Greisdorf,* 54 T.C. 1684 (1970), acq. 1970-2 C.B. xix.
[9] *Devora R. Shidler,* 1971 PH T.C. Memo ¶71,126, 30 TCM 529. See also *John A. Dreifus,* 1977 PH T.C. Memo ¶77,083, 36 TCM 368, and *Dr. Ernest M. Newkirk v. U.S.,* 40 AFTR 2d 77-5114, 77-1 USTC ¶9452 (D.C. Ohio, 1977).

tion are all deductible if the travel is incurred for medical reasons. However, no deduction is allowed if the travel is undertaken for recreational purposes or for the general improvement of the taxpayer's health.

In lieu of the actual cost of the use of an automobile, the IRS allows a deduction of ten cents for each mile that the automobile is driven for medical reasons. In addition to the standard mileage rate, the cost of tolls and parking may also be deducted.

Meals and Lodging En Route to a Medical Facility. Certain courts have held that the cost of meals and lodging while en route to a medical facility is part of travel costs incurred for medical purposes and, therefore, is deductible.[10] However, only 50% of the cost of meals may be deducted.[11] (See Chapter 19 for a discussion of the 50% disallowance rule for meals and entertainment.) The cost of meals eaten on trips that are too short to warrant a stop for meals is not deductible. Furthermore, the cost of lodging is limited to $50 per night and is deductible only if the travel is primarily for and essential to medical care, the medical care is provided in a licensed hospital (or a facility that is related or equivalent to a licensed hospital), and there is no significant element of personal pleasure or recreation in the travel.[12] For example, in one case, a woman moved from Michigan to Florida for the winter months. This move was undertaken on the advice of her physicians in Michigan. Furthermore, her husband returned to Michigan for the winter months. Her doctors in Michigan had not referred her to any physicians in Florida, and while in Florida she visited a doctor on only two occasions. Although her move was primarily for medical care and her condition prevented any significant element of personal recreation, while in Florida she received no medical care in a licensed hospital or equivalent facility. Thus, the medical deduction was denied.[13]

The $50 limitation on lodging is imposed on a per-individual basis. Thus, if the patient is unable to travel alone, an additional $50 per night may be deducted for the lodging costs of a nurse, parent, or spouse.

EXAMPLE 17-4 ▶ Lenea lives in a small town 50 miles from Billings, Montana. To receive treatment for a serious illness, she travels by automobile to the Mayo Clinic in Minnesota. The trip takes three days. The cost of the transportation and lodging incurred en route to Minnesota is deductible (subject to the appropriate limits). As previously discussed, some courts have ruled that the meals are also deductible when the trips are long enough to reasonably expect that meals must be eaten (subject to the limitations applicable to meals). ◀

KEY POINT

Meals and lodging for a patient being treated on an inpatient basis are deductible.

Meals And Lodging While At The Medical Facility. The rules for deducting the cost of meals and lodging while at the medical facility differ from those for en route costs. If an individual is hospitalized and treated on an inpatient basis, the costs of meals and lodging are deductible because they are considered part of the medical treatment. If the individual is treated on an outpatient basis, however, the cost of meals is not deductible[14] and the cost of the lodging is subject to the $50 per-person, per-night limitation.

EXAMPLE 17-5 ▶ Maxine's four-year old daughter, Sally, suffers from a specific medical ailment. On the advice of her local physician, Maxine takes Sally to a hospital in Houston that specializes in that type of

[10] *Morris C. Montgomery v. CIR*, 26 AFTR 2d 70-5001, 70-2 USTC ¶9466 (6th Cir., 1970). See also *William L. Pfersching*, 1983 PH T.C. Memo ¶83,341, 46 TCM 424. The cost of lodging and meals while en route to receive medical care are deductible as transportation that is essential to medical care. The IRS has argued that the term *transportation*, as opposed to "travel," excludes the cost of meals and lodging. This argument is manifest in the Regulations and in a private letter ruling (see Reg. Sec. 1.213-1(e)(1)(iv) and Ltr. Rul. 8336011). However, as indicated, at least two courts have specifically held that these expenses are deductible as medical expenses.
[11] The deductible limit of 50% of meals and entertainment is imposed by

Sec. 274(n), which imposes the limit on any meals that are deductible. Before 1994 the deductible limit was 80%. There is some indication that the IRS may not be enforcing the limit on deductible meals incurred as a medical expense or a charitable contribution. See IRS, Publication No. *502* [Medical and Dental Expenses], 1996, pp. 10–11, and IRS Publication No. *526* [Charitable Contributions], 1996.
[12] Sec. 213(d)(2).
[13] *Alex L. Polyak*, 94 T.C. 337 (1990).
[14] *Morris C. Montgomery v. CIR*, 26 AFTR 2d 70-5001, 70-2 USTC ¶9466 (6th Cir., 1970).

illness. It takes two days to drive the 500 miles to the hospital and two days to return to the taxpayer's home. At the hospital, Sally is treated on an outpatient basis for five days. Maxine and Sally share a motel room both en route and while at the hospital. In addition to the miles driven, Maxine incurs the following expenses on the trip:

Meals en route to and from the hospital:	
Maxine	$ 75
Sally	55
Motels en route to and from the hospital:	
$60 per night × four nights	240
Meals while in Houston:	
Maxine	95
Sally	70
Motel while at the hospital:	
$65 per night × five nights	325
Total	$860
Maxine may deduct the following expenses:	
Mileage (1,000 miles × 0.10)	$100
Meals en route ($75 + $55) × 0.50	65
Motels en route	240
Motel while in Houston	325
Total	$730

Because they shared the motel, the lodging cost for each person is below the $50 per-person, per-night limitation. ◄

Qualified Long-Term Care. Beginning in 1997, expenditures for qualified long-term care also are deductible as medical expenses subject to the 7.5% of AGI limitation. Long-term care is defined as medical services required by a chronically ill individual which are provided under a prescribed plan of care. Under Sec. 7702B, such items include expenditures for diagnostic, preventive, therapeutic, curing, treating, mitigating, rehabilitative, and personal care services. A chronically ill individual generally is someone who, for a period of at least 90 days, cannot perform at least two daily living tasks such as eating, toileting (including continence), transferring, bathing, or dressing.

Expenditures for long-term care insurance premiums also qualify as medical deductions, subject to an annual limit based upon the age of an individual.[15]

CAPITAL EXPENDITURES FOR MEDICAL CARE. Generally, capital expenditures are not deductible for federal income tax purposes. For assets used in a trade or business or held for the production of income, such costs are recovered through depreciation, cost recovery, or amortization. Capital expenditures incurred for personal medical purposes are not depreciable or amortizable. However, a current deduction is available when the capital expenditure is made to acquire an asset whose primary purpose is the medical care of the taxpayer, the taxpayer's spouse, or the taxpayer's dependents. To qualify as a deduction, the expenditure must be incurred as a medical necessity for primary use by the individual in need of medical treatment, and the expenditure must be reasonable in amount. Deductible capital expenditures for medical care are classified into three categories:[16]

---

[15] If the individual is 40 years of age or less, the annual deductible limit for the premiums is $200. For the individuals over 40 but less than 50 the limit is $375. For those over 50 but less than 60 the limit is $750; over 60 but less than 70 the limit is $2,000; and over 70 the limit is $2,500.

[16] Reg. Sec. 1.213-1(e)(1)(iii) and H. Rept. No. 99-841, 99th Cong., 2d Sess. p. II-22 (1986).

▶ Expenditures that relate only to the sick or handicapped person, not to the permanent improvement or betterment of the taxpayer's property (e.g., eyeglasses, dogs or other animals that assist the blind or the deaf, artificial teeth and limbs, wheelchairs, crutches, and portable air conditioners purchased for the sole use of a sick person)

▶ Expenditures that permanently improve or better the taxpayer's property as well as provide medical care (e.g., a swimming pool installed in the home of an individual suffering from arthritis)

▶ Expenditures incurred in removing structural barriers in the home of a physically handicapped individual

This last group of expenditures includes amounts spent on the physically handicapped individual's residence for

▶ Constructing entrance or exit ramps

▶ Widening doorways at entrances and exits

▶ Widening or modifying interior doorways and halls to accommodate a wheelchair

▶ Adding railings, support bars, or other modifications to bathrooms

▶ Lowering kitchen cabinets and equipment

▶ Adjusting electrical outlets and fixtures

▶ Installing porch lifts and other lifts (but not elevators)

▶ Modifying fire, smoke, and other alarm systems

▶ Modifying stairs, doors, and areas in front of entrance and exit doorways

REAL-WORLD EXAMPLE

The cost of installing an elevator in the home upon the recommendation of a physician to help a patient with a heart condition was deductible to the extent that it did not increase the value of the home. *James E. Berry v. Wiseman*, 2 AFTR 2d 6015, 58-2 USTC ¶9870 (D.C. Okla., 1958).

Capital expenditures that relate only to the sick person (the first category) are fully deductible in the year paid. Expenditures that improve the residence (the second category) are deductible only to the extent that the amount of the expenditure exceeds the increase in the fair market value (FMV) of the residence brought about by the capital expenditure. Expenditures incurred in removing physical barriers in the home of a physically handicapped individual (the third category) are deductible in full (i.e., the increase in the home's value is deemed to be zero). In addition, any costs of operating or maintaining the assets in all three categories are deductible as long as the medical reason for the capital expenditure continues to exist.[17] The deductibility of all of the above expenditures are subject to the 7.5% floor.

EXAMPLE I7-6 ▶

During the current year, Rita is injured in an industrial accident. As a result, she sustains a chronic disabling leg injury, which requires her to spend much time in a wheelchair. Rita's physician recommends that a swimming pool be installed in her backyard and that she devote several hours each day to physical exercise. During the year, Rita makes the following expenditures:

Wheelchair	$ 500
Swimming pool	12,000
Operation and maintenance of the pool	400
Entrance ramp and door modification	3,000

A qualified appraiser estimates that the swimming pool increases the value of Rita's home by only $8,000, because most homes in the neighborhood do not have a pool. Rita's medical expenses for the year include $500 for the wheelchair, $4,000 for the swimming pool (the excess of the cost of the pool over the increase in the FMV of the home), $400 for the operation and maintenance of the pool, and $3,000 for the ramp and door modification. ◀

---

[17] Rev. Rul. 87-106, 1987-2 C.B. 67.

EXAMPLE I7-7 ▶

COSTS OF LIVING IN INSTITUTIONS. The entire cost of in-patient hospital care, including meals and lodging, qualifies as a medical expense. However, if an individual is in an institution other than a hospital (e.g., a nursing home or a special school for the handicapped), the deductibility of the costs involved depends on the facts of the particular case. If the principal reason for the taxpayer's presence in an institution is the need for and availability of the medical care furnished by that institution, the entire costs of meals, lodging, and other services necessary for furnishing the medical care are all qualified medical expenditures. However, if an individual is in an institution primarily for considerations other than the furnishing of medical care, only costs directly attributable to furnishing medical care are deductible. The costs of the meals, lodging, and other services are not qualified medical expenditures.[18] ◀

MEDICAL INSURANCE PREMIUMS. Qualified medical expenses also include all premiums paid for medical insurance, including premiums paid for supplementary medical insurance for the aged under the Social Security Act. In many cases, premiums are paid for insurance coverage that extends beyond mere medical care. For example, in addition to the standard medical care coverage, an insurance policy may provide coverage for loss of income or loss of life, limb, or sight. In such cases, a deduction is allowed for the medical care portion of the premium only if the cost of each type of insurance is either separately stated in the contract or is furnished to the policyholder by the insurance company in a separate statement.[19]

Each month Malazia pays $300 for an insurance policy under which she is reimbursed for any doctor or hospital charges she incurs. In addition, the policy will pay two-thirds of her regular salary each month if she becomes disabled. Finally, the policy will pay her $10,000 for the loss of any limb. At the end of the year, her insurance company issues a statement that allocates two-thirds of the premiums to the medical insurance coverage. Malazia's medical care expenditure is $2,400 ($300 × 12 × 0.667). ◀

If the premiums attributable to an individual or group medical insurance plan are paid by the taxpayer, the payments are deductible as medical expenses which in most cases are itemized deductions. However, in 1997 self-employed individuals may deduct 40% of these amounts as deductions *for* AGI. The remainder is deductible as an itemized deduction. Any amounts paid by the taxpayer's employer are excluded from the employee's gross income and are not includible in the taxpayer's medical expenses.[20]

AMOUNT AND TIMING OF DEDUCTION
The amount and timing of the allowable medical expense deduction depend on when the medical expenses are actually paid, the taxpayer's AGI, and whether any reimbursement is received for the medical expenses.

OBJECTIVE 2

Determine the timing of a medical expense deduction and the effect of a reimbursement

TIMING OF THE PAYMENT. In general, a deduction for medical expenses is allowed only in the year in which the expenses are actually paid. This rule applies regardless of the taxpayer's method of accounting or when the event that caused the expenditure occurs.[21] Thus, if medical care is received during the year but remains unpaid as of the end of the

---

[18] Reg. Sec. 1.213-1(e)(1)(v).
[19] Sec. 213(d). See also Rev. Ruls. 66-216, 1966-2 C.B. 100, and 79-175, 1979-1 C.B. 117.
[20] Sections 162 and 106. The amount self-employed individuals may deduct as *for* AGI increases to 45% for the years 1998 through 2002 and increases each year thereafter until it reaches 80% in the year 2006.

[21] Reg. Sec. 1.213-1(a)(1). However, medical expenses paid within one year from the day following the taxpayer's death are treated as paid at the time they are incurred (see Sec. 213(c)).

year, the deduction for that care is deferred until the year in which payment occurs. If the obligation is charged on a credit card, payment is deemed to have been made on the date of the charge, not on the later date when the credit card balance is paid. Conversely, if medical care is prepaid, the deduction is deferred until the year the care is actually rendered unless there is a legal obligation to pay or unless the prepayment is a requirement for the receipt of the medical care.[22]

LIMITATION ON AMOUNT DEDUCTIBLE. As previously noted, a medical expense deduction is allowed only for the years in which the taxpayer itemizes his or her deductions and the taxpayer's expenditures for medical care exceed 7.5% of AGI.

EXAMPLE I7-8 ▶ During the current year, Kelly incurs qualified medical expenditures of $3,000. Her AGI for the year is $30,000. After subtracting the floor, she has $750 ($3,000 − [0.075 × $30,000]) of deductible medical expenses. These medical expenses are added to Kelly's other itemized deductions to determine whether they exceed the standard deduction. ◀

MEDICAL INSURANCE REIMBURSEMENTS. A tax deduction is only available for unreimbursed medical expenditures. It does not matter whether the reimbursement is from an insurance plan purchased from an insurance company, a medical reimbursement plan of an employer, or a payment resulting from litigation.

If reimbursement is received in the same year the medical expenses are paid, the deduction is reduced by the amount of the reimbursement. If reimbursement is received in a year subsequent to the year of payment, the taxpayer is required to include the reimbursement in gross income for the year the payment is received to the extent that a tax benefit was derived from the deduction in the previous year. If no deduction was taken in the prior year, the reimbursement need not be reported as income. This may occur when the taxpayer's total itemized deductions do not exceed the standard deduction or when the total medical expenses do not exceed 7.5% of AGI. If a deduction was taken in the prior year, however, the taxpayer must report as income the lesser of the amount of the reimbursement or the amount by which the taxable income of the prior year was reduced because of medical expenses.

SELF-STUDY QUESTION

Why does the IRS not require that the taxpayer file an amended return when a reimbursement is received in a later year?

ANSWER

The administrative burden on the IRS of processing additional returns would be too great.

EXAMPLE I7-9 ▶ During 1997, Diane, a single taxpayer under age 65, reports the following items of income and expense:

AGI	$35,000
Total qualified medical expenses	3,500
Itemized deductions other than medical	3,350

Diane's taxable income for 1997 is calculated as follows:

AGI			$35,000
Reduction: larger of itemized deductions or standard deduction			
Medical expenses	$3,500		
Minus: 7.5% of AGI	(2,625)	875	
Other itemized deductions		3,350	
Total itemized deductions		$4,225	
Standard deduction		$4,150	<4,225>
Personal exemption			<2,650>
Taxable income			$28,125

---

[22] Rev. Rul. 78-38, 1978-1 C.B. 67 and *Robert M. Rose v. CIR*, 26 AFTR 2d 70-5653, 70-2 USTC ¶9646 (5th Cir., 1970). See also Rev. Ruls. 75-302, 1975-2 C.B. 86, and 75-303, 1975-2 C.B. 87.

If during 1998 Diane receives a reimbursement of $1,000 for medical expenses incurred the prior year, she must include $75 ($4,225 − $4,150) in the gross income for 1998 (the amount of the tax benefit from the medical expense deduction for the prior year). This amount can be calculated by comparing the actual taxable income for 1997 with what would have been the 1997 taxable income if the reimbursement had been received that year.

AGI			$35,000
Reduction: larger of itemized deductions or standard deduction			
Medical expenses	$3,500		
Minus: Reimbursement	(1,000)		
7.5% of AGI	(2,625)		
Excess medical expenses		0	
Plus: Other itemized deductions		3,350	
Total itemized deductions		$3,350	
Standard deduction		$4,150	<4,150>
Personal exemption			<2,650>
Taxable income (assuming reimbursement was received in 1997)			$28,200
Minus: Actual 1997 taxable income			<28,125>
Tax benefit			$ 75 ◄

Topic Review I7-1 highlights the principal requirements for the medical expense deduction previously discussed.

STOP & THINK

Question: Vince and Diane are married and file a joint tax return. For the current year they estimate their AGI at $100,000. They also estimate their itemized deductions for taxes, interest, and charitable contributions total $9,000. Up to the current date they have incurred $7,000 in deductible medical expenses. For several months they have been considering radial kerototomy on Diane's eyes. The total expenditure for the operations will be $4,000 and is not covered by their medical insurance. Since they already have spent so much this year on medical expenses and they do not anticipate such large expenses next year they are considering delaying the eye operation until next year. They estimate next year's AGI to be approximately $110,000. Does this decision make sense from a tax point of view?

Solution: From a tax point of view, Diane should consider having and paying for the operation this year. If so, $4,000 is added to the prior $7,000 medical expenditures for a total of $11,000 for the year. After applying the 7.5% of AGI limitation, $3,500 [$11,000 − ($100,000 × 0.075)] of the medical expenses is deductible. If they wait until next year and if their estimates are correct, none of the medical expenses in either year are deductible.

Taxes

OBJECTIVE 3

Identify taxes that are deductible as itemized deductions

Section 164 provides taxpayers with a federal income tax deduction for specifically listed taxes that are paid or accrued during the taxable year. Generally, cash-method taxpayers are entitled to the deduction when the taxes are paid, whereas taxpayers using the accrual method deduct taxes in the year they accrue. Other taxes are specifically listed as nondeductible. To be deductible as a tax, the assessment in question must be a tax rather than a fee or charge imposed by a government for providing specific goods or services.

Topic Review I7-1

Medical Expense Deduction

Items	Deduction Rules and Limitations
Types of expenditures mitigation, treatment, or prevention of disease.	(a) Expenditures for the diagnosis, cure, that qualify (b) Transportation at $0.10 per mile and lodging limited to $50 per-night, per-person, and 50% of meals. (c) Medical insurance premiums. (d) Capital expenditures (subject to specific limitations).
Qualifying individuals	Taxpayer, spouse, dependents, and children of divorced parents even if not a dependent.
Amount and timing of the deduction	Deduct in the year paid unless prepayment is required or there is a legal obligation to pay. Medical expenses are subject to a 7.5% of AGI nondeductible limitation.
Treatment of insurance reimbursements	The deduction is reduced if the reimbursement is received in the year of payment. Reimbursements received in a subsequent year are included in gross income if tax benefit was received in the earlier year.

ADDITIONAL COMMENT

In 1993 the deduction for taxes represented 34.9% of the dollar amount of all itemized deductions, making it the second largest itemized deduction.

DEFINITION OF A TAX

A **tax** is a mandatory assessment levied under the authority of a political entity for the purpose of raising revenue to be used for public or governmental purposes. Thus, fees, assessments, or fines imposed for specific privileges or services are not deductible as taxes under Sec. 164. These nontax items include

▶ Vehicle registration and inspection fees

▶ Registration tags for pets

▶ Toll charges for highways and bridges

▶ Parking meter charges

▶ Charges for sewer, water, and other services

▶ Special assessments against real estate for items such as sidewalks, lighting, and streets

However, if these nontax fees and charges are incurred in a business or income-producing activity, they may be either capitalized or deducted as ordinary and necessary business expenses or ordinary and necessary expenses incurred for the production of income.

EXAMPLE I7-10 ▶ During the year, Bruce renews his automobile license at a cost of $150. In addition, Bruce pays $300 personal property taxes on the automobile based on its value. Bruce also incurs a total of $100 in highway toll charges. The $300 personal property tax is the only item that is deductible as a tax under Sec. 164. The license fee and the toll charges are deductible only if he uses the automobile for business or for the production of income. ◀

ADDITIONAL
COMMENT

In general, only taxes imposed
on the taxpayer are deductible.

DEDUCTIBLE TAXES

Section 164 specifically identifies the following taxes as deductible:

▶ State, local, and foreign real property taxes

▶ State and local personal property taxes if based on value

▶ State, local, and foreign income, war profits, and excess profits taxes

▶ The federal environmental tax (imposed on corporations)

▶ The federal generation-skipping transfer tax on income distributions

▶ Other state, local, and foreign taxes that are paid or incurred in either a trade or business or an income-producing activity

KEY POINT

All state, local, and foreign taxes paid or incurred in a trade
or business or in an income-
producing activity can be either deducted or capitalized.

Except for the environmental tax and the generation-skipping transfer tax, all of these taxes are imposed by a government body other than the federal government.[23] A foreign tax includes taxes imposed by a foreign country, including any political subdivision of that country.

Federal taxes other than the ones listed generally are not deductible for federal income tax purposes. However, federal customs and excise taxes incurred in the taxpayer's business or income-producing activity are deductible as ordinary and necessary expenses under Secs. 162 or 212. Likewise, the *employer's* portion of federal Social Security taxes and federal and state unemployment taxes are deductible by the employer as ordinary and necessary business expenses if the employee works in the employer's business or income-producing activity.

NONDEDUCTIBLE TAXES

The following taxes are not deductible under Sec. 164:

▶ Federal income taxes

ADDITIONAL
COMMENT

Sales and property taxes are
even more unpopular than the
federal income taxes according
to a poll conducted by Louis
Harris & Associates.

▶ Federal estate, inheritance, legacy, succession, and gift taxes

▶ Federal import or tariff duties and excise taxes unless incurred in the taxpayer's business or for the production of income

▶ Employee's portion of Social Security and other payroll taxes

▶ State and local sales taxes and state inheritance, legacy, succession, and gift taxes

▶ Foreign income taxes if the taxpayer elects to take the taxes as a credit against his or her federal income tax liability

▶ Property taxes on real estate to the extent that the taxes are treated as imposed on another taxpayer[24]   ◀

STATE AND LOCAL INCOME TAXES

State and local income taxes are normally an itemized (*from* AGI) deduction. Thus, a taxpayer does not receive any federal income tax benefit if these taxes, in addition to the other itemized deductions, do not exceed the standard deduction. Cash-method taxpayers deduct all state and local income taxes paid or withheld during the year even if the taxes are attributable to another tax year.

EXAMPLE I7-11 ▶ During 1997, Rita had $1,500 in state income taxes withheld from her salary. On April 15, 1998, Rita pays an additional $400 when she files her 1997 state income tax return. On her 1997 federal income tax return, Rita may deduct the $1,500 in state income taxes withheld

---

[23] The environmental tax is a tax imposed by the United States on corporations with modified alternative minimum taxable income in excess of $2 million (see Sec. 59A). The generation-skipping transfer tax is imposed by the United States on certain distributions from a trust (see Sec. 2601). Furthermore, under Sec. 691(c) a taxpayer who includes income in respect of

a decedent in taxable income may deduct estate tax attributable to that amount.
[24] Sec. 275(a)(5). For a discussion of when and how these taxes are to be apportioned between different taxpayers, see the Real Estate Taxes section of this chapter.

SELF-STUDY QUESTION

Would a taxpayer normally prefer to deduct foreign taxes or take a foreign tax credit?

ANSWER

Normally the foreign tax credit is better because a credit provides a direct dollar-for-dollar reduction of the tax liability rather than a reduction of taxable income.

ADDITIONAL COMMENT

Every state except Alaska, Florida, Nevada, South Dakota, Texas, Washington, and Wyoming has some type of income tax.

from her salary as an itemized deduction. The $400 that she pays on April 15, 1998 is deductible on Rita's 1998 federal income tax return, even though the liability relates to her 1997 state income tax return. ◄

If the taxpayer receives a refund of state income taxes deducted in a prior year, the refund must be included as income in the year of the refund to the extent that the taxpayer received a tax benefit from the prior deduction. This calculation is done in the same way the tax benefit from a medical expense reimbursement was calculated in Example I7-9.

PERSONAL PROPERTY TAXES

Many state and local governments impose personal property taxes. For individuals, the key issue is whether the levy is a deductible tax under Sec. 164 or a nondeductible fee. To qualify as a deductible personal property tax, the levy must meet two basic tests:

▶ The tax must be an ad valorem tax on personal property. In other words, the amount of the tax is determined by the property's value rather than some other measure such as a vehicle's weight or model year.

▶ The tax must be imposed on an annual basis, even if it is not collected annually.[25]

If a personal property tax is based partly on value and partly on some other basis, the ad valorem portion is deductible.

EXAMPLE I7-12 ▶

ADDITIONAL COMMENT

Several states impose a tax on the value of a taxpayer's investment portfolio. This is an example of a deductible intangible personal property tax.

Banner County imposes a property tax of 1% of value plus 20 cents per hundredweight on all passenger automobiles. Clay's automobile has a value of $10,000 and weighs 1,500 pounds. Clay may deduct $100 ($10,000 × 0.01) under Sec. 164. The remaining $300 (1,500 × 0.20) is not deductible under Sec. 164; however, it may be deductible as an ordinary business expense if the automobile is used in his business. ◄

For individuals, personal property taxes are *from* AGI (itemized) deductions unless they are incurred in an individual's trade or business or for the production of rental income.

REAL ESTATE TAXES

Apportionment of Taxes. When real estate is sold during the year, the federal income tax deduction for taxes imposed on that real estate is allocated between the seller and the purchaser based on the amount of time each taxpayer owns the property during the real property tax year. The real property tax year may or may not coincide with the taxpayer's tax year. The apportionment, based on the number of days each party holds the property during the real property tax year of sale, assumes that the purchaser owns the property on the date of the sale.[26] If the other party to the transaction (e.g., the buyer of the property) is liable for the payment of the tax, both cash and accrual method taxpayers who buy or sell real estate during the year are treated as having paid, on the date of the sale, their proportionate share of the real estate taxes attributable to the property. The party who actually pays the taxes (either the buyer or the seller) deducts his or her share of the taxes in the year the taxes are paid unless an election is made under Sec. 461(c) to accrue the taxes. The tax consequences do not depend on who actually pays the real estate taxes or whether the real estate taxes are prorated under the agreement.

ADDITIONAL COMMENT

Many companies are challenging state and local property tax assessments. A recent Coopers & Lybrand survey found that more than 75% of the companies surveyed challenged their assessments, and almost 90% viewed their challenge as successful.

EXAMPLE I7-13 ▶

The real property tax year for Bannock County is the calendar year. Property taxes for a particular real property tax year become a lien against the property as of June 30 of that year,

---

[25] Reg. Sec. 1.164-3(c).   [26] Sec. 164(d)(1)(A).

and the owner of the property on that date becomes liable for the tax. However, the taxes are not payable until February 28 of the subsequent year. On May 30 of the current year, Sandy, a cash-method taxpayer, sells a building to Roger, who is also a cash-method taxpayer. The real estate taxes on the property for the current year are $1,095. Because Roger is liable for the payment of the tax, Sandy is treated as having paid $447 ($1,095 × 149/365 [the numerator of 149 is the number of days from January 1 through May 29 and the denominator is the entire real property tax year]) on the date of the sale. Roger's share of the taxes equaling $648 ($1,095 × 216/365) is deductible in the subsequent year (i.e., the year during which Roger actually pays the taxes). On the other hand, if the taxes become a lien against the property on April 1, Sandy is the owner of the building on that date and she is liable for the tax. Under these circumstances, the result is the same except that Roger may take the $648 deduction in the year of sale rather than in the year of payment. ◄

ADDITIONAL COMMENT

Delinquent taxes of the seller that are paid by the buyer as part of the contract price are not deductible.

Generally, the apportionment of taxes is included as part of the sales agreement, and the amount of the taxes apportioned to each party is stated separately from the selling price of the property. However, if the agreement does not provide for an apportionment of taxes, the seller's gain or loss on the sale (and the purchaser's basis in the property) must be adjusted either upward or downward, depending on which party actually pays the taxes. For example, a buyer who pays all of the real estate taxes has, in effect, paid the seller's portion of the taxes. The purchase price must be increased by this amount.

EXAMPLE I7-14 ▶

TYPICAL MISCONCEPTION

It is common to fail to differentiate between assessments for new construction and for repairs. For example, an assessment for street repairs is deductible, but an assessment for the construction of a new street is not deductible.

On March 15 of the current year, William sells a tract of land to Ken for $100,000. On the date of sale, William's basis in the land is $45,000. The real estate taxes attributable to the property for the year are $2,000. The county in which the property is located uses the calendar year, and the taxes are due on February 28 of the following year. The sales agreement does not provide for apportionment of real estate taxes between the buyer and the seller.

Even though Ken pays the full amount of the taxes, $400 ($2,000 × 73/365 [the numerator is the number of days from January 1 through March 14]) is treated as having been paid by William (the seller). Only $1,600 of deductible taxes are treated as having been paid by Ken (the buyer). This, in essence, represents an increase of $400 in the selling price of the property, and William's gain on the sale is increased by that amount. In addition, Ken's basis in the property is increased by $400.

On the other hand, assume that William (the seller) pays the taxes before the sale. Because $1,600 of the taxes actually paid by William is treated as having been paid by Ken, this represents a decrease in the selling price by that amount. Thus, William's gain on the sale and Ken's basis in the property are both decreased by $1,600. ◄

REAL PROPERTY ASSESSMENTS FOR LOCAL BENEFITS. Assessments are often made against real estate for the purpose of funding local improvements. These assessments may be for such things as street improvements, sidewalks, lighting, drainage, and sewer improvements. If the tax is assessed only against the property that benefits from the improvement, it is not deductible, even though the general public may also be incidentally benefited.[27] Such assessments are capitalized as part of the property's adjusted basis.

Real property taxes incurred on personal-use assets are deductible *from* AGI. Real property taxes incurred on business property or property held for the production of rental income are deductions *for* AGI.

---

[27] Reg. Sec. 1.164-4. However, if the assessment against the local benefits is made for maintenance, repair, or interest charges on the benefits, the assessment is deductible. The burden of proof to show how much of the assessment is deductible falls on the taxpayer (see Sec. 164(c)(1)).

GENERAL SALES TAX

Before 1987, Sec. 164 allowed a deduction for sales taxes. However, that deduction was eliminated by the Tax Reform Act of 1986 for 1987 and subsequent years. Instead, the sales tax is treated as part of the purchase price of the property, increasing its basis.

SELF-EMPLOYMENT TAX

Self-employed individuals are subject to a tax on their self-employment income in lieu of the payment of a Social Security payroll tax on salary. The self-employment tax rate and total amount of tax are equal to the combined employee and employer Social Security tax (i.e., 12.4% with a ceiling of $65,400 in 1997; and no ceiling for the 2.9% additional Medicare hospital insurance premium for self-employed individuals). However, self-employed individuals can deduct one-half of the self-employment taxes paid as a *for* AGI deduction.[28]

INTEREST

OBJECTIVE 4

Identify different types of interest deductions

ADDITIONAL COMMENT

In 1993 the deduction for interest expense represented 40.6% of the total dollar amount of itemized deductions, making it the largest single itemized deduction.

KEY POINT

A taxpayer cannot deduct interest payments made for someone else if he or she is not legally liable to make them.

Section 163(a) states simply that taxpayers may take a deduction for all interest paid or accrued in the taxable year. This statement is deceptive for several reasons. First, distinguishing between interest expense and a charge for services rendered may be difficult. Furthermore, the deductibility of interest incurred for certain purposes is limited or disallowed. In some cases special rules apply in determining the timing of the deduction for interest expense. Thus, the proper classification of interest expense is critical in determining the amount of interest expense deduction. These categories include

▶ Active trade or business

▶ Passive activity

▶ Investment

▶ Personal

▶ Qualified residence

DEFINITION OF *INTEREST*

Interest is defined as "compensation for the use or forbearance of money."[29] Thus, finance charges, carrying charges, loan discounts, premiums, loan origination fees, and points are all deductible as interest if they represent a cost for the use of money.

CHARGE FOR SERVICES. In some instances, it is difficult to determine whether an item is interest or a charge for services rendered (e.g., a recording fee). For example, points are often charged when property is sold or purchased. A point is equal to 1% of the loan amount. Thus, two points paid on a $60,000 mortgage equal $1,200 ($60,000 × 0.02). These points may represent either additional interest expense (because the stated rate of interest for the loan is lower than the current market rate of interest), or service charges, such as fees for appraisals or title searches. Only the first category is interest.

Generally, prepaid interest paid in the form of points must be capitalized and amortized over the life of the loan. However, points paid on a loan incurred to purchase

---

[28] Sec. 164(f). (See Chapter I14 for a discussion of the self-employment tax.)
[29] *Deputy v. Pierre S. DuPont,* 23 AFTR 808, 40-1 USTC ¶9161 (USSC, 1940).

or improve the taxpayer's principal residence are deductible when paid if the loan is secured by the residence, the payment of points is an established business practice in the geographic area where the debt is incurred, and the points do not exceed the amount generally charged. Furthermore, the IRS has stated that if certain requirements are met the points are automatically currently deductible as interest.[30] The IRS has also indicated that points paid on VA and FHA loans are also currently deductible as interest if they are clearly designated as points incurred in connection with the indebtedness.[31]

EXAMPLE I7-15 ▶

During the current year, Kevin and Donna purchase a new home for $300,000, putting $100,000 down and borrowing $200,000. At the closing, they are required to pay one and one-half points as a loan discount in connection with the loan, which is secured by a mortgage against the home. The practice of charging points is an established business practice where they live.

These points represent prepaid interest on the purchase of a principal residence. Thus, in addition to the interest portion of every payment they make during the year, Kevin and Donna may also deduct $3,000 ($200,000 × 0.015) as interest paid during the year of purchase. ◀

Points paid on a loan to purchase property other than a principal residence or for refinancing a mortgage on a principal residence must be capitalized. If the property is business, investment, or a qualified residence (the taxpayer's principal residence and one other that the taxpayer chooses) the points may be amortized over the life of the loan.[32]

In order for the points to be currently deductible, the purchaser of the principal residence (borrower) must have paid for them with unborrowed funds. However, amounts provided by the borrower as down payments, escrow deposits, earnest money, or other funds are treated as paid for the points. Furthermore, as long as the borrower provides sufficient funds in these other categories, he or she is treated as having paid the points even if the seller has paid for them on behalf of the borrower.[33]

BANK SERVICE CHARGES AND FINANCE CHARGES. Bank service charges incurred on checking accounts are nondeductible expenses for services rendered rather than interest. The annual service charge on credit cards is also a charge for services rather than interest. However, finance charges on credit cards are interest. Late payments charged by public utilities are interest expense because they are not incurred for any specific service.[34] Of course, if these expenses are incurred in a trade or business, they are deductible.

CLASSIFICATION OF INTEREST EXPENSE

KEY POINT

The classification of interest expense depends on the use to which the borrowed money is put, not on the nature of the property used to secure the loan.

The deductibility of interest generally depends on the purpose for which the indebtedness is incurred because interest incurred in certain activities is subject to limitation and disallowance. For example, interest expense allocated to the taxpayer's active business is deductible in full against the business income (a deduction *for* AGI, taken on Schedule C), whereas interest expense allocated to the purchase of the taxpayer's residence is

---

[30] These requirements, mentioned in Chapter 16, are as follows: The points must be paid in connection with the purchase (not the improvement) of the taxpayer's principal residence, the closing agreement must clearly designate the amounts as points paid in connection with the acquisition debt, the amount must be computed as a percentage of the amount borrowed, the points must conform with established business practices, and the loan must be secured by the residence. See Rev. Proc. 94-27, I.R.B. 94-15, 17.

[31] Rev. Proc. 92-12A, 1992-1 C.B. 664.

[32] Rev. Rul. 87-22, 1987-1 C.B. 146, and Rev. Proc. 87-15, 1987-1 C.B. 624. The Tax Court has held in one case that points paid on refinancing a

"bridge" or temporary loan are currently deductible. *James R. Huntsman v. CIR,* 66 AFTR 2d 90-5020, 90-2 USTC ¶ 50,340 (8th Cir., 1990) rev'g 91 TC 57 (1988). However, the IRS has announced that it will not follow *Huntsman* in circuits other than the circuit in which the case was decided (IRS Action on Decision CC-1991-02, Feb. 11, 1991).

[33] Reg. Sec. 1.6050H-1(f)(3). See also Rev. Proc. 94-27, I.R.B. 94-15, 17.

[34] Rev. Rul. 73-136, 1973-1 C.B. 68 and Rev. Rul. 74-187, 1974-1 C.B. 48. However, interest on a credit card or interest charged by a public utility is not deductible if it is personal interest.

subject to the limitations applicable to that type of interest and is an itemized deduction (a deduction *from* AGI). No deduction is allowed for interest allocated to personal-use expenditures.

Pursuant to the Treasury Regulations, interest expense generally is allocated to the different interest expense categories by identifying the use of the borrowed money. With two exceptions, what the taxpayer uses as collateral in securing the debt has no bearing on the allocation of the interest expense.[35]

EXAMPLE I7-16 ▶ Cathy pledges some stock and securities as collateral for a $30,000 loan. She then purchases an automobile with the proceeds of the loan. The automobile is used 100% of the time for personal use. Even though the collateral for the loan consists of investment property, the interest expense is allocated to a personal-use asset and is not deductible. ◀

If the borrowed funds are deposited in a bank rather than spent immediately, the deposit is considered an investment, and the interest on the loan is investment interest until the funds are withdrawn and expended. Then the interest expense is allocated to the category for which the expenditure is made, regardless of when the interest expense for the debt is actually paid. This reallocation occurs as of the date the check is written on the account as long as the check is delivered or mailed within a reasonable period of time.[36]

EXAMPLE I7-17 ▶ On March 1 of the current year, José borrows $100,000 and immediately deposits the funds into an account that contains no other funds. No other funds are deposited into the account, and no payment is made on the loan balance. On May 1 of the current year, he withdraws $40,000 from the account and purchases a sailboat to be used for personal purposes. On July 1, José withdraws an additional $50,000 and purchases a passive activity. For the current year, the interest expense on the loan is categorized as follows: from March 1 through April 30, all of the expense is investment interest expense. 40% ($40,000/$100,000) of the interest expense attributable to the period May 1 through June 30 is classified as personal interest and the remainder is investment interest. The interest expense attributable to the period from July 1 to the end of the year is classified as 40% personal interest, 50% passive activity interest, and 10% investment interest. ◀

If both borrowed and personal funds are mingled in the same account, expenditures from that account are treated as coming first from the borrowed funds.[37]

EXAMPLE I7-18
KEY POINT

The attempt to classify interest expense correctly has resulted in significant additional record-keeping costs for many taxpayers.

▶ On April 1 of the current year, Diane borrows $30,000 and deposits it into a checking account that contains $10,000 of personal funds. On May 1 of the current year, Diane purchases a passive activity for $15,000, and on June 1 she purchases a personal automobile for $20,000. The $15,000 expended for the passive activity on May 1 is treated as coming from the borrowed funds. Thus, as of that date, one-half of the interest expense on the debt is reallocated from investment interest to passive activity interest. $15,000 of the funds expended for the personal automobile on June 1 is treated as coming from the borrowed funds, and the remaining $5,000 is treated as coming from the personal funds. Thus, as of that date, the remaining interest expense on the debt is reallocated to personal interest. ◀

---

[35] Temp. Reg. Sec. 1.163-8T. The exceptions deal with qualified residence interest attributable to home equity indebtedness and loans secured by tax-exempt securities. Qualified residence interest is explained later in this chapter in the Home Equity Indebtedness section. Interest on loans secured by tax-exempt securities is not deductible.
[36] Temp. Reg. Sec. 1.163-8T(c). If during any one month several expenditures are made from an account, the taxpayer may elect to treat all the expenditures as if made on the first day of the month. However, this election is made on each account separately and is available only for accounts where

the borrowed funds are already in the account as of the first day of the month. If the funds are not in the account as of the first day of the month, the expenditures may be treated as made on the date that the borrowed funds are deposited in the account. See Temp. Reg. Sec. 1.163-8T(c)(4)(iv).
[37] Temp. Reg. Sec. 1.163-8T(c)(4)(ii). However, if an expenditure is made out of the mingled funds within 15 days of the deposit of the borrowed funds into the account, the taxpayer may designate the expenditure to which the borrowed funds are allocated.

When a debt is repaid, the repayment is allocated to the expenditures made with that debt in the following order: (1) personal expenditures, (2) investment expenditures and passive activity expenditures other than rental real estate, (3) passive activity expenditures in rental real estate, and (4) trade or business expenditures.

EXAMPLE I7-19 ▶ Assume the same facts as in Example I7-18. In addition, assume that on October 31 of the current year, Diane repays $10,000 of the $30,000 debt incurred on April 1 of the current year. Even though the expenditure for the passive activity was made first, the repayment of the debt is first allocated to the expenditure for the personal automobile. Thus, beginning on November 1 of the current year, of the remaining $20,000 debt outstanding $15,000 is allocated to the passive activity and $5,000 is allocated to the expenditure for the personal automobile. ◀

ACTIVE TRADE OR BUSINESS. Interest expense incurred in a taxpayer's active trade or business generally is fully deductible without limitation. As explained in Chapter I6, the determination of whether a particular activity constitutes a trade or business or an investment depends on an examination of all the relevant facts and circumstances. For individuals, estates, trusts, and certain corporations, however, it is not sufficient that the interest be incurred in the taxpayer's trade or business. In addition, the taxpayer must *materially participate* in the business. If not, the activity is considered passive, and losses from the activity (including the interest expense) are subject to the passive loss limitation rules (see Chapter I8 for a discussion of these rules). Interest incurred in an active trade or business is a deduction *for* AGI.

PASSIVE ACTIVITY. Individuals, estates, trusts, and certain corporations that incur losses from passive activities are subject to the passive loss limitation rules explained in Chapter I8. These rules prevent taxpayers from offsetting passive activity losses against other income such as salary, interest, dividends, and income from an active business. Interest expense attributable to the passive activity is included in computing the net income or loss generated from the activity, and thus may not be deductible under these limitation rules (see Chapter I8 for a discussion of these rules).

OBJECTIVE 5

Compute the amount of investment interest deduction

INVESTMENT INTEREST. Since 1972, individuals and other noncorporate taxpayers have been limited on the deductibility of interest expense attributable to investments. Without this limitation, high-income taxpayers could realize significant tax savings by borrowing money to invest in assets that are appreciating in value but produce little or no current income. This would enable the taxpayer to offset current highly taxed income with a current interest deduction, while deferring the taxable income from the investment until it is sold at a later date. This technique also often enables taxpayers to increase their capital gain income and reduce their ordinary income, that is favorable to taxpayers because the tax on capital gains is, in many cases, less than the tax on ordinary income.

Because of these concerns, Sec. 163(d) limits the current deduction for investment interest expense to the taxpayer's net investment income for the taxable year. Any investment interest expense disallowed as a current deduction is carried over and treated as investment interest expense incurred in the following year.

EXAMPLE I7-20 ▶ In the current year, Rita earns $27,000 in net investment income and incurs $40,000 investment interest expense. Rita's interest expense deduction for the year is limited to $27,000, the amount of her net investment income.

The remaining investment interest expense of $13,000 ($40,000 − $27,000) may be carried over and deducted in a subsequent year. This carryover amount is treated as paid or accrued in the subsequent year and is subject to the disallowance rules that pertain to the subsequent year. ◀

Investment Interest. **Investment interest** is interest expense on indebtedness properly allocable to property held for investment. This includes property that generates portfolio types of income such as interest, dividends, annuities, and royalties. It does not include business interest, personal interest, qualified residence interest, or interest incurred in connection with any activity that is determined to be passive. Under Sec. 469, all rental activities are deemed to be passive (see Chapter I8 for a discussion of the passive loss limitation rules). Thus, interest incurred in owning and renting property is subject to the passive loss limitation rather than the investment interest limitation.

EXAMPLE I7-21 ▶ Paul owns a duplex that he rents out. The rental of the duplex is a passive activity. During the year, he incurs $7,000 in interest expense on the duplex. The $7,000 interest expense (along with the other expenses and the income from the property) is a *for* AGI deduction, but is subject to the passive loss limitation rather than the investment interest limitation. ◀

Investment interest also does not include interest expense incurred to purchase or carry tax-exempt securities. This interest is not deductible at all. Without this disallowance, a taxpayer could, in certain circumstances, actually borrow funds at a higher rate of interest than the rate at which they were reinvested, while still generating a positive net cash flow because the government would be subsidizing the transaction through the interest deduction on the borrowings.

Net Investment Income. For purposes of the investment interest limitation, the term **net investment income** means the excess of the taxpayer's investment income over investment expenses. Investment income is gross income from property held for investment, including items such as dividends, interest, annuities, and royalties (if not earned in a trade or business). Investment income also includes net gain (all gains minus all losses) on the sale of investment property, but only to the extent that the net gain exceeds the net capital gain (net long-term capital gains in excess of net short-term capital losses).

As explained in Chapter I5, net capital gain is generally taxed at a 28% maximum rate. Including net capital gain in the definition of investment income would increase the amount of deductible investment interest expense, which might offset other income that is taxed at rates higher than 28%. Thus, net capital gain attributable to the disposition of property held for investment is excluded from the definition of investment income. However, net capital gain from the disposition of investment property is included in the definition to the extent that the taxpayer elects to subject the gain from the disposition of investment property to the regular tax rates.[38] Gains on business and personal-use property are not included in the calculation of investment income.

EXAMPLE I7-22 ▶ During the current year, Michael incurs $15,000 investment interest expense, earns $7,000 of dividends and has $3,000 interest income. He also reports the following gains and losses from the sale of stocks and bonds during the year:

Short-term capital gains	$4,000
Short-term capital losses	(3,000)
Long-term capital gains	5,000
Long-term capital losses	(2,000)

Considering all of Michael's other income and deductions for the year, assume that he has a 39.6% marginal tax rate. Michael's net capital gain is $3,000 (net long-term capital gain of $3,000 in excess of net short-term capital losses of $0). He also has a $1,000 ($4,000 − $3,000) net short-term capital gain. Thus, his net gain is $4,000 ($9,000 of total gains − $5,000 of total losses) and only $1,000 ($4,000 net gain − $3,000 net capital gain) is included in investment income. If Michael does not make an election, his investment income is $11,000

ADDITIONAL COMMENT

A provision in the Revenue Reconciliation Act of 1993 eliminates net capital gain in the calculation of net investment income. Congress believed that it was inappropriate for a taxpayer to be taxed on net capital gain at a favorable 28% rate and to also be able to use that gain to deduct otherwise nondeductible investment interest against ordinary income that might otherwise be taxed at a higher rate.

---

[38] Secs. 1(h) and 163(d)(4)(B).

($10,000 of dividends and interest plus $1,000 net short-term capital gain). He may deduct $11,000 of the investment interest expense in the current year. The $4,000 ($15,000 − $11,000) is carried over to the next year. The $3,000 net capital gain is subject to the 28% ceiling tax rate on net capital gain. If Michael makes the election, his investment income is $14,000 (the $3,000 net capital gain is included), and he may deduct $14,000 of the investment interest expense. Thus, only $1,000 ($15,000 − $14,000) of investment interest expense is not currently deductible and is carried over to the next year. However, his $3,000 net capital gain is subject to the 39.6% ordinary income tax rate. ◀

ADDITIONAL COMMENT

Investment expenses are those which are deductible on the tax return, after the 2% limitation.

Investment expenses include all deductions (except interest) that are directly connected with the production of investment income. These expenses include rental fees for safe-deposit boxes, fees for investment counsel,[39] and subscriptions to investment and financial planning journals. As explained later in this chapter (see the section of this chapter titled Miscellaneous Itemized Deductions), these investment expenses are deductible only to the extent they exceed 2% of the taxpayer's AGI for the year. Only the investment expenses remaining after application of this limitation are used in computing the net investment income. Furthermore, in computing the amount of the disallowed investment expenses, the 2% of AGI limitation is applied to the noninvestment expenses first.[40] Any remaining 2% of AGI limitation is then used to reduce the noninterest investment expenses.

EXAMPLE I7-23 ▶

Kevin's AGI for the current year is $200,000. Included in his AGI is $175,000 salary and $25,000 of investment income. In earning the investment income, Kevin paid investment interest expense of $33,000. He also incurred the following expenditures subject to the 2% of AGI limitation:

Investment expenses:	
Subscriptions to investment journals	$ 700
Investment counseling	2,000
Safe-deposit box rental	300
Noninvestment expenses:	
Unreimbursed employee business expenses	1,500
Tax return preparation fees (non–business-related)	500

Kevin's investment interest expense deduction for the year is computed by first determining the deductible investment expenses (other than interest) and the net investment income.

Investment expenses:		
Subscriptions	$ 700	
Investment counseling	2,000	
Safe-deposit box rental	300	$3,000
Disallowed by the 2% limitation:		
2% of AGI ($200,000 × 0.02)	$4,000	
Unreimbursed employee expenses	(1,500)	
Tax return preparation fees	(500)	
Investment expenses (remainder of 2% limit allocated to investment expenses)		(2,000)
Deductible investment expenses		$1,000
Net investment income		
($25,000 − $1,000)		$24,000

---

[39] Sec. 163(d)(4)(C). Not included here are commissions for the sale or purchase of investment property. A commission paid on the purchase of property is added to the purchase price (and the basis) of the property. A commission paid on the sale of property reduces the amount realized.

[40] H. Rept. No. 99-841, 99th Cong., 2d Sess., pp. II-153 and 154 (1986). The noninvestment expenses subject to the 2% of AGI limitation include unreimbursed employee business expenses, hobby expenses up to the income from the hobby, and tax return preparation fees.

The investment interest expense deduction is limited to $24,000. The remaining investment interest of $9,000 ($33,000 − $24,000) is carried over and deducted in a subsequent year (subject to the disallowance rules that pertain to the subsequent year). ◀

OBJECTIVE 6

Compute the deduction for qualified residence interest

ADDITIONAL COMMENT

Banks and other financial institutions that have received mortgage interest from homeowners are required to report interest of $600 or more to the IRS and to the homeowners on Form 1098.

PERSONAL INTEREST. For years after 1990, no deduction is allowed for personal interest. **Personal interest** is defined as all interest other than interest incurred in a trade or business, investment interest, interest incurred in a passive activity, qualified residence interest, and interest incurred when paying estate taxes on installment.

QUALIFIED RESIDENCE INTEREST. Subject to certain limitations discussed below, individuals may deduct **qualified residence interest**. In order to be qualified residence interest the interest payment must be for either acquisition indebtedness or home equity indebtedness with respect to a qualified residence of the taxpayer. In all cases the debt must be secured by the residence.[41] A qualified residence (discussed below) may consist of the taxpayer's principal residence and a second residence.

ACQUISITION INDEBTEDNESS. Acquisition indebtedness is any debt that is secured by the residence and is incurred in acquiring, constructing, or substantially improving the qualified residence. Debt may be treated as qualified acquisition indebtedness if the residence is acquired within 90 days before or after the date that the debt is incurred. In the case of the construction or substantial improvement of a residence, debt incurred before the completion of the construction or improvement can qualify as acquisition debt to the extent of construction expenditures that are made no more than 24 months before the date the debt is incurred. Furthermore, debt incurred after construction is complete and within 90 days of the completion date may qualify as acquisition indebtedness to the extent of any construction expenditures made within the 24-month period ending on the date the debt is incurred.[42] As payments of principal are made on the loan, the amount of acquisition debt is reduced and cannot be increased unless the residence is substantially improved. Acquisition indebtedness may be refinanced (and therefore treated as acquisition indebtedness) to the extent that the principal amount of the refinancing does not exceed the principal amount of the acquisition debt immediately before the refinancing.

EXAMPLE I7-24 ▶

Kay acquired a personal residence in 1989 for $100,000 and borrowed $85,000 on a mortgage that was secured by the property. In the current year the principal balance of the mortgage has been reduced to $60,000. Kay's acquisition indebtedness in the current year is only $60,000 and cannot be increased above $60,000 (except by indebtedness incurred to substantially improve the residence). If she refinances the existing mortgage in the current year and the refinanced debt is $70,000, only $60,000 (the principal balance of the existing acquisition indebtedness) qualifies as acquisition indebtedness. ◀

Limitations on Acquisition Indebtedness. Qualified acquisition indebtedness is limited to $1,000,000 ($500,000 for a married individual filing a separate return). Qualified acquisition indebtedness incurred before October 13, 1987 (pre-October 13, 1987

---

[41] Sec. 163(h). If the loan is not secured by the residence, it does not qualify. In one instance the taxpayer agreed to purchase her ex-husband's interest in their residence. The terms of the sale were $10,000 down plus an unsecured $25,000 note. In a private ruling, the IRS ruled that because the note was not secured by the residence, the interest on the note was not qualified residence interest. Thus the deductibility of the interest is subject to the personal interest deduction limitations (See Ltr. Rul. 8752010 September 18, 1987). However, if under any state or local homestead law the security interest is

ineffective or unenforceable, the interest expense still qualifies as qualified residence interest. See Sec. 163(h)(4)(C). In another letter ruling the taxpayer borrowed money to purchase a residence securing the debt by pledging stock and bonds. Here also, the IRS denied the deduction because the loan was not secured by the residence. (See Ltr. Rul. 8906031 November 10, 1988).

[42] Notice 88-74, 1988-2 C.B. 385.

indebtedness) is not subject to any limitation.[43] However, the aggregate amount of pre-October 13, 1987 indebtedness reduces the $1,000,000 limitation on the indebtedness incurred after October 13, 1987.

Home Equity Indebtedness. Taxpayers may also deduct interest incurred on home equity indebtedness (so-called home equity loans). Subject to certain limits, home equity indebtedness is any indebtedness (other than acquisition indebtedness) that is secured by a qualified residence of the taxpayer. The proceeds of the loan may be used for any purpose (including purchasing or improving a qualified residence), as long as the loan is secured by the taxpayer's qualified residence. However, home equity indebtedness is limited to the lesser of:

▶ The FMV of the qualified residence in excess of the acquisition indebtedness with respect to that residence, or

▶ $100,000 ($50,000 for a married individual filing a separate return)

The $1,000,000 limit on acquisition indebtedness and the $100,000 limit on home equity indebtedness are two separate limits. The maximum amount of indebtedness on which a taxpayer may deduct qualified residence interest is generally limited to $1,100,000 if an individual has $100,000 or more equity in the property.

EXAMPLE I7-25 ▶

On April 23 of the current year, Kesha borrows $125,000 to purchase a new sailboat. The loan is secured by her personal residence. On that date, the outstanding balance on the original debt Kesha incurred to purchase the residence is $400,000 and the FMV of the residence is $900,000. The original debt is also secured by Kesha's residence. Kesha may deduct the interest paid on the $400,000 of acquisition indebtedness, plus the interest paid on $100,000 of the home equity loan. The interest on $25,000 ($125,000 − $100,000) is treated as personal interest and is, therefore, not deductible. The home equity loan is limited to the lesser of $100,000 or the FMV of the residence in excess of the outstanding acquisition indebtedness (the lesser of $100,000 or ($900,000 − $400,000)). ◀

QUALIFIED RESIDENCE. For any tax year, a taxpayer may have two qualified residences:

▶ Taxpayer's principal residence

▶ One other residence selected by the taxpayer, with regard to which the taxpayer meets the residence test of Sec. 280A(d)(1).

In order to meet this residence test, the taxpayer must have personally used the property more than the greater of 14 days or 10% of any rental days during the year.[44]

EXAMPLE I7-26 ▶

Fred owns a lakeside cabin, which he uses for vacations. He also rents the cabin out to others when he is not using it. During the year the cabin is rented at a fair rental for 90 days. Fred personally uses the cabin for a total of 22 days. Because Fred's personal use for the year (22 days) exceeds 14 days [the greater of 14 days or 9 days (10% of the rental days)], the cabin qualifies as his residence for purposes of deducting qualified residence interest for the year. ◀

---

[43] Sec. 163(h)(3). If the acquisition indebtedness exceeds the $1,000,000 limitation, the committee reports to the Revenue Act of 1987 indicate that a reasonable method of allocation between the debt should be used in order to determine which debt exceeds the limitation. This may be done by taking debt into account in the chronological order in which it is incurred, with the most recently incurred debt treated as the debt that exceeds the limit.

[44] Sec. 280A(d)(1). Use by the taxpayer's family, as defined in Sec. 267(c)(4), other individuals under a reciprocal-use arrangement, and anyone when a fair rental is not charged is counted as a day of personal use by the taxpayer (see Sec. 280A(d)(2) and Chapter I6).

Despite the residence test, a property that has not been rented by the taxpayer at any time during the year may be selected by the taxpayer as the second residence on which qualified residence interest may be deducted.

STOP & THINK

Question: Jana is about to purchase a new sport utility vehicle for $35,000. If she pays $5,000 down, the dealer is prepared to offer her a loan for the remaining $30,000 at 8% interest. In investigating other possible sources of funds, she found out that her brokerage firm would lend her the $30,000 at 9% interest if she pledged her stock as collateral. At her local credit union, she found that she could borrow the $30,000 at 10% interest if she took out a home equity loan by using her home as security. Jana is confused about which loan she should take.

Solution: The best way to analyze this problem is by comparing the after-tax interest rates of the loans. Interest paid to the car dealer is not deductible because it is personal interest. Thus, its after-tax interest rate remains at 8%. Furthermore, even though Jana uses her stock holdings as collateral, the interest on the loan from the brokerage firm is non-deductible personal interest because the proceeds of the loan are used to purchase personal property rather than investment property. Its after-tax interest rate remains at 9%. Only the interest on the home equity loan from the credit union is potentially deductible. This depends, of course, on the amount of Jana's total itemized deductions. Assuming that Jana's total itemized deductions exceed the standard deduction and that Jana is in the 31% marginal tax bracket, the after-tax interest rate of the home equity loan drops from 10% to 6.9% [$10\% \times (1 - 0.31)$].

TIMING OF THE INTEREST DEDUCTION

Section 163 allows a deduction for all interest paid or accrued during the tax year. This generally means that cash-method taxpayers deduct interest in the year it is paid, whereas accrual-method taxpayers deduct interest as it accrues. However, there are exceptions to this general rule.

ADDITIONAL COMMENT

Points paid on the refinancing of an existing mortgage must be written off over the life of the new mortgage.

PREPAID INTEREST. If a cash method taxpayer prepays interest and the prepayment relates to a loan that extends beyond the end of the tax year, the payment must be capitalized and amortized over the periods to which the interest relates (i.e., the accrual method is applied to cash-method taxpayers). As previously discussed, there is one exception to this rule involving interest paid in the form of points charged in connection with the purchase or improvement of the taxpayer's principal residence. If these points represent prepaid interest, they may be deducted in the year paid.[45]

INTEREST PAID WITH LOAN PROCEEDS. If an individual borrows money from a third party rather than from the original lending institution and uses the funds to make a payment on a previously outstanding loan, an interest deduction generally is allowed for the interest portion of the payment. However, if the funds used to pay the interest on the first loan are borrowed from the same lender to whom the interest is due, and either the purpose of the second loan is to pay the interest on the first, or the borrower does not have unrestricted control of the funds, no interest deduction is available.[46]

---

[45] Sec. 461(g). In order for the exception to apply, the home must be used to secure the loan, and the charging of points must be an established business practice in the area where the loan is granted. (See the discussion of the deductibility of points in this chapter under the heading Definition of *Interest* as well as the discussion in Chapter 16.)

[46] *H. C. Franklin v. CIR,* 50 AFTR 2d 82-5551, 82-2 USTC ¶9532 (5th Cir., 1982) and *Newton A. Burgess,* 8 T.C. 47 (1947). See also *Norman W. Menz,* 80 T.C. 1174 (1983). The IRS has also announced that it will disallow a deduction for interest paid with funds obtained through a second loan from the same lender (see IRS News Release 83-93, July 6, 1983).

DISCOUNTED NOTES. Lending institutions often discount notes. In effect, the borrower pays the interest by repaying more money than is received when the note is signed. A cash-basis taxpayer can deduct this interest at the time the note is repaid, whereas an accrual-method taxpayer must deduct the interest as it accrues over the term of the loan.

EXAMPLE I7-27 ▶

On December 1, 1997, Stan borrows $1,000 from his credit union to use in his business. Under the terms of the contract, Stan actually receives $970 but is required to repay $1,000 on February 28, 1998 (three months later). Because Stan is a cash method taxpayer, the full $30 interest can be deducted in 1998 only when the note is repaid. If he were an accrual-method taxpayer, he could deduct $10 ($30 × 0.333) in 1997, and $20 ($30 × 0.667) in 1998. ◀

TYPICAL MISCONCEPTION

It is sometimes mistakenly assumed that any interest paid on loans between related taxpayers is not deductible. However, if the taxpayers are not governed by the Sec. 267 limitation and the interest is paid on a bona fide loan, it is deductible.

INTEREST OWED TO A RELATED PARTY BY AN ACCRUAL METHOD TAXPAYER. One of the purposes of Sec. 267 is to require related cash-method lenders and accrual method borrowers to report the results of their joint transaction in the same year. Thus, a deduction for any expense (including interest) accrued by an accrual method taxpayer must be deferred until the year in which it is actually paid and is reported as income by a cash method creditor who is related to the debtor. Section 267 also disallows losses on the sale of property between related parties. The disallowance of such losses is discussed in Chapter I6.

The relationships covered by this rule are quite extensive. Some of the more common relationships include the following:

▶ Members of a family (defined as an individual's brothers, sisters, spouse, ancestors, and lineal descendants)

▶ An individual and a C corporation in that the individual owns directly or indirectly more than 50% of the outstanding stock

▶ A corporation and a partnership which are both over 50% owned directly or indirectly by the same people

▶ A partnership and any partner of the partnership

▶ An S Corporation and any shareholder of the S Corporation[47]

EXAMPLE I7-28 ▶

During the current year, Lisa, a cash method taxpayer, loans some money to her 100%-owned corporation, which uses the accrual method of accounting. As of December 31 of the current year, the corporation owes Lisa $3,000 in interest. However, because of a shortage of funds, the corporation does not actually pay the interest until February 15 of the following year. Despite the fact that the corporation uses the accrual method of accounting, the $3,000 cannot be deducted until it is actually paid to Lisa in the subsequent year. The result would be the same if the corporation were an S Corporation even if Lisa owned 50% or less of the outstanding stock. ◀

IMPUTED INTEREST. Under certain circumstances, if less than an adequate rate of interest is charged, the IRS is authorized to impute an interest charge. This may cause the lender to have additional interest income and the borrower to have additional interest expense.

---

[47] Secs. 267(b) and (e). The list of relationships is much more extensive than those mentioned. An S Corporation is one that meets certain requirements and has made an election to have its income taxed directly to its shareholders. A C Corporation is one that has not made an S election. (See Chapter C11 of the *Prentice Hall's Federal Taxation: Corporations, Partnerships, Estates, and Trusts* text or Chapter C11 of the *Prentice Hall's Federal Taxation: Comprehensive* text.)

The deductibility of this imputed interest expense also depends on how the expense is classified (i.e. personal, investment, etc.). (See Chapter I11 for a discussion of imputed interest.)

The rules for deducting various types of interest are summarized in Topic Review I7-2.

CHARITABLE CONTRIBUTIONS

Under Sec. 170, corporations and individuals who itemize their deductions can deduct **charitable contributions** to qualified organizations. With the exception of certain contributions made by corporations,[48] the deduction is taken in the year the contribution is made, regardless of the taxpayer's method of accounting. The amount of the deduction depends on the type of charity receiving the contribution, the type of property contributed, and the applicable limitations.

QUALIFYING ORGANIZATION

To be deductible for federal income tax purposes, a contribution must be made to or for the use of a qualified organization.[49] Contributions made directly to individuals, even though they may be needy, are generally not deductible.[50] Under Sec. 170, qualified organizations include the following:

▶ The United States, the District of Columbia, a state or possession of the United States, or a political subdivision of a state or possession

Topic Review I7-2

Deductibility of Interest Expense

Type of Interest	Rules
Business	Deductible in full as a *for* AGI deduction.
Passive	Subject to the passive loss limits (see Chapter I8).
Investment	Deductible as an itemized deduction to the extent of the taxpayer's net investment income for the year. Any amount not deductible is carried over to subsequent years.
Personal	Not deductible.
Qualified residence	(a) Must be attributable to debt secured by the taxpayer's principal residence and one other residence selected by the taxpayer.
	(b) Interest on up to $1,000,000 of home acquisition indebtedness is deductible as an itemized deduction.
	(c) Interest on home equity debt is deductible as an itemized deduction. Home equity debt is limited to the lesser of $100,000 or the excess of the FMV of the residence over the home acquisition indebtedness.

---

[48] This exception is explained later in this chapter in the Special Rules for Charitable Contributions Made by Corporations section.

[49] The Supreme Court has ruled that in order for a contribution to be for the use of a qualifying organization, the gift must be held either in a legally enforceable trust or in a similar legal arrangement. (See *U.S. v. Harold Davis,* 65 AFTR 2d 90-1051, 90-1 USTC ¶50,270 (USSC, 1990).)

[50] Under certain circumstances, a taxpayer may take a deduction (limited to $50 per month) for maintaining a student as a member of his or her household. The student may not be a dependent or relative of the taxpayer and must be placed in the taxpayer's home under an arrangement with a qualifying organization (see Sec. 170(g)).

▶ A corporation, trust, community chest, fund or foundation created or organized under the laws of the United States, a state, possession, or the District of Columbia[51]

▶ A post or organization of war veterans

▶ A domestic fraternal society, order, or association[52]

▶ Certain cemetery companies

Because of the restrictions and limitations examined later in this chapter, these qualifying organizations are further classified into public charities and private nonoperating foundations. Different restrictions and limitations apply to each type of organization.

REAL-WORLD EXAMPLE

The American Red Cross, Boy Scouts, United Fund, Goodwill, and Indiana University are examples of public charities.

Public charities include:

▶ Churches or a convention or association of churches

▶ Educational institutions that normally maintain a regular faculty, curriculum, and regularly enrolled students

▶ Organizations such as hospitals and medical schools whose principal function is medical care or medical education and research

▶ Government-supported organizations that exist to receive, hold, invest, and administer property for the benefit of a college or university

▶ Any qualified governmental unit

▶ Organizations that normally receive a substantial part of their support from either a governmental unit or the general public

▶ Certain private operating foundations[53]

ADDITIONAL COMMENT

The list of qualifying organizations is published in a book, IRS Pub. No. 78, Cumulative List of Organizations, 1994, that rivals the size of a big-city telephone directory.

Because several thousand organizations meet these requirements, the IRS publishes a list of many of the organizations that have applied for and received tax-exempt status.[54] Although this publication is frequently updated, an organization need not be listed in order to qualify.

TYPE OF PROPERTY CONTRIBUTED

If a contribution is made in cash, the amount of the deduction is easily determinable. However, if noncash property is donated, the amount of the contribution is not as easy to identify. In the case of noncash property, the amount of the donation depends on two factors: the type of property donated and the type of qualifying organization (public charity or private nonoperating foundation) to whom the property is given. Furthermore, a gift of property that consists of less than the donor's entire interest in the property is not usually considered a contribution of property. Thus, for example, no charitable contribution is made when an individual donates the use of a vacation home for a charitable fund-raising auction.[55]

SELF-STUDY QUESTION

Doug purchases an item having a FMV of $75 for $100 in a charity auction. How much can he deduct?

ANSWER

Doug can deduct only $25 because the cash paid must be reduced by the value of the property received.

CONTRIBUTION OF CAPITAL GAIN PROPERTY. In general, the amount of a donation of capital gain property is its FMV. A property's FMV is defined as the price at which the property would change hands between a willing buyer and a willing seller, neither being under any compulsion to buy or sell and both having reasonable

---

[51] These organizations must be organized and operated exclusively for religious, charitable, scientific, literary, or educational purposes; to foster national or international amateur sports competition; or for the prevention of cruelty to children or animals.

[52] Furthermore, gifts to these organizations must be made by individuals and must be used exclusively for religious, charitable, scientific, literary, or educational purposes, or for the prevention of cruelty to children or animals.

[53] Sec. 170(b)(1)(E). The distinction between a private operating foundation and a private nonoperating foundation generally depends on the way the foundation spends or distributes its income and contributions. The details of this distinction are beyond the scope of this text.

[54] IRS, Pub. No. 78, Cumulative List of Organizations, 1996. This publication is updated and reissued annually.

[55] Sec. 170(f)(3), Reg. Sec. 1.170A-7(a)(1) and Rev. Rul. 89-51, 1989-1 C.B. 89. Note, however, that certain transfers of partial interests in property do qualify (e.g., the contribution of certain remainder interests to a trust, the transfer of a remainder interest in a personal residence or a farm, or a contribution of an undivided interest in property). These exceptions are beyond the scope of this text.

knowledge of relevant facts.[56] **Capital gain property** is defined as property on which a long-term capital gain would be recognized if it were sold at its FMV on the date of the contribution. If a long-term capital loss or a short-term capital gain or loss would be recognized, the property is considered to be ordinary income property for purposes of the charitable contribution deduction.

Contribution to a Private Nonoperating Foundation. An exception to this general rule is provided for contributions of property to private nonoperating foundations. In general, a private nonoperating foundation is an organization that does not receive funding from the general public (e.g., the Carnegie Foundation). Private nonoperating foundations distribute funds to various charitable organizations that actually perform the charitable services. The amount of the contribution to a private nonoperating foundation is the property's FMV, reduced by the long-term capital gain that would be recognized if the property were sold at its FMV on the date of the contribution.[57] This means that generally the deductible amount of the contribution will be the property's adjusted basis.

EXAMPLE I7-29 ▶ Betty purchases land in 1986 for $10,000. In the current year, she contributes the land to the United Way. At the time of the contribution, the FMV of the property is $25,000. Because the land is capital gain property donated to a public charity, the amount of the contribution is $25,000 (its FMV).

On the other hand, if Betty donates the land to Cherry Foundation, a private nonoperating foundation, the amount of the contribution is $10,000 ($25,000 − $15,000 long-term capital gain that would be recognized if the land were sold). ◀

TYPICAL MISCONCEPTION

Many people do not understand that the unrelated use restriction applies only to tangible personal property. A gift of shares of stock (intangible property) would not be a gift of unrelated use property where the stock is sold by the donee.

Unrelated Use Property. A second exception applies to capital gain property (that is also tangible personal property) contributed to a public charity and used by the organization for purposes unrelated to the charity's function. In such cases, the amount of the contribution deduction is equal to the property's FMV minus the long-term capital gain that would be recognized if the property were sold at its FMV. This amount generally is the property's adjusted basis. Tangible property is all property that is not intangible property (e.g., property other than stock, securities, copyrights, patents, and so on). Personal property is all property other than real estate. The taxpayer is responsible for proving that the property was not put to unrelated use. However, this burden of proof is met if at the time of the contribution it is reasonable to anticipate that the property would not be put to unrelated use. The immediate sale of the property by the charitable organization is considered to be a use unrelated to its tax-exempt purpose.

EXAMPLE I7-30 ▶ Laura purchases a painting for $3,000. Several years later she contributes the painting to a local college. The FMV of the painting is $5,000 at the time the property is contributed. The painting is both tangible personal property and capital gain property. The college places the painting in the library for display and study by art students. Because the college does not use the painting for purposes unrelated to its function as an educational institution, the amount of Laura's contribution is equal to its FMV ($5,000).[58] ◀

CONTRIBUTION OF ORDINARY INCOME PROPERTY

General Rule. If ordinary income property is contributed to a charitable organization, the deduction is equal to the property's FMV minus the amount of gain that would be recognized if the property were sold at its FMV on the date of the contribution.[59] In most

---

[56] Reg. Sec. 1.170A-1(c)(2).
[57] Sec. 170(e)(1)(B).

[58] Reg. Sec. 1.170A-4(b)(3).
[59] Sec. 170(e)(1).

cases, this deduction is equal to the property's adjusted basis. This rule applies regardless of the type of charitable organization to which the property is donated.

Ordinary income property is defined as any property that would result in the recognition of ordinary income if the property were sold. Thus, ordinary income property includes inventory, works of art or manuscripts created by the taxpayer, capital assets that have been held for one year or less, and Sec. 1231 property that results in the recognition of ordinary income due to depreciation recapture.[60]

EXAMPLE I7-31 ▶ During the current year Bart purchases land as an investment for $10,000. Five months later he contributes the land to the United Way. At the time of the contribution the property's FMV is $15,000. The amount of Bart's contribution is $10,000 ($15,000 − [$15,000 − $10,000]) because he held the land for less than one year. ◀

EXAMPLE I7-32 ▶ Paul purchased a truck a few years ago for $20,000. During the current year, Paul donates the truck previously used in his business to a local community college. At the time of the contribution, the truck's adjusted basis is $5,000 and its FMV is $8,000. Because Paul would have recognized a $3,000 gain (all ordinary income under Sec. 1245) if the truck were sold at its FMV, the amount of the contribution is $5,000 ($8,000 − $3,000), which is equal to the truck's adjusted basis. ◀

Donation of Inventory by a Corporation. Under certain circumstances the donation of inventory by a corporate taxpayer to certain public charities gives rise to a contribution that is valued at more than the adjusted basis of the inventory. One exception is available if the inventory is to be used by the charity solely for the care of the ill, needy, or infants.[61] The other exception involves the donation of scientific equipment constructed by the taxpayer and donated to a college, university, or qualified research organization to be used for research, experimentation, or research training in the physical or biological sciences. In both cases, the amount of the charitable contribution is the property's FMV, reduced by 50% of the ordinary income that would be recognized if the property were sold at its FMV. However, the amount of the contribution is limited to twice the basis of the property.

EXAMPLE I7-33 ▶ During the current year, Able Corporation, a manufacturer of medical supplies, donates some of its inventory to the American Red Cross. The Red Cross intends to use the inventory for the care of the needy and ill. At the time of the contribution, the FMV of the inventory is $10,000. Able's basis in the inventory is $3,000. Because this transaction qualifies under the exception, the amount of Able's contribution (before any limitations are applied) is $6,500 [$10,000 − (0.50 × $7,000)] but the actual amount of the contribution is limited to $6,000 (2 x the $3,000 basis in the property). ◀

CONTRIBUTION OF SERVICES. When services are rendered to a qualified charitable organization, only the unreimbursed expenses incurred incident to the rendering of the services are deductible. These items include out-of-pocket transportation expenses, the cost of lodging and 50% of the cost of meals while away from home, and the cost of a uniform without general utility that is required to be worn in performing the donated services. The out-of-pocket expenses are deductible only if they are incurred by the taxpayer who actually renders the services to the charity. No deduction is allowed for traveling expenses while away from home unless there is no significant element of

---

[60] Reg. Secs. 1.170A-4(b)(1) and 1.170A-4(d). Sec. 1231 property includes property used in a trade or business that is subject to depreciation. If it is sold at a gain, part or all of the gain is treated as ordinary income. Any remaining gain is subject to the Sec. 1231 rules. (See Chapter I13 for an explanation of the depreciation recapture and Sec. 1231 rules.)

[61] Sec. 170(e). These charitable organizations are known as Sec. 501(c)(3) charities.

personal pleasure, recreation, or vacation in such travel. Instead of the actual costs of operating an automobile while performing the donated services, the law permits a deduction of 12 cents per mile.[62]

EXAMPLE I7-34 ▶
REAL-WORLD EXAMPLE

The cost of newspaper advertising, paper, pencils, and other supplies purchased by volunteers in connection with their involvement in the Volunteer Income Tax Assistance Program (VITA) is deductible. Rev. Rul. 80-45, 1980-1 C.B. 54.

During the current year, Tony spends a total of 100 hours developing an accounting system for the local council of the Boy Scouts of America. As an accountant, Tony earns $75 per hour. During the year, Tony also drives his car a total of 500 miles in performing the services for the Boy Scouts of America. If he uses the automatic mileage method to compute the amount of the charitable contribution, he can deduct $60 (0.12 × 500). No deduction is available for the value of 100 hours of Tony's contributed services. ◀

DEDUCTION LIMITATIONS

OVERALL 50% LIMITATION. The charitable contribution deduction available for any tax year is subject to certain limitations. For individuals, the general overall limitation applicable to public charities is 50% of the taxpayer's AGI for the year.[63] Any contributions in excess of the overall limitation may be carried forward and deducted in the subsequent 5 tax years. In addition, contributions of capital gain property to either a public charity or a private nonoperating foundation and all types of property contributions to private nonoperating foundations may be subject to further limitation.

KEY POINT

The charitable contribution deduction can never exceed 50% of AGI.

KEY POINT

The generosity of Congress in permitting individuals to use FMV is tempered by the 30% of AGI limitation.

30% LIMITATION. Under certain circumstances a special 30% of AGI limitation applies. Contributions of capital gain property to public charities are generally valued at the property's FMV but are subject to an overall limit of 30% of AGI instead of a 50% limit. This limit does not apply, however, in the following situations:

▶ Capital gain property (which is tangible personal property) donated to a public charity that does not put the property to its related use. In such cases, the amount of the contribution is scaled down by the long-term capital gain that would be recognized if the property were sold.

▶ The taxpayer elects to reduce the amount of the charitable contribution deduction by the long-term capital gain that would be recognized if the property were sold.

EXAMPLE I7-35 ▶

Joy donates a painting to the local university during a year in which she has AGI of $50,000. The painting, which cost $10,000 several years before, is valued at $30,000 at the time of the contribution. The university exhibits the painting in its art gallery. Because the painting is put to a use related to the university's purpose, the amount of her contribution is $30,000. The amount of the charitable deduction for the year, however, is limited to $15,000 (0.30 × $50,000 AGI) unless Joy elects to reduce the amount of the contribution by the long-term capital gain. ◀

The overall deduction limitation of 30% of AGI also applies to the contribution of all types of property other than capital gain property (e.g., cash and ordinary income property) to a private nonoperating foundation. However, the deductibility of certain contributions to this type of charity may be subject to even further restrictions.

REAL-WORLD EXAMPLE

The largest private nonoperating foundation ranked by the FMV of total assets is the Ford Foundation.

20% LIMITATION ON CAPITAL GAIN PROPERTY CONTRIBUTED TO PRIVATE NONOPERATING FOUNDATIONS. Contributions of capital gain property to private nonoperating foundations are limited to the lesser of 20% of the taxpayer's AGI or 30% of the taxpayer's AGI, reduced by any contributions of capital gain property donated to a public charity.

---

[62] Sec. 170(i).

[63] A 10% of taxable income limitation is placed on corporate taxpayers. For purposes of this limitation, a corporation's taxable income is computed without regard to any deduction for charitable contributions, dividends received, a net operating loss carryback, or a capital loss carryback.

CONTRIBUTIONS FOR ATHLETIC EVENTS. If a taxpayer makes a contribution to a college or university and in return receives the right to purchase tickets to athletic events, only 80% of the payment may be deducted.[64]

APPLYING THE DEDUCTION LIMITATIONS. Contributions subject only to the 50% of AGI limitation are accounted for before the contributions subject to the 30% of AGI limitation.

EXAMPLE I7-36 ▶ During a year when Ted's AGI is $70,000, he donates $22,000 to his church and $18,000 to a private nonoperating charity. The church contribution is initially subject to the 50% limitation and is fully deductible because the $22,000 contribution is less than the limitation amount of $35,000 (0.50 × $70,000). Ted's deduction for the contribution to the private nonoperating charity (a 30% charity) is limited to $13,000 (the lesser of the following three amounts):

The actual contribution	$18,000
The remaining 50% limitation after the contribution to Ted's church [(0.50 × $70,000) − $22,000]	$13,000
30% of AGI (0.30 × $70,000)	$21,000 ◀

APPLICATION OF CARRYOVERS

As noted earlier, any contributions that exceed the 50% limitation may be carried over and deducted in the subsequent five years. These carryovers are subject to the limitations that apply in subsequent years. Thus, carryovers may be deducted only to the extent that the limitation of the subsequent year exceeds the contributions made during that year.

ADDITIONAL COMMENT

If a taxpayer has contribution carryovers that are about to expire, the taxpayer should consider reducing the current year's contribution so that the carryovers can be deducted.

These general rules also apply with regard to the special limitations. For example, if property subject to the 30% limitation is donated during the current year and the amount of the contribution exceeds the limitation, the excess may be carried over to the five subsequent years subject to the 30% limitation in the carryover years. In the carryover year, a deduction may be taken for the excess contribution to the extent that the 30% limitation of the subsequent year exceeds the amount of the property donated during the subsequent year subject to the 30% limitation. Excess contributions of property subject to the 20% limitation may also be carried over to the subsequent five years. This carryover is also subject to the special restrictions noted above for the 30% limitation. The carryovers are used in chronological order.

EXAMPLE I7-37 ▶ Assume that for the years 1995 through 1997, Joan reports AGI and makes charitable contributions in the following amounts:

	1995	1996	1997
AGI	$40,000	$40,000	$60,000
Cash contributions subject to the 50% of AGI limitation	25,000	23,000	24,000
50% of AGI limitation	20,000	20,000	30,000

The amount of the charitable contribution deduction for each year and the order in which the deduction and carryovers are used are as follows:

	1995	1996	1997
Amount of deduction	$20,000	$20,000	$30,000
Amount of carryover			
From 1995	5,000	5,000	0
From 1996		3,000	2,000 ◀

---

[64] Sec. 170(b)(1)(D) and Sec. 170(l)(1).

SPECIAL RULES FOR CHARITABLE CONTRIBUTIONS MADE BY CORPORATIONS

The rules governing charitable contributions made by corporations are generally the same as those pertaining to contributions made by individuals. However, certain differences do exist.

KEY POINT

In effect, accrual basis taxpayers are placed on the cash method with respect to their charitable contributions.

ETHICAL POINT

A tax practitioner should not be a party to the backdating of a Board of Director's authorization of a charitable contribution pledge so that the corporation may improperly deduct the contribution in the earlier year.

PLEDGES MADE BY AN ACCRUAL METHOD CORPORATION. Generally, deductions are allowed only for actual contributions (but not pledges) made during the tax year. This rule applies to both cash and accrual method taxpayers. A major exception to this general rule exists for accrual method corporations. Such corporations may elect to claim a charitable deduction for the year in which a pledge is made as long as the actual contribution is made by the fifteenth day of the third month following the close of the year in which the pledge is made.[65]

LIMITATION APPLICABLE TO CORPORATIONS. Corporate charitable deductions are limited to 10% of the corporation's taxable income for the year. This amount is computed without regard to the dividends-received deduction, net operating loss or capital loss carrybacks, or any deduction for the charitable contribution itself. Excess contributions may be carried forward for five years and are deductible only if the current-year contributions are less than the current year's 10% limitation. The carryovers are used in chronological order.

SUMMARY OF DEDUCTION LIMITATIONS

The rules governing the deduction for charitable contributions are summarized in Topic Review I7-3.

STOP & THINK

Question: During the current year, Kim has pledged to contribute $10,000 to both her church and to a private nonoperating foundation. She wants to satisfy those pledges before the end of the year in order to take a deduction this year. She has enough cash to satisfy one of the pledges, but must either sell or donate some stock in order to satisfy the other. The stock she has in mind has a fair market value of $10,000 and a cost basis of $2,000. She purchased the stock four years ago. Kim estimates that she will have AGI of $300,000 and will be in the 39.6% marginal tax bracket. Assuming that both charities would gladly accept either contribution, how should Kim satisfy these pledges?

Solution: The amount of contribution of long-term capital gain property to a public charity is the property's fair market value. Such contributions are subject to a 30% of AGI limitation. However, a contribution of long-term capital gain property to a private non-operating private foundation is the property's fair market value, reduced by the gain that would be recognized if the property were sold (generally the property's basis). These contributions are subject to a 50% of AGI limitation. Since Kim's AGI for the year is so high, the limitations do not apply. Thus, Kim should contribute the stock to her church and the cash to the private non-operating foundation, for a total charitable contribution of $20,000.

CASUALTY AND THEFT LOSSES

Generally, losses on personal-use property are not deductible. However, under Sec. 165 individuals can deduct a casualty or theft loss on personal-use property as an itemized

[65] Sec. 170(a)(2).

Topic Review I7-3

Deduction Rules for Charitable Contributions

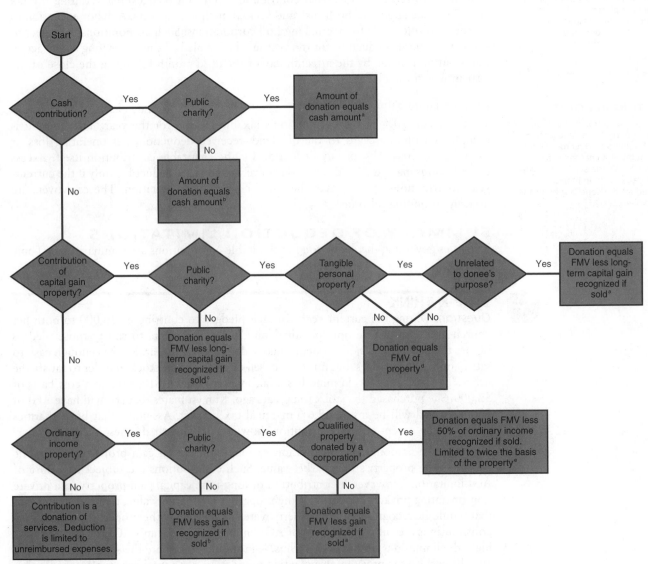

[a] Limited to 50% of AGI.
[b] Limited to lesser of (1) 30% of AGI or (2) remaining 50% of AGI after accounting for donations to public charities.
[c] Limited to lesser of (1) 20% of AGI or (2) 30% of AGI less capital gain contributions to public charities.
[d] Taxpayer may elect to scale down the amount of donation by long-term capital gain. If the election is made, limited to 50% of AGI. If no election is made, limited to 30% of AGI.
[e] Limited to 10% of the corporation's taxable income without regard to any deduction for charitable contributions, dividends received, a net operating loss carryback or a capital loss carryback.
[f] Qualified property consists of either (1) inventory or property used in a trade or business which will be used by a Sec. 501 (c) (3) charity for the care of the ill, needy, or infants, or (2) inventory constructed by the corporation which will be used by a qualified research institution in the physical or biological sciences.

deduction on Schedule A of Form 1040. Losses on business and investment properties held for the production of rents or royalties are deductible *for* AGI. Other casualty losses on investment property are itemized deductions. These casualty losses are studied in greater depth in Chapter I8.

MISCELLANEOUS ITEMIZED DEDUCTIONS

KEY POINT

Miscellaneous itemized deductions are limited to 2% of AGI.

Various expenses are deductible as miscellaneous itemized deductions. These deductions include employment-related expenses of employees, certain investment-related expenses, and the cost of tax advice. However, as explained in Chapter I9, generally these items are deductible only to the extent that, in the aggregate, they exceed 2% of AGI.

CERTAIN EMPLOYEE EXPENSES

Certain employment-related expenses of employees are also deductible as itemized deductions on Schedule A. These expenses include *unreimbursed* expenditures for travel and transportation, dues to professional organizations, costs of job hunting, items of protective clothing or uniforms not suitable for everyday wear, union dues, subscriptions to trade journals, and so on. A more detailed discussion of this topic is included in Chapter I9.

EXPENSES TO PRODUCE INCOME

REAL-WORLD EXAMPLE

A taxpayer was allowed to deduct traveling expenses to Dublin and attorney fees to collect the proceeds of a winning lottery ticket in the Irish Sweepstakes. *Harry Kanelos,* 1943 PH T.C. Memo ¶43, 429, 2 TCM 808.

Under Sec. 212, individuals may deduct expenses incurred to produce income. If these expenses arise in an activity that produces either rental or royalty income, they are deductions *for* AGI (see the explanation in Chapter I6). However, if the expenses are incurred in generating other types of investment income, they are deducted on Schedule A as itemized deductions. These investment-related expenditures include items such as rental fees for safe-deposit boxes used to hold investment property, subscriptions to investment and trade journals, bank service charges on checking accounts used in an investment activity, and fees paid for consulting advice. These expenses are all subject to the 2% of AGI reduction explained in Chapter I9. Certain investment income and expenses are earned by taxpayers in mutual funds and other publicly offered regulated investment companies. These items generally flow through and are reported by the shareholders or owners of the fund. Because typically these entities simply report the net income (income minus expenses) to the owners, Sec. 67(c)(2) exempts these investment-related expenses from the 2% of AGI limitation. Other types of flow-through entities (e.g., partnerships and S corporations) must report these expenses to their owners as separately stated items so that the 2% of AGI reduction may be applied to these expenses also.

ETHICAL POINT

If a client furnishes a handwritten list of his or her miscellaneous itemized deductions to a CPA, the CPA may in good faith rely on the information without verification. However, the CPA should not ignore the implications of information that is provided and should make reasonable inquiries if the information furnished appears to be incorrect, incomplete, or inconsistent.

COST OF TAX ADVICE

Section 212 provides individuals with a deduction for expenses incurred in connection with the determination, collection, or refund of any tax, including federal, state, local, and foreign income taxes as well as estate, gift, and inheritance taxes. These items include tax return preparation fees, appraisal fees incurred in determining the amount of a casualty loss, certain capital improvements for a medical deduction, or the FMV of property donated to a qualified charity, fees paid to an accountant for representation in a tax audit, long-distance telephone calls responding to IRS questions, costs of tax return preparation materials and books, and legal fees incurred in planning the tax consequences dealing with estate planning. If these items are incurred in connection with the taxpayer's (1) trade or business (reported on Schedule C), (2) farm income (reported on Schedule F), or (3) an activity which produces rents or royalties (reported on Part I of Schedule E), they are *for* AGI deductions.[66] All other expenses incurred for tax advice are miscellaneous itemized deductions subject to the 2% of AGI limitation.

Fees that are not directly connected with the determination, collection, or refund of a tax, however, are personal expenses and are not deductible. Thus, legal fees incurred for drafting wills or obtaining other legal advice or incurred in tax fraud cases in connection with the filing of a fraudulent return have been found nondeductible.[67] Legal fees relating to a divorce generally are not deductible, unless they deal with tax-related items such as determining who will receive the exemption for dependent children. These fees are discussed in greater detail in Chapter I3.

REDUCTION OF CERTAIN ITEMIZED DEDUCTIONS

Because of concerns with the budget deficit, Congress enacted Sec. 68 which provides for a reduction in the total amount of certain itemized deductions for high-income taxpayers. This reduction applies only to individuals with AGI in excess of a certain threshold amount. This AGI threshold amount for 1997 is $121,200 ($60,600 for married people filing separate returns), and will be adjusted by an inflation factor for subsequent years. The reduction of the itemized deductions is 3% of the amount that the individual's AGI for the year exceeds the threshold amount. However, two limitations apply. First, the reduction in the itemized deductions cannot exceed 80% of the total itemized deductions other than medical expenses, investment interest, casualty losses, and wagering losses. Second, the 3% reduction is applied after taking into account the other limitations on itemized deductions (e.g., the 2% of AGI limitation on miscellaneous itemized deductions).

EXAMPLE I7-38 ▶

During 1997, John and Sue (a married couple filing a joint return) report AGI of $250,000. In addition, their itemized deductions consist of $10,000 charitable contributions, $4,000 real property taxes, and $8,000 state income taxes. Because their AGI exceeds $121,200, their itemized deductions for the year are limited to $18,136 ($22,000 − $3,864), computed as follows:

AGI	$250,000
Threshold	<121,200>
Excess	$128,800
Times: Reduction percentage	× 0.03
Potential reduction	$ 3,864
Limit to reduction:	
Charitable contributions	$ 10,000
Property taxes	4,000
State income taxes	8,000
Total	$ 22,000
Times: Limitation percentage	× 0.80
Overall limit on reduction	$ 17,600

The 80% limitation does not apply because the $3,864 reduction is less than $17,600. ◀

---

[66] Rev. Rul. 92-29, 1992-1 C.B. 20.

[67] Rev. Rul. 68-662, 1968-2 C.B. 69.

EXAMPLE I7-39 ▶ Assume the same facts as Example I7-38 except that the $10,000 charitable contributions were instead medical expenses in excess of 7.5% of AGI and that the state income taxes were instead a deductible casualty loss (i.e., the amount in excess of the 10% of AGI limitation). Now John and Sue's allowable itemized deductions for the year are $18,800 ($22,000 − $3,200), computed as follows:

AGI	$250,000
Threshold	<121,200>
Excess	$128,800
Times: Reduction percentage	× 0.03
Potential reduction	$ 3,864
Limit to reduction:	
Real property taxes	$ 4,000
Times: Limitation percentage	× 0.80
Overall limit on reduction	$ 3,200 ◀

TAX PLANNING CONSIDERATIONS

MEDICAL EXPENSE DEDUCTION

WORKING WITH THE 7.5% OF AGI FLOOR. As explained previously, a deduction for medical expenses is available to individuals only to the extent that those expenditures exceed 7.5% of the taxpayer's AGI for the year. Thus, many individuals find that no deduction is available, even though their medical expenses are relatively high. In these cases, some benefit may be obtained if a portion of the medical expenses can be bunched into one year. Orthodontic work, certain orthopedic treatment, noncosmetic elective surgery, and new eyeglasses are all examples of medical expenditures that may be either accelerated or delayed into a year in which other medical expenses are high or AGI is lower.

Generally, a deduction for medical expenses is allowed only in the year in which the expense is actually paid. The mere prepayment of future expenses usually does not accelerate the deduction. However, if there is a legal obligation to pay or if the prepayment is a requirement for the receipt of the medical care, a deduction is available in the earlier year of payment.[68] If the medical treatment has already been received, but the taxpayer does not have sufficient cash to pay the bill, a deduction for the current year may be preserved by either borrowing the cash to satisfy the bill or by using a credit card.

ADDITIONAL COMMENT

In 1997, self-employed taxpayers can deduct as a business expense up to 40% of the amount paid for medical insurance. The balance is included with the other medical expenses.

EXAMPLE I7-40 ▶ During the current year, Marty's estimated AGI is $50,000. Marty has already incurred $2,000 in medical expenses for himself and his family during the year. Because 7.5% of AGI for the year is $3,750, he receives no medical expense deduction. Marty plans to incur $2,400 in medical expenses for orthodontic work for his son next year. No other major medical expenses are anticipated, and Marty expects his AGI in the following year to remain the same. If these estimates are accurate, he will receive no medical deduction in either year. However, if the orthodontic work is started in the current year and Marty pays for the work, he will incur a

---

[68] *Robert M. Rose v. CIR*, 26 AFTR 2d 70-5653, 70-2 USTC ¶9646 (5th Cir., 1970). See also Rev. Ruls. 75-302, 1975-2 C.B. 86, and 75-303, 1975-2 C.B. 87.

total of $4,400 in medical expenses in the current year. Thus, $650 ($4,400 − $3,750) of the medical expenses may be deducted.

Mere prepayment in this case is not sufficient. Marty must have a portion of the orthodontic services performed in the earlier year. If he does not have sufficient cash to pay the bill in the current year, he could borrow the money or use a bank credit card. ◄

MULTIPLE SUPPORT AGREEMENTS. An individual may deduct medical expenses incurred for him- or herself, his or her spouse, and any dependents. In cases where a multiple support agreement has been filed, the individual who is the subject of the agreement is treated as the dependent of the taxpayer who is entitled to the dependency exemption. Thus, in order to preserve the medical expense deduction, the taxpayer who is entitled to the dependency exemption should pay all medical expenditures for the dependent individual.

EXAMPLE I7-41 ► Amy, Bart, Clay, and Donna each provide 25% of the support of their father, Eric. Under the terms of a multiple support agreement, Bart, Clay, and Donna all agree to allow Amy to claim the dependency exemption with respect to Eric. During the year, $3,000 in medical expenses are incurred on Eric's behalf. If Amy pays these expenses, she may deduct them (subject to limitations). However, if Bart, Clay, or Donna pays these expenses, no one may claim the medical expenses as a deduction. ◄

INTEREST EXPENSE DEDUCTION

A taxpayer may deduct qualified residence interest incurred on a principal residence and one other qualified residence that is selected by the taxpayer. This choice is made annually. In order for the second residence to qualify, it must have been used personally by the taxpayer for more than the greater of 14 days or 10% of the rental days during the year. If this test is met, however, the rental of vacation home limitations of Sec. 280A also apply. As explained in Chapter I6, these rules require the expenses to be allocated between the rental use and the personal use. The expenses allocated to the rental use are deductible only to the extent of the rental income. Of the expenses allocated to the personal use, only the taxes and interest (if the residence is selected and if the loan is secured by the residence) are deductible as itemized deductions.

If the personal use by the taxpayer does not meet the test mentioned above, the interest allocated to the personal use cannot qualify as residence interest and it becomes nondeductible personal interest. Furthermore, the rental income and expenses allocated to the rental use of the property generally are subject to the passive loss rules (see Chapter I8). Under these rules, individuals generally can deduct losses generated from a passive activity only to the extent of the individual's passive income. Certain individuals, however, may deduct up to $25,000 of losses from the rental of real estate. Thus, the two alternatives and their consequences are as follows:

► Meet the test. No loss from the rental portion of the property may be deducted. However, the interest allocated to the personal use portion may be fully deductible as qualified residence interest.

► Do not meet the test: The interest allocated to the personal use portion is nondeductible personal interest. However, all of the passive loss from the rental portion is deductible against passive income. Furthermore, certain individuals may deduct up to $25,000 additional passive loss.

The alternative a taxpayer chooses depends on several factors such as the amount of the taxpayer's passive income, the total amount of itemized deductions, and whether the loan is secured by the vacation home, etc.

DEDUCTION FOR CHARITABLE CONTRIBUTIONS

ELECTION TO REDUCE THE AMOUNT OF A CHARITABLE CONTRIBUTION. The election to reduce the contribution of capital gain property to public charities by the long-term capital gain that would be recognized if the property were sold is an annual election that applies to all capital gain property donated to public charities during the year. Because the election increases the ceiling limitation from 30% to 50%, under certain circumstances a taxpayer may actually receive a larger deduction for the year than would normally be available if the election were not made.

EXAMPLE I7-42 ▶ During the current year, Jane has AGI of $50,000. She donates a painting to the local university during the same year. The painting, valued at $30,000 at the time of contribution, cost her $25,000 several years before. The university displays the painting in its art museum. If Jane does not make the election, the amount of the contribution is equal to its FMV ($30,000). However, Jane's charitable contribution deduction for the year is limited to $15,000 ($50,000 × 0.30). If Jane makes the election to scale down the contribution amount, the deduction is reduced to $25,000 ($30,000 − $5,000 LTCG). The deduction limitation, however, increases to $25,000 for the year because the limitation is now based on 50% of AGI instead of 30%. In this case, Jane will receive a larger deduction for the year by making the election. However, the cost associated with this election is the loss of $5,000 of deduction because the total deduction is reduced from $30,000 to $25,000 if she makes the election. ◀

Many tax practitioners make this election only when preparing the taxpayer's final tax return. The election is made at this time because charitable contribution carryovers to the decedent's estate are not permitted.

DONATION OF APPRECIATED CAPITAL GAIN PROPERTY. Instead of selling substantially appreciated capital gain property and donating the cash proceeds, the taxpayer should donate the property directly to charity. If property is donated in this way, the donor receives a deduction equal to the FMV of the property and does not recognize any gain on the disposition.

EXAMPLE I7-43 ▶ Colleen wishes to satisfy a pledge of $100,000 made to a local university. She owns $100,000 worth of marketable securities purchased ten years ago for $30,000. Because the securities are marketable, the university is indifferent as to whether Colleen donates cash or the securities. Although her marginal tax rate is 31%, Colleen would be subject to a tax rate of 28% on the sale of the securities because long-term capital gains are subject to a maximum tax rate of 28%. She has enough AGI to be able to deduct the full contribution in the current year. The following chart summarizes the cash flows to Colleen under two different alternatives:

	Donate Securities	Sell Securities and Donate Cash
Proceeds of sale	0	$100,000
Tax on gain	0	(19,600)[a]
Cash payment to charity		(100,000)
Tax savings from the contribution deduction	$31,000[b]	31,000
Net tax benefit	$31,000	$ 11,400

[a] ($100,000 − $30,000) × 0.28 = $19,600.
[b] $100,000 × 0.31 = $31,000.

◀

In order to take a tax loss on business or investment property, a taxpayer should not donate property that has decreased in value. Rather, the property should be sold and the cash proceeds donated.

COMPLIANCE AND PROCEDURAL CONSIDERATIONS

MEDICAL EXPENSES

ADDITIONAL COMMENT

If the taxpayer incurs capital expenditures for medical care, a written recommendation should be obtained from the physician.

In certain cases, expenditures qualify as both a medical care expense and a dependent care expense (i.e., expenses for household and dependent care services that the taxpayer must pay to be gainfully employed). A taxpayer who incurs an expense that qualifies under both provisions may choose to take either a medical expense deduction or a tax credit under Sec. 21.[69] However, if a taxpayer takes a credit for these expenses, they are not deductible as medical expenses.

EXAMPLE I7-44 ▶

Joel's daughter, Debbie, is physically handicapped. As a result, Joel hires a nurse, who provides daily care while he is employed. During the year, Joel pays the nurse a total of $3,000. This amount qualifies for both the dependent care credit and the medical expense deduction. If Joel takes the dependent care credit, the $3,000 may not be deducted as a medical expense. Because of the limitations imposed on each, the determination of which treatment is more advantageous depends on items such as the taxpayer's AGI, other medical expenses, and total itemized deductions. ◀

CONTRIBUTION OF PROPERTY

ADDITIONAL COMMENT

On Form 8283, the charitable organization is required to acknowledge receipt of the gift and to file an information return if the property is sold or disposed of within two years.

When property other than cash is donated to a qualifying charity, proper determination of the property's FMV is a critical issue. Because of actual and perceived abuses in this area, the IRS often scrutinizes and, if necessary, challenges the valuation of contributed property. This is especially true of property for which no published market quotes exist. If contributions of property exceed $500, Form 8283 (see Appendix B), which requires information about the type, location, holding period, basis, and FMV of the property, must be submitted with the taxpayer's return. This information must also be retained by the taxpayer. If the noncash contributions exceed $5,000, an appraisal by a qualified appraiser must be obtained,[70] and an appraisal summary, signed by the appraiser and an authorized officer of the charitable organization, must be submitted with Form 8283. Taxpayers should keep a copy of completed Form 8283 and any attachments for their records. Publicly traded securities need not be appraised. Nonpublicly traded stock must be appraised only if its value exceeds $10,000.

CHARITABLE CONTRIBUTIONS

Individuals report their charitable contribution deductions on Schedule A of Form 1040. Out-of-pocket expenses and contributions by cash or check are all reported on line 15. All contributions of property are included on line 16. As previously mentioned, if noncash property contributions exceed $500, Form 8283 (Noncash Charitable Contributions) must be attached to the return. The IRS has announced that if taxpayers do not attach Form 8283 to their tax returns in support of their noncash contributions, the deduction will be disallowed.[71]

If the contribution is made in cash, the taxpayer must retain evidence of the donation by keeping a cancelled check or a receipt from the charitable organization. In the absence of a cancelled check or receipt, other reliable written records showing the charity's name and the date and amount of the contribution will be accepted. If

---

[69] A credit of 30% of expenses for household and dependent care services is allowed if the dependent is under age 13 or a spouse or dependent who is mentally or physically incapable of caring for himself or herself. The credit is reduced 1% for every $2,000 (or portion thereof) of AGI over $10,000. (See the discussion on Personal Tax Credits in Chapter I14 for a more detailed explanation of the child and dependent care credit.)

[70] Reg. Sec. 1.170A-13(c). However, the requirement for an appraisal may be waived for contributions of inventory for the care of the ill, needy, or infants if the contribution is made by a closely held corporation or a personal service corporation. See Notice 89-56, 1989-1 C.B. 698.

[71] IRS Announcement 90-25, I.R.B. 1990-8, 25.

the contribution is in the form of noncash property, the taxpayer is required to maintain records containing the

ADDITIONAL COMMENT

If the taxpayer's total deduction for art is $20,000 or more, it is necessary to include an 8 × 10 inch color photograph or a color transparency no smaller than 4 × 5 inches.

▶ Name and address of the charity to which the contribution was made

▶ Date and location of the contribution

▶ Description of the property

▶ FMV of the property

▶ Method of determining the property's FMV

▶ Signed copy of the appraisal report if an appraiser was used[72]

For charitable contributions of $250 or more, no deduction is allowed unless the contribution is substantiated by a contemporaneous, written acknowledgment by the donee organization. Separate payments generally are treated as separate contributions for purposes of applying the $250 threshold. This acknowledgment must contain the following information:

▶ The amount of cash and a description of any property contributed

▶ Whether or not the organization provided any goods or services in consideration for the cash or property received, including a description and good faith estimate of the value of any goods or services provided by the organization.

The acknowledgment is considered contemporaneous if it is obtained by the earlier of the date the taxpayer files a return for the year in question or the extended due date for filing such a return. This substantiation requirement is waived if the donee organization files a return that contains the required information.[73]

Additionally, certain disclosure requirements must be met by charitable organizations for a quid pro quo contribution in excess of $75. This $75 limit is applied separately on each transaction. A quid pro quo contribution is a transaction that is partly a contribution and partly a payment for goods and services. In order for such payments to be deductible, the donee organization must provide the donor with a written statement indicating

▶ That the amount of the deduction is limited to the excess of the cash and value of the contributed property over the value of the goods and services provided by the charitable organization.

▶ A good faith estimate of the value of the goods and services provided to the donor by the charitable organization.

Failure to make the required disclosure subjects the charitable organization to a $10 per contribution penalty unless the failure is due to reasonable cause. The penalty is capped at $5,000 per fund-raising event.[74]

EXAMPLE I7-45 ▶ During the current year, Peter Smith (Soc. Sec. no. 276-31-7242) reports AGI of $100,000. Smith also makes the following charitable contributions during the year:

▶ Smith performs voluntary dental work three days each month in rural areas of the state. Smith drives a total of 4,000 miles on these trips during the year.

▶ Smith makes the following contributions by cash or check: $750 to the city library, $2,000 to the United Way, $500 to a local community college, and $4,000 to his church.

▶ Smith contributes a tract of land to a small rural town. The town plans to erect a public library on the site. Smith purchased the land in 1982 for $5,000. Its appraised value at the time of the contribution is $8,000.

---

[72] Reg. Sec. 1.170A-13.
[73] Sec. 170(f)(8) and Temp. Reg. Sec. 1.170A-13T.
[74] Sec. 6115.

Smith's contributions are reported on the partially completed Schedule A shown in Figure I7-1. The out-of-pocket expenses of $480 (4,000 miles × $0.12) and the contributions by cash or check of $7,250 (library, United Way, church, and community college) are totaled and reported on line 15. The property contribution of $8,000 is separately stated on line 16. Because Smith contributes property with a value exceeding $500, Form 8283, an appraisal summary, and signed statements by the qualified appraiser and an authorized official of the organization that received the property must be attached to the return. In addition, for the donations that separately exceed $250, Peter must obtain and retain written acknowledgments from the donee organizations in order for the contributions to be deductible. ◀

TAXES

ADDITIONAL COMMENT

Taxes incurred in the taxpayer's farming business are reported on Schedule F.

Individuals generally report their deduction for property taxes on Schedule A of Form 1040. However, if the taxes are incurred in the taxpayer's business, they are reported on Schedule C. Taxes incurred for the production of rents and royalties are reported on Schedule E. State and local income taxes imposed on individuals are always reported on Schedule A even if the individual is self-employed.

Real estate brokers are required to report any real estate tax allocable to the purchaser of a residence. (See the discussion in this chapter regarding the allocation of real estate taxes between the seller and buyer of a residence.)[75] This information is reported by the broker on Form 1099-S (Proceeds from Real Estate Transactions).

EXAMPLE I7-46 ▶

During the year, Andrea incurs $1,500 in property taxes on a two-family house. Andrea lives in one unit and rents out the other. She also pays $100 in registration fees and $600 in personal property taxes on her automobile, based on its value. Andrea uses the automobile 80% of the time in an unincorporated business. During the current year, she also pays $2,000 in state income taxes, all of which is attributable to her income of the prior year from the unincorporated business.

Because one-half of the real estate taxes are attributable to property used to produce rental income, $750 (0.50 × $1,500) is reported on Schedule E, and the remaining personal-use portion ($750) is reported on Schedule A. Because 80% of the use of the automobile is in Andrea's business, $80 (0.80 × $100) of the registration fee is deductible as a business expense on Schedule C. The remaining $20 is not deductible because the registration fee is not a tax. However, $480 (0.80 × $600) of the personal property tax on the automobile is

---

WHAT WOULD YOU DO IN THIS SITUATION?

GIVING TO BOTH: GOODWILL AND THE IRS

Much has been written about abusive practices concerning the valuation of noncash property donated to qualified charities. Under Sec. 170, both corporations and individuals may deduct the FMV of property contributed to charitable organizations. Of course, a number of valuation and percentage limitations and carryover rules are applicable to both individual and corporate taxpayers.

Assume your clients, Mr. and Mrs. Nicholas Nice, come into your office on December 27 for some year-end tax planning. Your review of their tax situation

indicates that they have made substantial donations of clothing and household goods to Goodwill Industries. They have obtained proper documentation for donations made during the year but do not know how to qualify for taking a charitable deduction vis-à-vis valuation, forms, and the like. They do know that their original cost basis in the donated goods was $15,000 and that the goods were in usable condition at the time of the donation. What tax and ethical issues should be considered?

---

[75] Sec. 6015(4).

Schedule A - Itemized Deductions
(Schedule B is on page 2)
► Attach to Form 1040.   ► See Instructions for Schedule A (Form 1040).

OMB No. 1545-0074

1996
Attachment
Sequence No. **07**

Name(s) shown on Form 1040

Peter Smith

Your social security number

276 31 7246

Medical and Dental Expenses		**Caution:** *Do not include expenses reimbursed or paid by others.*			
	1	Medical and dental expenses (see page A-1)	1		
	2	Enter amount from Form 1040, line 32	2		
	3	Multiply line 2 above by 7.5% (.075)	3		
	4	Subtract line 3 from line 1. If line 3 is more than line 1, enter -0-		4	
Taxes You Paid (See page A-1.)	5	State and local income taxes	5		
	6	Real estate taxes (see page A-2)	6		
	7	Personal property taxes	7		
	8	Other taxes · List type and amount ►			
			8		
	9	Add lines 5 through 8		9	
Interest You Paid (See page A-2.)	10	Home mortgage interest and points reported to you on Form 1098	10		
	11	Home mortgage interest not reported to you on Form 1098. If paid to the person from whom you bought the home, see page A-2 and show that person's name, identifying no., and address ►			
Note: Personal interest is not deductible.			11		
	12	Points not reported to you on Form 1098. See page A-3.	12		
	13	Investment interest. If required, attach Form 4952. (See page A-3.)	13		
	14	Add lines 10 through 13		14	
Gifts to Charity If you made a gift and got a benefit for it, see page A-3.	15	Gifts by cash or check. If you made any gift of $250 or more, see page A-3	15	7,730	
	16	Other than by cash or check. If any gift of $250 or more, see page A-3. If over $500, you **MUST** attach Form 8283	16	8,000	
	17	Carryover from prior year	17		
	18	Add lines 15 through 17		18	15,730
Casualty and Theft Losses	19	Casualty or theft loss(es). Attach Form 4684. (See page A-4.)		19	
Job Expenses and Most Other Miscellaneous Deductions (See page A-4 for expenses to deduct here.)	20	Unreimbursed employee expenses · job travel, union dues, job education, etc. If required, you **MUST** attach Form 2106 or 2106-EZ. (See page A-4.) ►			
			20		
	21	Tax preparation fees	21		
	22	Other expenses · investment, safe deposit box, etc. List type and amount ►			
			22		
	23	Add lines 20 through 22	23		
	24	Enter amount from Form 1040, line 32	24		
	25	Multiply line 24 above by 2% (.02)	25		
	26	Subtract line 25 from line 23. If line 25 is more than line 23, enter -0-		26	
Other Miscellaneous Deductions	27	Other · from list on page A-4. List type and amount ►			
				27	
Total Itemized Deductions	28	Is Form 1040, line 32, over $117,950 (over $58,975 if married filing separately)?			
		NO. Your deduction is not limited. Add the amounts in the far right column for lines 4 through 27. Also, enter on Form 1040, line 34, the **larger** of this amount or your standard deduction.		28	
		YES. Your deduction may be limited. See page A-5 for the amount to enter.			

LHA   **For Paperwork Reduction Act Notice, see Form 1040 instructions.**

619501
11-01-96

Schedule A (Form 1040) 1996

FIGURE 17-1   ►   PARTIALLY COMPLETED SCHEDULE A

deductible as a business expense on Schedule C. The remaining $120 is deductible as a tax on Schedule A. Finally, even though the tax is related to Andrea's business income, all $2,000 of the state income tax is reported on Schedule A. Because the state income tax is paid in the current year, it is deductible in the current year. ◀

PROBLEM MATERIALS

DISCUSSION QUESTIONS

I7-1 **a.** A taxpayer may deduct medical expenses incurred on behalf of which people?

b. In the case of children of divorced parents, must the parent who is entitled to the dependency exemption pay the medical expenses of the child to ensure that the expenses are deductible? Explain.

I7-2 What is the definition of medical care for purposes of the medical care deduction?

I7-3 **a.** What is the definition of cosmetic surgery under the Internal Revenue Code?

b. Is the cost of cosmetic surgery deductible as a medical expense? Explain.

I7-4 **a.** If a taxpayer must travel away from his or her home in order to obtain medical care, which en route costs, if any, are deductible as medical expenses?

b. Are there any limits imposed on the deductibility of these expenses?

I7-5 What are the rules dealing with the deductibility of the cost of meals and lodging incurred while away from home in order to receive medical treatment as an outpatient?

I7-6 **a.** Which types of capital expenditures incurred specifically for medical purposes are deductible?

b. What limitations, if any, are imposed on the deductibility of these expenditures?

I7-7 Bill, a plant manager, is suffering from a serious ulcer. Bill's doctor recommends that he spend three weeks fishing and hunting in the Colorado Rockies. Can Bill deduct the costs of the trip as a medical expense?

I7-8 In what cases are medical insurance premiums paid by an individual not deductible as qualified medical expenses?

I7-9 What is the limit placed on medical expense deductions? When can a deduction be taken for medical care? What if the medical care is prepaid?

I7-10 **a.** Which taxes are specifically deductible for federal income tax purposes under Sec. 164?

b. If a tax is not specifically listed in Sec. 164, under what circumstances may it still be deductible?

I7-11 What is an ad valorem tax? If a tax that is levied on personal property is not an ad valorem tax, under what circumstances may it still be deductible?

I7-12 When real estate is sold during a year, why is it necessary that the real estate taxes on the property be apportioned between the buyer and seller?

I7-13 If Susan overpays her state income tax due to excess withholdings, can she deduct the entire amount in the year withheld? When Susan receives a refund from the state how must she treat that refund for tax purposes?

I7-14 At times, the term *points* is used to refer to different types of charges. Define the term and describe when points are deductible.

I7-15 In which year or years are points (representing prepaid interest on a loan) deductible?

I7-16 **a.** Identify the different categories of interest expense that an individual may incur.

b. If interest expense is incurred in an unincorporated business owned by an individual, on which schedule is it deductible? (Assume that the passive loss rules do not apply.)

I7-17 Why does Sec. 267 impose a restriction on the deductibility of expenses accrued and payable by an accrual-method taxpayer to a related cash-method taxpayer?

I7-18   **a.** What is the amount of the annual limitation placed on the deductibility of investment interest expense?

    b. Explain how net investment income is calculated.

    c. Is any disallowed interest expense for the year allowable as a deduction in another year? If so, when?

I7-19   **a.** What are the different classifications of interest expense? How is the classification of the interest determined?

    b. How, if at all, are these different categories of interest expense deductible?

I7-20   Explain what acquisition indebtedness and home equity indebtedness are with respect to a qualified residence of a taxpayer, and identify any limitations on the deductibility of interest expense on this indebtedness.

I7-21   Explain what a qualified residence is for purposes of qualified residence interest.

I7-22   Why is interest expense disallowed if it is incurred to purchase or carry tax-exempt obligations?

I7-23   When is interest generally deductible for cash-method taxpayers? Explain if the general rule applies to prepaid interest, interest paid with loan proceeds, discounted notes, and personal interest. If the general rule does not apply, explain when these interest expenses are deductible.

I7-24   **a.** For purposes of the charitable contribution deduction, what is capital gain property? Ordinary income property?

    b. What is the significance of classifying property as either capital gain property or ordinary income property?

I7-25   How is the *amount* of a charitable contribution of capital gain property determined if it is donated to a private nonoperating foundation? How does this determination differ if capital gain property is donated to a public charity?

I7-26   May an individual who is married and files a joint return deduct any charitable contributions if the itemized deductions total only $3,000 (of which $1,000 are qualified charitable contributions)?

I7-27   For individuals, what is the overall deduction limitation on charitable contributions? What is the limitation for corporations?

I7-28   If a taxpayer's charitable contributions for any tax year exceed the deduction limitations, may the excess contributions be deducted in another year? If so, in which years may they be deducted?

I7-29   How are charitable contribution deductions reported on the tax return for individuals? What reporting requirements must be met for the contribution of property?

I7-30   List some of the more common miscellaneous itemized deductions and identify any limitations that are imposed on the deductibility of these items.

I7-31   Certain itemized deductions of high-income taxpayers must be reduced. Which itemized deductions are subject to this reduction and when does the reduction apply?

ISSUE IDENTIFICATION QUESTIONS

I7-32   Wayne and Maria file a joint tax return on which they itemize their deductions and report AGI of $50,000. During the year they incurred $1,500 of medical expenses when Maria broke her leg. Furthermore, their dentist informed them that their daughter, Alicia, needs $3,000 of orthodontic work to correct her overbite. Wayne also needs a new pair of eyeglasses that will cost $300. What tax issues should Wayne and Maria consider?

I7-33   During the current year, George made contributions totaling $40,000 to an organization called the National Endowment for the Preservation of Liberty (NEPL). Later during the year, the NEPL started giving money to a political candidate to help with his campaign expenses. What tax issues should George consider?

I7-34 Martha contributed a large pipe organ to the local university. Martha didn't have any documents stating the value of the organ or any facts about its condition. What tax issues should Martha consider?

I7-35 During the current year, Bob has AGI of $100,000. He donates stock to his church that was purchased two years ago for $55,000. The FMV of the stock is $60,000. Bob has $5,000 of unused excess contributions from a prior year. What tax issues should Bob consider?

PROBLEMS

I7-36 *Medical Expense Deduction.* During 1997, Liz is involved in an automobile accident and incurs the following expenditures:

Item	Amount
Doctor bills	$11,000
Hospital bills	13,000

Liz is single and has no dependents. In 1997, her salary is $30,000, and itemized deductions other than medical expenses are $1,500. During the year Liz also receives a reimbursement of $18,000 from the insurance company for medical expenses incurred in connection with the accident. What is Liz's taxable income for 1997?

I7-37 *Reimbursement of Previously Deducted Medical Expenses.* Assume the same facts as in Problem I7-36. In addition, assume that in 1998, Liz receives an additional $10,000 in a settlement of a lawsuit arising because of the automobile accident. $6,000 of the settlement is to pay Liz for the medical expenses incurred because of the accident that were not covered by insurance. What is the proper tax treatment of this $10,000 settlement?

I7-38 *Medical Expense Deduction.* Dan lives in a small town in Arizona. Because of a rare blood disease, Dan is required to take special medical treatments once a month. The closest place these treatments are available to Dan is in Phoenix, 200 miles away. The treatments are provided on an outpatient basis but require him to stay overnight in Phoenix. During the year, Dan makes 12 trips to Phoenix by automobile to receive the treatments. The motel he always stays in charges $85 per night. For the year, Dan also spends a total of $250 for meals on these trips. $100 of this $250 is spent while en route to Phoenix. What is the amount of Dan's qualified medical expenses for the year?

I7-39 *Medical Expense Deduction.* Kelly is divorced and has custody of Mike, his 17-year-old son. Kelly's ex-wife has custody of their daughter, Diana. During the year, Kelly incurs $2,000 for orthodontic work for Diana to correct a severe overbite and $1,500 in unreimbursed medical expenses associated with Mike's broken leg. Kelly also pays $900 in health insurance premiums. Both Mike and Diana are covered under Kelly's medical insurance plan. In addition, Kelly incurs $400 for prescription drugs and $600 in doctor bills for himself. Kelly's AGI is $35,000. What is Kelly's medical expense deduction for the year?

I7-40 *Medical Expense Deduction.* In 1997, Russ, a single taxpayer, was severely hurt in a construction accident. The accident left Russ's leg 70% paralyzed. After incurring $7,000 of medical expenses at the hospital, the doctor recommended that Russ install a jacuzzi at his home for therapy. The jacuzzi cost $8,000 to install and increased the value of his home by $5,000. He spent $300 maintaining the jacuzzi in 1997 and $500 in 1998. Russ also purchased a $500 wheelchair in 1997 but did not pay for the chair until 1998. In December 1997, Russ paid his physical therapist $4,000 for services to be performed in 1998. Russ paid $1,000 in medical insurance premiums in both 1997 and 1998. In 1998, the insurance company reimbursed Russ $5,000 for his hospital stay in 1997. His AGI for 1997 is $25,000. For 1998 his AGI is $24,000, not considering any of the above items. Russ has no other itemized deductions in either year.

a. What is the amount of his medical expense deduction in 1997?
b. What is the amount of his medical expense deduction in 1998?

I7-41 *Deduction of Taxes.* During 1997, Wendy has $1,100 in state income taxes withheld from her paycheck. Additionally, on April 15, 1997, she pays $200 in state income taxes when she files her state income tax return for 1996. In 1998 when she files her 1997 state income tax return, she will owe an additional $400 for her 1997 taxes. Wendy is a single, cash-method taxpayer who has total (excluding state income taxes) itemized deductions for 1997 of $1,300. What is the amount of state income taxes Wendy may include as an itemized deduction for 1997?

I7-42 *Refund of Previously Deducted Taxes.* Assume the same facts as Problem I7-41, except that Wendy receives a $600 refund of 1997's state income taxes in 1998. What is the proper tax treatment of the refund?

I7-43 *Deduction of Taxes.* Dawn, a single, cash method taxpayer, paid the following taxes in 1997: Dawn's employer withheld $5,400 for federal income taxes, $2,000 for state income taxes, and $3,800 for FICA from her 1997 paychecks. Dawn purchased a new car and paid $600 in sales tax and $70 for the license. The car's FMV was $10,000 and weighed 3,000 pounds. The county also assessed a property tax on the car. The tax was 2% of its value and $10 per hundredweight. The car is used 100% of the time for personal purposes. Dawn sold her house on April 15, 1997. The county's property tax on the home for 1997 is $1,850, payable on February 1, 1998. Dawn's AGI for the year is $50,000 and her other itemized deductions exclusive of taxes are $4,000.

a. What is Dawn's deduction for taxes in 1997?
b. Where on Dawn's tax return should she report her deduction for taxes?

I7-44 *Apportionment of Real Estate Taxes.* On May 1 of the current year, Tanya sells a building to Brian for $100,000. Tanya's basis in the building is $60,000. The county in which the building is located has a real property tax year that ends on June 30. The taxes are payable by September 1 of that year. On September 1, Brian pays the annual property taxes of $3,000. Both Tanya and Brian are calendar-year, cash-method taxpayers.

a. What amount of real property taxes may Brian deduct in the current year?
b. What amount of real property taxes may Tanya deduct in the current year?
c. If no apportionment on the real property taxes is made in the sales agreement, what is Tanya's total selling price of the building? Brian's basis for the building?

I7-45 *Classification of Interest Expense.* On January 1 of the current year, Scott borrowed $80,000, pledging the assets of his business as collateral. He immediately deposited the money in an interest-bearing checking account. Scott already had $20,000 in this account. On April 1, Scott invests $75,000 in a limited real estate partnership. On July 1, he buys a new ski boat for $12,000. On August 1, he makes a $10,000 capital contribution to his unincorporated business. Scott repays $50,000 of the loan on November 30 of the current year. Classify Scott's interest expense for the year.

I7-46   *Investment Interest.* During the current year, David reports interest and dividend income of $20,000, net short-term capital gains of $5,000, and net long-term capital gains of $8,000. His AGI is $100,000. His investment expenses, exclusive of interest, are $5,000. During the year David also pays a total of $50,000 interest on debt incurred in his investment activities. David is married and files a joint return.

    a. What is the total amount of deduction David may take with respect to his investment interest expense if he does not make a special election?

    b. What is the treatment of any disallowed investment interest expense?

    c. What is the total amount of deduction David may take with respect to his investment interest expense if he elects to have his net capital gain taxed at the regular marginal tax rates?

I7-47   *Qualified Residence Interest.* During the current year, Tina purchases a beachfront condominium for $600,000, paying $150,000 down and taking out a $450,000 mortgage, secured by the property. At the time of the purchase, the outstanding mortgage on her principal residence is $700,000. This debt is secured by the residence and the FMV of the principal residence is $1,400,000. She purchased the principal residence in 1989. What is the amount of qualified indebtedness on which Tina may deduct the interest payments?

I7-48   *Interest Between Related Parties.* King Corporation is an accrual-method taxpayer owned 60% by Jack and 40% by Kathy. The JR Partnership is owned 75% by Jack and 25% by Ron and uses the cash-method of accounting. On January 2 of the current year, King Corporation borrows $100,000 from the JR Partnership. Interest is charged at 9%, and both interest and principal are to be paid in full on December 31 of the current year. Because of a cash-flow problem arising late in the year, however, the loan and interest are not repaid until March 31 of the following year.

    a. What amount of interest expense may King Corporation deduct in the current year? in the following year?

    b. Assume the same facts except that on December 30 of the current year, King Corporation borrows cash from its bank to pay off the loan. What amount of interest expense may King Corporation deduct in the current year?

I7-49   *Timing of Interest Deduction.* On April 1 of the current year, Henry borrows $12,000 from the bank for a year. Because the note is discounted for the interest charge and Henry receives proceeds of $10,200, he is required to repay the face amount of the loan ($12,000) in four equal quarterly payments beginning on July 1 of the current year. Henry is a cash-method individual.

    a. What is the amount of Henry's interest expense deduction in the current year with respect to this loan?

    b. Assume the same facts except that the initial starting date when the repayments begin is April 1 of the following year. What is the amount of Henry's interest expense deduction in the current year?

    c. Assume the same facts as in Part b, except that Henry is an accrual method taxpayer. What is the amount of his interest expense deduction in the current year?

I7-50 *Charitable Contributions: Services.* Pauline is an attorney who renders volunteer legal services to a Legal Aid Society, which provides legal advice to low-income individuals. The Legal Aid Society is a qualified charitable organization. During the current year she spends a total of 200 hours in this volunteer work. Her regular billing rate is $100 per hour. In addition, she spends a total of $600 in out-of-pocket costs in providing these services. She receives no compensation and is not reimbursed for her out-of-pocket costs. What is Pauline's charitable contribution for the year because of these activities?

I7-51 *Itemized Deductions.* During 1997, Doug incurs the following deductible expenses: $1,000 in state income taxes, $1,200 in local property taxes, $800 in medical expenses, and $500 in charitable contributions. He is single, has no dependents, and has $30,000 AGI for the year. What is the amount of Doug's taxable income?

I7-52 *Computation of Taxable Income.* During 1997, James, a single, cash method taxpayer incurred the following expenditures:

Qualified medical expenses	$ 8,000
Investment interest expense	16,000
Other investment activity expenses	15,000
Qualified residence interest	12,000
Interest on loan on personal auto	2,000
Charitable contributions	3,000
State income tax paid	7,000
Property taxes	4,000
Tax return preparation and consulting fees	5,000

James's income consisted of the following items:

Salary	$70,000
Interest and Dividend income	20,000
Long-term Capital gains	23,000
Long-term Capital losses	(15,000)

Compute James's taxable income for the year (assuming that he makes an election to have the net capital gain taxed at the regular tax rates).

I7-53 *Computation of Taxable Income.* Assume all the same facts as in Problem I7-52 except that James's salary income is $100,000 instead of $70,000 and that he does not make the election. Compute James's taxable income for the year.

I7-54 *Charitable Contribution Limitations.* In each of the following independent cases, determine the amount of the charitable contribution and the limitation that would apply. In each case, assume that the donee is a qualified public charity.
a. Sharon donates a tract of land to a charitable organization. She has held the land for seven years. Her basis in the land is $10,000 and its FMV is $40,000.
b. Assume the same facts in Part a, except that Sharon has held the land for only 11 months and that its FMV is $23,000.
c. Jack purchases a historical document for $50,000. He donates the historical document to a charitable organization two years later. The organization plans to use it for research and study. Its FMV at the time of the donation is $100,000.

d. Assume the same facts in Part c, except that the organization plans to sell the document and put the money into an endowment fund.

e. Valerie donates some inventory to a charitable organization. The inventory is purchased for $500 and its FMV is $1,200 at the time of the donation. She held the inventory for seven months.

I7-55 *Charitable Contributions to Private Nonoperating Foundations.* Assume the same facts as Problem I7-54, except that the qualified organization is a private nonoperating foundation. Determine the amount of the charitable contribution for Parts a through e.

I7-56 *Charitable Contributions—Tax Planning.* Dean makes a pledge of $30,000 to a local college. The college is willing to accept either cash or marketable securities in fulfillment of the pledge. Dean owns stock in Ajax Corporation worth $30,000. The stock was purchased five years ago for $10,000, Dean's marginal tax rate is 28%. Should Dean sell the stock and then donate the cash, or should he donate the stock directly? Compute the net tax benefit from each alternative and explain the difference.

I7-57 *Charitable Contribution Limitations.* During the current year, Helen donates stock worth $50,000 to her local community college. Two years ago the stock cost Helen $40,000. Her AGI for the current year is $100,000. Beginning next year, the bulk of her income will be from tax-exempt municipal securities. Thus, she is not interested in any carryover of excess charitable contribution. What is the maximum charitable contribution deduction Helen may take this year?

I7-58 *Corporate Charitable Contributions.* Circle Corporation, an accrual method taxpayer, manufactures and sells mainframe computers. In January of the current year, Circle Corporation donates a mainframe that was part of its inventory to City College. City will use the computer for physical science research. Circle's basis in the mainframe is $300,000. The computer's FMV is $650,000. On December 15 of the current year, Circle also pledged stock to the Red Cross and promised delivery of the stock by March 1 of the following year. The stock's FMV is $100,000 and Circle's adjusted basis in the stock is $50,000. Circle's taxable income (before deducting any charitable contributions) for the current year is $4,000,000.

a. What is the amount of Circle's charitable contribution for the current year?

b. How much of the contribution can Circle deduct in the current year and how much may be carried over, if any?

I7-59 *Charitable Contribution Carryovers.* Bonnie's charitable contributions and AGI for the past four years were as follows:

	1994	1995	1996	1997
AGI	$50,000	$55,000	$58,000	$60,000
Contributions subject to the 50% limitation	40,000	29,000	25,000	10,000

What is the amount of the charitable deduction for each year and the order in which the deduction and carryovers are used?

TAX FORM/RETURN PREPARATION PROBLEMS

I7-60 Following is a list of information for Steven and Marcia Johnson for the current tax year. Steven and Marcia are married; have three children, Ryan, Casey and Lindsey; and live at 221 Elm St. in San Diego, California 90056. Steven is a computer programmer and Maria is a salesperson. The Johnsons' Social Security numbers and ages are as follows:

Name	S.S. No.	Age
Steven	215-60-1989	45
Marcia	301-60-2828	43
Ryan	713-84-5555	17
Casey	714-87-2222	14
Lindsey	430-89-1111	11

Receipts

Steven's salary	$35,000
Marcia's salary	28,000
Interest income on municipal bonds	2,000
Interest income on certificate of deposit (Universial Savings)	1,400
Dividends on GM stock	600

Disbursements

Eyeglasses and exam for Ryan	300
Orthodontic work for Casey to correct a congenital defect	2,000
Medical insurance premiums	1,000
Withholding for state income taxes	3,000
Withholding for federal income taxes	6,000
State income taxes paid with last year's tax return (paid when the return was filed in the current year)	400
Property taxes on home	1,000
Property taxes on automobile	100
Interest on home	9,000
Interest on automobile	500
Interest on credit cards	100
Cash contribution to church	2,400

In addition to the above, Steven and Marcia donate some stock to their local community college. The FMV of the stock at the time of the donation is $500. They purchased the stock 3 years before for $200.

Compute Steven and Marcia's income tax liability on Form 1040 for the current year.

I7-61 George and Martha Adams are married and reside at 291 Paul Revere Blvd., Boston, Massachusetts 02116. George's social security number is 222-33-4444 and Martha's is 222-34-5678. The Adamses have two children: Sherry, age 23, and Sean, age 19. Their Social Security numbers are 222-12-9876 and 222-57-6543, respectively. Sherry is a single college student and earned $8,000 during the summer. George and Martha help Sherry through school by paying for her room, board, and tuition. Sherry lives at home during the summer. Sean has a physical handicap and lives at home. He earned $2,500 addressing envelopes for a marketing firm.

George is a manager in a manufacturing plant. His salary is $80,000, from which $16,000 of federal income tax, $8,000 of state income tax, and $3,924 of Social Security taxes were withheld. George also pays premiums for health, disability, and life insurance. $2,000 of the premium was for health insurance, $400 for life insurance, and $250 for disability.

Martha owns Link Networks, a network consulting company. During the year, Martha's gross revenues were $12,000. She incurred the following expenses in her business:

Liability insurance	$ 500
Software rental	3,500
Journals and magazines	150
Training seminars	1,000
Supplies	800
Donations to a political campaign fund	600

George enjoys sculpting and this year he sold a few of his sculptures. His gross revenues were $1,500. He incurred the following expenses:

Studio rent expense	$1,300
Utilities	150
Clay and other supplies	400

George's father passed away during the year. George and Martha received $100,000 from the life insurance policy. Neither George nor Martha paid any of the premiums.

Martha purchased 100 shares of Kelly Co. stock on May 1, 1987 for $800. Kelly Co. was declared bankrupt during the current year.

Sean's physician recommended that he see a physical therapist to help with his disability. George paid the therapist $7,000 during the year because his insurance would not cover the bills.

George and Martha went to Atlantic City and won $4,000 at the blackjack table. The following night they lost $5,000.

George and Martha also gave $500 to their church.

During the year the Adamses had the following other income and expenses:

Real estate taxes	$1,000
Property taxes on car (determined by weight)	500
Home mortgage interest	5,000
Credit card finance charges	3,000
Tax return preparation fees ($500 is allocable to Martha's business)	1,000
Sales tax on purchases during the year	5,500
Interest from a savings account	400
Interest from City of Boston Bonds	300
Dividend from General Motors Stock	95

Prepare George and Martha's tax return Form 1040 and accompanying schedules for the current year.

CASE STUDY PROBLEMS

I7-62 Brian Brown, an executive at a manufacturing enterprise, comes to you on December 1 of the current year for tax advice. He has agreed to donate a small tract of land to the Rosepark Community College. The value of the land has been appraised at $53,000. Mr. Brown purchased the land 14 months ago for $50,000. Mr. Brown's estimated AGI for the current year is $100,000. He plans to retire next year and anticipates that his AGI will fall to $30,000 for all subsequent years. He does not anticipate making any additional large charitable contributions. He understands that there are special rules dealing with charitable contributions, and wants your advice in order to get the maximum overall tax benefit from his contribution. Because the college plans to use the property, selling the land is not an alternative. You are to prepare a letter to Mr. Brown explaining the tax consequences of the different alternatives. His address is 100 East Rosebrook, Mesa, Arizona 85203. For purposes of your analysis, assume that Mr. Brown is married and files a joint return. Also assume that Mr. Brown feels that an appropriate discount rate is 10%. In your analysis, use the tax rate schedules for the current year.

I7-63

For several years, you have prepared the tax return for Alpha Corporation, a closely held corporation engaged in manufacturing garden tools. On February 20 of the current year, Bill Johnson, the president of Alpha Corporation, delivered to your office the files and information necessary for you to prepare Alpha's tax return for the immediately preceding tax year. Included in this information were the minutes of all meetings held by Alpha's Board of Directors during the year in question.

Then on February 27, Bill stops by your office and hands you an "addendum" to the minutes of the director's meeting held December 15 of the tax year for which you are preparing the tax return. The addendum is dated the same day of the director's meeting, and authorizes a charitable contribution pledge of $20,000 to the local community college. With a wink and a big smile, Bill explains that the addendum had been misplaced. In reviewing the original minutes, you find no mention of a charitable contribution pledge.

What should you do? (See Appendix E and the *Statements on Responsibilities in Tax Practice* section in Chapter I1 for a discussion of these issues.)

TAX RESEARCH PROBLEM

I7-64

Last year Mr. Smith was involved in an automobile accident, severely injuring his legs. As part of a long-term rehabilitation process, his physician prescribes a daily routine of swimming. Because there is no readily available public facility nearby, Smith investigates the possibility of either building a pool in his own back yard or purchasing another home with a pool. In the current year he finds a new home with a pool and purchases it for $175,000. He then obtains some estimates and finds that it would cost approximately $20,000 to replace the pool in the home he has just purchased. He also obtains some real estate appraisals, which indicate that the existing pool increases the value of the home by only $8,000. During the current year, Smith also expends $500 in maintaining the pool and $1,800 in other medical expenses. What is the total amount of medical expenses he may claim in the current year? Smith's AGI for the year is $60,000.

A partial list of research sources is

- Sec. 213
- Reg. Sec. 1.213-1(e)(1)(iii)
- *Richard A. Polacsek*, 1981 PH T.C. Memo ¶81,569, 42 TCM 1289
- *Paul A. Lerew*, 1982 PH T.C. Memo ¶82,483, 44 TCM 918
- *Jacob H. Robbins*, 1982 PH T.C. Memo ¶82,565, 44 TCM 1254

CHAPTER 8

LOSSES AND BAD DEBTS

LEARNING OBJECTIVES

After studying this chapter, you should be able to

1. ▶ Identify transactions that may result in losses

2. ▶ Determine the proper classification for losses

3. ▶ Calculate the suspended loss from passive activities

4. ▶ Identify what constitutes a passive activity loss

5. ▶ Determine when a taxpayer has materially participated in a passive activity

6. ▶ Identify and calculate the deduction for a casualty or theft loss

7. ▶ Compute the deduction for a bad debt

8. ▶ Compute a net operating loss deduction

Taxpayers often sustain losses on property that is sold, exchanged, or otherwise disposed of. If the property on which the loss is sustained is used in a trade or business or held for investment, the tax law generally provides a deduction for these losses. The tax law also provides a limited deduction for losses on personal-use property that is either stolen or damaged in a casualty. Other losses on personal-use property (e.g. a sale of a personal residence at a loss) are not deductible. A deduction is also provided for losses that taxpayers may incur because of uncollectible business or nonbusiness debts.

This chapter discusses the rules dealing with the deductibility of these types of losses.

TRANSACTIONS THAT MAY RESULT IN LOSSES

OBJECTIVE 1

Identify transactions that may result in losses

In order for a loss on property to be deductible, it must be both realized and recognized for tax purposes. Generally, *realization* occurs in a completed (closed) transaction evidenced by an identifiable event. Realized losses are generally recognized unless a specific provision holds otherwise (see page I8-7).

EXAMPLE I8-1 ▶

Anita purchased 500 shares of Data Corporation stock for $10,000 on February 22 of the current year. By October 31 of the same year, the price of the stock declines to $8,000. Even though Anita realizes an economic loss on the stock, no realization event has occurred, and she may not deduct the $2,000 loss. However, if Anita sells the stock for $8,000 on October 31, the loss is realized for tax purposes in the current year. ◀

Losses on property may arise in a variety of transactions, including

▶ Sale or exchange of the property

▶ Expropriation, seizure, confiscation, or condemnation of the property by a government

▶ Abandonment of the property

▶ Worthlessness of stock or securities

▶ Planned demolition of the property in order to construct other property in its place

▶ Destruction of the property by fire, storm, or other casualty

▶ Theft

▶ Deductible business expenses exceeding business income, giving rise to a net operating loss (NOL)

SALE OR EXCHANGE OF PROPERTY

The amount of the loss incurred in a sale or exchange of property equals the excess of the property's adjusted basis on the sale or exchange date over the amount realized for the property.[1] The amount realized for the property equals the sum of the money received plus the fair market value (FMV) of any other property received in the transaction. If the property sold or exchanged is subject to a mortgage or other liability, the amount realized also includes the amount of the liability.[2] The treatment of any

ADDITIONAL COMMENT

If property is used partly for business and partly for personal use, the loss attributable to the business portion is deductible but the loss on the personal-use portion is not unless the loss was sustained in a casualty.

KEY POINT

Anticipated losses, including those for which reserves have been established, are not deductible.

REAL-WORLD EXAMPLE

A taxpayer whose truck was repossessed was required to treat as an amount realized the unpaid indebtedness on the truck. The taxpayer failed to prove that he was required to pay a portion of the indebtedness after repossession. *Billie J. Ledbetter v. CIR*, 61 AFTR 2d 88-638, 88-1 USTC ¶9183 (5th Cir., 1988).

---

[1] Sec. 1001.
[2] *Beulah B. Crane v. CIR*, 35 AFTR 776, 47-1 USTC ¶9217 (USSC, 1947); and Reg. Sec. 1.1001-2.

selling costs depends on the type of property being sold or exchanged. If the property is inventory, the selling costs are deductible expenses in the year in which they are paid or incurred. However, if the sale involves property that is not normally held for sale by the taxpayer, the selling costs merely reduce the amount realized from the sale or exchange.

EXAMPLE I8-2 ▶ Four years ago, Louis purchased a plot of land as an investment for $50,000. Unfortunately, local economic conditions worsened after the land was purchased, and its value declined to $35,000. Becoming discouraged, Louis sells the property in the current year. At the time of the sale, the land is subject to a $10,000 mortgage. The terms of the sale are $25,000 being paid in cash with the purchaser assuming the mortgage. Louis also incurs $2,000 in sales commissions. The amount realized is $33,000 ($25,000 cash + $10,000 mortgage assumed by the buyer − $2,000 commissions). The loss on the sale is $17,000 ($50,000 basis − $33,000 amount realized). ◀

Only losses incurred in the sale or exchange of property used in a trade or business or held for investment are deductible. Losses incurred in the sale or exchange of personal-use property are not deductible. Furthermore, the type of deduction that may be taken for a loss realized on the sale or exchange of business or investment property depends on the type of property sold. For example, if the asset is a capital asset, the loss is a capital loss (see Chapter I5). If the sale is of property used in a trade or business (a Sec. 1231 asset), the type of loss depends on the total gain or loss realized on all the taxpayer's Sec. 1231 assets sold during the year (see Chapter I13). If the sale is of inventory, the loss is an ordinary loss.

EXPROPRIATED, SEIZED, OR CONFISCATED PROPERTY

A taxpayer may own property that is expropriated, seized, confiscated, or condemned by a government. In these cases, a deductible loss is incurred if the property is used in a trade or business or is held for investment. However, the Tax Court has held that the confiscation, seizure, condemnation, or expropriation of property does not constitute a theft or a casualty. Rather, it is treated as a sale or exchange. Thus, no deductible loss arises if the seized property is personal-use property.[3] If the seized or condemned property is business or investment property, the classification of the loss depends on the type of property. (See the section in this chapter titled Classifying the Loss on the Taxpayer's Return.) The deduction may be taken only in the year in which the property is actually seized. It is irrelevant whether formal expropriation or nationalization occurs in a later year.[4] A gain is realized if the taxpayer receives compensation for the property in excess of its basis. Under certain circumstances this gain may be deferred. (See Chapter I12 for a discussion of the nonrecognition of gain in an involuntary conversion.)

ABANDONED PROPERTY

If the taxpayer's property has become worthless or if it is not worth placing into a serviceable condition, the taxpayer may simply abandon the property. If the property still has basis, a loss is realized. Such losses are not deductible if the property is personal-use property. However, business or investment property losses are deductible. Furthermore, because the abandonment of property is not a sale or exchange, the loss is an ordinary

REAL-WORLD EXAMPLE

Domestic confiscation losses may not be deductible even if the property was used in business. For example, a taxpayer who had been engaged in the business of trafficking in marijuana was arrested. As a result of the arrest, the taxpayer's truck and horse trailer were confiscated. The taxpayer was not entitled to a loss deduction, because losses from illegal activities are disallowed under Sec. 165. *Bill D. Holt,* 69 T.C. 75 (1977). See also Sec. 280E.

---

[3] *William J. Powers*, 36 T.C. 1191 (1961).
[4] Rev. Rul. 62-197, 1962-2 C.B. 66 as modified by Rev. Rul. 69-498, 1969-2

C.B. 31. See also *Estate of Frank Fuchs v. CIR*, 24 AFTR 2d 69-5077, 69-2 USTC ¶9505 (2nd Cir., 1969).

loss. The amount of the loss is the property's adjusted basis on the date of abandonment. The burden of proof to show that the property was actually abandoned rests with the taxpayer. If the property is depreciable (e.g., machinery and buildings), it must actually be physically abandoned in order for the taxpayer to take the full amount of the loss.[5]

WORTHLESS SECURITIES

A taxpayer may take a deduction for securities that become completely worthless during the tax year.[6] Because the deduction is only available in the year the security actually becomes worthless, a major problem for both the taxpayer and the IRS is determining the year in which the security becomes worthless. A mere decline in value is not sufficient to create a deductible loss if the stock has any recognizable value. Furthermore, the sale of the stock for a nominal amount such as $1 does not necessarily establish that the stock became worthless in the year of the sale. The burden of proof rests with the taxpayer to show that the security is completely worthless and that the security became worthless during the year.

Once the year of worthlessness is determined, Sec. 165(g) provides that any loss incurred by an investor is treated as a loss from the sale of a capital asset on the last day of the tax year. Although this provision does not help in determining the year of worthlessness, it does establish a definite date for purposes of measuring whether the loss is short- or long-term. In some cases, this provision causes the loss to be long-term because the time period is extended to the end of the year in which the worthlessness occurs.

EXAMPLE I8-3 ▶

On March 14 of the current year, Control Corporation enters into bankruptcy with no possibility for the shareholders to receive anything of value. Because the amount of Control Corporation's outstanding liabilities exceeds the FMV of its assets on that date, the stock of the corporation becomes worthless. Janet, a calendar-year taxpayer, owns 500 shares of Control's common stock, which she had purchased for $10,000 through her broker on December 12 of the prior year. Under Sec. 165(g), the loss is treated as having arisen from the sale of a capital asset on the last day of the current year. Thus, Janet incurs a $10,000 long-term capital loss because the holding period for the stock is more than one year. On the other hand, if Janet had received the stock directly from Control Corporation in exchange for either money or other property, and if certain other requirements are met, the stock may qualify as Sec. 1244 stock. Individuals who sustain losses on Sec. 1244 stock receive ordinary loss treatment rather than capital loss treatment. (See the discussion in this chapter under the heading Losses on Sec. 1244 Stock.) ◀

Under certain circumstances, if the worthless securities consist of securities of an affiliated corporation that are owned by a domestic corporation, the loss is treated as having arisen from a sale of a noncapital asset. This allows the loss to be treated as an ordinary loss rather than as a capital loss.[7] For this exception to apply, the following percentage ownership requirements must be met:

---

[5] Reg. Sec. 1.167(a)-8(a)(4).

[6] For this purpose, a *security* is defined in Sec. 165(g)(2) as stock in a corporation, the right to subscribe for or receive a share of stock in a corporation, or a bond, debenture, note, or certificate of indebtedness issued by a corporation or a government either in registered form or with interest coupons.

[7] As explained in Chapter I5, the deductibility of capital losses is limited. For corporate taxpayers, capital losses must initially be offset against capital gains of the current year, and any excess amount is not deductible but must be carried back 3 years and forward for 5 years. Individuals may offset capital losses against capital gains and any excess amount is deductible up to $3,000 per year as an offset to ordinary income. Capital losses in excess of this amount for an individual are carried forward for an indefinite period. Thus, taxpayers generally prefer ordinary losses rather than capital losses.

▶ At least 80% of the voting power of all classes of the affiliated corporation's stock (and 80% of all classes of nonvoting stock) must be owned by the domestic corporation that is deducting the ordinary loss.

▶ More than 90% of the affiliated corporation's gross receipts for all its taxable years must be from nonpassive income.[8]

DEMOLITION OF PROPERTY

At times taxpayers, intent on building their own facilities, purchase land that contains an existing structure. Taxpayers may also demolish a structure they are currently using in order to construct new facilities. In both cases, no deduction is allowed for any demolition costs or any loss sustained on account of the demolition. Instead, under Sec. 280B, these amounts are added to the basis of the land where the demolished structure was located.

CLASSIFYING THE LOSS ON THE TAXPAYER'S TAX RETURN

OBJECTIVE 2

Determine the proper classification for losses

KEY POINT

The distinction between ordinary losses and capital losses is important because for individuals only $3,000 of capital losses can be offset against ordinary income each year. In addition, for individuals a 28% maximum tax rate applies to net capital gains.

If a loss is deductible, the taxpayer must determine whether the loss is an ordinary loss or a capital loss and individual taxpayers must identify the amount as either a deduction *for* or *from* AGI.

ORDINARY VERSUS CAPITAL LOSS

Whether a deductible loss is ordinary or capital depends on the type of property involved and the transaction in which the loss is sustained. To have a capital loss, a sale or exchange of a capital asset must occur. If both elements (i.e., a sale or exchange and a capital asset) are not present, the deduction is an ordinary loss. In general, all assets except inventory, notes and accounts receivable, and depreciable property and land used in a trade or business (i.e., property, plant, and machinery) are classified as **capital assets**.[9]

Because a casualty is not a sale or exchange, the destruction of a capital asset by a casualty creates an ordinary rather than a capital loss. Likewise, a deductible loss realized on the abandonment of property is an ordinary loss because an abandonment is not a sale or exchange.

EXAMPLE 18-4 ▶

On July 24 of the current year, Jermaine sells some investment property for $75,000. The property's adjusted basis is $85,000. The investment property is a capital asset. Jermaine realizes a $10,000 ($75,000 − $85,000) capital loss. If, instead, the property had been destroyed by fire and Jermaine had received $75,000 in insurance proceeds, the $10,000 loss would have been an ordinary loss. ◀

Certain transactions, though not actually constituting a sale or exchange, are treated as a sale or exchange. For example, if a security owned by an individual investor becomes worthless during the year, the loss is treated as a loss from the sale of a capital asset on the last day of the tax year, even though no sale actually occurs. Thus, the loss is a capital loss. Likewise, the seizure or condemnation of property is treated as a sale or exchange.

---

[8] Sec. 165(g)(3). *Nonpassive income* includes all income other than royalties, rents, dividends, interest, annuities, and gains from the sale or exchange of stocks and securities.

[9] Sec. 1221. The definition of a capital asset is more fully examined in Chapter 15.

SECTION 1231 PROPERTY. Whether a loss on a particular transaction is treated as a capital loss may also depend on the gains and losses reported from other property transactions for the tax year. For instance, under Sec. 1231, certain gains and losses are netted together. If the Sec. 1231 gains exceed the Sec. 1231 losses, both the gains and losses are treated as long-term capital gains and losses. However, if the losses equal or exceed the gains, both the gains and the losses are treated as ordinary. **Section 1231 property** includes real property or depreciable property used in a trade or business that is held for more than one year. (See Chapter I13 for a discussion of the netting procedure under Sec. 1231.)

HISTORICAL NOTE

Section 1244 was enacted in 1958 in order to encourage investment in small business enterprises. This was the same year that the original S corporation provisions were enacted.

LOSSES ON SEC. 1244 STOCK. Capital gain or loss is generally recognized upon the sale of stock or securities. An exception is provided for losses from the sale or worthlessness of small business corporation (Sec. 1244) stock. These losses are deductible as ordinary losses up to a maximum of $50,000 per tax year ($100,000 for married taxpayers filing a joint return). Any remaining loss for the year is capital loss.

To qualify the loss as ordinary under Sec. 1244, the following requirements must be met:

▶ The stock must be owned by an individual or a partnership.

▶ The stock must have been originally issued by the corporation to the individual or to a partnership in which an individual is a partner.[10]

ADDITIONAL COMMENT

Stock qualifying as small business corporation stock under Sec. 1244 can be either preferred or common and either voting or nonvoting.

▶ The stock must be stock in a domestic (U.S.) corporation.

▶ The stock must have been issued for cash or property other than stock or securities. Stock issued for services rendered is not eligible for Sec. 1244 treatment.

▶ The corporation must not have derived over 50% of its gross receipts from passive income sources during the five tax years immediately preceding the year of sale or worthlessness.[11]

KEY POINT

Casualty losses incurred on property used to produce rental or royalty income are deductible *for* AGI even though the property is investment property and not used in a trade or business.

▶ At the time the stock is issued, the amount of money and property contributed to both capital and paid-in surplus may not exceed $1 million.

Note that the last test listed above is made *at the time the stock is issued*. Thus, even though at the time the loss is realized the corporation has capital and paid-in surplus in excess of the $1 million limit, the individual may still report an ordinary loss as long as the test is met when the stock is issued.

STOP & THINK

Question: Tony, a single taxpayer, incorporated Waffle, Inc. three years ago by contributing $70,000 in exchange for the stock. Waffle, Inc. owns and operates a small restaurant. Unfortunately, Waffle, Inc.'s business never really became profitable. Tony has been trying to sell the Waffle, Inc. stock since July of last year, but because the corporation had become insolvent, he couldn't find any buyers. In February of the current year Waffle, Inc. was judged to be bankrupt. Tony didn't receive anything for his stock. What issues should Tony's tax advisor address with regard to the Waffle, Inc. stock?

Solution: Tony's tax advisor must determine (1) the amount of any realized loss, (2) the year in which the loss is recognized, and (3) the character of the realized loss. The Waffle, Inc. stock is considered a security under Sec. 165. Whenever a security becomes completely

---

[10] Stock received in certain reorganizations of corporations in exchange for Sec. 1244 stock is also considered Sec. 1244 stock. Section 1244 does not apply to stock that the individual has received through other means such as purchase in a secondary market, exchange, gift, or inheritance.
[11] For this purpose, passive income sources include royalties, rents, divi-

dends, interest, annuities, and sales or exchanges of stocks and securities. If the corporation has not been in existence for a full five years, the gross receipts test is applied to the shorter period. If the corporation has not been in existence for an entire taxable year, the test is applied to the time period up to the date of the loss (see Sec. 1244(c)(2)).

worthless and it is determined that the owner will receive nothing for it, the owner realizes a loss to the extent of the security's basis ($70,000). The loss is deemed to be realized in the year in which the security becomes worthless. While the stock was judged to be worthless by the bankruptcy court in February of the current year, the fact that Tony could not find any buyers last year because the corporation was insolvent may indicate that the stock really became worthless last year. This determination is important because its loss must be taken in the year in which the stock becomes worthless. Furthermore, the stock is deemed to become worthless on the last day of that year. Since Tony received the stock directly from the corporation in exchange for contributed cash, Waffles, Inc.'s gross receipts are from business operations, and the capitalization is less than $1,000,000, the stock qualifies as Sec. 1244 stock. Thus, $50,000 of the loss is characterized as ordinary loss. The remaining $20,000 is a long-term capital loss.

DISALLOWANCE POSSIBILITIES

Losses incurred in certain transactions and activities may be disallowed or deferred. These include

▶ Transfers of property to a controlled corporation in exchange for stock of the corporation (see the discussion in Chapter C2 of *Prentice Hall's Federal Taxation: Corporations, Partnerships, Estates, and Trusts* text and Chapter C2 of the *Comprehensive* volume)

▶ Exchanges of property for other property that is considered to be like-kind to the property given up (see the discussion in Chapter I12)

▶ Property sold to certain related parties (see the discussion in Chapter I6)

▶ Wash sale transactions (see the discussion in Chapter I6)

▶ Losses limited because the losses exceed the amount for which the taxpayer is at risk (see the discussion in Chapter C9 of *Prentice Hall's Federal Taxation: Corporations, Partnerships, Estates, and Trusts* text and Chapter C9 of the *Comprehensive* volume)

In addition, individuals and certain corporations may be limited on the amount of deductible losses because of the passive loss rules.

Topic Review I8-1 contains a summary of loss transactions.

PASSIVE LOSSES

HISTORICAL NOTE

Before the passive activity loss limits became effective in 1987, most tax shelters were concentrated in the areas of real estate, oil and gas, equipment leasing, farming, motion pictures, timber, and research and development. Many tax shelters took advantage of liberal depreciation rules during the early 1980's such as the rapid depreciation of real estate over a 15-year period.

Before 1987, taxpayers had been able to reduce their income tax liability on income from one business or investment activity with deductions, losses, and credits arising in another activity. Thus, taxpayers often invested in activities, called **tax shelters**, that would spin off tax deductions and credits. Many of these tax shelters were simply *passive investments* because they did not require the taxpayer's involvement or participation. In some situations, tax shelters had real economic substance other than the mere creation of tax benefits. A taxpayer's investment in this type of shelter was not based solely on the tax benefits that the activity generated. In many cases, however, tax shelters had no real economic substance other than the creation of deductions and credits that enabled taxpayers to reduce and sometimes eliminate the income tax liability from their other business activities. In an effort to prevent these perceived and real abuses, Congress enacted Sec. 469, which restricts the current use of losses and credits that arise in activities in which the taxpayer does not materially participate in the business and any rental activities. These activities are described as passive activities. (See the Definition of a Passive Activity section in this chapter for an extended discussion of what constitutes a passive activity.)

Topic Review I8-1

Transactions That May Result In Losses

Type of Transaction	Result
Sale or exchange	A loss on personal-use property is not deductible. The tax treatment of a loss on business or investment property depends on the type of property. Losses on capital assets result in capital losses. Losses on Sec. 1231 assets are subject to the Sec. 1231 netting rules discussed in Chapter I13.
Seizure or condemnation	Treated as a sale or exchange.
Abandonment	Not treated as a sale or exchange. No deduction is allowed for a loss on personal-use property. Business or investment property is given ordinary loss treatment.
Worthless securities	Treated as a loss from the sale of the securities on the last day of the year in which the securities become worthless. This generally will result in a capital loss. However, if the requirements of Sec. 1244 are met, at least part of the loss may be treated as an ordinary loss. (See Sec. 1244 stock below.) A loss on worthless securities of an affiliated corporation results in an ordinary loss.
Demolition	No deductible loss is allowed. Instead, losses and costs of demolition are added to the basis of the land where the demolished structure was located.
Sec. 1244 stock	An ordinary loss is allowed for individuals up to $50,000 per year ($100,000 for married filing jointly). The remaining loss is capital. The stock must have been originally issued to the individual for property or cash, and the corporation must meet the requirements to be a small business corporation.

COMPUTATION OF PASSIVE LOSSES AND CREDITS

OBJECTIVE 3

Calculate the suspended loss from passive activities

In enacting the passive loss rules, Congress did not want to prevent taxpayers from currently deducting or using losses and credits generated in active business endeavors of the taxpayer. At the same time, Congress realized that certain investments (such as investments that generate interest or dividend income) normally give rise to taxable income, which could itself be sheltered by losses and credits that arise in other passive activities. Thus, Sec. 469 requires taxpayers to classify their income into three categories: *active income* (such as wages, salaries, and active business income), *portfolio (or investment) income,* and *passive income.* **Portfolio income** includes dividends, interest, annuities, and royalties (and allocable expenses and interest expense) that are not derived in the ordinary course of a trade or business. Gains and losses on property that produces these types of income also are included in portfolio income if the disposition of the property does not occur in the ordinary course of business.[12] Portfolio income becomes

---

[12] Sec. 469(e)(1). Gain or loss on property dispositions occuring in the ordinary course of business is either passive or active business income, depending on the taxpayer's level of involvement (i.e., material participation) in the activity.

part of net investment income, which is used in computing the deduction limit for investment interest expense. (See Chapter I7 for a discussion of the investment interest expense limitation.)

PASSIVE INCOME AND LOSSES. Income and loss in the passive category are computed separately for each passive activity in which the taxpayer has invested. In general, for any tax year, losses generated in one passive activity may be used to offset income from other passive activities, but may not offset either active or portfolio income.

EXAMPLE I8-5 ▶

During the year, Kasi, a CPA, reports $100,000 of active business income from his CPA practice. He also owns two passive activities, from which he earned $10,000 of income from activity A, and incurred a $15,000 loss from activity B. $10,000 of the loss from activity B may offset the $10,000 of income from activity A. However, the $5,000 excess loss is not deductible in the current year, even though Kasi must report $100,000 of active business income. ◀

CARRYOVERS

Passive activity losses that are disallowed as deductions for the year in which they are incurred are carried over indefinitely and treated as losses allocable to that activity in the following tax years.[13] These losses, known as **suspended losses,** may offset passive activity income of the subsequent year, but generally may not offset other types of income. If a taxpayer has invested in several passive activities, and for the year some of the activities generate income while others generate losses, the loss carried over for each loss activity is a pro rata portion of the total passive loss for the year.

EXAMPLE I8-6 ▶

Tammy reports the following income and loss for the year:

Salary	$200,000
Loss from activity X	(40,000)
Loss from activity Y	(10,000)
Income from activity Z	30,000

X, Y, and Z are all passive activities. The losses generated in activities X and Y offset the income from activity Z, but none of the salary income is offset. Thus, Tammy has a net passive loss for the year of $20,000 ($40,000 + $10,000 − $30,000), which must be carried over to subsequent years. The amount of the carryover attributable to each activity is as follows:

Activity X: $20,000 \times \dfrac{\$40,000}{\$50,000} = \$16,000$

Activity Y: $20,000 \times \dfrac{\$10,000}{\$50,000} = \$ 4,000$ ◀

TAXABLE DISPOSITION OF INTEREST IN A PASSIVE ACTIVITY. When a taxpayer disposes of a passive activity in a taxable transaction, the economic gain or loss generated by the activity can be computed, and the suspended losses of that activity may be deducted against the taxpayer's other income. However, the amount of the total net economic loss from the asset that is disposed of must first offset any passive income from other passive activities.[14]

EXAMPLE I8-7 ▶

During the current year, Pam realizes $6,000 of taxable income from activity A, $1,000 of loss from activity B, and $8,000 of taxable income from activity C. All three activities are passive

---

[13] Sec. 469(b).
[14] Sec. 469(g). Income from the activity for prior years may also be taken into

account in arriving at the net income from all passive activities for the year if it is necessary to prevent avoidance of the passive loss rules.

activities with regard to Pam. In addition, $30,000 of passive losses from activity C are carried over from prior years. During the current year, Pam sells activity C for a $15,000 taxable gain. Pam reports salary income of $90,000 for the year. Because activity C is disposed of in a fully taxable transaction, Pam may deduct $2,000 of loss against the salary income:

Income for the year from C	$ 8,000	
Gain from the sale of C	15,000	
Suspended losses from C	(30,000)	
Total loss from C		($7,000)
Income for the year from A	$ 6,000	
Loss for the year from B	(1,000)	5,000
Pam's deduction against salary income		($2,000) ◄

If the passive activity is sold to a related party, the suspended loss is not deductible until the related party sells the activity to a nonrelated person. The definition of *related persons* includes spouse, brothers and sisters, ancestors, lineal descendants, and corporations or partnerships in which the individual has a greater than 50% ownership.[15]

Although the death of a taxpayer is not a taxable disposition of the asset, some of the suspended losses may be deducted when this event occurs. The amount of the deduction allowed is the amount by which the suspended losses exceed the increase in basis of the property. These losses generally are deducted on the decedent's final income tax return. Any suspended losses up to the amount of the increase in basis are lost.[16]

EXAMPLE I8-8 ▶ At the time that John died during the current year, he owned passive activity property with an adjusted basis of $20,000 and a FMV of $35,000. There were $25,000 in suspended losses attributable to the property. Because the increase in the basis of the property is $15,000 ($35,000 − $20,000), $15,000 of the suspended losses are lost. However, $10,000 ($25,000 suspended losses − $15,000 increase in basis) of the suspended losses are deductible on John's final income tax return. ◄

In general, the suspended losses of a passive activity become deductible only when the taxpayer completely disposes of his or her interest in the activity. However, in Treasury Reg. 1.469-4(g) the government has stated that taxpayers may treat the disposition of a substantial part of an activity as the disposition of a separate activity. This treatment is only available, however, if the taxpayer can establish with reasonable certainty the amount of income, deductions, credits, and suspended losses and credits that are allocable to that part of the activity.

CARRYOVERS FROM A FORMER PASSIVE ACTIVITY. The determination of whether an activity is passive with respect to a taxpayer is made annually. Thus, an activity that previously was considered passive may not be passive with respect to the taxpayer for the current year. This is called a **former passive activity**.[17] Any loss carryover from a former passive activity is deductible against the current year's income of that activity even though the activity is not a passive activity in the current year. However, any suspended loss in excess of the activity's income for the year is still subject to the carryover limitations. Since the activity is no longer passive for the year, the current year's loss is deductible against active business income.

---

[15] Other relationships described in Secs. 267(b) and 707(b) are also considered related parties for this purpose.

[16] Sec. 469(g)(2). Generally, the basis of inherited property is its FMV on the date of death (see Chapter I5).

[17] Sec. 469(f)(3).

EXAMPLE I8-9 ▶ Kris owns activity A, which, for the immediately preceding tax year, was considered a passive activity with regard to Kris. $10,000 in losses from activity A were disallowed and carried over to the current year. Because of Kris' increased involvement in activity A in the current year, it is not considered passive with regard to Kris for that year. During the current year, activity A generates a $5,000 loss. During the current year, she also has an investment in activity B, a passive activity. Her share of activity B's income is $7,000. Kris reports $60,000 in salary. Because for the current year activity A is not a passive activity, the $5,000 current year loss is fully deductible against her salary. However, the $10,000 loss carryover from the prior year is deductible only against the $7,000 of income from passive activity B. The $3,000 ($10,000 − $7,000) excess is carried over to the subsequent year. ◀

Credits. Credits generated in a passive activity are also limited and may be used only against the portion of the tax liability that is attributable to passive income. This amount is determined by comparing the tax liability on all income for the year with the tax liability on all income excluding the passive income.

EXAMPLE I8-10 ▶ Dale invests in a passive activity. For the year, he must report $10,000 of taxable income from the passive activity. Dale's share of tax credits generated by the passive activity is $5,000. Assume Dale's precredit tax liability on all income (including the $10,000 from the passive activity) is $25,000, and his precredit tax liability on all income excluding the passive activity income is $22,000. He may use only $3,000 ($25,000 − $22,000) of the tax credits generated by the passive activity. The remaining $2,000 of tax credits is carried forward and may be used in a subsequent year against the portion of the tax liability attributable to passive activity income in that year. However, these credits may never offset any portion of the tax liability attributable to nonpassive activities. (See Chapter I14 for a discussion of credits and their carryovers.) ◀

DEFINITION OF A PASSIVE ACTIVITY

The term *passive activity* includes any rental activity or any trade or business in which the taxpayer does not materially participate.[18] The definition of a passive activity is based on two critical elements: an identification of exactly what constitutes an activity and a determination of whether the taxpayer has materially participated in that activity.

IDENTIFICATION OF AN ACTIVITY. Identifying whether an activity is either passive or active becomes critical for several reasons. Whether a taxpayer materially participates in an activity is determined separately for each activity. Suspended losses of a passive activity are deductible when the taxpayer's ownership of the activity is completely terminated. As explained in a subsequent section of this chapter, up to $25,000 of passive losses may be deducted currently if they are from rental real estate activities. Thus, losses from passive business and rental real estate activities must not be combined into one activity.

The way operations are combined or separated into activities can have a significant impact on the deductibility of losses that are generated. One or more activities may be treated as a single activity only if they constitute an "appropriate economic unit."[19] Although this determination is made by examining all the relevant facts and circumstances, the following factors are given the greatest weight:

---

[18] Secs. 469(c)(1) and (c)(2). Sec. 469(c)(6) also includes investment (production of income) activities under Sec. 212 as a passive activity. Section 469(j)(8) defines the term *rental activity* as any activity where payments are principally for the use of tangible property. Pursuant to the Regulations, there are six exceptions to this general rule. These exceptions include providing the use of tangible property where the average period of customer use is seven days or less, the average period of customer use is 30 days or less and significant personal services are provided by the owner in conjunction with the use of the property, extraordinary personal services are provided by

the owner in conjunction with the use of the property, the rental of the property is incidental to a nonrental activity of the taxpayer, the property is customarily made available during defined business hours for nonexclusive use by various customers, or the property is provided for use in a nonrental activity conducted by a partnership, S corporation, or joint venture in which the taxpayer owns an interest. The details of these exceptions are beyond the scope of this text. See Temp. Reg. Sec. 1.469-1T(e)(3)(ii).

[19] Reg. Sec. 1.469-4(c).

ADDITIONAL COMMENT

Tax year 1991 gave a clearer review of the impact of the passive loss provisions that were enacted in 1986. Net losses of limited partnerships, the types that are used as tax shelters, declined to $16.7 billion in 1991 from $35.5 billion in 1986.

▶ Similarities and differences in the types of business

▶ The extent of common control

▶ The extent of common ownership

▶ The geographical location, and

▶ Any interdependencies between the operations (i.e. the extent to which they purchase or sell goods between themselves, have the same customers, are accounted for with a single set of books, etc.).

Not all of these factors are necessary for a taxpayer to treat more than one operation as a single activity. Furthermore, a taxpayer may use any reasonable method of applying the relevant facts and circumstances in grouping the activities.

EXAMPLE I8-11 ▶ Carla owns a bakery and a movie theater in each of two different shopping malls, one located in Baltimore and the other in Philadelphia. Depending on other relevant facts and circumstances, a reasonable grouping of the operations may result in any of the following:

▶ One activity involving all four operations

▶ Two activities: a bakery activity and a theater activity

▶ Two activities: a Baltimore activity and a Philadelphia activity

▶ Four activities ◀

Under the Treasury Regulations, taxpayers apparently have some degree of flexibility in determining how different business operations are grouped into activities. However, once the activities are established, taxpayers must be consistent in grouping their activities in subsequent years unless material changes in the facts and circumstances clearly make the groupings inappropriate.

In identifying separate activities, rental operations generally may not be grouped with trade or business operations. However, a combination is allowed if either the rental operation is insubstantial in relation to the business operation or vice versa. Unfortunately, the Treasury Regulations do not give any guidance with regard to what is insubstantial.[20] Furthermore, because of the special rules dealing with real estate rental activities (explained later in this chapter), rental activities involving real estate may not be combined with rental activities involving personal property.

EXAMPLE I8-12 ▶ Sandy owns a building in which she operates a restaurant and leases out apartments to tenants. Generally the tenants sign apartment leases of one year or longer. Of the total gross income derived from the building, 15% comes from the apartment rentals and 85% comes from the restaurant operation. If the apartment rental operation is considered insubstantial in relation to the restaurant operation, the two may be combined into one activity. If it is not insubstantial, the two operations are considered two separate activities: a business activity and a rental real estate activity. ◀

Partnerships and S corporations (pass-through entities) are to identify their business and rental activities by applying these rules at the partnership or S corporation level and then should report the results of their operations by activity to the partners or shareholders. Each partner or shareholder must then take these activities and, using these same rules, combine them where appropriate with operations conducted either directly or through other pass-through entities. In fact, many real estate passive activities are held as either partnerships or S corporations.

---

[20] Reg. Sec. 1.469-4.

MATERIAL PARTICIPATION. Once each activity has been identified, a determination must be made as to whether the activity is passive or active with respect to the taxpayer. If the taxpayer does not **materially participate** in the activity, it is deemed to be a passive activity with respect to that taxpayer. Pursuant to the Treasury Regulations,[21] taxpayers are deemed to materially participate in an activity if they meet at least one of the following tests:

▶ The individual participates in the activity for more than 500 hours during the year.

▶ The individual's participation in the activity for the year constitutes substantially all of the participation in the activity by all individuals, including individuals who do not own any interest in the activity.

▶ The individual participates in the activity for more than 100 hours during the year, and that participation is more than any other individual's participation for the year (including participation by individuals who do not own any interest in the activity).

▶ The individual participates in "significant participation activities" for an aggregate of more than 500 hours during the year.[22] Thus, an individual who spends over 100 hours each in several separate significant participation activities may aggregate the time spent in these activities in order to meet the 500-hour test.

▶ The individual materially participated in the activity in any five years during the immediately preceding ten taxable years. These five years need not be consecutive.

▶ The individual materially participated in the activity for any three years preceding the year in question, and the activity is a personal service activity.[23]

▶ Taking into account all the relevant facts and circumstances, the individual participates in the activity on a regular, continuous, and substantial basis during the year.

Note that the first four tests are based on the number of hours the taxpayer spent in the activity during the year. The fifth and sixth tests are based on the material participation of the taxpayer in prior years and are designed to prevent taxpayers from asserting that retirement income is passive and offsetting it with passive losses from tax shelters. To determine whether a taxpayer materially participates in an activity, the participation of the taxpayer's spouse is taken into account.[24]

LIMITED PARTNERSHIPS. A limited partner has a limited liability for his or her investment in the partnership without assuming any active involvement; thus, the material participation test is not met and the limited partner's investment is generally considered passive. However, a limited partner can meet the material participation test if the individual meets either the 500 hour test or the fifth and sixth tests above (prior year tests).[25] It is rare for a limited partner to meet the material participation test because limited partners are generally not involved in the operation of the business. Thus, most income and deductions from limited partnerships are considered passive.

WORKING INTEREST IN AN OIL AND GAS PROPERTY. A working interest is an interest that is responsible for the cost of development or operation of the oil and gas property. This type of interest in an oil and gas property is not a passive activity as long as the taxpayer's liability in the interest is not limited.[26] Thus, even though a taxpayer may

---

[21] Temp. Reg. Sec. 1.469-5T(a).

[22] A significant participation activity is a trade or business in which the individual participates for more than 100 hours during the year but for which the individual does not meet the material participation test alone (i.e., with respect to that activity, the individual does not meet one of the other material participation tests.). See Temp. Reg. Sec. 1.469-5T(c).

[23] A personal service activity involves rendering personal services in the fields of health, law, engineering, architecture, accounting, actuarial science, performing arts, or consulting. It also includes any other trade or business in which capital is not a material income-producing factor. See Temp. Reg. Sec. 1.469-5T(d).

[24] Sec. 469(h).

[25] Temp. Reg. Sec. 1.469-5T(e)(2).

[26] Sec. 469(c)(3).

ADDITIONAL COMMENT

Congress excluded a working interest in an oil or gas property from the material participation requirement in those cases where the taxpayer's liability is not limited because Congress concluded that financial risk was a more relevant standard. At the time (1986) the oil and gas industry was suffering severe hardship due to the worldwide decline in oil prices.

KEY POINT

The passive loss limitations do not apply to partnerships and S corporations, but they apply to partners and shareholders of S corporations.

not materially participate in the activity, the passive loss rules do not apply. This is so even if the taxpayer holds the interest through an entity such as a partnership.

TAXPAYERS SUBJECT TO PASSIVE LOSS RULES

The passive loss limitation rules are applicable for

▶ Individuals, estates, trusts

▶ Any closely held C corporation

▶ Any personal service corporation

▶ Certain publicly traded partnerships

Because the income and losses of partnerships and S corporations are taxed directly to the partners and shareholders, the passive loss rules do not apply to these entities.[27] Rather, they are applied directly at the partner or shareholder level. Thus, the situation may arise where one partner or shareholder is subject to the passive loss rules while the others are not.

Generally, the passive loss limitation rules do not apply to regular corporations (i.e., C corporations) as opposed to S corporations. However, in order to prevent certain individuals from avoiding the passive loss rules through the use of a regular corporation, closely held C corporations and personal service corporations are also subject to these rules.

ADDITIONAL COMMENT

Because a closely held C corporation's passive losses may offset its income from active business operations, some tax professionals advise their clients to transfer their investments that generate passive losses to their profitable corporations.

CLOSELY HELD C CORPORATIONS. The passive loss rules apply to closely held C corporations but only on a limited basis. **A closely held C corporation** is a C corporation where more than 50% of the stock is owned by five or fewer individuals at any time during the last half of the corporation's taxable year.[28] The concern that Congress had regarding closely held C corporations was that without this special rule, taxpayers would be motivated to transfer their investments (both portfolio investments and passive activities) to a C corporation where the portfolio income could be offset by the corporation's passive losses. Thus, as applied to a closely held C corporation, the passive loss rules prevent passive activity losses from offsetting portfolio income. However, a closely held C corporation's passive losses may offset its income from active business operations.

EXAMPLE I8-13 ▶

All of the outstanding stock of Delta Corporation is owned equally by individuals Allen and Beth. During the current year, Delta generates $15,000 taxable income from its active business operations. It also earns $10,000 of interest and dividends from investments and reports a $30,000 loss from a passive activity. Because Delta is a closely held C corporation, the $15,000 of taxable income from the active business is offset by $15,000 of the passive loss. However, the $10,000 of portfolio income may not be offset. Thus, for the current year, Delta reports $10,000 of taxable income from its portfolio income and has a $15,000 passive loss carryover. ◀

PERSONAL SERVICE CORPORATION. **A personal service corporation (PSC)** is a regular C corporation whose principal activity is the performance of personal services that are substantially performed by owner-employees.[29] However, a corporation is not a PSC unless more than 10% of the value of the stock is held by owner-employees. In

---

[27] An S corporation is a corporation that has elected for federal income tax purposes to be treated basically like a partnership. Thus, the income or losses and separately stated items of an S corporation flow through to the shareholders and are reported on their individual tax returns.
[28] Secs. 469(j)(1) and 465(a)(1)(B).

[29] Secs. 469(j)(2) and 269A(b)(1). For this purpose any employee who owns any stock of the corporation is an owner-employee. This stock ownership is determined by using the Sec. 318 constructive ownership rules as modified by Sec. 469(j)(2).

contrast with a non-PSC closely held C corporation, the passive loss limitation rules apply in their entirety.[30] Thus, passive losses of a PSC may not offset the PSC's active business income or portfolio income.

MATERIAL PARTICIPATION BY PSCs AND CLOSELY HELD C CORPORATIONS. Special rules apply for determining whether closely held C corporations or PSCs materially participate in an activity. These corporations are deemed to materially participate in an activity only if one or more shareholders who own more than 50% in value of the outstanding stock materially participate in the activity. In addition, a closely held C corporation (other than a PSC) is deemed to materially participate in an activity if it meets *all* of the following tests with regard to that activity:

1. A substantial portion of the services of at least one full-time employee is in the active management of the activity.
2. A substantial portion of the services of at least three full-time nonowner employees is directly related to the activity.
3. The Sec. 162 business deductions of the activity exceed 15% of the activity's gross income for the period.[31]

HISTORICAL NOTE

Shortly after the passive loss limitations were enacted as part of the Tax Reform Act of 1986, some tax advisors recommended that individuals should purchase units in a PTP because it produced passive activity income that could be offset through the use of the individual's passive activity losses. However, the Tax Reform Act of 1987 changed net income from a PTP from passive income to portfolio income.

PUBLICLY TRADED PARTNERSHIPS

Generally, a **publicly traded partnership (PTP)** is treated for tax purposes as a corporation. For purposes of the passive loss rules, a PTP is defined as any partnership if interests in the partnership are either traded on an established securities market or readily tradable on a secondary market.[32] If a PTP is treated for tax purposes as a corporation, the passive loss rules generally do not apply. However, PTPs that existed on December 17, 1987 are still treated as partnerships until their first tax year beginning after 1997. Because under the partnership rules the partnership's income and losses flow through to the partners, the passive loss rules apply to these existing PTPs. However, these rules are applied separately to each existing PTP. Partners treat losses from a PTP as separate from any other type of income (passive, active business, or portfolio), as well as separate from any income from other PTPs. These losses can only be carried forward and be offset against income generated by that particular PTP in a subsequent year. Furthermore, the loss may not offset any portfolio income that the PTP might generate.[33] Any net income from PTPs is treated as portfolio income.

EXAMPLE I8-14 ▶ Mark owns interests in partnerships A and B, both of which are PTPs that existed on December 17, 1987. During the current year, Mark's share of the income from A is $2,000. Mark's share of B's loss is $1,200. B also generated some portfolio income. Mark's share of B's portfolio income is $800. The $1,200 loss from B may not offset any of B's $800 portfolio income. Furthermore, it may not offset any of the $2,000 income from A. The $2,000 income from A is treated as portfolio income. Thus, Mark reports $2,800 portfolio income and has a $1,200 suspended loss from B. In a subsequent year, Mark's share of any income from B can be offset by the $1,200 of suspended loss that is carried forward. ◀

Suspended losses from a PTP may be deducted only in the year the partner disposes of his or her interest in the PTP. No loss is recognized in the year that the PTP itself sells a passive activity.

---

[30] If a corporation is both a PSC and a closely held C corporation, the more restrictive rules for PSCs apply.
[31] Secs. 469(h)(4) and 465(c)(7). Tests 1 and 2 must be met for the 12-month period ending on the last day of the tax year. Test 3 must be met for the tax year. Furthermore, the Sec. 404 deductions are also included in the 15% of gross income test.

[32] Sec. 469(k)(2). See Chapter C10 of *Prentice Hall's Federal Taxation: Corporations, Partnerships, Estates, and Trusts* and Chapter C10 of the *Comprehensive* volume for a definition and discussion of publicly traded partnerships.
[33] Conf. Rept. No. 100-495, 100th Cong., 1st Sess., pp. 231–233 (1987).

RENTAL REAL ESTATE TRADE OR BUSINESS

In general, rental activities are considered passive activities. However, for tax years beginning after December 31, 1993, the passive activity loss rules no longer apply to certain taxpayers that are involved in real property trades or businesses. Instead, these activities are treated as active businesses. Under the new law, a real property trade or business means any development, redevelopment, construction, reconstruction, acquisition, conversion, rental, operation, management, leasing, or brokering of real property.[34]

This exception applies to taxpayers if both the following requirements are met:

▶ More than one-half of the personal services performed in all trades or businesses by the taxpayer during the year must be performed in real property trades or businesses in which the taxpayer materially participates.

▶ The taxpayer must perform more than 750 hours of work during the taxable year in real property trades or businesses in which the taxpayer materially participates.

In meeting these tests, personal services rendered by a taxpayer in his or her capacity as an employee are not treated as performed in real property trades or businesses unless the employee owns at least 5% of the employer. Furthermore, for married taxpayers filing a joint return, the exception applies only if one of the spouses separately meets both requirements. The time spent in the activity by both spouses is used in determining whether or not the material participation test is met.

EXAMPLE I8-15 ▶ Anwar and Anya are married and file a joint return. Anwar's only job is renting and maintaining four large apartment complexes that he owns. Anwar and Anya manage the buildings themselves. During the current year, Anya spent 500 hours keeping records and corresponding with tenants. Anwar spent 700 hours during the year maintaining and repairing the apartments. Even though all of Anya and Anwar's personal services are connected with a real property trade or business in which they materially participate, this rental activity is considered passive because neither Anwar nor Anya alone spends more than 750 hours doing services related to the rental activity. ◀

In order for a closely held C corporation to meet this rental real estate business exception, more than one-half of the gross receipts of the corporation must be derived from real property trades or businesses in which the corporation materially participates.

Any deduction allowed under the previously discussed exception for taxpayers who are involved in real property trades or businesses is not taken into consideration in determining the taxpayer's AGI for purposes of the phase-out of the $25,000 deduction available for taxpayers who actively participate in a rental real estate activity. (See the following section in this chapter for a discussion of the $25,000 active participation exception.)

OTHER RENTAL REAL ESTATE ACTIVITIES

Many rental real estate activities are not considered rental real estate businesses, and are therefore subject to the passive loss rules. However, if an individual taxpayer meets certain requirements, up to $25,000 of annual losses from these passive rental real estate activities may still be deducted against the taxpayer's other income. In order to meet this exception, an individual must do both of the following:

▶ *Actively* participate in the activity[35]

▶ Own at least 10% of the value of the activity for the entire tax year

---

[34] Sec. 469(c)(7).

[35] In order for a deduction to be taken in the current year for a loss sustained in a prior year, the taxpayer must actively participate in the activity during both years. See Sec. 469(i)(1).

ACTIVE PARTICIPATION. *Active participation,* as opposed to material participation, can be achieved by the taxpayer without regular, continuous, and material involvement in the activity and without meeting any of the material participation tests. However, the taxpayer still must participate in the making of management decisions or arranging for others to provide services in a significant and bona fide sense. This includes approving new tenants, deciding on rental terms, approving expenditures, and other similar decisions. Active participation may be achieved even if the taxpayer hires a rental agent and others provide the services.[36] In general, a limited partner is not able to participate actively in any activity of a limited partnership.

LIMITATION ON DEDUCTION OF RENTAL REAL ESTATE LOSS. Rental real estate losses are first applied against other net passive income for the year and then may be used to reduce portfolio or active business income up to $25,000. The $25,000, however, is reduced by 50% of the taxpayer's AGI in excess of $100,000. For this purpose, AGI is determined without regard to any passive activity loss or to any loss allowable to taxpayers who materially participate in real property trades or businesses (e.g., a real estate developer). Thus, if a taxpayer has AGI of $150,000 or more, all of the rental real estate losses must be suspended and carried over with the taxpayer's other passive losses.

EXAMPLE I8-16 ▶

During the current year, Penny, a married individual who files a joint return, reports the following items of income and loss:

Salary income	$120,000
Activity A (passive)	15,000
Activity B (nonbusiness rental real estate)	(50,000)

Penny owns over 10% and actively participates in Activity B. Her AGI for the year is as follows:

Salary		$120,000
Passive income from Activity A	$15,000	
Minus: Passive loss from Activity B ($50,000, but limited to $15,000)	(15,000)	
Minus: Maximum rental real estate loss (from Activity B)	$25,000	
Reduced by phase-out: [($120,000 − $100,000)× 0.50]	(10,000)	
Deductible amount (but not to exceed actual loss)		(15,000)
AGI		$105,000

Penny may deduct $30,000 ($15,000 deductible amount + $15,000 as an offset to the income from activity A) of the loss from activity B during the year. Penny has $20,000 ($35,000 − $15,000) of suspended passive losses from activity B that are carried over to the following year. ◀

The $25,000 limit applies to the sum of both deductions and credits. Thus, in order to properly apply the limit, the credits must be converted into deduction equivalents. A *deduction equivalent* is an amount that if taken as a deduction, would reduce the tax liability by an amount equal to the credits. The amount of deduction equivalents can be computed by dividing the amount of the credit by the taxpayer's marginal tax rate. If the

---

[36] S. Rept. No. 99-313, 99th Cong., 2d Sess., pp. 737–738 (1986). However, a lessor under a net lease will probably not be deemed to achieve active participation.

sum of the deductions and the deduction equivalents exceeds the $25,000 limit, the deductions are used first.

EXAMPLE I8-17 ▶ Hal owns over 10% and actively participates in activity A, which is a passive real estate rental activity. Hal's marginal tax rate is 28% and he has AGI of less than $100,000. For the year, activity A generates a $20,000 net loss and $10,000 in tax credits. After deducting the $20,000 net loss against his active business and portfolio income, Hal has a remaining real estate deduction of $5,000 ($25,000 − $20,000). Thus, Hal may use $1,400 ($5,000 × 0.28) of the credits. The remaining $8,600 ($10,000 − $1,400) of tax credits must be carried over to subsequent years. ◀

If deductions and credits exceeding the $25,000 limit arise from more than one passive activity, they must be allocated between the activities.

EXAMPLE I8-18 ▶ Mary has AGI of less than $100,000 and a 28% marginal tax rate. During the year she reports a $30,000 loss from activity A and a $10,000 loss from activity B. Additionally, activity A generates $5,000 of tax credits. Both activities A and B are passive real estate rental activities in which Mary actively participates and owns over 10% of each activity. The $25,000 deduction is first allocated to the losses. Because the sum of the losses ($40,000) exceeds the limit, the deductible loss must be allocated ratably between the activities as follows:

Activity A: $25,000 × $30,000 ÷ $40,000 = $18,750
Activity B: $25,000 × $10,000 ÷ $40,000 = $6,250

Activity A has an $11,250 ($30,000 − $18,750) suspended loss, and activity B has a $3,750 ($10,000 − $6,250) suspended loss. In addition, activity A has $5,000 of suspended tax credits. ◀

A summary of the passive activity loss rules is presented in Topic Review I8-2.

STOP & THINK

Question: Jana is a business woman who has successfully invested in various stock and bond funds. Now she is considering diversifying her holdings by investing in real estate. One of the alternatives she is considering is purchasing an interest in a limited partnership that invests in real estate. A friend is also urging Jana to go into a partnership with him in order to purchase a small office building they would rent out. Assume that the size of Jana's investment in the two alternatives would be exactly the same and that Jana estimates the economic results to be equivalent (e.g., she expects both to spin off equivalent losses for the first few years and then begin turning a profit.) What tax issues should Jana consider when making her investment decision?

Solution: In comparing alternatives such as these, of course, the most important considerations should be the non-tax factors such as, cash flow from the investment, the capital appreciation of the assets, the marketability of the investment, and the risk. For example, as a limited partner, Jana will not personally be liable for debts of the partnership or lawsuits filed against the partnership. Purchase of the office building as a general partner with her friend will cause her to be personally liable. However, in comparing these two alternatives, certain tax issues may come into play. Both alternatives are investments in rental real estate. However, Jana is not eligible to deduct up to $25,000 of the passive losses from the limited partnership because she will not actively participate in the partnership. On the other hand, if she is involved in management decisions regarding the office building, she will be actively participating and will be eligible for the $25,000 passive loss deduction exception. Of course, the benefit of this exception is phased-out if her AGI exceeds $100,000.

Topic Review I8-2

Passive Losses

Topic	Summary
Taxpayers covered	Individuals, estates, trusts, closely held C corporations, personal service corporations, certain publicly traded partnerships.
Definition	Any trade or business activity in which the taxpayer does not materially participate. Includes all rental activities except for certain rental real estate activities and exceptions contained in regulations. Does not include working interests in oil and gas property.
Limitation	Passive losses are deductible against passive income, but not against active or portfolio income. Disallowed losses are carried over to subsequent years (suspended losses). Losses must be accounted for separately by activity. Activities are identified by examining the taxpayer's undertakings.
Suspended losses	Must be allocated and attributed among the passive activities that generated the losses.
Disposition of interest	Suspended losses may be deducted in the year of a taxable disposition. For inherited property, suspended losses in excess of the increase in basis may be deducted on the final return of a decedent. Losses up to the amount of the basis increase are lost.
Material participation	Must be regular, continuous, and substantial. The regulations contain seven separate tests; four based on current-year participation; two based on participation in prior years; and one based on facts and circumstances.
Real property trades or businesses	Passive activity loss rules do not apply to taxpayers who materially participate in real property trade or business activities constituting more than 750 hours. Additionally, more than one-half of the taxpayer's personal services must be performed in real property trades or businesses in which the taxpayer materially participates.
Rental of real estate	Individuals may deduct losses up to $25,000 against active and portfolio income if they actively particpate in the activity. This is a lesser standard than material participation, but the taxpayer must still participate in management decisions or arranging for others to provide services. The deduction phases out at a 50% rate for AGI in excess of $100,000.

KEY POINT

In order to deduct a loss on personal-use property, it is crucial that the taxpayer establish that the loss was caused by a casualty. Otherwise, the loss is not deductible.

CASUALTY AND THEFT LOSSES

OBJECTIVE 6

Identify and calculate the deduction for a casualty or theft loss

Deductions for losses on personal-use property are generally disallowed. However, under Sec. 165 a limited deduction is available to an individual if the loss arises from a fire, storm, shipwreck, other casualty, or theft. Similar losses for business and investment property are also deductible. In order for an event to qualify as a casualty, certain requirements must be met.

CASUALTY DEFINED

According to the IRS, a deductible **casualty loss** is one that has occurred in an identifiable event that was sudden, unexpected, or unusual.[37]

IDENTIFIABLE EVENT. Because the event that causes the loss must be *identifiable,* the act of losing or misplacing property is generally not considered a casualty.

However, in some cases taxpayers have been able to prove that the loss of the property was the result of an identifiable event.

One evening Troy and his wife, Lynn, go to the theater. Troy accidentally slams the car door on Lynn's hand. The impact breaks the flanges holding the diamond in her ring. As a result, the diamond falls from the ring and is lost. In this case, a deductible casualty loss has occurred.[38] ◀

KEY POINT

The taxpayer has the burden of proof to establish that a loss was caused by a casualty. The taxpayer should gather as much evidence as possible. Newspaper clippings, police reports, photographs, and insurance reports can be helpful in establishing the cause of the loss.

SUDDEN, UNEXPECTED, OR UNUSUAL EVENTS. According to the IRS, a *sudden event* is one that is swift, not gradual or progressive. An *unexpected event* is one that is ordinarily unanticipated and not intended. An *unusual event* is one that is not a day-to-day occurrence and that is not typical of the activity in which the taxpayer is engaged.

Thus, the IRS has ruled that a deductible casualty loss was sustained when a taxpayer went ice fishing and his automobile fell through the ice.[39] A taxpayer whose automobile was damaged as the result of an accident also sustained a deductible casualty loss. However, if the accident is caused by the taxpayer's willful negligence or willful act, no deduction is allowed.[40] Damage sustained as the result of an accident in an automobile race was held nondeductible because accidents occur often and are not unusual events in automobile races.

The following are a few examples of events that have been held to constitute a deductible casualty loss:

ADDITIONAL COMMENT

Sudden, unexpected, or unusual events must also be accompanied by an external force. For example, a blown engine in an automobile is a sudden event but because no external force caused the event, the loss is not a casualty loss.

▶ Rust and water damage to furniture and carpets caused by the bursting of a water heater

▶ Damage to the exterior paint of a residence caused by a severe, sudden, and unexpected concentration of chemical fumes in the air

▶ Loss caused by fire (unless the taxpayer sets the fire, in which case no deduction is available)[41]

▶ Damage to a building caused by an unusually large blast at a nearby quarry or a jet sonic boom[42]

▶ Death of trees just a few days after a sudden infestation of pine beetles[43]

The following are examples of events that have been held *not* to be a casualty:

▶ Water damage to the walls and ceiling of a taxpayer's personal residence as the result of the gradual deterioration of the roof[44]

---

[37] IRS *Publication No. 547* (Nonbusiness Disasters, Casualties, and Thefts), 1996, p. 1.
[38] *John P. White*, 48 T.C. 430 (1967), *acq.* 1969-2 C.B. xxv. In another case, the taxpayer convinced the Tax Court to allow a deduction for a lost diamond, even though the taxpayer could not remember a specific blow to the ring. In this instance, the taxpayer obtained an expert witness to testify that the flanges of the ring were strong enough and in good enough repair that the loss of the diamond had to have been caused by a sudden, unexpected blow rather than by progressive deterioration.
[39] Rev. Rul. 69-88, 1969-1 C.B. 58.
[40] *Willie C. Robinson*, 1984 PH T.C. Memo ¶84,188, 47 TCM 1510 and

Reg. Sec. 1.165-7(a)(3).
[41] Ltr. Rul. 8227010 (March 30, 1982) contains the above examples.
[42] *Ray Durden*, 3 T.C. 1 (1944), *acq.* 1944 C.B. 8 and Rev. Rul. 60-329, 1960-2 C.B. 67.
[43] Rev. Rul. 79-174, 1979-1 C.B. 99. See also *Charles A. Smithgall v. U.S.*, 47 AFTR 2d 81-695, 81-1 USTC ¶9121 (D.C.-Ga., 1980). However, the IRS has ruled in Ltr. Rul. 8544001 (July 12, 1985) that no casualty loss results when the time interval between the infestation and the death of the trees was too long.
[44] *Lauren Whiting*, 1975 PH T.C. Memo ¶75,038, 34 TCM 241.

▶ Trees dying because of gradual suffocation of the root systems

▶ The loss of trees and shrubs because of disease[45]

▶ Damage to carpet and clothing caused by moths and carpet beetles[46]

▶ Damage to a road due to freezing, thawing, and gradual deterioration[47]

▶ Damage to a residence caused by the gradual sinking of the land underneath the home[48]

▶ Damage caused by drought because it occurs through progressive deterioration

▶ The steady weakening of a building caused by normal wind and weather conditions

▶ The rusting and deterioration of a water heater[49]

At times it is very difficult to determine under the particular facts whether the necessary incidents of suddenness, unexpectedness, or unusualness exist. For example, damage caused by the sudden infestation of pine beetles in some instances has been held to be a casualty, but in other instances it has not constituted a casualty.[50]

THEFT DEFINED

Under Sec. 165, a loss sustained as the result of a theft is also deductible. This includes theft of business, investment, or personal-use property. The Treasury Regulations state that "the term theft shall be deemed to include, but shall not necessarily be limited to, larceny, embezzlement, and robbery."[51] A determination whether other actions also constitute theft often depends on whether criminal intent was involved and the action is illegal under the state law where the action has occurred. Thus, the IRS has stated that blackmail, extortion, and kidnapping for ransom may also constitute theft.[52]

DEDUCTIBLE AMOUNT OF CASUALTY LOSS

The amount of a casualty loss deduction depends on the amount of the loss sustained, any insurance or other reimbursement received; and, in the case of personal-use property, the limitations imposed under the tax law.

MEASURING THE LOSS. In general, the amount of loss sustained in a casualty is the amount by which the property's FMV is reduced as a result of the casualty. This is measured by comparing the property's FMV immediately before and immediately after the casualty.[53] Any reduction in the FMV of the taxpayer's surrounding but undamaged property is disregarded.

EXAMPLE I8-20 ▶ Gail purchased a vacation home for $110,000. Shortly after she purchased the property, a mudslide completely destroyed several neighboring cabins. There was no damage to Gail's cabin. After the slide, an appraisal reveals that the FMV of the cabin has declined to $80,000

[45] *William R. Miller*, 1970 PH T.C. Memo ¶70,167, 29 TCM 741 and Rev. Rul. 57-599, 1957-2 C.B. 142, *modified by* Rev. Rul. 79-174, 1979-1 C.B. 99. See also *Howard F. Burns v. U.S.*, 6 AFTR 2d 6036, 61-1 USTC ¶9127 (6th Cir., 1960).

[46] Rev. Rul. 55-327, 1955-1 C.B. 25. See also *J. P. Meersman v. U.S.*, 18 AFTR 2d 6152, 67-1 USTC ¶9125 (6th Cir., 1966).

[47] *Howard Stacy*, 1970 PH T.C. Memo ¶70,127, 29 TCM 542. However, the breaking up of a road over a 4-month period because of extreme weather conditions was held to be a casualty. See *Emmett J. O'Connell v. U.S.*, 29 AFTR 2d 72-596, 72-1 USTC ¶9312, (D.C. Cal., 1972). See also *Stephen L. Shaffer*, 1983 PH T.C. Memo ¶83,677, 47 TCM 285.

[48] *Henry W. Berry*, 1969 PH T.C. Memo ¶69,162, 28 TCM 802. See also *David McDaniel*, 1980 PH T.C. Memo ¶80,557, 41 TCM 563.

[49] IRS *Publication No. 547* (Nonbusiness Disasters, Casualties, and Thefts), 1996, p. 1 contains the above examples.

[50] Rev. Rul. 79-174, 1979-1 C.B. 99 and *George K. Notter*, 1985 PH T.C.

Memo ¶85,391, 50 TCM 614. A graphic illustration of the controversy that may arise when determining whether an event is a casualty can be made by comparing the following two cases. In one case the taxpayer was washing dishes. Seeing a glass of water on the windowsill, he quickly dumped the contents down the drain and turned on the garbage disposal, not realizing that his wife's rings were in the glass. Damage to the rings in this case was deemed to be a casualty (*William H. Carpenter*, 1966 PH T.C. Memo ¶66,228, 25 TCM 1186). In the second case, the taxpayer gathered up some tissues from the night stand and flushed them down the toilet, not knowing that his wife's rings were wrapped in one of them. This event was held not to be a casualty (*W.J. Keenan, Jr. v. Bowers*, 39 AFTR 849, 50-2 USTC ¶9444 (D.C.-S.C., 1950)).

[51] Reg. Sec. 1.165-8(d).

[52] Rev. Rul. 72-112, 1972-1 C.B. 60 and IRS *Publication No. 547* (Nonbusiness Disasters, Casualties, and Thefts), 1996, p. 1.

[53] Reg. Sec. 1.165-7(a)(2).

because of fears that other mudslides might occur. The $30,000 reduction in the FMV of the cabin does not constitute a deductible casualty loss. ◄

Actual market value, not sentimental value, is used to compute the reduction in the FMV. Additionally, the cost of protecting property to prevent damage from a casualty is not a deductible loss.

If the property involved in the casualty is only partially destroyed, the amount of the loss is the lesser of the reduction in the property's FMV or the taxpayer's adjusted basis in the property.

EXAMPLE I8-21

TYPICAL MISCONCEPTION

It is sometimes thought that a taxpayer's loss should be based on the total economic loss rather than just the property's basis. It should be remembered that a taxpayer has not paid a tax on the appreciation in value, and therefore, should not be entitled to a deduction for a loss on the unrealized gain.

Troy purchased a home for $25,000 several years ago. Through the years, the value of the home appreciated until it was appraised at $125,000 in the current year. Shortly after the appraisal, a flood sweeps through the area, severely damaging Troy's home and reducing its value to $90,000. Troy does not have any flood insurance. His loss is limited to the $25,000 basis in the home even though the economic loss is $35,000 ($125,000 − $90,000). ◄

If business or investment property is totally destroyed in a casualty, the amount of the loss is the taxpayer's adjusted basis in the property, even if it is greater than the property's FMV. However, if personal-use property is totally destroyed, the amount of the loss is limited to the lesser of the reduction in the property's FMV or the property's adjusted basis.

EXAMPLE I8-22

A machine that Beth uses in her business is completely destroyed by fire. At the time of the fire, the adjusted basis of the machine is $5,000 and its FMV is $3,000. Because the machine is a business property, Beth's loss is $5,000. If the machine were a personal-use asset, the amount of the loss would be $3,000. ◄

The rules concerning deductibility of losses described above are summarized as follows:

	Deduction Based on Type of Property	
Result of Casualty	*Business or Investment*	*Personal-Use*
Total destruction	Basis of property	Lesser of basis or reduction in FMV
Partial destruction	Lesser of basis or reduction in FMV	Lesser of basis or reduction in FMV

Generally, the reduction in the FMV of the property is established by an appraisal. If an appraisal is difficult or impossible to obtain, the cost of the repairs may be used instead. All of the following requirements must be met before this alternative can be used:

▶ The repairs will bring the property back to its condition immediately before the casualty.

▶ The cost of the repairs is not excessive.

▶ The repairs do no more than repair the damage incurred in the casualty.

▶ The repairs do not increase the value of the property over its value immediately before the casualty.

If more than one property is destroyed in the same casualty, the loss on each property must be calculated separately.[54] Thus, each property's basis is compared with the

---

[54] Reg. Sec. 1.165-7(b)(2). For personal-use property, losses on real property and improvements to the property are computed in the aggregate. Thus, no separate basis need be apportioned to the improvements. See Reg. Secs. 1.165-7(b)(2)(ii) and 1.165-7(b)(3) Example (3).

reduction in the FMV of that property, rather than aggregating the basis and FMV amounts for all the properties destroyed in the casualty.

If the taxpayer receives insurance or any other type of recovery, the amount of the loss must be reduced by these amounts. In some cases these payments may actually exceed the taxpayer's basis in the property, causing the realization of a gain. If certain requirements are met, the recognition of these gains may be deferred or excluded. (See the detailed discussion of involuntary conversions in Chapter I12.)

LIMITATIONS ON PERSONAL-USE PROPERTY

HISTORICAL NOTE

The reduction in the amount of a taxpayer's casualty losses by 10% of AGI became effective in 1983.

The deductibility of casualty losses on personal-use property is subject to two limitations: the losses sustained in each separate casualty are reduced by $100, and the total amount of all net casualty losses for personal-use property is reduced by 10% of the taxpayer's AGI for the year.

EXAMPLE I8-23 ▶

A windstorm blows over a large tree in front of Cathy's house, damaging the house and totally destroying her automobile. After the insurance reimbursement, the loss on the house amounts to $3,000, and the loss on the automobile is $2,500. Because the losses occur in the same casualty, the total amount of the loss is reduced to $5,400 ($3,000 + $2,500 − $100). If the damage to the car was sustained in a separate event such as an automobile accident, the total amount of the casualty losses incurred by Cathy during the year would have been $5,300 ($3,000 + $2,500 − $200). This $5,300 loss is then further reduced by 10% of Cathy's AGI for the year. ◀

EXAMPLE I8-24
KEY POINT

Many taxpayers will not be able to deduct their casualty losses because of the $100 floor and 10% of AGI limitation.

As the result of a storm, Liz incurs a $4,500 casualty loss on personal-use property during the current year. She also sustains a $600 theft loss. Liz's AGI for the year is $50,000. She receives no tax deduction for the casualty and theft losses because they do not exceed the following limitations:

	Storm	Theft	Total
Loss before limitations	$4,500	$600	$5,100
Minus: $100 floor	(100)	(100)	(200)
	$4,400	$500	$4,900
Minus: 10% of AGI (0.10 × $50,000)			(5,000)
Deductible loss			0 ◀

ADDITIONAL COMMENT

Sometimes individuals fail to file insurance claims for damage to their personal automobile for fear that their insurance rates will increase, and hoping instead to deduct the loss. Because of this limitation, no deduction is available.

As a result of these limitations, many taxpayers who sustain casualty and theft losses on personal-use property do not receive a tax deduction. Furthermore, if the property is covered by insurance, no deduction is available for a casualty loss of personal-use property unless the taxpayer timely files an insurance claim for the loss.[55] This disallowance relates only to the portion of the loss that was covered by the insurance.

NETTING CASUALTY GAINS AND LOSSES ON PERSONAL-USE PROPERTY

TYPICAL MISCONCEPTION

The concept of a gain on a casualty is sometimes confusing. Nevertheless, if the insurance proceeds exceed the basis, a gain results.

Casualty gains and losses incurred during the year on personal-use assets are netted against each other rather than being combined with casualty gains and losses on business and investment property. For purposes of the netting process, the losses should be reduced by any insurance reimbursements and the $100 limitation, but not the 10% of AGI floor. If the gains exceed the losses for the year, all the gains and losses are treated as capital gains and losses. If the property has been held for one year or less, the gain or loss

---

[55] Sec. 165(h).

is short-term. If the property has been held for more than one year, the gain or loss is long term.

EXAMPLE I8-25 ▶ During the current year, Pat incurs the following casualty gains and losses on personal-use assets. Assets W and X are destroyed in one casualty, and asset Y is destroyed in another. Assets X and Y were acquired in the current year, whereas asset W was acquired several years ago.

Asset	Reduction in FMV	Adjusted Basis	Insurance	Holding Period
W	$10,000	$3,000	$10,000	More than one year
X	4,000	5,000	2,000	Less than one year
Y	2,000	3,000	0	Less than one year

A $7,000 ($10,000 − $3,000) gain is realized on asset W because the insurance proceeds received for the asset exceed its basis. A $2,000 ($4,000 reduction in FMV − $2,000 insurance) loss is realized on asset X. Because an overall gain of $5,000 ($7,000 gain for asset W and $2,000 loss on asset X) is realized as a result of the one casualty, the loss on asset X is not reduced by the $100 limitation. A $2,000 loss is realized on asset Y. Because an overall loss of $2,000 is realized as a result of the second casualty, the $100 limitation is deducted, resulting in a $1,900 loss from that casualty. A $3,100 ($5,000 − $1,900) net gain for the year has been realized. Thus, the gain or loss on each asset is treated as a capital gain or loss. Pat must report a $7,000 long-term capital gain on asset W, a $2,000 short-term capital loss on asset X, and a $1,900 short-term capital loss on asset Y. ◀

If the casualty losses on personal-use property exceed the casualty gains for the year, the net loss is further reduced by 10% of AGI. All of these calculations (the netting process and reductions) are done on Form 4684. If any loss remains after the netting and reductions, the loss is reported as an itemized deduction on Schedule A of Form 1040.

EXAMPLE I8-26 ▶ Assume the same facts as in Example I8-25, except that the loss on asset X amounts to $12,000 and that Pat's AGI for the year is $50,000. Because a $5,000 ($12,000 loss on asset X − $7,000 gain on asset W) loss is incurred in the first casualty, it must also be reduced by the $100 limitation. For the year, Pat has incurred a total loss of $6,800 ($4,900 + $1,900) due to the destruction by casualty of personal-use property. This loss is further reduced by 10% of AGI, or $5,000 (0.10 × $50,000). Pat's deductible loss for the year is $1,800 ($6,800 − $5,000), which is reported as an itemized deduction. The result would be the same if assets W and X were destroyed in separate casualties. ◀

CASUALTY GAINS AND LOSSES ATTRIBUTABLE TO BUSINESS AND INVESTMENT PROPERTY

Casualty gains and losses on business and investment property are netted. (See Chapter I13 for a discussion of the netting procedure under Sec. 1231.) If the losses exceed the gains, the business losses and losses on investment property that generate rents or royalties are *for* AGI deductions. Losses on other investment property (e.g., the theft of a security) are miscellaneous itemized deductions. Losses on business and investment property are not subject to the $100 or 10% of AGI limitations.

WHEN LOSSES ARE DEDUCTIBLE

In general, casualty losses must be deducted in the tax year in which the loss is sustained. In the following instances, however, the loss may be deducted in another year:

- ▶ Theft losses
- ▶ The receipt of insurance or other reimbursements that are reasonably expected to be received in a subsequent year
- ▶ Certain disaster losses (discussed later in this chapter)

THEFT. A theft loss is deducted in the tax year in which the theft is discovered. This rule is equitable and practical because a theft may not be discovered until a subsequent year.

EXAMPLE I8-27 ▶ Dale owns a hunting lodge in upstate New York. Sometime after his last trip to the lodge in November 1997, the lodge is broken into and several guns and paintings are stolen. The loss is discovered when Dale returns to the lodge on May 19, 1998. Dale's insurance does not cover the entire cost of the items. The loss is deductible in 1998, even though the theft may have occurred in 1997. ◀

INSURANCE AND OTHER REIMBURSEMENTS. Any reimbursement received as compensation for a loss must be subtracted in arriving at the amount of the loss. This is necessary even when the reimbursement has not yet been received, as long as there is a reasonable prospect that it will be received in the future. Thus no deduction is allowed in the year of loss if in that year a reasonable expectation of full recovery exists.[56] If full recovery is not anticipated, a loss may be deducted in the year the casualty occurs for the estimated unrecovered amount. As previously mentioned, no deduction is allowed to the extent the personal-use property is covered by insurance and the taxpayer does not file a timely insurance claim.

EXAMPLE I8-28 ▶ In December of the current year, Andrea suffers a $10,000 casualty loss when her personal automobile is struck by a city bus. Although she does not receive any reimbursement from the insurance company by December 31, there is a reasonable expectation that the full amount of the loss will be recovered. Andrea may not deduct a casualty loss in the current year. ◀

EXAMPLE I8-29 ▶ Assume the same facts as in Example I8-28, except that Andrea reasonably anticipates that her reimbursement from the insurance company will amount to only $7,000. In this case, her casualty loss in the current year is $3,000 (before reduction by the limitations). ◀

If the full amount of the anticipated recovery is not received in the subsequent year, the unrecovered portion may be deducted. However, rather than filing an amended return for the year of loss, the taxpayer deducts the loss in the subsequent year.[57] Thus in some cases, the income tax effects for a single casualty loss may be spread over two years.

EXAMPLE I8-30 ▶ During the current year, Javier's home is damaged by an exceptionally severe blast at a nearby stone quarry owned by Acme Corporation. Although the amount of the damage is properly appraised at $20,000, Javier can reasonably anticipate a recovery of only $15,000 from Acme Corporation at the end of the current year. He does not receive any recovery from Acme during the current year. Unfortunately, in the subsequent year Acme Corporation is declared bankrupt, and Javier does not receive any reimbursement. Javier's AGI is $40,000 in the current year and $45,000 in the subsequent year. During the current year, Javier may deduct $900 [$5,000 loss reasonably anticipated in the current year − [$100 limitation + (0.10 × $40,000)]] In the subsequent year, Javier may deduct an additional casualty loss of $10,500 [$15,000 additional loss − (0.10 × $45,000)]. ◀

---

[56] Reg. Sec. 1.165-1(d)(2)(i).　　　　[57] Reg. Sec. 1.165-1(d)(2)(ii).

If a subsequent recovery is received for a loss that is previously deducted, the reimbursement is included in income in the year of recovery. An amended return is not filed.[58] However, the amount that the taxpayer must include in income is limited to the amount of tax benefit the taxpayer received for the previous deduction.

EXAMPLE I8-31 ▶ During the current year, Becky's automobile sustains $5,000 in damages when it is struck by another automobile. The driver of the other automobile is at fault and is uninsured, and there is no reasonable prospect that Becky will recover any of the loss. Becky's AGI for the current year is $35,000. Becky deducts $1,400 ($5,000 loss − [$100 + $3,500]). During the subsequent year, the other driver reimburses Becky for the full amount of the damage. Because Becky received a tax benefit of only $1,400 for the loss in the year of the accident, only $1,400 must be included in gross income in the subsequent year, even though she receives a $5,000 reimbursement. Becky does not file an amended return for the year of the accident. ◀

REAL-WORLD EXAMPLE

Losses due to Hurricane Andrew in portions of southern Florida on August 24, 1992 and portions of Louisiana on August 26, 1992, qualified as disaster losses.

DISASTER LOSSES. Under certain circumstances, a taxpayer may elect to deduct a casualty loss in the year preceding the year in which the loss actually occurs. This election is available to taxpayers who suffer losses attributable to a disaster that occurs in an area subsequently declared by the President of the United States as a disaster area.[59] Thus, an individual can elect to deduct a disaster loss occurring in 1997 on his or her 1996 tax return or report it in the regular way on his or her 1997 return. An amended return (Form 1040X) must be filed unless the prior year's return has not been filed when the disaster occurs. This allows taxpayers the possibility of receiving financial help from potential tax refunds by filing an amendment to the prior year's return.

Casualty loss deduction rules are summarized in Topic Review I8-3.

STOP & THINK

Question: Due to unusually heavy rainfall in the Pacific Northwest during the current year, many homes, roads and other property were destroyed. Because of the tremendous destruction, the President of the United States declared the area a disaster area. One of the properties totally destroyed in a mudslide was Jack's mountain cabin in Oregon. Jack used the cabin exclusively for vacationing. The value of the cabin was $110,000. Unfortunately, the cabin was not insured against a mudslide. What issues must be considered in determining the year in which to take the casualty loss?

Solution: Since the property was destroyed in a disaster and is located in an area which the President subsequently declared as a disaster area, Jack may take the casualty deduction either in the year of the casualty or in the previous year. Which year is most beneficial is based on several factors. The destroyed property was personal use property, causing the deduction to be an itemized deduction subject to the 10% of AGI limitation. Thus, Jack must compare his estimated AGI for the current year with his AGI in the last year. He also should consider his other itemized deductions, including any other casualty losses. In addition, his marginal tax rates in the two years must be compared. Jack must consider the time value of money, since by taking the deduction on his prior year return, he will receive the tax benefit earlier than if he takes the deduction on the current year return.

---

[58] Reg. Sec. 1.165-1(d)(2)(iii).
[59] Sec. 165(i). Additionally, the same treatment may apply under Sec. 165 to taxpayers who live in a disaster area and who are ordered by a state or local government to move from or relocate their residence because the disaster caused the residence to be unsafe. In order to qualify for this treatment, the order to move must come from the state or local government within 120 days of the date that the President determines the area to be a disaster area. If the property destroyed in a presidentially declared disaster area is the taxpayer's principal residence and the casualty results in a gain, a portion of the gain may be excluded if certain conditions are met (see Chapter I12).

Topic Review I8-3

Casualty Losses

Type of Property	Limitation and Treatment
Personal-use	The amount of the loss is the lesser of the property's adjusted basis or the reduction of the asset's FMV. This amount is reduced by any insurance reimbursement. If the insurance reimbursement exceeds the property's basis, a gain is realized. To the extent the property is insured, a claim must be filed or the loss is disallowed.
	The amount of loss incurred in each separate casualty event during the year is reduced by $100.
	All casualty gains and losses for the year are netted. If the gains exceed the losses, all gains and losses are treated as either long-term or short-term capital gains and losses, depending on the holding period of the asset. If the losses exceed the gains, the net loss is reduced by 10% of AGI. Any remaining loss is an itemized deduction.
Business or investment	If the property is totally destroyed, the amount of the loss is the adjusted basis of the property. If only partially destroyed, the amount of the loss is the lesser of the property's adjusted basis or the reduction of the asset's FMV. This amount is reduced by any insurance reimbursement. A gain is realized if the insurance reimbursement exceeds the property's basis.
	For property held one year or less, the losses and gains are ordinary losses and gains. For property held over one year, the casualty gains and losses for the year are netted. The treatment depends on the total of the taxpayer's other Sec. 1231 transactions (see Chapter I13). Business casualty losses and losses on investment property that generate rents or royalties are not subject to the $100 or 10% of AGI limitations.

BAD DEBTS

In addition to losses on property, taxpayers may also sustain losses because of uncollectible debts. In dealing with a deduction for **bad debts,** taxpayers must address the following requirements and issues:

▶ A bona fide debtor-creditor relationship must exist between the taxpayer and some other person or entity.

▶ The taxpayer must have basis in the debt.

▶ The debt must actually have become worthless during the year.

▶ The type and timing of a bad debt deduction depend on whether the debt is a business or nonbusiness bad debt.

▶ Generally, only the specific write-off method of accounting may be used in deducting the bad debt.

▶ A partial or complete recovery of a debt that was previously deducted may occur. In many cases a recovery of this type causes income recognition in the year of the recovery.

BONA FIDE DEBTOR-CREDITOR RELATIONSHIP

Only items constituting bona fide debt are eligible to be deducted as a bad debt. A **bona fide debt** is one that arises from a valid and enforceable obligation to pay a fixed or determinable sum of money and results in a debtor-creditor relationship.[60]

RELATED-PARTY TRANSACTIONS. Determining whether a bona fide loan transaction has actually taken place is especially critical when the transaction is between the taxpayer and a family member or other related party (e.g., a controlled corporation). All the facts and circumstances surrounding the transaction must be carefully examined because a gift does not constitute a debt. The taxpayer's intent is critical here. For example, if the taxpayer's intent is to provide property, cash, or services to someone else without receiving any consideration in return, a gift—not a loan—has been made. Some tests used to determine the taxpayer's intent include the following:

▶ Is there a note or other written instrument evidencing the obligation to repay?[61]

▶ Has a definite schedule of repayment been established?

▶ Is a reasonable rate of interest stated?

▶ Would a person who is unrelated to the debtor make the loan?[62]

EXAMPLE I8-32

During the current year Maria loaned $20,000 to her son Sam, who used the money in his business. Although no written note or contract was signed, Sam orally promised to repay Maria as soon as his business became profitable. No rate of interest was stated. Unfortunately, the business failed and Sam went out of business in the subsequent year. No repayment of the loan principal or interest was ever made.

In this case, no valid debt exists because neither an interest rate nor a repayment schedule was established. An unrelated person would not have made a loan to Sam under these conditions. In addition, Maria does not receive any consideration in return for the "loan." Because the facts indicate that the transaction is actually a gift, Maria may not claim a bad debt deduction because of Sam's failure to repay. ◀

Other related party transactions must also be closely examined. For example, a loan from a shareholder to a controlled corporation may actually be an additional contribution to capital disguised as a loan. Thus, a transfer of cash by a shareholder who owns a controlling (i.e., more than 50%) interest in the stock of a corporation may indicate a capital contribution rather than a loan. Likewise, a loan from a corporation to a controlling shareholder may actually be a disguised dividend or a salary payment.

---

[60] Reg. Sec. 1.166-1(c).

[61] A written note or other instrument is an evidence of a bona fide debtor-creditor relationship. However, if the note or other instrument is registered or has interest coupons and is issued by a corporation or a government, the bad debt provisions of Sec. 166 do not apply. Instead, the worthless security provisions of Sec. 165 (previously discussed) apply.

[62] *Jean C. Tyler v. Tomlinson*, 24 AFTR 2d 69-5426, 69-2 USTC ¶9559 (5th Cir., 1969). See also, *C. L. Hunt*, 1989 PH T.C. Memo ¶89,335, 57 TCM 919, where certain loans that the taxpayer made to his children were treated as bona fide loans, whereas others were treated as gifts. In that case, the children had been trading in silver futures and were required to make margin calls. Because they could not make the calls, the children's positions were involuntarily liquidated. Up to the date of the liquidation, the taxpayer had made loans to the children that were payable on demand and were subject to the prime rate of interest. These loans were evidenced by promissory notes. After the liquidation, the taxpayer continued to make loans to the children. However, these loans were not evidenced by notes. The loans up to the time of the liquidation were treated as bona fide loans and the subsequent loans were treated as gifts.

THIRD PARTY DEBT. Generally, a taxpayer may deduct a bad debt only when a debtor-creditor relationship exists. However, in some cases a taxpayer will guarantee or endorse someone else's obligation. If the taxpayer is forced to pay the third party's debt under the terms of the guarantee, the guarantor may actually be treated as the creditor. If the original debtor does not repay the taxpayer who guarantees and pays the debt, the guarantor may deduct the loss. Any accrued interest that the guarantor pays may also be deductible as a bad debt. However, the interest is not deductible as interest when paid by the guarantor because it accrued on someone else's debt. Here, too, the taxpayer's intent must be examined to determine whether the guarantee and payment constitute a gift.

EXAMPLE I8-33 ▶ Ron is the sole shareholder and a full-time employee of Zip Corporation. In order for Zip Corporation to obtain a bank loan, Ron personally signs a guarantee that the loan would be repaid. Unfortunately, Zip Corporation defaults on the loan and Ron is required to repay the loan. In this case, Ron signed the guarantee to preserve his job and enhance his investment in Zip Corporation. Although Ron receives no direct consideration for having signed the note, he does receive indirect consideration in the form of continued job security and protection of his investment. Because the loan guarantee was motivated by a business or investment purpose, Ron may deduct the bad debt. ◀

TAXPAYER'S BASIS IN THE DEBT

TYPICAL MISCONCEPTION

It is sometimes mistakenly assumed that a cash method taxpayer can take a bad debt deduction on a debt that arose from services rendered by the taxpayer.

For a bad debt to be deductible, the creditor must have a basis in the debt. This basis may be acquired in different ways. If a taxpayer loans money, the taxpayer's basis in the debt is the amount loaned. If the debt arises because the taxpayer provides property or services for the other party, basis is established only if the taxpayer has previously included the FMV of the property or services in income. This often depends on the taxpayer's method of accounting. An accrual-method taxpayer generally reports income in the year the services are performed or the property is provided. (See the discussion in Chapter I11.) Thus, an accrual-method taxpayer has a basis in either a note receivable or an open account receivable equal to the amount included in gross income (i.e., the FMV of the services). A cash-method taxpayer, however, reports income only in the year in which payment in the form of cash or property is received. Because a note constitutes the receipt of property, a cash-basis taxpayer reports income in the year the note is received, and therefore has a basis in the note receivable.[63] However, if no note is received and the receivable is an open account item, a cash-method taxpayer reports no income until the receivable is collected. Thus, no basis is established in the receivable, and if it cannot be collected, no bad debt deduction is available.

EXAMPLE I8-34 ▶ In October of the current year, Jim performs some legal services for Joy. Jim bills Joy for $1,000. Joy does not sign a note for the debt. As a cash-method taxpayer, Jim does not include the $1,000 in his current year's income. After repeated efforts to collect the fee, Jim discovers in June of the subsequent year that Joy has left the city and cannot be found. Thus, Jim may not deduct a bad debt for the uncollected amount in the subsequent year. If Joy had signed a note for the debt, Jim would have reported income in the current year in an amount equal to the note's FMV and could have deducted the loss when the note became uncollectible in the subsequent year. ◀

DEBT MUST BE WORTHLESS

To deduct a bad debt, the taxpayer must show that the debt is worthless. This determination is made by reference to all the pertinent evidence, including the general financial condition of the debtor and whether the debt is secured by collateral.

---

[63] Reg. Sec. 1.166-1(e).

In proving the worthlessness of a debt, a taxpayer does not need to take legal action if the surrounding circumstances indicate that legal action probably would not result in the collection of the debt. Simply showing that legal action is not warranted is sufficient proof that the debt is worthless.[64] Indications that an unsecured debt is worthless include bankruptcy of the debtor, disappearance or death of a debtor, and repeated unsuccessful attempts at collection. Furthermore, if the surrounding circumstances warrant it, a debt may be deducted as worthless even before it comes due.[65] As will be explained later in this chapter, a nonbusiness debt must be totally worthless before a deduction is allowed. However, a current deduction is allowed for a partially worthless business bad debt.

NONBUSINESS BAD DEBTS

The distinction between a business bad debt and a nonbusiness bad debt is important because the character of the debt determines its tax treatment. A business bad debt gives rise to an ordinary deduction, whereas a nonbusiness bad debt is treated as a short-term capital loss. All loans made by a corporation are assumed to be associated with the corporation's business; therefore, the provisions for nonbusiness bad debts do not apply to corporations.

DEFINITION OF A NONBUSINESS BAD DEBT. A *nonbusiness debt* is defined as any debt other than (1) a debt created or acquired in connection with a trade or business of the taxpayer, or (2) a debt the loss from the worthlessness of which is incurred in the taxpayer's trade or business.[66] This determination depends on an examination of the facts and circumstances surrounding the debt in question.

A debt incurred in a taxpayer's business continues to be a business debt for that taxpayer even though at the time the debt goes bad, the taxpayer has ceased conducting that particular business. This is situation (1) above. If another taxpayer acquires a business, any outstanding debt at the time the business is acquired continues to be business debt as long as the purchaser continues the business. This is situation (2) above. The debt is a nonbusiness debt if the person who owns the debt when it becomes worthless is not engaged in the business in which the debt is incurred either at the time the debt arose or when it becomes worthless.

EXAMPLE I8-35 ▶

Matt, an individual who uses the accrual method of accounting, is engaged in the grocery business. During 1997, he extends credit to Jeff on an open account. In 1998 Matt sells his business to Joan, but retains Jeff's account. Jeff's account becomes worthless in 1998. Even though Matt is no longer engaged in the grocery business at the time the debt becomes worthless, he may deduct the loss as a business bad debt in 1998. If Joan purchases Jeff's account upon acquiring the grocery business, Joan is entitled to a business bad debt deduction in 1998 because the debt was incurred in the trade or business in which Joan is currently engaged. ◀

In addition, classification as a business debt requires a proximate relationship between the debt and the taxpayer's business.[67] According to the Supreme Court, this relationship exists if a business motive is the taxpayer's dominant motivation in incurring the debt. This determination must be made on a case-by-case basis. For example, when an individual stockholder who is also an employee of the corporation loans money to the corporation, is the loan a business or nonbusiness debt? Because an employee is considered to be engaged in the business of working for a corporation, a loan made to the corporation in an attempt to protect the

---

[64] Reg. Sec. 1.166-2.
[65] Reg. Sec. 1.166-1(c).

[66] Sec. 166(d)(2).
[67] Reg. Sec. 1.166-5(b)(2).

employment relationship may be held to be a business debt. However, if the individual's dominant motive is to protect his or her stock investment, the loan is a nonbusiness debt.[68]

EXAMPLE I8-36 ▶

Lisa is an individual engaged in the advertising business. If clients occasionally need additional funds to meet their cash-flow obligations, Lisa sometimes lends them money. Lisa's dominant motive for making the loans is to retain the clients. She has no ownership interests in these clients. Under these facts, if any of these loans becomes worthless, it would be considered a business bad debt.[69] ◀

KEY POINT

The nonbusiness bad debt of an individual is treated as a short-term capital loss regardless of how long the debt was outstanding.

TAX TREATMENT. Nonbusiness debts that become wholly worthless during the year are deductible by individuals as short-term capital losses.[70] The length of time the debt is outstanding has no bearing on this treatment.

For individuals, an ordinary deduction is generally preferable to a short-term capital loss because the tax deduction attributable to net capital losses is limited to $3,000 each year. Any loss in excess of this limit is carried over to subsequent years to be included in the capital gain and loss netting process in those years (see Chapter I5).

EXAMPLE I8-37

TYPICAL MISCONCEPTION

Partial worthlessness means that a debt is still partially recoverable. The term is sometimes erroneously applied to debt where there has been a partial recovery even though there is no prospect for further recovery.

During 1996, Kim loaned her friend $10,000. The friend used the funds to invest in commodities futures. The transaction had all the characteristics of a bona fide debt rather than a mere gift to a friend. Unfortunately, the commodities market prices declined, and Kim's friend incurred substantial losses. In 1997, Kim's friend declared personal bankruptcy and Kim was unable to collect any of the loan. Kim did not recognize any other capital gains or losses during 1997. The $10,000 bad debt loss recognized in 1997 is treated as a short-term capital loss. Thus, Kim may deduct only $3,000 in 1997. The remaining $7,000 is carried over indefinitely to 1998 and subsequent years. ◀

PARTIAL WORTHLESSNESS. As previously noted, no deduction is allowed for a partially worthless nonbusiness debt. Thus, no deduction is allowed for a nonbusiness debt that is still partially recoverable during the year.[71]

EXAMPLE I8-38 ▶

Gordon, an individual, made a $5,000, five-year interest-bearing loan to a small company in 1993. Gordon was not in the trade or business of making commercial loans. In 1997, Gordon received word from the attorney who was appointed trustee of the company that bankruptcy proceedings had been filed. The trustee indicated that although final disposition of the case will not occur until 1998, Gordon can reasonably expect to receive only 20 cents for every $1 invested. Because this is a nonbusiness bad debt that is still partly recoverable in 1997, Gordon may not deduct the partial loss as a short-term capital loss in 1997. ◀

BUSINESS BAD DEBTS

The tax treatment of losses from business bad debts differs substantially from the treatment of nonbusiness bad debts. As previously discussed, a business bad debt is deductible as an ordinary loss. Furthermore, a deduction may also be taken for a business debt that has become only partially worthless during the year.

EXAMPLE I8-39 ▶

Assume the same facts as in Example I8-38 except that Gordon's loan is made for business reasons (e.g., to provide assistance to a customer in financial difficulty). Because 80% of the

---

[68] *John M. Trent v. CIR*, 7 AFTR 2d 1599, 61-2 USTC ¶9506 (2nd Cir., 1961). See also *Charles L. Hutchinson*, 1982 PH T.C. Memo ¶82,045, 43 TCM 440 and *U.S. v. Edna Generes*, 29 AFTR 2d 72-609, 72-1 USTC ¶9259 (USSC, 1972).

[69] *Stuart Bart*, 21 T.C. 880 (1954), *acq.* 1954-1 C.B. 3.
[70] Sec. 166(d)(1).
[71] Reg. Sec. 1.166-5(a)(2).

loan is reasonably expected to be unrecoverable during 1997, Gordon may deduct $4,000 (0.80 × $5,000) as an ordinary loss in 1997. In 1998, when Gordon receives the $500 settlement, he may deduct an additional $500 of ordinary loss. ◄

ACCOUNTING FOR THE BUSINESS BAD DEBT

Before 1987, two basic methods were available to account for business bad debts: the specific write-off method and the reserve method. Except for certain specialized industries, however, only the specific write-off method may be used for tax years beginning after 1986. Under the **specific write-off method**, the taxpayer deducts each bad debt individually as it becomes worthless. This method is used for (1) business bad debts that are either totally or partially worthless and (2) nonbusiness bad debts that are totally worthless. However, as previously noted, no deduction is available for partially worthless nonbusiness bad debts.

In the case of a partially worthless business bad debt, only the worthless part of the debt is deductible. The taxpayer must prove to the satisfaction of the IRS the amount of the debt that has become worthless.[72]

RECOVERY OF BAD DEBTS

A taxpayer may collect a debt that was previously written off for tax purposes. As noted previously, the taxpayer must report the recovery as income in the year it is collected. The amount of the income that must be reported may depend on the tax benefit rule discussed in Chapter I4.

DEPOSITS IN INSOLVENT FINANCIAL INSTITUTIONS

At their election, qualified individuals may treat losses on deposits in qualified bankrupt or insolvent financial institutions as a personal casualty loss in the year in which the loss can be reasonably estimated. The recognized loss is the difference between the taxpayer's basis in the deposit and a reasonable estimate of the amount that will be received. This treatment allows the individual an ordinary loss deduction, but subjects the loss to the personal casualty loss limitations. In lieu of this election, qualified individuals may elect to treat these losses as if they were incurred in a transaction entered into for profit (but not connected with a trade or business). This election is available only with respect to deposits that are not insured under federal law, and is limited to $20,000 ($10,000 if married and filing separately) per institution per year. This limitation is reduced by any insurance proceeds expected to be received under state law. This election also allows the individual an ordinary loss deduction but subjects the loss to the $20,000 limitation as well as the 2% of AGI floor on miscellaneous itemized deductions. If neither of these elections is made, the loss may be claimed as a nonbusiness bad debt (a capital loss) in the year of worthlessness or partial recovery, whichever comes last.

A qualified individual is any individual *except* one who

▶ Owns at least 1% of the outstanding stock of the financial institution

▶ Is an officer of the financial institution

▶ Is a relative of an officer or a 1% owner of the financial institution[73]

Qualified financial institutions include banks, federal or state chartered savings and loans and thrift institutions, and federal or state insured credit unions.

---

[72] Reg. Sec. 1.166-3(a)(2).
[73] Sec. 165(l). A *relative* is defined as a sibling, spouse, aunt, uncle, nephew, niece, ancestor, or lineal descendant.

Topic Review I8-4

Bad Debts

Type of Debt	Results
Nonbusiness	Deductible as a short-term capital loss.
	Deductible only when the debt is totally worthless.
	The taxpayer must have basis in the debt.
Business	Deductible as an ordinary loss.
	Except for certain specialized exceptions, the specific write-off method must be used. The reserve method is not available.
	May deduct partial worthlessness.
	Must have basis in the debt.

This election applies to all losses sustained by the individual in the same institution and cannot be revoked unless the taxpayer receives IRS permission.[74]

The treatment of business and nonbusiness bad debts is summarized in Topic Review I8-4.

NET OPERATING LOSSES

A **net operating loss (NOL)** under Sec. 172 generally involves only business income and expenses and occurs when taxable income for any year is negative because business expenses exceed business income. A deduction for the NOL arises when it is carried to a year in which the taxpayer has taxable income and is deducted from that year's income. This is accomplished in one of two ways:

▶ The year's NOL is carried back and deducted from the income of a previous year. This procedure provides for a refund of some of the taxes previously paid for the prior year.

▶ The year's NOL is carried forward and deducted from the income of a subsequent year. This procedure provides a reduction in the taxable income of the subsequent year, thus reducing the tax liability associated with that year.

The NOL deduction is intended to mitigate the inequity caused by the progressive rate structure and the requirement to report income on an annual basis. This inequity arises between taxpayers whose business income fluctuates widely from year to year and those whose business income remains relatively constant.

KEY POINT

If taxpayers were not entitled to a deduction for net operating losses, taxpayers would actually pay a tax on an amount that exceeded their economic income over a period of time. The NOL deduction permits taxpayers to offset taxable income with losses incurred in other years.

EXAMPLE I8-40 ▶

Julie and Ken are both married (not to each other) and both file a joint return with their respective spouses. Over a two-year period they both report a total of $140,000 in taxable income. However, Julie reports $70,000 of taxable income each year; Ken reports $200,000 of taxable income in the first year and a $60,000 loss in the second year. Without the NOL provisions, Julie would report a $28,488 ($14,244 × 2) total tax liability for both years, whereas Ken would report a $56,069 (taxable income of $200,000) total liability.[75] However, Ken can carryback the $60,000 loss to recover a portion of the taxes paid on the $200,000 in

---

[74] The rules dealing with this special election are found in Notice 89-28, (1989-1 C.B. 667).

[75] Using the 1997 tax rate schedules.

the prior year. Based on 1997 rates, Ken would recover $21,013 of the $56,069 paid, resulting in a net tax liability for both years of $35,056 ($56,069 − $21,013). The ability to carryover NOL's provides some degree of fairness to the tax law.   ◄

COMPUTING THE NET OPERATING LOSS

The starting point in calculating an individual's NOL is generally taxable income. As mentioned earlier in this chapter, individuals may deduct three basic types of expenses to arrive at the amount of taxable income: business-related expenses, investment-related expenses, and certain personal expenses. The NOL, however, generally attempts to measure only the economic loss that occurs when business expenses exceed business income. Thus, several adjustments must be made to taxable income to arrive at the amount of the NOL for any particular year.[76] These include adjustments for an NOL deduction, a capital loss deduction, the deduction for personal exemptions, and the excess of nonbusiness deductions over nonbusiness income.

ADDITIONAL COMMENT

If taxpayers were permitted to calculate the NOL for the current year by including NOL carryovers from earlier years, it would be possible to extend the carryover period beyond 15 years.

ADD BACK ANY NOL DEDUCTION. Under certain circumstances, a deduction for an NOL arising from another tax year might have been taken in computing the taxable income for the current loss year. To allow this deduction to create or increase the NOL of the current loss year would provide an unwarranted benefit. Thus, taxable income for the current loss year must be increased for this deduction.[77]

ADD BACK ANY CAPITAL LOSS DEDUCTION. To compute taxable income, individuals may deduct up to a maximum of $3,000 capital losses in excess of capital gains in any year. Any capital loss in excess of this limit can be carried over and deducted in a subsequent tax year, subject to the same limitation. Because capital losses have their separate carryover provisions, any deduction associated with these losses must be added back to taxable income to arrive at the NOL for the current loss year. To make this adjustment, several steps must be followed:

Step 1:   A taxpayer must separate nonbusiness capital gains and losses from business capital gains and losses. The nonbusiness gains and losses are then netted, while the business gains and losses are netted separately.

Step 2:   If the nonbusiness capital gains exceed the nonbusiness capital losses, the excess, along with other types of nonbusiness income, is first used to offset any nonbusiness ordinary deductions. Any nonbusiness capital gain remaining is then used to offset any business capital loss in excess of the business capital gain for the year.[78]

Step 3:   If both groups of transactions result in net losses, the capital loss deduction provided by these transactions must be added back. For purposes of the NOL, no deduction is allowed for either business or nonbusiness net capital losses.

Step 4:   If the taxpayer's nonbusiness capital losses exceed the nonbusiness capital gains, the losses may not be offset against the taxpayer's excess business capital gains. Allowing this offset would provide an indirect deduction for a nonbusiness economic loss.[79]

EXAMPLE I8-41   ▶   During the current year, Nils recognizes a short-term capital loss of $10,000 on the sale of an investment capital asset. He also recognizes a $5,000 long-term capital gain on the sale of a

---

[76] In the case of a corporation, these adjustments are minor.

[77] Sec. 172(d)(1).

[78] Reg. Sec. 1.172-3. If the nonbusiness deductions exceed the nonbusiness income, the excess is added back. This adjustment is discussed later in the chapter.

[79] Sec. 172(d)(2). Note that all deductible nonbusiness capital losses involve investment property, because capital losses on personal-use assets are not deductible in arriving at taxable income. To make the adjustment for any capital loss, the exclusion under Sec. 1202 for gains from small business stock is not allowed (see Chapter I5).

business capital asset. For taxable income purposes, the loss is netted against the gain, leaving a $5,000 net short-term capital loss. This loss provides a $3,000 deduction from taxable income, with the remaining $2,000 being carried forward to the following year. To compute the NOL, however, none of the $10,000 nonbusiness capital loss is deductible. Thus, the $3,000 deduction as well as the $5,000 loss that offset the business capital gain must be added back. ◄

ADD BACK THE DEDUCTION FOR PERSONAL EXEMPTIONS. Because the deduction for personal and dependency exemptions is strictly a personal deduction, it must be added back to arrive at the year's NOL.

ADD BACK EXCESS OF NONBUSINESS DEDUCTIONS OVER NONBUSINESS INCOME. Because nonbusiness deductions do not reflect an economic loss from business, they are not deductible in arriving at the NOL. However, these deductions do offset any nonbusiness income reported during the year. Nonbusiness income includes sources of income such as dividends and interest, as well as nonbusiness capital gains in excess of nonbusiness capital losses.[80] Wages and salary, even if they are earned in part-time employment, are considered business income. Nonbusiness deductions include itemized deductions such as charitable contributions, medical expenses, and nonbusiness interest and taxes. Casualty losses on personal-use assets, however, are treated as business losses and are excluded from this adjustment.[81] If a taxpayer does not have itemized deductions in excess of the standard deduction, the standard deduction is used as the amount of the nonbusiness deductions.

Following are several independent examples demonstrating these required adjustments. In each case, assume that Nancy is a single taxpayer.

ADDITIONAL COMMENT

An excess of nonbusiness deductions over nonbusiness income cannot increase the NOL. However, an excess of nonbusiness income over nonbusiness expenses can reduce the NOL.

EXAMPLE 18-42 ▶

During 1997 Nancy, who is single, reports the following taxable income:

Gross income from business		$123,000	
Minus: Business expenses		(147,000)	($24,000)
Plus: Interest income			700
Dividend income			400
AGI			($22,900)
Minus: Greater of itemized deductions or standard deduction:			
Interest expense		$2,000	
Taxes		2,500	
Casualty loss (reduced by the $100 floor)		1,000	
Total itemized deductions		$5,500	
		or	
Standard deduction		4,150	(5,500)
Minus: Personal exemption			(2,650)
Taxable income			($31,050)

Nancy's NOL for the year is computed as follows:

Taxable income			($31,050)
Nonbusiness deductions:			
Itemized deductions	$5,500		
Minus: Casualty loss	(1,000)	$4,500	

---

[80] Reg. Sec. 1.172-3(c).   [81] Sec. 172(d)(4)(C).

Minus:	Nonbusiness income:			
	Interest	$700		
	Dividends	400	(1,100)	
Plus:	Excess of nonbusiness deductions over nonbusiness income			3,400
Plus:	Personal exemption			2,650
Net operating loss				($25,000)[a] ◄

[a]Note that the NOL equals the total of the $24,000 net business loss and the $1,000 casualty loss.

EXAMPLE I8-43 ▶ During 1997 Nancy, who is single, reports the following taxable income:

Gross income from business		$123,000		
Minus:	Business expenses	(147,000)		($24,000)
Plus:	Interest income			700
	Dividend income			400
AGI				($22,900)
Minus:	Greater of itemized deductions or standard deduction:			
	Interest expense		$ 2,000	
			or	
	Standard deduction		4,150	(4,150)
Minus:	Personal exemption			(2,650)
Taxable income				($29,700)

Nancy's NOL for the year is computed as follows:

Taxable income				($29,700)
Nonbusiness deductions:				
Standard deduction			$4,150	
Minus:	Nonbusiness income:			
	Interest	$700		
	Dividends	400	(1,100)	
Plus:	Excess of nonbusiness deductions over nonbusiness income			3,050
Plus:	Personal exemption			2,650
Net operating loss				($24,000)[a] ◄

[a]Note that the NOL equals the net business loss for the year.

EXAMPLE I8-44 ▶ During 1997 Nancy, who is single, reports the following taxable income:

Gross income from business		$123,000	
Minus:	Business expenses	(147,000)	($24,000)
Plus:	Interest income		700
	Dividend income		400
	Salary		6,000
	Nonbusiness LTCG		4,000
AGI			($12,900)
Minus:	Greater of itemized deductions or standard deduction:		

Interest expense		$ 2,000	
Taxes		2,500	
Casualty (reduced by the $100 floor)		1,000	
Total itemized deductions		$5,500	
		or	
Standard deduction		4,150	(5,500)
Minus: Personal exemption			(2,650)
Taxable income			($21,050)

Nancy's NOL for the year is computed as follows:

Taxable income			($21,050)
Plus: Nonbusiness deductions:			
Itemized deductions	$5,500		
Reduced by: Casualty loss	(1,000)	$4,500	
Minus: Nonbusiness income:			
Interest	$700		
Dividends	400		
LTCG	4,000	(5,100)	
Excess of nonbusiness deductions over nonbusiness income			0
Plus: Personal exemption			2,650
Net operating loss			($18,400)[a] ◀

[a]Note that the NOL can also be calculated as follows:

Loss from business	($24,000)
Salary	6,000
Casualty loss	(1,000)
Excess of nonbusiness income ($5,100) over nonbusiness deductions ($4,500)	600
NOL	($18,400)

CARRYBACK AND CARRYOVER PERIODS

HISTORICAL NOTE

The carryover period for an NOL was extended from five years to seven years in 1976 and from seven years to 15 years in 1981.

Under Sec. 172, an NOL is initially carried back for three years and is deductible as an offset to the taxable income of the carryback years. Except as noted below, the loss must be carried back first. If any loss remains, it may then be carried forward for a period of 15 years. Furthermore, in both the carryback and carryforward periods, the loss must be deducted from the years in chronological order. Thus, if an NOL is sustained in 1997, it first must be carried to 1994, then to 1995, followed by 1996, 1998, and so on until the loss is completely used. Any NOL that is not used during the carryover period expires and is of no further tax benefit.

If the NOL is carried back to a prior year, the taxpayer must file for a refund of taxes previously paid. If the NOL deduction is carried forward, it reduces the taxable income for the carryover year.

ADDITIONAL COMMENT

An election to forgo the carryback period for the NOL is irrevocable.

ELECTION TO FORGO CARRYBACK PERIOD. A taxpayer may elect not to carryback the NOL and to carry the loss forward.[82] This election, which is made with respect to the entire carryback period, does not extend the carryforward period beyond 15 years. This allows a taxpayer some degree of flexibility in using the NOL deduction to

[82] Sec. 172(b)(3)(C).

the greatest advantage. (See the Tax Planning Considerations section in this chapter for a discussion of this topic.)

LOSS CARRYOVERS FROM TWO OR MORE YEARS. At times, a taxpayer might have NOL carryovers that are incurred in two or more taxable years. Often these losses are carried to the same years in the carryover period. If such is the case, the loss of the earliest year is always completely used first before deducting any of the loss incurred in a subsequent year. Because of the limited carryover period, this rule is beneficial to the taxpayer.

RECOMPUTATION OF TAXABLE INCOME IN THE CARRYOVER YEAR

When the NOL deduction is carried back to a prior year, that year's taxable income must be recomputed. Because the NOL is attributable to a taxpayer's trade or business, it is deductible *for* AGI. As a result, the recomputation of taxable income for the carryback year may affect the deductible amount of certain itemized deductions because some of the deductions (e.g., the deductions for medical expenses, charitable contributions, and casualty losses) are limited or measured by reference to the taxpayer's AGI. All of these deductions except the deduction for charitable contributions must be recomputed using the reduced AGI amount.[83]

Once the tax refund for the carryback year is determined, the amount of the NOL available to be deducted in subsequent carryover years must be calculated. This is done by adjusting the recomputed income of the prior carryover year. Although certain differences exist, these adjustments are similar to those mentioned above.

The rules for computing and deducting NOLs are presented in Topic Review I8-5.

TAX PLANNING CONSIDERATIONS

BAD DEBTS

In order to deduct a bad debt, a taxpayer must show that the debt is worthless. At times the IRS might assert that the debt being written off is either not yet worthless or that it became worthless in a previous year. If the taxpayer is unable to overcome the IRS's assertion concerning the year of worthlessness, the taxpayer might be barred from filing an amended return for the prior year because of the statute of limitations.[84] Thus, taxpayers should carefully document all efforts at collection and other facts that show the debt is worthless.

As previously mentioned, a third-party guarantor of a loan who is required to repay the debt may, under certain circumstances, be entitled to a bad debt deduction. The guarantor must demonstrate that he or she received reasonable consideration in the form of cash or property in exchange for guaranteeing the debt. If proper consideration is not received, the guarantee and subsequent payment of the loan by the guarantor is considered to be a gift rather than a loan. Reasonable consideration is also deemed to have been received if the taxpayer enters into the agreement for a good faith business purpose or in accordance with normal business practice. However, if the taxpayer guarantees the debt of a spouse or a relative, the consideration must be received in the form of cash or property.

KEY POINT

If there is uncertainty as to the year in which a debt became worthless, it is possible that the issue will not be settled within the normal three-year statute of limitations. For this reason, a taxpayer may claim a deduction for a worthless debt at any time within seven years.

---

[83] Reg. Sec. 1.172-5(a)(3)(ii).
[84] However, the statute of limitations for claims for a refund or credit because of a bad debt is extended from three years to seven years under Sec. 6511(d)(1), thus giving the taxpayer additional time if this is the case.

Topic Review I8-5

Net Operating Losses

Item	Rules
Computation of NOL (adjustments to taxable income)	Add back any NOL deduction carried to the current year.
	Add back any capital loss deduction.
	Add back the deduction for personal and dependency exemptions.
	Add back the excess of nonbusiness deductions over nonbusiness income. For this purpose, casualty losses on personal-use property are treated as business losses.
Carryover period	May be carried back three years and forward fifteen years.
	Must be carried to the carryover years in chronological order: first carried back to the third prior year, then to the second prior year, then to the first prior year, then to the first succeeding year, etc.
	An election may be made to forgo the carryback. This does not extend the carryforward period.
	If losses from two or more years are carried to the same year, the losses from the earliest year are completely used first.

In the case of an outright loan between related taxpayers, the lender should always make sure that proper documentation is retained to substantiate the fact that the transaction is a loan. If such documentation is not kept, the IRS may assert that the transaction is a gift.

CASUALTIES

A deduction is allowed for stolen property, but no deduction is allowed for lost property. Thus, taxpayers should always carefully document losses of property through theft (e.g., the filing of police reports or claims with the taxpayer's insurance company). In addition, pictures and written appraisals may be helpful to prove the amount of the loss.

ADDITIONAL COMMENT

Normally, a taxpayer would want to carry back the NOL because he or she will receive a refund in a short time period from the filing of the amended return. The carryover of the NOL involves waiting for a year or more to receive a tax benefit.

NET OPERATING LOSSES

If a net operating loss is incurred, the taxpayer should carefully analyze whether to elect to forgo the carryback period. Situations under which a taxpayer might elect to only carry the loss deduction forward include the following:

▶ A taxpayer might anticipate being in a higher marginal tax rate in future years than in the carryback years. If such is the case, the value of the deduction is higher in the carryforward years than in the carryback years. Consideration should be given, however, to cash flows and the time value of money (e.g., the tax benefits from a refund of taxes are immediately available only if the NOL is carried back).

▶ General business and other tax credits that are nonrefundable (i.e., the credits are limited to the tax liability or some percentage thereof) may be reduced or eliminated for the carryback years because these credits must be recomputed based on the adjusted tax liability after applying the NOL carryback. (See Chaper 14 for a discussion of tax credits.)

COMPLIANCE AND PROCEDURAL CONSIDERATIONS

CASUALTY LOSSES

If a taxpayer sustains a casualty loss in a location that the President of the United States declares a disaster area, an election may be made to deduct the loss in the year preceeding the year in which the loss occurred. This election is made by either filing the return for the previous year and including the loss in that year (if the return has not already been filed) or filing an amended return or claim for refund for that year.[85] The return should clearly include all the following information:

▶ That the election is being made

▶ The date of the disaster giving rise to the loss

▶ The city, county, and state in which the damaged property is located

The election must be made before the due date of the return for the year in which the disaster actually occurs. Although the Regulations state that the election may not be revoked more than 90 days after it is made, the Tax Court has held that this part of the Regulation is invalid.[86]

NET OPERATING LOSSES

If a taxpayer carries an NOL deduction back to a prior year, a claim for refund of taxes is filed by either filing an amended return on Form 1040X or filing for a quick refund on Form 1045. Corporations use Form 1139. If Form 1045 is used, the IRS must act on the application for refund within 90 days of the later of the date of the application and the last day of the month in which the return of the loss year must be filed.[87] Form 1045 must be filed within a year after the end of the year in which the NOL arose. Additional information such as pages 1 and 2 of Form 1040 for the year of loss, a copy of the application for an extension of time to file the return for the year of loss, and copies of forms or schedules for items refigured in the carryback years must be attached.

WORTHLESS SECURITIES

As explained earlier in this chapter, securities that become worthless during the taxable year are deemed to have become worthless on the last day of the year. In most cases, this treatment causes the loss to be treated as a long-term capital loss. If the loss from the worthless security is long term, it is reported in Part II of Schedule D (Form 1040) along with the taxpayer's other long-term gains and losses for the year. Short-term capital losses are reported in Part I of Schedule D.

---

[85] Reg. Sec. 1.165-11(e).
[86] *Chester Matheson*, 74 T.C. 836 (1980), *acq.* 1981-2 C.B. 2.
[87] IRS, *Instructions for Filing Form 1045*, Revised, 1995.

PROBLEM MATERIALS

DISCUSSION QUESTIONS

I8-1 What is the closed transaction doctrine, and why does it exist for purposes of recognizing a loss realized on holding property?

I8-2 When property is disposed of, what factors influence the amount of the deductible loss?

I8-3 Describe the usual tax consequences that apply to a worthless security.

I8-4 Under what circumstances will a loss that is realized on a worthless security not be treated as a capital loss?

I8-5 What two general requirements must be met for a transaction to result in a capital loss?

I8-6 What requirements must be met for stock to be considered Sec. 1244 stock?

I8-7 What tax treatment applies to gains and losses on Sec. 1244 stock?

I8-8 Describe a situation where a loss on the sale of business or investment property is not currently deductible, and explain why.

I8-9 a. What is a passive activity?
b. Who is subject to the passive loss limitation rules?

I8-10 a. For purposes of the passive loss rules, what is a closely held C corporation?
b. In what way do the passive loss rules differ from the regular passive loss rules when applied to closely held C corporations?

I8-11 Why is it important to identify exactly what constitutes an activity for purposes of the passive activity rules?

I8-12 a. If a taxpayer is involved in several different business operations during the year, how is the determination made as to how many activities these operations constitute for purposes of the passive activity loss rules?

b. Can a business operation and a rental operation ever be combined into one activity? Explain.

I8-13 Which of the following activities are considered passive for the year? Explain. Consider each situation independently.
a. Laura owns a rental unit that she rents out to students. The rental unit is Laura's only business and she spends approximately 875 hours per year managing, collecting the rent, advertising, and performing minor repairs. At times she must hire professionals such as plumbers to do the maintenance. Is the rental unit a passive activity with respect to Laura?
b. Kami is a medical doctor who works four days a week in a medical practice that she and five other doctors formed. Last year she and her partners formed another partnership that owns and operates a medical lab. The lab employs ten technicians, one of whom also acts as manager. During the year Kami spent 120 hours in meetings, reviewing records, etc., for the lab. Is the lab a passive activity with respect to Kami?
c. Assume the same facts in part B. In addition, assume that the same group of doctors have formed two other partnerships. One is a medical supply partnership. Kami spent 150 hours working for this partnership. The medical supply partnership has five full-time employees. Kami also spent 250 hours during the year working for the other partnership. This partnership specializes in providing medical services to individuals from out of town who are staying at local hotels and motels. This partnership hires two full-time and six part-time nurses. Are the lab and the two other partnerships passive activities with respect to Kami?

I8-14 Explain the difference between materially participating and actively participating in an activity. When is the active participation test used?

I8-15 a. What requirements must be met in order for a taxpayer to deduct up to $25,000 of passive losses from rental real estate activities against active and portfolio income?

b. What requirements must be met in order for a real estate rental activity to be considered a real estate business that is not subject to the passive loss rules?

I8-16 Are the suspended losses under the passive loss rules lost forever? Explain.

I8-17 What tests must be met to qualify a loss as deductible under the casualty loss provisions? Discuss the application of each of these tests.

I8-18 Explain how a taxable gain on property can be realized because of a casualty event such as a fire or theft. How are these gains treated?

I8-19 During the current year, Bill completely destroyed his personal automobile in a one-car accident. Fortunately, he was not hurt. The FMV of the automobile at the time of the accident was $8,000. Because of a previous accident as well as several driving violations, Bill is afraid that if he files a claim with his insurance company, he will become uninsurable. Instead, Bill wants to deduct the loss as a casualty loss on his tax return. His AGI for this year is $40,000, and he has other itemized deductions of $5,000. Bill is single. What is the amount of casualty loss he may deduct?

I8-20 Compare and contrast the computational rules for deducting casualty losses on personal-use property with casualty losses incurred on business or investment property.

I8-21 Under what circumstances may a loss arising from a casualty or theft be deducted in a year other than the year in which the loss occurs?

I8-22 For individuals, how are casualty losses on personal-use property reported on the tax return? How are casualty losses on business property reported?

I8-23 Is the $100 floor on personal-use casualty losses imposed on each individual loss item if more than one item of property is destroyed in a single casualty? Is the floor imposed before or after the casualty gains are netted against the casualty losses?

I8-24 Steve loans $50,000 to his best friend, John. John uses the money to open a pizza parlor next to the local high school. Three years later, when John still owed Steve $15,000, John closed the pizza parlor and declared bankruptcy. Discuss the appropriate tax treatment Steve may take.

I8-25 Dana is an attorney who specializes in family law. She uses the cash method of accounting and is a calendar-year taxpayer. During the current year, she represented a client in a lawsuit and billed the client $5,000 for her services. Although she made repeated attempts during the current and subsequent year, Dana was unable to collect the outstanding receivable. Finally in November of the subsequent year she found out that the individual has moved without leaving any forwarding address. Dana's attempts to locate the individual were futile. What is the amount of deduction that Dana may take with respect to this bad debt?

I8-26 Under what circumstances may a taxpayer deduct a bad debt even though another party to the transaction is the creditor?

I8-27 What is the definition of a nonbusiness debt? What is the character of the deduction for a nonbusiness bad debt?

I8-28 a. What alternatives do individuals have in deducting a loss on a deposit in a qualifed financial institution?

b. Explain when it might be better to elect one over the other.

I8-29 A taxpayer collects a debt that was previously written off as a bad debt. What tax consequences arise if the recovery is received in a subsequent tax year?

I8-30 What is an NOL deduction, and why is it allowed?

I8-31 List the adjustments to an individual taxpayer's negative taxable income amount that must be made in computing a NOL for the year. What is the underlying rationale for requiring these adjustments for individuals?

I8-32 a. What is the NOL carryback and carryover period?
b. Does a taxpayer have any choice in deciding the years to which the NOL should be carried? If so, explain the circumstances under which a taxpayer might elect not to use the regular carryback or carryover period.

I8-33 Can a casualty loss on a personal-use asset create or increase an NOL? Explain.

I8-34 If an NOL is carried back to a prior year, what adjustments must be made to the prior year's taxable income? What are the possible results of the adjustments?

ISSUE IDENTIFICATION QUESTIONS

I8-35 On January 12 of the current year, Barney Corporation, a publicly-held corporation, files bankruptcy. During the bankruptcy proceedings it is determined that creditors will only receive 10% of what they are owed and that the shareholders will receive nothing. Sheryl, a calendar-year taxpayer, purchased 1,000 shares of Barney Corporation common stock for $7,000 on February 22 of the prior year. What are the tax issues that should be considered by Sheryl?

I8-36 Five years ago, Cora incorporated Gold, Inc., by contributing $80,000 and receiving 100% of the Gold common stock. Cora is single. Gold, Inc. experienced financial difficulties. On December 22 of the current year, Cora sold all of her Gold, Inc. stock for $5,000. What are the tax issues that should be considered by Cora?

I8-37 In a rage because of personal difficulties, Evan drove recklessly and crashed his automobile doing $8,000 damage. Fortunately, no one was injured. Since Evan received two speeding tickets during the past year, he is concerned about losing his insurance if he files an insurance claim. What are the tax issues that should be considered by Evan?

I8-38 Dan, a full-time employee of Beta, Inc., also owns 10% of its outstanding stock. The other 90% is owned by his three brothers. During the year, the president of Beta came to Dan, expressing grave concern about whether the company had the financial resources to remain in business. He mentioned specifically that a bank was threatening to force Beta to file bankruptcy if they didn't repay its $100,000 loan in full. After some negotiation, Dan agreed to loan Beta the $100,000 for one year until permanent financing could be obtained. A reasonable interest rate was set and a payment schedule was documented. Unfortunately, business did not improve, Beta discontinued its business, and the loan was not repaid. What are the tax issues that should be considered by Dan?

PROBLEMS

I8-39 *Sec. 1244 Losses.* During the current year Sally sells her entire interest in Central Corporation common stock for $10,000. She is the sole shareholder, and originally organized the corporation several years ago by contributing $80,000 in exchange for her stock, which qualifies as Sec. 1244 stock. Since its incorporation, Central has been involved in the manufacture of items that protect personal computers from static electricity. Unfortunately, this market is extremely competitive, and Central Corporation incurs substantial losses throughout its existence.

a. Assuming Sally is single, what are the amount and the character of the loss recognized on the sale of the Central Corporation stock?

b. Assuming Sally is married and files a joint return, what are the amount and the character of the loss recognized on the sale of the Central Corporation stock?

c. How would your answer to Part a change if Sally had originally purchased the stock from another shareholder rather than organizing the corporation?

d. How might Sally have structured the transaction in Part a to receive a greater tax advantage?

I8-40 *Amount and Character of Loss Transactions.* On February 2 of the current year, Madison Corporation files for bankruptcy. At the time, it is estimated that the total FMV of its assets is $800,000, whereas the total amount of its outstanding debt amounts to $1,000,000. Madison has been engaged for several years in a gold mining operation in Montana.

a. At the time of the bankruptcy Madison is owned 100% by Barry, who purchased the stock from an investor for $300,000 several years ago. Barry is married and files a joint return. What are the amount and character of the loss sustained by Barry upon Madison's bankruptcy?

b. How would your answer to Part a change if Barry originally organized Madison Corporation capitalizing it with $300,000? Madison Corporation qualifies as a small business corporation.

c. How would your answer to Part a change if Barry were a corporation instead of an individual?

d. How would your answer to Part b change if Barry were a corporation instead of an individual?

I8-41 *Character of Losses.* During the current year, Joe sold the following stocks:

Stock	Gain (Loss)	When Acquired
Acme	$6,000	5 years ago
Beta	(3,000)	3 years ago
Canary	25,000	8 years ago
Delta	(8,000)	8 months ago
Echo	2,000	3 months ago

In addition, on July 22, Joe received word that his Foxtrot, Inc. stock had gone bankrupt during the year and that Joe's entire $5,000 investment is lost. Joe purchased Foxtrot on December 5 of the prior year. All of the above corporations are large publicly-held companies. Joe asked his attorney to begin collection procedures on a $4,000 loan that was made to a friend two years ago, but the attorney informed Joe that the friend had skipped town and could not be found. Compute Joe's short-term and long-term capital gains and losses from the above transactions.

I8-42 *Passive Losses.* In the current year Alice reports $150,000 of salary income, $20,000 of income from activity X, and $35,000 and $15,000 losses from activities Y and Z, respectively. All three activities are passive with respect to Alice and are purchased during the current year. What is the amount of loss that may be deducted and that must be carried over with respect to each of these activities?

I8-43 *Passive Losses.* In the current year Clay reports income and losses from the following activities:

Activity X	$ 25,000
Activity Y	(10,000)
Activity Z	(20,000)
Salary	100,000

Activities X, Y, and Z are all passive with respect to Clay. $40,000 in passive losses from activity Z are carried over from the prior year. In the current year Clay sells activity Z for a taxable gain of $30,000. What is the amount of loss that Clay may deduct and that must be carried over in the current year?

I8-44 *Passive Losses: Rental Real Estate.* During the current year, Irene, a married individual who files a joint return, reports the following items of income and loss:

Salary	$130,000
Activity X (passive)	10,000
Activity Y (nontrade or business rental real estate)	(30,000)
Activity Z (nontrade or business rental real estate)	(20,000)

Irene actively participates in activities Y and Z and owns 100% of both Y and Z.
a. What is Irene's AGI for the year?
b. What is the amount of losses that may be deducted and must be carried over with respect to each activity?

I8-45 *Passive Losses.* In 1996, Martha purchased two separate activities. Information regarding these activities for 1996 and 1997 is as follows:

Activity	1996 Status	Income (Loss)	Activity	1997 Status	Income (Loss)
A	Passive	($12,000)	A	Active	$ 5,000
B	Passive	(4,000)	B	Passive	10,000

During 1997, Martha also reports salary income of $60,000 and interest and dividend income of $10,000. Compute the amount (if any) of the suspended losses attributable to activities A and B that are carried to 1998.

I8-46 *Passive Losses.* During the current year, Jim has AGI of $130,000 before taking into account any passive activity losses. He also actively participates and owns 100% of activity A, which is a real estate rental activity. For the year, activity A generates an $8,000 net loss and $5,000 in tax credits. Jim is in the 31% tax bracket. What is the amount of suspended loss and credit from activity A that must be carried to subsequent years?

I8-47 *Passive Losses.* In 1997, Julie, a single individual, reported the following items of income and deduction:

Salary	$120,000
Dividend income	11,000
Short-term capital gain from sales of stock	18,000
Short-term capital losses from sales of stock	(15,000)
Loss from a passive real estate activity	(18,000)
Interest expense on loan to purchase stock	(17,000)
Qualified residence interest on residence	(10,000)
Charitable contributions	(7,000)
Property taxes on residence	(3,000)
Tax return preparation fees	(2,000)
Unreimbursed employee business expenses	(3,000)

Julie owns 100% and is an active participant in the real estate activity. What is Julie's taxable income in 1996?

I8-48 ***Casualty Losses.*** Antonio, a mechanic, owns his own auto repair business. In the current year a fire starts in his garage, destroying the following property:

Asset	Adjusted Basis	FMV Before Casualty	FMV After Casualty	Insurance Recovery
A	$15,000	$25,000	—0—	$10,000
B	7,000	10,000	$2,000	5,000
C	12,000	8,000	1,000	3,000

Assets A and B are both machines that Antonio had used in his business for several years. Asset C is Antonio's personal automobile. Because of the fire, Antonio has to close the garage for 2 weeks. He estimates $5,000 lost in income while he is closed, none of which is compensated by insurance. Antonio's AGI for the year, not including the items mentioned above, is $30,000. What are the amount and character of Antonio's deduction as a result of the items noted above?

I8-49 ***Theft Losses.*** On December 17 of the current year, Kelly's business office safe is burglarized. The theft is discovered a few days after the burglary. $1,000 cash from the cash registers is stolen. A diamond necklace and a ring that Kelly frequently wore are also stolen. The necklace cost Kelly $1,500 many years ago and is insured for its $5,000 FMV. Kelly purchased the ring for $1,000 just two weeks before the burglary. Unfortunately, the ring and the cash are not insured. Kelly's AGI for the year, not including the items noted above, is $60,000.
a. What is Kelly's deductible theft loss in the current year?
b. What is Kelly's deductible theft loss in the current year if the theft is not discovered until January of the following year?

I8-50 ***Casualty Losses: Year of Deduction.*** Greg sprayed all of the landscaping around his house with a pesticide in June 1997. Shortly thereafter, all of the trees and shrubs unaccountably died. The FMV and the adjusted basis of the plants were $8,000. Later that year, the pesticide manufacturer announced a recall of the particular batch of pesticide that Greg used. It also announced a program whereby consumers would be repaid for any damage caused by the improper mixture. Greg is single and reports $30,000 AGI in 1997 and $32,000 in 1998.
a. Assume that in 1997 Greg files a claim for his losses and receives notification that payment of $8,000 will be received in 1997. Greg receives full payment for the damage in 1998. How should the loss and the reimbursement be reported?
b. How will your answer to Part a change if in 1998 the manufacturer files bankruptcy and Greg receives $2,000 in total and final payment for his claim?
c. How will your answer to Part a change if the announcement and the reimbursement do not occur until late in 1998, after Greg has already filed his tax return for 1997?

I8-51 ***Personal-Use Casualty Losses.*** In the current year Neil completely destroys his personal automobile (purchased two years earlier for $12,000) in a traffic accident. Fortunately none of the occupants are injured. The FMV of the car before the accident is $8,000; after the accident it is worthless. Neil receives a $5,000 settlement from the insurance company. Later in the same year his house is burglarized, and several antiques are stolen. The antiques were purchased a number of years earlier for $3,000. Their value at the time of the theft is estimated at $5,000. They are not insured. Neil's AGI for the current year is

$45,000. What is the amount of Neil's deductible casualty loss in the current year, assuming the thefts are discovered in the same year?

I8-52 ***Casualty Losses.*** During 1997, Pam incurred the following casualty losses:

Asset	FMV Before	FMV After	Basis	Insurance
Business 1	$18,000	$ 0	$15,000	$ 4,000
Business 2	25,000	10,000	8,000	3,000
Business 3	20,000	0	18,000	19,000
Personal 1	12,000	0	20,000	2,000
Personal 2	8,000	5,000	10,000	0
Personal 3	9,000	0	6,000	8,000

All of the items were destroyed in the same casualty. Before considering the casualty items, Pam reports business income of $80,000, qualified residential interest of $6,000 property taxes on her personal residence of $2,000, and charitable contributions of $4,000. Compute Pam's taxable income for 1997.

I8-53 ***Business Bad Debt.*** Elaine is a physician who uses the cash method of accounting for tax purposes. During the current year, Elaine bills Ralph $1,200 for office visits and outpatient surgery. Unfortunately, unknown to Elaine, Ralph moves away, leaving no payment and no forwarding address. What is the amount of Elaine's bad debt deduction with respect to Ralph's debt?

I8-54 ***Nonbusiness Bad Debt.*** During 1994, Becky loans her brother Ken $5,000, which he intends to use to establish a small business. Because Ken has no other assets and needs cash to expand the business, the agreement provides that Ken will repay the debt if (and when) sufficient funds are generated from the business. No interest rate is agreed upon. The business is unsuccessful, and Ken is forced to file for bankruptcy in 1997. By the end of 1997, it is estimated that the creditors will receive only 20% of the amount owed. In 1998 the bankruptcy proceedings are closed, and the creditors receive 10% of the amount due on the debt. What is Becky's bad debt deduction for 1997? for 1998?

I8-55 ***Bad Debt Deduction.*** Assume the same facts as in Problem I8-54, except that Becky and Ken are not related and that under the terms of the loan Ken agrees to repay Becky the $5,000 plus interest (at a reasonable stated rate) over a five-year period. What is Becky's bad debt deduction for 1997? for 1998?

I8-56 ***Net Operating Loss Deduction.*** Jeff and Julie are married and file a joint income tax return. Jeff owns an unincorporated landscaping business; Julie is employed as a bank loan officer. They have no dependents. During 1997, they report the following items of income and expense:

Revenue from landscaping business	$40,000
Expenses of landscaping business	94,000
Julie's salary	30,000
Dividends	800
LTCG on stock	2,000
Interest on personal residence	4,000
Itemized deductions for state and local taxes	5,000

a. What is Jeff and Julie's taxable income or loss for 1997?
b. What is Jeff and Julie's NOL for 1997?

I8-57   *Net Operating Loss Deduction.* Assume the same facts as in Problem I8-56, except that in addition to the other itemized deductions Jeff and Julie suffer a $3,000 deductible casualty loss (after limitations).
a. What is Jeff and Julie's taxable income or loss for 1997?
b. What is Jeff and Julie's NOL for 1997?

I8-58   *Net Operating Loss Deduction.* Assume the same facts as in Problem I8-56, except that instead of $5,000 itemized deductions for state and local taxes, Jeff and Julie's itemized deductions consist of a $5,000 casualty loss (after limitations).
a. What is Jeff and Julie's taxable income or loss for 1997?
b. What is Jeff and Julie's NOL for 1997?

I8-59   During 1997, Kim, a single taxpayer, reports the following:
   Revenue from business $ 65,000
   Expenses from business   105,000
Kim also worked part time during the year, earning a salary of $12,000. She reported dividends of $1,000 and interest of $500; but she had a long-term capital loss of $5,000 on the sale of some stock she had held for investment. Her itemized deductions total $3,000.
a. What is Kim's taxable income for 1997?
b. What is Kim's NOL for 1997?

TAX FORM/RETURN PREPARATION PROBLEMS

TAX CUT

I8-60   Hal and Jane Weeks are married and file a joint income tax return. Their address is 444 West Walnut Circle, Tempe, Arizona, 00000. Hal's social security number is 123-45-6789, and Jane's is 234-56-7890. Hal is employed as a steelworker, and Jane is self-employed as a financial planner. They report all of their income and expenses on the cash basis. For 1996 they report the following items of income and expense:

Gross receipts from Jane's business	$55,000
Rent on Jane's office	6,500
Receivables written off during the year (received for Jane's financial services)	900
Subscriptions to investment journals for Jane	200
Salary for Jane's secretary-receptionist	9,600
Hal's salary	40,000
Qualified medical expenses	9,000
Property taxes on their personal residence	1,500
State income tax refund received this year (the tax benefit was received in the prior year from the state income tax deduction)	600
State income taxes withheld on Hal's salary	1,200
Federal income taxes withheld on Hal's salary	7,000
Jane's estimated tax payments were	10,000
Interest paid on residence	8,000
Income tax preparation fee for the prior year's return paid this year ($400 is allocated to preparation of Schedule C)	600

Hal and Jane sold the following assets:

Asset	Acquired	Sold	Sales Price	Cost
A stock	2/15/90	3/13/96	$12,000	$ 7,000
B stock	3/2/96	7/7/96	18,000	19,000
C stock	6/8/90	4/10/96	8,000	12,000
Snowmobile	12/3/89	3/3/96	4,000	5,500

The C stock was owned by Jane and was sold to her brother. The snowmobile was used for personal recreation.

In addition to the items above, they donate Real Corporation stock to their church. The FMV of the stock on the date it is donated (7/24/96) is $5,000. It cost $2,000 when purchased on 2/12/87. Hal and Jane's residence is burglarized during the year. The burglar stole a stereo component system (FMV $2,000; cost $3,000), a diamond necklace (FMV $10,000; cost $9,000), and a painting (FMV $2,500; cost $1,500). The insurance company pays $1,000 for the stereo, $3,000 for the necklace, and $1,000 for the painting. Compute Hal and Jane's federal income tax liability, using the currently available income tax rates.

TAX CUT

I8-61 Doug and Elaine Graves are married and file a joint return. Their Social Security numbers are 098-76-5432 and 987-65-4321. They live at 427 So. Geneva Rd., Duncan, Arizona, 00001. They report their income on the cash basis. During 1996, they report the following items:

Salary	$80,000
Rental of a condominium at Vail, Co.:	
Rental income (30 days)	9,000
Interest expense	4,000
Property taxes	2,100
Maintenance	1,000
Depreciation (entire year)	6,000
Insurance	1,400
Days of personal use	16

During the year the following events also occur:

a. In 1993 Doug had loaned a friend $2,000 to help pay medical bills. During 1996 he discovers that his "friend" has skipped town.

b. On July 15, 1996 Doug sells West Corporation stock for $18,000. He purchased the stock on December 14, 1986 for $25,000.

c. On September 21, 1996 Elaine discovers that the penny stock of First Corp. she purchased on May 30 of the prior year is completely worthless. She paid $2,000 for the stock.

d. Rather than accept the $50 the repairperson offers for their old dishwasher, they donate it to Goodwill Industries on November 15, 1996. They purchased the machine for $600 on February 2, 1990. The new dishwasher cost $780.

e. They purchased a new residence for $120,000. As part of the closing costs, they pay two points, or $2,000 on the $100,000 mortgage, which are interest rather than loan processing fees. This payment enables them to obtain a more favorable interest rate for the term of the loan.

f. Paid $2,700 in property taxes on their residence and $5,000 in state income taxes.

g. On July 12, 1996 they donated an antique automobile to the local community college. The value of the automobile was $8,000. They purchased the automobile for $1,000 on November 15, 1987 and fixed it up themselves. They estimated they had put in approximately $5,000 worth of labor into the project. The college auctioned the car for $7,500.

h. $12,000 in federal income tax was withheld during the year.

Compute Doug and Elaine's federal income tax liability for 1996 using the currently available tax rates. Complete Form 1040 and accompanying schedules.

CASE STUDY PROBLEMS

I8-62 Dr. John Brown is a physician who expects to make $150,000 this year from his medical practice. In addition, Dr. Brown expects to receive $10,000 dividends and interest income.

Last year, on the advice of a friend, Dr. Brown invested $100,000 in Limited, a limited partnership. He spends no time working for Limited. Limited's operations did not turn out exactly as planned, and Dr. Brown's share of Limited's losses last year amounted to $15,000. Dr. Brown has already been informed that his share of Limited's losses this year will be $10,000.

In January of the current year, Dr. Brown set up his own laboratory. Originally he intended to have the lab only do the work for his own practice, but other physicians in the area were impressed with the quick turnaround and convenience that the lab provided, and began sending their work. This year Dr. Brown estimates that the lab will generate $30,000 of taxable income. The work in the lab is done by 2 full-time qualified laboratory technicians. A part-time bookkeeper is hired to keep the books. Dr. Brown has spent 320 hours to date establishing and managing the lab. He plans to hire another technician, who will also manage the lab so that it can operate on its own.

In November, Dr. Brown calls you requesting some tax advice. Specifically, he would like to know what actions he should take before the end of the year in order to reduce his tax liability for the current year.

Write a memo to Dr. Brown, detailing your suggestions. His address is: Dr. John Brown, 444 Physician's Drive, Suite 100, Anytown, USA, 88888.

I8-63 In preparing the tax return for one of your clients, Jack Johnson, you notice that he has listed a deduction for a large business bad debt. Jack explains that the loan was made to his corporate employer when the corporation was experiencing extreme cash flow difficulties. In fact, Jack was very concerned at the time he made the loan that the corporation would go bankrupt. This would have been extremely bad, because not only would he have lost his job, but he also would have lost the $80,000 he had invested in the common stock of the corporation.

You know that if the loan is a business loan Jack will receive an ordinary deduction. However, if the loan is a nonbusiness debt, it becomes a short-term capital loss (and Jack can only currently deduct $3,000).

After thoroughly reviewing all of the facts you do a complete search of the relevant judicial and administrative authority. There you find that the courts are split as to whether under these circumstances the loan should be treated as a business or nonbusiness bad debt.

What position should you take on Jack's federal income tax return? (See the *Statements on Responsibilities in Tax Practice* section in Chapter I15 and Appendix E for a discussion of this issue.)

TAX RESEARCH PROBLEM

I8-64 Early in 1997, Kay meets Dan through a business associate. Dan tells Kay that he is directing a business venture that purchases poorly managed restaurants in order to turn them around and make them profitable. Dan mentions that he is currently involved in acquiring a real "gold mine" but needs to raise additional cash in order to purchase it. On the strength of Dan's representations, Kay loans Dan $30,000 for the venture. An agreement is written up between Kay and Dan, wherein Dan agrees to repay Kay the entire amount over a 5-year period plus 14% interest per annum on the unpaid balance. Later in the year, however, Kay discovers that Dan had never intended to purchase the restaurant and, in fact, had used most of the money for his own benefit. Upon making this discovery, Kay sues Dan for recovery of the money, alleging that Dan falsely, fraudulently, and deceitfully represented that the money would be invested and repaid, in order to cheat and defraud Kay out of her money. Unfortunately for Kay, she is never able to recover any amount of the loan. Discuss the tax treatment that Kay may claim with regard to the loss.

A partial list of research sources is

- *Robert S. Gerstell*, 46 T.C. 161 (1966)
- *Michele Monteleone*, 34 T.C. 688 (1960)

CHAPTER 9

EMPLOYEE EXPENSES AND DEFERRED COMPENSATION

LEARNING OBJECTIVES

After studying this chapter, you should be able to

▶ 1   Determine the proper classification and deductibility of travel and transportation expenses

▶ 2   Determine the proper deductible amount for entertainment expenses under the 50% disallowance rule

▶ 3   Identify deductible moving expenses and determine the amount and year of deductibility

▶ 4   Describe the requirements for deducting education expenses

▶ 5   Determine whether the expenses of an office in home meet the requirements for deductibility and apply the gross income limitations

▶ 6   Discuss the tax treatment and requirements for various deferred compensation arrangements

**ADDITIONAL
COMMENT**

"The income tax has made
more liars out of the American
people than golf has. Even
when you make a tax form on
the level, you don't know
when its through if you are a
crook or a martyr." Will Rogers.

This chapter discusses the tax consequences that arise from two types of expenditures:

▶ Employment-related expenditures

▶ Deferred compensation payments made to employees

Employees routinely incur expenses in connection with their jobs, such as travel, entertainment, professional journals, etc. The tax law considers employee expenses to be incurred in connection with a trade or business and are, therefore, deductible under Sec. 162. However, employee expenses are subject to a myriad of special rules and limitations. Because of the large number of taxpayers who are employees and therefore subject to these rules, this chapter discusses the rules as well as tax planning opportunities.

Deferred compensation refers to methods of compensating employees that are based on their current service but the actual payments are deferred until future periods. Deferred compensation arrangements are very popular and widely used in business. The two principal types of deferred compensation methods are qualified plans and nonqualified plans. Qualified plans, such as pension and profit-sharing plans, have very favorable tax benefits but also impose strict eligibility and coverage requirements. Nonqualified plans, while not as tax advantageous as qualified plans, are very useful for highly compensated employees. Both of these types of deferred compensation arrangements are discussed later in this chapter.

CLASSIFICATION OF EMPLOYEE EXPENSES

Section 62(a)(2) provides that an employee may deduct reimbursed employee expenses *for* AGI. This presumes, of course, that the employee has included the reimbursement in his gross income. However, subject to certain limitations, unreimbursed employee expenses are generally deductible *from* AGI.

Some of the more frequently encountered employee expenses discussed in this chapter include

▶ Travel

▶ Transportation

▶ Moving

▶ Entertainment

▶ Education

▶ Office in home

NATURE OF THE EMPLOYMENT RELATIONSHIP

KEY POINT

The business expenses of a
self-employed individual and
the reimbursed business expenses of an employee are deductible *for* AGI. The unreimbursed business expenses of an
employee are deductible *from*
AGI.

The nature of the employment relationship hinges on whether an individual is classified as an employee or is engaged in a self-employed trade or business activity. A self-employed individual who incurs a trade or business-related expenditure may deduct the expense *for* AGI under Sec. 162, and it is reported on Schedule C of Form 1040. In contrast, unreimbursed expenses incurred by an employee are deductible *from* AGI and are subject to separate tax rules and restrictions. Certain items such as moving expenses are deductible *for* AGI if they are incurred by an employee or a self-employed individual, but are nondeductible personal expenditures if an individual is not employed or is not self-employed.

EMPLOYER-EMPLOYEE RELATIONSHIP DEFINED. The Regulations provide that an employer-employee relationship generally exists where the employer has the right to control and direct the individual who provides services with regard to the end result and the means by which the result is accomplished.[1]

EXAMPLE I9-1 ▶ Carmen is a nurse who assists a group of doctors in a clinic. Carmen is under the direct supervision of the doctors and is told what procedures to perform and when to perform them. Therefore, Carmen is classified as an employee. ◀

EXAMPLE I9-2 ▶ Carol is a live-in nurse who is paid by the patient and receives instructions from the patient's doctor regarding such items as medications and diet. Carol is directly responsible for the delivery of nursing care and is in control of the end result. Thus, Carol is self-employed. ◀

IMPORTANCE OF PROPER CLASSIFICATION. Proper classification is particularly important to employers because employers owe payroll taxes (e.g., the employer portion of Social Security [FICA] taxes and unemployment taxes) for individuals who are classified as employees. Individuals may prefer to be classified as employees because the employee portion of the social security and hospital (Medicare) taxes (7.65% in 1997) is less than the self-employment tax rate (15.3% in 1997). Of the 7.65%, 6.2% (12.4% for self-employed individuals) is for the old age, survivors and disability insurance (OASDI) portion of the FICA tax and is assessed on a maximum income amount of $65,400 (1997). The remaining 1.45% (2.9% for self-employed individuals) portion of the FICA tax is for hospital insurance and has no ceiling limitation.[2]

LITIGATION ISSUES AND ADMINISTRATIVE ENFORCEMENT. The determination as to whether an individual who performs services is either an employee or an independent contractor has been a major area of contention between the IRS and taxpayers. In Rev. Rul. 87-41, 1987-1 CB 296, the IRS enumerated 20 factors as guides for determining whether an individual is an employee or an independent contractor. These factors are designed to help determine whether the person or persons for whom the services are performed exercises sufficient **control** over the individual for the individual to be classified as an employee. Some of the factors include, instructions, set hours of work, work on employer's premises, and method of payment (hourly versus commission, for example).

Substantial litigation has occurred in the interpretation of these factors. For example, truck drivers who were owner-operators and were engaged under contract by an interstate trucking company were considered independent contractors because they also selected their own routes and were paid a percentage of the company's receipts for shipment.[3] However, drivers for a moving van company were considered employees because the company exercised control over their assignments.[4]

KEY POINT

Even if the employee expenses exceed 2% of AGI, the employee may not derive a tax benefit if the deductible employee expenses, when added to the other itemized deductions, do not exceed the standard deduction.

LIMITATIONS ON UNREIMBURSED EMPLOYEE EXPENSES

2% NONDEDUCTIBLE FLOOR. Section 67 imposes a nondeductible floor of 2% of AGI to the following types of itemized deductions:

---

[1] Reg. Sec. 31.3401(c)-1(b).

[2] For years before 1994, a ceiling limitation ($135,000 in 1993) applied to earnings and self-employment income subject to the hospital insurance portion of the FICA tax. (See Chapter I14 for a discussion of these rules.)

[3] Rev. Rul. 76-226, 1976-1 CB 332

[4] R. N. *Smith v. U.S.*, 78-1 USTC ¶9263 (CA-5, 1978).

1) Unreimbursed employee business expenses,

2) Investment expenses, and

3) Other miscellaneous itemized deductions

Investment expenses include expenses connected with the earning of investment income, such as publications and safe deposit box rentals. Other miscellaneous itemized deductions include items such as fees for tax return preparation and appraisal fees for charitable contributions. All of these types of expenses are referred to as **miscellaneous itemized deductions** in Sec. 67.[5]

Other unreimbursed employee expenses that are classified as miscellaneous itemized deductions include

▶ The cost and maintenance of special clothing (e.g., uniforms for an airline pilot)[6]

▶ Job-hunting expenses for seeking employment in the same trade or business (e.g., employment agency fees)[7]

▶ Professional journals, professional dues, union dues, small tools and supplies.

EXAMPLE I9-3
SELF-STUDY QUESTION

Before the Tax Reform Act of 1986, unreimbursed employee business expenses were not subject to the 2% nondeductible floor. Why did Congress decide to subject these expenses to this floor?

▶ Charles incurs $3,000 unreimbursed employee expenses in 1997. Charles also incurs $1,000 of investment counseling fees and $500 for the preparation of his 1996 tax return and pays these amounts in 1997. Charles's AGI is $100,000. The total of miscellaneous itemized deductions is $4,500 ($3,000 + $1,000 + $500). Charles is limited to a $2,500 itemized deduction ($4,500 − $2,000) because of the application of the 2% nondeductible floor (0.02 × $100,000 AGI = $2,000). ◀

EXCEPTIONS TO THE 2% FLOOR. Other itemized deductions such as charitable contributions, mortgage interest and real estate taxes on a principal residence are not subject to the 2% nondeductible floor.

EXAMPLE I9-4
ANSWER

Prior law required extensive recordkeeping with regard to items that were commonly small expenditures. These small amounts presented significant administrative and enforcement problems for the IRS. The use of a floor also takes into account the fact that some expenses are sufficiently personal in nature that they might be incurred apart from any business activities.

▶ In the current year Carmelia, who is single, incurs $1,500 of unreimbursed employee expenses, $3,000 of charitable contributions, and $4,000 of mortgage interest and real estate taxes on her principal residence. She has no other miscellaneous itemized deductions or investment expenses, and her AGI is $100,000. The $1,500 of employee expenses are not deductible because the 2% nondeductible floor ($2,000 in this case) is higher than the $1,500 of expenses. The $3,000 of charitable contributions and $4,150 of mortgage interest and real estate taxes are fully deductible as itemized deductions because Carmelia's itemized deductions exceed the standard deduction amount ($4,150 for a single taxpayer in 1997). The charitable contributions, mortgage interest, and real estate taxes are not subject to the 2% nondeductible floor. ◀

TRAVEL EXPENSES

DEDUCTIBILITY OF TRAVEL EXPENSES

The deductibility of travel expenses depends on the nature of the expenditure and whether the employee receives a reimbursement from the employer. If the taxpayer is

---

[5] The 2% disallowance applies before considering the 3% scale down of total itemized deductions under Sec. 68 for upper-income individuals with AGI in excess of $117,950. See Chapter I7 for a discussion of these rules. The 2% floor does not apply to certain other miscellaneous itemized deductions, including impairment-related work expenses for handicapped employees, amortizable bond premiums, certain short sale expenses, terminated annuity payments, and gambling losses to the extent of winnings.

[6] Rev. Rul. 70-474, 1970-2 C.B. 34.

[7] Rev. Rul. 75-120, 1975-1 C.B. 55, as clarified by Rev. Rul. 77-16, 1977-1 C.B. 37. The expenses are deductible even if the new position is not obtained. However, job-hunting expenses are not deductible if the taxpayer has been unemployed for an extended period or if the employee is seeking to enter a new trade or business.

engaged in a trade or business activity as a self-employed individual or is engaged in an activity for the production of rental and royalty income (e.g., an owner of rental property), the travel-related expenditures are deductible *for* AGI and the 2% nondeductible floor is not applicable. If the taxpayer is an employee and incurs travel expenses in connection with his job, the expenses are deductible either *for* AGI or *from* AGI depending on whether the expenses are reimbursed by the employer. In general, if the travel expenses are not reimbursed by his employer, the expenses are a deduction from AGI subject to the 2% floor. If the travel expenses are reimbursed and the reimbursement is included in the employee's gross income, the expenses are deductible *for* AGI. The tax rules for reporting reimbursed employee business expenses are discussed in more detail later in this chapter. Personal travel is not deductible. Table I9-1 illustrates these tax consequences.

DEFINITION OF TRAVEL EXPENSES

Travel expenses include transportation, meals, lodging, and other reasonable and necessary expenses incurred by a taxpayer while "away from home" in the pursuit of a trade or business, or an employment-related activity. The term *travel expense* is more broadly defined in the IRC than is the term **transportation expense**. If an individual is not away from home, expenses related to local transportation may still be deductible but are classified as transportation expenses rather than travel expenses. Transportation expenses for employees are discussed later in this chapter.

▼ TABLE I9-1
Classification of Travel Expenses

Situation Facts	Deductible *for* AGI	Tax Treatment Deductible *from* AGI	Not Deductible
1. Cindy is a self-employed attorney who incurs travel expenses related to her business.	X[a]		
2. Jose, who lives in Dallas, is the owner of several apartment buildings in Denver. Periodically he travels to Denver to inspect and manage the properties.	X[a]		
3. Clay is an employee who is required to travel to company facilities throughout the U.S. in the conduct of his management responsibilities. Clay is not reimbursed by his employer.		X[b]	
4. Same as Situation 3, except that Clay is fully reimbursed by his employer.	X		
5. Colleen is a student who travels to her parents' home during the holidays.			X

[a] The 2% nondeductible floor is not applicable.
[b] The 2% nondeductible floor is applicable and the expenses are only deductible in excess of the floor.

EXAMPLE 19-5 ▶ Ahmed is away from home overnight on an employment-related business trip and incurs air fare, hotel, and taxi fares amounting to $800. Because Ahmed is away from home, the $800 is deductible as travel expenses. ◀

EXAMPLE 19-6 ▶ Charlotte uses her personal automobile to make deliveries of company products to customers in the same local area of her employer's place of business. Charlotte's automobile expenses are classified as transportation expenses (rather than travel expenses), because she was not away from home when they were incurred. As is discussed later in this chapter, transportation expenses are deductible but are subject to strict recordkeeping rules. ◀

HISTORICAL NOTE

The partial disallowance of business meals (and entertainment) was enacted because Congress believed that prior law had not focused sufficiently on the personal consumption element of deductible business meal and entertainment expenses. Congress felt that taxpayers who could arrange business settings for personal consumption were unfairly receiving a federal tax subsidy for such consumption.

TYPICAL MISCONCEPTION

There is a tendency to erroneously assume that a taxpayer's tax home is the location of the primary personal residence.

REAL-WORLD EXAMPLE

A taxpayer was employed by a traveling circus with headquarters in Chicago. The Tax Court held that the taxpayer's home was wherever he happened to be with the circus. Therefore, the cost of his meals and lodging was not deductible. *Nat Lewis*, 1954 PH T.C. Memo ¶54,233, 13 TCM 1167.

GENERAL QUALIFICATION REQUIREMENTS

To qualify as a travel expense deduction, the following requirements must be met:

▶ The purpose of the trip must be connected with a trade or business or be employment-related (e.g., personal vacation trips or commuting to and from a job location are nondeductible personal expenses).[8]

▶ The taxpayer must be away from his tax home overnight or for a sufficient duration to require rest before returning home.

AWAY-FROM-TAX-HOME REQUIREMENT. Travel expenses are deductible if the taxpayer is temporarily away from his tax home overnight. The IRS's position is that a person's tax home is the location of his principal place of employment regardless of where the family residence is maintained. Reassignments of more than one year are treated as indefinite.[9] Work assignments for one year or less are classified as either temporary or indefinite depending on the facts and circumstances of each case. If an employee is reassigned only for a temporary period, then his tax home does not change and the travel expenses are deductible. However, if the assignment is for an indefinite period, the individual's tax home shifts to the new location.

The following bulleted items and examples are taken from Rev. Rul. 93-86[10] and are used to illustrate the IRS's position concerning whether a taxpayer is away from home temporarily for purposes of deducting travel expenses:

▶ A taxpayer accepts away-from-home employment where it is realistically expected that the work will be completed in six months. The actual employment period lasts ten months. Because the employment period is realistically expected to last (and does in fact last) for one year or less, the IRS's position is that the employment is temporary and the taxpayer's travel expenses are deductible.

▶ A taxpayer accepts away-from-home employment where it is realistically expected that the work will be completed in 18 months but the work is actually completed in ten months. In such case the IRS's position is that the employment is treated as indefinite, regardless of whether it actually exceeds one year or not.

▶ A taxpayer accepts away-from-home employment where it is realistically expected that the work will be completed in nine months. After eight months the taxpayer is asked to remain for seven more months or a total period of more than one year. Based on these facts, the IRS's position is that the employment is temporary for eight months and the travel expenses are deductible for the eight-month period. The job is considered indefinite for the remaining seven months and no travel expense deduction is allowed for the travel expenses during this period.

---

[8] Travel expenses incurred in the production or collection of income are also deductible from AGI under Sec. 212(l), even though the travel is not connected with employment or with the conduct of a trade or business. See Rev. Rul. 84-113, 1984-2 C.B. 60.

[9] Sec. 162(a).
[10] Rev. Rul. 93-86, 1993-2 C.B. 71.

BUSINESS VERSUS PLEASURE

Travel expenses are deductible only if they are incurred in the pursuit of a trade or business activity or are related to the taxpayer's employment. Thus, if a taxpayer takes a trip that is primarily personal in nature but some business is transacted, the only deductions allowed are those that are directly related to the business activity.[11] In such event, all of the traveling expenses to and from the destination are treated as nondeductible personal expenditures. However, if the trip is primarily related to business or employment, all of the traveling expenses to and from the destination are deductible, and meals and lodging, local transportation, and incidental expenses are allocated to the business and personal activities respectively. In effect, an all-or-nothing approach is applied to the deductibility of traveling expenses to and from the destination depending upon the primary purpose for making the trip.

In determining the primary purpose for a trip, the amount of time spent on personal activities compared to the time spent on business activities is an important factor. However, the fact that a taxpayer may spend slightly more time on personal activities than business activities will not automatically prohibit the deductibility of the transportation expenses to and from the destination. The taxpayer must clearly show that the purpose of the trip was **primarily business** even though slightly more time may have been spent on personal activities.

EXAMPLE I9-7 ▶ Dana travels to New York on a business trip for her employer. She is not reimbursed for the travel expenses. Dana spends three days in business meetings and vacations for two days. Because the trip is primarily business, the traveling expenses to and from the destination (e.g., airfare) are fully deductible by Dana. If Dana's meals, lodging, and incidental expenses amount to $100 per day, only $300 ($100 × 3 business days) of such travel expenses is also deductible. The deductible business meal expenses are reduced by 50%, and the total amount of deductible travel expenses are subject to the nondeductible 2% floor on miscellaneous itemized deductions. A proration of the meals, lodging, and incidental expenses based on the number of days may not be appropriate if the expenses are uneven or are directly related to either business or personal activities. ◀

EXAMPLE I9-8 ▶ Assume that the facts in Example I9-7 are reversed (i.e., that two days are employment-related and three days are personal). Because more time was spent on personal activities, the general rule would hold that the trip is primarily personal and the traveling expenses to and from the destination are not deductible. Thus, only $200 ($100 × two business days) of travel expenses related to meals, lodging, and incidental expenses are deductible (subject to the limitations previously discussed). None of the traveling expenses to and from the destination (i.e., the airfare) are deductible. ◀

EXAMPLE I9-9 ▶ Carroll, who lives and works in St. Louis, is required by his employer to attend a sales meeting in San Francisco. The meeting lasts two days. Carroll decides to take three days of vacation and sightsee in the San Francisco area. Even though Carroll spent more days on personal activities than business activities, Carroll's airfare would be deductible assuming he can clearly show that the primary purpose of the trip was business. ◀

The IRS has ruled that the incremental expenses of an additional night's lodging and an additional day's meals that are incurred to obtain "excursion" air fare rates with respect to employees whose business travel extends over Saturday night are deductible business expenses.[12] The reimbursement for these expenses is deductible by the employer (subject to the 50% disallowance for meals). The employer is not required to report the

[11] Reg. Sec. 1.162-2(b)(1).

[12] Ltr. Rul. 9237014 (June 10, 1992).

REAL-WORLD
EXAMPLE

A movie executive's wife accompanied him on business trips in the U.S. and abroad. She helped promote the movie company's image of a "family-type movie company." She also helped arrange his personal schedule. A deduction for her costs was allowed. *U.S. v. Roy O. Disney*, 24 AFTR 2d 69-5123, 69-2 USTC ¶9494 (9th Cir., 1969). As a result of the Revenue Reconciliation Act of 1993, the wife's travel costs would no longer be deductible unless she were an employee.

SELF-STUDY
QUESTION

Would the cost of going on a safari in Africa be deductible if the taxpayer were in the business of selling guns?

ANSWER

In an actual case, the Court held that the safari expenses were not sufficiently connected to the taxpayer's gun-selling business. Therefore, the safari costs were not deductible. *Vincent W. Eckel*, 1974 PH T.C. Memo ¶74,033, 33 TCM 147.

reimbursement on the employee's Form W-2 as gross income or withhold employment taxes.

Stringent rules are applied if the taxpayer is accompanied by family members because of the likelihood that the trip is primarily for personal reasons. No deduction is permitted for travel expenses of a spouse or dependent (or other person accompanying the taxpayer) unless the person is an employee, the travel is for a bona fide business purpose, and the expenses would be otherwise deductible.[13]

FOREIGN TRAVEL

Due to the potential for abuse, special rules apply to foreign travel and foreign convention expenses.[14] Travel expenses related to foreign conventions, seminars, or similar types of meetings are disallowed unless it can be shown that the meeting is directly related to the taxpayer's trade or business (including employment) activity and that it is reasonable for the meeting to be held outside North America. In addition, complex expense allocation rules are applied to business trips made outside the United States.[15]

ADDITIONAL LIMITATIONS ON TRAVEL EXPENSES

Additional limitations restrict the deductibility of certain types of travel expenses, including the following:

▶ Travel deductions are disallowed if the expenses are deductible only as a form of education.[16] For example, a French language professor cannot deduct travel expenses to France if the purpose of the trip is to maintain a general familiarity with the French language and customs.

▶ Deductions allowed for luxury water travel (i.e., ocean liners, cruise ships, or other forms of water transportation) are limited to twice the highest per diem amount allowable for a day of domestic travel by employees in the executive branch of the federal government.[17]

▶ Travel deductions to attend a convention, seminar, or meeting are disallowed if they are related to income-producing activities coming under Sec. 212.[18] Expenses to attend a convention, seminar, or meeting are deductible if directly connected with a taxpayer's trade or business. However, expenses to attend such meetings on a U.S. cruise ship are deductible but only to a maximum amount of $2,000.[19]

EXAMPLE 19-10 ▶ Danielle is an investor in real estate who attends real estate investment counseling seminars. During the current year, she incurs $4,000 travel expenses to attend the seminars. None of the travel expenses are deductible because the expenses are related to income-producing activities coming under Sec. 212. ◀

EXAMPLE 19-11 ▶ Dawn travels on a cruise ship to attend a business meeting in Bermuda. The round-trip cost of the cruise is $4,000, and the travel is for a period of four days. If the daily per diem amount is $150 for a government employee, the travel expenses related to the cruise ship are limited to $1,200 ($300 per day × 4 days travel). ◀

---

[13] Sec. 274(m)(3).

[14] Secs. 274(c) and (h).

[15] Reg. Sec. 1.274-4. No allocation of total expenses is made to the personal-use (nondeductible) element if an individual is away from home for seven days or less or if less than 25% of the time is devoted to personal purposes. In all other cases, all of the foreign travel expenses (including transportation costs) must be apportioned between business and personal activities based on the relative percentage of time devoted to each activity.

[16] Sec. 274(m)(2).

[17] Sec. 274(m)(1).

[18] Sec. 274(h)(7).

[19] Sec. 274(h)(2).

TRANSPORTATION EXPENSES

ADDITIONAL COMMENT

The IRS takes the position that the hauling of equipment, tools, etc., in an automobile for business purposes does not make the commuting expenses deductible. This position is based on the Supreme Court's decision in *Donald W. Fausner v. CIR*, 32 AFTR 2d 73-5202, 73-2 USTC ¶9515 (USSC, 1973). The Court held that it was not possible to allocate the automobile expenses between nondeductible commuting expenses and deductible business expenses. However, if the taxpayer incurs additional costs, such as in renting a trailer, these additional costs are deductible.

The deductibility and classification of transportation expenses also depends on the nature of the expenditure, as follows:

▶ Trade or business-related transportation expenses are deductible *for* AGI and are not subject to specific limitations.

▶ Transportation expenses related to the production of rental and royalty income (e.g., an owner-investor in rental properties) are deductible *for* AGI and are not subject to specific limitations.

▶ Reimbursed transportation expenses are deductible *for* AGI (assuming that an adequate accounting is made to the employer).

▶ Unreimbursed employee transportation expenses are deductible *from* AGI as itemized deductions subject to the 2% nondeductible floor for miscellaneous itemized deductions.

▶ Commuting expenses are nondeductible personal expenses.

DEFINITION AND CLASSIFICATION

Transportation costs include taxi fares, automobile expenses, airfares, tolls, parking fees, and so on incurred in a trade or business or employment-related activity. The cost of commuting to and from an employee's job location are nondeductible personal expenditures regardless of the length of the trip. Transportation expenses are treated as travel expenses only if the employee meets the away-from-home requirements previously discussed. Otherwise, they are deducted separately as transportation expenses. Both unreimbursed employment-related travel and transportation expenses for employees are subject to the 2% nondeductible limitation on miscellaneous itemized deductions. If a reimbursement is received, such expenses would be deductible *for* AGI.

EXAMPLE 19-12 ▶ Eurie's employer requires her to visit several customers at different locations in the metropolitan area during the course of the workday. Her transportation expenses (e.g., auto expenses, tolls, and parking) are deductible as transportation expenses because they are related to providing services as an employee. If Eurie is required to travel away from home overnight, the transportation costs are included with meals and lodging and deducted as a travel expense. In either situation, the unreimbursed employment-related expenses are treated as miscellaneous itemized deductions and are subject to the 2% nondeductible floor limitation. If the expenses were reimbursed by Eurie's employer and an adequate accounting is made to the employer, the expenses would be deductible *for* AGI. ◀

EXAMPLE 19-13 ▶ David accepts a permanent job with a company located 80 miles from his principal residence. He decides not to move to the new location. None of David's transportation costs are deductible because they are personal commuting expenses. (Note: Because the job is a permanent assignment, it is for an indefinite period rather than a temporary period and the transportation expenses are not deductible as travel expenses.) ◀

The following exceptions or unusual circumstances should be noted:

▶ Transportation expenses to travel from one job to another are deductible if an employee has more than one job. If the employee goes home between jobs, the deduction is only the amount it would have cost him to go directly from the first location to the second.[20]

---

[20] IRS, *Publication No. 917* (Business Use of a Car), 1996, p. 3

▶ Transportation expenses from an employee's regular place of employment to a distant temporary work site are deductible.[21]

▶ Certain transportation expenses related to income-producing activities are deductible under Sec. 212. Expenses are deductible *for* AGI if they are related to the production of rental or royalty income; expenses connected with other investment-related activities are deductible as miscellaneous itemized deductions subject to the 2% floor.

▶ Transportation expenses related to medical treatment may be deductible from AGI as a medical expense (subject to the limitations on the deductibility of medical expenses discussed in Chapter I7).

▶ Transportation expenses related to charitable activities may be deductible as a charitable contribution (subject to the limitations on the deductibility of charitable contributions discussed in Chapter I7).

▶ Transportation expenses incurred in going between the taxpayer's residence and a temporary work location outside the metropolitan area are deductible.[22] However, if the temporary work location is in the metropolitan area, the expenses are nondeductible (i.e., commuting expenses) unless the taxpayer has one or more regular work locations away from the residence or the taxpayer's residence is his or her principal place of business. Thus, a self-employed CPA operating her business from her home may deduct transportation expenses to clients located in the metropolitan area. Also, a CPA who is employed by a CPA firm and who maintains a regular work location (e.g., an office is provided at the CPA firm work location) may deduct transportation expenses for trips from home to clients in the metropolitan area. Unreimbursed transportation costs for an employee are deductible *from* AGI as unreimbursed employee expenses that are subject to the 2% nondeductible floor. Transportation expenses for a self-employed individual are deductible *for* AGI.

EXAMPLE I9-14 ▶ As shown in Figure I9-1 on page I9-11, Dick has two jobs that are 10 miles apart. Dick lives 5 miles from the first job site and 8 miles from the second job site. If Dick drives directly from one job to the other, he may deduct the automobile costs associated with the 10-mile trip. If he goes home before driving to the second job, the deduction is limited to 10 miles, even though he actually travels 13 miles. ◀

EXAMPLE I9-15 ▶ Diana owns a duplex, which she rents to tenants. She periodically drives from her place of business to this income-producing property to collect the rents and to inspect the property. The transportation expenses are deductible *for* AGI as an expense related to the production of rental income under Sec. 212. ◀

EXAMPLE I9-16 ▶ Donna, an accountant who is employed by a CPA firm, travels from her home to an audit client located in the local metropolitan area. The firm maintains an office for Donna at their business location. She is not reimbursed for her transportation costs. The transportation costs are deductible *from* AGI as unreimbursed employee expenses that are subject to the 2% nondeductible floor. If Donna were instead a self-employed CPA operating a business from her home, her transportation expenses would be deductible *for* AGI. ◀

---

[21] Rev. Rul. 190, 1953-2 C.B. 303.

[22] Rev. Rul. 90-23, 1990-1 C.B. 28 as amplified by Rev. Rul. 94-47, 1994-29, 6.

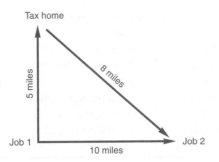

FIGURE I9-1 ▶ ILLUSTRATION FOR EXAMPLE I9-14

ADDITIONAL COMMENT

The Revenue Reconciliation Act of 1990 provided for an excise tax on the first retail sale of any passenger vehicle of 10% of the sales price over $30,000. The Revenue Reconciliation Act of 1993 provides that the $30,000 threshold is indexed annually for inflation and is $32,000 for 1995. This tax is capitalized as a component of the cost basis of the automobile.

TREATMENT OF AUTOMOBILE EXPENSES

An employee or self-employed person may deduct actual automobile expenses, including gas, oil, repairs, depreciation, interest, license fees, insurance, and so on based on the percentage of business miles to total miles. Detailed records to support the expenses are necessary in order to properly claim the deduction. To help reduce the burden of detailed recordkeeping, an alternative method, the standard mileage rate method, is available to taxpayers.

The standard mileage rate method permits a deduction based on a standard mileage rate, which is currently 31.5 cents per mile for 1997 (31 cents for 1996). Parking and tolls are allowed as an addition to this deduction.[23] The following restrictions apply when the standard mileage rate is used:

▶ The standard mileage rate method cannot be used if two or more automobiles are used simultaneously for business purposes.

▶ If a taxpayer changes from the standard mileage rate method rate in one year to the actual expense method in a later year, the basis of the used automobile must be reduced by 12 cents per mile for years 1994–1997 (11.5 cents per mile in 1993 and 1992) for years in which the standard mileage rate method was used. The modified accelerated cost-recovery system (MACRS) rules (discussed in Chapter I10) cannot be used for computing depreciation in the year of the change and for the remaining useful life of the automobile. In such case, only the straight-line method under the alternative depreciation system (ADS) may be used (see Chapter I10).

ADDITIONAL COMMENT

It should be remembered that in many cases the taxpayer can choose between the automatic mileage method and calculating the actual costs of operating the car. Although the automatic mileage method has the advantage of convenience, a calculation of the actual costs might produce a larger deduction.

▶ A change to the standard mileage rate method is not allowed for an automobile that was previously depreciated under the MACRS rules or where an election was made under Sec. 179 to expense part or all of the automobile's cost in the year of acquisition. (See Chapter I10 for a discussion of the Sec. 179 election.)

▶ The actual expense method is based on the ratio of business or employment-related miles to total miles. (See Chapter I10 for a discussion of specific restrictions on the computation of depreciation where mixed business- and personal-use automobiles are acquired.)

 STOP & THINK

Question: Assume a taxpayer uses his car (original cost, $20,000) in his business, drives a total of 25,000 miles per year, and can substantiate 80% of the mileage as business use. In general, will the taxpayer benefit more from the standard mileage method of deducting automobile expenses or from the actual expenses method?

---

[23] Rev. Proc. 96-63, I.R.B. 1996-53, 47.

Solution: In general, the actual expenses method will yield a higher deduction. The American Automobile Association estimates that it costs approximately $0.50 per mile to operate a $20,000 car. Therefore, the actual cost of operating the automobile would be approximately $12,500 (25,000 miles × $0.50). The deductible amount for tax purposes would be 80% of $12,500, or $10,000 for the actual expenses method. Compare this amount with the standard mileage amount of $6,200 (25,000 miles × 80% business usage × $0.31/mile) and the actual expenses method yields a higher deduction. Of course, each individual situation is different and the actual results can vary based on circumstances such as the amount of repairs, depreciation, and so on.

EXAMPLE I9-17 ▶ Danielle owns two automobiles that are used at the same time in her small unincorporated business. One automobile is driven by an employee of the business, and Danielle drives the other vehicle for business use. Danielle cannot use the standard mileage rate method for either automobile because both cars are used in the business simultaneously. ◀

EXAMPLE I9-18 ▶ Doug used the standard mileage rate method in 1996, the year the automobile was acquired for use in his unincorporated business. The automobile was used in the business for the entire year. If the actual expense method is used for 1997 and later years, the automobile's adjusted basis (for depreciation purposes) must be reduced by 12 cents per mile for its 1996 business usage. Thus, if the automobile originally cost $20,000 in 1996 and was used 10,000 miles for business purposes during the initial year, the adjusted basis for computing depreciation in 1997 is reduced to $18,800 [$20,000 − (0.12 × 10,000)]. The remaining $18,800 basis can be depreciated using straight-line depreciation over the automobile's estimated useful life if the actual expense method is used. ◀

EXAMPLE I9-19 ▶ Edith uses her automobile 50% of the time for business and employment-related use and 50% for personal use. These percentages are substantiated by records that document the total usage for the automobile. During 1997 Edith drives a total of 40,000 miles. If the standard mileage rate method is used, she can deduct $6,300 (0.315 × 20,000 miles) for the business and employment-related use. Additionally, Edith may deduct any business-related parking fees and tolls. ◀

KEY POINT

The Tax Reform Act of 1984 imposed a "contemporaneous" records test for substantiating expenses for automobiles and certain other activities. Public outcry caused Congress to repeal this requirement in 1985. Now the business use of an automobile can be substantiated either by keeping adequate records or by sufficient corroborating evidence, oral or written.

REIMBURSEMENT OF AUTOMOBILE EXPENSES

An employee is entitled to deduct actual automobile expenses (or amounts derived under the standard mileage rate method if applicable) in excess of reimbursed amounts received from the employer. The computation is made on Form 2106 (Employee Business Expenses) and is reported on Schedule A of Form 1040.

EXAMPLE I9-20

ADDITIONAL COMMENT

The kind of written record that could corroborate the business use of an automobile would include account books, diaries, logs, trip sheets, expense reports, or written statements from witnesses.

▶ Elizabeth, who makes an adequate accounting to her employer, receives a $2,000 (20,000 miles at 10 cents per mile) reimbursement in 1997 for employment-related business miles. She incurs the following expenses related to both business and personal use:

Gas and oil	$4,400
Repairs and maintenance	2,700
Depreciation	3,000
Insurance	1,800
Parking and tolls	100
Total	$12,000

Elizabeth drives a total of 40,000 miles during the year. Thus, 50% (20,000 ÷ 40,000) of the $12,000 in automobile expenses is deductible. After subtracting the employer's $2,000 reimbursement, Elizabeth may deduct $4,000 [($12,000 × 0.50) − $2,000] as a miscellaneous itemized deduction (subject to the 2% nondeductible floor). Alternatively, if 1997 is the first year she used the car in her business, she could have claimed a deduction using the standard mileage rate method if the amount were in excess of the actual expenses. In this case the $6,000 of actual expenses is less than the $6,350 permitted under the standard mileage rate method [(20,000 × 0.315) + $50 business-related tolls]. ◄

ENTERTAINMENT EXPENSES

Entertainment of business customers and clients is a routine and, in many cases, an essential practice in business. Because entertainment expenses are considered ordinary and necessary practices of a business, they are deductible under either Sec. 162 or Sec. 212. However, the nature of entertainment expenses lend themselves to abuse by taxpayers. There certainly is an element of personal pleasure in taking a client to a hockey game or a Philharmonic orchestra performance and allowing taxpayers to deduct such expenses creates serious enforcement problems for the IRS.

For the reasons above, Congress enacted Sec. 274, which is strictly a disallowance section and contains classification rules, restrictive tests, and specific recordkeeping requirements. To deduct entertainment expenses, taxpayers must first show that the expenditure qualifies for a deduction under Sec. 162 (trade or business expense) or Sec. 212 (investment-type expense). Then the various requirements of Sec. 274 must be adhered to in order for an entertainment expense to be deductible. Over the years, Congress has continued to tighten the rules for the deductibility of entertainment expenses.

50% DISALLOWANCE FOR MEAL AND ENTERTAINMENT EXPENSES

Sec. 274 (n) provides that any expense incurred for either business meals or entertainment must be reduced by 50%.[24] Business meals may be deductible either as travel expenses or as entertainment, depending on the nature of the expenditure. In either case, the 50% limit applies to the cost of food and beverages including tips and taxes but is not applicable to transportation expenses incurred going to and from a business meal. Further, any portion of a business meal that is considered lavish or extravagant is disallowed.[25] In such a situation, the 50% reduction rule is applied to the allowable portion of the business meal.

> Krishna, a self-employed individual, pays $40 for a business meal plus $2 sales tax and an $8 tip. The total cost of the meal is $50. Assuming that no portion of the $50 cost is deemed to be lavish or extravagant, $25 ($50 × 0.50) is deductible. ◄

If an employee incurs entertainment or business meal expenses that are fully reimbursed by the employer, it is the employer rather than the employee who is limited to a deduction for 50% of the expenses. The employee merely includes the reimbursement in gross income and deducts the full amount of the entertainment or business meal expenses as a *for* AGI deduction, thus resulting in no overall tax effect to the employee (i.e., such amounts are not reported on the employee's tax return).

---

[24] For pre-1994 tax years, the disallowance was 20%.

[25] Sec. 274(k).

EXAMPLE 19-22 ▶
ADDITIONAL
COMMENT

Entertainment expenses are not considered "directly related" if there are substantial distractions. Therefore, if a meeting takes place at a sporting event, theater, or night club, the entertainment cannot be "directly related." This type of entertainment could qualify as an "associated with" expense. An example of a "directly related" expense would be the costs related to a hospitality room at a convention.

Gordon incurs employment-related entertainment expenses of $1,000 and is fully reimbursed by his employer after an adequate accounting has been made. The employer may deduct $500 [$1,000 − ($1,000 × 0.50)] of entertainment expenses. Gordon includes the $1,000 reimbursement in gross income and deducts $1,000 as a *for* AGI deduction. Thus, there is no overall tax effect to Gordon. ◀

CLASSIFICATION OF EXPENSES

If an individual is engaged in a trade or business or is self-employed, allowable entertainment expenses are deductible *for* AGI. Employees, however, may deduct entertainment expenses only as a miscellaneous itemized deduction (subject to the 2% nondeductible floor) unless the expenses are reimbursed. The tax rules for reimbursements of employee business expenses are discussed more fully later in this chapter.

EXAMPLE 19-23 ▶

Helen is a self-employed attorney who entertains clients and prospective clients. To the extent that these expenditures meet the Sec. 274 requirements, they are deductible by Helen as a *for* AGI expense on Schedule C of Form 1040 because Helen is engaged in a trade or business activity. The entertainment expenses are subject to the 50% limit but are not subject to the 2% nondeductible floor because the entertainment is deductible when determining AGI as a trade or business expense. ◀

EXPENSE CATEGORIES. To be deductible as an entertainment expense, the expenditure must be either **directly related** to the active conduct of a trade or business or **associated with** the active conduct of a trade or business. Different restrictions apply to each of these categories. The Regulations under Sec. 274 provide the substantive rules for the two types of entertainment expenses.

"Directly Related" Expenses. To meet the requirements for a "directly related" **entertainment expense**, some business benefit must be expected from the business conducted other than goodwill and the expense must be incurred in a clear business setting (i.e., where there are no substantial distractions). In other words, business in anticipation of a business benefit must actually be conducted during the entertainment period.

ADDITIONAL
COMMENT

With respect to the "associated with" type of expense, there is *no* requirement that the business discussion last for any specified period, or that more time be devoted to business than to entertainment.

"Associated With" Expenses. To qualify an expense as an "associated with" entertainment expenditure, the taxpayer must show a clear business purpose, such as obtaining new business or encouraging the continuation of an existing business relationship. An added restriction is placed on "associated with" entertainment in that the entertainment must directly precede or follow a bona fide business discussion. This means that the entertainment generally must occur on the same day that business is discussed.

EXAMPLE 19-24 ▶

Holly is a lawyer who hosts a birthday party in her home. Most of the guests are law partners or clients. No formal business discussions are conducted either before or immediately following the party. The expenditures for the birthday party are not deductible because no business discussions are conducted either before or after the party. ◀

Substantiation Requirements. In addition to both the directly related and associated with requirements, Sec. 274 imposes stringent substantiation requirements for entertainment expenses. In order to deduct entertainment expenses, taxpayers are required to substantiate each expenditure for which a deduction is claimed. Lack of documentation alone will cause the disallowance of a deduction.

BUSINESS MEALS

Business meals related to both travel and entertainment activities are subject to the same business-connection requirements as other types of entertainment expenses. Thus, a deduction is allowed only if the meal meets the "directly related" or "associated with" tests previously discussed. In addition, the expense must not be lavish or extravagant under the circumstances, and the taxpayer (or an employee of the taxpayer) must generally be present when the food or beverages are furnished.[26] Thus, a business meal is not currently deductible unless there is a substantial and bona fide business discussion (i.e., a discussion associated with the taxpayer's active trade or business) during, directly preceding, or immediately following the meal. This requirement does not apply to a business meal associated with travel where the taxpayer claims a deduction only for his or her own expenses.

EXAMPLE I9-25 ▶ Hank is a salesman for a manufacturing supply company. Hank meets Harold, a purchasing agent who is a substantial customer, for lunch during a normal business day. Business is actually conducted during the lunch, and the lunch expenses are not lavish or extravagant under the circumstances. Hank is fully reimbursed by his employer for the $30 lunch expenses after an adequate accounting of the expenses is submitted. The business meal qualifies as "directly related" entertainment because the entertainment involved the actual conduct of business where some business benefit is reasonably expected and a business discussion was conducted during the meal. Hank's employer may deduct $15 ($30 × 0.50) of entertainment expenses because the meal was not lavish or extravagant. ◀

EXAMPLE I9-26 ▶ Assume the same facts as in Example I9-25, except that the purchasing agent is a prospective customer and no business is actually discussed either during, directly preceding, or immediately following the meal. Thus, no deduction is allowed because no business is discussed either before, during, or after the meal. ◀

The Regulations provide that the surroundings in which food or beverages are furnished must be in an atmosphere where there are no substantial distractions to the discussion (e.g., a floor show).[27]

EXAMPLE I9-27 ▶ Harry is a salesman who takes a customer to a local nightclub to watch a floor show and to have a few drinks. No business is discussed either before, during, or after the entertainment. The expenses for the beverages and floor show are not deductible because neither of the business meal requirements are met (i.e., the floor show produced substantial distractions, and no business was discussed). Even if business was actually discussed, no deduction would be allowed because there were substantial distractions. ◀

ENTERTAINMENT FACILITIES AND CLUB DUES

KEY POINT

Subject to a very few exceptions, no deduction is permitted for costs related to yachts, swimming pools, fishing camps, tennis courts, bowling alleys, vacation resorts, etc. This highly visible type of entertainment contributed to the public perception that the tax system was unfair.

No deduction is permitted for costs (e.g., depreciation, maintenance, repairs, and so on) related to the maintenance of facilities that are used for entertainment, amusement, or recreation. Facilities include yachts, hunting lodges, country clubs, and so on.

No deduction is permitted for any type of club dues (including business, social, athletic, luncheon, and sporting clubs, as well as airline and hotel clubs).[28] Professional, civic and public service organizations (e.g., business leagues, trade associations, chambers of commerce, boards of trade, and real estate boards) are generally not subject to the dues disallowance rules. Initiation fees that are paid only upon joining a club are treated

---

[26] Sec. 274(k).
[27] Reg. Sec. 1.274-2(f)(2)(i)(b).

[28] Sec. 274(a)(3).

WHAT WOULD YOU DO IN THIS SITUATION?

You have recently acquired a new individual tax client, Joe Windsack, who is a manufacturer's representative for a local tool and die company. You have been engaged by Windsack to prepare his individual income tax return for the current year. Before the current tax year is over, you are at a party where Windsack is also a guest. You overhear Windsack bragging to a group of people that he substantially reduces his income tax liability by overstating meal and entertainment expenses. He indicated that he overstates the deductions in several ways, (1) when he goes out to lunch or dinner that is personal in nature, such as with his family, he always uses a credit card and fictitiously writes the name of a client or prospective client on the charge card receipt,

(2) when he goes out to lunch with several colleagues from his office (not business related), he charges the entire amount on his credit card (for everyone at the table), collects the cash from his colleagues for the cost of their meals, and then writes the entire amount off as a business-related meal, and (3) whenever he goes to any entertainment event, such as a ballgame, he always says that he took a client to the game with him and deducts the cost of the ticket as a business expense. When Windsack brings his tax information to you a couple of months later and you see a substantial amount of meal and entertainment expenses, what should you do?

as nondeductible capital expenditures. While club dues are not deductible, other business expenses (e.g., business meals) are deductible if the general requirements for entertainment deductions are met.

EXAMPLE I9-28 ▶ Heidi is a self-employed CPA who entertains clients at her country club. Her club expenses include the following:

Annual dues	$4,000
Meal and entertainment charges related to business use	3,000
Personal-use meal charges	2,500
Initiation fee	10,000
Total expenses	$19,500

The only expense that is deductible is 50% of the specific business charges relating to the meals and entertainment. Thus, Heidi may deduct $1,500 ($3,000 × 0.50) *for* AGI as a business expense because she is a self-employed CPA. ◀

BUSINESS GIFTS

Business gifts are subject to an annual ceiling amount of $25 per donee.[29] Amounts in excess of the $25 limit per donee are disallowed. The following rules and exceptions apply to determine the business gift deduction:

▶ Multiple gifts to each donee are aggregated for purposes of applying the $25 per donee annual limitation. Husbands and wives and other family members are treated as a single donee.

▶ Husbands and wives who make gifts to a particular donee are treated as a single taxpayer and are subject to a single $25 limit.

▶ Incidental costs such as gift wrapping, mailing, and delivery of gifts and certain imprinted gift items costing $4 or less are excluded.

---

[29] Sec. 274(b)(1).

▶ Employee achievement awards made for length of service or safety that are under $400 per individual are excluded.[30]

▶ A gift from an employee to his or her supervisor does not qualify as a business gift because such gifts are personal rather than business related and are, therefore, not deductible.

EXAMPLE I9-29 ▶

Jack, an employee, makes the following gifts during the year, none of which are reimbursed by his employer:

Jack's immediate supervisor	$20
Jack's secretary	15
Jeff (a customer of Jack's)	24
Jeff's wife (a noncustomer)	26
Gift-wrapping for the gift to Jeff	6
Total	$91

REAL-WORLD EXAMPLE

A taxpayer who had deducted the full cost of two wedding gifts, both of which were in excess of $25 apiece, was able to deduct only $25 for each gift. *Jack R. Howard,* 1981 PH T.C. Memo ¶81,250, 41 TCM 1554.

Jack's total deduction for business gifts is $46 ($15 + $25 + $6) and is classified as a miscellaneous itemized deduction subject to the 2% nondeductible floor because Jack is an employee. The $20 gift to Jack's immediate supervisor is not deductible. The gifts of $24 and $26 to Jeff and Jeff's wife must be aggregated and are limited to $25. The gift-wrapping charge is fully deductible because it is an incidental cost. ◀

LIMITATIONS ON ENTERTAINMENT TICKETS

In addition to the general 50% meals and entertainment limitation, the cost of a ticket for any entertainment activity or facility is limited to the ticket's face value. Thus, the 50% limit applies to the face value of the ticket. Further restrictions are placed on the rental of skyboxes that are leased for more than one event.[31]

EXAMPLE I9-30 ▶

Able Corporation acquires four tickets to a football game for $500 that are used for entertaining customers. The face amount of the tickets is only $100. Able's deduction for entertainment is initially limited to the $100 face value of the tickets. The deductible amount is $50 ($100 × 0.50) after applying the 50% limit on entertainment expenses. ◀

REIMBURSED EMPLOYEE BUSINESS EXPENSES

The tax treatment of reimbursements received by an employee from his employer for employment-related expenses depends upon whether the reimbursement is made pursuant to an **accountable** or **nonaccountable** plan. An accountable plan is a reimbursement arrangement that meets both of the following two tests.[32]

1. Substantiation—the employee must make an adequate accounting of expenses to his employer, that is, substantiate each business expense (an expense report, for example);

2. Return of excess reimbursement—within a reasonable period of time, the employee is required to return to the employer any portion of the reimbursement in excess of the substantiated expenses.

---

[30] Sec. 274(j). The total limit including both qualified and nonqualified plan awards is $1,600 per individual (see Chapter I4).

[31] Sec. 274(l)(2). The cost of a skybox is disallowed to the extent that it exceeds the cost of the highest-priced nonluxury box seat tickets multiplied by the number of seats in the skybox (e.g., if a skybox contains 30 seats and the cost of the highest-priced nonluxury box seat for a particular event is $40, the deduction for the skybox is limited to $1,200 ($40 × 30). The deduction would be also reduced by the 50% limitation applicable to entertainment expenses.

[32] Reg. Sec. 1.62-2(c).

If both of these tests are not met, all amounts paid to an employee are treated as paid under a nonaccountable plan.

ACCOUNTABLE PLAN. Under an accountable plan, reimbursements are excluded from the employee's gross income and the expenses are not deductible by the employee. Because of this netting of reimbursement and expense, nothing is reported on the employee's return. In the event, however, that an excess reimbursement is not returned to the employer, the excess reimbursement is included in the employee's gross income.

EXAMPLE I9-31 ▶ Antoine is an employee of the Bluechip Corporation, which maintains an accountable plan for purposes of reimbursing employee expenses. During the current year, Antoine went on a business trip and incurred $1,500 of expenses as follows: airfare, $800; lodging, $450; meals, $200; and tips $50. Bluechip reimbursed him $1,500. Because the reimbursement is pursuant to an accountable plan, Antoine will not include the $1,500 reimbursement in his gross income and he is not allowed to deduct any of the business expenses. ◀

EXAMPLE I9-32 ▶ Using the same facts as in Example I9-31, assume Bluechip advanced Antoine $1,800 for his business trip and his expenses were the same as above. If Antoine returned the excess $300 to Bluechip within a reasonable period of time, the result would be the same as in Example I9-31. However, if Antoine did not return the excess reimbursement (even though he is required to under the terms of the plan), Antoine must include the $300 in his gross income. ◀

If an employee receives a reimbursement that is not as much as his expenses, a proration is required.[33]

EXAMPLE I9-33 ▶ Fred, an employee, incurs employment-related expenses of $4,500 consisting of $1,200 business meals, $1,800 local transportation, and $1,500 entertainment of customers. He receives a $3,000 reimbursement from his employer that is intended to cover all of the expenses. Since the reimbursement is less than the amount of expenses, Fred must prorate the expenses as follows:

Expense	Total Amount	Reimbursed Expense	Unreimbursed Expense
Business meals	$1,200	$ 800	$ 400
Local transportation	1,800	1,200	600
Entertainment	1,500	1,000	500
Total	$4,500	$3,000	$1,500

The reimbursed expenses of $3,000 are not deductible by Fred and the $3,000 reimbursement is not reportable as income. The $1,500 of unreimbursed expenses are deductible *from* AGI (subject to 2% of AGI) as follows

Business meals ($400 × 50%)	$200
Local transportation	600
Entertainment ($500 × 50%)	250
	$1,050 ◀

NONACCOUNTABLE PLAN. Under a nonaccountable plan, reimbursements are included in the employee's gross income and the expenses are deductible by the

[33] Temp. Reg. Sec. 1.62-IT(e).

employee as miscellaneous itemized deductions, subject to the 2% of AGI floor and the 50% disallowance for meals and entertainment expenses.

EXAMPLE I9-34 ▶ Using the same facts as in Example I9-31 except that Bluechip maintains a nonaccountable plan for purposes of reimbursing employee expenses. Bluechip's plan is a nonaccountable plan because Antoine is not required to submit an accounting of his expenses to the company. Antoine must include the $1,500 in his gross income and may deduct the expenses as miscellaneous itemized deductions, subject to the 2% of AGI floor, in the amount of $1,400 [$800 + 450 + (200 × 50%) + 50]. ◀

Table I9-2 summarizes the concepts relating to employee business expenses and reimbursements.

MOVING EXPENSES

Moving expenses are generally nondeductible personal expenditures. However, most moves for employees and self-employed people are deductible under Sec. 217. The underlying rationale for this deduction is that such moves are similar to business expenditures because they are often either employment-related job transfers or necessary to obtain employment.

EXAMPLE I9-35 ▶ Ken retires from his job and moves from Ohio to Arizona. His moving expenses are nondeductible personal expenditures because the move is not employment-related and he is not moving to look for a new job. ◀

▼ Table I9-2
TREATMENT OF EMPLOYEE REIMBURSEMENTS

TYPE OF PLAN	TAX EFFECT
Accountable Plan	
Reimbursement = Expense	No effect, amounts are netted and not reported on employee's return.
Reimbursement > Expense	Not permissible under plan, but should it occur, excess reimbursement is included in employee's gross income.
Reimbursement < Expense	Expenses are prorated to amount of reimbursement. Reimbursed expenses–no effect; Unreimbursed expenses are deductible as miscellaneous itemized deductions subject to 2% of AGI
Nonaccountable Plan	
Reimbursements	Always included in employee's gross income.
Expenses	Deductible as miscellaneous itemized deductions subject to 2% of AGI.

OBJECTIVE **3**

Identify deductible moving expenses and determine the amount and year of deductibility

ADDITIONAL COMMENT

The time requirement test ensures that taxpayers cannot use temporary jobs as a pretext for deducting the cost of moving for personal reasons.

EXAMPLE I9-36 ▶

EXAMPLE I9-37 ▶

ADDITIONAL COMMENT

The individual need not be employed at the location that he or she is leaving. For example, a graduating college student who has not been employed for the most recent four years could deduct moving costs if the distance requirement is satisfied and if he or she has been employed at the *new* location for the minimum time period.

KEY POINT

The standard mileage rate for purposes of the moving expense deduction is only 10 cents per mile, compared to the 1997 standard business mileage rate of 31.5 cents per mile.

The following two conditions must be met for a moving expense to be deductible:[34]

▶ *Distance requirement.* The new job location must be at least 50 miles farther from the taxpayer's old residence than the old residence was from the former place of employment. If an individual has no former place of employment, the new job must be at least 50 miles from the old residence.

▶ *Time requirement.* A new or transferred employee must be employed on a full-time basis at the new location for at least 39 weeks during the 12-month period immediately following the move. More stringent requirements must be met by self-employed people who either work as an employee at the new location or continue to be self-employed. Such individuals are subject to a 78-week minimum work period during the first two years following the move. At least 39 of the 78 weeks must be in the first 12-month period. The Regulations provide for a waiver of the time requirements for both employees and self-employed individuals if the taxpayer becomes disabled, dies, or is involuntarily terminated (other than for willful misconduct).[35]

Ellen is employed by the Able Company in Dallas, Texas. She lives 30 miles from her place of employment in Dallas. If Ellen accepts a new job in Houston, the new job location is 270 miles from her former residence in Dallas. The 50-mile distance requirement is satisfied because the distance from her old residence to her new job in Houston (270 miles) exceeds the distance from her old residence to her old job by 240 miles (270 − 30). ◀

Assume the same facts as in Example I9-36, except that Ellen accepts a new job and moves to a new residence in a small town outside of Dallas. Her new job location is 55 miles from her former residence. The 50-mile distance requirement is not met because the distance from her old residence to her new job only exceeds the 30-mile distance from her old residence to her old job by 25 miles (55 − 30). ◀

EXPENSE CLASSIFICATION

Moving expenses of an employee or a self-employed individual are deductible *for* AGI.[36] Thus, a taxpayer may receive a tax benefit from the deduction of moving expenses even if the standard deduction is used in lieu of itemizing deductions.

DEFINITION OF MOVING EXPENSES

DIRECT MOVING EXPENSES. Only direct moving expenses are deductible. These expenses are deductible without limit as long as they are reasonable in amount and include:

▶ The cost of moving household goods and personal effects from the former residence to the new residence (e.g., moving van).

▶ The cost of traveling (including lodging but excluding meals) from the former residence to the new residence. If the trip is by personal automobile, a deduction of ten cents per mile (or actual expenses) is allowed for each automobile that is driven.[37]

The expenses of moving household goods and personal effects do not include storage charges in excess of 30 days, penalties for breaking leases, mortgage penalties, expenses of refitting drapes, or losses on deposits and club memberships.[38]

---

[34] The requirements for deducting moving expenses are contained in Sec. 217 and the Regulations thereunder.
[35] Reg. Sec. 1.217-2(d)(1).
[36] Sec. 62(a)(15). For years before 1994 moving expenses were deductible *from* AGI as an itemized deduction (not subject to the 2% nondeductible floor).

[37] Rev. Proc. 96-63, I.R.B. 1996-53, 48.
[38] Reg. Sec. 1.217-2(b)(3). In-transit storage charges for up to 30 consecutive days are allowable moving expenses.

EXAMPLE I9-38 ▶ Gail, a resident of California and a college student in that state, graduates from college and accepts a new position with an accounting firm in Atlanta. Thus, Gail is an employee of the Atlanta firm. Because the move meets the distance requirement (i.e., more than 50 miles), Gail qualifies for the deduction if she also meets the 39-week time requirement. Gail incurs the following expenses pursuant to the move: moving van, $1,200; lodging en route, $400; automobile expenses, $250 (2,500 miles × $0.10 cents per mile); and tolls and parking, $25. Assuming these expenses are reasonable, they qualify as direct moving expenses and are deductible without limitation. The cost of any meals incurred by Gail en route is not deductible. ◀

Otherwise allowable expenses of any individual other than the taxpayer are taken into account only if the individual has both the former residence and the new residence as his principal place of abode and is a member of the taxpayer's household.

EXAMPLE I9-39 ▶ Assume the same facts as in Example I9-38 except that Gail's son Paul is a member of her household. Additional automobile expenses (including tolls and parking) of $275 are incurred during the move because Paul owns an automobile which is driven to the new location. The $275 of additional automobile expenses are deductible as moving expenses because Paul is a member of Gail's household and his principal place of abode includes both the former and the new residences. ◀

KEY POINT

Indirect moving expenses are not deductible after December 31, 1993. In the Revenue Reconciliation Act of 1993 Congress eliminated the deduction for costs associated with pre-move househunting trips, temporary quarters, and selling the old residence. Congress felt that a deduction was not justified for expenses that were not directly related to the move.

NONDEDUCTIBLE INDIRECT MOVING EXPENSES. In addition to the disallowed moving expenses previously discussed (e.g., meals en route, storage charges etc.), the following indirect or moving-related expense items are not deductible:[39]

▶ Househunting trips including meals, lodging, and transportation.

▶ Temporary living expenses at the new job location.

▶ Qualified expenses related to a sale, purchase, or lease of a residence (e.g., attorney's fees, points, or payments to a lessor to cancel a lease).

TREATMENT OF EMPLOYER REIMBURSEMENTS

Moving expense reimbursements made by an employer, paid directly or through reimbursement, are excluded from the employee's gross income as a qualified fringe benefit under Sec. 132 to the extent that the expenses meet the requirements for deductibility (i.e., the reimbursement is for moving expenses that are otherwise deductible under Sec. 217). Moving expense reimbursements must be included in gross income if the employee actually deducted the expenses in a prior tax year or if the expenses are otherwise not deductible under Sec. 217.[40]

EXAMPLE I9-40 ▶ In 1997, Ralph incurs $2,400 of otherwise deductible moving expenses related to moving household effects and traveling to his new residence. He also incurs $2,600 of nondeductible moving-related expenses (e.g., househunting trips and temporary living expenses). Ralph receives a $5,000 reimbursement from his employer. Of the total reimbursement, $2,400 is excluded from gross income as a Sec. 132 fringe benefit. However, $2,600 of the reimbursement for nondeductible moving-related expenses is included in Ralph's gross income under Sec. 82. None of the $2,400 otherwise deductible moving expenses may be deducted by Paul because they were reimbursed by his employer. ◀

---

[39] Before 1994, indirect moving expenses were deductible subject to a $1,500 limit for househunting trips and temporary living expenses and a $3,000 overall limitation was applied to all indirect moving expenses.

[40] Sec. 82.

EDUCATION EXPENSES

ADDITIONAL COMMENT

Attendance at a convention or professional meeting is one of the most common deductible education expenses. Almost every profession or occupation has its own society or association. Often these organizations sponsor local, regional, or national meetings. Training sessions or other types of educational activities are normally included on the program.

TYPICAL MISCONCEPTION

Education costs include more than the cost of books, tuition, registration fees, and supplies. Transportation costs and travel costs are also included.

ETHICAL POINT

A client asks advice from his CPA as to whether certain educational expenses are deductible. The CPA should inform the client that the advice reflects professional judgment based on an existing situation. The CPA should use cautionary language to the effect that the advice is based on facts as stated and authorities that are subject to change.

Generally, education expenses are considered personal expenses and, therefore, are not deductible despite the obvious social benefits that accrue to society from the pursuit of such activities. However, certain education expenses that are necessary in the pursuit of an employment-related or trade or business activity are deductible (e.g., employees or self-employed individuals may need to pursue certain continuing education activities to maintain or improve their employment or professional skills). It would be inequitable if such educational expenditures were not deductible because they are incurred to produce income from employment or professional service activities. Educational expenses incurred by employees or self-employed individuals may be contrasted with scholarship and fellowship grants under Sec. 117 and educational assistance payments under Sec. 127 made by employers. Both of these latter types of payments generally can be excluded from gross income. (See Chapter I4 for a discussion of scholarship and fellowship grants and educational assistance payments.)

CLASSIFICATION OF EDUCATION EXPENSES

Depending on the nature of the education-related activity, educational expenses may be either personal and nondeductible, deductible *for* AGI, deductible *from* AGI (as a miscellaneous itemized deduction), or reimbursed by an employer and excluded from gross income. Table I9-3 illustrates the tax consequences that are accorded to various types of education expenses depending on the facts and circumstances and the type of expenditure for each case.

GENERAL REQUIREMENTS FOR A DEDUCTION

An employee may generally deduct education expenses if either of the following two requirements are met:[41]

▶ The expenditure is incurred to maintain or improve skills required by the individual in his or her employment, trade, or business; or

▶ The expenditure is incurred to meet requirements imposed by law or by the employer for retention of employment, rank, or compensation rate.

Even if one of the two requirements above are met, education expenses are not deductible if:

▶ The education is required to meet minimum educational requirements for qualification in the taxpayer's employment; or

▶ The education qualifies the taxpayer for a new trade or business (or employment activity).

The deductibility of education expenses has been a frequent source of controversy and litigation because of the uncertainty in interpreting the above Regulations. The principal area of disagreement has been the interpretation of the term "qualifies the taxpayer for a new trade or business." If a taxpayer undertakes education and that education will **qualify** her for a new trade or business, then her expenses will not be deductible. For example, several courts have disallowed deductions to IRS agents and accountants for educational expenses incurred in obtaining a law degree, even though such training is helpful in the taxpayer's employment.[42] The courts reasoned that the taxpayers were qualifying for a new profession (i.e., the practice of law). However, the

---

[41] Reg. Sec. 1.162-5

[42] *Jeffry L. Weiler*, 54 T.C. 398 (1970).

▼ TABLE I9-3

Classification and Tax Treatment of Educational Expenses

Situation Facts	Classification and Tax Treatment
Jeremy is a college student who is not classified as an employee and is pursuing a general course of study.	The expenses are nondeductible personal expenditures regardless of whether Jeremy or his parents pay them.
Irene is an employee who incurs certain employment-related educational expenses including travel, transportation, tuition, and books. Her expenses are not reimbursed by her employer.	If the expenses meet the two general deduction requirements, the education expenses are deductible *from* AGI as a miscellaneous itemized deduction (subject to the 2% nondeductible floor).
Jesse is an employee who receives educational assistance payments from his employer to reimburse him certain educational expenses incurred in attending college at the undergraduate level.	Educational assistance payments up to $5,250 per year are excluded from Jesse's gross income and are deductible by the employer as trade or business expenses if the requirements of Sec. 127 are met.[43]
Jackie is a self-employed CPA who incurs education expenses including travel, transportation, books, registration fees, and so on to attend a continuing education conference.	All of the education expenses are deductible as trade or business expenses.
Jim is an employee who incurs education expenses for a continuing education course related to his employment, and the expenses are reimbursed by the employer.	The reimbursement is deductible by the employer as a trade or business expense. There is no tax effect to the employee because the education expenses are offset by the reimbursement.

IRS has ruled that a practicing dentist may deduct educational expenses in becoming an orthodontist under the theory that a dentist becoming an orthodontist is not a new trade or business.[44]

STOP & THINK

Question: The Regulations clearly provide that if the education "qualifies" a taxpayer for a new trade or business, the cost of such education is not deductible. If taken to the extreme, could the IRS argue that *any* course would qualify an individual for a new trade or business? For example, if a person took a basket weaving course, could not the IRS argue that the person is now qualified for the new trade or business of basket weaving? How can a taxpayer support his position that the education does not qualify him for a new trade or business in order to meet the deductibility requirements?

Solution: This is a difficult question and many commentators have written that the Regulations are unfairly harsh toward taxpayers. The courts have required that the IRS be "reasonable" in its interpretations of qualification of a new trade or business. The best way for a taxpayer to support his position is to find a case where the facts are approximately the same as the taxpayer's and where the court has upheld the taxpayer's position in that case.

---

[43] The Sec. 127 exclusion is scheduled to expire for tax years beginning after May 31, 1997. However, for tax years beginning in 1997, only expenses paid for courses beginning before July 1, 1997, are excludable. Finally, the exclusion is not available for any expenses related to graduate-level courses beginning after June 30, 1996.

[44] Rev. Rul. 74-78, 1974-1 C.B. 44.

Generally, a taxpayer must be employed or self-employed to be eligible for an education expense deduction. However, some courts have permitted individuals to qualify if they are unemployed for a temporary period.[45] School teachers have generally qualified for an education expense deduction in situations where the public school system requires advanced education courses as a condition for retention of employment or renewal of a teaching certificate or where state law imposes similar requirements. However, college instructors who are working on a doctorate in a college where the Ph.D. is the minimum degree for holding a permanent position generally have not been permitted to deduct the expenditures made to obtain the degree.[46]

EXAMPLE 19-41 ▶ Jane is a self-employed dentist who incurs education expenses attending a continuing education conference on new techniques in her field. Such expenditures are incurred to maintain or improve her skills as a practicing dentist (a trade or business activity). All of her educational expenses are deductible *for* AGI because Jane is engaged in a trade or business activity. ◀

EXAMPLE 19-42 ▶ Juan is a business executive who incurs education expenses in the pursuit of an MBA degree in management. None of the expenses are reimbursed by Juan's employer. The expenses are deductible because they are incurred to maintain or improve Juan's skills as a manager and do not qualify Juan for a new trade or business. All of Juan's education expenses (e.g., travel, transportation, tuition, books, and word processing) are deductible *from* AGI as a miscellaneous itemized deduction (subject to the 2% nondeductible floor). ◀

EXAMPLE 19-43 ▶ Janet is a high school teacher who is required by state law to complete a specified number of additional graduate courses to renew her provisional teaching certificate. None of the expenses are reimbursed by Janet's employer. The educational expenses are deductible *from* AGI as a miscellaneous itemized deduction (subject to the 2% nondeductible floor) because the expenditures are incurred to meet the requirements imposed by law to retain her job and do not qualify her for a new trade or business. ◀

EXAMPLE 19-44 ▶ Jean is an accountant with a public accounting firm who incurs expenses in connection with taking the CPA examination (e.g., CPA review course fees, travel, and transportation). None of the expenses are reimbursed by Jean's employer. Even though the expenditures may improve her employment-related skills, they are not deductible because they are incurred to meet the minimum educational standards for qualification in Jean's accounting position.[47] ◀

EXAMPLE 19-45 ▶

KEY POINT

The deduction for travel expenses is not permitted if the travel itself is the educational activity. Therefore, a high school teacher who teaches Spanish cannot deduct expenses incurred in living in Madrid during the summer.

Joy is a tax accountant who incurs expenses to obtain a law degree. Despite the fact that the law school courses may be helpful to Joy to maintain or improve her skills as a tax practitioner, such expenses are not deductible because the taxpayer is qualifying for a new trade or business. If Joy were not a degree candidate at the law school and merely took a few tax law courses for continuing education, the educational expenses would be deductible because they are incurred to maintain or improve Joy's skills as a tax specialist. In such a case, the expenses are deductible *for* AGI if Joy is self-employed and *from* AGI as a miscellaneous itemized deduction (subject to the 2% nondeductible floor) if Joy is an employee. ◀

---

[45] *Robert J. Picknally*, 1977 PH T.C. Memo ¶77,321, 36 TCM 1292. The IRS has conceded that a deduction may be warranted in periods where the cessation of business activity was for periods of a year or less (Rev. Rul. 68-591, 1968-2 C.B. 73).

[46] *Kenneth C. Davis*, 65 T.C. 1014 (1976).

[47] Rev. Rul. 69-292, 1969-1 C.B. 84.

OFFICE IN HOME EXPENSES

OBJECTIVE 5

Determine whether the expenses of an office in home meet the requirements for deductibility and apply the gross income limitations

Employees or self-employed individuals who use a portion of their home for trade or business or employment-related activities should be entitled to a deduction because of the relationship between the use of the property for trade or business or employment-related activities. However, it is often difficult to determine whether a taxpayer is using a portion of the home such as a den for business or personal use.

Before 1976, lenient standards were applied to determine whether a deduction should be permitted. For example, some courts permitted employees to deduct office-in-home expenses even if the taxpayer's use of the facilities was not in the exclusive conduct of a trade or business activity but was merely appropriate and helpful to the taxpayer's employment activity. In 1976 the office-in-home rules were substantially restricted by the enactment of Code Sec. 280A. These restrictions were further tightened by the Tax Reform Act of 1986.

ADDITIONAL COMMENT

Approximately 24 million individuals, or 23% of the work force, work at least part-time at home.

GENERAL REQUIREMENTS FOR A DEDUCTION

Employees and self-employed individuals are permitted to deduct office-in-home expenses only if the office is used under either of the following conditions:

▶ The office is used exclusively on a regular basis as the principal place of business for *any* trade or business of the taxpayer;[48] or

▶ The office is used as a place for meeting or dealing with patients, clients, or customers in the normal course of business.[49]

In addition to meeting either of these tests, an employee must further prove that the exclusive use is for the convenience of the *employer*. It is not enough that it is merely helpful or appropriate to the employee.

EXAMPLE 19-46 ▶

Nader is a self-employed anesthesiologist who performs medical services at three hospitals, none of which provides him with an office. He spends approximately two hours per day in his home office where he maintains patient records, correspondence, and performs billing procedures. The office was not used as a place for meeting with or dealing with patients, clients, or customers in the normal course of business. The Supreme Court denied a deduction in this situation because the words "principal place of business" was interpreted to mean the "most important or significant place for the business." The Court concluded that the essence of the professional service rendered by the doctor was the actual medical treatment in the hospitals.[50] A second factor that was considered to be important by the Supreme Court was the amount of time spent at the office relative to the total work effort. Thus, the office-in-home deduction was denied on the basis of both of these factors. ◀

REAL-WORLD EXAMPLE

Most teachers have been denied a home office deduction because the home office is not the principal place of business. Also, most teachers cannot demonstrate that their office in the home is for the convenience of the employer because the employer typically provides an office at the school.

The IRS's position is that it will first apply the "relative importance" test to determine whether an office in the taxpayer's home is a principal place of business.[51] If the relative importance test is inconclusive, the "time" test is then applied.

EXAMPLE 19-47 ▶

David is a self-employed retailer of costume jewelry who sells the jewelry at craft shows, on consignment, and through mail orders. A substantial amount of income is generated both from the sales at craft shows and from mail order sales made from his office in his home. David

---

[48] The exclusive use requirement does not prevent taxpayers from using a single home office for two or more businesses or require physical segregation of such activities. See *Alfred W. Hamacher*, 94 T.C. 348 (1992).
[49] Sec. 280A(c)(1).

[50] *CIR v. Nader E. Soliman*, 71 AFTR 2d 93-463, 93-1 USTC ¶50,014 (USSC, 1993).
[51] Rev. Rul. 94-24, 1994-5, I.R.B. 15.

KEY POINT

The office-in-home deduction is available only where the office is being used for trade or business purposes. No deduction is permitted if the office is used to carry on investment activities.

spends 25 hours per week in his home filling and shipping mail orders and attending to administrative matters. Approximately 15 hours per week is devoted to craft show and consignment sales activities. Because the "relative importance" test (e.g., the relative importance of the sales activities) is inconclusive, the "time" test is then applied. Because David devotes significantly more time to the activities in his home office, he can deduct expenses for the business use of his home. ◀

Because of these strict statutory requirements, this deduction is generally restricted to professionals such as attorneys, medical doctors, and accountants, and so on, who do not maintain a permanent place of business elsewhere and employees who conduct a separate trade or business exclusively in a portion of their personal residence. If an employee is engaged in the conduct of a separate trade or business, the allowable expenses are deductible *for* AGI as trade or business expenses. Otherwise, allowable office-in-home expenses are treated as miscellaneous itemized deductions (subject to the 2% nondeductible floor).

EXAMPLE I9-48 ▶

Joel, a teacher, uses his den to prepare lesson plans, grade papers, and perform other incidental tasks for his employer. Joel's employer provides office space at the school, but the den is helpful to the completion of these tasks because Joel prefers to be at home during the evening. No deduction for a home office, including depreciation, real estate taxes, mortgage interest, repairs, and utilities, is deductible as employment-related business expenses because the requirements listed above are not met. In addition, the use of the den is not for "the convenience of the employer" but is merely appropriate or helpful for the employee. However, real estate taxes and mortgage interest are deductible *from* AGI if Joel itemizes his deductions. ◀

STOP & THINK

Question: Charley is a self-employed electrician who works out of his home. He maintains an office in his home where he maintains his records and answers telephone calls. He only keeps on hand a limited amount of parts and keeps these items in his truck. He obviously performs all of his electrician services at the site of his customers. Since Charley's only office is the one in his home and he performs important administrative duties from the office, can Charley deduct the cost of maintaining his office in the home?

Solution: Under current law, Charley cannot deduct the cost of his office in the home. While this seems totally unfair, based on the recent *Soliman* decision of the Supreme Court, current law would deny a deduction for Charley because his principal place of business is at the customer locations, not his office.

DEDUCTION AND LIMITATIONS

The deduction for home office expenses is computed using the following two categories of expenses:

1. Expenses directly related to the office, and
2. Expenses indirectly related to the office.

Direct expenses include operating expenses (supplies, etc.) that are used in the business as well as other expenses that relate solely to the office, such as painting and wallpaper. Indirect expenses are the prorata share of expenses that benefit the entire house or apartment, such as mortgage interest (or rent), real estate taxes, insurance, utilities, and maintenance. The office in the home expense is the sum of the direct expenses plus the prorata share (generally based on square footage) of indirect expenses.

EXAMPLE I9-49 ▶ Julie works as a full-time employee for a local company. She also operates a mail order business out of her home and maintains an office in her home that is used exclusively for business. The size of her home in total is 2,400 square feet and her office is 300 square feet. During the current year, the following expenses were incurred in connection with the office in her home:

Painting of office	$ 600
Decorations in office	900
Mortgage interest (total)	3,200
Real estate taxes (total)	1,800
Insurance (total)	600
Utilities (total)	2,400
Depreciation (total)	800

Julie's home office expense for the current year would be computed as follows:

Direct expenses:		
Painting	$600	
Decorations	900	$1,500
Indirect expenses:		
Mortgage interest	3,200	
Real estate taxes	1,800	
Insurance	600	
Utilities	2,400	
Depreciation	800	
	8,800	
Business percentage ($300/$2,400)	12.5%	1,100
Total expense for office in home		$2,600	◀

TYPICAL MISCONCEPTION

Where a taxpayer is not entitled to an office-in-home deduction, the taxpayer can still deduct directly related business expenses (e.g., the cost of office supplies, and an MACRS deduction on filing cabinets and other equipment).

The total allowable office-in-home expenses may not exceed the taxpayer's gross income from the business (or rental) activity.[52] This ceiling limitation on otherwise qualifying office-in-home deductions is intended to prevent taxpayers from recognizing tax losses if the business (or rental) activity does not produce sufficient amounts of gross income. Expenses disallowed because of the gross income limitation can be carried forward but are subject to the gross income limitation in the later year.

Employee expense classifications and deduction limitations are summarized in Topic Review I9-1.

DEFERRED COMPENSATION

OBJECTIVE 6

Discuss the tax treatment and requirements for various deferred compensation arrangements

Various types of benefit plans providing favorable tax treatment are available to employees and self-employed individuals. These tax benefits were provided to stimulate savings accumulations for retirement as a supplement to the social security system. Favorable tax consequences generally include the following benefits:

▶ Deferral of taxes for employee or employer contributions to retirement plans until the individual retires or receives a distribution from the plan

▶ An immediate deduction for contributions to qualified retirement plans for the employer or self-employed individual

---

[52] Sec. 280A(c)(5).

Topic Review I9-1

Classification and Deductibility of Exployee Expenses

Type of Expenditure	50% Disallowance	For or From AGI	Other Limitations
Miscellaneous itemized deductions	Applies to unreimbursed meals and entertainment	*From* AGI	Subject to 2% of AGI nondeductible floor.
Reimbursed travel expenses (adequate accounting is made)	Applies to the employer for meals portion of the travel only	*For* AGI	2% of AGI nondeductible floor applies only to employee expenses that exceed the reimbursement.
Unreimbursed travel expenses	Applies to meals portion of travel only	*From* AGI	Subject to the 2% of AGI nondeductible floor. Employee must be away from his or her tax home overnight.
Automobile expenses	Not applicable	*From* AGI	Subject to the 2% of AGI nondeductible floor. The standard mileage rate method may be used.
Moving expenses	Not applicable because meals are not deductible	*For* AGI;	Indirect moving-related expenses are not deductible.
Entertainment expenses	Applies to all entertainment expenses	*From* AGI	Subject to the 2% of AGI nondeductible floor. Club dues and initiation fees are not deductible.
Education expenses	Applies to meal portion of education expenses	*From* AGI	Qualifying expenses are subject to the 2% of AGI nondeductible floor.
Office-in-home	Not applicable	*From* AGI; If trade- or business-related, the expenses are for AGI	Employment-related expenses (other than real estate taxes and interest) are subject to the 2% of AGI nondeductible floor. Gross income limitations apply to allowable expenses.

▶ Deferral of taxation on the income earned on amounts contributed to the retirement plan

▶ Special forward income-averaging or rollover benefits for lump-sum distributions from certain retirement plans

The following types of *deferred compensation arrangements* are discussed here:

▶ Qualified pension and profit-sharing plans

▶ Nonqualified deferred compensation arrangements including restricted property and employee stock option plans

▶ Self-employed (H.R. 10) retirement plans and individual retirement accounts (IRAs)

QUALIFIED PENSION AND PROFIT-SHARING PLANS

ADDITIONAL COMMENT

The Staff of the Joint Committee on Taxation estimates the revenue loss resulting from the deferral of taxes on contributions and earnings for qualified pension and profit-sharing plans for the period from 1994 through 1998 will approximate $311.1 billion. The provision is designed to encourage employers to establish pension plans for their employees. The employer receives a deduction for the contribution, but the employee is not taxed currently. The repeal of this provision would substantially reduce the budget deficit.

The federal tax law provides favorable tax benefits for employers (i.e., through an immediate tax deduction for amounts contributed) and employees (i.e., through a deferral of taxes on contributions and earnings) provided the plan meets certain qualification requirements. For example, qualified plans must not discriminate in favor of highly compensated individuals, must be formed and operated for the exclusive benefit of employees, and must meet certain vesting requirements. A distinguishing feature of a qualified plan is that the employer receives an immediate tax deduction for pension contributions. Under a nonqualified plan, the employer's deduction is generally deferred until the employee recognizes the income.

TYPES OF PLANS. Qualified plans include

▶ Pension plans

▶ Profit-sharing plans

▶ Stock bonus plans, including employee stock ownership plans (ESOPs)

Pension Plans. The features that distinguish a **qualified pension plan** include the following:

▶ Systematic and definite payments are made to a pension trust (without regard to profits) based on actuarial methods.

▶ A pension plan may provide for incidental benefits such as disability, death, or medical insurance benefits.

A pension plan may be either contributory or noncontributory. Under a **noncontributory pension plan**, the contributions are made solely by the employer. Under a **contributory pension plan**, the employee also makes voluntary contributions that supplement those made by the employer.

Pension plans are either defined benefit plans or defined contribution plans. In a **defined contribution pension plan**, a separate account is established for each participant and fixed amounts are contributed based on a specific formula (e.g., a specified percentage of compensation). The retirement benefits are based on the value of a participant's account (including the amount of earnings that accrue to the account) at the time of retirement.

EXAMPLE I9-50 ▶

Alabama Corporation establishes a qualified pension plan for its employees that provides for employer contributions equal to 8% of each participant's salary. Retirement payments to each participant are based on the amount of accumulated benefits in the employee's account at the retirement date. The pension plan is a defined contribution plan, because the contribution rate is based on a specific and fixed percentage of compensation. ◀

KEY POINT

All qualified plans can be classified into two broad categories. They are either defined contribution plans or defined benefit plans. An understanding of the distinction between these two broad categories is important because some rules will apply to one type of plan but not the other.

Defined benefit plans establish a contribution formula based on actuarial techniques that are sufficient to fund a fixed retirement benefit amount. For example, a defined benefit plan might provide fixed retirement benefits equal to 40% of an employee's average salary for the five years before retirement.

A distinguishing feature of a defined benefit plan is that forfeitures of unvested amounts (e.g., due to employee resignations) must be used to reduce the employer contributions that would otherwise be made under the plan. In a defined contribution plan, however, the forfeitures related to unvested amounts may either be reallocated to the other participants in a nondiscriminatory manner or used to reduce future employer contributions.[53]

---

[53] Sec. 401(a)(8).

Profit-Sharing Plans. A qualified profit-sharing plan may also be established by an employer in addition to, or in lieu of, a qualified pension plan arrangement. **Profit-sharing plans** include the following distinguishing features:

▶ A definite, predetermined formula must be used to allocate employer contributions to individual employees and to establish benefit payments.

▶ Annual employer contributions are not required, but substantial and recurring contributions must be made to satisfy the requirement that the plan be permanent.[54]

▶ Employees may be given the option to receive cash that is fully taxable as current compensation or to defer taxation on employer contributions by having such amounts contributed to the profit-sharing trust.[55] Plans of this type are called Sec. 401(k) plans.

▶ Forfeitures arising under the plan may be reallocated to the remaining participants to increase their profit-sharing benefits, provided that certain nondiscrimination requirements are met.

▶ Lump-sum payments made to an employee before retirement may be provided following a prescribed period for the vesting of such amounts.

▶ Incidental benefits such as disability, death, or medical insurance may also be provided in a profit-sharing arrangement.

Stock Bonus Plan. A **stock bonus plan** is a special type of defined contribution plan whereby the investments of the plan are in the employer-company's own stock. The employer makes his contribution to the trust either in cash or in stock. If in cash, the amounts are invested in the company's stock. The stock is allocated and subsequently distributed to the participants. Stock bonus plan requirements are similar to profit-sharing plans. An **employee stock ownership plan (ESOP)** is a type of qualified stock bonus plan.[56] An ESOP, funded by a combination of employer and employee contribution and plan loans, invest primarily in employer stock. The stock is held for the benefit of the employees. ESOPs are attractive because the employer is allowed to reduce taxable income by deducting any dividends that are paid to the participants (or their beneficiaries) in the year such amounts are paid and are taxable to the participant.[57] For employer securities acquired by the ESOP, the dividends-paid deduction is limited to dividends paid on employer stock acquired with an ESOP loan.

QUALIFICATION REQUIREMENTS FOR A QUALIFIED PLAN

Qualified pension, profit-sharing, and stock plans must meet complex qualification rules and requirements to achieve and maintain their favored qualifying status.

▶ Section 401(a) requires that the plan must be for the employee's exclusive benefit. For example, the trust must follow prudent investment rules to ensure that the pension benefits will accrue for the employees' benefit.

▶ The plan may not discriminate in favor of highly compensated employees. Highly compensated employees are employees who meet either of two tests, (1) own 5% or more of the corporation's stock, or (2) receive compensation of greater than $80,000.[58]

▶ Contributions and plan benefits must bear a uniform relationship to the compensation payments made to covered employees. For example, if contributions for the

KEY POINT

The tax law with respect to qualified pension and profit-sharing plans is extremely complex. A detailed study of these provisions is beyond the scope of this text.

---

[54] Reg. Sec. 1.401-1(b).
[55] Sec. 401(k).
[56] Secs. 409(a) and 4975(e)(7).

[57] Sec. 404(k).
[58] Sec. 414(q). The $80,000 amount is subject to annual indexing for inflation.

benefit of the participants are based on a fixed percentage of the employee's compensation (e.g., 4%), the plan should not be disqualified despite the fact that the contributions for highly-compensated employees are greater on an actual dollar basis than those for lower paid individuals.

▶ Certain coverage requirements that are expressed in terms of a portion of the employees covered by the plan must be met.

▶ An employee's right to receive benefits from the employer's contributions must vest (i.e., become nonforfeitable) after a certain period or number of years of employment. The vesting requirement is intended to ensure that a significant percentage of employees will eventually receive retirement benefits. Employer-provided benefits must be 100% vested after 5 years of service.[59] In all cases, any employee contributions to the plan must vest immediately.

EXAMPLE I9-51 ▶ Ken is a participant in a noncontributory qualified pension plan that provides for no vesting until an employee completes five years of service. Ken terminates his employment with the company after four years of service. Because Ken has not met the minimum vesting requirements, he is not entitled to receive any of the employer contributions that are made on his behalf. If the plan adopted the alternative three- to seven-year vesting schedule (see footnote 59), 40% of the employer-provided benefits would be vested at the time of his termination and would provide Ken with future retirement benefits. ◀

TAX TREATMENT TO EMPLOYEES AND EMPLOYERS

Employer contributions to a qualified plan are immediately deductible (subject to specific limitations on contribution amounts), and such amounts are not taxable to an employee until the pension payments are received.[60] Earnings on pension fund investments are tax-exempt to the trust. These amounts are taxable to the employee only when the pension benefits are paid. If an employee contributes to the qualified plan, such amounts are generally treated as having been made from after-tax earnings (i.e., the employee-contributed amounts are taxed to the employee when such amounts are earned.[61] Thus, when pension benefits are received, the employee's portion of the contributions is treated as a tax-free return of capital to prevent double taxation of such amounts.

EMPLOYEE RETIREMENT PAYMENTS. An employee's retirement benefits are generally taxed under the Sec. 72 annuity rules (see Chapter I3). If the plan is noncontributory (i.e., no employee contributions are made to the plan), the pension benefits when received by the employee are fully taxable. If the plan is contributory, each payment is treated, in part, as a tax-free return of the employee's contributions and the remainder is taxable. The excluded portion is based on the ratio of the employee's investment in the contract to the expected return under the contract.[62] However, the total amount that may be excluded is limited to the amount of the employee's contributions to the plan. If the employee dies before the entire investment in the contract is recovered, the unrecovered amount is allowed as an itemized deduction in the year of death.

---

[59] Sec. 411(a). An alternative vesting schedule may also be used that provides for 20% vesting after three years and increases by 20% per year until the employee is fully vested after seven years.
[60] Sec. 402(a)(1).
[61] Section 403(b) provides an exception to the general rule for employees of public educational organizations and certain other tax-exempt entities, whereby the amounts contributed by the employee to a tax-deferred annuity are treated as a reduction of the employee's gross income in the year the contributions are made.
[62] Sec. 72(b)(1). Employees whose annuity starting date is before July 1, 1986 may exclude all pension benefits paid by the plan up to the amount of the employee's contributions to the plan if the pension amounts received during the first three years exceed the total employee contributions. Any pension benefits received thereafter are fully taxable.

Kevin retires in 1996 and receives annuity payments for life from his employer's qualified pension plan of $24,000 per year beginning in 1997. Kevin's investment in the contract (represented by his contributions) is $100,000, and the total expected return (based on his life expectancy) is $300,000. The exclusion ratio is one-third, so that $8,000 ($24,000 × 0.333) is excluded from Kevin's income and $16,000 ($24,000 − $8,000) is taxable in 1997. After Kevin receives payments for 12.5 years, his investment in the contract is recovered ($8,000 × 12.5 = $100,000), and all subsequent payments are fully taxable. (See Chapter I3 for a discussion of the annuity formula and related rules.) ◀

ADDITIONAL COMMENT

Many individuals have the option of taking their retirement savings from traditional pensions, profit-sharing plans, and 401(k)s as a lump sum or an annuity. Those who want to take a lump-sum distribution can delay taxes by transferring the money directly into a tax-deferred IRA.

KEY POINT

For purposes of the limitation on employer contributions, all defined contribution plans maintained by one employer are treated as a single defined contribution plan. Furthermore, under some circumstances a group of employers can be treated as a single employer.

If an employee age 59½ or older receives a lump-sum distribution from a qualified plan, a five-year forward income-averaging technique is generally available to mitigate the effects of receiving a large amount of income in the year of the distribution.[63]

LIMITATION ON EMPLOYER CONTRIBUTIONS. The Code places the following limitations on the amounts an employer may contribute to qualified pension, profit-sharing, and stock bonus plans:

▶ Defined contribution plan contributions are limited to the lesser of $30,000 and 25% of the employee's compensation.[64]

▶ Defined benefit plans are restricted to an annual benefit to an employee equal to the greater of $120,000 or 100% of the participant's average compensation for the highest three years.[65]

▶ An overall maximum annual employer deduction of 15% of compensation paid or accrued to plan participants is placed on profit-sharing and stock bonus plans.[66] If an employer has more than one qualified plan (e.g., a defined benefit pension plan and a profit-sharing plan), a maximum deduction of 25% of compensation is allowed.

The distinguishing features and major requirements for qualified pension and profit-sharing plans are summarized in Topic Review I9-2.

NONQUALIFIED PLANS

Nonqualified deferred compensation plans are often used by employers to provide incentives or supplementary retirement benefits for executives. Common forms of nonqualified plans include the following:

▶ An unfunded, nonforfeitable promise to pay fixed amounts of compensation in future periods.[67]

▶ Restricted property plans involving property transfers (usually in the form of the employer-company stock), where the property transferred is subject to a substantial risk of forfeiture and is nontransferable.[68]

KEY POINT

Although the nonqualified plans are not subject to the same restrictions imposed upon qualified plans, they do not receive the same tax benefits as are available under qualified plans. For example, the employer may not be able to deduct amounts that are set aside or placed in an escrow account.

DISTINGUISHING CHARACTERISTICS OF NONQUALIFIED PLANS. Nonqualified plans are not subject to the same restrictions imposed on qualified plans (such as the nondiscrimination and vesting rules). Thus, such plans are particularly suitable for use in executive compensation planning. In general, nonqualified plans impose certain restrictions on the outright transfer of the plan's benefits to the employee. This avoids immediate taxation under the constructive receipt doctrine, which does not apply if the

---

[63] Sec. 402(e). Under the Small Business Act of 1996, the five-year forward averaging provision has been repealed for tax years beginning after December 31, 1999.

[64] Sec. 415(c). The $30,000 amount is the lesser of (1) $30,000 or (if greater, one-fourth of the maximum defined benefit plan annual addition) and (2) 25% of the employee's compensation. For 1997, the $30,000 amount is not increased because the maximum defined benefit plan limit is $125,000. An increase occurs only when the cost-of-living adjustment exceeds $5,000.

Thus, the $30,000 amount will not be increased until the defined benefit plan limit is increased to an amount greater than $125,000.

[65] Sec. 415(b)(1). The $120,000 is effective for 1997 and is subject to indexing each year.

[66] Sec. 404(a)(3)(A).

[67] Rev. Rul. 60-31, 1960-1 C.B. 174.

[68] Sec. 83.

Topic Review I9-2

Qualified Pension and Profit-Sharing Plans

Distinguishing Features and Major Requirements

▶ Employer contributions and earnings on contributed amounts are not taxed to employees until distributed or made available. The contributions are immediately deductible by the employer.

▶ Pension plans can be established as either defined contribution or defined benefit plans in which systematic and definite payments are made to a pension trust. Incidental benefits (e.g., death and disability payments) can be provided under the plan.

▶ Profit-sharing plans require the use of a predetermined formula and substantial and recurring contributions must be made although annual employer contributions are not required and the contributions need not be based on profits. Section 401(k) plans can be established where employees have the option to receive cash or to have such amounts contributed to the profit-sharing trust. The employer may also establish an ESOP where the plan is funded by a contribution of the employer's stock.

▶ Qualified plans must be created for the employees' exclusive benefit.

▶ The plans may not discriminate in favor of highly compensated employees.

▶ Contributions and plan benefits must bear a uniform relationship to the compensation of covered employees.

▶ Minimum vesting requirements must be met (e.g., 100% vesting after five years).

▶ Employee benefits are taxed under the Sec. 72 annuity rules.

▶ Total employer contributions to the plan are subject to specific ceiling limitations.

benefits are not yet credited, set apart, or made available so that the employee may draw on them.[69] The employee is taxed upon the lapse of such restrictions, and the employer receives a corresponding deduction in the same year.

UNFUNDED DEFERRED COMPENSATION PLANS. **Unfunded deferred compensation plans** are often used to compensate highly compensated employees who desire to defer the recognition of income until future periods (e.g., a professional athlete or a business executive who receives a signing bonus may prefer to defer the recognition of income from the bonus). In general, if the promise to make the compensation payment in a future period is nonforfeitable, the agreement must not be funded (e.g., the transfer of assets to a trust for the employee's benefit) or evidenced by a negotiable note. The employer, however, may establish an *escrow account* on behalf of the employee. Such an account is used to accumulate and invest the deferred compensation amounts.[70] If the requirements for deferral are met, the employee is taxed when the amounts are actually paid or made available, and the employer receives a corresponding deduction in the same year.[71]

EXAMPLE I9-53 ▶ In 1997 Kelly signs an employment contract to play professional football for the Chicago Skyhawks. The contract includes a $500,000 signing bonus that is payable in five annual installments beginning in 2004. The bonus agreement is nonforfeitable and is unfunded. The Skyhawks have agreed to place sufficient amounts of money into an escrow account to fund

---

[69] *George C. Martin*, 96 T.C. 39 (1991).
[70] Rev. Rul. 55-525, 1955-2 C.B. 543.

[71] Reg. Sec. 1.451-2(a).

the future payments to Kelly. None of the $500,000 bonus is deductible by the employer or taxable to Kelly when the agreement is signed in 1997. The Skyhawks do not receive a deduction for any amounts that are deposited into the escrow account during the 1997–2003 period. In 2004, Kelly receives $100,000 taxable compensation (interest, if any, that accrued and was paid to Kelly is also taxable) upon receipt of the initial payment, and the Skyhawks receive a corresponding tax deduction. ◀

RESTRICTED PROPERTY PLANS. **Restricted property plans** are used to attract and retain key executives. Under such arrangements, the executive generally obtains an ownership interest (i.e., stock) in the corporation. Restricted property plans are governed by the income recognition rules contained in Sec. 83. Under these rules, the receipt of restricted property in exchange for services rendered is not taxable if the property is nontransferable and subject to a substantial risk of forfeiture.[72]

The employee is treated as receiving taxable compensation based on the amount of the property's fair market value (FMV) (less any amount paid for the property) at the earlier of the time the property is no longer subject to a substantial risk of forfeiture or is transferable. The employer receives a corresponding compensation deduction at the same time the income is taxed to the employee.

EXAMPLE I9-54 ▶ In the current year, Allied Corporation transfers 1,000 shares of its common stock to employee Karen as compensation pursuant to a restricted property plan. The FMV of the Allied stock is $10 per share on the transfer date. The restricted property agreement provides that the stock is nontransferable by Karen until the year 2002 (i.e., Karen cannot sell the stock to outsiders until year 2002). The stock is also subject to the restriction that if Karen voluntarily leaves the company before the year 2002, she must transfer the shares back to the company and will receive no benefit from the stock other than from the receipt of dividends. The FMV of the stock is $100 per share in year 2002 when the forfeiture and nontransferability restrictions lapse. Because the stock is both nontransferable and subject to a substantical risk of forfeiture from the issue date to year 2002, the tax consequences from the stock transfer are deferred for both Karen and Allied Corporation until the lapse of the nontransferability or forfeiture restrictions in year 2002. In year 2002, Karen must report ordinary (compensation) income of $100,000 ($100 × 1,000 shares), and Allied Corporation is entitled to a corresponding compensation deduction of the same amount. Karen is taxed currently on the dividends she receives because they are not subject to any restrictions. ◀

KEY POINT

If an employee makes the election to be taxed immediately, he or she should be aware of the adverse consequences of leaving the company before the forfeiture restrictions lapse. The employee will not receive the property, and no deduction is allowed on the forfeiture.

Election to Be Taxed Immediately. An exception which permits an employee to elect (within 30 days after the receipt of restricted property) to recognize income immediately upon receipt of the restricted property is provided in Sec. 83(b). If the election is made, the employer is entitled to a corresponding deduction at the time the income is taxed to the employee. This election was frequently made for years prior to 1987 because an eventual sale of the restricted stock at a gain resulted in favorable long-term capital gain treatment (i.e., a 60% long-term capital gain deduction was applicable to pre-1987 years). For post-1986 years, the 60% long-term capital gain deduction was eliminated, which reduced the attractiveness of the Sec. 83(b) election. The increase in marginal tax rates for high-income taxpayers from 31% to 39.6% for taxpayers with substantial taxable income, along with the availability of a 28% maximum capital gain rate, may increase the attractiveness of this election.

---

[72] Regulation Sec. 1.83-3(c)(2) provides several examples of what constitutes a substantial risk of forfeiture.

EXAMPLE I9-55 ▶ Assume the same facts as Example I9-54, except that Karen elects to recognize income on the transfer date. Karen must include $10,000 ($10 × 1,000 shares) in gross income as compensation in the current year, and Allied Corporation is entitled to a corresponding deduction in the same year. If Karen sells the stock for $100,000 in the year 2002 after the restrictions lapse, Karen reports a $90,000 ($100,000 − $10,000) long-term capital gain on the sale.[73] If Karen voluntarily leaves the company before the forfeiture restrictions lapse, no deduction is allowed when the forfeiture occurs, despite the fact that Karen is previously taxed on the stock's value on the transfer date (i.e., $10,000 of income is recognized by Karen in the current year). In such event, Allied Corporation must include $10,000 in gross income in the year of the forfeiture (i.e., the amount of the deduction that is taken in the year of the transfer to the extent of any previous tax benefit).[74] ◀

Nonqualified plan features and requirements are summarized in Topic Review I9-3.

EMPLOYEE STOCK OPTIONS

Stock option plans are used by corporate employers to attract and retain key management employees. Both stock option and restricted property arrangements using the employer's stock permit the executive to receive a proprietary interest in the corporation. Thus, an executive may identify more closely with shareholder interests and the firm's long-run profit-maximization goals. The tax law currently includes two types of stock-option arrangements: the incentive stock option and the nonqualified stock option.[75] Each type is treated differently for tax purposes.

Before the passage of the Tax Reform Act of 1986, incentive stock-option arrangements were often used because the employee could receive favorable long-term capital gain treatment (i.e., a 60% long-term capital gain deduction) if certain requirements were met. The nonqualified stock-option arrangement has become increasingly popular for years after 1986 because of the elimination of favorable capital gain treatment for incentive stock options for the 1987–1990 period. The enactment of a 28% maximum

Topic Review I9-3

Nonqualified Plans

Distinguishing Features and Major Requirements

1. The employee is taxed upon the lapse of restrictions imposed on the availability or withdrawal of funds and the employer receives a corresponding deduction in the same year.
2. Nonqualified plans may discriminate in favor of highly compensated employees and no minimum vesting rules are required.
3. Restricted property (usually employer stock) may be offered to executives where the incidents of taxation are deferred if the property is nontransferable and subject to a substantial risk of forfeiture. An election may be made under Sec. 83(b) to recognize income immediately upon the receipt of the restricted property.
4. Restrictions must be imposed to avoid immediate taxation to the employee under the constructive receipt doctrine.
5. To avoid immediate taxation, restricted property plans must be both nonforfeitable and subject to a substantial risk of forfeiture.

---

[73] Sec. 1223. The holding period originates on the day following the transfer date because Karen made the election to be taxed immediately under Sec. 83(b).

[74] Reg. Sec. 1.83-6(c). A deduction would be available to Karen for any

amounts she paid for the Allied stock.

[75] The incentive stock option rules are provided in Sec. 422, whereas the rules governing nonqualified stock options are contained in Reg. Sec. 1.83-7.

capital gain rate combined with increased marginal tax rates for high-income taxpayers may increase the use of incentive stock option arrangements. However, an employer is more favorably treated under the nonqualified stock-option rules (i.e., the employer receives a tax deduction for the compensation related to a nonqualified stock option but does not receive a corresponding deduction if an incentive stock-option plan is adopted) and may therefore still prefer to continue to use nonqualified stock options.

INCENTIVE STOCK OPTION PLANS.

Employer Requirements. An **incentive stock option (ISO)** must meet the following plan or employer requirements:[76]

▶ The option price must be equal to or greater than the stock's FMV on the option's grant date.

▶ The option must be granted within ten years of the date the plan is adopted, and the employee must exercise the option within ten years of the grant date.

▶ The option must be both exercisable only by the employee and nontransferable except in the event of death.

▶ The employee cannot own more than 10% of the voting power of the employer corporation's stock immediately before the option's grant date.

▶ The total FMV of the stock options that become exercisable to an employee in any given year may not exceed $100,000 (e.g., an employee can be granted ISOs to acquire $200,000 of stock in one year, provided that no more than $100,000 is exercisable in any given year).

▶ Other procedural requirements must be met (e.g., shareholder approval of the plan).

Employee Requirements. In addition to the above plan requirements, the employee must meet the following requirements:

▶ The employee must not dispose of the stock within two years of the option's grant date nor within one year after the option's exercise date.

▶ The employee must be employed by the issuing company on the grant date and continue such employment until within three months before the exercise date.

If an employee meets the requirements listed above, no tax consequences occur on the grant date or on the exercise date. However, the excess of the FMV over the option price on the exercise date is a tax preference item for purposes of the alternative minimum tax (see Chapter I14). When the employee sells the optioned stock, a long-term capital gain or loss is recognized. If the employee meets the two requirements, the employer does not receive a corresponding compensation deduction.[77] If the requirements are not met, the option is treated as a nonqualified stock option.

EXAMPLE I9-56 ▶ American Corporation grants an incentive stock option to Kay, an employee, on January 1, 1997. The option price is $100, and the FMV of the American stock is also $100 on the grant date. The option permits Kay to purchase 100 shares of American stock. Kay exercises the option on June 30, 1999, when the stock's FMV is $400. Kay sells the 100 shares of American stock on January 1, 2001, for $500 per share. Because Kay holds the stock for the required period (at least two years from the grant date and one year from the exercise date) and because Kay is employed by American Corporation on the grant date and within three months before the exercise date, all of the requirements for an ISO have been met. No income is recognized on the grant date or on the exercise date, although $30,000 [($400 − $100) × 100 shares] is a tax preference item for the alternative minimum tax in 1999. Kay recognizes a

---

[76] Sec. 422.   [77] Sec. 421(a)(2).

$40,000 [($500 − $100) × 100 shares] long-term capital gain on the sale date in 2001. American Corporation is not entitled to a compensation deduction in 2001 or in any other year. ◄

Assume the same facts as Example I9-56, except that Kay disposes of the stock on August 1, 1999, thus violating the one-year holding period requirement. Kay must recognize ordinary income on the sale date equal to the spread between the option price and the exercise price, or $30,000 [($400 − $100) × 100 shares]. The $30,000 spread between the FMV and the option price is no longer a tax preference item because the option ceases to qualify as an ISO. American Corporation can claim a $30,000 compensation deduction in 1999. Kay also recognizes a $10,000 [($500 − $400 adjusted basis) × 100 shares] short-term capital gain on the sale date, which represents the appreciation of the stock from the exercise date to the sale date. The gain is short-term because the holding period from the exercise date to the sale date does not exceed one year. ◄

KEY POINT

With ISO the employee does not recognize income when the option is exercised; income is recognized only when the stock is sold. With nonqualified stock options, income is recognized when the option is exercised or on the grant date and when the stock is sold at a gain.

NONQUALIFIED STOCK OPTION PLANS. Stock options that do not meet the plan requirements for incentive stock options are referred to as **nonqualified stock options**. The tax treatment of nonqualified stock options depends on whether the option has a **readily ascertainable fair market value** (e.g., whether the option is traded on an established options exchange).

Readily Ascertainable Fair Market Value. If a nonqualified stock option has a readily ascertainable FMV (e.g., the option is traded on an established options exchange), the employee recognizes ordinary income on the grant date equal to the difference between the stock's FMV and the option's exercise price. The employer receives a compensation deduction on the grant date equal to the same amount of income that is recognized by the employee. In such case, no tax consequences occur on the date the option is exercised, and the employee recognizes capital gain or loss upon the sale or disposition of the stock.

No Readily Ascertainable Fair Market Value. If a nonqualified stock option has no readily ascertainable FMV, no tax consequences occur on the grant date. On the exercise date the employee recognizes ordinary income equal to the spread between the FMV of the stock and the option price, and the employer receives a corresponding compensation deduction. When the stock option is exercised, the employee's basis in the stock is equal to the option price plus the amount reported as ordinary income on the exercise date. Capital gain or loss is recognized upon the subsequent sale of the stock by the employee.

The alternative minimum tax does not apply to nonqualified stock options regardless of whether the option has a readily ascertainable FMV. Table I9-4 illustrates the tax consequences to employees and employers for such options.

As illustrated in Table I9-4, Kim reports a total gain of $11,000 from the option transaction under both circumstances. However, the character of her profit (i.e., ordinary income or capital gain) and the timing of the profit recognition (i.e., grant date or exercise date) depends on whether the option's FMV is readily ascertainable.

The distinguishing features and major requirements for employee stock options are summarized in Topic Review I9-4.

PLANS FOR SELF-EMPLOYED INDIVIDUALS

ADDITIONAL COMMENT

If you are self-employed and establish a Keogh plan, you must include any employees in the plan.

Self-employed individuals such as sole proprietors and partners who practice a trade or business are not classified as employees and are subject to special retirement plan rules known as **H.R. 10 plans** (also called **Keogh plans**). Retirement plans of self-employed people are generally subject to the same contribution and benefit limitations as other qualified corporate plans. An employee who is covered under a qualified pension or

▼ **TABLE I9-4**

Taxation of Nonqualified Stock Options

Situation Facts	Readily Ascertainable FMV	No Readily Ascertainable FMV
Grant date: On January 1, 1997, Kim is granted a nonqualified stock option to purchase 100 shares of stock from Apple Corporation (Kim's employer) at $90 per share. The stock's FMV is $100 on the grant date.	Ordinary income of $1,000 is recognized [($100 − $90) × 100 shares] by Kim. Apple Corporation receives a corresponding $1,000 compensation deduction.	No tax consequences to Kim or Apple Corporation.
Exercise date: On January 31, 1998, Kim exercises the option and acquires the 100 shares of Apple Corporation stock for the $90 option price when the FMV is $190.	No tax consequences to Kim or Apple Corporation.	Kim recognizes ordinary income of $10,000 [($190 − $90) × 100 shares], and Apple Corporation receives a $10,000 compensation deduction.
Sale date: On February 1, 1999, Kim sells the stock for $200 per share and realizes $20,000 ($200 × 100 shares).	Kim recognizes a $10,000 ($20,000 − $10,000 basis) long-term capital gain.[a]	Kim recognizes a $1,000 ($20,000 − $19,000 basis) long-term capital gain.[b]

[a] Kim's basis includes the amount paid for the optioned stock of $9,000 plus ordinary income of $1,000 recognized on the grant date. Kim's holding period commences on the January 1, 1997 grant date for determining whether the gain is long-term.

[b] Kim's basis includes the $9,000 paid for the option stock plus the $10,000 ordinary income recognized on the exercise date. Kim's holding period commences on the January 31, 1998 exercise date for determining whether the gain is long-term.

KEY POINT

Keogh plans can be either defined benefit or defined contribution plans. Many individuals avoid the defined benefit type of Keogh plan due to the extra paperwork and administrative costs.

profit-sharing plan for wages earned as an employee and who is also self-employed may establish an H.R. 10 plan for earned income derived from self-employment activities.

For a **defined contribution H.R. 10 plan**, a self-employed individual may contribute the smaller of $30,000 and 25% of earned income from the self-employment activity.[78] *Earned income* refers to net earnings from self-employment. To compute the limitations for 1997, only $160,000 ($150,000 for 1996) of earned income may be taken into account for any one individual.[79] For purposes of the 25% calculation, earned income is reduced by the contribution made on behalf of the self-employed individual.

EXAMPLE I9-58 ▶

Larry is a self-employed CPA whose 1997 net earnings from his trade or business (before the H.R. 10 plan contribution but after the deduction for one-half of the self-employment taxes paid under Sec. 164(f) [see Chapter I14]) is $100,000. The 25% contribution limitation is computed as follows: $100,000 − 0.25x = x, where x equals Larry's net earned income after the contribution deduction. Thus, under this formula, Larry's net earned income is $80,000. Therefore, Larry may contribute $20,000 to the plan for 1997 ($80,000 × 0.25), because this amount is less than the $30,000 ceiling. Larry must also provide coverage for all of his eligible full-time employees under the general rules provided in the law for qualified plans (e.g., nondiscrimination, vesting, and so on).[80] ◀

---

[78] Sec. 415(c)(1). A 15% deduction limit applies if the defined contribution plan is a profit sharing plan.
[79] Secs. 401(a)(17) and 404(1). For years beginning after 1994 the $160,000

ceiling will be adjusted for inflation in increments of $10,000.
[80] Sec. 401(d).

Topic Review I9-4

Employee Stock Options

Distinguishing Features and Major Requirements

▶ For an incentive stock option (ISO) plan no tax consequences occur on the grant or the exercise date (except for the recognition of a tax preference item under the AMT provisions on the exercise date). Capital gain or loss is recognized by the employee upon the sale or exchange of the stock. No deduction is allowed to the employer.

▶ ISOs and nonqualified stock options may be issued to highly compensated employees without regard to nondiscrimination rules.

▶ If a nonqualified stock option has a readily ascertainable FMV, the employee recognizes ordinary income equal to the spread between the FMV of the stock and the option price on the grant date and the employer receives a corresponding deduction. If the option has no readily ascertainable FMV, income is recognized on the exercise date equal to the spread between the FMV of the stock and the option price and a corresponding deduction is available to the employer.

▶ For an ISO, the option price must be equal to or greater than the FMV of the stock on the grant date, employees cannot own more than 10% of the voting power of the employer's stock, and restrictions are placed on the total FMV of stock options that may be issued.

▶ To qualify under the ISO rules, a two-year holding period from the grant date is required (and at least one year after the exercise date) and the employee must continue to be employed by the company until within three months of the exercise date.

KEY POINT

A Keogh plan must be created no later than the last day of your tax year.

REAL WORLD EXAMPLE

The IRA savings provisions were originally enacted in 1974 to provide a tax-favored retirement savings arrangement to individuals who were not covered under a qualified plan. Beginning in 1982, Congress extended IRA availability to all taxpayers. It was hoped that the extended availability would increase the level of savings and provide a discretionary retirement savings plan that was uniformly available. However, Congress in the Tax Reform Act of 1986 restricted the availability of IRAs because there was no discernible impact on aggregate personal savings.

An H.R. 10 plan must be established before the end of the tax year, but contributions may be made up to the due date for the tax return (including extensions). All H.R. 10 pension contributions made by a self-employed individual for employees are deductible for AGI on Schedule C. The H.R. 10 contribution for the self-employed individual is deductible *for* AGI on page 1 of Form 1040.

INDIVIDUAL RETIREMENT ACCOUNTS (IRAS)

Before 1987, an employee or a self-employed individual could establish an IRA even though he or she was also covered under an employer-sponsored qualified plan or an H.R. 10 plan. The Tax Reform Act of 1986 severely curtailed the availability of deductible IRA plans for many individuals. Effective for 1987 and subsequent years, an individual may make deductible contributions equal to the lesser of $2,000 or 100% of compensation only if either of the following conditions exists:

▶ The individual or his or her spouse is *not* an active participant in an employer-sponsored retirement plan, including tax-sheltered annuities, government plans, simplified employee pension plans, and H.R. 10 plans.

▶ Individuals who are active participants in an employer-sponsored retirement plan must have an AGI equal to or below the following applicable dollar limits: [81] $25,000 for an unmarried individual; $40,000 for a married couple filing a joint return; Zero for a married individual filing separately.

---

[81] Sec. 219(g).

If the dollar limitations apply, the deductible IRA contribution amounts are phased out on a pro rata basis as AGI increases from $25,000 to $35,000 for unmarried taxpayers and from $40,000 to $50,000 for married taxpayers filing a joint return.

EXAMPLE I9-59 ▶

Laura is an unmarried taxpayer who is not an active participant in an employer-sponsored retirement plan (or other qualified plan). In the current year, Laura's AGI is $60,000, consisting of earned income from wages. Laura is not subject to the dollar limitations because she is not an active participant in a qualified plan, and may, therefore, contribute up to $2,000 to a deductible IRA. Laura's AGI is reduced to $58,000 ($60,000 − $2,000) if the IRA contribution is made because the amount is deductible *for* AGI. ◀

EXAMPLE I9-60 ▶

ADDITIONAL COMMENT

Banks, savings and loan associations, insurance companies, and stock brokerage firms make IRAs available to taxpayers. Usually, the amounts are invested in long-term savings accounts. However, self-directed plans are offered by some stock brokerage firms. In this type of IRA, the taxpayer can specify how the contributions will be invested.

Judy is a married taxpayer who is an active participant in an employer-sponsored retirement plan. Judy files a joint return with her spouse. Judy and her spouse have $46,000 of AGI, consisting of $40,000 earned income from wages and $6,000 of dividends and interest. The ceiling amount is exceeded by $6,000 ($46,000 AGI − $40,000). Thus, the maximum deductible IRA contribution is reduced by 60%. If Judy and her spouse both have earned income of more than $2,000, each may make a deductible contribution of $800 ($2,000 × 0.40). ◀

If only one spouse is employed and such individual is otherwise eligible to make deductible IRA contributions, the nonworking spouse may contribute up to $2,000 per year to a deductible IRA. Thus, a total of $4,000 may be deductible by a married couple even though only one spouse has earned income. Under prior law (years beginning before 1997), the total amount the couple could contribute and deduct was $2,250. Under the new rules, the nonworking spouse's IRA deduction must be reduced in the same manner as the working spouse. ◀

EXAMPLE I9-61 ▶

Anne and David are married and file a joint return for the current year. Anne earns $42,000 in 1997 from her job; David has no income as he is a full-time student. They have no other income. Anne is covered under her employer's qualified plan. For 1997, both Anne and David can contribute and deduct $1,600 into their IRAs. Both are eligible to contribute $2,000 to their IRAs, but since Anne is an active participant in an employer-sponsored plan and their AGI is over $40,000, the deductible amount must be reduced by 20% ($2,000)/$10,000. These reductions apply to both spouses even though all of the income is earned by only one spouse. ◀

ADDITIONAL COMMENT

A 1997 contribution to an IRA can be made as late as the due date for filing the 1997 return.

The following significant tax rules apply to an IRA:

▶ Nondeductible contributions (maximum of $2,000 per year) to an IRA are permitted when an individual is ineligible to make deductible contributions.[82]

▶ An IRA plan may be established between the end of the tax year and the due date for the tax return (not including any extensions that are permitted). Any deductible contributions made during this time period are treated as a deduction for the prior year. For established plans, contributions are deductible if made by the due date for the tax return (i.e., contributions for 1997 must be made no later than April 15, 1998 for cash method individuals).

▶ Withdrawals by a participant before age 59½ are subject to a nondeductible 10% penalty tax.[83]

▶ Withdrawals must begin no later than April 1 of the year following the end of the tax year in which the individual reaches age 70½. Deductible IRA contributions are fully

---

[82] Sec. 408(o).
[83] Sec. 72(t). The amount subject to the 10% penalty is the portion of the amount that must be included in gross income. Exceptions are also provided in the event of death, disability, and for certain non–lump-sum distributions.

KEY POINT

Nondeductible contributions may still be advantageous because the income earned in the IRA is not subject to current taxation. However, it is important to keep track of the dollar amount of deductible and nondeductible IRA contributions so that the tax consequences of retirement payments can be determined. Some taxpayers consider the recordkeeping requirements to be too severe.

taxable as ordinary income when the amounts are distributed. If an individual has made both deductible and nondeductible IRA contributions, all IRA contracts are treated as one contract. The annuity rules under Sec. 72 are then used to determine the taxable and nontaxable portion of the distribution. Nondeductible IRA contributions are treated as nontaxable because these amounts were contributed with after-tax dollars.

▶ A nondeductible 6% penalty tax is levied on excess contributions to an IRA.[84]

Topic Review I9-5 contains a summary of H.R. 10 and IRA plan features and requirements.

SIMPLIFIED EMPLOYEE PENSIONS

Due to the administrative complexity associated with qualified pension and profit-sharing plans, small businesses often establish simplified employee pension (SEP) plans for their employees. In an SEP, the employer makes contributions to the IRAs of its employees.[85] The following is a summary of the tax rules that apply to an SEP:

▶ The employer receives an immediate tax deduction for contributions made under the plan. The annual deductible contributions for each participant are limited to the lesser of 15% of the participant's compensation (up to a ceiling of $160,000) and the dollar limitations for defined contribution plans.[86]

▶ Contributions are treated as being made on the last day of the tax year if they are made by the due date of the tax return (including extensions).

▶ Employer contributions must be nondiscriminatory.

▶ Participants may elect to receive cash or have the employer make contributions to the SEP (i.e., a salary reduction agreement). If an employee elects to receive cash, such amounts are immediately taxable to the recipient. Employer contributions to the SEP are excluded from gross income up to $9,500 in 1997.[87] Such amounts are subject to taxation when the funds are withdrawn by the employee.

▶ Distributions from an SEP are subject to taxation based on the IRA rules (previously discussed) including the penalty tax for premature distributions.

Topic Review I9-5

H.R. 10 (Keogh) Plans

Distinguishing Features and Major Requirements

1. Self-employed retirement plan contribution and benefit limitations correspond to those offered to employees under the qualified pension and profit-sharing arrangements.
2. The annual contribution limit is the smaller of $30,000 or 25% of earned income.
3. An employee who is also self-employed may establish an H.R. 10 plan based on the self-employment income.
4. H.R. 10 plan contributions are deductible *for* AGI.
5. To compute the allowable maximum H.R. 10 contribution, only $160,000 ($150,000 for 1996) of earned income may be taken into account.
6. Self-employed individuals must cover all eligible full-time employees under the plan.
7. An H.R. 10 plan must be established before the end of the tax year but contributions may be made up to the due date for the tax return (including extensions).

---

[84] Sec. 4973(b).
[85] Sec. 408(k).

[86] Sec. 402(h)(2).
[87] Sec. 408(k)(6).

Individual Retirement Accounts (IRAS)

Distinguishing Features and Major Requirements

1. Fully deductible contributions may be made only by an individual (or his or her spouse) who is *not* an active participant in an employer-sponsored retirement plan or by an individual (or spouse) who has AGI of $25,000 or less (or $40,000 or less for a married couple filing jointly). The deductible amounts are phased out on a pro-rata basis as AGI increases from $25,000 to $35,000 ($40,000 to $50,000 for married taxpayers filing a joint return).
2. Contributions to an IRA can be made as late as the due date for filing the tax return (excluding extensions) (e.g., by April 15, 1997 for a deduction on the 1996 tax return for a calendar-year taxpayer).
3. Nondeductible contributions to an IRA may be made by ineligible individuals.
4. The working spouse may contribute up to $2,250 per year if only one spouse is employed provided that a maximum of $2,000 is designated to the account of the working spouse.
5. Withdrawals before age 59½ are subject to a nondeductible 10% penalty unless due to death, disability, and certain non-lump-sum distributions.
6. Deductible contributions are generally limited to the lesser of $2,000 and 100% of compensation.

▶ A self-employed person (i.e., a partner or sole proprietor) may establish an SEP rather than using an H.R. 10 plan arrangement because of reduced administrative complexity associated with an SEP.

SIMPLE RETIREMENT PLANS

Under the Small Business Act of 1996, a new type of retirement savings plan for small businesses was created called the savings incentive match plan for employees (SIMPLE). This new type of plan can be adopted by employers who have 100 or fewer employees who received at least $5,000 in compensation from the employer in the preceding year. A SIMPLE plan may be set up either as an IRA for each employee or part of a qualified cash or deferred arrangement (401(k) plan). Essentially, employees are allowed to make elective contributions of up to $6,000 per year and requires employers to make matching contributions.

The unique features of the new SIMPLE plans are (1) that elective contributions by employees must be matched by the employer or the employer has the option of making nonelective contributions, (2) that all contributions to an employee's SIMPLE account must be fully vested and (3) the SIMPLE plans are not subject to the special nondiscrimination rules generally applicable to qualified plans. This last feature is important in that there is no requirement that a set number of employees *participate* in the plan, the only requirement is that all employees who had $5,000 in compensation in the previous year and are reasonably expected to have $5,000 in compensation in the current year must be eligible to participate.

TAX PLANNING CONSIDERATIONS

MOVING EXPENSES

To be eligible for the moving expense deduction, the moving expenses must be paid in connection with the commencement of work by the taxpayer as a full-time employee or self-employed individual. Therefore, it is important to secure full-time employment or to carry on a trade or business as a self-employed individual at the new location. Taxpayers who are approaching retirement are eligible for a moving expense deduction only if they continue to work in the new location before their actual retirement (e.g., 39 weeks in the 12-month period following the move).

EXAMPLE I9-62 ▶ Louis decides to quit his job and return to school as a full-time graduate student. Louis incurs substantial long-distance moving expenses that would otherwise be deductible to relocate to the university where the education is to be taken. No deduction is allowed unless Louis is employed on a full-time basis or is engaged in a self-employment activity at the new location. ◀

REIMBURSED AMOUNTS. Moving expense reimbursements are often greater than the amounts allowable as a deduction. This is caused by the common practice of reimbursing nondeductible items (e.g., an employer may reimburse an employee for the cost of certain indirect moving expenses such as househunting trips, which do not qualify as deductible moving expenses). This results in an increase in the employee's gross income to the extent of the excess reimbursement. From a tax planning standpoint, the employer may provide an additional payment to compensate the employee for the additional tax cost associated with the move (commonly referred to as a "gross-up".

EXAMPLE I9-63 ▶ Austin Corporation has a policy of reimbursing transferred employees for 30% of their moving reimbursement that exceeds their deductible expenses to cover the federal and state tax costs associated with the excess reimbursement. Kathy, an employee, is transferred by the company to a new job location and incurs $6,000 of otherwise deductible moving expenses and receives an $8,000 reimbursement. Austin also will make an additional payment to Kathy of $600 (0.30 × $2,000) to cover the additional federal and state income tax costs. Kathy must include $2,600 ($2,000 + $600) of the reimbursement in gross income. ◀

MAXIMIZING EMPLOYEE TRAVEL AND TRANSPORTATION EXPENSE DEDUCTIONS

Corporate officers who are also key shareholders in a closely held corporation often incur substantial travel and transportation expenses in connection with their employment activities. Such expenditures are usually subject to close scrutiny by the IRS due to possible abuse (i.e., such reimbursements may be treated as constructive dividends if the travel or transportation is personal rather than business-related).

If an officer-shareholder makes frequent use of an automobile in employment-related activities, it may be desirable to have the corporation acquire the automobile and provide a company car to the employee. If the automobile is also used for personal commuting, the employee should be required to reimburse the company for the personal-use mileage. In such cases, the documentation of business and personal use is particularly important to avoid constructive dividend treatment. It is generally preferable for an employee to be fully reimbursed for travel and transportation expenses because of the 2% nondeductible floor on miscellaneous itemized deductions.

In addition, only 50% of business meals incurred as a component of travel expense or as an entertainment activity is allowed. If business meals are reimbursed by the employer, only 50% of such amounts are deductible by the employer. If the expenses are reimbursed, the employee expenses (including business meals) are fully deductible *for* AGI and are used to offset the reimbursements includible in the employee's gross income. Unreimbursed employee expenses are combined with investment expenses and other nonbusiness itemized deductions (e.g., tax return preparation fees) and are treated as miscellaneous itemized deductions. They are subject to the nondeductible 2% floor. In many instances, these expenses do not exceed 2% of AGI or an employee will use the standard deduction and will, therefore, receive limited or no tax benefit. In addition, the remaining allowable miscellaneous itemized deductions may be subject to the 3% scale

TYPICAL MISCONCEPTION

It is sometimes mistakenly believed that if the standard mileage rate method is used to calculate automobile costs, then no other auto costs can be deducted. In fact, interest, state and local taxes (other than gasoline taxes), parking fees, and tolls can be deducted in addition to the standard mileage rate. This maximizes the travel or transportation expense deduction. Nevertheless, the interest on the car loan of an employee is considered personal interest.

down of total itemized deductions if the individual's AGI for 1997 exceeds $121,200 ($60,600 for married individuals filing separately).

EXAMPLE I9-64 ▶ Mark is an employee of the Bass Corporation and incurs $3,000 of travel expenses (including $1,000 in business meals) that are not reimbursed by his employer. Mark also incurs $1,000 other miscellaneous itemized deductions (e.g., safe-deposit box rentals, tax return preparation fees, and professional dues and subscriptions). Mark's AGI is $100,000. Only $500 ($1,000 × 0.50) of Mark's unreimbursed business meals are deductible (before the 2% limitation is applied). Thus Mark's total travel expenses are reduced to $2,500 ($3,000 − $500). Mark's total miscellaneous itemized deductions (before the 2% limitation) are $3,500 ($2,500 travel expenses plus $1,000 other miscellaneous itemized deductions). Mark may deduct only $1,500 [$3,500 − (0.02 × $100,000)] of miscellaneous itemized deductions if he does not use the standard deduction. Because Mark's AGI is only $100,000, his itemized deductions are not subject to the overall limitation on itemized deductions (i.e., total itemized deductions are reduced by 3% of AGI in excess of $121,200). (See Chapter I7 for a discussion of this limitation.) ◀

PROVIDING NONTAXABLE COMPENSATION TO EMPLOYEES

Employers should consider the tax consequences to employees when changes in fringe benefit and deferred compensation arrangements are evaluated. For example, it is preferable for an employer to pay for fringe benefit items such as group term life insurance (up to $50,000 in coverage), health and accident insurance, employee parking, and so on rather than to give cash raises of a comparable amount. Such payments are nontaxable to the employee up to certain limits, whereas a comparable salary increase is fully taxable. Both types of payments are deductible by the employer.

Consideration should also be given to increased deferred compensation benefit programs for employees, particularly highly compensated individuals. The use of nonqualified deferred compensation plans, restricted property, and stock options result in tax deferrals and may result in the eventual recognition of capital gains that may be used to offset capital losses or that are taxed at a maximum 28% marginal tax rate.

All eligible employees should consider establishing an individual retirement account (IRA) because of the available tax deferral benefits. Even if a premature withdrawal (i.e., before age 59½ occurs), the time value of the deferred benefits for the plan contributions and the earnings may be greater than the penalty tax imposed. Employees who are not eligible to make deductible IRA contributions should consider making nondeductible contributions because the income that is earned on such accounts can be deferred until distributions are received from the IRA.

REAL WORLD EXAMPLE

Banks and other financial institutions in their ads sometimes compare the accumulated wealth in an IRA to the accumulated wealth in a fully taxable investment. Although the IRA is generally advantageous, the ads sometimes overstate the advantages because they fail to deduct the tax that will be paid when amounts are withdrawn from the IRA.

COMPLIANCE AND PROCEDURAL CONSIDERATIONS

SUBSTANTIATING TRAVEL AND ENTERTAINMENT EXPENSES

Travel and entertainment expenses are disallowed if the taxpayer does not maintain adequate records or documentary proof of the expenditures.[88] Normally, documentation includes expense statements (diary or account book) and proof of the amount, time, place, and business purpose. Strict substantiation rules are enacted in the law to curb widespread abuses in the so-called expense account living practices engaged in by some taxpayers.

KEY POINT

It is extremely important to be able to substantiate travel and entertainment expenses. The *Cohan* Rule that permits a reasonable deduction when substantiation is lacking does not apply to travel and entertainment expenses (see Chapter I6).

---

[88] Sec. 274(d).

To make compliance easier, the IRS formulated the following administrative procedural rules:

▶ If an employee makes an adequate accounting of the expenditures to the employer, it is not necessary to submit a detailed statement on the employee's tax return unless the expenses exceed the reimbursements.

Form **2106**	**Employee Business Expenses**	OMB No. 1545-0139
Department of the Treasury Internal Revenue Service	▶ See separate instructions ▶ Attach to Form 1040	**1996** Attachment Sequence No. **54**

Your name	Social security number	Occupation in which expenses were incurred
Eric Graber	231 54 9876	Salesman

Part I   **Employee Business Expenses and Reimbursements**

STEP 1 **Enter Your Expenses**		**Column A** Other than Meals and Entertainment	**Column B** Meals and Entertainment
1 Vehicle expense from line 22 or line 29	1	7,161.00	
2 Parking fees, tolls, and transportation, including train, bus, etc., that **did not** involve overnight travel or commuting to and from work	2	250.00	
3 Travel expense while away from home overnight, including lodging, airplane, car rental, etc. **Do not** include meals and entertainment	3	3,050.00	
4 Business expenses not included on lines 1 through 3. **Do not** include meals and entertainment	4	0	
5 Meals and entertainment expenses (see instructions)	5		950.00
6 **Total expenses.** In Column A, add lines 1 through 4 and enter the result. In Column B, enter the amount from line 5	6	10,461.00	950.00

NOTE: *If you were not reimbursed for any expenses in Step 1, skip line 7 and enter the amount from line 6 on line 8.*

STEP 2   **Enter Amounts Your Employer Gave You For Expenses Listed In STEP 1**

7 Enter amounts your employer gave you that were **not** reported to you in box 1 of Form W-2. Include any amount reported under code "L" in box 13 of your Form W-2.	7	3,465.00	

STEP 3   **Figure Expenses To Deduct on Schedule A (Form 1040)**

8 Subtract line 7 from line 6	8	6,996.00	950.00
Note: *If **both columns** of line 8 are zero, **stop here.** If Column A is less than zero, report the amount as income on Form 1040, line 7.*			
9 In Column A, enter the amount from line 8. In Column B, multiply the amount on line 8 by 50% (.50). If either column is zero or less, enter -0- in that column	9	6,996.00	475.00
10 Add the amounts on line 9 of both columns and enter the total here. **Also, enter the total on Schedule A (Form 1040).** (Qualified performing artists and individuals with disabilities, see the instructions for special rules on where to enter the total.) ▶	10	7,471.00	

LHA   **For Paperwork Reduction Act Notice, see instructions.**   Form **2106** (1996)

FIGURE I9-2   ▶   PAGE 1 OF FORM 2106 FOR EXAMPLE I9-65

Part II   **Vehicle Expenses** (See instructions to find out which sections to complete.)

Section A. - General Information

			(a) Vehicle		(b) Vehicle	
11	Enter the date vehicle was placed in service	11				
12	Total miles vehicle was driven during 1996	12	33,000	miles		miles
13	Business miles included on line 12	13	23,100	miles		miles
14	Percent of business use. Divide line 13 by line 12	14	70	%		%
15	Average daily round trip commuting distance	15		miles		miles
16	Commuting miles included on line 12	16	3,000	miles		miles
17	Other personal miles. Add lines 13 and 16 and subtract the total from line 12	17	6,900	miles		miles

18 Do you (or your spouse) have another vehicle available for personal purposes? .... ☐ Yes ☒ No

19 If your employer provided you with a vehicle, is personal use during off-duty hours permitted? .... ☐ Yes ☐ No ☐ Not applicable

20 Do you have evidence to support your deduction? .... ☒ Yes ☐ No

21 If "Yes," is the evidence written? .... ☒ Yes ☐ No

Section B. - Standard Mileage Rate (Use this section only if you own the vehicle.)

22 Multiply line 13 by 31¢ (.31). Enter the result here and on line 1. (Rural mail carriers, see instructions.)	22	7,161.00

Section C. - Actual Expenses

			(a) Vehicle		(b) Vehicle	
23	Gasoline, oil, repairs, vehicle insurance, etc.	23	5,000	00		
24a	Vehicle rentals	24a				
b	Inclusion amount	24b				
c	Subtract line 24b from line 24a	24c				
25	Value of employer-provided vehicle (applies only if 100% of annual lease value was included on Form W-2.)	25				
26	Add lines 23, 24c, and 25	26	5,000	00		
27	Multiply line 26 by the percentage on line 14	27	3,500	00		
28	Depreciation. Enter amount from line 38 below	28	1,610	00		
29	Add lines 27 and 28. Enter total here and on line 1	29	5,110	00		

Section D. - Depreciation of Vehicles (Use this section only if you own the vehicle.)

			(a) Vehicle		(b) Vehicle	
30	Enter cost or other basis	30				
31	Enter amount of section 179 deduction	31				
32	Multiply line 30 by line 14	32				
33	Enter depreciation method and percentage	33				
34	Multiply line 32 by the percentage on line 33	34	1,610	00		
35	Add lines 31 and 34	35	1,610	00		
36	Enter the limitation amount from the table in the line 36 instructions	36	4,900 00			
37	Multiply line 36 by the percentage on line 14	37	3,430	00		
38	Enter the **smaller** of line 35 or line 37. Also, enter this amount on line 28 above	38	1,610	00		

612002
10-11-96

FIGURE 19-2   ▶   PAGE 2 OF FORM 2106 FOR EXAMPLE 19-65

ETHICAL POINT

The CPA has a responsibility to make sure that proper documentation has been furnished by the taxpayer to substantiate travel and entertainment expenses according to the provisions in Sec. 274(d). The CPA cannot rely on the use of estimates for these expenses despite the fact that the *AICPA's Statements on Responsibilities in Tax Practice No. 4* (see Appendix E) permits the use of estimates if it is impractical to obtain exact data and the estimated amounts appear to be reasonable.

▶ The standard mileage rate may be used to compute automobile expenses in lieu of actual expenses and is reported on Form 2106 (Employee Business Expenses).

▶ Taxpayers may elect an optional method for computing deductions for business travel and meal expenses in lieu of using actual costs. If a per diem allowance is paid by an employer in lieu of reimbursing actual expenses, the reimbursement is deemed to be substantiated if it does not exceed a federal per diem rate for the travel locality. In lieu of using actual expenses an employee or self-employed individual may use the applicable federal per diem rate.[89] The taxpayer must still provide documentation of time, place, and business purpose for the expenditures.

REPORTING EMPLOYEE BUSINESS EXPENSES

Form 2106 (Employee Business Expenses) is used to report employee business expenses (see Appendix B). Part I of Form 2106 is a recap of travel and transportation expenses. Part II includes a computation of automobile expenses using either actual expenses or the standard rate mileage method. Employer reimbursements must be included in the employee's wages on Form W-2 if an adequate accounting of the expenses is not made. Employer withholding of federal income tax is also required for nonaccountable plan reimbursements. Form 2106-EZ may be used by employees who do not receive an employer reimbursement, and where the standard mileage rate is used for the current year and for the year the taxpayer's automobile was first placed in service.

Moving expenses are reported on Form 3903 (Moving Expenses) instead of Form 2106 because they are treated differently from other employee expenses (e.g., unreimbursed moving expenses are deductible *for* AGI). Expenses such as entertainment, union dues, business gifts, and education expenses are reported on Schedule A of Form 1040 as itemized deductions (see Appendix B).

A filled-in copy of Form 2106 is shown in Figure I9-2. It includes the computations relating to the information in Example I9-65.

EXAMPLE I9-65 ▶

ADDITIONAL COMMENT

Many of the provisions related to employee business expenses are very complex. It has been said of the general complexity of the tax law that: "If Patrick Henry thought taxation without representation was bad, he should have seen taxation with representation."

Eric Graber, SSN 231-54-9876, is single and employed as a salesman by the Houston Corporation. Eric is required to use his personal automobile for employment-related business. He uses only one automobile for business purposes. During 1996, Eric drives his automobile 70% of the time for business use and incurs the following total expenses:

Gas and oil	$3,000
Repairs	600
Depreciation	2,300
Insurance	1,400
Parking and tolls (all business related)	250
Total	$7,550

During the year, Eric drives a total of 33,000 miles, of which 23,100 are business miles. Of the 9,900 personal miles, 3,000 miles are commuting to and from work. Eric receives a reimbursement of 15 cents per business mile from his employer. Eric also incurred $4,000 of unreimbursed employment-related travel and entertainment expenses. These expenses include the following:

Airfare	$2,500
Car rental	250
Business meals at which business was discussed	150
Laundry	100
Lodging	200
Entertainment of customers	800
Total	$4,000

---

[89] Rev. Proc. 96-64, I.R.B. 1996-53, 52, 53.

Step 1, line 1: Vehicle expense (23,100 × 0.31)	$7,161
Step 2, line 7: (23,100 miles × 0.15)	$3,465
Section C, line 23: Actual Expenses:	
Gas and oil	$3,000
Repairs	600
Insurance	1,400
Total	$5,000
Section C, line 28: Depreciation ($2,300 × .70)	$1,610 ◀

REPORTING MOVING EXPENSES

Employer reimbursements for qualifying moving expenses reduce the otherwise deductible amount for the employee. Reimbursements for nondeductible moving expenses are included in gross income and should be included in total wages on the employee's Form W-2 and reported on page 1 (line 7) of Form 1040. Employers should complete Form 4782 (Employee Moving Expense Information) which summarizes the moving expense payments made to the employee and to third parties for post-1993 and pre-1994 tax years. The form is provided to an employee to properly report his moving expenses and reimbursements. Form 3903 (Moving Expenses) is used to compute the allowable moving expenses and is attached to the employee's tax return (see Appendix B). Moving expenses are deductible *for* AGI on line 24 of page 1 of Form 1040. Moving expenses are not subject to federal income tax withholding if it is reasonable to believe that an employee will be entitled to a deduction for such amounts. Reimbursements in excess of the deductible amounts, however, are subject to the withholding of income and social security taxes.

KEY POINT

If a taxpayer who is an employee moves in early December, the earliest that the 39-week test could be met would be early September of the following year. This is well after the April 15 due date for the individual return. The taxpayer may nevertheless deduct the moving expenses in the earlier year.

A taxpayer may deduct moving expenses, even though the tests for qualification have not been met (e.g., the 39-week test). If the individual subsequently fails to satisfy the requirements, gross income for the subsequent year must be increased by the previous tax benefit.[90] Another alternative is to wait until the tests have been met and then file an amended return (Form 1040X–see Appendix B) for the prior year.

REPORTING OFFICE IN HOME EXPENSES

Form 8829 (Expenses for Business Use of Your Home) must be used to figure the allowable expenses for business use that are reported on Schedule C (Profit or Loss from Business) or Schedule C-EZ and the carryover of any nondeductible amounts from prior years. Form 4562 (Depreciation and Amortization) must also be used to compute depreciation on the office portion of the residence. These tax forms are reproduced in Appendix B.

QUALIFICATION OF PENSION AND PROFIT-SHARING PLANS

The reporting requirements to establish and maintain a qualified pension or profit-sharing plan are too complex for this text. However, it should be noted that it is generally advisable for a taxpayer to obtain advance approval of the plan from the district director of the IRS by requesting a determination letter that all requirements for qualification have been met. A new determination letter should generally be requested when any material (e.g., substantial) modification is made to a plan. Material changes are frequently required when major tax legislation is enacted. In addition, several reports must be filed with the IRS and the U.S. Department of Labor.

---

[90] Secs. 217(d)(2) and (3).

PROBLEM MATERIALS

DISCUSSION QUESTIONS

I9-1 Why is it important to distinguish whether an individual is an employee or an independent contractor (self-employed)?

I9-2 Matt is a CPA engaged in a tax practice and has several small clients. He is also employed as a tax accountant for a major company. Matt incurs local transportation and unreimbursed travel expenses for both his business and employment activities. How does Matt report these expenses on his tax return?

I9-3 Determine whether the following expenses are either deductible *for* AGI or *from* AGI or nondeductible on an employee's return. Indicate whether the expenses are subject to the 2% nondeductible floor for miscellaneous itemized deductions and whether the 50% meals and entertainment deduction limit applies.

  a. Reimbursed business meals (an adequate accounting is made to the employer and any excess reimbursement must be repaid)

  b. Automobile expenses associated with commuting to and from work

  c. Legal expenses incurred to prepare the taxpayer's income tax return

  d. Unreimbursed travel and transportation expenses (including meals)

  e. Unreimbursed entertainment expenses

  f. Qualified moving expenses of an employee

  g. Education-related expenses involving tuition and books

I9-4 Which of the following deduction items are subject to the 2% nondeductible floor applicable to miscellaneous itemized deductions?

  a. Investment counseling fees

  b. Fees for tax return preparation

  c. Unreimbursed professional dues for an employee

  d. Gambling losses

  e. Interest on a personal residence

  f. Unreimbursed employee travel expenses

  g. Reimbursed employee travel expenses (an adequate accounting is made to the employer and any excess reimbursement must be repaid)

  h. Safe-deposit box rental expenses for an investor

I9-5 In each of the following cases involving travel expenses, indicate how each item is reported on the taxpayer's tax return. Include any limitations that might affect its deductibility.

  a. Marilyn, who lives in Houston, owns several apartments in Denver. To supervise the management of these properties, Marilyn incurs travel expenses including airfare, lodging, and meals while traveling to and from the apartment site.

  b. Marc is an employee who incurs travel expenses as a salesperson. The expenses are fully reimbursed by his employer after an adequate accounting has been made.

  c. Assume the same facts as in Part b, except that the expenses are not reimbursed.

  d. Kay is a self-employed attorney who incurs travel expenses (including meals) to prepare a court case in a nearby city.

I9-6 Kelly is an employee who incurs $2,000 of business meal expenses in connection with business entertainment and travel, none of which are reimbursed by her employer. $500 of the business meal costs are lavish or extravagant. How much can Kelly deduct before applying the 2% nondeductible floor on miscellaneous itemized deductions?

I9-7 Latoya is a college professor who takes a nine-month leave of absence from her employment at a college in Ohio and accepts a temporary assignment at a college in Texas. Latoya leaves her husband and children in Ohio and incurs the following expenses in connection with the temporary assignment:

Airfare to and from the temporary assignment	$ 1,000
Living expenses in the new location (including meals of $1,000)	8,000
Personal clothing	1,500
Total	$10,500

a. Which (if any) of these items can Latoya deduct?

b. If Latoya quit her job in Ohio and accepted a two-year assignment with a college in Texas, which (if any) of the items listed above would be deductible?

c. How would your answer to Part b change if the two-year assignment lasted for only nine months? Assume that it was realistic to expect the assignment to be for a two-year period.

I9-8 Larry is an investor in real estate who attends several investment counseling seminars on how to invest in real estate. In the current year, Larry incurs $4,000 of related travel expenses and registration fees. He deducts the expenses on his income tax return as a *for* AGI expense related to the production of income. Are the travel expenses and registration fees deductible? Should they be classified as *for* AGI or *from* AGI?

I9-9 If an employee receives a specific monthly amount from his or her employer as a reimbursement for employment-related entertainment, travel, and transportation expenses, why is it necessary to allocate a portion of the total reimbursement to each expense category?

I9-10 If an employee receives a reimbursement of 15 cents a mile from her employer for employment-related transportation expenses, is the employee permitted to deduct the difference between the standard mileage rate and the reimbursement rate as an unreimbursed employee expense? What other alternative is available for claiming the transportation deduction?

I9-11 If an employee (or self-employed individual) uses the standard mileage rate method for the year in which an automobile is acquired, may the actual expense method be used in a subsequent year? If

so, what restrictions are imposed (if any) on depreciation methods? What adjustments to basis are required?

I9-12 What reporting procedures should be followed by an employee who deducts unreimbursed employee expenses on his or her tax return?

I9-13 Discuss the reporting procedures that should be followed by an employee to report employment-related expenses on his or her tax return under the following conditions:

a. Expenses are less than reimbursements, and no accounting is made to the employer.

b. Expenses equal reimbursements, and an adequate accounting is made to the employer.

c. Expenses exceed reimbursements, and an adequate accounting is made to the employer.

d. Expenses are less than reimbursements. An adequate accounting is made to the employer and the employee is required to repay any excess amount.

I9-14 Why were distance and time requirements legislated as conditions for eligibility for a moving expense deduction?

I9-15 Does it matter whether a moving expense is incurred by an employee, a self-employed individual, or an unemployed person?

I9-16 Len incurs $2,000 of allowable moving expenses in the current year and is fully reimbursed by his employer in the same year.

a. How are the expense deduction and the reimbursement reported on Len's tax return if he uses the standard deduction?

b. What tax consequences occur if the reimbursement is instead $3,000?

I9-17 Why are strict recordkeeping requirements required for the deduction of entertainment expenses?

I9-18 Louis incurs "directly related" entertainment expenses of $4,000, but he is reimbursed by his employer for only $3,000 after an adequate accounting is made.

a. How are these amounts reported on Louis's tax return?

b. What are the tax consequences if Louis is unable to provide adequate documentation of the expenditures during the course of an IRS audit of his tax return?

I9-19 Latesha is a self-employed attorney who entertains clients and potential clients in her home.

a. What requirements must be met to qualify the outlays as deductible entertainment expenses?

b. If the expenses qualify, are they classified as "directly related" or "associated with" entertainment?

I9-20 Liz is an employee who entertains customers. In the current year, Liz incurs $6,000 in business meal expenses that are connected with entertainment. Liz's expenses are not lavish or extravagant. She itemizes her deductions in the current year.

a. If none of these expenses are reimbursed by Liz's employer, what amounts are deductible and how are they classified?

b. How are these amounts reported by Liz and her employer if all of her expenses are reimbursed and an adequate accounting is made by Liz?

I9-21 Atlantic Corporation provides a cafeteria for its employees. The meal charges are set at a sufficiently high level that the employees are not taxed on the subsidized eating facilities. Are Atlantic's cafeteria-related costs subject to the 50% disallowance for business meals?

I9-22 Lynn is a salesperson who entertains clients at business luncheons. A business relationship exists for the entertainment, and there is a reasonable expectation of business benefit. However, no business discussions are generally conducted before, during, or immediately following the meals. Do the business meal expenditures qualify as entertainment expenses?

I9-23 If an individual belongs to a country club and uses the facility primarily for business entertainment of customers, what portion of the club dues is deductible?

I9-24 Bass Corporation purchases 10 tickets to the Super Bowl in January 1997 for entertaining its customers. Due to unusually high demand, the tickets have to be purchased from scalpers for $6,000 (10 × $600). The face value of the tickets is only $900 (10 × $90). What amount is deductible by Bass in 1997?

I9-25 a. Discuss the two requirements for an employee expense reimbursement plan to be treated as an accountable plan.

b. How are expenses and reimbursements treated under an accountable plan?

c. How are expenses and reimbursements treated under a nonaccountable plan?

I9-26 Martin is a tax accountant employed by a public accounting firm. He incurs the following expenses:

CPA review course	$ 400
Law school tuition and books	4,000
Accounting continuing education course (travel, fees, and transportation, (including meals of $200)	600
Total	$5,000

Martin is a degree candidate at the law school. Which (if any) of these expenditures qualify as deductible education expenses? How are they reported?

I9-27 Why are public school teachers generally allowed a deduction for education expenses related to graduate school or advanced courses?

I9-28 Discuss whether each of the following individuals is entitled to an office-in-home deduction:

a. Maggie is a self-employed management consultant who maintains an office in her home exclusively used for client meetings and other business-related activities. Maggie has no other place of business and her office is the most significant place for her business. She has substantial income from the consulting practice.

b. Marty is a college professor who writes research papers for academic journals in his office at home which is used exclusively for this purpose. Although Marty has an office at his place of employment, he finds it very convenient to maintain an office at home to avoid distractions from students and colleagues. Marty receives no income from the publication of the research articles for the year in question.

I9-29 Compare and contrast the tax advantages accruing to employers and employees from the establishment of a qualified pension or profit-sharing plan versus a nonqualified deferred compensation arrangement (e.g., a restricted property plan).

I9-30 What is the difference between a defined benefit pension plan and a defined contribution pension plan?

I9-31 Austin Corporation is proposing the establishment of a pension plan that will cover only employees with salaries in excess of $70,000. No other employees are covered under comparable qualified plans. What problems (if any) do you envision regarding the plan's qualification with the IRS?

I9-32 Babson Corporation is proposing the creation of a qualified profit-sharing plan for its employees. The proposed plan provides for vesting of employer contributions after 20 years because the company wants to discourage employee turnover and does not feel that short-term employees should qualify for benefits. Will this plan qualify? Why or why not?

I9-33 Explain how distributions from a qualified pension plan, which are made in the form of annuity payments, are reported by an employee under the following circumstances:
a. No employee contributions are made to the plan.
b. The pension plan provides for matching employee contributions.

I9-34 Discuss the limitations and restrictions that the Code places on employer contributions to qualified pension and profit-sharing plans.

I9-35 Why are nonqualified deferred compensation plans particularly well-suited for use in executive compensation arrangements?

I9-36 If a newly formed corporation is considering going public and anticipates substantial future appreciation in its stock, would it be advisable for an executive receiving restricted property to elect to recognize income immediately under Sec. 83(b)? Contrast the tax consequences of a restricted property arrangement for both the employer and employee when this election is made versus when it is not made.

Consider the effect of the subsequent lapsing of the restrictions and the employee's sale of the stock.

I9-37 List and discuss the qualification requirements for an incentive stock option plan (ISO). Describe the advantages and disadvantages of ISOs compared to nonqualified stock option plans.

I9-38 What difference does it make if a nonqualified stock option has a readily ascertainable FMV on the grant date?

I9-39 Is a self-employed individual, who is also employed and covered by an employer's qualified pension plan, eligible to establish an H.R. 10 or an SEP plan his or her self-employment income?

I9-40 What limitations are placed on self-employed individuals for contributions made to defined contribution H.R. 10 plans? Must self-employed individuals cover their full-time employees if an H.R. 10 plan is established?

I9-41 Would you be more favorably inclined to advise a 50-year-old individual or a 30-year-old individual to establish a deductible IRA? Why? A nondeductible IRA? Why? Consider any tax problems involved if the IRA funds are needed before age 59½.

I9-42 Sally, age 30, has previously made deductible IRA contributions for years before 1987 and is no longer eligible to make deductible IRA contributions. Would you advise Sally to make nondeductible IRA contributions? Explain.

I9-43 The owner of an unincorporated small business is considering whether to establish a simplified employee pension (SEP) plan for its employees.
a. What nontax factors might make an SEP attractive as an alternative to establishing a qualified pension or profit-sharing plan?
b. Is the owner of the small business eligible to make contributions on his or her behalf to the SEP?
c. Would you advise the owner to establish a salary reduction agreement SEP? Explain.

ISSUE IDENTIFICATION QUESTIONS

I9-44 Georgia is an executive who is considering whether to accept an assignment with her employer at an away-from-home location. It is realistically expected that the assignment will be completed in 15 months but the actual time period was only 11 months. Georgia incurred $15,000 of away-from-home expenses during the 11-month period none of which were reimbursed by her employer. What tax issues should Georgia consider?

I9-45 Jeremy is an executive for Columbia Corporation, which is going through a restructuring of its corporate headquarters operations. Columbia has offered to relocate Jeremy from its New York headquarters to its divisional operation in South Carolina and will reimburse him for both direct and indirect moving expenses. What tax issues should Jeremy consider?

I9-46 Juan is a medical doctor who maintains an office in his home where he maintains patient records and performs billing procedures. Most of his time is spent visiting patients and performing surgical procedures in the operating room at several local hospitals. What tax issues should Juan consider?

I9-47 David is on the audit staff of a national accounting firm. He has been with the firm for three years and is a CPA. David has applied and been accepted into a prestigious MBA program. The program is two years in duration. David has decided to resign from the accounting firm even though the firm has indicated that it would very much like David to return to work for the firm after he receives his MBA degree. David is somewhat interested in returning to public accounting but will certainly look at all of his options when he completes the program. David wants to deduct his education expenses, what are the relevant tax issues in this case?

PROBLEMS

I9-48 *Employment-Related Expenses.* Matt incurs the following employment-related expenses in the current year:

Actual automobile expenses	$1,000
Moving expenses (deductible under Sec. 217)	1,000
Entertainment expenses	2,000
Travel expenses (including $500 of business meals)	2,500
Professional dues and subscriptions	500
Total	$7,000

Matt's AGI is $100,000 before the above expenses are deducted. None of the expenses listed above are reimbursed by Matt's employer. He has no other miscellaneous itemized deductions and does not use the standard deduction.
a. What is the amount of Matt's deduction for employment-related expenses?
b. How are these items reported in Matt's tax return?

I9-49 *Travel and Entertainment.* Monique is a self-employed manufacturer's representative who solicits business for clients and receives a commission based on sales. She incurs the following expenditures during the current year:

Airfare and lodging while away from home overnight	$ 4,000
Business meals while traveling at which business is discussed	1,000
Local transportation costs for automobile, parking, tolls, etc.	2,000
Commuting expenses	1,000
Local entertainment of customers	2,000
Total	$10,000

a. Which of the expenditures listed above (if any) are deductible by Monique?

b. Are each of these items classified as *for* AGI or *from* AGI deductions?

c. How would your answers to Parts a and b change if Monique were an employee rather than self-employed and none of the expenses were reimbursed by her employer?

I9-50   *Unreimbursed Employee Expenses.* In the current year Mary incurs $2,000 of unreimbursed employment-related travel and entertainment expenses. These expenses include the following:

Airfare	$1,000
Taxi fare	100
Business meals at which business is discussed	200
Laundry	50
Lodging	150
Entertainment of customers	500
Total	$2,000

Mary also pays $1,000 of investment counseling fees and $500 of tax return preparation fees in the current year. Mary's AGI is $40,000.

a. What is the total amount of Mary's deductible expenses?

b. Are the deductible expenses classified as *for* AGI or *from* AGI?

I9-51   *Travel Expenses.* Marilyn is a business executive who accepts a temporary out-of-town assignment for a period of ten months. Marilyn leaves her husband and children in Miami and rents an apartment in the new location during the ten-month period. Marilyn incurs the following expenses, none of which are reimbursed by her employer:

Airfare to and from the new location	$ 800
Airfare for weekend trips to visit her family	6,200
Apartment rent	7,000
Meals at the temporary location	8,500
Entertainment of customers	2,000
Total	$24,500

a. Which of the expenditures listed above (if any) are deductible by Marilyn (before any limitations are applied)?

b. Are each of these expenditures classified as *for* AGI or *from* AGI deductions?

c. If Marilyn's AGI is $60,000, what is the amount of the deduction for the expenditures?

d. Do the tax consequences change if Marilyn's assignment is for a period of more than one year and is for an indefinite period rather than a temporary period?

e. Do the tax consequences in Parts a through c change if it was realistically expected that the work would be completed in ten months but after the ten-month period Marilyn is asked to continue for seven more months and if an additional $10,000 of travel expenses is incurred during the extended period?

I9-52 ***Business/Personal Travel Expenses.*** In the current year Mike's AGI is $50,000. Mike has no miscellaneous itemized deductions other than the employment-related expenses on the list below. Mike attends a professional trade association convention in Los Angeles. He spends three days at the meeting and two days vacationing before the meeting. Mike was unable to obtain excursion airfare rates despite the fact that he was on vacation immediately before the meeting. Mike's total expenses, of which the business-related expenses are fully reimbursed by his employer after an adequate accounting is made, include the following:

Airfare	$ 450
Meals ($30 per day)	150
Hotel ($60 per day)	300
Entertainment of customers (business is discussed)	500
Total	$1,400

a. How much can Mike deduct for employment-related expenses?

b. How is the reimbursement reported on Mike's tax return?

c. Is the reimbursement fully deductible by Mike's employer?

I9-53 ***Employment-Related Expenses and Reimbursements.*** Maxine incurs the following employment-related business expenses in the current year:

Professional dues and subscriptions	$1,000
Airfare and lodging	2,000
Local transportation for employment-related business activities	1,000
Customer entertainment (business lunches where business is discussed)	1,000
Total	$5,000

After making an adequate accounting of the expenses, Maxine receives a fixed reimbursement of $3,000 from her employer. Assume that Maxine's AGI is $50,000, she has other miscellaneous itemized deductions of $1,000, and she does not use the standard deduction.

a. What amount of the expenses are deductible by Maxine?

b. Are each of these expenditures classified as *for* AGI or *from* AGI deductions?

c. How would your answers to Parts a and b change if Maxine instead received a $6,000 reimbursement?

I9-54 ***Miscellaneous Itemized Deductions.*** In the current year, Melissa, a single employee whose AGI is $100,000, incurs the following expenses:

Safe deposit box rental for investments	$ 200
Tax return preparation fees	500
Moving expenses (otherwise deductible under Sec. 217)	2,000
Mortgage interest on Melissa's principal residence	12,000
Real estate taxes on Melissa's principal residence	3,000
Unreimbursed employment-related expenses (other than business meals and entertainment)	6,000
Unreimbursed employment-related expenses for business meals and entertainment (business is discussed)	400
Total	$24,100

a. What is the amount of Melissa's total miscellaneous itemized deductions (after deducting the 2% floor)?

b. What is the amount of Melissa's total itemized deductions?

c. What is the amount of Melissa's total itemized deductions if her AGI is instead $150,000?

I9-55 *Transportation Expenses.* Jose, an employee of a law firm, maintains an office at the principal business location of his firm. He frequently travels from his home to client locations within and outside the metropolitan area. Jose is not reimbursed for his transportation expenses and has incurred the following:

Transportation expenses associated with trips to clients within the metropolitan area	$2,000
Transportation expenses associated with trips to clients located outside the metropolitan area	3,000
Total	$5,000

a. What is the amount of Jose's deduction for transportation expenses?

b. How is the deduction reported on Jose's tax return?

c. What is the amount of Jose's deduction for transportation expenses and its classification if he is self-employed and operates his office from his home? Assume that the requirements of Sec. 280A are satisfied.

I9-56 *Auto Expenses.* Michelle is an employee who must use her personal automobile for employment-related business trips. During the current year Michelle drives her car 60% for business use and incurs the following total expenses (100% use of car):

Gas and oil	$2,000
Repairs	400
Depreciation	2,200
Insurance and license fees	1,300
Parking and tolls (business related)	100
Total	$6,000

Michelle drives 20,000 business miles during the current year and receives a reimbursement of 10 cents per mile from her employer. Assume that the 2% nondeductible floor on miscellaneous itemized deductions is not applicable and that an adequate accounting is made to Michelle's employer.

a. What amount is deductible if Michelle elects to use the standard mileage method?

b. What amount is deductible if Michelle uses the actual cost method?

I9-57 *Entertainment Expenses.* Milt, a self-employed attorney, incurs the following expenses in the current year:

Dues paid to the local chamber of commerce	$ 1,000
Business lunches for clients and prospective clients (Milt does not believe in conducting business discussions during lunch)	4,000
Entertainment of professional associates in his home (immediately following business meetings)	2,000
Country club dues (the club is used exclusively for business)	2,500
Entertainment of clients and prospective clients at the country club	1,500
Total	$11,000

a. Which of the expenditures listed above (if any) are deductible by Milt?
b. Are each of these items classified as *for* AGI or *from* AGI deductions?

I9-58 *Entertainment Expenses.* Beach Corporation purchases tickets to sporting events and uses them to entertain customers. In the current year Beach Corporation purchases the following tickets:

100 tickets to football games (face value of the tickets is $3,600)	$6,000
A skybox rented for six athletic events (seating capacity of the skybox is 30, and the highest price of a nonluxury box seat is $40)	18,000

What amount of the entertainment expenses is deductible in the current year?

I9-59 *Reimbursed Employee Expenses.* Latrisha is an employee of the Cooper Company and incurs significant employment-related expenses. During the current year, she incurred the following expenses in connection with her job:

Travel: Airfare	$ 5,850
Lodging	1,800
Meals	1,200
Entertainment of customers	2,400
Total	$11,250

a. Determine the amount of deductible expenses and whether they are deductible *for* AGI or *from* AGI assuming Cooper Company maintains an accountable plan for employee expense reimbursements, if the reimbursements are:

      1. $11,250
      2. $9,000
      3. $14,000

b. What would be the result in a. for each of the three situations if the plan was a nonaccountable plan?

I9-60 *Moving Expenses.* Michael graduates from City College of New York and on February 1, 1997 accepts a position with a public accounting firm in Chicago. Michael is a resident of New York. In March, Michael travels to Chicago to locate a house and starts to work in June. He incurs the following expenses, none of which are reimbursed by the public accounting firm:

Automobile expense enroute		
(1,000 miles 10 cents per mile standard mileage rate)	$	100
Cost of meals en route		100
Househunting trip travel expenses		1,400
Moving van rental		2,000
Commission on the sale of		
Michael's New York condominium		3,500
Points paid to acquire a mortgage on		
Michael's new residence in Chicago		1,000
Temporary living expenses for one week		
in Chicago (hotel and $100 in meals)		400
Expenses incurred in decorating the new residence		500
Total expenses		$9,000

a. What is Michael's moving expense deduction?

b. How are the deductible expenses classified on Michael's tax return?

c. How would your answer to Part a change if all of Michael's expenses were reimbursed by his employer?

I9-61 *Education Expenses.* For each of the following independent situations, determine whether any of the expenditures qualify as deductible education expenses. Are the expenditures classified as *for* AGI or *from* AGI deductions?

a. Law school tuition and books for an IRS agent: $2,000.

b. Continuing professional accounting education expenses of $1,900 for a self-employed CPA: travel, $1,000 (including $200 meals); registration fees, $800; books, $100.

c. MBA education expenses totaling $5,000 for a business executive of a major corporation: tuition, $4,000; transportation, $800; and books, $200.

d. Tuition and books acquired for graduate education courses required under state law for a schoolteacher in order to renew a provisional certificate: $1,000.

e. Bar review courses for a recent law school graduate: $1,000.

I9-62 *Office-in-Home.* Nancy is a self-employed artist who uses 10% of her residence as a studio. The studio portion is used exclusively for business and is frequented by customers on a regular basis. Nancy also uses her den as an office (10% of the total floor space of her home) to prepare bills and keep records. However, the den is also used by her children as a TV room. Nancy's income from the sale of the artwork amounts to $40,000 in the current year. She also incurs $2,000 of expenses directly related to the business other than home office expenses (e.g., art supplies and selling expenses). Nancy incurs the following expenses in the current year related to her residence:

Real estate taxes	$ 2,000
Mortgage interest	5,000
Insurance	500
Depreciation	3,500
Repairs and utilities	1,000
Total	$12,000

a. Which of the expenditures above (if any) are deductible? Are they *for* AGI or *from* AGI deductions?

b. Would your answer to Part a change if Nancy's income from painting were only $2,500 for the year? What is the amount of the office-in-home deduction and the amount of the carryover (if any) of the unused deductions? (Assume that Nancy is not subject to the hobby loss restrictions.)

I9-63 Dawn is a self-employed author who uses 10% of her home as an office to write novels. She spends 30 to 35 hours per week in her home office writing and another 15 hours per week at other locations conducting research, meeting with publishers, and attending promotional events. Dawn's royalty income from the writing is $60,000 in the current year. She incurs $6,000 of expenses directly related to her writing (e.g., supplies and transportation expenses). The following current year expenses relate to her residence:

Real estate taxes	$ 4,000
Mortgage interest	6,000
Insurance	1,000
Depreciation	4,000
Repairs and utilities	1,000
Total expenses for the residence	$16,000

a. Which of the above expenditures (if any) are deductible? Are they *for* AGI or *from* AGI deductions?

b. Would your answer to Part a change if Dawn's income were from sales and she devoted 70% of her time to sales-related activities at client's offices?

I9-64 *Deferred Compensation Plan Requirements.* Identify whether each of the following plan features is associated with a qualified pension plan, a qualified profit-sharing plan, an employee stock ownership plan, a nonqualifed plan, or none of these plans.

a. Annual employer contributions are not required, but substantial and recurring contributions must be made based on a predetermined formula.

b. Annual, systematic, and definite employer contributions are required without regard to profits but based on actuarial methods.

c. Forfeitures must be used to reduce contributions that would otherwise be made under the plan.

d. The plan may discriminate in favor of highly compensated individuals.

e. The trust is funded with the contribution of employer stock, which is subsequently distributed to employees.

I9-65 *Taxability of Pension Payments.* Pam is a participant in a qualified pension plan. She retires on January 1, 1997, and receives pension payments beginning in January 1997. Her pension payments, which will be received monthly for life, amount to $1,000 per month. Pam contributed $30,000 to the pension plan, and her life expectancy is 15 years from the date she starts receiving payments.

a. What gross income will Pam recognize in 1997 and each year thereafter?

b. How would your answer to Part a change if Pam did not make any contributions to the plan?

c. If Pam dies in December 1998 after receiving pension payments for two full years, what tax consequences occur in the year of death?

d. If Pam outlives her 15-year life expectancy, what amount of the pension payments are taxable in year 16 and subsequent years?

I9-66

Restricted Property. In 1997, Bear Corporation transfers 100 shares of its stock to its employee Patrick. The stock is valued at $10 per share on the issue date. The stock is subject to the following restrictions:

- Patrick cannot transfer the stock by sale or other disposition (except in the event of death) for a five-year period.
- The stock must be forfeited to Bear Corporation if Patrick voluntarily terminates his employment with the company within a five-year period.

In year 2002, the Bear stock is worth $100 per share when the restrictions expire.

a. Assuming that no Sec. 83(b) election is made, what are the tax consequences to Patrick and Bear Corporation in 1997?

b. What are the tax consequences to Patrick and Bear Corporation if Patrick makes a valid Sec. 83(b) election in 1997?

c. What are the tax consequences to Patrick and Bear Corporation if Patrick forfeits the stock back to the company in 1998 when the stock is worth $20 per share if an election has been made under Sec. 83(b)? What would happen if no Sec. 83(b) election were made?

d. What are the tax consequences to Patrick and Bear Corporation upon the lapse of the restrictions in year 2002 if an election has been made under Sec. 83(b)? What would the results be if no Sec. 83(b) election were made?

e. What are the tax consequences to Patrick and Bear Corporation if Patrick sells the Bear stock in year 2003 for $120 per share if a Sec. 83(b) election is made? if no Sec. 83(b) election is made?

I9-67

IRAs. On February 15, 1997, Phong, who is single and age 30, establishes an IRA and contributes $2,000 to the account. Phong's gross income is $31,000 in both 1996 and 1997. Phong is an active participant in an employer-sponsored retirement plan.

a. What amount of the contribution is deductible? In what year is it deductible?

b. How is the deduction (if any) reported (i.e., *for* AGI or *from* AGI)?

c. What tax treatment is accorded to Phong if he withdraws the $2,000 contribution plus $150 of accrued interest on the IRA in 1998 due to a need for cash to pay unexpected medical bills?

d. How would your answer to Part a change, if at all, if Phong were not an active participant in an employer-sponsored retirement plan?

e. How would your answer to Part a change if Phong were married and files a joint return with his spouse, who has no earned income? (Assume their combined AGI is $31,000.)

I9-68

IRAs. Phil, age 30, is married and files a joint return with his spouse. On February 15, 1998, Phil establishes a spousal IRA with a $4,000 contribution, $2,000 for himself and $2,000 for his wife. Phil's spouse earns $1,000 in 1997 from a part-time job, and their combined AGI is $40,000. Neither Phil nor his spouse is an active participant in an employer-sponsored retirement plan.

a. What amount of the contribution is deductible?

b. To what year does the contribution apply? (Assume that an election is made to treat Phil's spouse as having no compensation.)

c. Is the deduction reported as *for* AGI or *from* AGI?

d. How would your answer to Part a change, if at all, if Phil and his spouse were active participants in an employer-sponsored retirement plan?

e. If a portion of the contribution is nondeductible in Part d, is it possible for Phil to make a deductible and a nondeductible contribution in the same year? Explain.

f. How would your answer to Part a change if Phil and his spouse's combined AGI were $70,000 in 1997 and 1998 and Phil were an active participant in an employer-sponsored retirement plan?

I9-69   *H.R. 10 Plans.* Paula is a self-employed doctor who is considering whether to establish a defined contribution H.R. 10 plan. Paula's only employee is a full-time nurse who has been employed by Paula for seven years. Paula's net earnings from self-employment (before the H.R. 10 plan contribution but after the deduction for one-half of self-employment taxes paid) is expected to be $100,000 during the current year and in future years.

a. If the H.R. 10 plan is established, what is the maximum amount Paula can contribute for the nurse's benefit?

b. What is the maximum amount Paula can contribute for herself? Is the amount reported as a *for* AGI or *from* AGI deduction?

c. Is Paula's nurse required to be included in the plan?

d. What are the tax consequences if Paula makes a premature withdrawal from the plan before reaching age 59½?

I9-70   *Stock Options.* Bell Corporation grants an incentive stock option to Peggy, an employee, on January 1, 1997, when the option price and FMV of the Bell stock is $80. Peggy receives the option to buy 10 shares of Bell stock. Peggy exercises the option and acquires the stock on April 1, 1999, when the stock's FMV is $100. Peggy, while still employed by the Bell Corporation, sells the stock on May 1, 2001, for $120 per share.

a. What are the tax consequences to Peggy and Bell Corporation on the following dates: January 1, 1997; April 1, 1999; and May 1, 2001? (Assume all incentive stock option qualification requirements are met.)

b. How would your answer to Part a change if Peggy instead sold the Bell stock for $120 per share on May 1, 1999?

I9-71   *Stock Options.* Bender Corporation grants a nonqualified stock option to Penny, an employee, on January 1, 1997 that entitled Penny to acquire 10 shares of Bender stock at $80 per share. On this date, the stock has a $100 FMV and the option has a readily ascertainable FMV. Penny exercises the option on January 1, 1998 (when the FMV of the stock is $150) and acquires 10 shares of the stock for $80 per share. Penny later sells the Bender stock on January 1, 2000, for $200 per share.

a. What are the tax consequences to Penny and Bender Corporation on the following dates: January 1, 1997; January 1, 1998; and January 1, 2000?

b. How would your answer to Part a change if the Bender stock were instead closely held and the option had no readily ascertainable FMV?

TAX FORM/RETURN PREPARATION PROBLEMS

TAX CUT

I9-72 In the current year Dennis Johnson (SSN 277-33-7263) incurs the following unreimbursed employee business expenses:

Airplane and taxi fares	$ 3,000
Lodging away from home	4,000
Automobile expenses (related to 100% of the use of his personal automobile):	
Gasoline and oil	1,000
Repairs	200
Insurance	200
Depreciation	1,500
Parking and tolls (both equally allocable to business and personal use)	100
Total	$10,000

Johnson receives a $7,000 reimbursement for all of the expenses. He uses his personal automobile 80% for business use. Total business miles amount to 20,000. Johnson's AGI is $40,000, and he has no other miscellaneous itemized deductions.

a. Calculate Johnson's expense deduction using Form 2106 (Employee Business Expenses) based on actual automobile expenses and other employee business expenses.

b. Calculate Johnson's expense deduction using the standard mileage rate method and other employee business expenses. (Assume that none of the restrictions on the use of the standard mileage rate method are applicable.)

TAX CUT

I9-73 George Large (SSN 414-33-5688) and his wife Marge Large (SSN 555-81-9495), want you to prepare their income tax return based on the information below:

George Large worked as a salesman for Toyboat, Inc. He received a salary of $50,000 ($8,000 of income taxes withheld) plus an additional $5,000 to cover his out-of-pocket expenses. George must make an adequate accounting to his employer and return any excess reimbursement. Additionally, Toyboat provides George with medical insurance worth $3,500 per year. George drove his car 20,000 miles during the year. His log indicates that 17,000 miles were for sales calls to prospective customers at the customers' offices. George uses the standard mileage rate method. George is a professional basketball fan. He purchased two season tickets for a total of $2,000. He takes a customer to every game, and they usually discuss business at the games. George also takes clients to business lunches. His log indicates that he spent $1,500 on these business meals. George also took a five-day trip to the Toyboat headquarters in Musty, Ohio. He was so well-prepared that he finished his business in three days, so he spent the other two days sightseeing. He had the following expenses during each day of his trip:

Airfare	$200
Lodging	$85/day
Meals	$50/day
Taxicabs	$20/day

Marge Large is self-employed. She repairs rubber toy boats in the basement of their home, which is 25% of the house's square footage. She had the following income and expenses:

Income from rubber toy boat repairs	$11,000
Cost of materials	5,000
Contract labor	3,500
Long-distance phone calls (business)	500

The Larges incurred other expenses:

Utility bills for the house	$2,000
Real estate taxes	2,500
Mortgage interest	4,500
Cash charitable contributions	2,500

Prepare Form 1040, Schedules A and C for Form 1040, and Form 2106 for the current year. (Assume no depreciation for this problem and that no estimated taxes were paid by the Larges.)

CASE STUDY PROBLEMS

I9-74 Ajax Corporation is a young high-growth company engaged in the manufacture and distribution of automotive parts. Its common stock has doubled in value since the company was listed on the NASDAQ exchange about two years ago. Ajax currently has a high debt/equity ratio due to the issuance of debt to finance its capital expansion needs. Despite rapid growth in assets and profitability, Ajax has severe cash flow problems and a poor working capital ratio. The company urgently needs to attract new executives to the organization and to provide financial incentives to existing top management because of recent turnover and high growth. Approximately 55% of the common stock is owned by Andrew Ajax, who is the CEO, and his immediate family. None of the other officers own stock in the company.

You are a tax consultant for the company who has been asked to prepare suggestions after reviewing the compensation system. Your discussions with several top management individuals reveal the following aspects of corporate strategy and philosophy:

- The company needs to expand the equity capital base because of its concern for the high risk caused by large amounts of debt.

- Improvement in cash flow and liquidity would enhance its stock price and enable the company to continue its high growth rate.

- Top management feels that employee loyalty and productivity would be improved if all employees owned some stock in the company. The company currently offers a qualified pension plan to its employees and executives that provides only minimal pension benefits. No other deferred compensation or bonus arrangements are currently being offered.

- Andrew Ajax feels that the top management group should own a substantial amount of Ajax stock to ensure that the interests of management correspond with the shareholder interests (i.e., the maximization of shareholder wealth).

The following types of compensation arrangements have been discussed:

- Sec. 401(k) and ESOP plans for employees.

- Encourage all employees and executives to independently fund their retirement needs beyond any Social Security benefits by establishing IRA plans.

- Provide restricted property arrangements (using Ajax stock) to attract new top level executives and to retain existing executives.
- Offer nonqualified or incentive stock options to existing and new executives.

Required: Prepare a client memo that recommends revisions to Ajax Corporation's existing compensation system for both its employee and executive groups. Your recommendations should discuss the pros and cons of different deferred compensation arrangements and should consider both tax and nontax factors.

I9-75 Steve is part owner and manager of a small manufacturing company that makes keypads for alarm systems. The keypads are sold to several different alarm companies throughout the country. Steve must travel to several cities each year to meet with current customers and to attract new business. When you meet with Steve to obtain information to prepare his current year tax return, he tells you that he has spent about $5,000 during the current year on airfare and taking his customers out to dinner to discuss business. Because he took most of his trips in the summer and fall, and it is now April of the following year, Steve cannot remember the exact time and places of the business dinners and did not retain any receipts for the cash used to pay the bills. However he remembers the names of the customers he went to see and the business topics that were discussed. As Steve's tax consultant, what is your responsibility regarding the treatment of the travel and entertainment expenses under the mandates of the AICPA's *Statements on Responsibilities in Tax Practice?* Prepare a client letter explaining to Steve the requirements under Sec. 274(d) for sufficient substantiation of travel and entertainment expenses. (See the *Statements on Responsibilities in Tax Practice* section in Chapter I15 and Appendix E for a discussion of these issues.)

TAX RESEARCH PROBLEM

I9-76 Lou operates a small business that provides lawn maintenance services in his area. He is the sole owner of Lou's Landscaping and employs three employees. Lou rents a small warehouse in which he keeps all of his equipment but he maintains no office space in the warehouse. Because the equipment fills all of the warehouse, Lou has turned an extra room in his small house into an office where he keeps a computer and all the necessary paperwork for his customers. Lou spends a few hours each day keeping his customer billings up to date, making phone calls, and performing other activities related to his business. Lou deducted $1,000 last year as home office expenses. The IRS disallowed the deduction and Lou wants to pursue the matter further. Will Lou be entitled to the deduction as an office in home expense?

A partial list of research sources is:

- Sec. 280A
- *CIR v. Nader E. Soliman,* 71 AFTR 2d 93-463, 93-1 USTC ¶50,014 (USSC, 1993)
- Rev. Rul. 94-24, 1994-5, I.R.B. 15

CHAPTER 10

DEPRECIATION, COST RECOVERY, DEPLETION, AMORTIZATION, AND INVENTORY COSTS

LEARNING OBJECTIVES

After studying this chapter, you should be able to

1 ▸ Classify property and calculate depreciation under the pre-ACRS rules

2 ▸ Classify property and calculate cost recovery under the ACRS rules

3 ▸ Classify property and calculate depreciation under the MACRS rules

4 ▸ Apply cost and percentage depletion methods and understand the treatment for intangible drilling costs

5 ▸ Calculate amortization for intangible assets and understand the difference between amortizable and non-amortizable assets

6 ▸ Determine inventory cost and cost of goods sold under various methods

DEPRECIATION AND COST RECOVERY

TYPICAL MISCONCEPTION

It is easy to forget that the depreciation or cost-recovery system that applies to any one asset is the system that was in effect when the property was placed in service. Property acquired in 1986 is not affected by the MACRS rules that became effective in 1987.

REAL-WORLD EXAMPLE

Harrah's Club in Reno, Nevada, restores antique autos and displays them. The restoration costs cannot be depreciated because the autos have an indefinite life as museum pieces. *Harrah's Club v. U.S.*, 43 AFTR 2d 79-745, 81-2 USTC ¶9677 (Ct. Cls., 1981).

HISTORICAL NOTE

Before 1954, except for the limited use of a declining-balance method, taxpayers were required to use the straight-line method.

ADDITIONAL COMMENT

Property is considered to be "placed in service" when it is in a condition or state of readiness and is available for a specifically assigned function. This can be important in attempting to determine the first year that a depreciation deduction is available.

The tax law allows the write-off of certain assets that are used either in connection with a trade or business or held for the production of an income. These write-offs may be in the form of a direct write-off or through a systematic allocation of the cost of the asset over its estimated economic life. For example, inventory costs are charged to cost of goods sold in the period that the goods are sold to customers, whereas the cost of assets that benefit more than one period are recovered through depreciation, depletion, or amortization. This chapter discusses the income tax rules relating to depreciation, depletion, amortization, and certain inventory capitalization requirements. While the concepts in this chapter are similar to those in financial accounting, the specific rules relating to income taxes are unique.

Certain capital costs are neither depreciable nor amortizable under the tax law. Personal-use assets (e.g., a personal automobile or the taxpayer's personal residence) are not depreciable. In addition, no amortization or depreciation is permitted for land or assets that have an indefinite life (e.g., internally generated goodwill or a country club membership).

Three separate depreciation and cost-recovery systems are currently in place because Congress completely revamped the rules in 1981 as part of the Economic Recovery Tax Act of 1981 (ERTA), and substantial revisions were also made by the Tax Reform Act of 1986. The system that taxpayers must use depends on *when* the property was placed into service, as follows:

▶ Prior to 1981: use the rules contained in Sec. 167, these rules basically follow financial accounting.

▶ After December 31, 1980 and before January 1, 1987: use Accelerated Cost Recovery System (ACRS).

▶ After December 31, 1986: use the Modified Accelerated Cost Recovery System (MACRS).

Although the primary emphasis in this chapter is placed upon the MACRS rules, it is also important to understand the pre-ACRS rules and the ACRS rules because some assets (primarily real property) placed in service under these rules are still in service and not yet fully depreciated.

The terms *depreciation* and *cost recovery* are used interchangeably in the text. The Sec. 167 (or pre-ACRS) and the MACRS rules under Sec. 168 refer to depreciation. However, the Sec. 168 ACRS rules referred to cost recovery. In 1981 Congress initiated the original ACRS system to provide a stimulus for private investment. Therefore, less importance was placed on the financial accounting concept of matching costs and revenues, which is the primary theory that governed the Sec. 167 depreciation rules. The primary concern of Congress in 1981 was to allow businesses and investors to recover the cost of capitalized expenditures over a period of time that is substantially shorter than the property's economic useful life. Thus, the term *cost recovery* rather than *depreciation* was used under the ACRS system. The post-1986 MACRS rules more closely follow the concept of economic useful life. Thus, the MACRS rules refer to depreciation rather than cost recovery.

GENERAL RULES APPLYING TO ASSET ACQUISITIONS IN ALL PERIODS

Certain rules apply regardless of when an asset is acquired. For example, because neither the depreciation nor cost-recovery deductions are discretionary, certain prescribed accounting methods (e.g., straight-line or declining balance methods) must be used consistently from year to year. Also, the basis of the property must be reduced by the amount of depreciation that should be taken even if no depreciation is claimed. These requirements effectively prevent taxpayers from not claiming a depreciation deduction during years when little or no tax benefit is derived. For example, taxpayers might prefer not to deduct any depreciation in years they have low marginal tax rates or have NOL carryovers that are about to expire.

EXAMPLE I10-1 ▶

Maria acquires a business building for $300,000 on January 1, 1980 and claims straight-line depreciation based on a 30-year useful life with zero salvage value under the pre-ACRS rules. The allowable depreciation is $10,000 ($300,000 ÷ 30 years), and Maria deducts this amount each year during the 1980–1995 period.[1] Maria's business deteriorates after 1995, and large NOLs are incurred in 1996 and 1997 that cannot be carried back to earlier years. Maria also anticipates that the NOL carryovers will not be used in the immediate future because of the unlikelihood of earning substantial amounts of taxable income during the carryover period. Realizing that the depreciation would have little or no current tax benefit, Maria fails to claim any depreciation in 1996 and 1997. The building is sold for $200,000 on December 31, 1997. The basis of the building must be reduced by the full amount of the allowable depreciation of $180,000 ($10,000 × 18) for the 18-year period, and Maria must recognize a $80,000 gain on the sale of the building ($200,000 selling price − $120,000 adjusted basis), despite the fact that she claimed only $160,000 of depreciation during the 18-year period. ◀

ADDITIONAL COMMENT

A recent case held that a professional musician could depreciate a nineteenth-century violin bow. The IRS had argued the bow had an indeterminate life but the court ruled that the recovery period under ACRS represented the useful life of the bow. *Simon v. Comm.*, 95-2 USTC ¶50,552 (CA-2, 1995).

An important aspect of depreciation is determining when the deduction is *allowable* for an asset that a taxpayer has recently purchased. Depreciation is allowable in the year the asset is placed into service, not necessarily when purchased. For example, a taxpayer may purchase a depreciable asset in December, 1996, but not place it into service until January, 1997. Under this circumstance, depreciation is not allowable until 1997.

TYPES OF PROPERTY. Before examining the cost allocation rules, it is necessary to define certain terms relating to the various types of property. For both property law and income tax purposes, there are two basic types of property, tangible and intangible. **Tangible property** refers to property that has physical substance, such as land, buildings, natural resources, equipment, etc. **Intangible property** refers to property that does not have physical substance, such as goodwill, patents, and stocks and bonds. The cost of tangible property (other than land, of course) is systematically written off through depreciation or depletion. Natural resources, such as oil and gas reserves, are recovered through depletion. Intangible property is written off through amortization.

Tangible property is further classified as either real property or personal property. **Real property** (many times referred to as real estate) is defined as land or any structure permanently attached to the land, such as buildings. **Personal property** is any tangible property that is not real property, and includes items such as equipment, vehicles, furniture, etc. It is important to distinguish between personal property and personal-use property. **Personal-use property** is any property, tangible or intangible, real or personal, that is used by the taxpayer for his own personal use rather than in a trade or business or for the production of income.

CAPITALIZATION VERSUS EXPENSE. A frequent dilemma for taxpayers is whether an expenditure should either be capitalized (and depreciated) or expensed completely in the current year. As is discussed in Chapter I6, if an expenditure either improves the

---

[1] Allowable depreciation is the amount of depreciation permitted to be claimed under the tax law. The term *allowed depreciation* is the amount of depreciation that the taxpayer actually claims. In situations where the taxpayer has never taken depreciation, *allowable* is defined as the slowest possible method allowed by law (e.g., straight-line using the longest permissible recovery period). A taxpayer may file an amended tax return for the purpose of taking depreciation for all years that are not closed by the statute of limitations.

ADDITIONAL
COMMENT
The IRS recently issued a private letter ruling that required an airline to capitalize engine overhauls rather than expensing such amounts in the current year. The IRS position requires capitalization because the overhauls involve replacement or reconditioning of a large portion of the engine's parts. This ruling has been severely criticized by the airlines industry, saying that the decision could negatively impact passenger safety.

efficiency of an asset or extends the life of an asset beyond the end of the year, the expenditure should generally be capitalized. However, most taxpayers have established materiality limits in order to justify the expensing of small expenditures that technically should be considered a capital expenditure. Since the capitalization-expense decision many times is subjective in nature, disputes between the IRS and taxpayers are common.

CONVERSION OF PERSONAL-USE PROPERTY. If personal-use property is either converted to business use or held for the production of income (e.g., a rental house), the property's basis for depreciation purposes is the lesser of its adjusted basis or its fair market value (FMV) determined as of the conversion date.[2] This lower of cost or market rule is intended to prevent taxpayers from depreciating the portion of the cost that represents a nondeductible personal loss.

EXAMPLE I10-2 ▶ Marty acquires a personal residence for $115,000 in 1994. In 1997 he converts the property to rental use because he is unable to sell the house due to a depressed local real estate market. The property's FMV is only $100,000 when it is converted to rental status in 1997. The $15,000 ($115,000 − $100,000) decline in value represents a nondeductible personal loss and is not depreciable. The depreciable basis is $100,000 (minus the portion of the property's FMV that represents land that is not depreciable). ◀

PRE-ACRS DEPRECIATION (YEARS BEFORE 1981)

OBJECTIVE **1**

Classify property and calculate depreciation under the pre-ACRS rules.

The following depreciation methods are generally available for property that was placed in service before January 1, 1981:

▶ Straight-line method (SL)

▶ Double-declining balance method (DDB)

▶ 150% declining balance method (150% DB)

▶ Sum-of-the-year's digits method (SYD)[3]

Various restrictions were placed on the use of accelerated methods for new and used real estate (other than residential rental properties), used residential rental properties, and tangible personal property. Under the pre-ACRS rules, taxpayers could change from a declining balance method to the straight-line method without obtaining advance permission of the IRS.[4] Other changes fell under the general restrictions for changing from one accounting method to another and required approval of the IRS.

The useful life for depreciable properties was selected based on the individual taxpayer's prior experience and business practice regarding maintenance and asset use. Alternatively, taxpayers could have elected the **asset depreciation range (ADR) system**, which prescribed useful lives for various asset classes.[5]

The Code permitted taxpayers to disregard salvage value for amounts up to 10% of the basis of tangible personal property having a 3-year or longer useful life. Even though salvage value was disregarded in determining the depreciation deduction, an asset could not be depreciated below its salvage value.[6]

EXAMPLE I10-3 ▶ Boston Corporation acquired a business machine in 1980 (pre-ACRS period) for $20,000 with a $4,000 estimated salvage value and a 5-year useful life. Salvage value up to $2,000 (0.10 × $20,000) could be ignored in making the annual depreciation computation. However, if the

---

[2] Reg. Sec. 1.167(g)-1.

[3] Sec. 167(b). Certain additional depreciation methods not based on the passage of time (e.g., machine hours of usage and units of production) were also available.

[4] Sec. 167(e). See Chapter I11 for a discussion of accounting methods.

[5] For example, under the ADR system the guideline life for office furniture, fixtures, and equipment was 10 years, and the taxpayer could select any life within 20% of the guideline life. Thus, the lower limit for office furniture was 8 years and the upper limit was 12 years.

[6] Sec. 167(f) and Reg. Sec. 1.167(a)-(1)(c).

estimated salvage value did not change, Boston could not deduct total depreciation in excess of $16,000 ($20,000 cost − $4,000 estimated salvage value). ◀

In calculating current year depreciation on property placed into service before January 1, 1981, probably the most important piece of advice for taxpayers is to be consistent from year to year.

ACRS (1981 THROUGH 1986)

THE BASICS. As mentioned earlier, the ACRS rules enacted in 1981 were intended to stimulate private investment, improve business productivity, simplify taxpayer compliance, and facilitate IRS administration of the tax law. ACRS provided an economic stimulus because the cost-recovery amounts were based on accelerated methods and artificially shortened useful lives.

In 1986 Congress decided the cost-recovery system had provided too great a tax benefit. The ACRS deduction, when combined with an investment tax credit that was available for years before 1987, often provided a benefit greater than an immediate expensing of the asset. The MACRS system that applies to assets acquired after 1986 retains many of the original ACRS simplification features while returning to a recovery period that more nearly approaches a true economic life. This is accomplished by combining the former ADR system that was used for pre-1981 years with many of the features of the ACRS rules.

The features present in both the ACRS and MACRS systems that contribute to simplification and fewer disputes with the IRS include the following:

▶ Salvage value is not considered in the computation of the cost-recovery or depreciation amount. Under prior depreciation systems, disputes between taxpayers and the IRS over the use of a proper salvage value were common.

▶ Fewer asset classes are used. Both tangible personal property and real property must be placed into specific asset classes, depending on the date the asset is placed in service. Asset classes merely refer to the number of years over which the asset must be depreciated.

▶ Fewer cost-recovery methods are used and are built into the ACRS and MACRS tables. Initially, the tables for personal property provide for accelerated rates with an automatic change to the straight-line method when the latter method produces a greater deduction. The ACRS and MACRS tables are summarized in Appendix C.

CLASSIFICATION AND RECOVERY RATES FOR TANGIBLE PERSONAL PROPERTY. ACRS recovery property includes tangible personal property that is depreciable and used in a trade or business or held for the production of income (e.g., rental property held for investment).[7] Certain types of property are not considered recovery property and, therefore, are not depreciated under the ACRS system but are depreciated under the pre-ACRS rules. Property excluded from the ACRS rules include:

▶ Property depreciated using special depreciation methods, such as units of production;

▶ Intangible assets, such as goodwill or copyrights;

▶ Assets with no determinable life, such as land, securities, etc.;

▶ Personal-use assets.

Under the ACRS, the cost of recovery property was required to be recovered (depreciated) over either 3, 5, 10, or 15 years. Each individual property was classified into

---

[7] The rules for ACRS and MACRS depreciation are contained in Sec. 168 of the IRC.

one of the four categories and recovered using either Table I10-1 below or an optional straight-line method. The table incorporates an accelerated method of depreciation. As mentioned earlier, most types of tangible personal property are classified as either 3-year property (consisting principally of automobiles, light-duty trucks, and research and experimental equipment) or 5-year property (such as machinery, equipment, heavy-duty trucks, furniture and fixtures). Because ACRS is used only for assets placed into service between 1981 and 1986, most tangible personal property should be fully depreciated.

In using Table I10-1, the use of the **half-year convention** is required. The half-year convention is an assumption that all asset acquisitions or dispositions are made at the midpoint of the tax year, regardless when the actual acquisition or disposition is made. Thus, for a 3-year asset acquired during any month of the year, the cost recovery deduction would be 12.5% (25% times ½). Under ACRS, the half-year convention is modified in that no cost recovery is permitted for tangible personal property in the year of sale or disposition.

CLASSIFICATION AND RECOVERY RATES FOR REAL PROPERTY. The ACRS system applies to both residential and nonresidential depreciable real property used in a trade or business or held for the production of income (e.g., rental property held for investment). The recovery periods are 15, 18, or 19 years, depending on the date the property was placed in service. Different recovery periods are used because the law was amended three times after the original enactment of ACRS in 1981. The effective dates and recovery periods are provided below:

▶ 15 years: real estate placed in service after 1980 and before March 16, 1984

▶ 18 years: real estate placed in service after March 15, 1984, and before May 9, 1985

▶ 19 years: real estate placed in service after May 8, 1985, through December 31, 1986

▶ 15 years: low-income housing placed in service after 1980 and before December 31, 1986.

The tables for real estate assume a 175% DB rate (200% DB rate for low-income housing) and automatically convert to straight-line to maximize the allowable cost-recovery amount. For property placed in service after June 22, 1984, the tables assume a **mid-month convention** for real estate cost-recovery in the month of acquisition and in the month of disposition.[8] The mid-month convention is similar to the half-year

▼ TABLE I10-1

ACRS Cost-Recovery Rates for Tangible Personal Property

Recovery Year	Recovery Classes	
	3-Year	5-Year[a]
1	25%	15%
2	38	22
3	37	21
4	—	21
5	—	21
Totals	100%	100%

[a] The percentages that are applicable to each year for 10-year and 15-year property are presented in Appendix C.

[1] Fifteen-year property and 18-year property placed in service after March 15, 1984 and before June 23, 1984 are subject to a full-month convention.

convention except that all acquisitions and dispositions are assumed to be made at the mid-point of the month. Thus, if real property is acquired in October by a calendar-year taxpayer, only two and one-half months of cost recovery is allowed for the year. Similarly, nine and one-half months cost recovery is allowed if property is disposed of in October. For the year of acquisition the partial year amount is built into the tables but the partial year amount must be computed for the year of disposition. The ACRS tables for real estate acquired before 1987 are reproduced in Appendix C.

EXAMPLE I10-4 ▶ Cable Corporation acquires a commercial office building and land for $1,000,000 on April 1, 1986. The basis amount that is allocable to the land is $300,000. Cost recovery is based on a 19-year recovery period, and the mid-month convention is applied in the year of acquisition. The amount of cost recovery for 1986 is $45,500 (0.065 × $700,000 cost of the building). (See Table 13 in Appendix C.) ◀

EXAMPLE I10-5 ▶ Assume the same facts as in Example I10-4, except that the building is sold on December 30, 1997. The cost-recovery deduction for 1997 is $28,175 [0.042 × $700,000 × (11.5 ÷ 12)]. (See Table 13 in Appendix C.) ◀

USE OF THE STRAIGHT-LINE METHOD UNDER ACRS. Instead of using the statutory percentage methods previously described under the ACRS (pre-1987) rules, taxpayers could have elected to use the straight-line method for both tangible personal and real property. Under the straight-line method, the taxpayer could have used the same cost-recovery period or an extended period based on the following alternatives:

▶ 3-year ACRS personal property: 3, 5, or 12 years

▶ 5-year ACRS personal property: 5, 12, or 25 years

▶ 15-, 18-, or 19-year ACRS real property: basic ACRS recovery period (i.e., 15, 18, or 19 years), 35, or 45 years[9]

The following operating rules are used if the straight-line ACRS election is made for pre-1987 property:

▶ The half-year convention is used for tangible personal property in the year the property is acquired and placed into service.

▶ No cost recovery is permitted for personal property in the year of disposition.

▶ The mid-month convention is used for real estate in the year of acquisition and disposition. The deduction is based on the number of months the real estate is owned during the years of acquisition and disposition.

▶ For personal property, the straight-line election applies to all assets acquired during the year for a particular class (e.g., three-year recovery property). The election is made on a property-by-property basis for real estate.

EXAMPLE I10-6 ▶ Matt acquires and places into service on December 1, 1986 a business automobile costing $10,000. Matt elects straight-line depreciation using the longest possible recovery period (12 years). Matt's cost-recovery allowance in the initial year is $417 [($10,000 ÷ 12 years) × 0.50 year]. If Matt sells the automobile in a subsequent year, no cost-recovery deduction is allowed in the year of the sale. ◀

OBJECTIVE 3

Classify property and calculate depreciation under the MACRS rules

MACRS (1987 AND LATER YEARS)

CLASSIFICATION AND RECOVERY RATES FOR PERSONAL PROPERTY. MACRS generally follows the same rules originally provided by Congress for ACRS. However, class lives have been lengthened and depreciation methods are more rapidly accelerated.

---

[9] Sec. 168(b)(3). The recovery period for 10-year personal property is 10, 25, or 35 years and for 15-year personal property is 15, 35, or 45 years.

The following classifications apply to personal property placed in service after December 31, 1986 under the MACRS system.[10]

ADDITIONAL COMMENT

The depreciable life of an automobile has been extended from 3 years to 5 years under the MACRS rules.

▶ 3-Year   Property with an ADR life of 4 years or less, including tractor units, race horses over 12 years old, and special tools.

▶ 5-Year   Property with an ADR years life of more than 4 but less than 10 years including automobiles, light and heavy-duty, general purpose trucks, computers, and R&E equipment.

KEY POINT

Most depreciable personal property is classified as 7-year property under MACRS.

▶ 7-Year   Property with an ADR life of 10 years or more but less than 16 years, including office furniture and equipment, horses, single-purpose agricultural or horticultural structures, and property with no ADR class life and not classified elsewhere. Most types of machinery are included in this class.

▶ 10-Year Property with an ADR life of more than 16 years, but less than 20 years, including barges, vessels, and petroleum and food processing equipment.

ADDITIONAL COMMENT

The Tax Reform Act of 1986 increased the rate of acceleration on the declining-balance method from 150% to 200% for property in the 3-, 5-, 7-, and 10-year classes to compensate for the repeal of the investment tax credit.

▶ 15-Year Property with an ADR life of more than 20 years, but less than 25 years, including billboards, service station buildings, and land improvements.

▶ 20-Year Property with an ADR life of 25 or more years, including utilities and sewers.

The depreciation rates for the 3-year, 5-year, and 7-year recovery classes are provided in Table I10-2. The rates in Table I10-2 are based on the 200% DB method with a conversion to straight-line when it yields a larger amount. A half-year convention is used in the year of acquisition and zero salvage value is assumed.

EXAMPLE I10-7 ▶ Mary acquires and places into service a business machine in 1997 for $20,000. The machinery has a 7-year recovery period under the MACRS rules. The depreciation deduction for 1997 is $2,858 (0.1429 × $20,000). The rate that is applied (0.1429) is based on the 200% DB method and assumes a half-year convention and zero salvage value. The MACRS depreciation deduction for the year of acquisition can also be computed by applying the accelerated depreciation rate (using the half-year convention) to the basis of the assets. Thus the depreciation deduction for 1997 is $2,857 ($20,000 ÷ 7 years × 200% DB × 0.50 year). Minor differences between the two calculations are due to rounding. ◀

SELF-STUDY QUESTION

In Table I10-2, how has the 0.2000 first-year cost recovery rate for five-year property been calculated?

ANSWER

The 0.2000 rate is calculated by multiplying the double declining-balance rate of 0.4000 by ½ year of depreciation.

▼ **TABLE I10-2**

MACRS Rates for Tangible Personal Property (using half-year convention)

Recovery Year	Recovery Classes		
	3-Year	5-Year	7-Year
1	0.3333	0.2000	0.1429
2	0.4445	0.3200	0.2449
3	0.1481	0.1920	0.1749
4	0.0741	0.1152	0.1249
5	—	0.1152	0.0893
6	—	0.0576	0.0892
7	—	—	0.0893
8	—	—	0.0446

Source: Table 1 of Rev. Proc. 87-57, 1987-2 C.B. 687.

---

[10] Secs. 168(e)(1).

KEY POINT

Remember, the mid-quarter convention does *not* apply to real property.

Use of a Mid-Quarter Convention. The MACRS system requires the use of a mid-quarter convention if the aggregate basis of all personal property placed in service during the last three months of the year exceeds 40% of the cost of all personal property placed in service during the tax year.[11] Property placed in service and disposed of during the same tax year is not taken into account.[12] Also, property expensed under Sec. 179 is excluded in computing the 40% test for the applicability of the mid-quarter convention.[13]

The 40% rule prevents taxpayers from using the half-year convention and thereby obtaining one-half year's depreciation in the year of acquisition when a substantial portion of the assets are acquired during the last quarter of the tax year.

EXAMPLE I10-8 ▶ Michael acquires 5-year personal property in 1997 and places it in service on the following schedule:

Date Placed in Service	Acquisition Cost
January 20	$100,000
April 18	200,000
November 5	300,000
Total	$600,000

SELF-STUDY QUESTION

Under ACRS, no depreciation deduction was allowed in the year of disposition for personal property. Should taxpayers now be pleased that such a deduction is allowed under the MACRS system?

ANSWER

In general, there will not be a difference. The effect of the depreciation deduction is offset by the larger gain on the sale because the depreciation deduction reduces the basis of the property.

Because more than 40% of the property acquired during the year is placed in service in the last three months, the mid-quarter convention will apply for all property placed in service during the year. (See Tables 2 through 5 in Appendix C for the percentages that are used to make this calculation.)

Property Placed in Service	Year 1 Depreciation	
January 20	$100,000 × 35% =	$ 35,000
April 18	200,000 × 25% =	50,000
November 5	300,000 × 5% =	15,000
Total	$600,000	$100,000

Note that if the half-year convention had been applied in this example, $120,000 (0.2000 × $600,000) of depreciation could have been claimed. Generally, if larger depreciation deductions are desired, care should be exercised on asset acquisitions to prevent the application of the mid-quarter convention. ◀

STOP & THINK

Question: A common misconception of the mid-quarter convention is that it always yields a smaller depreciation deduction than the half-year convention. Consider the following situation where a business has placed into service the following assets (all 7-year property under MACRS) during the current year:

February	$300,000
June	10,000
November	200,000

The business needs an additional $10,000 of equipment (also 7-year property) in the current year, but the purchase could be delayed until early January of the next year. Assuming the business wants to *maximize* its depreciation deduction in the current year,

---

[11] Sec. 168(d)(3).
[12] Sec. 168(d)(3)(B) and Reg. Sec. 1.168(d)-1(b)(3).

[13] PLR 9126014 (March 29, 1991). Section 179 is discussed later in this chapter.

should the business purchase the additional $10,000 of equipment in the current year or delay the purchase until next year?

Solution: The business should purchase the equipment in the current year even though it will require the use of the mid-quarter convention.

Mid-quarter Test
Currently (before the purchase): $200,000/$510,000 = 39.2%

With the purchase: $210,000/$520,000 = 40.4%

Therefore, if the business purchases the additional $10,000 in the current year, the mid-quarter convention will apply. The depreciation for the current year assuming the purchase is made is:

First quarter:	$300,000 × 25% =	$75,000
Second quarter:	10,000 × 17.85% =	1,785
Fourth quarter:	210,000 × 3.57% =	7,497
TOTAL		$84,282

Compare this amount with the depreciation that would result under the half-year convention ($510,000 × 14.29% = $72,879) assuming the purchase *was not* made. (The mid-quarter convention produces a higher depreciation deduction even if the half-year convention is computed on $520,000, i.e., $520,000 × 14.29% = $74,308). It is clear that the mid-quarter convention actually maximizes depreciation for the current year. You should notice that the mid-quarter convention yields more than the half-year convention for the reason that virtually all of the equipment that was purchased (other than the fourth quarter) was in the first quarter and this equipment is depreciated using a 25% rate versus a 14.29% rate under the half-year convention.

Year of Disposition. The MACRS system allows depreciation to be taken in the year of disposition using the same convention that applied on acquisition (e.g., half-year, mid-month, or mid-quarter convention). Therefore, if property is disposed of during the year in which the half-year convention is applicable, the depreciation for the year of disposition will be one-half of the amount computed by using the table percentages.

EXAMPLE I10-9 ▶ Assume the same facts as in Example I10-8, except that the equipment purchased on April 18 is disposed of on August 14 in the following year. The midquarter convention must be used because it is used in the year of acquisition. Thus, $37,500 of depreciation is claimed in the year of disposition [($200,000 × 0.30) × (7.5 ÷ 12)]. (See Table 3 in Appendix C.) ◀

EXAMPLE I10-10 ▶ Michelle acquires machinery in 1997 that qualifies as seven-year MACRS property and has a $100,000 basis for depreciation. The half-year convention is applied in the year of acquisition. In December 1998 the machinery is sold. Michelle's depreciation deduction in 1998 is $12,245 [$100,000 × (0.2449 × 0.50)] for the equipment (see Table I10-2). ◀

KEY POINT

All depreciable real property can be classified in one of two classes.

CLASSIFICATION AND RECOVERY RATES FOR REAL PROPERTY. The MACRS recovery periods that apply to real property placed in service in years after 1986 have been lengthened as follows:

▶ Residential rental property: 27.5 years

▶ Nonresidential real property: 39 years[14]

---

[14] Sec. 168(c)(1). A 31.5-year recovery period applies to property placed in service on or after January 1, 1987 and before May 13, 1993. Certain exceptions permit the continued use of the 31.5-year recovery period for binding contracts entered into before May 13, 1993, and where the construction of the property commenced before May 13, 1993. See Table 8 in Appendix C for the 39-year property depreciation tables.

Depreciation must be calculated using the straight-line method. A mid-month convention is used in the year of acquisition and in the year of disposition. The tables for computing depreciation for real property are located in Tables 6, 7 and 8 in Appendix C.

Real properties are divided into two categories: residential rental property and nonresidential real property. **Residential rental property** is defined as property from which at least 80% of the gross rental income is rental income from dwelling units.[15] Dwelling units include houses, apartments, and manufactured homes that are used for residential purposes but not hotels, motels, or other establishments for transient use.

STRAIGHT-LINE (METHOD) ELECTION UNDER MACRS. Instead of using the accelerated methods previously described under the MACRS rules, taxpayers may elect to use the straight-line method for tangible personal property. If the straight-line election is made, the taxpayer must use either the same depreciation period or an extended period based on the alternative depreciation system.[16]

ALTERNATIVE DEPRECIATION SYSTEM. The MACRS system provides an alternative depreciation system (ADS) that is required for certain property and is also available for all other depreciable assets if the taxpayer so elects.[17] The principal type of property for which the ADS is required is any tangible property which is used predominantly outside the United States. The recovery periods are specified under the ADS and, many times, are longer than the recovery periods under MACRS. For example, personal property with no specific class life is assigned a 12-year life, and real property is assigned a 40-year life. Further, the ADS requires the use of the straight-line method with a half-year, mid-quarter, or mid-month convention, whichever is applicable. The election of the ADS is generally made by taxpayers who want to use the straight-line method over a longer recovery period. These taxpayers frequently have net operating losses or are subject to the alternative minimum tax (see Chapter I14 for a discussion of the alternative minimum tax).

The ADS is an elective provision made on a year-by-year basis. Once the election is made for specified property, it is irrevocable. Also, for personal property, the ADS election applies to all property within a class (all five-year property, for example); for real property, the ADS election may be made on an individual property basis.

EXAMPLE I10-11 ▶

In May, 1997, Bob Roaster purchased an office building for $300,000 ($50,000 allocated to the land) as rental property. Because he has substantial net operating losses from other business ventures, Roaster elects to depreciate the building using the ADS. Depreciation expense for 1997, using the mid-month convention and a 40-year life is $3,906 ($250,000 ÷ 40 years × 7.5/12). If Roaster had not elected the ADS, his depreciation would have been $4,013 [$250,000 × .01605 (from Table 8, Appendix C)]. ◀

The alternative depreciation system is also used to compute E&P for a corporation and to compute the alternative minimum tax for both individuals and corporations (see Chapter I14).

A comparison of the ACRS and MACRS rules is presented in Topic Review I10-1.

SECTION 179 EXPENSING ELECTION

In lieu of capitalizing the cost of new or used tangible personal business property, taxpayers may elect to expense up to $18,000 of the acquisition cost as an ordinary deduction in the year of acquisition.[18] To qualify for the deduction, the property must actually be placed into service during the year. The immediate expensing election is not

---

[15] Secs. 168(e)(2)(A) and 167(j)(2)(B).
[16] Sec. 167(j)(2)(B).
[17] Sec. 168(g).

[18] Sec. 179. The amount was increased from $10,000 to $17,500 for property placed in service in tax years beginning after December 31, 1992 and before January 1, 1997.

Topic Review I10-1

Comparison of ACRS and MACRS

	ACRS	MACRS
Useful lives:		
Automobiles	3 years	5 years
Computers	5 years	5 years
Office furniture and equipment	5 years	7 years
Residential rental property	15, 18, or 19 years	27.5 years
Nonresidential real property	15, 18, or 19 years	31.5 or 39 years
Conventions:		
Personal property	Mid-year	Mid-year or mid-quarter[a]
Real property	Mid-month[b]	Mid-month
Depreciation in year of sale:		
Personal property	No	Yes
Real property	Yes	Yes

[a] If more than 40% of personal property is placed in service during the last quarter of year.
[b] A full-month convention is used for property acquired before June 23, 1984.

applicable to real estate. The election is made on an annual basis, and the taxpayer must select the assets to which the $18,000 write-off applies. The MACRS rules apply to any amount of an asset's cost that is not expensed under Sec. 179.

The amount that may be expensed under Sec. 179 has been increased by the Small Business Job Protection Act of 1996 as follows:

▼ TABLE I10-3
Section 179 Expense Amounts

Tax Year Beginning In	Maximum Sec. 179 Expense
1996	$17,500
1997	18,000
1998	18,500
1999	19,000
2000	20,000
2001	24,000
2002	24,000
2003 and after	25,000

EXAMPLE I10-12 ▶ Tanya acquires and places into service a business machine (tangible personal property qualifying under Sec. 179) for $38,000 in July 1997. The machine has a 7-year MACRS recovery period. Tanya elects to immediately expense $18,000 of the asset's cost under Sec. 179. Tanya's remaining basis for calculating the MACRS depreciation deduction is $20,000 ($38,000 − $18,000). Tanya's 1997 depreciation allowance is $2,858 ($20,000 × 0.1429). Tanya's total capital recovery deductions for 1997 are $20,858 ($18,000 expensed under Sec. 179 + $2,858 MACRS depreciation). ◀

The following limitations and special rules apply to the Sec. 179 election:

► The property must be purchased for use in an active trade or business as distinguished from property that is acquired for the production of income (e.g., personal property used in a rental activity held by an investor does not qualify).

► The property cannot be acquired from a related party under Sec. 267 or by gift or inheritance.

► The Sec. 179 tax benefits are recaptured if the property is no longer predominantly used in a trade or business (e.g., the property is converted to personal use) at any time.[19] In the year of recapture, the taxpayer must include in gross income the amount previously expensed reduced by the amount of depreciation that would have been allowed for the period the property was held for business use.[20]

► If the total cost of qualified property placed into service during the year is more than $200,000, the $18,000 ceiling is reduced on a dollar-for-dollar basis by the excess amount. Thus, no deduction is permitted for the 1997 tax year in which $218,000 or more of Sec. 179 property is placed into service.

► A second limitation on the total Sec. 179 deduction is that it cannot exceed the taxpayer's taxable income (before deducting the Sec. 179 expense) from the trade or business.[21] Any acquisition cost that is unable to be deducted because of the limitation based on taxable income is carried forward for an unlimited number of years and is added to the other amounts eligible for the Sec. 179 deduction in the future year. The carryover amount is subject to the taxable income limitation in the carryover year.

EXAMPLE I10-13 ►

Pam owns an unincorporated manufacturing business. In 1997 she purchases and places in service $213,000 of qualifying equipment for use in her business. Pam's taxable income from the business (before deducting any Sec. 179 amount) is $4,000. The $18,000 ceiling amount is initially reduced by $13,000 ($213,000 − $200,000) to reflect the fact that the qualified property placed in service during the year exceeded $200,000. The remaining $5,000 Sec. 179 deduction is further reduced by $1,000 ($5,000 − $4,000) to reflect the taxable income limitation. Pam's Sec. 179 deduction is $4,000; $1,000 is available for use as a carryover to 1998. The cost basis of the equipment for MACRS purposes is reduced by $5,000 in 1997 despite the fact that only $4,000 was immediately deductible under Sec. 179. ◄

MACRS RESTRICTIONS

PERSONAL-USE ASSETS. The personal use portion of an asset's cost is not depreciable. For example, if a taxpayer owns a duplex and uses one unit as a personal residence, only the portion of the unit that is rented to tenants qualifies for depreciation.

LISTED PROPERTY RULES. Because Congress was concerned about taxpayers claiming large depreciation deductions (using accelerated methods) on certain types of assets that are conducive to mixed business/personal use, restrictions are placed on assets that are classified as *listed property*. Listed property includes automobiles, computers and peripheral equipment, cellular telephones, and property generally used for purposes of entertainment, recreation, or amusement (for example, a video recorder). If a listed property's business usage is greater than 50% of its total usage, the taxpayer may use the

---

[19] Sec. 179(d)(10).
[20] Reg. Sec. 1.179-1(e).
[21] Sec. 179(b)(3). Under Reg. Sec. 1.179-2(c)(5)(iv), employees are considered to be engaged in the active conduct of the trade or business from their employment. Thus, a small business person who is also an employee may include wages and salary derived from employment in determining taxable income for purposes of this limitation. Such amounts are considered derived from the conduct of a trade or business. For an individual, taxable income is also computed without regard to the deduction for one-half of self-employment taxes paid under Sec. 164(f) (see Chapter I14).

regular MACRS tables for the business-use portion of the asset's cost. However, if the business use is 50% or less, the taxpayer must use the alternative depreciation system (e.g., five-year straight-line cost recovery period for automobiles and computers).

EXAMPLE I10-14 ▶ Patrick acquires an automobile for $10,000 in June 1997. It is used 60% for business. The depreciation deduction on the business-use portion of the automobile's cost is based on the MACRS system and five-year recovery class because the automobile is predominantly used in business (i.e., more than 50%). The MACRS depreciation allowance in 1997 is $1,200 ($10,000 × 0.20 MACRS rate × 0.60 business percentage use). See Table I10-2 for the MACRS rate. ◀

EXAMPLE I10-15 ▶ Paula acquires an automobile for $10,000 in 1997. It is used only 40% for business. Paula may claim depreciation allowances on the business portion of the automobile only by using the alternative depreciation system. The business portion is $4,000 ($10,000 × 0.40). Paula's depreciation allowance in 1997 is $400 [($4,000 ÷ 5 years) × 0.50] the half-year convention. ◀

Additional restrictions apply to employees who acquire listed property (e.g., an automobile, personal computer, and so on) for use in employment-related activities. In addition to the "more than 50% test," the use must be for the convenience of the employer and be required as a condition of employment.[22] Apparently this rule is interpreted very strictly by the IRS.

EXAMPLE I10-16 ▶ Raul, a college professor, acquired a personal computer for use at home. He used the computer 60% of the time on teaching- and research-related activities associated with his job. The remaining usage was for personal activities. Raul's employer finds that it is helpful for employees to own a personal computer but does not require them to purchase a computer as a condition of employment. Raul meets the first requirement (i.e., the 60% business usage is greater than the 50% threshold). However, the second requirement for employees (that the use must be for the convenience of the employer and required as a condition of employment) is not met. Thus, no depreciation may be taken because the employment-related use is not deemed to be business use. ◀

RECAPTURE OF EXCESS COST-RECOVERY DEDUCTIONS. For listed property, if the MACRS rules were used and the business-use percentage decreases to 50% or less in a subsequent year, the property is subject to depreciation recapture. The depreciation deductions for all years are recomputed using the alternative depreciation system. The excess depreciation that has been taken is recaptured as ordinary income by including the excess amount in the taxpayer's gross income in the year the business-use percentage first falls to 50% or below.[23] Once the business use falls to 50% or below, the alternative depreciation system must be used for the current year and for all subsequent years, even if the business-use percentage increases to more than 50% in a subsequent year.

EXAMPLE I10-17 ▶ Peggy, a self-employed attorney, acquires an automobile in 1997 for $10,000. The automobile's business usage is 60% in 1997 but declines to 40% in 1998. In 1997 Peggy is eligible to use the regular MACRS depreciation rates because the business use was greater than 50%. The MACRS deduction in 1997 is $1,200 ($10,000 cost × 0.60 business use × 0.20). The straight-line depreciation method using the five-year life specified for the alternative depreciation system and the half-year convention would have resulted in a deduction of only $600

---

[22] Sec. 280F(d)(3). Any other property used for transportation (e.g., a pickup truck) qualifies as listed property if the nature of the property lends itself to personal use. See Sec. 280F(b)(4).

[23] Sec. 280F(b)(3).

ADDITIONAL
COMMENT

The limitations on luxury automobiles mean that the depreciation deductions are limited
during the normal five-year recovery period on business automobiles costing more than
$15,800 (for 1997).

[($10,000 cost × 0.60 business use ÷ 5 years) × 0.50 year] in 1997. Thus, $600 ($1,200 − $600) of the previously claimed depreciation is recaptured as ordinary income in 1998. Peggy's depreciation deduction for 1998 and subsequent years is limited to the straight-line method and a five-year recovery period. Her depreciation deduction for 1998 is $800 [($10,000 cost × 0.40 business use) ÷ 5 years]. ◄

LIMITATIONS ON LUXURY AUTOMOBILES. Additional MACRS depreciation deduction restrictions are placed on the purchase of so-called luxury automobiles.[24] The limitations apply even if such automobiles are used 100% of the time for business. The MACRS depreciation for automobiles placed into service in 1997 is subject to a $3,160 ceiling limitation for the first year, $5,000 for the second year, $3,050 for the third year, and $1,775 for each succeeding year in the recovery period.[25] In the years following the end of the depreciation period (e.g., in year six and subsequent years), additional depreciation up to $1,775 per year is allowed in taxable years commencing after the end of the recovery period until the business use portion of the automobile is fully depreciated. Luxury automobile limitations for the past several years are contained in Table I17 of Appendix C. These amounts are adjusted for inflation each year. These ceilings are reduced by the percentage of personal use and also apply to amounts that are expensed under Sec. 179. The effect of these ceilings is to extend the basic MACRS depreciation period from six to seven years or longer depending on the automobile's acquisition cost.

EXAMPLE I10-18 ▶

TYPICAL
MISCONCEPTION

It is sometimes mistakenly believed that the $18,000 expen-
sing allowance can be used to
boost the first-year write-off
on luxury automobiles.

Phil acquires an automobile for $20,000 in 1997. The automobile is used 80% for business and 20% for personal activities during the year. Table I10-4 lists the depreciation amounts for a six-year period, assuming that the 80% business use continues for the life of the automobile and that no amount is expensed under Sec. 179. At the end of the regular six-year depreciation period, the unrecovered cost in the business use portion of the automobile may be recovered in year 2003 and succeeding years at an annual rate not to exceed $1,420 ($1,775 × 0.80). ◄

ADDITIONAL COMPUTATIONS FOR LEASED LUXURY AUTOMOBILES. If a taxpayer leases an automobile for business purposes, the deduction for rental payments is reduced to reflect the limitations on depreciation deductions that are imposed on owners of automobiles under Sec. 280F. If these restrictions were not applied to leased automobiles, the limitations could be avoided by leasing instead of purchasing an automobile. The leasing restriction is accomplished by requiring taxpayers to include in their gross income an "inclusion amount" obtained from an IRS table.[26] This amount is based on the automobile's FMV and the tax year in which the lease commences, and is prorated for the percentage of business use and number of days used during the year.

ADDITIONAL
COMMENT

The amount that can be deducted for leased automobiles
is also limited.

EXAMPLE I10-19 ▶

On April 1, 1997 Jim leases and places into service an automobile with a FMV of $40,000. Business use is 60%. The "inclusion amount" for the initial year of the lease (1997) from the table contained in Rev. Proc. 97-20 is $194. This amount is prorated for the number of days the automobile is leased (275/365) and is then multiplied by the percentage of business use (60%). Jim is entitled to deduct 60% of the lease payments but must include $88 [($194 × 275/365) × 60%] in his gross income for the current year. ◄

Special elections and restrictions are summarized in Topic Review I10-2.

---

[24] Sec. 280F. The term "luxury automobile" may be an overstatement as the limitations begin for automobiles acquired in 1997 which cost in excess of $15,800.
[25] Sec. 280F(a)(2). The ceiling imitation for the first year includes any

amounts that are immediately written off under Sec. 179. The Sec. 280F limitations restrict the deductibility of lease payments for automobiles in the same way that depreciation is restricted.
[26] Rev. Proc. 97-20, 1997-11, I.R.B. 1997-11.

▼ TABLE I10-4
Depreciation Amounts for Example I10-18

	MACRS Deduction Before Limitation	Ceiling Limit	Deduction Allowed
1997			
Regular calculation			
($20,000 × 0.80 × 0.20)	$3,200		
Ceiling limit			
($3,160 × 0.80)		$2,528	$2,528
1998			
Regular calculation			
($20,000 × 0.80 × 0.32)	5,120		
Ceiling limit			
($5,000 × 0.80)		4,000	4,000
1999			
Regular calculation			
($20,000 × 0.80 × 0.192)	3,072		
Ceiling limit			
($3,050 × 0.80)		2,440	2,440
2000			
Regular calculation			
($20,000 × 0.80 × 0.1152)	1,843		
Ceiling limit			
($1,775 × 0.80)		1,420	1,420
2001			
Regular calculation			
($20,000 × 0.80 × 0.1152)	1,843		
Ceiling limit			
($1,775 × 0.80)		1,420	1,420
2002			
Regular calculation			
($20,000 × 0.80 × 0.0576)	922		
Ceiling limit			
($1,775 × 0.80)		1,420	922
2003 and later years until fully depreciated			
Ceiling limit			
($1,775 × 0.80)		1,420	1,420

DEPLETION AND INTANGIBLE DRILLING AND DEVELOPMENT COSTS

The exploration, development, and operation of oil and gas properties require an outlay of various types of expenditures. These expenditures must be properly classified to

Topic Review I10-2

Special Elections and Restrictions

Section 179 Expensing Election

Deduction: $18,000 for 1997 on the purchase of new or used tangible personal business property used in the conduct of a trade or business.

Limitations:

Asset purchases: The $18,000 limit is reduced by the excess of qualified purchases over $200,000.

Taxable income limitation: Limited to taxable income before the Sec. 179 deduction.

Basis reduction: The depreciable basis is reduced by the amount of the Sec. 179 deduction.

Recapture: Occurs when the asset is no longer predominantly used in a trade or business. The recapture amount equals the excess of the Sec. 179 expense amount minus the amount that would have been claimed as depreciation if no Sec. 179 election were made.

Business Use Restriction

Listed property: Business use must be more than 50% to use the regular MACRS rules. If business use is less than 50%, the alternative depreciation system's straight-line method must be used.

Recapture: If business use falls below 50%, the taxpayer must recompute depreciation using the alternative depreciation system's straight-line method and recapture the difference between the prior depreciation taken and straight-line depreciation. The straight-line method is continued for the remaining useful life even if business use subsequently exceeds 50%.

Luxury Automobile Limitations

Sum of depreciation and Sec. 179 expense limits:

	1996	1997
1st year	$3,060	3,160
2nd year	4,900	5,000
3rd year	2,950	3,050
4th and later years	1,750	1,775

Leased Luxury Automobile Limitations

An "inclusion amount" is added to gross income based on the automobile's FMV on the date placed in service to approximate the depreciation restrictions. Special tables that are revised annually are used to calculate the inclusion amount.

OBJECTIVE 4

Apply cost and percentage depletion methods and understand the treatment for intangible drilling costs

determine the correct income tax treatment of such expenditures. Below are the four major types of expenditures of an oil and gas property and their income tax treatment.

▶ Payments for the mineral interest. These costs are capitalized and recovered through depletion.

▶ Intangible drilling and development costs (e.g., labor and other operating costs to clear land, erect a derrick, and drill the well). Taxpayers elect to either capitalize or immediately write off these expenditures.

▶ Tangible asset costs (e.g., machinery, pipe). These expenditures must be capitalized and depreciated under the MACRS rules.

▶ Operating costs after the well is producing. These expenditures are deductible under Sec. 162 as ordinary and necessary business expenses.

TREATMENT OF INTANGIBLE DRILLING AND DEVELOPMENT COSTS

Intangible drilling and development costs (IDCs) may either be deducted as an expense or capitalized.[27] IDCs apply only to oil, gas, and geothermal wells and basically include all expenditures, other than the acquisition costs of the underlying property, that are incurred for the drilling and preparation of wells. If the IDCs are capitalized, the amounts are added to the property's basis for determining cost depletion, and the costs are written off through cost depletion. For a well that is nonproductive (i.e., a dry hole), an ordinary loss is allowed for any IDC costs that have been capitalized and not recovered through depletion. The amount of depletion claimed in a tax year equals the greater of the percentage depletion and cost depletion amounts. An increase in the amount of cost depletion due to the capitalization of IDCs may produce limited or no tax benefits when percentage depletion is claimed by the taxpayer. Therefore, it is generally preferable to expense the IDCs if the percentage depletion is expected to be more than the cost depletion and is used to compute the depletion allowance.

EXAMPLE I10-20 ▶ Penny acquires certain rights to oil and gas property in the current year for $1,000,000. In the current year Penny incurs $300,000 of IDCs. If the IDCs are capitalized, the basis for cost depletion purposes is $1,300,000. Assume that the cost depletion amounts are $100,000 in the current year if the IDCs are expensed and $130,000 if IDCs are capitalized. If the percentage depletion amount is $150,000, percentage depletion will be used because it is greater than either of the cost depletion amounts. Thus, the expensing of the IDCs permits the taxpayer to deduct the entire $300,000 of IDCs in the current year plus $150,000 of percentage depletion. ◀

DEPLETION METHODS

KEY POINT

A depletion deduction is available in the case of mines, oil and gas wells, other natural resources, and timber. However, the percentage depletion method is not available in the case of timber.

Depletion is similar to depreciation but refers to natural resources, such as oil and gas, timber, and coal. Depletion is the using up of natural resources by the process of mining (coal, for example) or drilling (oil and gas) and is calculated under the **cost depletion method** or the **percentage depletion method** for each period. The method that is used in any year is the one that results in the largest deduction. Thus, percentage depletion may be used in one year and cost depletion may be used in the following year.

COST DEPLETION METHOD. The cost depletion method is similar to the units-of-production method of depreciation. The adjusted basis of the asset is divided by the estimated recoverable units to arrive at a per-unit depletion cost. This per-unit cost is then multiplied by the number of units sold to determine the cost depletion amount.[28] If percentage depletion is used in any one year because it is greater than the cost depletion amount, the property's adjusted basis for purposes of determining cost depletion in the following year and the gain or loss on disposition of the property is reduced by the amount of percentage depletion claimed. If the original estimate of recoverable units is subsequently determined to be incorrect, the per-unit cost depletion rate must be revised and used on a prospective basis to determine cost depletion in future years.[29] It is not proper to file an amended return for the years in which the incorrect estimated unit cost was used.

---

[27] Sec. 263(c).
[28] Sec. 612.

[29] Sec. 611(a).

EXAMPLE I10-21 ▶

Ralph acquires an oil and gas property interest for $100,000 in 1997. The estimate of recoverable units is 10,000 barrels of oil. The per-unit cost depletion amount is $10 ($100,000 ÷ 10,000). If 3,000 units are produced and 2,000 units are sold in 1997, the cost depletion amount is $20,000 (2,000 units × $10 per unit). If cost depletion is used because it exceeds the percentage depletion amount, the cost basis of the property is reduced to $80,000 ($100,000 − $20,000) at the beginning of 1998. If the estimate of remaining recoverable units is revised downward from 8,000 units in 1998 (10,000 − 2,000 units sold in 1997) to 5,000 units (including the 1,000 barrels produced but not sold in 1997), the property's $80,000 adjusted basis is divided by 5,000 units to arrive at a new per-unit cost depletion amount of $16 for 1998. This process is continued each year until the oil and gas property interest is fully depleted. ◀

SELF-STUDY QUESTION

Why is the percentage depletion method not available in the case of timber?

ANSWER

Timber is considered a renewable natural resource.

PERCENTAGE DEPLETION METHOD. Percentage depletion generally offers substantial tax benefits for taxpayers in the natural resources industry. The purpose of allowing percentage depletion is to encourage persons to invest and/or operate in an industry that is both capital intensive and high risk but is also vital to our national interests. The percentage depletion method has not been available to large oil and gas producers since 1974. However, it is still available to small oil and gas producers and royalty owners under a specific exemption in the law[30] and for several types of mineral properties (e.g., coal, iron, gravel).[31] *Percentage depletion* for oil and gas properties is 15% times the gross income from the property.[32] However, it may not exceed 100% of the taxable income (before depletion is deducted) for oil and gas properties and 50% for property other than oil and gas under Sec. 613A.[33] Percentage depletion may not be calculated on any lease bonus, advance royalty, or other amount payable without regard to production from property.

EXAMPLE I10-22 ▶

HISTORICAL NOTE

An Arab oil embargo to the United States in 1973 created a situation where oil prices increased significantly. Consequently, most domestic U.S. oil producers reported huge profits. This situation contributed to the repeal of the percentage depletion allowance for large oil and gas producers.

KEY POINT

The use of the percentage depletion method permits recovery of more than the cost of the property.

Carmen acquires an oil and gas property interest for $400,000 in the current year. During the year, 10,000 barrels of oil are sold for $250,000. Intangible drilling and development costs amount to $100,000 and are expensed in the current year. Other expenses are $50,000. Cost depletion is $20,000 in the current year. The computation of percentage depletion is as follows:

(1) Percentage depletion before taxable income limitation	
$250,000 × 0.15	$ 37,500
(2) Taxable income ceiling:	
Gross income	$250,000
Minus: Intangible drilling costs	(100,000)
Other expenses	(50,000)
Taxable income before depletion	$100,000
(3) Percentage depletion (lesser of (1) or (2))	$ 37,500

Carmen's depletion deduction is $37,500 because the percentage depletion amount is greater than the $20,000 of cost depletion. ◀

---

[30] Sec. 613A(c). To be classified as a small oil and gas producer or royalty owner, the maximum depletable quantity is based on average daily production of not more than 1,000 barrels of oil or 6 million cubic feet of natural gas.
[31] Sec. 613. The rates vary from 5% to 22% depending on the type of resource being mined or extracted.
[32] Under Sec. 613A(c) the statutory percentage depletion rate for marginally

producing oil and gas wells is increased if the price of crude oil is less than $20 per barrel during the immediately preceding calendar year. The statutory rate is increased by 1 percentage point for each dollar below $20.
[33] For small producers and royalty owners of oil and gas properties, there is a further limitation: the percentage depletion deduction may not exceed 65% of taxable income from all sources before the depletion deduction, Sec. 631A(d)(1).

AMORTIZATION

An amortization deduction is allowed for a variety of intangible assets. While the amortization period varies greatly depending on the type of asset, a characteristic of all intangible assets is that they are amortized on a *straight-line basis*. The major intangible assets that may be amortized are as follows:

▶ Goodwill and Other Purchased Intangibles, Sec. 197

▶ Research and Experimental Expenditures, Sec. 174

▶ Start-up Expenditures, Sec. 195

▶ Organizational Expenditures, Sec. 248

▶ Pollution Control Facilities, Sec. 169

Several of the above intangibles are discussed below.

SEC. 197 INTANGIBLES

Sec. 197 was enacted in 1993 to provide greater certainty as to the amortization of many acquired intangible assets, and to specifically allow the amortization of *purchased goodwill*. An amortization deduction is permitted for certain acquired Sec. 197 intangible assets. The amortization is deducted on a ratable basis over a 15-year period beginning with the month of acquisition.[34] In general, Sec. 197 applies only to intangible assets that are *acquired* in connection with a transaction that involves the acquisition of a trade or business or a substantial portion of a trade or business. For example, Sec. 197 does not apply to an intangible asset that is internally created by the taxpayer, such as a patent resulting from the taxpayer's research and development lab. Internally-created patents and copyrights both have definite and limited lives and are therefore amortizable over the defined period.[35] Additionally, Sec. 197 does not apply to intangibles that are acquired independent of an acquisition (e.g., a formula, software, or a customer list). Such intangibles are subject to amortization if a definite and limited life can be established.

EXAMPLE I10-23 ▶

On January 1, 1997 Central Corporation receives patent approval on an internally created process improvement. Legal costs associated with the patent are $100,000 and the patent has a legal life of 17 years. The patent has a definite and limited life and is amortizable ratably over its legal life of 17 years beginning with the month of its creation. ◀

DEFINITION OF A SEC. 197 INTANGIBLE ASSET. Sec. 197 intangibles (i.e., intangible assets that are subject to 15-year ratable amortization) include the following:

▶ Goodwill and going concern value. Conceptually, goodwill is an intangible asset that is neither separately identified or valued but possesses characteristics that allow a business to earn greater returns than would be possible without such characteristics. The characteristics that make-up goodwill include many items, such as a superior management team, loyal customer base, strategic location, etc. For income tax purposes, however, goodwill is determined in a much more practical manner. **Goodwill** is defined as the excess of the purchase price of a business over the fair market value of all identifiable assets acquired. Going concern value is the added value that attaches to acquired property because it is an integral part of a going concern.[36]

---

[34] Sec. 197(a). The amortization rules apply to property acquired after August 13, 1993 unless an election is made to apply Sec. 197 to all property acquired after July 25, 1991.

[35] Reg. Sec. 1.167(a)-3. Internally created patents are generally amortized over 17 years; internally created copyrights over 28 years.

[36] Goodwill and going concern value that had an indefinite life were not amortizable for periods before the enactment of Sec. 197.

▶ Intangible assets relating to the workforce, information base, know-how, customers, suppliers, or similar items, (e.g., the portion of the purchase price of an acquired business that is attributable to an existing employment contract for a key employee) may be amortized over a 15-year period. An example of an information base intangible would be a customer list. Know-how related intangibles include patents, copyrights, formulas, and processes.

▶ Licenses, permits, or other rights granted by a governmental unit or agency (e.g., the capitalized cost of acquiring a radio broadcasting license).

▶ Covenants not to compete. A covenant not to compete represents an agreement between a buyer and seller of a business that the seller (i.e., the selling corporation and/or its shareholders) will not compete with the buyer for a limited period. The covenant may also be limited to a geographic area.

▶ Franchises, trademarks, and tradenames. A franchise includes any agreement that gives one of the parties the right to distribute, sell, or provide goods, services, or facilities, within a specified area.

EXAMPLE I10-24 ▶ During the current year, Chicago Corporation acquires all of the net assets of Coastal Corporation for $1,000,000. The following intangible assets are included in the purchase agreement:

Assets	Acquisition Cost
Goodwill and going concern value	$100,000
Licenses	55,000
Patents	45,000
Covenant not to compete for five years	100,000

All of the intangible assets qualify as Sec. 197 intangible assets and are amortizable on a ratable basis over 15 years beginning with the month of the acquisition. ◀

STOP & THINK

Question: When one company purchases the assets of another company, the purchasing company may acquire goodwill. Since purchased goodwill is a Sec. 197 intangible asset and may be amortized over 15 years, the determination of the cost of goodwill is important. How is the "cost" of goodwill determined when the purchasing company purchases many assets in the acquisition?

Solution: The IRS requires that taxpayers use the "residual method" as prescribed in Sec. 1060. Under this method, all of the assets except for goodwill are valued. The total value of these assets are then subtracted from the total purchase price and the residual value is the amount of the purchase price that is allocated to goodwill.

CLASSIFICATION AND DISPOSITION OF INTANGIBLE ASSETS. A Sec. 197 intangible asset is treated as depreciable property so that Sec. 1231 treatment is accorded the disposition if the intangible asset is held for more than one year.[37] Gain from the disposition of a Sec. 197 intangible is subject to depreciation recapture under Sec. 1245 (see Chapter I13).[38] A loss on the disposition of a Sec. 197 intangible asset, however, is not deductible if other intangibles acquired in the same asset acquisition of a trade or

---

[37] Sec. 197(f)(7).

[38] Sec. 1245(a)(2)(C).

business are retained. In such case, the bases of the retained Sec. 197 intangibles are increased by the unrecognized loss.[39]

EXAMPLE I10-25 ▶ Assume the same facts as in Example I10-24 except that after five years the covenant not to compete expires when its adjusted basis is $66,667 [$100,000 − (0.333 × $100,000)]. The loss is not deductible and the $66,667 disallowed loss is allocated to the retained Sec. 197 assets based on their respective FMVs. ◀

EXAMPLE I10-26 ▶ Assume the same facts as in Example I10-24 except that after one year the patent is sold for $50,000. In the initial year, $3,000 of amortization was deducted. The recognized gain is $8,000 ($50,000 − $42,000) and $3,000 of the gain is recaptured as ordinary income under Sec. 1245. The remaining $5,000 of gain is classified as Sec. 1231 gain. ◀

RESEARCH AND EXPERIMENTAL EXPENDITURES

In general, research and experimental (R&E) expenditures, as defined in Sec. 174, include experimental and laboratory costs incidental to the development of a product.[40] Sec. 174 was enacted to clarify the income tax treatment of research and experimental expenditures. Without statutory guidance, the decision to either capitalize or currently expense such expenditures would be in doubt. The Regulations define items that do and do not qualify as research and experimental expenditures. These items are summarized in Table I10-5. For income tax purposes, the following alternatives are available for R&E expenditures:

▶ Expense in the year paid or incurred

▶ Defer and amortize the costs as a ratable deduction over a period of 60 months or more

TYPICAL MISCONCEPTION

It is sometimes mistakenly believed that if a company constructs a new building to be used entirely as a research facility, the entire cost of the building can be expensed. However, the expensing election applies only to the depreciation allowances on the building.

▼ **TABLE I10-5**

Research and Experimental Expenditures

Items That Qualify	Items That Do Not Qualify[a]
▶ Costs incident to the development of an experimental or pilot model, a plant process, a product, a formula, an invention ▶ Costs associated with product improvements ▶ Costs of obtaining a patent, such as attorney fees ▶ Research contracted to others ▶ Depreciation or cost-recovery amounts attributable to capitalized R&E items (e.g., research laboratory and equipment)	▶ Expenditures for ordinary testing or inspection of materials or products for quality control purposes ▶ Efficiency surveys and management studies ▶ Marketing research, advertising, and so on ▶ Cost of acquiring another person's patent, model, production, or process ▶ Research incurred in connection with literary, historical, or similar projects

[a] Certain of these expenses may be deductible as trade or business expenses under Sec. 162, subject to amortization under Sec. 197, or treated as start-up expenditures under Sec. 195.

---

[39] Sec. 197(f)(1).

[40] Reg. Sec. 1.174-2(a)(2). The Regulations define the term "product" to include any pilot model, formula, invention, technique, patent, or similar product.

▶ Capitalize and write off the costs only when the research project is abandoned or is worthless[41]

A taxpayer must make an election to expense or defer and amortize the costs in the initial year the R&E expenditures are incurred. If no election is made, the costs must be capitalized. The taxpayer must continue to use the same accounting method for the R&E expenditures unless IRS approval to change methods is obtained.

The following points are significant regarding the computation of the deduction for R&E expenditures:

▶ Most taxpayers elect to expense the R&E expenditures because they prefer the immediate tax benefit.

▶ The deferral and amortization method is desirable if the taxpayer is currently in a low tax rate situation or expects initial NOLs during a start-up period.

▶ If the deferral and amortization method is used, the amortization period of 60 or more months commences with the month in which the benefits from the expenditures are first realized.

▶ R&E expenses include depreciation allowances related to capitalized expenditures. Thus, if the deferral and amortization method is used, depreciation allowances are deferred as part of the R&E expenditures that are amortized over a period of at least 60 months. Capital expenditures made in connection with R&E activities cannot be expensed when they are incurred merely because an election to expense R&E costs are made.

WHAT WOULD YOU DO IN THIS SITUATION?

Your CPA firm has a long-standing tax client named Widgets R Us, Incorporated (WRU). WRU has been a worldwide leader in widget technology for years and continues to expand its global market share of Class A Crystal Widgets through a substantial program of basic research and development of widget crystallization processes. You have always advised WRU as to which of these expenditures qualify as research and experimental (R&E) expenditures. In addition, you have always given timely advice as to when to expense rather than capitalize these expenditures.

You are having your monthly tax conference with Ms. Ima Worthmore, president of WRU, and Mr. Stan Cunning, tax counsel of WMU, and Ms. Worthmore relates to you a conversation she had with the local manager of a competitor CPA firm, Ms. Ruth Less. Ms Less told Ms. Worthmore that she had discovered that WRU was one of the top spenders on research and

development in the area and that her firm was "certified" to practice before the IRS and had experienced great success in gaining better R&E write-offs for comparable firms. Ms. Less went on to say that, "For you, for this one year only, we offer to prepare your tax returns on a contingent basis. We promise to save you at least $1 million dollars from what you are now paying the IRS through our better use of R&E write-offs and our fee will only be 30% of the tax savings!"

Ms. Worthmore was excited that WRU might pay such a considerably less amount of taxes under the plan of Ruth Less and is somewhat perturbed at you because you had not brought this tax opportunity to her attention. She wants your firm to provide her with a counteroffer. How do you ethically respond to your client's request to match or better Ms. Ruth Less' proposal?

---

[41] Sec. 174.

▶ A 20% tax credit applies to certain incremental research expenditures, even if they are immediately expensed under Sec. 174. (See Chapter I14 for a discussion of the research activities credit.)

EXAMPLE I10-27 ▶

In 1997 Control Corporation leases a research laboratory to develop new products and to improve existing products. Control Corporation, a calendar-year taxpayer that uses the accrual method of accounting, incurs the following expenditures during 1997:

Laboratory supplies and materials	$ 40,000
Laboratory equipment	60,000[a]
Utilities and rent	50,000
Salaries	50,000
Total expenditures	$200,000

[a] The MACRS recovery period is 5 years at a 20% rate for the initial year.

REAL-WORLD EXAMPLE

An airline company made payments to an aircraft manufacturer to help defray the cost of designing, developing, producing, and testing a supersonic transport prototype aircraft. These payments were considered R&E expenditures. Rev. Rul. 69-484, 1969-2 C.B. 38.

The benefits from the R&E expenditures are first realized in January, 1998. If Control Corporation elects to expense the R&E expenditures, the deduction in 1997 is $152,000 ($40,000 laboratory supplies and materials + $12,000 depreciation on the equipment + $50,000 utilities and rent + $50,000 salaries). If the deferral and amortization method is elected, none of the expenditures above are deductible in 1997 because the benefits of the R&E activities are not first realized until January, 1998. If the 60-month minimum amortization period is elected, the monthly amortization commencing in January, 1998 is $2,533 ($152,000 ÷ 60 months). The $48,000 ($60,000 − $12,000) of laboratory equipment cost is depreciated over the remaining MACRS recovery period beginning in 1998. ◀

NVENTORY COSTS

OBJECTIVE 6

Determine inventory cost and cost of goods sold under various methods

Cost of goods sold is often the most significant expense claimed in determining gross income. Inventory costs and costing methods affect the determination of that cost. In many situations, the tax and financial accounting inventory rules parallel each other because of the general requirement in the tax law that inventories must conform to the best accounting practice and clearly reflect income.[42] Other restrictions and conformity requirements with respect to inventories also apply, as follows:

▶ Taxpayers must use the accrual method of accounting for purchases (accounts payable) and sales (accounts receivable) if inventories are a material, income-producing factor.

▶ If the last-in, first-out (LIFO) inventory method is used for tax purposes, it must generally be used for all other financial reporting purposes.[43]

Taxpayers who use LIFO for tax purposes must use the same method in their primary financial reports to shareholders and creditors. This requirement has discouraged many companies from adopting LIFO because it would cause lower amounts of net income and earnings per share to be reported for financial reporting purposes during periods of inflation. Thus, despite LIFO's potential for tax savings, approximately two-thirds of the inventories in the United States are reported under the FIFO method.[44]

If a taxpayer violates the conformity requirements, the election to use LIFO is involuntarily terminated and the taxpayer loses the benefits from the LIFO method. However, the LIFO conformity requirement has been relaxed somewhat in recent years.

[42] Sec. 471.
[43] Sec. 472(c). Exceptions are provided for in Reg. Sec. 1.472-2(e) relating to disclosures in supplementary financial reports.
[44] U.S., Treasury Department, "Tax Reform for Fairness, Simplicity, and Economic Growth," in *The Treasury Department Report to the President* (Washington, DC: U.S. Government Printing Office, November 1984), vol. 2, p. 191.

The Regulations now permit footnote disclosure in supplementary reports to the financial statements of the effect on net income if a method other than LIFO is used.[45] In addition, the financial income statement supplements or other reports must be clearly identified as being supplementary or explanatory.

These restrictions and conformity requirements do not mean that a method that is used and is preferable under **generally accepted accounting principles (GAAP)** will automatically be acceptable for tax purposes. The courts have generally held that the IRS has broad discretion as to whether the taxpayer's method of accounting is a clear reflection of taxable income. For example, the Supreme Court held that a taxpayer could not deduct the cost of excess inventory that was deemed to exceed normal demands, even though the inventory method was in conformity with GAAP.[46] Thus, inventory write-downs to reflect obsolescence are not generally permitted for tax purposes unless the merchandise is either 1) offered at the lower price, or 2) defective. The following inventory methods are also unacceptable for income tax purposes:

▶ Deduction of a reserve for price changes or estimated depreciation (i.e., decline in value) from the value of inventories[47]

▶ Valuation of work in process at a nominal price

▶ Omission of portions of inventory

▶ Use of a constant price or nominal value for a normal quantity of goods in stock

▶ Inclusion of goods in transit in inventory

▶ Use of the direct costing method (i.e., treating fixed overhead costs as deductible period costs)

▶ Use of the prime costing method (i.e., exclusion of both fixed and variable overhead costs from inventory and treating these costs as period costs)[48]

The last two prohibited methods are also unacceptable for GAAP reporting purposes, although some companies prepare internal reports for management use based upon these methods.

DETERMINATION OF INVENTORY COST AND COST OF GOODS SOLD

Inventory cost includes the invoice price less trade discounts. It also includes freight-in and other handling costs. The treatment of cash discounts (representing an adjustment to the purchase price for prompt payment) depends on whether the taxpayer customarily expenses or capitalizes such amounts. Thus, cash discounts may either be charged directly to expense and excluded from the inventory or included in the inventory, provided a consistent practice is followed.[49] If the cost of goods purchased is not reduced by the amount of cash discounts received, another alternative is to credit the cash discount amounts to an income account and include such amounts in gross income.

Inventory costs include direct materials, direct labor, and manufacturing overhead based on the full absorption costing method. With some exceptions, all indirect production costs must be included in the inventory.[50] The use of standard costing methods is acceptable if standard costs are periodically revised to reflect actual costs and if the overhead variances are not significant.[51]

---

[45] Reg. Sec. 1.472-2(e)(1)(i).
[46] *Thor Power Tool Co. v. CIR*, 43 AFTR 2d 79-362, 79-1 USTC ¶9139 (USSC, 1979).
[47] The IRS has also ruled that a home builder may not depreciate houses that are temporarily used as models or sales offices because depreciation is not permitted for inventories (see Rev. Rul. 90-25, 1990-1 C.B. 79). A similar rule has been applied to automobile demonstrators (see Rev. Rul. 75-538, 1975-2 C.B. 35).
[48] Reg. Sec. 1.471-2(f).

[49] Reg. Sec. 1.471-3(b) and Rev. Rul. 73-65, 1973-1 C.B. 216.
[50] Sec. 263A contains the **uniform capitalization rules**, which require certain period costs to be capitalized and included in cost of goods sold. Some of these costs include those incident to purchasing inventory, repackaging, and assembly and others incurred in processing goods, storage costs, general and administrative costs allocable to pension and profit-sharing costs, and interest expense. These rules apply only to inventories valued at cost. (See Chapter I11 for a discussion of these requirements.)
[51] Reg. Sec. 1.471-11(d)(3).

EXAMPLE I10-28 ▶

Compact Corporation uses standard costs for direct labor and material costs and omits all manufacturing overhead costs from its inventory. The total unit cost for inventory on hand at the end of the year is $4 ($2 direct material cost + $2 direct labor cost). Variable and direct overhead costs would amount to $3 per unit if the costs were capitalized as part of the inventory. Compact must value its ending inventory at $7 per unit by including the manufacturing overhead costs and must place its beginning and ending inventory amounts on the same basis, because full absorption costing procedures are required for income tax purposes. Cost of goods sold is determined as follows:

Inventory at the beginning of the year			$ 1,000
Plus:	Merchandise purchased	$10,000	
	Labor	15,000	
	Materials and supplies	8,000	
	Overhead costs	2,000	35,000
Goods available for sale			$36,000
Minus:	Inventory at the end of the year		(2,000)
Cost of goods sold			$34,000

For an individual taxpayer who maintains inventory as part of his or her business, the cost of goods sold amount is reported on Schedule C. ◀

INVENTORY VALUATION METHODS

Taxpayers may value inventories based on the cost or the **lower of cost or market (LCM) methods.** However, if the LIFO method is used, only the cost method is allowed. If the LCM method is used, each inventory item is considered separately in the calculation of the total LCM inventory amount. Once an item is reduced to market, this amount becomes the cost of the inventory item in the subsequent period. The market inventory amount usually means replacement cost (i.e., the bid price) for purchased goods or the reproduction cost for manufactured goods on the inventory date.[52] Merchandise can be written down only to the offering price, and goods that are unsalable at normal prices or are unusable due to damage, imperfections, and so on are valued at selling price less any direct cost of disposal.[53] Before the inventory can be written down to market, the goods must actually be offered for sale at the reduced price.

EXAMPLE I10-29 ▶

Crane Corporation has the following items in its ending inventory:

Item	Cost	Market	Lower of Cost or Market
X	$ 600	$ 650	$ 600
Y	400	350	350
Z	1,000	800	800
Total	$2,000	$1,800	$1,750

If Crane Corporation inventories its goods at cost, the inventory is valued at $2,000. If the LCM method is used, the inventory is valued at $1,750 because each item is considered separately rather than using the aggregate market value of $1,800. The method selected must be used consistently for all periods and may not be changed without IRS consent. For financial accounting purposes, it is acceptable to use the aggregate LCM method, which would result in a valuation of $1,800 and would produce a difference between the financial accounting and taxable income amounts. ◀

---

[52] Reg. Sec. 1.471-4.
[53] Reg. Sec. 1.471-2(c).

COST-FLOW ASSUMPTIONS

It is usually not feasible or practical to specifically identify each item in the inventory, although the specific identification inventory method is acceptable for tax purposes if this method is in fact used by the taxpayer. For example, an automobile dealer may use the specific identification method to value its automobile inventory. In most cases, however, a cost-flow assumption (e.g., LIFO, FIFO, or average cost) must be used to determine the cost of goods sold and the ending inventory amounts.

The use of a particular cost-flow assumption affects the determination of taxable income. The LIFO method usually results in lower taxable income during inflationary periods if inventory levels remain stable or are increasing, because the LIFO cost-flow assumption matches the most recently incurred inventory costs (and higher-priced items) against sales for the period. For example, the application of a last-in, first-out assumption generally results in the ending inventory including the "oldest" inventory costs (and lowest priced items), since the most recent costs are charged to cost of goods sold.

THE FIFO METHOD. The **FIFO method** assumes that the first goods purchased are sold to customers during the period and, therefore, these costs enter into the determination of cost of goods sold. The ending inventory consists of the last goods purchased during the year.

SELF-STUDY QUESTION

Why do many companies in the computer and electronics industry use the FIFO method to minimize their tax liability?

ANSWER

The cost of many of the component parts purchased by these companies has declined over time.

TYPICAL MISCONCEPTION

Neither LIFO nor FIFO must be selected on the basis of the actual flow of goods.

EXAMPLE I10-30 ▶

Dakota Corporation uses the FIFO inventory method and reports the following purchase and sales transactions during the current year:

▶ Purchases: 100 units @ $12 = $1,200

▶ Sales: 90 units @ $20 = $1,800

Dakota's beginning inventory consists of 20 units costing $10 each. Cost of goods sold consists of 90 units. Twenty of these units are deemed to have come from the beginning inventory that cost $10, and 70 units are from the purchases made in the current year that cost $12. The cost of goods sold is $1,040 [(20 units × $10) + (70 units × $12)]. Ending inventory consists of the 30 most recently purchased units in the current year, which are valued at $12 per unit, or $360 (30 units × $12). ◀

THE LIFO METHOD. Under the **LIFO method,** the cost of the most recently acquired goods is charged to the cost of goods sold. Conversely, the ending inventory consists of the first items that are purchased. In a period of rapidly increasing prices, the LIFO method may result in substantial tax savings because the more recent, higher costs are charged to cost of goods sold. Taxable income is understated relative to the amount of taxable income that would have been reported under the FIFO method. However, the tax advantages of LIFO may be seriously eroded if prices decrease or if there is a reduction in the quantity of inventory resulting in a liquidation of a LIFO layer.

EXAMPLE I10-31 ▶

Data Corporation uses the LIFO method and reports the following purchases and sales transactions during 1997:

▶ Purchases: 800 units @ $12 = $9,600

▶ Sales: 750 units @ $20 = $15,000

Data's beginning inventory consists of 50 units purchased 8 years ago costing $4 each. 1997's cost of goods sold consists of 750 units. Under the LIFO method, all of the units sold are deemed to come from 1997's purchases, thereby producing a $9,000 (750 × $12) cost of goods sold amount. The ending inventory under LIFO is deemed to consist of 50 units from the beginning inventory costing $4, and a new LIFO "layer" of 50 units costing $12 from 1997's purchases, or $800 [(50 × $4) + (50 × $12)]. If the FIFO inventory method had been used, cost of goods sold would consist of 50 units from the beginning inventory costing $4 each and 700 units from 1997 purchases costing $12. Under FIFO, 1997's cost of goods sold is only $8,600 (instead of the $9,000 calculated under the LIFO method). ◄

EXAMPLE I10-32 ▶ Assume the same facts as in Example I10-31, except that Data's inventory is partially liquidated in 1998 because the units sold exceed the units purchased. Data reports the following purchase and sale transactions during 1998:

▶ Purchases: 900 units @ $14

▶ Sales: 975 units @ $20

1998's cost of goods sold under the LIFO method is determined as follows:

$$
\begin{array}{lr}
900 \text{ units @ \$14} = & \$12,600 \\
50 \text{ units @ \$12} = & 600 \\
25 \text{ units @ \$4} = & 100 \\
\hline
975 \text{ units} & \$13,300 \\
\end{array}
$$

Under the LIFO method, a portion of the cost of goods sold is priced using "old" costs because of the liquidation of the inventory layers, and taxable income is, therefore, increased accordingly. ◄

The following methods are available for applying LIFO:

▶ Specific goods method. Under this method (used above in Examples I10-31 and I10-32), like-kind items are grouped into separate pools and inventory changes are

Topic Review I10-3

Comparison of LIFO and FIFO Methods

	LIFO	FIFO
Valuation methods	Only the cost method is allowed.	Either the cost method or the LCM method is allowed.
Cost-flow assumptions	The cost of the most recently acquired goods is charged to cost of goods sold.	The cost of the first goods purchased is charged to cost of goods sold.
Inventory value	Ending inventory consists of the first items that are purchased.	Ending inventory consists of the last items purchased during the year.
Effects of inflation	In periods of rising prices and stable or increasing inventories, taxable income is lower under LIFO.	If the prices of inventory components decrease, taxable income is lower under FIFO.
Special rules	LIFO must be used for financial reporting purposes if it is used for tax purposes.	If the LCM method is used, each inventory item is considered separately.

measured in terms of physical units for each pool. This method often requires extensive record-keeping. It may also result in the liquidation of one or more inventory layers if a company has several inventory pools and significant differences exist between production and sales among product lines.

▶ Dollar-value method. This method uses dollar-value pools rather than physical unit pools, and the dollar cost for similar items are aggregated to form inventory pools. Dollar-value LIFO may be computed by using either the double-extension method, the index method, or the link-chain method. Further discussion of these methods is beyond the scope of this text.[54]

▶ Simplified LIFO method. The complexity of the LIFO calculation and its record-keeping requirements prevented many small businesses from adopting it until the simplified LIFO method was enacted in 1981. This method is available only to small businesses (i.e., businesses with $5 million or less average gross receipts for the three preceding years).[55] Under this method, inventory pools are established by general categories of items that are also contained in the producer and consumer price indexes prepared by the Bureau of Labor Statistics (BLS). The pools are then indexed for price changes by using the BLS indexes. This method is designed to allow small businesses to use LIFO without undue complexities or excessive compliance costs.

A comparison of the LIFO and FIFO methods is presented in Topic Review I10-3.

TAX PLANNING CONSIDERATIONS

ALTERNATIVE DEPRECIATION SYSTEM UNDER MACRS

In some instances, it may be preferable to elect to use the alternative depreciation system rather than the regular MACRS rules. For example, a taxpayer who anticipates losses during the next few years or who currently has NOL carryovers may elect to use the alternative depreciation system, which employs the straight-line method of depreciation over a longer recovery period.

EXAMPLE I10-33 ▶

Delta Corporation has substantial NOL carryovers that will expire if not used during the next few years. Delta Corporation anticipates it will not have taxable income for each of the next seven years if the regular MACRS rules are used to depreciate its fixed asset additions. In the current year, Delta Corporation acquires new machinery and equipment at a cost of $100,000. Depreciation deductions using the MACRS rules and a seven-year recovery period are $14,290 (0.1429 × $100,000). Depreciation deductions under the straight-line method using the alternative depreciation system (a 12-year life) and the half-year convention are only $4,167 [($100,000 ÷ 12 years) × 0.50 year]. The alternative depreciation system election increases taxable income in the current year by $10,123 and allows Delta Corporation to offset additional loss carryovers (which might otherwise expire) against this income amount. ◀

IDCs: CAPITALIZATION VERSUS EXPENSING ELECTION

Although most taxpayers elect to expense intangible drilling costs (IDCs), sometimes capitalization and amortization are preferable because of the effect of IDCs on the depletion deduction.

---

[54] See discussion of dollar-value LIFO in Donald E. Kieso and Jerry J. Weygandt, *Intermediate Accounting*, 8th ed. (New York: John Wiley, 1995), Ch. 8.

[55] Sec. 474(c).

If IDCs are expensed, taxable income from the property is reduced. This may result in a smaller percentage depletion deduction because the percentage depletion claimed is limited to 100% of pre-depletion taxable income.

EXAMPLE I10-34 ▶ Gross income from an oil and gas property is $500,000. Expenses of $450,000 are incurred including $200,000 of IDCs. The percentage depletion deduction (before the 100% limitation) is $75,000 (0.15 × $500,000). The percentage depletion limitation is $50,000 (1.00 × $50,000 net income before depletion). Thus, the percentage depletion that is allowed is limited to the lesser of the percentage depletion earned ($75,000) or the limitation ($50,000), or $50,000. If the IDCs are capitalized, the percentage depletion deduction limitation is $250,000 (1.00 × $250,000 net income before depletion) and the taxpayer could claim the full $75,000 of percentage depletion earned. ◀

If the IDCs are capitalized, the property's basis for cost depletion purposes is increased and the IDCs are amortized as part of the cost depletion. However, if cost depletion is less than percentage depletion, the benefits from IDC amortization may be lost because percentage depletion is used.

EXAMPLE I10-35 ▶ Assume the same facts as in Example I10-34, except that the IDCs are capitalized and assume that cost depletion is increased from $20,000 to $45,000 due to the capitalization of the IDCs. Because percentage depletion is $75,000 and cost depletion is only $45,000, percentage depletion is used and the benefits from capitalizing IDCs (i.e., $25,000 increase in cost depletion) are lost. The election to capitalize the IDCs did result in an increase in the amount of percentage depletion from $50,000 to $75,000. ◀

USE OF UNITS OF PRODUCTION DEPRECIATION

Many times, the MACRS depreciation system requires taxpayers to use a recovery period that is much longer than the actual useful life of the asset. For example, assume a taxpayer uses a machine in her business that is required to be classified as 7-year property under MACRS. However, the machine is operated 24 hours a day, seven days a week and will completely wear out in two years. The use of the 7-year recovery period substantially understates the depreciation for the machine. Under Sec. 168(f), taxpayers may exclude property from the MACRS system if the property is depreciated under the unit-of-production method or any other method not expressed in terms of years. Therefore, if a taxpayer can express the useful life of the machine in terms of some other base than years (such as machine hours, units produced, etc.), it may be possible for the taxpayer to depreciate the machine over a much shorter period than the seven years required under MACRS.

STRUCTURING A BUSINESS COMBINATION

Tax planning needs to be conducted to ensure favorable tax consequences for the acquiring company if the assets of the acquired company are purchased as part of a business combination. The sales agreement must specify the amounts that have been paid for the tangible depreciable and nondepreciable assets and the intangible assets and the reporting requirements of Sec. 1060 must be complied with. Under the requirements of Sec. 1060, both the transferor and the transferee are bound by their written agreement as to the allocation of the purchase price to individual assets unless the IRS determines that such allocation is not appropriate. The amounts paid for the tangible assets should be documented by appraisals and evidence of negotiations between the buyer and seller. Within reason, the purchaser should attempt to allocate as much of the total price to the tangible depreciable assets. The purchaser should also consider allocating part of the purchase price to amortizable Sec. 197 intangible assets such as goodwill, a covenant not to compete, patents, copyrights, licenses, and customer lists because such asset costs are recovered over a 15-year period.

COMPLIANCE AND PROCEDURAL CONSIDERATIONS

IDC ELECTION PROCEDURES

The IDC election is made in the initial year that the expenditures are incurred. No formal statement or form is required. The expensing election is made by merely deducting the IDCs on the tax return.[56] If the costs are capitalized, cost depletion merely reflects the capitalized IDC costs.

PROCEDURES FOR CHANGING TO LIFO

The LIFO method may be adopted in the initial year that inventories are maintained by merely using the method in that year. In addition, advance approval (e.g., within 180 days following the start of the year) from the IRS is not required for an adoption of the LIFO method in the initial year that inventories are maintained on the LIFO method. However, Form 970 should be filed along with the taxpayer's tax return for the year of the change.[57] The application must include an analysis of the beginning and ending inventories. Further, if a taxpayer is changing to the LIFO method from another method (e.g., FIFO), advance approval from the IRS is also not required. Form 970 must be filed with the return and the beginning inventory for LIFO purposes is the same as under the former inventory method.[58]

If the former inventory is valued based on the lower of cost or market (LCM) method, an adjustment is required to restate the beginning inventory to cost because the LCM method cannot be used under LIFO. Generally, the beginning LIFO inventory is the same as the closing inventory for the prior year, except for the required restatement of previous writedowns to market. This adjustment to the beginning inventory can be spread ratably over the year of the change and the next two years.[59]

EXAMPLE I10-36 ▶ Delaware Corporation elects to change to the LIFO inventory method for 1997. In 1996 Delaware's inventories are valued using the LCM method based on the FIFO cost-flow assumption. The FIFO cost for the ending inventory in 1996 is $50,000, and its LCM amount is $35,000. The initial inventory for 1997 under LIFO must be restated to its cost, or $50,000. The $15,000 ($50,000 cost − $35,000 LCM value) difference can be included in taxable income over the current year and next two years. $5,000 is added to taxable income in 1997, 1998, and 1999. ◀

REPORTING COST RECOVERY, DEPRECIATION, DEPLETION, AND AMORTIZATION DEDUCTIONS

If an individual is engaged in a trade or business as a sole proprietor, depreciation, cost recovery, depletion, and amortization deductions are initially computed and reported on Form 4562 (Depreciation and Amortization) and the totals are then carried to Schedule C. Depletion and depreciation on rental properties are reported on Schedule E instead of

---

[56] Reg. Sec. 1.612-4(d).
[57] An acceptable election is considered to have been made even if Form 970 is not filed as long as all of the information required by Reg. Sec. 1.472-3(a) is provided by the taxpayer.

[58] Reg. Sec. 1.472-2(c).
[59] Sec. 472(d).

Schedule C if the taxpayer is an investor. Depreciation on employee business property is reported on Form 2106. Separate Form 4562s are required for each different activity.

The election to expense property under Sec. 179 is made by claiming the deduction on Part I of Form 4562. The taxpayer must specify the items of property and the portion of the cost for each asset being expensed. Form 4562 is not required of individuals and noncorporate taxpayers (including S corporations) when filing their 1996 tax returns if the depreciation deduction is for assets, other than listed property, placed in service before 1996. In such cases, the depreciation deduction is entered directly on Form 1040 or other equivalent tax forms.

EXAMPLE I10-37 ▶ George Jones, SSN 277-32-6542, is a building trade contractor who acquires the following properties in September, 1996:

▶ Specialized utility repair truck (5-year property that is not listed property under Sec. 280F(d)(4)), costing $20,000.

▶ Office equipment (7-year property), costing $22,500. The election to expense under Sec. 179 is made for $17,500.

▶ Patent, costing $10,000, that was acquired in 1996 when it had a remaining legal life of 17 years.

▶ ACRS deduction for assets placed into service before 1987 is $2,000.

▶ MACRS deduction for assets placed into service before 1996 is $8,000.

Jones has taxable income (before the Sec. 179 deduction and the deduction for one-half of self-employment taxes paid under Sec. 164(f)) of $60,000. The cost-recovery, depreciation, and amortization amounts are reported on Form 4562 and Schedule C, respectively, and are shown in Figures I10-1 and I10-2. ◀

RESEARCH AND EXPERIMENTAL EXPENDITURES

ADDITIONAL COMMENT

Once the election to expense R&E expenditures has been made, it is applicable to all R&E expenditures paid or incurred in the current year and all subsequent years.

The election to expense or to defer R&E expenditures is made by attaching a statement to the tax return for the first tax year in which the expenditures are incurred.[60] As previously discussed in the text, the capitalization method is not an election and applies only if no election is made in the initial year. Once a method has been adopted, the taxpayer is required to obtain the permission of the IRS to change to another method.

PROBLEM MATERIALS

DISCUSSION QUESTIONS

I10-1 Which of the following assets are subject to either amortization, depreciation, or cost recovery?
a. An automobile held for personal use.
b. Excess amounts paid in a business combination that are attributable to goodwill.
c. Excess amounts paid in a business combination that are attributable to customer lists that have a limited useful life.
d. A patent that has been created internally and has a legal life of 17 years.

---

[60] Reg. Sec. 1.174-3(b)(1).

Depreciation and Amortization
(Including Information on Listed Property)
▶ **Attach this form to your return.**

OMB No. 1545-0172

1996

Attachment
Sequence No. **67**

Name(s) shown on return	Business or activity to which this form relates	Identifying number
George Jones	*Building Trade Contractor*	*277-32-6542*

Part I Election To Expense Certain Tangible Property (Section 179) (Note: If you have any "listed property," complete Part V before you complete Part I.)

1	Maximum dollar limitation. If an enterprise zone business, see instructions	1	
2	Total cost of section 179 property placed in service	2	*42,500*
3	Threshold cost of section 179 property before reduction in limitation	3	$200,000
4	Reduction in limitation. Subtract line 3 from line 2. If zero or less, enter -0-	4	*0*
5	Dollar limitation for tax year. Subtract line 4 from line 1. If zero or less, enter -0-. If married filing separately, see instructions	5	*17,500*

6	(a) Description of property	(b) Cost (business only)	(c) Elected cost	
	Office Equipment	*22,500*	*17,500*	

7	Listed property. Enter amount from line 27	7	
8	Total elected cost of section 179 property. Add amounts in column (c), lines 6 and 7	8	*17,500*
9	Tentative deduction. Enter the smaller of line 5 or line 8	9	*17,500*
10	Carryover of disallowed deduction from 1995	10	*0*
11	Business income limitation. Enter the smaller of business income (not less than zero) or line 5	11	*20,000*
12	Section 179 expense deduction. Add lines 9 and 10, but do not enter more than line 11	12	*17,500*
13	Carryover of disallowed deduction to 1997. Add lines 9 and 10, less line 12 ▶	13	

Note: *Do not use Part II or Part III below for listed property (automobiles, certain other vehicles, cellular telephones, certain computers, or property used for entertainment, recreation, or amusement). Instead, use Part V for listed property.*

Part II MACRS Depreciation For Assets Placed in Service ONLY During Your 1996 Tax Year (Do Not Include Listed Property.)

Section A - General Asset Account Election

14 If you are making the election under section 168(i)(4) to group any assets placed in service during the tax year into one or more general asset accounts, check this box. See instructions ▶ ☐

Section B - General Depreciation System (GDS) (See instructions.)

(a) Classification of property	(b) Month and year placed in service	(c) Basis for depreciation (business/investment use only - see instructions)	(d) Recovery period	(e) Convention	(f) Method	(g) Depreciation deduction
15 a 3-year property						
b 5-year property		*20,000*	*5 yr*	*Half yr*	*MACRS*	*4,000*
c 7-year property		*5,000*	*7 yr*	*Half yr*	*MACRS*	*715*
d 10-year property						
e 15-year property						
f 20-year property						
g 25-year property			25 yrs.		S/L	
h Residential rental property	/		27.5 yrs.	MM	S/L	
	/		27.5 yrs.	MM	S/L	
i Nonresidential real property	/			MM	S/L	
	/			MM	S/L	

Section C - Alternative Depreciation System (ADS) (See instructions.)

16 a Class life					S/L	
b 12-year			12 yrs.		S/L	
c 40-year	/		40 yrs.	MM	S/L	

Part III Other Depreciation (Do Not Include Listed Property)

17	GDS and ADS deductions for assets placed in service in tax years beginning before 1996	17	*8,000*
18	Property subject to section 168(f)(1) election	18	
19	ACRS and other depreciation	19	*2,000*

Part IV Summary

20	Listed property. Enter amount from line 26	20	
21	**Total.** Add deductions on line 12, lines 15 and 16 in column (g), and lines 17 through 20. Enter here and on the appropriate lines of your return. Partnerships and S corporations - see instructions	21	*32,215*
22	For assets shown above and placed in service during the current year, enter the portion of the basis attributable to section 263A costs	22	

LHA **For Paperwork Reduction Act Notice, see page 1 of the separate instructions.**

Form **4562** (1996)

616251
10-04-96

FIGURE I10-1 ▶ FORM 4562

Part V Listed Property - Automobiles, Certain Other Vehicles, Cellular Telephones, Certain Computers, and Property Used for Entertainment, Recreation, or Amusement

Note: For any vehicle for which you are using the standard mileage rate or deducting lease expense, complete **only** 23a, 23b, columns (a) through (c) of Section A, all of Section B, and Section C if applicable.

Section A - Depreciation and Other Information (Caution: See instructions for limitations for automobiles.)

23a Do you have evidence to support the business/investment use claimed? ☐ Yes ☐ No **23b** If "Yes," is the evidence written? ☐ Yes ☐ No

(a) Type of property (list vehicles first)	(b) Date placed in service	(c) Business/ investment use percentage	(d) Cost or other basis	(e) Basis for depreciation (business/investment use only)	(f) Recovery period	(g) Method/ Convention	(h) Depreciation deduction	(i) Elected section 179 cost
24 Property used more than 50% in a qualified business use:								
	: :	%						
	: :	%						
	: :	%						
	: :	%						
25 Property used 50% or less in a qualified business use:								
	: :	%			S/L ·			
	: :	%			S/L ·			
	: :	%			S/L ·			
	: :	%			S/L ·			

26 Add amounts in column (h). Enter the total here and on line 20, page 1 .... **26**

27 Add amounts in column (i). Enter the total here and on line 7, page 1 .... **27**

Section B - Information on Use of Vehicles

Complete this section for vehicles used by a sole proprietor, partner, or other "more than 5% owner," or related person.

If you provided vehicles to your employees, first answer the questions in Section C to see if you meet an exception to completing this section for those vehicles.

	(a) Vehicle	(b) Vehicle	(c) Vehicle	(d) Vehicle	(e) Vehicle	(f) Vehicle
28 Total business/investment miles driven during the year (DO NOT include commuting miles)						
29 Total commuting miles driven during the year ...						
30 Total other personal (noncommuting) miles driven..........						
31 Total miles driven during the year. Add lines 28 through 30						

	Yes	No	Yes	No	Yes	No	Yes	No	Yes	No	Yes	No
32 Was the vehicle available for personal use during off-duty hours?												
33 Was the vehicle used primarily by a more than 5% owner or related person?												
34 Is another vehicle available for personal use?												

Section C - Questions for Employers Who Provide Vehicles for Use by Their Employees

Answer these questions to determine if you meet an exception to completing Section B for vehicles used by employees who **are not** more than 5% owners or related persons.

	Yes	No
35 Do you maintain a written policy statement that prohibits all personal use of vehicles, including commuting, by your employees?.........		
36 Do you maintain a written policy statement that prohibits personal use of vehicles, except commuting, by your employees? See instructions for vehicles used by corporate officers, directors, or 1% or more owners		
37 Do you treat all use of vehicles by employees as personal use?		
38 Do you provide more than five vehicles to your employees, obtain information from your employees about the use of the vehicles, and retain the information received?		
39 Do you meet the requirements concerning qualified automobile demonstration use?		

Note: If your answer to 35, 36, 37, 38, or 39 is "Yes," you need not complete Section B for the covered vehicles.

Part VI Amortization

(a) Description of costs	(b) Date amortization begins	(c) Amortizable amount	(d) Code section	(e) Amortization period or percentage	(f) Amortization for this year
40 Amortization of costs that begins during your 1996 tax year:					
Patent	6 - 95	10,000	197	15	$389
	: :				
41 Amortization of costs that began before 1996				**41**	
42 Total. Enter here and on "Other Deductions" or "Other Expenses" line of your return				**42**	$389

616252
10-04-96

FIGURE I10-1 ▶ FORM 4562 (CONTINUED)

SCHEDULE C
(Form 1040)
Department of the Treasury
Internal Revenue Service (99)

Profit or Loss From Business
(Sole Proprietorship)

▶ Partnerships, joint ventures, etc., must file Form 1065.

▶ Attach to Form 1040 or Form 1041. ▶ See Instructions for Schedule C (Form 1040).

1996

Attachment
Sequence No. **09**

Name of proprietor: **George Jones**

Social security number (SSN): **277 32 6542**

A Principal business or profession, including product or service
Building Trade Contractor

B Enter principal business code (see page C-6) ▶ **0 8 8 5**

C Business name. If no separate business name, leave blank.

D Employer ID number (EIN), if any

E Business address (including suite or room no.) ▶ **2240 88th St Miami, FL 33124**
City, town or post office, state, and ZIP code

F Accounting method: (1) ☐ Cash (2) ☐ Accrual (3) ☐ Other (specify) ▶

G Did you "materially participate" in the operation of this business during 1996? If "No," see page C-2 for limit on losses .... ☒ Yes ☐ No

H If you started or acquired this business during 1996, check here .... ▶ ☐

Part I   Income

1	Gross receipts or sales. **Caution:** If this income was reported to you on Form W-2 and the "Statutory employee" box on that form was checked, see page C-2 and check here ▶ ☐	1	
2	Returns and allowances	2	
3	Subtract line 2 from line 1	3	
4	Cost of goods sold (from line 42 on page 2)	4	
5	**Gross profit.** Subtract line 4 from line 3	5	
6	Other income, including Federal and state gasoline or fuel tax credit or refund	6	
7	**Gross income.** Add lines 5 and 6. ▶	7	

Part II   Expenses. Enter expenses for business use of your home **only** on line 30.

8	Advertising	8		19	Pension and profit-sharing plans	19	
9	Bad debts from sales or services (see page C-3)	9		20	Rent or lease (see page C-4):		
10	Car and truck expenses (see page C-3)	10		a	Vehicles, machinery, and equipment	20a	
11	Commissions and fees	11		b	Other business property	20b	
12	Depletion	12		21	Repairs and maintenance	21	
13	Depreciation and section 179 expense deduction (not included in Part III)	13	32,215	22	Supplies (not included in Part III)	22	
				23	Taxes and licenses	23	
				24	Travel, meals, and entertainment:		
14	Employee benefit programs (other than on line 19)	14		a	Travel	24a	
15	Insurance (other than health)	15		b	Meals and entertainment		
16	Interest:			c	Enter 50% of line 24b subject to limitations (see page C-4)		
a	Mortgage (paid to banks, etc.)	16a		d	Subtract line 24c from line 24b	24d	
b	Other	16b		25	Utilities	25	
17	Legal and professional services	17		26	Wages (less employment credits)	26	
18	Office expense	18		27	Other expenses (from line 48 on page 2)	27	389

28	**Total expenses** before expenses for business use of home. Add lines 8 through 27 in columns ▶	28	32,604
29	Tentative profit (loss). Subtract line 28 from line 7	29	
30	Expenses for business use of your home. Attach **Form 8829**	30	
31	**Net profit or (loss).** Subtract line 30 from line 29.		
	• If a profit, enter on **Form 1040, line 12,** and ALSO on **Schedule SE, line 2** (statutory employees, see page C-5). Estates and trusts, enter on Form 1041, line 3.	31	
	• If a loss, you MUST go on to line 32.		
32	If you have a loss, check the box that describes your investment in this activity (see page C-5).		
	• If you checked 32a, enter the loss on **Form 1040, line 12,** and ALSO on **Schedule SE, line 2** (statutory employees, see page C-5). Estates and trusts, enter on Form 1041, line 3.	32a ☐ All investment is at risk.	
	• If you checked 32b, you MUST attach **Form 6198.**	32b ☐ Some investment is not at risk.	

LHA   **For Paperwork Reduction Act Notice, see Form 1040 Instructions.**

Schedule C (Form 1040) 1996

620001
01-06-97

FIGURE I10-2 ▶ FORM 1040, SCHEDULE C

Part III **Cost of Goods Sold** (see page C-5)

33 Method(s) used to
value closing inventory: **a** ☐ Cost   **b** ☐ Lower of cost or market   **c** ☐ Other (attach explanation)

34 Was there any change in determining quantities, costs, or valuations between opening and closing inventory? If "Yes," attach explanation .... ☐ Yes ☐ No

35 Inventory at beginning of year. If different from last year's closing inventory, attach explanation	**35**	
36 Purchases less cost of items withdrawn for personal use	**36**	
37 Cost of labor. Do not include salary paid to yourself	**37**	
38 Materials and supplies	**38**	
39 Other costs	**39**	
40 Add lines 35 through 39	**40**	
41 Inventory at end of year	**41**	
42 **Cost of goods sold**. Subtract line 41 from line 40. Enter the result here and on page 1, line 4	**42**	

Part IV **Information on Your Vehicle.** **Complete this part ONLY** if you are claiming car or truck expenses on line 10 and are not required to file Form 4562 for this business. See the instructions for line 13 on page C-3 to find out if you must file.

43 When did you place your vehicle in service for business purposes? (month, day, year) ▶ ____/____/____ .

44 Of the total number of miles you drove your vehicle during 1996, enter the number of miles you used your vehicle for:

a Business _____ **b** Commuting _____ **c** Other _____

45 Do you (or your spouse) have another vehicle available for personal use? .... ☐ Yes ☐ No

46 Was your vehicle available for use during off-duty hours? .... ☐ Yes ☐ No

47a Do you have evidence to support your deduction? .... ☐ Yes ☐ No
  b If "Yes," is the evidence written? .... ☐ Yes ☐ No

Part V **Other Expenses.** List below business expenses not included on lines 8-26 or line 30.

Patent Amortization	_389_
48 **Total other expenses.** Enter here and on page 1, line 27	**48** _389_

620002
10-14-96

FIGURE I10-2   ▶   FORM 1040, SCHEDULE C (CONTINUED)

e. Land that is being held for investment purposes.

f. A covenant not to compete which is entered into by the buyer and seller of a business.

I10-2 Rick is a sole proprietor who has a small business that is currently operating at a loss. He would like to discontinue depreciating the fixed assets of the business for the next few years in order to carry the deductions over to a future period. What tax consequences would result if Rick implements the plan to discontinue depreciation and then sells some of the depreciable assets several years later?

I10-3 Rita acquired a personal residence two years ago for $120,000. In the current year she purchases another residence and attempts to sell her former residence. Due to depressed housing conditions in the town where she used to live, Rita is unable to sell the house. Her former residence is now being offered for sale at $100,000 (its current FMV according to real estate appraisal experts). Rita has decided to rent the house rather than "give it away." She states that the rental for an indefinite period will permit her to write off the original $120,000 investment over its useful life and to, therefore, recoup her investment. What restrictions in the tax law may prevent her from accomplishing this objective? Explain.

I10-4 Contrast and compare the ACRS and MACRS rules with the pre-ACRS rules regarding the ease of administering the tax law (e.g., mitigating disputes between taxpayers and the IRS regarding the appropriate amount of cost-recovery or depreciation deductions).

I10-5 Daytona Corporation, a manufacturing corporation, acquires the following business assets in 1997.

• Furniture
• Plumbing fixtures
• Land
• Goodwill and a trademark acquired in the acquisition of a business
• Automobile
• Heavy truck
• Machinery
• Building used in manufacturing activities

a. Which of the assets above are eligible for depreciation under the MACRS rules or amortization under Sec. 197?

b. What recovery period should be used for each of the assets above that come under the MACRS rules or under Sec. 197?

I10-6 Robert, a sole proprietor who uses the calendar year as his tax year, acquires a business machine on December 31, 1997 for $10,000 and sells certain business equipment on the same date for $2,000. The equipment that is sold was acquired on January 1, 1993 for $20,000. What amount (if any) of depreciation deductions should be allowed under MACRS for the newly acquired machine and for the equipment that is sold in 1997?

I10-7 Is a depreciation deduction allowed under the MACRS rules for depreciable real estate (used in a business or held for investment) in the year the property is sold? If so, explain how it is calculated.

I10-8 Jose is considering acquiring a new luxury automobile costing $38,000 for use in his business (100%). The salesperson at the automobile dealership states that Jose will be entitled to both of the following tax benefits in the initial year (1997):

• A deduction for $18,000 of the acquisition cost under Sec. 179.

• A $4,000 ($20,000 × 0.20) MACRS depreciation deduction.

a. Are the salesperson's assertions relative to the tax benefits accurate? Explain.

b. How would your answer to Part a differ (if any) if the automobile were used only 60% for business purposes?

c. How would your answer to Part a differ (if any) if Jose instead was to lease the automobile?

I10-9 Explain why the straight-line MACRS method might be preferable over the regular MACRS method under the following circumstances:

a. Ray incurs NOLs in his business for a number of years and has NOL carryovers he would like to use.

b. Rhonda's marginal tax rate is 15% but is expected to increase to 36% in three years.

I10-10 Rudy is considering whether to make the election under Sec. 179 to expense $18,000 of the acquisition cost related to certain fixed asset additions. What advantages are associated with the Sec. 179 election?

I10-11 Your client is a self-employed attorney who is considering the purchase of a $12,000 automobile that will be used 80% of the time for business and a $4,000 personal computer that will be used 100% of the time for business but is located in his home.

    a. What depreciation methods and recovery periods may be used under MACRS for the automobile and the personal computer?

    b. How would your answer to Part a change if your client were an employee and the computer and automobile were not required as a condition of employment?

    c. What tax consequences occur in Part a if the business use of the personal computer or the automobile decreases to 50% or less in a succeeding year? Explain.

I10-12 Sarah enters into a three-year lease of an automobile in the current year that is used exclusively in her business. The automobile's FMV was $40,000 at the inception of the lease. Sarah made ten monthly lease payments of $600 each during the current year. Is Sarah able to avoid the luxury automobile restrictions on depreciation by leasing instead of purchasing the automobile? Explain. (The inclusion amount for Sarah's automobile under the current Rev. Proc. 97 is $194.)

I10-13 Simon acquires an interest in an oil property for $50,000. Intangible drilling costs (IDCs) in the initial year are $10,000. Cost depletion is $5,000 if the IDCs are expensed and $6,000 if the costs are capitalized. Percentage depletion is $15,000 if the IDCs are expensed and $20,000 if the costs are capitalized. The difference in the percentage depletion amounts is due to the 100% taxable income limitation.

    a. What method (i.e., immediate write-off or capitalization and amortization) should be elected for the treatment of the IDCs in the initial year?

    b. Why are intangible drilling costs expensed by most taxpayers?

I10-14 What difference does it make for income tax purposes whether an intangible asset is acquired in connection with a business acquisition, is acquired by the purchase of an individual asset (e.g., a patent), or is created internally? Explain.

I10-15 In January of the current year, Park Corporation incurs $34,000 of legal costs associated with the obtaining of a patent that was developed inter-

nally and has a legal life of 17 years. Park also acquired for cash the net assets of Central Corporation on January 1, for $1,000,000. The following assets are specified in the purchase agreement:

Land	$200,000
Goodwill and going concern value	100,000
Covenant not to compete	50,000
Licenses	125,000
Customer lists	25,000
Inventory	100,000
Equipment and other tangible depreciable business assets	400,000
Total	$1,000,000

    a. What tax treatment should be accorded the intangible assets?

    b. Assuming that you were advising Park Corporation during the negotiations before the drafting of the purchase agreement, what suggestions would you make regarding the allocation of the total purchase price to the individual assets? How could the purchase price of individual assets be substantiated?

I10-16 Why do most taxpayers prefer to expense research and experimental expenditures?

I10-17 Hill Corporation uses the lower of cost or market (LCM) method to value its inventory. The company accountant has advised that major write-downs are now required to reflect inventory obsolescence due to an excess supply of spare parts and that a reserve should be reflected on the books of the company.

    a. Should the inventory be written down for financial reporting purposes?

    b. Is an inventory write-down permitted for income tax purposes? (Assume that the write-down is made so that the financial reports can reflect GAAP.)

I10-18 Large Corporation uses direct costing in valuing its inventory for its internal management reports and full absorption costing for reports issued to creditors and shareholders. Which method is required for income tax purposes?

I10-19 Is the lower of cost or market (LCM) method allowed if a company uses the LIFO cost-flow assumption?

I10-20 Why does the LIFO method usually result in lower reported profits and taxable income during inflationary periods?

I10-21 Inflation is generally measured in terms of a general purchasing power index (i.e., consumer price index). The prices of a company's inventory more closely follow the wholesale price index, which is not expected to increase in future years. Explain how these facts could affect a company's decision to switch to the simplified LIFO method.

I10-22 What factors have discouraged many small companies from adopting LIFO? What special LIFO rules have encouraged more small companies to switch to LIFO for tax purposes?

I10-23 The Indiana Corporation is considering the adoption of the LIFO inventory method for the current year. The company currently values its inventory using the lower of cost or market (LCM) method based on the FIFO cost-flow assumption. Indiana's inventory cost at the end of the prior year is $800,000 using the FIFO method. The inventory is stated at $700,000 due to Indiana's use of the LCM method. The company wants to switch to the LIFO method because it expects substantial inflation during the next five years. However, the controller of the company states that the company would prefer to continue to use the FIFO method for financial reporting purposes because in two years the company plans to go public (i.e., issue stock to the public in a secondary offering).

a. What procedures are required to change from FIFO to LIFO?

b. What adjustment (if any) must be made to the current year's beginning inventory?

c. Why does Indiana Corporation want to switch to LIFO for tax purposes?

d. Can the company continue to use its existing inventory method for financial reporting to shareholders and creditors? Explain.

e. Is it possible to issue supplementary financial statement information regarding the effect of LIFO on reported earnings without violating the financial accounting conformity requirement? Explain.

I10-24 In a business combination, why does the buyer generally prefer to allocate as much of the purchase price to short-lived depreciable assets, ordinary assets such as inventory, and Sec. 197 intangible assets?

ISSUE IDENTIFICATION QUESTIONS

I10-25 Georgia Corporation acquires a business automobile for $30,000 on December 31 of the current year but does not actually place the automobile into service until January 1 of the following year. What tax issues should Georgia Corporation consider?

I10-26 Paula is planning to acquire by purchase or by lease a $50,000 luxury automobile. She anticipates that the business use will be 60% for the first two years but will decline to 40% in years three through five. Currently, Paula's marginal tax rate is 15% but she anticipates that her marginal tax rate will be 36% after a few years. What tax issues should Paula consider relative to the decision to purchase or lease the automobile?

I10-27 In the current year Coastal Corporation acquires all of the net assets of Acorn Corporation for $2,000,000. The purchase agreement allocated the following amounts to the individual assets and liabilities:

Land and building	$1,400,000
Accounts receivable	200,000
Inventory	300,000
Goodwill	400,000
Patents (remaining legal life of ten years)	100,000
Covenant not to compete	200,000
Liabilities	(600,000)
Total	$2,000,000

What tax issues should Coastal Corporation consider relative to the asset acquisitions?

I10-28 Weiskopf, a sole proprietor and a calendar-year taxpayer, purchased $100,000 of equipment during the current year, as follows:

	Cost	Recovery Period
March 1	$25,000	7 years
September 18	$40,000	7 years
October 2	$35,000	5 years

Weiskopf's CPA, to maximize the depreciation deduction, elected to take Sec. 179 depreciation on the March 1 property of $18,000. What tax issue should be considered with respect to the total depreciation deduction for the current year?

PROBLEMS

I10-29 *Allowed Versus Allowable Depreciation.* Sandy acquires business machinery (which qualifies as 7-year MACRS property) on July 15, 1997 for $10,000. In 1997 Sandy claims a $1,429 depreciation deduction, but Sandy fails to claim any depreciation deduction in 1998 or 1999. The machine is sold on July 1, 1999 for $6,000.
a. What is the adjusted basis of the machine on the sale date?
b. How much gain or loss is recognized on the sale of the machine?

I10-30 *ACRS-Straight-Line Depreciation.* Tess acquires and places in service on November 1, 1986 a business machine costing $20,000. Tess elects straight-line depreciation using the longest possible recovery period. The machine is sold on April 1, 1997 for $18,000. (Assume that no amount is expensed under Sec. 179.)
a. What is the amount of cost-recovery deduction for 1986 through 1997?
b. What is the amount of Tess's recognized gain or loss from the sale of the machine in 1997?

I10-31 *Conversion of Personal Asset to Business Use.* Sid purchased an automobile for personal use on January 1, 1995 for $10,000. On January 1, 1997, Sid starts a small business and begins to use the automobile exclusively in the business. The automobile's FMV on this date is $6,000. MACRS depreciation deductions are taken in 1997 based on a 5-year recovery period.
a. What is the automobile's basis for depreciation purposes when converted to business use in 1997?
b. What is Sid's depreciation deduction in 1997?

I10-32 *MACRS Depreciation.* Small Corporation acquires and places in service the following business assets in the current year (no other assets were placed in service during the year):
- Light truck costing $10,000 (on December 15) with a 5-year MACRS recovery period
- Machinery costing $50,000 (on February 1) with a 7-year MACRS recovery period
- Land costing $60,000 (on July 1)
- Building costing $100,000 (on December 1) with a 39-year MACRS recovery period
- Equipment costing $40,000 (acquired on December 24, but not placed in service until January of the following year) with a 5-year MACRS recovery period
a. What is the MACRS depreciation deduction for each asset in the current year (assume Sec. 179 was not elected for any asset)?
b. What is the MACRS deduction for each asset in the current year if the machinery is instead acquired on October 1?

I10-33 *MACRS Depreciation.* Ted purchases 5-year recovery period personal property costing $30,000 on April 1 of the current year, and 7-year recovery period personal property costing $40,000 on November 1 of the current year. (Assume that Ted does not elect the Sec. 179 expensing election and uses the MACRS rules.) What is the amount of the MACRS depreciation deduction for each asset in the current year?

I10-34 *Sec. 179 Expensing Election and MACRS Depreciation.* Tish acquires and places in service a business machine with a 7-year MACRS recovery period in July 1997. The machine costs $25,000, and Tish elects to expense the maximum amount allowable under Sec. 179. The total cost of qualifying property placed in service during the year amounts to $214,000. Tish's taxable income (before deducting the Sec. 179 amount and one-half of self-employment taxes paid) is $3,000.

a. What is the amount Tish can deduct under Sec. 179 in 1997?

b. What is the amount of MACRS depreciation deduction for the machine in 1997?

I10-35 *ACRS and MACRS Dispositions.* Tampa Corporation disposes of the following assets in 1997:

	Date Acquired	Date Sold	Original Cost Basis	Depreciation/ Cost-Recovery Method	Recovery Period (Years)
Truck	1/15/86	8/14/97	$ 10,000	SL-ACRS	12
Auto	1/1/95	12/1/97[a]	9,000	MACRS	5
Equipment	1/6/95	9/1/97[a]	20,000	MACRS	7
Building	4/1/86	12/15/97	100,000	ACRS	19

[a] Assume that the half-year convention was used in the year of acquisition.

What is the amount of cost recovery or depreciation deduction for each asset in 1997?

I10-36 *Sec. 179 and MACRS Depreciation.* Thad acquires a machine for use in his business in the current year for $28,000. The MACRS rules with a 7-year recovery period are used, and Thad elects to expense $18,000 of the acquisition cost under Sec. 179. What is the machine's basis for depreciation purposes and the depreciation deduction in its initial year?

I10-37 *Sec. 179 and Mid-Quarter Convention.* Todd acquired two pieces of equipment for use in his business during the year as follows:

Item	Date Acquired	Recovery Period	Cost
Equipment A	April, 1997	5-year	$50,000
Equipment B	November, 1997	7-year	$50,000

Todd elects to expense $18,000 of the acquisition cost under Sec. 179 and wants to maximize the amount of depreciation for the year. Compute Todd's depreciation in order to yield the highest depreciation possible. (Hint: The mid-quarter convention is calculated after taking Sec. 179 on any asset or assets)

I10-38 *Straight-Line Depreciation.* Long Corporation has been unprofitable for several years and has substantial NOL carryovers. Therefore, the company policy has been to use the straight-line ACRS or MACRS rules for property acquisitions. The following assets are acquired, held, or sold in 1997:

	Date Acquired	Date Sold	Original Cost Basis	Selling Price	Depreciation Method	Recovery Period (Years)
Equipment	7/1/97	—	$40,000	—	SL	7
Light truck	7/1/86	12/1/97	30,000	$12,000	SL	12
Furniture	3/1/86		10,000		SL	12
Automobile	7/1/95	12/1/97	12,000	10,000	SL	5

Assume the expensing election under Sec. 179 is not made.

a. What is the depreciation deduction for each asset in 1997?

b. What amount of gain or loss is recognized on the properties sold in 1997?

I10-39 *Mixed Personal/Business Use.* Trish, a self-employed CPA and calendar-year taxpayer, acquires an automobile and a personal computer in 1996. Pertinent data include the following:

Asset	Date Acquired	Original Cost Basis	Portion of Business Usage	Sec. 179 Election
Automobile	1/1/97	$11,000	60%	No
Personal computer	7/1/97	4,000	40	No

For each asset calculate the MACRS current year depreciation deduction.

I10-40 *Employee Listed Property.* Assume the same facts as in Problem I10-39, except that Trish is an employee and uses the automobile and personal computer on employment-related activities. While both assets are helpful to Trish in performing her job duties, her employer does not require employees to purchase a car or a personal computer as a condition of employment. What is the amount of depreciation for each asset?

I10-41 *Recapture of Depreciation Deductions Due to Personal Use.* Tammy acquires an automobile for $10,000 on July 1, 1995. She uses the automobile partially for business purposes during the 1995–1997 period. The percentage of business use is as follows: 1995, 70%; 1996, 70%; 1997, 40%. The MACRS rules with a 5-year recovery period are used in 1995 and 1996.
a. What is the amount of the MACRS depreciation deduction for 1995? 1996? 1997?
b. What is the amount of recapture of previously claimed depreciation deductions (if any) that must take place in 1997?

I10-42 *Luxury Auto Limitations.* Lutz Corporation acquires a luxury automobile on July 1, 1997 for $20,000 that is used 100% for business-use. The Sec. 179 expensing election is not made but the company chooses to claim the maximum amount of MACRS depreciation deductions available. What is the depreciation deduction amount for 1997, 1998, 1999, and any subsequent years?

I10-43 *Luxury Auto Limitations.* Tracy acquires a luxury automobile on January 1, 1997, for use 80% of the time in his business and 20% of the time for personal use. The automobile cost $30,000, and no amounts are expensed under Sec. 179. What is the depreciation amount for 1997–1999 and any subsequent years?

I10-44 *Luxury Auto Limitations—Leasing.* Troy enters into a 3-year lease of a luxury auto on January 1, 1997, for use 80% in business and 20% for personal use. The FMV of the automobile at the inception of the lease is $40,000 and twelve monthly lease payments of $600 were made in 1997. (The "inclusion amount" under Rev. Proc. 97-20 is $194.)
a. What is the amount of lease payments that are deductible in 1997?
b. What portion, if any, of the "inclusion amount" must be included in gross income in 1997?
c. How would your answers to Parts a and b change if the FMV of the auto were instead $10,000?

I10-45 *Cost Depletion.* Tina acquires an oil and gas property interest for $200,000 in the current year. The following information about current year operations is supplied for purposes of computing the amount of Tina's depletion and IDC deductions:

Estimated recoverable units	20,000
Units produced	6,000
Units sold	4,000
IDCs	$20,000
Percentage depletion (after limitations)	$25,000

a. What is the cost depletion amount if the IDCs are expensed?

b. What is the cost depletion amount if the IDCs are capitalized?

c. How much depletion is deducted on the tax return?

d. Should the IDCs be capitalized or expensed? Explain.

I10-46 ***Percentage Depletion.*** Tony has owned an oil and gas property for a number of years. The following information is provided about the property's operations in the current year:

Gross income	$500,000
Minus: Expenses (including IDCs of $100,000)	(300,000)
Taxable income (before depletion)	$200,000
Cost depletion (if IDCs are expensed)	$ 20,000
Cost depletion (if IDCs are capitalized)	$ 30,000

a. What is the percentage depletion amount if the IDCs are expensed?

b. What is the percentage depletion amount if the IDCs are capitalized?

c. What is the depletion deduction amount assuming that the IDCs are expensed?

d. Based on the information above, which method should be used for the IDCs? Explain.

I10-47 ***Goodwill.*** On January 1 of the current year, Palm Corporation acquires the net assets of Vicki's unincorporated business for $600,000. The tangible net assets have a $300,000 book value and $400,000 FMV. The purchase agreement states that Vicki will not compete with Palm Corporation by starting a new business in the same area for a period of five years. The stated consideration received by Vicki for the covenant not to compete is $50,000. Other intangible assets included in the purchase agreement are as follows:

- Goodwill: $70,000

- Patents (12-year remaining legal life): $30,000

- Customer list: $50,000

a. How would Vicki's assets be recorded for tax purposes by Palm Corporation?

b. What is the amortization amount for each intangible asset in the current year?

I10-48 ***R&E Expenditures.*** Park Corporation incurs the following costs in the initial year of doing business:

Materials and supplies for research laboratory	$ 80,000
Utilities and depreciation on research laboratory and equipment	40,000
Costs of acquiring another person's patent for a new product	20,000
Market research salaries for surveys relative to proposed new products	60,000
Labor and supplies for quality control tests	50,000
Research costs subcontracted to a local university	35,000
Total	$285,000

Park's controller states that all of these costs are qualifying R&E expenditures and that the company policy is to expense such amounts for tax purposes in the year they are incurred. Which of these expenditures are deductible as R&E costs under Sec. 174?

I10-49 ***R&E Expenditures.*** In 1997 Phoenix Corporation acquires a new research facility and hires several scientists to develop new products. No new products are developed until 1998, although the following expenditures were incurred in 1997:

Laboratory materials	$ 40,000
Research salaries	80,000
Overhead attributable to the research facility	30,000
R&E equipment placed into service (5-year MACRS recovery period)	100,000
Total	$250,000

a. What is Phoenix Corporation's deduction for R&E expenditures in 1997 and 1998 if the expensing method is elected?

b. How would your answer to Part a change if the deferral and amortization method were elected and the amortization period were 60 months?

I10-50 ***Inventory Costs: LCM, Financial Accounting, and Adoption of LIFO Methods.*** Red Corporation uses the LCM method to value its inventory. Cost is determined by using the FIFO cost-flow assumption. The following items are included in 1997's ending inventory:

Item	Cost	Market
X	$ 400	$300
Y	300	500
Z	300	150
Total	$1,000	$950

Red Corporation uses the aggregate market value to determine its inventory under GAAP.

a. What is the amount of Red Corporation's ending inventory for financial accounting purposes for 1997?

b. What is the amount of Red Corporation's ending inventory for tax purposes in 1997?

c. Assume Red Corporation decides to adopt the LIFO inventory method in 1998. What adjustment must be made (if any) to the beginning 1998 inventory in order to use the LIFO method?

I10-51 ***Inventory Costs: LCM Method.*** Star Corporation uses the LCM method to value its inventory. Cost is determined by using the FIFO cost-flow assumption. The company reports the following purchases and sales in the current year:

Purchases: 100 units @ $8.00	$ 800
Sales: 120 units @ $20.00	$2,400

Its inventory includes the following:

Beginning inventory: 40 units @ $5.00	$ 200
Ending inventory: 20 units @ ?	

The market value of the ending inventory is $9.00 per unit.

a. What is the cost of goods sold amount for the current year?

b. What is Star's ending inventory amount?

I10-52 ***Inventory Costs: LIFO Method.*** Small Corporation uses the LIFO inventory method. During the year Small Corporation is unable to meet its production schedules due to production problems in the plant and high product demand. Consequently, inventories decline to low levels. Inflation is rampant during the year, and the company controller states that footnote disclosure will be made in its financial statements to show the amount of net income under the FIFO method. Small Corporation has the following purchases, sales, and inventories during the year:

Beginning inventory: 1,000 units @ $2.00	$ 2,000
Purchases: 1,000 units @ $20.00	$20,000
Sales: 1,800 units @ $30.00	$54,000

a. What is the amount of Small Corporation's ending inventory and cost of goods sold?

b. What are the effects of liquidating the beginning inventory LIFO layer less upon the amount of reported earnings and taxable income?

c. Does footnote disclosure of the reported net income if the FIFO method is used constitute a violation of the financial accounting conformity requirement found in the LIFO rules?

TAX FORM/RETURN PREPARATION PROBLEMS

TAX CUT

I10-53 Thom Jones (SSN 277-31-7253) is an unincorporated manufacturer of widgets. He uses the LCM method to value his inventory and has the following transactions during the year:

Sales (less returns and allowances)	$800,000
Costs of goods sold	500,000
Office expenses	10,000
Depreciation and Sec. 179 deduction (see the schedule of asset acquisitions below)[a]	
Legal services	4,000
Salary expenses	36,000
Travel expenses	30,000
Repairs	20,000

[a] Assume that the cost of Sec. 179 property placed into service during the year is $150,000.

Mr. Jones's depreciation schedule is as follows:

Office furniture held for business use is purchased and an election is made to expense the acquisition cost under Sec. 179.	$17,500
Depreciation on recovery property acquired and placed into service in 1996:	
5-year recovery period property	6,000
7-year recovery period property	14,000
Other 12-year recovery period property using the straight-line method under the alternative depreciation system	20,000
Total depreciation allowance	$40,000

Complete Form 4562 and Schedule C of Form 1040 for 1996 for Mr. Jones.

I10-54 John and Ellen Brite (SSN 265-32-1497 and 571-07-7345, respectively) own an unincorporated specialty electrical lighting retail store, Brite-On. Brite-On had the following assets on January 1, 1996:

Assets	Cost
Building purchased April 1, 1986	$100,000
7-year recovery period equipment purchased January 1, 1993	30,000
Inventory valued using LIFO method:	
Oldest inventory: 4,000 light bulbs	$4/bulb
Newest inventory: 5,000 light bulbs	5/bulb

The Brites purchased a competitor's store on March 1, 1996 for $89,000. The purchase price included the following:

	FMV
Store building	$60,000
Land	18,000
5-year recovery period equipment	11,000
Inventory: 3,000 light bulbs	6/bulb

On June 30, 1996 the Brites sold the 7-year recovery period equipment for $12,000. Brite-On leased a $30,000 car for $500/month beginning on January 1, 1996. The car is used 100% for business. Brite-On sold 8,000 light bulbs at $15/bulb during the year. Brite-On had the following revenues and additional expenses:

Service revenues	$40,000
Interest on business loans	4,000
Auto expenses (gas, oil, etc.)	3,800
Taxes and licenses	3,300
Utilities	2,800

John and Ellen also had some personal expenses:

Medical bills	$ 4,500
Real property taxes	3,800
Home mortgage interest	9,000
Charitable contributions (cash)	600

John and Ellen made four $3,750 quarterly estimated tax payments.

Additional Facts:

- Assume that an election is made under Sec. 179 to expense the cost of the 5-year equipment that was acquired in 1996.

- Rev. Proc. 96-20 requires the Brites to include $114 in their gross income due to the leased automobile restrictions.

Complete Forms 4562, 4797, and 1040, pages 1 and 2 and Schedules A and C for 1996. (Omit any self-employment tax computation.)

CASE STUDY PROBLEMS

I10-55 Able Corporation is a manufacturer of electrical lighting fixtures. Able is currently negotiating with Ralph Johnson, the owner of an unincorporated business, to acquire his retail electrical lighting sales business. Johnson's assets that are to be acquired include the following:

Assets	Adjusted Basis	FMV
Inventory of electrical fixtures	$30,000	$ 50,000
Store buildings	80,000	100,000
Land	40,000	100,000
Equipment: 7-year recovery period	30,000	50,000
Equipment: 5-year recovery period	60,000	100,000
Total	$240,000	$400,000

Mr. Johnson indicates that a total purchase price of $1,000,000 in cash is warranted for the business because of its high profitability and strategic locations and Able has agreed that the business is worth $1,000,000. Despite the fact that both parties attribute the excess payment to be for goodwill, Able would prefer that the $600,000 excess amount be designated as a 5-year covenant not to compete so that he can amortize the excess over a 5-year period.

You are a tax consultant for Able who has been asked to make recommendations as to the structuring of the purchase agreement and the amounts to be assigned to individual assets. Prepare a client memo to reflect your recommendations.

I10-56 The Margate Corporation acquired an automobile with an acquisition cost of $30,000 for use in its business in 1994. During this time, Margate Corporation was experiencing a seasonal decline in sales. Several employees were laid off and the automobile was not immediately needed for any of the sales personnel. Instead of letting the new automobile sit in the corporate lot, the president decided to permit a corporate officer to use the automobile for personal use. The officer used the automobile in 1995 and 1996 only. In 1997, Margate Corporation has hired you as their new CPA (tax consultant). You learn about the officer's personal use of the corporate automobile that took place for the two prior years without proper accounting of the automobile to the IRS. As Margate Corporation's tax consultant, what actions (if any) should you take regarding the proper treatment of the automobile? What are your responsibilities as a CPA regarding this matter under the rules of the AICPA's *SRTP* No. 6? (See the *Statements on Responsibilities in Tax Practice (SRTP)* section in Chapter I15 and Appendix E for a discussion of *SRTP* No. 6.)

TAX RESEARCH PROBLEM

I10-57 Apple Corporation has never been audited before the current year. An audit is now needed from a CPA because the company is in a rapid expansion period and is planning to issue stock to the public in a secondary offering. A CPA firm has been doing preliminary evaluations of the Apple Corporation's accounts and records. One major problem involves the valuation of inventory under GAAP. Apple Corporation has been valuing its inventory under the cost method and no write-downs have been made for obsolescence. A review of the inventory indicates that obsolescence and excess spare parts in the inventory are two major problems. The CPA states that for GAAP the company will be required to write down its inventory by 25% of its stated amount, or $100,000, and charge this amount against net income from operations for the current period. Otherwise, a "clean opinion" will not be rendered. The company controller asks your advice regarding the tax consequences from the obsolescence and spare parts inventory write-downs for the current year and the procedures for changing to the LCM method for tax purposes. Apple Corporation is on a calendar year, and the date of your contact with the company is December 1 of the current year.

A partial list of research sources is

- Secs. 446 and 471

- Reg. Secs. 1.446-1(e)(3), 1.471-2 and 1.471-4

- *American Liberty Pipe Line Co. v. CIR*, 32 AFTR 1099, 44-2 USTC ¶9408 (5th Cir., 1944)

- *Thor Power Tool Co. v. CIR*, 43 AFTR 2d 79-362, 79-1 USTC ¶9139 (USSC, 1979)

CHAPTER 11

ACCOUNTING PERIODS AND METHODS

LEARNING OBJECTIVES

After studying this chapter, you should be able to

1. Explain the rules for adopting and changing an accounting period

2. Explain the difference between cash and accrual accounting

3. Determine whether specific costs must be included in inventory

4. Determine the amount of income to be reported from a long-term contract

5. Compute the gain to be reported from an installment sale

6. Compute the amount of imputed interest in a transaction

7. Determine the tax treatment of duplications and omissions that result from changes of accounting methods

An **accounting method** is a rule that is used to determine the year in which income and expenses are reported for tax purposes. The accounting methods used in computing income for tax purposes generally must be the same as those used in keeping the taxpayer's books and records. The accounting rules determine when income and expenses are reported, not whether they are reported. Although the accounting methods used by a taxpayer do not necessarily affect the amount of income reported over the life of a business, they do affect the tax burden in two ways. Selecting the appropriate accounting method can accelerate deductions or defer income recognition in order to postpone tax payments, and because of the progressive tax rate structure, taxpayers can save by spreading income over several accounting periods rather than having income bunched into one period.

EXAMPLE I11-1 ▶

Jane, a taxpayer using the cash method of accounting, has a 28% marginal tax rate for 1997 and expects to have a 15% marginal tax rate in 1998. Jane plans to make a charitable contribution of $1,000 in January 1998. A contribution in 1998 will reduce Jane's tax by $150 (0.15 × $1,000), whereas a contribution in 1997 will reduce Jane's tax by $280 (0.28 × $1,000). Obviously Jane may wish to accelerate the contribution in order to reduce her tax liability. ◀

ACCOUNTING PERIODS

OBJECTIVE 1

Explain the rules for adopting and changing an accounting period

TYPICAL MISCONCEPTION

It is sometimes mistakenly believed that a tax year can end on a day in the middle of the month.

SELF-STUDY QUESTION

Assume that the ABC partnership is permitted to adopt a tax year ending October 31. Alice, a partner who uses a calendar year, has $12,000 of income from ABC for the year ended October 31, 1997. How much income has Alice been able to defer?

ANSWER

Assuming that the income was earned ratably throughout the year, Alice has deferred $2,000 of income, which represents the income earned in November and December of 1996.

Taxable income is computed on the basis of the taxpayer's annual **accounting period**, which is ordinarily 12 months (either a calendar year or a fiscal year). A **fiscal year** is a 12-month period that ends on the last day of any month other than December. The tax year must coincide with the year used to keep the taxpayer's books and records. Taxpayers who do not have books (e.g., an individual with wage income) must use the calendar year.[1] A taxpayer with a seasonal business may find a fiscal year to be advantageous. During the slow season inventories may be lower and employees are available to take inventory and perform other accounting duties associated with the year-end. The tax year is elected on the first tax return that is filed by a taxpayer and cannot be changed without consent from the IRS.[2]

A partnership must use the same tax year of the partners who own the majority of partnership income and capital. If the majority does not have the same year, the partnership must use the tax year of its principal partners (those with more than a 5% interest in the partnership). If the principal partners do not have the same tax year, the partnership must use the calendar year.[3] An exception is made for partnerships that can establish to the satisfaction of the IRS a business purpose for having a different year.

The purpose of the rule is to prevent partners from deferring partnership income by choosing a different tax year for the partnership. For example, calendar-year partners might select a partnership year that ends on January 31. Because partnership income is considered to be earned by the partners on the last day of the partnership's tax year, reporting the profits would thus be deferred 11 months because the partnership year would end after the partner's year. (See the section entitled Required Payments and Fiscal Years in this chapter for further discussion of the calendar-year requirement.)

A similar rule generally requires S corporations and personal service corporations to adopt a calendar year unless the corporation has a business purpose for electing a fiscal year.[4] Taxpayers willing to make required payments or distributions may choose a fiscal year. (See the Required Payments and Fiscal Years section in this chapter.)

---

[1] Sec. 441(g).
[2] Reg. Sec. 1.441-1(b)(4).
[3] Sec. 706(b).
[4] Sec. 1378(a).

STOP & THINK

Question: The accounting period rules result in most partnerships, S corporations, and personal service corporations reporting on the calendar year basis. Of course, almost all individual taxpayers also report on the calendar year basis. What impact does this have on accountants?

Solution: The main result is a compression of tax compliance work into the "accounting busy season." A substantial portion of auditing and other accounting work also takes place following the year end. As a result, these services are also compressed into the accounting busy season. The accounting profession has sought to have these tax rules changed, but has, at least so far, been unsuccessful.

An improper election to use a fiscal year automatically places the taxpayer on the calendar year.[5] Thus, if the first return is filed late because of oversight, the option to choose a fiscal year is lost.

EXAMPLE I11-2 ▶

City Corporation receives its charter in 1995 but does not begin operations until 1997. Tax returns are required for 1995 and 1996 as well as for 1997. Timely returns are not filed because the City's officers are unaware that returns must be filed for inactive corporations. Thus, City Corporation must use the calendar year. City Corporation must petition the IRS for approval to use a fiscal year. ◀

ADDITIONAL COMMENT

The use of a 52- to 53-week year aids in budgetary matters and statistical comparisons because a four-week period, unlike a calendar month, is a uniform, fixed period.

Taxpayers who regularly keep their books over a period that varies from 52 to 53 weeks and that always ends on the same day of the week may elect the same period for tax purposes. The year must end either the last time a particular day occurs during a calendar month (e.g., the last Thursday in October) or the occurrence of the particular day that is closest to the end of a calendar month (e.g., the Friday closest to the end of November).[6] Under the first alternative, the year may end as many as six days before the end of the month, but must end within the month. Under the second alternative, the year may end as many as three days before or after the end of the month.[7]

REAL-WORLD EXAMPLE

Merrill Lynch & Company uses a 52- to 53-week year ending on the last Friday in December.

The 52- to 53-week year is especially useful to businesses with inventories. For example, a manufacturer might choose a 52- to 53-week year that ends on the last Friday in December to permit inventory to be taken over the weekend without interfering with the company's manufacturing activity. Similarly, wage accruals would be eliminated for a company with a weekly payroll if the payroll period always ends on Friday.

Although the 52- to 53-week year may actually end on a day other than the last day of the month, it is treated as ending on the last day of the calendar month for "effective date" changes in the tax law that would otherwise coincide with the year-end.[8]

EXAMPLE I11-3 ▶

KEY POINT

The use of a natural business year helps in the matching of revenue and expense because the business is normally in a maximum state of liquidity and the problems associated with making estimates involving uncompleted transactions are reduced to a minimum.

Eagle Corporation has adopted a 52- to 53-week year. Eagle's tax year begins on December 29, 1997. Assume that a new tax rate schedule applies to tax years beginning after December 31, 1997. The new tax rate schedule is applicable to Eagle because, in the absence of the 52- to 53-week year, its tax period would have started on January 1, 1998. ◀

CHANGES IN THE ACCOUNTING PERIOD

Once adopted, an accounting period cannot normally be changed without approval of the IRS.[9] The IRS will usually approve a change only if the taxpayer can establish a substantial business purpose for the change (i.e., changing to a natural business year).[10] A

---

[5] *Q.A. Calhoun v. U.S.,* 33 AFTR 2d 74-305, 74-1 USTC ¶9104 (D.C. Va., 1973).
[6] Sec. 441(f).
[7] Reg. Sec. 1.441-2(a)(ii).

[8] Reg. Sec. 1.441-2(b).
[9] Sec. 442.
[10] Rev. Procs. 74-33, 1974-2 C.B. 489, and 87-32, 1987-2 C.B. 32.

natural business year ends at or soon after the peak income earning period (e.g., the natural business year for a department store that has a seasonal holiday business may be on January 31). A business without a peak income period may not be able to establish a natural business year and may, therefore, be precluded from changing its tax year. In general, at least 25% of revenues must occur during the last two months of the year in order to qualify as a natural business year.

EXAMPLE I11-4 ▶

USA Department Store's sales reach their peak during the holiday season in December. During January the department store further reduces its inventory through storewide clearance sales. USA elects a "natural" business year-end of January 31 because its inventory levels are lowest at the end of January. ◀

REAL-WORLD EXAMPLE

J.C. Penney, K mart, and Wal-Mart all use an accounting period ending January 31.

In a few instances IRS approval is not required to change to another accounting period.

▶ A newly married person may change tax years to conform to that of his or her spouse so that a joint return may be filed. The election must be made in either the first or second year after the marriage date.[11]

▶ A change to a 52- to 53-week year that ends with reference to the same calendar month in which the former tax year ended.[12]

▶ A taxpayer who erroneously files tax returns using an accounting period other than that on which his or her books are kept is not required to obtain permission to file returns for later years based on the way the books are kept.[13]

▶ A corporation meeting the following specified conditions may change without IRS approval: (1) There has been no change in its accounting period within the past ten calendar years, (2) the resulting year does not have a net operating loss (NOL), (3) the taxable income for the resulting short tax year when annualized is at least 90% of the taxable income for the preceding full tax year, and (4) there is no change in status of the corporation (such as an S corporation election).[14]

▶ An existing partnership can change its tax year without prior approval if the partners with a majority interest have the same tax year to which the partnership changes or if all principal partners who do not have such a tax year concurrently change to such a tax year.[15]

There is one instance, however, when a change in tax years is required: A subsidiary corporation filing a consolidated return with its parent corporation must change its accounting period to conform with its parent's tax year.[16]

Application for permission to change accounting periods is made on Form 1128 (Application for Change in Accounting Period) on or before the fifteenth day of the second calendar month following the close of the resulting short period. The application must be sent to the Commissioner of the IRS, Washington, D.C.[17]

The IRS may establish certain conditions for the taxpayer to meet before it approves the change to a new tax year. For example, the IRS has ruled that if the short period that results from a change involves a NOL greater than $10,000, the taxpayer must agree to spread the loss over six years.

RETURNS FOR PERIODS OF LESS THAN 12 MONTHS

Most income tax returns cover an accounting period of 12 months. On two occasions, however, a taxpayer's accounting period may be less than 12 months:

---

[11] Reg. Sec. 1.442-1(e). A statement should be attached to the resulting short period return indicating that the change is being made.
[12] Reg. Sec. 1.441-2(c)(2). A statement should be attached to the first return filed under the election indicating that the change is being made.
[13] Rev. Rul. 58-256, 1958-1 C.B. 215.

[14] Reg. Sec. 1.442-1(c). A statement should be attached to the return indicating that each condition is met.
[15] Reg. Sec. 1.442-1(b)(2).
[16] Reg. Sec. 1.442-1(d).
[17] Reg. Sec. 1.442-1(b)(1).

when the taxpayer's first or final return is filed and when the taxpayer changes accounting periods.

Taxpayers filing an initial tax return and executors filing a taxpayer's final return or corporations filing their last return are not required to annualize the year's income, nor are personal exemptions or tax credits prorated. These returns are prepared and filed, and taxes are paid as though they are returns for a 12-month period ending on the last day of the short period. An exception permits the final return of a decedent to be filed as though the decedent lived throughout the entire tax year.[18]

EXAMPLE I11-5 ▶ ABC Partnership, which has filed its returns on a calendar-year basis, terminates on June 30, 1997. ABC's final return is due on October 15, 1997. ◀

EXAMPLE I11-6 ▶ Joy, a single individual who has filed her returns on a calendar-year basis, dies on June 30, 1997. Joy's final return is due on April 15, 1998. ◀

Taxpayers who change from one accounting period to another must annualize their income for the resulting short period. This prevents income earned during the resulting short period from being taxed at lower rates. Income is annualized as follows:

1. Determine modified taxable income. Individuals must compute their taxable income for the short period by itemizing their deductions (i.e., the standard deduction is not allowed) and personal and dependency exemptions must be prorated.[19]
2. Multiply modified taxable income by the following fraction:

$$\frac{12}{\text{Number of months in short period}}$$

3. Compute the tax on the resulting taxable income using the appropriate schedule.
4. Multiply the resulting tax by the following fraction:

$$\frac{\text{Number of months in short period}}{12}$$

EXAMPLE I11-7 ▶ Pat, a single taxpayer, obtains permission to change from a calendar year to a fiscal year ending on June 30, 1997. During the six months ending June 30, 1997, Pat earns $25,000 and has $5,000 in itemized deductions.[20]

Gross Income	$25,000
Minus: Itemized deductions	(5,000)
Personal exemption [(6 ÷ 12) × $2,650]	(1,325)
Modified taxable income	$18,675
Annualized income [(12 ÷ 6) × $18,675]	$37,350
Tax on $37,350 annualized income	7,254
Current tax [(6 ÷ 12) × $7,254]	3,627 ◀

Topic Review I11-1 summarizes the available accounting periods and the rules for changing accounting periods.

---

[18] Reg. Sec. 1.443-1(a)(2).
[19] The exemptions are prorated as follows: exemptions × (number of months in the short period ÷ 12).
[20] An alternative method to compute the tax is provided in Sec. 443(b)(2) and

Reg. Sec. 1.443-1(b)(2) whereby the taxpayer can elect to compute the tax for a 12-month period beginning on the first day of the short period and then convert the tax to a short-period tax.

Topic Review I11-1

Accounting Periods and Changes

Available Years

▶ Available tax years include the calendar year, a fiscal year (a year that ends on the last day of any month other than December), and a 52- to 53-week year (a year that always ends on the same day of the week).

▶ A partnership must use the tax year of its partners unless the partnership can establish a satisfactory business purpose for having a different year or if the partnership makes required payments.

▶ Similar rules generally require S corporations and personal service corporations to adopt a calendar year unless the corporation has a business purpose for electing a fiscal year. Taxpayers willing to make required payments or distributions may choose a fiscal year ending on September 30, October 31, or November 30.

Change in Accounting Periods

▶ Once adopted, an accounting period normally cannot be changed without approval by the IRS. The IRS is more likely to approve a change to a natural business year. In general, at least 25% of revenues must occur during the last two months of the year in order to qualify as a natural business year.

▶ Taxpayers who change from one accounting period to another must annualize their income for the resulting short period. This prevents income earned during the resulting short period from being taxed at lower rates.

STOP & THINK

Question: Why are taxpayers required to annualize when they change tax years? What provision of the tax law creates this need?

Solution: A change of tax years results in a shortened filing period during the period the change takes place. For example, a taxpayer who changes from a calendar year to a June 30 year end reports income for only a 6-month period on the first return following the change. Less income is reported, and that income would be taxed at lower rates without annualization. Annualization is necessary because of the progressive tax rate structure.

REQUIRED PAYMENTS AND FISCAL YEARS

Although taxpayers may use a fiscal year if they have an acceptable business purpose for doing so, most businesses are unable to meet the rather rigid business purpose requirements outlined by the IRS. As a result, most businesses report using the calendar year concentrating most tax work during the early months of the year. Concern over this problem led Congress to enact Sec. 444 which allows partnerships, S corporations, and personal service corporations (such as incorporated medical practices) to elect a taxable year that results in a tax deferral of three months or less (e.g., a partnership with calendar-year partners may elect a September 30 year end). Furthermore, partnerships, S corporations, and personal service corporations may continue using the fiscal year they were using when the current law was passed in 1986 even if that fiscal year results in a deferral beyond three months.

Electing partnerships and S corporations, however, must make annual required payments by April 15 of the following year. The purpose of the required payment is to offset the tax deferral advantage obtained when fiscal years are used.

The amount of the required payment is determined by multiplying the maximum tax rate for individuals plus 1% (i.e., 40.6% in 1997) times the previous year's taxable income times a deferral ratio.[21] The deferral ratio is equal to the number of months in the deferral period divided by the number of months in the taxable year. An adjustment is made for deductible amounts distributed to the owners during the year. If the amount due is $500 or less, no payment is required.

EXAMPLE I11-8 ▶ ABC Partnership begins operations on October 1, 1997. The partnership's net income for the fiscal year ended September 30, 1998 is $100,000. ABC must make a required payment of $10,150 ($100,000 × 40.6% × 3/12) on or before April 15, 1999. ◀

The owners of businesses making such payments do not claim a credit for the amount paid. Instead, the partnership or S Corporation subtracts the previous year's required payment from the current year's required payment. If the result is negative, then the entity is entitled to a refund.

EXAMPLE I11-9 ▶ Assume the same facts as in Example I11-8 except that ABC Partnership's required payment for the year ended September 30, 1999 is $6,000. ABC is entitled to a refund of the difference of $4,150 ($10,150 − $6,000). ◀

Personal service corporations may elect a fiscal year if they make minimum distributions to shareholders during the deferral period.[22] Personal service corporations are incorporated medical practices and other similar businesses owned by individuals who provide their services through the corporation. In general, the rules prevent a distribution pattern that creates a tax deferral. This is achieved by requiring that the deductible payments made to owners during the deferral period be at a rate no lower than during the previous fiscal year.

EXAMPLE I11-10 ▶ Austin is a personal service corporation of attorneys with a fiscal year ending September 30. For the year ended September 30, 1997 the company earned a profit of $480,000 before any salary payments to the owners. The entire profit, however, was paid out as wages to the owners, resulting in a taxable income of zero. To avoid penalty, Austin must pay salaries to its owners of $120,000 ($480,000 × 3/12) during the period October 1, 1997 to December 31, 1997. ◀

An option allows personal service corporations to compute the amount of the minimum distribution by using a three-year average of income and distributions.

OVERALL ACCOUNTING METHODS

OBJECTIVE **2**

Explain the difference between cash and accrual accounting

A taxpayer's method of accounting determines the year in which income is reported and expenses are deducted. Taxable income must be computed using the method of accounting regularly used by the taxpayer in keeping his or her books if that method clearly reflects income.[23] Permissible overall accounting methods are

▶ Cash receipts and disbursements method (often called the cash method of accounting)

---

[21] Sec. 7519(b).
[22] Sec. 280H(k).

[23] Sec. 446.

▶ Accrual method

▶ A combination of the first two methods, often called the hybrid method

New taxpayers may generally choose any of the accounting methods listed above. However, the accrual method must be used for sales and cost of goods sold if inventories are an income-producing factor to the business. This assumes, of course, that the chosen method clearly reflects income. The fact that an overall accounting method is used in one trade or business does not mean that the same method must be used in a second trade or business[24] or for nonbusiness income and deductions.[25]

EXAMPLE I11-11 ▶

Troy, a practicing CPA, also owns an appliance store. The fact that Troy uses the accrual method of reporting income from the appliance store, where inventories are an income-producing factor, does not preclude Troy from reporting income from his service-based accounting practice by using the cash method. Troy could also use the cash method for reporting nonbusiness income (such as dividends) and nonbusiness expenses (such as itemized deductions). ◀

The term *method of accounting* is used to include not only overall methods of accounting listed above but also the accounting treatment of any item.[26]

CASH RECEIPTS AND DISBURSEMENTS METHOD

Most individuals and service businesses use the cash receipts and disbursements method of accounting. Taxpayers cannot use the cash method in a business for sales and cost of goods sold if inventories are an income-producing factor.[27] C corporations and partnerships with a corporate partner may use the cash method only if their average annual gross receipts for the three preceding tax years do not exceed $5 million or if the business meets the requirements associated with providing personal services (i.e., if it is owned by professionals who are using the business to provide professional services).[28] Thus, a law or accounting firm can use the cash method even if its average receipts exceed $5 million.

Under the cash receipts and disbursements method of accounting, a taxpayer is required to report income for the tax year in which payments are actually or constructively received. While it might seem that receipts under the cash method of accounting should only be recognized if the taxpayer receives cash, this is not the case. The Regulations clearly provide that gross income under the cash method includes cash, property, or services.[29] Thus, if a CPA accepts a set of golf clubs as payment from a client for services rendered, the CPA must include the fair market value of the golf clubs in his gross income. However, an accounts receivable or other unsupported promise to pay is considered to have no value and, as a result, no income is recognized until the receivable is collected. Expenses are deducted in the year paid. Because the recognition of expense is measured by the flow of cash, a taxpayer can determine the year in which an expense is deductible by choosing when to make the payment. Individual taxpayers do not have the same opportunity to determine the year in which income is recognized, because the constructive receipt rule requires taxpayers to recognize income if a payment is available,

---

[24] Sec. 446(d).

[25] Reg. Sec. 1.446-1(c)(1)(iv)(b).

[26] Reg. Sec. 1.446-1(a)(1). Examples of accounting methods for specific items include Sec. 174, relating to research and experimentation expenses; Sec. 451, relating to reporting income from long-term contracts; and Sec. 453, relating to reporting income from installment sales.

[27] Reg. Sec. 1.471-1. However, Sec. 448(b) permits farmers to use the cash method even though they have inventories. Sec. 448(a) denies tax shelters the right to use the cash method even if they do not have inventories.

[28] Secs. 448(b) and (c).

[29] Reg. Sec. 1.446-1(c)(1)(i).

even if actual payment has not been received. (See Chapter I3 for a discussion of constructive receipt.)

CAPITALIZATION REQUIREMENTS FOR CASH-METHOD TAXPAYERS. Taxpayers who use the cash receipts and disbursements method are required to capitalize fixed assets and to recover the cost through depreciation or amortization. The Regulations state that prepaid expenses must be capitalized and deducted over the life of the asset if the life of the asset extends substantially beyond the end of the tax year.[30] Typically, capitalization is required only if the life of the asset extends beyond the close of the tax year following the year of payment.[31]

EXAMPLE I11-12 ▶

On July 1, 1997, Acme Corporation, a cash basis, calendar-year taxpayer, pays an insurance premium of $3,000 for a policy that is effective July 1, 1997 to June 30, 1998. The full $3,000 is deductible in 1997. ◀

EXAMPLE I11-13 ▶

Assume the same facts as in Example I11-12, except that the premium covers a three-year period beginning July 1, 1997 and ending June 30, 2000. Acme Corporation may deduct $500 in 1997, $1,000 in 1998 and 1999, and $500 in 2000. ◀

One notable exception to the one-year rule denies a deduction for prepaid interest. Cash-method taxpayers must capitalize such amounts and allocate interest over the prepayment period. A special rule allows homeowners to deduct points paid on a mortgage used to buy or improve a personal residence. The payment must be an established business practice in the area and not exceed amounts generally charged for such home loans. (See Chapter I7 for a discussion of the deductibility of points.)

To be deductible, a payment must be more than just a refundable deposit. A taxpayer who has an option of cancelling delivery and receiving a refund of amounts prepaid is not normally entitled to deduct the amount of the deposit.

Payments can be made either by a check that is honored in due course or by the use of a credit card.[32] Payment by credit card is considered to be the equivalent of borrowing funds to pay the expense. However, a taxpayer's note is not the equivalent of cash, so if a cash method taxpayer gives a note in payment, he or she cannot take the deduction until the note is paid, even if the note is secured by collateral.[33]

ACCRUAL METHOD

There are two tests used to determine when an item of income must be reported or an expense deducted: the **all-events test** and the **economic performance test**.

ALL-EVENTS TEST. An accrual-method taxpayer reports an item of income when "all events" have occurred that fix the taxpayer's right to receive the item of income and the amount can be determined with reasonable accuracy.[34] Similarly, an expense is deductible when all events have occurred that establish the fact of the liability and the amount of the expense can be determined with reasonable accuracy. For deductions, the all-events test is not satisfied until economic performance has taken place.

ECONOMIC PERFORMANCE TEST. Economic performance (of services or property to be provided to a taxpayer) occurs when the property or services are actually provided by the other party.

---

[30] Reg. Sec. 1.461-1(a)(1).
[31] *Bonaire Development Co.*, 76 T.C. 789 (1981), and *Martin J. Zaninovich v. CIR*, 45 AFTR 2d 80-1442, 80-1 USTC ¶9342 (9th Cir., 1980).
[32] Rev. Rul. 78-39, 1978-1 C.B. 73.

[33] *Frank D. Quinn Exec. v. CIR*, 24 AFTR 927, 40-1 USTC ¶9403 (5th Cir., 1940).
[34] Reg. Sec. 1.451-1(a). See Chapter I3 for a discussion of the all-events test as it applies to gross income.

EXAMPLE I11-14 ▶ The owner of a professional football team provides medical benefits for injured players through insurance coverage. Economic performance occurs over the term of the policy rather than when the team enters into a binding contract with the insurance company or during the season when the player earns the right to medical benefits. Thus, a one-year premium is deductible over the year of the insurance coverage rather than over the term of the player's contract under which the benefit is earned. ◀

Similarly, if a taxpayer is obligated to provide property or services, economic performance occurs in the year the taxpayer provides the property or service.

EXAMPLE I11-15 ▶ Assume the same facts as in Example I11-14 except that medical benefits are required under the terms of a player's contract. Also, the team decides to pay medical costs directly. Economic performance occurs as the team actually provides the benefits. Thus, the deduction is permitted only as medical care is provided. ◀

The requirement that economic performance take place before a deduction is allowed is waived if all of the following five conditions are met:

▶ The all-events test, without regard to economic performance, is satisfied.

▶ Economic performance occurs within a reasonable period (but in no event more than 8½ months) after the close of the tax year.

▶ The item is recurring in nature, and the taxpayer consistently treats items of the same type as incurred in the tax year in which the all-events test is met.

▶ The taxpayer is not a tax shelter.

▶ Either the amount is not material or the earlier accrual of the item results in a better matching of income and expense.[35]

EXAMPLE I11-16 ▶ To promote sales, Bass Corporation (a used car sales company) offers buyers coupons for three free car washes. Bass purchases the coupons from a local car wash. The coupons must be used within six months after the purchase of an automobile. If Bass uses the cash method, it could deduct the cost of the coupons at the time the payment for the coupons is made to the car wash. Under the accrual method and assuming the five conditions listed above are met, Bass could deduct the cost of the coupons as they are given to buyers (instead of having to wait until the coupons are used by the purchasers). ◀

TYPICAL MISCONCEPTION

It is sometimes mistakenly believed that taxpayers can deduct warranty expenses and bad debts using the allowance method instead of the direct write-off method.

Reserves for items such as product warranty expense are commonly encountered in financial accounting. The all-events and economic performance tests prevent the use of such reserves for tax purposes. This is because the amount of such expense is not usually determinable with sufficient accuracy. Under prior law, taxpayers were permitted to use the allowance method for bad debts, but that method is no longer allowed for tax purposes.

HYBRID METHOD

Taxpayers may use a combination of accounting methods as long as income is clearly reflected.[36] Taxpayers with inventories are required to use the accrual method to report sales and purchases. These taxpayers may use the cash method to report other items of income and expense. To ensure that income is clearly reflected, certain restrictions have been placed on combining accounting methods.

Taxpayers who use the cash method of accounting in determining gross income from a trade or business must use the cash method for determining expenses of the same trade

---

[35] Sec. 461(h). [36] Sec. 446(c).

KEY POINT

A taxpayer who uses the cash method in computing gross income from his or her business must use the cash method in computing expenses of such business.

or business. Similarly, taxpayers who use the accrual method of accounting for expenses must use the accrual method in computing gross income from the trade or business.

The basic rules relating to accounting methods, the all-events test, and economic performance are summarized in Topic Review I11-2.

STOP & THINK

Question: If an accountant does tax work for an automobile dealer, in exchange for free use of an automobile, does the accountant have to report any income? Does it make a difference whether the accountant uses the automobile in her business? When is any taxable income reported?

Solution: The rental value of the automobile must be included in gross income. If the automobile is used in the accountant's business, a portion of the rental value is deductible as a business expense. Although it is not entirely clear, it seems that an accrual basis accountant would report income as tax services are provided to the dealer. A cash basis taxpayer would report income over the time the automobile is used.

INVENTORIES

Manufacturing and merchandising companies are required to use the accrual method of accounting for purchases and sales of merchandise. The inventory method used by a taxpayer must conform to the best accounting practice in the trade or business, and it must clearly reflect income. However, best accounting practices (synonymous with generally accepted accounting principles) and clear reflection of income (which is determined by the IRS) occasionally conflict. The Supreme Court has held that the standard of clear reflection of income prevails in a case where the two standards conflict. In the *Thor Power Tool Co.* case, the company for both tax and financial accounting

Topic Review I11-2

Accounting Methods

Available Methods

▶ Permissible overall accounting methods are the cash receipts and disbursements method, the accrual method, and the hybrid method.

▶ Taxpayers cannot use the cash method in a business for sales and cost of goods sold if inventories are an income-producing factor. C corporations may not use the cash method if their gross receipts in the three preceding tax years equal or exceed $5 million. An exception allows personal service corporations to use the cash method of reporting even if their receipts exceed the $5 million threshold.

All-Events Test and Economic Performance Test

▶ An accrual-method taxpayer reports an item of income when all events have occurred that fix the taxpayer's right to receive the item of income and when the amount of the item can be determined with reasonable accuracy.

▶ An expense is deductible when all events have occurred that establish that there is a liability and when the amount of the expense can be determined with reasonable accuracy. The all-events test is not satisfied until economic performance has taken place.

▶ Economic performance takes place when property or services are actually provided.

OBJECTIVE **3**

Determine whether specific costs must be included in inventory

KEY POINT

Taxpayers cannot always use inventory methods for tax purposes that conform with generally accepted accounting principles.

purposes wrote off the cost of obsolete parts even though they were kept on hand and their selling price was not reduced.[37] Regulation Sec. 1.471-4(b) states that obsolete or other slow-moving inventory cannot be written down unless the selling price is also reduced.

Although the company's practice conformed with generally accepted accounting principles, it did not, according to the Supreme Court, clearly reflect income. Hence, generally accepted accounting principles are used only when the Regulations do not specify the treatment of an item or, alternatively, when the Regulations provide more than one alternative accounting method.

Taxpayers who value inventory at cost may write down goods that are not salable at their normal price (e.g., damaged, obsolete, or shopworn goods) only after the selling price has been reduced. Items may be valued at a bona fide selling price reduced by the direct cost of disposal.[38] The option to write down this type of merchandise is available even if the taxpayers use the LIFO inventory method.

EXAMPLE I11-17 ▶

Stone Corporation publishes books for small academic audiences in Sanskrit and other ancient languages. There is typically one printing of a few hundred or perhaps a thousand copies of each book. Stone may sell a few copies a year of each book. Only after several years can the Corporation determine whether they will ever sell all copies of a given work. Based upon the *Thor Power Tool Co.* case, Stone Corporation cannot write off unsold copies unless they are destroyed or otherwise disposed of, and they cannot write down unsold copies unless the asking price is reduced below cost. ◀

KEY POINT

The uniform capitalization rules, included in the Tax Reform Act of 1986, require the capitalization of significant overhead costs that previously were expensed.

DETERMINATION OF INVENTORY COST

Inventories may be valued at either cost or at the lower of cost or market value. Taxpayers who use the LIFO inventory valuation method (discussed later in this chapter) may not use the lower of cost or market method. In the case of merchandise purchased, cost is the invoice price less trade discounts, plus freight and other handling charges.

Unlike financial accounting, purchasing costs (e.g., salaries of purchasing agents), warehousing costs, packaging, and administrative costs related to these functions must be allocated between cost of goods sold and inventory. This requirement is applicable only to taxpayers whose average gross receipts for the three preceding years exceed $10 million.[39]

ETHICAL POINT

The UNICAP rules must be followed by taxpayers. To bring a business into compliance with these rules, the taxpayer may need to make certain estimates. SRTP No. 4 provides that a CPA may use a client's estimates if such use is generally acceptable or if it is impractical to obtain exact data. If a change in the overhead application rate is contemplated, it may be desirable to request IRS approval.

In the case of goods manufactured by the taxpayer, cost is determined by using the Uniform Capitalization rules (UNICAP), which may be thought of as an expanded version of the full absorption costing method. Thus, direct costing and prime costing are not acceptable inventory methods. Direct labor and materials along with manufacturing overhead must be included in inventory. Under UNICAP, the following overhead items are included in inventory:

▶ Factory repairs and maintenance, utilities, rent, insurance, small tools, and depreciation (including the excess of tax depreciation over accounting depreciation)

▶ Factory administration and officers' salaries related to production

▶ Taxes (other than the income tax)

▶ Quality control and inspection

▶ Rework, scrap, and spoilage

▶ Current and past service costs of pension and profit-sharing plans

▶ Service support such as purchasing, payroll, and warehousing costs

---

[37] *Thor Power Tool Co. v. CIR,* 43 AFTR 2d 79-362, 79-1 USTC ¶9139 (USSC, 1979).

[38] Reg. Sec. 1.471-2(c).

[39] Sec. 263A(b)(2)(B).

Nonmanufacturing costs (e.g., advertising, selling, and research and experimental costs) are not required to be included in inventory. Interest must be inventoried if the property is real property, long-lived property, or property requiring more than two years (one year in the case of property costing more than $1 million) to produce.

The main difference between full absorption costing traditionally used for financial accounting purposes and UNICAP costing required for tax purposes is that UNICAP expands the list of overhead costs to include certain indirect costs that have not always been included in overhead for financial accounting purposes. For example, for financial accounting purposes the costs of operating payroll and personnel departments have sometimes been considered sufficiently indirect or remote to justify omitting them from manufacturing overhead. This is true even though much of the effort of the payroll and personnel departments was directed toward manufacturing operations. For simplicity and other reasons, overhead costs included in inventory for financial purposes are often limited to those incurred in the factory. UNICAP requires that the costs associated with these departments must be allocated between manufacturing and nonmanufacturing functions (e.g., sales, advertising, research and experimentation).

EXAMPLE I11-18 ▶ Best Corporation manufactures traditional style rocking chairs in a small factory with 34 employees. The office staff consists of four employees who handle payroll, receivables, hiring, and other office responsibilities. The sales staff includes three employees who travel the region selling to furniture and craft stores. The remaining 27 employees all work in the factory. Under UNICAP, factory costs including the wages of the 27 factory workers are generally all manufacturing costs. The costs associated with the sales staff are not manufacturing costs. This would include their compensation along with related costs such as travel. Office expenses including the wages paid to the four office workers can be allocated between manufacturing overhead and sales. Reasonable allocation methods are acceptable. One possiblility might be to allocate office overhead between sales and manufacturing on a basis as simple as the number of employees in sales (3) and the number in manufacturing (27). Thus, 90% of the cost of the office operation could be treated as manufacturing-related and 10% sales-related. In such case, 90% of the office expenses would be allocated to inventory cost and 10% deducted as a period cost (i.e., selling expenses). ◀

A manufacturer may use standard costs to value inventory if any significant variance is reallocated pro rata to ending inventory and cost of goods sold.[40] Taxpayers may determine inventory costs by the following methods: specific identification method; first-in, first-out method (FIFO); last-in, first-out method (LIFO); or average cost method. A few taxpayers, such as an automobile or large applicance dealer, may find it practical to determine the specific cost of items in inventory. Most taxpayers, however, must rely on a flow of goods assumption (e.g., FIFO or LIFO). (See Chapter I10 for a more detailed discussion of inventory costs.) A discussion of the LIFO method is presented below.

LIFO METHOD. Many taxpayers use the LIFO cost flow assumption because, during inflationary periods, LIFO normally results in the lowest inventory value and hence the lowest taxable income. Once LIFO has been elected for tax purposes, the taxpayer's financial reports must also be prepared using LIFO.[41] This requirement to conform financial reporting often discourages companies from electing LIFO because lower earnings must be reported to shareholders. However, taxpayers may make footnote disclosure of the amount of net income that would have been reported under FIFO or other inventory methods.[42] Taxpayers may adopt LIFO by attaching a completed Form

---

[40] Reg. Sec. 1.471-11(d)(3).
[41] Sec. 472(c).

[42] Reg. Sec. 1.472-2(e).

970 (or by a statement acceptable to the IRS) to the return for the tax year in which the method is first used.

Recordkeeping under LIFO can be cumbersome. For this reason taxpayers are permitted to determine inventories using "dollar-value" pools and government price indexes rather than by maintaining a record of actual costs.[43] Retailers use appropriate categories in the Consumer Price Index; other taxpayers use categories in the Producer Price Index. Taxpayers using the index method must divide their inventories into one or more pools (groups of similar items). Thus, a department store might create separate pools for automobile parts, appliances, clothing, furniture, and other products. Dividing inventory into pools can be critical because of the different inflation rates associated with various goods and because, if a particular pool is depleted, the taxpayer loses the right to use the lower prices associated with past layers. An important exception permits taxpayers with average annual gross receipts of $5 million or less for the current and two preceding tax years to use the **simplified LIFO method.**[44] The simplified LIFO method uses a single LIFO pool, thereby avoiding problems with multiple pools.

REAL-WORLD EXAMPLE

An automobile dealer, using the dollar-value LIFO method in maintaining its inventory, was required to use one pool for new automobiles and a separate pool for new trucks. *Fox Chevrolet, Inc.,* 76 T.C. 708 (1981).

EXAMPLE I11-19 ▶

In 1997 King Department Store changes its inventory method from FIFO to LIFO. Because King's gross receipts have never exceeded $5 million, the simplified LIFO method is available. King's year-end inventories under FIFO are as follows:

1996	$100,000
1997	$130,000

Assume the 1996 price index is 120% and the 1997 index is 125%. King must convert its 1997 inventory to 1996 prices.

$$\frac{120\%}{125\%} \times \$130,000 = \$124,800$$

A base period inventory of $100,000 is established. The increase in inventory (the 1997 layer) is valued at 1997 prices.

Base inventory (1996)	$100,000
Plus: 1997 layer [(125% ÷ 120%) × ($124,800 − $100,000)]	25,833
1997 ending inventory	$125,833

Assume the 1998 inventory valued under FIFO is $136,000 and the 1998 price index is 130%. The 1998 inventory is converted to 1996 prices.

$$\frac{120\%}{130\%} \times \$136,000 = \$125,538$$

The 1998 increase in inventory (the 1998 layer) is valued at 1998 prices.

Base inventory (1996)	$100,000
1997 layer	25,833
1998 layer	800[a]
1999 ending inventory	$126,633

[a] [(130% ÷ 120%) × ($125,538 − $124,800)]. ◀

LOWER OF COST OR MARKET METHOD. Inventory may be valued at the **lower of cost or market.** This option is available to all taxpayers other than those who determine

---

[43] Sec. 472(f).   [44] Sec. 474(c).

ADDITIONAL COMMENT

For tax purposes the lower of cost or market method must ordinarily be applied to each separate inventory item, but for financial accounting purposes it can be applied using an aggregate approach.

cost using the LIFO method.[45] The term *market* refers to replacement cost. On the date an inventory is valued, the replacement cost of each item in the inventory is compared with its cost. The lower figure is used as the inventory value. The lower of cost or market method must ordinarily be applied to each separate item in the inventory.

Recall the *Thor Power Tool* case (discussed earlier in this chapter) in which the Supreme Court distinguished market value from expected selling price. **Market value** is the price at which the taxpayer can replace the goods in question. Replacement cost is used in the lower of cost or market determination. Obsolete or other slow-moving inventory can be written down below replacement cost only if the selling price has been reduced.

WHAT WOULD YOU DO IN THIS SITUATION?

INVENTORY VALUATION

Jack is a new tax client. He says he and his previous accountant did not get along very well. Jack owns an automobile dealership. He has provided you with most of the information you need to prepare his tax return, but he has not yet given you the year end inventory value. You have completed much of the work on his return, but cannot complete it without the inventory figure. You have called Jack three times and asked about the inventory. Each time he has interrupted, and asked you what his tax liability will be. What problem do you see?

SPECIAL ACCOUNTING METHODS

The term *method of accounting* is used to include not only overall methods of accounting (i.e., cash, accrual, and hybrid) but also the accounting treatment of specific items. Special rules have been established for two types of transactions that cover long time spans. One rule applies to installment sales (a sale in which final payment is not received until a subsequent tax year) and a separate set of rules applies to long-term contracts (construction and similar contracts that are not completed in the same year they are started). These special rules permit taxpayers to report income from this type of transaction when they have the wherewithal to pay the tax (i.e., the year in which payment is received).

LONG-TERM CONTRACTS

OBJECTIVE 4

Determine the amount of income to be reported from a long-term contract

Long-term contracts include building, installation, construction, or manufacturing contracts that are not completed in the same tax year in which they began.[46] A manufacturing contract is long-term only if the contract involves the manufacture of either a unique item not normally carried in finished goods inventory or items that normally require more than 12 calendar months to complete. Contracts for services (architectural, accounting, legal, and so on) do not qualify for long-term contract treatment.[47]

---

[45] Reg. Secs. 1.471-2(b) and (c).
[46] Reg. Sec. 1.451-3(b).
[47] Rev. Proc. 71-21, 1971-2 C.B. 549, does establish rules for service

contracts that extend into the year following the receipt of payment. These rules are discussed in Chapter I3.

EXAMPLE I11-20 ▶ Diamond Corporation manufactures two planes: a small, general aviation plane that requires six months to complete and a large jet aircraft sold to airlines that requires two years to complete. Diamond carries an inventory of the small plane but manufactures the large plane to specification. Diamond can use long-term contract accounting only for the large plane. Assume Diamond also offers aircraft design assistance to the government and others who seek such services. The long-term contract method of accounting is not available for such services. ◀

HISTORICAL NOTE

The use of the completed contract method was severely restricted in the Tax Reform Act of 1986 because Congress found that several large corporations, particularly those with large defense contracts, had significant deferred taxes attributable to this method. Many of these companies had extremely low or negative tax rates for several years.

The accounting method selected by a taxpayer must be used for all long-term contracts in the same trade or business.[48] In general, the income and expenses associated with long-term contracts may be accounted for by using either the **percentage of completion method** or the **modified percentage of completion method**. In limited instances (explained below), taxpayers may use the **completed contract method**. Under the percentage of completion method, income from a project is reported in installments as the work progresses. Under the completed contract method, income from a project is recognized upon completion of the contract. The modified percentage of completion method is a hybrid that combines two methods (discussed below). Alternatively, taxpayers may use any other accounting method (e.g., the accrual method) that clearly reflects income.

ADDITIONAL COMMENT

In general, a construction contract must involve what has historically been thought of as construction which includes erecting buildings, building dams, roads, and power plants.

COSTS SUBJECT TO LONG-TERM CONTRACT RULES. Direct contract costs are subject to the long-term contract rules. Labor, materials, and overhead costs must be allocated to the contract and accounted for accordingly. Thus, under the completed contract method, such costs are capitalized and deducted from revenue in the year the contract is completed. Selling, marketing and advertising expenses, expenses for unsuccessful bids and proposals, and research and development costs not associated with a specific contract may be deducted currently.[49]

In general, administrative overhead must be allocated to long-term contracts. (See the earlier list of overhead items that must be included in inventory.) This is not required of taxpayers (other than homebuilders) using the completed contract method, but as noted below, the use of the completed contract method is limited.[50]

As previously mentioned, interest must be capitalized if the property being produced is real property, long-lived property, or property requiring more than two years (one year in the case of property costing more than $1 million) to produce. Interest costs directly attributable to a contract and those that could have been avoided if contract costs had not been incurred must be allocated to long-term contracts.

COMPLETED CONTRACT METHOD. Under the completed contract method of accounting, income from a contract is reported in the taxable year in which the contract is completed. This is true without regard to whether the contract price is collected in advance, upon completion of the contract, or in installments. Costs associated with the contract are accumulated in a work-in-progress account and deducted upon completion. The courts are in conflict with regard to determining when a contract is completed. Some courts have required total completion and acceptance of the contract.[51] Other courts have held the contract to have been completed when the only work remaining consists of correcting minor defects or furnishing incidental parts.[52]

---

[48] Reg. Sec. 1.451-3(a)(1).
[49] Sec. 460(c)(4).
[50] Sec. 460(e)(1).
[51] *E. E. Black Limited v. Alsup*, 45 AFTR 1345, 54-1 USTC ¶9340 (9th Cir.,

1954), and *Thompson-King-Tate, Inc. v. U.S.*, 8 AFTR 2d 5920, 62-1 USTC ¶9116 (6th Cir., 1961).
[52] *Ehret-Day Co.*, 2 T.C. 25 (1943), and *Nathan Wohlfeld*, 1958 PH T.C. Memo ¶58,128, 17 TCM 677.

The use of the completed contract method is severely restricted in two situations. The method can be used by smaller companies (those whose average gross receipts for the three preceding tax years is $10 million or less) for construction contracts that are expected to take two years or less to complete and other taxpayers for home construction contracts.[53] It cannot be used by larger companies for manufacturing, or for other long-term contracts other than construction or for construction contracts expected to last longer than two years.

PERCENTAGE OF COMPLETION METHOD. Under the percentage of completion method of reporting income, the taxpayer reports a percentage of the gross income from a long-term contract based on the portion of work that has been completed. The portion of the total contract price reported in a given year is determined by multiplying the total contract price by the percentage of work completed in the year. The percentage is determined by dividing current year costs by the expected total costs.

MODIFIED PERCENTAGE OF COMPLETION METHOD. At the beginning of a contract, it is difficult to estimate total costs. For this reason, taxpayers may elect to defer reporting any income from a contract until they have incurred at least 10% of the estimated total cost.[54] This is called the modified percentage of completion method. Under this method, if a contract has just been started as of the end of the year, the taxpayer does not have to estimate the profit on the contract during that year. The next year the taxpayer will report profit on all work that has been completed, including work done during the first year. Of course, this assumes that at least 10% of the work has been completed as of the end of the taxable year. If more than 10% of the costs are incurred during the first year, the modified percentage of completion method is identical to the regular percentage of completion method.

The completed contract method, the percentage of completion method, and the modified percentage of completion method are compared in Example I11-21.

KEY POINT

In general, taxpayers with long-term contracts must compute income under the percentage of completion method for contracts entered into after July 10, 1989.

KEY POINT

After a taxpayer has adopted an accounting method for long-term contracts, he or she must continue to use that method unless permission to change methods is granted.

EXAMPLE I11-21 ▶

In 1997, a contractor enters into a contract to construct a bridge for $1,400,000. At the outset, the contractor estimates that it will cost $1,200,000 to build the bridge. Actual costs in 1997 are $540,000 (45% of the $1,200,000 total estimated costs). Actual costs in 1998 are less than expected and total $600,000. The profits reported in both years of the contract are illustrated below.

	1997	*1998*
Completed contract		
Revenue	0	$1,400,000
Costs incurred	0	(1,140,000)
Gross profit	0	$ 260,000
Percentage of completion		
Revenue	$630,000[a]	$ 770,000[b]
Costs incurred	(540,000)	(600,000)
Gross profit	$ 90,000	$ 170,000

[a] 0.45 × $1,400,000 = $630,000.
[b] $1,400,000 − $630,000 = $770,000.

◀

---

[53] Sec. 460(e).

[54] Sec. 460(a).

In Example I11-21, the modified percentage of completion method results in the same income being reported each year as the percentage of completion method because more than 10% of the estimated costs were incurred during the first year. Note that the completed contract method defers reporting income until the contract is completed, causing all income from the project to be reported in a single year. Thus, the tax is deferred but the taxpayer may end up being taxed at higher rates. As noted, the completed contract is available only for home construction contracts and to certain smaller contractors for projects of two years or less.

LOOK-BACK INTEREST. Certain contracts (or portions of a contract) accounted for under either the regular or modified percentage of completion method are subject to a **look-back interest** adjustment. When a contract is completed, a computation is made to determine whether the tax paid each year during the contract is more or less than the tax that would have been paid if the actual total cost of the contract had been used rather than the estimated cost.[55] Interest is paid on any additional tax that would have been paid. The taxpayer receives interest on any additional tax that was paid.

Look-back interest is applicable only to contracts completed more than two years after the commencement date. Furthermore, look-back interest is applicable only if the contract price equals or exceeds either 1% of the taxpayer's average gross receipts for the three taxable years preceding the taxable year the contract was entered into or $1 million.[56]

EXAMPLE I11-22 The contractor in Example I11-21 is exempt from the look-back rule because the contract is completed within two years after the commencement date. On the other hand, if the contract took more than two years to complete, interest would be owed on the underpaid taxes for the first and subsequent contract years. The underreported income for the first year would be $33,158 [($260,000 profit × $540,000 first year's costs ÷ $1,140,000 total costs) − $90,000 first year reported income]. Assuming a 35% tax bracket, the underpaid tax for the first year is $11,605. Upon completion of the contract, interest would be paid on this amount and underpaid taxes for other years. ◀

INSTALLMENT SALES METHOD

OBJECTIVE 5

Compute the gain to be reported from an installment sale

KEY POINT

The installment sales method allows either a cash or an accrual method taxpayer to spread the gain from the sale of property over the period during which payments are received.

In general, the gain or loss from the sale of property is reported in the year the property is sold. If the sales proceeds are collected in years after the sale, the taxpayer may find it difficult to pay the tax on the entire amount of the gain in the year of sale. To reduce the burden, the tax law permits taxpayers to spread the gain from installment sales over the collection period. The installment method is applicable only to gains and is used to report income from an installment transaction unless the taxpayer elects not to use the installment method.[57] An **installment sale** is any disposition of property where at least one payment is received after the close of the taxable year in which the disposition occurs.[58] The installment method is not applicable to sales of:

▶ inventory by dealers[59]

▶ publicly traded property (e.g., stock listed on an exchange).

COMPUTATIONS UNDER SEC. 453. Income under the installment sales method is computed as follows:

---

[55] Sec. 460(b)(3).
[56] Sec. 460(b)(3).
[57] Sec. 453(d).
[58] Sec. 453(b)(1).
[59] Sec. 453(b)(2)(A). Exceptions permit the use of the installment method for

sales of residential lots, timeshares, and property used or produced in the business of farming [Sec. 453(l)(2)]. Taxpayers who use the installment method in connection with the sale of residential lots and timeshares, however, must agree to pay interest to the government on the amount of deferred tax attributable to the use of the installment method.

STEP 1: Compute the gross profit from the sale.

Selling price	$xx,xxx
Minus: Adjusted basis	(x,xxx)
Selling expenses	(x,xxx)
Depreciation recapture[60]	(x,xxx)
Gross profit	$ x,xxx

STEP 2: Determine the contract price.

Contract price (greater of the gross profit from above or the selling price reduced by any existing mortgage assumed or acquired by the purchaser)	$xx,xxx

STEP 3: Compute the gross profit percentage.

$$\text{Gross profit percentage} = \frac{\text{Gross profit}}{\text{Contract price}} = xx\%$$

STEP 4: Compute the gain to be reported in the year of sale.

Collections of principal received during year (exclusive of interest)	$xx,xxx
Plus: Excess mortgage (if any)[a]	x,xxx
Total	$xx,xxx
Times: Gross profit percentage	× xx%
Net gain recognized in year of sale	$ x,xxx
Plus: Depreciation recapture	x,xxx
Gain reported in year of sale	$ x,xxx

STEP 5: Compute the gain to be reported in subsequent years.

Collections of principal received	$ x,xxx
Times: Gross profit percent	× xx%
Gain reported in each of the subsequent years	$ x,xxx

[a] Mortgage − Basis − Selling expense − Depreciation recapture = Excess mortgage.

Note that depreciation recapture (see Chapter I13) must be reported in the year of the sale even if no payment is received.

EXAMPLE I11-23 ▶ Gina, a cash basis taxpayer, sells equipment for $200,000. The equipment originally cost $70,000, and $10,000 of MACRS depreciation has been deducted before the sale. The $10,000 of depreciation must be recaptured as ordinary income under Sec. 1245. The buyer assumes the existing mortgage of $50,000, pays $10,000 down, and agrees to pay $10,000 per year for 14 years plus interest at a rate acceptable to the IRS. Selling expenses are $13,000. Using the steps listed above, calculations are made as follows:

STEP 1: Compute the gross profit from the sale.

Selling price	$200,000
Minus: Adjusted basis	(60,000)
Selling expenses	(13,000)
Depreciation recapture	(10,000)
Gross profit	$117,000

---

[60] For a discussion of depreciation recapture, see Chapter I13.

STEP 2:   Determine the contract price.

Greater of gross profit of $117,000 or selling price
minus mortgage assumed by purchaser ($150,000
= $200,000 − $50,000) $150,000

STEP 3:   Compute the gross profit percentage.

$$\frac{\text{Gross profit}}{\text{percentage}} = \frac{\text{Gross profit (\$117,000)}}{\text{Contract price (\$150,000)}} = 78\%$$

STEP 4:   Compute the gain to be reported in the year of sale.

Principal received during year	$ 10,000
Plus: Excess mortgage	0
Total amount realized	$ 10,000
Times: Gross profit percentage	× 0.78
Gross profit	$ 7,800
Plus: Depreciation recapture	10,000
Gain reported in year of sale	$ 17,800

STEP 5:   Compute the gain to be reported in subsequent years.

Principal received	$ 10,000
Times: Gross profit percentage	× 0.78
Gain reported in each subsequent year	$ 7,800

Thus, the total gain reported is $127,000 [$17,800 + ($7,800 × 14)]. This is equal to the gross profit of $117,000 (which is the amount of Sec. 1231 gain reported on the sale) plus the $10,000 of depreciation recapture. As a cash basis taxpayer Gina will report the interest income as it is collected. See Figure I11-1 which illustrates this computation on Form 6252, Installment Sale Income. ◄

REAL-WORLD EXAMPLE

When an installment obligation is assigned as collateral for a loan, the transaction is treated as a disposition of the obligation. Rev. Rul. 65-185, 1965-2 C.B. 153.

DISPOSITION OF INSTALLMENT OBLIGATIONS. A taxpayer who sells property on the installment basis may decide not to hold the obligation until maturity. For example, the holder may sell the obligation to a financial institution for the purpose of raising cash. Alternatively, the holder may not be able to collect the full amount of the installments because of the inability of the buyer to make payments. Thus, the holder must determine the adjusted basis of the obligation in order to compute the gain or loss realized on the disposition. The adjusted basis of an installment obligation is equal to the face amount of the obligation reduced by the gross profit that would be realized if the holder collects the face amount of the obligation. In general, this means the adjusted basis of an obligation is equal to

Face amount × (100% − Gross profit percentage)

EXAMPLE I11-24 ▶   Assume the same facts as in Example I11-23 except that Gina immediately sells a single $10,000 installment to a bank for $9,700. Gina reports a gain of $7,500 computed as follows:

Selling price	$9,700
Minus: Adjusted basis of installment	(2,200)[a]
Recognized gain	$7,500

[a] $10,000 face amount × (100% − 78% gross profit percentage) = $2,200

Gina would have reported a gain of $7,800 had she decided not to sell the installment but to collect the face amount. Because the obligation is discounted by $300 ($10,000 − $9,700), the reported gain is reduced by $300. If the installment had not been sold immediately, the bank would probably also pay to Gina an amount for the accrued interest. In such a situation Gina would report the gain from the sale and the accrued interest as income. ◄

EXAMPLE I11-25 ▶

Assume that Gina in Example I11-24 is unable to collect the final $10,000 installment because the individual who purchases the property declares bankruptcy. Gina would be entitled to a bad debt deduction of $2,200, the basis of the installment. Gina does not receive a bad debt deduction for the accrued interest because the interest has not been included in her gross income. ◄

KEY POINT

A donor of property does not normally recognize gain, but a gift of certain installment obligations causes the recognition of gain.

Certain dispositions of installment obligations, including giving them as gifts, are taxable events.[61] The main objective of this rule is to prevent income from being shifted from one taxpayer to another. Thus, if a corporation distributes an installment obligation as a dividend or if a father gives his daughter an installment obligation, gain or loss is recognized. In general, the gain or loss recognized is equal to the difference between the FMV of the obligation and its adjusted basis. In the case of a gift, the gain recognized is equal to the difference between the face of the obligation and its adjusted basis. However, certain exceptions to this rule exist. Transfers to controlled corporations under Sec. 351, certain corporate reorganizations and liquidations, transfers on the taxpayer's death, transfers incident to divorce, distributions by partnerships, and contributions of capital to a partnership are exceptions to this rule. In these cases, the recipients of the obligations report income when the installments are collected.[62]

REPOSSESSIONS OF PROPERTY SOLD ON THE INSTALLMENT BASIS. In general, the repossession of property sold on the installment basis is a taxable event. The gain or loss recognized is generally equal to the difference between the value of the repossessed property (reduced by any costs incurred as a result of the repossession) and the adjusted basis of any remaining installment obligations.

EXAMPLE I11-26 ▶

Yuji sells stock of a non–publicly traded corporation with a $7,000 adjusted basis for $10,000. Yuji receives a $1,000 down payment, and the balance of $9,000 is due the following year. In the year of the sale Yuji reports a capital gain of $300 (0.30 × $1,000) under the installment method of accounting. Yuji is unable to collect the $9,000 note, and after incurring legal fees of $500, he repossesses the stock. When Yuji repossesses the stock it is worth $8,700. The adjusted basis of the note is $6,300 (0.70 × $9,000). Yuji must report a capital gain of $1,900 ($8,700 − $500 − $6,300). The basis of the stock to Yuji is its FMV at the time it is repossessed ($8,700). ◄

The amount of gain recognized from the repossession of real property is limited to the lesser of (1) the gross profit in the remaining installments reduced by the costs incurred as a result of the repossession or (2) the cash and FMV of other property received from the buyer in excess of the gain previously recognized.[63] In the case of the repossession of either real or personal property, the gain or loss retains the same character as the gain or loss on the original sale.

EXAMPLE I11-27 ▶

Assume the same facts as in Example I11-26, except that the property sold is land. Yuji reports a capital gain of $700, which is the lesser of $2,200 [(0.30 × $9,000)− $500] or $700 ($1,000 − $300). The basis of the land is $7,500 [$9,000 − (0.30 × $9,000) unrealized profit + $700 gain previously recognized + $500 legal fees]. ◄

---

[61] Sec. 453B(a).
[62] Sec. 453B.

[63] Sec. 1038.

INSTALLMENT SALES FOR MORE THAN $150,000. Special rules apply to non-dealers who sell property for more than $150,000. The special rules do not apply to sales of personal use property, to sales of property used or produced in the trade or business of farming, or to sales of timeshares or residential lots.

First, if the taxpayer borrows funds using the installment obligations as security, the amount borrowed is treated as a payment received on the installment obligation.[64] This prevents the taxpayer from using the installment method to defer tax and yet obtain cash by borrowing against the installment obligation. Second, if the installment method is used, interest must be paid to the government on the deferred tax.[65] This rule, however, applies only to deferred principal payments over $5 million.[66]

INSTALLMENT SALES BETWEEN RELATED PERSONS. Installment sales between related persons are subject to the same rules as other installment sales except when the property is resold by the related purchaser. The primary purpose of the resale rule is to prevent the original owner from deferring gain recognition by selling the property to a related person who, in turn, resells the property.

Sec 453(e) requires the first seller to treat amounts received by the related person (second seller) as having been personally received. Thus, the first seller would be required to report the gain in the year (or years) in which proceeds are received by the second seller. This acceleration provision is applicable only if the resale takes place within two years of the initial sale. For purposes of Sec. 453(e), the term *related person* includes a spouse, children, grandchildren, and parents. Controlled corporations, partnerships, estates, and trusts are also covered.

DEFERRED PAYMENT SALES

The installment sale rules are not applicable to all sales involving future payments. The installment method cannot be used when the sale of property produces a loss. Also a taxpayer can elect out of the installment method when a sale results in a gain. How these transactions are reported depends on the taxpayer's accounting method. For accrual method taxpayers, the total *amount receivable* from the buyer (exclusive of interest) is treated as part of the amount realized. Thus, the entire gain or loss is reported in the year of sale. For cash method taxpayers, the FMV of the installment obligation is treated as part of the amount realized in the year of sale. The amount realized, however, cannot be considered to be less than the FMV of the property sold minus any other consideration received (e.g., cash).[67]

EXAMPLE I11-28 ▶ USA Corporation, an accrual method taxpayer, sells land for $100,000. USA receives $50,000 down and a $50,000 note payable in 12 months plus 14% interest. Assume the basis of the land is $80,000 and that it is a capital asset. Because of the buyer's poor credit, the value of the note is only $45,000. USA affirmatively elects not to report the installment sale on the installment method. USA reports a capital gain of $20,000 ($100,000 − $80,000). If USA collects the face of the note at maturity, no additional gain or loss is recognized. If USA sells the note for $45,000, a $5,000 capital loss is recognized. ◀

EXAMPLE I11-29 ▶ Assume the same facts as in Example I11-28, except that USA is a cash method taxpayer. If the FMV of the land is $100,000 (the stated selling price), the treatment of the transaction is exactly the same as it is using the accrual method. If the FMV of the land is assumed to be $95,000 (cash received plus FMV of the note received), USA recognizes a $15,000 ($95,000 − $80,000) capital gain in the year of the sale. If USA collects the face of the note at maturity, $5,000 of ordinary income is recognized. If USA sells the note for $45,000, no gain or loss is recognized. ◀

---

[64] Sec. 453A(d).
[65] The interest computation is described in Sec. 453A(c).

[66] Sec. 453A(b)(2)(B).
[67] Temp. Reg. Sec. 15A.453-1(d)(2)(ii)(A).

ADDITIONAL COMMENT

A contingent payment sale is a sale or other disposition of property in which the aggregate selling price cannot be determined by the close of the tax year in which the sale took place.

INDETERMINATE MARKET VALUE. In certain transactions, the value of obligations received cannot be determined (e.g., a mineral interest is sold for an amount equal to 10% of the value of future production). Under the Regulations, the value of obligations with an **indeterminate market value** is assumed to be no lower than the value of the property sold less the value of other property received.[68] Hence, if the value of property sold is determinable, the recognized gain equals the excess of the value of the property sold over its basis. On occasion, however, neither the value of the obligation received nor the value of property sold can be determined.

Temporary regulations specify how these types of transactions are to be treated.[69] The basic rules relating to special accounting methods are summarized in Topic Review I11-3.

IMPUTED INTEREST

OBJECTIVE 6

Compute the amount of imputed interest in a transaction

Before the enactment of Sec. 1274 and the amendment of Sec. 483, property could be sold on an installment basis in a contract providing for little or no interest. Instead of charging interest, the seller charged a higher price for the property. If the property sold was a capital asset, the result of the arrangement was to reduce the interest income reported by the seller and to increase the amount of favorably taxed capital gain. Sections 483 and 1274 now *impute* interest in a deferred payment contract

Topic Review I11-3

Special Accounting Methods

Long-Term Contracts

▶ Long-term contracts include building, installation, construction, or manufacturing contracts that are not completed in the same tax year in which they are entered into. A manufacturing contract is long-term only if the contract involves the manufacture of either a unique item not normally carried in inventory or an item that normally requires more than 12 calendar months to complete.

▶ Long-term contracts may be reported under the regular or the modified percentage of completion method. Under both methods income is reported as work is completed, except that under the modified percentage of completion method no income is reported until at least 10% of the work is completed.

▶ The completed contract method is available only for home construction contracts, for construction contracts expected to take two years or less to complete, and for use by smaller companies (those whose average gross receipts for the three preceding tax years are $10 million or less).

Installment Method

▶ Under the installment method gain is reported as the sales proceeds are collected. The installment method is generally not available for sales of inventory or publicly traded property. Furthermore, the method is available only for gains.

▶ Gain is reported as sales proceeds are collected. However, both depreciation recapture and any mortgage in excess of basis must be reported in the year of sale. Gain recognition is also accelerated in certain situations if the seller borrows against the installment obligation or if a related buyer resells the property within two years.

---

[68] Reg. Sec. 1.453-1(d)(3)(iii).   [69] Temp. Reg. Sec. 15A.453-1(c).

where no interest or a low rate of interest is provided. Another impact of the **imputed interest rules** on sellers is to reallocate payments received between interest (which is fully taxable) and principal (only the gain portion of which is taxable). The result is often an increase in the income reported in early years and a decrease in later years. The rules are generally applicable to both buyers and sellers. In certain instances, the buyer may want interest to be imputed in order to increase his interest deduction in early years.

The following transactions are exempt from the rules:

▶ Debt subject to original issue discount provisions (basically bonds issued for less than face where amortization of the discount is required under Sec. 1274, see Chapter I5)

▶ Sales of property for $3,000 or less

▶ Any sales where all of the payments are due within six months

▶ Sales of patents to the extent the payment is contingent on the use or disposition of the patent

▶ Certain carrying charges for personal property or educational services covered by Sec. 163(b) when the interest charge cannot be ascertained

▶ Charges for the purchase of personal-use property (purchaser only)[70]

EXAMPLE I11-30 ▶

Joan is involved in several transactions during the current year. No interest is stated on any of the transactions. The terms of the transactions and the applicability of the imputed interest rules are summarized below:

Transaction	Imputation of Interest
Purchases furniture costing $8,000 for her residence. Full price is payable within four months.	Not applicable because property is for personal use. Also, all payments are due within six months.
Sells a boat for $2,000. Payment is due in a year.	Not applicable because sales price is not more than $3,000.

Transaction	Imputation of Interest
Sells land for $100,000. Payment is due in five years.	Interest must be imputed because no exception is applicable.
Purchases a newly issued bond for $650 (face of $1,000).	Not applicable because transaction is subject to the original issue discount rules in Sec. 1274. Also, the price is not more than $3,000. ◀

IMPUTED INTEREST COMPUTATION

In order to avoid the imputation of interest, the stated interest rate must be at least equal to 100% of the applicable federal rate (110% of the applicable federal rate in the case of sale–lease back arrangements). Lower rates are specified for two types of transactions: (1) If the stated principal amount for qualified debt obligations that are issued in exchange for property under Sec. 1274A does not exceed $2,800,000, the interest rate is limited to 9% compounded semiannually; and (2) the interest rate is limited to 6% compounded

---

[70] Sec. 483(d). The rule lowers the basis of a personal-use asset in order to increase any gain on the future sale of the property.

semiannually in the case of sales of land between related individuals (unless the sales price exceeds $500,000).

The **applicable federal rate** is determined monthly and is based on the rate paid by the federal government on borrowed funds. The rate varies with the terms of the loan. Loans are divided into short-term (not over three years), mid-term (over three years but not over nine years), and long-term (over nine years).

EXAMPLE I11-31 ▶

Kasi sells land for $100,000 to Bill, an unrelated person. The sales price is to be paid to Kasi at the end of five years in a single installment with no stated interest. Kasi paid $60,000 for the land. Assume the current federal rate is 10%. Because the amount of the stated principal is less than $2,800,000, interest is imputed at a rate not to exceed 9% compounded semiannually. As a result, the effective rate is 9.2025% (9% compounded semiannually), and the present value factor is .64393 (1 ÷ 1.092025^5). Thus, the present value of the final payment is $64,393 (0.64393 × $100,000). Kasi reports a $4,393 ($64,393 − $60,000) gain on the sale of the land and $35,607 ($100,000 − $64,393) interest income instead of a $40,000 gain and no interest income. The buyer is treated as incurring $35,607 in interest and has a $64,393 basis in the land. Whether the interest is deductible depends on a variety of other factors (see Chapter I7). ◀

ACCRUAL OF INTEREST

ADDITIONAL COMMENT

The $2,000,000 limit on the stated principal is subject to inflation adjustments for calendar years beginning after 1989.

Is imputed interest reported under the cash or the accrual method? In other words, is imputed interest reported when it accrues or when it is paid? In general, imputed interest is reported as it accrues. However, there are some major exceptions, as follows:

▶ Sales of personal residences

▶ Most sales of farms for $1,000,000 or less

▶ Sales involving aggregate payments of $250,000 or less

▶ Sales of land between related persons unless the sales price exceeds $500,000[71]

In addition, if the borrower and lender jointly elect, and if the stated principal does not exceed $2,000,000, accrual of interest is not required. This election is not available if the lender is an accrual method taxpayer or a dealer with respect to the property sold or exchanged.[72]

EXAMPLE I11-32 ▶

Assume the same facts as in Example I11-31. Because the aggregate payments do not exceed $250,000, the transaction is exempt from the requirement that interest be accrued. As a result, Kasi reports interest income and Bill reports interest expense in the fifth year when the final payment is made on the transaction. Under the installment method, $4,393 gain on the sale is recognized in the fifth year. ◀

GIFT, SHAREHOLDER, AND OTHER LOANS

Imputed interest rules are not limited to installment transactions. Sec. 7872 applies to transactions involving related parties whose taxes are lowered as a result of low interest or interest-free loans. These situations include

▶ *Gift loans.* For example, parents in higher tax brackets may loan money to their children without charging interest. If the children invest the borrowed money and are taxed on the income at a lower rate, the family has reduced its total tax liability in the absence of imputed interest rules.

▶ *Corporation shareholder loans.* In the absence of imputed interest rules, taxes may be saved by a corporation that makes an interest-free loan to a shareholder. If the corporation had invested the money and paid out the resulting income as a dividend,

---

[71] Sec. 1274(c)(4).   [72] Sec. 1274A(c).

it would have first been taxed on the profit. By making the interest-free loan, the corporation could, in the absence of imputed interest rules, reduce its taxes by avoiding the otherwise taxable income.

▶ *Compensation-related loans.* Employers may loan money to employees without charging interest. Without the requirement to impute interest, this could produce tax savings if the employer was unable to deduct additional compensation because of the reasonable compensation limitation or if the employee was unable to deduct the interest, say, because the borrowed funds were used to purchase personal use property.

▶ *Other tax avoidance loans.* Any other low-interest or interest-free loan that produces tax savings may be subject to the imputed interest rules. For example, a club may offer its members a choice of either paying dues or making a large refundable deposit. The club can invest the money and earn interest perhaps equal to the dues. In the absence of imputed interest rules, the member avoids taxes by not having to report the income that would have been earned if the member personally invested the funds. The club is indifferent between the alternatives because both the dues and the interest income are taxable.

In general, interest is imputed on the above loans by applying the applicable federal rates discussed earlier. The resulting interest income is taxable to the lender. Whether the interest expense is deductible by the borrower is determined by applying the usual interest deduction rules (see Chapter I7).

The imputation process involves a second step. The lender is treated as returning the imputed interest to the borrower. This is necessary because the interest was not actually paid. For example, in the case of a gift loan, the lender is treated as giving the imputed interest back to the borrower. This would not normally have income tax implications, but if the imputed interest were large enough, it could result in a gift tax. In the case of the corporation-shareholder loan, the corporation is treated as paying the imputed interest back to the shareholder as a dividend. Typically, this does not increase the corporation's tax, but it results in the recognition of dividend income to the shareholder. For compensation-related loans, the second step is to impute compensation paid by the employer and received by the employee. The compensation is taxable to the employee and, if reasonable in amount, is deductible by the employer.

There are several important exceptions intended to limit the application of imputed interest in situations where tax avoidance may be immaterial:

▶ Interest is not imputed on gift loans between two individuals totaling $10,000 or less, except when the borrowed funds are used to purchase income-producing property.

▶ If the gift loans between two individuals total $100,000 or less, the imputed interest is limited to the borrower's "net investment income" as defined by Sec. 163(d)(4). (See Chapter I7 for a discussion of net investment income). If the net investment income is $1,000 or less, it is not necessary to impute interest.

▶ Interest is not imputed on compensation-related and corporate shareholder loans totaling $10,000 or less.

These exceptions do not apply when tax avoidance is one of the principal purposes of the loans.

EXAMPLE I11-33 ▶ Linda made interest-free gift loans to each of her four children: Andy, Bob, Cathy, and Donna. Andy borrowed $9,000 to purchase an automobile. Bob borrowed $25,000 to buy stock. Bob's net investment income is $800. Cathy also borrowed $25,000 to buy stock, but her net investment income is $1,100. Donna borrowed $120,000 to purchase a residence, and her net investment income is $500. Tax avoidance is not a motive for any of the loans. Imputation of interest is not required for the loans to Andy or Bob. The loan to Andy is exempt because the amount is less than $10,000, and the loan to Bob is exempt because his net investment

Topic Review I11-4

Imputed Interest

Purpose

The imputed interest rules are intended to prevent taxpayers from reducing their taxes by charging little or no interest on installment payment transactions and loans.

Applies to

In most cases applies to both parties, the debtor and the creditor. The result is to impute interest income to the lender and interest expense to the borrower. Several exceptions exempt small transactions from imputed interest. For example, sales involving payments of $3,000 or less are generally exempt as are loans of less than $10,000.

Rate

Interest is imputed at the applicable federal rate if the stated interest rate is lower. The applicable federal rate is the rate the federal government pays on borrowed funds and is determined monthly. In general, the current rate at the time of the transaction is used throughout the term of the loan. The rate varies with the term of the loan. Loans are divided into short-term (not over three years), mid-term (over three years but not over nine years), and long-term (over nine years).

income is under $1,000. Imputation of interest is required for the loans to Cathy and Donna. In the case of Cathy, the amount of imputed interest is limited to her net investment income of $1,100. The imputed interest for Donna, however, is not limited to her net investment income because the amount of the loan is over $100,000.   ◄

The imputed interest rules are summarized in Topic Review I11-4.

CHANGE IN ACCOUNTING METHODS

In general, a new taxpayer elects an accounting method by simply applying the selected method when computing income for the initial tax return.[73] If a particular item does not occur in the first year, the accounting method is elected the first year in which the item occurs.

EXAMPLE I11-34 ▶

OBJECTIVE 7

Determine the tax treatment of duplications and omissions that result from changes of accounting methods

Gordon opened a beauty shop several years ago. Because he had no inventory, no inventory method was selected. In the current year, Gordon expanded his business to offer beauty supplies to his customers. Gordon can delay electing the FIFO inventory method until the current year, the first year in which he has an inventory.   ◄

In general, once an accounting method is chosen, it cannot be changed without IRS approval. There are a few exceptions. For example, taxpayers may adopt the LIFO inventory method without prior IRS approval.[74] Once such methods are adopted, however, they cannot be changed without IRS approval.

---

[73] Reg. Sec. 1.446-1(e)(1).
[74] A taxpayer may adopt LIFO by merely determining year-end inventory by that method and attaching Form 970 to the tax return for the year (Reg. Sec. 1.472-3(a)).

REAL-WORLD EXAMPLE

The write-down of soil aggregate to its market value by a paving company was a change in accounting method rather than the mere correction of an accounting error. The soil aggregate was included in its election to adopt the LIFO inventory method, and the use of this method required that the soil aggregate be included at cost regardless of market value. *First National Bank of Gainesville, Trustee*, 88 T.C. 1069 (1987).

REAL-WORLD EXAMPLE

An extension of time to file the application for change of accounting method was granted because of the death of the accountant in charge of filing the application. Rev. Rul. 79-417, 1979-2 C.B. 202.

As previously noted, the term *accounting method* indicates not only the overall accounting method used by the taxpayer, but also the treatment of any item of income or deduction.[75] A change of accounting methods should not be confused with the correction of an error. Errors include mathematical mistakes, posting errors, deductions of the wrong amount for an expense, omission of an item of taxable income, or incorrect computation of a credit. An error is normally corrected by filing an amended return for the tax year or years in which the error occurs. In general, there is a three-year statute of limitations on the correction of errors. After three years, the tax year is closed and changes cannot be made.[76]

Taxpayers wishing to change accounting methods must pay a $500 fee and file Form 3115 with the IRS during the first 180 days of the tax year in which the change is made.[77] The deadline may be extended to nine months if good cause can be shown for the delay. For the change to be approved, the proposed method must, in the opinion of the IRS, clearly reflect income. Permission is required even if the taxpayer has been using an erroneous method of accounting. For example, the use of prime costing to compute inventory is an erroneous accounting method because manufacturing overhead must be included in the valuation of inventories. Thus, a change from prime costing to "full absorption costing" requires the permission of the IRS, even though the method has been erroneously applied. The IRS can, however, require a taxpayer to change accounting methods if the method that has been used does not clearly reflect income, even if the taxpayer does not propose the change. The authority to require a taxpayer to adopt any accounting method necessary to clearly reflect income does not include the authority to require an arbitrary change. If the accounting methods used by a taxpayer clearly reflect income, the IRS cannot require a change to another method that would also clearly reflect income.

AMOUNT OF CHANGE

A change in accounting methods usually results in duplications or omissions of items of income or expense.

EXAMPLE I11-35 ▶

Bonnie, a practicing CPA, has been reporting income using the cash method. In the current year, Bonnie obtains permission to change to the accrual method. At the beginning of the current year, Bonnie has $80,000 of receivables that have not been reported in prior years. The receivables were not reported in prior years because they were not collected. Although the receivables are collected in the current year, they are not taxable because, under the accrual method, Bonnie now reports income as it is earned and the income is not earned in the current year. In this case, the income was earned in prior years.

Also, assume Bonnie has accounts payable of $15,000 at the beginning of the current year. The accounts payable were not deducted in prior years because the expenses had not been paid. Furthermore, the accounts payable are not deductible in the current year even if they are paid. This is because the expenses were incurred in prior years. Obviously, the IRS expects to collect the tax on the $80,000 of receivables, and Bonnie is entitled to deduct the $15,000 of payables. In the absence of any special provision, both amounts would be omitted from the computation of taxable income. If the change is from the accrual method to the cash method, both amounts would be reported twice (in the year prior to the change because they had accrued and in the year of the change because they are collected or paid). Thus, a special provision is also needed for duplications. ◀

---

[75] Reg. Sec. 1.446-1(e)(2)(ii)(b).
[76] Exceptions are applicable when the taxpayer omits from the return an amount of income that is over 25% of the gross income stated on the return

(6 years) or where fraud occurs (no limitation).
[77] Reg. Sec. 1.446-1(e)(3).

REPORTING THE AMOUNT OF THE CHANGE

The net amount of the change must be taken into account.[78] A positive adjustment is added to income, whereas a negative adjustment is subtracted from income. This adjustment can, of course, be made in the year of the change. If the amount is small, recognizing the full amount of the net adjustment in the year of the change is both simple and equitable. Reporting a large positive adjustment in one year could push the taxpayer into a higher marginal tax bracket and result in a significant tax increase. Because the extra income is due to changing accounting methods, not increasing cash flows, the taxpayer may not have the wherewithal to pay the additional tax.

As a result, there are alternative methods that may be used to report the amount of the change. The alternative methods all have one thing in common: They spread the amount of the change over a period of more than one year. The spread may be over the current and prior tax years or the current and future tax years. The methods that are available depend on whether the change is voluntary (a change that is initiated by the taxpayer) or involuntary (a change from an unacceptable to an acceptable method that is required by the IRS).

REAL-WORLD EXAMPLE

A trucking company had been inventorying its used trailers at a cost of $1 per trailer. The change to a policy of inventorying the used trailers on the basis of lower of cost or market was an involuntary change from an unacceptable to an acceptable method that was required by the IRS. *Fruehauf Trailer Co.*, 42 T.C. 83 (1966).

INVOLUNTARY CHANGES. In the case of an involuntary change involving a negative adjustment or a positive adjustment of $3,000 or less, taxpayers are required to report the entire amount in the year of the change. In the case of positive adjustments over $3,000, two alternative relief provisions are available. The alternative methods allow the taxpayer to redetermine the tax on the amount of the change. If the amount so determined is lower, the taxpayer is obligated to pay only the lesser amount.

Three-year Method. Under the three-year method, the amount of the change is divided by three. This amount is then added to the taxable income for the current year and each of the two preceding years.[79] This often produces a lower tax because the amount is taxed at lower rates.

EXAMPLE I11-36 ▶

In 1997 Chris is required to change from the cash to the accrual method. His taxable income for 1997 is $10,000 (not including the amount of the adjustment). The net adjustment attributable to the change is $30,000. Under the one-year method, Chris adds the amount of the change ($30,000) to his income ($10,000) and computes the tax on the total ($40,000). Because the amount of the change is positive and is more than $3,000, Chris has the option of applying the three-year method. Assume his taxable income for 1995 is $90,000 and for 1996, $100,000. Under the three-year method, Chris would compute the tax by adding $10,000 to the income for each year (1995, 1996, and 1997). The result is to compute the tax on $100,000, $110,000, and $20,000, as opposed to $90,000, $100,000, and $40,000. In this instance, the one-year method is more beneficial because the current income (and tax rates) are lower than the income (and tax rates) for the two prior years. If the reverse were true (i.e., taxable income was lower in prior years than the current year), Chris would prefer to spread the amount of the change over three years and apply the lower tax rates. ◀

Reconstruction of Income. When reconstructing income, the income for prior years is recomputed using the new method of accounting. Thus, if a taxpayer is changing from the cash to the accrual method, income is reconstructed for the prior years using the accrual method.[80] Obviously, if a taxpayer has been in existence for decades, recon-

---

[78] Sec. 481.
[79] Sec. 481(b)(1).

[80] Sec. 481(b)(2).

structing income can be a complicated, time-consuming procedure. Hence, this method is not often used. Amounts that cannot be assigned to a particular year (e.g., because of a lack of records) are included in the income for the year of the change.

The reconstruction of income method, like the three-year method, is a relief provision that applies if the redetermined tax is less than the tax that is computed under the three-year alternative or the regular one-year method.

In the case of changes initiated by the IRS, any portion of the adjustment that is attributable to years before 1954 is excluded from income.[81] This is because under pre-1954 law, duplications and omissions were not taken into account when a taxpayer changed accounting methods. If a taxpayer voluntarily initiates the change, the pre-1954 exclusion from income is not available.

VOLUNTARY CHANGES. The three-year method and the reconstruction of income method are not explicitly limited to involuntary changes. Nevertheless, Rev. Proc. 84-74 specifies that in order to obtain IRS consent to change, taxpayers must agree to report the adjustment over a period not to exceed six years (not to exceed three years in the case of a change from an erroneous accounting method to a method that clearly reflects income).[82] In the case of a change spread over six years, equal portions of the change are reported in each of the six years beginning with the year of the change.

EXAMPLE I11-37 ▶

In 1997 Diana obtains permission to change from the accrual to the cash method of reporting income. The change results in a $45,000 negative adjustment to income. The IRS requires Diana to spread the adjustment over six years. As a result, she may deduct $7,500 in 1997 and $7,500 per year through year 2002. Note that because the amount of the adjustment is spread over the current and future years, the tax savings associated with the deduction are deferred.

◀

In general, the amount of the adjustment cannot be spread over a period longer than the method being changed has been used. The alternative methods for reporting the amount of a change are summarized in Topic Review I11-5.

OBTAINING IRS CONSENT

Most changes in accounting method require IRS approval. Sec. 446(e) states that a taxpayer changing the method of accounting "on the basis of which he regularly computes his income in keeping his books" must obtain consent before computing taxable income under the new method. This implies that a taxpayer who has been computing taxable income on a method other than that used in computing book income does not need approval to conform the computation of taxable income to the method regularly used on the taxpayer's books. This conclusion is supported by Sec. 441(a), which requires that the same method of accounting be used in computing taxable income as is used in keeping the books. The alternative might be to require the taxpayer to conform his or her book accounting method with the tax accounting method. The answer may well be in how one defines "books." The IRS has ruled that a reconciliation of taxable income with accounting income was a part of the taxpayer's auxiliary records.[83] Hence, the taxpayer was using the same accounting method for book and tax reporting. As a result, a taxpayer who changes the method of accounting used for financial reporting may not be required to change the method of accounting used for tax reporting as long as financial income and book income are reconciled.

The Regulations provide that IRS consent is required to change accounting methods even when the taxpayer has been using an improper accounting method.[84] It is not clear

---

[81] Reg. Sec. 1.481-1(a)(2).
[82] 1984-2 C.B. 736.

[83] Rev. Rul. 58-601, 1958-2 C.B. 81.
[84] Reg. Sec. 1.446-1(e)(2)(i).

Topic Review I11-5

Reporting the Amount of the Change

Section	Method of Reporting the Change	Years Involved	Conditions	Comments
481(a)	One-year	Year of change	Must be used for involuntary changes involving either a negative adjustment or a positive adjustment of $3,000 or less. Available for other changes	Simple, but can force taxpayers into higher tax rates
481(b)(1)	Three-year	Year of change and two prior years	Available for involuntary changes involving positive adjustment of over $3,000	Provides relief by helping taxpayers who are in a high tax bracket in the current year
481(b)(2)	Reconstruction of income	All years involved	Available for involuntary changes involving positive adjustment of over $3,000	Involves reconstructing income for prior years using the new method (seldom used because it is difficult and time-consuming)
481(c)	Six-year	Year of change and up to five subsequent years	Available for voluntary changes (either positive or negative)	Sec. 481(b)(2) grants the IRS authority to determine how amounts arising from voluntary changes are to be reported. The current IRS position is that such amounts should be spread over a period of no longer than six years. Desirable from the taxpayer's point of view in the case of positive adjustments because it defers tax into future.

whether the IRS, by declining to approve a change, can require a taxpayer to continue to use an improper accounting method indefinitely. Clearly, the IRS can require adjustments to prevent duplications and omissions. Further, the IRS may be able to require the taxpayer to use a proper method that is acceptable to the IRS even if the method is not the one preferred by the taxpayer. Presumably, if the first tax return for the taxpayer is still open under the statute of limitations, the taxpayer can change accounting methods by amending all prior returns and computing taxable income by using a proper accounting method.[85]

Tax Planning Considerations

ACCOUNTING PERIODS

New corporations often routinely adopt a calendar year. Consideration should be given, however, to adopting a tax year for the initial reporting period that ends before the amount of taxable income exceeds the amount that is taxed at the lowest tax rates (e.g., when taxable income is $50,000 or less). This is less critical for a corporation suffering losses because the NOLs may be carried forward for a 15-year period.

In the past, taxpayers were able to defer income by selecting different tax years for partners and partnerships or S corporations and shareholders. Current law limits this opportunity. Nevertheless, partnerships and S corporations may adopt a tax year that differs from that of their owners if that year qualifies as a natural business year (i.e., at least 25% of revenues occur during the last two months of the year). Furthermore, deferral is possible in the case of estates, because they are not subject to similar restrictions on the choice of tax years.

ACCOUNTING METHODS

New businesses should consider the tax implications of electing an accounting method. For example, taxpayers may benefit from the LIFO inventory method because LIFO typically reduces gross profit and defers the payment of taxes during inflationary periods. Similarly, service companies usually choose the cash method of reporting income because it permits receivables to be reported when collected rather than when the income is earned. Choosing an accounting method requires an understanding not only of the available accounting methods, but also the nature of the taxpayer's business. Will a specific election be to the tax advantage of the taxpayer? LIFO inventory is often recommended because, during inflationary periods, it tends to reduce inventory values and increase the cost of goods sold. In certain industries, such as the computer industry, however, costs are declining, and LIFO actually may result in a higher inventory value.

In other industries, inventories may fluctuate widely from one year to the next because of changing demand, shortages of materials, strikes, or other causes. LIFO layers may have to be depleted simply to continue business operations. This can cause one of two things to happen: (1) incurring extra recordkeeping costs of LIFO for little or no benefit because the inventories are depleted before they produce significant tax deferrals or (2) depleting low-cost layers from years past, resulting in a substantial increase in taxable income in the year of occurrence.

INSTALLMENT SALES

Taxpayers normally choose the installment method of reporting income from casual sales of property. By spreading the gain from a sale over more than one tax year, the taxpayer normally remains in lower tax brackets and defers the tax. A taxpayer with low current taxable income may elect not to use the installment sale method in order to take advantage of the lower current tax rates.

---

[85] Rev. Ruls. 70-539, 1970-2 C.B. 70, 75-56, 1975-1 C.B. 98, and 77-236, 1977-2 C.B. 84.

COMPLIANCE AND PROCEDURAL CONSIDERATIONS

REPORTING INSTALLMENT SALES ON FORM 6252

Form 6252 (Installment Sale Income) is used to report income under the installment method from sales of real property and casual sales of personal property other than inventory. Figure I11-1 illustrates how an installment sale transaction is reported. The illustration is based on Example I11-23. A separate Form 6252 is normally used for each installment sale. Form 6252 is used in the year of the sale and any year in which the taxpayer receives a payment from the sale. Taxpayers who do not wish to use the installment method may report the transaction on either Schedule D or on Form 4797.

PROBLEM MATERIALS

DISCUSSION QUESTIONS

I11-1 Do accounting rules determine the amount of income to be reported by a taxpayer?

I11-2 How does a taxpayer's tax accounting method affect the amount of tax paid?

I11-3 Most individuals use the calendar year as their tax year. What requirement, if any, in the tax law causes this?

I11-4 Why is it desirable for a new taxpayer to select an appropriate tax year?

I11-5 What restrictions apply to partnerships selecting a tax year?

I11-6 Does a similar restriction apply to S corporations? Explain.

I11-7 How could the 52-53 week year prove to be beneficial to taxpayers? Explain.

I11-8 Under what circumstances can an individual taxpayer change tax years without IRS approval?

I11-9 Is there any instance in which a change in tax years is required? Explain.

I11-10 a. In what situations will a tax year cover a period of less than 12 months?
b. Under what conditions is a taxpayer required to annualize income?
c. Does annualizing income increase or decrease the taxpayer's tax liability? Explain.

I11-11 When is a final tax return due for an individual who uses a calendar year and who dies during the year?

I11-12 a. Is it correct to say that businesses with inventories must use the accrual method?
b. What other restrictions apply to taxpayers who are choosing an overall tax accounting method?
c. Why is the cash method usually preferred to the accrual method?

I11-13 a. Does the term *method of accounting* refer only to overall methods of accounting? Explain.
b. Does a taxpayer's accounting method affect the total amount of income reported over an extended time period?
c. How can the use of an accounting method affect the total amount of tax paid over time?

I11-14 a. When are expenses deductible by a cash method taxpayer?
b. Are the rules that determine when interest is deductible by a cash method taxpayer the same as for other expenses?
c. Is a cash method taxpayer subject to the same rules for depreciable assets as accrual method taxpayers?

I11-15 Who may use the completed contract method of reporting income from long-term contracts?

I11-16 When is a cash method taxpayer allowed to deduct deposits?

I11-17 What constitutes a payment in determining when a cash-basis taxpayer is entitled to deduct an expense?

Form **6252**

Department of the Treasury
Internal Revenue Service

Installment Sale Income

▶ Attach to your tax return.

▶ Use a separate form for each sale or other disposition of property on the installment method.

OMB No. 1545-0228

1996

Attachment
Sequence No. **79**

Name(s) shown on return	Identifying number
Gina Green	*123-45-6789*

1 Description of property ▶ *Equipment*

2a Date acquired (month, day, and year) ▶ _____ **b** Date sold (month, day, and year) ▶ *8-31-96*

3 Was the property sold to a related party after May 14, 1980? If "No," skip line 4 .... ☐ Yes ☒ No

4 Was the property you sold to a related party a marketable security? If "Yes," complete Part III. If "No," complete
Part III for the year of sale and the 2 years after the year of sale .... ☐ Yes ☐ No

Part I Gross Profit and Contract Price. Complete this part for the year of sale only.

5	Selling price including mortgages and other debts. Do not include interest whether stated or unstated	5	*200,000*
6	Mortgages and other debts the buyer assumed or took the property subject to, but not new mortgages the buyer got from a bank or other source	6 *50,000*	
7	Subtract line 6 from line 5	7 *150,000*	
8	Cost or other basis of property sold	8 *70,000*	
9	Depreciation allowed or allowable	9 *10,000*	
10	Adjusted basis. Subtract line 9 from line 8	10 *60,000*	
11	Commissions and other expenses of sale	11 *13,000*	
12	Income recapture from Form 4797, Part III	12 *10,000*	
13	Add lines 10, 11, and 12	13	*83,000*
14	Subtract line 13 from line 5. If zero or less, **stop here.** Do not complete the rest of this form	14	*117,000*
15	If the property described on line 1 above was your main home, enter the total of lines 14 and 22 from Form 2119. Otherwise, enter -0-	15	
16	**Gross profit.** Subtract line 15 from line 14	16	*117,000*
17	Subtract line 13 from line 6. If zero or less, enter -0-	17	*0*
18	**Contract price.** Add line 7 and line 17	18	*150,000*

Part II Installment Sale Income. Complete this part for the year of sale and any year you receive a payment or have certain debts you must treat as a payment on installment obligations.

19	Gross profit percentage. Divide line 16 by line 18. For years after the year of sale, see instructions	19	*78%*
20	**For year of sale only:** Enter amount from line 17 above; otherwise, enter -0-	20	*0*
21	Payments received during year. Do not include interest whether stated or unstated	21	*10,000*
22	Add lines 20 and 21	22	*10,000*
23	Payments received in prior years. Do not include interest whether stated or unstated	23	
24	**Installment sale income.** Multiply line 22 by line 19	24	*7,800*
25	Part of line 24 that is ordinary income under recapture rules	25	*10,000*
26	Subtract line 25 from line 24. Enter here and on Schedule D or Form 4797	26	*17,800*

Part III Related Party Installment Sale Income. Do not complete if you received the final payment this tax year.

27 Name, address, and taxpayer identifying number of related party _____

28 Did the related party, during this tax year, resell or dispose of the property ("second disposition")? .... ☐ Yes ☐ No

29 If the answer to question 28 is "Yes," complete lines 30 through 37 below unless one of the following conditions is met. Check only the box that applies.

a ☐ The second disposition was more than 2 years after the first disposition (other than dispositions of marketable securities). If this box is checked, enter the date of disposition (month, day, year) .... ▶ _____

b ☐ The first disposition was a sale or exchange of stock to the issuing corporation.

c ☐ The second disposition was an involuntary conversion where the threat of conversion occurred after the first disposition.

d ☐ The second disposition occurred after the death of the original seller or buyer.

e ☐ It can be established to the satisfaction of the Internal Revenue Service that tax avoidance was not a principal purpose for either of the dispositions. If this box is checked, attach an explanation.

30	Selling price of property sold by related party	30	
31	Enter contract price from line 18 for year of first sale	31	
32	Enter the **smaller** of line 30 or line 31	32	
33	Total payments received by the end of your 1996 tax year	33	
34	Subtract line 33 from line 32. If zero or less, enter -0-	34	
35	Multiply line 34 by the gross profit percentage on line 19 for year of first sale	35	
36	Part of line 35 that is ordinary income under recapture rules	36	
37	Subtract line 36 from line 35. Enter here and on Schedule D or Form 4797	37	

619491
10-22-96 LHA **For Paperwork Reduction Act Notice, see separate Instructions.**

Form **6252** (1996)

FIGURE I11-1 ▶ REPORTING INSTALLMENT SALE INCOME ON FORM 6252 (BASED ON EXAMPLE I11-23)

I11-18 What is meant by economic performance?

I11-19 What conditions must be met if the economic performance test is to be waived for an accrual-method taxpayer?

I11-20 When is an accrual method taxpayer permitted to deduct estimated expenses? Explain.

I11-21 What is the significance of the *Thor Power Tool Co.* decision?

I11-22 **a.** How are overhead costs treated in determining a manufacturing company's inventory?
b. Do retailers have a similar rule?
c. Are these rules the same as for financial accounting? If not, explain.

I11-23 What transactions are subject to the long-term contract method of reporting?

I11-24 **a.** What conditions must be met in order to use the installment method?
b. Why would a taxpayer elect not to use the installment method?

I11-25 What is the impact of having the entire gain on an installment sale consist of ordinary income from depreciation recapture?

I11-26 What impact does the gifting of an installment obligation have on the donor?

I11-27 What treatment is given to an installment sale involving related people?

I11-28 What is the primary impact of the imputed interest rules on installment sales?

I11-29 What changes in accounting method can be made without IRS approval?

I11-30 **a.** Can the IRS require a taxpayer to change accounting methods?
b. If the IRS requires a change in accounting methods, how will the amount of the change be handled?

I11-31 Explain the purpose of the three-year method and the income reconstruction method in computing the tax resulting from a net adjustment due to a change in accounting methods.

I11-32 If a taxpayer changes the method of accounting used for financial reporting purposes, must the taxpayer also change his or her method of accounting for tax purposes?

ISSUE IDENTIFICATION QUESTIONS

I11-33 Judy's Cars, Inc. sells collectible automobiles to consumers. She employs the specific identification inventory valuation method. Prices are negotiated by Judy and individual customers. Judy accepts trade-ins when she sells an automobile. Judy negotiates the allowance for trade with the customer. Occasionally, Judy finds that it can take two or three years to sell a given automobile. Judy now has four automobiles that she has held for over two years. She expects to eventually sell those automobiles, but expects that they will sell for less than their original cost. What tax issues should Judy consider?

I11-34 Lana operates a real estate appraisal service business in a small town serving local lenders. After noting that lenders must pay to bring in a surveyor from out of town, she completes a course and obtains a surveyor's license that enables her to provide this service also. She now provides both services as a proprietor. What tax issues should Lana consider?

I11-35 John owns a small farm on a lake. A local developer offers John $400,000 cash for his farm. The developer believes John's farm will be very attractive to home buyers because it is on a lake. After John turns down the initial offer, the developer offers to pay John $250,000 plus an amount equal to 10% of the selling price for the homes that are developed and sold. Identify the tax issues John should consider if he accepts the offer.

I11-36 Lee is starting a small lawn service. On the advice of his accountant, Lee has formed a corporation and made an S corporation election. The accountant has asked Lee to consider electing a fiscal year ending on the last day in February. The accountant pointed out that Lee's business is likely to slow down in the winter. Also, the accountant indicated that the February year end would permit the accountant to do Lee's accounting work after the busy season in accounting is over. What tax issues should Lee consider?

PROBLEMS

I11-37   *Allowable Taxable Year.* For each of the following cases, indicate whether the taxpayer has selected an allowable tax year in an initial year. If the year selected is not acceptable, indicate what an acceptable year would be.

a. A corporation selects a January 15 year-end.

b. A corporation selects a March 31 year-end.

c. A corporation selects a year that ends on the last Friday in March.

d. A partnership selects a year that ends on December 31 and has three equal partners whose years end on March 31, April 30, and June 30.

e. An S corporation selects a December 31 year-end.

I11-38   *Change in Accounting Period.* In which of the following instances is a taxpayer permitted to change accounting periods without IRS approval?

a. A calendar-year taxpayer who wishes to change to a year that ends on the last Friday in December.

b. ABC Partnership has filed its tax return using a fiscal-year ending on March 31 for over 40 years. The partnership wishes to change to a calendar year-end that coincides with its partners' year-end.

c. Iowa Corporation, a newly acquired subsidiary, wishes to change its year-end to coincide with its parent.

I11-39   *Annualization.* Each of the following cases involves a taxable year of less than 12 months. In which situations is annualization required?

a. A new corporation formed in September elects a calendar year.

b. A calendar-year individual dies on June 15.

c. Jean, who has been using a calendar year, marries Hank, a fiscal-year taxpayer. Soon after the marriage, Jean changes her tax year to coincide with her husband's tax year.

d. A calendar-year corporation liquidates on April 20.

I11-40   *Short Period Return.* Lavanya, a single taxpayer, is a practicing accountant. She obtains permission to change her tax year from the calendar year to a year ending July 31. Her practice income for the seven months ending July 31 is $40,000. In addition, Lavanya has $3,000 of interest income and $6,454 of itemized deductions. She is entitled to one exemption. What is her tax for the short period?

I11-41   *Cash Basis Expenses.* How much of the following expenses are currently deductible by a cash basis taxpayer?

a. Medical prescriptions costing $20 paid by credit card (medical expenses already exceed the 7.5% of AGI floor).

b. Prepaid interest (not related to points) of $200 on a residential loan.

c. Taxpayer borrows $300 from the bank to make a charitable contribution. The $300 is paid to the charitable organization before the end of the tax year.

d. Taxpayer gives a note to his church indicating an intent to contribute $300.

e. A calendar-year individual mails a check for $200 to his church on December 31. The check is postmarked December 31 and clears the bank on January 4.

I11-42   *Economic Performance.* In light of the economic performance requirement, how much is deductible by the following accrual-basis corporate taxpayers in 1997?

a. Camp Corporation sells products with a one-year warranty. In 1997 Camp estimates that the warranty costs on products sold during the year will amount to $80,000. In 1997 Camp performs $38,000 of warranty work on products sold during 1996 and $36,000 of warranty work on products sold in 1997.

b. Data Corporation agrees to pay $10,000 per year for two years to a software developer. The developer has completed all work on the software and delivers the product to Data before the end of 1997.

c. In 1997 Palm Corporation pays $5,000 to a supplier to guarantee delivery of raw materials. The $5,000 is refundable if Palm decides not to acquire the materials.

d. In 1997 North Corporation pays a $1,000 security deposit on space it rents for a new office. In addition, North pays 1997 rent of $18,000. The security deposit is refundable if the property is returned in good condition.

I11-43 **Manufacturing Inventory.** Which of the following costs must be included in inventory by a manufacturing company?
a. Raw materials
b. Advertising
c. Payroll taxes
d. Research and experimental costs
e. Factory insurance
f. Repairs to factory equipment
g. Factory utility costs
h. Factory rent

I11-44 **Single Pool LIFO.** Prime Corporation begins operations in late 1997. Prime decides to use the single pool LIFO method. Year-end inventories under FIFO are as follows:

1997	$110,000
1998	134,000
1999	125,000

The price index for 1997 is 130%; for 1998, 134%; and 1999, 140%. What are 1998 and 1999 inventories?

I11-45 **Installment Sale.** In 1997 Ace Construction Company sells a used crane to Go Construction Company. The crane, which cost $87,000 in 1989, sells for $80,000. Ace has deducted the entire cost of the crane under ACRS depreciation. Ace receives $20,000 down and is to receive $20,000 per year plus 10% interest for four years. Under the Sec. 1245 depreciation recapture rules, the entire gain is taxable as ordinary income. There is no applicable installment obligation. How much of the gain is taxable in 1997? 1998?

I11-46 **Installment Sale.** In 1997 Fast Corporation sells land held as an investment. The land, which cost $87,000 in 1993, sells for $180,000. Fast incurs selling expenses of $12,000. The mortgage on the property at the time of the sale is $100,000. The buyer assumes the mortgage, pays $20,000 down, and agrees to pay $20,000 per year for three years plus interest at an acceptable rate to the IRS. How much of the gain is taxable in 1997? 1998?

I11-47 **Installment Sale Collections.** During 1997, Bear Corporation collects $240,000 of 1997 installment sales, $150,000 of 1996 installment sales, and $40,000 of 1995 installment sales. Actual 1997 sales total $450,000. The gross profit percentage is 32% for 1997, 33% for 1996, and 35% for 1995. What gross profit must Bear report in 1997?

I11-48 **Installment Sale.** On December 31, 1997, Dan sells unlisted stock with a cost of $14,000 for $20,000. Dan collects $5,000 down and is scheduled to receive $5,000 per year for three years plus interest at a rate acceptable to the IRS.
a. How much gain must Dan recognize in 1997? Assume Dan uses the installment method to report the gain.
b. In early January 1998, Dan sells the three installments for a total of $13,800. How much gain or loss must Dan recognize from the sale?

I11-49 **Repossession.** Liz sells for $50,000 stock not listed on any exchange having a $36,000 adjusted basis. Liz receives $10,000 down and a one-year interest-bearing note for the balance. Liz is unable to collect the balance, and after incurring $1,000 in legal fees, repossesses the stock. When Liz repossesses the stock, it is worth $49,000.

a. How much gain must Liz recognize in the year of the sale?

b. How much gain must Liz recognize when she repossesses the stock?

c. What is the basis of the stock after the repossession?

d. How would your answers to Parts b and c differ if the property sold were land instead of stock?

e. What would be the basis of the land?

I11-50   *Deferred Payment Sale.* Joe sells land with a $40,000 adjusted basis for $32,000. He incurs selling expenses of $3,000. The buyers pay $8,000 down and agree to pay him $8,000 per year for three years plus interest at a rate acceptable to the IRS. Because of the buyers' poor credit rating, the installments are worth only $20,000 ($7,200, $6,600, and $6,200, respectively).

a. What gain or loss is reported in the year of the sale? Assume Joe is an accrual method taxpayer.

b. How would the answer to Part a change if Joe had instead been a cash method taxpayer? Assume the land is worth $32,000.

c. How would your answer to Part a change if Joe had been a cash method taxpayer and the land were worth only $28,000?

d. What is the tax impact of collecting the installments in Parts a through c?

I11-51   *Imputed Interest.* On January 30, 1997, Amy sells land to Bob for a stated price of $200,000. The full $200,000 is payable on January 30, 1999. No interest is stated. Amy, a cash-method taxpayer, purchased the land in 1993 for $130,000.

a. How much interest income must be reported by Amy on the sale? Assume a 9% rate compounded semiannually. The present value factor is 0.83856.

b. In what year is the interest reported?

c. How much gain is reported by Amy on the sale?

d. In what year is the gain reported?

e. What is Bob's basis in the land?

I11-52   *Change of Accounting Method.* Dana owns a small retail store and is a cash method taxpayer. The IRS requires her to change to the accrual method in 1998. Dana's business income for 1998 is $30,000 computed on the accrual method. Her books show the following:

	December 31, 1997	December 31, 1998
Accounts receivable	$ 6,000	$ 5,300
Accounts payable	15,200	11,800
Inventory	12,000	12,400

a. What adjustment is necessary to Dana's income?

b. How should Dana report the adjustment?

I11-53   *Required Payment.* BCD Partnership has, for many years, had a March 31 year end. The Partnership's net income for the fiscal year ended March 31, 1998 is $400,000. Because of its fiscal year, BCD has $100,000 on deposit with the IRS from 1997.

a. How much must BCD add to the deposit?

b. When must BCD make the addition?

c. Will the partners receive any credit for the deposit? That is, are they permitted to treat the amount as estimated payments?

I11-54   *Imputed Interest.* Lorenzo sells land to Jan, an unrelated person, for $500,000. Jan pays $200,000 down and agrees to pay the remaining $300,000 one year after the purchase. No interest is provided for in the contract of sale. Lorenzo had purchased the land for $400,000 several years earlier. Assume the applicable rate is 8% compounded semiannually and the relevant present value factor is 0.92456.

a. What is Jan's basis in the land?

b. How much interest income must Lorenzo report and when?

c. How much gain must Lorenzo report from the sale?

d. Is the installment method available to Lorenzo?

I11-55 ***Imputed Interest.*** Jane loans $80,000 to John, her son, to permit him to purchase a principal residence. The loan principal is secured by John's residence, but the agreement does not specify any interest. The applicable federal rate for the year is 8%. John's net investment income is $800.

a. How much interest is imputed on the loan each year?

b. Assume that the amount of the loan is $125,000. How much interest is imputed on the loan?

c. Is John allowed to deduct the imputed interest?

d. What other tax implications are there for the loan?

I11-56 ***Long-Term Contract.*** King Construction Company is engaged in a road construction contract to build a highway over a three-year period. King will receive $11,200,000 for building five miles of highway. King estimates that it will incur $10,000,000 of costs before the contract is completed. As of the end of the first year King incurred $3,000,000 of costs allocated to the contract.

a. How much income from the contract must King report during the first year?

b. Assume King incurs an additional $5,000,000 of costs during the second year. How much income is reported during that year?

c. Assume that King incurs an additional $2,500,000 of costs in the third and final year of the contract. How much does King report during the third year?

d. Will King receive or pay look-back interest? Explain.

TAX FORM/RETURN PREPARATION PROBLEM

I11-57 Barbara B. Kuhn (Social Security number 987-65-4321) purchases a fourplex on January 8, 1993 for $175,000. She allocates $25,000 of the cost to the land, and she deducts MACRS depreciation totaling $16,364. Barbara sells the fourplex on January 6, 1996, for $225,000. The buyer assumes the existing mortgage of $180,000, pays $15,000 down, and agrees to pay $15,000 per year for two years plus 12% interest. Barbara incurs selling expenses of $18,000. Complete Form 6252.

CASE STUDY PROBLEMS

I11-58 Lavonne just completed medical school and residency. She plans to open her medical practice soon. She is not familiar with the intricacies of accounting methods and periods. On advice of her attorney, she plans to form a professional corporation (a form of organization permitted under the laws of most states that does not have the usual limited liability found with business corporations, but is taxed as a corporation). She has asked you whether she should elect a fiscal year and whether she should use the cash or accrual method of reporting income. Discuss whether the options are available to her and the implications of available choices.

I11-59 Don owns an office building that he purchased several years ago. He purchased the building for $400,000, allocated $280,000 of the purchase price to the structure, and over the years properly deducted $110,000 of depreciation. The depreciation will have to be recaptured as ordinary income on the sale. There is a $90,000 mortgage on the property. Don has an offer to purchase the building from an individual who says he will pay $100,000 down and $100,000 per year for five years. There is no mention of interest. As the mortgage is nonassumable, Don will pay off the mortgage using most of the down payment. Don is age 61, and proceeds from the sale along with a pension from his employer will provide for his retirement. Don plans to retire next year. He currently has a 28% marginal tax rate. Discuss the tax implications of the sale. Is there anything Don can do to improve his situation?

I11-60 Troy Tools manufactures over one hundred different hand tools used by mechanics, carpenters, and plumbers. Troy's cost accounting system has always been very simple. The costs allocated to inventory have included only materials, direct labor, and factory overhead. Other overhead costs such as costs of the personnel department, purchasing, payroll, and computer services have never been treated as manufacturing overhead even though many of the activities of the departments relate to the manufacturing operations. You are preparing Troy's tax return for the first time and determine that the company is not following the uniform capitalization rules prescribed in the tax law. You have explained to the company's president that there is a problem, and she is reluctant to change accounting methods. She says allocating these costs to the many products the company makes will be a time-consuming and expensive process. She feels that the cost of determining the additional amounts to include in inventory under the uniform capitalization rules will probably be more than the additional tax that the company will pay. What is the appropriate way to handle this situation? (See the *Statements on Responsibilities in Tax Practice* section in Chapter I15 for a discussion of these issues.)

TAX RESEARCH PROBLEMS

I11-61 Eagle and Hill Corporations discuss the terms of a land sale in December 1997, and they agree to a price of $230,000. Eagle wants to use the installment sale method, but is not sure Hill is a reliable borrower. As a result, Eagle requires Hill to place the entire purchase price in escrow to be released in five yearly installments by the escrow agent. Is the installment method available to Eagle?

A partial list of research sources is

- Rev. Rul. 77-294, 1977-2 C.B. 173
- Rev. Rul. 79-91, 1979-1 C.B. 179
- *H. O. Williams v. U.S.*, 46 AFTR 1725, 55-1 USTC ¶9220 (5th Cir., 1955)

I11-62 Texas Corporation disassembles old automobiles for the purpose of reselling their components (i.e., different types of metals, plastics, rubber, and other materials). Texas sells some of the items for scrap, but must pay to dispose of environmentally hazardous plastics and rubber. At year-end, Texas Corporation has a difficult time determining the cost of the individual parts that are stacked in piles. In fact, it would be very expensive to even weigh some of the materials on hand. Texas has followed the practice of having two experienced employees estimate the weight of different stacks and then pricing them based on quotes found in trade journals. If Texas must pay to dispose of an item, it is assigned a value of zero. In other words, Texas does not value its inventory using standard FIFO or LIFO methods. Is such a practice acceptable?

A partial list of research sources is

- Reg. Secs. 1.471-2(a) and 1.471-3(d)
- *Morrie Chaitlen*, 1978 PH T.C. Memo ¶78,006, 37 TCM 17
- *Justus & Parker Co.*, 13 BTA 127 (1928)

CHAPTER 12

PROPERTY TRANSACTIONS: NONTAXABLE EXCHANGES

LEARNING OBJECTIVES

After studying this chapter, you should be able to

1 ▶ Understand the tax consequences arising from a like-kind exchange

2 ▶ Determine the basis of property received in a like-kind exchange

3 ▶ Determine whether gain from an involuntary conversion may be deferred

4 ▶ Determine the basis of replacement property in an involuntary conversion

5 ▶ Determine when a gain resulting from the sale of a principal residence is deferred and the basis for replacement property

6 ▶ Determine when a gain resulting from the sale of a principal residence may be excluded

KEY POINT

The transactions examined in this chapter override the normal rule that provides for the recognition of realized gains and realized losses on property used in a business or held for investment.

Taxpayers who sell or exchange property for an amount greater or less than their basis in that property have a realized gain or loss on the sale or exchange. Almost any transfer of property is treated as a sale or other disposition (see Chapter I5). The realized gain or loss must be recognized unless a specific Code section provides for nonrecognition treatment. If the realized gain or loss is not recognized at the time of the transaction, the nonrecognized gain or loss may be deferred in some cases and excluded in others.

The general rules related to the computation of realized and recognized gains or losses are covered in Chapter I5. This chapter discusses three of the most common transactions that may result in *nonrecognition* of a realized gain or loss:

▶ Like-kind exchanges under Sec. 1031 (deferred gain or loss)

▶ Involuntary conversions under Sec. 1033 (deferred gain)

▶ Sales of a personal residence under Sec. 1034 (deferred gain) or Sec. 121 (excluded gain)

Nonrecognition of gain treatment for like-kind exchanges, involuntary conversions, and the sale of a residence may be partially justified by the fact that taxpayers may lack the wherewithal to pay the tax despite the existence of a realized gain. For example, a taxpayer who realizes a gain due to an involuntary conversion of property (damage from fire, storm, etc.) may have to use the amount received to replace the converted property.

A typical requirement in a nontaxable exchange is that the taxpayer is required to maintain a continuing investment in comparable property (e.g., a building is exchanged for another building). In essence, a change in form rather than a change in substance occurs.

A transaction that is generally considered to be nontaxable may be taxable in part. In a like-kind exchange, for example, the taxpayer may also receive money or property that is not like–kind property. If non-like-kind property or money is received, the realized gain is taxable to the extent of the sum of the money and the fair market value (FMV) of the non–like-kind property received.[1]

LIKE-KIND EXCHANGES

OBJECTIVE 1

Understand the tax consequences arising from a like-kind exchange

Section 1031(a) provides that "No gain or loss shall be recognized on the exchange of property held for productive use in a trade or business or for investment if such property is exchanged solely for property of like-kind which is to be held either for productive use in a trade or business or for investment."[2]

In a **like-kind exchange**, both the property transferred and the property received must be held either for productive use in the trade or business or for investment.

EXAMPLE I12-1 ▶

Tom owns land used in his trade or business. He exchanges the land for other land, which is to be held for investment. No gain or loss is recognized by Tom because he has exchanged property used in a trade or business for like-kind property to be held for investment. ◀

EXAMPLE I12-2
REAL-WORLD
EXAMPLE

An exchange or trade of professional football player contracts qualifies as a like-kind exchange. Rev. Rul. 71-137, 1971-1 C.B. 104.

Dawn's automobile is held only for personal use. She exchanges the automobile, which has a $10,000 basis, for stock of AT&T with a $12,000 FMV. The stock will be held for investment. A $2,000 gain is recognized because the automobile is not used in Dawn's trade or business or held for investment. The exchange is not a like-kind exchange because neither personal-use assets nor stock qualify as like-kind property. ◀

---

[1] Sec. 1031(b).

[2] Sec. 1031(a).

ADDITIONAL
COMMENT

The mandatory nonrecognition of loss under Sec. 1031 can be avoided by selling the old property in one transaction and buying the new property in a separate, unrelated transaction.

Section 1031 is not an elective provision. If the exchange qualifies as a like-kind exchange, nonrecognition of gain or loss is mandatory. To qualify for like-kind exchange treatment, a direct exchange must occur and the property exchanged must be like-kind. A taxpayer who prefers to recognize a loss on an exchange must structure the transaction to avoid having the exchange qualify as a like-kind exchange.

LIKE-KIND PROPERTY DEFINED

CHARACTER OF THE PROPERTY. To be a nontaxable exchange under Sec. 1031, the property exchanged must be like-kind. The Treasury Regulations specify that "the words 'like-kind' have reference to the nature or character of the property and not to its grade or quality."[3] Thus, exchanges of real property qualify even if the properties are dissimilar.

EXAMPLE I12-3 ▶ Eric owns an apartment building that is held for investment. Eric exchanges the building for farmland to be used in his trade or business. The exchange is a like-kind exchange because both the building and the farmland are classified as real property and both properties are used either in business or held for investment. ◀

EXAMPLE I12-4 ▶ Trail Corporation exchanges improved real estate for unimproved real estate, both of which are held for investment. The exchange is a like-kind exchange.[4] ◀

ADDITIONAL
COMMENT

Real property is often referred to as real estate.

PROPERTY MUST BE THE SAME CLASS. An exchange is not a like-kind exchange when property of one class is exchanged for property of a different kind or class.[5] For example, if real property is exchanged for personal property (or vice versa), no like-kind exchange occurs.[6]

EXAMPLE I12-5 ▶ Gail exchanges an office building with a $400,000 adjusted basis for an airplane with a $580,000 FMV to be used in business. This is not a like-kind exchange because the office building is real property and the airplane is personal property. Gail must recognize a $180,000 ($580,000 − $400,000) gain. ◀

EXAMPLE I12-6 ▶ Gary exchanges a business truck for another truck that will be used in his business. This is an exchange of like-kind property because both properties are personal property and are used in business. ◀

ADDITIONAL
COMMENT

The rules in the Regulations dealing with exchanges of personal property are not interpreted as liberally as the rules relating to real property.

PROPERTY OF A LIKE CLASS. The Treasury Regulations provide that personal property of a **like class** meets the definition of *like-kind*.[7] Like class property is defined as depreciable tangible personal properties that are within the same General Asset Class or within the same Product Class.[8] Property within a General Asset Class consists of depreciable tangible personal property described in one of the asset classes provided in Rev. Proc. 87-56 for depreciation.[9] Some of the General Asset Classes are as follows:

▶ Office furniture, fixtures, and equipment (Asset Class 00.11)

▶ Information systems such as computers and peripheral equipment (Asset Class 00.12)

▶ Automobiles and taxis (Asset Class 00.22)

---

[3] Reg. Sec. 1.1031(a)-1(b). Section 1031(h) provides an exception for exchanges of real property located in the U.S. and real property located outside the U.S. For transfers on or after July 10, 1989 the like-kind exchange rules do not apply.
[4] *Ibid.*
[5] *Ibid.*
[6] Real property includes land and property attached to land in a relatively

permanent manner. Personal property that is affixed to real property in a relatively permanent manner is a fixture and is considered part of the real property. Personal property is all property that is not real property or a fixture.
[7] Reg. Sec. 1.1031(a)-2.
[8] Reg. Sec. 1.1031(a)-2(b).
[9] 1987-2 C.B. 674.

- Buses (Asset Class 00.23)
- Light general purpose trucks (Asset Class 00.231)
- Heavy general purpose trucks (Asset Class 00.242)
- Vessels, barges, tugs, and similar water-transportation equipment except those used in marine construction (Asset Class 00.28)

For purposes of the like-kind exchange provisions, a single property may not be classified in more than one General Asset Class or more than one Product Class. Furthermore, property in any General Asset Class may not be classified in a Product Class. A property's General Asset Class or Product Class is determined as of the exchange date.

EXAMPLE I12-7 ▶ Wint transfers a personal computer used in his trade or business for a printer to be used in his trade or business. The exchange is a like-kind exchange because both properties are in the same General Asset Class (00.12). ◀

EXAMPLE I12-8 ▶ Renee transfers an airplane (Asset Class 00.21) that she uses in her trade or business for a heavy general purpose truck to use in her trade or business. The properties are not of a like class because they are in different General Asset Classes. The heavy general purpose truck is in Asset Class 00.242. ◀

Example I12-8 is taken from the Treasury Regulations, which further state: "Because each of the properties is within a General Asset Class, the properties may not be classified within a Product Class. The airplane and heavy general purpose truck are also not of a like kind. Therefore, the exchange does not qualify for nonrecognition of gain or loss under Sec. 1031."[10]

If two properties are not within a General Asset Class, it still may be possible to be considered like-kind if the properties are within the same Product Class. Property in a Product Class consists of depreciable tangible personal property listed in a 4-digit product class in Division D of the **Standard Industrial Classification (SIC)** codes set forth in the *Standard Industrial Classification Manual*.[11] The Regulations state that an exchange of a grader for a scrapper is an exchange of properties of like class because neither property is in a General Asset Class and both properties are listed in the same Product Class (SIC code 3533).[12]

There are no like classes for intangible personal property, nondepreciable personal property, or personal property held for investment. To have a like-kind exchange of property held for investment, the property must be exchanged for like-kind property. To determine whether an exchange of intangible personal property is a like-kind exchange, one must consider the type of right involved as well as the underlying property to which the intangible property relates. An exchange of a copyright for a novel for a copyright on a different novel is a like-kind exchange, but the exchange of a copyright on a novel for a copyright on a song is not a like-kind exchange.[13]

NON–LIKE-KIND PROPERTY EXCHANGES. An exchange of inventory or securities does not qualify as a like-kind exchange.[14]

EXAMPLE I12-9 ▶ Antonio, a dealer in farm equipment, exchanges a new combine for other property in the same General Asset Class to be used in Antonio's trade or business. Because Antonio is a dealer, the new combine is inventory and the exchange does not qualify as a like-kind exchange. ◀

ADDITIONAL COMMENT

An exchange can be a like-kind exchange for one party to the transaction but not qualify as a like-kind exchange for the other party.

---

[10] Reg. Sec. 1.1031(a)-2(b)(7) Ex. 2.
[11] Reg. Sec. 1.1031(a)-2(b)(3).
[12] Reg. Sec. 1.1031(a)-2(b)(7) Ex. 3.
[13] Reg. Sec. 1.1031(a)-2(c)(1).

[14] Sec. 1031(a)(2). An exchange of stock is not a like-kind exchange. However, an exchange of stock is a nontaxable exchange if the exchange is related to a tax-free reorganization.

EXAMPLE I12-10 ▶ Nancy owns Able Corporation stock as an investment. Nancy exchanges the stock for antiques to be held as investments. This exchange is taxable because stock does not qualify as like-kind property. ◀

In most cases, to qualify as a like-kind exchange of personal property, the property must be nearly identical. For example, livestock of different sexes are not like-kind property.[15] An exchange of gold bullion held for investment for silver bullion held for investment is not a like-kind exchange. Silver and gold are intrinsically different metals and primarily are used in different ways.[16] Currency exchanges are not like-kind exchanges,[17] and the exchange of a partnership interest for an interest in another partnership is not a like-kind exchange.[18]

EXCHANGE OF SECURITIES. The like kind exchange rules also do not apply to stocks, bonds, or notes.[19] However, Sec. 1036 provides that no gain or loss is recognized on the exchange of common stock for common stock or preferred stock for preferred stock in the same corporation. Common stock for preferred stock of the same corporation or any kind of stock in different corporations may not be exchanged tax-free. Sec. 1036 applies even if voting common stock is exchanged for nonvoting stock of the same corporation. The nontaxable exchange of stock of the same corporation may be between two stockholders or a stockholder and the corporation.[20]

EXAMPLE I12-11 ▶ Kelly owns common stock of Best Corporation. Best issues class B common stock to Kelly in exchange for her common stock. No gain or loss is recognized because this is an exchange of common stock for common stock in the same corporation. ◀

EXAMPLE I12-12 ▶ Shirley owns 100 shares of Top Corporation common stock. The stock has a $40,000 adjusted basis and a $50,000 FMV. Bob owns 100 shares of Star Corporation common stock with a $50,000 FMV. If Shirley and Bob exchange their stock, the exchange is taxable, and Shirley has a $10,000 ($50,000 − $40,000) recognized gain. The exchange is neither a like-kind exchange nor an exchange of stock for stock of the same corporation. ◀

A DIRECT EXCHANGE MUST OCCUR

To qualify as a like-kind exchange, a direct exchange of property must occur.[21] Thus, the sale of property and the subsequent purchase of like-kind property does not qualify as a like-kind exchange unless the two transactions are interdependent.

EXAMPLE I12-13 ▶ Karen sells a lathe used in her business to Rashad for an amount greater than the lathe's adjusted basis. After the sale, Karen purchases another lathe from David. The gain is recognized because these two transactions do not qualify as an exchange of like-kind property. ◀

KEY POINT

Transfers of property in a three-party exchange must be part of a single, integrated plan. It is important that the taxpayers can show their intent to enter into a like-kind exchange even though contractual interdependence is not necessary to the finding of an exchange.

A sale and a subsequent purchase may be treated as an exchange if the two transactions are interdependent. The IRS indicates that a nontaxable exchange may exist when the taxpayer sells property to a dealer and then purchases like-kind property from the same dealer.[22]

THREE-PARTY EXCHANGES

The typical two-party exchange is not always practical. If both parties do not own like-kind property that meets each other's needs, a three-party exchange might be necessary.

---

[15] Sec. 1031(e).
[16] Rev. Rul. 82-166, 1982-2 C.B. 190.
[17] Rev. Rul. 74-7, 1974-1 C.B. 198.
[18] Sec. 1031(a)(2).

[19] Reg. Sec. 1.1031(a)-1(a)(1)(ii).
[20] Rev. Rul. 66-248, 1966-2 C.B. 303.
[21] Sec. 1031(a).
[22] Rev. Rul. 61-119, 1961-1 C.B. 395.

A three-party exchange is also useful when the taxpayer is willing to exchange property for like-kind property but is not willing to sell the property to a prospective buyer. The taxpayer's unwillingness to sell the property may be motivated by the desire to avoid an immediate tax on a gain resulting from the sale of the property. Therefore, the taxpayer may arrange to have the prospective buyer purchase property from a third party that fulfills his or her needs. The three-party exchange can be an effective way of allowing the taxpayer to consummate a like-kind exchange.

EXAMPLE I12-14 ▶ Kathy owns a farm in Nebraska, which Dick offers to purchase. Kathy is not willing to sell the farm but is willing to exchange the farm for an apartment complex in Arizona. The complex is available for sale. Dick purchases the apartment complex in Arizona from Allison and transfers it to Kathy in exchange for Kathy's farm. The farm and the apartment complex each have a $900,000 FMV. For Kathy, the transaction qualifies as a like-kind exchange because it is a direct exchange of business real property (the farm) for investment real estate (the apartment complex). For Dick and Allison, the exchange is not a like-kind exchange. ◀

In the example above, the exchange is convenient for all the parties. However, it is not always this convenient to execute a three-party exchange. For example, Kathy may want to own an apartment complex in Arizona, but the property she prefers may not be currently available. In this case, a nonsimultaneous exchange may occur.

ADDITIONAL COMMENT

The property to be received in the exchange can be identified as late as 45 days after the transfer of the property given up in the exchange.

NONSIMULTANEOUS EXCHANGE. As a result of the Tax Reform Act of 1984, a nonsimultaneous exchange is a like-kind exchange if the exchange is completed within a specified time period. The property to be received in the exchange must be identified within 45 days after the date of the transfer of the property relinquished in the exchange. The replacement property must be received within the earlier of 180 days after the date the taxpayer transfers the property relinquished in the exchange and the due date for filing a return (including extensions) for the year in which the transfer of the relinquished property occurs.[23]

EXAMPLE I12-15 ▶ On May 5, 1997, Joel transfers property to Lauren, who transfers cash to an escrow agent. The escrow agent is to purchase suitable like-kind property for Joel. Joel does not have actual or constructive receipt of the cash during the delayed period. To be a like-kind exchange for Joel, the suitable like-kind property must be identified by June 19, 1997 (45 days after the transfer) and Joel must receive the property by November 1, 1997 (180 days after the transfer). ◀

EXAMPLE I12-16 ▶ Assume the same facts as Example I12-15 except that the transfer by Joel occurs on November 10, 1997. To be a like-kind exchange for Joel, the suitable like-kind property must be identified by December 25, 1997 and Joel must receive the property by April 15, 1998 unless Joel files an automatic four-month extension for the filing of his return (i.e., the due date is extended until August 15, 1998). In such a case, the property must be received no later than 180 days following the transfer of the property relinquished in the exchange, or by May 8, 1998 (i.e., 180 days after November 10, 1997). ◀

RECEIPT OF BOOT

TYPICAL MISCONCEPTION

In calculating the amount of gain to be recognized when boot is received, it is important not to apply financial accounting principles, which use a proportionate approach.

Taxpayers who want to exchange property do not always own property of equal value. To complete the exchange, non–like-kind property or money may be given or received. Cash and non–like-kind property constitute **boot**.

Gain is recognized to the extent of the boot received. However, the amount of recognized gain is limited to the amount of the taxpayer's realized gain.[24] In effect, the

---

[23] Secs. 1031(a)(3)(A) and (B).

[24] Sec. 1031(b).

realized gain serves as a ceiling for the amount of the recognized gain. The receipt of boot as part of a nontaxable exchange does not cause a realized loss to be recognized.[25]

EXAMPLE I12-17 ▶ Mario exchanges business equipment with a $50,000 adjusted basis for $10,000 cash and business equipment with a $65,000 FMV. The realized gain is $25,000 ($75,000 − $50,000). Because the $10,000 of boot received is less than the $25,000 of realized gain, the recognized gain is $10,000. ◀

EXAMPLE I12-18 ▶ Mary exchanges business equipment with a $70,000 adjusted basis for $20,000 cash and business equipment with a $65,000 FMV. Her realized gain is $15,000 ($85,000 − $70,000). Because the $20,000 of boot received is more than the $15,000 of realized gain, only $15,000 of gain is recognized. ◀

TYPICAL MISCONCEPTION

It is possible to erroneously assume that the receipt of boot causes the recognition of loss.

Taxing part or all of the gain when cash is received in like-kind exchanges is consistent with the wherewithal-to-pay concept. However, boot may not always be in the form of a liquid asset. If non-like-kind property other than cash is received as boot, the amount of the boot is the property's FMV.

EXAMPLE I12-19 ▶ Jane exchanges land held as an investment with a $70,000 basis for other land with a $100,000 FMV and a motorcycle with a $2,000 FMV. The acquired land is to be held for investment, and the motorcycle is for personal use. Personal-use property is non-like-kind property and is classified as boot. The realized gain is $32,000 [($100,000 + $2,000) − $70,000]. The amount of boot received is equal to the FMV of the motorcycle. The recognized gain is $2,000, the lesser of the amount of boot received ($2,000) or the realized gain ($32,000). ◀

EXAMPLE I12-20
SELF-STUDY QUESTION

Why is the relief of a liability treated as if one has received cash?

ANSWER

If it were not treated as such, a taxpayer could receive cash shortly before the exchange by borrowing from a bank, using the property as collateral. Then, if the taxpayer is relieved of the debt in the like-kind exchange, he or she would still have the cash without having paid a tax on the gain.

▶ Assume the same facts in Example I12-19 except that Jane uses the motorcycle in a business. The motorcycle is boot, and a $2,000 gain is still recognized because the exchange of real property for personal property is not a like-kind exchange. ◀

PROPERTY TRANSFERS INVOLVING LIABILITIES. If a liability is assumed (or the property is taken subject to a liability), the amount of the liability is considered money received by the taxpayer on the exchange.[26] One who assumes the debt or takes the property subject to a liability is treated as having paid cash, while the party that is relieved of the debt is treated as having received cash. If each party assumes a liability of the other party, only the net liability given or received is treated as boot.[27]

EXAMPLE I12-21 ▶ Mary exchanges land with a $550,000 FMV that is used in her business for Doug's building, which has a $450,000 FMV. Mary's basis in the land is $400,000, and the land is subject to a liability of $100,000, which Doug assumes. Mary's realized gain is $150,000 [($450,000 + $100,000) − $400,000]. Because assumption of the $100,000 liability is treated as boot, Mary recognizes a $100,000 gain. ◀

EXAMPLE I12-22 ▶ Matt owns an office building with a $700,000 basis, which is subject to a liability of $200,000. Susan owns an apartment complex with a $900,000 FMV, which is subject to a $150,000 liability. Matt and Susan exchange buildings. Matt's realized gain is $250,000 [($900,000 + $200,000) − ($700,000 + $150,000)]. Matt receives boot of $50,000 ($200,000 − $150,000) and recognizes a $50,000 gain. ◀

---

[25] Sec. 1031(c).
[26] Sec. 1031(d). If a liability is assumed, the taxpayer agrees to pay the debt. If property is taken subject to the liability, the taxpayer is responsible for the

debt only to the extent that the property could be used to pay the debt.
[27] Reg. Sec. 1.1031(b)-1(c).

BASIS OF PROPERTY RECEIVED

LIKE-KIND PROPERTY RECEIVED. The basis of property received in a nontaxable exchange is equal to the adjusted basis of the property exchanged increased by gain recognized and reduced by any boot received or loss that is recognized on the exchange.[28]

Basis of property received in a non-taxable exchange	=	Basis of property exchanged	−	Boot received	+	Gain recognized	−	Loss recognized[29]

EXAMPLE I12-23 ▶

Chuck, who is in the business of racing horses, exchanges a racehorse with a $30,000 basis for $10,000 cash and a trotter with an $80,000 FMV. Chuck's realized gain is $60,000 [($80,000 + $10,000) − $30,000], and $10,000 of the gain is recognized because the boot received is less than the realized gain. Chuck's basis for the replacement property (i.e., the trotter) is $30,000 ($30,000 basis of property exchanged − $10,000 of boot received + $10,000 of gain recognized). ◀

The basis of the like-kind property received can also be computed by subtracting the unrecognized gain from its FMV or by adding the unrecognized loss to its FMV. Chuck's $30,000 basis for the trotter in Example I12-23 may be computed by subtracting the $50,000 of unrecognized gain from the $80,000 FMV.

EXAMPLE I12-24 ▶

Pam, who operates a circus, exchanges an elephant with a $15,000 basis for $3,000 cash and a tiger with a $10,000 FMV. The $2,000 realized loss [($10,000 + $3,000) − $15,000] is not recognized. The receipt of boot does not cause a realized loss to be recognized. Pam's basis for the replacement property (i.e., the tiger) is $12,000 ($15,000 basis of property exchanged − $3,000 boot received). ◀

As indicated earlier, realized gains and losses resulting from nontaxable exchanges are deferred. This deferral is reflected in the basis of property received and is illustrated in the two preceding examples. In Example I12-23, the $50,000 ($60,000 − $10,000) unrecognized gain may be recognized when the trotter is sold or exchanged in a taxable transaction, because the basis of the replacement property is less than its FMV by the amount of the deferred gain. For example, if the trotter is sold in a taxable transaction for its $80,000 FMV, the $50,000 ($80,000 − $30,000 basis) of previously unrecognized gain would be recognized. In Example I12-24, the $2,000 unrecognized loss is reflected in the basis of the tiger. If Pam sells the tiger for its $10,000 FMV, a $2,000 loss ($10,000 − $12,000 basis) is recognized.

If more than one item of like-kind property is received, the basis is allocated among the properties in proportion to their relative FMVs on the date of the exchange.

EXAMPLE I12-25 ▶

Saul, who operates a zoo, exchanges a boa constrictor with a $300 basis for a python with a $400 FMV and an anaconda with a $600 FMV. The $700 realized gain [($400 + $600) − $300] is not recognized. The total bases of the properties received is $300. This amount is allocated to the properties (i.e., the python and the anaconda) based on their relative FMVs. Saul's basis for the python is $120 [($400 ÷ $1,000) × $300], and the basis for the anaconda is $180 [($600 ÷ $1,000) × $300]. ◀

NON–LIKE-KIND PROPERTY RECEIVED. The basis of non–like-kind property received is "an amount equivalent to its FMV at the date of the exchange."[30]

---

[28] Sec. 1031(d).
[29] A loss is recognized only when the taxpayer transfers boot with a basis greater than its FMV. Transfers of non–like-kind property (i.e. boot) are discussed in a separate section of this chapter.
[30] Reg. Sec. 1.1031(d)-1(c).

EXAMPLE I12-26 ▶

KEY POINT

Steve had basis of $20,000 before the exchange. Since he recognized gain of $5,000, the total basis of the two assets should be $25,000.

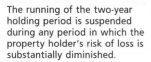

ADDITIONAL COMMENT

The running of the two-year holding period is suspended during any period in which the property holder's risk of loss is substantially diminished.

Steve exchanges a punch press with a $20,000 adjusted basis for a press brake with a $50,000 FMV and $5,000 of marketable securities. Steve's realized gain is $35,000 [($50,000 + $5,000) − $20,000], and $5,000 of the realized gain is recognized due to the receipt of boot. Steve's basis for the marketable securities is $5,000, and the basis for the press brake is $20,000 ($20,000 basis of property exchanged − $5,000 boot received + $5,000 gain recognized). ◀

STOP & THINK

Question: Chris Reedy owns 40 houses that he uses as rental property. All houses have a FMV greater than their adjusted basis. Chris wishes to diversify his investments and is considering selling ten of his houses and using the proceeds to purchase other types of investment assets such as stocks, bonds, commercial parking lots and land near town that he expects to increase in value. He asks you for advice.

Solution: If he sells the ten houses, he will have a gain and have to pay taxes on the gain. He could defer the gain by exchanging the houses for like-kind property. Stocks and bonds are not like-kind property, but the commercial parking lots and the land should qualify as like-kind property, therefore the tax law encourages him to exchange the houses for the commercial parking lot and/or the land.

EXCHANGES BETWEEN RELATED PARTIES

Before the Revenue Reconciliation Act of 1989, related taxpayers could often use the like-kind exchange provisions to lower taxes because the tax basis for the property received is determined by the basis of the property exchanged. Related taxpayers could take advantage of the shift in tax basis to transfer a gain on a subsequent sale to a related party.[31] However, exchanges of property between related parties are not like-kind exchanges under current law if either party disposes of the property within two years of the exchange. Any gain resulting from the original exchange is recognized in the year of the subsequent disposition.[32] Dispositions due to death or involuntary conversion, or for non–tax avoidance purposes are disregarded.[33]

EXAMPLE I12-27 ▶

Melon Corporation, which is 100% owned by Linda, owned land with a basis of $200,000 that was held for investment. Rick wanted to purchase the land for $900,000. Linda owned an office building with a basis of $750,000 and a FMV of $900,000. Instead of selling the land to Rick, Melon Corporation exchanged the land for Linda's office building in December, 1996.

Two months later, Linda sells the land to Rick for $900,000. The exchange of the land for the office building is not a like-kind exchange because one of the related parties disposes of the property within two years of the exchange. In 1997, Melon's recognized gain on the exchange of the land is $700,000 ($900,000 − $200,000) and Linda's recognized gain on the exchange of the office building is $150,000 ($900,000 − $750,000). Because Linda's basis for the land is now $900,000, no gain is recognized on the sale of the land to Rick. ◀

If the parties in Example I12-27 were not related, a like-kind exchange occurred in 1996 and Linda's gain on the sale of the land to Rick would be $150,000 ($900,000 − $750,000). Of course, the exchange is not a like-kind exchange if Linda does not hold the land for investment or for use in her trade or business after receiving it from Melon.

REMINDER

Most exchanges of non-personal use assets result in recognized gains or losses.

TRANSFER OF NON–LIKE-KIND PROPERTY

In all of the preceding examples that include a transfer of boot, the transferor (i.e., the taxpayer) received boot. If the taxpayer transfers non–like-kind property, gain or loss

---

[31] The definition of *related parties* is the same as those for Sec. 267(a) which is discussed in Chapter I6, and includes brothers, sisters, parents, children, and corporations where the taxpayer owns at least 50% in value. See Sec. 1031(f)(3).

[32] Sec. 1031(f)(1)(C).
[33] Secs. 1031(f)(2).

equal to the difference between the FMV and the adjusted basis of the non–like-kind property surrendered must be recognized. However, if the non–like-kind property is a personal use asset, the loss is not recognized.

EXAMPLE I12-28 ▶ Shirley exchanges land with a $30,000 basis and marketable securities with a $10,000 basis to David for land with a $60,000 FMV in a transaction that otherwise qualifies as a like-kind exchange. The FMV of the marketable securities and the land surrendered by Shirley is $14,000 and $46,000 respectively. Because the non–like-kind property that Shirley transfers has a FMV greater than its basis, she recognizes $4,000 ($14,000 − $10,000) of gain. Shirley's basis for the land received is $44,000 ($30,000 + $10,000 + $4,000), which is the basis of both assets exchanged plus the gain recognized on the exchange. ◀

EXAMPLE I12-29 ▶
KEY POINT

Before the exchange in Example I12-28, Shirley owned two assets with a total basis of $40,000 and potential gain of $20,000 ($60,000 − $40,000). After the exchange, she owns one asset with potential gain of $16,000 ($60,000 FMV − $44,000 basis) and has recognized a $4,000 gain.

Paul exchanges timberland held as an investment for undeveloped land with a $200,000 FMV. Paul's basis for the timberland is $125,000. His tractor with a $6,000 basis and a $4,000 FMV is also transferred. Because the non–like-kind property (i.e., the tractor) that Paul transfers has a FMV less than its basis, he recognizes a $2,000 ($4,000 − $6,000) loss. Paul's basis for the undeveloped land is $129,000 ($125,000 + $6,000 − $2,000). ◀

In Example I12-29, Paul recognizes a loss on the non–like-kind property he surrenders, despite receiving property in the aggregate with a FMV greater than the total adjusted basis of the transferred assets. Paul is actually making two exchanges. His exchange of timberland with a basis of $125,000 for undeveloped land with a $196,000 FMV is a like-kind exchange, but his exchange of the tractor with a basis of $6,000 for undeveloped land with a $4,000 FMV is a taxable exchange. In Example I12-30, Ed also makes two exchanges. He has a realized and recognized gain as well as a realized but unrecognized loss.

EXAMPLE I12-30 ▶
KEY POINT

A taxpayer who exchanges like-kind property and non-like-kind property is actually making two exchanges.

Ed owns equipment used in business with a $20,000 adjusted basis and a $15,000 FMV and marketable securities with a $10,000 basis and an $18,000 FMV. Ed exchanges the marketable securities and the equipment for business equipment in the same General Asset Class with a $33,000 FMV. Although the net realized gain is $3,000 [$33,000 − ($20,000 + $10,000)], Ed recognizes an $8,000 gain because he has transferred non–like-kind property with a $10,000 basis and an $18,000 FMV. The $5,000 realized loss on the transfer of equipment is not recognized due to the nonrecognition of gain or loss rules of Sec. 1031. Ed's basis for the equipment received is $38,000 ($20,000 + $10,000 + $8,000). ◀

ADDITIONAL COMMENT

The holding period is relevant only when the asset is a capital asset or a Sec. 1231 asset.

HOLDING PERIOD FOR PROPERTY RECEIVED

LIKE-KIND PROPERTY. The holding period of like-kind property received in a nontaxable exchange includes the holding period of the property exchanged if the like-kind property surrendered is a capital asset or an asset that is Sec. 1231 property. In essence, the holding period of the property exchanged carries over to the holding period of the like-kind property received.[34] The rule regarding the holding period carryover is consistent with the notion of a continuing investment in the underlying property that has been transferred.

BOOT. The holding period for the boot property received begins the day after the date of the exchange.[35]

EXAMPLE I12-31 ▶ Mario owns a Van Gogh painting he acquired on May 1, 1987 as an investment. He exchanges the painting on April 10, 1997 for a Picasso sculpture and marketable securities to be held as

---

[34] Sec. 1223(1) and Reg. Sec. 1.1223-1(a).   [35] Sec. 1223 and Reg. Sec. 1.1223-1(a).

Topic Review I12-1

Section 1031—Like-Kind Exchanges

▶ Gains and losses are not recognized for like-kind exchanges.

▶ Nonrecognition of gains and losses is mandatory if the exchange is a like-kind exchange.

▶ Section 1031 applies to exchanges of property used in a trade or business or held for investment.

▶ Property exchanged and received must be like-kind.

▶ Subject to certain time constraints, a nonsimultaneous exchange may qualify as a like-kind exchange.

▶ Some gain may be recognized if the taxpayer receives or gives non–like-kind property (boot) in an otherwise like-kind exchange.

▶ A loss may be recognized if the taxpayer transfers non–like-kind property (boot) in an otherwise like-kind exchange.

▶ The basis of property received in an exchange is the basis of the property exchanged less the boot received plus the gain recognized less any loss recognized.

▶ The nonrecognized gain or loss is deferred.

▶ The holding period of like-kind property received includes the holding period of the property exchanged.

investments. The holding period for the sculpture begins on May 1, 1987, and the holding period for the marketable securities starts on April 11, 1997. ◀

The like-kind exchange provisions are summarized in Topic Review I12-1.

INVOLUNTARY CONVERSIONS

OBJECTIVE 3

Determine whether gain from an involuntary conversion may be deferred

KEY POINT

Unlike the like-kind exchange provisions which are mandatory, the involuntary conversion provisions are elective. Further, the involuntary conversion rules apply only to gains, not losses.

Taxpayers who realize a gain due to the involuntary conversion of property may elect to defer recognition of the entire gain if qualifying replacement property is acquired within a specified time period at a cost equal to or greater than the amount realized from the involuntary conversion. No gain is recognized if the property is converted "into property similar or related in service or use to the property so converted."[36]

The opportunity provided in Sec. 1033 to defer recognition of the gain reflects the fact that the taxpayer maintains a continuing investment and may lack the wherewithal to pay the tax on the gain that would otherwise be recognized. Furthermore, the involuntary conversion is beyond the taxpayer's control.

Note that the gain is deferred, not excluded. The basis of the replacement property is the property's cost reduced by the amount of gain that is deferred. This is similar to the treatment of a like-kind exchange.

EXAMPLE I12-32 ▶ Lenea's warehouse with a $500,000 basis is destroyed by a hurricane. She collects $650,000 from the insurance company and purchases a new warehouse for $720,000. Lenea may elect to defer recognition of the $150,000 gain ($650,000 − $500,000). If the election is made, the

---

[36] Sec. 1033(a)(1).

ADDITIONAL
COMMENT

Property involved in an involuntary conversion need not be used in a trade or business or held for investment to qualify for the deferral of gain.

TYPICAL
MISCONCEPTION

Occasionally, taxpayers fail to realize that Sec. 1033 applies only to gains, not losses.

basis of the new warehouse is $570,000 ($720,000 − $150,000). The $150,000 gain is merely deferred rather than excluded, because an immediate sale of the replacement property at its $720,000 FMV results in a recognized gain equal to the deferred gain on the involuntarily converted property. For example, if the new warehouse is sold for $720,000, the recognized gain is $150,000 ($720,000 − $570,000). ◄

Section 1033 does not apply to losses realized from an involuntary conversion. A taxpayer may not elect to defer recognition of a loss resulting from an involuntary conversion.

EXAMPLE I12-33 ▶

Barry's offshore drilling rig with an $800,000 basis is destroyed by a typhoon. He collects $700,000 from the insurance company and purchases a new drilling rig for $760,000. The $100,000 loss ($700,000 − $800,000) is recognized as a casualty loss, and the basis of the new drilling rig is its purchase price of $760,000. ◄

INVOLUNTARY CONVERSION DEFINED

ADDITIONAL
COMMENT

Typically, an involuntary conversion consists of either a casualty or a condemnation.

For Sec. 1033 to apply, property must be compulsorily or involuntarily converted into money or other property. An **involuntary conversion** may be due to theft, seizure, requisition, condemnation, or destruction of the property. The destruction of the property may be complete or partial.[37] For purposes of Sec. 1033, destruction of property does not have to meet the "suddenness" test if the cause of destruction otherwise falls within the general concept of a casualty.[38]

An involuntary conversion occurs when a governmental unit exercises its power of eminent domain to acquire the taxpayer's property without the taxpayer's consent. Furthermore, the threat or imminence of requisition or condemnation of property may permit a taxpayer to defer the recognition of gain from the sale or exchange of property under the involuntary conversion rules. Taxpayers who transfer property due to such a threat must be careful to confirm the fact that a decision to acquire their property for public use has been made.[39] Written confirmation of potential condemnation is particularly helpful.[40]

EXAMPLE I12-34 ▶

Bruce owns an automobile dealership near a state university campus. On a number of occasions, the president of the university has expressed an interest in acquiring Bruce's property for additional parking space. The president is not certain about the availability of funds for the purchase, and the university is reluctant to have the property condemned for its use. Based on the university's interest in the property, Bruce sells the property to the Jet Corporation. The threat or imminence of conversion does not exist merely because the property is being considered for acquisition. The sale does not constitute an involuntary conversion.[41] ◄

THREAT OF CONDEMNATION. If a threat of condemnation exists and the taxpayer has reasonable grounds to believe that the property will be condemned, Sec. 1033 applies even if the taxpayer sells the property to an entity other than the governmental unit that is threatening to condemn the property.[42]

EXAMPLE I12-35 ▶

At its regular meeting on Tuesday night, the city commission authorized the city attorney to start the process of condemning two lots owned by Beth for use as a public park. On

---

[37] Reg. Sec. 1.1033(a)-1.
[38] Rev. Rul. 59-102, 1959-1 C.B. 200.
[39] Rev. Rul. 63-221, 1963-2 C.B. 332, and *Joseph P. Balistrieri*, 1979 PH T.C. Memo ¶79,115, 38 TCM 526.

[40] Rev. Rul. 63-221, 1963-2 C.B. 332.
[41] *Forest City Chevrolet*, 1977 PH T.C. Memo ¶77,187, 36 TCM 768.
[42] Rev. Rul. 81-180, 1981-2 C.B. 161, and *Creative Solutions, Inc. v. U.S.*, 12 AFTR 2d 5229, 1963-2 USTC ¶9615 (5th Cir., 1963).

ADDITIONAL COMMENT

If the property in Example I12-35 is later condemned, Marty may be able to defer part or all of the gain.

Wednesday afternoon, Beth sells the two lots to Marty at a gain. The sale of property to Marty is an involuntary conversion, and Beth may elect to defer recognition of the gain if she satisfies the Sec. 1033 requirements. ◀

CONVERSION MUST BE INVOLUNTARY. The conversion must be involuntary. For example, an involuntary conversion does not occur when a taxpayer pays someone to set fire to his or her building.[43] An involuntary conversion does not occur when a taxpayer who is developing a subdivision, voluntarily reserves property for a school site, which is later sold to the school district under condemnation proceedings. In this situation, to receive zoning approval for development of the subdivision, the taxpayer was required to reserve property for a school site.[44]

Although the typical involuntary conversion generally results from a casualty or condemnation, Sec. 1033 provides that certain transactions involving livestock are to be treated as involuntary conversions.[45] For example, the destruction or sale of livestock because of disease is an involuntary conversion.

TAX TREATMENT OF GAIN DUE TO INVOLUNTARY CONVERSION INTO BOOT

Gain may be deferred if the property is involuntarily converted into money or property that is not similar or related in service or use to the converted property.[46] The taxpayer must make a proper replacement of the converted property within a specific time period and elect to defer the gain.

REALIZED GAIN. The taxpayer's realized gain is the excess of the amount received due to the involuntary conversion over the adjusted basis of the property converted. The total award or proceeds received are reduced by expenses incurred to determine the amount realized (e.g., attorney's fees incurred in connection with determining the settlement to be received from a condemnation). If the payment of the award or proceeds is delayed, any amounts paid as interest are not included in determining the amount realized.[47] Amounts received as interest on an award for property condemned are taxed as ordinary income even if the interest is paid by a state or political subdivision.[48]

REAL-WORLD EXAMPLE

Because of mounting losses and declining property values, a taxpayer decided to burn down his building in order to collect the fire insurance proceeds. Although the building was converted into money (insurance proceeds) as a result of its destruction, this conversion was not involuntary within the meaning of Sec. 1033. Rev. Rul. 82-74, 1982-1 C.B. 110.

EXAMPLE I12-36 ▶

Richard's property with a $100,000 basis is condemned by the city of Phoenix. Richard receives a $190,000 award and pays $1,000 legal expenses for representation at the condemnation proceedings and $800 for an appraisal of the property. The amount realized is $188,200 [$190,000 − ($1,000 + $800)]. The gain realized is $88,200 ($188,200 − $100,000). Part or all of the realized gain may be deferred if the requirements of Sec. 1033 are satisfied and an election is made to defer the gain. ◀

GAIN RECOGNIZED. To defer the entire gain, the taxpayer must purchase replacement property with a cost equal to or greater than the amount realized from the involuntary conversion. If the replacement property is purchased for an amount less than the amount realized, that portion of the realized gain that is equal to the excess of the amount realized from the conversion over the cost of the replacement property must be recognized.[49]

ADDITIONAL COMMENT

The gain recognized is limited to the lesser of the gain realized or the excess of the amount realized from the conversion over the cost of the qualified replacement property.

EXAMPLE I12-37 ▶

Bob owns a restaurant with a $200,000 basis. The restaurant is destroyed by fire, and he receives $300,000 from the insurance company. Bob's realized gain is $100,000 ($300,000 −

---

[43] Rev. Rul. 82-74, 1982-1 C.B. 110.
[44] Rev. Rul. 69-654, 1969-2 C.B. 162.
[45] Secs. 1033(d) and (e). If a taxpayer sells or exchanges more livestock than normal because of a drought, the sale or exchange of the excess amount is treated as an involuntary conversion. The livestock must be other than poultry and be held by the taxpayer for draft, breeding, or dairy purposes.

[46] Sec. 1033(a)(2).
[47] *Flushingside Realty & Construction Co.*, 1943 PH T.C. Memo ¶43,286, 2 TCM 259.
[48] *Spencer D. Stewart v. CIR.*, 52 AFTR 2d 83-5885, 83-2 USTC ¶9573 (9th Cir., 1983).
[49] Sec. 1033(a)(2)(A).

$200,000). He purchases another restaurant for $275,000. Bob may elect to defer $75,000 of the gain under Sec. 1033; $25,000 ($300,000 − $275,000) of Bob's gain must be recognized because he failed to reinvest all of the $300,000 insurance proceeds in a suitable replacement property. ◀

EXAMPLE I12-38 ▶

Stacey owns a racehorse with a $450,000 basis that is used for breeding purposes. The racehorse is killed by lightning, and she collects $800,000 from the insurance company. Stacey's realized gain is $350,000 ($800,000 − $450,000). She purchases another racehorse for $430,000. The entire $350,000 of gain is recognized, because the cost of the replacement property is $370,000 ($800,000 − $430,000) less than the amount realized from the involuntary conversion. ◀

OBJECTIVE 4

Determine the basis of replacement property in an involuntary conversion

BASIS OF REPLACEMENT PROPERTY. If replacement property is purchased, the basis of the replacement property is its cost less any deferred gain. If the taxpayer elects to defer the gain, the holding period of the replacement property includes the holding period of the converted property.[50]

EXAMPLE I12-39 ▶

Tracy owns a yacht that is held for personal use and has a $20,000 basis. The yacht is destroyed by a storm, and Tracy collects $24,000 from the insurance company. She purchases a new yacht to be held for personal use for $35,000 and elects to defer the $4,000 ($24,000 − $20,000) gain. The basis of the new yacht is $31,000 ($35,000 − $4,000). The holding period for the new yacht includes the holding period of the yacht that was destroyed. ◀

SEVERANCE DAMAGES. If a portion of the taxpayer's property is condemned, the taxpayer may receive **severance damages** as compensation for a decline in the value of the retained property. For example, if access to the retained property becomes difficult or if the property is exposed to greater damage from flooding or erosion, its value may decline.

The IRS considers severance damages to be "analogous to the proceeds of property insurance; they represent compensation for damages to the property."[51] Amounts received as severance damages reduce the basis of the retained property, and any amount received in excess of the property's basis is treated as gain.[52]

EXAMPLE I12-40 ▶

Cindy owns a 500-acre farm with a $200 basis per acre (a total of $100,000). The state condemns ten acres across the northwest corner of her farm to build a major highway. Cindy receives a condemnation award of $500 per acre for the ten acres. The highway separates the farm into a 25-acre tract and a 465-acre tract. Because her ability to efficiently use the 25-acre tract for farming is reduced because of the highway, the state pays additional severance damages of $90 per acre for the 25 acres. Cindy's gain realized from the condemnation of the ten acres is $3,000 [$5,000 − ($200 × 10 acres)]. The $2,250 ($90 × 25 acres) of severance damages reduce the basis of the 25-acre tract from $5,000 ($200 × 25 acres) to $2,750 [($200 × 25) − $2,250]. The reduction in basis is applied solely to the 25 acres because of its decline in value as farmland. ◀

REAL-WORLD EXAMPLE

Seven of the 18 holes of a golf course were condemned. Although 11 holes remained, it was anticipated that the course would have to be reduced to 9 holes. Therefore, $21,000 of the condemnation award was allocated to severance damages to reflect the decline in value of the two lost holes. *Marco S. Marinello Associates, Inc.,* 1975 PH T.C. Memo ¶75,078, 34 TCM 392.

The Sec. 1033 provisions concerning nonrecognition of gain may apply to severance damages. For instance, if severance damages are used to restore the retained property, only that portion of severance damages not spent for restoration reduces the basis of the retained property. A taxpayer who uses severance damages to purchase adjacent farmland to replace the portion of the farm condemned may use Sec. 1033 to defer a gain due to the receipt of the severance damages.[53]

---

[50] Sec. 1223(1)(A).
[51] Rev. Rul. 53-271, 1953-2 C.B. 36.
[52] Rev. Rul. 68-37, 1968-1 C.B. 359.

[53] Rev. Ruls. 69-240, 1969-1 C.B. 199, 73-35, 1973-1 C.B. 367, and 83-49, 1983-1 C.B. 191.

TAX TREATMENT OF GAIN DUE TO AN INVOLUNTARY CONVERSION DIRECTLY INTO SIMILAR PROPERTY

ADDITIONAL COMMENT

The direct conversion of property into similar property is rarely encountered.

Nonrecognition of gain is mandatory if property is involuntarily converted directly into similar property rather than money.[54] The basis of the replacement property is the same as the basis of the converted property, and the holding period for the converted property carries over to the replacement property.[55]

EXAMPLE I12-41 ▶

Ed's farm with a $200,000 basis is condemned by the state. The state transfers other farmland with a $280,000 FMV to Ed. The $80,000 ($280,000 − $200,000) of realized gain is not recognized, and the basis of the farmland received is $200,000. Nonrecognition of gain is mandatory. Direct conversions are rarely encountered because the usual payment procedure for insurance companies and governmental agencies involves a payment of cash. ◀

REPLACEMENT PROPERTY

To qualify for nonrecognition of gain due to an involuntary conversion, the taxpayer must acquire qualified replacement property. With some exceptions, the **replacement property** must be "similar or related in service or use to the property so converted."[56] Taxpayers who own and use the property must use the functional use test although replacement may be made with like-kind property in certain cases. A taxpayer who owns and leases the property that is involuntarily converted may use the taxpayer-use test.

FUNCTIONAL-USE TEST. The **functional-use test** is more restrictive than the like-kind test. To be considered similar or related in service or use, the replacement property must be functionally the same as the converted property. For example, the exchange of a business building for land used in business qualifies as a like-kind exchange. Replacing a building with land does not qualify as replacement property under the involuntary conversion rules. The building must be replaced with a building that is functionally the same as the converted building.

EXAMPLE I12-42 ▶

REAL-WORLD EXAMPLE

The replacement of bowling alleys destroyed in a fire with a recreational billiards center did not pass the functional-use test. Rev. Rul. 76-319, 1976-2 C.B. 242.

Julie owns a movie theater that is destroyed by fire. She uses the insurance proceeds to purchase a skating rink. The converted property has not been replaced with property that is similar or related in service or use under the functional-use test. The election to defer gain under Sec. 1033 is not available. ◀

REPLACEMENT WITH LIKE-KIND PROPERTY. If real property held for productive use in a trade or business or for investment is **condemned**, a proper replacement may be made by acquiring like-kind property.[57] This exception to the functional use test applies only to real property used in a trade or business or held for investment but not to real property held as inventory.

EXAMPLE I12-43 ▶

Ken owns a building used in his business that is condemned by the state to widen a highway. He uses the proceeds to purchase land to be held for investment. The land is a qualified replacement property because the condemned building is real property used in a trade or business, and the like-kind exchange rule may be applied to the condemnation. ◀

EXAMPLE I12-44 ▶

Assume the same facts as in Example I12-43 except that the building is destroyed by a violent windstorm. Ken's purchase of the investment land is not qualified replacement property

---

[54] Sec. 1033(a).
[55] Sec. 1033(b).
[56] Secs. 1033(a)(2)(A) and 1033(f). The replacement of property requirement is modified when proceeds from the involuntary conversion of livestock may not be reinvested in property similar or related in use to the converted

livestock because of soil contamination or other environmental contamination. Sec. 1033(f) permits the livestock to be replaced with other property, including real property, used for farming purposes.
[57] Sec. 1033(g)(1).

because the more flexible like-kind exchange rules apply only to condemnations. He must purchase property with the same functional use as the business building. ◀

If business or investment property is involuntarily converted as a result of a Presidentially declared disaster after 1994, the taxpayer may replace the property with any tangible property that is held for productive use in a trade or business.

TAXPAYER-USE TEST. The **taxpayer-use test** applies to the involuntary conversion of rental property owned by an investor. This test permits greater flexibility than the functional use test. The principal requirement is that the owner-investor must lease out the replacement property that is acquired. However, the lessee is not required to use the leased property for the same functional use.[58]

EXAMPLE I12-45 ▶

Sally owns an apartment complex that is rented to college students. The apartment complex is destroyed by fire. She uses the insurance proceeds to purchase a medical building that is leased to physicians. This is a qualified replacement property by Sally under the taxpayer-use test, and the gain, if any, may be deferred if an election is made under Sec. 1033. ◀

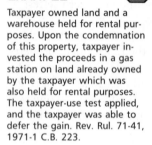

STOP & THINK

Question: Greg Stacey's motel was destroyed by fire on March 10 of the current year. The basis of the property is $400,000 and he received $2,000,000 from the insurance company. Greg is concerned about the possibility of having to pay income tax on the $1,600,000 gain and is aware of the tax rules relating to involuntary conversions. Greg is considering replacing the destroyed motel by building either a new motel or an ice skating rink on the vacant lot. The cost of a new motel or an ice skating rink is expected to be $2,500,000, and he expects to borrow 60% of the cost. What tax advice would you give him?

Solution: Greg can defer the $1,600,000 gain if the involuntary conversion requirements are met and he makes a proper election. The principal issue in this case is whether the replacement property is considered to be "similar in service or use" to the converted property. Because the functional-use test is applicable in this case, an ice skating rink would not be considered as similar property and the gain of $1,600,000 must be recognized. Conversely, the new motel would be similar property and, since Greg is reinvesting an amount greater than $2,000,000, none of the gain is recognized. His basis in the new motel would be $900,000 ($400,000 plus the extra $500,000 that Greg invested over and above the $2,000,000 insurance proceeds). The fact that he borrows money and does not spend the $2,000,000 insurance proceeds does not prevent him from electing to defer the gain. The tax requirement is only that he must reinvest an amount equal to or greater than the $2,000,000 insurance proceeds. In this case, the tax law clearly encourages the taxpayer to build a new motel rather than an ice skating rink.

OBTAINING REPLACEMENT PROPERTY

The general rule is that the taxpayer must purchase the replacement property.[59] Taxpayers may purchase replacement property indirectly by purchasing control (i.e., 80% or more of the stock) of a corporation that owns the replacement property.[60] However, this exception is not applicable to the purchase of like-kind property to replace condemned real property used in a trade or business or held for investment.[61]

[58] Rev. Rul. 64-237, 1964-2 C.B. 319.
[59] To qualify as a purchase of property or stock under Sec. 1033(a)(2)(A)(ii), the unadjusted basis of the property or stock must be its cost within the meaning of Sec. 1012 without considering the basis adjustment for the deferred gain. Property acquired by inheritance, gift, or a nontaxable

exchange does not qualify as replacement property (see Reg. Sec. 1.1033(a)-2(c)(4)).
[60] Sec. 1033(a)(2)(A) and Reg. Sec. 1.1033(a)-2(c).
[61] Sec. 1033(g)(2).

EXAMPLE I12-46 ▶ Hank's airplane, which is used in business, is hijacked and taken to a foreign country. He uses the insurance proceeds to purchase 80% of the Fast Corporation stock. Fast Corporation owns an airplane which is qualified replacement property. The involuntary conversion requirements are satisfied if Hank elects to defer any gain realized. ◀

EXAMPLE I12-47 ▶ Lynn's farm is condemned by the state for public use. She used the proceeds to purchase 80% of Vermont Corporation stock. Vermont Corporation owns eight parking lots. A qualified replacement property has not been obtained through the stock purchase because the farm was condemned real property. ◀

TYPICAL MISCONCEPTION

The first taxable year in which any part of the gain on the conversion is realized is the year in which the insurance proceeds are received not the year in which the involuntary conversion took place.

TIME REQUIREMENTS FOR REPLACEMENT

To qualify for nonrecognition of gain treatment, the converted property must be replaced within a specified time period. The general rule is that the period begins with the date of disposition of the converted property and ends "two years after the close of the first taxable year in which any part of the gain upon the conversion is realized."[62] If the involuntary conversion is due to condemnation or requisition, or the threat of such, the replacement period begins on the date of the threat or imminence of the requisition or condemnation. The replacement period may be extended by obtaining permission from the IRS.[63]

EXAMPLE I12-48 ▶ On December 8, 1997, Craig's business property was destroyed by fire. Craig receives insurance proceeds in 1998 and elects to defer recognition of the gain. He must replace the property between December 8, 1997 and December 31, 2000. The two-year time period includes 1999 and 2000 because the gain is realized when the insurance proceeds are received in 1998. ◀

KEY POINT

The replacement period is three years instead of two years on the condemnation of real property used in a business or held for investment.

The replacement period is longer if the involuntary conversion is due to the condemnation of real property (excluding inventory) held for productive use in a trade or business or for investment. The replacement period ends three years after the close of the first tax year in which any part of the gain is realized.[64] This provision for a longer replacement period applies to the same type of real property that may be replaced with like-kind property.

EXAMPLE I12-49 ▶ Beth owns a building used in her dry cleaning business. In 1997, the state condemns the building and awards Beth an amount greater than the adjusted basis of the building. Beth may replace the property with like-kind property, and the replacement period ends on December 31, 2000. ◀

The involuntary conversion rules are summarized in Topic Review I12-2.

SALE OF PRINCIPAL RESIDENCE: DEFERRAL OF GAIN

Congress uses the tax law to encourage home ownership in many ways: (1) Real estate taxes and interest on a mortgage used to acquire a principal or second residence are deductible (see Chapter I7), (2) taxpayers can defer any gain on the sale of a principal residence if a new principal residence is acquired within a certain time period at a

---

[62] Sec. 1033(a)(2)(B).
[63] Sec. 1033(a)(2)(B)(ii).

[64] Sec. 1033(g)(4).

Topic Review I12-2

Section 1033: Involuntary Conversions

1. Section 1033 applies only to gains, not losses.
2. Nonrecognition of gain under Section 1033 is elective. (Nonrecognition of gain is mandatory in a direct conversion, but direct conversions seldom occur.)
3. Section 1033 applies to involuntary conversions of all types of properties.
4. Some gain may be recognized if the taxpayer replaces the involuntarily converted property with property that costs less than the amount realized in the involuntary conversion.
5. The nonrecognized gain is deferred.
6. The basis of property acquired to replace the involuntarily converted property is the cost of the property less the deferred gain.
7. Property acquired to replace the involuntarily converted property generally must be functionally related property.
8. The required replacement period generally begins with the date of disposition of the converted property and ends two years after the close of the first taxable year in which any part of the gain on the conversion is realized. (A three-year period applies to condemnations of real property used in a trade or business or held for the production of income.)

OBJECTIVE 5

Determine when a gain resulting from the sale of a principal residence is deferred and the basis for replacement property

KEY POINT

The nonrecognition of gain under Sec. 1034 results only in the deferral of gain, but if the gain can be deferred until the taxpayer reaches age 55, the deferred gain can be permanently excluded in an amount up to $125,000.

TYPICAL MISCONCEPTION

The nonrecognition of gain is mandatory, not elective, as is sometimes believed.

cost equal to or greater than the adjusted sales price of the old principal residence,[65] and (3) taxpayers who are at least 55 years old may elect to exclude part or all of the gain from the sale of a principal residence.[66]

Section 1034(a) provides, "If property [in this section called 'old residence'] used by the taxpayer as his principal residence is sold by him and, within a period beginning two years before the date of such sale and ending two years after such date, property [in this section called 'new residence'] is purchased and used by the taxpayer as his principal residence, gain [if any] from such sale shall be recognized only to the extent that the taxpayer's adjusted sales price . . . of the old residence exceeds the taxpayer's cost of purchasing the new residence."[67]

Section 1034 applies only to gains. A loss on the sale of a personal residence is not deductible because the residence is personal-use property.[68] If Sec. 1034 applies, the nonrecognition of gain treatment is mandatory.

A gain realized on the sale of a principal residence that does not qualify under the Sec. 1034 deferral provisions or the Sec. 121 exclusion rule is treated as a capital gain because a personal residence is a capital asset.

PRINCIPAL RESIDENCE DEFINED

For Sec. 1034 to apply, taxpayers must sell property that qualifies as their principal residence and purchase property that is used as a new principal residence. Whether property is used as the taxpayer's principal residence is determined on a case-by-case basis.[69]

---

[65] Sec. 1034. The provision for deferral of gain recognition from the sale of a personal residence was first enacted in the Revenue Act of 1951. Congress created the provision in recognition of the fact that disposition of one's residence and acquisition of another residence were often necessitated by an increase in the size of the taxpayer's family or a change in the taxpayer's place of employment. Although primarily concerned with providing relief for a forced type of sale such as the above, Congress recognized the administrative burden of confining the provision's application to specific fact

situations and, therefore, extended relief to all sales of personal residences that meet certain requirements. S. Rept. No. 781, 82d Cong., 1st Sess., p. 482 (1951).
[66] Sec. 121.
[67] Sec. 1034(a).
[68] Reg. Secs. 1.165-9(a) and 1.262-1b)(4).
[69] Reg. Sec. 1.1034-1(c)(3).

Len, a 40-year-old college professor, owns and occupies a house in Oklahoma. During the summer, he lives in a cabin in Idaho. After owning the cabin for eight years, Len sells it for $50,000 and realizes a gain. He purchases a new cabin in Alaska for $60,000. Gain on the sale of the cabin in Idaho must be recognized because Len's principal residence is in Oklahoma. ◀

Condominium apartments, houseboats, and housetrailers may qualify as principal residences.[70] Stock held by a tenant-stockholder in a cooperative housing corporation is a principal residence if the dwelling that the taxpayer is entitled to occupy as a stockholder is used as his or her principal residence.[71]

DETERMINING WHETHER THE PROPERTY IS THE TAXPAYER'S PRINCIPAL RESIDENCE. To qualify for the favorable tax treatment provided by Sec. 1034, both the sold and acquired residences must be the taxpayer's principal residence.[72] Controversy often exists as to whether a residence qualifies as the taxpayer's principal residence, and the IRS will not issue rulings or determination letters concerning whether property qualifies under Secs. 121 or 1034.[73]

Property that is not being used as a principal residence when sold may have lost its character as the taxpayer's residence. A taxpayer's residence that is abandoned before its sale does not qualify as the taxpayer's principal residence.[74] In a case where taxpayers had not occupied their residence for more than ten years, the court disallowed the use of Sec. 1034 to the sale of the residence. The taxpayers were in the process of remodeling the property when they received and accepted an unsolicited offer.[75]

While attempting to sell the residence, the taxpayer may rent the property to another party. This action may jeopardize the taxpayer's ability to use Sec. 1034, although temporary rental before the sale does not always indicate a conversion to business use.[76]

In December 1996, Sandy discovered that her "dream house" was available for purchase. Sandy purchased the house and immediately occupied it as her new principal residence. She lives in a college town and knows that the market for housing becomes active in the spring. She lists her vacated house for sale with a realtor and agrees to allow two college students to rent the property on a month-to-month basis. Sandy retains the right to show the house to prospective buyers while the students are tenants. In April 1997, she sells the property. Because the conversion to rental property status is temporary, the residence is still Sandy's principal residence and Sec. 1034 is applied to defer recognition of gain from the sale of the former residence. ◀

If rental of the property constitutes abandonment of the residence, Sec. 1034 may not be used by the taxpayer.

In 1991, Sam and his wife moved from their residence in New Orleans to a home in Mobile. After renting the house in New Orleans for six years, they sell it in 1997. Section 1034 does not apply to the sale of the residence in New Orleans because the extended rental period constitutes an abandonment of the principal residence.[77] ◀

TIME REQUIREMENTS FOR REPLACEMENT OF PRINCIPAL RESIDENCE

The new principal residence must be acquired and used by the taxpayer during the period of time beginning two years before the date of sale of the old residence and ending two

---

[70] Rev. Rul. 64-31, 1964-1 C.B. 300.
[71] Reg. Sec. 1.1034-1(c)(3).
[72] Sec. 1034(a) and *Anne F. Stanley*, 33 T.C. 614 (1959).
[73] Rev. Proc. 92-3, 1992-1 C.B. 561.
[74] *William C. Stolk v. CIR*, 13 AFTR 2d 535, 64-1 USTC ¶9228 (2nd Cir.,

1964).
[75] *Ann K. Demeter*, 1971 PH T.C. Memo ¶71,209, 30 TCM 863.
[76] Rev. Rul. 78-146, 1978-1 C.B. 260.
[77] *Rene A. Stiegler, Jr.*, 1964 PH T.C. Memo ¶64,057, 23 TCM 412.

ADDITIONAL
COMMENT

The taxpayer does not have to be occupying the old residence at the date of sale. The taxpayer may have already moved to a new residence and be renting the old residence temporarily before its sale.

EXAMPLE I12-53 ▶
REAL-WORLD
EXAMPLE

The replacement period was not extended even when the new home that was being constructed was destroyed by fire. Rev. Rul. 75-438, 1975-2 C.B. 334.

TYPICAL
MISCONCEPTION

It is easy to become confused about the opportunity to purchase a new residence during the two-year period before the sale of the old one. At times taxpayers are compelled to relocate on short notice and may not be able to sell the house at the old location before buying another residence.

EXAMPLE I12-54 ▶

KEY POINT

The taxpayer must physically live in the replacement home before the expiration of the two-year period.

EXAMPLE I12-55 ▶

years after the date of sale.[78] The new residence must be used as a principal residence within this time period to avoid recognition of the gain realized on the sale of the old residence.[79] Even when failure to occupy the new residence within the required time is beyond the taxpayer's control, the benefits of Sec. 1034 are denied.[80] However, the two-year period is extended for members of the U.S. Armed Forces serving on extended active duty after the date of sale.[81]

After selling her home on June 10, 1995, Nancy, age 32, agreed to purchase a residence on August 5, 1995. Unfortunately, the real estate agent lacked proper authority to bind the seller, and Nancy was not able to acquire the residence. Nancy, unable to find another suitable house, signs a contract on July 2, 1996, to have a new residence constructed. Due to a strike by the carpenters' union and unusually bad weather, the house is not completed until July 25, 1997. Because Nancy does not occupy the new principal residence within two years of the date of sale, her realized gain on the sale must be recognized. ◀

The new residence may be purchased by the taxpayer during the two-year period before the sale of the old residence. If such a purchase does occur, the purchased residence is not treated as the new residence if it is sold or otherwise disposed of before the old residence is sold.[82]

If a taxpayer acquires more than one principal residence during the two-year period after the date of sale of the old residence, only the last residence purchased qualifies as the new residence.[83] This limitation is modified in certain situations involving business transfers as discussed below.

Joel's principal residence was sold for $50,000 in February 1996. He realized a gain. In September 1996, Joel purchased a principal residence for $70,000. The property is converted to rental property in March 1997 and Joel purchases another principal residence in a new neighborhood in May 1997. To determine whether Joel must recognize a gain on the sale of the principal residence occurring in February 1996, the residence purchased in May 1997 is considered to be the new principal residence, because it is the last residence purchased during the two-year period after the sale of the residence in February 1996. ◀

SALE OF MORE THAN ONE PRINCIPAL RESIDENCE WITHIN A TWO-YEAR PERIOD

A taxpayer who sells a principal residence within a two-year period after the sale of another principal residence may not be able to defer the gain resulting from the second sale if Sec. 1034 was used to defer any part of a gain realized on the first sale.[84] This restriction prevents taxpayers from avoiding the recognition of economic gains earned from frequent sales of personal residences.

Gail, age 40, sells her principal residence at a profit on May 10, 1997. The gain is not recognized because she purchased a new principal residence in the same neighborhood on March 5, 1997 at a cost greater that the adjusted sales price of the residence sold on May 10, 1997. If Gail sells the residence acquired on March 5, 1997, or any other principal residence acquired during the two-year period after May 10, 1997, any gain on the sale is recognized. The gain is not deferred under Sec. 1034 unless the moves are necessitated by business (i.e., the business move exception discussed below applies). ◀

---

[78] Sec. 1034(a).
[79] Rev. Rul. 69-434, 1969-2 C.B. 163.
[80] *Joseph T. Gelinas*, 1976 PH T.C. Memo ¶76,103, 35 TCM 448.
[81] Sec. 1034(h)(1). The period of time is not to extend longer than four years after the date of sale of the old residence. For sales of old residences after July 18, 1984, Sec. 1034(h)(2) provides that the extended time period may be

as long as eight years for certain members of the armed forces. The two-year period is also extended by Sec. 1034(k) for an individual whose tax home is outside the United States after the date of the sale of the old residence.
[82] Sec. 1034(c)(3).
[83] Sec. 1034(c)(4).
[84] Sec. 1034(d)(1).

THE BUSINESS MOVE EXCEPTION. The *business move exception* recognizes that business reasons may necessitate multiple sales of personal residences within a two-year period. An employment-related move is considered to be a business reason. Thus, if the sale of a personal residence within two years of the sale of another personal residence is due to a work-related move, Sec. 1034 may apply to the sale. The Sec. 217(c) time and distance tests used to determine the deductibility of moving expenses must be satisfied in order to use this exception.[85] (These tests are discussed in Chapter I9.)

EXAMPLE I12-56 ▶ In April 1996, Helen, who lived in Texas, sold her principal residence and purchased a new principal residence. Gain on the sale was deferred under Sec. 1034. In June 1997, Helen sells the residence located in Texas for $80,000 and moves to Florida to accept a new job. Her moving expenses are deductible. In July 1997, Helen purchases a new residence in Florida for $140,000. Even though she sells more than one principal residence within a two-year period, any gain on the sale of the first replacement residence (i.e., the residence sold in June 1997) is deferred because the business move exception applies. ◀

COMPUTING THE DEFERRED GAIN AND THE BASIS OF THE NEW RESIDENCE

No gain is recognized on the sale of a principal residence if a new principal residence is acquired at a cost equal to or greater than the adjusted sales price of the old residence. The new residence must be acquired and used as the taxpayer's personal residence during the specified two-year replacement period. If the cost of the new residence is less than the adjusted sales price of the old residence, part or all or the realized gain is recognized. The realized gain is recognized to the extent that the adjusted sales price exceeds the taxpayer's cost of purchasing the new residence.[86]

EXAMPLE I12-57 ▶ Judy sells her personal residence and has a $40,000 realized gain. The adjusted sales price is $94,000. She purchases a new residence two months later for $100,000. No gain is recognized because the cost of the new principal residence is greater than the adjusted sales price of the old principal residence and the other requirements of Sec. 1034 are met. ◀

EXAMPLE I12-58 ▶ Assume the same facts as in Example I12-57 except that the adjusted sales price is $105,000. Judy recognizes a $5,000 ($105,000 − $100,000) capital gain. The adjusted sales price is $5,000 more than the cost of the new principal residence, and the excess is not greater than the $40,000 realized gain. ◀

DETERMINING THE REALIZED GAIN. Gain realized is the excess of the amount realized over the property's adjusted basis.[87] The amount realized on the sale of the property is equal to the selling price less selling expenses.[88] Selling expenses include commissions, advertising, deed preparation costs, and legal expenses incurred in connection with the sale.[89]

EXAMPLE I12-59 ▶ Kirby sells his personal residence, which has a $100,000 basis, to Maxine. To make the sale, Kirby pays a $7,000 sales commission and incurs $800 of legal costs. Maxine pays $30,000 cash and assumes Kirby's $90,000 mortgage. The amount realized is $112,200 [($30,000 + $90,000) − ($7,000 + $800)]. The realized gain is $12,200 ($112,200 − $100,000). ◀

ADJUSTED SALES PRICE. The **adjusted sales price** is the amount realized, reduced by fixing-up expenses.[90] **Fixing-up expenses** are expenses incurred to assist in the sale of the

---

[85] Sec. 1034(d)(2).
[86] Sec. 1034(a).
[87] Reg. Sec. 1.1034-1(b)(5).

[88] Reg. Sec. 1.1034-1(b)(4).
[89] Reg. Sec. 1.1034-1(b)(4)(i).
[90] Reg. Sec. 1.1034-1(b).

old residence. Normal repairs and painting costs are examples of fixing-up expenses. Fixing-up expenses must be incurred during the 90-day period ending on the day the taxpayer enters into a contract to sell the old residence. The expenses must be paid within 30 days after the sale. Capital expenditures are not fixing-up expenses.

EXAMPLE I12-60 ▶

Dale sells a personal residence with a $100,000 adjusted basis for $140,000. Selling expenses amount to $10,000. He pays $4,000 of fixing-up expenses. The amount realized is $130,000 ($140,000 − $10,000). The adjusted sales price is $126,000 ($130,000 − $4,000). The realized gain is $30,000 ($130,000 − $100,000). ◀

EXAMPLE I12-61 ▶

SELF-STUDY QUESTION

How do fixing-up expenses affect the total amount of gain that a taxpayer will eventually recognize

ANSWER

Fixing-up expenses may reduce the amount of gain recognized but do not affect the amount of gain realized.

On February 10, 1997, David lists his house for sale with a broker. David pays $100 to a carpenter for minor repairs made on February 2, 1997. On April 25, 1997, he pays $6,000 to install central air conditioning. He also pays $40 to replace a broken window on May 12, 1997. David signs a contract to sell the house to Edith on June 14, 1997. Fixing-up expenses amount to $40. The $6,000 payment for central air conditioning is capitalized and increases the basis of the residence. The $100 payment to the carpenter is for work performed outside the 90-day period ending on the date a contract of sale was entered into (June 14, 1997). ◀

Fixing-up expenses are personal in nature and do not affect the realized gain. They are considered only when determining the amount of gain to be recognized. Payment of fixing-up expenses reduces the adjusted sales price. Adjusted sales price is then compared with the cost of the new residence to determine whether any of the realized gain should be recognized.

EXAMPLE I12-62 ▶

Milton sells a personal residence for $90,000. The property has a $60,000 adjusted basis. Selling expenses amount to $7,000, and the realized gain is $23,000 [($90,000 − $7,000) − $60,000]. Milton purchases a new residence four months later for $70,000. Because the adjusted sales price of $83,000 ($90,000 − $7,000) is more than the $70,000 cost of the new residence, he recognizes a $13,000 ($83,000 − $70,000) gain. If Milton incurs $1,000 of fixing-up expenses, the adjusted sales price is $82,000 [$90,000 − ($7,000 + $1,000)] and the recognized gain is $12,000 ($82,000 − $70,000). Although the realized gain is not affected by the fixing-up expenses, the recognized gain is reduced from $13,000 to $12,000. ◀

KEY POINT

In computing the cost of a new residence, the taxpayer can include additional expenditures for improving the property, such as the cost of remodeling a kitchen, if the expenditures are made within the replacement period.

COST OF REPLACEMENT RESIDENCE. The cost of purchasing a new residence includes all amounts attributable to the acquisition, including partial or total construction and reconstruction and improvements constituting capital expenditures made during the replacement period.[91] The mere improvement of a residence is not considered to be a purchase of a residence.[92] Commissions and other purchasing expenses paid to acquire the new residence are included in determining the cost of the residence.[93] Capital improvements are included in determining the cost of the replacement residence only if they are incurred during the period beginning two years before the date of sale of the former residence and ending two years after that date.

EXAMPLE I12-63 ▶

On March 10, 1995, Susan purchased a lot for $15,000 to use as the site of a new residence. Construction of the new house started on November 20, 1996 and is completed by April 4, 1997. Total construction costs of $70,000 (excluding the lot) are paid. On May 1, 1997, Susan sells her old personal residence at a $20,000 gain. The adjusted sales price is $74,000. Susan recognizes a $4,000 ($74,000 − $70,000) gain. The cost of the lot was not included because it is not incurred within the replacement period (i.e., within two years before or after the sale of the former residence). ◀

---

[91] Reg. Sec. 1.1034-1(b)(7).
[92] Reg. Sec. 1.1034-1(b)(9).

[93] Reg. Sec. 1.1034-1(c)(4).

If the old principal residence is exchanged for a new principal residence, the cost of the new residence is its FMV. The value of any part of the new residence acquired by the taxpayer other than by purchase is not included in determining the taxpayer's cost of the new residence.[94] A taxpayer who inherits a residence or receives one as a gift has not made a purchase under Sec. 1034 and may not, therefore, include the value of the gift in determining the cost of the new residence.

EXAMPLE I12-64 ▶ On April 10, 1997, Carol's uncle dies. She inherits her uncle's house, which has a $100,000 FMV. On May 1, 1997, Carol sells her former residence and has a $38,000 realized gain. The adjusted sales price is $75,000. Carol incurs $60,000 of reconstruction costs to modernize the inherited house and occupies the residence on July 5, 1997. Carol's cost of the new principal residence is only $60,000 because the FMV of the inherited house is excluded in determining the cost of the new residence for the purpose of determining the recognized gain under Sec. 1034. She recognizes a $15,000 ($75,000 − $60,000) gain. ◀

BASIS OF REPLACEMENT RESIDENCE. The basis of the new residence is its cost less the unrecognized gain on the sale of the old residence.[95] As with both the provisions under like-kind exchanges and involuntary conversions, the deferred gain may be taxed at a later date. If the purchase of a new residence results in the nonrecognition of any part of a gain on the sale of an old residence, the holding period of the old residence carries over to the new residence.[96]

EXAMPLE I12-65 ▶ Mark owns a personal residence with a $40,000 basis. Its holding period starts on April 10, 1980. On August 20, 1997, Mark sells the residence and has a $50,000 realized gain. The adjusted sales price is $88,000. Mark purchases and occupies a new residence on September 5, 1997. The cost of the new residence is $82,000. The recognized gain is $6,000 ($88,000 − $82,000), and the unrecognized gain is $44,000 ($50,000 − $6,000). Mark's basis in the new residence is $38,000 ($82,000 − $44,000), and its holding period begins on April 10, 1980. ◀

STOP & THINK

Question: Rebecca's uncle told her that she could purchase his house for $150,000 in five years provided that she could pay at least $30,000 of the purchase price in cash. Rebecca has $15,000 and is considering two alternative methods to raise the remaining $15,000 in five years. The first alternative would be to purchase $15,000 of non-dividend paying stock that she expects to increase in value to $30,000 within five years. The second alternative would be to purchase an $80,000 residence by paying $15,000 and borrowing $65,000. Payments on the mortgage will be interest only for five years and amount to $540 per month. She expects the house to be worth $95,000 at the end of five years. She will rent an apartment for $540 per month if she buys the stock. Ignoring transaction costs and assuming that she does not itemize deductions, should Rebecca purchase the stock or the house?

Solution: The $15,000 gain resulting from sale of the stock is gross income and subject to tax. The gain is probably LTCG and taxed at a maximum rate of 28%. If the rate is 28%, she must pay taxes of $4,200 and has only $25,800 available to use for the purchase of her uncle's house. She will have a gain of $15,000 if she sells the house but the gain is deferred since the $150,000 cost of the house is greater than the adjusted sales price for the house she sells. She has $30,000 of cash and is able to buy her uncle's house. The tax law encourages Rebecca to buy a principal residence.

---

[94] Reg. Sec. 1.1034-1(c)(4)(i).
[95] Sec. 1034(e).

[96] Sec. 1223(7).

ADDITIONAL
COMMENT

A factor that should be considered in electing to treat the condemnation of a personal residence as a voluntary sale under Sec. 1034 (in lieu of an involuntary conversion under Sec. 1033) is the replacement period. The replacement period varies depending on whether Sec. 1033 or Sec. 1034 applies.

INVOLUNTARY CONVERSION OF A PRINCIPAL RESIDENCE

Ordinarily, the involuntary conversion of a principal residence is governed by Sec. 1033, which was discussed earlier in this chapter. A gain due to an involuntary conversion of a personal residence may be deferred if the requirements of Sec. 1033 are satisfied. The functional use test must be satisfied regardless of the type of involuntary conversion. The like-kind test for replacement property may not be used because the personal residence is not used in a trade or business or held for investment.

If the gain is due to "the seizure, requisition, or condemnation of a residence, or the sale or exchange of a residence under threat or imminence thereof," the taxpayer may elect to use the provisions of Sec. 1034 in lieu of Sec. 1033.[97] If the involuntary conversion is a casualty, taxpayers may defer the gain only under Sec. 1033.

A loss due to a condemnation of a personal residence is not recognized. If the loss is due to a casualty, the loss is deductible and is treated like other casualty losses of nonbusiness property (see Chapter I8).

ADDITIONAL
COMMENT

Because of the tremendous damage and hardships produced by Hurricane Andrew in Florida and the flooding of the Mississippi River, Congress responded with substantial tax relief for taxpayers who received insurance proceeds for damaged personal property, and made the favorable tax treatment retroactive to disasters after August 31, 1991.

PRESIDENTIALLY DECLARED DISASTER OF A PRINCIPAL RESIDENCE. Special treatment is provided when a taxpayer's principal residence or any of its contents is compulsorily or involuntarily converted and the residence is located in an area which is determined by the President to be in an area that warrants assistance by the federal government under the Disaster Relief and Emergency Assistance Act. Part of the gain resulting from the receipt of insurance proceeds is excluded and part may be deferred if the President's declaration is after August 31, 1991.[98]

No gain is recognized due to the receipt of insurance proceeds for damaged personal property located in the residence if the property was unscheduled property for the purpose of such insurance. Although proceeds received for property that is not separately scheduled are excluded from gross income, other proceeds received, including those received for scheduled property, are treated as being received as a common fund for a single item of property. Separately scheduled property typically consists of items such as computers, jewelry, artwork, and pianos.

If insurance proceeds received due to damages to the house and separately scheduled property are used to purchase any property similar or related in service or use to the converted residence or its contents, the taxpayer may elect to defer any gain realized. Gain is recognized only to the extent that the cost of the replacement property is less than the amount of insurance funds received. The replacement period is extended to four years after the close of the first taxable year in which any part of the gain on the conversion is realized.[99]

EXAMPLE I12-66 ▶

Nora's principal residence, with an adjusted basis of $70,000, was destroyed by a flood in May 1997. The area was declared by the President to be a federal disaster area. All of the contents of her home, including a Steinway grand piano with a basis of $25,000 and a FMV of $30,000, were destroyed. Nora received the following payments from the insurance company in July 1997: $200,000 for the house, $25,000 for personal property contents with an adjusted basis of $15,000, and $30,000 for the piano, which was separately scheduled property in the insurance policy. In December 1997, Nora pays $248,000 for a new house and does not replace the piano. The $10,000 ($25,000 − $15,000) gain on the unscheduled personal property is excluded from gross income. Because she paid at least $230,000 ($200,000 +

---

[97] Sec. 1034(i) and Reg. Sec. 1.1034-1(h).

[98] The Revenue Reconciliation Act of 1993 granted retroactive tax relief for taxpayers because of the mass destruction in Florida caused by Hurricane Andrew and the flooding in several midwest states that occurred in 1993.

[99] Sec. 1033(h)(1)(B). As noted in Chapter I8, taxpayers who suffer losses attributable to a disaster that occurs in an area subsequently declared by the President to be a disaster area may elect to deduct the loss in the year preceding the year in which the loss actually occurs.

$30,000) for the replacement residence, the gain attributable to the house and the piano is deferred. ◀

SALE OF PRINCIPAL RESIDENCE: EXCLUDED GAIN

OBJECTIVE 6

Determine when a gain resulting from the sale of a principal residence may be excluded

KEY POINT

This provision is different from the like-kind exchange or the involuntary conversion in that the gain is excluded instead of deferred.

A taxpayer may elect to exclude gain from the sale of a principal residence under Sec. 121. However, the taxpayer must be at least 55 years of age and the amount of gain excluded may not exceed $125,000. A married individual filing a separate return may not exclude more than $62,500.

As indicated in Table I12-1, significant differences exist between the deferral of gain on the sale of a principal residence under Sec. 1034 and the exclusion of gain under Sec. 121. The major difference is that an excluded gain is never subject to tax, whereas a deferred gain may be recognized upon the subsequent sale of the replacement residence. The basis of the replacement residence is reduced by the amount of gain deferred upon the sale of the former residence.

▼ **TABLE I12-1**

Comparison of Secs. 1034 (Deferral of Gain on Sale of Principal Residence) and 121 (Exclusion of Gain From Sale of Principal Residence)

	Section 1034	Section 121
Definition of principal residence.	Determined on a case-by-case basis.	Same as Sec. 1034.
Must property have been used as a principal residence before sale?	Yes.	Yes, for at least three years during the five-year period ending on the date of sale.
Treatment of realized gain.	All or part of the gain may be deferred depending on the relationship between the adjusted sales price of the old residence and the cost of the new principal residence.	Excluded up to $125,000 ($62,500 for a married individual filing a separate return).
Availability of election	No election required because the treatment is mandatory.	Election filed with tax return for year of sale.
Does taxpayer need to acquire and use new residence to replace residence sold?	Yes, within a period beginning two years before the date of sale and ending two years after that date.	No.
Are there any restrictions on age of taxpayer?	No.	Yes, must be at least 55 years of age before the date of sale.
Are there any restrictions on number of times section may be used?	No.	Yes, once a lifetime.

REQUIREMENTS TO QUALIFY FOR THE EXCLUSION

To qualify for the Sec. 121 exclusion, the taxpayer must be at least 55 years of age before the date of the sale or exchange of the principal residence and must own and use the property as a principal residence for at least three years of the five-year period ending on the date of sale.[100] "Short temporary absences such as for vacation or other seasonal absence . . . are counted as periods of use."[101]

A married couple that holds the property jointly and file a joint return meets the age, holding, and use requirements discussed above if only one spouse satisfies them.[102] A taxpayer, age 55 or older, who inherits property from a deceased spouse may be able to exclude the gain even if the taxpayer does not satisfy the holding and use requirements. If the holding and use requirements are satisfied by the deceased spouse, these requirements are deemed to be satisfied by the surviving spouse.[103]

KEY POINT

In general, the IRS considers the taxpayer's age at December 31 to be his or her age for the entire year. In this case, however, the taxpayer must be age 55 before the date of sale.

EXAMPLE I12-67

ADDITIONAL COMMENT

To qualify for the Sec. 121 exclusion, the taxpayer must own and use the property for at least three years of the five-year period ending on the date of sale. However, the ownership test and the use test do not have to be met simultaneously during the five-year period ending on the date of sale.

Dorothy purchased a house in Iowa on April 10, 1994 and occupied it until July 1, 1995, when she accepted a six-month job assignment in Alaska. While in Alaska, Dorothy rented the house to an elderly couple for five months. Dorothy returned to the house in Iowa on January 1, 1996, and sold the house, realizing a $110,000 gain on September 1, 1997. Dorothy is 55 years old and has never elected to exclude a gain under Sec. 121. The gain resulting from the sale on September 1, 1997, may be excluded because Dorothy used the house as a principal residence for at least three years of the five-year period ending September 1, 1997 (i.e., the five month temporary absence is counted in the required three-year period of use). Because the realized gain is less than $125,000, Dorothy may exclude the entire gain. ◀

EXAMPLE I12-68

Clay and Kathryn live in a community property state. Kathyrn owns a residence that is separate property because she acquired it before their marriage. The house's FMV is much greater than its adjusted basis. Clay and Kathyrn have occupied the house for nine years. Clay is 55 years old, but Kathryn is 51 years old. Kathryn wants to transfer title to the house from her sole ownership to joint ownership and then Clay and Kathyrn will sell the residence shortly thereafter. None of the gain may be excluded under Sec. 121. Neither spouse meets all the requirements for an exclusion of the gain under Sec. 121. Clay has not owned the property as his principal residence for three years, and Kathryn is less than 55 years old.[104] ◀

If the taxpayer sells a principal residence that is purchased as a new replacement residence under Sec. 1034, the use and ownership test period begins on the day the replacement residence is acquired.

EXAMPLE I12-69

In April, 1995, Vince, age 54, sold a residence used as his principal residence for six years. Two months later, he purchased a new residence at a cost greater than the adjusted sales price for the old residence and deferred the realized gain. Vince uses the replacement residence as a principal residence until April 10, 1997, when the residence is sold at a gain. Vince may not elect to exclude the gain under Sec. 121 because the replacement residence is not used as his principal residence for three years of the five-year period ending on April 10, 1997. ◀

INVOLUNTARY CONVERSION. For purposes of Sec. 121, the destruction, theft, seizure, requisition, or condemnation of property is treated as a sale.[105] Thus, taxpayers

---

[100] Sec. 121(a). Section 121(d)(9) provides an exception for a taxpayer who becomes physically or mentally incapable of self-care if the property is used as a principal residence for at least one year during the five-year period. In such case, the period that the taxpayer resides in a state-licensed facility (including a nursing home) is counted for the three-year-out-of-five-year required use requirement.

[101] Reg. Sec. 1.121-1(c).
[102] Sec. 121(d)(1)(C).
[103] Sec. 121(d)(2).
[104] Ltr. Rul. 8909020 (December 2, 1988) and Reg. Sec. 1.121-1(d) Ex. 3.
[105] Sec. 121(d)(4).

may elect to exclude a gain due to the involuntary conversion of a principal residence if the use and ownership test is satisfied.

If gain due to the involuntary conversion of a principal residence is deferred under Sec. 1033, the holding period of the replacement residence includes the holding period of the converted property for purposes of satisfying the use and ownership tests of Sec. 121.[106] Thus, when there is a choice, it might be preferable to defer a gain under Sec. 1033 instead of Sec. 1034.

EXAMPLE I12-70 ▶

SELF-STUDY QUESTION

Assume that Rick sells his principal residence and elects to exclude the $10,000 gain under Sec. 121. What happens to the remaining $115,000 ($125,000 − $10,000) limitation?

ANSWER

It is lost and has no future tax benefit for Rick.

In 1997, Gina's principal residence of ten years was destroyed by fire. She replaced the principal residence on June 5, 1997 and elected to defer the gain under Sec. 1033.[107] After using the replacement residence as a principal residence for only two years, Gina, age 55, sells the residence at a gain. She elects to exclude the gain under Sec. 121. The use and ownership test is satisfied because her use and ownership of the converted property is also counted toward satisfying the three-year requirement. ◀

ELECTION

The election to exclude the gain on the sale or exchange of a principal residence is a once-in-a-lifetime exclusion.[108] The election "may be made or revoked at any time before the expiration of the period for making a claim for credit or refund."[109]

A married taxpayer may elect or revoke under Sec. 121 if the taxpayer's spouse joins in such election or revocation.[110] An election by one spouse eliminates the opportunity for either spouse to make a subsequent election.

EXAMPLE I12-71 ▶

Roy, age 55, marries Lois, who is Jack's widow. While married, Jack and Lois sold their principal residence and elected to exclude the gain. Roy, now married to Lois, sells his principal residence of 20 years at a gain. Under Sec. 121, Roy may not elect to exclude the gain because he is married to Lois, who made a previous election with Jack. If Roy wanted to exclude the gain, he should have sold the residence before he married Lois. ◀

COMBINATION OF EXCLUSION AND DEFERRAL PROVISIONS

Sections 121 and 1034 may apply to the same sale of a principal residence. If the realized gain exceeds $125,000, the excess amount of realized gain may be deferred under Sec. 1034. However, for Sec. 1034 to apply, the taxpayer must purchase and occupy a new principal residence during the four-year replacement period (i.e., two years before the sale or two years after the sale). To defer all of the remaining gain, the cost of the new residence must be equal to or greater than the adjusted sales price of the old residence. When computing the adjusted sales price, the amount realized from the sale or exchange of the residence is reduced by any gain excluded under Sec. 121.[111]

EXAMPLE I12-72 ▶

ADDITIONAL COMMENT

In determining the lowest price of a new residence that will result in the recognition of no gain under Sec. 1034, the adjusted selling price is reduced by the $125,000 gain excluded under Sec. 121.

During the current year, Amy, age 55, sells a principal residence and purchases a new residence. The requirements for Sections 121 and 1034 are both satisfied, and Amy elects to exclude the gain. The deferral of gain under Sec. 1034 is mandatory. The following information pertains to the sale and purchase:

Basis of old residence	$ 60,000
Selling price of old residence	300,000
Selling expenses	18,000
Fixing-up expenses	3,000
Purchase price of new residence	150,000

---

[106] Sec. 121(d)(8).
[107] Section 1034 does not apply when the involuntary conversion of a principal residence is due to a casualty.
[108] Sec. 121(b)(2).
[109] Sec. 121(c).
[110] Ibid.
[111] Sec. 121(d)(7).

The tax consequences of Amy's sale of her principal residence are as follows:

Selling price	$300,000
Minus: Selling expenses	(18,000)
Amount realized	$282,000
Minus: Adjusted basis	(60,000)
Realized gain	$222,000
Minus: Excluded gain	(125,000)
Balance of realized gain	$ 97,000
Selling price	$300,000
Minus: Selling expenses	(18,000)
Fixing-up expenses	(3,000)
Excluded gain	(125,000)
Adjusted sales price	$154,000
Adjusted sales price	$154,000
Minus: Cost of replacement residence	(150,000)
Recognized gain	$ 4,000[a]
Cost of replacement residence	$150,000
Minus: Deferred gain ($97,000 − $4,000)	(93,000)
Basis of replacement residence	$ 57,000

[a] Limited to the balance of realized gain, $97,000.

Section 121 allows Amy to exclude $125,000 of the $222,000 realized gain. To compute the adjusted sales price, the excluded portion of the realized gain is deducted to determine the amount realized. Thus, the adjusted sales price is the selling price less selling expenses, the excluded gain and fixing-up expenses. Because the cost of the new residence does not exceed the adjusted sales price, not all of the remaining gain of $97,000 ($222,000 − $125,000) is deferred. A $4,000 gain is recognized. The remaining $93,000 gain is deferred. The $150,000 cost of the new residence is reduced by the $93,000 deferred gain to determine the $57,000 basis for the new residence. ◀

TAX PLANNING CONSIDERATIONS

AVOIDING THE LIKE-KIND EXCHANGE PROVISIONS

In some cases, a taxpayer may prefer a taxable exchange to a nontaxable like-kind exchange. For instance, if the gain is taxed as a capital gain and the taxpayer has capital losses to offset the gain, the taxpayer may prefer to recognize the gain during the current year. If the gain on the exchange is recognized instead of deferred, the basis of the property received in the exchange is higher.

EXAMPLE I12-73 ▶ Connie owns land with a $20,000 basis. The land is held as an investment. Connie exchanges the land for a duplex with a $100,000 FMV. Because the exchange qualifies as a like-kind exchange, no gain is recognized and Connie's basis for the duplex is $20,000. If the exchange does not qualify as a like-kind exchange (e.g., the land is a personal-use asset), Connie recognizes an $80,000 capital gain. Connie's basis for the duplex is

$100,000. The basis of the duplex, except for the portion allocable to land, is eligible for depreciation. ◄

If an exchange qualifies as a like-kind exchange, no loss on the exchange is recognized. A taxpayer who prefers to recognize a loss should avoid making a like-kind exchange. It may be advantageous to sell the property to recognize the loss and then purchase the replacement asset in two independent transactions. If the sale and purchase transactions are with the same party, the IRS may maintain that the like-kind exchange rules apply because the two transactions are in substance a like-kind exchange (i.e., the judicial doctrine of substance over form might be applied).

SALE OF A PRINCIPAL RESIDENCE

DEFERRAL PROVISIONS. It is unlikely that a taxpayer will ever have an incentive to avoid the mandatory tax treatment provided by Sec. 1034 because

▶ When the taxpayer is at least age 55, up to $125,000 of the gain may be excluded.

▶ A personal residence is not subject to depreciation and thus, a step-up in basis has less value as a tax benefit.

▶ The residence may eventually be transferred to the taxpayer's heirs as a result of the taxpayer's death and no income taxes will be paid on the unrealized appreciation as of the date of death. In addition, the heirs will receive a step-up in basis of the property to its FMV.

IDENTIFYING THE PRINCIPAL RESIDENCE. In view of the advantages of deferring the gain on the sale of a principal residence, a taxpayer contemplating a sale should satisfy all requirements of Sec. 1034. A taxpayer who owns and occupies more than one residence may have difficulty identifying which is the principal residence. However, the *principal residence* is defined as the one that the taxpayer occupies most of the time.[112]

EXAMPLE I12-74 ▶ Paula, a business consultant, owns residences in Boston and Philadelphia. She plans to sell both residences in two years and purchase a new residence in California. The Boston residence has a FMV that is $200,000 greater than its basis. The residence in Philadelphia has not appreciated. Paula should plan her activities in a manner that will allow her to occupy the Boston residence more than the Philadelphia residence so the Boston residence will qualify as her principal residence. ◄

HISTORICAL NOTE
The replacement period was increased for sales after July 20, 1981 from a period that began 18 months before and that ended 18 months after the sale.

TIMING THE SALE AND PURCHASE. Because Sec. 1034 requires that the purchase and use of the new residence must occur within a period beginning two years before the date the old residence is sold and ending two years after that date, the taxpayer must consider the timing of the sale and purchase. A taxpayer who purchases a new residence before selling the old residence may lose the advantage of Sec. 1034 if it takes more than two years to sell the old residence.

To defer all of the gain, the cost of the new residence must equal or exceed the adjusted sales price of the old residence. When the cost of the new residence is determined, only capital costs incurred during the four-year replacement period are used.

EXAMPLE I12-75 ▶ Eventually, Gary expects to sell his principal residence and build a new one. On March 10, 1997, Gary pays $25,000 for a lot in a new subdivision. If Gary plans to include the $25,000 as part of the cost of the new residence to defer a gain on the sale of the old residence, the old residence should be sold no later than March 10, 1999. ◄

---

[112] Rev. Rul. 77-298, 1977-2 C.B. 308.

The taxpayer may find it beneficial to postpone the sale of a principal residence if Sec. 1034 was recently used to defer the gain on the sale of a previous residence. Unless the business move exception applies, Sec. 1034 cannot be applied more than once within a two-year period.

EXAMPLE I12-76 ▶

On June 5, 1997, Kristie offers to purchase Tony's principal residence. Because of the attractive purchase offer, Tony is willing to sell the residence and purchase a new one. The basis of Tony's current residence was reduced by the gain deferred on the sale of Tony's previous residence on August 12, 1995. Section 1034 will not apply to the sale on June 5, 1997, because only one principal residence may be sold during the two-year period ending on August 12, 1997. To obtain the tax deferral benefit of Sec. 1034, Tony should delay the closing of the sale of his current residence until after August 12, 1997. ◀

EXCLUSION PROVISIONS. A taxpayer who is eligible to use the $125,000 exclusion under Sec. 121 must decide whether to make the election. Careful consideration must be given to this decision because the election is available only once in a person's lifetime, no unused portion of the $125,000 exclusion may be used at a later date, and the use of the exclusion precludes the taxpayer's spouse from using the exclusion in a subsequent year even if the spousal relationship no longer exists.

Thus, if the taxpayer has the opportunity to choose whether to defer all of the gain under Sec. 1034 or exclude it under Sec. 121, the choice should probably be deferral. However, consideration should be given to the fact that the holding period for the use and occupancy requirement (i.e., three years out of the five years preceding the sale) does not carry over to the new principal residence if Sec. 1034 is used to defer the gain on the sale of the old residence.

The size of the realized gain and the likelihood of selling another principal residence at a gain are two factors that must also be considered by the taxpayer who is making the election. Despite the time value of money, a taxpayer with a small gain might not elect to exclude the gain currently if the anticipated gain on a subsequent sale of a principal residence is substantially larger than the current gain. If the taxpayer does not expect to sell another principal residence (e.g., the individual plans to rent an apartment and has no desire to be a homeowner again), the exclusion of gain provision should be elected.

As with any election provided in the Code, there is a risk that the law will change. To date, the only major change in Sec. 121 has been to increase the amount of the exclusion from $100,000 to $125,000.[113] During the 1996 campaign for President, both President Clinton and candidate Bob Dole advocated major changes in the taxation of principal residences.

PROPERTY CONVERTED TO BUSINESS USE. If a residence is converted to business use at the time of the sale, it does not qualify as a principal residence.[114] A principal residence converted to business use may subsequently become the taxpayer's principal residence if the business use is discontinued for a period of time.[115]

EXAMPLE I12-77 ▶

Brad, a college professor, uses 20% of his residence as an office from 1972 until 1997. Brad deducted expenses related to the office portion of the residence for the years 1972 through 1977. After 1977, no deduction was allowed because Brad no longer met the eligibility requirements for an office-in-home deduction. (See Chapter I9 for a discussion of the office-in-home deduction.) If Brad sold the property before 1978, only 80% of the property would have qualified as a principal residence and 20% would be considered business property. Alternative-

---

[113] The increase to $125,000 is effective for residences sold or exchanged after July 20, 1981.

[114] Reg. Sec. 1.1034-1(a)(3)(ii).
[115] Rev. Rul. 82-26, 1982-1 C.B. 114.

ly, if he sells the residence in 1997, the entire residence is considered to be his principal residence because the business use has been discontinued. The basis of the residence is reduced by the depreciation allowed from 1972 through 1977. ◀

COMPLIANCE AND PROCEDURAL CONSIDERATIONS

ADDITIONAL COMMENT

The failure to include gain from an involuntary conversion in gross income is deemed to be an election even though the details are not reported.

REPORTING OF INVOLUNTARY CONVERSIONS

The election to defer recognition of the gain from an involuntary conversion is made by not reporting the gain as income for the first year in which gain is realized. All details pertaining to the involuntary conversion (including those relating to the replacement of the converted property) should be reported for the taxable year or years in which any of the gain is realized.[116]

A taxpayer who elects to defer recognition of the gain but does not make a proper replacement of the property within the required period of time must file an amended return for the year or years for which the election was made. An amended return may be needed if the cost of the replacement property is less than expected at the time of the election. All details pertaining to the replacement of converted property must be reported in the year in which replacement occurs.[117]

EXAMPLE I12-78 ▶

Bob's property, with a $40,000 adjusted basis, was destroyed by a storm in 1996. Bob received $45,000 insurance proceeds in 1996 and planned to purchase property similar to the converted property in 1997 at a cost of $47,000. Bob elected to defer recognition of the gain in 1996. In 1997 the replacement property is purchased for $44,500. Bob must file an amended return for 1996 and recognize a $500 ($45,000 − $44,500) gain. ◀

ADDITIONAL COMMENT

The replacement period may be extended if special permission is obtained from the IRS.

A taxpayer who either is ineligible or does not want to defer the gain must report the gain in the usual manner. If a taxpayer does not elect to defer the gain in the year the gain is realized and the replacement period has not expired, a subsequent election may be made. In such an event, a refund claim should be filed for the tax year in which the gain was realized and previously recognized.[118]

Taxpayers who do not initially elect to defer the gain from an involuntary conversion may later make the election, but the election may not subsequently be revoked. The Tax Court has ruled that the Treasury Regulations allow the filing of an amended return for a year in which the election is made only if proper replacement is not made within the specified time period or the replacement is made at a cost lower than anticipated at the time of the election.[119] The IRS takes the position that taxpayers who designate qualifying property as replacement property may not later designate other qualifying property as the replacement property.[120]

EXAMPLE I12-79 ▶

In 1995 Troy collected $200,000 from an insurance company as the result of the destruction of rental property with a $140,000 basis. He made the election to defer the gain realized in 1995 and attached a supporting schedule of details regarding the involuntary conversion including a designation of replacement property to be acquired in 1996. In 1996 Troy purchased the designated replacement rental property for $225,000. In 1997 Troy purchases other rental property for $400,000 and now wants to designate that property as the replacement property

---

[116] Reg. Sec. 1.1033(a)-2(c)(2).
[117] *Ibid.*
[118] *Ibid.*

[119] *John McShain*, 65 T.C. 686 (1976).
[120] Rev. Rul. 83-39, 1983-1 C.B. 190.

for the property destroyed in 1995. Troy may not designate the property acquired in 1997 as the replacement property because the rental property purchased in 1996 was already designated as such. ◀

REPORTING OF SALE OR EXCHANGE OF A PRINCIPAL RESIDENCE

Form 2119 is used to report the sale or exchange of a principal residence. That form reports the date of the sale and the date the new residence is occupied. Any portion of the old or new residence that is not used as a principal residence is not used to determine the deferred gain. For this reason, the taxpayer must indicate whether any rooms in either residence are rented out or used for business. If a gain is recognized, the gain is reported on Schedule D of Form 1040.

EXAMPLE I12-80 ▶

Amy's house, which is used as a principal residence, contains a home office. Depreciation deductions are allowed for the portion of the house used as an office. The basis of the principal residence portion of the house is $50,000 and the adjusted basis of the office is $5,000.

Amy sells the house for $80,000, and 10% of the selling price is allocated to the office portion of the house. No selling or fixing-up expenses are incurred. The gain realized on the sale of the principal residence is $22,000 ($72,000 − $50,000). The gain realized on the sale of the office portion of the house is $3,000 ($8,000 − $5,000).

Amy purchases a new residence for $100,000, and 12% of the new residence is used for an office. The $22,000 gain realized due to the sale of a principal residence is deferred because the $88,000 cost [$100,000 − (0.12 × $100,000)] allocated to the new residence exceeds the $72,000 adjusted sales price of the old residence. The $3,000 gain on the sale of the office portion of the residence is recognized. Amy's basis for the principal residence is $66,000 ($88,000 − $22,000). The basis for the office is $12,000. ◀

FORM 2119 ILLUSTRATED. Part I of Form 2119, which is shown in Figure I12-1, is used to report the taxpayer's realized gain. The amount realized is $183,000, and the gain realized is $93,000.

In Part III of Form 2119, the adjusted sales price is computed and compared with the cost of the new residence to determine the recognized gain. The excess of the realized gain over the recognized gain (i.e., the deferred gain), if any, is subtracted from the cost of the new residence to determine the adjusted basis of the new residence.

As illustrated in Part III of Form 2119, the recognized gain is $60,000. The $183,000 adjusted sales price ($185,000 selling price − $2,000 of sales commissions) exceeds the $123,000 cost of the new residence by $60,000. The $33,000 ($93,000 − $60,000) deferred gain is subtracted from the $123,000 cost to determine the $90,000 adjusted basis of the new residence.

Part II of Form 2119 is used by taxpayers who are at least 55 years old before the principal residence is sold. If the taxpayer in the illustration is eligible to elect to exclude the gain and makes the election, the $93,000 gain realized, or $125,000 if less, is reported on line 14. Because the gain realized is less than $125,000, no gain is recognized. Although it is not necessary to purchase a new principal residence to use the election, Part III is used to report the purchase of a new residence, the possible deferral of a realized gain in excess of $125,000, and the adjusted basis of the new residence.

NEW RESIDENCE IS NOT ACQUIRED IN YEAR THE OLD RESIDENCE IS SOLD. Often a taxpayer may sell a principal residence in one tax year and purchase a new residence in either the following tax year or the second tax year following the year of sale. If an individual plans to replace his or her principal residence, Form 2119 should

Form 2119

Department of the Treasury
Internal Revenue Service

Sale of Your Home

▶ Attach to Form 1040 for year of sale.
▶ Please print or type.

OMB No. 1545-0072

1996

Attachment
Sequence No. **20**

Your first name and initial. If a joint return, also give spouse's name and initial. | Last name | Your social security number

Fill in Your Address Only If You Are Filing This Form by Itself and Not With Your Tax Return

Present address (no., street, and apt. no., rural route, or P.O. box no. if mail is not delivered to street address) | Spouse's social security no.

City, town or post office, state, and ZIP code

Part I Gain on Sale

1	Date your former main home was sold (month, day, year) ▶	1	1-10-95
2	Have you bought or built a new main home?		☒ Yes ☐ No
3	If any part of either main home was ever rented out or used for business, check here ▶ ☐		
4	Selling price of home. Do not include personal property items you sold with your home	4	185,000
5	Expense of sale	5	2,000
6	Subtract line 5 from line 4	6	183,000
7	Adjusted basis of home sold	7	90,000
8	**Gain on sale.** Subtract line 7 from line 6	8	93,000

Is line 8 more than zero?
— Yes ——▶ If line 2 is "Yes," you **must** go to Part II or Part III, whichever applies. If line 2 is "No," go to line 9.
— No ——▶ **Stop** and attach this form to your return.

9	If you haven't replaced your home, do you plan to do so within the **replacement period**? ☐ Yes ☐ No
	• If line 9 is "Yes," stop here, attach this form to your return, and see **Additional Filing Requirements.**
	• If line 9 is "No," you **must** go to Part II or Part III, whichever applies.

Part II One-Time Exclusion of Gain for People Age 55 or Older - By completing this part, you are electing to take the one-time exclusion. If you are not electing to take the exclusion, go to Part III now.

10	Who was age 55 or older on the date of sale?	☐ You ☐ Your spouse ☐ Both of you
11	Did the person who was 55 or older own and use the property as his or her main home for a total of at least 3 years of the 5-year period before the sale? If "No," go to Part III now	☐ Yes ☐ No
12	At the time of sale, who owned the home?	☐ You ☐ Your spouse ☐ Both of you
13	Social security number of spouse at the time of sale if you had a different spouse from the one above. If you were not married at the time of sale, enter "None". ▶	13	
14	**Exclusion.** Enter the **smaller** of line 8 or $125,000 ($62,500 if married filing separate return). Then, go to line 15	14	

Part III Adjusted Sales Price, Taxable Gain, and Adjusted Basis of New Home

15	If line 14 is blank, enter the amount from line 8. Otherwise, subtract line 14 from line 8	15	93,000
	• If line 15 is zero, stop and attach this form to your return.		
	• If line 15 is more than zero and line 2 is "Yes," go to line 16 now.		
	• If you are reporting this sale on the installment method, stop and see instructions.		
	• All others, stop and **enter the amount from line 15 on Schedule D, col. (g), line 4 or line 12.**		
16	Fixing-up expenses	16	0.
17	If line 14 is blank, enter amount from line 16. Otherwise, add lines 14 and 16	17	0.
18	**Adjusted sales price.** Subtract line 17 from line 6	18	183,000
19a	Date you moved into new home ▶ 10-22-95 **b** Cost of new home	19b	123,000
20	Subtract line 19b from line 18. If zero or less, enter -0-	20	60,000
21	**Taxable gain.** Enter the **smaller** of line 15 or line 20	21	60,000
	• If line 21 is zero, go to line 22 and attach this form to your return.		
	• If you are reporting this sale on the installment method, see the line 15 instructions and go to line 22.		
	• All others, **enter the amount from line 21 on Schedule D, col. (g), line 4 or line 12,** and go to line 22.		
22	Postponed gain. Subtract line 21 from line 15	22	33,000
23	**Adjusted basis of new home.** Subtract line 22 from line 19b	23	90,000

Sign Here Only If You Are Filing This Form by Itself and Not With Your Tax Return

Under penalties of perjury, I declare that I have examined this form, including attachments, and to the best of my knowledge and belief, it is true, correct, and complete.

Your signature | Date | Spouse's signature | Date

▶ If a joint return, both must sign.

LHA **For Paperwork Reduction Act Notice, see separate instructions.**

Form **2119** (1996)

612701
11-13-96

FIGURE I12-1 ▶ FORM 2119

be attached to the taxpayer's Form 1040 for the year of sale. Only lines 1 through 9 are completed, and no gain is reported on Schedule D.

If the taxpayer purchases a new residence within the replacement period at a cost greater than the adjusted sales price, the taxpayer should notify the IRS by providing a new Form 2119 for the year of sale. If the taxpayer does not purchase a new residence within the replacement period or if a new residence is purchased at a cost less than the adjusted sales price, an amended return should be filed for the year of sale.

The statute of limitations with respect to any gain due to the sale of a principal residence does not expire before the three-year period beginning on the day the IRS receives written notification of

▶ The taxpayer's cost of the new residence used to defer any part of the gain

▶ The taxpayer's intention not to purchase a new residence within the replacement period, or

▶ The taxpayer's failure to purchase a new residence within the replacement period[121]

ETHICAL POINT

Tax preparers should inform the client if there is an error in a previously filed return or if the client fails to file a required return. (See the discussion of this topic in Chapter I15 in the *Statements on Responsibilities in Tax Practice* section.)

WHAT WOULD YOU DO IN THIS SITUATION?

You are a CPA who specializes in taxation and has a substantial list of clients. One of your clients, Sam Shaver, age 45, sold his principal residence on April 25, 1995 for $400,000 and realized a gain of $120,000. He indicated to you that he intended to purchase a replacement residence for at least $400,000 within the required two-year period of time. Therefore, when you filed Shaver's 1995 income tax return, you attached Form 2119 showing the sales price and gain, but, based on Shaver's statement to you about his intention to purchase a replacement residence within the requisite time period, you did not include the $120,000 gain in his 1995 return. In March,

1998, at a meeting with Shaver to gather his tax information for his 1997 income tax return, you discover that Shaver did not purchase a replacement residence during the two-year period ending on April 25, 1997. You inform Shaver that he should file an amended 1995 return and report the $120,000 gain and that you would be happy to assist him in the preparation of this return. Shaver tells you that he does not intend to file an amended return and will only file the amended return if the IRS notifies him that such a return is required. What should you do in this situation with respect to both the 1995 amended return and the 1997 return that you are about to prepare?

BASIS OF PRINCIPAL RESIDENCE

The normal rules for determining basis are applied when ascertaining the basis of a principal residence. The basis of property is a function of how the property is obtained (e.g., purchase, gift, or inheritance).

Although the basis of property purchased is usually its cost, the basis of a new principal residence is reduced by any gain deferred on the sale of the old principal residence under Sec. 1034.[122] Expenses incurred to purchase the residence (such as legal fees, commissions, survey costs, title search, and appraisal fees) are added to the basis of the residence.

The basis of the residence is increased by the cost of capital improvements. Thus, the cost of adding a room, installing an air conditioning system, finishing a basement, and landscaping are capital improvements that are added to the basis of the residence. Expenses incurred to protect the taxpayer's title in the residence are also added to the basis.[123]

---

[121] Sec. 1034(j) and Reg. Sec. 1.1034-1(i).
[122] Sec. 1034(e).
[123] Reg. Sec. 1.212-1(k).

EXAMPLE I12-81 ▶ Joe purchased a principal residence in 1980 at a cost of $100,000. As a result of the purchase, a gain of $20,000 on the sale of Joe's old principal residence was deferred. In 1983, Joe paid $900 to enlarge the patio and $100 to repair broken drainage gutters. In 1986, Joe added a family room to the residence at a $14,000 cost. His basis for his residence is $94,900 ($100,000 − $20,000 + $900 + $14,000). The basis is reduced by the deferred gain on the sale of the old residence and increased by the capital expenditure items. The cost of repairing the gutters is not a capital expenditure. ◀

PROBLEM MATERIALS

DISCUSSION QUESTIONS

I12-1 Evaluate the following statement: The underlying rationale for the nonrecognition of a gain or loss resulting from a like-kind exchange is that the exchange constitutes a liquidation of the taxpayer's investment.

I12-2 Why might a taxpayer want to avoid having an exchange qualify as a like-kind exchange?

I12-3 Debbie owns office equipment with a basis of $300,000 that was acquired on May 10, 1990. Debbie exchanges the equipment for other office equipment owned by Doug on July 23, 1997. Doug's equipment has an FMV of $500,000. Both Debbie and Doug use the equipment in their businesses.
a. What is Debbie's basis for the office equipment received in the exchange and when does the holding period start for that equipment?
b. If Debbie and Doug are related taxpayers, explain what action could occur that would cause the exchange not to qualify as a like-kind exchange.

I12-4 Kay owns equipment used in her business and exchanges the equipment for other like-kind equipment and marketable securities.
a. Will Kay's recognized gain ever exceed the realized gain?
b. Will Kay's recognized gain ever exceed the FMV of the marketable securities?
c. What is the basis of the marketable securities received?
d. When does the holding period of the marketable securities begin?

I12-5 Demetrius sells word processing equipment used in his business to Edith. He then purchases new word processing equipment from Zip Corporation.
a. Do the sale and purchase qualify as a like-kind exchange?
b. When may a sale and a subsequent purchase be treated as a like-kind exchange?

I12-6 When determining whether property qualifies as like-kind property, is the quality or grade of the property considered?

I12-7 When does a nonsimultaneous exchange qualify as a like-kind exchange?

I12-8 Does the receipt of boot in a transaction that otherwise qualifies as a like-kind exchange always cause the exchange to be at least partially taxable?

I12-9 When must a taxpayer who gives boot recognize a gain or loss?

I12-10 What is the justification for Sec. 1033, which allows a taxpayer to elect to defer a gain resulting from an involuntary conversion? May a taxpayer elect under Sec. 1033 to defer the recognition of a loss resulting from an involuntary conversion?

I12-11 Must property be actually condemned for the conversion of property to be classified as an involuntary conversion? Explain.

I12-12 What are severance damages? What is the tax treatment for severance damages received if the taxpayer does not use the severance damages to restore the retained property?

I12-13 The functional use test is often used to determine whether the replacement property is similar or related in service or use to the property converted. Explain the functional use test.

I12-14 In what situations can a gain due to an involuntary conversion of real property be deferred if like-kind property is purchased to replace the converted property?

I12-15 What is the justification for Sec. 1034, which results in nonrecognition of gain on the sale or exchange of a principal residence?

I12-16 For an expense to qualify as a fixing-up expense, when must the expense be incurred? When must the expense be paid?

I12-17 Which of the following statements are true?
a. Fixing-up expenses reduce the realized gain.
b. Capital expenditures qualify as fixing-up expenses.
c. Fixing-up expenses reduce the amount realized to arrive at the adjusted sales price.

I12-18 A taxpayer sells her principal residence on November 15, 1997 for $100,000 and realizes a gain. She purchases a new principal residence for $150,000. In which of the following independent cases will Sec. 1034 apply?
a. The new residence is occupied on March 10, 1996.
b. The new residence is occupied on December 2, 1999.
c. The new residence is occupied on February 19, 1999.

I12-19 Harold's principal residence has an $80,000 basis. It is involuntarily converted, and he receives $95,000 because of the conversion. Harold pays $112,000 for a new principal residence within a month after the involuntary conversion. Under what conditions may Harold use Sec. 1033 or 1034 to defer the gain?

I12-20 Steve maintains that the cost of wallpapering his three-bedroom house is a capital expenditure while Martha maintains that the cost of wallpapering her three-bedroom house is an expense. Comment on the following statements:
a. For both Steve and Martha, the house is their personal residence.
b. Martha's house is used as rental property.

I12-21 In 1996, Diane sold her principal residence at a $40,000 gain. Because she expected to pay $150,000 for a new principal residence, and the adjusted sales price for the old residence was $146,000, Diane did not report a gain in 1996. In 1997 she purchases a new principal residence for $140,000.
a. What is the amount of gain recognized because of the sale?
b. Must Diane file an amended return for 1996 and recognize the gain in 1996?

I12-22 Gordon sells his principal residence and defers the gain realized on the sale under Sec. 1034.
a. Why is the basis of his new principal residence adjusted downward?
b. Provide two reasons why the deferred gain may never be subject to tax.

I12-23 What requirements must be satisfied by a taxpayer under Sec. 121 in order to be eligible for the election to exclude a gain up to $125,000 on the sale or exchange of a principal residence?

I12-24 Which of the following statements are true?
a. A new principal residence must be purchased in order to exclude a gain under Sec. 121.
b. Sections 121 and 1034 may apply to the same sale of a principal residence.
c. If Secs. 121 and 1034 apply to the same sale of a principal residence, the amount realized from the sale of the residence is reduced by the excluded gain to determine the adjusted sales price.

ISSUE IDENTIFICATION QUESTIONS

I12-25 John owns 25% of the ABC Partnership and Jane owns 25% of the XYZ Partnership. The ABC Partnership owns a farm and produces corn and the XYZ Partnership owns a farm and produces soybeans. John and Jane agree to exchange their partnership interests. What tax issues should John and Jane consider?

I12-26 Natalya and Larry divorced in January and Larry moved out of the house they own jointly. It was agreed that Natalya would offer the house for sale after their eight-year-old daughter's school year ended in May and the proceeds from the sale would be divided equally. In October, the house was sold for $200,000 and a $85,000 gain was realized. Natalya purchased another residence in September for $167,000 and Larry purchased another residence in November for $124,000. What tax issues should Natalya and Larry consider?

I12-27 In March 1995, Jennifer and Harry sold their jointly owned residence for $300,000. The adjusted sales price was $280,000 and the realized gain was $125,000. Jennifer and Harry did not recognize the gain on their 1995 joint income tax return because they intended to purchase another residence for more than $280,000. In July 1996 they divorced. Harry purchased another residence in January, 1997 for $132,000. As of the end of 1997, Jennifer had not purchased another residence. What tax issues should Jennifer and Harry consider?

I12-28 Tatyana's principal residence was destroyed by a tornado and she received the following insurance proceeds: $200,000 for the house; $35,000 for personal belongings including furniture; and $28,000 for a piano. She plans to replace the residence within six months but not the piano. Before determining any gain or loss that she must recognize, what questions would you ask and why?

PROBLEMS

I12-29 *Like-Kind Property.* Which of the following exchanges qualify as like-kind exchanges under Sec. 1031?
 a. Acme Corporation stock held for investment purposes for Mesa Corporation stock also held for investment purposes
 b. A motel used in a trade or business for an apartment complex held for investment
 c. A pecan orchard in Texas used in a trade or business for an orange grove in Florida used in a trade or business
 d. A one-third interest in a general partnership for a one-fourth interest in a limited partnership
 e. Inventory for equipment used in a trade or business
 f. Unimproved land held as an investment for a warehouse used in a trade or business
 g. An automobile used as a personal-use asset for marketable securities held for investment

I12-30 *Like-Kind Property.* Which of the following exchanges qualify as like-kind exchanges under Sec. 1031?
 a. A motel in Texas for a motel in Italy
 b. An office building held for investment for an airplane to be used in the taxpayer's business
 c. Land held for investment for marketable securities held for investment
 d. Land held for investment for a farm to be used in the taxpayer's business

I12-31 *Like-Kind Exchange: Boot.* Determine the realized gain or loss, the recognized gain or loss, and the basis of the equipment received for the following like-kind exchanges:

Basis of Equipment Exchanged	FMV of Boot Received	FMV of Equipment Received
$40,000	$-0-	$75,000
50,000	10,000	70,000
60,000	20,000	65,000
70,000	30,000	60,000
80,000	20,000	50,000

I12-32 *Like-Kind Exchange: Personal Property.* Beach Corporation owns a computer with a $40,000 adjusted basis. The computer is used in the company's trade or business. What is the realized and recognized gain or loss for each of the following independent transactions?

a. The computer is exchanged for a used computer with a $70,000 FMV plus $8,000 cash.

b. The computer is exchanged for a used computer with a $25,000 FMV plus $7,000 cash.

c. The computer is exchanged for marketable securities with a $57,000 FMV.

I12-33 *Like-Kind Exchange: Personal Property.* Boise Corporation exchanges a machine with a $14,000 basis for a new machine with an $18,000 FMV and $3,000 cash. The machines are used in Boise's business and are in the same General Asset Class.

a. What are Boise Corporation's recognized gain and the basis for the new machine?

b. How would your answer to Part a change if the corporation's machine is also subject to a $6,000 liability, and the liability is assumed by the other party?

I12-34 *Like-Kind Exchange: Liabilities.* Paul owns a building used in his business with an adjusted basis of $500,000 and an $800,000 FMV. He exchanges the building for a building owned by David. David's building has a $950,000 FMV but is subject to a $150,000 liability. Paul assumes David's liability and uses David's building in his business.

a. What is Paul's realized gain?

b. What is Paul's recognized gain?

c. What is Paul's basis for the building received?

I12-35 *Like-Kind Exchange: Liabilities.* Helmut exchanges his apartment complex for Heidi's farm, and the exchange qualifies as a like-kind exchange. Helmut's adjusted basis for the apartment complex is $600,000 and the complex is subject to a $180,000 liability. The FMV of Heidi's farm is $770,000 and the farm is subject to a $100,000 liability. Each asset is transferred subject to the liability. What is Helmut's recognized gain and the basis of the new farm?

I12-36 *Like-Kind Exchange: Liabilities.* Sheila owns land with a basis of $100,000 and FMV of $220,000. The land is subject to an $80,000 liability. Sheila plans to exchange the land for land owned by Tony that has a $250,000 FMV but is subject to a liability of $150,000. Sheila plans to assume Tony's debt and Tony will assume her $80,000 debt. Because the exchange is not of equal value, how much cash must Tony transfer to equalize the exchange?

I12-37 *Like-Kind Exchange: Transfer of Boot.* Wayne exchanges unimproved land with a $40,000 basis and marketable securities with a $10,000 basis for an eight-unit apartment building having a $150,000 FMV. The land and marketable securities are held by Wayne as investments, and the apartment building is held as an investment. The marketable securities have a $25,000 FMV. What is his realized gain, recognized gain, and the basis for the apartment building?

I12-38 *Like-Kind Exchange: Related Parties.* Bob owns a duplex used as rental property. The duplex has a basis of $86,000 and $300,000 FMV. He transfers the duplex to Cindy, his sister, in exchange for a triplex that she owns. The triplex has a basis of $279,000 and a $300,000 FMV. Two months after the exchange, Cindy sells the duplex to a business associate for $312,000.
a. What is Bob's realized and recognized gain on the exchange?
b. What is Cindy's realized and recognized gain on the exchange?

I12-39 *Like-Kind Exchange: Related Parties.* Assume the same facts as in I12-38 except Cindy sells the duplex to a nonrelated individual more than two years after the exchange with Bob. Ignore any changes in adjusted basis due to depreciation that would have occurred after the exchange.
a. What is Bob's realized and recognized gain on the exchange?
b. What is Cindy's realized and recognized gain on the exchange?
c. What is Cindy's realized and recognized gain on the sale?

I12-40 *Involuntary Conversion.* Duke Corporation owns an office building with a $400,000 adjusted basis. The building is destroyed by a tornado. The insurance company paid $750,000 as compensation for the loss. Eight months after the loss, Duke uses the insurance proceeds and other funds to acquire a new office building for $682,000 and machinery for one of the company's plants at a $90,000 cost. Assuming that Duke elects to defer as much of the gain as possible, what is the recognized gain, the basis for the new office building, and the basis for the machinery acquired?

I12-41 *Involuntary Conversion: Replacement Period.* The Madison Corporation paid $3,000 for several acres of land in 1989 to use in its business. The land is condemned and taken by the state in March 1997. The company receives $25,000 from the state. Whenever possible, the corporation elects to minimize taxable income. For each of the following independent cases, what is the recognized gain or loss in 1997 on the conversion and the tax basis of the replacement property (whenever the property is replaced)?
a. The land will not be replaced.
b. Replacement land will be purchased in July 1998 for $22,500.
c. Replacement land will be purchased in July 1999 for $28,500.
d. Replacement land will be purchased in July 2000 for $23,600.

I12-42 *Involuntary Conversion of Real Property.* On April 27, 1997, an office building owned by Newark Corporation, an offshore drilling company that is a calendar-year taxpayer, is destroyed by a hurricane. The basis of the office building is $700,000, and the corporation receives $910,000 from the insurance company.
a. To defer the entire gain due to the involuntary conversion, what amount must the corporation pay for replacement property?
b. To defer the gain due to the involuntary conversion, by what date must the corporation replace the converted property?
c. If Newark replaces the office building by purchasing a 900,000 gallon storage tank at an $850,000 cost, may it defer any of the gain due to the involuntary conversion?

d. How would your answers to Parts b and c change if the office building had been condemned by the state? Explain.

I12-43 *Involuntary Conversion: Different Methods of Replacement.* On September 3, 1997, Federal Corporation's warehouse is totally destroyed by fire. $800,000 of insurance proceeds are received, and the realized gain is $300,000. Whenever possible, Federal elects to defer gains. For each of the following independent situations, what is the amount of gain recognized? Explain why the gain is not deferred, if applicable.

a. On October 23, 1997, Federal purchases a warehouse for $770,000.

b. On February 4, 1998, Federal purchases 100% of the Park Corporation, which owns a warehouse. Federal pays $895,000 for the stock.

c. On March 10, 1998, Federal receives a capital contribution from its majority shareholder. The shareholder transfers a warehouse to the corporation. The warehouse's FMV is $975,000. The shareholder's basis in the warehouse is $635,000.

d. On November 20, 1999, Federal purchases an apartment complex for $900,000.

e. On March 26, 2000, Federal purchases a warehouse for $888,000.

I12-44 *Severance Damages.* Twelve years ago, Marilyn purchased two lots in an undeveloped subdivision as an investment. Each lot has a $10,000 basis and a $40,000 FMV when the city condemns one lot for use as a municipal sewage treatment plant. As a result of the condemnation, Marilyn receives $40,000 from the city. Because the value of the other lot is reduced, the city pays $7,500 severance damages. She does not plan to replace the condemned lot.

a. What is her recognized gain due to the condemnation?

b. What is her recognized gain from the receipt of the severance damages?

c. What is her basis for the lot she continues to own?

I12-45 *Sale of a Principal Residence.* Louis is 40 years old, single, and owns a principal residence acquired for $71,000 in 1987. During the current year he sells the residence for $90,000 and purchases a new principal residence for $78,000. In order to sell the former residence, he spends $6,100 to sell the home and $300 to fix it up.

a. What is the realized and recognized gain from the sale of the principal residence?

b. What is the basis of the new residence?

I12-46 *Sale of a Principal Residence.* Marc, age 45, sells his personal residence in May of the current year for $70,000. He pays $5,000 in selling expenses and $600 in fixing-up expenses. He has lived in the residence since 1980, when he purchased it for $40,000. In 1984, he paid $4,000 to install central air conditioning. If Marc purchases a new principal residence in December of the current year for $62,000, what is the realized gain, recognized gain, and the basis for the new residence?

I12-47 *Sale of a Principal Residence: Cost of New Residence.* Laurie sells her personal residence for $50,000 in January of the current year and purchases a new residence in the following October. Her old residence has a $34,000 basis and she incurs $1,500 fixing-up expenses to prepare the house for sale. She pays $4,000 of selling expenses. As a result of the sale, Laurie recognizes a $1,700 gain in the current year. What is the cost of the new residence?

I12-48 *Sale of a Principal Residence.* In August, Rob and Maria, who are married, sell their principal residence and realize a $30,000 gain. It is the first house Rob and Maria ever owned, and the adjusted sales price is $75,000. In September of the same year Rob and Maria purchase a new residence for $92,000. What is the gain recognized and the basis of the new residence?

I12-49 *Definition of a Principal Residence.* Ken's parents lived with him until 1995 in a house on 23rd Street purchased by Ken in 1984 for $30,000. In 1995 Ken married Beth and moved to a rented apartment. In 1997 they purchase a house on 42nd Street for $90,000 and Ken sells the house on 23rd Street for $60,000 when his parents move into a nursing home. Ken pays $4,000 selling expenses and $1,000 fixing-up expenses. How much of the realized gain on the sale of the house on 23rd Street may be deferred?

I12-50 *Sale of a Principal Residence: Rental Property.* For the last several years, Mr. and Mrs. Cockrell have rented their furnished basement to local college students. When determining their taxable income each year, they have deducted a portion of the utilities, property taxes, interest, and depreciation based on the fact that 15% of the house is used for rental purposes. The original basis of the property is $100,000, and depreciation of $4,000 has been allowed on the rental portion of the property. During the current year, Mr. and Mrs. Cockrell sell the house for $300,000. No selling expenses or fixing-up expenses are incurred. Neither individual is 55 years old or older. They plan to purchase a new principal residence and will no longer rent any portion of their house to college students.
a. What is the amount realized on the sale of the principal residence?
b. What is the realized gain on the sale of the principal residence?
c. What is the amount realized on the sale of the portion of the residence not considered to be the principal residence?
d. What is the realized gain on the sale of the portion of the residence not considered to be the principal residence?
e. If a new principal residence is purchased for $340,000 and occupied within the next two months, what is the maximum gain that may be deferred?
f. If Mr. and Mrs. Cockrell wish to defer all of their gain, what must be the minimum cost of the new principal residence?

I12-51 *Multiple Sales of a Principal Residence.* Consider the following information for Mr. and Mrs. Di Palma:

- On June 10, 1996, they sold their principal residence for $80,000 and incur $6,000 of selling expenses and $1,000 of fixing-up expenses. The basis of the residence, which was acquired in 1988, is $50,000.

- On June 25, 1996, they purchased a new principal residence for $90,000 and occupied it immediately.

- May 10, 1997, they purchase their neighbor's residence for $115,000 and occupy the residence immediately.

- August 29, 1997, they sell the residence purchased on June 25, 1996 for $108,000. They pay $7,000 of selling expenses and $500 of fixing-up expenses.

a. What is the realized gain on the sale of the residence in 1996 and the adjusted sales price?
b. What is the recognized gain on the sale of the residence in 1996? Which residence is considered to be the new principal residence: the one purchased in 1996 or the one purchased in 1997?
c. What is the realized gain on the sale of the residence in 1997?
d. What is the recognized gain on the sale of the residence in 1997?

I12-52   *Multiple Sales of a Principal Residence.* Consider the following information for Mr. and Mrs. Gomez:

- On May 6, 1996, they sold their principal residence, acquired in 1987, for $100,000. They paid $8,000 of selling expenses and $1,500 of fixing-up expenses. Their basis in the residence was $70,000.
- On July 2, 1996, they purchased a new principal residence for $105,000.
- On June 9, 1997, Mr. Gomez, a bank officer, is transferred to another bank in the northern part of the state.
- On July 1, 1997, they purchase a new principal residence for $120,000.
- On October 6, 1997, they sell the residence that was purchased on July 2, 1996 for $118,000. They pay $10,000 of selling expenses and $1,000 of fixing-up expenses.

a. What is the realized gain on the sale of the residence in 1996 and the adjusted sales price?

b. What is the recognized gain on the sale of the residence in 1996? Which residence is considered the new principal residence: the one purchased in 1996 or the one in 1997?

c. What is the realized gain on the sale of the residence in 1997 and the adjusted sales price?

d. What is the recognized gain on the sale of the residence in 1997?

I12-53   *Involuntary Conversion of Principal Residence.* As a result of a hurricane, Gail's house, with an adjusted basis of $136,000, is destroyed during the current year. After viewing the damaged area, the President declares it to be a disaster area. Gail's insurance policy specifies coverage for artwork that she has collected. She receives the following payments from the insurance company: $200,000 for the house, $26,000 for the unscheduled personal property contents with an adjusted basis of $6,000, and $50,000 for the artwork. Her basis for the artwork is $17,500. Three months after the hurricane, she purchases another residence.

a. If the purchase price of the new residence is $270,000 and she does not replace the artwork, how much of the $32,500 gain ($50,000 − $17,500) on the artwork must be recognized?

b. What amount of gain is recognized, if any, from the receipt of insurance proceeds relative to the unscheduled personal property contents?

c. Assume Gail has not purchased another residence and receives the insurance proceeds in August of the current year. How long does she have to acquire the replacement property and still be eligible to defer the gain?

I12-54   *Sale of a Principal Residence: Sec. 121 Exclusion.* After owning their principal residence for 15 years, Mr. and Mrs. Hall sell their personal residence and realize a $170,000 gain. He is 77 years old, and she is 54 years old. Mr. and Mrs. Hall do not plan to purchase another residence.

a. If Mr. and Mrs. Hall file a joint return and both consent to make the election to exclude the gain under Sec. 121, what is the maximum amount of the gain they may exclude?

b. If they file a joint return but Mrs. Hall refuses to consent to the election under Sec. 121, what is the maximum amount of the gain they may exclude?

c. If Mrs. Hall will not consent to filing the election and Mr. Hall files a separate return, what is the maximum amount of the gain that may be excluded?

I12-55 *Sale of Principal Residence: Sec. 121 Exclusion.* Russ and Sandy, who are married and file a joint return, are both more than 55 years old and are eligible to use Sec. 121. During the current year, they sell their old residence and purchase a new principal residence. They elect to exclude as much of the gain as possible. The following information is provided about the sale and repurchase:

Basis of old residence	$ 40,000
Selling price of residence	280,000
Selling expenses	20,000
Fixing-up expenses	3,000
Purchase price of new residence	127,000

a. What is their realized gain?
b. What is their excluded gain?
c. What is their recognized gain?
d. What is their basis for the new residence?

TAX FORM/RETURN PREPARATION PROBLEMS

I12-56 On October 29, 1996, Miss Joan Seely (Social Security no. 123-45-6789), age 32, sells her principal residence for $150,000 cash. She purchased the residence on May 12, 1989 for $85,000. She spent $12,000 for capital improvements in 1990. To help sell the house, she pays $300 on October 2, 1996 for minor repairs made on that date. The realtor's commission amounts to $7,500. On February 3, 1997, she purchases a new principal residence for $130,000. Her old residence is never rented out or used for business, and she does not plan to rent out or use the new residence for business. Prepare Form 2119 for Miss Seely.

I12-57 At the beginning of the current year, Donna Harp was employed as a cinematographer by Farah Movie, Inc., a motion picture company in Los Angeles, California. In June, she accepted a new job with Ocala Production in Orlando, Florida. Donna is single, age 35, and her social security number is 223-77-6793. She sold her house in California on August 10 for $300,000. She paid a $14,000 sales commission and fixing-up expenses of $500. The house was acquired on March 23, 1987 for $140,000. The house in California is the first house she has ever owned.

The cost of transporting her household goods and personal effects from California to Orlando amounted to $2,350. To travel from California to Florida, she paid travel and lodging costs of $370 and $100 for meals.

On July 15, she purchased a house for $270,000 on 1225 Minnie Lane in Orlando. To purchase the house, she incurred a 20-year mortgage for $170,000. To obtain the loan, she paid points of $3,400. The $3,600 of property taxes for the house in Orlando were prorated with $1,950 being apportioned to the seller and $1,650 being apportioned to the buyer. In December of the current year she paid $3,600 for property taxes.

Other information related to her return:

Salary from Farah Movie, Inc.	$30,000
Salary from Ocala Production, Inc.	50,000
Federal income taxes withheld by Farah	6,000
Federal income taxes withheld by Ocala	12,000
FICA taxes withheld by Farah	2,295
FICA taxes withheld by Ocala	3,825
Dividend income	10,000

Interest paid for mortgage:	
Home in California	2,780
Home in Orlando	3,800
Property taxes paid in California	4,100
Sales taxes paid in California and Florida	3,125
State income taxes paid in California	2,900
Interest income from Sun National Bank	1,800

Prepare Form 1040 including Schedules A, B, and D and Forms 2119 and 3903.

I12-58 Jim Sarowski (Social Security no. 344-77-9255) is 70 years old and single. He received social security benefits of $16,000. He works part-time as a greeter at a local discount store and received wages of $7,300. Federal income taxes of $250 were withheld from his salary. Jim lives at Rt. 7 in Daingerfield, Texas.

In March of the current year, he purchased a duplex at 2006 Tennessee Street to use as rental property for $100,000, with 20% of the price to be allocated to land. During the current year, he had the following receipts and expenditures with respect to the duplex:

Rent receipts	$8,800
Interest paid	5,900
Property taxes	1,400
Insurance	800
Maintenance	300

Other expenditures during the current year:

Contributions to the church	$2,600
Personal property taxes	225
Sales tax	345

On July 24 of the current year, he exchanged ten acres of land for a car with a $16,500 FMV to be held for personal use. The land was purchased on November 22, 1990 for $18,000 as an investment. Because of some pollution problems in the area, the value of the land declined.

On December 1 of the current year, he sold his residence, which had been his home for 30 years, for $275,000. Sales commissions of $16,000 were paid, and the adjusted basis for his home is $110,000. He plans to rent an apartment and does not plan to purchase another home. His only other sale of a principal residence occurred 32 years ago.

Prepare Forms 1040, 2119, and 4562 and Schedules D and E.

CASE STUDY PROBLEMS

I12-59 The Electric Corporation, a publicly held corporation, owns land with a $1,600,000 basis that is being held for investment. The company is considering exchanging the land for two assets owned by the Quail Corporation: land with a FMV of $3,000,000 and marketable securities with a $1,000,000 FMV. Both assets will be held by the Electric Corporation for investment, although the corporation is considering the possibility of developing the land and building residential houses. The president of the corporation has hired you to prepare a report explaining how the exchange will affect the corporation's reported net income and its tax liability. The corporation has a tax rate of 34%.

I12-60   Monique Srivastava, a CPA, is a self-employed tax professional who specializes in preparing tax returns for individuals and small businesses. Two weeks ago, she prepared a return for a new client, Bruce Duncan. Bruce claimed a deduction for points paid to purchase a new residence on October 24, 1997 and Monique agreed that the deduction was appropriate. Bruce did not provide any information about the sale of a residence, and Monique did not ask about a possible sale of a residence.

In a recent conversation with Tasha Short, a realtor, Monique learned that Bruce sold a residence during the summer of 1995. Given the substantial appreciation for real estate in the subdivision where Bruce's home was located, Monique estimates that the house was sold at a substantial gain.

As a normal practice, Monique always requests tax returns for at least three previous years from new clients. In reviewing the three returns, she finds that Bruce did not file Form 2119 or report a gain on the sale of a residence in 1995. What action should Monique take? (See the *Statements on Responsibilities in Tax Practice* section in Chapter I1 and Appendix E for a discussion of this issue.)

TAX RESEARCH PROBLEMS

I12-61   For the last nine years, Mr. and Mrs. Orchard, age 42 and 40, respectively, live in a residence located on eight acres. In January of the current year they sell the home and two acres of land. The purchaser of the residence does not wish to own the entire eight acres of land. In December they sell the remaining 6 acres of land to another individual for $60,000. The house and the land have never been used by the Orchards in a trade or business or held for investment. The realized gains resulting from the two sales are computed as follows:

	House and Two Acres January Sales	Eight Acres December Sale
Selling price	$140,000	$60,000
Minus: selling expenses	(8,000)	(3,000)
Amount realized	$132,000	$57,000
Minus: Basis	(80,000)	(18,000)
Realized gain	$ 52,000	$39,000

In March they purchase a new residence for $225,000. As a result of the sales described above, what is the amount of realized gain that must be recognized during the current year?

A partial list of research sources is

- Sec. 1034
- Reg. Sec. 1.1034-1(c)(3)
- Rev. Rul. 76-541, 1976-2 C.B. 246

I12-62   George, age 68, decides to retire from farming and is considering selling his farm. The farm has a $100,000 basis and a $400,000 FMV. George's two sons are not interested in farming. Both sons have large families and would like to own houses suitable for their needs. The Iowa Corporation is willing to purchase George's farm. George's tax advisor suggests that Iowa Corporation should buy the two houses the sons want to own for $400,000 and then exchange the houses for George's farm. After the exchange, George could make a gift of the houses to the sons.

a. If the transactions are executed as suggested by the tax advisor, George's recognized gain will be $300,000. The transaction does not qualify as a like-kind exchange. Explain why.

b. George wants the exchange to qualify as a like-kind exchange and still help his sons obtain the houses. What advice do you have for him?

A partial list of research sources is

- *Dollie H. Click,* 78 T.C. 225 (1982)

- *Fred S. Wagensen,* 74 T.C. 653 (1980)

I12-63 On January 14, 1995, the Kelders sold their personal residence for $120,000 to Mr. and Mrs. Clancy. Although the Kelders did not have the house listed for sale, the Clancys fell in love with the house while driving through the neighborhood and made an offer the Kelders could not refuse. Both Kelders are less than 55 years old.

The Kelders moved to a townhouse and negotiated a renewable three-month rental agreement. In November 1995, the Kelders were still living in the townhouse due to their inability to locate a house they wanted to buy. Finally, they decided to build a new house. They purchased a lot in December and construction was scheduled to start during the spring of 1996. However, the builder declared bankruptcy and construction of the home was not started until October 1996. The Kelders agreed to pay the new builder a $2,000 premium if the house was completed within 60 days. Because of bad weather, the house was not completed until January 10, 1997 at a total cost of $129,000. On January 11, one day before the Kelders planned move into the house, the house was totally destroyed by fire. The Kelders purchased another home for $130,000 on January 23, 1997, and occupied the residence as of February 1, 1997.

May the Kelders defer the gain on the sale of the residence to the Clancys?

A partial list of resource sources is

- Rev. Rul. 75-438, 1975-2 C.B. 334

- *Joseph T. Gelinas,* 1976 P.H. T.C. Memo 76,103, 35 TCM 448

I12-64 On March 1, 1993, Jeremy, who was 53 years old, purchased a principal residence for $90,000. He has never been married. Except for two months in 1993 when Jeremy was on vacation in Hawaii, he owned and used the house as his principal residence until January 4, 1996, when he suffered a massive stroke. He was in the hospital until February 10, 1996, when he was moved to a nursing home because he was incapable of self-care.

If he sells the house on April 12, 1997 for $160,000, may Jeremy elect to exclude the gain?

A partial list of research sources is

- Sec. 121(d)(9)

- Reg. Sec. 1.121-1(c)

CHAPTER 13

PROPERTY TRANSACTIONS: SECTION 1231 AND RECAPTURE

LEARNING OBJECTIVES

After studying this chapter, you should be able to

1. Identify Sec. 1231 property

2. Understand the tax treatment for Sec. 1231 transactions

3. Apply the recapture provisions of Sec. 1245

4. Apply the recapture provisions of Sec. 1250

5. Describe other recapture applications

KEY POINT

If a taxpayer has gains, it is preferable to have the gains treated as capital gains; if a taxpayer has losses, it is preferable to have the losses treated as ordinary losses. Because Sec. 1231 property receives the preferable treatment for both net gains and losses, it has been said that this property enjoys the best of both worlds.

Chapter 15 states that all recognized gains and losses must eventually be designated as either capital or ordinary. However, gains or losses on certain types of property are designated as Sec. 1231 gains or losses, which are given preferential treatment under the tax law. Ordinary loss treatment is accorded to a net Sec. 1231 loss, which is defined as the excess of Sec. 1231 losses over Sec. 1231 gains.[1] Net Sec. 1231 gain, which is the excess of Sec. 1231 gains over Sec. 1231 losses, is generally treated as long-term capital gain.[2] However, as with many provisions of the tax law, the preferential treatment of Sec. 1231 gains has been gradually diminished, principally by the so-called "depreciation recapture rules." This chapter discusses the important rules dealing with Sec. 1231 gains and losses and depreciation recapture.

HISTORY OF SEC. 1231

During the depressed economy of the early and mid-1930s, business property was classified as a capital asset. Many business properties were worth less than their adjusted basis. Instead of selling business properties, taxpayers found it advantageous to retain assets that had declined in value because they could recover the full cost as depreciation. Capital losses had only limited deductibility during this period. To encourage the mobility of capital (i.e., the replacement of business fixed assets), the Revenue Act of 1938 added business property to the list of properties not considered to be capital assets.

During the period from 1938 to 1942, gains and losses on the sale or exchange of business property were treated as ordinary gains and losses. Favorable capital gain treatment was eliminated and taxpayers with appreciated business properties were reluctant to sell the assets because of the high tax cost. This restriction on the mobility of capital was more significant than usual because business assets had to be shifted into industries that were more heavily involved in the production of military goods. Furthermore, taxpayers were often forced to recognize ordinary gains because the government used the condemnation process to obtain business property for the war effort. In 1942 Congress created the predecessor of Sec. 1231, which allowed taxpayers to treat net gains from the sale of business property as capital gains and net losses as ordinary losses. Before 1987, only 40% of an individual's net capital gain might be subject to tax because of the 60% long-term capital gain deduction.

The Tax Reform Act of 1986 eliminated the 60% long-term capital gain deduction for net long-term capital gains. Favorable long-term capital gain treatment was reinstated into the tax law in 1991 in the form of a 28% maximum tax rate applying to net capital gains for noncorporate taxpayers. It may also be advantageous to have the gain classified as capital or Sec. 1231 if taxpayers have capital losses or capital loss carryovers because of the limitations imposed on the deductibility of capital losses. Furthermore, there are other situations where it may be important for the property to be Sec. 1231 property (e.g., a contribution of appreciated property to a charitable organization).

OVERVIEW OF BASIC TAX TREATMENT FOR SEC. 1231

NET GAINS

At the end of the tax year, Sec. 1231 gains are netted against Sec. 1231 losses. If the overall result is a net Sec. 1231 gain, the gains and losses are treated as long-term capital gains (LTCGs) and long-term capital losses (LTCLs) respectively.[3] For the sake of expediency, it is often stated that a net Sec. 1231 gain is treated as a LTCG. For tax years

---

[1] Secs. 1231(c)(4) and (a)(2).

[2] Secs. 1231(c)(3) and (a)(1). There are several exceptions to this rule that are covered later in this chapter.

[3] Sec. 1231(a)(1).

beginning after 1984, however, a portion or all of the net Sec. 1231 gain may be treated as ordinary income because of a special five-year lookback rule.

EXAMPLE I13-1 ▶ Dawn owns a business that has $20,000 of Sec. 1231 gains and $12,000 of Sec. 1231 losses during the current year. Because the Sec. 1231 gains exceed the Sec. 1231 losses, the gains and losses are treated as LTCGs and LTCLs. After the gains and losses are offset, there is an $8,000 net long-term capital gain (NLTCG). ◀

EXAMPLE I13-2 ▶ Assume the same facts as in Example I13-1 except that Dawn also recognizes a $7,000 LTCG from the sale of a capital asset. After considering the $8,000, net Sec. 1231 gain, which is treated as a LTCG, Dawn has a $15,000 NLTCG ($8,000 + $7,000). ◀

NET LOSSES

If the netting of Sec. 1231 gains and losses at the end of the year results in a net Sec. 1231 loss, the Sec. 1231 gains and losses are treated as ordinary gains and losses.[4] For expediency, it is often stated that the net Sec. 1231 loss is treated as an ordinary loss.

EXAMPLE I13-3 ▶ David owns an unincorporated business and has $30,000 of Sec. 1231 gains and $40,000 of Sec. 1231 losses in the current year. Because the losses exceed the gains, they are treated as ordinary losses and gains. ◀

EXAMPLE I13-4 ▶ Assume the same facts as in Example I13-3 except that David receives a $37,000 salary as a corporate employee. David has no other income, losses, or deductions affecting his adjusted gross income (AGI). The Sec. 1231 gains and losses are treated as ordinary gains and losses, and David's AGI is $27,000 ($37,000 salary − $10,000 of ordinary loss). The $40,000 of ordinary losses offsets the $30,000 of ordinary gains and $10,000 of David's salary. ◀

TYPICAL MISCONCEPTION

It is sometimes erroneously thought that each Sec. 1231 gain should be treated as a LTCG and each Sec. 1231 loss as an ordinary loss. However all Sec. 1231 gains and losses must be combined to determine whether the Sec. 1231 gains and losses are LTCGs and LTCLs or ordinary gains and losses.

ADDITIONAL COMMENT

A taxpayer's share of a Sec. 1231 loss from a partnership or S Corporation may be subject to the passive activity loss rules.

One important advantage of Sec. 1231 is illustrated in Example I13-4. Because the Sec. 1231 gains and losses are treated as ordinary, the $10,000 net Sec. 1231 loss is fully deductible in the current year. If the gains and losses were classified as long-term capital gains and losses, David would have a $10,000 NLTCL. Only $3,000 of the $10,000 NLTCL would have been deductible against David's other income. As explained in Chapter I5, only $3,000 of net capital losses may be deducted from non-capital gain income.

The Tax Reform Act of 1984 reduced the benefits of Sec. 1231. For tax years beginning after 1984, any net Sec. 1231 gain is ordinary gain to the extent of any nonrecaptured net Sec. 1231 losses from the previous five years.[5] In essence, net Sec. 1231 losses previously deducted as ordinary losses are recaptured by changing what would otherwise be a LTCG into ordinary income.

EXAMPLE I13-5 ▶

HISTORICAL NOTE

Congress reduced the benefits of Sec. 1231 by requiring the recapture of any nonrecaptured net Sec. 1231 loss. This recapture is required because taxpayers have a certain amount of control over the timing of the recognition of Sec. 1231 gains or losses. Taxpayers had attempted to recognize Sec. 1231 losses in one year and Sec. 1231 gains in another year to avoid the netting process.

In 1997, Craig recognizes $25,000 of Sec. 1231 gains and $15,000 of Sec. 1231 losses. In 1993, Craig reported $14,000 of Sec. 1231 losses and no Sec. 1231 gains. No other Sec. 1231 gains or losses were recognized by Craig during the 1992–1996 period. The $10,000 ($25,000 − $15,000) of net Sec. 1231 gain in 1997 is treated as ordinary income due to the $14,000 of nonrecaptured net Sec. 1231 losses. ◀

To determine the amount of nonrecaptured net Sec. 1231 losses, compare the aggregate amount of net Sec. 1231 losses for the most recent preceding five tax years with the amount of such losses recaptured as ordinary income for those preceding tax years. The excess of the aggregate amount of net Sec. 1231 losses over the previously

---

[4] Sec. 1231(a)(2).

[5] Sec. 1231(c)(1). This provision is referred to as the *five-year lookback rule*.

recaptured loss is the nonrecaptured net Sec. 1231 loss. In Example I13-5, $4,000 of nonrecaptured net Sec. 1231 losses remain that can be recaptured in 1998. In 1998, the preceding five-year period includes 1993 through 1997.

SECTION 1231 PROPERTY

SECTION 1231 PROPERTY DEFINED

OBJECTIVE 1

Identify Sec. 1231 property

Section 1231 property is real property or depreciable property used in a trade or business that is held for more than one year.[6] Certain types of property do not qualify as Sec. 1231 property, even if used in a trade or business. For example, inventory is not Sec. 1231 property. Thus, a sale of inventory results in ordinary gain or loss. Publications of the U.S. Government received other than by purchase at its regular sale price; a copyright; literary, musical, or artistic compositions; letters or memorandums; or similar properties held by certain taxpayers are not classified as Sec. 1231 property.[7]

EXAMPLE I13-6 ▶

KEY POINT

Only property used in a trade or business is included in the definition of Sec. 1231 property. Gains and losses on property held for investment may be included only if the result of a condemnation or casualty.

KEY POINT

Inventory, free publications of the U.S. government, and copyrights, literary, musical, or artistic compositions are not capital assets.

Carl, who owns a recording studio, writes a musical composition to be sold to a record company. Because the musical composition is created by the personal efforts of the taxpayer, the musical composition is not Sec. 1231 property, and the sale results in ordinary gain from the sale of an ordinary asset. ◀

RELATIONSHIP TO CAPITAL ASSETS

As noted in Chapter I5, the Code does not provide a definition of a capital asset. Instead, Sec. 1221 provides a list of noncapital assets. This list includes both depreciable property and real property used in a trade or business.[8] These properties are treated as Sec. 1231 properties if held for more than one year. Depreciable property and real property used in a trade or business and held for **one year or less** are neither capital assets nor Sec. 1231 property. Any gain or loss resulting from the disposition of such assets is ordinary.

EXAMPLE I13-7 ▶

The Prime Corporation owns land held as an investment and land used as an employee parking lot. The land held as an investment is a capital asset. The land used as a parking lot is real property used in a trade or business and is not a capital asset. The land used as a parking lot is a Sec. 1231 asset if held for more than one year. ◀

EXAMPLE I13-8 ▶

Dale, a self-employed plumber, owns an automobile held for personal use and a truck used in his trade. The automobile is a capital asset because it is held for personal use. The truck is a Sec. 1231 asset if held for more than one year. As described later, a portion or all of any gain realized on the sale of the truck may be taxed as ordinary income due to the Sec. 1245 depreciation recapture provisions. ◀

NATURAL RESOURCES AND FARMING

Congress extended Sec. 1231 treatment to transactions involving timber, coal, domestic iron ore, livestock, and land with unharvested crops. These extensions reflect Congress's concern for developing natural resources and its recognition of farming as a rather unique type of business.

REAL-WORLD EXAMPLE

Christmas trees can be included in the definition of Sec. 1231 property, and this opportunity to convert ordinary income into capital gains has resulted in the use of Christmas tree tax shelters.

TIMBER. Section 631 allows taxpayers to elect to treat the cutting of timber as a sale or exchange of such timber. To be eligible to make this election, the taxpayer must own the timber or hold the contract right on the first day of the year and for more than one year.

---

[6] This holding period requirement coincides with the holding period requirement for LTCGs.

[7] Sec. 1231(b)(1).

[8] Sec.1221(2).

Furthermore, the timber must be cut for sale or for use in the taxpayer's trade or business.[9]

The gain or loss is determined by comparing the timber's adjusted basis for depletion with its fair market value (FMV) on the first day of the tax year in which it is cut. If the timber is eventually sold for more or less than its FMV (determined on the first day of the year the timber is cut), the difference is ordinary gain or loss.

EXAMPLE I13-9 ▶

Vermont Corporation owns timber with a $60,000 basis for depletion. The timber, acquired four years ago, is cut during the current year for use in the corporation's business. The FMV of the timber on the first day of the current year is $200,000. Vermont Corporation may elect to treat the cutting of the timber as a sale or exchange and recognize a $140,000 ($200,000 − $60,000) gain. ◀

If the election is made to treat the cutting of timber as a sale or exchange, the timber is considered Sec. 1231 property.[10] Thus, the $140,000 of gain in Example I13-9 is a Sec. 1231 gain. If the taxpayer does not make the election, the character of any gain or loss depends on whether the timber is held for sale in the ordinary course of the taxpayer's trade or business, held for investment, or held for use in a trade or business.

COAL OR DOMESTIC IRON ORE. An owner who disposes of coal (including lignite) or domestic iron ore while retaining an economic interest in it must treat the disposal as a sale.[11] The coal or iron ore is considered Sec. 1231 property.[12] The owner must own and retain an economic interest in the coal or iron ore in place.[13] An economic interest is owned when one acquires by investment any interest in mineral in place and seeks a return of capital from income derived from the extraction of the mineral.[14]

LIVESTOCK. Livestock held by the taxpayer for draft, breeding, dairy, or sporting purposes is considered Sec. 1231 property. However, to qualify for such treatment, cattle and horses must be held for 24 months or more from the date of acquisition and other livestock must be held for 12 months or more from the date of acquisition.[15]

UNHARVESTED CROPS AND LAND. An unharvested crop growing on land used in a trade or business is considered Sec. 1231 property if the crop and the land are both sold at the same time to the same person and the land is held more than one year.[16] Section 1231 does not apply to the sale or exchange of an unharvested crop if the taxpayer retains any right or option to reacquire the land.[17]

If Sec. 1231 applies to the sale or exchange of an unharvested crop sold with the land, no deductions are allowed for expenses attributable to the production of the unharvested crop.[18] Instead, costs of producing the crop must be capitalized.

SELF-STUDY QUESTION

Is the possible inclusion of timber and coal or domestic iron ore in the definition of Sec. 1231 property favorable to the taxpayers who produce these items?

ANSWER

Yes, it can result in income being taxed as long-term capital gain instead of ordinary income from the sale of inventory.

ADDITIONAL COMMENT

Livestock includes cattle, hogs, horses, mules, donkeys, sheep, goats, fur-bearing animals, and other mammals, but excludes poultry, fish, frogs, and reptiles.

ADDITIONAL COMMENT

The treatment of unharvested crops as a Sec. 1231 asset is largely a rule of convenience. If the taxpayer were not permitted to treat the crops in this fashion, it would be necessary to allocate the selling price between the land and crops.

INVOLUNTARY CONVERSIONS

Gains and losses from involuntary conversions of property used in a trade or business generally are classified as Sec. 1231 gains and losses. Involuntary conversions of capital assets that are held in connection with a trade or business or in a transaction entered into for profit also generally qualify for Sec. 1231 treatment. The property that is involuntarily

---

[9] Sec. 631(a) and Reg. Sec. 1.631-1.
[10] Sec. 1231(b)(2) and Reg. Sec. 1.631-1(d)(4).
[11] Sec. 631(c) and Reg. Sec. 1.631-3(a)(1).
[12] Sec. 1231(b)(2) and Reg. Sec. 1.631-3(a)(2).
[13] Reg. Sec. 1.631-3(b)(4).

[14] Reg. Sec. 1.611-1(b)(1).
[15] Sec. 1231(b)(3).
[16] Sec. 1231(b)(4) and Reg. Secs. 1.1231-1(c)(5) and 1(f).
[17] Reg. Sec. 1.1231-1(f).
[18] Sec. 268 and Reg. Sec. 1.268-1.

converted must be held for more than one year. Certain involuntary conversions are treated differently for income tax purposes. For example, the tax rules are different for condemnations and casualties, even though both are involuntary conversions of property.

CONDEMNATIONS

Gains and losses resulting from condemnations of Sec. 1231 property and capital assets held more than one year are classified as Sec. 1231 gains and losses. As indicated above, the capital assets must be held in connection with a trade or business or with a transaction entered into for profit.[19]

EXAMPLE I13-10 ▶ Kathryn owns land with a $20,000 basis and a $30,000 FMV as well as a capital asset with a $40,000 basis and a $26,000 FMV. Both assets are used in her trade or business and have been held for more than one year. As a result of the state exercising its powers of requisition or condemnation, Kathryn is required to transfer both properties to the state for cash equal to their FMVs. No other transfers of assets occur during the current year. The $10,000 gain due to condemnation of the land is a Sec. 1231 gain and the $14,000 loss due to condemnation of the capital asset is a Sec. 1231 loss. ◀

OTHER INVOLUNTARY CONVERSIONS

Gains or losses resulting from an involuntary conversion arising from fire, storm, shipwreck, other casualty, or theft are not classified as Sec. 1231 gains or losses if the recognized losses from such conversions exceed the recognized gains.[20] In such a case, the involuntary conversions are treated as ordinary gains and losses. However, if the gains from such involuntary conversions exceed the losses, both are classified as Sec. 1231 gains and losses.

EXAMPLE I13-11 ▶ Jose owns equipment having a $50,000 basis and a $42,000 FMV and a building having a $30,000 basis and a $35,000 FMV which are used in Jose's trade or business. The straight-line method of depreciation is used for the building. Both assets are held for more than a year. As a result of a fire, both assets are destroyed, and Jose collects insurance proceeds equal to the assets' FMV. No other transfers of assets occur during the current year. Because the $8,000 ($42,000 − $50,000) recognized loss exceeds the $5,000 ($35,000 − $30,000) recognized gain, the recognized loss and gain are both treated as ordinary. ◀

PROCEDURE FOR SEC. 1231 TREATMENT

After determining the recognized gains and losses from transfers of property qualifying for Sec. 1231 treatment, it is necessary to determine whether any gain must be recaptured as ordinary income under Secs. 1245 and 1250. The recaptured gain, discussed later in this chapter, is not eligible for Sec. 1231 treatment. After eliminating the gain recaptured as ordinary income due to the recapture of depreciation, the procedure for analyzing Sec. 1231 transactions is as follows:

STEP 1. Determine all gains and losses resulting from casualties or thefts of Sec. 1231 property and non–personal-use capital assets held for more than one year. Gains and losses are netted and treated as Sec. 1231 gains and losses if the gains exceed the losses.

---

[19] Secs. 1231(a)(3)(A) and (4)(B).

[20] Sec. 1231(a)(4)(C).

If the losses exceed the gains, both are treated as ordinary losses and gains and do not, therefore, enter into the Sec. 1231 netting procedure. Recall from Chapter I8 that business casualty losses are deductible *for* AGI and other casualty losses are deductible *from* AGI.

STEP 2. Combine the following gains and losses to determine whether Sec. 1231 gains exceed Sec. 1231 losses or vice versa:

▶ Net casualty and theft gains resulting from Step 1, if any

▶ Gains and losses resulting from the sale or exchange of Sec. 1231 property

▶ Gains and losses resulting from the condemnation of Sec. 1231 property and non–personal-use capital assets held more than one year.

If a net Sec. 1231 loss is the result, the losses and gains are treated as ordinary losses and gains. If a net Sec. 1231 gain is the result, the gains and losses are treated as LTCGs and LTCLs, although a portion or all of the capital gain may be recaptured as ordinary income as outlined in Step 3 below.

STEP 3. If a net Sec. 1231 gain is the result of Step 2, the amount of nonrecaptured net Sec. 1231 losses must be determined. Net Sec. 1231 gains to the extent of any nonrecaptured net Sec. 1231 losses are treated as ordinary income. Any net Sec. 1231 gain in excess of nonrecaptured net Sec. 1231 loss is treated as a LTCG. Nonrecaptured net Sec. 1231 losses are the excess of aggregate net Sec. 1231 losses for the preceding five years over losses previously recaptured as ordinary income due to the recapture provision of Sec. 1231.

EXAMPLE I13-12 ▶ The following gains and losses pertain to Danielle's business assets that qualify as Sec. 1231 property. Danielle does not have any nonrecaptured net Sec. 1231 losses from previous years, and the portion of gain recaptured as ordinary income due to the depreciation recapture provisions has been eliminated.

Gain due to an insurance reimbursement for fire damage	$10,000
Loss due to condemnation	19,000
Gain due to the sale of Sec. 1231 property	22,000

The $10,000 casualty gain is classified as a Sec. 1231 gain. Danielle has $32,000 ($10,000 + $22,000) of Sec. 1231 gains and a $19,000 Sec. 1231 loss. Danielle's $13,000 net Sec. 1231 gain is treated as a LTCG. No portion of the $13,000 LTCG is recaptured as ordinary income because Danielle does not have any nonrecaptured net Sec. 1231 losses during the preceding five-year period. ◀

EXAMPLE I13-13 ▶ Assume the same facts as in Example I13-12 except that Danielle has a $10,000 loss because of the fire instead of a $10,000 gain. The $10,000 casualty loss is an ordinary loss, not a Sec. 1231 loss. Because the loss is a business loss, it is deductible *for* AGI. Due to the $19,000 condemnation loss and the $22,000 of Sec. 1231 gain, she has a $3,000 net Sec. 1231 gain that is treated as a LTCG. ◀

EXAMPLE I13-14 ▶ The following gains and losses recognized in 1997 pertain to Fred's business assets that were held for more than one year. The assets qualify as Sec. 1231 assets.

Gain due to an insurance reimbursement for a casualty	$15,000
Gain due to a condemnation	25,000
Loss due to the sale of Sec. 1231 property	12,000

A summary of Fred's net Sec. 1231 gains and losses for the previous five-year period is as follows:

Year	Sec. 1231 Gain	Sec. 1231 Loss	Cumulative Nonrecaptured Net Sec. 1231 Losses (from 5 Prior Years)
1992	$ 5,000		—0—
1993		$2,000	$2,000
1994		6,000	8,000
1995	13,000		—0—
1996		9,000	9,000

The $15,000 gain due to the insurance reimbursement for a casualty is treated as a Sec. 1231 gain. The $25,000 gain from the condemnation is also a Sec. 1231 gain. Fred's net Sec. 1231 gain in 1997 is $28,000 [($15,000 + $25,000) − $12,000]. However, $9,000 of the Sec. 1231 gain is recaptured as ordinary income due to the $9,000 of nonrecaptured Sec. 1231 loss from 1996. The remaining $19,000 of net Sec. 1231 gain is a LTCG.   ◀

RECAPTURE PROVISIONS OF SEC. 1245

OBJECTIVE 3

Apply the recapture provisions of Sec. 1245

In 1962, Congress enacted Sec. 1245, which substantially reduced the advantages of Sec. 1231. A gain from the disposition of Sec. 1245 property is treated as ordinary income to the extent of the total amount of depreciation (or cost-recovery) deductions allowed since January 1, 1962. The gain recaptured as ordinary income cannot exceed the amount of the realized gain.

EXAMPLE I13-15 ▶

TYPICAL MISCONCEPTION

It is sometimes thought that only tangible property is subject to Sec. 1245 recapture. In fact, both tangible and intangible personal property are included.

Adobe Corporation sells equipment used in its trade or business for $95,000. The equipment was acquired several years ago for $110,000 and is Sec. 1245 property.[21] The equipment's adjusted basis is reduced to $60,000 because $50,000 of depreciation was deducted. The entire $35,000 ($95,000 − $60,000) of gain is treated as ordinary income because the total amount of depreciation taken ($50,000) is greater than the $35,000 realized gain.   ◀

The recapture provisions of Sec. 1245 apply to the total amount of depreciation (or cost recovery) allowed or allowable for Sec. 1245 property. It makes no difference which method of depreciation is used.[22]

Generally, the entire gain from the disposition of Sec. 1245 property is recaptured as ordinary income because the total amount of depreciation (or cost recovery) is greater than the gain realized. A portion of the gain will receive Sec. 1231 treatment if the realized gain exceeds total depreciation or cost recovery.

EXAMPLE I13-16 ▶

ADDITIONAL COMMENT

Section 1245 does not apply to losses because in these cases the taxpayers have taken too little depreciation rather than too much depreciation.

Assume the same facts as in Example I13-15 except that the asset is sold for $117,000. Because the $57,000 ($117,000 − $60,000) realized gain is greater than the $50,000 of total depreciation, $50,000 of the gain is ordinary income and the remaining $7,000 is a Sec. 1231 gain.   ◀

PURPOSE OF SEC. 1245

The purpose of Sec. 1245 is to eliminate any advantage taxpayers would have if they were able to reduce ordinary income by deducting depreciation and subsequently receive Sec. 1231 treatment when the asset was sold. The effect of Sec. 1245 is not as significant after

---

[21] Throughout this chapter, property is considered to be placed in service when it is purchased or acquired. The term *Sec. 1245 property* is used here to refer to either recovery property under the ACRS or MACRS rules or nonrecovery property that falls outside of the ACRS or MACRS rules.

[22] As explained later in this chapter, the method of cost recovery used determines whether certain real property is treated as Sec. 1245 recovery property.

the Tax Reform Act of 1986, because the preferential treatment for long-term capital gain has been eliminated for corporate taxpayers. For individuals, Sec. 1245 recapture prevents net Sec. 1231 gain from being treated as net long-term capital gain and being taxed at a maximum 28% rate. An increase in the maximum tax rates for high-income individuals in 1993 and subsequent years from 31% to 36% or 39.6% has increased the importance of the Sec. 1245 recapture provisions for such individuals. The conversion of Sec. 1231 gain to Sec. 1245 ordinary income also prevents taxpayers from offsetting Sec. 1231 gains against net capital losses when offsetting capital gains do not exist.

EXAMPLE I13-17 ▶

KEY POINT

On the sale of Sec. 1245 property, a portion of the gain is treated as Sec. 1231 gain only if the property is sold for more than the original cost. This is very unlikely for factory equipment, trucks, office equipment, and other Sec. 1245 property.

During the current year, Coastal Corporation has capital losses of $50,000 and no capital gains for the current year or the preceding three years. The corporation owns equipment that was purchased several years ago for $90,000, and depreciation deductions of $48,000 have been allowed. If Coastal sells the equipment for $72,000, the entire $30,000 ($72,000 − $42,000) gain, which is due to the depreciation deductions, is Sec. 1245 ordinary income. Without Sec. 1245, the $30,000 gain is a Sec. 1231 gain that could be offset by $30,000 of the corporation's capital loss. ◀

Note that Sec. 1245 does not apply to losses. If Coastal Corporation sells the equipment in Example I13-17 for $40,000, a $2,000 ($40,000 − $42,000 basis) Sec. 1231 loss is recognized.

KEY POINT

Property must be depreciable or amortizable to be considered Sec. 1245 property.

SECTION 1245 PROPERTY. **Section 1245 property** is certain property subject to depreciation and, in some cases, amortization. The most common example of Sec. 1245 property is depreciable personal property such as equipment. Automobiles, livestock, railroad grading, and single-purpose agricultural or horticultural structures are Sec. 1245 properties as well as intangible assets that are subject to amortization under Sec. 197 (see Chapter I10).[23] Except for certain buildings placed in service after 1980 and before 1987, buildings and structural components are generally not Sec. 1245 property.[24]

EXAMPLE I13-18 ▶

Buckeye Corporation owns the following assets acquired before 1981: equipment, a patent, an office building (including structural components), and land. The equipment and patent are Sec. 1245 property. The office building and the land are not Sec. 1245 property. ◀

REAL WORLD EXAMPLE

Pipelines, electric transmission towers, blast furnaces, greenhouses, and oil tanks are examples of real property that are included in the definition of Sec. 1245 property.

In many cases, taxpayers are allowed preferential treatment with respect to amortizing certain costs. For example, taxpayers may elect to expense up to $35,000 of the cost of making any business facility more accessible to handicapped and elderly people,[25] or to amortize pollution control facilities over 60 months[26] and reforestation expenditures over 84 months.[27] If taxpayers have amortized the costs of any real property under the special provisions, Sec. 1245 applies to the gain resulting from the disposition of such property.[28]

If taxpayers elect to expense certain depreciable property under Sec. 179, the amount deducted is treated as a depreciation deduction for purposes of the Sec. 1245 recapture provisions.[29]

EXAMPLE I13-19 ▶

Compact Corporation purchased $90,000 of equipment in 1996 and elected to expense $17,500 under Sec. 179. Compact sells the equipment in 1997 for $95,000. Depreciation allowed for 1996 and 1997 is $14,500 and $11,600 respectively. The adjusted basis of the

---

[23] Sec. 1245(a)(3).
[24] Sec. 1245(a)(3)(B)(i). Tangible real property "used as an integral part of the manufacturing, production, extraction, or furnishing of transportation, communication, electrical energy, gas, water, or sewage disposal services" is Sec. 1245 property.
[25] Sec. 190.

[26] Sec. 169(a).
[27] Sec. 194(a).
[28] Sec. 1245(a)(3)(C). The Sec. 1245 rules recapture amortization deductions claimed on real property under Secs. 169, 179, 185, 188, 190, 193 and 194.
[29] Sec. 1245(a)(2)(C).

equipment on the date of sale is $46,400 ($90,000 − $17,500 − $26,100 depreciation). The realized gain is $48,600 ($95,000 − $46,400), and $43,600 ($17,500 + $26,100) of the gain is Sec. 1245 ordinary income. The remaining $5,000 is Sec. 1231 gain.   ◄

APPLICATION OF SEC. 1245 TO NONRESIDENTIAL REAL ESTATE. Most real property is not affected by Sec. 1245. However, Sec. 1245 does apply to nonresidential real estate that qualified as recovery property under the ACRS rules (i.e., placed in service after 1980 and before 1987) unless the taxpayer elected to use the straight-line method of cost recovery.[30] Section 1245 does not apply to nonresidential real estate acquired after 1986. Only straight-line depreciation may be used for nonresidential real estate acquired after 1986 (see Chapter I10).

EXAMPLE I13-20 ▶

Brad sells the following two warehouses during the current year:

	Warehouse 1	Warehouse 2
Year of purchase	1984	1984
Cost	$720,000	$900,000
Cost recovery—straight line ACRS	200,000	
Cost recovery—ACRS statutory rates (accelerated)		360,000
Adjusted basis	520,000	540,000
Selling price	700,000	800,000

Both warehouses were acquired after 1980 and qualified as recovery property. The $180,000 ($700,000 − $520,000) gain on the sale of Warehouse 1 is a Sec. 1231 gain. Section 1245 does not apply because the straight-line method of cost recovery is used. Section 1245 applies to the sale of Warehouse 2 because ACRS is used and the property is nonresidential real estate. Therefore, the $260,000 ($800,000 − $540,000) gain is ordinary income because the $260,000 gain is less than the $360,000 total ACRS cost-recovery allowance.   ◄

If the properties in Example I13-20 were acquired before 1981, they would not be subject to the Sec. 1245 recapture rules regardless of the method of depreciation used. However, nonresidential real estate (e.g., a warehouse) acquired before 1981 and after 1963 is subject to the Sec. 1250 recapture rules, and a portion of the gain from its disposition may be treated as ordinary income.

The Sec. 1245 recapture rules are summarized in Topic Review I13-1.

RECAPTURE PROVISIONS OF SEC. 1250

OBJECTIVE 4

Apply the recapture provisions of Sec. 1250

In 1964, Sec. 1250 was enacted to extend the recapture concept to include most depreciable real property. Unlike Sec. 1245, where the recapture is based upon the total amount of depreciation (or cost recovery) allowed, Sec. 1250 applies solely to additional depreciation. **Additional depreciation**, also referred to as **excess depreciation**, is the excess of the actual amount of accelerated depreciation (or cost-recovery deductions under ACRS) over the amount of depreciation that would be deductible under the straight-line method. For property held a year or less, additional depreciation is the total amount of depreciation taken on the property.[31] Although Sec. 1250 was enacted in 1964, it is no longer necessary to consider additional depreciation for pre-1970 years.[32]

---

[30] Sec. 1245(a)(5), before being eliminated by the Tax Reform Act of 1986.
[31] Sec. 1250(b)(1).

[32] Recapture of additional depreciation allowed before 1970 is avoided under Sec. 1250(a)(3) if the property is held for more than ten years.

Topic Review I13-1

Section 1245 Recapture

▶ Section 1245 affects the character of the gain, not the amount of gain.

▶ Section 1245 does not apply to assets sold or exchanged at a loss.

▶ Section 1245 ordinary income is never more than the realized gain.

▶ Section 1245 recapture applies to the total depreciation or amortization allowed or allowable.

▶ Section 1245 property includes depreciable personal property.

▶ Section 1245 property includes nonresidential real estate placed in service after 1980 and before 1987 under the ACRS rules **unless** the taxpayer elected to use the straight-line method of cost recovery.

▶ Section 1245 does not apply to nonresidential real estate acquired after 1986 because only straight-line depreciation may be used.

PURPOSE OF SEC. 1250

Section 1250 has the effect of converting a portion of the Sec. 1231 gain into ordinary income when real property is sold or exchanged. The incremental benefits from using accelerated depreciation or ACRS cost recovery may be recaptured when the property is sold. Noncorporate taxpayers can avoid Sec. 1250 recapture by either using the straight-line method of depreciation or cost recovery or holding the Sec. 1250 property for its entire useful life or recovery period.

When the Sec. 1250 recapture rules are applied solely to the additional depreciation amount instead of to the total depreciation claimed (as is the case for Sec. 1245 property), real property that is not Sec. 1245 property gets more favorable treatment. Despite a number of changes making Sec. 1250 more restrictive, Sec. 1250 still affords taxpayers more favorable tax treatment than Sec. 1245.

SECTION 1250 PROPERTY DEFINED

Section 1250 property is any depreciable real property other than Sec. 1245 property and includes the following:[33]

▶ All other depreciable real property except nonresidential real estate that qualifies as recovery property (i.e., placed in service after 1980 and before 1987) unless the straight-line method of cost recovery is elected

▶ Low-income housing

▶ Depreciable residential rental property

Depreciation recapture is not required on real property placed in service after 1986 because such property must be depreciated under the straight-line modified ACRS rules.[34]

RECAPTURE RULES FOR RESIDENTIAL RENTAL PROPERTY

All residential rental property is Sec. 1250 property. For a building or structure to qualify as residential rental property, 80% or more of the gross rental income from the building or structure must be rental income from dwelling units. Residential rental property does not include any unit in a hotel, motel, inn, or other establishment if more than one-half of the units are used on a transient basis.[35]

ADDITIONAL COMMENT

Elevators and escalators were defined as Sec. 1245 property if placed in service before 1987, but as Sec. 1250 property if placed in service after 1986.

KEY POINT

An apartment building is the most common type of property classified as residential real estate.

---

[33] Sec. 1250(c).
[34] As explained in the Additional Recapture for Corporations section for this chapter, corporations may have depreciation recapture under Sec. 291(a)

despite the use of straight-line depreciation.
[35] Reg. Sec. 1.167(j)-3(b)(1)(i).

For depreciable residential rental property, Sec. 1250 recapture applies only to additional depreciation allowed after 1975.[36]

EXAMPLE I13-21 ▶

ADDITIONAL COMMENT

If the selling price in Example 13-21 is $600,000, all of the gain is Sec. 1250 ordinary income.

Selling Price	$600,000
Adjusted Basis	391,000
Realized Gain	$209,000
Ordinary Gain	$209,000

Buddy sells an apartment complex used as residential rental property and placed in service on January 1, 1976. The cost of the apartment complex is $900,000, and the complex is sold on January 1, 1997, for $700,000. Depreciation claimed by Buddy on the property is as follows:

Time Period	Depreciation Allowed	Straight-Line Depreciation	Additional Depreciation
Jan. 1, 1976–Jan. 1, 1997	$509,000	$286,000	$223,000

On the date of sale, the adjusted basis of the apartment is $391,000 ($900,000 − $509,000) and the realized gain is $309,000 ($700,000 − $391,000). All $223,000 of additional depreciation allowed is recaptured as ordinary income because the additional depreciation is less than the realized gain. The remaining $86,000 ($309,000 − $223,000) of gain is a Sec. 1231 gain. ◀

RESIDENTIAL RENTAL PROPERTY THAT IS RECOVERY PROPERTY

For residential rental property that is cost-recovery property (i.e., property placed in service after 1980 and before 1987), all of the **additional depreciation** is recaptured as ordinary income to the extent of gain. Additional depreciation is the excess of the ACRS deduction using the percentages provided in the ACRS tables over a hypothetical cost recovery amount based upon the straight-line ACRS method using the length of the recovery period (i.e., 15, 18, or 19 years).

EXAMPLE I13-22 ▶

Joel purchased depreciable residential rental property for $700,000 on January 1, 1986. The property is 19-year recovery property and accelerated cost recovery was used. Joel sells the property for $800,000 on January 1, 1997.

Cost Recovery Deductions Allowed	Cost Recovery with Straight-Line	Additional Depreciation
$406,000	$333,200	$72,800

Joel's realized gain is $506,000 [$800,000 − ($700,000 − $406,000)] and $72,800 is recaptured as Sec. 1250 ordinary income. The remaining $433,200 of gain is Sec. 1231 gain. ◀

RECAPTURE RULES FOR NONRESIDENTIAL REAL ESTATE

Nonresidential real property is Sec. 1250 property if placed in service before 1981 or after 1986. Nonresidential real property placed in service after 1980 and before 1987 is subject to Sec. 1245 recapture if accelerated cost recovery was taken on the property.[37] There is no depreciation recapture if the taxpayer elected to use the straight-line method of cost recovery[38] for nonresidential ACRS property.[39]

EXAMPLE I13-23 ▶

The AB partnership purchased an office building in 1981 and a warehouse in 1982. The statutory percentages provided in the ACRS table are used to determine cost-recovery deductions for the office building. The straight-line method is used to determine cost-recovery

---

[36] For additional depreciation after December 31, 1969, and before January 1, 1976, the recapture percentage is 100% minus 1% for each full month over 100 months the property is held. If the residential rental property is held for at least 200 months, none of the additional depreciation is recaptured for the 1970-1975 period. Secs. 1250(a)(1)(B)(v) and (a)(2)(B)(iii).

[37] Sec. 1245(a)(5), before amendment by the Tax Reform Act of 1986.
[38] The cost of 18-year recovery property may be recovered under Sec. 168(b)(3)(A) over a period of 18, 35, or 45 years.
[39] Sec. 1245(a)(5)(C), before being repealed by the Tax Reform Act of 1986.

deductions for the warehouse. The office building is subject to the Sec. 1245 recapture rules, and the warehouse is Sec. 1250 property. Even though the warehouse is Sec. 1250 property, the gain realized on the sale is Sec. 1231 gain because the straight-line ACRS method was used. ◄

PRE-ACRS NONRESIDENTIAL REAL ESTATE. All additional depreciation allowed after December 31, 1969 is subject to recapture as ordinary income under Sec. 1250.[40] The recaptured amount is limited to the realized gain.

EXAMPLE I13-24 ▶ Wayne sells his manufacturing plant during the current year. The plant was purchased in 1972 for use in his business. Additional depreciation (excess of accelerated depreciation under ACRS over straight-line) of $375,000 has been taken on the building. Information pertaining to the sale is as follows:

	Original Cost	Total Depreciation	Adjusted Basis	Selling Price
Plant	$3,000,000	$2,400,000	$600,000	$1,100,000
Land	300,000		300,000	900,000

The realized gain from the sale of the plant is $500,000 ($1,100,000 − $600,000) and $375,000 of the gain is recaptured as ordinary income under Sec. 1250. The remaining $125,000 of gain and the $600,000 of realized gain from the sale of the land are Sec. 1231 gains. ◄

EXAMPLE I13-25 ▶

TYPICAL
MISCONCEPTION

It is easy to forget that the amount recaptured as ordinary income under either Sec. 1245 or Sec. 1250 can never exceed the realized gain.

Assume the same facts as in Example I13-24 except that the selling price of the plant is $850,000. All of the $250,000 realized gain ($850,000 − $600,000) is recaptured as ordinary income because the $375,000 of additional depreciation is greater than the $250,000 of realized gain. ◄

RECAPTURE FOR ACRS NONRESIDENTIAL REAL ESTATE. Section 1245 applies to nonresidential real property placed in service after December 31, 1980 and before January 1, 1987, if the ACRS statutory rates are used to determine the cost-recovery deductions. For Sec. 1245 recovery property, all gain to the extent of the lesser of the gain realized or the cost recovery deductions claimed is ordinary income. If the straight-line method of cost recovery is elected, the property is Sec. 1250 and none of the cost-recovery deductions are recaptured under Sec. 1250.[41]

EXAMPLE I13-26 ▶

SELF-STUDY
QUESTION

If the asset in Example I13-22 is an office building, how much ordinary income must Joel recognize?

ANSWER

$406,000
The office building is Sec. 1245 property. Joel must recognize ordinary income of $406,000 and a $100,000 Sec. 1231 gain.

Larry owns the following two buildings that are used in his business. Both buildings qualify as recovery property under the ACRS rules. Larry uses the ACRS statutory rates to determine cost-recovery deductions for building 1 and the straight-line method for building 2.

	Original Cost	Cost-Recovery Deductions	Adjusted Basis
Building 1	$1,000,000	$420,000	$580,000
Building 2	1,000,000	300,000	700,000

If building 1 is sold for $1,200,000, the realized gain is $620,000 ($1,200,000 − $580,000). Section 1245 applies, and $420,000 is recaptured as ordinary income. The remaining $200,000 is Sec. 1231 gain. If building 2 is sold for $1,200,000, the realized gain is $500,000 ($1,200,000 − $700,000). All of the gain is Sec. 1231 gain because the straight-line cost recovery method is used and Sec. 1245 does not apply unless the ACRS statutory rates are used. ◄

---

[40] Secs. 1250(a)(1)(B)(v) and (a)(2)(B)(v).
[41] An exception is provided for corporate taxpayers under Sec. 291 (See the Additional Recapture for Corporations section in this chapter.)

LOW-INCOME HOUSING

Congress has provided incentives for the construction and rehabilitation of low-income housing. For tax years after 1986, a low-income housing credit is available to owners of qualified low-income housing projects.[42]

The depreciation recapture provisions of Sec. 1250 also favor low-income housing. The recapture percentage applied to the amount of additional depreciation allowed for low-income housing after 1975 is 100% less one percentage point for each full month the property is held for more than 100 months.[43] If the low-income housing unit is held for 16 years and 8 months, none of the additional depreciation is subject to recapture as ordinary income. To illustrate the more favorable treatment provided in Sec. 1250 for low-income housing, consider Example I13-27.

EXAMPLE I13-27 ▶ On January 1, 1982, Priscilla acquired two apartment buildings for $3,000,000 each. Building 1 qualifies as low-income housing, and building 2 is residential rental property but not low-income housing. Accelerated depreciation is used for both buildings, and $300,000 in additional depreciation has been deducted with respect to each building. Each building is sold on January 1, 1997, for $2,650,000.

Apartment Building	Cost	Total Depreciation	Adjusted Basis
Building 1	$3,000,000	$1,000,000	$2,000,000
Building 2	3,000,000	1,000,000	2,000,000

Gain realized from the sale of each apartment building is $650,000 ($2,650,000 − $2,000,000). Whereas 100% of the additional depreciation for building 2 is recaptured as ordinary income under Sec. 1250, only 20% of the additional depreciation for building 1 is recaptured as ordinary income. The low-income housing unit has been held for 180 months. For the first 100 months, the recapture percentage is 100%. Then the recapture percentage decreases by 1% each month for the next 80 months. $60,000 (0.20 × $300,000 additional depreciation) of the $650,000 gain realized from the sale of building 1 is recaptured as ordinary income. The remaining $590,000 ($650,000 − $60,000) of gain is Sec. 1231 gain. Of the $650,000 gain realized from the sale of building 2, $300,000 is recaptured as ordinary income and $350,000 is Sec. 1231 gain. ◀

The Sec. 1250 recapture rules for noncorporate taxpayers are summarized in Topic Review I13-2.

ADDITIONAL RECAPTURE FOR CORPORATIONS

KEY POINT

Section 291 has no effect on Sec. 1245 property because gain is already recaptured to the extent of all depreciation.

Corporations are subject to additional recapture rules under Sec. 291 if depreciable real estate is sold or otherwise disposed of. This recapture is in addition to the normal recapture rules under Sec. 1250. The additional ordinary income that is recaptured effectively reduces the amount of the Sec. 1231 gain.

The additional recapture amount under Sec. 291 is equal to 20% of the difference between the amount that would be recaptured under Sec. 1245 and the actual recapture amount under Sec. 1250.[44]

EXAMPLE I13-28 ▶ In 1980 Orlando Corporation purchased an office building for $500,000 for use in its business. The building is sold during the current year for $480,000. Total depreciation allowed for the

---

[42] Sec. 42.
[43] Secs. 1250(a)(1)(B)(i), (ii), (iii), and (iv).
[44] Sec. 291(a)(1).

Topic Review I13-2

Section 1250 Recapture for Noncorporate Taxpayers

▶ Section 1250 affects the character of the gain, not the amount of gain.

▶ Section 1250 does not apply to assets sold or exchanged at a loss.

▶ Section 1250 ordinary income is never more than the realized gain.

▶ Section 1250 ordinary income is never more than the *additional* depreciation allowed. (Note, that this statement is not true for corporate taxpayers.)

▶ Section 1250 property includes depreciable real property unless the real property is nonresidential real estate placed in service in 1980 and before 1987 under the ACRS rules and the straight-line method is not elected.

▶ Section 1250 ordinary income does not exist if the straight-line method of depreciation is used. (Note that this statement is not true for corporate taxpayers because of the additional recapture requirements under Sec. 291.)

SELF-STUDY QUESTION

If the taxpayer in Example I13-28 is a noncorporate taxpayer, how much of the gain is Sec. 1250 ordinary income?

ANSWER

$45,000

building is $170,000. Total depreciation of $125,000 would have been allowed if the straight-line method of depreciation has been used. The property's adjusted basis is $330,000 ($500,000 − $170,000) and the realized gain is $150,000 ($480,000 − $330,000). Under Sec. 1250, the ordinary income recaptured amount is equal to 100% of the additional depreciation, which is $45,000 ($170,000 − $125,000). Under Sec. 1245, the ordinary income recapture amount would be $150,000. The amount of Sec. 1250 ordinary income under Sec. 291 is $21,000 [0.20 × ($150,000 − $45,000)]. To summarize, the total amount recaptured as Sec. 1250 ordinary income is $66,000 ($45,000 + $21,000) and the Sec. 1231 gain is $84,000 ($150,000 − $66,000). ◀

EXAMPLE I13-29 ▶

SELF-STUDY QUESTION

If the taxpayer in Example I13-29 was a noncorporate taxpayer, how much of the gain is Sec. 1250 ordinary income?

ANSWER

Zero

Pacific Corporation purchased an office building in 1981 for $800,000 for use in its trade or business. The building is sold during the current year for $850,000. Pacific elected to use the straight-line method of cost recovery and $320,000 cost-recovery deductions have been allowed. The realized gain is $370,000 ($850,000 − $480,000). Because the straight-line method was elected, none of the gain is ordinary income under Sec. 1250 if Sec. 291 is not considered. If the building were instead Sec. 1245 recovery property, $320,000 of the gain would be treated as ordinary income. The amount of Sec. 1250 ordinary income under Sec. 291 is $64,000 [0.20 × ($320,000 − $0)]. The remaining $306,000 ($370,000 − $64,000) gain is Sec. 1231 gain. ◀

OBJECTIVE 5

Describe other recapture applications

RECAPTURE PROVISIONS— OTHER APPLICATIONS

The Secs. 1245 and 1250 recapture provisions take precedence over other provisions of the tax law.[45] Unless an exception or limitation is specifically stated in Secs. 1245 or 1250, gain is recognized under Secs. 1245 or 1250 despite the existence of provisions elsewhere in the Code that allow nonrecognition of gain.[46]

---

[45] Secs. 1245(d) and 1250(i).

[46] Reg. Secs. 1.1245-6(a) and 1.1250-1(c)(1).

GIFTS OF PROPERTY SUBJECT TO RECAPTURE

A gift of appreciated depreciable property does not result in the recapture of depreciation or cost-recovery deductions under Secs. 1245 or 1250.[47] The donee must consider the recapture potential when disposing of the property. The recapture amount for the donee is computed by including the recaptured amount attributable to the donor.[48]

EXAMPLE I13-30 ▶ Ashley makes a gift of equipment with an $8,200 FMV to Helmut. Ashley paid $10,000 for the equipment and deducted $4,000 of depreciation before making the gift. Ashley does not have to recapture any depreciation when making the gift. Helmut's basis for the equipment is $6,000 and the potential depreciation recapture carries over to Helmut. ◀

EXAMPLE I13-31 ▶ Assume the same facts as in Example I13-30 except that Helmut uses the equipment in a trade or business, deducts $1,500 of depreciation, and sells the equipment for $7,100. When determining the amount of depreciation subject to recapture, Helmut must also consider the depreciation allowed to Ashley. The entire $2,600 [$7,100 − ($6,000 − $1,500)] of gain is recaptured as ordinary income because it is less than the $5,500 ($4,000 + $1,500) of depreciation claimed. ◀

TRANSFER OF PROPERTY SUBJECT TO RECAPTURE AT DEATH

KEY POINT

Death is one of the few ways to avoid the recapture provisions.

The transfer of appreciated property at death does not cause a recapture of depreciation deductions to the decedent's estate under Secs. 1245 and 1250.[49] In addition, recapture potential does not carry over to the person who receives the property from the decedent.

EXAMPLE I13-32 ▶ Nancy dies while owning a building with a $900,000 FMV. The building is Sec. 1245 property acquired in 1982 for $800,000 on which cost-recovery deductions of $680,000 have been claimed. Pam inherits the building from Nancy. Pam's basis for the building is $900,000, and the $680,000 of cost-recovery deductions are not recaptured. If Pam immediately sells the building, there is no depreciation recapture attributable to the $680,000 of cost-recovery deductions taken by the decedent. ◀

CHARITABLE CONTRIBUTIONS

As discussed in Chapter I7, the deduction for a charitable contribution of ordinary income property is generally limited to its adjusted basis (i.e., the amount of the contribution deduction is equal to the FMV of the property less the amount of gain that would not have been LTCG [or Sec. 1231 gain] if the contributed property had been sold by the taxpayer at its FMV).[50] Thus, the contribution deduction for recapture property is generally scaled down to reflect the ordinary income that would be recognized if the property were sold rather than contributed to the charity.

EXAMPLE I13-33 ▶ Ralph makes a gift of an organ to a church. The organ is used in Ralph's trade or business and has a $6,300 FMV. Ralph paid $10,000 for the organ, and $8,000 depreciation has been claimed. If the organ were sold for its $6,300 FMV, the realized and recognized gain would be $4,300 ($6,300 − $2,000) and all of the gain would be ordinary income due to the recapture of depreciation under Sec. 1245. The charitable contribution deduction is limited to $2,000 ($6,300 − $4,300), because none of the $4,300 gain would be taxed as a LTCG if the organ were sold. ◀

---

[47] Secs. 1245(b)(1) and 1250(d)(1).
[48] Reg. Secs. 1.1245-2(a)(4) and 1.1250-2(d).

[49] Secs. 1245(b)(2) and 1250(d)(2).
[50] Sec. 170(e)(1)(A).

LIKE-KIND EXCHANGES

A taxpayer who receives boot (i.e., non–like-kind property) in a transaction that otherwise qualifies as a like-kind exchange recognizes gain equal to the lesser of the realized gain and the amount of boot received. If the property is Sec. 1245 or 1250 property, the gain is first considered to be ordinary income up to the maximum amount of the gain that is subject to the recapture provisions.

EXAMPLE I13-34 ▶

Virginia owns a duplex that is residential rental property. The duplex cost $300,000 in 1979 and has a $140,000 adjusted basis. Additional depreciation of $22,000 has been deducted. Virginia exchanges the duplex for a four-unit apartment building with a $250,000 FMV and $25,000 in cash. Gain realized on the exchange is $135,000 [($250,000 + $25,000) − $140,000)], and the recognized gain is $25,000. Gain recognized is the lesser of the $25,000 boot received or the $135,000 of gain realized. Because additional depreciation is recaptured as ordinary income under Sec. 1250, $22,000 of the gain is ordinary income and $3,000 of the gain is Sec. 1231 gain. ◀

If gain is not recognized in a like-kind exchange, the recapture potential carries over to the replacement property (i.e., any recapture potential associated with the property exchanged attaches to the property received in the exchange).[51]

EXAMPLE I13-35 ▶

Melissa owns a Chevrolet pickup truck used in her trade or business that cost $10,000 and has a $6,000 adjusted basis due to $4,000 in depreciation deductions she has claimed. The truck is exchanged for a Ford pickup truck with a $9,000 FMV. The Ford truck is used in Melissa's business. Melissa does not recognize any portion of the $3,000 realized gain because the exchange qualifies as a like-kind exchange and no boot is received. Her basis for the Ford truck is $6,000 (i.e., a substituted basis).

After deducting $2,000 of depreciation, Melissa sells the Ford truck for $7,300. All of the recognized gain of $3,300 ($7,300 − $4,000) is ordinary income. The depreciation recapture amount under Sec. 1245 is equal to the total $6,000 in depreciation (including $4,000 on the Chevrolet pickup truck) but the recognized gain is only $3,300.[52] ◀

INVOLUNTARY CONVERSIONS

If an involuntary conversion of Sec. 1245 property occurs and all or a portion of the gain is not recognized,[53] the amount of gain that is considered to be Sec. 1245 ordinary income is limited. Ordinary income under Sec. 1245 may not exceed the sum of (1) the recognized gain and (2) the FMV of acquired property that is not Sec. 1245 property but is qualifying property under Sec. 1033.[54] A similar provision exists for the involuntary conversion of Sec. 1250 property.[55]

EXAMPLE I13-36 ▶

Joan owns an office building with a $600,000 adjusted basis. The building was originally purchased in 1978, and additional depreciation amounts to $60,000. The building is destroyed by fire, and she receives insurance proceeds of $800,000. Joan purchases another office building for $750,000 and elects to defer as much of the gain as possible. Joan must recognize $50,000 of the $200,000 ($800,000 − $600,000) realized gain because the cost of the replacement property is $50,000 ($800,000 − $750,000) less than the insurance proceeds. The amount of ordinary income under Sec. 1250 is limited to $50,000 because Sec. 1250 property is purchased to replace the Sec. 1250 property destroyed by the fire. ◀

---

[51] Reg. Sec. 1.1245-2(c)(4).
[52] Reg. Sec. 1.1245-2(a)(4).
[53] As discussed in Chapter I12, one may elect to defer recognition of the gain if the Sec. 1033 requirements are satisfied.

[54] Sec. 1245(b)(4) and Reg. Sec. 1.1245-4(d)(1).
[55] Sec. 1250(d)(4) and Reg. Sec. 1.1250-3(d).

INSTALLMENT SALES

As discussed in Chapter I11, gain resulting from an installment sale is generally recognized as payments are received. Thus, the gain may be spread over more than one accounting period. An installment sale of depreciable property may result in all of the recaptured gain being taxed in the year of the sale.[56] Recapture income is "the aggregate amount which would be treated as ordinary income under Sec. 1245 or 1250 for the taxable year of the disposition if all payments to be received were received in the taxable year of disposition."[57] Recapture income must be recognized in the year of sale, even if no payments are received.

EXAMPLE I13-37 ▶

KEY POINT

In the case of an installment sale of Sec. 1245 or 1250 property, it is possible to report a large taxable gain even though the taxpayer has not yet received the cash to pay the tax on such gain.

Pat owns equipment with a $100,000 acquisition cost and a $50,000 adjusted basis. Depreciation of $50,000 has been allowed. In 1997, Pat sells the property for $30,000 cash and a $60,000 ten-year interest-bearing note. The realized gain is $40,000 ($90,000 − $50,000), and the recapture income amount is $40,000 (the lesser of total depreciation deductions of $50,000 or the $40,000 of realized gain). The $40,000 of gain is all recognized as ordinary income in 1997, despite the fact that the transaction qualifies as an installment sale and only $30,000 of cash is received in the year of sale. ◀

If the gain realized from the installment sale exceeds the recapture income, the excess gain is reported under the installment method.[58] The amount of recapture income recognized is added to the adjusted basis to determine the gross profit ratio.

EXAMPLE I13-38 ▶

SELF-STUDY QUESTION

What method of cost recovery is Bob using in Example I13-38?

ANSWER

Accelerated cost recovery. The office building is subject to Sec. 1245 recapture.

Bob owns an office building acquired for $700,000 in 1986 and subject to the Sec. 1245 recapture rules. After claiming $120,000 of cost recovery deductions, Bob sells the building to Judy in 1997 for $1,000,000. Bob receives $200,000 in cash and an $800,000 interest-bearing note. The note is to be paid with annual principal payments of $100,000 beginning in 1998. The total amount of realized gain is $420,000 ($1,000,000 − $580,000). In 1997 Bob recognizes $120,000 of Sec. 1245 ordinary income. The gross profit ratio is determined by adding $120,000 recapture income to the $580,000 basis. The gross profit ratio is 30% [($1,000,000 − $700,000) ÷ $1,000,000]. In addition to recognizing $120,000 of ordinary income, Bob recognizes $60,000 (0.30 × $200,000) Sec. 1231 gain in 1997 because a $200,000 cash down payment was received in the year of the sale. In 1998 and in each subsequent year, $30,000 (0.30 × $100,000) of Sec. 1231 gain is recognized as the cash payments on the principal are received. ◀

SECTION 179 EXPENSING ELECTION

In lieu of capitalizing the cost of new or used tangible personal business property, taxpayers may elect to expense up to $18,000 of the acquisition cost[59] (see Chapter I10). If the property is subsequently converted to nonbusiness use, previous tax benefits derived from the immediate expensing election must be recaptured and added to the taxpayer's gross income in the year of the conversion.[60] The recaptured amount equals the difference between the amount expensed under Sec. 179 and the total depreciation that would otherwise have been claimed for the period of business use.

EXAMPLE I13-39 ▶

Joel purchased business equipment last year for $18,000 and elected to expense the entire amount under Sec. 179. In the current year, he converts the equipment to nonbusiness use. Depreciation of $3,600 (0.20 × $18,000) based on a five-year recovery period under the MACRS rules would have been allowed during the period the equipment was held for business use. Joel must include $14,400 ($18,000 − $3,600) in his gross income for the current year. This amount represents the previous tax benefit obtained from the immediate expensing election. ◀

---

[56] Sec. 453(i)(1).
[57] Sec. 453(i)(2).
[58] Sec. 453(i)(1)(B).

[59] Secs. 179(a) and (b)(1).
[60] Sec. 179(d)(10) and Reg. Sec. 1.179-1(e).

WHAT WOULD YOU DO IN THIS SITUATION?

You recently graduated with an advanced degree in taxation and have accepted a job with a CPA firm in the tax department. One of the firm's clients, a wealthy individual, was in need of cash and decided to sell some assets to raise the cash. The client asked the firm to advise him, from a tax standpoint, which assets he should sell. The client is in the 39.6% tax bracket. You suggested in a written memo that the client sell one of the client's jet airplanes. The plane you recommended to be sold had originally cost $16 million and now had an adjusted basis of $6 million. A buyer had offered to buy the plane for $12 million on the installment basis, paying $4 million per year for three years plus interest at 9%. The principal reason for selling that particular plane is that it would raise $12 million over three years, but the tax could be spread over three years by using the installment sale method. The client took your advice and sold the plane in the current year.

Later, when preparing the client's tax return, you realize that depreciation recapture must be recognized in the year of sale, even if the property is sold under the installment sale method. Thus, *all* of the gain on the sale of the plane must be recognized in the year of sale, not spread over three years. You go to your manager and tell him about your major mistake. Your manager, who reviewed your original memo, indicates that he thinks that the two of you should not tell anyone about the mistake as it will negatively impact both of your careers. The manager thinks that because the client has such a large amount of income, reporting the entire gain on the sale of the plane on the client's return might not be detected by the client. Thus, the manager instructs you to prepare the current year return with the entire $6 million of gain and to not tell anyone about the mistake. What should you do in this situation?

CONSERVATION AND LAND CLEARING EXPENDITURES

Taxpayers engaged in the business of farming may deduct expenditures paid or incurred during the taxable year for soil and water conservation or the prevention of erosion. The expenditures must be made with respect to land used in farming and would be capital expenditures except for this provision.[61]

The deductions for conservation expenditures may be partially or fully recaptured as ordinary income if the farmland is disposed of before the land is held for ten years.[62] The amount of deductions recaptured as ordinary income under Sec. 1252 is a percentage of the aggregate deductions allowed for conservation expenditures. The amount of ordinary income recognized under Sec. 1252 is limited to the lesser of the taxpayer's realized gain or the applicable recapture percentage times the total conservation expenditures.

The recapture percentage is 100% if the farmland is disposed of within five years after the date it is acquired. The percentage declines by 20 percentage points for each additional year the property is held. If the land is disposed of after being held for ten years or more, none of the expenses are recaptured.[63]

KEY POINT

There is no recapture of conservation costs if the farmland has been held for at least 10 years.

EXAMPLE I13-40 ▶

Paula owns farmland with a $400,000 basis. She has deducted $50,000 for soil and water conservation expenditures. After farming the land for six years and five months, Paula sells the land for $520,000. The realized gain is $120,000 ($520,000 − $400,000) and the recapture percentage is 60%, because the farmland is disposed of within the seventh year after it was acquired. The amount of ordinary income due to recapture under Sec. 1252 is $30,000, the lesser of the $120,000 realized gain or the $30,000 (0.60 × $50,000) recapture amount. ◀

---

[61] Sec. 175(a).
[62] Sec. 1252(a)(1).

[63] Sec. 1252(a)(3).

INTANGIBLE DRILLING COSTS AND DEPLETION

ADDITIONAL
COMMENT

Intangible drilling and development costs represent the major cost of operations and can provide investors with working interests in oil and gas properties with a first-year write-off of substantially all of their investment.

Taxpayers may elect to either expense or capitalize intangible drilling and development costs (IDC).[64] If the election to expense is not made, the costs are capitalized and recovered through additional cost depletion deductions. Intangible drilling and development costs include "all expenditures made by an operator for wages, fuel, repairs, hauling, supplies, etc., incident to and necessary for the drilling of wells and the preparation of wells for the production of oil or gas."[65]

Part or all of the gain from the sale of oil and gas properties may be recaptured as ordinary income due to the recapture of the IDC deduction and the deduction for depletion. However, the amount of ordinary income recognized from the recapture of IDC and depletion is limited to the gain realized from the disposition of the property.[66]

EXAMPLE I13-41 ▶ In 1987 Marty purchased undeveloped property for the purpose of drilling for oil and gas. Intangible drilling and development costs of $400,000 were paid in 1987. Marty elected to expense the IDC. During the current year, Marty sells the property and realizes a $900,000 gain. $300,000 of cost depletion was allowed. Marty must recognize $700,000 of ordinary income because of the recapture of IDC ($400,000) and the recapture of depletion ($300,000). The remaining $200,000 ($900,000 − $700,000) gain is Sec. 1231 gain. ◀

EXAMPLE I13-42 ▶ In 1988 Tina acquired oil and gas properties for $700,000. During 1988, she elected to expense $200,000 of IDC. Total depletion allowed was $80,000. During the current year, Tina sells the property for $840,000 and realizes a $220,000 [($840,000 − ($700,000 − $80,000)] gain. The amount of ordinary income due to recapture is $220,000, because both IDC and depletion must be recaptured only to the extent of the gain. ◀

GAIN ON SALE OF DEPRECIABLE PROPERTY BETWEEN RELATED PARTIES

All of the gain recognized on the sale or exchange of property between related parties is ordinary income if the property is subject to depreciation in the hands of the transferee (i.e., the person who purchases the property). The sale or exchange may be direct or indirect.[67]

EXAMPLE I13-43 ▶ Phil owns a building with a $500,000 adjusted basis and $800,000 FMV. The building, which cost $700,000, is used in his business, and the straight-line method of depreciation is used. $200,000 of depreciation deductions were allowed. If the building is sold to Phil's 100%-owned corporation for $800,000, the $300,000 realized gain ($800,000 − $500,000) is treated as ordinary income under Sec. 1239, because the property is subject to depreciation in the hands of the transferee and the corporation and Phil are related parties. ◀

A sale or exchange of property could be subject to depreciation recapture under Sec. 1245 or 1250 as well as the Sec. 1239 related party rules. If so, recapture under Sec. 1245 or 1250 is considered before recapture under Sec. 1239.[68]

EXAMPLE I13-44 ▶ Assume the same facts as in Example I13-43 except that Phil sells equipment to the corporation instead of a building. All of the $300,000 realized gain is treated as ordinary income. The recapture amount under Sec. 1245 is $200,000, and Sec. 1239 applies to the remaining $100,000 gain. ◀

---

[64] Sec. 263(c).
[65] Reg. Sec. 1.612-4(a).
[66] Sec. 1254(a)(1).

[67] Sec. 1239(a).
[68] Reg. Sec. 1.1245-6(f).

PURPOSE OF SEC. 1239. Without Sec. 1239, a taxpayer could transfer appreciated depreciable property to a related party and recognize a Sec. 1231 gain on the sale. Net Sec. 1231 gain is treated as LTCG. The related purchaser of the property would receive a step up in the depreciation basis of the property to its FMV and be able to claim a larger amount of depreciation. In Example I13-43, Phil might prefer to recognize a $300,000 Sec. 1231 gain if the 100%-owned corporation was able to obtain a step-up in the property's basis to $800,000. Because Sec. 1239 applies, Phil must recognize $300,000 of ordinary income rather than Sec. 1231 gain. This rule prevents an individual taxpayer from receiving favorable Sec. 1231 gain treatment and prevents all taxpayers having large capital loss carryovers from using a related party to recognize a Sec. 1231 or capital gain which can be offset against their capital losses.

RELATED PARTIES. A person is related (1) to any corporation if the individual owns (directly or indirectly) more than 50% of the value of the outstanding stock and (2) to any partnership in which the person has a capital or profits interest of more than 50%.[69] Constructive ownership rules apply when determining whether the person owns more than 50% of the corporation or has more than a 50% interest in the partnership. Thus, an individual is considered to own stock that is owned by other family members and related entities (e.g., corporations, partnerships, estates, and trusts).

EXAMPLE I13-45 ▶ Tony sells a truck, which he has used for nonbusiness purposes, to the Able Corporation for $15,000. The adjusted basis of the truck is $12,000 on the date of the sale.

Tony owns 60% of the Able stock and his spouse owns the remaining 40% of the Able stock. Tony and Able are related parties because Tony is deemed to own all of the Able stock under the constructive ownership rules and $3,000 of ordinary income must be recognized under Sec. 1239 unless the overriding recapture rules of Sec. 1245 apply. ◀

A person is related to any trust in which such a person or the person's spouse is a beneficiary.[70] Section 1239 also applies to a sale or exchange of depreciable property between two corporations if the same individual owns more than 50% of each corporation.[71]

TAX PLANNING CONSIDERATIONS

For noncorporate taxpayers, net Sec. 1231 gains are generally preferable to ordinary gains because of the 28% maximum tax rate that is applicable to net capital gains. For corporate taxpayers, however, after 1986 it usually does not make any difference whether a gain is classified as Sec. 1231 or ordinary.

EXAMPLE I13-46 ▶ Western Corporation sells equipment for $400,000 during the current year. The equipment originally cost $500,000 and has a $350,000 adjusted basis after deducting depreciation. The corporation has no other gains and losses during the year or any capital loss carryovers from previous years. For Western Corporation, it does not make any difference whether the gain is Sec. 1245 ordinary income or Sec. 1231 gain. The effect on the corporation's taxable income and tax liability is the same regardless of how the gain is classified. ◀

The avoidance of the recapture provisions is important to both corporate and noncorporate taxpayers if capital loss carryovers exist. For example, if Western

---

[69] Sec. 1239(c).
[70] Sec. 1239(b)(2).

[71] Rev. Rul. 79-157, 1979-1 C.B. 281.

Corporation has a capital loss carryforward of $40,000 in Example I13-46, the corporation's taxable income is increased by $10,000 ($50,000 − $40,000) if the $50,000 gain is Sec. 1231 gain. However, because the gain is Sec. 1245 ordinary income, the corporation's taxable income is increased by $50,000. The $40,000 capital loss carryforward is not deductible unless it can be offset by a capital gain or a net Sec. 1231 gain.

AVOIDING THE RECAPTURE PROVISIONS

In view of the pervasiveness of the recapture provisions discussed in this chapter, recapture is difficult to avoid. In some cases, recapture can be avoided by holding the property a specific length of time before disposing of it (e.g., the recapture of conservation and land clearing expenses can be avoided by holding the farmland for at least ten years).[72] Contributing appreciated property to a qualified charitable organization cannot be used to circumvent the recapture provisions because in such case the amount of the charitable contribution is reduced by the amount of the gain that would not be a LTCG if the property were sold by the taxpayer.[73]

Although it is often difficult to avoid the recapture provisions, taxpayers may dispose of the property and defer recapture if the disposition is a nontaxable exchange. In a like-kind exchange where no boot is received, the recapture potential is carried over to the property received in the exchange. In a tax-free incorporation under Sec. 351, the recapture potential is transferred to the corporation receiving the recapture property. Recapture may also be avoided in situations involving a transfer of property to a partnership in exchange for a partnership interest.

Proper timing of the asset's disposition may be advantageous. Disposition may be delayed until the taxpayer's tax rate is low or the property can be sold in the same year that the taxpayer has an NOL that is about to expire.

Taxpayers can shift the recapture potential to other taxpayers by making a gift of property subject to recapture. The recapture potential remains with the property and must be considered when the donee disposes of the property.

RESIDENTIAL RENTAL PROPERTY. Noncorporate taxpayers can avoid the recapture provisions for residential rental property by using the straight-line method of depreciation.[74] The recapture provisions do not apply to residential rental property acquired after 1986 because only the straight-line depreciation method may be used. Recapture can also be avoided if the asset is fully depreciated at the date of disposal because no additional depreciation or cost recovery exists.

EXAMPLE I13-47 ▶ Vincent owns a building used as residential rental property. The building was purchased before 1981 and is not ACRS recovery property. Vincent could avoid depreciation recapture at the time of disposing of the asset by using the straight-line method of depreciation. If Vincent uses an accelerated method of depreciation, recapture is avoided if the disposition does not occur until the asset is fully depreciated. ◀

EXAMPLE I13-48 ▶ Assume the same facts as in Example I13-47 except that Vincent purchased the building after 1980 and before 1987 and the building is ACRS recovery property. Vincent could avoid recapturing cost recovery deductions when he disposes of the asset by using the straight-line method of cost recovery. If Vincent uses the accelerated method of cost recovery and disposes of the residential rental property at a gain, he cannot avoid recapture unless the asset's cost is fully recovered (i.e., no additional cost recovery exists). ◀

---

[72] Sec. 1252(a)(1).
[73] Sec. 170(e)(1)(A).

[74] Corporate taxpayers must consider Sec. 291(a). (See the Additional Recapture for Corporations section in this chapter.)

NONRESIDENTIAL REAL PROPERTY. For noncorporate taxpayers, the Sec. 1250 recapture provisions do not apply to nonresidential real property acquired after 1986 because only the straight-line method may be used. However, to avoid recapture on the disposition of appreciated nonresidential real property acquired after 1980 and before 1987 noncorporate taxpayers must use the straight-line method of depreciation. Nonresidential real property acquired before 1987, which is recovery property subject to ACRS, is subject to the Sec. 1245 recapture rules unless the straight-line method is used. If the accelerated method of cost recovery is used, recapture cannot be avoided by waiting until the asset's cost is fully recovered before disposing of the asset.

EXAMPLE I13-49 ▶

Christine purchased an office building in 1986 for $225,000 for use in her trade or business. The property is ACRS recovery property, and she uses the accelerated method to compute the cost-recovery deductions. Cost-recovery deductions taken before the sale of the building amount to $140,000. If she sells the building for $250,000, $140,000 of the $165,000 ($250,000 − $85,000) realized gain is recaptured as ordinary income under Sec. 1245. The remaining gain of $25,000 is Sec. 1231 gain. Recapture could have been avoided if Christine had instead used the straight-line method of cost recovery. If the straight-line method were used instead, she would report a smaller realized gain, all of which is Sec. 1231 gain. ◀

EXAMPLE I13-50 ▶

Bryce purchased an office building in 1986 for $300,000 for use in his trade or business. The property is 19-year recovery property, and he used the accelerated method of cost recovery. If Bryce sells the building for $250,000 after all of the cost has been recovered (i.e., the adjusted basis is zero), the realized gain of $250,000 is recaptured as ordinary income under Sec. 1245. ◀

TRANSFER PROPERTY AT DEATH. One of the most effective ways to avoid the recapture provisions is to transfer the property at death. No recapture occurs at the time of the transfer, and the basis of property received from a decedent is generally the FMV of the property at the date of the decedent's death.[75] The property's recapture potential does not carry over to the beneficiary as in the case of a gift made to a donee.

COMPLIANCE AND PROCEDURAL CONSIDERATIONS

Form 4797, Supplemental Schedule of Gains and Losses, is used to report gains and losses from sales or exchanges of assets used in a trade or business (see Figures I13-1 through I13-3). The form is also used to report gains or losses resulting from involuntary conversions, other than casualties or thefts, of property used in the trade or business and capital assets held more than a year. If gains or losses due to casualties or thefts of property used in a trade or business or property held to produce income are recognized, they are reported on Form 4684, Casualties and Thefts (see Figure I13-3). If such casualties or thefts occur, Form 4684 is prepared either before or at the same time as Form 4797.

REPORTING SEC. 1231 GAINS AND LOSSES ON FORM 4797

Part I of Form 4797, which is reproduced in Figure I13-1, is used to report gains and losses resulting from

▶ The sale or exchange of Sec. 1231 property

---

[75] Sec. 1014(a).

▶ An involuntary conversion, other than a casualty or theft, of Sec. 1231 property

▶ An involuntary conversion, other than a casualty or theft, of capital assets held more than one year and used to produce income.

As indicated on lines 3 through 6 in Part I of Form 4797, gains and losses recorded on other forms and in Part III of Form 4797 are reported in Part I. The netting of Sec. 1231 gains and losses occurs in Part I of Form 4797. If Sec. 1231 gains exceed Sec. 1231 losses, the net gain is reported on line 8 and then recorded on Schedule D, unless the taxpayer has nonrecaptured net Sec. 1231 losses from prior years. Net Sec. 1231 gain to the extent of any nonrecaptured net Sec. 1231 losses, as reported on line 9, is ordinary and is reported on line 13 of Part II. If Sec. 1231 losses exceed Sec. 1231 gains, the loss is reported on line 8 and on line 12 of Part II. Part II of Form 4797, which is reproduced in Figure I13-1, is used to report ordinary gains and losses.

Ordinary gains and losses recognized including those recorded on other forms and in Parts I and III of Form 4797 are reported on lines 11 through 18 in Part II of Form 4797.

REPORTING GAINS RECAPTURED AS ORDINARY INCOME ON FORM 4797

Part III of Form 4797, reproduced in Figure I13-2, is used to determine and report ordinary income due to the recapture provisions of Secs. 1245, 1250, 1252, 1254, and 1255. Part III is completed before Parts I and II. To illustrate the use of Part III, assume an individual sells equipment used in a trade or business for $20,000 on April 30, 1996. The equipment cost $18,000 on March 10, 1994 and depreciation deductions of $3,000 were allowed. The $5,000 ($20,000 − $15,000) total gain is reported on line 26. The $3,000 of depreciation allowed is reported on lines 27(a) and (b). On line 32, total gains resulting from the sale of all properties ($5,000 in this illustration) reported in Part III are combined. The total amount of ordinary income due to the recapture provisions ($3,000 in this illustration) is reported on line 33 and then reported as ordinary income on line 14 in Part II. The excess of the gain over the amount of ordinary income is reported on line 34. The portion of this gain not due to casualty or theft ($2,000 in this illustration) is a Sec. 1231 gain and is reported on line 6 of Part I of Form 4797. If any of the gain is due to casualty or theft, that portion of the gain is reported on Section B of Form 4684.

REPORTING CASUALTY OR THEFT GAIN OR LOSS ON FORM 4684

Section A of Form 4684 is used to report gains and losses resulting from a casualty or theft of personal-use property. These gains and losses are not Sec. 1231 transactions. Thus Sec. A of Form 4684 is not discussed in this chapter.

Section B of Form 4684, which is reproduced in Figure I13-3, is used to report gains and losses resulting from a casualty or theft of property used in a trade or business or held for the production of income. Note that a separate Part I is used for each different casualty or theft. Gains are reported on line 22, and losses are reported on line 28. For properties held a year or less, the gains and losses are reported on lines 29 through 32 of Part II. These gains and losses are either recorded as ordinary gains and losses on line 15 of Part II of Form 4797 or as itemized deductions on Schedule A of Form 1040.

For properties held more than a year, the gains and losses are reported on lines 33 and 34. If gains exceed losses, the net gain is reported on line 39 and then on line 3 of Part I of Form 4797 (i.e., the gains and losses are treated as Sec. 1231 gains and losses). If the losses exceed the gains, all or part of the gains and losses are reported as ordinary in Part II of Form 4797 and/or on Schedule A of Form 1040.

PROBLEM MATERIALS

DISCUSSION QUESTIONS

I13-1 Explain how the gain on the sale or exchange of land could be classified as either ordinary income, a Sec. 1231 gain, or a LTCG, depending on the facts and circumstances.

I13-2 Why were taxpayers reluctant to sell appreciated business property between 1938 and 1942? What effect did this reluctance have on the tax law?

I13-3 Alice owns timber, purchased in 1991, with an adjusted basis of $50,000. The timber is cut for use in her furniture business on October 1, 1997, when the FMV of the timber is $200,000. The FMV of the timber on January 1, 1997 is $190,000. May Alice treat any of the gain as Sec. 1231 gain? If so, how much?

I13-4 Explain how the gain from an involuntary conversion of business property held more than one year is taxed if the involuntary conversion is the result of a condemnation. Explain the tax treatment if the involuntary conversion is due to a casualty.

I13-5 When is livestock considered Sec. 1231 property?

I13-6 When is a net Sec. 1231 gain treated as ordinary income?

I13-7 Why is it unlikely that gains due to the sale of equipment will be treated as Sec. 1231 gains?

I13-8 Hank sells equipment used in a trade or business for $25,000. The equipment costs $30,000 and has an adjusted basis of $25,500. Why is it important to know the holding period?

I13-9 Jackie purchases equipment during the current year for $800,000 that has a seven-year MACRS recovery period. She expects to sell the property after three years. Jackie anticipates that her marginal tax rate in the year of sale will be significantly higher than her current marginal tax rate. Why might it be advantageous for her to use the straight-line method of depreciation?

I13-10 Karen purchased a computer three years ago for $4,500 to use exclusively in her business. She expensed the entire cost of the computer under Sec. 179. If she sells the computer during the current year for $1,622, what is the amount and character of her recognized gain?

I13-11 Sheila owns a motel that is used in a trade or business. If she sells the motel, the gain will be Sec. 1245 ordinary income. During what period of time was the motel placed into service?

I13-12 How may a taxpayer avoid having additional depreciation?

I13-13 Marty sells his fully depreciated building at a gain to an unrelated party. The building is purchased before 1981. Is any of the gain taxed as ordinary income?

I13-14 Which of the following assets (assume all assets have a holding period of more than one year) do not qualify as Sec. 1231 property: inventory, a pig held for breeding, land used as a parking lot for customers, and marketable securities?

I13-15 When is an office building subject to the depreciation recapture rules of Sec. 1245?

I13-16 Does a building that is 60% rented for residential use and 40% for commercial use qualify as residential rental property?

I13-17 Roger owns an apartment complex with a FMV of $2 million. If he sells the apartment complex, $700,000 of the gain is ordinary income. If he dies before selling the apartment complex and his estate sells the property for $2 million, how much ordinary income must the estate recognize?

I13-18 Rashad owns a duplex that is used 100% as residential rental property. Under what conditions, if any, will any gain that he recognizes be Sec. 1245 ordinary income?

I13-19 Why may a corporation recognize a greater amount of ordinary income due to the sale of Sec. 1250 property than a noncorporate taxpayer?

Form **4797**

Department of the Treasury
Internal Revenue Service   (99)

Sales of Business Property
(Also Involuntary Conversions and Recapture Amounts
Under Sections 179 and 280F(b)(2))

▶ Attach to your tax return.

OMB NO. 1545-0184

1996

Attachment
Sequence No. **27**

Name(s) shown on return

Identifying number

1 Enter here the gross proceeds from the sale or exchange of real estate reported to you for 1996 on Form(s) 1099-S
(or a substitute statement) that you will be including on line 2, 11, or 22 .... | **1** |

Part I   **Sales or Exchanges of Property Used in a Trade or Business and Involuntary Conversions From Other Than Casualty or Theft - Property Held More Than 1 Year**

2 **(a)** Description of property	**(b)** Date acquired (mo., day, yr.)	**(c)** Date sold (mo., day, yr.)	**(d)** Gross sales price	**(e)** Depreciation allowed or allowable since acquisition	**(f)** Cost or other basis, plus improvements and expense of sale	**(g)** LOSS If (f) is more than (d) plus (e), subtract the sum of (d) and (e) from (f)	**(h)** GAIN If (d) plus (e) is more than (f), subtract (f) from the sum of (d) and (e)

3	Gain, if any, from Form 4684, line 39	**3**	
4	Section 1231 gain from installment sales from Form 6252, line 26 or 37	**4**	
5	Section 1231 gain or (loss) from like-kind exchanges from Form 8824	**5**	*2,000*
6	Gain, if any, from line 34, from other than casualty or theft	**6**	*2,000*
7	Add lines 2 through 6 in columns (g) and (h)	**7**	*2,000*

8 Combine columns (g) and (h) of line 7. Enter gain or (loss) here, and on the appropriate line as follows: .... | **8** |

  Partnerships - Enter the gain or (loss) on Form 1065, Schedule K, line 6. Skip lines 9, 10, 12, and 13 below.

  S corporations - Report the gain or (loss) following the instructions for Form 1120S, Schedule K, lines 5 and 6.
  Skip lines 9, 10, 12, and 13 below, unless line 8 is a gain and the S corporation is subject to the capital gains tax.

  All others - If line 8 is zero or a loss, enter the amount on line 12 below and skip lines 9 and 10. If line 8 is a gain
  and you did not have any prior year section 1231 losses, or they were recaptured in an earlier year, enter the
  gain as a long-term capital gain on Schedule D and skip lines 9, 10, and 13 below.

9 Nonrecaptured net section 1231 losses from prior years .... | **9** |

10 Subtract line 9 from line 8. If zero or less, enter -0-. Also enter on the appropriate line as follows: .... | **10** |

  S corporations - Enter this amount on Schedule D (Form 1120S), line 13, and skip lines 12 and 13 below.

  All others - If line 10 is zero, enter the amount from line 8 on line 13 below. If line 10 is more than zero, enter the
  amount from line 9 on line 13 below, and enter the amount from line 10 as a long-term capital gain on Schedule D.

Part II   **Ordinary Gains and Losses**

11 Ordinary gains and losses not included on lines 12 through 18 (include property held 1 year or less):

12	Loss, if any, from line 8	**12**		
13	Gain, if any, from line 8, or amount from line 9 if applicable	**13**		*3,000*
14	Gain, if any, from line 33	**14**		
15	Net gain or (loss) from Form 4684, lines 31 and 38a	**15**		
16	Ordinary gain from installment sales from Form 6252, line 25 or 36	**16**		
17	Ordinary gain or (loss) from like-kind exchanges from Form 8824	**17**		
18	Recapture of section 179 expense deduction for partners and S corporation shareholders from property dispositions by partnerships and S corporations	**18**		*3,000*
19	Add lines 11 through 18 in columns (g) and (h)	**19**		*3,000*

20 Combine columns (g) and (h) of line 19. Enter gain or (loss) here, and on the appropriate line as follows: .... | **20** |
  a For all except individual returns: Enter the gain or (loss) from line 20 on the return being filed.
  b For individual returns:
  (1) If the loss on line 12 includes a loss from Form 4684, line 35, column (b)(ii), enter that part of the loss
       here and on line 22 of Schedule A (Form 1040). Identify as from "Form 4797, line 20b(1)." .... | **20b(1)** |
  (2) Redetermine the gain or (loss) on line 20, excluding the loss, if any, on line 20b(1). Enter here and on Form 1040, line 14 | **20b(2)** | *3,000* |

618011
11-12-96   **LHA   For Paperwork Reduction Act Notice, see page 1 of separate Instructions.**   Form **4797** (1996)

FIGURE I13-1   ▶   PART I AND PART II OF FORM 4797

Part III Gain From Disposition of Property Under Sections 1245, 1250, 1252, 1254, and 1255

21	(a) Description of section 1245, 1250, 1252, 1254, or 1255 property:			**(b)** Date acquired (mo., day, yr.)	**(c)** Date sold (mo., day, yr.)
A	*Equipment*			3-10-93	4-30-95
B					
C					
D					

	Relate lines 21A through 21D to these columns ▶		Property A	Property B	Property C	Property D
22	Gross sales price (**Note:** See line 1 before completing.)	22	20,000			
23	Cost or other basis plus expense of sale	23	18,000			
24	Depreciation (or depletion) allowed or allowable ..	24	3,000			
25	Adjusted basis. Subtract line 24 from line 23	25	15,000			
26	Total gain. Subtract line 25 from line 22	26	5,000			
27	**If section 1245 property:**					
a	Depreciation allowed or allowable from line 24 ...	27a	3,000			
b	Enter the **smaller** of line 26 or 27a	27b	3,000			
28	**If section 1250 property:** If straight line depreciation was used, enter -0- on line 28g, except for a corporation subject to section 291.					
a	Additional depreciation after 1975	28a				
b	Applicable percentage multiplied by the **smaller** of line 26 or line 28a	28b				
c	Subtract line 28a from line 26. If residential rental property or line 26 is not more than line 28a, skip lines 28d and 28e	28c				
d	Additional depreciation after 1969 and before 1976	28d				
e	Enter the **smaller** of line 28c or 28d	28e				
f	Section 291 amount (corporations only)	28f				
g	Add lines 28b, 28e, and 28f	28g				
29	**If section 1252 property:** Skip this section if you did not dispose of farmland or if this form is being completed for a partnership.					
a	Soil, water, and land clearing expenses	29a				
b	Line 29a multiplied by applicable percentage	29b				
c	Enter the **smaller** of line 26 or 29b	29c				
30	**If section 1254 property:**					
a	Intangible drilling and development costs, expenditures for development of mines and other natural deposits, and mining exploration costs	30a				
b	Enter the **smaller** of line 26 or 30a	30b				
31	**If section 1255 property:**					
a	Applicable percentage of payments excluded from income under section 126	31a				
b	Enter the **smaller** of line 26 or 31a	31b				

Summary of Part III Gains. Complete property columns A through D through line 31b before going to line 32.

32	Total gains for all properties. Add property columns A through D, line 26	32	5,000
33	Add property columns A through D, lines 27b, 28g, 29c, 30b, and 31b. Enter here and on line 14	33	3,000
34	Subtract line 33 from line 32. Enter the portion from casualty or theft on Form 4684, line 33. Enter the portion from other than casualty or theft on Form 4797, line 6	34	2,000

Part IV Recapture Amounts Under Sections 179 and 280F(b)(2) When Business Use Drops to 50% or Less
See instructions.

			(a) Section 179	**(b) Section 280F(b)(2)**
35	Section 179 expense deduction or depreciation allowable in prior years	35		
36	Recomputed depreciation	36		
37	Recapture amount. Subtract line 36 from line 35.	37		

FIGURE I13-2 ▶ PART III OF FORM 4797

Name(s) shown on tax return.	Identifying number

SECTION B - Business and Income-Producing Property
(Use this section to report casualties and thefts of property used in a trade or business or for income-producing purposes.)

Part I   Casualty or Theft Gain or Loss (Use a separate Part I for each casualty or theft)

19 Description of properties (show type, location, and date aquired for each):

Property **A** ....

Property **B** ....

Property **C** ....

Property **D** ....

Properties (Use a separate column for each property lost or damaged from one casualty or theft.)

		A	B	C	D
20 Cost or adjusted basis of each property	20				
21 Insurance or other reimbursement (whether or not you filed a claim) **Note:** If line 20 is **more than** line 21, skip line 22.	21				
22 Gain from casualty or theft. If line 21 is **more than** line 20, enter difference here and on line 29 or line 34, column **(c)**, except as provided in the instructions for line 33. Also, skip lines 23 through 27 for that column. See the instructions for line 4 if line 21 includes insurance or other reimbursement you did not claim, or you received payment for your loss in a later tax year	22				
23 Fair market value **before** casualty or theft	23				
24 Fair market value **after** casualty or theft	24				
25 Subtract line 24 from line 23	25				
26 Enter the **smaller** of line 20 or line 25 **Note:** If the property was totally destroyed by casualty or lost from theft, enter on line 26 the amount from line 20.	26				
27 Subtract line 21 from line 26. If zero or less, enter -0-	27				

28 Casualty or theft loss. Add the amounts on line 27. Enter the total here and on line 29 **or** line 34. (see instructions) .... | 28 |

Part II   Summary of Gains and Losses (from separate Parts I)

(a) Identify casualty or theft	(b) Losses from casualties or thefts		(c) Gains from casualties or thefts includible in income
	(i) Trade, business, rental or royalty property	(ii) Income-producing property	

Casualty or Theft of Property Held One Year or Less

29		( )	( )	
		( )	( )	
30 Totals. Add the amounts on line 29 30		( )	( )	

31 Combine line 30, columns (b)(i) and (c). Enter the net gain or (loss) here and on Form 4797, line 15. If Form 4797 is not otherwise required, see instructions | 31 |

32 Enter the amount from line 30, column (b)(ii) here and on Schedule A (Form 1040), line 22. Partnerships, S corporations, estates and trusts, see instructions | 32 |

Casualty or Theft of Property Held More Than One Year

33 Casualty or theft gains from Form 4797, line 34 | 33 |

34		( )	( )	
		( )	( )	

35 Total losses. Add amounts on line 34, columns (b)(i) and (b)(ii) .... 35 | ( ) | ( ) |

36 Total gains. Add lines 33 and 34, column (c) | 36 |

37 Add amounts on line 35, columns (b)(i) and (b)(ii) | 37 |

38 If the loss on line 37 is **more than** the gain on line 36:

  a Combine line 35, column (b)(i) and line 36, and enter the net gain or (loss) here. Partnerships and S corporations see the note below. All others enter this amount on Form 4797, line 15. If Form 4797 is not otherwise required, see instructions. | 38a |

  b Enter the amount from line 35, column (b)(ii) here. Partnerships and S corporations see the note below. Individuals enter this amount on Schedule A (Form 1040), line 22. Estates and trusts, enter on the "Other deductions" line of your tax return | 38b |

39 If the loss on line 37 is **equal to** or **less than** the gain on line 36, combine these lines and enter here. Partnerships see the note below. All others enter this amount on Form 4797, line 3 | 39 |

617402
11-02-96

Note: Partnerships, enter the amount from line 38a, 38b, or line 39 on Form 1065, Schedule K, line 7. S corporations, enter the amount from line 38a or 38b on Form 1120S, Schedule K, line 6.

FIGURE I13-3   ▶   SECTION B OF FORM 4684

I13-20 Assume a taxpayer sells equipment used in a trade or business for a gain that is less than the depreciation allowed. If the taxpayer is a corporation, will a greater amount of Sec. 1245 income be recognized than if the taxpayer is an individual? Explain.

I13-21 Dale owns business equipment with a $100,000 FMV and an adjusted basis of $60,000. The property was originally acquired for $150,000. Which one of the following transactions would result in recognition of $40,000 ordinary income by Dale due to the depreciation recapture rules of Sec. 1245?
a. He makes a gift of the property to a daughter.
b. He contributes the property to a qualified charitable organization.
c. He disposes of the equipment in an installment sale and receives $10,000 cash in the year of sale.

I13-22 Carlos owns an office building with a $700,000 acquisition cost, a $250,000 adjusted basis, and a $500,000 FMV. The office building was acquired before 1981, and additional depreciation amounts to $110,000. Carlos makes a gift of the building to a charitable organization. What is the amount of his charitable contribution deduction?

I13-23 Ted owns a warehouse that cost $650,000 in 1984 and is subject to depreciation recapture under Sec. 1245. The warehouse, which has an adjusted basis of $300,000, is destroyed by a tornado and Ted receives $510,000 from the insurance company. Within 9 months, he pays $450,000 for a new warehouse and an election is made to defer the gain under Sec. 1033. What is the amount and character of Ted's recognized gain?

I13-24 When a taxpayer disposes of oil, gas, or geothermal property, part or all of the gain may be recaptured as ordinary income. Explain how the recapture amount is determined for oil and gas and geothermal properties.

I13-25 William owns two appreciated assets, land and a building, which have been used in his trade or business for several years. The straight-line method of depreciation is used for the building. If he sells the two assets to his 100%-owned corporation, will William have to recognize any ordinary income? Explain.

ISSUE IDENTIFICATION QUESTIONS

I13-26 Six years ago Joelle started raising chinchillas. She separates her chinchillas into two groups, a breeding group and a market group. During the year, she had the following sales of chinchillas from her market group: 400 to producers of fur products; 100 to pet stores; and 25 to individuals to use as pets. From her breeding stock, she sold six chinchillas to Rebecca, an individual who is starting a chinchilla ranch, and five to Fur Pelts, a producer of fur products. All 11 chinchillas from the breeding group have been held for at least 22 months, and the five sold to Fur Pelts were poor performers.

I13-27 Green Acres, Inc. owns 1,400 acres adjacent to land owned by the U.S. government. The government, wanting to sell timber from its land, had to assure prospective bidders of access to the timber. The government entered into an agreement with Green Acres for a logging road easement across land owned by Green Acres. The government agreed to pay $2 per thousand board feet of timber removed up to a maximum of $130,000. Bidders for the rights to obtain the government's timber had to agree to pay the fee to Green Acres as part of their bids for the timber. Stanley Lumberyard, Inc. provided the highest bid and paid $80,000 to Green Acres during the first year of cutting and removing the timber and $50,000 during the second year. What tax issues should Green Acres and Stanley Lumberyard consider?

I13-28 Sarah, who has been in the business of erecting, maintaining, and renting outdoor advertising displays for 18 years, has an offer to purchase her business. Two basic types of advertising displays are used in her business: structure X and structure Y. Structure X consists of a single sign face nailed to a wooden support frame and attached to wooden poles 30 feet long. Its structure is rather easy to dismantle and move from one location to another. In contrast, structure Y is a permanent sign that is designed to withstand winds of up to 100 miles per hour. None of the Structure Y signs have ever been moved. What tax issues should Sarah consider?

I13-29 Sylvester owns and operates an unincorporated pizza business that delivers pizza to customers. Three years ago, he acquired an automobile for $10,000 to provide delivery service. Recently, Sylvester hired an employee who prefers to use his personal automobile to make the deliveries. Thus, Sylvester decided to permit his 18-year old daughter to use the automobile for her personal use. The automobile's adjusted basis is $3,080 and its FMV is $4,700. What tax issues should Sylvester consider?

PROBLEMS

I13-30 *Sec. 1231, 1245, and 1250 Transactions.* All assets listed below have been held for more than one year. Which assets might be classified as Sec. 1231, Sec. 1245, or Sec. 1250 property? An asset may be classified as more than one type of property.
a. Land on which a factory is located
b. Equipment used in the factory
c. Raw materials inventory
d. Patent purchased to allow use of a manufacturing process
e. Land held primarily for sale
f. Factory building acquired in 1986 (the straight-line ACRS recovery method is used)

I13-31 *Sec. 1231 Gains and Losses.* Vivian's AGI is $40,000 without considering the gains and losses below. Determine her revised AGI after the inclusion of any applicable gains or losses for the following independent cases. Assume she has no unrecaptured net Sec. 1231 losses at the beginning of the year.

	Case A	Case B	Case C	Case D
Sec. 1231 gain	$15,000	$10,000	$20,000	$ 5,000
Sec. 1231 loss	5,000	18,000	25,000	12,000
LTCG	—0—	—0—	4,000	—0—
LTCL	—0—	—0—	—0—	4,200

I13-32 *Sec. 1231 Transactions.* Which of the following transactions or events is treated as a Sec. 1231 gain or loss? Assume all assets are held for more than one year.
a. Theft of uninsured diamond ring, with an $800 basis and a $1,000 FMV.
b. Gain due to condemnation of land used in business.
c. Loss on the sale of a warehouse.
d. Gain on the sale of equipment. The gain recognized amounts to $4,000 and the depreciation deductions allowed amount to $10,000.

I13-33 *Capital Loss Versus Sec. 1231 Loss.* Vicki has an AGI of $60,000 without considering the sale of a nondepreciable asset for $19,000. The asset was acquired six years ago and has an adjusted basis of $27,000. She has no other sales or exchanges. Determine her AGI for the following independent situations:
a. The asset is a capital asset.
b. The asset is Sec. 1231 property.

I13-34 *Ordinary Income Versus Sec. 1231 Gain.* At the beginning of 1997, Silver Corporation has a $95,000 capital loss carryforward from 1996. During 1997, the corporation sells land, held for four years, and realizes a $80,000 gain. Silver has no unrecaptured Sec. 1231 losses, and it made no other sales during the current year. Determine the amount of capital loss carryforward that Silver can use in 1997 if

a. The land is Sec. 1231 property.

b. The land is not a capital asset or Sec. 1231 property.

I13-35 *Sec. 1231 Transactions.* During the current year, Sean's office building is destroyed by fire. After collecting the insurance proceeds, Sean has a $50,000 recognized gain. The building was acquired in 1978, and the straight-line method of depreciation has been used. He does not plan to acquire a replacement building. Consider the following independent cases and determine his net capital gain. For each case, include the $50,000 casualty gain described above.

a. Land used in his trade or business and held more than a year is condemned by the state. The recognized gain is $60,000.

b. Assume the same facts as in Part a, except the condemnation results in a $60,000 loss.

c. An apartment building used as residential rental property and held more than one year is destroyed by a sudden, unexpected mudslide. The building is not insured, and the loss amounts to $200,000.

I13-36 *Nonrecaptured Net Sec. 1231 Losses.* Consider the following summary of Sec. 1231 gains and losses recognized by Janet during the period 1992–1997. If Janet has no capital gains and losses during the six-year period, determine her net capital gain for each year.

	Sec. 1231 Gains	Sec. 1231 Losses
1992	$9,000	$ 7,000
1993	20,000	24,000
1994	12,000	20,000
1995	9,000	5,000
1996	25,000	12,000
1997	10,000	17,000

I13-37 *Sec. 1245.* The Pear Corporation owns equipment with a $200,000 adjusted basis. The equipment was purchased six years ago for $650,000. If Pear sells the equipment for the selling prices given in the three independent cases below, what are the amount and character of Pear's recognized gain or loss?

Case	Selling Price
A	$395,000
B	680,000
C	145,000

I13-38 *Sec. 1245.* Elizabeth owns equipment that cost $500,000 and has an adjusted basis of $230,000. If the straight-line method of depreciation had been used, the adjusted basis would be $300,000.

a. What is the maximum selling price that she could sell the equipment for without having to recognize Sec. 1245 ordinary income?

b. If she sold the equipment and had to recognize $61,000 of Sec. 1245 ordinary income, what was the selling price?

I13-39 *Secs. 1231, 1245, and 1250.* Betty is in the business of breeding and racing horses. Consider the following transactions that occur during the year:

- A building with an adjusted basis of $300,000 is destroyed by fire. Insurance proceeds of $500,000 are received, but Betty does not plan to replace the building. The building was built 12 years ago at a cost of $430,000 and straight-line depreciation has been used. The building was used to provide lodging for her employees.

- Four acres of the farm are condemned by the state to widen the highway and Betty receives $50,000. The adjusted basis of the four acres is $15,000 and the land was inherited from her mother 15 years ago. She does not plan to purchase additional land.

- A racehorse purchased four years ago for $200,000 was sold for $550,000. Total depreciation allowed using the straight-line method amounts to $160,000.

- Equipment purchased three years ago for $200,000 is exchanged for $100,000 of IBM common stock. The adjusted basis of the equipment is $120,000. If straight-line depreciation had been used, the adjusted basis would be $152,000.

- A pony, with an adjusted basis of $20,000 and FMV of $35,000, that her daughter uses only for personal use is injured while attempting a jump. Because of the injury, the uninsured pony has to be destroyed by a veterinarian.

a. What amount of Sec. 1245 ordinary income must be recognized?
b. What amount of Sec. 1250 ordinary income must be recognized?
c. Will the loss resulting from the destruction of her daughter's pony be used to determine net Sec. 1231 gains or losses?
d. After all of the netting of gains or losses is completed, will the gain resulting from the involuntary conversion of the building be treated as LTCG?
e. What is the amount of the net Sec. 1231 gain or loss?

I13-40 *Sale of Business and Personal-Use Property.* Arnie, a college student, purchased a new truck in 1995 for $6,000. He used the truck 70% of the time as a distributor for the local newspaper and 30% of the time for personal use. The truck has a five-year recovery period, and he claimed depreciation deductions of $840 in 1995 and $1,344 in 1996. Arnie sells the truck on June 20, 1997 for $3,000.
a. What is the amount of allowable depreciation in 1997?
b. What are the amount and character of Arnie's realized and recognized gain or loss?

I13-41 *Like-Kind Exchange of Sec. 1245 Property.* General Corporation owns equipment costing $50,000 in 1991 currently having a $31,000 adjusted basis. General exchanges the equipment for other equipment with a $45,000 FMV and marketable securities with a $20,000 FMV. Determine the following:
a. Realized gain
b. Recognized gain
c. Gain treated as ordinary income
d. Gain treated as Sec. 1231 gain
e. Basis of marketable securities received
f. Basis of equipment received

I13-42 *Purpose of Sec. 1245.* Assume the year is 1986 when noncorporate taxpayers are allowed to deduct 60% of net capital gains to determine their AGI. Martin owns equipment used in his trade or business that was purchased in 1979 for $200,000. Allowed depreciation deductions amount to $160,000. Martin sells the equipment in 1986 for $110,000. No other sales or exchanges are made in 1986 or the preceding five years.
a. Determine the increase in Martin's 1986 AGI as a result of the sale if Sec. 1245 did not exist.
b. Given that Sec. 1245 does exist, what is the increase in his AGI as a result of the sale?
c. How would your answers to Parts a and b change if the asset were sold in 1997?

I13-43 *Secs. 1231 and 1250.* Charles owns an office building and land that are used in his trade or business. The office building and land were acquired in 1978 for $800,000 and $100,000, respectively. During the current year, the properties are sold for $900,000 with 20% of the selling price being allocated to the land. The assets as shown on the taxpayer's books before their sale are as follows:

Building	$800,000	
Accumulated depreciation	185,000[a]	$615,000
Land		100,000

[a] If the straight-line method of depreciation had been used, the accumulated depreciation would be $120,000.

a. What is the recognized gain due to the sale of the building?

b. What is the character of the recognized gain due to the sale of the building?

c. What is the recognized gain and character of the gain due to the sale of the land?

d. If the taxpayer is a corporation, how will the answers to Parts a–c change?

I13-44 ***Sec. 1250.*** Maggie owns a motel that is operated as a trade or business adjacent to an interstate highway. The motel was purchased in March 1965 for $2,000,000, and she used an accelerated method of depreciation. The motel is sold during the current year for $975,000. The adjusted basis of the motel is $600,000. Additional depreciation is deducted as follows:

	Additional Depreciation
March 1965 to January 1, 1970	$ 95,000
January 1, 1970 to current date	205,000

a. What is the amount of realized gain?

b. What is the amount, if any, of ordinary income that Maggie must recognize as a result of the additional depreciation deducted before January 1, 1970?

c. What is the amount of ordinary income that Maggie must recognize as a result of selling the motel?

I13-45 ***Sec. 1250.*** Ken purchased an office building on January 1, 1980, for $360,000 (40-year life and a $32,000 salvage value) and he elected to use the sum-of-the-years' digits method of depreciation. Total depreciation allowed at the time of sale is $217,600. If the building is sold on January 1, 1997, for $340,000, what is the amount of gain recognized and the character of the gain?

I13-46 ***Sec. 1250.*** Assume the same facts as Problem I13-45 except that the taxpayer is a corporation instead of an individual. What is the amount and character of the corporation's recognized gain or loss?

I13-47 ***Sec. 1250 Residential Rental Property.*** Assume the same facts as Problem I13-45 except that the building is an apartment complex that qualifies as residential rental property. What is the amount and character of Ken's recognized gain or loss?

I13-48 ***Sec. 1250 Residential Rental Property.*** Assume the same facts as in Problem I13-46 except that the building is an apartment complex that qualifies as residential rental property. What is the amount and character of the corporation's recognized gain or loss?

I13-49 ***Sec. 1250 Residential Rental Property.*** Jesse owns a duplex that he uses as residential rental property. The duplex cost $100,000 nine years ago, and 10% of the cost was allocated to the land. Total cost-recovery deductions allowed amount to $36,000. The statutory percentages were used to compute cost-recovery deductions. If the straight-line method of cost recovery were used instead, $25,000 of cost-recovery deductions would have been allowed.

a. What is the amount of recognized gain and the character of the gain if Jesse sells the duplex for $125,000?

b. What is the amount of recognized gain in the year of sale and the character of the gain if Jesse sells the property under the installment sale method? Terms of the installment sale are as follows: $25,000 in the year of sale and a $100,000 note to be paid in four annual payments. The note is an interest-bearing note at the market rate of interest.

I13-50 ***Sec. 1250.*** Rosemary owns an office building that cost $625,000 and has an adjusted basis of $227,000. If the straight-line method of depreciation were used, the adjusted basis would be $300,000.

a. What is the maximum selling price that she could sell the building for without having to recognize Sec. 1250 ordinary income?

b. If she sold the building and had to recognize $51,000 of Sec. 1250 ordinary income, what was the selling price?

I13-51 *Recapture of Soil and Water Conservation Expenditures.* Bob owns farmland with a $600,000 basis, and he elects to expense $100,000 of expenditures incurred for soil and water conservation purposes. After farming for seven years and four months, Bob sells the farmland for $825,000.

a. What is the amount of the recognized gain and the character of the gain?

b. What is the amount of recognized gain and the character of the gain if the farmland is sold for $615,000?

I13-52 *Recapture of Intangible Drilling Costs.* Jeremy purchased undeveloped oil and gas property in 1990 and paid $300,000 for intangible drilling and development costs. He elected to expense the intangible drilling and development costs in 1990. During the current year, Jeremy sells the property, which has an $800,000 adjusted basis, for $900,000. What is the amount of gain treated as ordinary income under Sec. 1254 because of the election to expense intangible drilling and development costs?

I13-53 *Recapture of Intangible Drilling Costs and Depletion.* In 1992, Jack purchased undeveloped oil and gas property for $900,000 and paid $170,000 for intangible drilling and development costs. He elected to expense the intangible drilling and development costs. During the current year he sells the property for $950,000 when the property's adjusted basis is $700,000. Depletion of $200,000 was allowed on the property.

a. What is the realized gain and how much of the gain is ordinary income?

b. For Jack to have a Sec. 1231 gain, the selling price must exceed what amount?

I13-54 *Related Party Transactions.* Ed operates a storage business as a sole proprietorship and owns the following assets acquired in 1977:

Warehouse	$400,000	
Minus: Accumulated depreciation (straight-line method)	(190,000)	
Adjusted basis		$210,000
Land		75,000

The FMV of the warehouse and the land are $500,000 and $200,000, respectively. Ed owns 75% of the stock of the Crane Corporation. If he sells the two assets to Crane at a price equal to the FMV of the assets, determine the following:

a. Recognized gain due to sale of the building and character of the gain.

b. Recognized gain due to the sale of the land and character of the gain.

I13-55 *Timing of Sec. 1231 Transactions.* Russ has never recognized any Sec. 1231 gains or losses. In December 1997, Russ is considering the sale of two Sec. 1231 assets. The sale of one asset will result in a $20,000 Sec. 1231 gain while the sale of the other asset will result in a $20,000 Sec. 1231 loss. Russ has no other capital or Sec. 1231 gains and losses in 1997 and does not expect to have any other capital or Sec. 1231 gains and losses in 1997. He is aware that it might be advantageous to recognize the Sec. 1231 gain and the Sec. 1231 loss in different tax years. However, he does not know whether he should recognize the Sec. 1231 gain in 1997 and the Sec. 1231 loss in 1998 or vice versa. His marginal tax rate for each year is expected to be 31%. Advise the taxpayer with respect to these two alternatives:

a. Recognize the $20,000 Sec. 1231 loss in 1997 and the $20,000 Sec. 1231 gain in 1998.

b. Recognize the $20,000 Sec. 1231 gain in 1997 and the $20,000 Sec. 1231 loss in 1998.

I13-56 *Timing of Sec. 1231 Transaction.* Holly has recognized a $9,000 STCL. She has no other recognized capital gains and losses in 1997. She is considering the sale of a Sec. 1231 asset at a $5,000 gain in 1997. She had not recognized any Sec. 1231 losses during the previous five years and does not expect to have any other Sec. 1231 transactions in 1997. Her marginal tax rate for 1997 is 31%. What is the amount of increase in her 1997 taxes if Holly recognizes the $5,000 Sec. 1231 gain in 1997?

TAX FORM/RETURN PREPARATION PROBLEMS

TAX CUT

I13-57 George Buckner, Soc. Sec. no. 267-31-7251, sells an apartment building during the current year for $1,750,000. The building was purchased on January 1, 1978 for $2,000,000. An accelerated method of depreciation has been used, and depreciation of $880,000 has been taken. If the straight-line method of depreciation had been used, depreciation of $600,000 would have been allowed. The figures given above do not include the purchase price or the selling price of the land. Mr. Buckner's adjusted basis for the land is $200,000, and the sales price is $300,000. Mr. Buckner, who owns and operates a taxi business, sells one of the automobiles for $1,800. The automobile's adjusted basis is zero, and the original cost is $5,000. The automobile was purchased on April 25, 1990. Mr. Buckner has no other gains and losses during the year, and nonrecaptured net Sec. 1231 losses amount to zero. Prepare Form 4797 for the current year.

I13-58 Julie Hernandez is single and has no dependents. She operates a dairy farm and her social security number is 510-88-6387. She lives at 1325 Vermont Street in Costa, Florida. Consider the following information for her tax return for the current year:

- Schedule C was prepared by her accountant and the net profit from the dairy operations for the current year is $48,000.

- Itemized deductions amount to $3,185.

- Dividend income amounts to $280.

- State income tax refund received during the year is $125. She did not itemize her deductions last year.

- In June, a burglar broke into her house and stole the following two assets, which were acquired in 1984:

	Basis	FMV	Insurance Proceeds Received
Painting	$2,000	$10,000	$9,000
Sculpture	1,700	1,500	0

The following assets used in her business were sold during the year:

	Acquisition Date	Original Cost	Depreciation to Date of Sale	Date of Sale	Selling Price
Tractor	June 10, 1982	$25,000	$25,000	Oct. 20	$ 8,300
Barn	May 23, 1980	90,000	36,000[a]	May 13	87,000
Land	May 23, 1980	15,000	—0—	May 13	27,000
Cows	Sept. 7, 1992	20,000	13,000	Nov. 8	21,000

[a] $25,000 if the straight-line method had been used.

In August, three acres of the farm were taken by the state under the right of eminent domain for the purpose of building a highway. The basis of the three acres is $1,500 and the state paid the FMV, $22,000, on February 10. The farm was purchased on August 12, 1968.

Nonrecaptured net Section 1231 losses from the five most recent tax years preceding the current year amount to $7,000. Estimated taxes paid during the year amount to $38,200.

Prepare Forms 1040, 4684, 4797, Schedule D, and a Schedule D Tax Worksheet in the Instructions to Form 1040 for the current year. (Do not consider self-employment taxes discussed in Chapter I14.)

CASE STUDY PROBLEMS

I13-59 Your client, Kent Earl owns a bowling alley and has indicated that he wants to sell the business for $1,000,000 and purchase a minor league baseball franchise. His business consists of the following tangible assets:

	Acquisition Date	Original Cost	Adjusted Basis
Equipment	1984	$600,000	$150,000
Building	1978	900,000	400,000[a]
Land	1978	100,000	100,000
Inventory	Current year	50,000	50,000

[a] $480,000 if straight-line depreciation had been used.

Because you have another client, Tom Quick, who is interested in purchasing a business, you informed Tom of Kent's interest in selling. Tom wants to purchase the bowling alley, and the price sounds right to him. The bowling alley business has been very profitable in the last few years because Kent has developed a loyal group of customers by promoting bowling leagues during the week days and a special Saturday afternoon session for children in the elementary school grades. Kent and Tom have come to you and want to know how the transaction should be handled for the best tax results. You know, of course, that the $1,000,000 purchase price will have to be allocated among the assets and it will be necessary to estimate the FMV of all assets. Because FMV is often subjective, Kent and Tom recognize that some flexibility might exist in allocating the purchase price. For example, it might be just as easy to justify a FMV of $300,000 or $325,000 for the equipment.

a. What advice do you have for Kent with respect to the allocation (i.e., should he be interested in allocating more to some assets than others)? Explain the reasoning for your advice.

b. Would your advice to Kent be different if he had a large amount of capital losses and no nonrecaptured net Sec. 1231 losses?

c. What advice do you have for Tom with respect to the allocation (i.e., should he be interested in allocating more of the purchase price to some assets than to others)? Explain the reasoning for your advice.

d. What advantages might result from having Kent sign an agreement not to compete (i.e., operate a bowling alley)?

e. Should you have a concern about the ethical implications of advising both Kent and Tom?

I13-60 Assume the same facts as in Case Study Problem I13-59 except you have the following market values as a result of an appraisal:

Equipment	$ 250,000
Building	500,000
Land	140,000
Inventory	110,000
Total	$1,000,000

Tom insists that $150,000 of the purchase price should be allocated to inventory and $100,000 should be allocated to land. He refuses to complete the purchase unless the allocation is made as he requests. What action should you take with respect to Tom's request? (See Chapter I10 for a discussion of valuation issues in the purchase and sale of a business.)

TAX RESEARCH PROBLEM

I13-61 Berkeley Corporation has a policy of furnishing new automobiles to the athletic department of the local university. The automobiles are used for short periods of time by the extremely popular head basketball coach. When the automobiles are returned to Berkeley Corporation, they are sold to regular customers. The owner of Berkeley Corporation maintains that any such cars held for more than one year should qualify as Sec. 1231 property. Do you agree?

Research sources include

- Rev. Rul. 75-538, 1975-2 C.B. 34.

CHAPTER 14

SPECIAL TAX COMPUTATION METHODS, PAYMENT OF TAX, AND TAX CREDITS

LEARNING OBJECTIVES

After studying this chapter, you should be able to

1 Calculate the alternative minimum tax

2 Describe what constitutes self-employment income and compute the self-employment tax

3 Understand the mechanics of the federal withholding tax system and the requirements for making estimated tax payments

4 Describe the various business and personal tax credits

OBJECTIVE 1

*Calculate the
alternative minimum
tax*

Chapter I2 discussed the basic tax computation for individuals using the tax table and tax rate schedules. This chapter completes the discussion of tax computation by examining three principal topics;

1. Two special methods of tax computation, the alternative minimum tax and self-employment tax,

2. Methods for payment of an individual's tax liability, including the pay-as-you-go withholding rules and estimated tax payment requirements, and

3. Various tax credits that are available to reduce a taxpayer's tax liability.

ALTERNATIVE MINIMUM TAX

Over the years, Congress has used the income tax law for a variety of purposes other than just the raising of revenue to fund government operations, such as enacting provisions to promote economic and social goals. As the number of special tax provisions increased, many taxpayers were able to carefully plan their financial affairs so as to use these special tax provisions to substantially reduce or eliminate their entire income tax liability. As a result, a new set of rules were implemented in 1969 to ensure that all taxpayers would pay at least a minimum amount of income tax. Thus was born what is known today as the **alternative minimum tax** (**AMT**).

The original minimum tax was referred to as an add-on minimum tax because it was added to the taxpayer's regular income tax liability. The amount of the tax was 10% times the taxpayer's tax preferences in excess of a $30,000 statutory exemption. The present AMT system, originally created in 1978, is no longer an add-on tax but is actually a separate and parallel tax system. Taxpayers are first required to compute their regular income tax liability and then compute their tax under the AMT system. The AMT system essentially requires taxpayers to adjust their regular taxable income by a number of adjustments and preferences, then subtract an exemption amount to arrive at the AMT base. The AMT base is then multiplied by the special AMT rates to compute the AMT.

The present AMT applies to individuals, corporations, estates, and trusts.[1] Most individual taxpayers are actually not subject to the AMT because their regular income tax is greater than the AMT. This is caused primarily because many taxpayers do not have substantial adjustments and preferences and the AMT exemption is liberal in amount (i.e., $45,000 for married individuals filing a joint return and $33,750 for single individuals).

EXAMPLE I14-1 ▶

Ricardo and Sue are married and file a joint return for the current year with taxable income of $30,000 and $12,000 of tax preferences and other adjustments. Their alternative minimum taxable income (AMTI) is $42,000 ($30,000 + $12,000), but the alternative minimum tax base is zero because of the $45,000 exemption. Thus, their tax liability is based on the regular tax computation and no AMT liability is owed. ◀

COMPUTATIONAL ASPECTS

The formula for computing the alternative minimum tax for the tax year is to apply a two-tiered graduated rate schedule. The tax base consists of the following items:[2]

---

[1] The AMT applicable to corporations is discussed in *Prentice Hall's Federal Taxation: Corporations, Partnerships, Estates, and Trusts* text and in the

Comprehensive volume.
[2] Sec. 55(b)(1).

Taxable income
Plus: Tax preference items[3]
Plus: Personal and dependency exemptions
        The standard deduction if the taxpayer does not itemize
Plus or minus: Adjustments required because different rules are used for calculating the alternative minimum taxable income as compared with taxable income (e.g., special AMT limitations on certain itemized deductions)

Equals: Alternative minimum taxable income (AMTI)
Minus: Exemption amount ($45,000 for a married couple filing a joint return and surviving spouses, $33,750 for single individuals, and $22,500 for a married individual filing separately). The exemption amount is reduced by 25% of AMTI in excess of $150,000 for a married couple filing a joint return and surviving spouses, $112,500 for single individuals, and $75,000 for a married individual filing separately.[4]

Equals: Alternative minimum tax base
Times: Tax rate (26% of first $175,000; 28% of amounts in excess of $175,000)

Equals: Tentative minimum tax
Minus: Regular tax

Equals: Alternative minimum tax

EXAMPLE I14-2 ▶

Rita, a single taxpayer, has a regular tax liability of $37,876 and taxable income of $138,300, a positive adjustment due to limitations on itemized deductions of $30,000, and tax preferences of $40,000 in 1997. Rita's alternative minimum tax for 1997 is calculated as follows:

Taxable income		$138,300
Plus:	Tax preferences	40,000
Plus:	Personal exemption	2,650
Plus:	Adjustments related to itemized deductions	30,000
Alternative minimum taxable income		$210,950
Minus:	Exemption	(9,137)[a]
Alternative minimum tax base		$201,813
Tax on first $175,000: $175,000 × 0.26 =		$ 45,500
Tax on excess over $175,000: $26,813 × 0.28 =		$ 7,508
Tentative minimum tax		$ 53,008
Minus: Regular tax		(37,876)
Alternative minimum tax		$ 15,132

Rita will pay a total of $53,008 ($37,876 regular tax + $15,132 AMT). ◀

[a] $33,750 − [0.25 × ($210,950 − $112,500)].

TAX PREFERENCE ITEMS

Tax preferences are provisions in the Code granting favorable treatment to taxpayers. For example, accelerated depreciation allowed for real property placed in service before 1987 is a tax preference item. (See Chapter I10 for a discussion of ACRS depreciation.) To compute the tax base for the AMT, the tax preferences designated in Sec. 57 must be added to taxable income. Some of the most common tax preference items include the following:

[3] Sec. 57.   [4] Sec. 55(d)(3).

▶ Excess of accelerated depreciation (or ACRS cost recovery) claimed over a hypothetical straight-line depreciation amount for real property placed in service before 1987 computed on an item-by-item basis.

▶ Tax-exempt interest on certain private activity bonds.

▶ Exclusion of gain on the sale of certain small business stock. The exclusion is 50% of the gain on the disposition of qualified small business stock under Sec. 1202[5] (See Chapter I15).

It should be noted, however, that not all items receiving preferential treatment are tax preference items. For example, most municipal bond interest income is exempt from the federal income tax but is not a tax preference item. Only tax-exempt interest on private activity bonds (e.g., bonds issued by a municipality to fund certain nongovernmental activities such as industrial parks) issued after August 7, 1986 are subject to the AMT.

EXAMPLE I14-3 ▶ Richard, a single taxpayer, has the following tax preference items for the current year:

▶ $15,000 ACRS cost-recovery deduction on real property placed in service before 1987 and held for investment. The straight-line ACRS deduction would have been $10,000.

▶ $10,000 of tax-exempt interest on private activity bonds.

Richard's total tax preferences are $15,000, consisting of $5,000 excess cost recovery deductions and $10,000 tax-exempt interest on the private activity bonds. ◀

AMT ADJUSTMENTS

As previously discussed, AMTI equals taxable income as modified by certain adjustments and increased by tax preference items. For most individual taxpayers AMT adjustments represent itemized deductions that are not allowed in computing AMTI or timing differences relating to the deferral of income or the acceleration of deductions under the regular tax rules. These adjustments generally increase the AMT tax base, although the netting of timing differences may result in an overall reduction of the AMT tax base when the timing differences reverse. Some of the more important adjustments are included below.

ADDITIONAL COMMENT

In the Revenue Reconciliation Act of 1993 Congress repealed the AMT preference for donated appreciated capital gain property. Congress felt that the repeal would induce additional charitable giving.

LIMITATION ON ITEMIZED DEDUCTIONS. Only certain itemized deductions are allowed in computing AMTI. Additionally, the standard deduction is not allowed if an individual does not itemize deductions. The following items are deductible for AMT purposes:

▶ Casualty and theft losses in excess of 10% of AGI

▶ Charitable contributions (but not in excess of the 20%, 30%, and 50% of AGI limitation amounts)

▶ Medical expenses in excess of 10% of AGI (a 7.5% ceiling applies to the regular tax computation)

▶ Qualified housing interest and certain other interest up to the amount of qualified net investment income included in the AMT base

▶ Estate tax deduction on income in respect of a decedent

▶ Gambling losses

Some of the more significant itemized deductions that are not deductible for the AMT include miscellaneous itemized deductions (e.g., unreimbursed employee expenses), state, local, and foreign income taxes, and real and personal property taxes. The 3% disallowance rule for itemized deductions of high-income taxpayers does not apply to the AMT.

---

[5] Sec. 57(a)(7). As a sidenote, this tax preference item will not occur until 1998 because qualified stock must have been purchased after August 10, 1993 and the stock held for more than five years.

EXAMPLE I14-4 ▶ Robin, a single taxpayer, has AGI of $100,000 and the following itemized deductions in 1997:

Personal casualty loss, net of insurance	$22,000
Charitable contributions	4,000
Medical expenses in excess of 7.5% of AGI ($10,000 actual expenses − $7,500)	2,500
Mortgage interest on Robin's personal residence	18,850
Real estate taxes	4,000
State income taxes	6,000

From the information above, Robin's taxable income is $50,000. Assume she has $20,000 of tax preferences. Robin's AMT adjustments for disallowed itemized deductions include $2,500 of medical expenses, because the 10% AMT limitation eliminates the medical expense deduction [$10,000 − (0.10 × $100,000 AGI) = $0] and $10,000 of real estate and state income taxes ($4,000 + $6,000). Thus, Robin's total AMT adjustment for disallowed itemized deductions is $12,500 ($2,500 + $10,000). Robin's AMTI is $85,150 ($50,000 taxable income + $20,000 tax preferences + $12,500 disallowed itemized deductions + her $2,650 personal exemption). ◀

AMT ADJUSTMENTS DUE TO TIMING DIFFERENCES. Other adjustments are required when the rules for calculating taxable income permit the taxpayer to temporarily defer the recognition of income or to accelerate deductions. This temporary benefit is caused by applying different accounting methods that result in timing differences when income or expenses are recognized. When an AMT liability is paid, an AMT tax credit is available for the portion of the tax attributable to timing differences to reduce the taxpayer's regular tax liability in subsequent years.[6] The most common AMT adjustments for individuals that represent timing differences include

KEY POINT

The 40-year life that is used to calculate the AMT adjustment for real property placed in service after 1986 causes taxpayers to maintain two separate depreciation schedules.

▶ For real property placed in service after 1986, the difference between the MACRS depreciation claimed using the property's actual recovery period and a hypothetical straight-line depreciation amount calculated using a 40-year life (see Chapter I10 for a discussion of the alternative depreciation system).

▶ For personal property placed in service after 1986, the difference between the MACRS deduction and the amount determined by using the 150% declining balance method under the alternative depreciation system with a switch to the straight-line method.

▶ For research and experimental (R&E) expenditures, the difference between the amount expensed and the deduction that would have been allowed if the expenditures were capitalized and amortized over a ten-year period.[7]

EXAMPLE I14-5 ▶ Rob has the following AMT adjustments caused by timing differences in the current year:

▶ Depreciation on residential rental property costing $100,000 and placed in service in January of the current year is $3,485 using the straight-line method and a 27½-year recovery period, based on the MACRS rules. The depreciation for AMT purposes is $2,396 based on the straight-line method and a 40-year recovery period under the alternative depreciation system. Thus, the positive AMT adjustment is $1,089 ($3,485 − $2,396).

▶ Depreciation on an automobile used in business costing $10,000 and placed in service in the current year is $2,000 based on the MACRS rules (i.e., 200% DB method, a half-year convention, and a five-year recovery period). The depreciation for AMT purposes is $1,500 based on the alternative depreciation system (i.e., 150% DB method, half-year convention and a five-year recovery period). Thus, the positive AMT adjustment is $500 ($2,000 − $1,500).

---

[6] Sec. 53. The AMT credit may be carried forward indefinitely against the regular tax liability but is limited to the excess of the taxpayer's regular tax (reduced by nonrefundable credits) over the tentative minimum tax for the year. Detailed discussion of the rules for computing the AMT credit is beyond the scope of the text.

[7] Sec. 56(a).

ADDITIONAL COMMENT

For corporate taxpayers only, there is a 0.12% environmental tax imposed on the excess of the corporation's modified alternative minimum taxable income over $2 million.

▶ R&E expenditures amounting to $50,000 are expensed in the current year. The R&E deduction would be $5,000 ($50,000 ÷ 10 years) if the expenditures are capitalized and amortized over a 10-year period. Thus, the positive AMT adjustment is $45,000 ($50,000 − $5,000).

Rob's total positive AMT adjustment to his taxable income to arrive at AMTI is $46,589 ($1,089 + $500 + $45,000). ◀

CREDIT THAT REDUCES THE AMT. As we will discuss later in this chapter, there are a number of credits that are allowed to reduce a taxpayer's regular tax liability. However, for purposes of the AMT, only the foreign tax credit is allowed to reduce the tentative minimum tax. Further, the foreign tax credit that may be deducted from the AMT is a specially computed credit, called the "alternative minimum tax foreign tax credit." It is basically computed using the various amounts used in computing alternative minimum taxable income instead of taxable income. Thus, the AMT is likely to apply to a taxpayer who uses credits (other than the foreign tax credit) to reduce his regular tax liability.

STOP & THINK

Question: What are the most common characteristics of taxpayers who are subject to the AMT?

Solution: While each situation is certainly unique, there are certain taxpayers who are more likely to be subject to the AMT. First, taxpayers who materially invest in real estate are likely candidates for the AMT because they will have a large positive adjustment caused from the differences in depreciation. Second, as discussed above, taxpayers who use credits to reduce their regular tax liability may well be subject to the AMT because only the foreign tax credit can reduce the AMT. Third, taxpayers who have very large itemized deductions, primarily from large deductions from state and local taxes, may be subject to the AMT because state and local taxes are not deductible for AMT purposes.

SUMMARY ILLUSTRATION OF THE AMT COMPUTATION

The AMT formula is illustrated in the following example:

EXAMPLE I14-6 ▶

ADDITIONAL COMMENT

Some tax advisors recommend that cash basis taxpayers prepay their local property taxes or state income taxes before the end of the year in order to reduce the current year's tax liability. However, if the taxpayer is subject to the AMT, this may not be a valid strategy.

Roger and Kate are married and file a joint return. They have the following items (including $25,000 in tax preference items from interest income earned on private activity bonds) that are used to compute taxable income in 1997:

Gross income:		
Salary		$ 60,000
Dividends and interest		10,000
Business income		30,000[a]
AGI		$100,000
Minus: Itemized deductions:		
State and local property taxes	$10,000	
Mortgage interest on their personal residence	12,000	
Charitable contributions	3,000	(25,000)
Minus: Personal and dependency exemptions ($2,650 × 2)		(5,300)
Taxable income		$ 69,700

[a] MACRS depreciation deductions of $70,000 on personal property placed in service after 1986 were claimed in arriving at business income. Only $50,000 of depreciation would be claimed under the alternative depreciation system using the 150% declining balance method.

Roger's AMT is computed as follows:

Taxable income			$ 69,700
Plus:	Tax preferences		25,000
	Personal and dependency exemptions		5,300
	AMT adjustments:		
	Excess depreciation	$20,000	
	State and local property taxes	10,000	30,000
AMTI			$130,000
Minus: AMT exemption			(45,000)
Tax base			$ 85,000
Times: Tax rate			× 0.26
Tentative minimum tax			$ 22,100
Minus: Regular tax (based on taxable income of $69,700)			(14,160)
Alternative minimum tax			$ 7,940[a]

[a] An AMT credit may be available in future years to offset any regular tax that is owed. However, the AMT credit applies only to the AMT that results from timing differences such as depreciation adjustments and not from exclusions (e.g., personal exemptions and taxes).

The total tax liability for Roger and Kate is $22,100 ($14,160 + $7,940). ◀

SELF-EMPLOYMENT TAX

OBJECTIVE 2

Describe what constitutes self-employment income and compute the self-employment tax

ETHICAL POINT

An employer must have a reasonable basis for treating a worker as an independent contractor or meet the general common law rules for determining whether an employer-employee relationship exists. Otherwise, the employer is liable for federal and state income tax withholding, FICA and FUTA taxes, interest, and penalties associated with the misclassification.

Most individuals are classified as employees and are not subject to the self-employment tax. Employees are covered under the Federal Insurance Contributions Act (FICA) through the payment of payroll taxes. The employer must withhold the employee's share of the FICA tax and provide a matching amount. Employees are not subject to an additional employment tax upon the filing of their federal income tax return.

The self-employment tax is imposed to finance Social Security coverage for self-employed individuals. Thus, the distinction between an independent contractor (i.e., a self-employed individual) and an employee is important because no employer FICA contribution is required if the payee is deemed to have independent contractor status. Independent contractors are subject to self-employment tax on the amount of net earnings from the self-employment activity. Employees who have a small business in addition to their regular employment (e.g., an accountant, who is an employee for a large corporation, also prepares tax returns as a consultant) may also be subject to the self-employment tax in addition to the FICA tax.

COMPUTING THE TAX

Individuals having net earnings from self-employment of $400 or more are subject to the self-employment tax.[8] The FICA tax imposed on both wages and self-employment income includes a 6.2% (12.4% for self-employed individuals) tax for the old-age, survivors and disability insurance (OASDI) component up to a $65,400 ceiling amount in 1997 ($62,700 in 1996). The second component of the FICA tax is a 1.45% (2.9% for self-employed individuals) tax for the hospital insurance (HI) portion. No ceiling amount applies to the HI component for wages and self-employment income. For employee wages the 6.2 and 1.45 percentages (totaling 7.65%) must be matched by the employer.

---

[8] Sec. 6017.

HISTORICAL NOTE

The ceiling amount on income from self-employment was $7,800 in 1971.

One-half of the self-employment tax imposed is allowed as a *for* AGI deduction and is reported on page 1 of Form 1040.[9] Net earnings from self-employment are determined by multiplying self-employment income by 0.9235 (which is equivalent to 100% of self-employment income minus one-half of self-employment taxes, or 7.65%, resulting in net earnings from self-employment of 92.35%) to compute the amount that is subject to self-employment tax.

EXAMPLE I14-7 ▶

ADDITIONAL COMMENT

The Revenue Reconciliation Act of 1993 eliminated the wage cap on the hospital insurance component of wages. Though presented as a tax increase for high-income individuals, it also increases the tax burden for employers of high-income individuals.

Rose has $80,000 of earnings from self-employment in 1997. Her net earnings from self-employment is $73,880 ($80,000 × 0.9235). The OASDI portion of the tax is $8,110 ($65,400 × 0.124). The amount of self-employment income that is subject to the hospital insurance portion of the tax is $73,880 and the HI tax is $2,143 ($73,880 × 0.029). Thus, the total self-employment tax reported on Schedule SE is $10,253. Rose also receives a *for* AGI tax deduction of $5,127 ($10,253 × 0.50), which is reported on page 1 of Form 1040. ◀

If an individual is an employee and also has income from self-employment, the tax base for computing the self-employment tax is reduced by the wages that are subject to the FICA tax. The self-employment tax base for the OASDI component is equal to the lesser of the primary ceiling ($65,400 in 1997) reduced by the FICA wages or the self-employment income multiplied by 0.9235.

EXAMPLE I14-8 ▶

Sandy receives wages as an employee of $35,000 in 1997 that are subject to FICA tax. In addition, Sandy has a small consulting practice that generates $10,000 of income from self-employment. The tentative tax base for computing the self-employment tax is $9,235 ($10,000 × 0.9235) net earnings from self-employment. Thus, the tax base for computing the OASDI portion of the tax is the lesser of $9,235 net earnings from self-employment or $30,400 ($65,400 ceiling − $35,000 FICA wages). Sandy's self-employment tax for the OASDI portion is $1,145 ($9,235 × 0.124) and the HI component is $268 ($9,235 × 0.029) The total amount of self-employment tax is therefore $1,413 ($1,145 + $268) and Sandy also receives a *for* AGI deduction of $707 ($1,413 × 0.50), which is reported on page 1 of Form 1040. ◀

EXAMPLE I14-9 ▶

Assume the same facts as in Example I14-8 except that Sandy's wages are $100,000. Sandy's taxable self-employment income for the OASDI portion of the tax is zero because her FICA wages exceed the $65,400 primary ceiling amount. However, she is subject to self-employment tax with respect to the HI portion. The tax base for the HI portion is the $9,235 net earnings from self-employment because no ceiling amount is applicable. The HI portion of the self-employment tax is $268 ($9,235 × 0.029) and Sandy also receives a *for* AGI deduction for $134 ($268 × 0.50). ◀

KEY POINT

In the case of married taxpayers filing joint returns, it is important on Schedule SE of Form 1040 to fill in the name and Social Security number of the spouse with the self-employment income. This information is used to establish benefit eligibility.

WHAT CONSTITUTES SELF-EMPLOYMENT INCOME

Individuals who carry on a trade or business as a proprietor or partnership are considered to render services as independent contractors and are, therefore, subject to the self-employment tax. If an individual has two separate self-employment activities, the *net* earnings from each activity are aggregated. However, where a husband and wife file a joint return and both have self-employment income, the self-employment tax must be computed separately.

EXAMPLE I14-10 ▶

Russ and Ruth are married and file a joint return. Russ has $13,000 net earnings from a consulting business and a $4,000 net loss from a retail store that is operated as a sole proprietorship. Ruth has wages of $50,000 from her employer that are subject to FICA taxes. Russ's net earnings from self-employment are $8,312 ($9,000 × 0.9235). No reduction in the

---

[9] Sec. 164(f).

Topic Review I14-1

Self-Employment Tax Summary

▶ The self-employment tax is imposed on net earnings from self-employment over $400.

▶ The tax base for computing the self-employment tax is generally the amount of self-employment income multiplied by 0.9235.

▶ A $65,400 ceiling applies to the old age survivors and disability (OASDI) portion. However, no ceiling applies to the hospital insurance (HI) portion of the tax.

▶ Self-employment tax is computed separately for married individuals filing joint returns.

▶ One-half of the self-employment tax that is imposed is allowed as a business deduction *for* AGI.

▶ The self-employment tax rate is 15.3% which includes 12.4% for the OASDI portion and 2.9% for the hospital insurance (HI) portion.

self-employment tax base is allowed for Ruth's wages as an employee because Ruth is not self-employed and the tax is computed separately for Russ and Ruth.   ◀

Among the items that constitute earnings that are subject to the self-employment tax are:

▶ Net earnings from a sole proprietorship

▶ Director's fees[10]

▶ Taxable research grants

▶ Distributive share of partnership income plus guaranteed payments from the partnership

The self-employment tax is computed on Schedule SE of Form 1040 (see Appendix B). The rules for computing the self-employment tax are summarized in Topic Review I14-1.

PAYMENT OF TAXES

OBJECTIVE 3

Understand the mechanics of the federal withholding tax system and the requirements for making estimated tax payments.

The IRS collects federal income taxes during the year either through withholding on wages or quarterly estimated tax payments. If the withholdings and estimated taxes are less than the amount of tax computed on the tax return, the taxpayer must pay the balance of the tax due when the tax return is filed. If there has been an overpayment of tax, the taxpayer may either request a refund or choose to apply the overpayment to the following year's quarterly estimated taxes.

Substantial penalties are imposed if an employer fails to withhold federal income tax and pay such amounts to the IRS.[11] In addition, a taxpayer may be subject to a nondeductible penalty upon an underpayment of estimated tax.[12]

---

[10] Rev. Rul. 57-246, 1957-1 C.B. 338. It is a factual question whether an officer who also serves as a director is performing services as an employee or as an independent contractor. The courts have recognized that an individual can perform services as a director and also perform employment-related services but the director fees may be recharacterized by the courts if the fees are in reality compensation for services rendered as an employee. See *Peter H. Jacobs* 1993 RIA T.C. Memo ¶ 93, 570, 66 TCM 1470.

[11] Sec. 3403. Employers are liable for payment of the full amount of

withholdings that must be withheld and paid to the IRS. In addition, responsible individuals (e.g., corporate officers, directors, and consultants) may be held personally liable for payment of the tax. (See *Renate Schiff v. U.S.,* 69 AFTR 2d 92-804, 92-1 USTC ¶50,248 (D.C. NV, 1992), *Ted E. Tsouprake v. U.S.,* 69 AFTR 2d 92-821, 92-1 USTC ¶50,249 (D.C. FL, 1992), and *Ralph M. Guito, Jr. v. U.S.,* 67 AFTR 2d 91-1066, 92-1 USTC ¶ 50,231 (D.C. FL, 1991).

[12] Sec. 6654.

WITHHOLDING OF TAXES

An employer must withhold federal income taxes and FICA taxes from an employee's wages. No withholdings are required if an employer-employee relationship does not exist (e.g., if the individual who performs the services is an independent contractor).Generally, unless a specific exemption is provided under the Code, withholding is required on all forms of remuneration paid to an employee. Thus, salaries, fees, bonuses, dismissal payments, commissions, vacation pay, and taxable fringe benefits are subject to withholding.[13] Special rules are provided for the following:

▶ *More than one employer during the same year.* Each employer must withhold FICA and federal income taxes without regard to the fact that the employee has more than one employer. This requirement may result in an overwithholding of FICA taxes if the ceiling amount on the OASDI portion of the tax is exceeded. In the event of an overwithholding of FICA taxes, the employee may credit the excess amount as an additional payment of tax on line 58 on page 2 of Form 1040 (see Appendix B). However, the excess FICA contributions related to the matching employer contributions are not refundable or creditable against the tax liabilities of either employer.

▶ *Exemptions for certain employment activities.* Certain employees such as agricultural laborers, ministers, domestic servants, newspaper carriers under age 18, and tips of less than $20 per month from an employer are exempt from income tax withholding. Note, however, that the earnings of such individuals are fully taxable and that an employer may be liable for FICA tax payments on these earnings.[14]

▶ *Exemptions for certain fringe benefits.* Fringe benefits such as moving expense reimbursements, payments under a self-insured medical reimbursement plan, meals and lodging, travel expense reimbursements, and payments under a qualified educational assistance program are not subject to withholding if it is reasonable to believe that an employee can deduct the item or the item is nontaxable. Any excess reimbursements are subject to withholding. For example, the portion of moving expenses that is not deductible by an employee (e.g., nondeductible indirect moving expenses) is subject to withholding.

▶ *Backup withholding.* Backup withholding rules were enacted to prevent abusive noncompliance situations. Taxpayers who give false information to avoid backup withholding are subject to both civil and criminal penalties.[15] A 31% withholding rate is required on most types of payments that are reported on Form 1099 (e.g., interest, dividends, royalties, etc.) under the following circumstances:

  ▶ The taxpayer does not provide the payor with the taxpayer identification number in the required manner.

  ▶ The taxpayer is required to certify that she is not subject to backup withholding but fails to do so.

  ▶ The IRS notifies the payor that the taxpayer gave an incorrect taxpayer identification number.

  ▶ The IRS notifies the payor that the taxpayer has failed to report the item of income on his or her return.[16]

▶ *Special rules for lump-sum pension plan or annuity payments.* Federal income tax withholding is mandatory for such payments unless the individual elects to have no tax withheld.[17] These requirements are intended to increase the level of taxpayer

---

[13] Reg. Sec. 31.3401(a)-1(a)(2).
[14] Reg. Sec. 31.3401(a)-4(b)(1). An employer is liable for FICA tax payments for domestic servants if $1,000 or more is paid to an individual in any calendar year. Beginning in 1995 employers will be allowed to pay the employment taxes annually when they file their own tax return on Form 1040.
[15] Sec. 6682.

[16] Sec. 3406.
[17] Sec. 3405. Withholding is imposed at a 20% rate on any distribution eligible for tax deferral rollover treatment (e.g., a distribution from a qualified pension plan to an IRA) unless the funds are transferred directly to the eligible plan (see Sec. 3405(c)). The percentage withholding rate on supplemental wage payments (e.g., bonuses, commissions, overtime pay) was increased from 20% to 28% for payments made after December 31, 1993.

compliance and alleviate the need for retired people to pay quarterly estimated taxes, which would otherwise be necessary to avoid an underpayment penalty.

If the pension payments are periodic (i.e., received as an annuity), the withholding is figured using the same procedures that are used for salary and wages. The retiree merely fills out a withholding certificate (Form W-4P). If this form is not filled out, the withholding is based on the tables for a married individual claiming three withholding allowances.[18] A 10% withholding rate is generally used for nonperiodic payments (e.g., lump-sum distributions). Withheld amounts are based on the taxable portion of a pension payment.[19]

EXAMPLE I14-11 ▶

Roy, a married taxpayer with four dependents, retires in the current year and receives taxable pension income from a qualified pension plan of $600 per month. He also receives a lump-sum distribution of $50,000 from a qualified profit-sharing plan. The trustees of both plans notify Roy that amounts will be withheld unless he elects not to have any amount withheld. If Roy elects not to have any taxes withheld, he may be required to make quarterly estimated tax payments to the extent that the pension payments are taxable to avoid an underpayment penalty. If Roy does not make an election and files two withholding certificates, regular withholding procedures will apply to the periodic pension payments and a 10% withholding rate will apply to the lump-sum distribution. ◀

HISTORICAL NOTE

The withholding of federal income taxes by employers began during World War II.

▶ *Special rules for supplemental wage payments.* A 28% rate is used for compensation paid in addition to the employee's regular wages. They include, but are not limited to, bonuses, commissions, overtime, accumulated sick pay, severance pay, awards, prizes, back pay, and retroactive pay increases.

WITHHOLDING ALLOWANCES AND METHODS. Every employee must file an employee's withholding allowance certificate (Form W-4), which lists the employee's marital status and number of withholding allowances and becomes the basic source of input for the computation of the amount to be withheld. If an employee's circumstances

WHAT WOULD YOU DO IN THIS SITUATION?

THE NANNY TAX: DON'T PAY NOW, WORRY LATER

You are a CPA engaged in tax practice and one of your clients is Mr. Throckmorton D. Princeton IV, J.D. He is a senior partner in the prestigious employment litigation firm of Huey, Dewey and Fooey. Mr. Princeton is known for his ruthless style of litigation services.

Things were really rosy for Mr. Princeton until last week, when there was some speculation in the press about his being appointed to a cabinet-level position by the President. A TV news magazine show looked into Mr. Princeton's domestic worker situation. It appears that Mr. Princeton has long engaged in the practice of hiring part-time workers in his household to clean his house, tend to his gardens, walk his dogs, cook his meals, service his car, and nurse him when he is ill. All told, he used over twenty-five people at one time or another over the past year. These workers were all paid as little as possible, and all were asked to sign a contract with Mr. Princeton that declared that they were to be classified as independent contractors. The total amount paid out to these workers added up to $50,000. No payroll taxes of any kind were paid by Mr. Princeton, although he did file Forms 1099 with the IRS. What tax and ethical issues should be considered?

---

[18] Sec. 3405(a)(4).
[19] Pension payments are subject to tax under the Sec. 72 annuity rules (see Chapter I3).

change (e.g., a married taxpayer is divorced or the amount of allowances claimed is reduced), an amended Form W-4 must be filed within 10 days. In general, the employee's Form W-4 is not sent to the IRS unless the number of withholding allowances exceeds 10 or an employee claims an exemption from withholding when his earnings are more than $200 per week.[20] This procedure is intended to prevent employees from avoiding the withholding of income tax on amounts that are otherwise due.

The following procedural rules apply to withholding:

▶ A $500 civil penalty is imposed for filing false statements (e.g., claiming excessive numbers of withholding allowances).[21]

▶ An employee may claim an exempt status on Form W-4 if he or she has no income tax liability in the prior year and anticipates none in the current year. High school or college students with jobs earning less than the minimum dollar amount required to file a tax return should take advantage of this exemption. Otherwise, it may be necessary to file a return to obtain a tax refund in the following year. In such a case, the student has, in effect, made an interest-free loan to the government.

▶ Income tax withholding tables result in a lower amount being withheld if the taxpayer is married.

▶ An individual may request that additional amounts be withheld if it is anticipated that taxes will be owed at the end of the year and the person does not want to make quarterly estimated payments. It is also possible to claim fewer withholding allowances in order to increase the amount withheld.

▶ Each additional withholding allowance that is claimed reduces the amount withheld.

Withholding allowances on Form W-4 may be claimed for the same number of personal and dependency exemptions that will be taken on the employee's tax return for the year. An additional special withholding allowance that reflects the standard deduction may be claimed by a taxpayer who has one job or, if married, has a spouse who is unemployed.[22] Additional withholding allowances may be claimed if an individual who has deductions, losses, or credits from a wide variety of sources, including itemized deductions, alimony payments, moving expenses, and losses from a trade or business, rental property, or farm. Tables and a worksheet are provided to compute the amount of the additional withholding allowances.[23]

EXAMPLE I14-12 ▶ Sam and Sally are married and have three dependent children. They file a joint return. Sally is not employed, and Sam does not claim additional withholding allowances for unusually large deductions or tax credits. Sam may claim six allowances (two personal exemptions [for Sam and Sally]) plus three dependency exemptions plus one special withholding allowance to reflect the standard deduction). The special allowance is available because Sally is not employed and Sam has only one job. ◀

STOP & THINK

Question: Many taxpayers believe that they must claim the same number of withholding allowances for withholding purposes as the number of personal exemptions on their income tax return. Why is this not correct?

Solution: While the starting point for determining withholding allowances is taxpayer's marital status and number of personal exemptions, taxpayers are allowed to claim more

---

[20] Reg. Sec. 31.3402(f)(2)-1. A $500 civil penalty may be imposed when a taxpayer claims withholding allowances based on false information (see Sec. 6682).
[21] Sec. 6682(a).

[22] Sec. 3402(f)(1)(E).
[23] Married taxpayers who are both employed may allocate withholding allowances as they see fit as long as the same allowance is not claimed more than once.

or less withholding allowances based on their individual situations. According to the IRS, taxpayers may claim additional withholding allowances for two principal reasons: (1) a taxpayer has high deductions, losses, or credits, or (2) an unmarried taxpayer qualifies for head of household filing status. The withholding tables are constructed by assuming that the taxpayer's deductions will be equal to the standard deduction. Therefore, if a taxpayer has much higher itemized deductions than the standard deduction, the withholding tables may prescribe too much tax to be withheld and the taxpayer would have a large refund at the end of the year. To alleviate this situation, taxpayers are allowed to claim additional withholding allowances so as to prevent a large overpayment. Similarly, the withholding tables only have two categories of marital status, single or married. Thus, if an unmarried taxpayer qualifies for the head of household status, the "single" withholding tables may cause over-withholding of tax.

COMPUTATION OF FEDERAL INCOME TAX WITHHELD. The computation of the amount to be withheld is made by using wage bracket tables or by an optional percentage method of withholding. Both methods produce approximately the same results. Wage bracket tables are available for daily, weekly, biweekly, and monthly payroll periods. Separate tables are used for single (including heads-of-household) and married individuals. The wage bracket table for married persons using a monthly payroll period for wages from $0 through $3,239.99 is reproduced in Figure I14-1.

EXAMPLE I14-13 ▶ Henry is married and claims six withholding allowances. His monthly salary is $3,000. The federal income tax withheld for 1997 using the wage bracket table in Figure I14-1 is $174. ◀

ESTIMATED TAX PAYMENTS

Certain types of income are not subject to withholding (e.g., investment income, rents, income from self-employment, and capital gains). Taxpayers who earn this type of income must make quarterly estimated tax payments.

The purpose of the estimated tax system is to ensure that all taxpayers have paid enough tax by the end of the tax year to cover most of their tax liability. Thus, estimated tax payments may also be required if insufficient tax is being withheld from an individual's salary, pension, or other income (although many taxpayers prefer to file an amended Form W-4 instead and request additional withholding amounts or reduce the number of withholding allowances). The amount of estimated tax is the taxpayer's tax liability (including self-employment tax and alternative minimum tax) reduced by withholdings, tax credits, and any excess FICA amounts.[24]

REQUIRED ESTIMATED TAX PAYMENTS. For calendar-year individuals, required quarterly payments are due by April 15, June 15, September 15 of the current year, and January 15 of the following year. The estimated tax payments must be the lesser of the following amounts to avoid the imposition of a penalty[25] on the underpaid amount:

▶ 90% of the tax liability shown on the return for the current year;

▶ 100% of the tax liability shown on the return for the prior year (110% for taxpayers whose AGI on the prior year's return exceeded $150,000); or

▶ 90% of the tax liability shown on the return for the current year computed on an annualized basis.

ADDITIONAL COMMENT

The IRS does not mail reminder statements for the required quarterly estimated payments.

ADDITIONAL COMMENT

Red Skelton on the IRS: "I get even with them. I send in an estimated tax form, but I don't sign it. If I've got to guess what I'm making, let them guess who's making it."

---

[24] Excess FICA payments will occur if an employee has more than one employer during the year and the total FICA payments exceed in the aggregate the ceiling on FICA taxes.

[25] Sec. 6654.

If the wages are—		And the number of withholding allowances claimed is—										
At least	But less than	0	1	2	3	4	5	6	7	8	9	10
		The amount of income tax to be withheld is—										
$0	$540	0	0	0	0	0	0	0	0	0	0	0
540	560	2	0	0	0	0	0	0	0	0	0	0
560	580	5	0	0	0	0	0	0	0	0	0	0
580	600	8	0	0	0	0	0	0	0	0	0	0
600	640	12	0	0	0	0	0	0	0	0	0	0
640	680	18	0	0	0	0	0	0	0	0	0	0
680	720	24	0	0	0	0	0	0	0	0	0	0
720	760	30	0	0	0	0	0	0	0	0	0	0
760	800	36	3	0	0	0	0	0	0	0	0	0
800	840	42	9	0	0	0	0	0	0	0	0	0
840	880	48	15	0	0	0	0	0	0	0	0	0
880	920	54	21	0	0	0	0	0	0	0	0	0
920	960	60	27	0	0	0	0	0	0	0	0	0
960	1,000	66	33	0	0	0	0	0	0	0	0	0
1,000	1,040	72	39	6	0	0	0	0	0	0	0	0
1,040	1,080	78	45	12	0	0	0	0	0	0	0	0
1,080	1,120	84	51	18	0	0	0	0	0	0	0	0
1,120	1,160	90	57	24	0	0	0	0	0	0	0	0
1,160	1,200	96	63	30	0	0	0	0	0	0	0	0
1,200	1,240	102	69	36	3	0	0	0	0	0	0	0
1,240	1,280	108	75	42	9	0	0	0	0	0	0	0
1,280	1,320	114	81	48	15	0	0	0	0	0	0	0
1,320	1,360	120	87	54	21	0	0	0	0	0	0	0
1,360	1,400	126	93	60	27	0	0	0	0	0	0	0
1,400	1,440	132	99	66	33	0	0	0	0	0	0	0
1,440	1,480	138	105	72	39	6	0	0	0	0	0	0
1,480	1,520	144	111	78	45	12	0	0	0	0	0	0
1,520	1,560	150	117	84	51	18	0	0	0	0	0	0
1,560	1,600	156	123	90	57	24	0	0	0	0	0	0
1,600	1,640	162	129	96	63	30	0	0	0	0	0	0
1,640	1,680	168	135	102	69	36	3	0	0	0	0	0
1,680	1,720	174	141	108	75	42	9	0	0	0	0	0
1,720	1,760	180	147	114	81	48	15	0	0	0	0	0
1,760	1,800	186	153	120	87	54	21	0	0	0	0	0
1,800	1,840	192	159	126	93	60	27	0	0	0	0	0
1,840	1,880	198	165	132	99	66	33	0	0	0	0	0
1,880	1,920	204	171	138	105	72	39	6	0	0	0	0
1,920	1,960	210	177	144	111	78	45	12	0	0	0	0
1,960	2,000	216	183	150	117	84	51	18	0	0	0	0
2,000	2,040	222	189	156	123	90	57	24	0	0	0	0
2,040	2,080	228	195	162	129	96	63	30	0	0	0	0
2,080	2,120	234	201	168	135	102	69	36	3	0	0	0
2,120	2,160	240	207	174	141	108	75	42	9	0	0	0
2,160	2,200	246	213	180	147	114	81	48	15	0	0	0
2,200	2,240	252	219	186	153	120	87	54	21	0	0	0
2,240	2,280	258	225	192	159	126	93	60	27	0	0	0
2,280	2,320	264	231	198	165	132	99	66	33	0	0	0
2,320	2,360	270	237	204	171	138	105	72	39	5	0	0
2,360	2,400	276	243	210	177	144	111	78	45	11	0	0
2,400	2,440	282	249	216	183	150	117	84	51	17	0	0
2,440	2,480	288	255	222	189	156	123	90	57	23	0	0
2,480	2,520	294	261	228	195	162	129	96	63	29	0	0
2,520	2,560	300	267	234	201	168	135	102	69	35	2	0
2,560	2,600	306	273	240	207	174	141	108	75	41	8	0
2,600	2,640	312	279	246	213	180	147	114	81	47	14	0
2,640	2,680	318	285	252	219	186	153	120	87	53	20	0
2,680	2,720	324	291	258	225	192	159	126	93	59	26	0
2,720	2,760	330	297	264	231	198	165	132	99	65	32	0
2,760	2,800	336	303	270	237	204	171	138	105	71	38	5
2,800	2,840	342	309	276	243	210	177	144	111	77	44	11
2,840	2,880	348	315	282	249	216	183	150	117	83	50	17
2,880	2,920	354	321	288	255	222	189	156	123	89	56	23
2,920	2,960	360	327	294	261	228	195	162	129	95	62	29
2,960	3,000	366	333	300	267	234	201	168	135	101	68	35
3,000	3,040	372	339	306	273	240	207	174	141	107	74	41
3,040	3,080	378	345	312	279	246	213	180	147	113	80	47
3,080	3,120	384	351	318	285	252	219	186	153	119	86	53
3,120	3,160	390	357	324	291	258	225	192	159	125	92	59
3,160	3,200	396	363	330	297	264	231	198	165	131	98	65
3,200	3,240	402	369	336	303	270	237	204	171	137	104	71

FIGURE I14-1 ▶ WITHHOLDING TABLES: MONTHLY PAYROLL PERIOD—MARRIED PEOPLE (FOR WAGES PAID IN 1997)

Further, no penalty is imposed if (1) the estimated tax for the current year is less than $500 or (2) the individual had no tax liability for the prior year.

It should be noted that no penalty is imposed for failure to file quarterly estimated tax payments, even though the Code includes specific filing requirements. A penalty is imposed only if the taxpayer fails to meet the minimum payment requirements or one of the previously mentioned exceptions does not apply.

EXAMPLE I14-14 ▶ Sarah does not make quarterly estimated tax payments for 1997, even though she has a substantial amount of income not subject to withholding. Her actual tax liability (including self-employment taxes and the alternative minimum tax) for 1997 is $10,000. Withholdings from her salary are $7,000. She pays the $3,000 balance due to the IRS with the filing of the return on April 3, 1998. Sarah's tax liability for 1996 was only $6,000. There is no penalty for failure to make the quarterly estimated tax payments because she meets one or more of the exceptions relating to the minimum payment requirement. Although the first exception is not met because her $7,000 of withholdings (plus zero estimated tax payments) is less than 90% of her $10,000 tax liability for 1997 ($7,000 ÷ $10,000 = 70%), she meets the second exception because the $7,000 of withholdings is more than 100% of her $6,000 tax liability for 1996. If Sarah's AGI for 1996 was more than $150,000, the second exception safe harbor amount would be 110% (instead of 100%) of the prior year's tax or $6,600 ($6,000 × 1.10). Because the $7,000 of withholding is still more than 110% of her $6,000 tax liability, Sarah would also meet the second exception and would not be subject to the underpayment penalty. ◀

Form 2210 (see Appendix B) should be completed and submitted with the tax return if a possible underpayment of tax is indicated. This form is used to determine whether one of the exceptions is applicable and, if not, to compute the amount of the underpayment penalty. The actual computation of the underpayment penalty is not shown here because of the length and complexity of the rules. Topic Review I14-2 summarizes the withholding tax and estimated payment requirements.

OVERVIEW AND GENERAL TREATMENT FOR TAX CREDITS

OBJECTIVE 4

Describe the various business and personal tax credits

USE AND IMPORTANCE OF TAX CREDITS

Tax credits are often used to implement tax policy objectives. For example, tax credits are provided to increase employment, encourage energy conservation and research and experimental activities, encourage certain socially desired activities, and provide tax relief for low-income taxpayers and working couples with dependent children. Tax credits are also used to mitigate the effects of double taxation on income from foreign countries. Credits may be classified into two broad categories, **nonrefundable** and **refundable.** Nonrefundable credits may only be used to offset a taxpayer's tax liability. Refundable credits, on the other hand, not only offset a taxpayer's tax liability but if the credits exceed the tax liability, the excess will be paid (refunded) directly to the taxpayer. Topic Review I14-3 provides a summary of selected tax credits and the rationale for their inclusion in the tax law. Note that most tax credits are nonrefundable. The principal refundable credits include taxes withheld on wages and the earned income credit.

VALUE OF A CREDIT VERSUS A DEDUCTION

Tax credits are extremely valuable for taxpayers as they reduce the tax liability on a dollar-for-dollar basis. This is in contrast to a tax deduction which reduces taxable

Topic Review I14-2

Withholding Taxes and Estimated Payments

Withholding of Taxes

	FICA	Income Tax
When to withhold	All employee earnings up to $65,400 (in 1997) per employer. No ceiling applies to the 1.45% hospital insurance portion of the tax.	All employee wages. salaries, fees, bonuses, commissions, taxable fringe benefits, and so on.[a]
Amount to withhold	7.65% of FICA wages including 1.45% for the hospital insurance portion of the tax. 1.45% for amounts in excess of $65,400 is withheld from the employee's earnings.	Determined by using withholding tables or the percentage method based on an individual's filing status and number of exemptions.

[a]Exceptions are provided for certain nontaxable fringe benefits.

Estimated Tax Payments

▶ To avoid an underpayment penalty, the estimated tax payments and withholdings for the year must be equal to or exceed any one of the following:
90% of the tax liability shown on the return for the current year, or 100% of the tax liability shown on the return for the prior year (110% if AGI for the prior year exceeds $150,000), or 90% of the tax liability shown on the return for the current year computed on an annualized basis.

▶ The underpayment penalty is not deductible for income tax purposes.

▶ Form 2210 should be completed and submitted with the tax return if an underpayment is indicated.

income and the value of a tax deduction is limited to the taxpayer's marginal tax rate. Thus, tax deductions are more valuable to high-income taxpayers than lower-income taxpayers because their marginal tax rate is higher. Tax credits, however, benefit all taxpayers the same regardless of their marginal tax rate.

EXAMPLE I14-15 ▶ If Tasha's marginal tax rate is 15%, a $100 deduction produces a tax benefit of $15 ($100 × 0.15). If Sean's marginal tax rate is 28%, a $100 deduction produces a tax benefit of $28 ($100 × 0.28). However, a tax credit provides the same benefit to both Tasha and Sean. ◀

LIMITATION ON GENERAL BUSINESS CREDIT AND PRIORITY OF CREDITS

The tax credits commonly available to businesses are grouped into a special credit category called the **general business credit**. The more significant items included in the general business credit are the investment tax credit, targeted jobs credit, research credit,

ADDITIONAL COMMENT

The total amount of tax credits claimed by individual taxpayers increased by 1.5% in 1992.

low-income housing credit, Empowerment Zone employment credit, and the disabled access credit.[26] The general business credits are combined for the purpose of computing an overall dollar limitation on their use because these credits are not refundable. The general business credit may not exceed the *net income tax* minus the greater of the tentative minimum tax or 25% of the *net regular tax liability* above $25,000.[27]

Nonrefundable personal tax credits are allowed against the taxpayer's tax liability before all other credits up to the amount of the taxpayer's tax liability for the year.[28] Certain other business tax credits (items 2 through 5 below) are also nonrefundable and are offset against the taxpayer's tax liability before the general business credit is offset. These credits are used after the personal tax credits are offset but before the general business credit. Nonrefundable credits are offset against the taxpayer's tax liability in the following order of priority:

1. Personal tax credits
2. Foreign tax credit
3. Drug testing credit
4. Nonconventional source fuel credit
5. Qualified electric vehicles credit
6. General business credit

ADDITIONAL COMMENT

The general business credit fell from $4.8 billion in 1985 to $0.5 billion in 1992. The decrease is attributable to the phasing out in 1986 of the major component of the general business credit, the investment tax credit.

EXAMPLE I14-16 ▶ Steve's general business tax credit includes a $40,000 research credit and a $10,000 work opportunity credit. Steve's regular tax liability (before credits) is $45,000, and his tentative minimum tax is $10,000 (thus, Steve is not subject to the AMT). Nonrefundable tax credits also include a $2,000 child and dependent care credit (a nonrefundable personal tax credit) and a $1,000 foreign tax credit. Steve's dollar limitation on the general business tax credit is initially limited by the amount of net income tax of $42,000 ($45,000 regular tax minus $3,000 other nonrefundable credits). This amount is reduced by the $10,000 tentative minimum tax because this amount is greater than the net regular tax ceiling of $4,250 [0.25 × ($45,000 regular tax − $3,000 nonrefundable credits − $25,000)]. Thus, the limitation upon the $50,000 of general business tax credits ($40,000 + $10,000) is $32,000 ($42,000 − $10,000). ◀

CARRYBACK AND CARRYFORWARD OF UNUSED CREDITS

Initially, unused general business tax credits are carried back 3 years. Any remaining unused credits are then carried forward for 15 years.[29] The entire amount of unused credit is first carried to the earliest year.

EXAMPLE I14-17 ▶ Eagle Corporation has unused general business tax credits of $50,000 in 1997. The following is a schedule showing the use of the excess credits in the carryback years:

---

[26] Sec. 38. Also included in the general business credit is the alcohol fuels credit, enhanced oil recovery credit, renewable electricity production credit, Indian employment credit, and the employer Social Security credit for employee tips. For property placed into service after 1990, the investment tax credit has been reconstituted as the sum of the following three components: the rehabilitation credit, the business energy credit, and the reforestation credit.

[27] Sec. 38(c). The term *net income tax* is the sum of the regular tax plus the alternative minimum tax reduced by other nonrefundable credits. The term *net regular tax liability* means the regular tax liability reduced by nonrefundable credits.

[28] Nonrefundable personal tax credits include the child and dependent care credit, credit for the elderly, the residential mortgage interest credit, and the adoption credit. For the purpose of deducting these credits, the tax liability does not include special taxes such as the alternative minimum tax. Refundable personal tax credits include the earned income credit and federal income taxes withheld (including quarterly estimated taxes). In such case an individual may receive a tax refund from the IRS equal to the amount of the credit even if no tax is owed.

[29] Sec. 39(a)(1).

ADDITIONAL COMMENT

A provision in Sec. 6411 permits a quick refund of taxes resulting from the carryback of an unused general business credit. An individual uses Form 1045 to file for the quick refund.

	Credits Used in Carryback Year	Credit Limitation in Carryback Year	Carryback Applied
1994	$40,000	$60,000	$20,000
1995	70,000	70,000	—0—
1996	30,000	50,000	20,000

Eagle Corporation carries back $20,000 of its unused general business tax credit to 1994 and an additional $20,000 to 1996. The tax liability for the carryback years is recomputed, and Eagle files amended tax returns in order to obtain a refund of the taxes paid in 1994 and 1996. The remaining $10,000 of unused credit is carried forward to 1997 and the 14 succeeding years. ◄

During the carryover years, the unused credits from prior years are first applied (commencing with the earliest carryover year) before the current year credits that are earned are used (i.e., a first-in, first-out [FIFO] method is applied). This method permits the use of credits from the earliest of the carryover years and may prevent such carryovers from expiring.

EXAMPLE I14-18 ▶ Eastern Corporation has unused general business tax credits of $10,000 in 1996 that are carried forward to 1997. Eastern earns $5,000 of additional credits in 1997 and has a $12,000 limitation. The $12,000 of credits that are used consist of the $10,000 carryover from 1996 and $2,000 from 1997. The remaining $3,000 ($5,000 − $2,000) of 1997 credits are carried forward to 1998. ◄

FOREIGN TAX CREDIT

KEY POINT

The foreign tax credit is available only on income, war profits, and excess profits taxes or taxes paid in lieu of such taxes. It is sometimes difficult to determine whether a particular foreign tax falls into the qualifying category.

U.S. citizens, resident aliens, and U.S. corporations are subject to U.S. taxation on their worldwide income.[30] To reduce double taxation, the tax law provides a foreign tax credit for income taxes paid or accrued to a foreign country or a U.S. possession.[31]

Taxpayers may elect to take a deduction for the taxes paid or accrued in lieu of a foreign tax credit.[32] In general, the foreign tax credit results in greater tax benefit because (as previously discussed) a credit is fully offset against the tax liability, while a deduction merely reduces taxable income.

COMPUTATION OF ALLOWABLE CREDIT

ADDITIONAL COMMENT

In 1993, 1 million individual taxpayers claimed foreign tax credits totaling $1.82 billion.

The **foreign tax credit** amount equals the lesser of the foreign taxes paid or accrued in the tax year or the portion of the U.S. income tax liability attributable to the income earned in all foreign countries.[33] This limitation, which restricts the claiming of foreign tax credit if the effective foreign tax rate on the foreign earnings exceeds the effective U.S. tax rate on these earnings, may result in double taxation if the unused credit cannot be used as a carryback or carryover (see discussion under the next heading). The foreign tax credit limitation is based on the following formula:

$$\frac{\text{Foreign source taxable income}}{\text{Worldwide taxable income}} \times \frac{\text{U.S. income tax}}{\text{before credits}} = \frac{\text{Foreign tax credit}}{\text{limitation}}$$

---

[30] Certain exceptions are provided by treaty agreements between the United States and foreign countries whereby certain types of foreign-source income may be exempt from taxation in the foreign country.

[31] Under Sec. 911, U.S. citizens and resident aliens may elect to exclude from gross income up to $70,000 of foreign-earned income and certain housing

cost amounts. The foreign taxes that are attributable to the excluded income cannot be taken as a credit. (See Chapter 14 for a discussion of these exclusions.)

[32] Sec. 164(a)(3).

[33] Sec. 904.

EXAMPLE I14-19 ▶ Edison Corporation has $200,000 U.S. source taxable income and $100,000 of foreign source taxable income from country A. Total worldwide taxable income is $300,000 ($200,000 + $100,000). Country A levies a total of $40,000 in foreign income taxes upon the foreign source taxable income (i.e., a 40% effective tax rate). The U.S. tax before credits is $100,250 on the $300,000 of taxable income. Using the formula given above, the overall foreign tax credit limitation is computed as follows:[34]

$$\frac{\$100,000}{\$300,000} \times \$100,250 = \$33,417$$

Because the foreign tax payments ($40,000) exceed the U.S. tax attributable to the foreign source income ($33,417), the limitation applies. Thus, $6,583 ($40,000 − $33,417) of foreign tax credit cannot be used in the current year. ◀

STOP & THINK

Question: Since a credit is generally much more valuable than a deduction, under what circumstances would it be more beneficial for a taxpayer to take a deduction for foreign taxes in lieu of the foreign tax credit?

Solution: If a taxpayer has foreign source taxable income from one country and an equal loss from another foreign country, the foreign tax credit limitation is zero because the net foreign source taxable income is zero. Because none of the taxes paid in the foreign country in which taxable income was produced can be claimed as a credit, the taxpayer may choose to deduct them unless the credits are carried back or forward.

TREATMENT OF UNUSED CREDITS

Unused foreign tax credits are carried back two years and then forward for five years to years where the limitation is not exceeded (i.e., the foreign tax payment is lower than the U.S. taxes attributable to the foreign source income in the carryback or carryover years). The unused credits are lost if they are not used by the end of the five-year carryover period.

CREDIT FOR INCREASING RESEARCH ACTIVITIES

HISTORICAL NOTE

The research credit was enacted in 1981 because Congress was concerned about the substantial relative decline in total U.S. expenditures for research and development.

The tax law provides two means of encouraging research and experimental activities: (1) research and experimental expenditures may be either deducted immediately or capitalized and amortized over a period of 60 months or more under Sec. 174 (see Chapter I10 for a discussion of these rules) or (2) a tax credit for qualified research expenses is available under Sec. 41. Before July 1, 1995, the research credit was allowed in an amount equal to the sum of:

▶ 20% of qualified research expenses incurred in a tax year in excess of a base amount[35] for that tax year, plus

▶ 20% of basic research payments in excess of a base amount for that year.

---

[34] Certain types of income may have a separate foreign tax credit limitation. These types of income include passive income, high withholding tax interest, financial services income, shipping income, dividends from noncontrolled foreign (Sec. 902) corporations, dividends from domestic international sales corporations (DISCs), and foreign trade income from a foreign sales corporation.

[35] The base amount is defined in Sec. 41(c)(2) as the product of the fixed-base

percentage and the taxpayer's average annual gross receipts for the four tax years before the current (credit) year. All taxpayers are limited to a minimum base amount that may not be less than 50% of the qualified research expenses for the current year. The fixed-based percentage is the ratio of the taxpayer's total qualified research expenses to its total gross receipts for a specified base period (see Sec. 41(c)(3)).

However, the research credit expired effective June 30, 1995. Under the Small Business Job Protection Act of 1996, the research credit was restored in a modified form but only for the period of July 1, 1996 through May 31, 1997. Thus, no research credit was allowed for the period of July 1, 1995 through June 30, 1996.

The new Act allows taxpayers to elect to compute the credit in two alternative ways: (1) in a manner substantially similar to the law that existed prior to July 1, 1995, or (2) to elect to compute the credit under an alternative method that employs a three-tiered credit regime with reduced credit rates and fixed-based percentages. The second alternative is intended to benefit taxpayers whose base amount has gotten very high because of dramatically higher sales. Because the computation of the research credit is very complex, the details are not presented in this textbook. Readers are directed to Sec. 41 for additional details.

WORK OPPORTUNITY CREDIT

ADDITIONAL COMMENT

The employer must receive or request the certification in writing no later than the employee's first day of work.

The work opportunity credit is a new credit that replaces the targeted jobs credit and is effective for individuals beginning work for an employer after September 30, 1996. The targeted jobs credit had expired as of December 31, 1994 and was not extended by Congress. Thus, no credit is available for wages paid after December 31, 1994 and before October 1, 1996. Finally, the new credit is scheduled to expire for individuals beginning work after September 30, 1997. This constant reshuffling of effective dates creates considerable uncertainty and complexity for taxpayers. However, Congress wants to allow the credit on a year-by-year basis in order to evaluate its effectiveness in creating employment opportunities for economically disadvantaged individuals.

The work opportunity credit (WOC) is intended to reduce unemployment for individuals who are usually economically disadvantaged and includes the following targeted groups:[36]

(1) Qualified AFDC (Aid to Families with Dependent Children) recipient,
(2) Qualified veteran,
(3) Qualified ex-felon,
(4) High-risk youth,
(5) Vocational rehabilitation referral,
(6) Qualified summer youth employee, or
(7) Qualified food stamp recipient.

The credit is 35% of the first $6,000 of qualified wages paid to employees hired from one or more of the seven targeted groups. The new credit imposes a minimum employment period for qualified employees: employment for at least 180 days (20 days for qualified summer youth employee) or completes at least 400 hours of service for the employer (120 hours for a qualified summer youth employee). To qualify for the credit, the employer must obtain a certification from a local jobs service office of a state employment security agency stating that the unemployed individual is a qualified member of a targeted group on or before the day employment is offered. A disadvantage associated with the WOC is that the employer's deduction for wages must be reduced by the amount of the credit.

EXAMPLE I14-20 ▶ Jet Corporation hires two individuals in the current year, one a qualified ex-felon and the other a qualified food stamp recipient. Both individuals are properly certified by the state agency

---

[36] Sec. 51.

before being hired. One of the individuals is paid $8,000 of wages during the year, and the second individual is paid $4,000. The amount of wages eligible for the work opportunity credit is $10,000 ($6,000 ceiling limit for the first employee plus $4,000 actual wages paid to the second employee). The credit is $3,500 (35% × $10,000). Jet must reduce its $12,000 deduction for wages paid to the two individuals by $3,500 in the current year. ◄

The WOC is one of the items included in the general business credit. Thus, the limitation is based on the taxpayer's tax liability, and the carryback and carryover of excess credits are governed by the Sec. 38 rules.

EMPOWERMENT ZONE EMPLOYMENT CREDIT

The empowerment zone employment credit is an attempt to provide economic revitalization of distressed urban and rural areas. Empowerment zones and enterprise zones that have a condition of pervasive poverty, unemployment, and general distress are designated by the Secretary of Housing and Urban Development and the Secretary of Agriculture.

Employers are eligible for a 20% tax credit on the first $15,000 of wages per employee including training and educational costs paid to full- and part-time employees who are residents of an empowerment zone provided that the employer's trade or business and the employee's principal place of abode are within the empowerment zone.[37]

Qualified wages do not include wages taken into account for purposes of the targeted jobs credit (discussed above). The empowerment zone employment credit is one of the items included in the general business credit and the employer's deduction for wages is also reduced by the amount of the credit.

EXAMPLE I14-21 ▶ Ace Corporation is located in a designated empowerment zone and employs two eligible individuals who reside in the empowerment zone. One of the individuals is paid $12,000 in wages (plus $4,000 of training expenses are incurred for the employee) and the second employee is paid $10,000 in wages. $15,000 of wages and training expenses for the first employee and $10,000 of wages for the second employee are qualified wages. The credit is $5,000 ($25,000 × 0.20). Ace Corporation must reduce its $26,000 deduction for wages and training expenses by $5,000 (the credit amount for the year). ◄

DISABLED ACCESS CREDIT

A nonrefundable tax credit is available to eligible small businesses for expenditures incurred to make existing business facilities accessible to disabled individuals. Eligible access expenditures include payments for the purpose of removing architectural, communication, physical or transportation barriers that prevent a business from being accessible or usable by disabled individuals. Expenditures made in connection with new construction are not eligible for the credit. The disabled access credit is equal to 50% of eligible expenditures that exceed $250 but do not exceed $10,250.[38] Thus, the annual credit limitation is $5,000. The basis of the property is reduced by the allowable credit. An eligible small business is any business that either (1) had gross receipts of $1 million or less in the preceding year or, (2) in the case of a business failing the first test, had no more

---

[37] Sec. 1396. [38] Sec. 44.

than 30 full-time employees in the preceding year and makes a timely election to claim the credit.

EXAMPLE I14-22 ▶ Crane Corporation had 14 employees during the preceding tax year and $2 million of gross receipts. During the current year, Crane installed concrete access ramps at a total cost of $14,000. Crane is an eligible small business because the company had 30 or fewer full-time employees during the preceding year even though its gross receipts exceed the threshold amount (i.e., $1 million). Only $10,000 of eligible expenditures qualify for the credit, thereby limiting it to $5,000 ($10,000 × 0.50). The depreciable basis of the property is reduced by the credit amount to $9,000 ($14,000 − $5,000). ◀

The disabled access credit is also one of the items included in the general business credit. Thus, the limitation is based on the taxpayer's tax liability, and the carryback and carryover of excess credits are governed by the Sec. 38 rules.

TAX CREDIT FOR REHABILITATION EXPENDITURES

Congress has provided incentives for the rehabilitation of older industrial and commercial buildings and certified historic structures. A credit for rehabilitation expenditures is available subject to the following special rules and qualification requirements:[39]

▶ The credit is 10% for structures that were originally placed in service before 1936 and 20% for certified historic structures.[40]

▶ The credit applies only to trade or business property and property held for investment that is depreciable. Residential rental property does not qualify unless the building is a certified historic structure.

▶ At least 75% of the external walls, including at least 50% utilization of external walls, and at least 75% of the building's internal structural framework must remain in place.[41]

▶ Straight-line depreciation generally must be used with the applicable Sec. 168 recovery periods with respect to rehabilitation expenditures. The regular MACRS depreciation rules apply to the portion of the property's basis that is not eligible for the credit.

▶ The basis of the property for depreciation is reduced by the full amount of the credit taken.[42]

▶ The rehabilitation expenditures must exceed the greater of the property's adjusted basis or $5,000.

▶ The rehabilitation credit is recaptured at a rate of 20% per year if there is an early disposition of the property.

EXAMPLE I14-23 ▶ During the current year, Ted rehabilitates a certified historic structure used in his business at a cost of $40,000. The adjusted basis of the certified historic structure is $38,000 at the time the property is rehabilitated. The property qualifies for the rehabilitation credit because

---

[39] Sec. 47.
[40] Secs. 47(a)(1) and (2). A certified historic structure must be certified by the Department of Treasury and must be located in a registered historic district or listed in the *National Register.*

[41] Sec. 47(c)(1)(A). The percentage requirements for rehabilitation do not apply to a certified historic structure.
[42] Sec. 50(c)(1).

▶ It is used in Ted's trade or business and is depreciable.

▶ The property is a certified historic structure.

▶ The amount of the expenditure exceeds the greater of the property's $38,000 adjusted basis or the $5,000 statutory minimum.

The credit is $8,000 (0.20 × $40,000). The basis of the rehabilitation expenditures for depreciation purposes is reduced by the full amount of the credit to $32,000 ($40,000 − $8,000). If the property is disposed of after one year, $1,600 of the credit (0.20 × $8,000) is earned and $6,400 ($8,000 − $1,600) is recaptured. ◀

BUSINESS ENERGY CREDITS

To encourage energy conservation measures, additional credits are available to businesses that invest in energy-conserving properties (e.g., solar and geothermal property).[43] The business energy credit is 10%. The construction, reconstruction, or erection of the property must be completed by the taxpayer and its original use must commence with the taxpayer. This credit is part of the general business credit and is subject to the same limitations on deductibility and carryback and carryover rules as other general business credits.

PERSONAL TAX CREDITS

The two most common personal nonrefundable credits are the child and dependent care credit and credit for the elderly and disabled. These credits are allowed as an offset against an individual's tax liability before all other credits (e.g., the general business credit and the foreign tax credit) are offset. The earned income credit for certain low-income individuals is refundable (e.g., an individual may receive a tax refund equal to the amount of the credit even if no tax is owed). Most tax credits for individuals have been enacted for social welfare rather than economic reasons.

CHILD AND DEPENDENT CARE CREDIT

ADDITIONAL COMMENT

The dollar amount of the child and dependent care credit amounted to $2.5 billion in 1992.

The child and dependent care credit provides relief for taxpayers who incur child and dependent care expenses because of employment activities.[44] To qualify for the credit, an individual must meet two requirements: employment-related expenses (i.e., qualifying child or dependent care expenses) must be incurred to enable the taxpayer to be gainfully employed, and the taxpayer must maintain a household for a dependent under age 13 or an incapacitated dependent or spouse.[45]

EXAMPLE I14-24 ▶ Tim and Tina are married and have two children under age 13. They incur child care expenses (e.g., a housekeeper and nurse) to enable Tina to pursue non–employment-related social activities. The child care expenditures are not eligible for the child and dependent care credit because Tina is not employed or attending school as a full-time student. ◀

QUALIFYING EMPLOYMENT-RELATED EXPENSES. Eligible expenses include amounts spent for housekeeping, nursing, cooking, baby-sitting, etc. in the taxpayer's

---

[43] Sec. 48(a)(2). This credit has been permanently extended by the Energy Tax Act of 1992.

[44] Sec. 21.

[45] Secs. 21(b)(1) and (e)(1). Maintaining a household means that the individual

(or the individual and spouse if married) must provide over one-half of the cost of maintaining the home. Married individuals must generally file a joint return to obtain the credit.

ADDITIONAL
COMMENT

Qualifying child care expenses include amounts spent to send a child to nursery school or kindergarten, but not first grade.

home but do not include expenses for a chauffeur or gardener. If the child or dependent care is provided outside the home by a dependent care facility (e.g., a day care facility), the amounts will generally qualify only if the dependent care facility provides care for more than six individuals. Employment-related expenses do not include amounts paid for services outside of the taxpayer's household at a camp where the qualifying individual stays overnight. In addition, amounts paid for services outside of the taxpayer's household (e.g., adult day care) that are spent for the care of an incapacitated dependent or spouse qualify only if the individual lives in the taxpayer's home for at least eight hours a day.

EXAMPLE I14-25 ▶ Tony is divorced and has two children under age 13. He is employed and incurs child care expenses at a preschool nursery for one of the children. He also has a live-in nanny who provides housekeeping services and a gardener to care for his yard. The expenditures for the preschool nursery and the live-in nanny qualify because these services constitute eligible household services and care of a qualifying individual. However, the payments to the gardener do not constitute qualifying household services. ◀

The following special rules also apply:

▶ Payments to a relative qualify unless the relative is a dependent or a child (under age 19) of the taxpayer.[46]

ADDITIONAL
COMMENT

According to the Census Bureau, 58.4% of married women with preschoolers worked in the paid labor force in 1989, up from 35% in 1977.

▶ The maximum child and dependent care expenses cannot exceed the individual's earned income. For married individuals, the limitation is applied to the earned income of the spouse with the smaller amount of earned income.

▶ A spouse who either is a full-time student or is incapacitated is deemed to have earned income of $200 per month.[47] The amount is increased to $400 per month if there are two or more qualifying individuals (e.g., children under age 13) in the household.

▶ The ceiling amount on qualifying child and dependent care expenses is $2,400 for one qualifying individual and $4,800 for two or more individuals. These ceilings are reduced by the aggregate amount excludable from gross income due to the exclusion under Sec. 129 relating to dependent care assistance programs.

EXAMPLE I14-26 ▶ Troy and Tracy are married and incur qualifying child care expenses of $4,000 to take care of their two children, ages 1 and 3. Tracy's earned income is $20,000, and Troy's earned income from a part-time job is $3,000. The limitation on qualifying child care expenses is $3,000. The earned income limitation applies because Troy's earned income ($3,000) is less than the child care expenses ($4,000) and is also less than the overall limitation on such expenses for an individual with two qualifying children ($4,800). Therefore, the amount of eligible child-care expenses is limited to $3,000. ◀

KEY POINT

The percentage used to calculate the credit varies from 20% to 30% depending on the taxpayer's AGI.

COMPUTATION OF THE CREDIT RATE AND AMOUNT. The credit is 30% of the qualifying expenses (after the ceiling limitations of $2,400 or $4,800 have been applied). However, the credit rate is reduced by one percentage point for each $2,000 (or fraction thereof) of adjusted gross income (AGI) in excess of $10,000. The minimum credit (20%) is applied once a taxpayer's AGI exceeds $28,000.

EXAMPLE I14-27 ▶ Vincent and Vicki are married, file a joint return, and have three children under age 13. Vincent and Vicki's employment-related earnings are $25,000 and $10,000, respectively. Their AGI is $35,000. They incur $8,000 of child care expenses during the current

---

[46] Sec. 21(e)(6).
[47] Sec. 21(d)(2). To qualify as a full-time student, the individual must enroll in

an educational institution on a full-time basis for at least five calendar months of the year (Reg. Sec. 1.44A-2(b)(3)(B)(ii)).

year. The eligible child care expenses are limited to $4,800, because Vincent and Vicki have more than one child who is qualified and this limitation is less than Vicki's earned income or the actual expenses incurred. Because their AGI is greater than $28,000, the minimum 20% credit rate is applicable. The child and dependent care credit is $960 (0.20 × $4,800). ◀

DEPENDENT CARE ASSISTANCE. An employee may exclude amounts up to $5,000 from gross income for dependent care assistance payments made by the individual's employer and provided to the employee.[48] The exclusion amount is limited to the earned income of the employee (or in the case of a married taxpayer, the lesser of the employee's earned income or the earned income of the spouse). To avoid a double benefit, the otherwise eligible expenses for purposes of computing the child and dependent care credit are reduced by the amount of assistance that is excluded from gross income.[49]

EXAMPLE I14-28 ▶

Assume the same facts as in Example I14-27 except that Vincent was reimbursed $4,000 by his employer under a qualified dependent care assistance program and this amount was excluded from gross income. The earned income limitation for the dependent care assistance exclusion does not apply because both Vincent and Vicki have employment-related earnings in excess of $4,000. Thus, the eligible child care expenses are reduced to $800 ($4,800 − $4,000) and the child care credit is $160 (0.20 × $800). ◀

ADOPTION CREDIT

A new nonrefundable credit has been enacted for qualified adoption expenses for tax years beginning after 1996. The amount of the credit is limited to a maximum of $5,000 ($6,000 for a child with special needs) and is allowable in the year following the year the qualified adoption expenses are paid unless the expenses are incurred in the year the adoption becomes final. Further, there is a phase-out of the credit based on AGI. For taxpayers with AGI between $75,000 and $115,000, the credit is ratably phased out and is fully phased out when a taxpayer's AGI reaches $115,000.[50] The credit, except in the case of special needs adoptions, expires with respect to expenses paid or incurred after December 31, 2001.

Qualified adoption expenses include reasonable and necessary adoption fees, court costs, attorney fees, and other expenses that are directly related to the legal adoption by the taxpayer of an eligible child. An eligible child is defined as a child who has not reached 18 years old when the adoption takes place or is physically or mentally incapable of self-care.

EXAMPLE I14-29 ▶

Oscar and Betty began adoption proceedings in June, 1997 to adopt an infant child. They incurred attorney fees and adoption agency fees in 1997 of $3,000. In 1998, they incurred an additional $4,000 of qualified adoption expenses when the adoption became final. Oscar and Betty's AGI in 1998 is $100,000. The adoption credit is allowable in 1998 in the amount of $1,875, computed as follows:

Total qualified adoption expenses in 1997 and 1998	$7,000
Maximum credit	5,000
Phase-out percentage ($25,000/$40,000)	62.5%
Amount of credit disallowed	3,125
Amount of credit allowed	1,875

---

[48] Sec. 129. (See Chapter I4 for a discussion of the requirements for exclusion.)
[49] Sec. 21(c).
[50] For purposes of the phase-out of the credit, AGI must be modified. AGI

for this purpose is determined without regard to the exclusions from gross income for foreign earned income under Sec. 911 and after the application of the rules relating to the taxation of Social Security, as well as selected other items. See Sec. 23.

Oscar and Betty can only use $5,000 of expenses (maximum) and must claim the expenses in 1998, the year the adoption becomes final. Finally, the adoption is limited based upon the level of their AGI. ◀

The adoption credit, when combined with the child and dependent care credit and the credit for the elderly, is limited to the taxpayer's regular tax liability.[51] The portion of the credit which is limited may be carried forward for up to five years.

TAX CREDIT FOR THE ELDERLY

ADDITIONAL COMMENT

The tax credit for the elderly was claimed on 243,000 tax returns in 1992 and amounted to only $52 million.

A limited, personal, nonrefundable credit is provided for certain low-income elderly individuals who have attained age 65 before the end of the tax year and individuals who retired because of a permanent and total disability who receive insubstantial Social Security benefits. Most elderly taxpayers are ineligible for the credit because they receive Social Security benefits in excess of the ceiling limitations that apply to the credit (e.g., an initial amount of $5,000 per year for a single taxpayer) or they have AGI amounts in excess of the limitations, which effectively reduces or eliminates the allowable credit.

The maximum credit is 15% times an initial amount of $5,000 ($7,500 for married individuals filing jointly if both spouses are 65 or older).[52] This initial amount is reduced by

▶ Social Security, railroad retirement, or Veterans Administration pension or annuity benefits that are excluded from gross income

▶ One-half of AGI in excess of $7,500 for a single individual ($10,000 for married taxpayers filing a joint return).[53] All types of taxable income items are included in AGI (e.g., salaries, taxable pension and taxable Social Security benefits, and investment income).

EXAMPLE I14-30 ▶

Wayne and Tammy are both 65 years old and file a joint return. They have AGI of $11,000 and receive nontaxable Social Security payments of $3,000 during the current year. Their tax credit for the elderly is computed as follows:

Initial ceiling amount		$7,500
Minus: Nontaxable social security	$3,000	
One-half of AGI in excess of $10,000		
(0.50 × [$11,000 − $10,000])	500	(3,500)
Total credit base		$4,000
Times: Credit percentage		× 0.15
Tax credit		$ 600

The $600 credit is allowed only to the extent that Wayne and Tammy's total personal tax credits do not exceed the actual tax due before credits. ◀

EARNED INCOME CREDIT

ADDITIONAL COMMENT

The earned income credit was claimed on 14.4 million tax returns in 1992 and amounted to $13.4 billion.

The earned income credit is refundable (i.e., the individual receives a refund of tax even though no tax is due or paid). As such, the earned income credit is a special type of "negative income tax" or welfare benefit for certain low-income families. The credit is based on earned income that includes wages, salaries, tips, and other employee compensation plus net earnings from self-employment and is designed to encourage low-income individuals to become gainfully employed.

---

[51] Sec. 26.
[52] Sec. 22(c)(2). The initial ceiling amount is $5,000 if one spouse filing a joint return is less than age 65 and the limitation is $3,750 for a married individual filing a separate return. Unless married individuals are living apart for the

entire year, they must file a joint return in order to obtain the credit.
[53] The AGI ceiling is $5,000 for married individuals filing a separate return. To obtain the credit, however, a separate return can be filed only if both spouses live apart for the entire tax year.

ELIGIBILITY RULES. The credit is available to individuals with qualifying children and to certain individuals without children if the earned income and AGI thresholds are met.[54] The earned income credit applies to married individuals only if a joint return is filed. Individuals without children are eligible only if the following requirements are met:

KEY POINT

The Revenue Reconciliation Act of 1993 dramatically increased the benefits available from the earned income credit, which follows President Clinton's campaign promise to provide tax relief to the working poor.

▶ The individual's principal place of abode is in the United States for more than one-half of the tax year.

▶ The individual (or spouse if married) is at least age 25 and not more than age 64 at the end of the tax year.

▶ The individual is not a dependent of another taxpayer for the tax year.[55]

For tax years beginning after December 31, 1995, a taxpayer will become ineligible for the earned income credit if the taxpayer has excessive investment income. Excessive investment income is defined as disqualified income that exceeds $2,200 for the taxable year. Disqualified income includes:

1. Dividends;
2. Interest (both taxable and tax-free); and
3. Net rental income.
4. Capital gain net income.

COMPUTATION OF THE CREDIT AMOUNT. The earned income credit percentages and the maximum amount of earned income used to compute the credit for 1997 are summarized in Table I14-1. The basic percentage rate and the maximum amount of earned income used to compute the credit depend on the number of qualifying children (from none to two or more). The maximum allowable credit is then reduced by a phase-out percentage (see Table I14-2).[56]

EXAMPLE I14-31 ▶ Vivian is eligible for the earned income credit and has one qualifying child. In the current year she has $10,360 of earned income from wages and $2,000 of alimony. Vivian's AGI is, therefore, $12,360 ($10,360 wages + $2,000 alimony). The tentative credit is $2,210 (0.34 × the first $6,500 of earned income). This amount is reduced by $69 [0.1598 × ($12,360 − $11,930)].[57] The allowable credit is therefore $2,141 ($2,210 − $69), and this amount is refundable to Vivian. ◀

▼ **TABLE I14-1**

1997 Earned Income Credit Table

Number of Qualifying Children	Basic Percentage	Maximum Amount of Earned Income to Compute Credit	Maximum Tentative Credit
None	7.65%	$4,340	$ 332
One	34.0%	6,500	2,210
Two or more	40.0%	9,140	3,656

---

[54] Sec. 32(c). A qualifying child must be the taxpayer's child, stepchild, foster child, or a descendent of the taxpayer's child. The child must share the same principal place of abode with the taxpayer for more than one-half of the tax year and the child must be less than age 19 or be a full-time student under age 24 or be permanently and totally disabled.

[55] Sec. 32(d).

[56] The percentages are adjusted annually for inflation.

[57] Sec 32(b)(1). $12,360 is used in the formula because modified AGI of $12,360 is greater than $10,360 of earned income. Modified AGI is defined as the individual's AGI decreased by certain items, principally net capital losses (not over $3,000), net losses from nonbusiness rents and royalties, and 50% of net losses from a trade or business.

▼ TABLE I14-2

1997 Earned Income Credit Phase-Out Table

Number of Qualifying Children	Phase-Out Begins at[a]	Phase-Out Percentage	Phase-Out Ends at
None	$ 5,430	7.65%	$ 9,770
One	11,930	15.98%	25,760
Two or more	11,930	21.06%	29,290

[a]Larger of modified AGI or earned income.

TAX PLANNING CONSIDERATIONS

KEY POINT

The alternative minimum tax can be avoided or its impact lessened by various tax strategies.

AVOIDING THE ALTERNATIVE MINIMUM TAX

Taxpayers with substantial amounts of tax preference items and a corresponding low regular tax liability may be subject to the AMT. These taxpayers need to engage in tax planning in order to minimize or avoid the AMT. Because a liberal exemption is provided for most individuals (i.e., $45,000 for married individuals filing a joint return and $33,750 for single taxpayers and heads-of-households), the timing of certain income and deduction items may result in the full use of the exemption in each year. For example, planning to avoid the AMT may be accomplished by delaying the payment of certain itemized deductions (e.g., state and local taxes) that reduce the regular income tax but do not reduce the AMT. A cash method of accounting taxpayer who defers the payment of state income taxes into the following year triggers an increase in the regular tax for the current year. This increase can eliminate the AMT liability. However, it is necessary to consider the tax effects for both the current and following years because state income taxes are deductible for purposes of the regular tax calculation when the payment is made in the following year. This reduction may affect the AMT calculation in such a year and increase the amount of tax that is owed.

Certain tax-exempt investments generate additional tax preferences for the investor such as interest on private activity bonds. Before such investments are acquired, an investor should determine the impact on his or her AMT.

AVOIDING THE UNDERPAYMENT PENALTY FOR ESTIMATED TAX

Many taxpayers find it difficult to estimate their taxes for the purposes of making quarterly estimated payments and are uncertain whether their withholdings and estimated tax will equal or exceed 90% or more of their actual tax liability for the year. A common planning technique to avoid a possible underpayment tax penalty is to make estimated tax payments and withholdings in an amount that is at least 100% (or 110% if AGI was in excess of $150,000 for the prior year) of the actual tax liability for the prior year, thereby meeting one of the exceptions that prevents the underpayment penalty from being imposed. This technique is commonly referred to as a "safe estimate."

EXAMPLE I14-32 ▶ Yong expects his federal income tax withholdings to be $14,000 for the current year and estimates that his income tax liability will be $24,000. Last year Yong's actual federal income

Topic Review I14-3

Summary of Selected Tax Credits

Tax Credit Item	Rationale
Investment tax credit[a]	To encourage new private investment, which stimulates the economy and employment
Rehabilitation expenditure credit[a]	To encourage the rehabilitation of older buildings including certified historic structures
Business energy credits[a]	To encourage energy conservation measures and the use of fuel other than petroleum
Foreign tax credit	To mitigate the effects of double taxation on foreign source income
Credit for increasing research activities[a]	To encourage research and development activities to enhance our technological base
Work opportunity[a]	To encourage employers to hire unemployed people from disadvantaged groups
Low-income housing credit[a]	To encourage construction, rehabilitation, and ownership of qualified low-income housing projects (this credit is not discussed in the text due to its limited applicability)
Qualified electrical vehicles credit[a]	To encourage energy conservation (this credit is not discussed in the text due to its limited applicability)
Disabled access credit[a]	To encourage small businesses to provide access for disabled
Empowerment zone employment credit[a]	To reduce the level of unemployment in distressed urban and rural areas.
Child and dependent care credit[b]	To provide equitable relief for parents and other individuals who are employed and who must incur expenses for household and dependent care services
Adoption credit[b]	To provide relief for taxpayers who incur expenses in the adoption of children
Earned income credit[b]	To provide special tax breaks for certain low-income individuals who have earned income (e.g., salary and wages) and dependent children or other incapacitated individuals living in the household
Tax credit for the elderly[b]	To provide tax relief for elderly taxpayers who are not substantially covered by the Social Security system
Residential mortgage interest credit[b]	To encourage qualified first-time home buyers to purchase a principal residence (this credit is not discussed in the text due to its limited applicability)

[a]Part of the general business credit.
[b]Personal tax credits.

taxes were $20,000. If estimated taxes of at least $6,000 are paid during the year, Yong's estimated taxes plus withholding will be at least 100% of his prior year's tax liability ($14,000 + $6,000 = $20,000) and no underpayment penalty is due despite the fact that there is a $4,000 ($24,000 − $20,000) underpayment of the actual tax liability. If Yong's AGI was in excess of $150,000 for the prior year, his estimated taxes plus withholding must be at least 110% of his prior year's tax liability or $22,000 (1.10 × $20,000) to avoid the underpayment penalty. Thus, his estimated tax payments must be at least $8,000. ◄

CASH-FLOW CONSIDERATIONS

Assuming that the underpayment penalty can be avoided, it is generally preferable to have an underpayment of tax to the government at the time for filing the return rather

KEY POINT

A taxpayer should avoid making estimated payments that exceed the actual tax liability because the taxpayer is making an interest-free loan to the IRS. Nevertheless, many taxpayers deliberately have excess amounts withheld from their wages or make excessive estimated payments in order to receive a refund. These taxpayers view this strategy as a forced saving plan.

than to receive a refund resulting from an overpayment of tax. No interest is paid on a refund if the IRS pays the refund within 45 days from the later of the due date of the return or its filing date.[58] In addition, the IRS has, in effect, received an interest-free loan from the taxpayer during the period such overpayment is made. To avoid an overpayment, a taxpayer may file an amended W-4 form and claim additional withholding allowances if the requirements are met (e.g., the taxpayer has unusually large itemized deductions, tax credits, alimony payments, etc.).

If an individual anticipates that her estimated tax payments and withholdings are insufficient to avoid the underpayment penalty, it may be preferable to increase the amounts that are withheld before the end of the tax year (e.g., the amounts that are withheld in the fourth quarter) to avoid the penalty rather than to increase the estimated tax payments. This technique may be advantageous because the penalty is calculated on a quarterly basis, and the withholdings are spread evenly over the year, despite the fact that such increased withholding amounts are paid near the end of the year. The end result is cash-flow savings to the taxpayer. Another alternative means to avoid the underpayment penalty is to accelerate certain deductions (e.g., real estate taxes on a personal residence), by paying such amounts before the end of the tax year. Additionally, otherwise deductible contributions to an IRA made between the end of the tax year and the due date for the tax return may be treated as a deduction for the prior year, thereby avoiding the underpayment penalty (see Chapter I9).

USE OF GENERAL BUSINESS TAX CREDITS

Business tax credits (e.g., the disabled access credit and the targeted jobs credit) are combined for the purpose of computing an overall limitation based on the taxpayer's tax liability. Also, an individual's personal tax credits (e.g., the child and dependent care credit) and the foreign tax credit are deducted from the tax liability before the limitations are applied to the general business tax credit. Similarly, the nonrefundable personal tax credits reduce the tax liability before the foreign tax credit limitation is applied. Therefore, it is necessary to consider the priority and interrelated aspects of these credits to ensure that a particular credit is fully used.

FOREIGN TAX CREDITS AND THE FOREIGN EARNED INCOME EXCLUSION

Individuals who accept foreign job assignments should consider the federal income tax implications because U.S. citizens are subject to U.S. tax on their worldwide income. Assuming that certain requirements and limitations are met, an individual may elect to take either a foreign tax credit or a foreign-earned income exclusion of $70,000 with respect to salaries, allowances, and other forms of earned income that are earned while on extended non-U.S. assignments.[59] Any taxes that are paid or accrued with respect to the excluded income are not available as a foreign tax credit. In general, the exclusion is preferable if the effective foreign tax rate is less than the effective U.S. tax rate because the foreign tax credit that can be claimed does not equal the gross U.S. tax owed on the income. If the effective foreign tax rate on the earned income exceeds the effective U.S. tax rate, U.S. taxpayers ordinarily elect not to use the exclusion. Instead, the excess tax credits on earned income are used to offset the U.S. taxes owed on other types of foreign income. Detailed coverage of foreign tax credits and the exclusion is contained in Chapter C15 of the *Prentice Hall's Federal Taxation: Corporations, Partnerships, Estates and Trusts* text.

---

[58] Sec. 6611(e).
[59] Sec. 911(a). The foreign income exclusion requirements are discussed in Chapter I4.

CHILD AND DEPENDENT CARE CREDIT

ADDITIONAL COMMENT

If the employer provides a child care assistance plan, the taxpayer may lose the benefit of the child and dependent care credit because it is necessary to reduce the amount of expenses eligible for the credit dollar-for-dollar by the amount excluded from gross income under the employer's child care plan.

The child and dependent care credit is increasingly important because a greater percentage of both spouses are now in the labor force as well as the large number of single parent families. Nonworking spouses who are considering employment should evaluate the tax consequences arising from the child and dependent care credit.

It should be noted that certain child and dependent care expenses may qualify as a medical expense (e.g., nursing care for a disabled dependent). Therefore, it is necessary to compare the marginal tax benefit from the additional child and dependent care credit with the marginal tax benefit from the additional medical expense deduction to determine whether the credit is worth more than the deduction. Expenditures in excess of the child and dependent care ceiling amounts ($2,400 for one child or dependent and $4,800 for two or more children or dependents) may also qualify as medical expenses.

EXAMPLE I14-33 ▶

REAL WORLD EXAMPLE

Many taxpayers do not comply with the tax law when they hire people to care for their children. Zoe Baird withdrew as attorney general nominee when it was disclosed that she had hired illegal aliens to care for her children and had failed to withhold the FICA tax from the employee's wages and to pay the employer's FICA tax.

Stacey, a single taxpayer, maintains a household for an incapacitated dependent parent and two children under age 13. Stacey has AGI from alimony of $20,000 and could earn an additional $15,000 working as a secretary. To enable Stacey to be employed, assume that she would incur $4,000 of eligible child care expenses for the children and an additional $4,000 of nursing expenses for the care of her disabled parent. Before considering the tax effects, Stacey's net increase in income from being employed would only be $7,000 ($15,000 earnings − $8,000 of child and dependent care expenses). The tax credit for child and dependent care expenses is $960 ($4,800 × 0.20). The rate is scaled down from 30% to 20% because Stacey's AGI is $35,000 (i.e., the credit rate is reduced by one percentage point for each $2,000 of AGI in excess of $10,000 until it reaches 20% when AGI exceeds $28,000). A portion of the qualified nursing care expenses (i.e., $8,000 − $4,800 = $3,200) that is not used as child and dependent care expenditures may be deducted as medical expenses if they exceed the 7.5% of AGI nondeductible medical expense floor. If Stacey itemizes her deductions and has other medical expenses equal to or greater than 7.5% of AGI and has an average tax rate of 20%, the value of the additional medical deductions is $640 (0.20 × $3,200). Stacey's additional net cash flows from working are only $4,453, consisting of the following:

Gross earnings from employment		$15,000
Minus:	Federal income tax on earnings ($15,000 × 0.20)	(3,000)[a]
	Actual child and dependent care expenses	(8,000)
	FICA taxes (0.0765 × $15,000)	(1,147)
Plus:	Child and dependent care credit	960
	Medical expense tax benefit	640
Cash flow from employment		$ 4,453

[a] A 20% average tax rate was used because more than one tax rate is used to compute Stacey's tax liability.

Consideration should also be given to additional incremental work-related expenditures (e.g., clothing, meals, and commuting expenses) that are not deductible. The income tax and cash flow consequences arising from an employee assistance program for child care or medical expenses should also be considered if a plan is offered to employees. ◀

COMPLIANCE AND PROCEDURAL CONSIDERATIONS

ALTERNATIVE MINIMUM TAX FILING PROCEDURES

Form 6251 is used by individuals to compute the AMT, and corporations must use Form 4626 (see Appendix B for both forms). Form 6251 must be completed and attached to an individual's tax return in any of the following situations:

ADDITIONAL
COMMENT

The Revenue Reconciliation Act of 1993 raised the AMT rate from 24% to 26% on the first $175,000 of AMTI over the exemption amount and 28% on amounts over $175,000. Because the rate on net capital gains was capped at 28%, taxpayers whose income is primarily from net capital gains are more likely to fall into an AMT position.

▶ An AMT tax liability actually exists.

▶ The taxpayer has tax credits that are limited by the tentative minimum tax.

▶ The AMT base exceeds the exemption amounts and an individual has AMT adjustment or tax preference items.

IRS Publication 909 contains detailed information regarding filing considerations for individuals.

WITHHOLDING AND ESTIMATED TAX

Taxpayers who have income taxes withheld from wages, pensions, and so on should receive a Form W-2 (or Form 1099-R for pensions) by January 31. These forms should be attached to the tax return to substantiate the amount of the withholdings. If the form is incorrect, the taxpayer should request a corrected form from the payor.

If an individual makes quarterly estimated tax payments, Form 1040A or Form 1040EZ may not be used. Married individuals may make either joint estimated tax payments or separate estimated tax payments. If joint estimated tax payments are made and the married individuals subsequently file separate returns (e.g., in the case of a divorce that is pending or a divorce completed before the end of the year), the joint estimated tax payments are divided in proportion to each spouse's individual tax if no agreement is reached concerning an appropriate division.

EXAMPLE I14-34 ▶

Allen and Alice make joint estimated tax payments during 1997 of $10,000. Allen and Alice are separated in February 1998 and Alice refuses to file a joint return with Allen. Allen's tax liability for 1997 on his separate return is $20,000 and Alice's tax liability on her separate return is $5,000. Alice is entitled to claim $2,000 of the estimated tax payments to her return [($5,000 ÷ $25,000) × $10,000]. The remaining $8,000 is apportioned to Allen. ◀

GENERAL BUSINESS TAX CREDITS

The computation of the business energy credit is made on Form 3468. Individuals must transfer the totals to page 2 of Form 1040. Form 3800 must be filed if any other general business credits are claimed.

PERSONAL TAX CREDITS

KEY POINT

The earned income credit is available even in cases where the taxpayer has no tax liability.

Personal tax credits, including the credit for child and dependent care expenses and credit for the elderly (and the adoption credit in 1997), are reported on page 2 of Form 1040. These credits are deducted from the taxpayer's tax liability before other credits. The credits section on page 2 of Form 1040 limits the deduction for personal tax credits to the amount of the tax due. Form 2441 (see Appendix B) must be filed to claim the child and dependent care credit. Taxpayers who claim the child and dependent care credit must also include the care provider's name, address, and taxpayer identification number on their tax return. If the caregiver will not provide the required information, the taxpayer has the option to supply the name and address of the caregiver on Form 2441 and attach a statement explaining that the caregiver has refused to provide his or her identification number (TIN). Schedule R of Form 1040 (see Appendix B) is filed to claim the credit for the elderly. An elderly individual may elect to have the IRS compute the tax and the amount of the tax credit.[60]

The earned income credit is refundable to an individual even if no tax is owed. The IRS will automatically compute the credit amount. However, tax tables to assist in the process are included in IRS instructions to Forms 1040 and 1040A. Schedule EIC of Form 1040 (see Appendix B) is used to compute the credit if Form 1040 is used. Schedule 4 is used for Form 1040A. If an individual expects to be eligible for the earned income

[60] Sec. 6014. See Form 1040 instructions for more reporting details.

credit, he or she can obtain advance payments of the credit amount by filing Form W-5 (Earned Income Credit Advance Payment Certificate) with his or her employer, who will increase the employee's pay by the amount of the credit. Individuals who receive advance payments must file Form 1040 or Form 1040A to obtain the credit even if they are not required to file a tax return. Taxpayers who are eligible for the earned income credit can not use Form 1040-EZ (see Appendix B).

The foreign tax credit for individuals is computed on Form 1116 (see Appendix B). The foreign tax credit amount so determined is entered on page 2 of Form 1040.

PROBLEM MATERIALS

DISCUSSION QUESTIONS

I14-1 Why are most taxpayers not subject to the alternative minimum tax (AMT)?

I14-2 Does the AMT apply if an individual's tax liability as computed under the AMT rules is less than his or her regular tax amount?

I14-3 Which of the following are tax preference items for purposes of computing the individual AMT?
a. Net long-term capital gain
b. Excess depreciation for real property placed in service before 1987
c. Straight-line depreciation on residential real estate acquired in 1992
d. Appreciated element for charitable contributions of capital gain real property

I14-4 Which of the following are individual AMT adjustments?
a. Itemized deductions that are not allowed in computing AMTI
b. Excess of MACRS depreciation over depreciation computed under the alternative depreciation system for real property placed in service after 1986.
c. Excess of MACRS depreciation over depreciation computed under the alternative depreciation system for personal property placed in service after 1986
d. Tax-exempt interest earned on State of Michigan general revenue bonds.

I14-5 Which of the following itemized deductions are deductible when computing the alternative minimum tax for individuals?
a. Charitable contributions
b. Mortgage interest on a personal residence
c. State and local income taxes
d. Interest related to an investment in undeveloped land where the individual has no investment income
e. Medical expenses amounting to 8% of AGI

I14-6 Why are most individuals not subject to the self-employment tax?

I14-7 Tony, who is single and 58 years old, is considering early retirement. He currently has $70,000 salary and $50,000 of profits from a consulting business. What advice would you give Tony relative to the need to make Social Security tax payments if he retires and continues to be actively engaged as a consultant during his retirement?

I14-8 Theresa is a college professor who wants to work for a consulting firm during the summer. She will be working on special projects involving professional development programs. What advantages might accrue to the consulting firm if the engagement is set up as a consulting arrangement rather than an employment contract?

I14-9 Ted and Tina are both self-employed and file a joint return in 1997. Ted has self-employment income of $20,000 and receives a $30,000 salary from his employer. Tina's has no salary and self-employment income of $10,000.
a. How much self-employment tax is due for Ted and Tina on a joint return?
b. How much, if any, of the self-employment tax payments may be deducted on Ted and Tina's income tax return?

I14-10 If an employer fails to withhold federal income taxes and FICA taxes on wages or fails to make payment to the IRS, what adverse tax consequences may result? May corporate officers or other corporate officials be held responsible for the underpayment?

I14-11 Jet Corporation reimburses Tracy, an employee, for certain moving expenses. The reimbursement is $6,000. However, only $4,000 is deductible on Tracy's income tax return. Should Jet Corporation withhold federal income tax on the reimbursed amounts? If so, how much?

I14-12 When Vicki retires during the current year, she will receive a monthly pension of $800 and a fully taxable lump-sum distribution of $50,000 from her employer's qualified profit-sharing plan. She does not want the trustee of either plan to withhold any federal income tax because she expects that it will be difficult for her to live on the pension income and the investment income from the lump-sum distribution.
  a. What procedures should Vicki follow if she does not want the trustees to withhold on the periodic pension payments or the lump-sum distribution?
  b. What are the possible tax consequences that might occur if Vicki does not file estimated tax payments?
  c. What percentage rate is used to determine the amount withheld from periodic pension payments and lump-sum distributions?

I14-13 Although Virginia is entitled to five personal and dependency exemptions, she claims only one withholding allowance on Form W-4.
  a. Is it permissible to claim fewer allowances than an individual is entitled to?
  b. Why would an individual claim fewer allowances?

I14-14 Mario is a college student who had no income tax liability in the prior year and expects to have no tax liability for the current year.
  a. What steps should Mario take to avoid having amounts being withheld from his summer employment wages?
  b. What are the cash-flow implications to Mario if the employer withholds federal income taxes?

I14-15 What is backup withholding? What is its purpose?

I14-16 Under what circumstances may an individual claim additional withholding allowances on Form W-4?

I14-17 In April 1997, Vincent anticipates that his actual tax liability for 1997 will be $12,000 and that the federal income taxes withheld from his salary will be $11,600. His actual federal income tax liability for 1995 was $8,000 and his AGI for 1996 was not more than $150,000.
  a. Is Vincent required to make estimated tax payments in 1997?
  b. If no estimated tax payments are made, will Vincent be subject to an underpayment penalty if the actual tax liability for 1997 is $12,000? Why or why not?
  c. Will Vincent be subject to an underpayment penalty if his actual tax liability for 1997 is instead $25,000? Why?

I14-18 What tax planning strategy can you suggest to avoid the penalty for underpayment of estimated tax for an individual who has increasing levels of income each year and is uncertain regarding the amount of his or her estimated taxable income for any given year?

I14-19 From a cash-flow perspective, why is it generally preferable to have an underpayment of tax (assuming there is no underpayment penalty imposed) rather than an overpayment of tax?

I14-20 Why do many taxpayers intentionally overpay their tax through withholdings so as to obtain a tax refund?

I14-21 Discuss the underlying rationale for the following tax credit items:
  a. Foreign tax credit
  b. Research credit
  c. Business energy credit
  d. Work opportunity credit
  e. Child and dependent care credit
  f. Earned income credit
  g. Tax credit for the elderly
  h. Low-income housing credit
  i. Disabled access credit
  j. Empowerment Zone employment credit
  k. Adoption credit

I14-22 If Congress is considering a tax credit or deduction as an incentive to encourage certain activities, is a $40 tax credit more valuable than a $200 tax deduction for a taxpayer with a 15% marginal rate? a 28% marginal rate?

I14-23 What are the more significant tax credit items included in the computation of the general business tax credit?

I14-24 Discuss the limitations that have been imposed on the claiming of the general business tax credit including the following:
  a. Overall ceiling limitation based on the tax liability

b. Priority of general business and personal credits

c. Carryback and carryover of unused credits (including the application of the FIFO method).

I14-25 Wayne is considering a foreign assignment for two years. He will earn approximately $70,000 in the foreign country and will be eligible for the foreign tax credit or the earned income exclusion. The effective tax rate on Wayne's earnings if fully taxable under U.S. law would be 30%. The effective tax rate for the foreign salary is 20% under the foreign country's laws.

a. Discuss in general terms the computation of the foreign tax credit and its limitation.

b. Would Wayne be better off electing the foreign tax credit or the earned income exclusion? Explain.

I14-26 King Corporation is expanding its business and is planning to hire four additional employees at an annual labor cost of $12,000 each. What will the tax consequences be if King hires employees who are eligible for the work opportunity credit?

I14-27 Queen Corporation has been in business since 1979. During the preceding year the company had 25 full-time employees and gross receipts of $8,000,000. During the current year Queen spent $10,000 to install access ramps for disabled individuals. Is Queen Corporation eligible for the disabled access credit? If so, what is the credit amount and the basis reduction (if any) for the depreciable property?

I14-28 Discuss the special tax rules that apply to the tax credit for rehabilitation expenditures including the following:

a. Types of eligible expenditures

b. Applicable tax credit rates

c. Restrictions on depreciation methods

d. Calculation of basis for expenditures

e. Potential recapture of the credit

I14-29 What types of business property qualify for the business energy credit?

I14-30 What is the underlying reason for enactment of most of the personal tax credits?

I14-31 Discuss the difference between a refundable tax credit and a nonrefundable tax credit. Give at least one example of each type of credit.

I14-32 If an individual is unemployed and has no earned income, is it possible to receive a child and dependent care credit for otherwise qualifying child and dependent care expenses? Explain.

I14-33 What is the maximum child and dependent care credit available to an individual who has at least $4,800 of qualifying child care expenses and two or more qualifying children or incapacitated dependents?

I14-34 Vivian is a single taxpayer with two children who qualify for the child and dependent care credit. She incurred $5,000 of qualifying child care expenses during the current year. She also received $3,000 in reimbursements from her employer from a qualified employee dependent care assistance program. What is the maximum child and dependent care credit available to Vivian?

I14-35 The adoption credit is intended to assist taxpayers with the financial burden of adopting children.

a. Discuss how the credit is computed.

b. Why did Congress impose a phase-out of the credit for taxpayers based on AGI?

I14-36 Alice is single and is 37 years old with two qualifying children, ages 3 and 6. She receives $2,500 alimony and $8,000 of wages and has $10,500 of AGI. Is Alice eligible for the earned income credit? If so, is it possible for her to receive advance payments of the credit amounts rather than receiving a tax refund when the tax return is filed?

I14-37 Why are most elderly people unable to qualify for the tax credit for the elderly?

ISSUE IDENTIFICATION QUESTIONS

I14-38 Daryl is an executive who has an annual salary of $120,000. He is considering early retirement so that he can pursue a career as a management consultant. Daryl estimates that he could earn approximately $80,000 annually from his consulting business. What tax issues should Daryl consider?

I14-39 Jennifer recently received a check for $30,000 and securities with an FMV of $200,000 from her former husband. The $30,000 represents back alimony and the securities were transferred pursuant to the property settlement. What tax issues should Jennifer consider?

I14-40 Coastal Corporation is planning an expansion of its production facilities and is considering whether to hire additional employees from economically disadvantaged groups so as to be able to avail itself of the targeted jobs credit. The company plant is not located in an Empowerment Zone. New employees are paid approximately $18,000 per year. If economically disadvantaged employees are hired, additional job training expenses of $5,000 per employee will be required. What tax issues should Coastal consider with regard to the hiring and training of its new employees?

PROBLEMS

I14-41 *AMT Computation.* William, a married taxpayer who files a joint return with his spouse, reports the following items in the current year:

Taxable income	$50,000
Tax preferences	50,000
AMT adjustments related to itemized deductions	30,000
Regular tax liability	12,000

a. What is William's AMT liability in the current year?
b. What is William's AMT liability in the current year if he is instead a single taxpayer?
c. What is William's AMT liability if he files a joint return and his AMT adjustments are $60,000 instead of $30,000?

I14-42 *AMT Computation.* Jose, a single taxpayer with no dependents, reports the following items in the current year:

Taxable income	$130,000
Tax preferences	40,000
AMT adjustments related to itemized deductions	30,000
Regular tax liability	36,440

What is Jose's AMT liability in the current year?

I14-43 *AMT Tax Preferences.* Allison, a single taxpayer, reports the following items on her federal income tax return in the current year:

Excess depreciation on real property placed in service in 1986	$ 20,000
Excess depreciation on personal property placed in service in 1993	10,000
Net long-term capital gain	20,000
Charitable contribution of capital gain real property having a $100,000 FMV and a $70,000 basis	30,000
Tax-exempt municipal bond interest (private activity bonds)	30,000

What is the amount of Allison's tax preferences for purposes of computing the AMT in the current year?

I14-44 *AMT Adjustments and Computation of Tax.* Allen, a single taxpayer, reports the following items on his current year federal income tax return:

Adjusted gross income	$75,000
Taxable income	30,000
Regular tax liability	6,000
Tax preferences	25,000

Itemized deductions including:	
Charitable contributions	7,500
Medical expenses (before AGI floor)	10,000
Mortgage interest on personal residence	10,000
State income taxes	5,000
Real estate taxes	8,000

a. What is the amount of Allen's AMT adjustments related to the itemized deductions?

b. What is Allen's AMT liability for the current year?

I14-45 *Self-Employment Tax.* In the current year Amelia receives wages of $30,000 and net earnings from a small unincorporated business of $50,000. What is the amount of Amelia's self-employment tax and *for* AGI deduction relative to her self-employment tax?

I14-46 *Self-Employment Tax.* Arnie and Angela are married and file a joint return in the current year. Arnie is a partner in a public accounting firm. His share of the partnership's income in the current year is $40,000, and he receives guaranteed payments of $30,000. Angela receives wages of $50,000 from a large corporation. What is each taxpayer's self-employment tax amount?

I14-47 *Self-Employment Tax.* Anita, a single taxpayer, reports the following items for the current year:

Salary (subject to withholding)	$20,000
Director's fees	10,000
Consulting fees	10,000
Expenses related to consulting practice	(15,000)

a. What is the amount of Anita's self-employment tax?

b. How would your answer to Part a change if Anita's salary were instead $70,000?

I14-48 *Penalties for Nonpayment of Withholding and FICA Taxes.* Lake Corporation has some severe cash-flow problems. You are the company's financial and tax consultant. The treasurer of the company has informed you that the company has failed to make FICA and federal income tax withholding payments for both the employer and employee contributions to the IRS for a period of approximately six months.

a. What advice can you give to the company treasurer regarding the nonpayment of taxes?

b. Can the liability for payment of the taxes extend to parties other than the corporation? Explain.

I14-49 *Exemptions from Withholding.* Which of the following categories of individuals or income are exempt from the federal withholding tax requirements?

a. Domestic servants

b. Independent contractors

c. Newspaper carriers over age 18

d. Bonuses

e. Commissions

f. Vacation pay

g. Tips under $20 per month from a single employer

h. Nontaxable fringe benefits

i. Pensions

I14-50 *Withholding Exemptions.* Barry is a college student who is employed as a waiter during the summer. He earns approximately $1,500 during the summer and estimates that he will not be required to file a tax return and will have no federal income tax liability. Last year, however, he made $6,000 and was required to file a return and pay $400 in taxes. Barry is single and is supported by his parents. He has no dependents and does not have any other sources of income or deductions.

a. Can Barry claim an exempt status on Form W-4 for withholding purposes?

b. Can Barry claim more than one exemption on Form W-4 (e.g., additional withholding allowances or the standard deduction allowance) to minimize the amount withheld? Explain.

I14-51 *Witholding Allowances.* Bart's spouse is not employed. They plan to file a joint return. Bart obtains a new job and is asked to fill out a Form W-4. His monthly gross earnings will be $3,000. Bart, who has four dependent children, can claim three additional withholding allowances because he is obligated to pay substantial alimony to his ex-wife.

a. What is the correct number of withholding allowances that he may claim on Form W-4?

b. What is the amount of federal income tax to be withheld using the wage bracket tables (in Figure I14-1)?

c. What disclosure procedures must Bart's employer follow if Bart claims more than ten allowances?

I14-52 *Estimated Tax Requirements.* Anna does not make quarterly estimated tax payments even though she has substantial amounts of income that are not subject to withholding. Last year Anna's tax liability was $18,000. This year Anna's actual tax liability is $30,000, although only $18,200 was withheld from her salary. Anna's AGI for the prior year was not over $150,000.

a. Is Anna subject to the underpayment penalty? Why?

b. If Anna's withholdings were only $15,000, would she be subject to the underpayment penalty? Why?

c. If Anna is subject to an underpayment penalty, can she deduct this amount as interest? Explain.

I14-53 *Estimated Tax Underpayment Penalty.* Anne's estimated tax payments for the current year are $8,000. Her withholdings amount to $12,000. Anne's actual tax liability for the current year and for the prior year are $25,000 and $19,000, respectively. Her income is earned evenly throughout the current year. Anne's AGI for the prior year was $160,000. Is Anne subject to the underpayment penalty? Explain.

I14-54 *Computation of Tax Credits.* Becky's tentative tax credits for the current year include the following:

Targeted jobs credit	$ 1,000
Child and dependent care credit	960
Research credit	14,000
Business energy credit	600
Total	$16,560

Becky's regular tax liability before credits is $14,000. Assume that there is no alternative minimum tax liability.

a. What is the amount of allowable personal tax credits?

b. What is the amount of allowable business tax credits?

c. What treatment is accorded to the unused tax credits for the current year?

I14-55 *Business Tax Credit Carrybacks and Carryovers.* In 1997 Large Corporation, which was incorporated in 1991, has an unused general business tax credit of $40,000 in 1994. The following schedule shows the amount of business tax credits earned and used for the period 1991–1997:

	Credits Earned During the Year	Credit Limitation for the Carryback or Carryover Year
1991	$40,000	$40,000
1992	30,000	40,000
1993	25,000	25,000
1994	60,000	20,000
1995	20,000	22,000
1996	15,000	20,000
1997	15,000	15,000

The excess credits for 1994 were carried back to 1991, the initial year of operation.
a. How much of the unused 1994 credit is used in the carryback period?
b. What is the amount of the unused credit that is carried foward to 1995? In what years are the credits used?
c. What is the amount of the general business credit carryovers to 1998? Identify the tax years in which the credit carryovers are earned.

I14-56 *Foreign Tax Credit.* Laser Corporation has a foreign office that conducts business in France. Laser pays foreign taxes of $40,000 on foreign-source taxable income of $100,000. Its U.S.-source taxable income is $200,000 and the total U.S. tax liability (before reductions for the foreign tax credit) is $100,250. What is Laser's foreign tax credit? What is Laser's foreign tax credit carryback or carryover?

I14-57 *Work Opportunity Credit.* Last Corporation hires two economically disadvantaged youths (qualified for the work opportunity credit) in August of the current year. Each employee receives $8,000 of wages in the current year. Salaries and wages paid to other employees in the current year are $50,000. Last Corporation has a regular tax liability of $50,000 in the current year before deducting its tax credits assuming the appropriate deduction is claimed for the youths' salaries. Its tentative minimum tax is $10,000. Business tax credits other than the work opportunity credit amount to $50,000 in the current year.
a. What is Last Corporation's tentative work opportunity credit (before limitations) in the current year?
b. What is Last Corporation's total general business credit that is used in the current year? What amount is available for carryover or carryback?
c. What is Last Corporation's deduction for salaries and wages paid to the two youths?

I14-58 *Empowerment Zone Employment Credit.* Acorn Corporation operates its business in an Empowerment Zone and John, one of its employees, lives in the zone. In the current year John received $12,000 in wages. In addition, Acorn incurred $4,000 of training expenses related to John's employment.
a. What is Acorn Corporation's tentative Empowerment Zone credit (before any limitations on the general business credit are considered)?
b. What is Acorn Corporation's deduction for wages paid to John?

I14-59 *Rehabilitation Tax Credit.* Bob acquires a certified historic structure in the current year to be used as an office for his business. He pays $20,000 for the building (exclusive of the land) and spends $40,000 for renovation costs.
a. What is the rehabilitation tax credit (before limitations)?
b. What depreciation method(s) must be used for the property?
c. What is the basis of the building for MACRS depreciation purposes?

I14-60   *Child and Dependent Care Credit.* In each of the following independent situations, determine the amount of the child and dependent care tax credit. (Assume that both taxpayers are employed.)

    a. Brad and Bonnie are married and file a joint return. Brad and Bonnie have earned income of $40,000 and $14,000, respectively. Their combined AGI is $52,000. They have two children ages 10 and 12 and employ a live-in nanny at an annual cost of $9,000.

    b. Assume the same facts as in Part a, except that Brad and Bonnie employ Bonnie's mother as the live-in nanny. Bonnie's mother is not claimed as a dependent by her children.

    c. Bruce is divorced and has two children ages 10 and 16. He has AGI and earned income of $27,000. Bruce incurs qualifying child care expenses of $8,000 during the year which were incurred equally for both children. Bruce's employer maintains an employee dependent care assistance program. $1,000 was paid to Bruce from this program and excluded from Bruce's gross income.

    d. Buddy and Candice are married and file a joint return. Their combined AGI is $50,000. Buddy earns $46,000, and Candice's salary from a part-time job is $4,000. They incur $5,000 of qualifying child care expenses for a day-care facility for their two children, ages 2 and 4.

I14-61   *Adoption Credit.* Brad and Valerie decided to adopt a child and contacted an adoption agency in August, 1997. After extensive interviews and other requirements (such as financial status, etc.), Brad and Valerie were approved as eligible parents to adopt a child. The agency indicated that it might take up to two years to find a proper match. In November, 1998, Brad and Valerie adopted an infant daughter (not a special needs child). Below is a list of expenses that they incurred:

1997:	Agency fees (first installment)	$5,000
	Travel expenses for interviews, etc.	1,500
	Publications for prospective adoptive parents	300
	Legal fees connected with the adoption	1,000
	Kennel fees for dog while on adoption trips	250
1998:	Agency fees (final installment)	$3,000
	Travel expenses	400
	Court costs for adoption	200
	Kennel fees	100
	Nursery furniture (baby's room) and supplies	2,000

Brad and Valerie's AGI for 1997 was $70,000 and in 1998 was $90,000.

    a. Compute Brad and Valerie's qualified adoption expenses for 1997 and 1998.

    b. Compute Brad and Valerie's adoption credit. What year(s) may the credit be taken?

    c. Would your answer to b. change if the adopted child was a special needs child?

I14-62   *Earned Income Credit.* Carolyn has a dependent child, age 6, who lived with her for the entire year. She has earned income of $9,000 of wages and $4,000 of alimony in the current year. Her AGI is $13,000.

    a. What is Carolyn's tentative earned income credit (before the phase-out reduction is applied)?

    b. What is Carolyn's allowable earned income credit?

    c. If Carolyn has no income tax liability (before the earned income credit is subtracted), is she entitled to a tax refund in the current year?

I14-63   *Earned Income Credit.* Jose is single with no qualifying children. He has $7,000 of wages during the current year and is otherwise eligible for the earned income credit. Jose has $1,000 of interest income and no *for* AGI deductions. His AGI is $8,000.

a. What is Jose's tentative earned income credit before the phase-out reduction is applied?

b. What is Jose's allowable earned income credit?

c. If Jose has no income tax liability (before the earned income credit is subtracted), is he entitled to a refund for the current year?

I14-64 *Tax Credit for the Elderly.* Caroline, age 66 and single, receives the following income items for the current year:

Social Security payments	$ 3,000
Fully taxable pension	4,000
Dividend and interest income	4,500
Total	$11,500

Caroline's tax liability (before credits) is $300 in the current year.

a. What is Caroline's tentative tax credit for the elderly (before the tax liability limitation is applied) in the current year?

b. What is the amount of Caroline's allowable tax credit for the elderly in the current year?

COMPREHENSIVE PROBLEM

I14-65 Chuck's tax file reveals the following information for the current year:

Salary		$35,000
Net income from consulting (before deducting one-half of self-employment taxes paid)		30,000
Net loss from an unincorporated business		(10,000)
Itemized deductions:		
State and local taxes	$6,000	
Mortgage interest on personal residence	8,000	
Contributions	2,000	
Credit for child and dependent care		500
General business tax credits		500
Estimated taxes paid and withholdings from salary		7,500
Actual income tax liability for the current year (after credits)		10,000
Actual income tax liability for the prior year		7,000
AGI for the prior year		60,000
Personal and dependency exemptions		4
Filing status: Married filing jointly		

a. Is Chuck subject to the self-employment tax? If so, what are the self-employment tax liability and the amount of self-employment taxes that may be deducted on Chuck's income tax return?

b. Is Chuck subject to the estimated income tax underpayment penalty? Explain.

TAX FORM/RETURN PREPARATION PROBLEMS

TAX CUT

I14-66 Warren (SSN 123-45-6789) and Alice (SSN 987-65-4321) Williams have the following tax credits for the current year:

General business credits	$12,140
Child and dependent care credit	960
Total	$13,100

Warren and Alice Williams have two children, 5 and 7, and incur $5,000 of qualifying child care expenses ($2,500 for day care and $2,500 for a nurse). Each spouse had earned income of $25,000 and their AGI is $50,000. Their regular tax liability (before credits) is $20,000. Disregard any limitations that might be imposed by the tentative minimum tax.

Complete Form 2441 and the Tax Credits section on page 2 of Form 1040.

TAX CUT

I14-67 Harold Milton (Soc. Sec. no. 574-45-5477) is single. He had the following income and deductions for the current year:

Salary	$77,000	State income taxes	8,000
Interest income	12,000	Mortgage interest expense	
Dividend income	3,000	on residence	19,000
IRA contribution	2,000	Interest expense on car loan	3,000
Tax-exempt interest		Real estate taxes	
from private activity		on residence	2,000
bonds issued in 1990	24,000	Miscellaneous deductions	
Charitable contributions	27,000	(subject to the 2% AGI floor)	7,000
		Income taxes withheld	9,000

Complete Form 1040, Schedule A, and Form 6251.

CASE STUDY PROBLEMS

I14-68 Barbara was divorced in 1994. However, the final property settlement and determination of alimony payments was not made until February 1997 because of extended litigation. Barbara received a $20,000 payment of back alimony in March 1997 and will receive monthly alimony payments of $2,000 for the period April through December 1997. In 1996, Barbara's income consisted of $15,000 salary and $2,000 of taxable interest income. She uses the standard deduction and has no dependents. In 1996 Barbara's tax liability was $1,900. She expects to continue working at an annual salary of $15,000 and have $2,000 of interest income in 1997. Her monthly alimony payments of $2,000 are also expected to continue for an indefinite period.

In April 1997 Barbara requests your advice regarding the payment of quarterly estimated taxes for 1997. Prepare a memo to your client that discusses these requirements, including any possible penalties for not making quarterly payments and nontax issues such as cash-flow and investment income decisions.

I14-69 Chips-R-Us is a computer technology corporation that designs hardware and software for use in large businesses. The corporation regularly pays individuals to install programs and give advice to different companies that buy their software. In the current year, Simone, a computer expert, was sent to a customer of Chips-R-Us by the corporation to perform computer services. Simone is not a regular employee of the corporation and the corporation did not train Simone for the task. Simone keeps track of the time spent on the job at the customer and reports to the corporation, which pays Simone for her services. The corporation specifies the work to be done for their client. The corporation can also replace Simone with another individual if her work is not satisfactory. Chips-R-Us treats Simone as an independent contractor for employment tax purposes. In the current year the IRS challenges the corporation that it has failed to remit FICA taxes and income taxes that should have been withheld with respect to Simone's employment. Chips-R-Us refuses to pay the amount, stating that it is not required to do so because Simone is not an employee of the corporation. What will be the likely outcome of the

IRS's decision concerning the status of Simone as an employee or independent contractor? Who may be liable for payment of the employment taxes, interest, and penalties to the government? What ethical responsibilities should be followed in the remittance of taxes on behalf of an employee?

TAX RESEARCH PROBLEM

I14-70
Lean Corporation was incorporated in 1981 by Bruce Smith, who has served as an officer and member of the Board of Directors. Carl Jones has served as the secretary-treasurer of the company as a convenience to his friend Bruce Smith. He acted as a part-time bookkeeper but did not run the everyday business affairs and paid only the bills he was instructed to pay. Carl was an authorized signatory for the corporate bank accounts but had no final control over expenditures.

Beginning in the last quarter of 1996, the company failed to pay all of the taxes withheld from employees and the employer's share of FICA taxes to the IRS. Despite this delinquency, the corporation continued to pay other creditors, including its employees, in preference to the IRS.

In January 1997, Lean Corporation entered into an installment agreement with the IRS to keep current on its withholding taxes and to make payments on the past due balance until paid in full. The company subsequently defaulted on the agreement in April 1997. During this period, Bruce Smith was serving as chief financial officer and was a member of the Board of Directors. He had the authority to make policy decisions. He was responsible for negotiating the installment agreement with the IRS and the decision to default on the agreement.

Who is liable for the penalty for the nonpayment of the payroll tax withholdings? A partial list of research sources is

- Sec. 6672

- *Ernest W. Carlson v. U.S.*, 67 AFTR 2d 91-1104, 91-1 USTC ¶50,262 (D.C. UT, 1991)

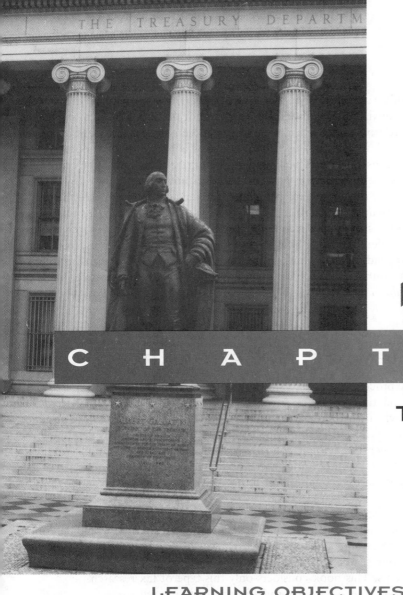

CHAPTER 15

TAX RESEARCH

LEARNING OBJECTIVES

After studying this chapter, you should be able to

1. Describe the steps in the tax research process

2. Explain how the facts affect the tax consequences

3. Enumerate the sources of tax law and understand the authoritative value of each

4. Use the tax services and/or electronic resources to research an issue

5. Use the citator to assess authorities

6. Understand the guidelines to which CPAs in tax practice should adhere

7. Prepare work papers and communications to clients

This chapter introduces the reader to the tax research process. Its major focus is the sources of the tax law (i.e., the statutory and other authorities that constitute the federal tax laws) and the relative weights that are given to these sources. The steps in the tax research process are described, and particular emphasis is placed on the importance of the facts to the tax consequences. The chapter also describes how to use the citator and the most frequently used tax services and computer resources.

The end product of the tax research process—written communication of the results to an interested party in the form of a client letter—is also discussed. This text uses a hypothetical set of facts to provide a comprehensive illustration of the research process. Sample work papers demonstrating how to document the results of the research efforts are included in Appendix A. In addition, the text discusses the American Institute of Certified Public Accountants' (AICPA's) guidelines for CPAs in tax practice, its *Statements on Responsibilities in Tax Practice*. These statements are included in Appendix E.

OVERVIEW OF TAX RESEARCH

Tax research is the process of solving a specific tax-related question on the basis of both tax law sources and the specific circumstances surrounding the particular situation. Sometimes this activity involves researching several issues. Tax research can also be aimed at determining tax policy. For example, policy-oriented research would determine the extent (if any) to which the amount contributed to charitable organizations would be likely to change if such contributions were no longer deductible. This type of tax research is usually done by economists in order to assess the effect of actions by the government.

Tax research can also be conducted to determine the tax consequences to a particular taxpayer of a certain transaction. For example, client-oriented research would determine whether Smith Corporation could deduct a particular expenditure as a trade or business expense. This type of research is generally conducted by accounting and law firms for the benefit of their clients. This book considers only this type of tax research.

Client-oriented tax research is performed in one of two contexts:

KEY POINT

Closed-fact situations allow the tax advisor the least amount of flexibility. Because the facts are already established, the tax advisor must develop the best solution possible within certain predetermined constraints.

1. **Closed-fact or tax compliance situations:** The client contacts the tax advisor after a transaction has occurred or a question arises while the tax return preparer is preparing the client's tax return. Unfortunately, in such situations, the tax consequences can be costly because the facts cannot be restructured to obtain more favorable tax results.

EXAMPLE I15-1 ▶

Tom advises Carol, his tax advisor, that on November 4 of the current year, he sold land held as an investment for $500,000 cash. His basis in the land was $50,000. On November 9, Tom reinvested the sales proceeds in another plot of investment land costing $500,000. This is a closed-fact situation. Tom wants to know the amount and the character of the gain (if any) he must recognize. Because the tax advisor's advice is solicited after the sale and reinvestment occur, the opportunity for tax planning is limited. The opportunity to defer taxes by using a like-kind exchange or an installment sale has been lost. ◀

KEY POINT

Open-fact or tax-planning situations allow a tax advisor the flexibility to help structure the transaction to accomplish the client's objectives. In this type of situation, a creative tax advisor can often save taxpayers considerable tax dollars through effective tax planning.

2. **Open-fact or tax-planning situations:** The client contacts the tax advisor before the transaction has been finalized. Sometimes, the tax advisor is even approached to discuss the available tax strategies before any particular transaction is decided upon. Tax-planning situations are generally more difficult and challenging because the tax advisor must keep in mind both the client's tax and nontax objectives. Most clients will not be interested in a transaction that minimizes their taxes if it is inconsistent with their nontax objectives.

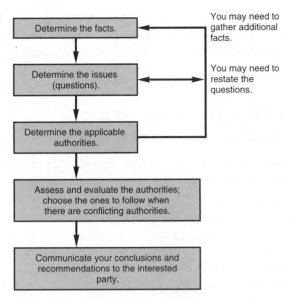

FIGURE I15-1 ▶ STEPS IN THE TAX RESEARCH PROCESS

EXAMPLE I15-2 ▶ Diane seeks advice from Carol, her tax advisor, about how to minimize her estate taxes and pass the most property to her descendants. Diane is a widow with three children and five grandchildren and at present has property valued at $10,000,000. This is an open-fact situation. Carol could advise Diane to leave all but a few hundred thousand dollars of her property to a charitable organization so that her estate would owe no estate taxes. Although this recommendation would minimize Diane's estate taxes, Diane would reject it because she wants her children or grandchildren to be her primary beneficiaries. Thus, reducing estate taxes to zero is inconsistent with her objective of allowing her descendants to receive as much after-tax wealth as possible. ◀

When doing tax research in the context of tax planning, the tax professional needs to keep a number of points in mind. First, the objective is not to minimize taxes per se but rather to maximize the after-tax return. For example, if the federal income tax rate is a constant 40%, an investor should not buy a tax-exempt bond yielding 5% when he could buy a corporate bond of equal risk that yields 9% before tax and 5.4% after tax, even though his explicit taxes (his actual tax liability) would be minimized with the investment in the tax-exempt bond.[1] Second, one does not engage in unilateral transactions; thus, the tax ramifications to all parties to a contract are relevant. For example, in the executive compensation context, employees may prefer to receive incentive stock options (because income recognition is postponed until the stock is sold), but the employer receives no tax deduction with respect to incentive stock options. Thus, the employer might grant a different number of options if it uses one type of stock option versus another as compensation. Third, taxes are but one cost of doing business. In deciding where to locate a manufacturing plant, for example, factors more important to some businesses than the amount of state and local taxes might be the proximity to raw materials and good transportation systems, the cost of labor, the quantity of skilled labor available, and the quality of life in the area. Fourth, the time for tax planning is not restricted to when one enters into an investment, contract, or other arrangement; the time extends

ADDITIONAL COMMENT

It is important to consider non-tax objectives as well as tax objectives. In many situations, the nontax considerations outweigh the tax considerations. Thus, the plan that is eventually adopted by a taxpayer may not always be the best when viewed strictly from a tax perspective.

---

[1] For an excellent discussion of explicit and implicit taxes and tax planning see Myron S. Scholes and Mark A. Wolfson, *Taxes and Business Strategy: A Planning Approach* (Englewood Cliffs, NJ: Prentice Hall, 1992), Chs. 1, 2, 5, and 7. See also Chapter I18. An example of an implicit tax is the excess of the before-tax earnings on a taxable bond over the risk-adjusted before-tax earnings on a tax-favored investment (e.g., a municipal bond).

throughout the life of the activity. As tax rules change or as the environment changes, the tax advisor needs to reevaluate whether the taxpayer should continue with an investment and determine the transaction costs of making changes.

STEPS IN THE TAX RESEARCH PROCESS

In both the open-fact and closed-fact situations, the tax research process consists of the following five basic steps:

1. Determine the facts.
2. Determine the issues (questions).
3. Determine which authorities are applicable.
4. Assess and evaluate the authorities and choose which to follow in situations where the authorities are in conflict.
5. Communicate your conclusions and recommendations to the client.

Although the listing of the steps suggests that you proceed from one step to the next and then the next, the tax research process is often circular. That is, it does not always proceed step-by-step from the first through the fifth step. Figure I15-1 illustrates the steps in the process.

ADDITIONAL COMMENT

The steps of tax research, as outlined on this page, also provide an excellent format for a written tax communication. For example, a good format for a client memo includes (1) statement of facts, (2) list of issues, (3) discussion of relevant authority, and (4) recommendations to the client of appropriate actions that are based on the results of the research.

In a closed-fact situation, the facts are often self-evident. But if one is researching the tax consequences in an open-fact context, a number of the facts have not yet occurred, and the tax advisor's task is to determine which facts are likely to result in a particular tax outcome. This goal is accomplished by reviewing the authorities, especially court cases, and denoting which facts accompanied a favorable outcome and which produced an unfavorable result. For example, if a client hopes to achieve ordinary loss treatment from the anticipated sale of several plots of land in the current year, the advisor might compare and contrast the facts that were present in cases addressing this type of situation. The advisor should consider cases won and lost by the taxpayer.

Often, the research deals with a gray area (i.e., an issue for which no clear-cut, unequivocally correct solution exists). In such situations, it is best to pursue the issue through a specifically tailored set of detailed questions. For example, in researching whether the taxpayer may deduct a loss as an ordinary loss instead of a capital loss, the tax advisor may need to investigate whether the presence of any investment motive precludes classifying a loss as ordinary.

TYPICAL MISCONCEPTION

Many taxpayers think that the tax law is all black and white. However, most tax research deals with gray areas. Ultimately, the ability, when confronted with tough issues, to develop strategies that favor the taxpayer and then to find relevant authority to support those strategies will make a successful tax advisor.

Deciding on the particular issues that must be researched is one of the most challenging aspects of the research process. At times, the client may raise an explicit question, such as "May I deduct the costs of a winter trip to Florida recommended by my physician?" Often, however, the tax advisor must read the pertinent documents and other papers submitted by the taxpayer to formulate the issues for which an investigation is appropriate. Thus, one needs a fairly extensive knowledge of tax law in order to be able to determine which issues must be researched.[2]

The following example illustrates that frequently the tax advisor, once he or she becomes more familiar with tax law, must request additional information from the client. Example I15-3 assumes that all of the tax authorities are in agreement.

EXAMPLE I15-3 ▶

Mark calls his tax advisor, Al, and states that (1) he incurred a loss on renting his beach cottage during the current year and (2) he wonders whether he may deduct the loss. He also states

---

[2] Often supervisors will explain to a relatively new staff person the questions they think are appropriate issues to be researched. Based on the supervisor's past experience and knowledge, he or she will indicate the specific authorities he or she thinks will offer insight with respect to the tax consequences.

that he, his wife, and their minor child occupied the cottage only eight days during the current year.

Assume that this is the first time that Al has worked with the Sec. 280A vacation home rules. On reading Sec. 280A, Al learned that a loss is *not* deductible if Mark used the cottage as a residence for personal purposes for longer than the greater of (1) 14 days or (2) 10% of the number of days the unit was rented at a fair rental value. He also learned that the property is *deemed* to be used by the taxpayer for personal purposes on any days on which it is used by any member of his or her family (as defined in Sec. 267(c)(4)). The Sec. 267(c)(4) definition of family members includes brothers, sisters, spouse, ancestors, or lineal descendants (i.e., children and grandchildren).

Mark's eight-day use is not long enough to make the rental loss nondeductible. However, Al must inquire about the number of days, if any, Mark's brothers, sisters, or parents used the property. (He already has information about use by Mark, his spouse, and his lineal descendants.) In addition, Al must find out how many days the cottage was rented to other persons at a fair rental value. On obtaining such additional facts, Al proceeds to determine how to calculate the deductible expenses. Al then reaches his conclusion concerning the deductible loss, if any, and communicates it to Mark. Assume that the passive activity and at-risk rules restricting a taxpayer's ability to deduct losses from real estate activities will not pose a problem for Mark. (See Chapter 18 **of** *Prentice Hall's Federal Taxation: Individuals* for a comprehensive discussion of these topics.) ◄

Many firms require that a researcher's conclusions be communicated to the client in writing. Members or employees of such firms can answer questions orally, but their oral conclusions must be followed up with a written communication. According to the AICPA's *Statements on Responsibilities in Tax Practice* (reproduced in Appendix E).

> Although oral advice may serve a client's needs appropriately in routine matters or in well-defined areas, written communications are recommended in important, unusual, or complicated transactions. In the judgment of the CPA, oral advice may be followed by a written confirmation to the client.[3]

IMPORTANCE OF THE FACTS TO THE TAX CONSEQUENCES

OBJECTIVE 2

Explain how the facts affect the tax consequences

At times, the statute is difficult to interpret, and a dilemma arises concerning the tax results. For example, one of the requirements a taxpayer must meet to claim a personal exemption for another person is to provide more than half of such person's support.[4] Neither the Code nor the Regulations define support. Consequently, if a taxpayer purchased a used automobile costing $5,000 for an elderly parent whose only source of income was $4,800 of social security, a question would arise concerning whether the expenditure for the car constitutes support. The tax advisor would need to consult court cases and revenue rulings to find an interpretation of the word support.

In other situations, the statutory language may be quite clear, but there might be a question as to whether the taxpayer's transaction falls within the realm of the facts necessary to obtain the favorable tax consequences. The following discussion of two actual cases focuses on the importance of facts in determining the tax results. In each case the taxpayer was arguing about the proper deduction for salary expense for payments made to the shareholder's spouse. Any amounts deemed "unreasonable" would not be deductible.

---

[3] AICPA, *Statements on Responsibilities in Tax Practice*, No. 8, "Form and Content of Advice to Clients," 1991, Sec. .06.   [4] Sec. 152(a).

FACTS OF CASE WHERE TAXPAYER PARTIALLY WON

Excerpts of the *Summit Publishing Company, Inc.* case appear below.[5] The Tax Court concluded that the corporation was entitled to a deduction for a portion of the purported salary payments to the shareholder's spouse. The taxpayer is referred to as the "petitioner" and the government as the "respondent."

FINDINGS OF FACT

At all times pertinent to this case, petitioner, Summit Publishing Company, Inc. (Summit) was a Texas corporation with its primary place of business in San Antonio, Texas. During the taxable years ended October 31, 1982, and October 31, 1983, Summit paid corporate officer and employee Marcia J. Mogavero (Mrs. Mogavero) compensation in the amounts of $72,780 and $183,910, respectively. These amounts were deducted in arriving at Summit's taxable income for the years in issue. Respondent determined that reasonable compensation for Mrs. Mogavero for the taxable years ended October 31, 1982 and 1983, was $41,050 and $50,083, respectively, and disallowed the difference between the amount claimed and the amount determined.

Summit was incorporated during 1977 by Alfred G. Mogavero, Sr. (Mr. Mogavero) who, at all pertinent times, was Summit's sole shareholder and president. Mr. and Mrs. Mogavero were married around the time of petitioner's incorporation and continued to be married throughout the taxable years in issue.

Summit's business activity involved the publishing of an in-flight magazine for Southwest Airlines (Southwest). Summit also did a limited amount of typesetting, production, layout, and art work for other companies. . . . Kenneth E. Lively (Lively) worked for Mr. Mogavero nearly from the beginning and his expertise related to the editing-publishing or creative side of the business activity. Mr. Mogavero's expertise related to sales and management.

During 1977, . . . Mrs. Mogavero began to work at Summit. Prior to that time she had no job experience, no formal education beyond high school, or any special skills, other than typing. Initially, Mrs. Mogavero performed routine clerical tasks. In time, and during the years in issue, she performed the role of an office manager. Lively and Mr. Mogavero were principally responsible for publishing and sales. . . .

Mrs. Mogavero supervised the clerical and support personnel, oversaw accounts receivable and payable, and reviewed the credit worthiness of advertisers. Although Summit had an accountant, Mrs. Mogavero did some of the bookkeeping and assisted in the compilation of certain of the financial information necessary for top management. She also assisted in the approval and location or layout of advertisements. . . .

During the years in issue, Summit generally employed between 16 and 25 employees. . . .

Mr. Mogavero, as owner-operator of Summit, decided to increase Mrs. Mogavero's salary because the business was doing well. . . . [Between the taxable years ended October 31, 1978 through October 31, 1983 the firm's gross profit rose from $484,680 to $3,409,438. Mr. Mogavero's compensation was $52,900 and $927,530 for the taxable years ended October 31, 1978 and October 31, 1983, respectively. Mrs. Mogavero's compensation increased from $16,715 for the fiscal year ended October 31, 1978 to $183,910 for the fiscal year ended October 31, 1983.]

During the taxable years ended October 31, 1982 and 1983, Summit paid cash dividends to its sole shareholder in the amounts of $232,690 and $382,359, respectively.

OPINION

. . . Many factors are relevant in determining whether compensation is reasonable, and no single factor is decisive; the totality of the facts and circumstances must be weighed. . . .

---

[5] 1990 PH T.C. Memo ¶90,288, 59 TCM 833. In this and all other Tax Court cases, the *petitioner* is the person who originates the case—the taxpayer—and the government is the *respondent*. For an excellent discussion of how critical facts are for the outcome, see Robert L. Gardner and Dave N. Stewart, *Tax Research Techniques,* 4th. Ed., Rev. (New York: AICPA, 1993), pp. 11–53.

The parties in this case have focused on about six of the factors enumerated in *Foos v. Commissioner*, TC Memo 1981-61 [Para. 81,061 PH Memo TC]. In *Foos v. Commissioner*, supra, the following factors were referenced:

1. Employee's qualifications and training.
2. Nature, extent, and scope of his duties.
3. Responsibilities and hours involved.
4. Size and complexity of business.
5. Results of the employee's efforts.
6. Prevailing rates for comparable employees in comparable business.
7. Scarcity of other qualified employees.
8. Ratio of compensation to gross and net income (before salaries and Federal income tax) of the business.
9. Salary policy of the employer to its other employees.
10. Amount of compensation paid to the employee in prior years.
11. Employee's responsibility for employer's inception and/or success.
   . . . .
14. Correlation between the stockholder-employees' compensation and his stockholdings.
15. Corporate dividend history.
   . . . .

Employee's Qualifications and Training

Respondent argues that Mrs. Mogavero's educational background and training were insufficient to justify the level of compensation claimed by Summit. Petitioner agrees that Mrs. Mogavero "had limited qualifications" when she began working for Summit in 1977, but that she acquired "extensive on-the-job training" qualifying her for the position held.

We agree with petitioner's analysis on this point. . . . [I]t is likely that actual experience is more significant than academic achievement in the operation and success of a particular business, especially one which is relatively small and unique requiring the personal service of the particular employee. Moreover, when measuring the value of education as opposed to actual experience, greater weight should usually be afforded to actual and successful experience in a particular position or discipline.

Nature, Extent, and Scope of Employee's Work

Petitioner contends that Mrs. Mogavero should be characterized as second-in-command of Summit. Respondent counters that Mrs. Mogavero was relegated to the more menial tasks and the major contributions that resulted in Summit's success were made by Mr. Mogavero and Lively. Respondent also argues that Mrs. Mogavero's position (second-in-command) with Summit is "primarily a function of her marriage to [Mr. Mogavero]."

To the extent that the subject employee has an ownership interest or is related to the owner, we should carefully scrutinize the question of the reasonableness of compensation. . . . In so doing we find that Mrs. Mogavero did not receive, relative to her experience, a large beginning salary when she began working at Summit at a time when all agree that her experience and skill levels were not great. . . .

Mrs. Mogavero was responsible for the day to day administrative and financial operations of Summit. In addition to playing a significant role in the business relationship with Southwest, she was also primarily responsible for matters which had a direct effect on Summit's success. . . .

Most importantly, Mrs. Mogavero acted on Mr. Mogavero's behalf while he was away on the business of Summit. . . .

In summary, we have found that Mrs. Mogavero's importance and contribution to the success and operation of Summit are somewhere between Lively's and Mr. Mogavero's.

Summit's Salary Scale and Policy

Here, respondent points to the wide disparity between owner, family members and other nonowner, nonfamily employees. . . .

During the 2 years in issue, total officers' compensation increased 15 and 74 percent and total employees' compensation increased 41 and 28 percent. . . . [W]e find that petitioner appears to have had a relatively generous policy regarding the increases of officer and employee compensation. We also note that, in a relative sense, it may be appropriate to give larger raises to the officers, as opposed to other employees, if the officers' efforts were more instrumental to the success of the business. . . .

Compensation in Prior Years Size and Complexity of the Business

Regarding this aspect, respondent argues that Mrs. Mogavero's "salary increased from $16,715.53 per year to $183,910.00 per year over a period of only five years." Respondent cites several cases for the proposition that increases in salary should be a result of increases in responsibility. . . . Petitioner agrees that Mrs. Mogavero's salary was low and her experience was limited when she started with petitioner. Petitioner, however, argues that Mrs. Mogavero's salary increased in accord with her increased responsibilities in subsequent years.

. . . Considering that Summit's business was so successful, the number of employees supervised increased, inflationary indexing may have played a role, and Mrs. Mogavero played a significant role in some areas of the business which helped the business success, we believe that respondent has not determined sufficient compensation to Mrs. Mogavero for the years before the Court.

Prevailing Rates of Compensation in the Industry

. . . Accordingly, neither petitioner nor respondent has established, by expert testimony, or otherwise, the prevailing rates of compensation in this industry. We are herein limited to considering whether Mrs. Mogavero's salary is reasonable based upon the facts in the record.

Comparison of Salaries Paid with Summit's Gross and Net Income

. . . Petitioner argues that Mrs. Mogavero's salary was 2.71 and 15.34 percent of gross income and 7.55 and 13.42 percent of net income for the taxable years in issue. For the same 2 years Summit paid dividends to Mr. Mogavero (its sole shareholder) in the amounts of $232,690 and $382,359, which represented 24.14 and 27.89 percent of net income in those same 2 taxable years.

The relatively sizable dividends paid by petitioner (in addition to a relatively large salary to its president and sole shareholder) substantially diminish respondent's argument that there was a motive of tax avoidance in this case.

Summary

Our view of the record in this case results in our conclusion that Mrs. Mogavero's responsibilities and contribution to the success of Summit fell somewhere between those of Lively and Mr. Mogavero. . . . Additionally, Mrs. Mogavero did have certain responsibilities that directly contributed to the success of the business. . . .

[The court decided that a reasonable salary for Mrs. Mogavero for the taxable years ended October 31, 1982 and October 31, 1983 was $70,000 and $85,000, respectively (compared with $72,780 and $183,910 deducted on Summit's tax return).]

FACTS OF CASE WHERE TAXPAYER LOST

J.B.S. Enterprises, Inc. lost its case dealing with the deductibility of payments made to the sole shareholder's former wife.[6] The Tax Court held that the payments could not be characterized as salary.

FINDINGS OF FACT

Petitioner was a Texas corporation with its principal place of business in Fort Worth, Texas. . . . Petitioner owned three bars and restaurants in Fort Worth during the years at issue. Among the three bars was the Blues Bar, which opened for business during 1982. James B. Schusler, Mary Schusler's ex-husband, is petitioner's president and sole stockhold-

---

[6] 1991 PH T.C. Memo ¶91,254, 61 TCM 2,829.

er. James . . . and Mary . . . were separated during the years at issue. During this period Mary had only two sources of income, part-time secretarial work . . . and payments from petitioner. She had two minor children to support, as well as a child in college and a grown child. . . . Mary received the payments [in question] from petitioner, at James' direction. . . .

Schedule E (Compensation of Officers) of petitioner's Federal income tax returns (Form 1120) for the years at issue reported that Mary devoted "0%" of her time to business. Nevertheless, the return for the fiscal year ending April 30, 1986, reported that petitioner paid Mary compensation of $26,600 during the year, and claimed a business expense deduction for that amount. . . .

On its Federal income tax return for the year ending April 30, 1987, petitioner stated that it paid Mary a salary of $35,910 and claimed a business expense deduction in that amount. . . .

[The IRS agent disallowed the deduction for the payments to Mary. In its initial petition to the Tax Court the petitioner stated that an error was made in showing that the payments were made to Mary and that such payments should have been shown as made to James. Several months later, however, the petitioner amended its petition to the court and stated that Mary was Vice President and did in fact perform valuable services for the Corporation. It stated, further, that the amounts Mary received were reasonable in light of the services Mary performed and her experience and expertise.]

OPINION

. . . As a preliminary matter, we note that we attach little weight to the testimony of James, Mary, and Sue Ratcliff [the tax advisor]. The testimony, and documents which they signed under oath, are replete with inconsistencies.

. . . The statements made to Gerald Yentes [the IRS agent] and the [first] protest letter . . . indicate that Mary performed no services for petitioner. The only explanation petitioner offered for the inconsistency in its current position is Sue Ratcliff's testimony that she thought it would be advantageous, with respect to taxes, to initially declare that Mary performed no services. It is clear to us that petitioner's position in the instant case has been motivated throughout by tax considerations. Because of inconsistencies in testimony and sworn documents, we do not accept petitioner's recantation of its original position. . . .

While petitioner did introduce documents showing that Mary reviewed petitioner's monthly profit and loss statement, given her marital status, her dependence on petitioner for support, and comments made to Revenue Agent Gerald Yentes, we conclude her review

▼ TABLE I15-1

Summary Comparison of Facts in *Summit* and *J.B.S.*

Situation	Decision	
	Summit	*J.B.S.*
Type of taxpayer	Corporation	Corporation
Person to whom "salary" was paid	Spouse of sole shareholder	Former spouse of sole shareholder
Dividend history of corporation	Substantial dividends had been paid	Not disclosed
Profit history of corporation	Substantial increase over the years	Not disclosed
Services performed by recipient of salary	Extensive, valuable services	None

of the statements was for her own benefit, rather than for petitioner's. Petitioner introduced no other relevant documentary evidence. We find that petitioner has failed to carry its burden of proof, and that respondent has established that the payments at issue were a personal expense intended to provide support for Mary and her children.

COMPARISON OF THE FACTS OF THE TWO CASES

Table I15-1 provides a summary comparison of the two cases. Both taxpayers were corporations that claimed a salary deduction for payments they made to the spouse or former spouse of the sole shareholder. In *Summit* the IRS contended that only a portion of the amount claimed as a salary expense was nondeductible whereas in the *J.B.S.* case the IRS argued that none of the purported salary payments should be deductible. In *Summit* the spouse performed extensive, valuable services for the firm. In *J.B.S.*, however, the former spouse appears to have performed no services for the corporation. In *Summit* the corporation's gross profit and net income increased substantially between the date the firm was founded and the years for which the salary deduction was in question. The court record for *J.B.S.* does not discuss the firm's profitability. In *Summit*, because rather large dividends were paid to the sole shareholder, it did not appear that the objective for the payments to the shareholder's spouse was to have dividends masquerade as salary. In *J.B.S.* the taxpayer did not present any documentation to prove that the ex-wife of the sole shareholder actually performed services for *J.B.S.* Moreover, some of the testimony presented indicated that positions were being taken on the tax return to achieve the lowest tax liability for the corporation.

The court allowed expense deductions in *Summit* for a portion of the payments that the IRS argued constituted unreasonable compensation. The court was impressed with how valuable the services of the shareholder-spouse were to the firm; it also noted that dividends had been paid to the shareholder. The *J.B.S.* case is a primer in how not to structure a transaction. The sole shareholder seemed to be attempting to disguise support payments made to his former wife as salary expense. However, the recipient performed no services for which she should receive compensation.

ABILITY TO DESIGN A FACTUAL SITUATION FAVORING THE TAXPAYER

By using tax research, a tax advisor can recommend to a taxpayer who is about to enter into a transaction a way to structure the facts that should increase the likelihood that his travel expenses will be deductible. For example, suppose a taxpayer is assigned to work in a different location from the city (City X) where he is currently employed. The taxpayer would like to deduct the meals and lodging expenses incurred at the new location and the cost of travel thereto. To do so, he must establish that City X is his tax home and that he is away from City X only temporarily. Incidentally, Sec. 162 precludes a taxpayer from being classified as away from home if the employment period at the new location exceeds one year. The taxpayer wonders what would happen if he was originally assigned away from City X for ten months and eventually accepted permanent employment in the new location. Tax research reveals an IRS ruling that states that in these circumstances the employment will be treated as temporary *until* the date that the realistic expectation about the temporary nature of the assignment changes.[7] Thus, if the taxpayer is offered a permanent job in the new location, it will be to his tax advantage to postpone making a decision to accept the job so that the expectation about the temporary nature of the employment will not change until near the end of the initial ten-month period. As a result, a greater amount will qualify for deduction as travel-away-from-home expenses.

TYPICAL MISCONCEPTION

Many taxpayers believe tax practitioners spend most of their time preparing tax returns. In reality, providing tax advice that accomplishes the taxpayer's objectives is one of the most important responsibilities of a tax advisor.

---

[7] Rev. Rul. 93-86, 1993-2 C.B. 71.

THE SOURCES OF TAX LAW

KEY POINT

One of the reasons the tax law is so complex is that it comes from a variety of sources. This chapter highlights the three principal sources of the tax law: statutory, judicial, and administrative.

When tax advisors speak of tax law, they generally refer to more than simply the tax statutes that are passed by Congress. For the most part, tax statutes (legislation) contain very general language. Congress is not capable of anticipating every type of transaction in which taxpayers might engage. Moreover, even if Congress could do so, it would not be feasible for the statute (known as the *Internal Revenue Code*) to contain details addressing the tax consequences of all such transactions.

Because the language contained in the statute generally does not provide detailed guidance about the tax treatment of a particular transaction, interpretations—both administrative and judicial—are necessary. Administrative interpretations include, for example, Treasury regulations, revenue rulings, and revenue procedures. Judicial interpretations consist of court decisions. The term *tax law* as used by most tax advisors encompasses administrative and judicial interpretations in addition to the statute. It also includes committee reports issued by the Congressional committees involved in the legislative process.

THE LEGISLATIVE PROCESS

Chapter I1 of *Prentice Hall's Federal Taxation: Individuals* describes the legislative process. That process is summarized here as well. All tax legislation must begin in the House of Representatives. The committee responsible for initiating statutory changes dealing with taxation is the Ways and Means Committee. Once proposed legislation is approved by the Ways and Means Committee, it goes to the floor of the House for consideration by the full membership. Legislation approved by a majority vote in the House then goes to the Senate, where it is considered by the Senate Finance Committee. The bill moves from the Finance Committee to the full Senate. Upon being approved by the Senate, the bill goes to the President for approval or veto, provided the House and Senate versions of the bill are in complete agreement. If the President signs the bill, it becomes law. If the President vetoes the bill, Congress can override the veto by a vote of at least two-thirds of the members of each house.

Often, the House and Senate versions are not in complete agreement. Whenever the two versions of a bill are not identical, the bill goes to a Conference Committee,[8] consisting of members of each house, and the revised bill goes back to the House and Senate for approval. For example, in 1990 the House and Senate disagreed about the earned income credit. The House approved a higher increase in the credit percentage than did the Senate. The Senate's provision provided one credit percentage for taxpayers with one qualifying child and a higher percentage for taxpayers with two or more children. The Conference Committee compromised by choosing a different rate from either of the two houses and approving different rates, depending on whether there was one child or two or more children. The House and Senate approved the Conference version.

Before embarking on drafting statutory changes, both the House of Representatives and the Senate often hold hearings at which various persons testify. Often the Secretary of the Treasury or another member of the Treasury Department offers extensive testimony. Generally, persons testifying express their opinions concerning provisions that should or should not be enacted. The U.S. Government Printing Office publishes the statements made at the hearings.

Most major legislation is also accompanied by Committee Reports. These reports, published by the U.S. Government Printing Office as separate publications and as part of the *Cumulative Bulletin*, explain Congress's purpose in drafting legislation.[9] Because

KEY POINT

Committee Reports can be very helpful in interpreting new legislation because these reports indicate the intent of Congress. Due to the proliferation of tax legislation, Committee Reports are especially important because the Treasury is often unable to draft the needed regulations in a timely manner.

---

[8] The size of the Conference Committee can vary. It is made up of an equal number of members from the House and the Senate.

[9] The *Cumulative Bulletin* is described in the discussion of revenue rulings on page I15-16.

Committee Reports give clues to Congressional intent, they can be invaluable aids in interpreting the statute, especially in situations where there are no regulations concerning the statutory language in question.

EXAMPLE I15-4 ▶ In 1984 Congress enacted Sec. 7872 of the Internal Revenue Code concerning the tax treatment of below-market-interest-rate loans. One subset of the rules applies to "gift loans," defined in Sec. 7872(f)(3) as "any below-market loan where the forgoing of interest is in the nature of a gift." The Conference Report elaborates on the transactions classified as gift loans as follows: "In general, there is a gift if property (including forgone interest) is transferred for less than full and adequate consideration under circumstances where the transfer is a gift for gift tax purposes. A sale, exchange, or other transfer made in the ordinary course of business . . . generally is considered as made for full and adequate consideration. A loan between unrelated persons can qualify as a gift loan."[10] This definition was quite important to a tax advisor because the Treasury did not issue proposed regulations on the Sec. 7872(f)(3) definition until ten months after the statute was enacted. Until such regulations were issued, this definition may have been the only "authoritative" interpretation available concerning the term "gift loans". ◀

THE INTERNAL REVENUE CODE

The Internal Revenue Code (the Code), which constitutes Title 26 of the federal statutes, is the foundation of all tax law. First codified (i.e., organized into a single compilation of the internal revenue statutes) in 1939, the law was recodified in 1954. The Code was known as the Internal Revenue Code of 1954 until 1986, when its name was changed to the Internal Revenue Code of 1986. Whenever changes to the statute are approved, the old language is deleted and the new language added. Thus, the statutes are organized as a single document, and a researcher does not have to read through the applicable parts of all previous tax bills to find the current version of the law.

The Code contains provisions addressing income taxes, estate and gift taxes, employment taxes, alcohol and tobacco taxes, and other excise taxes. For purposes of organization, the Code (Title 26) is subdivided into subtitles, chapters, subchapters, parts,

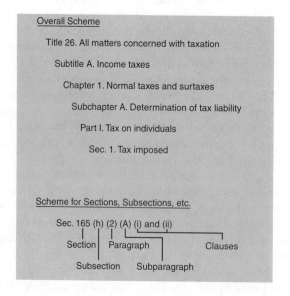

FIGURE I15-2 ▶ ORGANIZATIONAL SCHEME OF THE INTERNAL REVENUE CODE

---

[10] H. Rept. No. 98-861, 98th Cong., 2d Sess., p. 1,018 (1984).

subparts, sections, subsections, paragraphs, subparagraphs, and clauses. Subtitle A contains the rules concerning income taxes, and Subtitle B focuses on estate and gift taxes. A set of provisions concerned with one general area generally constitutes a subchapter. For example, the topics of corporate distributions and adjustments and partners and partnerships appear in Subchapters C and K, respectively. Figure I15-2 presents the organizational scheme of the Code.

A section is the organizational category that tax advisors refer to most often. For example, they speak of "Sec. 351 transactions," "Sec. 306 stock," and "Sec. 1231 gains and losses." Although it is generally not important to differentiate between a section and a paragraph or a part, one must be familiar with the Code's organizational scheme in order to read and interpret it correctly. The language of the Code is replete with cross-references to titles, paragraphs, subparagraphs, and so on.

EXAMPLE I15-5 ▶ Section 7701, a definitional section, begins by stating, "When used in this title . . ." and then lists a series of definitions. Thus, a definition in Sec. 7701 applies for all of Title 26; that is, it applies for purposes of the income tax, estate and gift tax, excise tax, and so on. ◀

EXAMPLE I15-6 ▶ Section 302(b)(3) allows taxpayers whose stock holdings are completely terminated in a redemption (a corporation's purchase of its stock from one of its shareholders) to receive capital gain treatment on the excess of the redemption proceeds over the stock's basis instead of ordinary income treatment on the entire proceeds. Section 302(c)(2)(A) states, "In the case of a distribution described in subsection (b)(3), section 318(a)(1) shall not apply if. . . ." Further, Sec. 302(c)(2)(C)(i) indicates "Subparagraph (A) shall not apply to a distribution to any entity unless. . . ." Thus, in determining whether a taxpayer will receive capital gain treatment for a stock redemption transaction, a tax advisor must be able to locate and interpret various Code sections, subsections, paragraphs, subparagraphs, and clauses. ◀

KEY POINT

When attempting to read a provision in the Code, the tax advisor must understand the organization of a Code section. Example I15-6 shows that in order to properly understand Sec. 302, the tax advisor must understand how references to terms such as subsections and subparagraphs can limit the application of the particular phrase being examined.

REGULATIONS

The Treasury Department (the Treasury) issues regulations as interpretations of the statute. The Regulations often give extensive examples, complete with computations providing invaluable assistance in understanding the statutory language.

Because of the frequency of statutory changes, the Treasury Department is not always able to update the regulations in a timely manner. Consequently, when referring to a regulation, a tax advisor should consult its introductory note to determine when the regulation was adopted. If the regulation was adopted before the most recent revision of this Code section, the regulation should be applied with the understanding that it does not reflect the most recent version of the statute. For example, a revised dollar amount stated in the Code would need to be substituted for an out-of-date amount in the regulation.

PROPOSED, TEMPORARY, AND FINAL REGULATIONS. Generally, regulations are first issued to the public in proposed form. The public is given the opportunity to comment on them and suggest changes. The individuals most likely to issue comments are tax accountants and tax attorneys. Organizations such as the American Bar Association, the Tax Division of the AICPA, and the American Taxation Association also regularly comment on proposed regulations. In general, such comments suggest that the proposed treatment affects the taxpayer more adversely than warranted by Congressional intent. In drafting final regulations, the Treasury usually takes the remarks into consideration and modifies the proposed regulations somewhat.

Proposed regulations are just that—proposed—and, consequently, have no more weight than the position the IRS argues for in a court brief. However, they do provide guidance concerning the Treasury's interpretation of the statute. Thus, if the proposed regulations take a fairly pro-taxpayer approach, one can be sure that tax advisors will not attack them as being too lenient. Therefore, the final regulations will probably take the same approach as the proposed regulations. On the other hand, if the Treasury receives considerable criticism about proposed regulations, it will probably adopt a more moderate approach in drafting the final regulations.

Often the Treasury issues **temporary regulations** (which generally are effective on publication) soon after a major statutory change in order to give taxpayers and their advisors guidance about procedural or computational matters. For example, in 1980 Congress essentially rewrote the law concerning the qualification for, and the tax results of, installment sales. In January 1981, the Treasury issued temporary regulations interpreting the amended statute. Temporary regulations have the same authoritative value as final regulations. According to the Technical Amendments and Miscellaneous Revenue Act of 1988, temporary regulations may remain effective for up to three years. Also, a temporary regulation must be issued concurrently as a proposed regulation.

KEY POINT

Temporary regulations have the force and effect of final regulations. However, they cannot remain effective for more than three years.

The Treasury drafts final regulations after the public has had time to comment on the proposed regulations. Most of the time, the final regulations differ at least slightly from the proposed version. As discussed under the next heading, final regulations have the same authoritative weight as the statute. Final regulations generally are retroactive to the effective date of the statutory language they interpret.

For changes to the Code enacted after July 29, 1996, the Treasury is generally precluded from issuing regulations with retroactive effect. In the case of final regulations, however, a regulation can be effective on the date proposed or temporary regulations are filed with the *Federal Register*. Regulations issued within 18 months of the date of a change to the statute can be issued with retroactive effect, however.

INTERPRETATIVE AND STATUTORY REGULATIONS. In addition to being classified as proposed, temporary, or final, regulations are categorized as interpretative or statutory. **Interpretative regulations** are issued under the general authority of Sec. 7805 and, as the name implies, merely make the statutory language easier to understand and apply. In addition, they may provide illustrations about how to perform certain computations. **Statutory (or legislative) regulations**, in comparison with interpretative regulations, are written in situations where Congress delegated its rule-making duties to the Treasury. Because Congress feels it lacks the expertise necessary to deal with a highly technical matter, it instructs the Treasury to write the rules in the form of statutory regulations.

KEY POINT

Regulations may be interpretative or legislative. Occasionally, Congress delegates its law-making responsibility to the Treasury. In such cases, the regulations are elevated from being an interpretation of the statute to being treated as the statute.

Whenever the statute contains language such as "The Secretary shall prescribe such regulations as he may deem necessary" or "under regulations prescribed by the Secretary," the regulations interpreting such a statute are legislative regulations. Perhaps the consolidated tax return regulations are the most dramatic example of statutory regulations. In Sec. 1502 Congress delegated to Treasury the responsibility for writing regulations that would enable the tax liability of a group of affiliated corporations filing a consolidated tax return to be determined. As a requirement of electing the privilege of filing a consolidated tax return, the corporations must consent to following the consolidated return regulations.[11] By consenting to follow the regulations, a taxpayer generally gives up the chance to argue that provisions in the regulations should be overturned by the courts.

AUTHORITATIVE WEIGHT. The presumption is that final regulations have the same authoritative weight as the statute. Section 7805 expressly grants to the Secretary of the Treasury the right to prescribe regulations for enforcing the tax laws and to prescribe the extent, if any, to which the regulations are to be applied without retroactive effect. Despite the presumption concerning the validity of final regulations, occasionally

---

[11] Sec. 1501.

taxpayers can successfully argue that a regulation is invalid and, consequently, should not be followed.

A court will not conclude that an interpretative regulation is invalid unless, in its opinion, such regulation is "unreasonable and plainly inconsistent with the revenue statutes."[12] The courts are less likely to conclude that a legislative regulation is invalid because Congress has abdicated its rule-making authority with respect to such regulations to the Treasury. However, the courts have held that legislative regulations were invalid in situations where the courts concluded the regulations exceeded the scope of the power delegated to the Treasury,[13] were contrary to the statute,[14] or were unreasonable.[15]

In assessing the validity of regulations, courts often apply the **legislative reenactment doctrine**. Under this doctrine, a regulation is deemed to have received Congressional approval if such regulation was finalized many years earlier and during the interim period Congress did not amend the statutory language that the regulation addresses. In other words, if Congress had deemed the regulatory language to be an inappropriate interpretation, it could have changed the words of the statute to achieve a different result. Congress's failure to change the wording in the Code signifies its approval of the regulatory provisions.

KEY POINT

The older a regulation becomes, the less likely a court is to invalidate the regulation. The legislative reenactment doctrine holds that if a regulation did not reflect the intent of Congress, lawmakers would have changed the statute in subsequent legislation to obtain their desired objectives.

STOP & THINK

Question: You are doing research about a certain calculation that affects a client's deductions. You consult the Regulations for guidance because the Code states that the calculation is to be done "in a manner prescribed by the Secretary." After studying the Code and the Regulations, you conclude that another way of doing the calculations is arguably correct under an intuitive approach. This intuitive approach would result in a lower tax liability for the client. Should you follow the Regulations or use the intuitive approach and argue that the Regulations are not valid?

Solution: Because of the language "in a manner prescribed by the Secretary," any Regulations dealing with the calculations are legislative (statutory) regulations. Because Congress explicitly asks the Treasury to write the "rules" whenever it calls for legislative Regulations, such regulations are more difficult than interpretative Regulations to get overturned by the courts as being invalid. Grounds for overruling legislative Regulations include exceeding the scope of the power that Congress delegated, being contrary to the statute, and being unreasonable. If based on your research you do not believe that the Regulations would be overturned by a court, you should follow them.

CITATIONS. Citations to regulations are relatively easy to understand. One or more numbers appear before a decimal place, and several numbers follow the decimal place. The numbers immediately following the decimal place indicate the Code section being interpreted. The numbers preceding the decimal place indicate the general subject matter of the regulation. Numbers that often appear before the decimal place and their general subject matter are as follows:

Number	General Subject Matter
1	Income tax
20	Estate tax
25	Gift tax
301	Administrative and procedural matters
601	Procedural rules

---

[12] *CIR v. South Texas Lumber Co.*, 36 AFTR 604, 48-1 USTC ¶5922 (USSC, 1948). In *U.S. v. Douglas B. Cartwright, Executor*, 31 AFTR 2d 73-1461, 73-1 USTC ¶12,926 (USSC, 1973), the Supreme Court concluded that a regulation dealing with the valuation of mutual fund shares for estate and gift tax purposes was invalid.

[13] *Panama Refining Co. v. U.S.*, 293 U.S. 388 (USSC, 1935).

[14] *M. E. Blatt Co. v. U.S.*, 21 AFTR 1007, 38-2 USTC ¶9599 (USSC, 1938).

[15] *Joseph Weidenhoff, Inc.*, 32 T.C. 1222 (1959).

The number following the Code section number indicates the number of the regulation, such as the fifth regulation. There is no relationship between this number and the subsection of the Code being interpreted. An example of a citation to a final regulation is

$$\underset{\text{Income tax}}{\text{Reg. Sec.}} \quad \underset{\text{Code section}}{1.165} \quad - \quad \underset{\text{Fifth regulation}}{5}$$

Citations to proposed or temporary regulations are in the same format. They are referenced as Prop. Reg. Sec. or Temp. Reg. Sec. For temporary regulations the numbering system following the Code section number always begins with the number of the regulation and an upper case T (e.g., -1T).

Section 165 itself addresses the broad topic of losses and is accompanied by several regulations. According to its caption, the topic of Reg. Sec. 1.165-5 is worthless securities, a topic addressed in subsection (g) of Code Sec. 165. Parenthetical information following the caption to this regulation indicates that this regulation was last amended December 5, 1972 by Treasury Decision (T.D.) 7224. Section 165(g) was last revised in 1971.

When referencing a regulation, the researcher should fine tune the citation as much as possible to indicate the precise wording that provides the basis for his or her conclusion. An example of such a detailed citation is Reg. Sec. 1.165-5(i), Ex. 2(i), which refers to the first portion of Example 2, an example contained in the ith portion of the fifth regulation interpreting Sec. 165.

ADMINISTRATIVE INTERPRETATIONS

The IRS uses several forums as means of interpreting the statute. The IRS's interpretations are referred to generically as **administrative interpretations**. After referring to the Code and the Regulations, tax advisors are likely to refer next to IRS interpretations for further authority for answering a tax question. Some of the most important categories of interpretations are discussed below.

REVENUE RULINGS. In **revenue rulings**, the IRS indicates the tax consequences of a particular transaction in which a number of taxpayers might be interested. For example, a revenue ruling might indicate whether certain expenditures constitute support for purposes of claiming a dependency exemption for another individual.

The IRS frequently issues more than one hundred revenue rulings a year. Revenue rulings do not rank as high as regulations and court cases in the hierarchy of authorities. They simply represent the viewpoint of the IRS. Taxpayers do not have to follow revenue rulings if they have sufficient authority for different treatment.[16] However, the IRS presumes that the tax treatment specified in a revenue ruling is correct. Consequently, if an examining agent discovers in an audit that a taxpayer did not adopt the position espoused in a revenue ruling, the agent will contend that the taxpayer's tax liability should be adjusted to reflect the tax results prescribed in the ruling.

Soon after the IRS issues a revenue ruling, it appears in the weekly *Internal Revenue Bulletin* (cited as I.R.B.), published by the U.S. Government Printing Office. Revenue rulings are also published in the *Cumulative Bulletin* (cited as C.B.), a bound publication issued semiannually by the U.S. Government Printing Office. An example of a citation to a revenue ruling appearing in the *Cumulative Bulletin* is as follows:

---

[16] Chapter C15 discusses in depth the authoritative support taxpayers and tax advisors should have for positions they adopt on a tax return.

Rev. Rul. 80-265, 1980-2 C.B. 378.

This is the 265th ruling issued during 1980, and it appears on page 378 of Volume 2 of the 1980 *Cumulative Bulletin*. Before the issuance of the appropriate volume of the *Cumulative Bulletin*, citations are given to the *Internal Revenue Bulletin*. An example of such a citation follows:

Rev. Rul. 97-1, I.R.B. 1997-2, 1.

The ruling is the first issued during 1997. It was published on page 1 of the *Internal Revenue Bulletin* for the second week of 1997. Once a revenue ruling is published in the *Cumulative Bulletin*, the citation to the *Cumulative Bulletin* should be used.

REVENUE PROCEDURES. As the name suggests, **revenue procedures** are pronouncements by the IRS that generally deal with the procedural aspects of tax practice. For example, in a revenue procedure the IRS provides guidance concerning the reporting of tip income. Another revenue procedure describes the requirements for reproducing paper substitutes for informational returns such as Form 1099.

Revenue procedures are published first in the *Internal Revenue Bulletin* and later in the *Cumulative Bulletin*. An example of a citation to a revenue procedure appearing in a *Cumulative Bulletin* is as follows:

Rev. Proc. 65-19, 1965-2 C.B. 1002.

This item was published in Volume 2 of the 1965 *Cumulative Bulletin* on page 1002; it was the nineteenth revenue procedure issued during 1965.

In addition to revenue rulings and revenue procedures, the *Cumulative Bulletin* includes IRS notices, as well as texts of proposed regulations, treaties and tax conventions, committee reports, and Supreme Court decisions.

SELF-STUDY QUESTION

Do letter rulings provide precedential value for clients?

ANSWER

Not really. A letter ruling is binding only on the taxpayer to whom the ruling was issued. However, letter rulings can be very beneficial in tax research because they provide insight as to the IRS's opinion about the tax consequences of various transactions.

LETTER RULINGS. **Letter rulings** are initiated by taxpayers who write and ask the IRS to explain the tax consequences of a particular transaction.[17] The IRS provides its explanation in the form of a letter ruling, that is, a personal response to the individual or corporation requesting an answer. Only the taxpayer to whom the ruling is addressed may rely on it as an authority. Nevertheless, letter rulings can furnish significant information to other taxpayers and to tax advisors because the rulings lend insight into the IRS's opinion about the tax consequences of particular transactions.

Originally the public did not have access to letter rulings issued to other taxpayers. As a result of Code Sec. 6110, enacted in 1976, letter rulings (with any confidential information deleted) are accessible to the general public. Commerce Clearing House publishes letter rulings in a letter rulings service titled *IRS Letter Rulings*. An example of a citation to a letter ruling appears below.

Ltr. Rul. 8511075.

The numbering system for all letter rulings consists of seven digits.[18] The first two digits indicate that this ruling was made public during 1985. The next two digits denote the week it was made public, here the eleventh. The last three numbers reflect that it was the seventy-fifth ruling that week.

---

[17] Chapter C15 of Prentice Hall's Federal Taxation Corporations, Partnerships, Estates and Trusts provides a more in-depth discussion of letter rulings.

[18] Sometimes letter rulings are cited as PLR (private letter ruling) instead of Ltr. Rul.

OTHER INTERPRETATIONS

Technical Advice Memoranda. When a taxpayer's return is being audited about a complicated, technical matter, the IRS district or appeals office may refer the matter to the IRS National Office in Washington, D.C., for technical advice concerning the appropriate tax treatment. The answer from the National Office, in the form of a **technical advice memorandum**,[19] is made available to the public as a letter ruling. Researchers are able to recognize which letter rulings are technical advice memos because they generally begin with language such as, "In response to a request for technical advice. . . ."

Information Releases. If the IRS thinks that vast numbers of the general public will be interested in a particular interpretation, it may issue an **information release**. Information releases are written in lay terms and are dispatched to thousands of newspapers throughout the United States for publication therein. The IRS may, for example, write an information release to announce the amount of the standard mileage rate applicable to taxpayers who deduct this standard allowance per mile instead of deducting their actual automobile expenses for business travel. An example of a citation to an information release is

I.R. 86-70.

This is the seventieth information release issued in 1986.

Announcements and Notices. The IRS also issues documents that are more technical in nature and generally aimed at tax practitioners. These documents are called **announcements** and **notices** and provide technical explanations of a tax issue that is of current importance. The IRS is bound to follow the guidance contained in announcements and notices in the same way as if contained in a revenue procedure or a revenue ruling. The IRS used a number of announcements to provide technical interpretations of the Tax Reform Act of 1986 before the Treasury was able to issue either proposed or temporary regulations. Examples of citations for announcements and notices are presented below.

Ann. 96-119, I.R.B. 1996-46, 13.
Notice 96-54, I.R.B. 1996-44, 13.

The first citation is for the 119th announcement issued in 1996. It can be found on page 13 of the forty-sixth *Internal Revenue Bulletin* of 1996. The second citation is for the 54th notice issued in 1996. It can be found on page 13 of the forty-fourth *Internal Revenue Bulletin* of 1996.

JUDICIAL DECISIONS

Judicial decisions constitute important sources of tax law. Judges are unbiased persons who decide questions of fact (the appropriate tax result for a given set of facts) or questions of law (the proper interpretation of ambiguous language in the statute). Judges, like other persons, do not always agree on the tax consequences; therefore, tax advisors must often reach their conclusions against the background of conflicting judicial authorities. For example, a district court decision may differ from a Tax Court decision, or different circuit courts may have disagreed on an issue.

OVERVIEW OF THE COURT SYSTEM. With respect to tax matters, there are three trial courts: the U.S. Tax Court, the U.S. Court of Federal Claims (formerly the U.S. Claims Court), and U.S. District Courts. The taxpayer may begin litigation in any of the

---

[19] Technical advice memoranda are discussed in more depth in Chapter C15 of Prentice Hall's Federal Taxation Corporations, Partnerships, Estates, and Trusts.

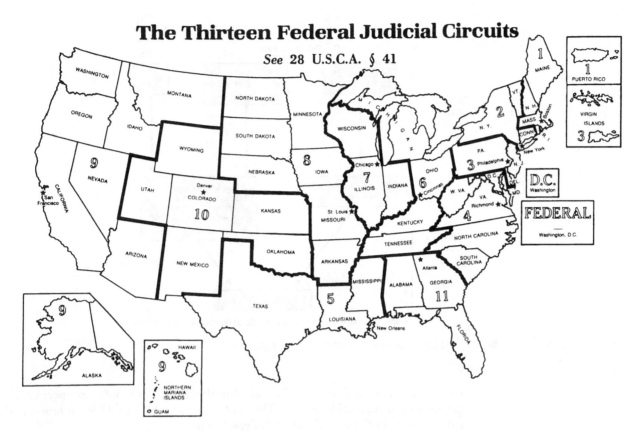

The Thirteen Federal Judicial Circuits

See 28 U.S.C.A. § 41

FIGURE I15-3 ▶ MAP OF THE GEOGRAPHICAL BOUNDARIES OF THE CIRCUIT COURTS OF APPEALS

Source: Reprinted with permission from *West's Federal Reporter,* Third Series, Copyright © by West Publishing Company.

SELF-STUDY QUESTION

What are some of the factors that should be considered when deciding in which court to initiate the litigation of a tax case?

ANSWER

(1) Each court's published precedent pertaining to the issue, (2) desirability of a jury trial, (3) tax expertise of each court, and (4) effect on cash flow.

three. Precedents of the various courts are an important factor in a taxpayer's decision process of where to begin litigation (see page I15-26 for a discussion of precedent). Another important influence is the timing of the cash flow to pay the deficiency. A taxpayer who wants to litigate either in a U.S. District Court or in the U.S. Court of Federal Claims must first pay the additional tax that the IRS contends is due. The taxpayer then files a claim for refund, which the IRS will deny. This denial must be followed by a suit for obtaining a refund of the taxes. If the taxpayer wins the refund suit, he or she receives a refund of the taxes in question plus interest thereon. If the taxpayer begins litigation in the Tax Court, however, payment of the deficiency need not occur until the case has been decided. If the taxpayer loses in the Tax Court, he or she must pay the deficiency plus any interest and penalties.[20] A taxpayer who thinks that a jury trial would be especially favorable should litigate in a U.S. District Court, the only place where a jury trial is possible.

Regardless of which party loses at the trial court level, such party can appeal the decision. Appeals from Tax Court and U.S. District Court decisions are made to the Court of Appeals for the taxpayer's circuit (i.e., geographical area). There are eleven numbered circuits plus the circuit for the District of Columbia. The map in Figure I15-3 shows which states lie in the various circuits. California, for example, is in the Ninth Circuit. Instead of saying "the Court of Appeals for the Ninth Circuit," one generally says "the Ninth Circuit." All decisions of the U.S. Court of Federal Claims are appealable

---

[20] Revenue Procedure 84-58, 1984-2 C.B. 501, provides procedures for taxpayers to make remittances in order to stop the running of interest on deficiencies. This action is more important now that the deduction for personal interest has been eliminated.

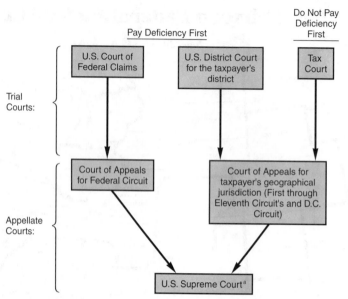

Do Not Pay
Deficiency
First

Pay Deficiency First

| U.S. Court of Federal Claims | U.S. District Court for the taxpayer's district | Tax Court |

Trial Courts:

| Court of Appeals for Federal Circuit | Court of Appeals for taxpayer's geographical jurisdiction (First through Eleventh Circuit's and D.C. Circuit) |

Appellate Courts:

U.S. Supreme Court[a]

[a] Cases are heard only if the Supreme Court grants a writ of certiorari.

FIGURE I15-4 ▶ OVERVIEW OF COURT SYSTEM—TAX MATTERS

to one court—the Court of Appeals for the Federal Circuit—irrespective of the taxpayer's geographical location.[21] The only cases that the Federal Circuit hears are those that originate in the U.S. Court of Federal Claims.

The party losing at the Court of Appeals level can petition by a **writ of certiorari** that the Supreme Court hear the case. If the Supreme Court agrees to consider the issue, it grants certiorari.[22] In recent years, the Court has heard only about six to ten tax cases per year. Figure I15-4 provides an overview of the court system with respect to tax matters.

THE U.S. TAX COURT. The U.S. Tax Court originated in 1942 as a successor to the Board of Tax Appeals. It is a court of national jurisdiction that hears cases dealing only with tax matters. Regardless of a taxpayer's state of residence, all litigated Tax Court cases end up in the same court. There are nineteen Tax Court judges, including one chief judge. The President, with the consent of the Senate, appoints the judges for fifteen years and may reappoint them for an additional term. The judges, specialists in issues concerning taxation, periodically travel to various major cities to hear cases. At present, the Tax Court hears cases in approximately 100 cities. In most instances, only one judge hears a particular case.

The Tax Court issues both regular and memorandum (memo) decisions. The chief judge decides whether to publish each opinion as a memo or regular decision. Generally, the first time the Tax Court decides a particular legal issue, its decision appears as a **regular decision. Memo decisions** usually deal with some factual variation on a matter for which an earlier case decided the interpretation of the law. Regular and memo decisions have the same precedential value.

KEY POINT

Because the Tax Court deals only with tax cases, the Tax Court presumably has a higher level of tax expertise than do other courts. Tax Court judges are appointed by the President, in part, due to their considerable tax experience. In July, 1996, the Tax Court judges faced a backlog of just under 28,000 cases. This is a marked improvement over its record 84,000 cases in 1986.

---

[21] The creation of the U.S. Court of Federal Claims in 1992 is the result of a name change. There is no change in the court's operations from its predecessor, the U.S. Claims Court, which operated from 1982 to 1992. Before the 1982 restructuring, this court was known as the U.S. Court of Claims; its decisions were appealable only to the U.S. Supreme Court.

[22] In granting certiorari, the Supreme Court denotes its granting of an appellate review. The denial of certiorari does not necessarily mean that the Supreme Court agrees with the lower court's decision. It simply decides not to hear the case.

At times the chief judge determines that a particular decision deals with a very important matter that the entire Tax Court should have a chance to consider. In such a situation, the words *reviewed by the court* will appear at the end of the majority decision. If there are any concurring or dissenting opinions, they will appear after the opinion of the majority.[23]

Other language sometimes appearing at the end of a Tax Court decision is *Entered under Rule 155*. These words signify that the court has reached a decision concerning the appropriate tax treatment of an issue but it has left the computation of the exact amount of the deficiency to the two litigating parties.

Small Cases Procedure. The Tax Court has a special policy concerning small cases. Taxpayers have the option of having their cases heard under the **small cases procedure** if the amount in question for a particular year does not exceed $10,000.[24] Such procedures are less formal than the regular Tax Court procedures, and taxpayers can appear without an attorney.[25] The cases are heard by special commissioners instead of by one of the nineteen Tax Court judges. For the losing party, a disadvantage of the small case procedure is that the decision cannot be appealed. The opinions in the small cases are not published and have no precedential value.

Acquiescence Policy. Years ago the IRS adopted the policy of announcing whether it agreed or disagreed with Tax Court cases decided in favor of the taxpayer. This policy is known as the **acquiescence policy**. If the IRS wants to announce that it agrees with a Tax Court decision, it acquiesces to the decision. If it wishes to go on record as disagreeing with a decision, it issues a nonacquiescence to such decision. The acquiescence policy extends only to regular Board of Tax Appeals and Tax Court decisions.[26] The IRS does not, however, make a formal statement, an acquiescence or nonacquiescence, to every regular decision decided in a taxpayer's favor.

The IRS's decision to acquiesce or nonacquiesce has important implications for taxpayers. For example, suppose the IRS has nonacquiesced to a particular decision, and another taxpayer in similar circumstances files a return that adopts the Tax Court position. If the taxpayer's return is audited and the examining agent discovers that the taxpayer's return was prepared on the basis of the Tax Court holding rather than the nonacquiescence statement, the agent must argue that the taxpayer owes more tax. Because an acquiescence or nonacquiescence statement is binding on the agent, about the only way the taxpayer can prevail is by litigation. If the IRS acquiesces to a decision, however, the implication is that the IRS will no longer oppose a pro-taxpayer position on this issue.

When the IRS issues an acquiescence or nonacquiescence, information to this effect appears in the weekly *Internal Revenue Bulletin*. Such information is also published near the front of the *Cumulative Bulletin* for the period in which the announcement was made. If the case dealt with more than one issue, the acquiescence or nonacquiescence may extend to only one issue. Sometimes the IRS acquiesces "in result only," meaning that it agrees with the ultimate outcome (for example, an expenditure is deductible) but not with the court's rationale. The *Cumulative Bulletin*, by way of footnotes, contains details about whether the IRS's acquiescence is complete, partial, or in result only.

---

[23] A judge who issues a concurring opinion agrees with the basic outcome of the majority's decision but not with its rationale. A judge who issues a dissenting opinion believes that the majority decided on an inappropriate outcome.

[24] Sec. 7463. The $10,000 limitation on the amount in dispute includes penalties but excludes interest.

[25] Taxpayers can represent themselves in regular Tax Court proceedings also,

even though they are not attorneys. In situations where taxpayers represent themselves, the words *pro se* appear after the taxpayer's name.

[26] Board of Tax Appeals decisions can serve as precedent for current Tax Court decisions, although it is less likely now that the cases are so old. It is also less likely that the IRS will acquiesce or nonacquiesce to a Board of Tax Appeals decision today.

Published Opinions and Citations. Regular decisions of the Tax Court are published by the U.S. Government Printing Office in a bound volume known as the *Tax Court of the United States Reports.* Soon after a decision is made public, it is also published by Research Institute of America and Commerce Clearing House in their looseleaf reporters of Tax Court decisions. An official citation to a Tax Court decision is as follows:[27]

> *J. Simpson Dean,* 35 T.C. 1083 (1961).

The information in the citation indicates that this case appears on page 1083 in Volume 35 of the official *Tax Court of the United States Reports* and that the case was decided in 1961.

Regular decisions of the Board of Tax Appeals were published by the U.S. Government Printing Office in the *United States Board of Tax Appeals Reports* from 1924 to 1942. A reference to a Board of Tax Appeals case can be cited as follows:

> *J. W. Wells Lumber Co. Trust A.,* 44 B.T.A. 551 (1941).

This case is printed in Volume 44 of the *United States Board of Tax Appeals Reports* on page 551. It is a 1941 decision.

If the IRS has acquiesced or nonacquiesced to a regular Tax Court or Board of Tax Appeals decision, information concerning the IRS's action should appear as part of the citation. At times the IRS's announcement may not occur until several years after the date of the court decision. An example of a citation involving an acquiescence is as follows:

> *Estate of John A. Moss,* 74 T.C. 1239 (1980), *acq.* 1981-1 C.B. 2.

The case appears on page 1239 of Volume 74 of the *Tax Court of the United States Reports* and the acquiescence is reported on page 2 of Volume 1 of the 1981 *Cumulative Bulletin.* The IRS acquiesced to this 1980 decision in 1981.

A citation to a decision to which the IRS has nonacquiesced is as follows:

> *Warren Jones Co.,* 60 T.C. 663 (1973), *nonacq.* 1980-1 C.B. 2.

The case appears in Volume 60 of the *Tax Court of the United States Reports* on page 663. The nonacquiescence is reported on page 2 of Volume 1 of the 1980 *Cumulative Bulletin.* The IRS nonacquiesced to this 1973 decision in 1980.

Tax Court memorandum decisions are not published by the U.S. Government Printing Office. The decisions are available in bound form from Research Institute of America in *RIA T.C. Memorandum Decisions* and from Commerce Clearing House in *CCH Tax Court Memorandum Decisions.* In addition, soon after an opinion is completed, it is published in loose-leaf form by the two publishers. Following are the citations to a Tax Court memorandum decision.

> *Edith G. McKinney,* 1981 PH T.C. Memo ¶81,181, 41 *TCM* 1272.

KEY POINT

Once the IRS has acquiesced to a Tax Court position, other taxpayers generally will not need to litigate the same issue. However, the IRS can change its mind and revoke a previous acquiescence or nonacquiescence. References regarding acquiescences or nonacquiescences to Tax Court decisions can be found in the citators.

---

[27] In a Tax Court case only the plaintiff (taxpayer) is listed. The defendant is understood to be the Commissioner of Internal Revenue and sometimes is not shown in the citation. In cases litigated outside the Tax Court, the plaintiff is listed first and the defendant second. The Commissioner of Internal Revenue is listed as *CIR* in our footnotes and text for cases outside of the Tax Court.

KEY POINT

To have access to all Tax Court cases, a tax advisor must refer to two different publications. The regular opinions are found in the *Tax Court of the United States Reports*, published by the U.S. Government Printing Office, and the memorandum decisions are published by both RIA (formerly PH) and CCH.

McKinney is reproduced in Prentice Hall's (now Research Institute of America's)[28] 1981 *PH T.C. Memorandum Decisions* reporter in paragraph 81,181, and in Volume 41, page 1272, of Commerce Clearing House's *Tax Court Memorandum Decisions*. The 181 in the PH citation denotes that the case is the Tax Court's 181st memorandum decision of the year. A more recent citation continues the same basic format to refer to Research Institute of America's (RIA) memorandum decisions.

Paul F. Belloff, 1992 RIA T.C. Memo ¶92,346, 63 TCM 3150.

U.S. DISTRICT COURTS. Each state has at least one U.S. district court, and more populous states have more than one. Each district court is a separate entity and is free to reach its own decision, subject to the precedential constraints discussed later (see page I15-26). Many different types of cases—not just tax cases—are heard in this forum. A district court is the only forum in which the taxpayer has an opportunity for a jury trial for questions of fact. Depending on the particular taxpayer and the circumstances involved, a jury trial might or might not be perceived as beneficial.[29]

District court decisions are officially reported in the *Federal Supplement* (cited as F. Supp.) published by West Publishing Co. However, some decisions are not officially reported and are referred to as **unreported decisions**. Decisions by U.S. district courts on the topic of taxation are also published by Research Institute of America and Commerce Clearing House in secondary reporters that include only tax-related cases. The Research Institute of America's reporter is called *American Federal Tax Reports* (cited as AFTR),[30] and the Commerce Clearing House reporter is known as *U.S. Tax Cases* (cited as USTC). Even though a case is not officially reported, it may nevertheless be published in the AFTR and USTC. An example of a citation to a U.S. district court decision is as follows:

Margie J. Thompson v. U.S., 429 F. Supp. 13, 39 AFTR 2d 77-1485, 77-1 USTC ¶9343 (D.C. PA., 1977).

KEY POINT

A cite, at a minimum, should contain the following information: (1) the name of the case, (2) the reporter that contains the case along with both a volume and page (or paragraph) number, (3) the year the case was decided, and (4) the court that decided the case.

In the example above, the citation to the *Federal Supplement* is referred to as the **primary cite**. The case appears on page 13 of Volume 429 of the *Federal Supplement*. **Secondary cites** are to Volume 39 of the second series of the AFTR, page 77-1485 (meaning page 1485 in the volume containing 1977 cases) and to Volume 1 of the 1977 USTC in paragraph 9343. The parenthetical information denotes that the case was decided by a district court in Pennsylvania in 1977. Because some judicial decisions have greater value as precedents (i.e., a Supreme Court decision versus a District Court decision), the reader finds it useful to know which court decided the case.

U.S. COURT OF FEDERAL CLAIMS. The U.S. Court of Federal Claims, another trial court that addresses tax matter, has nationwide jurisdiction. Originally this court was named the U.S. Court of Claims (cited as Ct. Cl.), and its decisions were appealable to the Supreme Court only. In a restructuring, effective as of October 1, 1982, the court was

---

[28] For a number of years the Prentice Hall Information Services division published its *Federal Taxes 2nd* tax service and a number of related publications such as the *PH T.C. Memorandum Decisions*. Changes in ownership occurred, and in late 1991 Thomson Professional Publishing added the former Prentice Hall tax materials to the product line of its Research Institute of America tax publishing division. Some products such as the *PH T.C. Memorandum Decisions* still have the Prentice Hall name on the spine of older editions.

[29] Taxpayers usually prefer to have a jury trial if they think that a jury will be sympathetic to their circumstances.

[30] The *American Federal Tax Reports* (AFTR) comes in two series. The first series is cited as AFTR. The second series, which includes decisions published after 1957, is cited as AFTR 2d. The *Margie Thompson* decision cited as an illustration of a District Court decision is from the second *American Federal Tax Reports* series.

renamed the U.S. Claims Court (cited as Cl. Ct.), and its decisions became appealable to the Circuit Court of Appeals for the Federal Circuit. In October 1992, the court's name was changed to the U.S. Court of Federal Claims (cited as Fed. Cl.).

Beginning in 1982, U.S. Claims Court decisions were reported officially in the *Claims Court Reporter*, a reporter published by West Publishing Co. from 1982 to 1992.[31] An example of a citation for a U.S. Claims Court decision appears below.

Benjamin Raphan v. U.S., 3 Cl. Ct. 457, 52 AFTR 2d 83-5987, 83-2 USTC ¶9613 (1983).

The *Raphan* case appears in Volume 3 of the *Claims Court Reporter* on page 457. Secondary cites are to Volume 52, page 83-5987 of the AFTR, second series, and to Volume 2 of the 1983 USTC in paragraph 9613.

Effective with the 1992 name change, decisions of the U.S. Court of Federal Claims are now reported in the *Federal Claims Reporter*. An example of the citation appears below.

Jeffrey G. Sharp v. U.S., 27 Fed. Cl. 52, 70 AFTR 2d 92-6040, 92-2 USTC ¶50,561 (1992).

The *Sharp* case appears in Volume 27 of the *Federal Claims Reporter* on page 52, on page 6040 of the 70th volume of the AFTR, second series, and in Volume 2 of the 1992 USTC reporter in paragraph 50,561. Note that even though the name of the reporter published by West Publishing Co. has changed, the volume numbers continue as if there were no name change.

CIRCUIT COURTS OF APPEALS. Trial court decisions are appealable by the losing party to a circuit court of appeals. The applicable circuit is a function of where the litigation originated. Generally, if the case began in the Tax Court or a U.S. district court, the case is appealable to the circuit for the taxpayer's residence as of the date of the appeal. In the case of a corporation, the case is appealable to the circuit where the corporation's principal place of business is located. As mentioned above, the Federal Circuit handles all appeals of cases originating in the U.S. Court of Federal Claims.

There are eleven geographical circuits designated by numbers, the circuit for the District of Columbia, and the Federal Circuit. A map of the circuits and their jurisdictions appears on page I15-19. The eleven numbered circuits and the D.C. circuit hear appeals of persons or firms from their locality. In October 1981, the Eleventh Circuit was created by moving Alabama, Georgia, and Florida from the Fifth to the new Eleventh Circuit. The Eleventh Circuit voluntarily adopted the policy that it will follow as precedent all decisions made by the Fifth Circuit during the time the states currently constituting the Eleventh Circuit were part of the Fifth Circuit.[32]

EXAMPLE I15-7 ▶ The Eleventh Circuit first faced a particular issue in 1997; the case concerns a Florida taxpayer. In 1980 the Fifth Circuit had ruled on this issue in a case involving a Louisiana taxpayer. Because Florida was part of the Fifth Circuit in 1980, under the policy adopted by the Eleventh Circuit, it will follow the Fifth Circuit's earlier decision. If the Fifth Circuit's decision had been

---

[31] Before the creation in 1982 of the U.S. Claims Court (and the *Claims Court Reporter*), the decisions of the U.S. Court of Claims were reported in either the *Federal Supplement* (F. Supp.) or the *Federal Reporter, Second Series* (F.2d). The *Federal Supplement* was used as the primary reference for the U.S. Court of Claims from 1932 through January 19, 1960. From January 20, 1960, to October 1982, these decisions were reported in the *Federal Reporter, Second Series*.

[32] *Bonner v. City of Prichard*, 661 F.2d 1206 (11th Cir., 1981).

rendered in 1982—after the creation of the Eleventh Circuit—the Eleventh Circuit would not have been bound by the Fifth Circuit's decision. ◀

As the later discussion of precedential value points out, different circuits may reach different conclusions concerning the same issue.

Circuit courts of appeals decisions—regardless of the topic (e.g., civil rights, securities law, taxation, etc.)—are now reported officially in the *Federal Reporter, Third Series* (cited as F.3d), published by West Publishing Co. The third series began in October 1993 after the volume number for the second series reached 999. The *Federal Reporter, Third Series* is the primary citation. In addition, tax decisions of the circuit courts appear in the *American Federal Tax Reports* and *U.S. Tax Cases*. Below is an example of a citation to a 1994 decision by a circuit court.

Leonard Greene v. U.S., 13 F.3d 577, 73 AFTR 2d 94-746, 94-1 USTC ¶50,022 (2nd Cir., 1994).

The *Greene* case appears on page 577 of Volume 13 of the *Federal Reporter, Third Series.* It is also reported in Volume 73, page 94-746 of the AFTR, second series, and in Volume 1, paragraph 50,022, of the 1994 USTC. Parenthetical information indicates that the Second Circuit decided the case in 1994. (A reference to a *Federal Reporter, Second Series* citation can be found in footnote 32 of this chapter.)

SUPREME COURT. Whichever party loses at the appellate court level can request that the Supreme Court hear the case. The Supreme Court, however, hears very few tax cases. Unless the circuits are divided on the proper treatment, or the issue is deemed to be of great significance, the Supreme Court probably will not hear the case.[33] Supreme Court decisions are the law of the land and supersede earlier cases. As a practical matter, a Supreme Court ruling on an interpretation of the Code has the same effect as if its interpretative language was added to the Code. If Congress does not approve of the Court's interpretation, it can amend the statutory language to achieve a result to the contrary. From time to time Congress has reacted to Supreme Court decisions by amending the Code.[34] If a Supreme Court decision concludes that a particular statute is unconstitutional, the provision is ineffective and must be revised.

All Supreme Court decisions, regardless of the subject matter, are published in the *United States Supreme Court Reports* (cited as U.S.), by the U.S. Government Printing Office, the *Supreme Court Reporter* (cited as S.Ct.), by West Publishing Co., and the *United States Reports, Lawyers' Edition* (cited as L. Ed.) by Lawyer's Co-Operative Publishing Co. In addition, the AFTR and USTC reporters published by Research Institute of America and Commerce Clearing House, respectively, contain Supreme Court decisions concerned with taxation. An example of a citation to a Supreme Court case appears below.

U.S. v. Maclin P. Davis, 397 U.S. 301, 25 AFTR 2d 70-827, 70-1 USTC ¶9289 (1970).

According to the primary cite, this case appears in Volume 397, page 301, of the *United States Supreme Court Reports.* It is also reported in Volume 25, page 70-827, of the AFTR, second series, and in Volume 1, paragraph 9289, of the 1970 USTC.

---

[33] *Vogel Fertilizer Co. v. U.S.*, 49 AFTR 2d 82-491, 82-1 USTC ¶9134 (USSC, 1982), is an example of a case the Supreme Court decided to hear to settle the controversy existing in the courts. The Fifth Circuit, the Tax Court, and the Court of Claims had reached one interpretation, whereas the Second,

Fourth, and Eighth Circuits had ruled to the contrary.

[34] For an example of a situation where Congress enacted legislation to achieve a result contrary to that of a Supreme Court decision, see *U.S. v. Marian A. Byrum*, 30 AFTR 2d 72-5811, 72-2 USTC ¶12,859 (USSC, 1972).

▼ **TABLE I15-2**

Summary of Format for Citations

Court Cases	
Court	Citation
Tax Court—regular decisions	*J. Simpson Dean*, 35 T.C. 1083 (1961)
Tax Court—memo decisions	*Paul F. Belloff*, 1992 RIA T.C. Memo ¶92,346, 63 TCM 3150
Board of Tax Appeals— regular decisions	*J. W. Wells Lumber Co. Trust A.*, 44 B.T.A. 551 (1941)
U.S. District Court	*Margie J. Thompson v. U.S.*, 429 F. Supp. 13, 39 AFTR 2d 77-1485, 77-1 USTC ¶9343 (DC PA, 1977)
U.S. Court of Federal Claims	*Jeffrey G. Sharp v. U.S.*, 27 Fed. Cl. 52, 70 AFTR 2d 92-6040, 92-2 USTC ¶50,561 (1992)
U.S. Claims Court	*Benjamin Raphan v. U.S.*, 3 Cl. Ct. 457, 52 AFTR 2d 83-5987, 83-2 USTC ¶9613 (1983)
Circuit Court of Appeals	*Leonard Greene v. U.S.*, 13 F.3d 577, 73 AFTR 2d 94-746, 94-1 USTC ¶50,022 (2nd Cir., 1994)
Supreme Court	*U.S. v. Maclin P. Davis*, 397 U.S. 301, 25 AFTR 2d 70-827, 70-1 USTC ¶9289 (1970)
ADMINISTRATIVE INTERPRETATIONS	
Revenue Rulings—prior to publication in *Cumulative Bulletin*	Rev. Rul. 97-1, I.R.B. 1997-2, 1
Revenue Rulings—after publication in *Cumulative Bulletin*	Rev. Rul. 80-265, 1980-2 C.B. 378
Revenue Procedures	Rev. Proc. 65-19, 1965-2 C.B. 1002
Letter Rulings	Ltr. Rul. 8511075
Information Release	I.R. 86-70
Announcement	Ann. 96-119, I.R.B. 1996-46, 13
Notice	Notice 96-54, I.R.B. 1996-44, 13

Table I15-2 provides a summary of how court decisions, revenue rulings, revenue procedures, and other administrative interpretations should be cited. Primary citations are to the reporters published by West Publishing Co. or the U.S. Government Printing Office, and secondary citations are to the AFTR and USTC reporters.

PRECEDENTIAL VALUE OF VARIOUS DECISIONS.

Tax Court. The Tax Court is a court of national jurisdiction. Consequently, in general it rules uniformly for all taxpayers, regardless of their geographical location. It follows Supreme Court decisions and its own earlier decisions. It is not bound by cases decided by the U.S. Court of Federal Claims or a U.S. district court, even if the district court is the court for the taxpayer's jurisdiction.

In 1970 the Tax Court voluntarily adopted what has become known as the *Golsen* rule.[35] Under the *Golsen* rule, the Tax Court departs from its general policy of ruling uniformly for all taxpayers and instead follows decisions to the contrary made by the court of appeals to which the case in question is appealable. Stated differently, the *Golsen* rule provides that the Tax Court rules consistently with decisions of the circuit court for the taxpayer's jurisdiction.

EXAMPLE I15-8 ▶ In 1991, the first time the issue was litigated, the Tax Court decided that an expenditure was deductible. The government appealed the case to the Tenth Circuit and won a reversal. This is the only appellate case that has been decided regarding this issue. If and when the Tax Court faces this issue again, it will hold, with one exception, that the expenditure is deductible. The sole exception involves taxpayers of the Tenth Circuit; for them the Tax Court applies the *Golsen* rule and denies the deduction. ◀

U.S. District Court. Because each U.S. district court is a separate court, district court decisions have precedential value only for subsequent cases before that same U.S. district court. District courts must follow decisions of the Supreme Court and the circuit court to which the case is appealable.

EXAMPLE I15-9 ▶ The U.S. District Court for Rhode Island, the Tax Court, and the Eleventh Circuit have ruled on a particular issue. Any U.S. district court within the Eleventh Circuit must follow that circuit's decision. Similarly, the U.S. District Court for Rhode Island must rule consistently with the way it ruled earlier. Tax Court decisions are not binding precedents for district courts. Thus, all district courts other than the one for Rhode Island and those within the Eleventh Circuit are free to reach their own independent decisions. ◀

U.S. Court of Federal Claims. In reaching decisions today, the U.S. Court of Federal Claims must rule consistently with Supreme Court cases, cases decided by the Circuit Court of Appeals for the Federal Circuit, and its own earlier decisions, including decisions rendered when the court had a different name. It need not follow decisions of other circuit courts, the Tax Court, or district courts.

EXAMPLE I15-10 ▶ Assume the same facts as in Example I15-9. In a later year the same issue is litigated in the U.S. Court of Federal Claims. This court is not bound by any of the authorities that have addressed the issue. Thus, it has complete flexibility to reach its own answer. ◀

Circuit Courts of Appeals. A circuit court is bound by Supreme Court cases and earlier cases decided by that particular circuit. If neither the Supreme Court nor the circuit in question has already faced the issue, there is no precedent that the circuit court must follow, regardless of whether other circuits have ruled on this point. In such a situation, the circuit court is said to be writing on a clean slate. In reaching a decision, the judges may adopt the viewpoint articulated in another circuit's opinion if they deem it appropriate.

EXAMPLE I15-11 ▶ Assume the same facts as in Example I15-9. Any circuit other than the Eleventh would be writing on a clean slate if it faced the same issue. After reviewing the Eleventh Circuit's decision, another circuit court might or might not decide to rule the same way. ◀

Forum Shopping. Not surprisingly, courts are not always unanimous in their conclusions concerning the appropriate tax treatment. Consequently, conflicts sometimes exist

---

[35] The *Golsen* rule is based on the decision in *Jack E. Golsen*, 54 T.C. 742 (1970).

among the courts—trial courts and appellate courts. Because taxpayers have the flexibility of choosing where to begin their litigation, part of their decision-making process should involve considering the precedents applicable in the various courts. The ability to consider differing precedents in choosing the forum for litigation is sometimes called **forum shopping**.

An example of a situation where until recently a conflict in the circuits existed was the issue of when it became too late for the IRS to question the proper treatment of items that flowed through from an S corporation's tax return to a shareholder's tax return. For example, if the time (statute of limitations) had already expired for the corporation's but not the shareholder's tax return, was the IRS precluded from collecting additional taxes from the shareholder? The Ninth Circuit in *Kelley*[36] held that the IRS would be barred from collecting from the shareholder if the statute of limitations was already up for the S corporation's information return. On the other hand, three other circuits held in *Bufferd*,[37] *Fehlhaber*,[38] and *Green*[39] that the statute of limitations for flow-through items did not expire until the statute of limitations for flow-through items was up for the shareholder. The Supreme Court affirmed the *Bufferd*[40] case and created certainty and uniformity for the interpretation of this important issue.

STOP & THINK

Question: You have been researching whether a certain amount received by your new client can be excluded from her gross income. The client's tax return for two years ago is being audited; another firm prepared the return. In a similar case decided a few years ago the Tax Court allowed an exclusion, but the IRS nonacquiesced to the case. The case involved a taxpayer from the Fourth Circuit. Your client is a resident of Maine, which is in the First Circuit. Twelve years ago in a case involving another taxpayer, the district court for the client's district ruled that this type of receipt was not excludable. There has been no other litigation. To sustain a deduction, will your client likely need to litigate? Explain. If your client litigates, in which trial court should she begin her litigation?

Solution: Because of the IRS's nonacquiescence, your client's exclusion is not likely to be sustained unless she litigates. She would not want to begin litigation in her district court because it would need to follow its earlier decision, which is unfavorable to taxpayers. A good place to begin would be the Tax Court because of its earlier pro-taxpayer position. There is no way to predict how the U.S. Court of Federal Claims would rule because there is no precedent it must follow.

Dictum. At times a court may comment on an issue or a set of facts that it did not face in the case being tried. Comments by a court on facts or an issue on which it does not have to rule are called *dictum*. In building an argument in favor of a particular tax result, a party may reference *dictum* as support for the argument. The *Central Illinois Public Service Co.*[41] case addressed whether lunch reimbursements received by employees constituted wages subject to withholding. In this case, Justice Blackman remarked that income in such forms as interest, rent, and dividends is not wages. This remark by Justice Blackman is *dictum* because the case concerned only reimbursements for expenditures for lunches.

---

[36] *Daniel M. Kelley v. CIR*, 64 AFTR 2d 89-5025, 89-1 USTC ¶9360 (9th Cir., 1989).
[37] *Sheldon B. Bufferd v. CIR*, 69 AFTR 2d 92-465, 92-1 USTC ¶50,031 (2nd Cir., 1992).
[38] *Robert Fehlhaber v. CIR*, 69 AFTR 2d 92-850, 92-1 USTC ¶50,131 (11th Cir., 1992).

[39] *Charles T. Green v. CIR*, 70 AFTR 2d 92-5077, 92-2 USTC ¶50,340 (5th Cir., 1992).
[40] *Sheldon B. Bufferd v. CIR*, 71 AFTR 2d 93-573, 93-1 USTC ¶50,038 (USSC, 1993).
[41] *Central Illinois Public Service Co. v. CIR*, 41 AFTR 2d 78-718, 78-1 USTC ¶9254 (USSC, 1978).

TAX TREATIES

The United States has reached treaty agreements with numerous foreign countries. These treaties address tax and other matters. As a result, a tax advisor addressing the U.S. tax results of a U.S. corporation's business operations in another country, for example, Sweden, should determine whether there is a treaty between Sweden and the United States and, if there is, the applicable provisions of the treaty. (See Chapter C16 for a more extensive discussion of treaties.)

TAX PERIODICALS

Writings of experts in tax periodicals can lend informative assistance for interpreting the tax law. For example, such writings can be especially helpful if they address a recently enacted statutory provision and it is too early for there to be any regulations, cases, or rulings on point.

Tax experts also often write articles in which they discuss the judicial authorities—often conflicting ones—with respect to a particular issue. The experts who most frequently write articles concerning technical tax matters are attorneys, accountants, and professors. Some periodicals that are devoted to providing in-depth discussions of tax matters are listed below.

> *The Journal of Taxation*
> *The Tax Adviser*
> *Taxation for Accountants*
> *Taxes—the Tax Magazine*
> *Tax Law Review*
> *The Journal of Corporate Taxation*
> *The Journal of Partnership Taxation*
> *The Journal of Real Estate Taxation*
> *The Review of Taxation of Individuals*
> *Estate Planning*
> *Tax Notes*

The first five journals listed above contain articles dealing with a variety of topical areas. As the titles of the next five suggest, these publications deal with specialized areas. All of these publications (other than *Tax Notes*, which is published weekly) are monthly or quarterly publications. Daily reports, such as the *Daily Tax Report,* published by the Bureau of National Affairs, are used by tax professionals when more timely updates on tax matters are needed than can be provided by monthly and quarterly publications.

Published articles and tax services are examples of secondary sources of authority. The Code and administrative and judicial interpretations are primary sources of authority. Your research efforts should always involve citing primary authorities.

TAX SERVICES

Multivolume commentaries on the tax law are published by several publishers. These commentaries are known generically as **tax services**. Each of these tax services is encyclopedic in scope and most come in looseleaf form so that information concerning current developments can be easily added. The organizational scheme differs from one service to another; some are updated more frequently than others. Each has its own special features and unique way of presenting certain material. The only way to become familiar with the various tax services is to use them in researching hypothetical or actual problems.

KEY POINT

Tax services are often where the research process begins. A tax service helps identify the tax authorities pertaining to a particular tax issue. The actual tax authorities, and not the tax service, are generally cited as support for a particular tax position.

KEY POINT

Both the *United States Tax Reporter* and the *Standard Federal Tax Reporter* services are organized by Code section. Accordingly, many tax advisors find both of these services easy to use. The other major tax services are organized by topic and offer more of a commentary style.

As with almost any other activity, the more familiar one becomes with the organizational scheme with which one is working, the more comfortable one feels. Knowledge of the organization is relevant even if the researcher is using the CD-ROM or the on-line version of a tax service. The following discussion provides an overview of the most commonly used tax services.

UNITED STATES TAX REPORTER

United States Tax Reporter, the tax reporter service published by Research Institute of America, consists of an eighteen-volume series devoted to income taxes, a two-volume series covering estate and gift taxes, and a single volume dealing with excise taxes. This service also contains two volumes that reproduce the Internal Revenue Code.

The *United States Tax Reporter* service is organized by Code section (i.e., its commentary begins with Sec. 1 of the Code and proceeds in numerical order through the last section of the Code). Researchers familiar with the Code section applicable to their problem can begin their research process by turning directly to the paragraphs discussing this section. For each Code section, a code-based paragraph sequencing is used for the Code text, the Regulations text, committee reports, editorial explanations, and digests of cases and rulings so that the researcher does not have to learn a different numbering system. Another technique for beginning the research process is to think of key words that capture the flavor of the problem and consult the index. The topical index appears in a separate volume. It refers the researcher to the paragraph number(s) of the service where the topics of interest are discussed. A researcher who knows which Code section addresses the issue (e.g., Sec. 280A) can go immediately to whichever volume provides commentary on that section.

For each Code section, the *United States Tax Reporter* service reproduces verbatim the statutory language and the regulations, provides an editorial explanation of the provisions, and furnishes brief summaries of cases and rulings interpreting the Code section. It provides citations to the full text of each case or ruling. The summaries are categorized into fairly explicit topical areas, such as the deductibility as a medical expense of the cost of special food and beverages and food supplements.

The *United States Tax Reporter* service is updated weekly; the most recent developments are highlighted in Volume 16 in a cross-reference table and regularly moved into the body of the text. The cross-reference table is organized by paragraph number. To determine whether any recent developments affect your question, look in the table for entries for the paragraph number where you found helpful information in the main body of the service. Because of the need to consult the cross-reference table, it is helpful to take note as you go along of the paragraph numbers that proved fruitful in your research process. The supplementary index in the Index Volume (Volume 1) of the service is updated monthly to reflect recent developments. Supplementary tables of cases and rulings in the Tables Volume (Volume 2) provide information on new authorities that have been incorporated into the main body of the service.

REAL WORLD EXAMPLE

The 1913 CCH explanation of the federal tax law was a single 400 page volume. The 1997 *Standard Federal Tax Reporter* is 22 volumes and 40,800 pages in length.

STANDARD FEDERAL TAX REPORTER

Commerce Clearing House (CCH) publishes the *Standard Federal Tax Reporter* (referred to in this text as the CCH service). This service is also organized by Code section. Separate services devoted to excise taxes and estate and gift taxes are available, as well as the multivolume income tax service. The CCH service reproduces the statute and the regulations for each Code section and summarizes and provides citations to other authorities in much the same way as the *United States Tax Reporter* service does.[42]

---

[42] Citations for the two primary tax services are not often used. If one wanted to cite these services, it might be as follows: (1997) 6 *United States Tax Reporter* (RIA) ¶3,025 and (1997) 8 *Std. Fed. Tax Rep.* (CCH) ¶22,609.01, where 6 and 8 are the volume numbers and the paragraph numbers refer to the cited portion of the volume.

An index volume contains a topical index that lists references by paragraph number. Because the volumes are organized by Code section number, a researcher who knows the number of the relevant Code section can bypass the index.

The approach for looking for any recent authorities on an issue is similar to the *United States Tax Reporter* service. Consult the Cumulative Index table in Volume 16 and search for entries applicable to the paragraph numbers in the main body of the service where you found relevant authorities. The CCH service publishes supplements with current developments weekly. Updates for court cases and revenue rulings are retained in Volume 16 until the end of the calendar year, when an entire new service is published. Major events such as new legislation and Supreme Court decisions are integrated into the service text throughout the year.

FEDERAL TAX COORDINATOR 2d

The *Federal Tax Coordinator 2d* is published by the Research Institute of America (RIA) and is referred to here as the *RIA* service. It covers all three areas of tax law: income tax analysis, estate and gift tax analysis, and excise tax analysis. The RIA income tax service is a multi-volume looseleaf publication organized by fairly broad topics. For example, Volume K explores the tax law with respect to the following deductions: taxes, interest, charitable contributions, medical, and other. The topical index, contained in a separate volume, refers to the chapter and paragraph numbers where the matters of interest are discussed. Another volume furnishes a finding table of where the various Code sections and regulations are discussed and where they are reproduced in the commentary volumes.

The RIA service reproduces all of the Code sections and regulations applicable to a particular volume behind a tab marker titled "Code & Regs." Using detailed captions, the various volumes provide an editorial-type commentary about the tax results. References to cases, including citations, appear in footnote form. The RIA service does not compile in a single volume information about new developments for all topics. Although, each volume has a tab marker titled "Developments," current developments for that volume are now included in the main body of the service. Originally, however, they appeared behind the "Developments" tab. Separate volumes are devoted to proposed regulations and revenue rulings and procedures. The RIA service publishes current developments weekly.

LAW OF FEDERAL INCOME TAXATION (MERTENS)

The *Law of Federal Income Taxation,* published by Clark Boardman & Callaghan, was originally edited by Jacob Mertens and is usually called Mertens by tax practitioners. Mertens is generally deemed to be the most authoritative tax service. It is the service most frequently cited by the courts and, in fact, the only service cited by the judiciary with any regularity. Like the RIA *Federal Tax Coordinator 2d* service, Mertens is organized by general topical area. Volume 7, for example, provides a comprehensive discussion of wages, travel, interest, taxes, and net operating losses. The commentary is in narrative form and reads like an article. References to the authorities appear in footnotes.

One volume is devoted to a topical index. References are to section numbers (assigned by Mertens) instead of to paragraph numbers. Another volume, titled *Tables,* discloses where Code sections, regulations, and rulings are discussed in the commentary volumes. The *Table of Cases* volume does the same with respect to cases.

Mertens is updated monthly to reflect current developments. Like the RIA *Federal Tax Coordinator 2d* service, the supplementary material for a particular volume is filed in that volume. The new material is organized by Mertens' section numbers and is reported under the section number assigned to the topic in question in the main body of the service. The volume titled *Highlights* contains in-depth articles on current developments as well as monthly updates that complement the supplementary material included in the treatise volumes.

Mertens devotes separate volumes to reproducing the Code and the regulations, and these items do not appear in the commentary volumes. A special feature of Mertens is its *Rulings Volume,* which contains a Code-Rulings Table organized by Code section number. The table lists the numbers of all of the revenue rulings that have been issued after 1953 with respect to a particular Code section. For example, for the period 1954 through 1994, the table lists one ruling interpreting Sec. 1034(b)(1). The post-1994 table lists no further rulings interpreting Sec. 1034(b)(1).

Another part of the rulings volume consists of a Rulings Status Table. For all post-1953 revenue rulings, this table denotes any subsequent action taken concerning each ruling. Examples of actions the IRS could have taken include revoking, modifying, and superseding a ruling. The Research Institute of America and Commerce Clearing House citator volumes contain the same information, but in a different format.[43]

TAX MANAGEMENT PORTFOLIOS

The Bureau of National Affairs (BNA) publishes booklets of approximately 100 pages each called *Tax Management Portfolios* (referred to as BNA portfolios by many practitioners and in this text). Each portfolio provides an in-depth discussion of a relatively narrow issue, such as involuntary conversions or the estate tax marital deduction. Thus, when the research question has been narrowed down to a very precise issue, consultation of a BNA portfolio can be quite helpful.

BNA provides a notebook that contains a Code section index and a key words list or topical index. Each index references appropriate page numbers.

Each portfolio contains a narrative discussion called *Detailed Analysis* and a section called *Working Papers.* In the Detailed Analysis portion, citations to authorities appear in the footnotes. The Working Papers section often contains items such as excerpts from committee reports, copies of tax forms applicable to the matter under discussion, and sample language for making a particular election. Each portfolio also has a bibliography and a list of references where relevant articles are listed and revenue rulings and letter rulings on the topic are summarized.

BNA portfolios are updated a few times a year with sheets filed in the front of the applicable booklet. The current developments material is organized according to the page number of the Detailed Analysis that it supplements. From time to time, a portfolio may be revised or a new portfolio published to reflect major changes in the law.

CCH FEDERAL TAX SERVICE

The newest of the major tax services is the *CCH Federal Tax Service,* which is published by Commerce Clearing House and was formerly published by Matthew Bender & Company. This service is a multi-volume looseleaf publication that, like the RIA *Federal Tax Coordinator 2d* and Mertens services, is organized by fairly broad topics. An analysis is provided of broad topical areas such as individuals, partnerships, sales and exchanges, and farming and natural resources.

The *CCH Federal Tax Service* does not reproduce the Code and Treasury Regulations in the volumes with the topical commentary or analysis. Instead, it devotes separate volumes to the Internal Revenue Code and proposed, temporary, and final Treasury Regulations. A Code section and the related Treasury Regulations appear together in the same volume.

The *CCH Federal Tax Service* is updated twice a month to reflect current develop-

---

[43] Citators are described elsewhere in this chapter.

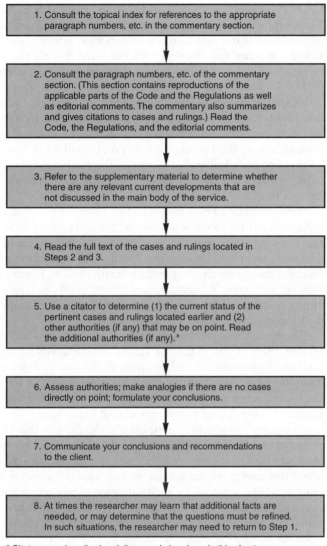

1. Consult the topical index for references to the appropriate paragraph numbers, etc. in the commentary section.

2. Consult the paragraph numbers, etc. of the commentary section. (This section contains reproductions of the applicable parts of the Code and the Regulations as well as editorial comments. The commentary also summarizes and gives citations to cases and rulings.) Read the Code, the Regulations, and the editorial comments.

3. Refer to the supplementary material to determine whether there are any relevant current developments that are not discussed in the main body of the service.

4. Read the full text of the cases and rulings located in Steps 2 and 3.

5. Use a citator to determine (1) the current status of the pertinent cases and rulings located earlier and (2) other authorities (if any) that may be on point. Read the additional authorities (if any).[a]

6. Assess authorities; make analogies if there are no cases directly on point; formulate your conclusions.

7. Communicate your conclusions and recommendations to the client.

8. At times the researcher may learn that additional facts are needed, or may determine that the questions must be refined. In such situations, the researcher may need to return to Step 1.

[a] Citators are described and discussed elsewhere in this chapter.

FIGURE I15-5 ▶ USE OF TAX SERVICES TO RESEARCH A TAX QUESTION

ments. In addition, a weekly newsletter is sent to subscribers. The current developments material is combined with the analysis to which it relates.

Figure I15-5 provides an overview of one approach for using the tax services to research a tax question.

CITATORS

OBJECTIVE 5

Use the citator to assess authorities

Citators serve two functions: they give a history of the case (i.e., if the case in question is an appeals court decision, the citator lists the trial court decision and the Supreme Court decision, if any, for the case); and they list the other authorities (i.e., cases and revenue rulings) that have cited the case in question. A citator of judicial decisions is included with the Commerce Clearing House tax service at no additional charge. The RIA citator is available separately from either of its basic tax services.

COMMERCE CLEARING HOUSE CITATOR

The Commerce Clearing House Citator (herein referred to as the CCH citator) consists of two loose-leaf volumes, one for cases with names beginning with the letters A through L and the other for cases with names starting with the letters M through Z, revenue rulings, and other government promulgations. This citator lists all cases reported in CCH's *Standard Federal Tax Reporter;* citations are also provided for cases in its *Excise Tax Reporter* and its *Federal Estate and Gift Tax Reporter.* Citing cases that comment on or add information relevant to a reported decision are determined by CCH editors and therefore reported on a selective basis. In the case of rulings and other government promulgations, the Finding Lists section provides full histories of all actions affected by or affecting each ruling. For example, the publication notes that a certain 1993 revenue ruling revokes a certain 1989 revenue ruling. A sample page from the CCH citator appears in Figure I15-6.

Refer to Figure I15-6 and find the *Leonarda C. Diaz* case. The information in bold print with bullets to the left denotes that *Diaz* was a decision of the Second Circuit and the Tax Court and that the Second Circuit affirmed (upheld) the Tax Court's decision. The two cases listed beneath the Second Circuit decision (i.e., *Kuh* and *Damm*) cited the *Diaz* decision. The six cases listed beneath the Tax Court decision (i.e., *German, Jr., Orr, Zeidler, Schwerm, Wassenaar,* and *Toner*) cited the Tax Court's opinion in *Diaz.* The abbreviation *Dec.* appearing in some of the citations stands for *decision.* CCH lists the decision numbers of the Tax Court cases.

The basic CCH citator is published once a year. The first volume contains an update section, titled "Current Citator Table," which shows listings for new court decisions and additional citations of earlier court decisions; updates supplement the Citator on a quarterly basis. The *Diaz* decision has not been cited by any additional decisions since the CCH citator was last published in late 1996. The appropriate page for *Diaz* in the Current Citator Table is not reproduced here.

The entry "¶5504.195" appearing to the right of the Alfonso Diaz case name denotes the paragraph number of the *Standard Federal Tax Reporter* (the CCH service) at which the *Diaz* case is summarized. In most situations, a researcher would have already read about this case in the tax service and decided it was helpful for the research issue before consulting the citator. In such situations, this paragraph reference is not necessary because the citator is used to determine whether there are other relevant cases. At other times, the reference to the paragraph in the CCH tax service summarizing the case in question can be helpful. For example, if a researcher learned about the case from a colleague and wants to read in the tax service about the general topical area of the case, the discussion of the case can be easily located.

Cases are included in the CCH citator even though they have not been cited by a later case. This point is illustrated by the entry for *Frank Diaz,* a Tax Court memo decision for which no subsequent case citations are listed. The citator also indicates whether the Commissioner has acquiesced or nonacquiesced to Tax Court decisions. For example, if you refer to the entry for *Alfonso Diaz* in Figure I15-6, you will note that the capital "A" following the Tax Court citation shows that the Commissioner's acquiescence is reported on page 2 of Volume 2 of the 1972 *Cumulative Bulletin.*

RESEARCH INSTITUTE OF AMERICA CITATOR 2ND SERIES

Like the CCH citator, the *Research Institute of America Citator 2nd Series*[44] (referred to here as the RIA citator) gives the history of each case and ruling and lists the cases and

---

[44] The *Research Institute of America Citator 2nd Series* is published currently by Research Institute of America, Inc. It was originally published by Prentice Hall's Information Services Division, which was acquired in 1990 by Maxwell Macmillan. *Prentice Hall* and/or *Maxwell Macmillan* appears on the spines and title pages of the older citators and will remain there because, unlike the CCH citator, the RIA citator is not republished each year.

—————CCH————— 93,223 **DIB**

Diamond Red Paint Co.—continued
Halters Co., BTA, Dec. 5124, 16 BTA 325
Fidelity Trust Co., BTA, Dec. 4285, 13 BTA 109
Diamond Shoe Co. . . . . . (Expired Excess Profits Tax)
● SCt—Cert. denied, 282 US 859; 51 SCt 34
● CA-2—(aff'g BTA), 5 ustc ¶ 1392; 42 F2d 144
● BTA—Dec. 5272; 16 BTA 1069
● BTA—Dec. 4939; 15 BTA 826
Diamond, Sol . ¶ 5508.085, 8470.517, 25,383.2683, 25,543.016, 25,543.08, 25,742.023
● CA-7—(aff'g TC), 74-1 ustc ¶ 9306; 492 F2d 286
Campbell, CA-8, 91-2 ustc ¶ 50,420
Rev. Proc. 93-27
Anderson, TC, Dec. 50,410(M), 69 TCM 1609, TC Memo. 1995-8
Banks, TC, Dec. 47,832(M), 62 TCM 1611, TC Memo. 1991-641
Pacheco, CA-9, 90-2 ustc ¶ 50,458
Vestal, CA-8, 74-2 ustc ¶ 9501, 498 F2d 487
St. John, DC-III, 84-1 ustc ¶ 9158
Campbell, TC, Dec. 46,493(M), 59 TCM 236, TC Memo. 1990-162
McNulty, TC, Dec. 44,857(M), 55 TCM 1138, TC Memo. 1988-274
Greater Display & Wire Forming, Inc., TC, Dec. 44,802(M), 55 TCM 922, TC Memo. 1988-231
National Oil Co., TC, Dec. 43,557(M), 52 TCM 1223, TC Memo. 1986-596
Hirst, TC, Dec. 43,215(M), 51 TCM 1597, TC Memo. 1986-321
Mouriz, TC, Dec. 42,851(M), 51 TCM 392, TC Memo. 1986-43
Parker, TC, Dec. 42,129(M), 50 TCM 14, TC Memo. 1985-263
Kenroy, Inc., TC, Dec. 41,186(M), 47 TCM 1749, TC Memo. 1984-232
Bertolini Trucking Co., TC, Dec. 39,474(M), 45 TCM 44, TC Memo. 1982-643
Kessler, TC, Dec. 39,226(M), 44 TCM 624, TC Memo. 1982-432
Tooke, TC, Dec. 34,336(M), 36 TCM 396, TC Memo. 1977-91
Pierson, TC, Dec. 34,009(M), 35 TCM 1256, TC Memo. 1976-281
● TC—Dec. 30,838; 56 TC 530
Manchester Music Co., Inc., DC-NH, 90-1 ustc ¶ 50,168, 733 FSupp 473
Miller, Jr., TC, Dec. 45,977(M), 57 TCM 1419, TC Memo. 1989-461
McNulty, TC, Dec. 44,857(M), 55 TCM 1138, TC Memo. 1988-274
Greater Display & Wire Forming, Inc., TC, Dec. 44,802(M), 55 TCM 922, TC Memo. 1988-231
National Oil Co., TC, Dec. 43,557(M), 52 TCM 1223, TC Memo. 1986-596
Goodwin, David C., TC, Dec. 36,413, 73 TC 215
Schaevitz, TC, Dec. 30,925(M), 30 TCM 823, TC Memo. 1971-197
Diamond, Solomon
● TC—Dec. 25,981(M); 22 TCM 229; TC Memo. 1963-57
Diamond T Motor Car Co.: Allen v. . . . . . ¶ 39,060.82
● CA-10—(rev'g DC), 61-1 ustc ¶ 9484; 291 F2d 115
Randall, CA-5, 76-2 ustc ¶ 9770, 542 F2d 270
Jefferson Bank and Trust, DC-Colo, 89-1 ustc ¶ 9221
Rodkey, DC-Okla, 87-1 ustc ¶ 9218
Nevada Rock & Sand Co., DC-Nev, 74-2 ustc ¶ 9617, 376 FSupp 161
Nomellini Construction Co., DC-Calif, 71-2 ustc ¶ 9510, 328 FSupp 1281
● DC-Colo—63-2 ustc ¶ 9557
Diamondhead Corp. v. Fort Hope Development, Inc.
. . . . ¶ 41,520.1945
● DC-Ga—78-2 ustc ¶ 9718
Diamondstone, I. A. (See Kann, William L.)
DiAndre, Anthony F. . . . . . . ¶ 37,894.7255, 42,358.30
● SCt—Cert. denied, 3/19/93
● CA-10—(rev'g and rem'g unreported DC), 92-2 ustc ¶ 50,373; 968 F2d 1049
Stewart, DC-Ohio, 95-1 ustc ¶ 50,004
Russell, DC-Mich, 95-1 ustc ¶ 50,029
Jones, DC-Neb, 94-2 ustc ¶ 50,562, 869 FSupp 747
Schachter, DC-Calif, 94-1 ustc ¶ 50,242
Fostvedt, DC-Colo, 93-1 ustc ¶ 50,299, 824 FSupp 978
Jones, DC-Neb, 95-2 ustc ¶ 50,567, 898 FSupp 1360
May, DC-Mo, 95-2 ustc ¶ 50,605
DiAndrea, Inc. . . . ¶ 16,233.25, 21,817.108, 45,257.09
● TC—Dec. 40,697(M); 47 TCM 731; TC Memo. 1983-768

DiAndrea, Inc.—continued
Johnson, TC, Dec. 47,836(M), 62 TCM 1629, TC Memo. 1991-645
Diaz, Alfonso . . . . ¶ 5504.195
● TC—Dec. 31,442; 58 TC 560; A. 1972-2 CB 2
Marrone, TC, Dec. 50,424(M), 69 TCM 1684, TC Memo. 1995-22
Sloan, TC, Dec. 50,305(M), 68 TCM 1489, TC Memo. 1994-628
Muniz, TC, Dec. 49,775(M), 67 TCM 2625, TC Memo. 1994-151
Drabiuk, TC, Dec. 50,692(M), 69 TCM 2890, TC Memo. 1995-260
Jackson, TC, Dec. 50,736(M), TC Memo. 1995-300, 70 TCM 12
Levin, TC, Dec. 51,326(M), 71 TCM 2938, TC Memo. 1996-211
Kong, TC, Dec. 46,090(M), 58 TCM 378, TC Memo. 1989-560
Caglia, E. Bonnie, TC, Dec. 45,585(M), 57 TCM 1, TC Memo. 1989-143
Ettig, TC, Dec. 44,736(M), 55 TCM 720, TC Memo. 1988-182
Heller, TC, Dec. 44,083(M), 53 TCM 1486, TC Memo. 1987-376
Anastasato, TC, Dec. 43,309(M), 52 TCM 293, TC Memo. 1986-400
Stevenson, TC, Dec. 43,068(M), 51 TCM 1050, TC Memo. 1986-207
Wilhelm, TC, Dec. 42,813(M), 51 TCM 261, TC Memo. 1986-12
Branson, TC, Dec. 38,026(M), 42 TCM 281, TC Memo. 1981-338
Calloway, TC, Dec. 37,019(M), 40 TCM 495, TC Memo. 1980-211
Greenfield, TC, Dec. 35,253(M), 37 TCM 1082, TC Memo. 1978-251
Leong, TC, Dec. 34,232(M), 36 TCM 89, TC Memo. 1977-19
Dougherty, TC, Dec. 32,138, 60 TC 917
Diaz, Antonio A. v. Southern Drilling Corp. . . . .
. . . . ¶ 42.299.45
● CA-5—(aff'g unreported DC), 71-1 ustc ¶ 9236
Diaz, Enrique . . ¶ 35,038.43, 40,375.65, 40,485.63, 42,288.377
● DC-Calif—90-1 ustc ¶ 50,209
Van Camp & Bennion, P.S., DC-Wash, 96-2 ustc ¶ 50,438
Diaz, Frank . . . . ¶ 29,762.9911
● TC—Dec. 42,922(M); 51 TCM 594; TC Memo. 1986-98
Diaz, Humberto (See Flicker, Marvin)
Diaz, Juan (See Setal, Manuel G.)
Diaz, Leonarda C.
● CA-2—(aff'g TC), 79-2 ustc ¶ 9473; 607 F2d 995
Kuh, TC, Dec. 40,461(M), 46 TCM 1405, TC Memo. 1983-572
Damm, TC, Dec. 37,861(M), 41 TCM 1359, TC Memo. 1981-203
● TC—Dec. 35,436; 70 TC 1067
German, Jr., TC, Dec. 48,867(M), 65 TCM 1931, TC Memo. 1993-59
Orr, TC, Dec. 48,532(M), 64 TCM 882, TC Memo. 1992-566
Zeidler, TC, Dec. 51,264(M), 71 TCM 2603, TC Memo. 1996-157
Schwerm, TC, Dec. 42,817(M), 51 TCM 270, TC Memo. 1986-16
Wassenaar, TC, Dec. 36,359, 72 TC 1195
Toner, TC, Dec. 35,877, 71 TC 772
Diaz, Miguel A. (See Powers (Belcher), Sandra L.)
Dibble, Leon N., Exr. . . . . ¶ 29,625.442
● BTA—Dec. 2320; 6 BTA 732; A. VI-2 CB 2
Dibble, Phillip A. . . . . ¶ 25,424.415
● TC—Dec. 41,602(M); 49 TCM 32; TC Memo. 1984-589
Ogden, CA-5, 86-1 ustc ¶ 9368, 788 F2d 252
Elrod,, TC, Dec. 43,486, 87 TC 1046
Dibblee, Isabel K. . . . . ¶ 32,263.381, 44,840.04
● SCt—(rev'g CA-9), 36-1 ustc ¶ 9008; 296 US 102; 56 SCt 54
● CA-9—(aff'g BTA), 35-1 ustc ¶ 9128; 75 F2d 617
● BTA—Dec. 8415; 29 BTA 1070
Di Benedetto, Frank R. . . . . ¶ 40,580.43
● DC-RI—75-1 ustc ¶ 9503
Carlucci, DC-NY, 93-1 ustc ¶ 50,211, 793 FSupp 482
Cook, DC-Pa, 91-1 ustc ¶ 50,284, 765 FSupp 217
Seachrist v. Riggs, DC-Va, 91-1 ustc ¶ 50,019
Continental Illinois Nat'l Bk. and Trust Co., Chicago, DC-III, 87-2 ustc ¶ 9442
Swift, DC-Conn, 86-1 ustc ¶ 9109, 614 FSupp 172
Rebelle, DC-La, 85-2 ustc ¶ 9493
Rebelle, III, DC-La, 84-2 ustc ¶ 9717, 588 FSupp 49

FIGURE I15-6 ▶ EXCERPT FROM COMMERCE CLEARING HOUSE CITATOR

rulings that have cited the authority in question. The RIA citator, however, conveys more extensive information than the CCH citator. Specifically, the citator includes information about the following:

1. Cases that have referenced the case in question, including whether the citing cases commented in a favorable or unfavorable manner or distinguished the cited cases.[45]
2. The specific issue in the case in question (the cited case) for which the citing authorities have referenced the case.

The RIA (formerly Prentice Hall) Citator consists of five hard-bound volumes plus softback cumulative supplements. The first hard-bound volume denotes citations made to cases during the period 1863 through 1941; the second volume contains citations made from 1942 through September 30, 1948; the third volume gives citations made from October 1, 1948 through July 29, 1954; the fourth volume contains citations made from July 30, 1954 through December 15, 1977; the fifth volume lists citations made from December 15, 1977 through December 20, 1989. The softback cumulative supplements contain citations made after December 20, 1989. Each year a revised cumulative supplement is prepared. In addition, monthly supplements are issued. A researcher interested in determining how the courts have subsequently evaluated a 1945 case should consult all volumes of the citator except the first. If the case in question is a 1980 case, the researcher need consult only the most recent bound volume plus the supplements.

As mentioned, the RIA citator discloses how the citing cases commented on the case in question. The nature of the comment is denoted by letters that appear to the left of the name of the citing case. Letters are also used to denote the history of the cited case (i.e., whether it was affirmed, etc.).[46] Figure I15-7 indicates what the various abbreviations symbolize.

The RIA citator is especially helpful if the cited case deals with more than one issue. As mentioned, the citator reports the issue(s) for which the case was cited. The numbers to the left of the citing authority denote the issue number of the cited case for which the citation is made. The number designation is not universally associated with a particular topic. Instead, the issue number refers to the number used to designate a particular issue in the cited case. Issue numbers appear in the headnotes to the case (at the top of the first page of the case). To save time, researchers should take note of the applicable issue number when reading cases.

Part of a sample page from the 1977–1989 citator appears in Figure I15-8. Refer to Figure I15-8 and locate the Tax Court decision for *Leonarda C. Diaz*. All of the cases citing the Tax Court's *Diaz* decision after 1977 and through 1989 are listed. (*Diaz* was decided by the Tax Court in 1978, so no earlier references will be found.) *Diaz* has been cited with respect to both the first and second issues in the case. If the case was concerned with additional issues, it has not been cited for them.

The "a" on the first line beneath the name of the case indicates that the Tax Court's decision was affirmed by the Second Circuit. The Tax Court's opinion has been explained and followed in various cases, but it has not been cited in an unfavorable manner. Thus, its authoritative value is strong.

The Second Circuit's decision appears as a separate entry. The letters "sa" signify that the circuit court affirmed the Tax Court decision in the *Diaz* case. The cases that have

---

[45] When a court distinguishes its conclusion in one case from an earlier decision, it points out that the two different outcomes are justifiable because the facts in the two cases are not the same.

[46] If a case is *affirmed,* the decision of the lower court is upheld. *Reversed* means that the higher court arrived at the opposite decision of the court from which the case was appealed. *Remanded* signifies that the higher court sent the case back to the lower court with instructions to address certain matters not earlier addressed.

Certain notations appear at the end of the cited case line. These notations include:

(A) the government has acquiesced in the reasoning or the result of the cited case

(NA) the government has refused to acquiesce or to adopt the reasoning or the result of the cited case, and will challenge the position adopted if future proceedings arise on the same issue

on rem the case has been remanded by a higher court and the case cited is the resulting decision

Evaluation of Cited Cases

c the citing case court has adversely commented on the reasoning of the cited case, and has criticized the earlier decision.

e the cited case is used favorably by the citing case court

f the reasoning of the court in the cited case is followed by the later decision

g the cited and citing cases are distinguished from each other on either facts or law

inap the citing case court has specifically indicated that the cited case does not apply to the situation stated in the citing case.

iv on all fours (both the cited and citing cases are virtually identical)

k the cited and citing case principles are reconciled

l the rationale of the cited case is limited to the facts or circumstances surrounding that case (this can occur frequently in situations in which there has been an intervening higher court decision or law change)

n the cited case was noted in a dissenting opinion

o the later case directly overrules the cited case (use of the evaluation is generally limited to situations in which the court notes that it is specifically overturning the cited case, and that the case will no longer be of any value)

q the decision of the cited case is questioned and its validity debated in relation to the citing case

The evaluations used for the court decisions generally are followed by a number. That number refers to the headnoted issue in the American Federal Tax Reports (AFTR) or Tax Court decision to which the citing case relates. If the case is not directly on point with any headnote, a bracketed notation at the end of the citing case line directs the researcher to the page in the cited case on which the issue appears.

---

a affirmed by a higher court (Note: When available, the official cite to the affirmance is provided; if the affirmance is by unpublished order or opinion, the date of the decision and the court deciding the case are provided.)

App auth appeal authorized by the Treasury

App appeal pending (Note: Later volumes may have to be consulted to determine if the appellate case was decided.)

cert gr petition for certiorari was granted by the U.S. Supreme Court

d appeal dismissed by the court or withdrawn by the party filing the appeal

(G) following an appeal notation, this symbol indicates that it was the government filing an appeal.

m the earlier decision has been modified by the higher court, or by a later decision.

r the decision of the lower court has been reversed on appeal

rc related case arising out of the same taxable event or concerning the same taxpayer.

reh den rehearing has been denied by the same court in which the original case was heard.

reinst a dismissed appeal has been reinstated by the appellate court and is under consideration again.

remd the case has been remanded for proceedings consistent with the higher court decision.

remg the cited case is remanding the earlier case

revg & remg the decision of the lower court has been reversed and remanded by a higher court on appeal

s same case or ruling

sa the cited case is affirming the earlier case

sm the cited case is modifying the earlier case

sr the cited case is reversing the earlier case

sx the cited case is an earlier proceeding in a case for which a petition for certiorari was denied

(T) an appeal was filed from the lower court decision by the taxpayer

vacd the lower court decision was vacated on appeal or by the original court on remand.

vacg a higher court or the original court on remand has vacated the lower court decision

widrn the original opinion was withdrawn by the court

x petition for certiorari was denied by the U.S. Supreme Court

● Supreme Court cases are designated by a bold-faced bullet (●) before the case line for easy location.

FIGURE I15-7 ▲ ABBREVIATIONS USED IN RIA CITATOR 2ND SERIES

Source: Reproduced with permission from Research Institute of America, Inc.

cited the circuit court's opinion are listed under the entry for such opinion. The appellate decision has not been questioned or criticized; thus, it is a relatively strong decision.

Recall that for the *Alfonso Diaz* case, the CCH Citator reported that in 1972 the Commissioner acquiesced to the decision. Because the page from the 1978–1989 PH *Federal Taxes 2nd* Citator reproduced in Figure I15-8 includes developments from December 15, 1977 through December 20, 1989, it does not report the 1972 acquiescence. The bound citator for 1954–1977 reports the 1972 acquiescence. In order to locate the most recent references to the *Leonarda C. Diaz* case, one would need to refer to the cumulative supplements. The appropriate excerpts from the 1990–1995 cumulative supplement is illustrated here and indicates one subsequent case that cites the Second Circuit's *Leonarda C. Diaz* decision and seven that cite the Tax Court decision.[47]

1990–1995 *Cumulative Supplement*	*January–November 1996* *Cumulative Supplement*

DIAZ, LEONARDA C., 70 TC 1067, ¶ 70.95 PH TC
  a—Diaz, Leonarda C. V Comm., 44 AFTR 2d 79-6027, (CA2)
  f—Wiertzema, Vance v U.S., 66 AFTR 2d 90-5371, 747 F Supp 1365, (DC ND), [See 70 TC 1074-1075]
  e—Barboza, David, 1991 TC Memo 91-1905, [See 70 TC 1074]
  e—Orr, J. Thomas, 1992 RIA TC Memo 92-2912, [See 70 TC 1073]
  e—German, Harry, Jr. & Carol, 1993 RIA TC Memo 93-261-93-262, [See 70 TC 1074-1075]
  e—Meredith, Judith R., 1993 RIA TC Memo 93-1247, [See 70 TC 1074, cited at 73 TC 726]
  e—Holmes, Lynn J., 1993 RIA TC Memo 93-1978, [See 70 TC 1072-1073]
  e—Kersey, Robert C., 1993 RIA TC Memo 93-3396, [See 70 TC 1072-1073]
DIAZ, LEONARDA C. v COMM., 44 AFTR 2d 79-6027, 607 F2d 995, (CA2, 6-25-79)
  e—Wiertzema, Vance v U.S., 66 AFTR 2d 90-5371, 747 F Supp 1363, (DC ND)

One additional case is shown in the January 1996–November 1996 Cumulative Supplement volumes as citing each of the *Leonarda C. Diaz* decisions.

COMPUTERS AS A RESEARCH TOOL

CD-ROM AND ONLINE RESEARCH

Computers are now being used by most tax professionals as a tax research tool. Three computer-based legal data bases for taxation are now available. These data bases cover federal and state tax matters as well as other federal and state legal matters. The names of the services and their providers are indicated below.

Name of Data Base	*Provider*
ACCESS	Commerce Clearing House
LEXIS	Mead Data Central
WESTLAW	West Publishing

Each of the above tax data bases includes the basic tax research sources: Code, regulations, government promulgations, private letter rulings, legislative histories, committee reports, treaties, and judicial decisions. In addition, the computerized tax data bases contain a number of tax services. For example, WESTLAW contains the index and

---

[47] No additional references have been reported as of January 17, 1997.

ADDITIONAL COMMENT

The RIA citator has the advantage of providing the most citations for a given case. This is obvious when one compares RIA's five volumes plus supplements with CCH's two volumes. Also, RIA numbers each tax issue litigated in a court case. This coding allows the tax advisor to identify cases dealing specifically with the issue being researched. For example, if one is interested in the 2nd issue in the *Leonarda Diaz* Tax Court decision, the citator reproduced in Figure I15-8 denotes five cases that deal specifically with issue 1 of which three follow the *Diaz* reasoning.

DIAZ, LEONARDA C. v COMM., 44 AFTR 2d 79-6027, 607 F2d 995, (CA2, 6-25-79)
e—Zeidler, Gerald L. & Joy M., 1996 RIA TC Memo 96-1151

DiBENEDETTO, FRANK R. v U.S., 35 AFTR 2d 75-1502, 75-1 USTC ¶ 9503, (DC RI, 11-7-74)
e-1—Padalino, Vincent v. U.S., 71A AFTR 2d 93-3016, (DC NJ)

DIBERT, BANCROFT & ROSS CO, LTD, IN RE, 77 AFTR 2d 96-1152, (DC LA, 2/12/96)
sa—Marrero, Robert L., Trustee v. Central Progressive Bank, et al, 74 AFTR 2d 94-6470, (Bktcy Ct LA)

DICARLO, STEPHEN ALAN, 1992 RIA TC Memo ¶ 92,280
e—Lisle, Helen v. U.S., 76 AFTR 2d 95-7886, (DC CA), [See 1992 RIA TC Memo 92-1385]
e—Talmage, Stephen V., 1996 RIA TC Memo 96-875, [See 1992 RIA TC Memo 92-1387]

DICKENS, JACK v U.S., 49 AFTR 2d 82-1238, 671 F2d 969, 82-1 USTC ¶ 16,377, (CA6, 3-1-82)
e—Houch, Buford F. v. U.S., 77 AFTR 2d 96-1947, (DC OH), [See 49 AFTR2d 82-1239, 671 F2d 971]
e—Kruzel, Dennis A. v. I.R.S., et al, 77 AFTR 2d 96-1978, (DC MI), [See 49 AFTR2d 82-1239, 671 F2d 971-972]

DICKERSON, M. ASHLEY, 1990 PH TC Memo ¶ 90,577
e-1—Bauman, Carl J. D. & Margaret A., 1996 RIA TC Memo 96-1595

DICKEY, RAYMOND L., 1985 PH TC Memo ¶ 85,478
e—Barnhill, Joseph L., Jr. & Cynthia A., 1996 RIA TC Memo 96-778, [See 1985 PH TC Memo 85-2145]

DICKEY, WILLIAM L., IN RE, 57 AFTR 2d 86-1101, 86-1 USTC ¶ 9424, (Bktcy Ct VA, 4-30-85)
k-1—Curasi, James B. v. U.S., 76 AFTR 2d 95-6407, 907 F Supp 378, (DC FL)

•DICKMAN, ESTHER C. v COMM., 53 AFTR 2d 84-1608, 465 US 330, 104 S Ct 1086, 79 L Ed 343, 84-1 USTC ¶ 9240, (2-22-84), [ro]reh den, 466 US 945, 104 S Ct 1932, 80 LE2d 477, 4-16-84
e—White, Clayton S. v. U.S., 71A AFTR 2d 93-3123, 93-3124, (DC NM), [See 53 AFTR2d 84-1612, 465 US 343]
e—Indianapolis Life Insurance Co v. U.S., 78 AFTR 2d 96-6150, (DC IN), [See 53 AFTR2d 84-1613—84-1614, 465 US 343]
f—Bankers Trust New York Corp & Consolidated Subsidiaries v. U.S., 78 AFTR 2d 95-5104, 36 Fed Cl 36, (Ct Fed Cl), [See 53 AFTR2d 84-1612, 465 US 343]
e—McLendon, Gordon B., Est of, 1996 RIA TC Memo 96-2223, [See 53 AFTR2d 84-1612, 465 US 343]
g-1—Miller, Elizabeth B., 1996 RIA TC Memo 96-19

DICKSON, ROBERT W. & JEANNE K., 1983 PH TC Memo ¶ 83,723
g-1—Ballard, Charles A., 1996 RIA TC Memo 96-571

DIEBOLD, INC. v U.S., 65 AFTR 2d 90-648, 891 F2d 1579, 90-1 USTC ¶ 50,003, (CA Fed Cir, 12-19-89)
e—Piccadilly Cafeterias Inc v. U.S., 78 AFTR 2d 96-6189, 96-6190, 36 Fed Cl 335, 336, (Ct Fed Cl), [See 65 AFTR2d 90-651, 891 F2d 1583]
e-1—Girling Health Systems, Inc v. U.S., 71A AFTR 2d 93-3308, (Cl Ct)

DIECKMANN, RICHARD R. v U.S., 39 AFTR 2d 77-845, 550 F2d 622, 77-1 USTC ¶ 9224, (CA10, 2-18-77)
e—Berlanga, Cristofora v. U.S., 71A AFTR 2d 93-3202, (DC MI), [See 39 AFTR2d 77-846, 550 F2d 624]
e—Southtrust Bank of Etowah County, N.P. v. Cheerzportz, Inc, et al, 71A AFTR 2d 93-3291, (DC AL), [See 39 AFTR2d 77-846, 550 F2d 624]
e—Pederson, Roland v. U.S., 71A AFTR 2d 93-3503, (DC MT), [See 39 AFTR2d 77-846, 550 F2d 624]
e-1—Sanders, Marjorie v. U.S., 77 AFTR 2d 96-1842, (DC CO)
e-1—Compagnoni, Jacqueline M. v. U.S., 78 AFTR 2d 96-6503, (DC FL)

DIEGO INVESTORS-IV, 1989 PH TC Memo ¶ 89,630
rc—Fox, Johana C. v. U.S., 78 AFTR 2d 96-5725, (DC CA)
e—Bealor, Barry B. & Nancy L., 1996 RIA TC Memo 96-3101

DIEHL, THOMAS C., 1990 PH TC Memo ¶ 90,048
e-1—McKee, Wayne Curtis, 1996 RIA TC Memo 96-1061
e-1—Cowan, Ted, 1996 RIA TC Memo 96-1206

DIELECTRIC MATERIALS CO., 57 TC 587, ¶ 57.61 PH TC, (A), 1972-1 CB 2
e—Wy'East Color Inc, 1996 RIA TC Memo 96-1031, [See 57 TC 591]

DIEMER, JAMES D.; U.S. v., 76 AFTR 2d 95-7587, 859 F Supp 126, 94-2 USTC ¶ 50420, (DC NJ, 8/1/94)
revg & remg—Avila, Fred A., et al; U.S. v., 78 AFTR 2d 96-5189, 88 F3d 229, (CA3)

DIERCKS, KENNETH W., 1996 RIA TC Memo ¶ 96,345

DIESCHER, ALFRED J., 18 BTA 353
e—Mullings, Manley v. Com., 78 AFTR 2d 96-6111, (DC NY), [See 18 BTA 358]

DIETRICH INDUSTRIES, INC. v U.S., 71 AFTR 2d 93-1623, 988 F2d 568, (CA5, 4-16-93)
e-1—Progressive Consumers Federal Credit Union v. U.S., 77 AFTR 2d 96-1427, 79 F3d 1237, (CA1)
g-1—First Federal Savings Bank of Wabash v. U.S., 78 AFTR 2d 96-6064, (DC IN)

DIETRICK, GERALD PATRICK & ANITA LEA, 1988 PH TC Memo ¶ 88,180
e-1—Zand, J.J., 1996 RIA TC Memo 96-201

DIETRICK, GERALD PATRICK v COMM., 64 AFTR 2d 89-5353, 881 F2d 336, 89-2 USTC ¶ 9469, (CA6, 8-10-89)
e-1—Zand, J.J., 1996 RIA TC Memo 96-201

DIETZ, C. RAYMOND, SR.; U.S. v, 75 AFTR 2d 95-1613, (CA4, 3/28/95)
rc—Dietz, C. Raymond, Sr. v. U.S., 78 AFTR 2d 96-5500, (DC MD)

DIETZ, C. RAYMOND, SR. v. U.S., 78 AFTR 2d 96-5500, (DC MD, 6/7/96)
rc—Dietz, C. Raymond, Sr.; U.S. v., 75 AFTR 2d 95-1613, (CA4)

DIETZ, MYRTLE V., ESTATE OF, 1996 RIA TC Memo ¶ 96,471

DIETZ, R.E., CORP. v U.S., 68 AFTR 2d 91-5238, 939 F2d 1, 91-2 USTC ¶ 50,375, (CA2, 7-22-91)
e—Bausch & Lomb Inc & Consol. Subs., 1996 RIA TC Memo 96-487, [See 68 AFTR 2d 91-5241-91-5242, 939 F2d 5]

DIFFERENTIAL STEEL CAR CO., 16 TC 413, ¶ 16.52 PH TC 1951
e—Medieval Attractions N.V., 1996 RIA TC Memo 96-3318, [See 16 TC 423-425]

DIGBY, DONALD R. & LYDIA, 103 TC 441, ¶ 103.24 TCR
e—Ackerman, Robert W. & Patricia A., 1996 RIA TC Memo 96-2267, [See 103 TC 447]

DiLEO, JOSEPH R. & MARY A., 96 TC 858, ¶ 96.42 PH TC
e—Lee, Chong-Kak & Sang-Ok, 1995 RIA TC Memo 95-3814, 95-3815, [See 96 TC 874]
e—Wynn, Eric, 1995 RIA TC Memo 95-3883, 95-3884, [See 96 TC 873]
e—Marason, Keith F., 1996 RIA TC Memo 96-34, [See 96 TC 867]
e—Rouzmehr, Yousef, 1996 RIA TC Memo 96-217, [See 96 TC 867]
e—Sharer, Mary Lee, 1996 RIA TC Memo 96-747, [See 96 TC 867]
e—Eresian, Ara & Evelyn, 1996 RIA TC Memo 96-1371, [See 96 TC 867]
e—Kale, William, 1996 RIA TC Memo 96-1459, [See 96 TC 873]
e—M.S. Food Stores, Inc., 1996 RIA TC Memo 96-1612, [See 96 TC 867, 868]
e—Sparrow, Robert D., 1996 RIA TC Memo 96-1927, [See 96 TC 874]
e—Van Heemst, John, 1996 RIA TC Memo 96-2206, 96-2210, 96-2211, [See 96 TC 871, 873-874]
e—McGirl, Richard K. & Christine M., 1996 RIA TC Memo 96-2256, [See 96 TC 867, 868]
e—Katerelos, Haralampos & Irene, 1996 RIA TC Memo 96-2428, [See 96 TC 872]
e—Wagner, Edward A. & Barbara, 1996 RIA TC Memo 96-2542, [See 96 TC 873]
e—DeCaprio, Ferdinand & Claire, 1996 RIA TC Memo 96-2584, [See 96 TC 880]
e—Harp, Charles R. & April B., 1996 RIA TC Memo 96-2657, 96-2659, 96-2664, [See 96 TC 868, 869]
e—Meilak, Inez, 1996 RIA TC Memo 96-2672, [See 96 TC 874]

FIGURE I15-8 ▶ EXCERPT FROM PRENTICE HALL FEDERAL TAXES 2ND CITATOR, 1978–1989

Reproduced with permission from Research Institute of America, Inc.

text for BNA's *Tax Management Portfolios.* LEXIS includes the TAXRIA data base, which has the index and text for RIA's *United States Tax Reporter* service and the RIA citator along with many other materials including state and international tax services. LEXIS also includes the *RIA Federal Tax Coordinator 2d* and BNA's *Tax Management Portfolios.* The ACCESS data base includes the CCH service and citator, as well as the *U.S. Master Tax Guide.* ACCESS also includes court cases, letter rulings, state tax reports, and BNA's *Tax Management Portfolios,* among other items. Each of these data bases also contains the text for a number of tax newsletters and some data bases include the text of tax journals and law reviews.

Unlike the tax services, some computerized data bases do not contain an index. Rather, the researcher locates applicable authorities by using key-word search requests. That is, he or she instructs the computer to locate all of the authorities containing certain words or phrases. Researchers need to be imaginative in thinking of search requests; under the key-word approach the computer will not locate an authority on point unless it contains the exact wording the researcher specifies, even though it contains synonymous terms.

EXAMPLE I15-12 ▶ A researcher is interested in whether a certain expenditure for clothing is deductible under Sec. 162 as a uniform expense. The researcher might instruct the computer to retrieve all cases containing the words *uniform* and *Sec. 162* in close proximity to each other. This search will turn up only cases containing those words if the system uses the key-word approach. Cases using the words *work clothing* will not be retrieved. A more comprehensive search will take place if the researcher instructs the computer to look for either *uniform* or *work clothing* in close proximity of *Sec. 162.* ◀

Use of these data bases can be especially valuable as a supplement to the research conducted manually through the tax services. After researchers have located some authorities through the tax services, they can use the computerized data base to

WHAT WOULD YOU DO IN THIS SITUATION?

You are a new associate of the accounting firm of Smith, Wesson, and Swilley, P.C., of Yuma, Arizona. Your undergraduate specialty was behavioral accounting, where you were constantly on the lookout for misbehaving accountants. But as you enter the real world, the specter of taxation over your practice and your clients' business and personal decisions has become a much more consuming passion. As a matter of fact, you have found that doing tax research gives you the opportunity to grow in the area of your first real intellectual love, the computer. You simply love to sit at the controls of your Super-duper Model XYZ, 1.3 giga-byte personal computer all day. Your colleagues have come to nickname you the "ROM-Roamer" because of your uncanny ability to locate the most insignificant minutiae at the push of a button.

Your managing partner, Ms. Sandra Smith, sees a wonderful potential in your computing research skills and assigns you to the firm's tax section. In a short time,

you have mastered the intricacies of all the major computer databases that provide tax research tools, including but not limited to ACCESS, LEXIS, and Westlaw, copyrighted by Commerce Clearing House, Mead Data Central, and West Publishing Company, respectively.

Assume that your firm's on-line cost for these research services is approximately $5 per minute. Because of your demonstrated expertise in the use of these research tools, in 15 minutes you are able to do tax research for a client that has historically taken and was billed for six hours. Given the fact that the end product to the client is the same in both cases, can you or your firm ethically continue to bill the client for six hours of research time? What other ethical issues are raised by this scenario? What guidelines are provided on this issue in the AICPA Code of Professional Conduct or the AICPA's Statements on Responsibilities in Tax Practice?

determine whether there are additional authorities on point. The data bases are updated for new developments on a very timely basis; for example, some court cases may appear within a few days of the decision.

A number of tax services, including CCH's *Federal Tax Service*, RIA's *Federal Tax Coordinator 2d (RIA On Point)*, CCH's *Standard Federal Tax Reporter (CCH Access)*, BNA's *Tax Management Portfolios*, RIA's *United States Tax Reporter*, and West's *Federal Taxation*, are available on CD-ROM (compact disc read-only memory). The material is organized the same as in the loose-leaf services. The compact discs allow pages and pages of information to be stored in practically no space. The compact discs generally are updated monthly, and the filing of supplementary pages is avoided. One way to retrieve information from the compact discs is to type key words into the computer. Alternatively, you could locate the index on the disk, consult the index, and then refer to the portion of the disk discussing your topic, for example, the deductibility of the cost of uniforms. Extensive material is available on the CCH ACCESS CD-ROM, including *Standard Federal Tax Reports, State Tax Reports,* Letter Rulings and IRS Positions, Revenue Rulings and Revenue Procedures, IRS Publications, Tax Forms and Instructions, and court cases dating back to 1913. Tax-oriented periodicals often provide listings and reviews of computer-based or CD-ROM research products.[48]

STATEMENTS ON RESPONSIBILITIES IN TAX PRACTICE

Tax advisors often wonder what they should do in certain circumstances and may turn to a professional organization for guidance. The standards set by professional organizations are not legally enforceable, although they have a great deal of moral clout. The most comprehensive guidelines for CPAs in tax practice were set forth by the Tax Division of the American Institute of Certified Public Accountants (AICPA) in their advisory **Statements on Responsibilities in Tax Practice (SRTP)** (reproduced in Appendix E).[49] The Tax Division articulated the following objectives for the SRTPs:

▶ To recommend appropriate standards of responsibilities . . . and to promote their uniform application by CPAs

▶ To encourage the development of increased understanding of the responsibilities of CPAs by the Treasury Department and Internal Revenue Service . . .

▶ To foster increased public understanding of, compliance with, and confidence in our tax system through awareness of the recommended standards of responsibilities of CPAs . . . [50]

The SRTPs are not enforceable standards, but rather are advisory guidelines. Some of the more important guidelines contained in the SRTP are highlighted below.

At times, a CPA may wonder whether it is appropriate to use an estimated amount on a tax return. *Statement No. 4* discusses the use of estimates in the following manner:

---

[48] For a discussion of the benefits of CD-ROM vs. hard copy research, the alternative CD-ROM products, and the structure of CD-ROM searches, see: Robert L. Black, "CD-ROM Tax Research: Tips, Tricks, and Traps," *The Tax Adviser*, Parts 1 (October, 1995, pp. 583-589) and 2 (January, 1996, pp. 23-27). Also, for a more detailed discussion of computerized tax research, see William A. Raabe, Gerald E. Whittenburg, and John C. Bost, *West's Federal Tax Research*, 3rd Edition (Minneapolis/St. Paul, MN: West

Publishing Co., 1994), Chapters 13 and 14.

[49] AICPA, *Statements on Responsibilities in Tax Practice, 1991 Revision*, Introduction, ¶.03. For a thorough discussion of ethical responsibilities in the tax context, see Bernard Wolfman, James P. Holden, and Kenneth Harris, *Standards of Tax Practice* (Boston, MA: Little, Brown and Company, 1995).

[50] Ibid.

▶ A CPA may prepare tax returns involving the use of the taxpayer's estimates if it is impracticable to obtain exact data, and the estimated amounts are reasonable under the facts and circumstances known to the CPA. When the taxpayer's estimates are used, they should be presented in such a manner as to avoid the implication of greater accuracy than exists.

Keep in mind, however, that certain expenses are not deductible unless the taxpayer has the proper documentation.[51] Thus, a CPA cannot use estimates for such amounts.

It is not unusual for a CPA to discover that a client's tax return for an earlier year contains one or more errors. *Statement No. 6* contains guidelines concerning what CPAs should do when they know about errors their clients, or prior return preparers, made. The recommendations are as follows:

▶ The CPA should inform the client promptly upon becoming aware of an error in a previously filed return or . . . a client's failure to file a required return. The CPA should recommend the measures to be taken. Such recommendation may be given orally. The CPA is not obligated to inform the Internal Revenue Service, and the CPA may not do so without the client's permission, except where required by law.

Statement No. 7 describes the CPA's responsibilities in an administrative proceeding (e.g., an audit) if the CPA is aware of an error on the return.

▶ [T]he CPA should inform the client promptly upon becoming aware of the error. The CPA should recommend the measures to be taken. Such recommendation may be given orally. The CPA is neither obligated to inform the Internal Revenue Service nor may the CPA do so without the client's permission, except where required by law.

▶ The CPA should request the client's agreement to disclose the error to the Internal Revenue Service.

Some CPAs, especially newer ones, may wonder about the advisability of giving advice orally. *Statement No. 8* makes the following comments about the form—oral or written—of the advice given by CPAs.

▶ Although oral advice may serve a client's needs appropriately in routine matters or in well-defined areas, written communications are recommended in important, unusual, or complicated transactions.

With respect to the procedural aspects of return preparation, including relying on the client's "numbers," *Statement No. 3* furnishes the guidance shown below.

▶ In preparing or signing a return, the CPA may in good faith rely without verification upon information furnished by the client or by third parties. Yet, the CPA should not ignore the implications of information furnished and should make reasonable inquiries if the information furnished appears to be incorrect, incomplete, or inconsistent either on its face or on the basis of other facts known to the CPA. In this connection, the CPA should refer to the client's returns for prior years whenever feasible.

▶ Where the Internal Revenue Code or income tax regulations impose a condition with respect to deductibility or other tax treatment of an item (such as taxpayer maintenance of books and records or substantiating documentation to support the reported deduction or tax treatment), the CPA should make appropriate inquiries to determine to his or her satisfaction whether such condition has been met.

---

[51] Section 274(d) precludes deductions for certain expenditures (e.g., travel expenses including meals and lodging) unless the taxpayer can substantiate them by "adequate records or sufficient" corroborating evidence.

▶ The individual CPA who is required to sign the return should consider information actually known to that CPA from the tax return of another client when preparing a tax return if the information is relevant to that tax return, its consideration is necessary to properly prepare that tax return, and use of such information does not violate any law or rule relating to confidentiality.

One should keep in mind that unlike an auditor, a tax practitioner should serve as an advocate for the client. Nevertheless, tax professionals should not adopt or recommend pro-taxpayer positions that lack sufficient support. *Statement No. 1* provides standards for taking pro-taxpayer positions on a tax return or in recommending such positions. The following guidance is given.

▶ A CPA should not recommend to a client that a position be taken . . . on a return unless the CPA has a good faith belief that the position has a realistic possibility of being sustained administratively or judicially on its merits if challenged.

▶ A CPA should not prepare or sign a return as an income tax return preparer if the CPA knows that the return takes a position that the CPA could not recommend under the standard expressed [above].

▶ Notwithstanding [the above], a CPA may recommend a position that the CPA concludes is not frivolous as long as the position is adequately disclosed on the return or claim for refund.

▶ In recommending certain tax return positions and in signing a return . . . a CPA should, where relevant, advise the client as to the potential penalty consequences of the recommended tax return position and the opportunity, if any, to avoid such penalties through disclosure.

Statement No. 1 elaborates on the "good faith" belief requirement for a pro-taxpayer position as follows:

▶ The standards suggested herein require that a CPA in good faith believe that the position is warranted in existing law or can be supported by a good faith argument for an extension, modification, or reversal of existing law. For example, the CPA may reach such a conclusion on the basis of well-reasoned articles, treatises, IRS General Counsel Memoranda, a General Explanation of a Revenue Act prepared by the staff of the Joint Committee on Taxation, and Internal Revenue Service written determinations (such as private letter rulings), whether or not such sources are treated as "authority" under Sec. 6661.[52]

STOP & THINK

Question: As described on page I1-15, you are researching a certain calculation that affects a client's deductions. The Code states that the calculation is to be done "in a manner prescribed by the Secretary." After studying the Code and the Regulations and the Committee Reports, you conclude that another way of doing the calculations is arguably correct under an intuitive approach. This intuitive approach would result in a lower tax liability for the client. According to the *Statements on Responsibilities in Tax Practice*, may you take a position contrary to the Regulations (which are final Regulations) on the basis that the Regulations are not valid?

Solution: You should not take a position that goes against the Regulations unless you have a "good faith belief that the position has a realistic possibility of being sustained administratively or judicially." However, you can take a position that does not meet the above standard, provided you adequately disclose the position and the position is not

---

[52] Chapter C15 of Prentice Hall's Federal Taxation Corporations, Partnerships, Estates, and Trusts provides a discussion of Sec. 6661, which has been renumbered as Sec. 6662. In the context of Sec. 6662 the taxpayer can potentially incur a penalty even if a position is disclosed on a tax return unless there is a reasonable basis (i.e., a higher standard than non-frivolous) for the position.

frivolous. We need more detailed information about the situation before we can definitively assess whether we meet the "good faith belief" test. Chapter 15 also discusses tax-return preparers taking positions contrary to the Regulations.

SAMPLE WORK PAPERS AND CLIENT LETTER

OBJECTIVE 7

Prepare work papers and communications to clients

A sample set of work papers, including a draft of a client letter and a memo to the file describing the facts on which the research is based, is presented in Appendix A. The purpose of the work papers is to denote the issues to be researched, the authorities addressing the issues, and the researcher's conclusions concerning the appropriate tax treatment, with rationale therefor.

The format and other details of a set of work papers differ from firm to firm. The sample in this text is designed to give general guidance concerning the content of work papers. In practice, work papers may include less detail.

PROBLEM MATERIALS

DISCUSSION QUESTIONS

I15-1 Explain the difference between closed-fact and open-fact situations.

I15-2 List the steps of the tax research process.

I15-3 Explain why the steps in the tax research process are sometimes circular.

I15-4 In what circumstances do the AICPA's *Statements on Responsibilities in Tax Practice* recommend that tax advisors communicate with their clients in writing instead of orally?

I15-5 Refer to the *Summit Publishing Company, Inc.* case reproduced in part on pages I15-6 to I15-8 and indicate whether the taxpayer had to pay any additional taxes.

I15-6 Refer to the *J.B.S. Enterprises, Inc.* case reproduced in part on pages I15-8 and I15-10 and indicate what information reported on the tax return probably triggered the audit.

I15-7 Explain what is encompassed by the term *tax law* when tax advisors use this phrase.

I15-8 The U.S. Government Printing Office publishes both hearings on proposed legislation and committee reports. Distinguish between these two publications.

I15-9 Explain why committee reports can be valuable research aids.

I15-10 Why has the tax researcher's job been simplified as a result of the codification of the tax statutes?

I15-11 A friend notices that you are reading from the *Internal Revenue Code of 1986*. Your friend inquires why you are consulting a 1986 publication, especially given that tax laws change so frequently. What is your response?

I15-12 Does Title 26 contain statutory provisions dealing only with income taxation? Explain.

I15-13 Refer to Sec. 301 of the Code.
a. Which subsection discusses the general rule for the tax treatment of a distribution of property?
b. Where should one look for exceptions to the general rule?
c. What type of Regulations would relate to subsection (e)?

I15-14 Why should tax researchers take note of the date on which a regulation was adopted?

I15-15 a. Distinguish between proposed, temporary, and final regulations.
b. Distinguish between interpretative and statutory regulations.

I15-16 Which type of regulation is more difficult for a taxpayer to successfully challenge, and why?

I15-17 Explain the legislative reenactment doctrine.

I15-18 a. Discuss the authoritative weight of revenue rulings.
   b. As a practical matter, what will happen if a taxpayer does not follow a revenue ruling and his or her return is audited?

I15-19 a. In which courts may litigation dealing with tax matters begin?
   b. Discuss the factors that would probably be important to a taxpayer who is deciding in which trial court to begin litigation.
   c. Describe the appeals court structure that exists for the various trial courts.

I15-20 May a taxpayer appeal a case litigated under the Small Cases Procedures of the Tax Court?

I15-21 Explain whether the following decisions have the same precedential value: (1) Tax Court regular decisions, (2) Tax Court memorandum decisions, (3) decisions under the Small Cases Procedures of the Tax Court.

I15-22 Does the IRS potentially issue acquiescences to decisions of a U.S. district court?

I15-23 Which courts' decisions are reported in the AFTR 2d? In the USTC?

I15-24 Who publishes regular decisions of the Tax Court? Memorandum decisions?

I15-25 Explain the *Golsen* rule. Design an example to illustrate its application.

I15-26 Assume that the only litigation to date on a particular issue is as follows:
Tax Court—decided for the taxpayer
Eighth Circuit Court of Appeals—decided for the taxpayer (affirming the Tax Court)
District Court of Louisiana—decided for the taxpayer

Fifth Circuit Court of Appeals—decided for the government (reversing the District Court of Louisiana)
   a. Discuss the precedential value of the cases listed above for your client, who is a California resident.
   b. If your client, a Texas resident instead, litigates in the Tax Court, how will the court rule? Explain.

I15-27 When might a tax advisor need to consult the provisions contained in a tax treaty?

I15-28 Compare the tax services listed below that are found in your tax library with respect to (a) how they are organized and (b) where current developments appear.
   a. *United States Tax Reporter*
   b. *Standard Federal Tax Reporter*
   c. *Federal Tax Coordinator 2d*
   d. *Law of Federal Income Taxation* (Mertens)
   e. BNA's *Tax Management Portfolios*
   f. CCH's *Federal Tax Service*

I15-29 What two functions does a citator serve?

I15-30 Describe two types of information reported in the *Research Institute of America Citator 2nd Series* but not in the Commerce Clearing House citator.

I15-31 Explain how your research approach might differ if you were using a computerized data base instead of a looseleaf tax service (e.g., the *Standard Federal Tax Reporter* service) at the beginning of your research.

I15-32 According to the *Statements on Responsibilities in Tax Practice,* how much support should exist before a CPA should take a pro-taxpayer position on a tax return?

PROBLEMS

I15-33 *Interpretation of the Code.* Under a divorce instrument executed in 1996, an ex-wife receives cash of $25,000 per year for eight years from her former husband. The instrument does not explicitly state that the payment is not includable in income.
   a. Does the ex-wife have gross income? If so, how much?
   b. Does the former husband receive a tax deduction? If so, is it for or from AGI? Refer only to the Internal Revenue Code in answering this problem. Start with Sec. 71.

I15-34 *Interpretation of the Code.* Refer to Code Sec. 385 and answer the questions below.
   a. Whenever regulations are adopted, what type will they be: statutory or interpretative? Explain.
   b. Assume regulations have been finalized for Sec. 385. Will they have any relevance to estate tax matters? Explain.

I15-35 *Using the Cumulative Bulletin.* Consult any *Cumulative Bulletin.* In what order are revenue rulings arranged?

I15-36 *Using the Cumulative Bulletin.* Which Code section does Rev. Rul. 85-44 interpret? (Hint: Consult the 1985-1 *Cumulative Bulletin.*)

I15-37 *Using the Cumulative Bulletin.* Refer to the 1989-1 *Cumulative Bulletin.*
a. What time period is covered by this bulletin?
b. What appears on page 1?
c. What items are printed in Part I of the bulletin?
d. In what order are the items presented in Part I?
e. What items are printed in Part II?
f. What items are printed in Part III?

I15-38 *Using the Cumulative Bulletin.* Refer to the 1990-1 *Cumulative Bulletin.*
a. For the time period covered by the bulletin, to which cases did the IRS issue a nonacquiescence?
b. What is the topical area of Rev. Rul. 90-10?
c. Does this bulletin contain any revenue ruling that interprets Sec. 162? If so, list it.

I15-39 *Determination of Acquiescence.*
a. What official action did the Commissioner take in 1986 concerning the Tax Court case of *John McIntosh?* (Hint: Consult the 1986-1 *Cumulative Bulletin.*)
b. Did such action concern *all* the issues in the case? If not, explain. (Consult the headnote to the case before answering this part of the question.)

I15-40 *Determination of Acquiescence.*
a. What original action (acquiescence or nonacquiescence) did the Commissioner take concerning *Streckfus Steamers, Inc.,* 19 T.C. 1 (1952)?
b. Was the action complete or partial?
c. Did the Commissioner subsequently change his mind? If so, when?

I15-41 *Determination of Acquiescence.*
a. What original action (acquiescence or nonacquiescence) did the Commissioner take concerning *Pittsburgh Milk Co.,* 26 T.C. 707 (1956)?
b. Did the Commissioner subsequently change his mind? If so, when?

I15-42 *Assessing a Case.* Look up the decision for *Everett J. Gordon,* 85 T.C. 309 (1985), and answer the questions below.
a. Was the decision reviewed by the court? If so, was it a unanimous decision? Explain.
b. Was the decision entered under Rule 155?
c. Consult a citator. Was the case heard by an appellate court? If so, which court?

I15-43 *Assessing a Case.* Look up the decision for *Bush Brothers & Co.,* 73 T.C. 424 (1979), and answer the questions below.
a. Was the decision reviewed by the court? If so, was it a unanimous decision? Explain.
b. Was the decision entered under Rule 155?
c. Consult a citator. Was the case heard by an appellate court? If so, which court?

I15-44 *Writing Citations.* Provide the proper citations (including both primary and secondary cites where applicable) for the authorities listed below. (For secondary cites, give both the AFTR and USTC cites.)
a. *Ruth K. Dowell v. U.S.,* a 10th Circuit decision
b. *Thomas M. Dragoun v. CIR,* a Tax Court memo decision
c. *John M. Grabinski v. U.S.,* a District Court of Minnesota decision
d. *John M. Grabinski v. U.S.,* an Eighth Circuit decision
e. *Rebekah Harkness,* a 1972 Court of Claims decision

f. *Hillsboro National Bank v. CIR,* a Supreme Court decision

g. Rev. Rul. 78-129

I15-45 ***Writing Citations.*** Provide the proper citations (including both primary and secondary cites where applicable) for the authorities listed below. (For secondary cites, give both the AFTR and USTC cites.)

a. Rev. Rul. 69-125

b. *Frank H. Sullivan,* a Board of Tax Appeals decision

c. *Lloyd Weaver,* a Tax Court decision

d. *Ralph L. Rogers v. U.S.,* an Ohio District Court decision

e. *Norman Rodman v. CIR,* a Second Circuit Court decision

I15-46 ***Interpreting Citations.*** Following are some actual citations. For each case, indicate which court decided the case. In addition, for each authority, indicate on which pages and in which publications the authority was reported.

a. *Lloyd M. Shumaker v. CIR,* 648 F.2d 1198, 48 AFTR 2d 81-5353 (9th Cir., 1981)

b. *Dean R. Shore,* 69 T.C. 689 (1978)

c. *Real Estate Land Title & Trust Co. v. U.S.,* 309 U.S. 13, 23 AFTR 816 (USSC, 1940)

d. *J. B. Morris v. U.S.,* 441 F. Supp. 76, 41 AFTR 2d 78-335 (D.C. TX, 1977)

e. Rev. Rul. 83-3, 1983-1 C.B. 72

f. *Malone & Hyde, Inc. v. U.S.,* 568 F.2d 474, 78-1 USTC ¶9199 (6th Cir., 1978)

I15-47 ***Using a Tax Service.*** Use the topical index of the *United States Tax Reporter* tax service to locate authorities dealing with the deductibility of the cost of a facelift.

a. In which paragraph(s) does the *United States Tax Reporter* service give a synopsis of these authorities and citations to them?

b. List the authorities.

c. Have there been any recent non-statutory developments concerning the tax consequences of facelifts? (*Recent* means authorities appearing in the cross-reference section.)

d. May a taxpayer deduct the cost of a facelift paid for in 1996? Explain.

I15-48 ***Using a Tax Service.*** Refer to Reg. Sec. 1.302-1 at ¶3022 of the *United States Tax Reporter* service. Does the regulation interpret today's version of the Code? Explain.

I15-49 ***Using a Tax Service.*** Use the topical index of the *Standard Federal Tax Reporter* to locate authorities dealing with whether termite damage qualifies for a casualty loss deduction.

a. In which paragraph(s) does the *Standard Federal Tax Reporter* service give a synopsis of these authorities and citations to them?

b. List the authorities.

c. Have there been any recent developments concerning the tax consequences of termite damage? (*Recent* means authorities appearing in the cumulative index section.)

I15-50 ***Using a Tax Service.***

a. Locate in the *Standard Federal Tax Reporter* service the place where Sec. 303(b)(2)(A) is reproduced. This provision states that Sec. 303(a) applies only if the stock meets a certain percentage test. What is the applicable percentage?

b. Locate Reg. Sec. 1.303-2(a) in the same tax service as in Part a. Does this regulation interpret today's version of the Code with respect to the percentage test addressed in Part a? Explain.

I15-51 ***Using a Tax Service.*** The questions below deal with the *Tax Management Portfolios* published by the Bureau of National Affairs.

a. What is the portfolio number of the volume that provides a detailed examination of only the topic of tax-free exchanges under Sec. 1031?

b. On which page does a discussion of "boot" begin?

c. What are the purposes of Worksheets 1 and 5 of this portfolio?

d. Refer to the bibliography and references at the back of the portfolio. List the numbers (e.g., 90-5) of the 1990 revenue rulings that, according to the portfolio, dealt with the sale or exchange of a personal residence.

I15-52 *Using a Tax Service.* This problem deals with the Mertens' *Law of Federal Income Taxation* tax service.

a. Refer to Volume 5. What broad, general topics does it discuss?

b. Which section of Volume 5 is devoted to a discussion of the principal methods of determining depreciation?

c. In Volume 5, what is the purpose of the yellow and white sheets appearing before the tab labeled "Text"?

d. Refer to the Ruling Status Table in the Rulings volume. What is the current status of Rev. Ruls. 79-433 and 75-335?

e. Refer to the Code-Rulings Tables in the Rulings volume. List the numbers (e.g., Rev. Rul. 84-88) of all 1984 revenue rulings and revenue procedures interpreting Sec. 121.

I15-53 *Using a Tax Service.* The questions below deal with the *Federal Tax Coordinator 2d* published by the Research Institute of America.

a. Use the topical index to locate authorities dealing with the deductibility of the cost of work clothing by ministers (clergymen). List the authorities.

b. Where does this tax service report new developments?

I15-54 *Using a Tax Service.* Refer to the *United States Tax Reporter* and *Standard Federal Tax Reporter* services. Then for each tax service, answer the following questions.

a. In which volume is the index located?

b. Is the index arranged by topic or by Code section?

c. If all you know is a Code section number, how do you locate additional materials?

d. If all you know is the name of a court decision, how do you locate additional materials?

I15-55 *Using a Citator.* Trace *Biltmore Homes, Inc.,* a 1960 Tax Court memorandum decision, through both citators described in the text.

a. According to the *RIA Citator 2nd Series,* how many times has the Tax Court decision been cited by other courts on Issue Number 5?

b. How many issues were involved in the trial court litigation? (Hint: Refer to the headnote of the case.)

c. Did an appellate court hear the case? If so, which court?

d. According to the CCH citator, how many times has the Tax Court decision been cited by other courts?

e. According to the CCH citator, how many times has the Circuit Court decision been cited by other courts on Issue Number 5?

I15-56 *Using a Citator.* Trace *Stephen Bolaris,* 776 F.2d 1428, through both citators described in the text.

a. According to the *RIA Citator 2nd Series,* how many times has the Ninth Circuit's decision been cited?

b. Did the case address more than one issue? Explain.

c. Was the case ever commented on in an unfavorable manner? Explain.

d. According to the CCH citator, how many times has the Ninth Circuit's decision been cited?

e. According to the CCH citator, how many times has the Tax Court's decision been cited for Issue Number 1?

I15-57   *Interpreting a Case.* Refer to the *Levin Metals Corporation* case (92 T.C. 307).
  a. In which year was the case decided?
  b. What controversy was litigated?
  c. Who won the case?
  d. Was the decision reviewed?
  e. Is there an appellate decision?
  f. Has the case been cited in other cases?

CASE STUDY PROBLEM

I15-58   A client, Mal Manley, fills out his client questionnaire for the year just past, and on it he provides you with information to be used in the preparation of his individual income tax return. Mal's returns have never been audited by the IRS. Mal reports that he made over a hundred relatively small cash contributions in the total amount of $24,785 to charitable organizations. In the last few years, Mal's charitable contributions have averaged about $15,000 per year. For the year just past, Mal's adjusted gross income is about $350,000, about a 10% increase from the preceding year.

   Required: According to the *Statements on Responsibilities in Tax Practice,* may you accept Mal's information concerning his charitable contributions at face value? Now assume, instead, that Mal's tax return for two years ago was audited recently and that 75% of the charitable contribution deduction claimed thereon were denied because of a lack of substantiation. Assume also that for the year just past Mal indicates he contributed $25,000 (instead of $24,785). How does this change in the information affect your earlier answer?

TAX RESEARCH PROBLEMS

I15-59   In answering these questions, refer only to *Thomas A. Curtis, M.D., Inc.,* 1994 RIA TC Memo ¶94,015. The purpose of this question is to enhance your skills in interpreting authorities that you locate while doing research.
  a. What is the general controversy being litigated in this case?
  b. Which party—the taxpayer or the goverment—won the case?
  c. Why is the plaintiff the corporation instead of Dr. and/or Ms. Curtis?
  d. What is the relationship between Ellen Barnert Curtis and Dr. Thomas A. Curtis?
  e. Approximately how many hours a week did Ms. Curtis work, and what are her credentials?
  f. For the fiscal year ended in 1989 how much salary did Ms. Curtis receive from the corporation? What amount did the court decide was a reasonable amount of compensation for her for that year?
  g. What dividends did the corporation pay for its fiscal years ended in 1988 and 1989?
  h. To which circuit would this case be appealable?
  i. According to the *Curtis* case, what five factors did the Ninth Circuit enumerate in *Elliotts, Inc.* as having relevance in determining reasonable compensation?

I15-60   Josh contributes $5,000 toward the support of his widowed mother, aged 69. His mother, a U.S. citizen and resident, has $2,000 of gross income and spends it all on her own support. In addition, $3,200 of her medical expenses are paid for by Medicare. She does not receive any support from sources other than those described above. Must the Medicare payments be counted as support that Josh's mother provides for herself?

   Prepare work papers and a client letter (to Josh) dealing with the question about the Medicare payments.

I15-61   Amy owns a vacation cottage in Maine. She estimates that use of the cottage during the current year will be as follows:

By Amy, solely for vacation	12 days
By Amy, making repairs ten hours per day and vacationing the rest of the day	2 days
By her sister, who paid fair rental value	8 days
By her cousin, who paid fair rental value	4 days
By her friend, who paid a token amount of rent	2 days
By three families from the Northeast, who paid fair rental value for forty days each	120 days
Not used	217 days

Determine the ratio to be used for allocating the following expenses against the rental income received from the cottage: interest, taxes, repairs, insurance, and depreciation. The ratio will affect the deductible expenses and, thus, Amy's taxable income for the year.

Prepare for the tax manager to whom you are regularly assigned work papers in which you address the ratios to be used in making the allocations. Also, draft a memorandum to the client's file dealing with the results of your tax research.

CHAPTER 16

CORPORATIONS

LEARNING OBJECTIVES

After studying this chapter, you should be able to

1. Define a corporation

2. Calculate the corporate income tax liability and explain specific tax rules

3. Apply the nonrecognition of gain or loss rules for corporate formations

4. Understand the significance of earnings and profits

5. Determine the consequences of distributions and stock redemptions

6. Understand the consequences of a corporate liquidation to shareholders and the liquidating corporation

KEY POINT

Income from sole proprietorships and flow-through entities is taxed once at the individual owner level while corporate income is taxed twice, once at the corporate level and again at the shareholder level upon dividend distributions or stock sales.

ADDITIONAL COMMENT

In 1960, corporate taxes produced over 20% of federal tax revenues. By 1993, that percentage dropped to 10%.

A business may be organized and operated as a **sole proprietorship, C corporation, S corporation, partnership, limited liability partnership,** or **limited liability company.** These forms of organizations fall into two major types: taxable entities and flow-through entities. This latter category also is referred to as conduit or pass-through entities. Sole proprietorships and regular C corporations fall into the taxable category although sole proprietorships are subject to a single level of tax, whereas C corporations entail two levels of tax. Sole proprietorships are relatively simple because they do not require a separate legal entity. The individual business proprietor is taxed directly and reports business income and expenses on Schedule C of Form 1040 (U.S. Individual Income Tax Return). The C corporation also is taxed directly and reports its tax results on Form 1120 (U.S. Corporate Income Tax Return). In addition, the corporate shareholders are taxed if the C corporation distributes dividends to them or if the shareholders sell their stock at a gain. Thus, the C corporation organizational form creates two levels of taxation: once at the corporate level and again at the shareholder level. Despite its double taxation and sometimes complicated legal form, the corporation has the advantages of raising outside capital and limiting the shareholders' legal liability.

Flow-through entities, like a sole proprietorship, entail only one level of taxation at the ownership level. Accordingly, the entities themselves are not taxed, and the income and losses pass through to the shareholders of an S corporation, the partners of a partnership, or the members of a limited liability company. The owners then report the pass-through income or losses in their individual tax returns. Some of these entities, such as S corporations, limited liability companies, and limited partnerships, also have the advantage of limiting their owners' legal liability. Nevertheless, flow-through entities entail certain complexities and restrictions, which is one disadvantage of this form of organization.

This chapter explores the basic tax consequences of forming, operating, and liquidating a regular C corporation. Chapter I17 discusses the basic tax rules pertaining to flow-through entities, and Table I17-2 at the end of that chapter compares the alternative forms of business organizations. Detailed coverage of these two areas of taxation are reserved for this text's companion volume titled *Prentice Hall's Federal Taxation: Corporations, Partnerships, Estates, and Trusts.*

DEFINITION OF A CORPORATION

OBJECTIVE 1

Define a corporation

Under Treasury Regulations,[1] a business entity with two or more owners is classified as either a corporation or a partnership. An entity having only one owner is classified as a corporation or a sole proprietorship. The business entity is a corporation if it is organized under a federal or state statute that refers to the entity as incorporated or as a corporation, body corporate, body politic, joint-stock company, or joint-stock association. Corporations also include insurance companies, state-chartered banks, and a business entity wholly owned by a state or political subdivision. In short, if a business entity incorporates, it is a corporation.

On the other hand, if the business entity has two or more owners and forms itself as a partnership, limited liability company, or limited liability partnership, the entity can elect to be *taxed* as either a partnership or corporation. These so-called "check-the-box" election rules replace prior entity classification procedures that involved much subjective judgement and manipulation.

EXAMPLE I16-1 ▶

Al and Jane form a business entity that incorporates in the state of Delaware. Because it is legally incorporated, the entity is taxed as a corporation. Bill and Max form a limited liability company in the state of Florida. The limited liability company can elect to be taxed as a corporation or it can elect to be treated as a partnership for federal tax purposes. ◀

---

[1] Reg. Secs. 301.7701-1, -2, and -3.

SIMILARITIES AND DIFFERENCES BETWEEN CORPORATIONS AND INDIVIDUALS

SIMILARITIES

The computation of corporate taxable income is similar to the computation of taxable income for an unincorporated business operating as a sole proprietorship. For example, corporations are permitted to deduct ordinary and necessary business expenses under Sec. 162 and may exclude items such as tax-exempt interest and life insurance proceeds from gross income. Corporations also are allowed to deduct interest, depreciation, and other business-related expenses in a manner similar to unincorporated taxpayers.

DIFFERENCES

One principal difference in computing corporate taxable income compared with an individual is that personal, consumption-type expenditures and exemptions apply solely to individuals. Certain specific differences should be noted before discussing the corporate provisions in greater detail:

▶ Computation of *adjusted gross income* (AGI) applies only to individuals.

▶ A corporation is not permitted to use the standard deduction or deduct personal and dependency exemptions.

▶ Corporations receive a dividends-received deduction of 70%, 80%, or 100% for qualifying dividends, whereas individuals are taxed on their total dividends with no exclusion or deduction.

▶ Corporate charitable contributions are limited in any given year to 10% of taxable income (with certain adjustments described on page I16-16 of this chapter), whereas individual contributions generally are limited to 50% of AGI.

COMPUTATION OF TAX

COMPUTATION OF TAXABLE INCOME

Table I16-1 illustrates the computation of *taxable income* for a C corporation.

COMPUTATION OF REGULAR TAX

The corporate tax rates reflect a stair-step pattern of progression as follows:[2]

If Taxable Income Is: Over...	But Not Over...	The Tax Is:	Of the Amount Over...
$0	$50,000	15%	$0
50,000	75,000	$7,500 + 25%	50,000
75,000	100,000	13,750 + 34%	75,000
100,000	335,000	22,250 + 39%	100,000
335,000	10,000,000	113,900 + 34%	335,000
10,000,000	15,000,000	3,400,000 + 35%	10,000,000
15,000,000	18,333,333	5,150,000 + 38%	15,000,000
18,333,333		6,416,667 + 35%	18,333,333

[2] Sec. 11(b)(1).

▼ TABLE I16-1

Computation of Corporate Taxable Income

Sales	$600,000
Minus: Cost of goods sold	(300,000)
Gross profit	$300,000
Plus: Other income	
Dividends from 25%-owned corporation	100,000
Interest	10,000
Net capital gain	90,000
Gross income	$500,000
Minus: Deductions:	
Salaries	$ 80,000
Repairs	20,000
Bad debts	30,000
Taxes	10,000
Contributions (subject to the 10% corporate limitations discussed on page I16-16)	5,000
Depreciation	20,000
Pension and profit-sharing contributions	35,000
Total deductions	$200,000
Taxable income before special deductions	$300,000
Minus: Special deductions:	
Net operating loss deduction	(15,000)[a]
Dividends-received deduction	(80,000)[b]
Taxable income	$205,000

ADDITIONAL COMMENT

Most states also impose an income tax on corporations.

[a] This amount represents an NOL carryover from a prior year.
[b] $0.80 \times \$100,000 = \$80,000$ dividends-received deduction.

EXAMPLE I16-2 ▶ Able Corporation's taxable income for the current year is $100,000. Its regular tax liability is computed as follows:

$0.15 \times \$50,000$	=	$ 7,500
$0.25 \times \$25,000$	=	6,250
$0.34 \times \$25,000$	=	8,500
Total tax		$22,250

The total tax due on the $100,000 of taxable income is $22,250. ◀

The 15% and 25% tax rates on the first $75,000 of taxable income provide a $11,750 benefit to corporations as compared to a flat 34% rate, computed as follows:

Tax on $75,000 at 34%	$25,500
Tax on $75,000 from tax rate schedule	13,750
Benefit of lower rates	$11,750

Congress, however, wanted only small corporations to obtain this benefit, so it imposed a 5% surtax on taxable income between $100,000 and $355,000. This 5% rate is reflected in the 39% (34% + 5%) marginal tax rate in the corporate tax rate schedule. Once taxable income reaches $335,000, the entire benefit is recaptured ($235,000 × 0.05 = $11,750).

Therefore, corporations with taxable income from $335,000 to $10,000,000 pay a flat tax equal to 34% times taxable income.

EXAMPLE I16-3 ▶ Ajax Corporation's taxable income for the current year is $335,000. Its tax liability is computed as follows:

$$
\begin{array}{lll}
0.15 \times \$\ 50,000 & = & \$\ 7,500 \\
0.25 \times \$\ 25,000 & = & 6,250 \\
0.34 \times \$260,000 & = & 88,400 \\
0.05 \times \$235,000 & = & 11,750 \\
\text{Total tax} & & \$113,900
\end{array}
$$

Alternatively, the $113,900 tax liability is 34% times $335,000. Thus, the benefit of the lower rates on the first $75,000 of taxable income is completely phased-out when taxable income reaches $335,000. ◀

KEY POINT

The corporation income tax is essentially a flat tax for large corporations.

A 35% rate applies to taxable income exceeding $10 million. An additional 3% surtax (reflected in the 38% rate) applies to taxable income from $15 million to $18,333,333, which eliminates the benefit of the 34% rate once taxable income equals or exceeds $18,333,333. Thus, a flat 35% rate applies to taxable income exceeding $18,333,333.

EXAMPLE I16-4 ▶ Ajax Corporation's taxable income for the current year is $18,333,333. Its tax liability is computed as follows:

$$
\begin{array}{lll}
0.34 \times \$10,000,000 & = & \$3,400,000 \\
0.35 \times \$5,000,000 & = & 1,750,000 \\
0.38 \times \$3,333,333 & = & 1,266,667 \\
\text{Total tax} & & \$6,416,667
\end{array}
$$

Alternatively, at $18,333,333 of taxable income, a flat 35% rate applies (0.35 × $18,333,333 = $6,416,667). ◀

SPECIAL RULE FOR CERTAIN PERSONAL SERVICE CORPORATIONS. Personal service corporations are denied the benefits of the corporate graduated rates.[3] Thus, a flat 35% rate is imposed on a personal service corporation that performs services in the fields of health, law, engineering, architecture, accounting, actuarial science, performing arts, or consulting where substantially all of the stock is held by employees or retired employees, or by their estates.

COMPUTATION OF CORPORATE ALTERNATIVE MINIMUM TAX (AMT)

KEY POINT

The AMT is designed to ensure that no corporation with substantial economic income can use exclusions, deductions, and credits to avoid significant tax liability.

The corporate alternative minimum tax (AMT) is similar to that applicable to individuals (see Chapter I14 for a discussion of the AMT for individuals).[4] The AMT ensures that corporations with substantial economic income pay a minimum amount of federal income tax. If a corporation's AMT liability is greater than its regular tax liability, the excess amount is payable in addition to the regular tax.

The corporate AMT is 20% of alternative minimum taxable income (AMTI) less an exemption amount. The exemption amount for corporations is $40,000 reduced by 25% of the excess of AMTI over $150,000.

EXAMPLE I16-5 ▶ Allied Corporation has $200,000 of AMTI before the exemption. The $40,000 exemption is reduced by $12,500 [0.25 × ($200,000 − $150,000)]. Thus, the tax base for the AMT is $172,500 ($200,000 − $27,500). ◀

---

[3] Sec. 11(b)(2).

[4] The AMT rules are in Secs. 55–58.

ADDITIONAL COMMENT

For AMTI through $150,000, the exemption amount is $40,000. For AMTI of $310,000 or more, the exemption amount is $0. Thus, the reduction formula need be applied only for AMTI between $150,000 and $310,000.

COMPUTATION OF AMTI. AMTI equals taxable income modified by certain adjustments and increased by tax preference items. Tax preferences are specific items that receive preferential tax treatment. As with the individual AMT, these tax preference items are *added* to taxable income to compute AMTI. Tax preferences are computed separately for each item of property. The most common tax preference item is the excess of accelerated depreciation over straight-line depreciation for real property placed in service before 1987.

AMT Adjustments. AMT adjustments are timing differences relating to deferred income or accelerated deductions. These adjustments generally increase the AMT tax base, although the netting of timing differences may result in an overall reduction of the AMT tax base when the timing differences reverse. When an AMT liability is paid, an AMT tax credit carryover is available to reduce the regular tax liability in subsequent years if the regular tax exceeds the tentative minimum tax in those years. (See Chapter I14 for a detailed discussion of this topic.) The most common AMT adjustments include

▶ For real property placed in service after 1986, the difference between tax depreciation claimed and a hypothetical straight-line depreciation amount computed under the alternative depreciation system using a 40-year life (see Chapter I10 for a discussion of the alternative depreciation system)

▶ For personal property placed in service after 1986, the difference between the MACRS depreciation deduction and the amount determined by using the 150% declining balance method under the alternative depreciation system

▶ 75% of the excess of the adjusted current earnings over AMTI (before this adjustment and the alternative tax NOL deduction but after all other adjustments and tax preference items)[5]

EXAMPLE I16-6 ▶

Beach Corporation's adjusted current earnings are $1,400,000 and its AMTI (before the adjustment amount) is $400,000. The AMT adjustment is $750,000 [0.75 × ($1,400,000 − $400,000)]. Thus, its AMTI is $1,150,000 ($400,000 + $750,000). ◀

EXAMPLE I16-7 ▶

In the current year, Camp Corporation has taxable income of $100,000, its tax preference items and adjustments total $200,000, and its regular tax liability is $22,250. Camp Corporation's AMT is computed as follows:

Taxable income	$100,000
Preference items and adjustments	200,000
AMTI	$300,000
Minus: Exemption [$40,000 − ($300,000 − $150,000) × .25]	(2,500)
AMT base	$297,500
Times: AMT rate	×0.20
Tentative minimum tax	$ 59,500
Minus: Regular tax	(22,250)
AMT	$ 37,250

ADDITIONAL COMMENT

Because of the AMT credit, the AMT essentially is a prepaid tax on preference items and adjustments; it affects the timing of tax payments.

Thus, Camp's total current year tax liability is $59,500 ($22,250 regular tax + $37,250 AMT). In effect, the taxpayer pays the greater of the regular tax or the tentative minimum tax. Camp also carries over the $37,250 to next year as an AMT credit. For example, if next year's regular tax liability is $30,000 and the tentative minimum tax is 20,000, Camp takes a $10,000 credit against next year's regular tax and carries over the remaining $27,250 ($37,250 − $10,000) AMT credit to the following year. ◀

---

[5] The term *adjusted current earnings* is a concept based on the traditional earnings and profits definition found in Sec. 312. (See Chapter C5 of *Prentice Hall's Federal Taxation: Corporations, Partnerships, Estates, and Trusts* for a detailed discussion of this AMT adjustment.)

STOP & THINK

Question: Corporations that are subject to AMT typically must alter their tax planning to minimize their overall tax liability. How might a corporation change its tax planning concerning the timing of income and deductions when the AMT applies?

Solution: When subject to the regular tax, a corporation prefers to accelerate deductions into the current year and defer income until a future year. However, while this technique reduces the regular tax, it increases the AMT and results in no overall tax benefit to the corporation. Therefore, when the AMT applies, the corporation should reverse its planning by accelerating income and deferring deductions. The interplay of regular tax planning and AMT planning thus creates a point at which the regular tax is reduced to as low an amount as possible without triggering the AMT.

SPECIAL TAXES

The following two penalty taxes are imposed to avoid otherwise abusive practices: the accumulated earnings tax and the personal holding company tax. The computation of both these penalty taxes involves a complex array of rules that are discussed in detail in the companion volume to this text, *Prentice Hall's Federal Taxation: Corporations, Partnerships, Estates, and Trusts.* Here, we present an overview of these complex subjects.

KEY POINT

When the highest marginal tax rate on individuals was considerably higher than the corporate tax rate, corporations commonly were used as tax shelters. From 1987 through 1992, corporate tax rates were higher than the individual tax rates, making the accumulated earnings tax and the personal holding company tax less important. In 1993 and subsequent years, the increase in the highest individual tax rate to 39.6% may increase the importance of the two penalty taxes to some degree because the top corporate tax rate is only 35%.

ACCUMULATED EARNINGS TAX. The **accumulated earnings tax** discourages companies from retaining excessive amounts of earnings if the funds are invested in assets unrelated to business needs.[6] Thus, a company may avoid the penalty tax if its earnings are reinvested in operating-type assets or retained for the reasonable needs of the business. If this tax were not imposed, closely held corporations might not pay dividends to their shareholders (thereby avoiding a double tax on the earnings). The retained earnings then could be reinvested in passive investments.

Reasonable needs of the business include

▶ Reasonably anticipated expansion of the business and plant replacement

▶ Acquiring the assets or stock (other than portfolio investments) of another business

▶ Providing working capital for the business

▶ Retiring debts

▶ Making investments or loans to suppliers or customers

The accumulated earnings tax generally is imposed on closely held corporations. However, the tax may be imposed on a publicly held company if effective control is in the hands of a few related shareholders.[7]

KEY POINT

The accumulated earnings tax can be avoided by the payment of a large enough dividend or by making an S corporation election. The accumulated earnings tax does not apply for the years the S corporation election is in effect.

Computation of Accumulated Earnings Tax. The accumulated earnings tax is imposed on a corporation's accumulated taxable income for a particular year. The accumulated earnings tax rate is 39.6%. Accumulated taxable income is computed as follows:

Taxable income
Plus: Dividends-received deduction
   Net operating loss deduction
Minus: Net capital losses
    Net long-term capital gains over net short-term capital
     losses (less federal income tax on such net gains)

---

[6] The basic rules for the accumulated earning tax are in Secs. 531–537.
[7] Sec. 532(c) and *Golconda Mining Corp. v. CIR*, 35 AFTR 2d 75-336, 74-2 USTC ¶9845 (9th Cir., 1974).

Federal income tax liability
Charitable contributions exceeding the 10% limit
Deductions for dividends paid or deemed paid[8]
Accumulated earnings credit

Accumulated taxable income

The accumulated earnings credit equals the greater of (1) $250,000 minus the accumulated earnings and profits (E&P) at the beginning of the year[9] or (2) the amount of E&P for the tax year retained for reasonable needs of the business. Reasonable needs of the business are determined at year end and are reduced by accumulated E&P at the beginning of the year. Thus, only the amount of E&P retained to meet the increase in reasonable business needs can be claimed as a credit. (The term earnings and profits (E&P) is formally defined later in this chapter.)

EXAMPLE I16-8 ▶ Compact Corporation has taxable income of $100,000 in the current year. Compact's federal income tax liability is $22,250, and the corporation paid $10,000 in dividends to its shareholders. Compact claims a dividends-received deduction of $80,000 on $100,000 of dividend income. Accumulated E&P at the beginning of the year retained for the reasonable needs of the business is $200,000, and Compact Corporation's reasonable needs of the business at year end amount to $220,000. The accumulated taxable income and the accumulated earnings credit are computed as follows:

Taxable income	$100,000
Plus: Dividends-received deduction	80,000
Minus: Federal income tax liability	(22,250)
Dividends paid deduction	(10,000)
Accumulated earnings credit—the greater of $250,000 (statutory exemption) − $200,000 (accumulated E&P at the beginning of the year) or E&P retained for the increased reasonable needs of the business ($220,000 − $200,000)	(50,000)
Accumulated taxable income	$ 97,750

The accumulated earnings tax is $38,709 (0.396 × $97,750). ◀

ADDITIONAL COMMENT

The personal holding company tax is imposed on the basis of mechanical criteria, whereas the accumulated earnings tax uses a subjective standard of purpose to avoid the tax.

PERSONAL HOLDING COMPANY TAX. A company must meet both of the following tests to be classified as a **personal holding company**:[10]

▶ More than 50% of the value of outstanding stock must be owned by five or fewer individuals at some time during the last six months of the tax year.

▶ 60% or more of adjusted ordinary gross income must be personal holding company income. Personal holding company income consists of passive types of income including dividends, interest, and under certain circumstances, rental income.

Most closely held companies have difficulty avoiding the 50% stock ownership test because of special family stock attribution rules. For example, 20 family members (e.g., spouses, children, and grandchildren) owning stock in a family corporation count as only one shareholder for purposes of applying the 50% and five or fewer shareholders test.

---

[8] Sec. 561. The deduction for dividends paid includes dividends actually paid during the tax year and consent dividends (e.g., a hypothetical dividend) where the shareholders agree to be taxed on such amounts. Under Sec. 563, dividends paid during the first 2½ months following the end of the tax year are considered paid during the last day of the preceding tax year.

[9] The $250,000 credit amount is reduced to $150,000 for service corporations engaged in the field of health. law, engineering, architecture, accounting, actuarial science, performing arts, or consulting.
[10] The basic rules for personal holding companies are in Secs. 541–547.

The personal holding company tax prevents closely held companies from converting an operating company into a nonoperating investment company by reinvesting substantial amounts of earnings into passive investments (e.g., stocks and bonds of other companies). The personal holding company tax forces a company to distribute its earnings to shareholders as dividends if the earnings are not invested in operating assets. This tax is imposed even if the corporation and shareholders have no tax-avoidance motive, whereas the intent to avoid tax on dividend distributions must be present under the accumulated earnings tax provisions.

The accumulated earnings tax, however, cannot be imposed in the same year the corporation qualifies as a personal holding company. In many instances, a corporation that is gradually converting itself into a nonoperating company by reinvesting its earnings in passive investments will have an accumulated earnings tax problem before being subjected to the personal holding company tax. However, this is not always the case. For example, a newly formed company that temporarily invests surplus funds in nonoperating assets may be classified as a personal holding company while the $250,000 accumulated earnings credit will temporarily shield the same company from the accumulated earnings tax.

Computation of Personal Holding Company Tax. The **personal holding company tax** is 39.6% times undistributed personal holding company income. Various adjustments are made to taxable income to arrive at the tax base. These adjustments are similar to those for the accumulated earnings tax as illustrated in Example I16-9.

EXAMPLE I16-9 ▶

Crane Corporation has four shareholders who together own more than 50% of the value of the stock at all times during the current year. In addition, 60% or more of adjusted ordinary gross income is personal holding company income (dividends, interest, etc.). Therefore, Crane is classified as a personal holding company for the current year because the stock ownership and income tests are met. Crane receives a $25,000 dividend for which a $20,000 dividends-received deduction is claimed and pays $18,750 of dividends to shareholders. Crane has $200,000 of taxable income and a $61,250 regular tax liability.

The personal holding company tax for Crane Corporation is computed as follows:

Taxable income	$200,000
Adjustments:	
Federal income tax liability	(61,250)
Dividends-received deduction	20,000
Dividends-paid deduction[11]	(18,750)
Undistributed personal holding company income	$140,000
Times: Personal holding company tax rate	× 0.396
Personal holding company tax	$ 55,440

Crane's total federal tax liability is $116,690 ($61,250 + $55,440). The $55,440 personal holding company tax may be avoided if Crane pays the undistributed personal holding company income amount to its shareholders. The Code contains special rules that allow personal holding companies to pay these dividends even after the corporation's year end. The shareholders then pay tax on the dividend distribution. ◀

---

[11] Secs. 547 and 561. The dividends-paid deduction is available for dividends paid during the tax year, dividends paid within 2½ months following the end of the tax year (subject to certain limitations), consent dividends, and dividends paid within 90 days following a determination that a personal holding company tax liability is owed (i.e., deficiency dividends). Deficiency dividends are not allowed for computing the accumulated earnings tax.

Topic Review I16-1 presents a comparison of the accumulated earnings tax and personal holding company tax rules.

COMPUTATION OF TAX FOR CONTROLLED GROUPS

Shareholders of a single corporation could recognize substantial tax savings by splitting the corporation into two or more corporations. This tax savings results from splitting the income of the single corporation among the separate corporations, allowing the separate corporations to take advantage of the lower corporate tax rates. To prevent this type of manipulation, however, a **controlled group** must apportion the lower tax rates among the group members as if only one corporation existed.[12] An equal apportionment to each member is required unless all the controlled group's members consent to an unequal allocation of such amounts. A controlled group, as discussed below, is a group of corporations that have an 80% common ownership.

EXAMPLE I16-10 ▶ West and East Corporations are members of a controlled group. West and East each have taxable income of $100,000. If each corporation were taxed separately, each corporation's tax

Topic Review I16-1

Comparison of Penalty Taxes

Item	Accumulated Earnings Tax—Sec. 531	Personal Holding Company (PHC) Tax—Sec. 541
Reason for imposing the penalty tax	To discourage companies from retaining excessive amounts of earnings if the funds are invested in nonoperating assets. A primary purpose is to force dividend payments of excess earnings.	To prevent closely held companies from converting an operating company into a passive investment company. A primary purpose is to force dividend payments of passive income.
Nature of the tax formula	The tax base is taxable income plus or minus certain adjustments. The tax computation is inherently subjective because the accumulated earnings credit (which often reduces the tax base to zero) is based on the retention of earnings for the reasonable needs of the business, which is a subjective determination.	The determination of whether a corporation is a personal holding company and the computation of the penalty tax is a mechanical process. Once the corporation is determined to be a PHC, the tax base is taxable income plus or minus certain adjustments.
Computation of tax	Adjustments are made to taxable income including such items as the dividends-received deduction, the dividends-paid deduction, the federal income tax liability, and the accumulated earnings credit (see Example I16-8). The tax is 39.6% of accumulated taxable income.	Adjustments, such as the dividends-received deduction, dividends-paid deduction, and the federal income tax liability, are made to taxable income to arrive at undistributed PHC income (see Example I16-9). The tax rate is 39.6% of undistributed PHC income.

---

[12] Sec. 1561.

WHAT WOULD YOU DO IN THIS SITUATION?

Scott, Steve, and Sean own 100% of the outstanding stock of Sofa Corporation for all of the current year. Sofa Corporation, a manufacturer of custom-made sofas, has never paid a dividend to its shareholders, preferring to retain earnings for working capital, capital additions, and marketable security investments. Scott and Steve would like to borrow money from Sofa before the end of the year because Scott is planning to open a florist shop as an additional business, and Steve needs a loan to pay off personal debts. For these reasons, Sofa Corporation will not pay a dividend in the current year. However, the company plans to start paying dividends next year. Sofa has accumulated E&P exceeding $250,000. As Sofa's tax consultant, you inform the shareholders of the possi-

bility that the company will be subject to the accumulated earnings tax. The shareholders ask you if they should inform the IRS, voluntarily pay the tax, or just wait to be audited by the IRS.

a. What advice would you give the shareholders regarding the reporting of the potential accumulated earnings tax problem to the IRS and the payment of the tax? (See the *Statements on Responsibilities in Tax Practice* section in Chapter I15 and Appendix E.)

b. What advice would you give to the shareholders if the corporation reported low operating profits from its sofa-making activities and met the requirements for a personal holding company during the current year?

liability would be $22,255, or a total of $44,500. However, because West and East are members of a controlled group, the reduced tax rate brackets must be apportioned to each corporation. The tax liability for each corporation assuming an equal apportionment is computed as follows:

ADDITIONAL COMMENT

A controlled group of corporations must apportion not only the lower tax rates but also the $250,000 accumulated earnings credit and the $40,000 exemption for the alternative minimum tax.

	Corporation	
	West	East
Tax on initial $50,000 of taxable income apportioned equally to West and East (0.15 × $25,000)	$ 3,750	$ 3,750
Tax on next $25,000 apportioned equally to West and East (0.25 × $12,500)	3,125	3,125
Tax on next $25,000 apportioned equally to West and East (0.34 × $12,500)	4,250	4,250
Tax on remaining $50,000 of taxable income for each corporation (0.39 × $50,000)	19,500	19,500
Tax on $100,000 taxable income for each corporation	$30,625	$30,625

The tax result of being a controlled group caused West and East Corporations to pay $16,750 ($61,250 − $44,500) more tax than if each were taxed as separate corporations. However, the total tax of $61,250 also would have been the total tax if West and East were, in fact, one corporation. ◀

If taxable income of the controlled group exceeds $10 million, a comparable allocation needs to occur to reflect the lower 34% rate applying to taxable income up to $10 million.

Controlled groups may be classified into two types: a brother-sister controlled group and a parent-subsidiary controlled group. These two groups are discussed below.

BROTHER-SISTER CORPORATIONS. A **brother-sister controlled group** exists if the following conditions are met:

▶ Five or fewer individuals, estates, or trusts own at least 80% of the voting power or value of all classes of stock of each corporation.[13]

▶ There is common ownership of more than 50% of the total voting power or value of all classes of stock. The stock is counted for this test only to the extent that each shareholder owns an identical interest in each corporation.[14]

EXAMPLE I16-11 ▶

The single class of outstanding stock of First, Second, and Third Corporations is owned by Amir, Beth, Carol, Dawn, and Edith as shown below.

| | Corporation | | | Identical |
Individuals	First	Second	Third	Interest
Amir	40%	20%	20%	20%
Beth	30	30	60	30
Carol	10	40	10	10
Dawn	10	10	—	—
Edith	10	—	10	—
Total	100%	100%	100%	60%

The 80% test is met because five or fewer individuals own at least 80% of First, Second, and Third stock. This test is met because Amir, Beth, and Carol own 80% of First stock and 90% of Second and Third stock. Dawn and Edith are not included for the 80% test because they do not have ownership in each of the three corporations. The 50% test also is met because common ownership exceeds 50% (60% total in Indentical Interest column). For the 50% test, the stock ownership of Dawn and Edith is not counted because they do not own shares in each of the three corporations. For example, if Dawn owned at least 10% of Third stock, the common ownership would increase from 60% to 70%. ◀

PARENT-SUBSIDIARY CONTROLLED GROUPS. A **parent-subsidiary controlled group** exists if the following conditions are met:

▶ A common parent corporation owns at least 80% of the stock of at least one subsidiary corporation.[15]

▶ At least 80% of the stock of each other member of the controlled group is owned by other members of the controlled group.

EXAMPLE I16-12 ▶

Federal Corporation owns 100% of Apex Corporation stock and 30% of Giant Corporation stock. Apex Corporation also owns 50% of Giant Corporation stock. Each corporation has only one class of stock outstanding. Owning at least 80% of Apex stock makes Federal Corporation the common parent corporation of the controlled group. Giant Corporation also is a member of the controlled group because at least 80% of Giant stock is owned by members of the controlled group (Federal and Apex own 30% + 50%). The parent-subsidiary controlled group consists of Federal, Apex, and Giant Corporations. ◀

---

[13] The 80% test is met if 80% or more of the total combined voting power of all classes of voting stock *or* at least 80% of the total value of all classes of stock of each corporation is held by five or fewer people on December 31. To be counted for the 80% test, a shareholder must own stock in each corporation of the brother-sister controlled group.

[14] Sec. 1563(a)(2).

[15] Sec. 1563(a)(1).

CONSOLIDATED RETURNS

Corporations that are members of a parent-subsidiary affiliated group are eligible to file a consolidated tax return if an election is made under the consolidated return regulations. Parent-subsidiary controlled groups generally are eligible to file a consolidated tax return, although the eligibility requirements for an affiliated group and a controlled group are slightly different (see Chapter C8 of the *Prentice Hall's Federal Taxation: Corporations, Partnerships, Estates, and Trusts* text for a detailed discussion of the requirements for filing a consolidated tax return). Once the election is made, IRS permission must be obtained to discontinue filing on a consolidated basis.[16]

STOP & THINK

Question: P Corporation owns 100% of S-1 Corporation and P and S-1 each own 50% of S-2 Corporation. Both P and S-1 are highly profitable (subject to a flat 34% corporate tax rate). S-2, however, has never earned a profit and has had a net operating loss (NOL) in each year of its existence. Would it be beneficial from a tax standpoint for P, S-1, and S-2 to file a consolidated tax return?

Solution: Filing a consolidated return would be highly beneficial because S-2's losses can offset profits of P and S-1. Because S-2 has never earned a profit, it would not be able to use the NOL if it filed a separate return. Therefore, filing a consolidated return allows NOLs of one or more members of an affiliated group to offset profits of other members and reduce the groups overall tax liability.

The consolidated return treats the affiliated group as a single entity, thereby allowing the following advantages: (1) net operating losses of one or more members can offset profits of other members; (2) capital losses of one or more members can offset capital gains of other members; and (3) profit and gains between members are eliminated in the consolidation and thus deferred until a transaction occurs outside the affiliated group.

SPECIFIC RULES APPLICABLE TO CORPORATIONS

CAPITAL GAINS AND LOSSES

The rules for netting long- and short-term capital gains and losses, the treatment of Sec. 1231 (i.e., business fixed assets) gains and losses, and the long-term capital gain and loss holding periods are the same for both corporations and individuals. The netting process consists of the following procedural rules (See Schedule D of Form 1120–Capital Gains and Losses in Appendix B):

▶ Long-term capital gains (LTCGs) are netted against long-term capital losses (LTCLs).

▶ Short-term capital gains (STCGs) are netted against short-term capital losses (STCLs).

▶ A net long-term capital gain (NLTCG) is then offset against a net short-term capital loss (NSTCL).

▶ A net long-term capital loss (NLTCL) is then offset against a net short-term capital gain (NSTCG).

▶ If a corporation reports both a NLTCG and a NSTCG after the netting procedure is completed, both the NSTCG and the NLTCG are taxed at the same rates as ordinary income.

---

[16] Reg. Sec. 1.1502-75(c).

▶ NSTCGs are netted against NLTCLs, and any excess amount is taxed at the same rates as ordinary income.

▶ NLTCLs and NSTCLs cannot be deducted from ordinary income.

EXAMPLE I16-13 ▶ Gulf Corporation has the following capital gains and losses during the current year:

LTCG	$15,000
LTCL	5,000
STCG	3,000
STCL	8,000

Gulf Corporation has a $10,000 NLTCG and a $5,000 NSTCL. The NLTCG is offset against the NSTCL, resulting in a $5,000 NLTCG that is taxed at the same rates as ordinary income. ◀

EXAMPLE I16-14 ▶ High Corporation has the following capital gains and losses during the current year:

LTCG	$15,000
LTCL	5,000
STCG	10,000
STCL	8,000

High Corporation has a $10,000 NLTCG and a $2,000 NSTCG. Both the $2,000 NSTCG and the $10,000 NLTCG are taxed at the same rates as ordinary income. ◀

EXAMPLE I16-15 ▶ Huge Corporation has the following capital gains and losses during 1997:

LTCG	$ 5,000
LTCL	15,000
STCG	8,000
STCL	10,000

Huge Corporation has a $10,000 NLTCL and a $2,000 NSTCL. Neither net loss is deductible against ordinary income in computing its 1997 taxable income. ◀

CORPORATE CAPITAL LOSS LIMITATIONS. Neither a NLTCL nor a NSTCL is deductible against ordinary income in the year it is incurred. Instead, they are subject to a 3-year carryback and 5-year carryover as an offset against capital gains for those years.[17] For corporations, both the NSTCL and the NLTCL are treated as STCLs for purposes of the carryback and carryover rules. The corporate capital loss limitations and carryback-carryover rules differ from the rules applicable to noncorporate taxpayers (see the discussion in Chapter I5).[18]

EXAMPLE I16-16 ▶ Assume the same facts as in Example I16-15. The $10,000 NLTCL and the $2,000 NSTCL are not deductible in 1997. The $12,000 ($10,000 + $2,000) total loss is carried back initially to 1994 as a STCL. If the net gains in the carryback years (1994 through 1996) are insufficient to absorb the $12,000 STCL carryback from 1997, the excess is carried over for up to 5 years (1998 through 2002). ◀

DIVIDENDS-RECEIVED DEDUCTION

Corporations may deduct 80% of dividends received from a domestic corporation if the recipient corporation owns 20% or more of the voting power and value of the issuing corporation's stock.[19] If a corporation owns less than 20% of the distributing corporation's stock, the dividends-received deduction is 70%. The percentage increases to 100%

---

[17] Secs. 1211(a) and 1212(a).
[18] Noncorporate taxpayers (e.g., individuals) can deduct up to $3,000 of net capital losses against ordinary income. Unused capital losses are carried over

(but not carried back) for an indefinite period and retain their character as long- or short-term capital losses.
[19] The dividend-received deduction rules are in Secs. 243 and 246.

if the dividend is received from an affiliated corporation for which a consolidated return election is not in effect. This seemingly liberal deduction mitigates the effects of triple taxation that would occur otherwise if one corporation paid dividends to another corporate shareholder, which in turn distributed such amounts to its shareholders.

The illustration below summarizes the amount of dividends-received deduction.

Percentage of Stock Owned	Dividends-Received Deduction
Less than 20%	70%
20% to less than 80%	80%
80% or more	100%

The 80% and 70% **dividends-received deduction** are subject to the following limitations:

▶ The dividends-received deduction is limited to 80% (or 70%) of taxable income (computed without regard to the net operating loss (NOL) deduction, the dividends-received deduction, and capital loss carrybacks to the limitation year).

▶ The limitation based on 80% (or 70%) of taxable income does not apply if the corporation has an NOL for the year after deducting the dividends-received deduction under the general rules.

▶ The dividends-received deduction is not available if the stock is held for 45 days or less.

EXAMPLE I16-17 ▶

King Corporation has the following income and expense items during the current year:

Net income from operations	$ 50,000
Dividend income from 20% (or more) owned corporations	200,000

The dividends-received deduction under the general rule is $160,000 (0.80 × $200,000 dividends). The deduction limitation is $200,000 (0.80 × $250,000 taxable income before the dividends-received deduction). Because the limitation ($200,000) exceeds the dividends-received deduction computed under the general rule ($160,000), the full $160,000 dividends-received deduction is allowed. ◀

EXAMPLE I16-18 ▶

Assume the same facts as in Example I16-17, except that the corporation incurred a $10,000 net loss from operations. The dividends-received deduction under the general rule is $160,000 (0.80 × $200,000 dividends). The limitation under the general rule based on taxable income before the dividends-received deduction is $152,000 (0.80 × $190,000). No NOL results after deducting the entire 80% dividends-received deduction computed under the general rule as shown below:

Net loss from operations	$ (10,000)
Plus: Dividends received	200,000
Minus: Dividends-received deduction (0.80 × $200,000)	(160,000)
Taxable income as computed under the general rule	$ 30,000

Because the dividends-received deduction is limited to $152,000 (0.80 × $190,000 taxable income before deducting the dividends-received deduction), the actual taxable income for the year is $38,000 ($190,000 − $152,000). ◀

EXAMPLE I16-19 ▶

Assume the same facts as in Example I16-18, except that the loss from operations is $50,000. The dividends-received deduction under the general rule is $160,000 (0.80 × $200,000 dividends). The limitation is $120,000 (0.80 × $150,000 taxable income before the dividends-received deduction). The limitation does not apply, however, because a $10,000 NOL results after subtracting the dividends-received deduction computed using the general rule as shown below:

SELF-STUDY QUESTION

Calculate the maximum tax rate on dividends received from a corporation that is less than 20%-owned.

ANSWER

The maximum rate is 10.5% (30% times the top corporate tax rate of 35%).

ADDITIONAL COMMENT

Although corporations are allowed a dividends-received deduction, they are not allowed a dividends-paid deduction for purposes of computing taxable income.

ADDITIONAL COMMENT

Even though the dividends-received deduction creates (or increases) a NOL, the corporation gets the full benefit of the deduction because it can carry back or carryover the NOL.

Net loss from operations	$ (50,000)
Plus: Dividends received	200,000
Minus: Dividends-received deduction (0.80 × $200,000)	(160,000)
Net operating loss	$ 10,000

Therefore, the full $160,000 dividends-received deduction is allowed. ◀

EXAMPLE I16-20 ▶ Lean Corporation acquires Madison Corporation stock on June 1. Madison Corporation pays a $100,000 cash dividend to Lean on June 15. On July 1, Lean sells the Madison stock. The dividends-received deduction is not allowed because Lean does not hold the Madison stock for the required 45-day holding period. ◀

NET OPERATING LOSSES

The computation of a corporate **net operating loss** (NOL) does not involve making adjustments for nonbusiness deductions and capital gains and losses as is required for individuals (see Chapter I8 for a discussion of these adjustments for individuals). Thus, the corporate rules are fairly straightforward.[20] In computing a corporation's NOL, the full dividends-received deduction is allowed. However, no deduction is permitted for an NOL carryover or carryback from a preceding or succeeding year.

EXAMPLE I16-21 ▶ Maine Corporation's NOL is computed from the following income and deduction items:

Operating income	$ 400,000
Plus: Dividends	300,000
Gross income	$ 700,000
Minus: Business operating expenses	(600,000)
Dividends-received deduction (0.80 × $300,000)	(240,000)
Net operating loss	$(140,000)

NOLs are carried back 3 years (beginning with the earliest tax year). Any excess amounts are carried forward up to 15 years to offset taxable income in those years. ◀

KEY POINT

In making the decision whether to forgo the NOL carryback, the corporation should compare the current refund from the potential carryback to the present value of any future benefit from a carryover.

A corporation may elect to forgo the NOL carryback and instead carry the unused loss forward. For example, if the corporation has taxable income less than $75,000 in the carryback year(s) subject to tax rates less than 34%, the tax benefit may be of limited value because the NOL carryback offsets income taxed at these lower rates. The NOL might be more valuable if the carryback is forgone and the NOL is carried over to a year in which the marginal tax rate may be as high as 35%. However, in this case the tax savings are deferred, whereas a carryback produces tax savings currently. The election, if made, applies to all carryback years, and the NOL carries forward for 15 years.

ADDITIONAL COMMENT

Taxable income for purposes of determining the charitable contribution limit is calculated without regard to NOL and capital loss carrybacks, but carryovers are reflected in calculating taxable income.

CHARITABLE CONTRIBUTIONS

Some of the rules governing charitable contributions for individuals also apply to corporations (e.g., the restriction imposed on contributions of ordinary income property, which is discussed in Chapter I7).[21] The following rules apply solely to corporations:

▶ Under the general rule, a payment must be made before a contribution deduction is allowed. However, accrual basis corporations may accrue a contribution deduction in the year preceding payment if the payment is authorized by the board of directors

---

[20] The NOL rules are in Sec. 172.

[21] Rules pertaining to charitable contributions are in Sec. 170.

before the end of the tax year and the contribution is made within 2½ months of the end of the tax year.

▶ Corporate charitable contributions are limited to 10% of taxable income (computed without regard to the charitable contribution deduction, NOL and capital loss carrybacks, or the dividends-received deduction).

▶ Unused contributions are carried forward 5 years. In the carryover year, the current year's contributions are deducted first in applying the 10% limitation. Any unused limitation is then applied to contribution carryovers from the earliest year.

EXAMPLE I16-22 ▶ During 1997, Mesa Corporation reports the following results:

Taxable income (before deducting the dividends-received deduction and charitable contributions)	$130,000
Dividends-received deduction	10,000
Charitable contributions	20,000

The limitation on contributions is $13,000 ($130,000 × 0.10), and taxable income is $107,000 ($130,000 − $13,000 − $10,000). The $7,000 ($20,000 − $13,000) of unused contributions carries forward for 5 years. ◀

EXAMPLE I16-23 ▶ Assume that the same facts as in Example I16-22 for 1997 also apply to 1998, except that taxable income (before deducting the dividends-received deduction and charitable contributions) is $220,000. The contribution limitation therefore is $22,000 ($220,000 × 0.10). The $20,000 charitable contribution from 1998 initially applies against the $22,000 limitation, leaving a $2,000 unused charitable contribution limitation. Thus, $2,000 of the carryover from 1997 is used against this limitation, leaving a $5,000 carryover from 1997, which can be used in tax years 1999 through 2002. ◀

COMPENSATION DEDUCTION LIMITATION FOR PUBLICLY HELD CORPORATIONS

A publicly held corporation is denied a deduction for compensation paid to its chief executive officer and its four highest compensated officers if the compensation amount for any individual exceeds $1 million per year.[22] Includible compensation includes both cash and noncash benefits. The following types of compensation are not taken into account for purposes of the $1 million limitation:

▶ Remuneration payable on a commission basis

▶ Compensation based on individual performance goals (if approved by certain outside directors and shareholders)[23]

▶ Payments to a qualified retirement plan

▶ Tax-free employee benefits (such as employer-provided health benefits and Sec. 132 fringe benefits)

EXAMPLE I16-24 ▶ Acorn Corporation is a publicly held company listed on the New York Stock Exchange. During the current year, its chief executive officer, Rodney, receives the following compensation from the corporation: salary, $1,200,000; commissions based on sales generated by Rodney, $400,000; payments to a qualified pension plan, $25,000; and tax free fringe benefits, $10,000. The commissions, payments to the qualified pension plan, and the fringe benefits are

---

[22] Sec. 162 (m). A publicly held corporation is any corporation issuing any class of securities required to be registered under Section 12 of the Securities Exchange Act of 1934. The Conference Committee Report indicates that this generally is a corporation listed on a national securities exchange, or one

that has at least $5 million or more of assets and 500 or more shareholders.
[23] See Reg. Sec. 1.162-27 for the requirements relating to the attainment of performance goals.

Topic Review I16-2

Summary of Capital Gain and Loss, Dividends-Received Deduction, Net Operating Loss Deduction, Charitable Contribution Deduction, and Compensation Deduction Limitation Rules for Corporations

▶ If a net loss results after netting long-term and short-term capital gains and losses, no amount can be deducted from ordinary income. Instead, net losses are carried back 3 years and forward 5 years as STCLs.

▶ The corporate net capital gain does not receive favorable tax treatment. The maximum 28% tax rate for net capital gains applies only to individuals.

▶ The dividends-received deduction for corporate shareholders is 80% if the corporate investor owns 20% or more of the stock and is 70% if the corporate investor owns less than 20%. A 100% dividends-received deduction is available for dividends from affiliated group members not filing consolidated tax returns.

▶ The dividends-received deduction is limited to 80% (or 70% as the case may be) of taxable income (after adjustments for the NOL deduction, the dividends-received deduction, and capital loss carrybacks) unless the corporate shareholder has an NOL after deducting the full amount of the dividends-received deduction.

▶ NOLs are carried back 3 years (beginning with the earliest year) and forward 15 years. However, the corporation may elect to forgo the 3-year carryback.

▶ Accrual-basis corporate donors may accrue a contribution deduction at the end of the tax year if authorized by the board of directors and paid within 2½ months following the end of the tax year.

▶ Contributions are limited to 10% of the taxable income (with certain adjustments).

▶ Unused charitable contributions are carried forward 5 years.

▶ Publicly held corporations are denied a deduction for compensation payments exceeding $1 million to certain key executives.

not subject to the $1 million annual deduction limitation for Rodney's compensation. Thus, $200,000 ($1,200,000 − $1,000,000) of Rodney's salary is not deductible by Acorn Corporation even though Rodney is taxed on the entire $1,200,000. ◀

For a summary of the capital gain and loss, dividends-received deduction, net operating loss, charitable contribution deduction, and compensation deduction rules for corporations, see Topic Review I16-2.

TRANSFERS OF PROPERTY TO CONTROLLED CORPORATIONS

OBJECTIVE 3

Apply the nonrecognition of gain or loss rules for corporate formations

Section 351 permits shareholders of a corporation to defer recognition of gain or loss on the transfer of assets to the corporation. The transfer of property may be made when a new corporation is formed or may reflect additional capital contributions to an existing corporation. Without Sec. 351, a sole proprietorship or a partnership would have difficulty adopting the corporate form of organization because the transfer of appreciated property would constitute a taxable transaction resulting in a recognized gain.

SECTION 351 NONRECOGNITION REQUIREMENTS

The deferral of gain or loss under Sec. 351 can be justified because realization has not occurred. The assets merely have been transferred to a corporation that is controlled by the transferors. In addition, the transferors do not have the wherewithal to pay the tax on the gains that otherwise would be recognized because the shareholders receive only stock of the transferee (controlled) corporation, rather than cash or liquid assets. Section 351 also prevents recognition of artificial losses on transfers of property that have declined in value.

Gain or loss is not recognized if the following conditions are met:

▶ Property (other than services) is transferred to the corporation solely in exchange for stock of the transferor corporation.[24]

▶ Immediately after the exchange, the transferor-shareholders in aggregate must control the transferee corporation by owning at least 80% of its stock.[25]

▶ If the transferor receives money or property (other than stock in the transferee corporation), the transferor recognizes gain (but not loss) equal to the lesser of the boot received (i.e., money plus the FMV of other property received) or the realized gain.[26] In addition, a corporation that transfers appreciated property (other than its own stock) to the transferor-shareholders also recognizes gain on the exchange.[27]

▶ The character of any gain recognized by the transferor depends on the type of asset transferred as follows: Capital gain on capital assets, Sec. 1231 gain on Sec. 1231 property, and ordinary income on other property (e.g., inventory).

▶ Depreciation recapture does not apply to a Sec. 351 transfer unless the transferor recognizes gain.[28]

EXAMPLE I16-25 ▶ Carlos and Fred combine their sole proprietorships by forming the Miami Corporation. Carlos transfers land and a building having a $50,000 adjusted basis and a $100,000 FMV to the corporation in exchange for 40% of the Miami stock. Fred transfers equipment with a $60,000 adjusted basis and a $150,000 FMV to the corporation in exchange for 60% of the Miami stock. Carlos and Fred receive stock of Miami Corporation, which is controlled by Carlos and Fred because they own at least 80% of the single class of stock immediately after the exchange. Carlos and Fred recognize no gain because the requirements of Sec. 351 are met and they received no property other than Miami stock. The depreciation recapture potential on the building and equipment carries over to the controlled corporation. ◀

EXAMPLE I16-26 ▶ Gail and Gary form Michigan Corporation. Gail transfers inventory with a $50,000 adjusted basis and a $100,000 FMV to Michigan Corporation in exchange for 50% of the stock worth $80,000 and $20,000 cash. The cash funds represent borrowings by Michigan Corporation from a bank. Gary transfers equipment with a $150,000 adjusted basis and a $100,000 FMV in exchange for 50% of the stock worth $80,000 and a Michigan Corporation 10-year note valued at $20,000. Section 351 applies to the exchange because property is transferred by transferors who control at least 80% of the stock of the corporation immediately after the exchange. The tax consequences to Gail and Gary are as follows:

---

[24] Section 351(d) provides that services do not qualify as property. Thus, if an individual transfers services in exchange for stock, the individual is not counted as a transferor for purposes of meeting the 80% control requirement unless the individual also transfers substantial other properties. In any event, the transfer of services results in the transferor recognizing ordinary income equal to the FMV of services rendered.

[25] Sec. 368(c). Control means the ownership of at least 80% of the total

combined voting power of all classes of stock and at least 80% of the total number of shares of all other classes of stock.

[26] Sec. 351(b).

[27] Secs. 351(f) and 311(b).

[28] Secs. 1245(b)(3) and 1250(d)(3). The corporation recognizes the depreciation recapture if it subsequently sells or disposes of the assets.

	Gail	Gary
FMV of stock received	$ 80,000	$ 80,000
Plus: Cash or note received	20,000	20,000
Amount realized	$100,000	$100,000
Minus: Adjusted basis of property transferred	(50,000)	(150,000)
Gain (loss) realized	$ 50,000	$ (50,000)
Gain (loss) recognized	$ 20,000	$ 0

Gail's gain recognized is the lesser of the boot received or gain realized. Moreover, her gain is ordinary income because she transferred inventory. Because Gary realized a loss, he recognizes no gain or loss even though he received boot. ◀

BASIS CONSIDERATIONS

In Sec. 351 transactions, substituted basis rules apply to stock received by the transferors and carryover basis rules apply to property transferred to the corporation. The basis formula for the transferor's stock is as follows:

	Basis of the property transferred to the corporation
Plus:	Any gain recognized by the transferor on the exchange (e.g., due to boot received)
Minus:	Amount of money received (including any liabilities transferred to the corporation) plus the FMV of any nonmoney boot property received
	Basis of the stock received[29]

ADDITIONAL COMMENT

When different classes of stock are received in a Sec. 351 exchange, the available basis must be allocated to the different classes in proportion to their relative FMVs when received.

In addition, any boot property received takes a basis equal to its FMV.

EXAMPLE I16-27 ▶

George and Gina form New Corporation. George transfers land and a building with a $60,000 adjusted basis and a $100,000 FMV in exchange for 50% of New stock. Gina transfers equipment with a $120,000 adjusted basis and a $100,000 FMV for 50% of the New stock. George realizes a $40,000 gain, and Gina realizes a $20,000 loss. However, George and Gina recognize no gain or loss because Sec. 351 applies. George's basis in the New stock is $60,000, and Gina's basis in the New stock is $120,000. ◀

STOP & THINK

Question: In Example I16-27, George and Gina recognized no gain or loss. Why is this treatment a deferral rather than permanent nonrecognition?

Solution: George's $40,000 nonrecognized gain is reflected in a $60,000 stock basis that is $40,000 *below* its $100,000 FMV. Thus, if George subsequently sells his stock for its FMV, he recognizes the $40,000 deferred gain ($100,000 selling price − $60,000 adjusted basis in his stock). Similarly, Gina's $20,000 nonrecognized loss is reflected in a $120,000 stock basis that is $20,000 *above* its $100,000 FMV. Thus, if Gina subsequently sells her stock for its FMV, she recognizes the $20,000 deferred loss ($100,000 selling price − $120,000 adjusted basis in her stock). In short, the substituted basis rules ensure that nonrecognized gains and losses are merely deferred.

PROPERTY RECEIVED BY TRANSFEREE CORPORATION. Carryover basis rules apply to the property received by the transferee corporation. The basis of property received by the transferee corporation is computed as follows:

---

[29] Sec. 358(a).

Adjusted basis of property in the transferor's hands
Plus: Gain recognized by the transferor

Basis of property to the transferee corporation[30]

EXAMPLE I16-28 ▶ North Corporation receives property having a $60,000 adjusted basis in the transferor's hands and a $100,000 FMV in an exchange qualifying under Sec. 351. Assume that the transferor recognizes a $10,000 gain because she receives boot (e.g., cash) from the transferee corporation. North Corporation's basis of the property is $70,000 ($60,000 adjusted basis in the transferor's hands + $10,000 gain recognized by the transferor). ◀

TREATMENT OF LIABILITIES

NONRECOGNITION OF GAIN. Section 357(a) permits the assumption of liabilities by the transferee corporation (or the corporation may take the property subject to the liability) without recognition of gain under the boot rules previously discussed. Thus, under the general rule, shareholders recognize no gain if they transfer liabilities to a controlled corporation. The shareholders, however, must reduce their stock basis by the amount of liabilities assumed or acquired. This rule is logical because, if a shareholder transfers net assets of $10,000 (i.e., gross assets of $100,000 and liabilities of $90,000), the contribution to capital is only $10,000 even though $100,000 in assets are transferred.

TYPICAL MISCONCEPTION

When a corporation assumes a shareholder's liabilities and the shareholder recognizes no gain, one can mistakenly assume that the shareholder's stock basis is not reduced by the liabilities assumed.

EXAMPLE I16-29 ▶ Ira transfers land with an $80,000 adjusted basis and a $100,000 FMV to a corporation in exchange for 100% of its stock having a $60,000 FMV in a transaction otherwise qualifying under Sec. 351. The transferred property is subject to a $40,000 liability that the corporation assumes. The tax consequences to Ira are as follows:

FMV of stock received	$ 60,000
Plus: Liability assumed by corporation	40,000
Amount realized	$100,000
Minus: Adjusted basis of property transferred	(80,000)
Gain realized	$ 20,000
Gain recognized	$ 0
Adjusted basis of property transferred	$ 80,000
Minus: Liability assumed by corporation	(40,000)
Adjusted basis of stock received	$ 40,000

In addition, the corporation takes an $80,000 carryover basis in the land. ◀

EXCEPTIONS. Two exceptions require gain recognition upon the transfer of liabilities to the corporation. The first exception relates to the nature of the exchange. If the principal purpose for the assumption of the liabilities is tax avoidance or if the transaction does not have a bona fide business purpose, all of the transferor's liabilities assumed by the transferee corporation are treated as boot, causing potential gain recognition.[31]

EXAMPLE I16-30 ▶ Helen transfers land and a building with a $70,000 adjusted basis and a $100,000 FMV to the Orlando Corporation in exchange for 100% of its stock in a transaction otherwise qualifying under Sec. 351. Shortly before the transfer, Helen obtains a $60,000 mortgage on the

---

[30] Sec. 362(a).   [31] Sec. 357(b).

property and uses the funds to pay off personal debts. The corporation then assumes the $60,000 mortgage and issues stock worth $40,000. The mortgage assumption lacks business purpose and is intended to get cash into Helen's hands without boot recognition. For this reason, Helen must treat the liability assumed as boot for determining gain recognized. Thus, the tax consequences to Helen are as follows:

FMV of stock received	$ 40,000
Plus: Liability assumed by corporation	60,000
Amount realized	$100,000
Minus: Adjusted basis of property transferred	(70,000)
Gain realized	$ 30,000
Gain recognized	$ 30,000
Adjusted basis of property transferred	$ 70,000
Plus: Gain recognized	30,000
Minus: Liability assumed by corporation	(60,000)
Adjusted basis of stock received	$ 40,000

Although the total boot is $60,000 (the liability assumed), Helen's gain recognized does not exceed her gain realized. In addition, the stock basis equals its FMV because Helen recognizes the entire gain realized, leaving no gain to defer. Finally, Orlando's basis in the land and building is $100,000 ($70,000 adjusted basis in the transferor's hands + $30,000 gain recognized by the transferor). ◄

A second exception applies to excess liabilities. If a transferor's total liabilities assumed by the corporation exceeds the total basis of assets (including cash) transferred by that transferor, the transferor must recognize gain to the extent of the excess.[32] Without this rule, the shareholder would have a negative basis in the stock received. In

Topic Review I16-3

Sec. 351 Requirements, Gain Recognition Rules, and Basis Rules

▶ Nonrecognition treatment under Sec. 351 requires an exchange of property solely for stock, and the transferor-shareholders must control (i.e., 80% stock ownership) the corporation immediately after the exchange.

▶ Nonqualifying property (e.g., cash or debt obligations of the transferee corporation) received by the transferors is treated as boot received.

▶ The transferors recognize gain equal to the lesser of boot received or the realized gain.

▶ Generally, the transferors recognize no gain if liabilities are transferred to a controlled corporation. Exceptions to the nonrecognition of gain rule apply if the principal purpose of the liability transfer is tax avoidance, if no bona fide business purpose exists, or if the total liabilities assumed by the corporation exceed the transferor's adjusted basis for the assets.

▶ Substituted basis rules apply to the stock received by the transferors, and carryover basis rules apply to property contributed to the transferee corporation.

---

[32] Sec. 357(c). Accounts receivable and accounts payable with a zero basis for a cash basis transferor are disregarded for purposes of applying the Sec. 357(c) rules. See Sec. 357(c)(3).

addition, gain is recognized because the transferor has received a net economic benefit to the extent the liabilities assumed exceed the adjusted basis of the transferred assets.

EXAMPLE I16-31 ▶ Jack transfers assets with a $60,000 adjusted basis and a $100,000 FMV, along with $75,000 of liabilities assumed by the transferee corporation in a transaction otherwise qualifying under Sec. 351. Jack recognizes a $15,000 gain because the liabilities assumed by the corporation exceed the basis of the assets transferred ($75,000 − $60,000). If the gain were not recognized, Jack's basis for his stock would be a negative $15,000 ($60,000 − $75,000). Jack's net economic benefit from the exchange also is $15,000 ($75,000 liabilities assumed by the corporation − $60,000 adjusted basis of assets transferred). Jack's basis in the stock received is zero ($60,000 adjusted basis of assets + $15,000 gain recognized − $75,000 liabilities assumed). Because Jack's realized gain is $40,000 and because he recognizes $15,000 of the gain, $25,000 of the gain is deferred. ◀

Topic Review I16-3 summarizes the general requirements relating to the transfer of property to controlled corporations.

CAPITALIZATION OF THE CORPORATION

A corporation may be capitalized with both equity securities (generally common or preferred stock) and long-term debt issued to the shareholders. Issuance of debt in the capital structure has the following advantages:

▶ The interest payments on the debt are deductible by the corporation, whereas dividends are not deductible.

▶ Redemptions of stock may result in dividend income treatment to the shareholders unless certain requirements are met (see page I16-28), whereas a repayment of debt is a tax-free return of capital.

If the corporation is too thinly capitalized (e.g., excessive amounts of debt are issued relative to the amount of equity capital), the IRS may attempt to recharacterize the debt as equity and deny an interest deduction to the corporation. Section 385 provides the following guidelines (or factors) for determining whether debt is recharacterized as equity:

▶ The legal form of the instrument and actual adherence to its terms: For example, if a reasonable interest rate is stated, the interest is currently being paid, a definite maturity date is stated, and the notes actually are repaid when due, then the evidence supports the taxpayer's contention that the instrument is debt.

▶ Excessive debt-equity ratio: The courts have not prescribed any exact mathematical formula although a debt-equity ratio that does not exceed 3 to 1 is likely to be acceptable.[33]

▶ Proportionality of debt and the shareholder's equity interests: If the shareholders own the same percentage of the debt as their percentage of common stock, the debt stands a greater likelihood of being reclassified as equity than if the debt is disproportionate.

▶ Convertibility of the debt into stock of the corporation or contingent interest payments based on corporate earnings: These features are more likely to be found in equity rather than in debt instruments.

ADDITIONAL COMMENT

The thin capitalization issue is primarily a problem for closely held corporations where the stockholders are also the ones holding the debt, and is not normally a problem for large publicly-held corporations.

ADDITIONAL COMMENT

A safe-harbor rule sets parameters that characterize a transaction one way if met and that characterize a transaction another way if not met.

---

[33] Boris I. Bittker and James S. Eustice, *Federal Income Taxation of Corporations and Shareholders* (Boston: Warren Gorham Lamont, 1994), p. 4-35.

Under Sec. 385, the issuing corporation must characterize the instrument as debt or stock. The shareholders or debtholders are prohibited from treating the instrument inconsistently with the issuer's characterization unless they disclose the inconsistent treatment on their tax returns. The issuer's characterization is not binding on the IRS.

EXAMPLE I16-32

Palm Corporation is formed with $90,000 of debt consisting of 3-year shareholder notes and $10,000 of common stock. The corporation issues $30,000 notes to each shareholder, Hank, Harold, and Antonio, who also own equal interests in the common stock. The interest payments are contingent on the earnings of the company, and the notes were not repaid at maturity. All of the factors above (i.e., high debt-equity ratio, proportionality of debt and equity interests, contingent interest payments, and the failure to observe the obligation's legal form) indicate that the debt probably will be reclassified by the IRS as equity. If the debt is treated as equity on audit, the interest payments are not deductible by the corporation over the life of the debt, and any repayments of debt are treated as a stock redemption and may represent dividends to the shareholders. ◀

EARNINGS AND PROFITS

CALCULATION OF EARNINGS AND PROFITS

OBJECTIVE 4

Understand the significance of earnings and profits

Earnings and profits (E&P) measure a corporation's economic ability to pay dividends from its current and accumulated earnings without impairment of capital. If the corporation has no earnings and profits, a distribution represents a tax-free return of capital, and possibly a capital gain, rather than a taxable dividend.

E&P is similar to retained earnings in financial accounting although numerous differences exist between the two accounts. For example, issuance of a stock dividend usually reduces retained earnings but does not affect E&P.

Current E&P is calculated by making various adjustments to the corporation's taxable income.[34] This computation and the addition to accumulated E&P are illustrated as follows:

Taxable income

Plus: Income excluded from taxable income:
    Tax-exempt interest income
    Life insurance proceeds where the corporation is the beneficiary
    Recoveries of bad debts and other prior-year deductions for which
        the corporation received no tax benefit
    Federal income tax refunds from prior years

Plus: Income deferred to a later year when computing taxable income:
    Deferred gain on installment sales

Plus or minus: Adjustments for items that must be recomputed:
    Income on long-term contracts must be based on percentage of
        completion method rather than completed contract method
    Excess of pre-ACRS accelerated depreciation over straight-line depreciation
    Excess of ACRS depreciation deductions claimed over straight-
        line ACRS calculation using an extended recovery period
    Excess of regular MACRS depreciation over depreciation calcu-
        lated using the alternative depreciation system (ADS).
    Excess of percentage depletion claimed over cost depletion

SELF-STUDY QUESTION

Should Sue, an individual, consider transferring her $100,000 municipal bond to her controlled corporation?

ANSWER

No; although the interest income on the municipal bond is excludable from the corporation's income, the tax-exempt interest creates E&P, which causes the cash distribution to Sue to be taxable as a dividend.

---

[34] These adjustments are enumerated in Sec. 312 and related Treasury Regulations.

Taxable income (continued)
Plus: Deductions not allowed in computing E&P:
           Dividends-received deduction
           NOL carryovers, charitable contribution carryovers, and capital
             loss carryovers used in the current year

KEY POINT

Several items that cannot be deducted in computing taxable income must be deducted in computing E&P.

Minus: Expenses and losses not deductible in computing taxable income:
           Federal income taxes
           Life insurance premiums where the corporation is the beneficiary
           Excess capital losses not deductible for taxable income
           Excess charitable contributions not deductible for taxable income
           Expenses related to production of tax-exempt income
           Nondeductible losses on sales to related parties
           Nondeductible penalties and fines
           Nondeductible political contributions

Current E&P (or E&P deficit)
Minus: Distributions to shareholders

Addition to accumulated E&P (if any)

EXAMPLE I16-33 ▶

Park Corporation has the following taxable income and adjustments to its current E&P:

Taxable income	$100,000
Plus:	
Tax-exempt bond interest	2,000
Key officer life insurance proceeds (nontaxable)	10,000
Dividends-received deduction	20,000
MACRS depreciation exceeding ADS depreciation	18,000
Percentage depletion exceeding cost depletion	10,000
	$160,000
Minus:	
Federal income tax liability	(22,250)
Net capital losses	(5,000)
Key officer life insurance premiums (not deductible because the corporation is the beneficiary)	(2,000)
Charitable contributions exceeding the 10% limitation	(3,000)
Disallowed expense (e.g., penalties and fines)	(5,000)
Current E&P	$122,750
Minus: Cash dividends	(5,000)
Addition to accumulated E&P	$117,750 ◀

CURRENT VERSUS ACCUMULATED E&P

Current and accumulated E&P must be differentiated because Sec. 316 provides specific tracing rules to determine whether a distribution is taxable as a dividend. For example, a distribution to shareholders is deemed to be made first out of current E&P and therefore results in a taxable dividend even if accumulated E&P at the beginning of the year shows a deficit. Accumulated E&P represents the total of all prior years' undistributed current E&P amounts as of the first day of the tax year. Distributions are deemed to be made out of accumulated E&P only after the current E&P (if any) is exhausted.

EXAMPLE I16-34 ▶

Pacific Corporation, a calendar-year taxpayer, has a $100,000 accumulated E&P deficit as of January 1. It reports $30,000 of current E&P. The corporation makes a $40,000 distribution to its shareholders. Of the $40,000 distribution, $30,000 is a taxable dividend to the extent of current E&P, and the remaining $10,000 is a tax-free return of capital (to the extent that Pacific's shareholders have basis in their stock) because of the accumulated E&P deficit. ◀

If a shareholder's basis is reduced to zero because of a tax-free return of capital distribution, any excess amounts received are treated as a capital gain.

EXAMPLE I16-35 ▶ Peach Corporation, a calendar-year taxpayer, has one shareholder, Georgia, who has owned the stock for several years. The corporation has $30,000 of current E&P and $20,000 of accumulated E&P at the beginning of the current year. Georgia's stock basis is $10,000. At the end of the current year, Peach distributes $65,000 to Georgia. The $65,000 distribution is treated as follows:

Taxable dividend out of current E&P	$30,000
Taxable dividend out of accumulated E&P	20,000
Total dividend	$50,000
Tax-free return of capital	10,000
Capital gain	5,000
Total distribution	$65,000

In addition, because of the $10,000 return of capital, Georgia's stock basis is reduced to zero. ◀

If the distributing corporation has a current E&P deficit and a positive accumulated E&P balance, the current deficit and accumulated E&P are netted on the date of the distribution.[35] The current E&P deficit for the year is prorated on a daily basis unless a nonratable allocation can be shown to be more appropriate.

EXAMPLE I16-36 ▶ Prime Corporation, a calendar-year taxpayer, has a $100,000 positive accumulated E&P balance and a $50,000 current E&P deficit. Prime makes a $30,000 distribution to its shareholders on June 30. E&P as of June 30 is $75,000 [$100,000 accumulated E&P − (0.50 × $50,000 current E&P deficit)] because the current deficit is allocated ratably during the year (i.e., 6 months out of 12 months, assuming that all months have 30 days) unless the corporation can show that a nonratable allocation is more appropriate. Therefore, the $30,000 distribution is fully taxable as a dividend. ◀

PROPERTY DISTRIBUTIONS

OBJECTIVE 5

Determine the consequences of distributions and stock redemptions

TAX CONSEQUENCES TO THE SHAREHOLDERS

Occasionally, a corporation distributes property (i.e., assets other than its stock or stock rights) instead of money to its shareholders. If property is distributed to the shareholders, the following tax consequences generally occur:

▶ The amount distributed equals the FMV of the property (reduced by any associated liabilities).

▶ The amount distributed is treated as a taxable dividend if the corporation has sufficient E&P.

▶ The basis of distributed property equals its FMV (without reduction for any associated liabilities).

[35] Reg. Sec. 1.316-2(b).

Red Corporation distributes land and a building having a $50,000 adjusted basis and a $100,000 FMV to its sole shareholder, Irene. Red has current and accumulated E&P exceeding $60,000. The property is subject to a $40,000 mortgage, which Irene assumes. The amount distributed to Irene is $60,000 ($100,000 FMV of the property − $40,000 liability). Irene has a $60,000 taxable dividend because the corporation has sufficient E&P. Irene's basis in the real estate is $100,000, its FMV. ◀

TAX CONSEQUENCES TO THE DISTRIBUTING CORPORATION

As a general rule, the corporation recognizes no gain or loss upon a property distribution to its shareholders.[36] However, if a corporation distributes appreciated property to its shareholders, the corporation is treated as if it sold the property to the shareholder for its FMV immediately before the distribution, and the corporation recognizes any realized gain.[37]

EXAMPLE I16-38 ▶ Rocket Corporation distributes $75,000 in cash along with land having a $50,000 adjusted basis and a $60,000 FMV to its shareholder. Rocket Corporation recognizes $10,000 ($60,000 − $50,000) of gain on the distribution of the land. ◀

If the property distributed is subject to a liability that exceeds its basis, the FMV of such property, for purposes of determining gain on the distribution, is the lesser of the actual FMV or the amount of the liability.[38]

EXAMPLE I16-39 ▶ Assume the same facts as in Example I16-38 except that Rocket Corporation also transfers a $70,000 mortgage attaching to the land to its shareholder. Rocket recognizes a $20,000 ($70,000 − $50,000) gain on the distribution of the land because the liability exceeds the property's FMV. ◀

STOP & THINK

Question: So far we have been describing cash and other property distributions. What are the tax consequences if a corporation instead makes a pro rata stock dividend, that is, if it issues additional shares of its own stock to existing shareholders?

Solution: The economic situation for the shareholders does not change as a result of the stock dividend. They each still own the same proportion of the corporation, but they have additional shares of stock. Consequently, shareholders recognize no income on receiving the stock dividend. Instead, they spread the basis of their old stock over the combined old and new stock, thereby causing the per share basis to decrease while the total basis remains unchanged. In addition, the corporation recognizes no gain and does not reduce its E&P.

STOCK REDEMPTIONS

Two possible tax consequences can result when a corporation repurchases (redeems) its outstanding stock from a shareholder:

▶ The redemption is treated as a taxable dividend (to the extent of E&P)

▶ The redemption is treated as an exchange of the stock, generally resulting in capital gain or loss treatment by the shareholder.

---

[36] Sec. 311(a).
[37] Sec. 311(b).

[38] Secs. 311(b)(2) and 336(b).

The dividend income rule prevents corporations from paying disguised dividends in the form of a stock redemption. For example, the corporation might redeem 10% of its sole shareholder's stock rather than pay a cash dividend to the shareholder. After the redemption, the shareholder continues to own all of the outstanding stock, retains the same amount of control over the corporation, and has received a substantial distribution of money or other property.

The tax advantage of capital gain treatment accorded to a stock redemption (compared with ordinary income treatment for dividends) is significant because individual shareholders are subject to a 28% maximum tax rate on their net capital gain. In addition, the exchange treatment is preferable if the shareholders have unused capital losses or capital loss carryovers that otherwise would be of limited tax benefit. Moreover, exchange treatment permits shareholders a tax-free recovery of their investment in the stock. A tax-free recovery of the shareholder's stock basis is not permitted if the distribution is a dividend.

EXAMPLE I16-40 ▶

Ajax Corporation has two equal shareholders, Rita and Harry. Each shareholder owns 10 shares of Ajax stock and has owned the stock for several years. Each share has a $100 basis and a $150 FMV. Ajax, which has sufficient E&P, redeems 5 shares from each shareholder at FMV. This redemption causes Rita and Harry each to recognize $750 ($150 FMV × 5 shares) of dividend income taxed at ordinary tax rates. Rita and Harry have dividend income in this case because they each still own 50% of Ajax after the redemption.

If instead, Ajax redeems 5 shares from Rita but none from Harry, Rita obtains exchange treatment and recognizes a $250 capital gain calculated as follows:

Proceeds of redemption ($150 × 5)	$750
Basis of stock redeemed ($100 × 5)	(500)
Capital gain	$250

The capital gain is taxed at the maximum 28% tax rate on capital gains. Moreover, only $250 is taxed as contrasted with $750 under dividend treatment. Example I16-41 on the next page explains why the first redemption causes dividend treatment while the second redemption provides exchange treatment. ◀

DETERMINING WHETHER A REDEMPTION IS A DIVIDEND OR CAPITAL GAIN

A redemption is treated as an exchange subject to capital gain or loss treatment if any of the following conditions or tests are met:[39]

▶ The redemption is not essentially equivalent to a dividend [Sec. 302(b)(1)].[40]

▶ The redemption is substantially disproportionate with respect to the shareholder's interest [Sec. 302(b)(2)].

▶ The redemption results in a complete termination of the shareholder's interest [Sec. 302(b)(3)].

▶ The redemption is made in partial liquidation of the corporation [Sec. 302(b)(4)].

SUBSTANTIALLY DISPROPORTIONATE RULE. If a redemption is substantially disproportionate, capital gain or loss (rather than dividend income) treatment results. Constructive stock ownership rules generally apply to determine whether a redemption is disproportionate.[41] **Constructive stock ownership** means that the redeemed shareholder is considered to own the stock of certain related parties. These related parties include

---

[39] Sec. 302.
[40] For example, exchange treatment has been allowed where the redeemed shareholder's voting control, right to share in current earnings, and rights to receive corporate assets upon liquidation have been significantly reduced.

Ordinarily, this occurs when a shareholder's majority interest is converted to a minority (less than 50%) interest, or a minority interest is reduced.
[41] Sec. 318.

family members, partnerships, corporations in which an ownership interest is held, and trusts and estates in which a beneficial interest is held.

For a redemption to qualify as substantially disproportionate, Sec. 302(b)(2) provides that the following tests must be met immediately after the redemption:

▶ The shareholder must own less than 80% of his or her former percentage interest in the voting stock (including stock held by related parties).

▶ The shareholder also must own less than 80% of his or her former percentage interest in the common (voting and nonvoting) stock (including stock held by related parties).

▶ The shareholder must own less than 50% of the voting stock (including stock held by related parties).

EXAMPLE I16-41 ▶ In Example I16-40, the redemption of both Rita and Harry's stock failed the substantially disproportionate test. For Rita and Harry to qualify, their ownership must be less than 80% of their prior ownership percentage, or 40% (80% × 50% prior ownership) and be less than 50%. However, after the redemption, Rita and Harry each still own exactly 50%, thereby failing both the 80% and 50% tests.

On the other hand, the redemption of only Rita's 5 shares qualifies for exchange treatment because, after the redemption, Rita owns 33⅓% (5 shares Rita still owns ÷ 15 total shares outstanding) of Ajax stock. Thus, Rita's post-redemption ownership is less than 40% and 50%, thereby making the redemption substantially disproportionate. ◀

EXAMPLE I16-42 ▶ Jane owns 60 shares of Slow Corporation's single class of stock, and her mother owns 20 additional shares of Slow stock. One hundred shares of the stock are outstanding. Slow Corporation redeems 30 shares of Jane's stock for $100,000. Jane's percentage interest before the redemption is 80% [(60 + 20 shares) ÷ 100 shares]. Immediately after the redemption, Jane's percentage interest is 71.4% [(30 + 20 shares) ÷ 70 shares]. To meet the 80% test, Jane's interest must be less than 64% (80% × 80%). Therefore, Jane does not meet the 80% test. Also, Jane does not meet the 50% test because she does not own less than 50% of the Slow stock after the redemption. Both tests must be met for the redemption to qualify as a substantially disproportionate redemption. Therefore, the $100,000 received is treated as a dividend and is taxable to Jane to the extent Slow has sufficient E&P. ◀

COMPLETE TERMINATION. Under Sec. 302(b)(3), a complete termination of a shareholder's stock interest also qualifies for capital gain or loss treatment. At first glance, this rule appears to be redundant because the substantially disproportionate redemption rule also should apply to a redemption that results in a complete termination of a shareholder's interest. However, the complete termination provision is important because a special rule permits a waiver of the constructive ownership rules for family members. The constructive ownership rules are waived in a complete termination if the former shareholder files an agreement with the IRS that he or she will have no interest other than a creditor interest in the corporation for 10 years.[42]

EXAMPLE I16-43 ▶ Assume the same facts as in Example I16-42 except that Slow Corporation redeems all 60 shares held by Jane for $200,000, and Jane's basis for her shares is $90,000. The constructive stock ownership rules are waived if Jane agrees not to acquire any interest in Slow Corporation for 10 years. Therefore, Jane's interest is deemed to be completely terminated, and the redemption is treated as a sale of stock qualifying for capital gain treatment. Jane has a capital gain of $110,000 ($200,000 − $90,000). If the waiver is not obtained, the substantially disproportionate tests are applied to determine whether the redemption qualifies as an exchange. Jane would be considered to own 50% of the stock (20 shares owned ÷ 40 outstanding shares) immediately after the redemption, and therefore the substantially

---

[42] Sec. 302(c)(2). The former shareholder cannot serve as an officer, director, or employee for at least 10 years and must notify the IRS if additional stock is acquired (other than by bequest or inheritance). If such stock is acquired, it usually causes the redemption to be taxed as a dividend.

disproportionate redemption test would not be met. The redemption does not qualify as a complete termination because Jane is deemed to own her mother's stock unless Jane obtains a waiver of the constructive ownership rules. Thus, without the waiver, the redemption would be treated as a dividend to Jane. ◀

REDEMPTION PROVISIONS FOR SPECIAL SITUATIONS

The following redemption rules cover special situations:

▶ Section 302(b)(4) provides exchange (rather than dividend) treatment for noncorporate shareholder redemptions in a partial liquidation. To qualify, the distribution must be made pursuant to the termination of an active trade or business.[43]

▶ Section 303 permits the executor of an estate or a beneficiary to have stock in a closely held corporation redeemed, whereby the redemption is treated as an exchange (rather than as a dividend) provided certain conditions are met.[44] The redemption amount is limited to the death taxes imposed and the amount of deductible funeral and administration expenses.

CORPORATE DISTRIBUTIONS IN COMPLETE LIQUIDATION

Sometimes shareholders may wish to terminate a corporation's existence. A complete liquidation is similar to a stock redemption except that all (rather than a portion) of the stock is redeemed. In a complete liquidation, the assets are either distributed in kind to the shareholders in exchange for their stock or sold and converted to cash, which is then distributed to the shareholders in exchange for their stock. The liquidated corporation usually is dissolved under state law.

Surprisingly, the reasons for a complete termination are not always associated with unprofitable operations. For example, a highly successful closely held company may have management continuity problems because the key officer-shareholder group is approaching retirement age. Also, a parent corporation, as a matter of organizational management policy, may wish to liquidate a subsidiary and continue its operations as a separate division.

TAX CONSEQUENCES TO THE LIQUIDATING CORPORATION

DISTRIBUTION OF ASSETS. The liquidating corporation recognizes gains and losses on distributions of property.[45] A corporation that makes the liquidating distribution is treated as if it had sold the assets for their FMV to the shareholders. If the distributed property is subject to a liability, the FMV of the property is treated as being the greater of the actual FMV or the amount of the liability.

EXAMPLE I16-44

Pursuant to a complete liquidation, Southern Corporation distributes the following assets to its shareholders:

▶ Inventory: $10,000 basis, $20,000 FMV

▶ Land held as an investment: $5,000 basis, $30,000 FMV, subject to a $40,000 liability

▶ Marketable securities: $20,000 basis, $15,000 FMV

---

[43] Secs. 302(b)(4) and 302(e). The distributions must be made pursuant to a plan and must occur within the same tax year in which the plan is adopted or within the next succeeding tax year. Immediately after the distribution, the distributing corporation must be actively engaged in the conduct of at least

one qualified trade or business.
[44] Sec. 303.
[45] Sec. 336.

Southern Corporation recognizes $10,000 ($20,000 − $10,000) of ordinary income on the distribution of the inventory, $35,000 ($40,000 − $5,000) of capital gain on the distribution of the land, and $5,000 ($15,000 − $20,000) of capital loss on the distribution of the marketable securities. ◀

SALE OF ASSETS. The tax consequences for an asset sale closely parallel a liquidating distribution. For example, if a corporation sells its assets pursuant to a complete liquidation and then distributes money to its shareholders, all gain or loss realized on the sale of the assets is recognized by the corporation.

LIMITATION ON LOSS RECOGNITION. Under the general rule, the corporation recognizes both gains and losses on liquidations. However, to prevent abuses, special rules limit the recognition of losses in certain situations. These special loss limitations are explained in Chapter C6 of *Prentice Hall's Federal Taxation: Corporations, Partnerships, Estates, and Trusts.*

TAX ATTRIBUTES. Tax attributes, such as NOL carryovers, earnings and profits, capital loss carryovers, and tax credits, disappear upon liquidation of the corporation.

TAX CONSEQUENCES TO THE SHAREHOLDERS

KEY POINT

An appraisal may be necessary to determine the FMV of distributed assets.

Under the general rule for complete liquidations, shareholders are deemed to have sold their stock to the corporation in exchange for money or other property.[46] If the stock is a capital asset, the shareholder recognizes capital gain or loss equal to the difference between (1) the money plus the FMV of other property distributed to the shareholder and (2) the adjusted basis of the shareholder's stock.[47] The basis of property distributed to a shareholder is its FMV on the distribution date.[48]

EXAMPLE I16-45 ▶

Sun Corporation makes a liquidating distribution of land with a $70,000 adjusted basis and a $100,000 FMV to shareholder John, who surrenders his Sun stock to the corporation. Joan, another shareholder, receives $100,000 cash for her shares. John's adjusted basis in the Sun stock is $40,000, and Joan's adjusted basis in her stock is $120,000. John recognizes a $60,000 capital gain ($100,000 − $40,000), and Joan recognizes a $20,000 capital loss ($120,000 − $100,000). The tax basis of the land received by John is $100,000 (the land's FMV on the distribution date). ◀

SECTION 332: LIQUIDATION OF A SUBSIDIARY CORPORATION

KEY POINT

Section 351 permits a parent corporation to incorporate a subsidiary corporation tax free. Section 332 permits a parent to liquidate a controlled subsidiary without incurring adverse tax results where the subsidiary's property has significantly appreciated in value.

GAIN AND LOSS CONSIDERATIONS. Section 332 provides an exception to the general rule that gain or loss is recognized in a liquidating distribution. Under this exception (along with Sec. 337) neither the parent nor the subsidiary recognize gain or loss if a parent corporation liquidates an 80%-owned subsidiary corporation.[49] In a Sec. 332 liquidation, the subsidiary corporation usually is dissolved, and the assets and liabilities transfer to the parent corporation. Section 332 nonrecognition rules are mandatory (rather than elective) if their requirements are satisfied.

The subsidiary corporation is required to do either of the following:

▶ Distribute all its property to the parent corporation in complete liquidation of its stock within a single tax year.

---

[46] Sec. 331(a)(1).

[47] Certain losses on small business stock receive ordinary loss treatment if the requirements of Sec. 1244 are met (see Chapter I8).

[48] Sec. 334(a).

[49] Pursuant to Sec. 1504(a)(2), 80% ownership means the parent corporation must own at least 80% of the total combined voting power of all classes of stock and at least 80% of the total value of all classes of stock.

▶ Make a series of liquidating distributions resulting in a complete liquidation over a 3-year period that commences with the close of the tax year in which the first liquidating distribution is made.

If a minority interest also is being liquidated, the general liquidation rules apply, and the subsidiary corporation recognizes gain (but not loss) on property distributed to a minority shareholder. In addition, the liquidation will be taxable to the minority shareholders with gain or loss being recognized under the general liquidation rules outlined above.

KEY POINT

A parent corporation whose basis for its subsidiary's stock exceeds the tax basis of its share of the subsidiary's net assets loses the tax benefit of the economic loss if the subsidiary is liquidated.

BASIS CONSIDERATIONS. The basis of the subsidiary's assets carry over to the parent corporation, and the adjusted basis of the parent corporation's interest in the subsidiary stock disappears.[50] This carryover basis rule may create certain inequities because the parent corporation may have paid an amount for the subsidiary stock that is greater (or less) than the tax basis of the parent corporation's share of the subsidiary's net assets.

EXAMPLE I16-46 ▶

Tampa Corporation acquired 100% of Top Corporation's stock several years ago for $100,000. In the current year, Top is liquidated, and assets having a $50,000 tax basis are transferred to Tampa Corporation. Tampa's $100,000 stock basis disappears, and Tampa takes only a $50,000 basis in Top's assets. ◀

If these carryover basis rules apply, the parent corporation inherits the tax attributes of the subsidiary.[51] For example, NOL and capital loss carryovers and the E&P balance of the liquidated subsidiary carry over to the parent corporation. In addition, the subsidiary does not recognize any depreciation or investment tax credit recapture. Instead, this recapture potential carries over to the parent corporation.

Topic Review I16-4 summarizes the complete liquidation rules.

TAX PLANNING CONSIDERATIONS

CAPITAL STRUCTURE AND SECTION 1244

As mentioned earlier in the chapter, the use of long-term debt to capitalize a closely held C corporation is an excellent choice assuming the corporation is profitable. However, if the corporation is not successful and goes defunct, the corporate debt to the shareholders becomes worthless and is treated by the shareholders as a nonbusiness bad debt. As is discussed in Chapter I8, nonbusiness bad debts are deductible as a short-term capital loss subject to the $3,000 per year limitation.

An alternative to using debt is to capitalize the corporation using stock (equity). Assuming the requirements are met, the corporation stock would be considered Sec. 1244 stock (small business corporation stock, see Chapter I8 for details). Upon the worthlessness of Sec. 1244 stock, an ordinary loss of up to $50,000 ($100,000 on a joint return) may be deducted in the year of loss. The ability to deduct up to $100,000 against ordinary income is much superior to the capital loss limitation that results with nonbusiness bad debts.

The two alternative capitalization methods clearly yield different results depending upon whether the corporation is ultimately successful or unsuccessful. Thus, the decision as to the method of capitalization of a closely held corporation involves an evaluation of the potential profitability of the corporation at the beginning of the business. For example, if the owners of a new corporation believe the venture is going to be very profitable, debt

---

[50] Sec. 334(b)(1).   [51] Sec. 381.

Topic Review I16-4

Distributions in Complete Liquidation

Sec. 331 Liquidation: General Liquidation Rules	Liquidating Corporation	Shareholders
Recognition of gain or loss	Gain or loss generally is recognized equal to the difference between the FMV of property distributed and the property's adjusted basis.	Gain or loss is recognized equal to the difference between the sum of money plus the FMV of other property received and the basis of the shareholder's stock in the liquidating corporation.
Exception to the gain or loss rule	Losses are not recognized on certain distributions of property to related parties, or property acquired in a carryover basis transaction where the principal purpose was tax avoidance.	Not applicable.
Basis considerations	Not applicable.	The basis of property received is its FMV.
Tax attributes	Tax attributes (e.g., NOL carryovers and E&P) disappear when the liquidation is completed.	Not applicable.

Sec. 332 Liquidation: Subsidiary Corporation	Parent Corporation	Subsidiary Corporation
General requirements	Sec. 332 is mandatory. The parent corporation must own at least 80% of the subsidiary corporation's stock.	The subsidiary corporation is dissolved, and its assets and liabilities transfer to the parent corporation.
Recognition of gain or loss	No gain or loss is recognized except for distributions to minority shareholders.	No gain or loss is recognized on the transfer of assets to the parent. Gain but not loss is recognized on distributions to minority shareholders.
Basis considerations	The basis of the subsidiary's assets carryover to the parent corporation.	Not applicable.
Tax attributes	Tax attributes (e.g., NOL carryovers and E&P) carry over to the parent corporation.	Not applicable.

may be the preferred method of capitalization. Because no one would go into a business believing that the business is going to be unsuccessful, it may be difficult to advise a taxpayer to capitalize a corporation using substantially more stock equity than debt.

One major alternative to avoid some of the problems discussed above is to organize the corporation as either an S corporation or a limited liability company (LLC) rather than as a C corporation. These types of flow-through entities are discussed in Chapter I17.

DIVIDEND POLICY

KEY POINT

Reasonableness of a salary payment is a question of fact to be determined for each case. No formula can be used to determine a reasonable amount.

Dividends paid from E&P are fully taxable to shareholders and not deductible by the corporation. Thus, in a closely held corporation where ownership and management are not separated, the parties may wish to increase salaries or rental payments to owner-shareholders rather than increase dividends. Even though the increased salary or rental payments are taxable to the shareholders (as are dividends), these payments are deductible as business expenses as long as the amounts are reasonable.

EXAMPLE I16-47 ▶ Mario and Nancy are equal owners of Texas Corporation, which is highly profitable and has substantial E&P. Mario and Nancy are the key officers and each are paid a $100,000 salary. A reasonable salary for each would be $150,000. To increase cash distributions to the owners, additional salary payments of $50,000 should be made to both Mario and Nancy (rather than increasing the dividend payments by the same amount) because the corporation can deduct salary payments, whereas the dividend payments are not deductible. The salary payments result in only a single level of taxation, while the dividend payments result in double taxation. Consideration also should be given to payroll taxes because the additional $50,000 compensation may subject the employer and the officers to additional payroll taxes (e.g., the hospitalization portion of the FICA tax). ◀

USE OF LOSSES

Net operating losses and capital losses may be of limited benefit due to the loss carryover limitations (i.e., NOL carryovers are limited to 15 years and net capital losses expire after 5 years). Therefore, attempts should be made to trigger the recognition of additional ordinary income or capital gains to use any expiring carryovers. The sale of appreciated business assets results in recognition of Sec. 1231 gain that can offset capital loss carryovers because net Sec. 1231 gains receive capital gain treatment. The sale or disposition of assets also may result in the recognition of ordinary income because of the depreciation recapture rules. This ordinary income can offset expiring NOLs.

If a business anticipates net operating losses or capital losses during its start-up phase, an S corporation election may be desirable because the losses can be used by the shareholders. The S corporation election may be terminated when the corporation becomes profitable. (See Chapter I17 for a discussion of S corporations.)

CHARITABLE CONTRIBUTIONS

Many owners of closely held corporations prefer to make charitable donations through their controlled corporation rather than as individuals because the corporation can deduct the contributions. Otherwise, to fund the contributed amounts, the controlled corporation may have to make nondeductible dividend payments to the shareholders. Also, an accrual basis corporation may accelerate a charitable contribution deduction if the board of directors approves the contribution before year-end, and the corporation makes payment within 2 1/2 months of year-end.

DIVIDENDS-RECEIVED DEDUCTION

Corporate shareholders may deduct 80% (or 70%) of dividends received. However, this deduction is limited to 80% (or 70%) of taxable income unless the deduction creates or increases an NOL. Thus, a substantial scale-down of the dividends-received deduction may result if taxable income (other than the dividend income) is negative and if the final result is a small amount of taxable income instead of an NOL. Therefore, if the limitation is expected to apply, the corporation should either accelerate deductions into the current year or postpone the recognition of income to a later year. Either action can result in an NOL that prevents the limitation on the dividends-received deduction from applying. (See Examples I16-18 and I16-19.)

COMPLIANCE AND PROCEDURAL CONSIDERATIONS

FILING REQUIREMENTS

A corporation must file Form 1120 (U.S. Corporation Income Tax Return) even if the corporation exists for part of the year. The basic return is supplemented with a separate Schedule D to report capital gains and losses. In addition, Form 4626 (Alternative Minimum Tax—Corporations) must be filed even if no alternative minimum tax is due (see Appendix B for sample Forms 1120, 1120—Schedule D, and 4626). Certain small corporations are eligible to file a simplified Form 1120-A (U.S. Corporation Short-Form Income Tax Return) if their gross receipts, total income, or total assets are less than $500,000. The Form 1120-A may not be filed in certain instances (e.g., the corporation is in the process of being liquidated or is a member of a controlled group).

The regular filing due date for the corporate return is the fifteenth day of the third month following the end of the tax year (e.g., March 15 for calendar-year corporations). The corporation can obtain an automatic 6-month extension by filing Form 7004 (Application for Automatic Extension of Time to File Corporation Income Tax Return), which is included in Appendix B. If an extension is obtained, the full amount of the estimated tax due must be paid on or before the due date of the return (e.g., March 15 for calendar-year corporations).

Quarterly estimated tax payments must be made on the fifteenth day of the fourth, sixth, ninth, and twelfth months of the tax year. In general, the total required estimated tax payments are the lesser of 100% of the corporation's tax liability for the current year or 100% of the tax shown on the preceding year's return.[52] However, a corporation may not base the installment payments of estimated tax on the preceding year's tax liability if that liability was zero.[53] The corporation is subject to a nondeductible underpayment penalty on the underpayment to the extent the quarterly payments are less than the required payments.

SCHEDULE M-1 AND M-2 RECONCILIATIONS

Schedule M-1 is used to reconcile financial accounting net income with taxable income (before the NOL and dividends-received deductions). Figure I16-1 shows a completed Schedule M-1 based on the following adjustments:

Net income per books	$100,000
Plus:	
Federal income tax liability	3,000
Net capital losses	2,000
Nondeductible premiums on key officers' life insurance	4,000
Minus:	
Tax-exempt interest	(9,000)
Excess of tax depreciation over financial accounting depreciation	(75,000)
Taxable income (before special deductions)	$ 25,000

Schedule M-2 reconciles the beginning of the year balance in retained earnings (for financial accounting purposes) with the balance in the account at year end. This reconciliation explains changes in the balance sheet reported on Schedule L or accounts for items of income, gain, or loss taken directly to retained earnings without being reported as part of net income. Figure I16-2 shows a completed Schedule M-2 based on the above facts and assuming a $140,000 balance for retained earnings on January 1, $100,000 of net income for financial accounting, and the payment of a $40,000 cash dividend.

MAINTENANCE OF RECORDS FOR E&P

Companies are not required to compute E&P on the tax return. Therefore, many companies do not maintain adequate records for this account. Detailed records of items that make up current and accumulated E&P, however, should be maintained because the statute of limitations remains open indefinitely on this determination, and the taxpayer

---

[52] Exceptions are provided for large corporations and corporations that earn their income unevenly during the tax year. Large corporations—those with taxable income exceeding $1 million in any of the three preceding tax years—must make quarterly estimated tax payments based on 100% of the tax shown on their current year return, although they are permitted to make

their first-quarter payment based on 100% of the preceding year's tax liability [Sec. 6655(d)]. Section 6655(e) permits corporations to use an annualized income installment or seasonally adjusted installment if it is less than the normally required installment [Sec. 6655(e)].

[53] Rev. Rul. 92-54 1992-2 C.B. 320.

Schedule M-1	Reconciliation of Income (Loss) per Books With Income per Return (See page 16 of instructions.)		
1	Net income (loss) per books	100,000	7	Income recorded on books this year not included on this return (itemize):
2	Federal income tax	3,000		Tax-exempt interest $ 9,000
3	Excess of capital losses over capital gains .	2,000		9,000
4	Income subject to tax not recorded on books this year (itemize):		8	Deductions on this return not charged against book income this year (itemize):
5	Expenses recorded on books this year not deducted on this return (itemize):		a	Depreciation $75,000
a	Depreciation . . . . $		b	Contributions carryover $
b	Contributions carryover $			
c	Travel and entertainment $ Premiums on Life Insurance			75,000
		4,000	9	Add lines 7 and 8	84,000
6	Add lines 1 through 5	109,000	10	Income (line 28, page 1)—line 6 less line 9	25,000

FIGURE I16-1 ▶ FORM 1120, SCHEDULE M-1

Schedule M-2	Analysis of Unappropriated Retained Earnings per Books (Line 25, Schedule L)		
1	Balance at beginning of year	140,000	5	Distributions: a Cash	40,000
2	Net income (loss) per books	100,000		b Stock	
3	Other increases (itemize):			c Property	
			6	Other decreases (itemize):	
			7	Add lines 5 and 6	40,000
4	Add lines 1, 2, and 3	240,000	8	Balance at end of year (line 4 less line 7)	200,000

FIGURE I16-2 ▶ FORM 1120, SCHEDULE M-2

has the burden of proof. Thus, if the IRS determines that a company has current or accumulated E&P and treats a distribution as a taxable dividend rather than a tax-free return of capital, the taxpayer must show that the IRS determination is erroneous.

Form 5452 (Corporate Report of Nondividend Distributions) must be filed by a corporation that makes a return-of-capital distribution. This form requires a computation of E&P for the tax year and a schedule of differences between taxable income and E&P. This form also requires a year-by-year computation of accumulated E&P.

PROBLEM MATERIALS

DISCUSSION QUESTIONS

I16-1 Under the present tax system, C corporation income is taxed twice, once when earned and again when the shareholders receive dividends or sell their stock. Nevertheless, the C corporation form is widely used in the United States, especially for large corporations. Why would an entity choose C corporation status instead of a flow-through organizational form?

I16-2 Anya is considering whether to become a limited partner in a real estate limited partnership by making an investment of $10,000. The limited partnership will generate substantial operating losses for the first 5 years. What are the tax consequences to Anya if the partnership elects to be taxed as a corporation? Is this election a good idea?

I16-3 Does a corporation really pay taxes? Who actually bears the corporate tax burden?

I16-4 The current corporate tax structure contains phaseouts (via surtaxes) at various levels of taxable income that eliminate the benefits of lower tax brackets. Identify the two phaseouts contained in the corporate tax rate structure. How do these phaseouts affect a corporation's marginal and average tax rates? In your opinion, should phaseouts be retained in the tax law or repealed?

I16-5 Describe the basic structure of the alternative minimum tax (AMT), including a discussion of the differences between tax preference items and AMT adjustments.

I16-6 Current tax law contains a dual tax system, the regular tax and alternative minimum tax. In effect, a corporation pays the greater of the regular tax or the tentative minimum tax. Why did Congress enact such a dual system of taxation? How could Congress replace the dual system with a single tax system?

I16-7 The accumulated earnings tax is a penalty tax on corporations.
a. What is the purpose of the accumulated earnings tax?
b. Why do "reasonable needs of the business" either reduce or eliminate the accumulated earnings tax?

I16-8 The personal holding company tax is a penalty tax on corporations.
a. What is the purpose of the personal holding company tax?
b. Two tests are used to classify a corporation as a personal holding company. What are these tests, and how do they accomplish the purpose of the personal holding company tax?

I16-9 Ace Corporation's taxable income is $20,000, and its tax preferences and positive adjustments for alternative minimum tax purposes are $100,000.
a. Is the corporation subject to the corporate alternative minimum tax?
b. What reporting requirements must be satisfied for the preparation of the corporation's tax return?

I16-10 Acme Corporation is a highly profitable closely held corporation that has never paid a dividend. During the past 5 years, earnings of $200,000 per year have been retained in the business. All of the earnings have been reinvested in operating assets to finance an expansion of the business. Is the corporation subject to possible attack by the IRS regarding the imposition of the accumulated earnings tax because no dividends have been paid?

I16-11 Why are controlled groups of corporations required to apportion the lower tax rates applicable to taxable income up to $75,000 among the group members?

I16-12 If a corporation has a net Sec. 1231 loss and a net long-term capital gains are the gain and loss netted against each other? What difference does it make whether the items are netted or treated separately?

I16-13 Acorn Corporation has a $5,000 NSTCG and a $9,000 NLTCL in the current year. Last year, Acorn Corporation had a $3,000 NLTCG. No other capital gains or losses were reported in prior tax years.
a. Do the NSTCG and NLTCL have to be offset in the current year?
b. Is any portion of the NLTCL deductible in the current year?
c. What loss carryback or carryover rules should be applied to any unused capital losses incurred in the current year?

I16-14 C corporations are allowed a dividends-received deduction (DRD) for dividends received from domestic corporations.
a. What is the purpose of the DRD?
b. Does the taxable income limitation on the DRD serve any useful function?

I16-15 Under what circumstances might a corporation elect not to carry back an NOL to the three carryback years?

I16-16 What requirements must be met for an accrual-basis corporation to deduct a charitable contribution in a year before its payment?

I16-17 Acorn Corporation is publicly traded on the American Stock Exchange. Its chief executive officer, Carl, currently receives an annual salary of $1 million. The Board of Directors is considering increasing his compensation level by $200,000.
a. What are the income tax consequences to Acorn if Carl's salary is increased to $1,200,000?
b. What alternatives might be considered to increase Carl's annual compensation that would produce more favorable tax consequences for Acorn Corporation?

I16-18 Current tax law imposes a $1 million limitation on the deductibility of executive compensation. Should such a limitation be retained or repealed? Give reasons for your opinion.

I16-19 Discuss the underlying rationale for the nonrecognition of gain or loss in a Sec. 351 transaction.

I16-20 Carmen transfers land and a building having a $60,000 adjusted basis and a $100,000 FMV to Bass Corporation in a transaction qualifying under Sec. 351. Immediately before the exchange, Carmen takes out a $50,000 mortgage on the property. The mortgage is assumed by the corporation, and the mortgage proceeds are used by Carmen to remodel her personal residence.
   a. What are the likely tax consequences of the asset transfer?
   b. What is the rationale for this result?

I16-21 Damien, Eric, and Fred form a new corporation. Each individual contributes $100,000 of property and receives a one-third ownership interest. Each individual is to receive $10,000 of common stock and a $90,000 20-year corporate note bearing an 8% annual interest rate.
   a. What are the advantages of capitalizing the corporation with a high percentage of debt?
   b. What are the income tax complications to Damien, Eric, and Fred if they transfer appreciated property to the newly formed corporation in a transaction that qualifies under Sec. 351?
   c. List the factors used to determine whether an instrument is debt or equity.
   d. What are the tax consequences if the notes are subsequently recharacterized as equity on an IRS audit of the corporation?

I16-22 Under current tax law, a corporation may deduct interest payments but not dividends paid to shareholders. What problems are created by this disparate treatment? Should the law be changed to either disallow the interest deduction or allow a dividends-paid deduction?

I16-23 Due to severe financial difficulties, Big Corporation has not paid a dividend to its shareholders for several years. Big has a $300,000 accumulated E&P deficit on January 1 of the current year but has sufficient liquidity to resume dividend payments. Current E&P is expected to be $10,000 in the current year and $50,000 in subsequent years.
   a. What are the income tax consequences for the shareholders if Big makes a $50,000 cash distribution in the current year?
   b. What are the income tax consequences for the shareholders if Big delays the $50,000 distribution until January of next year?
   c. In which year should Big make the distribution?

I16-24 Why is it generally preferable to structure the redemption of a shareholder's stock so that it meets the mechanical substantially disproportionate or complete termination test rather than to rely on the not essentially equivalent to a dividend provision?

I16-25 If the requirements for a complete termination of a shareholder's interest are met, shouldn't the substantially disproportionate redemption requirements also be met? What is the major difference between these two provisions?

I16-26 How does the liquidation of a controlled subsidiary differ from the liquidation of a corporation owned by an individual? What is the reason for the distinction?

I16-27 Why is Sec. 1244, which pertains to small business corporation stock, in the tax law?

I16-28 Why is it generally preferable to increase salaries or rental payments to employee-shareholders in a closely held corporation rather than to increase dividends?

I16-29 In many accounting firms, managers review the corporate tax return prepared by others. Why is the Schedule M-1 an important tool for this review?

ISSUE IDENTIFICATION QUESTIONS

I16-30 Acorn Corporation is a very profitable closely held company that is owned solely by Helen, age 55, who plans to retire in 10 years. Management continuity is a problem because neither the existing employees nor Helen's children are interested in or capable of managing the company. Acorn has never paid a dividend and does not intend to do so in the future because dividends are not deductible by the corporation and would be taxable to the shareholders. Helen does not wish to expand the business and plans to have the corporation reinvest its earnings in investment securities. What tax issues should Helen consider?

I16-31 Hugo and Helga each own unincorporated businesses. They plan to form a corporation. Under the plan, they would transfer all of their business assets and liabilities to the corporation in exchange for all of the corporation's stock. Because Hugo's assets are substantially appreciated, a transfer of all of the assets and liabilities would result in an excess of liabilities over the adjusted basis of the assets. On the other hand, Helga has substantial unrealized losses on certain business properties (e.g., land and a building). Her broker has recommended that she sell the properties to recognize capital losses that could be used to offset capital gains. The sales proceeds could then be invested in the new corporation. What tax issues should both individuals consider?

I16-32 Eastern Corporation is formed by John and Joy with an initial capitalization of $500,000. Two alternative capitalization plans are being considered: (1) John and Joy each would receive $200,000 of 8% 15-year bonds and $50,000 of Eastern stock or (2) John and Joy each would receive $250,000 of Eastern stock. John's business assets that would be transferred to Eastern are highly appreciated, and he does not want to recognize any gain on the transfer of these assets. What tax issues should John and Joy consider?

PROBLEMS

I16-33 *Corporate Tax Rates.* Calculate Ajax Corporation's regular tax liability for the following amounts of taxable income:
a. $90,000
b. $300,000
c. $5 million
d. $12 million
e. $17 million
f. $20 million
g. Alternatively, for Parts a, b, and c above, compute Ajax Corporation's regular tax liability if it were a personal service corporation.

I16-34 *Corporate Tax Rates.* In December of the current year, Colorado Corporation is considering selling certain corporate assets that would result in the recognition of a $50,000 LTCG. The company controller estimates that the taxable income for the current year will be $60,000 (before considering the LTCG). She also estimates that taxable income for the following year will be $200,000 (before considering the LTCG).
a. What is Colorado Corporation's tax liability in the current year if the assets are sold in the current year?
b. What is Colorado Corporation's tax liability in the following year if the assets are sold in the following year?
c. Should Colorado Corporation sell the assets in the current year or in the following year? Explain.

I16-35 *Alternative Minimum Tax.* Columbus Corporation reports the following results for the current year:

Taxable income	$100,000
Regular tax liability	22,250
Tax preferences	60,000
Positive AMT adjustments	40,000

Calculate the following amounts for Columbus Corporation:
- Alternative minimum taxable income (AMTI)
- AMT base
- Tentative minimum tax
- Alternative minimum tax
- Total tax liability

I16-36 *Tax Preferences and AMT Adjustments.* During an audit of Control Corporation, you have been assigned to review the company's current-year tax accrual (e.g., provision for federal income taxes and the related liability). The following information is made available for your review:

- Taxable income for regular income tax purposes is $100,000.
- Tax depreciation on real estate placed in service in 1990 is $90,000. Straight-line depreciation with a 40-year life would have been $50,000.
- Accelerated depreciation on real estate placed in service in 1986 is $2,000,000. Straight-line depreciation would have been $1,900,000.
- Adjusted current earnings is $340,000.

a. What is the total amount of Control Corporation's tax preferences and AMT adjustments for the current year?

b. What is Control Corporation's alternative minimum tax?

I16-37 *Accumulated Earnings Tax.* The IRS is auditing Crane Corporation, a manufacturer of widgets, to ascertain whether the company is subject to the accumulated earnings tax in the current year. Crane is widely owned and therefore is not a personal holding company. Crane reported the following results during the year:

Taxable income	$150,000
Federal income taxes	41,750
Dividends-received deduction	85,000
Dividends paid on June 1	20,000

The accumulated E&P balance on January 1 was $180,000, and the company can justify the retention of $80,000 of current earnings to meet its reasonable business needs.

a. What is Crane Corporation's accumulated taxable income?

b. What is Crane Corporation's accumulated earnings tax liability?

I16-38 *Personal Holding Company Tax.* Delta Corporation has been gradually converting its operating business into an investment company because its retained earnings have been invested in passive investments. The company is owned by three shareholders, and more than 60% of its income is personal holding company income. George, the president of Delta Corporation, however, feels that personal holding company status should not be detrimental because the company has paid dividends to its shareholders for several years and therefore should not be liable for any penalty tax.

Delta reports the following results for the current year:

Taxable income	$25,000
Federal income tax liability	3,750
Dividends paid	3,000
Dividends-received deduction	81,750

a. Do you agree or disagree with George? Explain.

b. What is the Delta Corporation's personal holding company tax liability for the current year?

c. How could Delta avoid being subject to the personal holding company tax?

I16-39 *Controlled Group.* Eagle and East Corporations are members of a controlled group. Eagle's taxable income is $50,000, and East's taxable income is $75,000.

a. What is the total federal income tax liability for Eagle and East Corporations?

b. What is the total federal income tax liability for Eagle and East Corporations if they are not members of a controlled group?

I16-40 **Brother-Sister Corporations.** Alfred, Barbara, and Cathy own stock in First, Second, and Third Corporations as follows:

Individuals	First	Second	Third
Alfred	40%	40%	40%
Barbara	30%	60%	30%
Cathy	30%	-0-	30%

Which corporations are members of a brother-sister controlled group?

I16-41 **Capital Gains and Losses.** First Corporation has the following capital gains and losses in the current year:

LTCG	$10,000
LTCL	4,000
STCG	8,000
STCL	20,000

Taxable income (exclusive of the capital gains and losses) is $30,000.
a. What is First Corporation's capital gain or loss position?
b. What is First Corporation's taxable income for the current year?
c. Explain the tax treatment for any unused capital losses.

I16-42 **Capital Loss Carrybacks and Carryovers.** Federal Corporation has the following net capital losses in 1997:

STCL	$ 80,000
LTCL	120,000

NLTCGs were incurred in 1994 through 1996 as follows:

1994	$20,000
1995	20,000
1996	60,000

a. What are the amount and character of the capital loss carryback to 1994 through 1996?
b. What treatment should be accorded to any unused capital losses after the carryback rules are applied?
c. What is the character of any unused capital loss carryovers?

I16-43 **Dividends-Received Deduction.** During the current year, Florida Corporation reports the following results:

Net income from operations	$100,000
Dividend income from a 20%-owned corporation (qualifying for the dividends-received deduction)	200,000

a. What is Florida Corporation's dividends-received deduction?
b. How would your answer to Part a change if Florida Corporation instead reported a $20,000 loss from operations?
c. How would your answer to Part a change if the dividend income were instead from a 10%-owned corporation?

I16-44 **Dividends-Received Deduction.** During the current year, Maine Corporation reports the following results:

Net income (loss) from operations	$(20,000)
Dividend income from a 10%-owned corporation	200,000
(qualifying for the dividends-received deduction)	

a. What is Maine Corporation's dividends-received deduction?

b. How would your answer to Part a change if Maine Corporation's dividend income were from a 25%-owned corporation and net income from operations were instead $90,000?

I16-45 *Net Operating Losses.* General Corporation reports the following results for its second year of operations (the current year):

Gross operating income	$300,000
Business operating expenses	500,000
Dividend income from a 20%-owned corporation	100,000
Dividends-received deduction	80,000

a. What is General Corporation's NOL for the current year?

b. What is the disposition of the NOL if General Corporation reported a $40,000 profit in its first tax year (last year) on which federal income taxes of $6,000 were paid and no special elections were made?

c. What is the best disposition of the NOL if General Corporation anticipates taxable income of $600,000 in the following year?

I16-46 *Charitable Contributions.* On May 15 of the current year, the board of directors of Georgia Corporation authorized a $40,000 donation to a qualified charity. The corporation made the $40,000 payment to the charity on December 1 of the current year. It made no other charitable contributions during the year. Georgia Corporation reports the following results for the current year:

Taxable income (before deducting the dividends-received deduction and charitable contributions)	$250,000
Dividends-received deduction	10,000

a. What amount of charitable contributions are deductible in the current year?

b. How are any unused contributions treated?

c. How would your answer to Part a change, if at all, if Georgia incurs a $30,000 capital loss next year that is carried back to the current year?

I16-47 *Corporate Formation.* In the current year, Jack, Karen, Latoya, and Marc transfer the following property to Giant Corporation (an existing corporation), which is owned equally by the transferors.

- Jack transfers land and a building with a $60,000 adjusted basis and a $100,000 FMV for 25% of Giant stock having an $80,000 FMV and $20,000 of marketable securities having an adjusted basis of $15,000 to Giant Corporation.

- Karen transfers equipment with a $120,000 adjusted basis and a $100,000 FMV for 25% of Giant stock having an $80,000 FMV and a $20,000 20-year Giant Corporation note.

- Latoya transfers inventory with a $70,000 adjusted basis and a $100,000 FMV for 25% of Giant stock having an $80,000 FMV and $20,000 cash.

- Marc transfers land with an $80,000 adjusted basis and a $100,000 FMV, subject to a $20,000 mortgage, which Giant Corporation assumes, for 25% of Giant stock having an $80,000 FMV.

a. How much gain or loss does Jack recognize? What is Jack's basis in the Giant stock and the marketable securities? What is Giant's basis in the land and building?

b. How much gain or loss does Karen recognize? What is Karen's basis in the Giant stock and note? What is Giant's basis in the equipment?

c. How much gain or loss does Latoya recognize? What is Latoya's basis in the Giant stock? What is Giant's basis in the inventory?

d. How much gain or loss does Marc recognize? What is Marc's basis in the Giant stock? What is Giant's basis in the land?

e. How much gain or loss, if any, does Giant Corporation recognize from the distribution of its assets to the shareholders?

I16-48 *Corporate Formation.* Gold Corporation receives land from Marty in a transaction qualifying for nonrecognition of gain or loss under Sec. 351. Marty's basis in the land was $80,000. The FMV of the land is $200,000. Marty receives $20,000 cash and 80% of Gold stock. Mary transfers inventory with a $50,000 adjusted basis and a $200,000 FMV to Gold in exchange for $200,000 of Gold Corporation's debt obligations. Mary acquired the remaining 20% of Gold stock for $45,000. Mary recognizes a $150,000 gain because she received debt obligations of Gold in addition to the Gold stock.

a. What is the basis of the land to Gold Corporation?

b. What is the basis of the building to Gold Corporation?

c. Under what circumstances might it be preferable for Sec. 351 *not* to apply?

I16-49 *Corporate Formations: Transfer of Liabilities.* Matt transfers land that was used in his business with a $600,000 adjusted basis and a $1,000,000 FMV to Hill Corporation in a transaction that otherwise qualifies under Sec. 351. The land is subject to an $800,000 mortgage, which Hill Corporation assumes. Matt receives 100% of the Hill stock.

a. What are the amount and character of the gain or loss (if any) recognized by Matt?

b. What is Matt's basis in the Hill stock?

c. What is Hill's basis in the land?

I16-50 *Debt/Equity.* Joe and Joy formed Huge Corporation 5 years ago with an initial total capitalization of $500,000. Joe received $80,000 of Huge stock and a $100,000, 12% 15-year Huge Corporation note. Joy received $20,000 of Huge stock and a $300,000 12% 15-year Huge Corporation note. During the next 5 years, the interest payments were made when due, and the corporation reinvested its retains earnings of $500,000 to finance operating needs. The IRS audits the company in the current year, and the IRS agent maintains that the debt should be reclassified as equity and that the interest payments on the notes should be treated as dividends.

a. List the factors that should be taken into consideration in determining whether debt should be reclassified as equity.

b. Present arguments the taxpayer should make to the IRS agent as to why the debt should not be reclassified as equity.

I16-51 *Earnings and Profits.* During the current year, Nevada Corporation distributed $100,000 to its sole shareholder. Because the corporation has a $300,000 accumulated earnings and profits deficit at the beginning of the current year and only $10,000 of taxable income in the current year, Nevada's controller feels that the distribution should be treated as a tax-free return of capital to the shareholder. Your investigation reveals the following items that may have an effect on the computation of current E&P:

Federal income tax liability	$ 1,500
Dividends-received deduction	60,000
MACRS depreciation deductions exceeding	
alternative depreciation system depreciation for E&P purposes	40,000
Excess charitable contributions	9,000

a. What is Nevada Corporation's current E&P?

b. How much (if any) of the $100,000 distribution is taxable as a dividend to the sole shareholder?

c. What is the amount of Nevada Corporation's accumulated E&P on the last day of the current year?

I16-52 *Earnings and Profits.* North Corporation has $200,000 of accumulated E&P at the beginning of the current year. North made cash distributions of $300,000 during the current year to its shareholders. The company's operating results on the last day of the current year are as follows:

Taxable income	$100,000
Tax-exempt bond interest	10,000
Dividends-received deduction	7,000
Federal income tax liability	22,250
Net capital losses	5,000

a. What is North Corporation's current E&P?

b. How much of the $300,000 distribution is taxable as a dividend?

c. What is North Corporation's accumulated E&P balance at the end of the current year?

I16-53 *Earnings and Profits.* Ohio Corporation has a $40,000 accumulated E&P balance at the beginning of the current year and a $75,000 current E&P deficit. The corporation makes a $60,000 cash distribution to its sole shareholder on April 30. The shareholder's tax basis in her Ohio stock is $15,000.

a. What amount of the $60,000 distribution is taxable as a dividend (assume that all months have 30 days and that a ratable allocation of the deficit is used)?

b. What are the amount and character of any nondividend amounts received by the shareholder?

I16-54 *Property Distributions.* Old Corporation has a severe liquidity shortage but desires to maintain its existing dividend payment policy. Therefore, Old distributes land that was being held as an investment to its two shareholders. The land has a $30,000 adjusted basis and a $100,000 FMV. Old Corporation has E&P of $300,000. Nancy receives 50% of the land, and Palm Corporation receives the remaining 50%.

a. What amount of the distribution is taxable to Nancy and Palm Corporation?

b. What is the basis of the property to Nancy and Palm Corporation?

c. What are the income tax consequences of the distribution to Old Corporation?

I16-55 *Property Distributions.* Park Corporation distributes equipment with a $60,000 adjusted basis and a $70,000 FMV as a nonliquidating distribution to Pam. The equipment is subject to a $40,000 mortgage note assumed by Pam. Park Corporation has $300,000 of E&P.

a. How much gain (if any) does Park Corporation recognize on the distribution of the equipment?

b. What amount of the distribution is taxable as a dividend to Pam?

c. What is Pam's basis in the equipment?

I16-56 *Stock Redemptions.* Private Corporation redeems some of its stock from Jane, a major shareholder in the company. Before the redemption Jane owns 50 of the 100 outstanding shares, and her daughter Jill owns 40 shares. The remaining ten shares are owned by unrelated individuals. Private Corporation redeems 40 of Jane's shares, having a $200,000 basis, for $600,000. Private Corporation has $900,000 of current and accumulated E&P. Jane's basis in her remaining ten shares of Private Corporation stock is $50,000.

a. What are the tax consequences of the redemption to Jane?

b. What is the basis of Jane's remaining ten shares of Private stock after her 40 shares are redeemed?

I16-57 ***Stock Redemption.*** Prime Corporation redeems some of its stock from two of its shareholders on the same date. Frank and Sam own 50 and 20 shares, respectively, of the 100 shares outstanding before the redemption. The remaining 30 shares are owned by unrelated individuals. Prime redeems ten of Frank's shares having a $15,000 basis for $50,000. All of Sam's shares, having a $30,000 basis are redeemed for $100,000. Frank and Sam are father and son. Sam files an agreement with the IRS that he will have no interest in the corporation other than as a creditor for 10 years. Prime Corporation has current and accumulated E&P totaling $200,000.

a. What are the tax consequences of the redemption to Frank and Sam?

b. What are the tax consequences of the redemption to Sam if he does not file an agreement with the IRS to waive the family attribution rules or if he violates the agreement during the 10-year period?

I16-58 ***Corporate Liquidation.*** Queen Corporation adopts a plan of complete liquidation on January 1 of the current year. The corporation sells the assets listed below during the current year, and this sale is followed by the payment of Queen's liabilities and a single liquidating distribution of $1,200,000 cash on December 12 of the current year to Ahmed (Queen's sole shareholder). Ahmed has a $400,000 basis for his Queen stock.

- Inventory costing $600,000 is sold to customers for $1,000,000.

- Depreciable fixed assets with a $2,000,000 adjusted basis are sold for $3,000,000. Depreciation recapture under Sec. 1245 is $800,000.

- Land with a $4,000,000 adjusted basis is sold for $5,000,000.

a. What are the tax consequences to Queen Corporation of the liquidation?

b. What are the tax consequences to Ahmed upon receiving the liquidating distribution?

I16-59 ***Corporate Liquidation.*** Tampa Corporation acquired 100% of Union Corporation's stock several years ago for $1,000,000. In the current year, Tampa liquidates Union Corporation, receiving all of its assets and liabilities. Tampa continues to operate it as a division. On the date of liquidation, the tax basis and FMV of Union Corporation's assets are $700,000 and $2,000,000, respectively. Union Corporation also has $100,000 of liabilities outstanding that were owed to third parties and E&P of $100,000 on the date of liquidation.

a. How much gain or loss does Union Corporation recognize as a result of the liquidation?

b. What is Tampa's basis for Union Corporation's assets?

c. What tax attributes of Union Corporation carry over to Tampa Corporation?

TAX FORM/RETURN PREPARATION PROBLEMS

I16-60 Zane Corporation's financial accounting balance sheet as of the end of the current year is as follows:

Cash	$ 50,000
Accounts receivable	30,000
Land	20,000
Buildings (net of $30,000 accumulated depreciation)	100,000
Equipment (net of $50,000 accumulated depreciation)	150,000
Total assets	$350,000

Accounts payable	$ 50,000
Mortgage payable	50,000
Capital stock	100,000
Retained earnings	150,000[a]
Total liabilities and stockholders' equity	$350,000

[a] The retained earnings balance at the beginning of the current year was $70,000.

Zane Corporation reports the following financial accounting operating results for the current year:

Sales	$500,000
Minus: Costs of goods sold	(300,000)
Gross profit	$200,000
Dividend income (from 20%-owned domestic corporations)	100,000
Net long-term capital gains	100,000
Total income	$400,000

Expenses:	
Salaries (including officer's salaries of $30,000)	$ 80,000
Repairs	20,000
Bad debts	30,000
State and local taxes	50,000
Contributions	60,000
Depreciation (straight-line for financial accounting purposes)	40,000
Total expenses (before federal income tax expense)	$280,000
Operating profit	$120,000
Minus: Provision for federal income taxes	(40,000)
Net income	$ 80,000

In addition, the following items should be taken into account in the preparation of Form 1120:

Current-year estimated tax payments	$20,000
Depreciation (MACRS for tax purposes)	60,000
Dividends-received deduction (20%-owned corporations)	80,000

Prepare Form 1120 (U.S. Corporation Income Tax Return) for Zane Corporation. Disregard beginning-of-the-year balance sheet amounts other than retained earnings. Also, leave spaces blank on Form 1120 if information is not provided.

I16-61 Huge Corporation has the following balance sheet information at the beginning and end of the current year:

	Beginning of Year	End of Year
Cash	$ 40,000	$ 50,000
Accounts receivable	23,000	21,500
Inventories	26,000	53,000
Marketable securities	30,000	30,000
Investment in 100% owned subsidiary	100,000	115,000
Depreciable assets	100,000	100,000
Accumulated depreciation	(20,000)	(30,000)
Total assets	$299,000	$339,500

Accounts payable	$ 50,000	$ 60,000
Short-term loans	20,000	35,000
Mortgage loan	80,000	79,000
Common stock	1,000	1,000
Additional paid-in capital	49,000	49,000
Retained earnings	99,000	115,500
Total liabilities and stockholders' equity	$299,000	$339,500

Huge Corporation had the following income and expense items for the year:

Sales	$665,000
Purchases	525,000
Dividend income from 100% owned subsidiary	30,000
Dividend income from less than 20%-owned corporations	10,000
Salaries (including officers' salaries of $20,000)	80,000
Repairs	12,000
Contributions	60,000
State and local taxes	7,500
Interest	11,000
MACRS depreciation (financial accounting depreciation is $10,000)	17,490
Federal income tax expense per books	10,000

In addition, Huge Corporation reported an NOL carryover of $12,000 from the preceding year and made estimated tax payments of $10,000.

Prepare Form 1120 (U.S. Corporation Income Tax Return) for Huge Corporation. Leave spaces blank on Form 1120 if information is not provided. Note: You need to prepare a schedule of net income per books to determine the number for Line 1 of Schedule M-1.

CASE STUDY PROBLEMS

I16-62 Frank, Paul, and Sam are considering whether to merge their respective unincorporated businesses and form a C corporation. Frank would transfer land and a building with a $50,000 adjusted basis and $100,000 FMV to the corporation in exchange for $100,000 of common stock in the newly formed FPS Corporation. Paul would transfer inventory with an adjusted basis of $60,000 and $100,000 FMV to FPS Corporation for $50,000 of FPS stock and $50,000 of FPS 10-year notes. Sam will contribute equipment with an adjusted basis of $80,000 and $60,000 FMV along with legal services for the creation of the business with a $40,000 FMV in exchange for $100,000 of FPS stock.

Prepare a client memo that details the tax consequences of the transaction to the newly formed corporation and to Frank, Paul, and Sam if the transaction is carried out as proposed.

I16-63 Beth is the sole shareholder of Pet Store, Inc., which is a regular C corporation. She also manages the store. She wishes to expand the business, but the corporation needs additional capital for her to do so. Fortunately, she has saved $50,000 cash and plans to contribute it to the corporation. However, she doesn't know whether to contribute the cash in exchange for additional stock, make a contribution to capital without receiving additional stock, or lend the $50,000 to the corporation. Prepare a client memo that explains the tax consequences and requirements of each alternative so that Beth can make an informed decision.

TAX RESEARCH PROBLEM

I16-64   Ted is the sole shareholder of Zero Corporation. Before his retirement from the company, he transferred 100 shares of Zero stock by gift to his son. A few months later, Ted sold the remaining 1,900 shares to Zero Corporation for $2,000,000. The company has E&P exceeding $2,000,000. Ted's basis for his 2,000 shares before the two transfers was $80,000. Ted then filed for a waiver of the attribution rules under Sec. 318 and treated the redemption of Zero stock as a long-term capital gain. He also signed a consulting contract with the company that provides him with consulting income of $5,000 per month for 5 years. The IRS audits Ted's return and argues that the redemption should be treated as a dividend under Sec. 301. Have the requirements for Sec. 302(c)(2) been met that would permit a waiver of the family attribution rules?

A partial list of research sources is

- Secs. 302(c)(2) and (b)(3)

- Reg. Sec. 1.302-4

- *William M. Lynch v. CIR*, 58 AFTR 2d 86-5970, 86-2 USTC ¶9731 (9th Cir., 1986)

CHAPTER 17

PARTNERSHIPS AND S CORPORATIONS

LEARNING OBJECTIVES

After studying this chapter, you should be able to

1. ▶ Determine the tax implications of a partnership formation

2. ▶ Apply the operating rules for partnerships

3. ▶ Understand the tax implications (to the partnership and its partners) of distributions to partners

4. ▶ Understand the requirements for S corporation status

5. ▶ Apply the operating rules for S corporations

6. ▶ Determine the tax treatment of an S corporation's shareholders

KEY POINT

Flow-through entities entail taxation only at the ownership level. This single level of taxation is achieved by (1) exempting the entity from taxation; (2) passing income, deductions, losses, and credit through to the owners; and (3) adjusting the basis of the owner's interest in the entity.

Flow-through or conduit entities, such as partnerships, S corporations, limited liability companies, and limited liability partnerships, have the major advantage of entailing only one level of taxation. These legal organizational forms thus represent an interesting blend of what tax theorists call the entity and aggregate theories of taxation. In some ways, they are treated as entities separate from their owners. For example, the entity files a tax return (for information purposes), makes elections pertaining to accounting periods and methods, and computes results of business operations. In other ways, however, a flow-through entity is treated as a mere aggregation of its owners. For example, the entity is not taxed, and the entity's income, deductions, losses, and credits are allocated to the owners based on their proportionate ownership or some other allocation arrangement. These allocated items then flow through to the owners to be reported in their own tax returns.

Aside from exempting flow-through entities from entity-level taxation, the tax law preserves the single-level of taxation in another important way: basis adjustments to the owner's interest in the entity. Each owner obtains an original basis in his ownership interest upon acquiring the interest via formation of the entity, purchase of the entity interest, gift of the entity interest, etc. Subsequently, the owner's basis increases if the entity earns income or if the owner contributes additional money or property to the entity. Conversely, the owner's basis decreases if the entity incurs a loss or if the entity distributes money or property to the owner. In short, the owner's basis increases as the entity expands, and the owner's basis decreases as the entity contracts. Without these basis adjustments, the owner could be subject to double taxation upon selling her interest or upon the dissolution of the entity.

EXAMPLE I17-1 ▶

Conduit Company is a flow-through entity with two owners, George and Flo. Each owner has a $10,000 original basis in the entity. In its first year of operations, Conduit Company earns $30,000, which is allocated $15,000 to each owner. Thus, each owner reports $15,000 in his or her individual tax return even though the company does not distribute the earnings to the owners. At the beginning of the second year, Flo sells her interest to Fred for $25,000. If Flo did not get an increased basis adjustment for her $15,000 of earnings, she would recognize a $15,000 ($25,000 selling price − $10,000 basis in the entity) gain on the sale of her interest, which taxes her twice on the $15,000. However, both George and Flo do increase their bases to $25,000 ($10,000 original basis + $15,000 share of entity earnings). Therefore, when Flo sells her interest for $25,000, she incurs no addition taxable gain ($25,000 selling price − $25,000 basis in the entity = $0 gain). ◀

The next section of this chapter briefly describes the four basic types of flow-through entities. Afterward, the chapter provides more detail on the tax treatment of partnerships and S corporations.

Types of Flow-Through Entities

PARTNERSHIPS

Of the flow-through entities, partnerships have been around the longest. The Code defines a **partnership** as "a syndicate, group, pool, joint venture, or other incorporated organization" that carries on any business, financial operation, or venture. The definition of a partnership, however, does not include a trust, estate, or corporation.[1] A partner is a member of such syndicate, group, pool, joint venture, or organization, and the partner

---

[1] Secs. 761(a) and 7701(a)(2).

can be an individual, corporation, trust, or estate. Unlike a corporation, which must file incorporation documents with the state, partnerships require no legal documentation although most states have laws that govern the rights and restrictions of partnerships. Moreover, most states model their laws on the Uniform Partnership Act (UPA) or the Uniform Limited Partnership Act (UPLA). A partnership must have at least two partners but can have an unlimited number beyond two.

A partnership can be either a general partnership or a limited partnership. In a general partnership, each partner has unlimited liability for partnership debts. Thus, these partners are at risk for more than their investment in the partnership. In a limited partnership, at least one partner must be a general partner, and at least one partner must be a limited partner. As in a general partnership, the general partners are liable for all partnership debts, but the limited partners are liable only to the extent of their investment plus any amount they commit to contribute to the partnership if called upon. Moreover, limited partners may not participate in the management of the partnership.

A major document for a partnership is the partnership agreement. In this agreement, the partners set out the terms of how the partnership will operate and how income, deductions, losses, and credits will be allocated to the partners. The partners, therefore, should take great care in drafting this agreement.[2]

A partnership files an annual information return with the IRS. This return, Form 1065 (U.S. Partnership Return of Income), reports the results of the partnership's operations and indicates the separate items of income, deductions, losses, and credits that flow through to the partners. Form 1065 is included in Appendix B.

S CORPORATIONS

An **S corporation** is so designated because rules pertaining to this entity are located in Subchapter S of the Code. S corporations are a special form of corporation treated as flow-through entities. Similar to partnerships, therefore, S corporations are not taxed, and income, deductions, losses, and credits flow through to the shareholders. These entities, however, still are corporations so that corporate tax rules apply to them unless overridden by the Subchapter S provisions.[3] As with regular C corporations, the shareholders enjoy limited liability, but S corporations offer less flexibility than do partnerships. For example, the number and type of shareholders are limited, and the shareholders cannot agree to allocate income, deductions, losses, and credits in a way that differs from their proportionate ownership.

To achieve S corporation status, the corporation must file an election, and its shareholders must consent to that election. An elected S corporation files an information return, Form 1120S (U.S. Income Tax Return for an S Corporation), which reports the results of the corporation's operations and indicates the separate items of income, deductions, losses, and credits that flow through to the shareholders. Form 1120S is included in Appendix B.

LIMITED LIABILITY COMPANIES

KEY POINT

LLCs and LLPs are recently developed legal forms that achieve partnership taxation while providing their members or partners with limited liability.

A qualifying **limited liability company (LLC)** combines the best features of a partnership and corportion even though it is neither.[4] Specifically, it is taxed like a partnership while providing the limited liability of a corporation. Moreover, this unlimited liability extends to all the LLC's owners, called members. Thus, the LLC is similar to a limited partnership with no general partners, and unlike an S corporation, it can have an unlimited number of members who can be individuals, corporations, estates, or trusts.

---

[2] For a recent article about partnership agreements, see T. Thorne-Thomsen and J.B. Truskowski, "The Importance of Partnership Agreements," *Journal of Accountancy*, January, 1994, pp. 92-96.

[3] Sec. 1371(a)(1).

[4] An LLC is a new type of entity that has been legislatively adopted by all 50 states.

As discussed in Chapter I16, the LLC elects to be taxed as either a corporation or partnership. Assuming the LLC elects partnership treatment, it files Form 1065 (U.S. Partnership Return of Income). Nevertheless, an LLC is not legally a partnership; it just is taxed as one.

LIMITED LIABILITY PARTNERSHIPS

Many states also have statutes that allow a business to operate as a **limited liability partnership (LLP)**. This partnership form is particularly attractive to professional service partnerships, such as public accounting firms. As a result, many firms have adopted the LLP form, primarily to limit legal liability. Under state LLP laws, partners are liable for their own acts and the acts of individuals under their direction. However, LLP partners are not liable for the negligence or misconduct of other partners. Thus, from a liability perspective, an LLP partner is like a limited partner with respect to other partners' acts but like a general partner with respect to his own acts.

TAXATION OF PARTNERSHIPS

FORMATION OF A PARTNERSHIP

OBJECTIVE 1

Determine the tax implications of a partnership formation

When a partnership is formed, the partners often contribute property (e.g., money, business equipment, and inventory previously used in a proprietorship) or services to the partnership. In exchange for this property and/or services, the partners receive an interest in the partnership. For each partner, a **partnership interest** is an investment security similar to corporate stock and thus is a capital asset.

KEY POINT

The nonrecognition provisions under Sec. 721 apply not only at the time of the formation of a partnership but also to subsequent capital contributions.

SECTION 721: NONRECOGNITION RULES. Section 721 prevents the recognition of gain or loss upon either the transfer of property in exchange for a partnership interest or subsequent transfers of property by the partners in exchange for a pro rata increase in their partnership interests. Without this nonrecognition provision, gain on a transfer of appreciated property would be recognized, and the partners might not have sufficient liquidity (e.g., cash) to pay the tax. In addition, the transfer of property to the partnership represents a mere change in ownership form, which is not a recognition event under the tax laws. Finally, the depreciation recapture rules do not apply if no gain is recognized under Sec. 721.

The following exceptions to the Sec. 721 nonrecognition rules should be noted:

▶ The Sec. 721 nonrecognition of gain or loss rules do not apply if the partner acts in a capacity other than as partner. For example, if a partner sells property to the partnership in an arm's-length transaction, the sale would be taxable.[5]

▶ If a partner contributes services instead of cash or property in exchange for an unrestricted partnership interest, the fair market value (FMV) of the services is taxed as compensation to the contributing partner because services do not qualify as property.[6]

▶ The contributing partner recognizes gain if liabilities transferred to the partnership exceed the partner's basis in the partnership.[7]

▶ The contributing partner recognizes gain if the partnership would be treated as an investment company had it incorporated under Sec. 351.[8]

---

[5] Reg. Sec. 1.721-1(a).
[6] Reg. Sec. 1.721-1(b)(1).
[7] See Example I17-5 and the discussion of the partnership basis rules.
[8] Sec. 721(b). The partnership is considered to be an investment company if 80% or more of the transferred assets (excluding cash and nonconvertible debt obligations) consists of marketable stocks or securities. This restriction prevents investors from diversifying their portfolios by creating a partnership through a tax-free transfer of securities in exchange for a partnership interest.

BASIS OF A PARTNERSHIP INTEREST. If the Sec. 721 nonrecognition rules apply, Sec. 722 provides a substituted basis rule for determining the basis of a partnership interest. Disregarding the effect of any liabilities, the basis of the contributing partner's partnership interest equals the sum of money contributed plus the adjusted basis of other property transferred to the partnership.

EXAMPLE I17-2 ▶

Allen contributes business equipment having a $10,000 FMV and a $4,000 adjusted basis to the ABC Partnership in exchange for a 30% interest in the partnership. The basis of Allen's partnership interest is $4,000 (a substituted basis) because he recognizes no gain or loss under Sec. 721. ◀

If a contributing partner renders services to the partnership in exchange for a partnership interest, the contributing partner's basis equals the amount of income recognized from rendering the services (i.e., the FMV of the services).[9] The FMV basis is permitted because the partner recognizes ordinary income equal to the FMV of the services.

EXAMPLE I17-3 ▶

Angela contributes property having a $10,000 FMV and a $4,000 adjusted basis and renders services valued at $10,000 in exchange for a 60% interest in the ABC Partnership. Section 721 prevents gain from being recognized on the transfer of the property. However, Angela recognizes $10,000 of ordinary income for the services rendered. Thus, the basis of Angela's partnership interest equals $14,000 ($4,000 adjusted basis of the property plus the $10,000 FMV of the services). ◀

Section 752 Adjustment. A partner's basis for his or her partnership interest includes the partner's ratable share of partnership liabilities as well as the basis attributable to any property and services contributed to the partnership. In addition, the following rules apply if a partnership assumes a partner's liability or if the partner transfers property to the partnership subject to a liability:

▶ The increase in partnership liabilities is treated as a cash contribution by all partners, which increases their bases by their ratable share of the assumed liabilities.

▶ The partnership's assumption of the liability is treated as a cash distribution to the partner whose liability is assumed, which decreases his basis in the partnership.

EXAMPLE I17-4 ▶

Brad contributes a building to a newly-formed partnership, BCD Partnership, in exchange for a one-third interest in the partnership. The building has a $90,000 FMV, an $80,000 adjusted basis, and is subject to a $60,000 mortgage. The partnership assumes the mortgage but has no other liabilities. Carol and Dale each contribute $30,000 of cash for a one-third interest in the partnership. After the contributions, the partners have the following bases in their partnership interests:

	Brad	*Carol*	*Dale*
Adjusted basis or cash contributed	$80,000	$30,000	$30,000
Plus: Share of mortgage assumed by the partnership ($60,000 × 1/3)	20,000	20,000	20,000
Minus: Decrease in Brad's individual liabilities	(60,000)	—0—	—0—
Basis in partnership interest	$40,000	$50,000	$50,000 ◀

Under the general rules of Sec. 752, a partner's basis in the partnership interest increases by the partner's share of any changes in the partnership's liabilities during the year. For example, if total partnership liabilities (including accounts and notes payable,

---

[9] Reg. Sec. 1.722-1.

mortgages, bank loans, etc.) increase during the year from $100,000 to $200,000, the basis of a partner with a 50% interest in the partnership increases by $50,000 ($100,000 increase in liabilities × 0.50).

Negative Basis Rule. The basis of a partnership interest cannot be negative. Therefore, Sec. 731 requires recognition of gain in situations where a negative basis would otherwise occur.

EXAMPLE I17-5 ▶ Becky transfers property having a $100,000 FMV and a $20,000 adjusted basis, which is subject to a $60,000 mortgage, in exchange for a one-third interest in the BCD Partnership. The partnership owes no other liabilities. Becky, Cindy, and Dan each has a one-third interest in the partnership. The $60,000 reduction in Becky's individual liabilities is treated as a distribution of money. Thus, Becky must recognize a $20,000 gain because the distribution exceeds her $40,000 basis in the partnership interest. Becky's basis in the partnership interest is zero after the distribution computed as follows:

Adjusted basis of property transferred	$20,000
Plus: Becky's share of the mortgage assumed by the partnership ($60,000 × ⅓)	20,000
Minus: Decrease in Becky's individual liabilities	(60,000)
Tentative basis of Becky's partnership interest	($20,000)
Plus: Gain recognized by Becky (to the extent of negative basis)	20,000
Becky's basis in the partnership interest	$ —0— ◀

STOP & THINK

Question: In Example I17-5, Becky transferred property subject to a liability exceeding the property's adjusted basis. How does the treatment of excess liabilites in a partnership differ from the treatment when such property is transferred to a corporation?

Solution: In the corporation situation, the shareholder recognizes gain to the extent that total liabilities exceed total basis of property transferred by that shareholder. Thus, had Becky transferred the same property to a corporation in a Sec. 351 transaction, she would have recognized gain for the entire $40,000 ($60,000 mortgage - $20,000 adjusted basis) excess liability. In a partnership, however, the transferor partner recognizes gain only if the deemed money distribution associated with the liability exceeds the partner's basis in the partnership interest. In Example I17-5, Becky recognized only a $20,000 gain. Had she already had substantial basis in an existing partnership, she would not have recognized any gain.

HOLDING PERIOD FOR A PARTNERSHIP INTEREST. If a partner contributes only cash to the partnership in exchange for a partnership interest, the holding period begins on the date the interest is acquired. If the partner contributes property, the holding period for the partnership interest generally includes the holding period of the contributed property. However, if the contributed property is other than a capital asset or Sec. 1231 property, the holding period begins on the date the partnership interest is acquired.[10]

EXAMPLE I17-6 ▶ In the current year, Johanna contributes business machinery to the JK Partnership in exchange for a partnership interest. Johanna originally acquired the machinery in 1993. Because the machinery is Sec. 1231 property, Johanna's holding period for her partnership interest begins

---

[10] Reg. Sec. 1.1223-1(a).

in 1993 (the date she acquired the machinery). If Johanna had contributed inventory instead of machinery, the holding period would begin on the contribution date). ◄

ADDITIONAL COMMENT

When property that has been held for personal use is contributed to a partnership, the basis equals the lesser of the property's FMV or adjusted basis.

BASIS OF PARTNERSHIP ASSETS. Section 723 provides a carryover basis rule for property contributed to the partnership. The partnership's basis in the property is the same as that of the transferor partner, even if the contributing partner recognizes gain. Without this rule, partners could increase the basis of their property for depreciation and subsequent sale purposes merely by contributing appreciated property to a partnership. Because the carryover basis rule applies, the holding period of the property includes the period the property was held by the contributing partner.[11]

EXAMPLE I17-7 ▶

In the current year, Carlos contributes equipment with a $6,000 adjusted basis and an $8,000 FMV to the CDE Partnership and receives a one-third interest in the partnership. Carlos acquired the equipment in 1993. CDE's basis for the equipment is $6,000, its adjusted basis in the hands of the contributing partner. Carlos recognizes no gain due to the Sec. 721 nonrecognition rules. CDE's holding period for the equipment begins in 1993 because it includes Carlos' holding period for the property. ◄

KEY POINT

For many items, the partnership must maintain separate sets of records for tax and financial accounting purposes.

FINANCIAL ACCOUNTING CONSIDERATIONS. Under generally accepted accounting principles (GAAP), the carryover basis and nonrecognition rules used in taxation do not apply. For example, if property is contributed to a partnership, its book value is recorded at the contributed property's FMV. This GAAP treatment results in a difference between tax basis and financial accounting book value of contributed assets.

EXAMPLE I17-8 ▶

Anwar contributes cash of $30,000 and Beth contributes land having a $30,000 FMV and a $20,000 adjusted basis to the AB Partnership. Each partner receives a 50% interest in the partnership. For financial accounting purposes, the land is recorded at $30,000. For tax purposes, the carryover basis of the land to the partnership is $20,000. No gain or loss is recorded for financial accounting purposes if the partnership later sells the land for $30,000. However, the partnership recognizes a $10,000 gain under the tax rules because the land's adjusted basis for tax purposes is only $20,000. The $10,000 pre-contribution gain is allocated to Anwar. (See the section titled Special Allocations on page I17-8 for a discussion of pre-contribution gains and losses.) ◄

Topic Review I17-1 highlights the nonrecognition of gain or loss provisions and basis rules.

ORGANIZATIONAL AND SYNDICATION FEES. The costs of organizing a partnership are not immediately deductible but must be capitalized by the partnership and amortized over a period of not less than 60 months beginning with the month in which the partnership begins business.[12] **Organizational expenses** include legal and accounting fees incident to organizing the partnership, filing fees, etc.

The partnership must capitalize expenses attributable to syndicating the partnership. These expenses, however, are *not* amortizable. **Syndication fees** are expenses incurred to promote and market partnership interests (usually associated with tax-sheltered limited partnership interests). Examples of nondeductible syndication fees include brokerage and registration fees, legal fees of the underwriter and issuer, and printing costs associated with the prospectus and promotional materials.

---

[11] Sec. 1223(2) and Reg. Sec. 1.723-1.

[12] These rules are contained in Sec. 709 and associated Treasury Regulations. The partnership makes the election to amortize organization costs by attaching a statement to the partnership's tax return that includes the month in which it begins business.

Topic Review I17-1

> ### Section 721 Formations: Nonrecognition of Gain or Loss Rules

> ▶ A transfer of property in exchange for a partnership interest or pro rata increase in a partnership interest causes nonrecognition of gain or loss treatment.

> ▶ The depreciation recapture rules do not apply to contributed property unless a gain is recognized, but the recapture potential carries over to the partnership.

> ▶ A partner's basis in her partnership interest is adjusted for the following:
> Cash contributed to the partnership
> Adjusted basis of noncash property contributed
> FMV of services contributed
> Sec. 752 adjustment for liabilities
> Gain recognized under Sec. 731 due to negative basis rule

> ▶ The partnership's basis in the transferred property carries over from the transferor partners.

> ▶ The partnership's holding period for the transferred property includes the contributing partner's holding period.

> ▶ The nonrecognition rules do not apply to services contributed. The contributing partner recognizes ordinary income equal to the FMV of the services, and the partner's basis in the partnership interest is increased by the amount of income recognized from rendering the services.

OBJECTIVE 2

Apply the operating rules for partnerships

ADDITIONAL COMMENT

Many states impose an income tax on each nonresident partner's share of income produced by the partnership in that state, which can cause a partner to file several state income tax returns where a partnership conducts business in those states.

PARTNERSHIP OPERATIONS

The partnership tax return (Form 1065) provides information regarding the measurement and reporting of income, deductions, losses, and credits that pass through to the partners. Certain separately stated items (e.g., capital gains and losses, charitable contributions, and Sec. 1231 gains and losses) are segregated and passed through to the partners without losing their identity. Such items must be separately stated because their tax effect depends on the partner's particular tax situation. These items are reported on Schedules K and K-1 of the partnership return. Schedule K reports tax information for the entire partnership, and a separate schedule K-1 summarizes the results for each partner (see Appendix B).

Items that do not have special tax effect are netted at the partnership level and are reported on page 1 of Form 1065. The netting of such items results in partnership ordinary income or ordinary loss, which then is allocated to the partners depending on the profit and loss sharing ratios contained in the partnership agreement. Table I17-1 contains a list of commonly encountered separately stated items and items that make up partnership ordinary income or loss.

ADDITIONAL COMMENT

In general, the partnership income or loss is allocated according to the provisions of the partnership agreement, and the partnership agreement can be amended any time up to the due date for filing the partnership return.

SPECIAL ALLOCATIONS

Section 704 permits partners some latitude to decide how income, deductions, losses, and credits are to be allocated among the individual partners. Special allocations are unique to partnerships and permit flexible arrangements among the partners for sharing specific items of income and loss. A partner's distributive share of such items generally is determined by the partnership agreement. However, the special allocations provisions restrict the partners' freedom to shift tax benefits among individual partners. For example, the special allocation must have substantial economic effect (e.g., it cannot be a

▼ **TABLE I17-1**

Segregation of Ordinary Income and Separately Stated Items

	Separately Stated Items (Schedules K and K-1)	Partnership Ordinary Income (or Loss) (Page 1 of Form 1065)
Sales minus cost of goods sold (gross profit)		X
Salaries and wages		X
Guaranteed payments to partners[a]	X	X
Taxes, bad debts, and repairs		X
Charitable contributions	X	
Tax preference items	X	
Investment interest income and expense	X	
Foreign income taxes paid or accrued	X	
Specially allocated items of income, deductions, and so on, that differ from the general profit and loss allocation ratios	X	
Tax-exempt interest income	X	
Capital gains and losses	X	
Tax credits	X	
Sec. 1245 and 1250 depreciation recapture		X
Sec. 1231 gains or losses	X	

[a] Guaranteed payments appear in both columns because the partnership deducts them to arrive at partnership ordinary income (or loss), and they are reported separately and are taxable to the partner who receives the payments.

tax sham). In addition, a special allocation must be made for property contributed by the partners when determining the allocation of depreciation deductions and the amount of gain or loss recognized when the partnership eventually sells the property. Essentially, the allocation of the depreciation deductions and the amount of recognized gain or loss must take into account the difference between the partnership's basis for the contributed property and the property's FMV at the time of the contribution.

EXAMPLE I17-9 ▶ Clay and Dana formed an equal partnership 5 years ago. Clay contributed cash of $100,000, and Dana contributed land having a $60,000 adjusted basis and a $100,000 FMV. The partnership's basis for the land is $60,000 (Dana's carryover basis). If the partnership sells the land in the current year for $110,000, it recognizes $50,000 ($110,000 − $60,000) of gain. If a special allocation of the gain were not required, $25,000 of the gain would be allocated to Clay and Dana based on their equal profit and loss sharing ratios. The special allocation rules, however, require $45,000 of the gain to be allocated to Dana ($40,000 appreciation accruing before her transfer of property to the partnership plus $5,000, which is one-half of the post-contribution appreciation). The remaining $5,000 of post-contribution gain is allocated to Clay [($110,000 − $100,000) × 0.50]. ◀

WHAT WOULD YOU DO IN THIS SITUATION?

Alex and Alicia plan to form a partnership with each partner making an equal capital contribution to the partnership. The partnership agreement will specify that the partners share equally in partnership profits and losses. Among other things, the partnership will invest in taxable and tax-exempt bonds. The partners expect the taxable and tax-exempt bonds each to generate $1,000 of interest per year. For the next several years, Alex expects to be in the 15% tax bracket and Alicia expects to be in the 39.6% tax bracket. Without a special allocation, each partner would be allocated $500 of each type interest. Instead, however, they want a special allocation in the partnership agreement that allocates (1) all $1,000 of taxable interest to Alex plus $75 of tax-exempt interest to compensate him for additional taxes on the extra $500 of taxable interest and (2) the remaining $925 of tax-exempt interest to Alicia. Alex and Alicia seek your advice on the propriety of this special allocation. Hint: Prepare a schedule of after-tax interest income to the partners with and without the special allocation.

ALLOCATION OF PARTNERSHIP INCOME, DEDUCTIONS, LOSSES, AND CREDITS TO PARTNERS

KEY POINT

The varying interest rule applies to any partner who sells or exchanges less than his or her entire interest, or whose interest is reduced either by the entry of a new partner who purchases his or her interest directly from the partnership, by partial liquidation, by gift, or otherwise.

If any partner's interest in the partnership changes during the year (e.g., due to the sale of a partnership interest or the entry of a new partner who contributes property to the partnership in exchange for an interest), all of the partners must determine their distributive share of the partnership income, deductions, losses, and credits according to their varying interests in the partnership during the year.[13] Retroactive allocations (e.g., of deductions or losses) may not be made to new partners admitted before the end of the partnership's tax year.

EXAMPLE I17-10 ▶

Colleen and Dan are equal partners in the CDE Partnership, which uses the calendar year as its tax year. On December 1 of the current year, Ed contributes $50,000 cash for a one-third interest in the partnership. The partnership reports a $9,000 ordinary loss for the current tax year ending on December 31. The partners must report their shares of the partnership loss based on their varying interests. A daily allocation of the loss (assuming all months have 30 days) takes place as follows:[14]

Partner		Loss Allocation
Colleen	½ × $9,000 × 11/12	$4,125
	⅓ × $9,000 × 1/12	250
		$4,375
Dan	Same as Colleen	4,375
Ed	⅓ × $9,000 × 1/12	250
		$9,000

Ed's loss is limited to his ratable share of the loss incurred after his entry into the partnership, or $250. This result occurs even if the partnership agreement provides that Ed would receive one-third of all losses for the entire year. ◀

---

[13] Sec. 706(d)(1).
[14] Regulation Sec. 1.706-1(c)(2) provides for alternative allocation methods.

The partners may elect to use the interim closing method as an alternative to the pro rata method used in Example I17-10.

BASIS ADJUSTMENTS FOR OPERATING ITEMS

Under Sec. 705, the basis of each partnership interest is adjusted to reflect the partner's share of income and deduction items. This basis adjustment is necessary to ensure the single level of taxation of partnerships. Basis adjustments for items of income and deduction are made currently regardless of whether an actual distribution is made to the partners. In addition, each partner's basis in the partnership interest is adjusted for capital contributions, withdrawals, and changes in liabilities that occur during the year. Each partner's basis is increased by the partner's distributive share of partnership ordinary income and separately stated income and gain items. The basis of the partnership interest is increased whether the income is taxable to the partners or is tax-exempt.[15]

A partner's basis is decreased (but not below zero) by partnership distributions and by the partner's distributive share of partnership ordinary loss, separately stated losses and deductions, and expenditures that are nondeductible in computing partnership ordinary income or loss (e.g., charitable contributions made by the partnership).

EXAMPLE I17-11 ▶

David and Edith form a partnership in the current year and share profits and losses equally. The partnership agreement provides for no special allocations. The following transactions occur during the year that affect David's basis in his partnership interest:

▶ David contributes land having a $60,000 basis and a $100,000 FMV in exchange for his initial partnership interest.

▶ The partnership liabilities increase from zero to $100,000 by the end of the tax year.

▶ The partnership earns $50,000 of ordinary income.

▶ The partnership earns $5,000 of tax-exempt interest income.

▶ The partnership incurs $10,000 of capital losses.

▶ David withdraws $20,000 in cash from the partnership.

▶ The partnership makes a $15,000 charitable contribution.

David's year-end basis is determined as follows:

Capital contribution of land	$60,000
Plus: Share of the increase in partnership liabilities ($100,000 × 0.50)	50,000
Share of ordinary income ($50,000 × 0.50)	25,000
Share of tax-exempt interest income ($5,000 × 0.50)	2,500
Minus: Share of capital losses ($10,000 × 0.50)	(5,000)
Withdrawals by David	(20,000)
Share of charitable contributions ($15,000 × 0.50)	(7,500)
David's basis at the end of the current year	$105,000 ◀

STOP & THINK

Question: Why do partners increase the basis of their partnership interests by their share of tax-exempt income?

Solution: Increasing the basis ensures that the tax-exempt income will retain its tax-free character when the income is distributed in the form of cash.

---

[15] If the partnership includes oil and gas properties, an increase in basis is made for the excess of percentage depletion claimed over the basis of the property subject to depletion, and a reduction in basis is made for the depletion deduction claimed under Sec. 611.

LIMITATIONS ON LOSSES AND RESTORATION OF BASIS

Although a partner's distributive share of the partnership's ordinary loss and any separately stated losses and deductions pass through to the partner, Sec. 704(d) limits deductibility of the losses to the partner's adjusted basis in her partnership interest as determined at the end of the partnership's tax year.[16] All positive and negative adjustments referred to in Example I17-11 (except the loss) are made before the limitation is considered. If the loss limitation rule did not apply, the partner's interest could have a negative basis. Any unused losses and deductions carry over indefinitely and are allowed in subsequent years when the partner again has a positive basis in her partnership interest.

EXAMPLE I17-12 ▶ Ellen, who has a 50% interest in the EF Partnership, has a $10,000 basis in her partnership interest at the end of 1997 (before deducting her share of losses). The EF Partnership incurs a $50,000 ordinary loss in 1997. Ellen's share of the loss is $25,000 ($50,000 × 0.50), but Ellen can deduct only $10,000 in 1997. The remaining $15,000 of loss carries over to 1998. The deductible loss reduces Ellen's partnership basis to zero at the end of 1997. ◀

EXAMPLE I17-13 ▶ Assume the same facts as in Example I17-12, except that in 1998 Ellen's share of partnership liabilities increases by $5,000, Ellen's share of 1998 ordinary income is $5,000, and Ellen makes a $5,000 additional capital contribution. Ellen's basis increases by $15,000 due to the three items. Therefore, she deducts the $15,000 loss carryover from 1997 in 1998. The deduction reduces Ellen's partnership basis to zero at the end of 1998. A zero tax basis for a partnership interest does not necessarily mean that the interest is worthless. The FMV of the partnership's net assets or their financial accounting book value, nevertheless, may be substantial. ◀

Topic Review I17-2 summarizes the special allocation and basis rules.

PASSIVE ACTIVITY LOSS LIMITATIONS. The passive activity loss limitations that were discussed in Chapter I8 apply to partners who do not materially participate in the business of the partnership. The passive activity loss rules are applied at the *partner* level, that is, each partner must determine whether he or she materially participates in the partnership. If a loss is determined to be passive, a partner may not deduct the loss against either earned income or portfolio income, but may deduct the loss only against other passive income. These rules are highly significant and play a major role in determining the deductibility of partnership losses by partners.

TRANSACTIONS BETWEEN A PARTNER AND THE PARTNERSHIP

Sometimes a partner may independently engage in transactions with the partnership. For example, a partner may sell property to the partnership rather than make a capital contribution of the property. In such transactions, the partner is treated as an outside independent party.[17] Thus, a partner recognizes gain or loss on the sale of property to the partnership, and the partnership receives a cost basis equal to the amount of consideration paid. Because the partner and the partnership are not truly independent parties, abuse of this provision is possible. For example, the partners might want to recognize losses by selling certain assets at a loss to the partnership while still retaining those assets in the partnership. Alternatively, a partner may wish to sell certain depreciable business

---

[16] Two other rules also restrict the deductibility of losses. The at-risk rules contained in Sec. 465 limit loss deductions to the partner's at-risk basis. In addition, Sec. 469 contains passive activity loss rules that disallow virtually all net passive activity losses. These restrictions are discussed in Chapter I8 of this text and in Chapter C9 of *Prentice Hall's Federal Taxation: Corporations, Partnerships, Estates, and Trusts.*

[17] Rules for transactions between a partner and the partnership are in Sec. 707.

Topic Review I17-2

Allocation Rules and Basis Adjustments

▶ When a partner contributes property to a partnership, any unrecognized gain or loss must be allocated to the contributing partner when the partnership sells the property.

▶ Partnership income, deductions, losses, and credits are allocated to the partners on a daily basis based on each partner's interest in the partnership.

▶ Special allocations of income, gains, deductions, losses, and credits are permitted as long as they have substantial economic effect.

▶ Basis in the partnership interest is increased by the partner's share of ordinary income, separately stated income items, and tax-exempt income. Basis is reduced by a partner's share of ordinary loss, separately stated deductions and losses, and nondeductible expenditures. Basis also is adjusted for capital contributions, withdrawals, and changes in partnership liabilities. Basis cannot be decreased below zero.

▶ Ordinary losses and separately stated items that exceed a partner's basis carry over indefinitely until the partner has a positive basis in his partnership interest.

assets (Sec. 1231 property) at a gain taxable to the partner at favorable capital gains rates while the partnership receives a stepped-up FMV basis in the assets for depreciation purposes. Section 707(b) forestalls such potential abuses by disallowing losses and by providing ordinary income (rather than capital gain) treatment under the following circumstances:

ADDITIONAL COMMENT

Defining a partner's interest in a partnership is not always an easy matter. These determinations become difficult if a partner has varying interests in different types of income.

▶ Losses are disallowed on sales or exchanges between a partner and the partnership if the partner owns more than a 50% interest in the partnership. A loss also is disallowed if a sale or exchange of property occurs between two partnerships in which the same partners own more than a 50% interest. The Sec. 267 constructive ownership rules apply to determine whether the 50% test is met. If the purchaser (i.e., the partner or the partnership) of the property later sells the asset to an outsider, the gain recognized is reduced by the previously disallowed loss.

▶ Gains are treated as ordinary income (rather than a capital gain) if the partner owns (directly or indirectly) more than a 50% interest in the partnership and if the exchanged asset is not a capital asset in the transferee's hands.[18] Again, the Sec. 267 constructive ownership rules apply.

EXAMPLE I17-14 ▶ Ira has a 60% interest in the HI Partnership. Ira sells land with a $100,000 adjusted basis to the partnership for its $60,000 FMV. Ira does not recognize the $40,000 ($60,000 − $100,000) loss, and the basis of the land to the partnership is $60,000 because Ira owns more than a 50% interest in the partnership. If the partnership later sells the land to an outsider for $110,000, the partnership recognizes only $10,000 of gain because the $50,000 ($110,000 − $60,000) realized gain is reduced by the $40,000 previously disallowed loss. ◀

EXAMPLE I17-15 ▶ Helen has a 90% interest in the HI Partnership. Helen sells a building (used in her business) with a $50,000 adjusted basis to the HI Partnership for $100,000. After the purchase, the partnership uses the building for business purposes, while before the sale Helen had taken straight-line depreciation. Therefore, had Helen sold the building to an outsider, she would have recognized a $50,000 Sec. 1231 gain with no depreciation recapture. Net Sec. 1231 gain

---

[18] Gains also are converted to ordinary income if the sale is between two partnerships in which the same partners owns directly or indirectly more than a 50% interest in the partnership. In determining the 50% ownership rule, the Sec. 267 constructive ownership rules apply.

is treated as capital gain so that the taxpayer may use the gain to offset capital losses. However, because Helen sells the building to a partnership in which she owns a more than 50% interest, and because the building is not a capital asset to the partnership, Helen's $50,000 gain is treated as ordinary income. HI Partnership's basis in the building is $100,000.

◀

GUARANTEED PAYMENTS. Even though a partner does not qualify as an employee of the partnership for tax purposes, the partnership agreement may provide for fixed salary payments that are not based on partnership income. Generally, the partnership deducts such payments as guaranteed payments to arrive at partnership ordinary income. They are includible in the partner's income in the tax year received. Guaranteed payments also can be made in lieu of interest payments on the amount of the partner's capital investment. Such payments also are deductible by the partnership to arrive at partnership ordinary income and are includible in the partner's income.

EXAMPLE I17-16 ▶

José owns a 40% interest in the JKL Partnership. The partnership agreement provides that José is to receive a fixed salary of $20,000 plus 10% interest on his average capital balance. No other guaranteed payments are made to the other partners. If his average capital balance is $50,000, $5,000 (0.10 × $50,000) of interest would be paid as a guaranteed payment. If partnership ordinary income is $10,000 before deducting the guaranteed payments, the partnership ordinary loss is $15,000 ($10,000 income − $25,000 of guaranteed payments to José). José reports $25,000 of ordinary income for the year, consisting of the $20,000 salary and the $5,000 interest. He also reports a $6,000 ($15,000 × 0.40) ordinary loss. The other partners report a $9,000 ($15,000 × 0.60) ordinary loss.

◀

OBJECTIVE 3

Understand the tax implications (to the partnership and its partners) of distributions to partners

PARTNERSHIP DISTRIBUTIONS

A distribution of cash or property from the partnership to a partner generally is treated as a tax-free return of capital. This treatment closely parallels the tax-free consequences resulting from a capital contribution of property made in exchange for a partnership interest under Sec. 721.

A distribution may result in a reduction of a partner's capital interest in the partnership. This type of distribution is called as a **nonliquidating distribution**. The partnership may desire to liquidate a partner's entire interest due to retirement, death, or other business reasons. These distributions are called **liquidating distributions**. In such cases, the liquidating distribution is treated as a sale or exchange of the partnership interest.

Due to the complex nature of this topic, this chapter includes only an abbreviated coverage of these materials, and the discussion of liquidating distributions is omitted. Comprehensive coverage of these topics is included in Chapter C9 of *Prentice Hall's Federal Taxation: Corporations, Partnerships, Estates, and Trusts.*

NONLIQUIDATING DISTRIBUTIONS. As a general rule, neither the partner nor the partnership recognize gain or loss if the partnership distributes money or other property to the partner.[19] Such nonliquidating distributions generally are treated as tax-free returns of capital. If the amount of money received by the partner exceeds the partner's basis for the partnership interest, the partner recognizes gain to the extent of the excess.[20] If property other than money (e.g., land and machinery) is distributed to the partner, the basis of the partnership interest is reduced by the adjusted basis of the distributed

---

[19] Distribution rules are in Sec. 731.
[20] Exceptions apply if unrealized receivables and inventory items, referred to as Sec. 751 assets, remain in the partnership or are distributed to the partner.

In such instances, the partnership and/or the partner may recognize gain on the distribution.

assets. As previously mentioned, no gain or loss is recognized by the partnership or by the distributee partner even if the adjusted basis of the distributed property exceeds the partner's basis in his or her partnership interest. In this case, the basis of the property to the partner is reduced to equal the basis of the partnership interest. If the partnership distributes both money and property, the money distribution reduces the basis of the partnership interest before any adjustment is made for the property distribution.

EXAMPLE I17-17 ▶ Jane receives a nonliquidating distribution of $10,000 in money from the JK Partnership. At the distribution date, Jane's basis in her partnership interest is $8,000. Of the $10,000 distribution, $8,000 is a tax-free return of capital, which reduces Jane's basis to zero. The remaining $2,000 is a capital gain.[21] ◀

EXAMPLE I17-18 ▶ Jeff receives a nonliquidating distribution of land having a $6,000 adjusted basis and a $10,000 FMV from the JK Partnership. When the distribution is made, Jeff's basis in his partnership interest is $8,000. Neither Jeff nor the partnership recognize gain or loss when the distribution is made. Jeff's basis in his partnership interest is reduced by $6,000 (the adjusted basis of the property distributed). Thus, Jeff's basis in his partnership interest is $2,000 ($8,000 − $6,000) following the distribution. His basis in the land is $6,000. ◀

EXAMPLE I17-19 ▶ Jean receives a nonliquidating distribution of $5,000 cash plus land having a $6,000 adjusted basis and a $10,000 FMV from the JK Partnership. When the distribution is made, Jean's basis in her partnership interest is $8,000. Her basis initially is reduced by the $5,000 money distribution to reflect its tax-free return of capital treatment. The remaining $3,000 basis in her partnership interest is allocated to the land, and neither Jane nor the partnership recognize gain or loss on the distribution. Jean's basis for her partnership interest is zero after the distribution. ◀

Topic Review I17-3 summarizes the gain or loss recognition rules relating to nonliquidating distributions.

SALE OF A PARTNERSHIP INTEREST

RECOGNITION OF GAIN OR LOSS. A partnership interest is a capital asset similar to a corporate security. It may be sold or exchanged as existing partners retire or withdraw from the buisness. The remaining partners may acquire the selling partner's interest, or the interest may be sold to an outsider.

Capital gain or loss generally arises from the sale of a partnership interest because the interest is a capital asset in the hands of the selling partner. In this case, a partnership is viewed as an entity separate and distinct from the partners. However, in some circumstances a partner is considered to own a proportionate interest in each partnership asset (i.e., the partnership is viewed as a conduit), which results in part capital gain and part ordinary income treatment depending on the character of the underlying assets.

Under the general rules of Sec. 741, gain or loss is measured by the difference between the amount realized and the selling partner's adjusted basis in the partnership interest. The amount realized includes the partner's share of partnership liabilities from which the partner is released as a result of the sale. The basis of the partnership interest also is adjusted by the selling partner's distributive share of partnership income or loss, which must be computed up to the sale date.

---

[21] A portion of this gain may be converted to ordinary income if Jane's share of any Sec. 751 assets (i.e., unrealized receivables and substantially appreciat- ed inventory items) held by the partnership changes as a result of the cash distribution.

Topic Review I17-3

Nonliquidating Distributions

▶ Generally, neither the partner nor the partnership recognize gain on loss upon a nonliquidating distribution of money or other property. However, if the distributed money exceeds the distributee partner's partnership basis, the partner recognizes gain on the excess. For this purpose, any release from partnership liabilities is treated as a distribution of money to the partner.

▶ The partner's basis in the partnership is reduced (but not below zero) by the amount of money distributed. If the partnership distributes other property, the following two points apply.

▶ If the adjusted basis of distributed property does not exceed the partner's basis in the partnership (after reduction for money distributions), the basis of the distributed property carries over to the partner, and the partner's partnership basis is reduced by the distributed property's adjusted basis.

▶ If the adjusted basis of distributed property exceeds the partner's basis in the partnership (after reduction for money distributions), the distributed property takes a basis equal to the partner's basis in the partnership, and the partner's partnership basis is reduced to zero.

EXAMPLE I17-20 ▶ On October 1, Jesse sells his interest in the JK Partnership to Paula, an outsider, for $150,000 cash plus the release from $30,000 of partnership liabilities. Jesse's basis in his partnership interest is $74,000 before taking into account his distributive share of partnership income for the period ending on the sale date and his share of any increase in partnership liabilities during the same period. For the current year, Jesse's share of the partnership income for the period up to the date of sale is $20,000, and his share of increased partnership liabilities is $6,000. Thus, Jesse's basis in his partnership interest is $100,000 ($74,000 basis on January 1 + $20,000 share of partnership income + $6,000 share of increased partnership liabilities). The amount realized on the sale is $180,000 ($150,000 selling price + $30,000 liabilities). Thus, Jesse recognizes $80,000 gain on the sale, which is capital gain unless ordinary income is triggered under Sec. 751. (See Example I17-21 for a discussion of Sec. 751.) ◀

SECTION 751 ORDINARY INCOME TREATMENT. Ordinary income rather than capital gain treatment may result under Sec. 751 if a partnership has unrealized receivables or substantially appreciated inventory when a partnership interest is sold. A sale of Sec. 751 assets by the partnership results in ordinary income, which eventually flows through to the partners. Thus, this rule prevents a partner from converting ordinary income into capital gain by selling or liquidating the partnership interest. Section 751 assets include the following:

▶ Substantially appreciated inventory, which means its FMV exceeds 120% of its adjusted basis

▶ Accounts receivable of a cash method partnership (i.e., receivables having a) zero basis

▶ Section 1245 and 1250 depreciation recapture potential (i.e., amounts that would be recaptured as ordinary income if Sec. 1245 or 1250 property were sold by the partnership)

EXAMPLE I17-21 ▶ Joy's basis in her partnership interest is $100,000, and the amount realized on its sale is $180,000, which results in an $80,000 gain. The cash method partnership has accounts receivable with a zero basis and a $30,000 FMV. Joy's share of these receivables is $10,000.

Thus, $10,000 of the amount realized on the sale of the partnership interest is attributed to Joy's share of the accounts receivable. Because her share of the receivables has a zero basis and a $10,000 FMV, $10,000 ($10,000 − $0) of the gain is ordinary income to Joy as though she sold her share of the receivables. The remaining $70,000 ($170,000 − $100,000) of gain from the sale of Joy's partnership interest is a capital gain. ◄

OPTIONAL BASIS ADJUSTMENTS

Section 754 provides an election that permits a basis adjustment to the assets of a continuing partnership when a partnership interest is sold or exchanged or when certain distributions take place. This election, which is made at the partnership level, prevents inequities that might arise because the basis of partnership assets are not adjusted under general partnership tax accounting rules. The election is binding for all future years unless the IRS consents to a revocation of the election.

EXAMPLE I17-22 ▶ Jim acquires Antonio's one-third partnership interest in the ABC Partnership for $40,000. The partnership's balance sheet on the sale date includes the following:

	Adjusted Basis	FMV
Assets:		
Cash	$20,000	$ 20,000
Accounts receivable	10,000	10,000
Inventory	15,000	20,000
Depreciable assets	15,000	85,000
Total	$60,000	$135,000
Liabilities	$15,000	$ 15,000
Capital:		
Antonio	15,000	40,000
Beth	15,000	40,000
Carmen	15,000	40,000
Total	$60,000	$135,000

Jim's basis adjustment equals the difference between his basis for the partnership interest of $45,000 ($40,000 amount paid + $5,000 of ABC's liabilities) and his $20,000 ($60,000 × ⅓) basis in the underlying partnership assets. Thus, if the partnership makes the optional basis adjustment election with respect to the sale or if a previous election is in effect on the sale date, Jim steps up the basis of his share of partnership assets from $20,000 to $45,000. The election does not affect the remaining partners' underlying basis in partnership assets.

The election would be favorable only to Jim because his share of the appreciated partnership assets (inventories and depreciable assets) would be stepped up by $25,000, based on the relative amounts of appreciation for each asset. Jim then would be entitled to additional depreciation deductions on the increased basis. In addition, Jim would receive an increased basis for calculating gain on the sale of the inventory. If this election were not in effect and the inventory were sold, Jim would report $1,667 (⅓ × $5,000) gain from the sale of his one-third interest in the inventory even though he paid $6,667 (⅓ × $20,000) for such interest. ◄

KEY POINT

The Sec. 754 election can be both an opportunity and a trap because both positive and negative basis adjustments are required.

ADDITIONAL COMMENT

Recordkeeping and administrative problems can increase substantially if the partnership makes the Sec. 754 election.

Once the election is in effect, its application may be detrimental because a downward adjustment is required if the amount paid for a partnership interest is less than the adjusted basis of the assets (i.e., the assets have declined rather than appreciated in value). The complexities of the basis adjustment rules relative to partnership distributions and sales of an interest to existing partners are discussed in Chapter C10 of *Prentice Hall's Federal Taxation: Corporations, Partnerships, Estates, and Trusts.*

PARTNERSHIP ELECTIONS

TAX YEAR RESTRICTIONS

When a partnership's tax year ends, each partner's distributive share of the partnership income (including guaranteed payments) is reported on each partner's Form 1040 (or Form 1120 for corporate partners). Thus, if the partnership's tax year ends on January 31, 1997 and the partners report on a calendar-year basis ending December 31, 1996, none of the partnership income for 1996 is reported on the partners' federal income tax returns until 1997. This situation results in an effective 11-month deferral of income.

EXAMPLE I17-23 ▶ Kim is admitted to the ABC Partnership on April 1, 1996. Kim is a calendar-year taxpayer who previously was employed by the partnership from January 1, 1996, until her admission to the partnership on April 1, 1996. Kim's earnings as an employee for the 3-month period are $8,000. She receives monthly distributions of $3,000 for the last 9 months of the year that represent her share of partnership income for the year ending January 31, 1997. ABC's tax year ends on January 31, 1997, and Kim's distributive share of the partnership income for the period April 1, 1996, through January 31, 1997, is $60,000. Because distributions to a partner are treated as made on the last day of the partnership's tax year (January 31, 1997) and because the partnership tax year ends after December 31, 1996, Kim's income for 1996 is only $8,000 (her salary as an employee for the first 3 months of 1996). Kim's $60,000 share of the partnership income for the year ending January 31, 1997, is reported on her 1997 tax return. ◀

To prevent or minimize opportunities for the deferral of partnership income as illustrated in Example I17-23, Sec. 706 provides the following restrictions on the selection of a tax year by the partners and the partnership:

▶ A partnership uses the tax year of the one or more partners who own a majority interest (more than 50%) in the partnership. This majority interest tax year rule is determined on the first day of the partnership's existing tax year.

▶ If partners having a majority interest in the partnership do not have the same tax year, the partnership uses the same tax year as all of its principal partners (a **principal partner** has a 5% or greater interest in the partnership).

▶ If the principal partners do not have the same tax year and no majority of its partners have the same tax year, the partnership uses the tax year that allows the "least aggregate deferral." (See Chapter C9 of *Prentice Hall's Federal Taxation: Corporations, Partnerships, Estates, and Trusts* for a detailed discussion of this requirement.)

EXAMPLE I17-24 ▶ ABC Partnership has one corporate partner, Ace Corporation, with a fiscal year-end of March 31. Ace Corporation has a 25% interest in the ABC Partnership. The other partners are individuals with a calendar year for tax purposes, none of whom has a 5% or more interest in the ABC Partnership. ABC Partnership must use a calendar year for tax purposes (the tax year of the individual partners who in aggregate own a majority interest). ◀

SELF-STUDY QUESTION

Ace and Buckeye, corporate partners in the ABC Partnership, have September 30 year-ends. Craig, an individual partner, uses the calendar year. Ace, Buckeye, and Craig have equal 1/3 interests in the partnership. What tax year must the newly organized partnership adopt?

The rules given above have three exceptions. First, a partnership with all calendar-year partners can adopt or change to a fiscal year if it can convince the IRS that a business purpose exists for the choice. For example, if the partnership owns a ski resort, it probably could make a good case for closing the partnership tax year on May 31, shortly after the ski season ends, rather than December 31, which is in the middle of the ski season. However, the IRS must agree that a valid business purpose exists for using the fiscal year.

Second, a partnership may adopt or change to a fiscal year-end if the business recognizes 25% or more of its annual gross receipts in the last 2 months of the fiscal year,

ANSWER

It must adopt a September 30 year-end because it must use the tax year of the two partners who own a majority interest.

with this being the case for three consecutive 12-month periods. Third, a partnership may elect a maximum 3-month deferral if it agrees to make a special tax payment each year that approximates the deferral benefit.[22] The net effect of these rules is to restrict any deferral opportunities for partnerships in choosing their year-end.

(See Chapter I11 of this text and Chapter C9 of *Prentice Hall's Federal Taxation, Corporations, Partnerships, Estates, and Trusts* for a detailed discussion of partnership tax years.)

CASH METHOD OF ACCOUNTING RESTRICTIONS

A partnership may elect with its first tax return any method of accounting that clearly reflects income. Unlike the tax year election, partnerships may elect an accounting method without regard to the methods used by its partners. The two most commonly used methods are the cash method and the accrual method. Under the *cash method*, the partnership reports income as received and expenses when actually paid. Under the *accrual method*, the partnership reports income when earned even if the cash has not yet been received. Similarly, the partnership reports expenses when incurred, not when actually paid.

Whenever Congress considers new tax legislation, it usually discusses the fact that the cash method does not always reflect the economic realities of a business. However, Congress concedes that the cash method is much simpler to use than the accrual method. Because of its simplicity, the cash method still is an option, but it has been restricted by Congress.

Partnerships that have a C corporation for a partner and that have average gross receipts exceeding $5,000,000 during the prior 3 years are not allowed to use the cash method of accounting.[23] Tax shelters, no matter what their size, may not use the cash method under any circumstances. (See Chapter I11 for a discussion of permissible accounting methods.)

TAXATION OF S CORPORATIONS

OBJECTIVE 4

Understand the requirements for S corporation status

ADDITIONAL COMMENT

Some states do not recognize the S corporation election for state income tax purposes, which results in the payment of state income taxes by the S corporation.

QUALIFICATION REQUIREMENTS

To qualify as an S corporation, a business must meet the definition of a small business corporation.[24] To meet this definition, the corporation

▶ Must be a domestic (U.S.) corporation rather than a foreign corporation

▶ Must not be an ineligible corporation[25]

▶ Must not have more than 75 shareholders[26]

▶ Must have only individuals, estates, certain kinds of trusts, and certain kinds of tax-exempt organizations as shareholders

▶ Must not have a nonresident alien as a shareholder

▶ Must issue only one class of stock

All of the above requirements must be met for the initial election to be made. Once an election is made, the requirements must be met on every day of each tax year that the S corporation election is in effect. Otherwise, the election terminates.

---

[22] Secs. 444 and 7519.

[23] Sec. 448(a)(2). Section 448(b) provides exceptions for farming businesses and certain qualified personal service corporations.

[24] These qualification rules are in Sec. 1361.

[25] Ineligible corporations include insurance companies, certain financial institutions, U.S. possessions corporations, and Domestic International Sales Corporations.

[26] The numbers of shareholders permitted by S corporations was formerly 35 shareholders. The Small Business Act of 1996 increased the number of shareholders to 75 for years beginning after December 31, 1996.

SEVENTY-FIVE SHAREHOLDER LIMITATION. The S corporation rules place no restriction on the amount of an S corporation's assets or income. Nevertheless, most large, publicly traded corporations have more than 75 shareholders and therefore are not eligible for S corporation treatment.

The following operating rules apply to S corporations:

▶ A husband and wife (each owning stock individually or jointly) are treated as one shareholder. This rule might create problems in a divorce situation if both individuals continue their ownership interests because the divorce results in two shareholders rather than one shareholder.

▶ If one spouse dies, the estate of the deceased spouse is not counted as an additional shareholder. Thus, the death of a spouse does not create problems if the estate distributes the stock to the surviving spouse. However, additional shareholders are created if the estate distributes the stock to heirs who do not already own any stock in the S corporation.

EXAMPLE I17-25 ▶

SELF-STUDY QUESTION

At any one time, how many different individuals could be shareholders in a single S corporation?

ANSWER

The S corporation could have as many as 150 shareholders in the case of 75 married couples.

Adobe Corporation, a qualifying S corporation, has 75 shareholders, including Brad and Bonnie, who are married and are counted as one shareholder. Brad dies and his stock is willed to his two children, who do not already own stock in Adobe. Before the distribution of the stock from the estate, the estate and Bonnie are counted as one shareholder, and the S corporation remains qualified under the 75-shareholder limitation. The S corporation is disqualified when the stock is distributed to the two children because the S corporation then has 76 shareholders. ◀

TYPE OF SHAREHOLDER RESTRICTIONS. A qualifying shareholder must be an individual (other than a nonresident alien), estate, qualifying trust, or qualifying tax-exempt organization.[27] Thus, a C corporation or a partnership may not own stock in the S corporation. If a C corporation or partnership were permitted to own stock, the 75-shareholder limitation easily could be avoided through indirect ownership of the S corporation stock through another corporation or partnership.

SUBSIDIARIES OF S CORPORATIONS. Although an S corporation may not have a corporate shareholder, it may own stock of a C corporation. If this stock ownership equals or exceeds 80%, however, the S corporation (parent) and the C corporation (subsidiary) are considered an affiliated group under Sec. 1504. Under tax law for years prior to 1997, the existence of an affiliated group would have terminated the S corporation election. However, under the Small Business Act of 1996, being a member of an affiliated group no longer terminates the S election. Nevertheless, an S corporation may not file a consolidated return with its 80%-owned subsidiaries.[28] In addition, and S corporation may have a Qualified Subchapter S Subsidiary (QSSS).[29] The subsidiary is a QSSS if the parent S corporation owns 100% of the QSSS stock and elects to treat the QSSS as such. Under this election, the QSSS is not treated as a separate corporation for income tax purposes. Instead, all assets, liabilities, income, deductions, and credits of the QSSS are treated as those of the parent S corporation.

ONE CLASS OF STOCK RESTRICTION. An S corporation can have only one class of stock outstanding. This requirement simplifies problems that otherwise would result from determining how corporate income and losses should be allocated to the shareholder.

---

[27] Qualifying trusts include voting trusts, Sec. 678 grantor trusts, electing small business trusts, and qualified Subchapter S trusts. Qualifying tax-exempt organizations include qualified retirement plan trusts and charitable organizations. See Chapter C11 of *Prentice Hall's Federal Taxation: Corpo-* *rations, Partnerships, Estates, and Trusts* for a discussion of these trusts.
[28] Sec. 1504(a)(8).
[29] Sec. 1361(b)(3).

The requirement for one class of stock, however, can be troublesome if an S corporation is thinly capitalized (i.e., significant amounts of debt exist in the capital structure) because the debt may in fact be equity and represent a second class of stock. To reduce the uncertainty regarding the second class of stock issue, a safe-harbor rule provides that straight debt shall not be treated as a second class of stock if it meets certain requirements. To qualify as straight debt, the interest rate cannot be contingent on profits,[30] the debt cannot be convertible into stock, and the creditor must be either a person otherwise eligible to be an S corporation shareholder or a person actively and regularly engaged in the business of lending money.

Aside from the debt issue, Treasury Regulations provide that a corporation is treated as having only one class of stock if all outstanding shares of stock confer identical rights to distribution and liquidation proceeds. This test is determined based on the corporate charter, articles of incorporation, bylaws, applicable state law, and any binding agreements relating to distribution or liquidation proceeds.[31] Nevertheless, shares of common stock can have different voting rights without violating the one-class-of-stock restriction.

EXAMPLE I17-26 ▶

Dale is the sole owner of an S corporation. For estate tax planning purposes, Dale desires to make gifts of certain shares of the corporation's stock to his children while still retaining control over the company. S corporation common stock with limited or no voting rights may be issued to Dale, who subsequently makes gifts of this stock to his children without disqualifying the S corporation status. ◀

ELECTION REQUIREMENTS

ADDITIONAL COMMENT

Because of the new higher individual income tax rates in the Revenue Reconciliation Act of 1993, the S corporation election and continued status may be less favorable than under prior law.

The corporation files an election for S corporation status, and all shareholders who own stock on the date the S corporation election is filed must consent to the election.[32] The election and consent are filed with the IRS on Form 2553 (Election by a Small Business Corporation to Tax Corporation Income Directly to Shareholders). Shareholders who own stock during any part of the current tax year preceding the election date must consent to the election even if they are not shareholders on the election date.

A corporation may make the election in the tax year preceding the election year or on or before the fifteenth day of the third month of the election year. An election after the fifteenth day of the third month of the election year is treated as made for the next tax year.

The tax law, however, provides some relief for improper elections. First, if the corporation misses the deadline for making the S corporation election, the IRS can treat the election as timely made if the IRS determines that the corporation had reasonable cause for making the late election. Second, if the election was ineffective because the corporation inadvertently failed to qualify as a small business corporation or because it inadvertently failed to obtain shareholder consents, the IRS can nevertheless honor the election if the corporation and shareholders take steps to correct the deficiency within a reasonable period of time.

EXAMPLE I17-27 ▶

Circle Corporation, a C corporation, uses the calendar year as its tax year. To file an S corporation election for 1997, the election may be filed anytime in 1996 or during the period that starts on January 1, 1997, and ends on March 15, 1997. If Circle Corporation makes the election on March 31, 1997, the corporation remains a C corporation in 1997 and becomes an S corporation in 1998. However, if Circle Corporation can show reasonable cause for making the late election, the IRS may allow the election to be effective for 1997. ◀

---

[30] The interest rate, however, may vary with the prime rate or a similar factor unrelated to the debtor corporation.

[31] Reg. Sec. 1.1361-1(l).

[32] Election and termination rules are in Sec. 1362.

TERMINATION CONDITIONS

REVOCATION OF S CORPORATION STATUS. An S corporation election may be terminated either voluntarily by the shareholders or involuntarily if the corporation fails to continue to meet the requirements for a small business corporation (e.g., if on any day in any year the S corporation has more than 75 shareholders or issues a second class of stock). Voluntary revocation is permitted if consents are obtained from shareholders owning more than 50% of the corporation's stock.

KEY POINT

An election to be taxed as an S corporation becomes effective only as of the beginning of a tax year, but a termination can become effective before the end of the normal tax year.

General Effective Date. Under the general rules, a revocation is effective for the entire tax year if the corporation files a statement on or before the fifteenth day of the third month of the tax year. If the corporation files the revocation after this date (e.g., after March 15 for a calendar-year S corporation), the effective date is the first day of the next tax year.

EXAMPLE I17-28 ▶ Shareholders owning more than 50% of the stock of a qualifying calendar-year S corporation consent to a voluntary revocation statement filed by the corporation on March 12, 1997. Because the corporation filed the revocation on or before March 15, it is taxed as a C corporation for all of 1997. If the corporation does not file the revocation until March 18, 1997, it continues to be taxed as an S corporation during 1997, and its special tax status is revoked for 1998. ◀

Specified Termination Date. The law provides an exception when the corporation and its shareholders specify a prospective termination date. In this case, the revocation takes effect as of the specified date. If a prospective date other than the first day of a tax year is specified, the revocation results in a short tax year for the final S corporation return and a short tax year for the initial C corporation return. In such a case, the income or loss is allocated between the two short years on a prorated daily basis.[33]

EXAMPLE I17-29 ▶ Assume the same facts as in Example I17-28, except that a prospective termination date of July 1, 1997, is specified. The termination is effective as of this date, and the corporation files an S corporation short-period return for the period January 1 through June 30, 1997 and files a C corporation short-period return for the period July 1 through December 31, 1997. The income or loss is prorated to each return on a daily basis. ◀

INVOLUNTARY AND INADVERTENT TERMINATIONS. An S corporation may involuntarily lose its special tax status and revert to a C corporation if it fails to meet the small business corporation requirements or if it has excessive amounts of passive (investment) income for each year in a 3-year period (i.e., more than 25% of gross receipts).[34] However, if the IRS deems that the termination was inadvertent and the S corporation or its shareholders take the necessary steps within a reasonable time period to restore its small business corporation status, the S corporation status is considered to have been continuously in effect.

EXAMPLE I17-30 ▶ A calendar-year S corporation adds a seventy-sixth shareholder on June 4. The S corporation status terminates on June 3. The corporation files a short-period S corporation return for the

---

[33] The first day of the C corporation tax year is the day on which the revocation occurs. Under Sec. 1377(a)(2), a special election may be made to use the interim closing method (i.e., the books are closed as of the termination date) if all affected shareholders consent to this method.

[34] The passive income restrictions apply solely to S corporations that were previously taxed as C corporations in pre-election years and have accumulated Subchapter C earnings and profits from those years on the last day of

three consecutive S corporation tax years. Thus, a corporation that elects S corporation status in its initial tax year is not subject to the restrictions. If the restrictions apply and the S corporation has passive income exceeding 25% of its gross receipts for three consecutive years, the S corporation election automatically terminates at the beginning of the fourth year. In addition, a penalty tax equal to 35% of the corporation's excess net passive income is imposed during each year of the 3-year period.

period January 1 through June 3 and files a C corporation return for the period from June 4 through December 31. Income or loss is prorated to the two tax returns on a daily basis. ◄

EXAMPLE I17-31 ▶ Assume the same facts as in Example I17-30 except that the termination is deemed to be inadvertent and the violation of the 75-shareholder requirement is corrected within a reasonable time period. The S corporation status is considered to have been continuously in effect, and no C corporation return is required. ◄

ELECTION AFTER TERMINATION. If an S corporation terminates its election either by ceasing to be a small business corporation or by revocation, the corporation may not reelect S corporation status for 5 years unless the IRS consents to such reelection. For purposes of the 5-year rule, tax years beginning before January 1, 1997 are not counted.[35] Thus, for example, corporations whose election terminated before this date can reelect S corporation status at any time without IRS consent.

Topic Review I17-4 summarizes the S corporation qualification, election, and termination rules.

OBJECTIVE 5

Apply the operating rules for S corporations

S CORPORATION OPERATIONS

Income, gains, losses, deductions, and credits pass through to the S corporation shareholders in a manner similar to the partnership rules. Some common separately stated items include

▶ Short-term and long-term capital gains and losses

▶ Sec. 1231 gains and losses

▶ Charitable contributions

▶ Credits

▶ Interest on investment indebtedness (see Chapter I7 for a discussion of this item)

▶ Tax preference items

▶ Foreign taxes paid or accrued

▶ Dividends and other portfolio income

(Table I17-1 on pg.17-9 provides a list of comparable items for partnerships.) These separately stated items are segregated from the computation of ordinary income (or loss) because each item affects the tax returns of the various shareholders differently, depending on their particular tax situation. The residual income or loss amount (i.e., the amount remaining after removing the separately stated items) represents the S corporation's ordinary income (or loss). Separately stated items and S corporation ordinary income (or loss) pass through to the shareholders as of the last day of the S corporation's tax year.[36] The S corporation computes its ordinary income (or loss) on page 1 of Form 1120S (U.S. Income Tax Return for an S Corporation), and it reports all items on Schedule K of that return. Then for each shareholder, the corporation prepares a Schedule K-1, which reports each shareholder's share of S corporation items. The shareholders use the Schedule K-1 information to prepare their individual tax returns (Form 1040). The forms are reproduced in Appendix B.

The tax treatment of some S corporation items is similar to that for C corporations. For example, S corporations can amortize organizational expenditures over a period of at least 60 months under general corporate taxation rules. However, S corporations are not

---

[35] P.L. 104-188, Sec. 1317(b), enacted August 20, 1996.   [36] Sec. 1363.

Topic Review I17-4

S Corporation Qualification, Election, and Termination Rules

Qualification Requirements

▶ An S corporation must be a domestic corporation.

▶ A maximum of 75 shareholders are allowed. A husband and wife count as one shareholder, and each beneficiary of a qualifying trust is a separate shareholder.

▶ Only individuals (citizens or resident aliens), estates, certain kinds of trusts, and certain kinds of tax-exempt organizations can be shareholders. No corporate or partnership shareholders are permitted.

▶ Only one class of stock may be issued and outstanding.

▶ Certain corporations that maintain special tax statuses are ineligible.

▶ If an S corporation has an 80%-owned subsidiary, it cannot file a consolidated tax return with that subsidiary.

Election Requirements

▶ All shareholders on the S election date must consent and the corporation must file Form 2553. To be effective for the election year, the S election and consent form must be filed on or before the fifteenth day of the third month of the election year. Otherwise, the election is effective for the subsequent tax year.

▶ The IRS can waive this deadline if the corporation shows reasonable cause for late filing.

▶ The IRS can grant relief for improper elections if they are inadvertent and subsequently corrected.

Termination Rules

▶ To effect a voluntary revocation, consent must be obtained from shareholders owning more than 50% of the S corporation's stock. The revocation is effective for the entire year if made on or before the fifteenth day of the third month of the tax year. Otherwise, the termination is effective the first day of the next tax year unless a prospective termination date is specified.

▶ An involuntary revocation takes place if (1) the S corporation fails to meet any of the small business corporation requirements (e.g., more than 75 shareholders) or (2) it has excessive passive investment income in a 3-year period (assuming the corporation has prior C corporation accumulated E&P). If the IRS deems the involuntary termination to be inadvertent, the S corporation status is considered to have been continuously in effect provided the corporation and shareholders correct the defect.

▶ Aside from the inadvertent termination exception, a corporation may not reelect S corporation status for 5 years after a termination or revocation. Years before 1997 do not count for the 5-year test.

entitled to other corporate deductions, such as the dividends-received deduction or the net operating loss deduction because dividends and net operating losses pass through to the S corporation's shareholders.

EXAMPLE I17-32 ▶ Ajax Corporation, an electing S corporation owned equally by Linda and Hal, reports the following operating results for the current year:

Sales	$10,000
Minus: Cost of goods sold	(2,000)
Gross profit	$ 8,000
Long-term capital gains	3,000
Total income	$11,000
Minus: Administrative expenses	(500)
Repairs	(500)
Sec. 1231 losses	(1,000)
Charitable contributions	(1,000)
Net income per books	$ 8,000

The individual items are reported on the S corporation tax return as follows:

	Ordinary Income	Separately Stated Items	Linda's K-1	Hal's K-1
Sales	$10,000			
Cost of goods sold	(2,000)			
Administrative expenses	(500)			
Repairs	(500)			
Total ordinary income	$ 7,000		$3,500	$3,500
Long-term capital gains		$3,000	1,500	1,500
Sec. 1231 losses		(1,000)	(500)	(500)
Charitable contributions		(1,000)	(500)	(500)

Linda and Hal each report $3,500 of ordinary income plus 50% of each separately stated item on their individual tax returns. ◀

SELF-STUDY QUESTION

Compare the manner in which income of an S corporation is allocated among the shareholders to the manner in which partnership income is allocated among the partners.

ANSWER

In the case of an S corporation, the income must be allocated based on the percentage of stock owned on a daily basis. Partners have much greater flexibility. The partnership agreement serves as the basis for allocation, with special allocations being permitted. No special allocations are permitted for an S corporation.

Income, gains, losses, deductions, credits, and other separately stated items are allocated to the shareholders based on the number of shares of stock owned on each day of the S corporation's tax year. Thus, if a shareholder sells S corporation stock during the year, ordinary income (or loss) and separately stated items are allocated on a daily basis to the seller and purchaser of the stock.[37]

EXAMPLE I17-33 ▶ Assume the same facts as in Example I17-32, except that Linda sells her stock to Marc on the 181st day of the tax year. Income through the day preceding the date of the transfer is allocated to Linda. Only $1,726 [0.50 × (180 ÷ 365)× $7,000] of the ordinary income and a similar portion of each separately stated item would be reported by Linda. The ordinary income and separately stated items attributable to Linda's one-half interest for the remainder of the year are reported by Marc. The sale does not affect Hal's reporting of his share of the income. ◀

OBJECTIVE 6

Determine the tax treatment of an S corporation's shareholders

BASIS ADJUSTMENTS TO S CORPORATION STOCK

Usually, a shareholder's original basis for S corporation stock is either the amount paid for the stock or a substituted basis from a nontaxable transaction (e.g., a Sec. 351 tax-free incorporation transaction).[38] Adjustments are subsequently made for ordinary income (or loss) and separately stated items that flow through to the shareholders, as well as additional capital contributions by shareholders and distributions to shareholders.[39]

---

[37] If a special election is made under Sec. 1377(a)(2), the income is allocated according to the accounting methods used by the S corporation (instead of on a daily basis) when a shareholder terminates his or her interest during the tax year.

[38] The death or gift tax basis rules also may be used to determine the initial basis for S corporation stock.
[39] Sec. 1367.

EXAMPLE I17-34 ▶ Juan acquires 100 shares of Allied Corporation stock during the current year for $40,000. Allied Corporation is a qualifying calendar-year S corporation. Juan's share of Allied's current year ordinary income is $10,000. In addition, his share of separately stated items includes $4,000 of long-term capital gains and $2,000 of Sec. 1231 losses. Allied Corporation also distributes $5,000 cash to Juan on November 9. Juan's basis in the S corporation stock on December 31 is computed as follows:

Original basis (cost)		$40,000
Plus:	Share of ordinary income	10,000
	Share of long-term capital gains	4,000
Minus:	Share of Sec. 1231 losses	(2,000)
	Cash distribution to Juan	(5,000)
Basis of stock on December 31		$47,000 ◀

The logic behind these basis adjustments can be explained by differentiating between the conduit (aggregate) and entity concepts. For example, C corporations are taxable as separate entities. Thus, corporate earnings are taxed at the corporate level, so no adjustments are made to a shareholder's C corporation stock basis for amounts earned by the corporation. The S corporation's shareholders would be subject to double taxation if the basis adjustments were not allowed because all corporate earnings (distributed and undistributed) flow through and are taxed to the individual shareholders on an annual basis.

KEY POINT

Adjustments to a shareholder's stock basis prevent double taxation of income or double deduction of losses.

EXAMPLE I17-35 ▶ Mary is the sole shareholder of Apple Corporation, an electing S corporation. Mary originally contributed $100,000 to the newly formed company. The funds were used to acquire various corporate assets. During the next 10 years, the corporation earned $900,000 of ordinary income and reinvested these earnings in corporate assets. After 10 years, Mary sells the stock for $1,000,000 (its tax basis). Mary's gain on the sale of her stock is as follows:

	With Stock Basis Adjustments	If No Basis Adjustments Were Permitted
Selling price of the stock	$1,000,000	$1,000,000
Minus: Original capital contribution	$ (100,000)	$ (100,000)
Share of ordinary income (taxed to Mary)	(900,000)	
Adjusted basis of stock	$(1,000,000)	$ (100,000)
Gain on sale	$ 0	$ 900,000

The $900,000 of earnings would be taxed twice to Mary if the positive basis adjustments were not permitted under the S corporation rules. With a C corporation, the $900,000 of earnings would be taxed at the corporate level and not to Mary. However, Mary would have an eventual $900,000 capital gain upon selling her stock after 10 years. ◀

S CORPORATION LOSSES AND LIMITATIONS
LIMITATIONS ON LOSS DEDUCTIONS. An ordinary loss and any separately stated loss and deduction items of an S corporation are allocated among the shareholders based on the number of shares of stock owned on each day of the S corporation's tax year.[40] The last day of the S corporation's tax year determines when the shareholders report the loss.[41]

---

[40] Sec. 1366(a)(1).
[41] The same rule is applied for the reporting of ordinary income and separately stated income and gain items.

EXAMPLE I17-36 ▶

KEY POINT

An S corporation shareholder gets debt basis, separate from stock basis, for amounts the shareholder lends directly to the corporation, but the shareholder gets no basis for corporate level liabilities.

KEY POINT

Unlike a partnership, a shareholder gets no basis for entity level liabilities other than debt basis for his or her direct loans to the corporation.

Adobe Corporation is an S corporation whose tax year ends on January 31, 1997. All of its shareholders report their taxes on a calendar year. Adobe reports a $100,000 ordinary loss for the 12-month period ending on January 31, 1997. The shareholders report this loss on their calendar-year 1997 returns. ◀

A shareholder's deduction for ordinary losses and separately stated items cannot exceed his or her basis for the S corporation stock plus the debt basis for any shareholder loans made to the S corporation.[42] The following rules apply when determining the deductibility of ordinary loss and separately-stated loss items:

▶ A positive basis adjustment is made to stock basis for ordinary income or separately stated income or gain items accruing during the year before the ordinary losses and separately stated loss and deduction items are used to reduce basis.

▶ The shareholder's deduction for pass-through losses is limited to (1) stock basis after the above positive adjustments and after distributions but before negative adjustments for losses and deductions and (2) the shareholder's debt basis.[43]

▶ A shareholder's pass-through loss first reduces the shareholder's stock basis (but not below zero).

▶ If the loss exceeds the shareholder's stock basis, the remaining pass-through loss then reduces the shareholder's debt basis (but not below zero).

▶ If the loss exceeds both the stock and debt basis, the shareholder carries over the excess loss and deducts it in a subsequent year when the shareholder again has basis in stock or debt. The carryover period is indefinite but does not transfer to another taxpayer if the shareholder disposes of all of the stock or if the shareholder dies. Furthermore, if the S corporation election is terminated, the loss must be used against any basis of the former S corporation stock by the end of a one-year post-termination transition period.

EXAMPLE I17-37 ▶

Matt owns 20% of the stock of an electing S corporation. His basis in the stock is $20,000 at the end of 1997 after adjustments for separately stated income and gain items. Matt also loans the S corporation $10,000 during 1997. The S corporation incurs a $200,000 ordinary loss in 1997. Matt's share of the ordinary loss is $40,000 (0.20 × $200,000). Matt's deduction and carryover of the unused loss are as follows:

Basis in stock	$20,000
Minus: Ordinary loss applied against stock basis	(20,000)
Basis in stock after ordinary loss	0
Debt basis in loan	$10,000
Minus: Ordinary loss applied against debt basis	(10,000)
Debt basis in loan after ordinary loss	0
Share of ordinary loss	$40,000
Minus: Deduction in 1997 ($20,000 + $10,000)	(30,000)
Carryover of ordinary loss to 1998	$10,000 ◀

If a shareholder's basis is insufficient to absorb the entire amount of ordinary loss (and separately-stated loss and deduction items), the flow-through of each item is determined

---

[42] Sec. 1366(d)(1). The deductible loss is treated as a deduction for AGI on an individual shareholder's return. S corporation shareholders also are subject to special limitations on losses and deductions that pass through from the S corporation (e.g., at-risk limitations under Sec. 465 and passive activity losses

under Sec. 469 (see Chapter C11 of *Prentice Hall's Federal Taxation: Corporations, Partnerships, Estates, and Trusts* for a discussion of these additional limitations.

[43] Secs. 1366(d)(1)(A) and 1367(a)(2).

on a pro rata basis. For example, if a shareholder's basis is $5,000 and he has a $6,000 ordinary loss and a $4,000 capital loss, his total deduction is limited to $5,000. This deduction consists of a $3,000 [($6,000 ÷ $10,000) × $5,000] ordinary loss and a $2,000 [($4,000 ÷ $10,000) × $5,000] capital loss. He also has a $3,000 ordinary loss and a $2,000 capital loss carryover.

RESTORATION OF BASIS. If a shareholder's debt basis in a loan made to the S corporation is reduced by a loss deduction, subsequent increases in basis resulting from S corporation income in a future year initially increase the debt basis until that basis reduction is fully restored. Any excess positive adjustment then increases the shareholder's stock basis.

EXAMPLE I17-38 ▶ Assume the same facts as in Example I17-37, except that in 1998 the S corporation's ordinary income is $140,000. Matt's share of the income is $28,000 (0.20 × $140,000). The $28,000 of income earned in 1998 permits Matt to deduct the $10,000 ordinary loss carryover from 1997. Stock and debt basis are adjusted as follows:

	Stock Basis	Debt Basis
Basis at beginning of year	$ 0	$ 0
Plus: Income for the year ($28,000)	18,000	10,000
Minus: Loss carryover from prior year.	(10,000)	–
Basis at end of year	$ 8,000	$10,000 ◀

If the debt basis is not fully restored, gain results when the loan is repaid. If the loan is in the form of a note, the repayment results in a capital gain because the note constitutes a capital asset.[44] However, ordinary income results if the loan is an unsecured advance.[45]

PASSIVE ACTIVITY LOSS LIMITATIONS. S corporation shareholders are subject to the passive activity loss limitations in the same manner as partners. Losses that pass through to a shareholder who does not materially participate in the S corporation's business may not be deducted against that shareholder's other earned income or against portfolio income (e.g., dividends and interest). Such passive losses can offset only other passive activity income. S corporation shareholders who materially participate (i.e., participate on a regular, continuous, and substantial basis) can avoid the passive activity loss limitations. (See Chapter I8 for a detailed discussion of the passive activity loss limitations rules.)

Topic Review I17-5 summarizes the basic tax rules for S corporation shareholders.

OTHER S CORPORATION CONSIDERATIONS

DISTRIBUTIONS OF CASH AND PROPERTY TO SHAREHOLDERS. A money or property distribution made by an S corporation to its shareholders is treated as a return of capital if the S corporation has no accumulated earnings and profits from pre-S corporation years.[46] As such, the money or FMV of the property distributed reduces the basis of the shareholders' S corporation stock. If distributions exceed the shareholders' basis, the excess is treated as a capital gain.[47]

KEY POINT

Another important difference between partnerships and S corporations involves the tax consequences of property distributions. An S corporation recognizes gain if it distributes appreciated property to its shareholders, but a partnership would not recognize gain.

---

[44] Rev. Rul. 64-162, 1964-1 C.B. 304.
[45] Rev. Rul. 68-537, 1968-2 C.B. 372.
[46] The tax consequences of property distributions to shareholders are discussed in Chapter C11 of *Prentice Hall's Federal Taxation: Corporations, Partnerships, Estates, and Trusts.*
[47] Sec. 1368(b). The S corporation also can have accumulated E&P from a

tax year in which it was taxed as a C corporation. The tax consequences of a distribution made by an S corporation having accumulated E&P are complex. These rules are beyond the scope of this text but are discussed in Chapter C11 of *Prentice Hall's Federal Taxation: Corporations, Partnerships, Estates, and Trusts.*

Topic Review I17-5

Basic Tax Rules for S Corporation Shareholders

▶ Ordinary losses and separately stated loss and deduction items are allocated to shareholders on a per share per day basis.

▶ The last day of the S corporation's tax year determines the year in which the shareholders report their share of income, gain, deductions, losses, credits, and other separately stated items.

▶ Basis cannot be reduced below zero. Positive basis adjustments are made for ordinary income and separately stated income or gain items before reduction for ordinary losses, separately stated loss and deduction items, and distributions.

▶ Losses initially reduce the shareholder's stock basis (but not below zero). Any excess losses then reduce the basis of shareholder loans.

▶ Unused losses are suspended and carried over until the shareholder again has basis to absorb the losses.

▶ Net positive basis adjustments in subsequent years initially increase the shareholder's loan basis until fully restored. Any additional net positive basis adjustments increase the basis of the shareholder's S corporation stock.

The S corporation recognizes gain if it distributes appreciated property to its shareholders.[48] The distribution is treated as if the corporation sold property to the shareholders at its FMV. The gain then passes through to the shareholders whose basis for the property is its FMV.

EXAMPLE I17-39 ▶ Austin Corporation, an electing S corporation, distributes land (a capital asset) to its shareholders. The land has a $10,000 basis and a $90,000 FMV. The S corporation recognizes an $80,000 capital gain, which passes through to its shareholders. The basis of the land to the shareholders is $90,000 (its FMV). ◀

TAX YEAR RESTRICTIONS. S corporations must use a calendar year unless a business purpose (i.e., a natural business year) can be established for choosing a fiscal year-end.[49] These year-end restrictions prevent shareholders from deferring pass-through income for up to 11 months (e.g., if a January 31 fiscal year-end were permitted). Also, like a partnership, an S corporation may elect a maximum 3-month deferral if it agrees to make a special tax payment each year that approximates the deferral benefit.

ADDITIONAL COMMENT

For purposes of calculating which shareholders own more than 2% of the outstanding stock, the Sec. 318 attribution rules apply.

TREATMENT OF FRINGE BENEFITS. S corporation shareholders who own more than 2% of the outstanding stock are not eligible for tax-free corporate employee fringe benefits, including the following:

▶ The group term life insurance exclusion under Sec. 79 for premiums paid for up to $50,000 coverage

---

[48] Sec. 311(b). [49] Sec. 1378(b).

▶ The exclusion from income for premiums paid for accident and health insurance and medical reimbursement plans under Secs. 105 and 106[50]

▶ The exclusion under Sec. 119 for meals and lodging furnished for the convenience of the employer

EXAMPLE I17-40 ▶ Bass Corporation is an electing S corporation. Health insurance and group term life insurance premiums are paid by the corporation for its employee-owner group, all of whom own more than 2% of the Bass stock. The premiums are included in the gross income of the owner-employees and are deductible by the S corporation. ◀

KEY POINT

The built-in gains tax was enacted in 1986 to prevent C corporations from avoiding double taxation in a corporate liquidation by electing S corporation status immediately before the liquidation.

CORPORATE TAX ON BUILT-IN GAINS. A 35% corporate tax on built-in gains applies if a corporation that previously was a C corporation elects S corporation.[51] The built-in gains tax does not apply to a corporation that always has been an S corporation or that elected S corporation status before 1987. A built-in gain exists if the FMV of an asset exceeds its adjusted basis on the first day the S corporation election is effective. If the corporation sells an asset with a built-in gain within the 10-year period beginning on the effective date for the election, the S corporation is taxed on the built-in gain. Any appreciation on the asset that occurs after conversion from a C corporation to an S corporation is subject to the regular S corporation pass-through rules but is not taxed under the built-in gains tax. Any asset not held on the first day of the S corporation election period also is exempt from the built-in gains tax.

EXAMPLE I17-41 ▶ Beach Corporation, an accrual method taxpayer incorporated 5 years ago, elects to be taxed as an S corporation as of January 1 of the current year. On January 1 of the current year, Beach owns land with a $50,000 basis and a $200,000 FMV. Beach sells the land next year for $225,000. Thus, Beach reports a total gain of $175,000 ($225,000 − $50,000). The first $150,000 is subject to the built-in gains tax and flows through to the shareholders. The other $25,000 of post-conversion appreciation also is subject to the regular S corporation pass-through rules but is not subject to the built-in gains tax. In addition, the built-in gains tax paid by the corporation flows through as a loss to the shareholders. ◀

TAX ON EXCESS NET PASSIVE INCOME. A 35% excess net passive income tax applies when an S corporation has passive investment income for the tax year that exceeds 25% of its gross receipts and, at the close of the tax year, the S corporation has accumulated Subchapter C E&P. Subchapter C E&P is the earnings and profits the corporation earned when it was taxed as a C corporation.[52]

EXAMPLE I17-42 ▶ Acorn Corporation made an S corporation last year after having been a C corporation for several years. Acorn has accumulated Subchapter C E&P at the end of the current year. During the current year, Acorn's excess net passive income is $10,000. The excess net passive income tax is $3,500 ($10,000 × 0.35). The tax reduces (on a pro rata basis) the passive income items (e.g., dividends and interest) that pass through to shareholders. ◀

---

[50] Rev. Rul. 91-26, 1991-1 C.B. 184. The IRS ruled that amounts paid on behalf of partners and more-than-2% shareholder-employees for accident and health premiums related to services rendered are treated like guaranteed payments—that is, the amounts are deductible by both a partnership and an S corporation and are included in the partner's or shareholder's gross income.

[51] Sec. 1374. This discussion is only a sketch of these complex rules.
[52] Sec. 1375(a). These rules are discussed in greater detail in Chapter C11 of *Prentice Hall's Federal Taxation: Corporations, Partnerships, Estates, and Trusts.*

STOP & THINK

Question: Suppose shareholders of an S Corporation wanted to convert the business into a limited liability company (LLC). What tax obstacles might they encounter?

Solution: The shareholders would have to liquidate the corporation and recontribute the assets to the LLC. Because the S corporation must comply with general corporate rules, the liquidation will cause gain recognition at the corporate level for appreciated property distributed. This gain will flow through to the shareholders and be taxable to them. In addition, the liquidation might trigger the corporate level tax on built-in gains. Thus, conversion from an S corporation to an LLC could have adverse tax consequences. Contrast these major tax obstacles above with the conversion of a partnership to an LLC. The IRS has ruled that the conversion of a partnership to an LLC is a nontaxable event.

TAX PLANNING CONSIDERATIONS

USE OF NET OPERATING LOSSES

Often, the decision to select a particular form of business organization involves both tax and nontax issues. For example, the corporate form may be preferred due to the availability of nontax attributes such as limited liability, the relative freedom to transfer ownership interests, and the ability to raise outside equity capital.

In many instances, however, the tax attributes dominate, making the partnership or S corporation form preferable to the C corporation. If the owners expect net operating losses in the initial years of operation, they may prefer the partnership form to either the C corporation or the S corporation form of organization. In a C corporation, the operating losses do not benefit the shareholders directly and may be of no benefit if the corporation cannot generate sufficient profits in future years to offset the loss carryovers.[53] In a partnership, the losses pass through to the partners, limited by their basis for the partnership interest. The basis of a partner's interest, however, includes his or her share of partnership liabilities. In contrast, an S corporation's ability to pass through losses is limited to the shareholder's basis in the stock and any shareholder loans. Other S corporation liabilities are not included in determining the shareholder's loss limitation. Thus, the partnership form may provide its owners a greater opportunity to deduct losses than does the S corporation form.

EXAMPLE I17-43 ▶ Mary and Marty are considering whether to operate a new business venture as a C corporation, S corporation, or a partnership. Mary and Marty plan to invest $50,000 of equity and raise an additional $50,000 from outside creditors (e.g., accounts payable, and mortgage). They expect initial losses of $20,000 per year for 5 years. If a C corporation is used, the corporate losses are not deductible (i.e., the corporation has net operating loss carryovers of $100,000 after the 5-year period). If an S corporation is formed, Mary and Marty can deduct only $50,000 due to the exclusion of general corporate debt from determining the basis for the shareholder's investment. The remaining $50,000 loss carries forward indefinitely at the sharholder level unless the shareholders choose to lend $50,000 of additional funds to the corporation (instead of having the corporation borrow these amounts from outside creditors) or make $50,000 of additional capital contributions. If a partnership is formed, Mary and

---

[53] In a corporation, net operating losses are carried back 3 years and forward 15 years. In a newly formed corporation, the carryback rules do not apply.

Marty can deduct the full $100,000 of losses because their basis includes the partnership's liabilities. Assuming Mary and Marty have sufficient other sources of income to absorb the losses, the value of these additional deductions in the first 5 years favors the partnership form of organization. ◄

STOP & THINK

Question: Paul owns a business that produces $50,000 of annual profits. If the business were incorporated, it could justify the retention of all of its earnings and pay little or no dividends. Paul also has $100,000 of taxable income from other sources. Should Paul organize the business as an S corporation or as a C corporation?

Solution: Although many factors could be involved, one important tax factor is that Paul's income from the business could be taxed at a 39.6% rate if it is an S corporation. The rate of taxation on a C corporation is 15% on the first $50,000 of taxable income. Double taxation would result, however, if the profits were withdrawn as a dividend.

INCOME SHIFTING AMONG FAMILY MEMBERS

Subject to gift tax rules and restrictions, an attractive tax planning strategy is to shift income from higher tax bracket family members to children or others who are subject to lower tax rates. In an S corporation, parents may gift nonvoting common stock to their children age 14 and older (subject to the gift tax rules and restrictions). Thus, a portion of the S corporation income is taxed to the children even though the parents retain all voting rights for the corporate stock. A partnership interest also may be gifted to other family members. However, the IRS generally does not recognize the family member as a partner in a partnership where capital (e.g., inventory, plant, and equipment) is a material income-producing factor unless the individual is the real owner of the interest and has dominion and control over it. In a service partnership (e.g., an accounting firm), the family member must provide vital or substantial services. If property is given to a child under age 14, the child's unearned income exceeding $1,300 is taxed at the parents' higher tax rate. Therefore, if S corporation stock or a partnership interest is given to a child under age 14, the child's share of S corporation or partnership income generally is taxed to the child at the parents' highest marginal tax rate. Essentially, the tax planning technique of income shifting from higher tax bracket family members to children under age 14 no longer exists. These rules do not apply to children age 14 and older (see Chapter I2).

With an S corporation or a partnership, family members (e.g., children) can be hired as employees. Thus, income may be shifted to lower tax bracket family members. The under-age-14 rules discussed previously have no effect on earned income even if derived from a parent's business. In a partnership and an S corporation, the IRS will reallocate income to reflect the value of the services and capital contributions if reasonable salaries are not paid.[54]

EXAMPLE I17-44 ▶ Paul, the sole owner of an electing S corporation, gifts 20% of the corporation's stock to his children age 14 and older. The S corporation's ordinary income is $100,000 after deducting a $10,000 salary paid to Paul. If a reasonable salary for Paul's services is $50,000, the IRS may reduce ordinary income to $60,000 ($100,000 − $40,000) and increase Paul's taxable compensation to $50,000. Thus, the share of income that passes through to the children is reduced from $20,000 (0.20 × $100,000) to $12,000 (0.20 × $60,000). ◄

---

[54] Secs. 1366(e) and 704(e).

OPTIONAL BASIS ADJUSTMENT ELECTION UNDER SEC. 754

A basis adjustment election under Sec. 754 usually is desirable for an incoming partner whose partnership interest cost more than the tax basis of his or her share of partnership's assets. The excess amount is added to the new partner's basis for his or her interest in the partnership's assets. If the partnership made a Sec. 754 election in a prior year, the election continues in effect and automatically applies to the current year. However, if the election was not previously made, all of the partners must agree to make the election because it is made at the partnership level rather than by the individual partner.

Therefore, before a sale is consummated, an incoming partner should attempt to obtain assurances from the remaining partners that the partnership will agree to make the election in the current year if the election is not already in effect. The election is made by attaching a statement to a timely filed tax return for the year the transaction occurs. A retroactive election cannot be made for prior years.[55] A Sec. 754 election, however, may have adverse effects in subsequent years if the amount paid for a partnership interest is less than the tax basis of partnership assets because the incoming partner must reduce her share of the basis of partnership assets.

COMPLIANCE AND PROCEDURAL CONSIDERATIONS

PARTNERSHIP FILING REQUIREMENTS AND ELECTIONS

Partnerships must file Form 1065 on or before the fifteenth day of the fourth month following the close of its tax year (by April 15 for a calendar-year partnership). The IRS can allow reasonable extensions of time up to 6 months although a partnership can obtain an automatic 3-month extension by filing Form 8736 (Application for Automatic Extension of Time To File U.S. Return for a Partnership, REMIC, or for Certain Trusts). If the partnership needs an additional extension, it can file Form 8800 (Application for Additional Extension of Time To File U.S. Return for Partnership, REMIC, or for Certain Trusts). Penalties are imposed for failure to file a timely or complete partnership return.

PARTNERSHIP ELECTIONS. The partnership makes most elections affecting the computation of partnership income. These elections include

▶ Selection of a tax year

▶ Selection of an overall accounting method

▶ Inventory valuation method

▶ Depreciation methods

▶ Amortization method for organization expenses

▶ Optional basis adjustments under Sec. 754

An election made at the partnership level is binding on all partners.

---

[55] Reg. Sec. 1.754-1(b).

Certain elections are made by each partner. The common elections are the partners' own accounting periods and methods and the election to take a credit or deduction for foreign income taxes.

REPORTING PARTNERSHIP ITEMS ON FORM 1065

The partnership ordinary income and deduction items are reported on page 1 of Form 1065 (see Appendix B). Schedule K summarizes all of the partner's share of separately stated items (e.g., capital gains and losses, tax credits, and charitable contributions). Schedule K also includes guaranteed payments made to partners and the ordinary income or loss, even though both items are reported on page 1. A separate Schedule K-1 is prepared for each partner. The Schedule K-1 represents each partner's share of the Schedule K items, depending on the agreed ratio for sharing income, deduction, loss, and credit items. This schedule becomes the primary input for preparation of each partner's federal income tax return.

A partnership also must prepare a balance sheet (Schedule L), a reconciliation of income per books with income per tax (Schedule M-1), and an analysis of capital accounts (Schedule M-2).

S CORPORATION FILING REQUIREMENTS AND ACCOUNTING METHOD ELECTIONS

An S corporation must file its corporate tax return no later than the fifteenth day of the third month following the end of the tax year. The S corporation reports its results on Form 1120 S (U.S. Income Tax Return for an S Corporation). An S corporation is allowed an automatic 6-month extension of time for filing its tax return by filing Form 7004 (Application for Automatic Extension of Time to File U.S. Corporation Income Tax Return). Both forms are included in Appendix B.

The S corporation, rather than the shareholders, make the accounting method elections used to compute ordinary income or loss and the separately stated items. As with a partnership, these elections are made independently of the accounting method elections made by its shareholders.

REPORTING S CORPORATION ITEMS ON FORM 1120S

Page 1 of Form 1120S summarizes the ordinary income and deduction items for the S corporation. If the corporation owes any tax due to the excess net passive income tax or the built-in gains tax, such amounts are reported on page 1 of the return. Schedule K lists the separately stated items and ordinary income or losses for the S corporation. A Schedule K-1 is prepared for each shareholder reflecting his or her share of the ordinary income (loss) and separately stated items. The Schedule K-1 becomes the basis for preparing each shareholder's federal income tax return. The S corporation also must prepare a balance sheet (Schedule L) and a reconciliation of income per books with income per tax (Schedule M-1).

COMPARISON OF ALTERNATIVE FORMS OF BUSINESS ORGANIZATIONS

Table I17-2 provides comparison of sole proprietorships, partnerships, S corporations, and C corporations.

▼ **TABLE I17-2**

Comparison of Alternative Forms of Business Organizations

Attributes	Sole Proprietorship	Partnership	S Corporation	C Corporation
Application of the separate entity versus the conduit (flow-through) concepts.	Single level of taxation. The proprietor is the same person as the individual taxpayer. The sole proprietor reports proprietorship income, expenses, losses, and credits in his individual tax return.	Conduit with a single level of taxation. The partnership is not taxed. Instead, its income, deductions, losses, and credits flow through to the partners to be taxed in their tax returns.	Conduit with a single level of taxation. Similar to a partnership in that its income deductions, losses, and credits flow through to the share-holders to be taxed in their tax returns. In special cases, the S corporation may pay entity level taxes on built-in gains and excess passive income.	Entity with double taxation. The corporation is taxed at the entity level, and its shareholders are taxed again when they receive dividends or sell their stock.
Applicable income tax rates	Individual tax rates apply to the proprietorship's income, which is included in the proprietor's total taxable income.	Individual tax rates apply to individual partners; corporate tax rates apply to corporate partners; and estate and trust tax rates apply to partners.	Individual tax rates apply to individual shareholders.	Corporate tax rates apply to the corporation's taxable income. Individual, corporate, or estate and trust tax rates apply to the shareholders depending on the type of shareholder.
Ownership restrictions	By definition, a sole proprietorship can have only one owner.	A partnership can have an unlimited number of partners, and these partners can be individuals, corporations, estates, or trusts.	An S corporation may have only 75 share-holders (with spouses counting as one). Shareholders are limited to individuals, estates, certain trusts, and certain tax-exempt organizations.	A C corporation can have an unlimited number of shareholders of any type.
Personal liability	The sole proprietor is liable for debts of the proprietorship.	General partners have unlimited liability. Limited partners have liability to the extent of their investment.	Shareholders have limited liability.	Shareholders have limited liability.
Other nontax factors	A sole proprietorship has management continuity problems and may have difficulty raising outside capital.	A partnership has management continuity problems and restrictions on the transfer of partnership interests. It may have difficulty raising outside capital although limited partners, who are pure investors, mitigate this problem.	S corporations have the same characteristics as C corporations. Problems, however, may arise if the state income tax law does not recognize the conduit form of taxation and taxes the S corporation as a C corporation.	Along with limited liability, C corporations have continuity of life, centralized management, and free transferability of interests. These factors may outweigh the disadvantages of double taxation.

▼ **TABLE I17-2**

Comparison of Alternative Forms of Business Organizations (Continued)

Attributes	Sole Proprietorship	Partnership	S Corporation	C Corporation
Basis	A sole proprietor has basis in the business's assets but has no basis in an entity.	A partnership has basis in its assets, and partners have basis in their partnership interests. The partners' basis includes their share of partnership liabilities. Partners' basis is adjusted annually for their share partnership transactions.	An S corporation has basis in its assets. Shareholders have basis in their stock and a separate debt basis in their loans to the corporation. The shareholders' basis does not include corporate level liabilities. Shareholder's stock basis is adjusted annually for their share corporate transactions. Debt basis is adjusted for offsetting flow-through losses and restorations.	A C corporation has basis in its assets, and shareholders have basis in their stock. Stock basis is adjusted only for additional contributions to the corporation and for distributions that exceed the corporation's E&P.
Treatment of losses	No limitations apply to the proprietor's NOLs assuming the at-risk and PAL limitations do not apply. Unused NOLs carry back 3 years and carry over 15 years.	Partners' flow-through loss deductions are limited to the basis of their partnership interests. At-risk and PAL limitations also may apply.	Shareholders' flow-through loss deductions are limited to their stock and debt basis. At-risk and PAL limitations also may apply.	C corporation losses do not flow through to its shareholders. Unused corporate level NOLs carry back 3 years and carry over 15 years at the corporate level.
Choice of accounting methods	The sole proprietor can elect the cash or accrual method for business items. However, the accrual method for sales and purchases is required if inventory is a material income producing factor.	Partnerships can elect the cash or accrual method unless they are tax shelters or have a C corporation as a partner, in which case they must use the accrual method. Also, the accrual method for sales and purchases is required if inventory is a material income producing factor.	S corporations can elect the cash or accrual method unless they are tax shelters, in which case they must use the accrual method. Also, the accrual method for sales and purchases is required if inventory is a material income producing factor.	C corporations must use the accrual method unless they are personal service corporations or meet other exceptions, in which case they can elect the cash or accrual method.
Choice of tax year	A sole proprietorship must use the same tax year as the sole proprietor, usually a calendar year.	The tax year is restricted to that of the majority partners, principal partners, or the least aggregate deferral. The partnership can use a fiscal year if it establishes a business purpose (e.g., a natural business cycle). Other special rules allow a tax year resulting in a maximum 3-month deferral.	The tax year is restricted to a calendar year unless the corporation establishes a business purpose (e.g., a natural business cycle) for a fiscal year. Other special rules allow a tax year resulting in a maximum 3-month deferral.	C corporations can use a calendar year or any fiscal year. Personal service corporations, however, face restrictions similar to those for S corporations.

▼ TABLE I17-2

Comparison of Alternative Forms of Business Organizations (Continued)

Attributes	Sole Proprietorship	Partnership	S Corporation	C Corporation
Employment related tax considerations	A sole proprietor is not considered an employee of the business and must pay self-employment taxes on business earnings. Corporate fringe benefits, such as group term life insurance, are not available.	A partner is not considered an employee of the partnership and must pay self-employment taxes on business earnings. Corporate fringe benefits, such as group term life insurance, are not available.	Same as for partnerships for shareholders owning more than 2% of the corporation's stock. S corporation shareholders may be treated as employees, however, for social security taxes if they receive salary.	A shareholder-employee may be treated as an employee for social security taxes and fringe benefits.

PROBLEM MATERIALS

DISCUSSION QUESTIONS

I17-1 Distinguish between the partnership, S corporation, and C corporation forms of organization regarding the following:
a. Incidence of taxation on business income of the organization
b. Taxation of distributions to owners
c. Application of the conduit and separate entity concepts of taxation

I17-2 Paula transfers the following assets to a partnership:
a. Land with a $60,000 adjusted basis and a $100,000 FMV in exchange for a 20% interest in the partnership
b. A machine with a $50,000 adjusted basis and a $40,000 FMV. The partnership signs a note for $40,000 as consideration for the exchange.
Explain whether Paula recognizes gain or loss for either of these transactions, and discuss the reason for any difference in tax treatment.

I17-3 Peggy agrees to act as a broker to arrange debt financing for the PQR Partnership. In exchange, the PQR Partnership offers Peggy, as compensation for the brokerage services rendered, a 25% interest in the partnership having a $50,000 value. Discuss the tax implications to Peggy.

I17-4 In the current year, Penny contributes machinery (Sec. 1231 property) that she acquired 5 years earlier and that has a $50,000 adjusted basis and an $80,000 FMV to a partnership in exchange for a partnership interest. What are Penny's basis and holding period for the partnership interest? Explain the reasons for this rule in the tax law.

I17-5 How is Mario's basis in his partnership interest affected by the following changes in partnership liabilities (assuming he has a 50% interest in the partnership)?
a. Mario contributes a building with a $70,000 basis subject to a $50,000 mortgage, which the partnership assumes.
b. The partnership's accounts payable increase by $50,000 during the tax year.
c. The partnership pays off a $50,000 bank note that was outstanding for several years.

I17-6 What are the tax consequences to a partner who contributes liabilities that exceed the basis of assets transferred to the partnership in exchange for a partnership interest?

I17-7 Why are certain special partnership income and deduction items (e.g., capital gains and losses, charitable contributions, etc.) reported separately on the Schedule K rather than being included in ordinary income on page 1 of Form 1065?

I17-8   What inequities might result if partners were not required to make special allocations for pre-contribution gains and losses when a contribution of noncash property is made to a partnership?

I17-9   Indicate whether a partner's basis in the partnership interest increases (+), decreases (−), or is not affected (0) by the partner's share of the following operating items:
a. Ordinary income
b. Ordinary loss
c. Tax-exempt income
d. Capital losses
e. Charitable contributions made by the partnership
f. Distributions of property to the partners

I17-10   Phyllis owns a 30% interest in the PQR Partnership and has a $20,000 basis in her partnership interest (before adjustments for Phyllis's share of partnership income or loss). During the current year, the PQR Partnership reports a $100,000 ordinary loss and no change in partnership liabilities, and Phyllis materially participates in the business in the current year.
a. What amount of the loss is deductible by Phyllis in the current year?
b. What is Phyllis's basis in her partnership interest at the end of the current year?
c. What happens to Phyllis's unused ordinary loss (if any)?

I17-11   Ralph sells an asset to the RST Partnership at a loss. In which of the following situations is the loss recognized?
a. Ralph owns a 20% direct interest in the partnership, and his son also owns a 20% interest.
b. Ralph owns a 35% direct interest in the partnership, and his daughter also owns a 35% interest.
c. Ralph owns a 35% direct interest in the partnership, and his 100%-owned corporation also owns a 35% interest.

I17-12   Jose owns a 60% interest in the JKL Partnership. What are the amount and character of the recognized gain or loss in each of the following situations?
a. Jose sells a security (e.g., common stock) with a $1,000 adjusted basis and a $2,000 FMV to the partnership.

b. Jose sells a parcel of land held for investment with a $10,000 adjusted basis and a $20,000 FMV to the partnership.
c. Jose sells a building used in his business with a $100,000 adjusted basis and a $60,000 FMV to the partnership.

I17-13   Ursula is a 30% partner in the UV Partnership. The partnership agreement states that she shall receive 30% of partnership profits computed before considering guaranteed payments. However, she is not to receive less than $10,000.
a. What is Ursula's income if the partnership earns $60,000? How much of her income is a guaranteed payment?
b. What is Ursula's income if the partnership earns $20,000? How much of her income is a guaranteed payment?

I17-14   Explain the circumstances that cause a partner to recognize gain or loss if money or other property is distributed in a nonliquidating partnership distribution.

I17-15   Explain why a partner who sells his or her interest in the partnership for cash must include his or her share of the partnership liabilities in the amount realized from the sale.

I17-16   What are the tax consequences to a partner who sells his or her partnership interest if the partnership has Sec. 751 assets (i.e., unrealized receivables or substantially appreciated inventory)? What is the reason for this result?

I17-17   What inequity might result if an incoming partner purchases a partnership interest for an amount exceeding his or her share of the tax basis of the partnership's assets? Assume that no basis adjustment election is made under Sec. 754.

I17-18   What are the tax consequences to an S corporation and its shareholders if one of the requirements for a small business corporation is not met at some point in a tax year?

I17-19   An S corporation issues straight debt obligations to its shareholders. Is it possible for the debt to be treated as a second class of stock, which would terminate the S corporation election? Explain.

I17-20   Andrew sells his Ajax Corporation stock to Angela on March 1. On March 15, Ajax Corporation elects S corporation status for the current year. Which shareholder(s) must consent to the election? Why?

I17-21 An S corporation's shareholder wants to voluntarily revoke the S corporation election. What percentage of stock interests must agree to the revocation? When is the revocation first effective?

I17-22 Under what conditions will an S corporation involuntarily lose its special tax status and revert to being a C corporation? What remedies are available if the S corporation termination is deemed to be inadvertent?

I17-23 Indicate whether the following items are reported on the tax return of an S corporation as part of ordinary income (or loss) or as a separately stated item:
a. Repairs
b. Long-term capital gains
c. Short-term capital losses
d. Sec. 1231 gains
e. Tax credits
f. Tax preference items

I17-24 Explain why the basis of S corporation stock is reduced by the stockholder's share of an ordinary loss.

I17-25 Anne's basis in her S corporation stock on January 1 of the current year is $10,000. On March 1 of the current year, Anne lends the corporation $8,000. Her share of the S corporation's ordinary loss for the current year (which has not yet ended) is expected to be $28,000. Anne expects her marginal tax rate to be 15% in the current year. She expects that her marginal tax rate will increase to 31% next year, and she anticipates substantial profits for the S corporation next year. Advise Anne regarding the deductibility of her share of the losses and the desirability of making additional capital contributions in either year.

I17-26 Allied Corporation, an electing S corporation, is considering making a distribution of land (acquired 3 years earlier and held for investment) having a $60,000 adjusted basis and a $120,000 FMV to its sole shareholder. Explain the tax consequences to the corporation and to the shareholder if the land is distributed.

I17-27 Barry and Bart are considering whether to start a new manufacturing business. Alternative forms of business organization being considered include operating as a partnership, an S corporation, or a C corporation. Barry and Bart are calendar-year taxpayers but would like to use a January 31 year-end for the business to obtain an 11-month deferral of the income. Discuss the implications and restrictions of operating under each alternative form of business organization being considered.

I17-28 Assume the same facts as in Problem I17-27, except that Barry and Bart are instead considering the treatment of fringe benefits. Barry and Bart want to provide group term life insurance and accident and health insurance for themselves and their employees and plan to make the premium payments from business funds. Explain any restrictions that apply to each form of business organization.

I17-29 Explain the circumstances in which an S corporation is subject to taxation at the corporate level.

ISSUE IDENTIFICATION QUESTIONS

I17-30 Bert and Jose plan to combine their unincorporated businesses by forming a partnership. Bert has substantially appreciated business assets. Moreover, if he transfers all of the liabilities of the business and all of the assets, the liabilities will exceed the adjusted basis of the assets. Jose will render services to the partnership in addition to transferring all of his business assets. What tax issues should Bert and Jose consider?

I17-31 Helen and Helga are equal partners in the HH Partnership. However, Helen devotes most of her time managing the business and feels that she should be given additional compensation in the form of a guaranteed payment. Currently, the partnership is operating at a break-even point (i.e., zero ordinary income and no separately stated items of income or loss). The basis of each partner's partnership interest also is negligible. Helen has requested an $80,000 guaranteed payment as compensation for her additional efforts. What tax issues should Helen and Helga consider?

I17-32 Coastal Corporation has been a C corporation for several years and has substantial earnings and profits. Its tangible business assets are highly appreciated, and the corporation has paid no dividends for several years. The Board of Directors and its key shareholders are now recommending making an S corporation election, selling the appreciated property, and paying a substantial cash distribution in the initial S corporation year. What tax issues should Coastal Corporation and its shareholders consider?

PROBLEMS

I17-33 *Formation of a Partnership.* Becky, Beth, and Bob form the BBB Partnership, and all the partners have an equal share in the partnership. Becky contributes cash of $100,000; Beth contributes land (acquired 5 years earlier and held for business use) with a $50,000 adjusted basis and a $100,000 FMV; and Bob contributes cash of $60,000 and legal and brokerage services with a $40,000 FMV.

    a. What are the amount and character of the gain or loss Beth must recognize on the land transfer to the partnership?

    b. What are the amount and character of the income Bob must recognize due to the services he performed?

    c. What is the basis of each individual's partnership interest?

    d. Beth sells her partnership interest 4 months after it is acquired and recognizes a capital gain. Is the gain long-term or short-term? Explain.

    e. What is the partnership's basis for each asset acquired?

    f. How is the land recorded on the partnership's books under generally accepted accounting principles?

I17-34 *Formation of a Partnership and Treatment of Liabilities.* Bonnie, Carlos, and Dale form the BCD Partnership as equal partners. Bonnie contributes land and a building with a $50,000 adjusted basis and a $200,000 FMV that is subject to a $100,000 mortgage assumed by the partnership. The land and the building originally cost $200,000, and straight-line depreciation of $150,000 has been claimed on the building. Carlos contributes cash of $100,000, and Dale contributes land (a capital asset) with a $200,000 adjusted basis and a $100,000 FMV. All assets have been held for more than one year.

    a. What are the amount and character of Bonnie's recognized gain or loss on the transfer?

    b. What is Bonnie's basis in her partnership interest?

    c. What is Carlos's basis in his partnership interest?

    d. What are the amount and character of Dale's recognized gain or loss on the transfer?

    e. What is Dale's basis in his partnership interest?

    f. What is the basis of the contributed properties to the BCD Partnership?

I17-35 *Formation of a Partnership and Excess Liabilities.* In the current year, Dana transfers to the DE Partnership land and a building having a $20,000 adjusted basis and an $80,000 FMV that is subject to a $70,000 mortgage. The land and the building cost $100,000 when acquired by Dana in 1970, and the building has been depreciated by $80,000 using the straight-line method. Dana receives a one-half interest in the partnership.

    a. What are the amount and character of Dana's recognized gain or loss on the transfer?

    b. What is Dana's basis in her partnership interest?

    c. When does Dana's holding period for the partnership interest begin?

    d. What is the basis of the contributed properties to the DE Partnership?

I17-36 *Formation of a Partnership and Loss Limitation.* Dan contributes $10,000 to the newly formed DEF Partnership for a 10% interest in the partnership. No liabilities are transferred to the partnership by any of the partners. During the partnership's first year, DEF borrows $100,000 from a bank and is liable for accounts payable amounting to $100,000 at the end of its tax year. The DEF Partnership incurs a $400,000 ordinary loss during the year.

a. How much of the ordinary loss may Dan deduct on his individual return?

b. What is Dan's basis in his partnership interest at the end of the year?

c. How much of the loss (if any) carries over to future years?

I17-37 *Expenses of Forming a Partnership.* The ABC Partnership, a calendar-year entity, is formed on July 1 of the current year and incurs the following expenditures on the date the partnership is formed:

Legal fees incident to the organization of the partnership	$3,000
Printing costs associated with the syndication of the partnership	6,000
Brokerage fees associated with underwriting efforts to sell limited partnership interests	5,000

a. What is the appropriate tax treatment (i.e., capitalization, capitalization subject to amortization, or immediate expensing) for each of these items?

b. How much amortization should be deducted for the current year?

I17-38 *Pass Through of Income and Separately Stated Items.* Damien and Donna are equal partners in the DD Partnership. The passive activity loss and the at-risk rules are not applicable to the partners. The partnership reports the following items on its Schedule K during the current year:

Ordinary loss	$10,000
Long-term capital gains	40,000
Research and experimentation credit	4,000
Tax preferences	6,000

Damien's basis in his partnership interest is $80,000 at the beginning of the current year. The DD Partnership liabilities increased by $20,000 during the current year.

a. What amounts should Damien report on his individual tax return as a result of DD Partnership's activities?

b. What is Damien's basis in his partnership interest after the adjustments for the Schedule K items?

I17-39 *Special Allocations on Contributed Property.* Ed contributes land (a capital asset) having an $80,000 adjusted basis and a $100,000 FMV, and Gail contributes $100,000 cash to the EG Partnership. Ed and Gail each receive 50% interests in the partnership. Two years later the partnership sells the land (still a capital asset) for $110,000. What are the amount and character of the EG Partnership's gain or loss? How much of EG's gain or loss is allocated to Ed? To Gail?

I17-40 *Loss Allocations.* Alice and Bruce are equal partners in the calendar-year AB Partnership. On December 1 of the current year, Carl is admitted to the partnership by making a $100,000 cash contribution in exchange for a one-third interest in the partnership. Alice and Bruce's partnership interests are each reduced to one-third. The partnership agreement is amended to provide that Carl will receive a retroactive allocation of one-third of all partnership profits and losses incurred for the entire year. The AB Partnership reports a $90,000 ordinary loss for the tax year ending on December 31. How much of the partnership's loss is allocated to Alice, Bruce, and Carl?

I17-41 *Basis of a Partnership Interest.* Anita has a one-half interest in the AB Partnership. Anita's basis in her interest at the beginning of the current year is $50,000. During the year, the following events occur:

- Partnership liabilities increase by $50,000.
- Partnership earns $60,000 of ordinary income.
- Partnership recognizes $20,000 of capital losses.
- Partnership earns $10,000 of tax-exempt interest.
- Anita withdraws $20,000 in cash.
- Anita contributes land having a $40,000 adjusted basis and a $100,000 FMV as an additional capital contribution without increasing her interest in the partnership.

What is Anita's basis in her partnership interest at the end of the current year?

I17-42 *Partnership Losses and Basis.* Ken has a one-half interest in the KL Partnership. His basis in the partnership interest at the end of the current year (before deducting his share of partnership losses) is $40,000. His share of the partnership's ordinary loss in the current year is $180,000. Next year, Ken makes a $50,000 additional capital contribution, and the partnership's ordinary income is $100,000. Assume that no change occurs in Ken's partnership interest as a result of the capital contribution and that he materially participates in the business.
a. How much ordinary loss can Ken deduct in the current year?
b. What is Ken's basis in his partnership interest at the end of the current year?
c. How much ordinary income or loss does Ken report next year?
d. What is Ken's basis in his partnership interest at the end of next year?

I17-43 *Transactions Between the Partners and the Partnership.* Kevin has a 30% interest in the KLM Partnership. Louis (Kevin's son) also has a 30% interest. The remaining 40% interest is owned by an individual unrelated to either Kevin or Louis. Kevin sells the following assets to the partnership during the year:

- Common stock having a $10,000 basis and a $20,000 FMV and selling price.
- Land having a $100,000 adjusted basis and a $60,000 FMV and selling price.
- Machine having a $50,000 adjusted basis and a $70,000 FMV and selling price. The original cost of the machine was $60,000, and $10,000 in MACRS depreciation allowances has been taken.

a. What are the amount and character of Kevin's recognized gain or loss on the sale of the common stock? The land? The machine?
b. What gain or loss would the partnership recognize if it sells the land 2 years later for $90,000?

I17-44 *Guaranteed Payments.* Laura and Mark are equal partners in the LM Partnership. Laura receives a $30,000 guaranteed payment in the current year and withdraws $20,000 of her partnership capital in cash. Partnership ordinary income is $100,000 for the current year. What amounts must be included in Laura's income for the current year?

I17-45 *Nonliquidating Distributions.* Lynn's basis in her partnership interest is $10,000 when she receives a nonliquidating distribution of $5,000 cash and land having a $6,000 adjusted basis and a $12,000 FMV.
a. What are the amount and character of the gain Lynn must recognize on the distribution?
b. What is Lynn's basis in the land?
c. What is Lynn's basis in her partnership interest after the distribution?

I17-46   *Sale of a Partnership Interest.* The balance sheet of the ABC Partnership at November 30 of the current year is as follows:

	Adjusted Basis	FMV
Assets:		
Cash	$ 10,000	$ 10,000
Accounts receivable	20,000	20,000
Inventory	15,000	16,000
Land, buildings, and machinery	60,000	74,000[a]
Total	$105,000	$120,000
Liabilities and capital:		
Accounts payable	$ 5,000	$ 5,000
Notes payable	10,000	10,000
Allen's capital (⅓)	30,000	35,000
Beth's capital (⅓)	30,000	35,000
Candace's capital (⅓)	30,000	35,000
Total	$105,000	$120,000

[a] Assume that $3,000 would be ordinary income under depreciation recapture rules if the assets were sold.

All partners have an equal interest in the partnership. Allen sells his partnership interest to an outsider on November 30 for $35,000. Allen's share of the partnership income for the 11-month period ending November 30 is $3,000, and his basis in the partnership interest is $38,000 (which includes Allen's share of the income and partnership liabilities for the period ending November 30).
a. What amount is realized by Allen on the sale?
b. What are the amount and character of the gain or loss Allen must recognize on the sale?

I17-47   *Reporting Partnership Income.* Rita, a calendar-year taxpayer, is an employee of the RST Partnership, which has an April 30 year-end. The partnership pays Rita a salary of $3,000 per month for the period from January 1 through April 30, 1997. On May 1, she is admitted to the partnership and receives monthly drawings of $3,000 for the 12-month period ending April 30, 1998. The drawings reflect her approximate share of the partnership income for the period from May 1, 1997 through April 30, 1998. On April 30, 1998, Rita's share of the partnership ordinary income is $40,000.
a. What amount of income does Rita report on her 1997 individual tax return?
b. What amount of income does Rita report on her 1998 individual tax return?

I17-48   *S Corporation Terminations.* Which of the following events will cause a termination of the S corporation election? When is the termination effective? (Assume that all other requirements for an S corporation election are met and that the termination is not inadvertent.)
a. Best Corporation has 75 qualifying S corporation shareholders. Sam dies on October 13, and his stock is held by the estate for the rest of the year.
b. Assume the same facts as in Part a, except that the estate distributes the stock to Sam's child before the end of the tax year. Sam's child did not previously own any Best stock.
c. Best Corporation issues nonvoting common stock to Susan's two children during the current year.

    d. Shareholders Susan, Ted, and Tim, who own 60% of the Best stock, file a revocation on October 1 to terminate the election as of this date.

I17-49   *S Corporation Ordinary Income and Separately Stated Items.* The income statement for Central Corporation, an electing S corporation, reflects the following:

Sales	$200,000
Cost of goods sold	(60,000)
Repair expense	(5,000)
Depreciation expense	(10,000)
Salary expense	(30,000)
Long-term capital losses	(10,000)
Charitable contributions	(5,000)
Sec. 1231 losses	(8,000)
Net income per books	$ 72,000

    a. What is Central's ordinary income (or loss) for the year?
    b. Which of the items above appear as separately stated items on Schedule K?
    c. Carol owns 50% of Central's stock, which has a $50,000 basis (before any of the items above are taken into account). What is Carol's adjusted basis for her stock after all adjustments are made for Carol's share of Central's ordinary income or loss and separately stated items?

I17-50   *Basis of S Corporation Stock.* Cathy is a 50% shareholder of City Corporation. City is an electing (calendar-year) S corporation. Cathy acquires her stock on January 1 of the current year for $50,000. In the current year, City reports the following results of operations, cash distributions, and salary payments:

Ordinary income allocable to Cathy	$30,000
Salary payments to Cathy	40,000
Long-term capital losses allocable to Cathy	5,000
Cash distributions to Cathy	10,000

    a. What is Cathy's basis in her stock at the end of the current year?
    b. What amounts should be included in Cathy's individual tax return for the current year?

I17-51   *S Corporation Losses and Stock Basis.* Chris owns one-third of the stock of Coastal Corporation, an electing S corporation, and he materially participates in the business. Coastal uses the calendar year as its tax year. On January 1 of the current year, Chris's basis in the stock is $25,000, and he has a $10,000 loan outstanding to the corporation. In the current year, Coastal Corporation reports a $180,000 ordinary loss.
    a. What amount of loss can Chris deduct on his individual tax return?
    b. What is Chris's basis in his stock and loan at December 31?
    c. How much of the loss is carried forward to subsequent years?

I17-52   *S Corporation Basis for Stock and Loans.* Because of earlier losses, Cindy has a zero basis in her S corporation stock and a zero basis in her $10,000 loan to the corporation. During the current year, Cindy acquires additional shares of the S corporation stock for $8,000, and her share of the S corporation income is $7,000.
    a. What is Cindy's basis in her loan and stock on December 31?
    b. What are the tax consequences to Cindy if her loan (secured by a note) is fully repaid on January 1 of the following year?

I17-53   *S Corporation Distributions and Basis of Property.* Compact Corporation, an electing S corporation, distributes land used in its business to Clay, its sole shareholder. The land has an $80,000 adjusted basis and a $100,000 FMV. Clay's basis in the Compact stock is $150,000, which includes his share of ordinary income and separately stated items for the current year (other than any gains or losses recognized because of the distribution). Compact has always been an S corporation.

a. What are the tax consequences of the distribution to Compact Corporation and Clay?

b. What is the basis of the land to Clay?

I17-54 *S Corporation Distributions and Basis of Stock.* Control Corporation distributes $10,000 cash to shareholder Craig whose stock basis is $8,000. Craig's share of ordinary income for the current year is $1,000, and the corporation has no separately stated items. Control Corporation always has been an electing S corporation.

a. What are the tax consequences of the distribution (i.e., amount and character of income or gain to Control Corporation and Craig)?

b. What is Craig's stock basis at the end of the tax year?

I17-55 *S Corporation Fringe Benefits.* Copper Corporation is formed in 1996 and immediately elects S corporation status. In the current year, the corporation pays the following insurance premiums for its employees:

Group term life insurance for shareholder-employees, all of whom own more than 2% of the stock	$3,000
Accident and health insurance premiums for shareholder-employees, all of whom own more than 2% of the stock	5,000
Accident, health, and group term life insurance premiums for employees who are not shareholders	2,000
Group term life insurance premiums for employees who are not shareholders	1,000

a. What tax consequences result from Copper Corporation's payment of the insurance premiums?

b. What are the tax consequences to the shareholder-employees and to employees who are not shareholders?

I17-56 *S Corporation Built-In Gains Tax.* Delta Corporation made an S corporation election on January 1 of the current year. Delta had been a C corporation since 1981. The corporation has the following operating results during the current year:

Ordinary income	$200,000
Long-term capital gains	130,000

The adjusted basis and FMV of capital assets held on January 1 and sold during the current year were $200,000 and $300,000, respectively, as of the January 1 beginning of the S election period.

a. Is Delta Corporation subject to the built-in gains tax under Sec. 1374? Explain.

b. What is the amount of corporate tax liability on the built-in gain (if applicable)?

c. How would your answers to Parts a and b change if Delta Corporation instead elected S corporation status on January 31, 1986?

COMPREHENSIVE PROBLEM

I17-57 Charles is a 50% partner in CD Partnership, a calendar-year partnership. For 1997, Charles received a Schedule K-1 that reported his share of partnership items as follows:

Partnership ordinary income	$100,000
Tax-exempt income	1,000
Dividend income	3,000
Short-term capital loss	10,000
Sec. 1231 loss	12,000
Charitable contributions	2,000
Cash distribution	60,000

In addition, Charles and his wife, Charlene, had the following items outside the partnership:

Charlene's salary	$110,000
Long-term capital gain	4,000
Interest income from corporate bonds	5,000
Mortgage interest expense	12,000
State income taxes	8,000
State sales taxes	5,000
Property taxes on home	3,000
Charitable contributions	5,500
Withholding on Charlene's salary	25,000
Estimate taxes payments	20,000

Charles and Charlene have two dependent children, ages 7 and 9, and file a joint tax return. Calculate the following items for Charles and Charlene:

- Adjusted gross income (AGI)
- Taxable income
- Tax liability
- Taxes due or refund

TAX FORM/RETURN PREPARATION PROBLEMS

I17-58 The XYZ Partnership reports the following items during the current year:

Sales	$200,000
Cost of goods sold	100,000
Dividends	10,000
Salaries to employees	20,000
Guaranteed payments to partners	30,000
Net long-term capital gain	15,000
Net short-term capital gain	5,000
Repairs	3,000
MACRS depreciation	8,000
Charitable contributions	2,000
Research and experimentation credit	3,000
Partner withdrawals	8,000

Compute ordinary income (or loss) by completing page 1 of Form 1065 and the Schedule K (Partners' Shares of Income, Credits, Deductions, etc.). Leave spaces blank on Form 1065 if information is not provided.

I17-59 Eagle Corporation, an electing S corporation, reports the following items during the current year:

Sales	$200,000
Cost of goods sold	100,000
Dividends	10,000
Officer salaries	20,000
Net short-term capital gain	2,000
Net long-term capital loss	1,000
Repairs	10,000
Depreciation	5,000
Sec. 1231 losses	15,000
Charitable contributions	8,000
Research and experimentation credit	4,000

Compute ordinary income (or loss) by completing page 1 of Form 1120S and Schedule K (Shareholders' Share of Income, Credits, Deductions, etc.). Leave spaces blank on Form 1120S if information is not provided.

CASE STUDY PROBLEMS

I17-60 Peggy, Phil, and Ralph each have unincorporated accounting practices, and they wish to pool their resources and operate as a single business entity. Peggy owns a building that has appreciated in value since she purchased it 8 years ago. They intend to use this building for their office. Other than the building, they own office and computer equipment and furniture, none of which is worth more than book value. They all have substantial outstanding accounts receivable with a zero basis because each individual uses the cash method of accounting. Each individual has substantial amounts of portfolio income (i.e., dividends and interest). Under the plan, accounts payable with a zero basis from the unincorporated accounting practices would be transferred to the new entity.

Each accountant has two or three employees each. They all agree that it is important to provide benefits to their employees, such as group health insurance, group term life insurance, and a retirement plan of some kind. Additionally, they wish to have their staff participate in the profits of the company and have some form of equity interest in the company.

Peggy, Phil, and Ralph use different computerized accounting and billing systems. They also have different documentation requirements for their client files. The computerized accounting records, billing records, and client files will all have to be consolidated from three systems to one system. The conversion will take place over a period of time. For this reason, they anticipate losses for the first tax year.

Peggy, Phil, and Ralph have agreed that they want to operate as a conduit-type entity because they wish to avoid double taxation, and they want to use the losses from the first year immediately. They have come to you for advice. Write a client memo comparing the pros and cons of operating the accounting practice as a partnership and an S corporation.

I17-61 Dan is the partial owner of an S corporation that currently has 75 shareholders. In March of the current year, Dan sold some of his S corporation stock to each of his two adult children. In August, Dan redeemed the stock he sold because he is in the midst of a divorce and was fearful of the consequences associated with giving voting rights of his business to his children. Dan informs you, his tax consultant, of the stock sale and subsequent redemption. You explain to Dan that by selling the stock he created 77 shareholders between the months of March and August and that the S corporation election had been terminated on the day preceding the date the corporation had more than 75 shareholders. Dan tells you that he sees no reason to inform the IRS of the termination because he bought back the stock within the year, and the IRS probably would not discover the event. What are your responsibilities as a CPA under the SRTP rules as mandated by the AICPA concerning the S election termination? (See the *Statements on Responsibilities in Tax Practice* section in Chapter I15 and Appendix E for a discussion of these issues.) What advice can you offer Dan concerning reinstatement of the S election under the rules for inadvertent terminations?

TAX RESEARCH PROBLEMS

I17-62 Sandee is an employee of the Beach Group, an organization active in the Florida real estate industry. Sandee performs the task of finding real estate property on Miami Beach and subsequently organizing partnerships to acquire and finance the property. Sandee was particularly interested in one building in the Art Deco district that was to be purchased and renovated. She gathered interested investors who formed the Deco Partnership, consisting of two general partners and several limited partners. In exchange for her services in organizing the partnership, Sandee received a 3% limited partnership interest in the profits of the Deco Partnership. As part of the agreement, the profits interest was transferable only at the discretion of the general partners. Based on the uncertainty in the South Florida real estate industry at the time, the partners could not estimate whether profits or losses would be generated when the renovation was completed in 3 years. Based on these facts, will Sandee's receipt of the limited partnership interest be a taxable event?

A partial list of research sources is

- Sec. 721

- Reg. Sec. 1.721-1(a)

- *William G. Campbell v. CIR*, 68 AFTR 2d 91-5425, 91-2 USTC ¶ 50,420 (8th Cir., 1991)

- *Sol Diamond v. CIR*, 33 AFTR 2d 74-852, 74-1 USTC ¶ 9306 (7th Cir., 1974)

- Rev. Proc. 93-27, 1993-2 C.B. 343

I17-63   Chuck, Cindy, and Clay are the three equal owners of Able Corporation common stock. Able was incorporated in the current year. Able elects to be taxed as an S Corporation starting in its initial year. Chuck, Cindy, and Clay each contributed $10,000 cash to Able in exchange for their common stock. Able borrows $60,000 from a bank, and Chuck, Cindy, and Clay personally guaranteed the loan. In the current year, Able suffers a $90,000 ordinary loss. How much of the loss will be deductible by Chuck, Cindy, and Clay? (Assume that the at-risk and passive activity loss limitation rules do not apply.)

A partial list of research sources is

- Sec. 1366(d)(1)

- *Estate of Daniel Leavitt v. CIR*, 63 AFTR 2d 89-1437, 89-1 USTC ¶9332 (4th Cir., 1989)

- *Edward M. Selfe v. U.S.*, 57 AFTR 2d 86-464, 86-1 USTC ¶9115 (11th Cir., 1986)

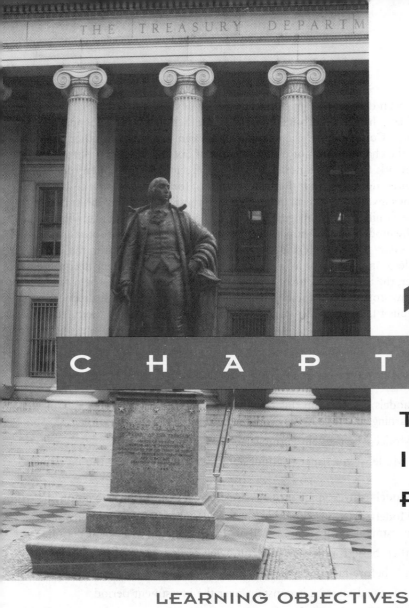

CHAPTER 18

TAXES AND INVESTMENT PLANNING

LEARNING OBJECTIVES

After studying this chapter, you should be able to

▶ 1 Apply the investment models to various investment alternatives

▶ 2 Use the investment models to make entity choices

▶ 3 Use the investment models to make current salary versus deferred compensation decisions

▶ 4 Understand the role of implicit taxes in investment decisions

This chapter has been derived from a book written by Myron S. Scholes and Mark A. Wolfson and takes what has become known as the Scholes-Wolfson approach to investment strategy.[1] Consequently, the chapter differs significantly from other chapters in this text. First, the chapter does not present details of tax law. Instead, it introduces a conceptual framework for understanding how taxes affect basic investment decisions. Second, the chapter develops and illustrates models for determining the after-tax outcomes of various investment alternatives. Although these models may look strange at first, they become familiar and manageable after some study and practice. Third, the chapter extends the models' application to the flow-through versus C corporation choice and the current salary versus deferred compensation decision. Fourth, the chapter introduces the role of implicit taxes as well as explicit taxes in investment decisions. As demonstrated later, the before-tax rate of return of a tax-favored asset will be reduced by market forces as investors increase their demand for these investments. This reduced rate of return is an implicit tax that investors need to consider when making their decisions.

INVESTMENT MODELS

OBJECTIVE 1

Apply the investment models to various investment alternatives

KEY POINT

Future values are necessary to compare all amounts at the same point in time. This is critical in evaluating alternative investment opportunities.

The investment models described in this chapter fall into four categories depending on how investment earnings are taxed. We refer to these models as:

▶ The Current Model—Investment earnings are taxed currently.
▶ The Deferred Model—Investment earnings are taxed at the end of the investment period.
▶ The Exempt Model—Investment earnings are exempt from explicit taxation.
▶ The Pension Model—The initial investment is deductible or excludable from gross income, and investment earnings are taxed at the end of the investment period.

These models in their basic form reflect the following assumptions:

▶ The investment's before-tax rate of return is constant over the investment period.
▶ The investor's marginal tax rate is constant over the investment period.
▶ Investment earnings are reinvested at the same rate of return as earned by the original investment.
▶ The investor knows future rates of returns and tax rates with certainty.
▶ The investor incurs no transaction costs.

The models can be modified, however, to accommodate changes to these assumptions. For example, we later show how to adapt the Current Model for changing tax rates (see Example I18-5).

THE CURRENT MODEL

The Current Model gives the future value of an investment having the following characteristics:

▶ Only after-tax dollars are invested.
▶ The earnings on the investment are taxed annually (currently); thus, the reinvested earnings grow at the after-tax rate of return.

Common examples of investments taxed this way are savings accounts, money market funds, and taxable bonds, if the investor reinvests the after-tax earnings annually.

[1] Myron S. Scholes and Mark A. Wolfson, *Taxes and Business Strategy: A Planning Approach* (Englewood Cliffs, NJ: Prentice Hall, 1992).

INVESTMENT WITH NO TAXATION. Before developing the Current Model, however, we first illustrate how an investment grows when compounded annually in a no-tax situation, and we introduce the notions of before-tax dollars and the before-tax rate of return. We then show the relationship between before-tax dollars and after-tax dollars and between before-tax and after-tax rates of return. Finally, we incorporate these concepts into the Current Model.

EXAMPLE I18-1 ▶ Carla, an individual investor, lives in a land of no taxation and earns $1,000 of salary. She invests this amount in a bond that pays interest at 10% per year and holds the bond for 3 years, reinvesting the interest annually at the same 10% return. The following schedule details the investment's cash flow over the 3 years:

(1) Year	(2) Cumulative Investment at Beginning of Year	(3) Interest Income[a]	(4) Cumulative Investment at End of Year[b]
1	$1,000	$100	$1,100
2	1,100	110	1,210
3	1,210	121	1,331

[a] Column 2 × 10%
[b] Column 2 + Column 3

Thus, at the end of 3 years, the $1,000 original investment accumulates to $1,331. ◀

The 3-year accumulation determined in Example I18-1 also can be calculated as follows: $1,000 (1.1)^3 = \$1,331$, which is $1,000 compounded at 10% for 3 years. Thus, the general form of the compounding formula is:

$$\text{Accumulation} = \text{BT\$} (1 + R)^n$$

In this formula, BT$ stands for before-tax dollars invested. For instance, in Example I18-1, Carla invested the entire $1,000 because her salary was not reduced by taxes. Also in the formula, R is the before-tax rate of return (BTROR). Again, this return is a before-tax percentage because, as in Example I18-1, the interest on the investment is not taxed. Consequently, all the interest can be reinvested; nothing is siphoned away as taxes. Finally, n equals the number of years the investor holds the investment or, in other words, n represents the investment horizon. Thus, the formula gives the future value (accumulation) of before-tax dollars invested for n years while earning a BTROR equal to R.

THE CURRENT MODEL. Now assume our investor is subject to taxation at marginal tax rate t. In this case, any earned income, such as salary, will be subject to taxes, leaving only after-tax dollars available for investment.

EXAMPLE I18-2
ADDITIONAL COMMENT

In this chapter, we primarily use only federal tax rates. However, in real life situations, all taxes must be considered.

▶ Assume that Carla's $1,000 salary is subject to tax and that her marginal tax rate is 40%. That is, t = 40% or 0.4. (For simplicity in this chapter, we use 40% instead of 39.6% as the top tax rate.) In this case, Carla has only $600 to invest. This amount is computed as follows:

Salary before taxes	$1,000
Minus: Taxes ($1,000 × 0.4)	(400)
After-tax dollars available to invest	$ 600 ◀

The $600 amount determined in Example I18-2 also can be calculated as follows:

$$
\begin{aligned}
\text{After-tax dollars} &= \$1,000 - (\$1,000 \times 0.4) \\
&= \$1,000 (1 - 0.4) \qquad \text{(Factoring out the \$1,000 salary)} \\
&= \$1,000 \times 0.6 = \$600
\end{aligned}
$$

In general, then, the relationship between before-tax dollars (BT$) and after-tax dollars (AT$) can be expressed as follows:

$$AT\$ = BT\$ (1 - t)$$

Now assume that the interest our investor earns also is taxed at her marginal tax rate. The following example shows the impact on the investor's after-tax cash flows.

EXAMPLE I18-3 ▶ Carla again earns $1,000 of salary, but because of taxation at 40%, she has only $600 to invest, as shown in Example I18-2. She invests the $600 in a bond for 3 years that yields 10% interest per year before taxes. However, in this case, the interest income also is taxed at 40%. The following schedule details the investment's cash flow over the 3 years:

(1) Year	(2) Cumulative Investment at Beginning of Year	(3) Before-Tax Interest Income[a]	(4) Tax on Interest[b]	(5) After-Tax Interest Income[c]	(6) Cumulative Investment at End of Year[d]
1	$600.00	$60.00	$24.00	$36.00	$636.00
2	636.00	63.60	25.44	38.16	674.16
3	674.16	67.42	26.97	40.45	714.61

[a] Column 2 × 10%
[b] Column 3 × 40%
[c] Column 3 − Column 4
[d] Column 2 + Column 5

◀

In Example I18-3, after-tax interest in Column 5 for Year 1 also can be calculated as follows:

$$
\begin{aligned}
\text{After-tax interest} &= \$600 (0.1) - \$600 (0.1) (0.4) \\
&= \$600 (0.1) (1 - 0.4) \quad \text{(Factoring out the \$600 after-tax salary} \\
&\qquad\qquad\qquad\qquad\qquad\text{and the 10\% before-tax rate of return)} \\
&= \$600 (0.1) (0.6) \\
&= \$600 (.06) = \$36
\end{aligned}
$$

Thus, although the BTROR is 10%, the after-tax rate of return (ATROR) is only 6%. In general, the relationship between the BTROR and the ATROR can be expressed as follows:

$$r = R (1 - t)$$

As before, R equals the BTROR, and t equals the investor's marginal tax rate. The new variable, r, equals the ATROR, which is easy to remember because taxes reduce big R to little r.

With knowledge of this ATROR, the 3-year accumulation in Example I18-3 also can be calculated as follows: After-tax accumulation (ATA) = $600 (1.06)^3 = 714.61, which is $600 compounded at 6% for 3 years. Thus, the general form of the after-tax compounding formula is:

The Current Model:
$$ATA = AT\$ (1 + r)^n \text{ or}$$

$$ATA = AT\$ [1 + R (1 - t)]^n$$

Note that, because of current taxation, investments conforming to the Current Model provides no deferral advantages because all earnings are taxed currently. As demonstrated later in this chapter, the other three models reflect certain tax advantages.

EXAMPLE I18-4 ▶ At the beginning of Year 1, Harry invests $5,000 (AT$) in a money market fund that pays a 5% annual return before taxes. Harry's marginal tax rate is 28%, and he allows all after-tax earnings to remain in the money market fund. That is, he withdraws only enough cash to pay taxes on the fund's annual earnings. The following table shows Harry's after-tax accumulation for various investment horizons. In this table, note that Harry's ATROR equals 3.6%, which is 5% $(1 - 0.28)$. Thus, the Current Model appears as $5,000 $[1 + 0.05 (1 - 0.28)]^n$ or $5,000 $(1.036)^n$.

Investment Horizon (n)	Computation	After-Tax Accumulation
5 years	$5,000 $(1.036)^5$	$ 5,967.18
10 years	$5,000 $(1.036)^{10}$	$ 7,121.44
20 years	$5,000 $(1.036)^{20}$	$10,142.97 ◀

Changes to Assumptions. As stated earlier, the Current Model (as well as other models) assumes that R and t are constant over the investment period. However, the model can be modified to accommodate changes to these assumptions. This modification is accomplished by breaking the model into separate components, as demonstrated in the next example.

EXAMPLE I18-5 ▶ At the beginning of Year 1, Dan invests $5,000 (AT$) in a money market fund that pays a 5% annual return before taxes. He plans to leave the after-tax earnings in the fund for 15 years. Dan expects his marginal tax rate to be 28% over the next 5 years but expects his tax rate to be 36% for the subsequent 10 years. Thus, his ATROR for the first 5 years equals 3.6%, which is 5% $(1 - 0.28)$. For the remaining 10 years, his ATROR equals 3.2%, which is 5% $(1 - 0.36)$. Dan's after-tax accumulation (ATA) after 15 years is calculated as follows:

$$\text{ATA} = \$5,000 \ (1.036)^5 \ (1.032)^{10} = \$8,176.47.$$

Note that the first part of this calculation, $5,000 $(1.036)^5$ = $5,967.18, gives the accumulation after the 5 years during which Dan's tax rate is 28%. This accumulation then continues to grow at the 3.2% ATROR for the remaining 10 years as follows: $5,967.18 $(1.032)^{10}$ = $8,176.47. ◀

THE DEFERRED MODEL

KEY POINT

Deferral is beneficial because the tax dollars not used currently to pay tax can be reinvested to help generate more earnings.

The Deferred Model gives the future value of an investment having the following characteristics:

▶ Only after-tax dollars are invested (as with the Current Model).

▶ The earnings on the investment are not taxed annually; thus, they grow at the BTROR.

▶ The accumulated earnings are taxed at the end of the investment horizon when the investor cashes out of the investment; thus, taxation of these earnings is deferred.

The nondeductible IRA described in Chapter I9 is a classic example of the Deferred Model. Recall that, if the taxpayer or the taxpayer's spouse is covered by an employer-sponsored qualified retirement plan and the taxpayer's AGI exceeds a specified amount, the taxpayer may not deduct contributions to the IRA. Nevertheless, the taxpayer may make nondeductible contributions up to $2,000 per year. These nondeductible contributions are after-tax dollars.

EXAMPLE I18-6 ▶ Marsha, who is in the 28% tax bracket, wishes to contribute $2,000 to a nondeductible IRA. She wants to know how much taxable salary she must earn to have $2,000 left for the contribution. Recall that AT$ = BT$ (1 − t). Rearranging these terms gives BT$ = AT$ / (1 − t). In words, we can "gross up" after-tax dollars by dividing after-tax dollars by one minus the tax rate. Accordingly, the before-tax dollars necessary to yield $2,000 after taxes equals $2,777.78, which is $2,000 / (1 − 0.28). Thus, Marsha must earn $2,777.78 of salary before taxes. The tax on this amount equals $777.78, which is $2,777.78 × 0.28, leaving $2,000 available for contribution to the IRA. ◀

EXAMPLE I18-7 ▶ Suppose Marsha makes the $2,000 contribution in the current year and makes no subsequent contributions. Suppose further that investments in the IRA yield 12% per year before taxes and that Marsha allows her investment to accumulate in the IRA for 15 years. At the end of 15 years, she withdraws all amounts from the IRA, at which time her marginal tax rate is 28%. The following calculation demonstrates one way to determine Marsha's after-tax accumulation in the IRA:

(1) Before-tax accumulation in the IRA [$2,000 $(1.12)^{15}$]	$10,947.13
(2) Minus: Original contribution	(2,000.00)
(3) Accumulated earnings before taxes	$ 8,947.13
(4) Times: Tax rate	0.28
(5) Tax on accumulated earnings	$ 2,505.20
(6) After-tax accumulation (Line 1 − Line 5)	$ 8,441.93 ◀

The calculation in Example I18-7 also can be formulated as follows:

$$ATA = \$2,000 \ (1.12)^{15} − [\$2,000 \ (1.12)^{15} − \$2,000] \times .028$$

The first term, $2,000 $(1.12)^{15}$, gives the total before-tax accumulation; the subtraction in brackets gives the accumulated before-tax earnings; and the multiplication by 28% gives the tax on the accumulated earnings. Subtracting these taxes from the first term gives the total after-tax accumulation. Factoring out the $2,000 investment yields the following expression:

$$ATA = \$2,000 \ \{(1.12)^{15} − [(1.12)^{15} − 1] \times .028\}$$

Substituting our general symbols into this expression yields the following model, the component parts of which are shown in Figure I18-1:

$$ATA = AT\$ \ \{(1 + R)^n − [(1 + R)^n − 1] \times t_n\}$$

The subscript n on the tax rate emphasizes that the rate in Year n applies rather than the rate in the investment year or any intervening year. To make the model easier to use computationally, we can simplify this model algebraically with the following three steps. Multiplying through by t yields:

$$ATA = AT\$ \ \{(1 + R)^n − [t_n \ (1 + R)^n − t_n]\}$$

Carrying the first minus sign through yields:

$$ATA = AT\$ \ [(1 + R)^n − t_n \ (1 + R)^n + t_n]$$

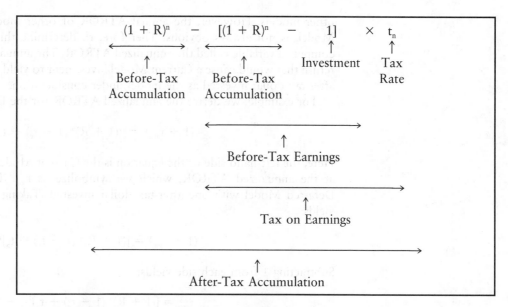

$$(1 + R)^n - [(1 + R)^n - 1] \times t_n$$

Before-Tax Accumulation   Before-Tax Accumulation   Investment   Tax Rate

Before-Tax Earnings

Tax on Earnings

After-Tax Accumulation

FIGURE I18-1 ▶ Deferred Model before Algebraic Simplification

Factoring out $(1 + R)^n$ yields:

The Deferred Model:
$$ATA = AT\$ [(1 + R)^n (1 - t_n) + t_n]$$

We call this model the Deferred Model because the tax on investment earnings is deferred until the investor cashes out of the investment. This characteristic causes the Deferred Model investment to outperform the Current Model investment given equal BTRORs and constant tax rates.

EXAMPLE I18-8 ▶ Phillip can invest $1,000 (AT$) directly in a taxable bond outside an IRA, or he can contribute the $1,000 to a nondeductible IRA and invest in the same bond through the IRA vehicle. In either case, the bond yields an annual 10% BTROR. Phillip's marginal tax rate is 28%, and he expects it to remain so for the entire investment horizon. The two alternatives give the following after-tax accumulations after 20 years:

Bond outside the IRA (Current Model):

$$\$1,000 [1 + 0.1 (1 - 0.28)]^{20} = \$1,000 (1.072)^{20} = \$4,016.94$$

Bond inside the IRA (Deferred Model):

$$\$1,000 \{(1.1)^{20} (1 - 0.28) + 0.28\} = \$5,123.80$$

The Deferred Model investment outperforms the Current Model investment because the interest on the bond grows at the BTROR (10%), with taxation deferred until Year 20. ◀

ANNUALIZED ATROR. As we explained earlier, the ATROR in the Current Model is $r = R (1 - t)$. That is, an investment that fits the Current Model yields this ATROR annually. The annual ATROR is a useful number for comparison to annual ATRORs of other models. However, the annual ATROR of other models, such as the Deferred Model, is not always obvious. Therefore, to determine this comparable number, we compute a variable called the annualized ATROR. The annualized ATROR is the rate of return that would cause a Current Model investment to yield the same accumulation per after-tax dollar invested as the model under consideration.

For example, we derive the annualized ATROR for the Deferred Model as follows:

$$(1 + r_{ann})^n = \{(1 + R)^n (1 - t_n) + t_n\}$$

Here, the left-hand side of the equation is the Current Model investment compounding at the annualized ATROR, which we symbolize as r_{ann}. The right-hand side is the Deferred Model with one after-tax dollar invested. Taking the nth root of each side yields:

$$(1 + r_{ann}) = [(1 + R)^n (1 - t_n) + t_n]^{1/n}$$

Subtracting 1 from each side yields:

$$r_{ann} = [(1 + R)^n (1 - t_n) + t_n]^{1/n} - 1$$

The general form for this relationship, which can be used for any model, is:

Annualized ATROR:
$$r_{ann} = [\text{Accumulation per AT\$ invested}]^{1/n} - 1$$

EXAMPLE I18-9 ▶

Consider the same facts as in Example I18-8. The annualized ATROR for the investment outside the IRA is 7.2%. No additional computation is necessary because the model already is in the Current Model form. The accumulation per AT$ invested inside the IRA (the Deferred Model) can be determined two ways. First, divide the total accumulation ($5,123.80) by the $1,000 (AT$) invested, which yields 5.1238. Alternatively, compute the accumulation per AT$, as follows: $[(1.1)^{20} (1 - 0.28) + 0.28] = 5.1238$. The annualized ATROR, then, is computed as follows: $r_{ann} = (5.1238)^{1/20} - 1 = .085125$ or 8.5125%. Thus, on an annualized basis, a 20-year investment outside the IRA (the Current Model) yields 7.2% after taxes, while a 20-year investment inside the IRA (the Deferred Model) yields 8.5125% after taxes. To check this result, simply put the 8.5125% annualized ATROR in the Current Model to see that it yields the same result as did the Deferred Model.

$$\text{ATA} = \$1,000 (1.085125)^{20} = \$1,000 (5.1238) = \$5,123.80$$ ◀

ADDITIONAL COMMENT

There are many policymakers who support increasing the benefits for capital gains. For example, one proposal would make the capital gain rate for all capital assets 50% of the ordinary income rate. This would reduce the top capital gain rate to 19.8%.

CAPITAL ASSETS. The Deferred Model also describes the after-tax growth of a capital asset. For example, suppose a stock grows annually at rate R and does not pay dividends, that is, the stock is strictly a growth stock. In n years, the stock will be worth $(1 + R)^n$. If the investor then sells the stock for its fair market value (FMV), the investor pays tax on the capital gain. Consequently, the tax on the gain is deferred until the investor sells the asset, which reflects the realization principle of taxation. Moreover, the capital gain may be taxed at a preferential tax rate, for example, the 28% maximum rate on long-term capital gains. Thus, when applied to capital assets, the Deferred Model provides two tax advantages: deferral and a preferential tax rate.

When Figure I18-1 is applied to this situation, the before-tax accumulation represents the selling price at the FMV, and the before-tax earnings represent the capital gain.

EXAMPLE I18-10 ▶ Brian purchases stock for $5,000. The stock appreciates (grows) at an 8% rate before taxes. Brian sells the stock 10 years later for $10,794.62, which is $5,000 $(1.08)^{10}$. At the time of sale, his regular tax rate is 40%, but his long-term capital gains tax rate is 28% (see Chapter I5). One way to calculate Brian's after-tax proceeds is as follows:

(1) Selling price [$5,000 $(1.08)^{10}$]	$10,794.62
(2) Minus: Original investment (basis)	(5,000.00)
(3) Long-term capital gain	$ 5,794.62
(4) Times: long-term capital gains tax rate	0.28
(5) Tax on capital gain	$ 1,622.49
(6) After-tax proceeds (Line 1 − Line 5)	$ 9,172.13

Alternatively, the after-tax proceeds can be determined quickly with the Deferred Model as follows:

$$\text{ATA} = \$5,000 \,[(1.08)^{10} \,(1 - 0.28) + 0.28] = \$9,172.13 \qquad ◀$$

COMPARING CURRENT AND DEFERRED MODELS. As mentioned earlier, a Deferred Model investment always outperforms a Current Model investment if BTRORs are constant over time and equal across models and if tax rates also are constant and equal. However, when these conditions are not present, the models must be compared to determine which is preferable. One way to make this comparison is to set up a spreadsheet of the various alternatives.

EXAMPLE I18-11 ▶ As in Example I18-8, assume that Phillip can invest $1,000 (AT$) in a taxable bond either outside or inside a nondeductible IRA. The bond yields 10% per year before taxes, and Phillip's marginal tax rate is 28%. Assume also that Phillip will be younger than 59½ when he withdraws the funds from the IRA. As described in Chapter I9, a taxpayer who withdraws amounts from an IRA before reaching age 59½ must pay a 10% penalty tax on the taxable portion of the withdrawal. This penalty, in effect, increases the applicable tax rate in the Deferred Model. Thus, the following models apply (the Deferred Model with no penalty is repeated for comparison):

Bond outside the IRA (Current Model):

$$\$1,000 \,[1 + 0.1 \,(1 - 0.28)]^n = \$1,000 \,(1.072)^n$$

Bond inside the IRA (Deferred Model)—No penalty:

$$\$1,000 \,[(1.1)^n \,(1 - 0.28) + 0.28]$$

Bond inside the IRA (Deferred Model)—With penalty:

$$\$1,000 \,[(1.1)^n \,(1 - 0.38) + 0.38]$$

Notice that the 10% penalty increases the effective tax rate to 38%. Given the 10% penalty, which investment is better, the Current Model or the Deferred Model? The answer depends on the length of the investment horizon. Table I18-1 schedules the after-tax accumulations and related annualized ATRORs for various investment horizons (n) from one to 20 years.

Before considering the penalty situation, observe the no penalty case. For all values of n above one, the Deferred Model investment produces a greater after-tax accumulation than does the Current Model investment (compare Columns 2 and 3). This result also is apparent in the annualized ATRORs. For all values of n above one, the Deferred Model investment produces

ADDITIONAL COMMENT

Minimum withdrawals must begin when a taxpayer reaches age 70½. Otherwise, the taxpayer faces a 50% penalty on the difference between the minimum required distribution and the actual distribution.

▼ **TABLE I18-1**

Comparison of Current and Deferred Models

(1)	After-Tax Accumulations			Annualized ATRORs[d]		
	(2)	(3)	(4)	(5)	(6)	(7)
		Deferred	Deferred		Deferred	Deferred
	Current	Model	Model	Current	Model	Model
n	Model[a]	No Penalty[b]	With Penalty[c]	Model	No Penalty	With Penalty
1	$1,072.00	$1,072.00	$1,062.00	7.2%	7.2000%	6.2000%
2	1,149.18	1,151.20	1,130.20	7.2	7.2940	6.3109
3	1,231.93	1,238.32	1,205.22	7.2	7.3852	6.4197
4	1,320.62	1,334.15	1,287.74	7.2	7.4735	6.5264
5	1,415.71	1,439.57	1,378.52	7.2	7.5589	6.6307
6	1,517.64	1,555.52	1,478.37	7.2	7.6414	6.7326
7	1,626.91	1,683.08	1,588.20	7.2	7.7210	6.8319
8	1,744.05	1,823.38	1,709.03	7.2	7.7978	6.9285
9	1,869.62	1,977.72	1,841.93	7.2	7.8716	7.0224
10	2,004.23	2,147.49	1,988.12	7.2	7.9427	7.1135
11	2,148.54	2,334.24	2,148.93	7.2	8.0110	7.2018
12	2,303.23	2,539.67	2,325.83	7.2	8.0765	7.2872
13	2,469.06	2,765.64	2,520.41	7.2	8.1395	7.3699
14	2,646.84	3,014.20	2,734.45	7.2	8.1998	7.4496
15	2,837.41	3,287.62	2,969.89	7.2	8.2577	7.5266
16	3,041.70	3,588.38	3,228.88	7.2	8.3131	7.6009
17	3,260.70	3,919.22	3,513.77	7.2	8.3663	7.6724
18	3,495.47	4,283.14	3,827.15	7.2	8.4171	7.7412
19	3,747.15	4,683.45	4,171.86	7.2	8.4658	7.8075
20	4,016.94	5,123.80	4,551.05	7.2	8.5125	7.8712

[a] $1,000 (1.072)^n$
[b] $1,000 [(1.1)^n (1 - 0.28) + 0.28]$
[c] $1,000 [(1.1)^n (1 - 0.38) + 0.38]$
[d] $[(ATA \ per \ AT\$)^{1/n} - 1] \times 100$

an annualized ATROR greater than 7.2% (compare Columns 5 and 6). Moreover, the greater n, the greater the annualized ATROR from the Deferred Model investment. This result occurs because tax deferral increases as the investment horizon lengthens. Thus, the longer the deferral, the better the annualized ATROR produced by the Deferred Model investment.

Now compare the Current Model to the Deferred Model with the 10% penalty. For investment horizons up to 10 years, the Current Model investment outperforms the Deferred Model investment, while for horizons greater than 10 years, the Deferred Model investment beats the Current Model investment (compare Columns 2 and 4). This result can be seen more easily with the annualized ATRORs, where beginning in Year 11, the annualized ATRORs for the Deferred Model investment exceed 7.2% (compare Columns 5 and 7). The Current Model investment is better for short horizons because the applicable tax rate is 28% rather than 38% (rate + penalty). However, after 10 years, the deferral benefit of the Deferred Model investment overcomes the detrimental effect of the penalty. Thus, if an investor has a long enough investment horizon, a nondeductible IRA subject to the 10% penalty may be the preferred method of accumulating savings. ◄

THE EXEMPT MODEL

The Exempt Model gives the future value of an investment having the following characteristics:

▶ Only after tax dollars are invested (as with the Current and Deferred Models).

▶ Earnings on the investment are exempt from explicit taxation (unlike the Current and Deferred Models).

In fact, the Exempt Model is a special case of the Current Model with the tax rate equal to zero. Consequently, the investment grows at the BTROR and appears as follows:

$$\text{The Exempt Model:}$$
$$\text{ATA} = \text{AT\$} (1 + R)^n$$

For now, we note that this tax benefit will be reduced or eliminated by market forces that drive down the BTROR. We will consider this point in some detail when we introduce implicit taxes later in the chapter.

State and local government obligations, such as municipal bonds, are classic examples of the Exempt Model. Under Sec. 103, interest on these instruments is excluded from gross income.

ADDITIONAL COMMENT

In 1993, individual taxpayers earned $46 billion of interest from tax-exempt investments.

EXAMPLE I18-12 ▶

Carmen invests $10,000 (AT$) in tax-exempt municipal bonds, which yield 5% per year. She reinvests the interest and holds the bonds for 10 years. Thus, the investment accumulates to $16,288.95, which is $10,000 $(1.05)^{10}$. ◀

Another example of the Exempt Model is an IRA that is not allowed by current tax law but that lawmakers have proposed numerous times to either supplement or replace deductible IRAs. We will call this type of IRA an exempt IRA. Like the nondeductible IRA, it does not allow a deduction for contributions. However, upon withdrawals, the accumulated earnings are not taxed. We will say more about the exempt IRA after developing the Pension Model.

THE PENSION MODEL

The Pension Model gives the future value of an investment in a qualified retirement plan having the following characteristics:

▶ Before-tax dollars are invested (unlike the previous three models).

▶ The annual earnings on the investment grow at the BTROR (as with the Deferred and Exempt Models).

▶ The entire accumulation, not just the earnings, is taxed at the end of the investment horizon when the investor cashes out of the plan.

Thus, the Pension Model provides two levels of tax deferral. First, salary or earned income contributed to the plan escapes taxation when contributed but is taxed later upon withdrawal. Second, earnings on the underlying investment are not taxed while in the plan but also are taxed later upon withdrawal. This double deferral contrasts with the Deferral Model, in which only the taxes on investment earnings are deferred.

Deductible IRAs and H.R. 10 plans described in Chapter I9 are classic examples of the Pension Model. The taxpayer deducts the IRA or H.R. 10 contribution from gross income, the underlying investments grow at before-tax rates of return, and the taxpayer later includes any withdrawals in gross income.

EXAMPLE I18-13 ▶ Frank, whose marginal tax rate is 40%, earns $1,000 of salary and wishes to contribute this amount to a deductible IRA (Pension Model). He may do so because he can deduct the $1,000 contribution from gross income, leaving the entire $1,000 available for contribution. If, instead, Frank contributes to a nondeductible IRA (Deferred Model), he can contribute only $600 because he must pay $400 of taxes on the $1,000 salary. Thus, Frank can contribute $1,000 before-tax dollars to a deductible IRA as contrasted with $600 after-tax dollars to a nondeductible IRA. ◀

Other examples of the Pension Model include cash or deferred arrangements, commonly known as Sec. 401(k) plans, and tax-deferred annuities, sometimes referred to as Sec. 403(b) plans. Both of these type plans operate through a salary reduction agreement whereby the employee elects to have a specified amount of his or her salary contributed to the plan. The amount of salary contributed to the plan is excluded from the employee's gross income. However, annual contributions are limited to $9,500 (in 1997), with this limitation adjusted each year for inflation.[2] As with IRA and H.R. 10 plans, the underlying investments in Sec. 401(k) and Sec. 403(b) plans grow at before-tax rates of return, and the employee later includes any withdrawals in gross income. Withdrawals before the employee reaches age 59½, however, are subject to a 10% penalty in addition to the tax. Although most employers can offer Sec. 401(k) plans, only educational institutions and certain tax-exempt organizations may provide Sec. 403(b) plans.

Employer-sponsored qualified retirement plans also fit the Pension Model. In this case, the employer makes a deductible contribution on the employee's behalf, and the employee excludes the contribution from gross income. Upon retirement, the employee's retirement payments are fully taxed.

EXAMPLE I18-14 ▶ Frank in Example I18-13 makes the $1,000 contribution to a deductible IRA. The investment in the IRA will earn 10% per year before taxes, and Frank will withdraw all accumulated amounts from the IRA after 20 years. He expects his tax rate to be 28% at that time, and he will not be subject to the 10% penalty for early withdrawals. The following calculation demonstrates one way to determine Frank's after-tax accumulation in the IRA:

Before-tax accumulation in the IRA [$1,000 $(1.1)^{20}$]	$6,727.50
Minus: Tax on withdrawn accumulation ($6,727.50 × 0.28)	(1,883.70)
Accumulated earnings after taxes	$4,843.80 ◀

The calculation in Example I18-14 also can be formulated as follows:

$$\text{ATA} = \$1,000\ (1.1)^{20} - [\$1,000\ (1.1)^{20}] \times 0.28$$

Factoring out the before tax accumulation of $1,000 $(1.1)^{20}$ yields the following expression:

$$\text{ATA} = \$1,000\ (1.1)^{20}\ (1 - 0.28)$$

Substituting our general symbols into this expression yields:

The Pension Model:
$$\text{ATA} = \text{BT\$}\ (1 + R)^n\ (1 - t_n)\ \text{or}$$
$$\text{ATA} = \text{AT\$}\left[\frac{1}{(1 - t_o)}\ (1 + R)^n\ (1 - t_n)\right]$$

---

[2] This dollar limitation is imposed by Sec. 402(g). Percentage of compensation limitations also apply to contributions to Sec. 401(k) and Sec. 403(b) plans, but these limitations are complex and beyond the scope of this chapter. See Chapter I9 and Secs. 403(b) and 415(c).

Recall that BT\$ = AT\$ / (1 − t). That is, before-tax dollars equals after-tax dollars grossed up by one minus the tax rate. Thus, the second form of the Pension Model is equivalent to the first form. The second form, however, has the same format as the other three models: AT\$ times a future value formula. This format allows the investor to compare all four models without considering a specific level of investment because each model in this format is stated in terms of the after-tax accumulation per AT\$ invested. In these models, t_o is the tax rate in Year o, and t_n is the tax rate in Year n.

EXAMPLE I18-15 ▶

Given four options listed below, Beth wants to know the after-tax accumulation and annualized ATROR of each.

▶ Current Model: R = 10%, t = 28%, n = 5

▶ Deferred Model: R = 9%, t_n = 28%, n = 5

▶ Exempt Model: R = 8%, n = 5

▶ Pension Model: R = 10%, t_o = 28%, t_n = 36%, n = 5

The results of the four options are as follows:

Model	Computation	After-Tax Accumulation	Annualized ATROR
Current	$[1 + 0.1 (1 − 0.28)]^5$	1.4157	7.20%
Deferred	$(1.09)^5 (1 − 0.28) + 0.28$	1.3878	6.77%
Exempt	$(1.08)^5$	1.4693	8.00%
Pension	$[1 / (1 − 0.28)] (1.1)^5 (1 − 0.36)$	1.4316	7.44% ◀

COMPARING EXEMPT AND PENSION MODELS. With equal BTRORs and constant tax rates (i.e., $t_o = t_n$), the Exempt and Pension Models are equivalent because the $1 / (1 − t_o)$ and $(1 − t_n)$ terms cancel out leaving the Pension Model (second form) to appear as AT\$ $(1 + R)^n$. However, if t_o and t_n differ, this equivalency disappears. Thus, the following relationships hold:

▶ If $t_o = t_n$, ATA per Exempt Model = ATA per Pension Model.

▶ If $t_o > t_n$, ATA per Exempt Model < ATA per Pension Model.

▶ If $t_o < t_n$, ATA per Exempt Model > ATA per Pension Model.

EXAMPLE I18-16 ▶

Consider the following situations:

▶ R = 10%, t_o = 28%, t_n = 28%, n = 10

▶ R = 10%, t_o = 40%, t_n = 28%, n = 10

▶ R = 10%, t_o = 28%, t_n = 40%, n = 10

The after-tax accumulations (ATAs) for the three situations are as follows:

Situation	Exempt Model	Pension Model
$t_o = 28\%, t_n = 28\%$	$(1.1)^{10} = 2.5937$	$[1 / (1 − 0.28)] (1.1)^{10} (1 − 0.28) = 2.5937$
$t_o = 40\%, t_n = 28\%$	$(1.1)^{10} = 2.5937$	$[1 / (1 − 0.40)] (1.1)^{10} (1 − 0.28) = 3.1125$
$t_o = 28\%, t_n = 40\%$	$(1.1)^{10} = 2.5937$	$[1 / (1 − 0.28)] (1.1)^{10} (1 − 0.40) = 2.1615$ ◀

Thus, if Congress enacted an exempt IRA, this new type IRA would provide the same result as a current-law deductible IRA as long as the investor's tax rate remained constant. With changing tax rates, however, the two types would not be equivalent. Specifically, a person who contributes to an IRA during his or her high tax rate years and retires in low tax rate years would be better off with a deductible IRA (Pension Model) than with an exempt IRA (Exempt Model). The Pension Model is better than the Exempt Model in this case because the investor deducts the contributions at high tax rates but includes income later at low tax rates.

ADDITIONAL
COMMENT
Placing the maximum $2,000
into an IRA for 40 years with
an earnings rate of 10% will
result in a pretax account balance of over $973,700. An IRA
earning 11% during the same
period will accumulate a balance of over $1,291,600.

MULTIPERIOD STRATEGIES

All previous examples assumed a single amount invested for a specified time period. However, suppose an investor wants to invest a certain amount each year over several years. In this case, the investor may optimize his or her after-tax accumulation by investing in one type of investment in early years and another type investment in late years.

EXAMPLE I18-17 ▶

For the next 15 years, Jack wishes to invest $10,000 (AT$) at the beginning of each year into either nondividend paying stock that increases in value at 9% per year before taxes or a taxable bond that yields 10% per year before taxes. Jack's regular tax rate is 31%, but he pays only 28% on long-term capital gains. Jack wants to know which asset to invest in for each of the 15 years. The following models apply to this situation:

Stock (Deferred Model):

$$\$10,000 \, [(1.09)^n \, (1 - 0.28) + 0.28]$$

Taxable bond (Current Model):

$$\$10,000 \, [1 + 0.1 \, (1 - 0.31)]^n = \$10,000 \, (1.069)^n$$

Table I18-2 schedules the alternatives for each year. The stock produces the larger after-tax accumulations for investments made in Years 1 through 9. For Years 10 through 15, however, the taxable bonds outperform the stock. Consequently, Jack should invest in stock for each of the first 9 years. For the remaining 6 years, he should invest in taxable bonds.

▼ TABLE I18-2

Multiperiod Investments

(1) Year	(2) n	(3) Amount Invested	(4) Stock[a] (Deferred Model)	(5) Taxable Bond[b] (Current Model)	(6) Greater of Column 4 or 5
1	15	$10,000	$29,025.87	$27,206.06	$29,025.87
2	14	10,000	26,860.43	25,450.01	26,860.43
3	13	10,000	24,873.79	23,807.30	24,873.79
4	12	10,000	23,051.19	22,270.63	23,051.19
5	11	10,000	21,379.07	20,833.14	21,379.07
6	10	10,000	19,845.02	19,488.44	19,845.02
7	9	10,000	18,437.63	18,230.53	18,437.63
8	8	10,000	17,146.45	17,053.82	17,146.45
9	7	10,000	15,961.88	15,953.06	15,961.88
10	6	10,000	14,875.12	14,923.35	14,923.35
11	5	10,000	13,878.09	13,960.10	13,960.10
12	4	10,000	12,963.39	13,059.03	13,059.03
13	3	10,000	12,124.21	12,216.12	12,216.12
14	2	10,000	11,354.32	11,427.61	11,427.61
15	1	10,000	10,648.00	10,690.00	10,690.00
Total after-tax accumulation					$272,857.54

[a] $10,000 [(1.09)^n (1 − 0.28) + 0.28]
[b] $10,000 (1.069)^n

The stock outperforms the taxable bonds for the first 9 years even though the taxable bonds yield a higher BTROR than does the stock. This result occurs because the deferral benefit outweighs the lower BTROR for long investment horizons. ◀

SUMMARY AND COMPARISON OF BASIC INVESTMENT MODELS

Topic Review I18-1 summarizes the models along with simple examples. In the examples, each model assumes an investment earning 10% before taxes and assumes a constant 28% tax rate. With these assumptions, the Exempt and Pension Models outperform the Current and Deferred Models, and the Deferred Model outperforms the Current Model.

OTHER APPLICATIONS OF INVESTMENT MODELS

In the previous section of this chapter, we developed four investment models and applied them to currently taxable investments, capital gains assets, tax-exempt bonds, and retirement plans. In this section, we present two additional applications: (1) the flow-through entity versus the C corporation form of business operations and (2) current salary versus deferred compensation.

OBJECTIVE 2

Use the investment models to make entity choices

FLOW-THROUGH ENTITY VERSUS C CORPORATION

Chapter I16 described how the government taxes C corporations and their shareholders, and Chapter I17 introduced the tax consequences of operating as a flow-through entity. Flow-through entities include partnerships, limited liability companies (LLCs), limited liability partnerships (LLPs), and S corporations. A flow-through entity's primary characteristic is that income escapes taxation at the entity level and flows through to be taxed at the ownership level. Corporate income, on the other hand, is taxed once at the entity level and again at the owner level. Taxation at the owner level occurs when the corporation distributes its earnings, when the shareholder sells his or her stock, or when the corporation liquidates.

In this section, we will show that the Current Model describes a flow-through entity and that a variation of the Deferred Model describes a C corporation. These models can be used to decide which form of business is best from a tax perspective. At first, one might think the flow-through entity is the better form because it avoids double taxation. But, in fact, the better alternative depends on a combination of factors, specifically, rates of returns, the corporate tax rate, the owner's tax rate, and the entity's expected life span (investment horizon).

THE FLOW-THROUGH MODEL. To keep matters simple, we assume an S corporation with only one shareholder. The one-owner assumption allows us to focus on the entity decision without worrying about distributive shares and differential individual tax rates among owners. The model also applies to an S corporation, a partnership, an LLC, or an LLP with more than one owner. In addition, the model applies to a sole proprietorship because that form of business also entails one level of taxation.

ADDITIONAL COMMENT

Remember from earlier chapters that as the income and deductions flow through to the owners of partnerships and S corporations, the character is retained. For example, ordinary income at the entity level is ordinary income to the owner; capital gains at the entity level flow through as capital gains.

EXAMPLE I18-18 ▶

Assume the following facts. Rebecca forms an S corporation by contributing $10,000 to the corporation in exchange for all of the corporation's stock. The S corporation invests in assets that produce a 10% BTROR per year. At the end of each year, the S corporation distributes cash to Rebecca equal to the taxes she must pay on the S corporation's flow-through earnings. The corporation reinvests the remaining earnings in its business. Rebecca's tax rate is 40%.

Topic Review I18-1

Summary of Investment Models

Investment Model	Initial Income	Investment Earnings or Capital Gain	Example[a]	ATA	ATA/AT$	r_{ann}
Current: $AT\$ [1 + R (1-t)]^n$ — or — $AT\$ (1+r)^n$	Taxed currently	Taxed annually	$720 (1.072)^5$	$1,019.31	1.4157[b]	7.20%
Deferred: $AT\$ [(1+R)^n (1-t_n) + t_n]$	Taxed currently	Tax deferred	$720 [(1.1)^5 (0.72) + 0.28]$	$1,036.49	1.4396[c]	7.56%
Exempt: $AT\$ (1+R)^n$	Taxed currently	Tax exempt	$720 (1.1)^5$	$1,159.57	1.6105[d]	10.00%
Pension: $BT\$ (1+R)^n (1-t_n)$ — or — $AT\$ \left[\dfrac{1}{(1-t_o)} (1+R)^n (1-t_n) \right]$	Tax deferred	Tax deferred	$1,000 (1.1)^5 (0.72)$ — or — $720 (1/0.72) (1.1)^5 (0.72)$	$1,159.57	1.6105[e]	10.00%

Definitions of Variables:

ATA = After-tax accumulation (future value of an investment)

BT$ = Before-tax dollars

AT$ = After-tax dollars

R = Before-tax rate of return (BTROR)

r = After-tax rate of return (ATROR)

r_{ann} = Annualized ATROR

n = Investment horizon

t = Marginal tax rate, generally and for Current Model

t_o = Marginal tax rate in the year of investment (Year o) for Pension Model

t_n = Marginal tax rate at the end of the investment horizon (Year n) for Deferred and Pension Models

[a] Initial before-tax income (BT$) = $1,000; AT$ = $1,000 (0.72) = $720; R = 10%; $t = t_o = t_n = 28\%$; n = 5

[b] Also: $(1.072)^5 = 1.4157$

[c] Also: $(1.1)^5 (0.72) + 0.28 = 1.4396$

[d] Also: $(1.1)^5 = 1.6105$

[e] Note that the $1,159.57 after-tax accumulation is divided by $720, not $1,000, because $720 is the after-tax dollar equivalent of $1,000 before taxes.
Also: $(1/0.72) (1.1)^5 (0.72) = 1.6105$

Immediately after the end of the second year, the S corporation liquidates, selling the assets and distributing the cash proceeds to Rebecca. Because the corporation reinvested its retained earnings, the basis of the assets on the sale date equals their FMV. Thus, the sale produces no realized gain at the entity level. The following schedule shows the results of these transactions at the entity and owner levels:

	Year 1	Year 2
Entity level:		
Investment at beginning of year	$10,000	$10,600
Plus: Earnings on investment (10% × investment)	1,000	1,060
Minus: Distribution to shareholder (40% × earnings)	(400)	(424)
Investment at end of year	$10,600	$11,236
Owner level:		
Stock basis at beginning of year	$10,000	$10,600
Plus: Increase due to flow-through income	1,000	1,060
Minus: Decrease due to distribution	(400)	(424)
Stock basis at end of year	$10,600	$11,236

Upon liquidation, the S corporation sells the assets and distributes the $11,236 to Rebecca. Because Rebecca's stock basis equals $11,236, she recognizes no additional gain on the liquidation. Thus, after 2 years, she ends up with $11,236 on a $10,000 original investment.

◀

In Example I18-18, the S corporation was able to reinvest only its earnings after paying the shareholder's tax. Thus, the investment grew at a 6% ATROR, which is 10% $(1 - 0.4)$. Consequently, the shareholder's after-tax accumulation also can be calculated as follows: ATA $= \$10,000 \ (1.06)^2 = \$11,236$. From the owner's viewpoint, then, the flow-through entity resembles the Current Model. In general terms, the owner's after-tax accumulation can be expressed as:

The Flow-Through Model:

$$\text{ATA} = \text{Contribution} \ [1 + R_f \ (1 - t_p)]^n$$

In this model, R_f equals the flow-through entity's BTROR, t_p is the owner's marginal tax rate (p is for personal), and n is the investment horizon. Although Example I18-18 assumes a liquidating distribution at the end of the investment, the same result would have occurred had the owner sold her ownership interest (stock in this case) to another party.

THE C CORPORATION MODEL. Again, to keep matters simple, we assume a C corporation with only one shareholder, and we further assume that the corporation retains all earnings after paying corporate level taxes. That is, the corporation pays no dividends. The model could be modified to reflect annual dividend payments, but such a model becomes extremely complicated and beyond the scope of this chapter.[3]

EXAMPLE I18-19 ▶ Assume the same facts as in Example I18-18 except that Rebecca forms a C corporation instead of an S corporation. In this case, the corporation makes no annual distributions to Rebecca. Instead, the corporation pays its own taxes at a 35% rate and reinvests the after-tax retained earnings. Thus, the shareholder has no owner-level taxes until the corporation liquidates. Rebecca's ordinary tax rate remains 40%, but her capital gains tax rate is the maximum 28%. As in Example I18-18, the sale prior to liquidation produces no realized gain at the entity level. The following schedule shows the results of these transactions at the entity and owner levels:

	Year 1	Year 2
Entity level:		
Investment at beginning of year	$10,000	$10,650
Plus: Earnings on investment (10% × investment)	1,000	1,065
Minus: Corporate taxes (35% × earnings)	(350)	(373)
Investment at end of year	$10,650	$11,342
Owner level:		
Stock basis	$10,000	$10,000
(1) Liquidation proceeds		$11,342
(2) Minus: Stock basis		(10,000)

---

[3] See Scholes and Wolfson, Chapter 4, footnote 22 for this expanded model.

(3) Capital gain on liquidation	$ 1,342
(4) Times: Long-term capital gains tax rate	0.28
(5) Tax on capital gain	$ 376
(6) After-tax proceeds (Line 1 − Line 5)	$10,996

Because the corporation is a C corporation, Rebecca makes no adjustments to her stock basis, which remains at $10,000. Consequently, she recognizes a capital gain upon liquidation, and after 2 years she ends up with $10,996 on a $10,000 original investment. ◀

In Example I18-19, the C corporation was able to reinvest only its after-tax earnings. Thus, at the corporate level, the investment grew at a 6.5% ATROR, which is 10% (1 − 0.35). Consequently, the corporate-level accumulation before distribution to the shareholders can be calculated as follows: $10,000 [1 + 0.1 (1 − 0.35)]^2 = $10,000 (1.065)^2 = $11,342. In general terms, this expression is: Contribution $[1 + R_c (1 - t_c)]^n$, or Contribution $[1 + r_c]^n$. This formulation is a variation of the Current Model, where R_c is the corporation's BTROR, r_c is the corporation's ATROR, and t_c is the corporation's marginal tax rate.

Upon liquidation, the shareholder receives the corporate-level accumulation and pays tax at rate t_p on the difference between the distribution and her stock basis. Thus, the shareholder's after-tax accumulation in Example I18-19 can be formulated as follows:

$$ATA = \$10,000 \, (1.065)^2 - [\$10,000 \, (1.065)^2 - \$10,000] \times .028$$

The first term, $10,000 (1.065)^2$, gives the corporate-level after-tax accumulation; the subtraction in brackets gives the shareholder's liquidation gain before shareholder-level taxes; and the multiplication by 28% gives the tax on the liquidation gain. Subtracting this tax from the first term gives the shareholder's total after-tax accumulation on the investment in the C corporation. Factoring out the $10,000 contribution yields the following expression:

$$ATA = \$10,000 \, \{(1.065)^2 - [(1.065)^2 - 1] \times 0.028\}$$

Substituting our general symbols into this expression yields the following model, which is a variation of the Deferred Model shown earlier in Figure I18-1:

$$ATA = \text{Contribution} \, \{(1 + r_c)^n - [(1 + r_c)^n - 1] \times t_p$$

As done earlier with the Deferred Model, we can simplify this model algebraically to obtain:

The C Corporation Model:

$$ATA = \text{Contribution} \, [(1 + r_c)^n \, (1 - t_p) + t_p] \text{ or}$$

$$ATA = \text{Contribution} \, \{[1 + R_c \, (1 - t_c)]^n \, (1 - t_p) + t_p\}$$

In the first form of this model, the corporation's ATROR (r_c) plays the same role as the BTROR plays in the Deferred Model developed earlier in this chapter. More specifically, in terms used in Example I18-10, r_c is the appreciation (growth) rate of the shareholder's stock investment, assuming the stock value reflects increases in the corporation's after-tax retained earnings. Thus, the corporation's ATROR functions as the shareholder's BTROR on his or her stock investment. The second form of the C Corporation Model emphasizes that the corporate-level accumulation (the Current Model) is embedded in the shareholder's after-tax accumulation model (the Deferred Model).

COMPARING THE FLOW-THROUGH AND C CORPORATION MODELS. Given these two models, an owner can compare whether operating as a flow-through entity or a C corporation provides the better result.

EXAMPLE I18-20 ▶

Assume the following facts. Mark forms Wolfson Corporation by contributing $5 million in exchange for the corporation's stock. The corporation expects to earn 20% per year before-taxes on this investment. The corporate tax rate is 34%, and Mark's individual tax rate on ordinary income is 40%. In addition, Mark's long-term capital gains tax rate is 28%. However, because Wolfson stock qualifies as small business stock under Sec. 1202, any gain recognized on disposition of the stock after a 5-year holding period qualifies for a 50% exclusion. This exclusion makes Mark's effective long-term capital gains rate 14% rather than 28%. Wolfson can operate either as an S corporation or a C corporation. If the corporation elects S corporation status, each year it will distribute exactly enough cash for Mark to pay taxes on any flow-through income, and it will reinvest the remaining earnings in the business. If the corporation operates as a C corporation, it will make no annual distributions, reinvesting all after-tax earnings in the business. In either case, the corporation will liquidate at the end of the investment horizon. Mark wants to know whether the corporation should operate as an S or a C corporation given each of the following investment horizons: 4 years, 8 years, or 12 years. The following schedule gives Mark's after-tax accumulation for each of these alternatives:

S Corporation:

4 years: $\text{ATA} = \$5,000,000 [1 + 0.2 (1 - 0.4)]^4 = \$7,867,597$

8 years: $\text{ATA} = \$5,000,000 [1 + 0.2 (1 - 0.4)]^8 = \$12,379,816$

12 years: $\text{ATA} = \$5,000,000 [1 + 0.2 (1 - 0.4)]^{12} = \$19,479,880$

C Corporation:

4 years: $\text{ATA} = \$5,000,000 \{[1 + 0.2 (1 - 0.34)]^4 (1 - 0.28) + 0.28\} = \$7,311,371$

8 years: $\text{ATA} = \$5,000,000 \{[1 + 0.2 (1 - 0.34)]^8 (1 - 0.14) + 0.14\} = \$12,294,176$

12 years: $\text{ATA} = \$5,000,000 \{[1 + 0.2 (1 - 0.34)]^{12} (1 - 0.14) + 0.14\} = \$19,738,187$

Thus, if Mark decides to operate the corporation for 4 or 8 years, the corporation should make the S corporation election. However, if he plans to operate for 12 years, the corporation should remain a C corporation. (In fact, the C corporation beats the S corporation for investment horizons above 9 years.) Note that Mark's capital gains tax rate drops to 14% for the 8- and 12-year investments because of the 50% small business stock exclusion. ◀

SUMMARY. The Flow-Through Model is an application of the Current Model, where taxation occurs only at the owner level. The C Corporation Model is a variation of the Deferred Model, where taxation occurs at both the entity and the owner levels. These models can help the planner decide whether the flow-through entity or the C corporation is the better alternative from a tax perspective. Topic Review I18-2 summarizes these models.

CURRENT SALARY VERSUS DEFERRED COMPENSATION

OBJECTIVE 3

Use the investment models to make current salary versus deferred compensation decisions

Chapter I9 introduced the characteristics of a nonqualified deferred compensation plan. This arrangement differs from current salary in that the employer's deduction and the employee's inclusion in gross income occur later than with current salary. The key question, then, is whether an employee should choose current salary or deferred compensation. The decision model developed in this section helps answer this question. Because both the employer and the employee are affected by the timing of compensation, the decision model must incorporate these dual effects. Specifically, the model includes the current and future tax rates of the employer and employee as well as the employer's and employee's ATRORs.

Topic Review I18-2

Flow-Through and C Corporation Models

Flow-Through Model:

$$\text{ATA} = \text{Contribution} [1 + R_f (1 - t_p)]^n$$

C Corporation Model:

$$\text{ATA} = \text{Contribution} [(1 + r_c)^n (1 - t_p) + t_p]$$

or

$$\text{ATA} = \text{Contribution} \{[1 + R_c (1 - t_c)]^n (1 - t_p) + t_p\}$$

Definitions of Variables:

R_f = Flow-through entity's BTROR
R_c = C corporation's BTROR
t_p = Owner's marginal tax rate
t_c = C corporation's marginal tax rate
r_c = C corporation's ATROR
n = Investment horizon

THE EMPLOYEE'S POINT OF VIEW. The employee can choose between current salary in Year o or deferred compensation in Year n. If the employee chooses current salary, he immediately pays taxes on the salary and invests the after-tax amount at his ATROR.[4] If, instead, the employee receives deferred compensation, he pays taxes on this compensation in Year n, leaving an after-tax amount of deferred compensation. These two alternatives are comparable because both are stated in terms of future values.

EXAMPLE I18-21 ▶ Bruce works for Xeron Corporation and is considering receiving either $10,000 of current salary or $25,000 of deferred compensation in 10 years. His current tax rate is 40%, but he expects his tax rate to be 28% 10 years from now. Bruce can invest any after-tax current salary at a 10% ATROR. If Bruce receives current salary and invests the after-tax amount, his investment will accumulate as follows:

$$\$10,000 (1 - 0.4) (1.1)^{10} = \$15,562$$

Bruce's after-tax salary is $6,000, which grows to $15,562 in 10 years if invested at a 10% ATROR. Thus, this calculation, which is an application of the Current Model, gives the future value of Bruce's after-tax current salary. Alternatively, if Bruce receives deferred compensation, his after-tax deferred compensation is calculated as follows:

$$\$25,000 (1 - 0.28) = \$18,000$$

In this case, Bruce prefers the deferred compensation alternative because he will have $18,000 in 10 years instead of $15,562 under the current salary alternative. ◀

---

[4] The employee also could spend the current salary. However, this current consumption is equivalent to the future consumption available if the employee invests and spends later. In this case, the investment assumption gives the future value of current consumption. Thus, whether the employee actually spends or invests, the investment assumption provides the future value of that decision.

Using general terms, we can state the employee's current salary and deferred compensation alternatives as follows:

$$CSI = BT\$ \, (1 - t_{po}) \, (1 + r_p)^n$$

$$DCI = BT\$ \, (D_n) \, (1 - t_{pn})$$

In these formulas, CSI stands for current salary income and is the employee's after-tax future value of current salary; DCI stands for deferred compensation income and is the employee's after-tax future value of deferred compensation; and BT$ stands for before-tax current salary. In the second formula, D_n is the amount of deferred compensation received in lieu of $1 currently. Accordingly, BT$ $\times$ D_n gives total deferred compensation before taxes. For example, in Example I18-21, BT$ = $10,000, and BT$ $\times$ D_n = $25,000. Thus, D_n = 2.50. In other words, Bruce could choose between $1 of current salary or $2.50 of deferred compensation, before taxes. The factor, BT$, converts these per dollar amounts to total dollars of current salary or deferred compensation. The other variables in the formulas are defined as follows:

▶ t_{po} = The employee's marginal tax rate in Year o

▶ t_{pn} = The employee's marginal tax rate in Year n

▶ r_p = The employee's ATROR

▶ n = The number of years until the employee receives the deferred compensation

The employee prefers deferred compensation if DCI exceeds CSI. From the previous formulas, this relationship can be expressed as follows:

$$DCI > CSI \text{ or}$$

$$BT\$ \, (D_n) \, (1 - t_{pn}) > BT\$ \, (1 - t_{po}) \, (1 + r_p)^n$$

Solving the second expression for D_n yields:

$$D_n > \frac{(1 - t_{po}) \, (1 + r_p)^n}{(1 - t_{pn})}$$

The level of D_n that exactly equals the right-hand side of this expression makes the employee indifferent to receiving current salary or deferred compensation. That is, at the indifference level of D_n, the employee's current salary income (CSI) equals the employee's deferred compensation income (DCI). Levels of D_n above the indifference level make deferred compensation more beneficial than current salary to the employee.

EXAMPLE I18-22 ▶ Assume the same facts as in Example I18-21. Bruce prefers deferred compensation rather than $1 of current salary if D_n exceeds 2.1615, calculated as follows:

$$D_n > \frac{(1 - 0.4) \, (1.1)^{10}}{(1 - 0.28)} = 2.1615$$

Therefore, D_n = 2.1615 is Bruce's indifference level, as shown by the following calculation for $1 of current salary:

$$CSI = \$1 \, (1 - 0.4) \, (1.1)^{10} = \$1.5562$$
$$DCI = \$1 \, (2.1615) \, (1 - 0.28) = \$1.5562$$

Given a choice between $10,000 of current salary (BT$) and deferred compensation, Bruce will prefer deferred compensation to current salary if the deferred compensation exceeds $21,615, which is $10,000 $\times$ 2.1615. ◀

THE EMPLOYER'S POINT OF VIEW. The issue from the employer's point of view is whether the employer is willing to pay deferred compensation in lieu of current salary. If the employer pays current salary, the employer takes a business deduction and obtains an immediate tax benefit. The current salary net of the tax benefit is the employer's after-tax salary expense. This after-tax amount must be projected to Year n to be comparable to the alternative deferred compensation expense. We compound the after-tax salary expense at the employer's ATROR because, if the employer does not pay the salary, the employer will have the after-tax amount available for investment in its business. This investment, in turn, grows at the employer's ATROR. Thus, compounding determines the future value of the employer's after-tax salary expense. If instead of paying salary the employer pays deferred compensation, the employer deducts the deferred compensation expense in Year n. The deferred compensation net of the Year n tax benefit is the employer's after-tax deferred compensation expense.

EXAMPLE I18-23 ▶

Again consider the facts in Example I18-21, that is, $10,000 of current salary versus $25,000 of deferred compensation in 10 years. In addition, the employer's current tax rate is 34%, but the employer expects its tax rate to be 25% 10 years from now. The employer's ATROR is 10%. If the employer pays current salary, its after-tax salary expense projected to Year n is calculated as follows:

$$\$10{,}000 \, (1 - 0.34) \, (1.1)^{10} = \$17{,}119$$

Alternatively, the after-tax deferred compensation expense is calculated as follows:

$$\$25{,}000 \, (1 - 0.25) = \$18{,}750$$

In this case, the employer's after-tax deferred compensation expense ($18,750) exceeds its after-tax salary expense ($17,119). Consequently, the employer is unwilling to pay Bruce the $25,000 of deferred compensation even though Bruce prefers that alternative. ◀

Using general terms, we can state the employer's current salary and deferred compensation alternatives as follows:

$$CSE = BT\$ \, (1 - t_{co}) \, (1 + r_c)^n$$
$$DCE = BT\$ \, (D_n) \, (1 - t_{cn})$$

In these formulas, CSE stands for current salary expense and is the employer's after-tax salary expense projected to Year n; DCE stands for deferred compensation expense and is the employer's after-tax deferred compensation expense in Year n; and BT$ stands for before-tax current salary. As before, D_n equals the amount of deferred compensation paid in lieu of $1 currently. Accordingly, $BT\$ \times D_n$ gives total deferred compensation before taxes. The other variables in the formulas are defined as follows:

▶ t_{co} = The employer's marginal tax rate in Year o
▶ t_{cn} = The employer's marginal tax rate in Year n
▶ r_c = The employer's ATROR
▶ n = The number of years until the employer pays the deferred compensation

The employer will pay deferred compensation only if DCE does not exceed CSE. From the previous formulas, this relationship can be expressed as follows:

$$DCE \leq CSE \text{ or}$$
$$BT\$ \, (D_n) \, (1 - t_{cn}) \leq BT\$ \, (1 - t_{co}) \, (1 + r_c)^n$$

Solving the second expression for D_n yields:

$$D_n \leq \frac{(1 - t_{co})(1 + r_c)^n}{(1 - t_{cn})}$$

The level of D_n that exactly equals the right-hand side of this expression makes the employer indifferent to paying current salary or deferred compensation. That is, at the indifference level of D_n, the employer's current salary expense (CSE) equals the employer's deferred compensation expense (DCE). Levels of D_n below the indifference level make deferred compensation more beneficial than current salary to the employer.

EXAMPLE I18-24 ▶ Assume the same facts as in Example I18-23. Compared to $1 of current salary, the employer will pay deferred compensation only if D_n does not exceed 2.2825, calculated as follows:

$$D_n \leq \frac{(1 - 0.34)(1.1)^{10}}{(1 - 0.25)} = 2.2825$$

Therefore, $D_n = 2.2825$ is the employer's indifference level, as shown by the following calculation for $1 of current salary:

$$CSE = \$1 (1 - 0.34)(1.1)^{10} = \$1.7119$$
$$DCE = \$1 (2.2825)(1 - 0.25) = \$1.7119$$

Given a choice between $10,000 of current salary (BT$) and deferred compensation, the employer will pay deferred compensation instead of current salary only if deferred compensation does not exceed $22,825, which is $10,000 × 2.2825. ◀

COMPARING THE EMPLOYEE'S AND EMPLOYER'S VIEWS. Knowledge of the employee's and employer's acceptable levels of D_n gives the two parties the necessary tools to decide whether deferred compensation is preferable to current salary. Specifically, the employee and employer can apply the following decision rules:

▶ If the employee's indifference level of D_n exceeds the employer's indifference level of D_n, the employee must accept current salary because the employer will not pay the employee's required deferred compensation.

▶ If the employee's indifference level of D_n is less than the employer's indifference level of D_n, the employer can pay deferred compensation up to its indifference level.

EXAMPLE I18-25 ▶ Marsha and Todd are employed by Omega Corporation. They want to compare deferred compensation to $10,000 of current salary. Assume the following tax rates and rates of return:

	Year o	Year n	ATROR
Marsha	$t_{po} = 0.28$	$t_{pn} = 0.15$	$r_p = 0.10$
Todd	$t_{po} = 0.40$	$t_{pn} = 0.15$	$r_p = 0.10$
Omega Corporation	$t_{co} = 0.39$	$t_{cn} = 0.25$	$r_c = 0.10$

The indifference level of D_n for each party is as follows:

Marsha:
$$D_n = \frac{(1 - 0.28)(1.1)^2}{(1 - 0.15)} = 1.0249$$

Todd:
$$D_n = \frac{(1 - 0.4)(1.1)^2}{(1 - 0.15)} = 0.8541$$

Omega Corporation:
$$D_n = \frac{(1 - 0.39)(1.1)^2}{(1 - 0.25)} = 0.9841$$

Compared to $10,000 of current salary, Omega Corporation will pay no more than $9,841 of deferred compensation. Consequently, Marsha must settle for $10,000 of current salary because she requires more than $10,249 of deferred compensation to make that alternative preferable, and this amount exceeds what Omega Corporation is willing to pay as deferred compensation.

Todd, on the other hand, can benefit from a deferred compensation arrangement. He requires deferred compensation exceeding $8,541, and Omega Corporation is willing to pay up to $9,841 of deferred compensation. ◀

We can provide additional insight into the salary versus deferred compensation decision by carrying Example I18-25 a bit further. If Omega Corporation pays Todd $9,841 of deferred compensation, Omega Corporation incurs the same after-tax expense it would have incurred had it paid $10,000 of current salary. Thus, Omega Corporation remains indifferent, and Todd obtains the full benefit of the deferred compensation arrangement. This outcome can be seen with the following income and expense amounts:

Todd:

$$CSI = \$10,000 (1 - 0.4) (1.1)^2 = \$7,260$$
$$DCI = \$10,000 (0.9841) (1 - 0.15) = \$8,365$$

Omega Corporation:

$$CSE = \$10,000 (1 - 0.39) (1.1)^2 = \$7,381$$
$$DCE = \$10,000 (0.9841) (1 - 0.25) = \$7,381$$

Because Omega Corporation pays its indifference level of D_n, its current salary and deferred compensation expenses are equal. Under the deferred compensation arrangement, however, Todd ends up with $8,365 rather than $7,260.

Suppose instead that Omega Corporation pays deferred compensation that makes Todd indifferent. In this case, Todd obtains the same amount of after-tax income as under the salary option, and Omega Corporation obtains the full benefit of the deferred compensation arrangement. This outcome can be seen with the following income and expense amounts:

Todd:

$$CSI = \$10,000 (1 - 0.4) (1.1)^2 = \$7,260$$
$$DCI = \$10,000 (0.8541) (1 - 0.15) = \$7,260$$

Omega Corporation:

$$CSE = \$10,000 (1 - 0.39) (1.1)^2 = \$7,381$$
$$DCE = \$10,000 (0.8541) (1 - 0.25) = \$6,406$$

Because Omega Corporation pays Todd's indifference level of D_n, Todd's current salary and deferred compensation income are equal. Under the deferred compensation arrangement, however, Omega Corporation's deferred compensation expense ($6,406) is less than the alternative current salary expense ($7,381).

In each case, one party was made indifferent while the other party benefited from the deferred compensation alternative. However, Omega Corporation also could pay deferred compensation somewhere between the two indifference levels of D_n. For example, suppose Omega Corporation chose $D_n = 0.92$. The following outcomes would occur:

Todd:

$$CSI = \$10,000 (1 - 0.4) (1.1)^2 = \$7,260$$
$$DCI = \$10,000 (0.92) (1 - 0.15) = \$7,820$$

Omega Corporation:

$$CSE = \$10,000 (1 - 0.39) (1.1)^2 = \$7,381$$
$$DCE = \$10,000 (0.92) (1 - 0.25) = \$6,900$$

In this case, Todd's deferred compensation income is $7,820 rather than $7,260 of current salary income. In addition, Omega Corporation's deferred compensation expense is $6,900 rather than the $7,381 current salary expense. Thus, both parties are better off with the deferred compensation arrangement than with current salary. However, neither party is as well off had the other party remained indifferent. In short, they share the benefit.

OTHER NONTAX ISSUES. The preceding analysis incorporated tax rates and ATRORs in the decision model for current salary versus deferred compensation. Other nontax factors, however, also may affect the decision. For example, the parties must consider their cash-flow requirements. If the employee needs cash now, he or she may be unwilling to defer income despite a better result from the decision model. Similarly, an employer short on current cash may prefer deferred compensation even though the decision model suggests current salary as the better alternative. Deferred compensation also carries some risk. Under nonqualified deferred compensation plans, the employee becomes a general creditor of the employer. Consequently, if the employer runs into financial difficulties later, the employer may not be able to pay the deferred compensation. The employee, therefore, may decide for the safe alternative, current salary, regardless of the decision model outcome. Finally, deferred compensation may lock the employee into continued employment unless the deferred compensation contract makes adequate provision for the employee's severance.

SUMMARY. The decision model developed in this section provides an analytic tool for employees and employers to plan current salary versus deferred compensation arrangements. The model takes into account the tax and ATROR attributes of both parties to the transaction. This approach prevents one party benefiting at the disadvantage of the other and therefore leads to the best overall solution. Topic Review I18-3 summarizes the decision model.

IMPLICIT TAXES AND CLIENTELES

OBJECTIVE 4

Understand the role of implicit taxes in investment decisions

Several of the investment vehicles we modeled earlier have certain tax benefits compared to other investments. For example, interest earned on tax-exempt investments, such as state and local bonds, is excluded from gross income. The Exempt Model reflects this tax benefit. As another example, assets that generate long-term capital gains also are tax favored. The taxation of the capital gain is deferred until realization, and then the realized gain may be subject to a preferential tax rate, specifically, the 28% maximum tax rate on long-term capital gains. The Deferred Model, when applied to capital gain assets, reflects this preferential taxation. For the sake of simplicity, however, this section focuses on tax-exempt bonds to introduce the concept of implicit taxes and clientele effects.

IMPLICIT TAXES. Consider what happens in the marketplace for tax-favored assets. Given a choice between a fully-taxable investment and a tax-favored investment, investors will prefer the tax-favored investment, assuming the two investments are equally risky. This preference manifests itself as an increased demand for the tax-favored investment, thereby driving up the asset's price. The increased price, in turn, causes the asset's BTROR to decrease. For example, the BTROR on a bond with an unlimited life (a perpetuity) is as follows:

$$BTROR = \frac{\text{Annual cash flow}}{\text{Bond's price}}$$

Topic Review I18-3

Current Salary Versus Deferred Compensation

Employee's Point of View	Employer's Point of View
$CSI = BT\$ \, (1 - t_{po}) \, (1 + r_p)^n$	$CSE = BT\$ \, (1 - t_{co}) \, (1 + r_c)^n$
$DCI = BT\$ \, (D_n) \, (1 - t_{pn})$	$DCE = BT\$ \, (D_n) \, (1 - t_{cn})$
$D_n = \dfrac{(1 - t_{po}) \, (1 + r_p)^n}{(1 - t_{pn})}$	$D_n = \dfrac{(1 - t_{co}) \, (1 + r_c)^n}{(1 - t_{cn})}$

Decision rules:

▶ If the employee's indifference level of D_n exceeds the employer's indifference level of D_n, the employee must accept current salary because the employer will not pay the employee's required deferred compensation.

▶ If the employee's indifference level of D_n is less than the employer's indifference level of D_n, the employer can pay deferred compensation up to its indifference level.

Definitions of Variables:

CSI = Current salary income; employee's after-tax future value of current salary, before taxes

DCI = Deferred compensation income; employee's after-tax future value of deferred compensation

CSE = Current salary expense; employer's after-tax salary expense projected to Year n

DCE = Deferred compensation expense; employer's after-tax deferred compensation expense in Year n

$BT\$$ = Before-tax current salary

D_n = Amount of deferred compensation paid in lieu of \$1 of current salary

t_{po} = Employee's marginal tax rate in Year o

t_{pn} = Employee's marginal tax rate in Year n

r_p = Employee's ATROR

t_{co} = Employer's marginal tax rate in Year o

t_{cn} = Employer's marginal tax rate in Year n

r_c = Employer's ATROR

n = Number of years until the deferred compensation

If the bond's price increases, the BTROR must decrease.

The difference between the BTRORs of the fully-taxable and tax-favored investments is an implicit tax, which can be expressed as follows:

$$IT = R_b - R_f$$

In this formula, IT stands for implicit tax, R_b is the BTROR on a fully-taxable benchmark investment, and R_f is the BTROR on a tax-favored investment having the same risk level as the benchmark. (Later in this chapter, we will show the problem with comparing investments of unequal risk.) Dividing the implicit tax by the benchmark BTROR (R_b) converts the implicit tax (IT) to an implicit tax *rate* (t_I), expressed as follows:

$$t_I = \frac{R_b - R_f}{R_b}$$

EXAMPLE I18-26 ▶ Maria invests $1,000 in a taxable bond that yields a 10% BTROR and another $1,000 in a tax-exempt bond that yields a 7.2% BTROR (i.e., R_b = 10%, and R_f = 7.2%). Maria's marginal tax rate is 28% (i.e., t = 28%). The two investments yield the following earnings each year:

	Taxable Bond	Tax-Exempt Bond
Before-tax interest	$100	$72
Minus: Tax on interest	(28)	0
After-tax interest	$ 72	$72

Although the tax-exempt bond is free from explicit taxation, it reflects a 2.8% implicit tax, which is $R_b - R_f$ = 10% − 7.2% = 2.8%. Here, we express the implicit tax as a 2.8% reduction in the BTROR. Stated in dollars, the implicit tax is $1,000 × 0.028 = $28. Thus, Maria incurs a $28 explicit tax on the taxable bond and a $28 implicit tax on the tax-exempt bond. Maria's implicit tax *rate* on the tax-exempt bond is 28%, calculated as follows:

$$t_I = \frac{R_b - R_f}{R_b} = \frac{10\% - 7.2\%}{10\%} = 0.28 \text{ or } 28\%$$

Thus, Maria incurs a 28% explicit tax *rate* on the taxable bond and a 28% implicit tax *rate* on the tax-exempt bond.

Maria's ATROR on each bond is 7.2%. For the taxable bond, the ATROR is calculated as follows: $r_b = R_b (1 - t) = 10\% (1 - 0.28) = 7.2\%$. For the tax-exempt bond, the ATROR is the same as the BTROR. ◀

ADDITIONAL COMMENT

Tax return filings show that higher income taxpayers do invest in tax-exempt bonds more than lower income taxpayers. For those returns reporting tax-exempt interest in 1993, taxpayers with AGI of over $1 million averaged 19 times more tax-exempt interest than taxpayers with AGI between $40,000 and $50,000.

EQUILIBRIUM CONDITION AND CLIENTELES. The degree to which R_f falls in relation to R_b depends on the marginal investor's tax rate. By definition, marginal investors are indifferent between fully-taxable and tax-favored investments. As marginal investors compete for a tax-favored investment, supply and demand forces drive up its price (and reduce its BTROR) to the point where the ATRORs of the fully-taxable and tax-favored investments are equal. That is, in equilibrium for marginal investors, the ATRORs for investments meet the following condition: $r_b = r_f$. For example, in Example I18-26, Maria is a marginal investor because $r_b = r_f = 7.2\%$. Thus, Maria is indifferent between the two investments.

In Example I18-26, Maria incurred a 28% tax rate on each investment, explicit on the fully-taxable bond and implicit on the tax-exempt bond. Thus, Maria did not realize a tax benefit on the tax-exempt bond. In fact, the term "tax-exempt" is a misnomer when implicit taxes are considered. The issuer of the tax-exempt bond, however, received a tax subsidy in the form of a reduced interest rate. Therefore, the transaction works as though Maria paid a tax while the bond issuer received a subsidy.

This result leads to the following question: Can any investor benefit from tax-exempt bonds? In a flat-rate tax system where only one tax rate prevails, the answer is no because all investors are marginal investors. In a progressive tax rate system, however, the answer is yes for an investor whose marginal tax rate exceeds that of the marginal investor. In this situation, investors form natural clienteles for the alternative investments.

EXAMPLE I18-27 ▶ Assume the same facts as in Example I18-26, where Maria is the indifferent marginal investor. Consider two other investors, Silvia and Bob. Silvia's tax rate is 40%, and Bob's tax rate is 15%. If Silvia invested in a fully-taxable bond, her ATROR would be as follows: $r_b = 10\% (1 - 0.4) = 6\%$. Consequently, Silvia will prefer the tax-exempt bond that yields a 7.2% ATROR (which also equals its BTROR). Silvia's high tax rate puts her in the clientele for tax-exempt bonds. By investing in the tax-exempt bond, Silvia converts her 40% explicit tax rate into a 28% implicit tax rate, thereby giving her the higher ATROR.

Topic Review I18-4

Implicit Taxes

Implicit tax:
$$IT = R_b - R_f$$

Implicit tax rate:
$$t_i = \frac{R_b - R_f}{R_b}$$

Equilibrium condition for marginal investor:
$$r_b = r_f.$$

Definitions of Variables:

IT = Implicit tax

t_i = Implicit tax rate

R_b = BTROR on a fully-taxable benchmark investment

R_f = Risk-adjusted BTROR on a tax-favored investment

r_b = ATROR on a fully-taxable benchmark investment

r_f = Risk-adjusted ATROR on a tax-favored investment

If Bob invests in the fully-taxable bond, his ATROR will be as follows: r_b = 10% (1 − 0.15) = 8.5%. Thus, Bob prefers the fully-taxable bond because he obtains an 8.5% ATROR rather than 7.2% from the tax-exempt bond. Bob's low tax rate puts him in the clientele for taxable bonds. If he mistakenly invests in the tax-exempt bond, he will convert a 15% explicit tax rate into a 28% implicit tax rate. Therefore, he should avoid the tax-exempt bond. ◄

Example I18-27 highlights a key planning concept. Investors must consider the ATRORs of investments in making their investment decisions. Doing so will ensure that all tax effects are accounted for, including implicit as well as explicit taxes.

RISKY ASSETS. A key requirement for calculating the implicit tax rate on a tax-favored investment is that the risk level be the same as the benchmark investment. The BTROR of a risky asset has two components, the riskless return and a risk premium. This relationship can be formulated as follows:

$$\tilde{R} = R + P$$

In this formula, $\tilde{R}$ is the risky return, R is the riskless return, and P is the risk premium. Investors who invest in risky assets require this premium as an incentive to make the investment. If the benchmark investment is a fully-taxable, riskless bond, the tax-favored investment's BTROR must be adjusted to remove this risk premium to obtain an accurate measure of the implicit tax rate.

EXAMPLE I18-28 ▶ A tax-exempt bond issued by Troubled City is highly risky and therefore yields a 12% BTROR, which is composed of a 6.9% riskless return and a 5.1% risk premium. A riskless benchmark investment yields a 10% BTROR. Computing the implicit tax rate with the 12% return yields the following incorrect (and negative) implicit tax rate:

$$t_i = \frac{R_b - \tilde{R}_f}{R_b} = \frac{10\% - 12\%}{10\%} = -0.2 \text{ or } -20\%$$

The correct implicit tax rate is calculated with the risk-adjusted return as follows:

$$t_I = \frac{R_b - R_f}{R_b} = \frac{10\% - 6.9\%}{10\%} = 0.31 \text{ or } 31\%$$ ◀

SUMMARY. Market forces drive down the BTRORs of tax-favored assets. This reduced return is an implicit tax. Thus, potential tax benefits to a marginal investor are competed away, thereby providing an implicit subsidy to the asset's issuer or seller. Investors whose tax rate exceeds that of the marginal investor, however, can still reap some benefit through the clientele effect. Topic Review I18-4 summarizes the implicit tax rate formula.

PROBLEM MATERIALS

DISCUSSION QUESTIONS

I18-1 What is the primary distinguishing feature that causes the Current Model, Deferred Model, and Pension Model to differ?

I18-2 What is an annualized ATROR, and why is it useful?

I18-3 Why might an investment in a capital asset be preferable to an investment that is fully taxed currently even though the capital asset's BTROR is less than that of the fully-taxable investment?

I18-4 Suppose a taxpayer is trying to decide between saving outside an IRA or saving through an IRA. If the taxpayer needs the savings before reaching age 59½, should he or she necessarily avoid the IRA because of the 10% early withdrawal penalty? Why or why not?

I18-5 How does the length of the investment horizon affect the annualized ATROR of an investment conforming to the Deferred Model?

I18-6 Under what conditions are the Exempt Model and Pension Model equivalent? Under what conditions would one model perform better than the other?

I18-7 What characteristics of a C corporation cause the shareholder's stock investment to conform to the Deferred Model?

I18-8 How does the tax treatment of deferred compensation differ from the tax treatment of current salary?

I18-9 What is the variable, D_n, and why is it important to the current salary versus deferred compensation decision?

I18-10 Why might the employee and/or employer prefer salary over deferred compensation even in cases where deferred compensation provides the better tax results?

I18-11 Why might an investment conforming to the Exempt Model have a lower BTROR than an equivalent-risk investment conforming to the Current Model?

I18-12 What is an implicit tax and how does it arise?

I18-13 What forces cause ATRORs of various investments to be equal for marginal investors?

I18-14 What is a clientele effect, and what conditions are necessary for it to occur?

I18-15 An article that appeared in the September 30, 1993 issue of *The Wall Street Journal* (p. A18) made the following statement:

At the highest federal tax rates . . . dividends and interest from private sector investments are taxed at 39.6%, capital gains at 28%, while interest from state and local debt instruments isn't taxed at all.

What problem do you see with the author's statement?

I18-16 Why would a flat-rate tax system eliminate clientele effects?

I18-17 Why might the BTROR on a tax-favored investment be higher than the BTROR on a fully-taxable investment even though implicit tax theory says that it should be lower?

I18-18 We have discussed implicit taxes using tax-exempt bonds as an example, and we have mentioned capital gains assets as another case where implicit taxes might occur. Give one or two other specific tax provisions that might cause implicit taxes to arise. In so doing, explain:

- How the implicit tax is manifested (e.g., increased prices, reduced returns, increased costs, etc.).

- Who "pays" the implicit tax.

- Who "receives" the implicit subsidy.

PROBLEMS

I18-19   *Tax-Exempt Bond.* Laura, who is in the 40% tax bracket, notices that tax-exempt municipal bonds are yielding a 7% return. What before-tax rate of return on a fully-taxable bond must Laura obtain to make her prefer the taxable bond over the tax-exempt bond?

I18-20   *After-Tax Rates of Return.* Suppose a bond is taxable for both federal and state purposes. Let R_b = the BTROR on the bond, t_{fed} = the federal tax rate, and t_{st} = the state tax rate. Determine the ATROR (i.e., after federal and state taxes) if:
a. The state tax is *not* deductible for either federal or state purposes.
b. The state tax *is* deductible for federal but not for state purposes.
After algebraic simplification, each answer should take the form: R_b [   ], with the rest of the answer inside the brackets.

I18-21   *Investment Models.* David can make a single investment in one of three alternatives. The first investment conforms to the Current Model, the second investment conforms to the Deferred Model, and the third investment conforms to the Pension Model. The investment horizon is 7 years, and the BTROR for each alternative is 10%. David will incur no penalties upon withdrawal.
a. Assuming David's tax rate will be 15% for all 7 years, what is the accumulation and annualized ATROR for each investment. Which alternative should David choose?
b. Assuming David's tax rate will be 15% for the first 6 years but will be 28% in the seventh year, what is the accumulation and annualized ATROR for each investment. Which alternative should David choose?

I18-22   *Investment Models.* Mark is considering investing in either a tax-exempt municipal bond that yields 7% or a nondeductible IRA that contains investments that yield 10% before taxes. Mark's current tax rate is 40%, and he plans to make a single investment now with a 15-year investment horizon.
a. Using after-tax accumulations and annualized ATRORs, show that the nondeductible IRA outperforms the municipal bonds assuming Mark's tax rate remains at 40%. Assume no additional penalty upon withdrawal from the IRA.
b. How high would Mark's tax rate have to rise in Year n to make the municipal bond more attractive than the nondeductible IRA. Assume the 7% and 10% BTRORs remain constant over time.

I18-23   *Investment Models and IRAs.* Brenda has $2,000 of before-tax dollars available for a one-time investment. She is in the 28% bracket and expects to remain in this bracket indefinitely. She can invest directly in a taxable bond yielding 8% before taxes, or she can open an IRA and invest in the bond within the IRA. She knows that she will need the accumulated funds before she reaches age 59½. Thus, if she invests in an IRA, she will incur a 10% penalty on taxable amounts withdrawn from the IRA. Note: The two parts to this problem are best solved using a spreadsheet.
a. If she invests in an IRA that allows immediate deduction of contributed amounts, how many years must she wait before the IRA is a better vehicle than direct investment in the bond outside the IRA?
b. How many years must she wait if she is allowed no deduction for IRA contributions?

I18-24 ***Investment Planning.*** Martha, who is in the 40% tax bracket, has $40,000 of before-tax income with which she wants to make a one-time investment. She wants to put $20,000 of this income in a deductible H.R. 10 plan, and she wants to invest any remaining after-tax income outside the H.R. 10 plan. Two investments are available: (1) a taxable bond yielding a 10% before-tax rate of return and (2) a nondividend paying stock that appreciates at a 10% annual rate before taxes. She is considering two alternatives:
1. Have the H.R 10 plan invest in the stock, and Martha will invest in the bond outside the H.R. 10 plan.
2. Have the H.R 10 plan invest in the bond, and Martha will invest in the stock outside the H.R 10 plan.

The investment horizon is 10 years with tax rates constant over this period. Capital gains upon sale of stock outside the H.R 10 plan are taxed at 28%. However, if the stock is placed in the H.R 10 plan, the H.R 10 plan will sell the stock after 10 years and distribute the proceeds to Martha, triggering ordinary income recognition to Martha. Assume no early withdrawal penalties on H.R 10 plan distributions. Determine the total after-tax accumulation of Alternative 1 and of Alternative 2. Which of the two alternatives should Martha choose?

I18-25 ***Multiperiod Investment Strategy.*** Given the following facts and assumptions, determine what investment strategy Karen should follow to maximize accumulations and how much she will have accumulated at the *beginning* of Year 10 (including her last paycheck).

- Karen's ordinary tax rate is 31%, and her long-term capital gains tax rate is 28%. These rates will remain constant over her investment horizon.

- Karen earns $20,000 per year, which she receives on the first day of each year.

- Karen saves all her income after paying income taxes on her earnings. Taxes are payable immediately upon receiving her paycheck.

- At the beginning of each year, Karen can invest her savings in any of three vehicles:
  1. A money market fund yielding 6% per year before taxes,
  2. An IRA that yields 6% per year before taxes, and/or
  3. Capital assets that grow at 5.6% per year before taxes.

- IRA contributions are limited to $2,000 per year and are deductible up to that amount.

- At the beginning of Year 10, Karen saves no more income. Instead, she withdraws any IRA and/or money market accumulations and sells her capital assets for their accumulated FMV before taxes. She also receives a $20,000 paycheck at the beginning of Year 10.

- IRA accumulations are taxable immediately upon withdrawal with no additional penalty.

- Ignore itemized deductions, standard deductions, exemptions, etc.

I18-26 ***Proprietorship versus C Corporation.*** Myron has $10,000 to invest in a business. He can either (1) operate as a sole proprietor or (2) form a regular C corporation by contributing the $10,000 in exchange for corporate stock. In either case, the $10,000 will be invested in business assets and will earn a 10% before-tax rate of return for the first 5 years and a 20% before-tax rate of return for years 6 through 15. All after-tax earnings will be reinvested in the business. If Myron uses the corporate form, the corporation will liquidate at the end of the investment horizon. Myron's personal tax rate is 40%; the corporate tax rate is 25%; and the maximum tax rate on capital gains for individuals is 28% (assume no 50% exclusion). Determine whether Myron should operate as a sole proprietor or form a C corporation if the investment horizon is 15 years. Show the after-tax accumulation for each alternative.

I18-27   *S Corporation versus C corporation.* Prior to 1993 Tax Act changes to tax rates, S corporations were very popular. Using the data below, compare S corporation status to C corporation status before and after the 1993 Tax Act.

Variable	Pre-1993 Act	Post-1993 Act	Description of Variables
R	12%	12%	BTROR to S or C corporation
t_p	31%	40%	Shareholder's ordinary tax rate
t_c	34%	34%	C corporation tax rate
t_g	28%	14%*	Long-term capital gains tax rate
n	30	30	Investment horizon

The C corporation pays no dividends, and the S corporation distributes annually only enough for the shareholder to pay current taxes. *Note: The 14% rate reflects the 28% maximum rate on long-term capital gains in conjunction with the 50% exclusion on certain small business investments held more than 5 years.

a. What is the shareholder's 30-year accumulation for a $1 investment under Pre-1993 law for S and C corporation status? Which is better?

b. What is the shareholder's 30-year accumulation for a $1 investment under Post-1993 law for S and C corporation status? Which is better?

I18-28   *Current Salary versus Deferred Compensation.* Consider Marsha and Todd from Example I18-25 in the text. Suppose these employees worked for Learned University, a tax-exempt organization, instead of a taxable corporation. Would the university be willing to pay deferred compensation to either employee? If so, how much? That is, what is the university's indifference level of D_n?

I18-29   *Current Salary versus Deferred Compensation.* Sandy will earn a $100,000 bonus that can be split between current and deferred compensation in any of the following ways:

Current (BT$)*	Deferred (BT$)*
$100,000	$ 0
80,000	20,000
60,000	40,000
40,000	60,000
20,000	80,000
0	100,000

* The numbers in the above lists are BT$ as in the text formulas. Thus, the numbers in the second column are not BT$ × D_n.

Assume that Sandy is subject to the following progressive tax rate schedule in the current and future years:

Income Range	Marginal Tax Rate	Computation of Tax
$ 0–$20,000	30.0%	0.30 × TI
20,001– 40,000	32.5	$ 6,000 + 0.325 (TI − $20,000)
40,001– 60,000	35.0	$12,500 + 0.35 (TI − $40,000)
60,001– 80,000	37.5	$19,500 + 0.375 (TI − $60,000)
Over $80,000	40.0	$27,000 + 0.4 (TI − $80,000)

- Corporate tax rates are as follows: t_{co} = .35, t_{cn} = .34.
- Rates of return are as follows: r_{cn} = .08; r_{pn} = .07.
- The length of deferral is 5 years, i.e., n = 5.

What is the best way for Sandy to split the $100,000 bonus given a level of D_n that makes the corporation indifferent?

I18-30 *Implicit Tax Rates and Clientele Effects.* Terry's marginal tax rate is 28%. He can invest in a taxable bond yielding 7.5% before taxes. What is the implicit tax rate on a tax-exempt bond of equivalent risk that yields 6%?

a. Which bond should Terry invest in? Why?

b. How would your answer to Part a change if Terry's statutory marginal tax rate were 15%?

I18-31 *Implicit Tax Rates and Clientele Effects.* Consider three taxpayers who are in the following tax brackets:

Alice	28%
Brad	36%
Camille	40%

The BTROR on a benchmark investment is 10% (i.e., $R_b = 10\%$). Compute the equilibrium BTROR and the implicit tax rate on a tax-exempt bond under each of the following three alternative assumptions.

a. Alice is the marginal investor.

b. Brad is the marginal investor.

c. Camille is the marginal investor.

d. Which taxpayer (Alice, Brad, or Camille) would Camille like to see be the marginal investor? Why?

1996 TAX TABLES
AND RATE SCHEDULES

Section 5.

1996 Tax Table

Use if your taxable income is less than $100,000.
If $100,000 or more, use the Tax Rate Schedules.

Example. Mr. and Mrs. Brown are filing a joint return. Their taxable income on line 37 of Form 1040 is $25,300. First, they find the $25,300–25,350 income line. Next, they find the column for married filing jointly and read down the column. The amount shown where the income line and filing status column meet is $3,799. This is the tax amount they should enter on line 38 of their Form 1040.

Sample Table

At least	But less than	Single	Married filing jointly *	Married filing separately	Head of a household
			Your tax is—		
25,200	25,250	3,943	3,784	4,457	3,784
25,250	25,300	3,957	3,791	4,471	3,791
25,300	25,350	3,971	(3,799)	4,485	3,799
25,350	25,400	3,985	3,806	4,499	3,806

If line 37 (taxable income) is—		And you are—				If line 37 (taxable income) is—		And you are—				If line 37 (taxable income) is—		And you are—			
At least	But less than	Single	Married filing jointly *	Married filing separately	Head of a household	At least	But less than	Single	Married filing jointly *	Married filing separately	Head of a household	At least	But less than	Single	Married filing jointly *	Married filing separately	Head of a household
		Your tax is—						Your tax is—						Your tax is—			
0	5	0	0	0	0	1,300	1,325	197	197	197	197	2,700	2,725	407	407	407	407
5	15	2	2	2	2	1,325	1,350	201	201	201	201	2,725	2,750	411	411	411	411
						1,350	1,375	204	204	204	204	2,750	2,775	414	414	414	414
15	25	3	3	3	3	1,375	1,400	208	208	208	208	2,775	2,800	418	418	418	418
25	50	6	6	6	6	1,400	1,425	212	212	212	212	2,800	2,825	422	422	422	422
50	75	9	9	9	9	1,425	1,450	216	216	216	216	2,825	2,850	426	426	426	426
75	100	13	13	13	13	1,450	1,475	219	219	219	219	2,850	2,875	429	429	429	429
100	125	17	17	17	17	1,475	1,500	223	223	223	223	2,875	2,900	433	433	433	433
125	150	21	21	21	21	1,500	1,525	227	227	227	227	2,900	2,925	437	437	437	437
150	175	24	24	24	24	1,525	1,550	231	231	231	231	2,925	2,950	441	441	441	441
175	200	28	28	28	28	1,550	1,575	234	234	234	234	2,950	2,975	444	444	444	444
200	225	32	32	32	32	1,575	1,600	238	238	238	238	2,975	3,000	448	448	448	448
225	250	36	36	36	36	1,600	1,625	242	242	242	242	**3,000**					
250	275	39	39	39	39	1,625	1,650	246	246	246	246	3,000	3,050	454	454	454	454
275	300	43	43	43	43	1,650	1,675	249	249	249	249	3,050	3,100	461	461	461	461
300	325	47	47	47	47	1,675	1,700	253	253	253	253	3,100	3,150	469	469	469	469
325	350	51	51	51	51	1,700	1,725	257	257	257	257	3,150	3,200	476	476	476	476
350	375	54	54	54	54	1,725	1,750	261	261	261	261	3,200	3,250	484	484	484	484
375	400	58	58	58	58	1,750	1,775	264	264	264	264	3,250	3,300	491	491	491	491
400	425	62	62	62	62	1,775	1,800	268	268	268	268	3,300	3,350	499	499	499	499
425	450	66	66	66	66	1,800	1,825	272	272	272	272	3,350	3,400	506	506	506	506
450	475	69	69	69	69	1,825	1,850	276	276	276	276	3,400	3,450	514	514	514	514
475	500	73	73	73	73	1,850	1,875	279	279	279	279	3,450	3,500	521	521	521	521
500	525	77	77	77	77	1,875	1,900	283	283	283	283	3,500	3,550	529	529	529	529
525	550	81	81	81	81	1,900	1,925	287	287	287	287	3,550	3,600	536	536	536	536
550	575	84	84	84	84	1,925	1,950	291	291	291	291	3,600	3,650	544	544	544	544
575	600	88	88	88	88	1,950	1,975	294	294	294	294	3,650	3,700	551	551	551	551
600	625	92	92	92	92	1,975	2,000	298	298	298	298	3,700	3,750	559	559	559	559
625	650	96	96	96	96	**2,000**						3,750	3,800	566	566	566	566
650	675	99	99	99	99	2,000	2,025	302	302	302	302	3,800	3,850	574	574	574	574
675	700	103	103	103	103	2,025	2,050	306	306	306	306	3,850	3,900	581	581	581	581
700	725	107	107	107	107	2,050	2,075	309	309	309	309	3,900	3,950	589	589	589	589
725	750	111	111	111	111	2,075	2,100	313	313	313	313	3,950	4,000	596	596	596	596
750	775	114	114	114	114	2,100	2,125	317	317	317	317	**4,000**					
775	800	118	118	118	118	2,125	2,150	321	321	321	321	4,000	4,050	604	604	604	604
800	825	122	122	122	122	2,150	2,175	324	324	324	324	4,050	4,100	611	611	611	611
825	850	126	126	126	126	2,175	2,200	328	328	328	328	4,100	4,150	619	619	619	619
850	875	129	129	129	129	2,200	2,225	332	332	332	332	4,150	4,200	626	626	626	626
875	900	133	133	133	133	2,225	2,250	336	336	336	336	4,200	4,250	634	634	634	634
900	925	137	137	137	137	2,250	2,275	339	339	339	339	4,250	4,300	641	641	641	641
925	950	141	141	141	141	2,275	2,300	343	343	343	343	4,300	4,350	649	649	649	649
950	975	144	144	144	144	2,300	2,325	347	347	347	347	4,350	4,400	656	656	656	656
975	1,000	148	148	148	148	2,325	2,350	351	351	351	351	4,400	4,450	664	664	664	664
1,000						2,350	2,375	354	354	354	354	4,450	4,500	671	671	671	671
1,000	1,025	152	152	152	152	2,375	2,400	358	358	358	358	4,500	4,550	679	679	679	679
1,025	1,050	156	156	156	156	2,400	2,425	362	362	362	362	4,550	4,600	686	686	686	686
1,050	1,075	159	159	159	159	2,425	2,450	366	366	366	366	4,600	4,650	694	694	694	694
1,075	1,100	163	163	163	163	2,450	2,475	369	369	369	369	4,650	4,700	701	701	701	701
1,100	1,125	167	167	167	167	2,475	2,500	373	373	373	373	4,700	4,750	709	709	709	709
1,125	1,150	171	171	171	171	2,500	2,525	377	377	377	377	4,750	4,800	716	716	716	716
1,150	1,175	174	174	174	174	2,525	2,550	381	381	381	381	4,800	4,850	724	724	724	724
1,175	1,200	178	178	178	178	2,550	2,575	384	384	384	384	4,850	4,900	731	731	731	731
1,200	1,225	182	182	182	182	2,575	2,600	388	388	388	388	4,900	4,950	739	739	739	739
1,225	1,250	186	186	186	186	2,600	2,625	392	392	392	392	4,950	5,000	746	746	746	746
1,250	1,275	189	189	189	189	2,625	2,650	396	396	396	396						
1,275	1,300	193	193	193	193	2,650	2,675	399	399	399	399						
						2,675	2,700	403	403	403	403						

Continued on next page

* This column must also be used by a qualifying widow(er).

1996 Tax Table—*Continued*

If line 37 (taxable income) is—		And you are—				If line 37 (taxable income) is—		And you are—				If line 37 (taxable income) is—		And you are—			
At least	But less than	Single	Married filing jointly *	Married filing separately	Head of a household	At least	But less than	Single	Married filing jointly *	Married filing separately	Head of a household	At least	But less than	Single	Married filing jointly *	Married filing separately	Head of a household
		Your tax is—						Your tax is—						Your tax is—			

5,000

At least	But less than	Single	MFJ	MFS	HoH	At least	But less than	Single	MFJ	MFS	HoH	At least	But less than	Single	MFJ	MFS	HoH
5,000	5,050	754	754	754	754	8,000	8,050	1,204	1,204	1,204	1,204	11,000	11,050	1,654	1,654	1,654	1,654
5,050	5,100	761	761	761	761	8,050	8,100	1,211	1,211	1,211	1,211	11,050	11,100	1,661	1,661	1,661	1,661
5,100	5,150	769	769	769	769	8,100	8,150	1,219	1,219	1,219	1,219	11,100	11,150	1,669	1,669	1,669	1,669
5,150	5,200	776	776	776	776	8,150	8,200	1,226	1,226	1,226	1,226	11,150	11,200	1,676	1,676	1,676	1,676
5,200	5,250	784	784	784	784	8,200	8,250	1,234	1,234	1,234	1,234	11,200	11,250	1,684	1,684	1,684	1,684
5,250	5,300	791	791	791	791	8,250	8,300	1,241	1,241	1,241	1,241	11,250	11,300	1,691	1,691	1,691	1,691
5,300	5,350	799	799	799	799	8,300	8,350	1,249	1,249	1,249	1,249	11,300	11,350	1,699	1,699	1,699	1,699
5,350	5,400	806	806	806	806	8,350	8,400	1,256	1,256	1,256	1,256	11,350	11,400	1,706	1,706	1,706	1,706
5,400	5,450	814	814	814	814	8,400	8,450	1,264	1,264	1,264	1,264	11,400	11,450	1,714	1,714	1,714	1,714
5,450	5,500	821	821	821	821	8,450	8,500	1,271	1,271	1,271	1,271	11,450	11,500	1,721	1,721	1,721	1,721
5,500	5,550	829	829	829	829	8,500	8,550	1,279	1,279	1,279	1,279	11,500	11,550	1,729	1,729	1,729	1,729
5,550	5,600	836	836	836	836	8,550	8,600	1,286	1,286	1,286	1,286	11,550	11,600	1,736	1,736	1,736	1,736
5,600	5,650	844	844	844	844	8,600	8,650	1,294	1,294	1,294	1,294	11,600	11,650	1,744	1,744	1,744	1,744
5,650	5,700	851	851	851	851	8,650	8,700	1,301	1,301	1,301	1,301	11,650	11,700	1,751	1,751	1,751	1,751
5,700	5,750	859	859	859	859	8,700	8,750	1,309	1,309	1,309	1,309	11,700	11,750	1,759	1,759	1,759	1,759
5,750	5,800	866	866	866	866	8,750	8,800	1,316	1,316	1,316	1,316	11,750	11,800	1,766	1,766	1,766	1,766
5,800	5,850	874	874	874	874	8,800	8,850	1,324	1,324	1,324	1,324	11,800	11,850	1,774	1,774	1,774	1,774
5,850	5,900	881	881	881	881	8,850	8,900	1,331	1,331	1,331	1,331	11,850	11,900	1,781	1,781	1,781	1,781
5,900	5,950	889	889	889	889	8,900	8,950	1,339	1,339	1,339	1,339	11,900	11,950	1,789	1,789	1,789	1,789
5,950	6,000	896	896	896	896	8,950	9,000	1,346	1,346	1,346	1,346	11,950	12,000	1,796	1,796	1,796	1,796

6,000 / **9,000** / **12,000**

At least	But less than	Single	MFJ	MFS	HoH	At least	But less than	Single	MFJ	MFS	HoH	At least	But less than	Single	MFJ	MFS	HoH
6,000	6,050	904	904	904	904	9,000	9,050	1,354	1,354	1,354	1,354	12,000	12,050	1,804	1,804	1,804	1,804
6,050	6,100	911	911	911	911	9,050	9,100	1,361	1,361	1,361	1,361	12,050	12,100	1,811	1,811	1,811	1,811
6,100	6,150	919	919	919	919	9,100	9,150	1,369	1,369	1,369	1,369	12,100	12,150	1,819	1,819	1,819	1,819
6,150	6,200	926	926	926	926	9,150	9,200	1,376	1,376	1,376	1,376	12,150	12,200	1,826	1,826	1,826	1,826
6,200	6,250	934	934	934	934	9,200	9,250	1,384	1,384	1,384	1,384	12,200	12,250	1,834	1,834	1,834	1,834
6,250	6,300	941	941	941	941	9,250	9,300	1,391	1,391	1,391	1,391	12,250	12,300	1,841	1,841	1,841	1,841
6,300	6,350	949	949	949	949	9,300	9,350	1,399	1,399	1,399	1,399	12,300	12,350	1,849	1,849	1,849	1,849
6,350	6,400	956	956	956	956	9,350	9,400	1,406	1,406	1,406	1,406	12,350	12,400	1,856	1,856	1,856	1,856
6,400	6,450	964	964	964	964	9,400	9,450	1,414	1,414	1,414	1,414	12,400	12,450	1,864	1,864	1,864	1,864
6,450	6,500	971	971	971	971	9,450	9,500	1,421	1,421	1,421	1,421	12,450	12,500	1,871	1,871	1,871	1,871
6,500	6,550	979	979	979	979	9,500	9,550	1,429	1,429	1,429	1,429	12,500	12,550	1,879	1,879	1,879	1,879
6,550	6,600	986	986	986	986	9,550	9,600	1,436	1,436	1,436	1,436	12,550	12,600	1,886	1,886	1,886	1,886
6,600	6,650	994	994	994	994	9,600	9,650	1,444	1,444	1,444	1,444	12,600	12,650	1,894	1,894	1,894	1,894
6,650	6,700	1,001	1,001	1,001	1,001	9,650	9,700	1,451	1,451	1,451	1,451	12,650	12,700	1,901	1,901	1,901	1,901
6,700	6,750	1,009	1,009	1,009	1,009	9,700	9,750	1,459	1,459	1,459	1,459	12,700	12,750	1,909	1,909	1,909	1,909
6,750	6,800	1,016	1,016	1,016	1,016	9,750	9,800	1,466	1,466	1,466	1,466	12,750	12,800	1,916	1,916	1,916	1,916
6,800	6,850	1,024	1,024	1,024	1,024	9,800	9,850	1,474	1,474	1,474	1,474	12,800	12,850	1,924	1,924	1,924	1,924
6,850	6,900	1,031	1,031	1,031	1,031	9,850	9,900	1,481	1,481	1,481	1,481	12,850	12,900	1,931	1,931	1,931	1,931
6,900	6,950	1,039	1,039	1,039	1,039	9,900	9,950	1,489	1,489	1,489	1,489	12,900	12,950	1,939	1,939	1,939	1,939
6,950	7,000	1,046	1,046	1,046	1,046	9,950	10,000	1,496	1,496	1,496	1,496	12,950	13,000	1,946	1,946	1,946	1,946

7,000 / **10,000** / **13,000**

At least	But less than	Single	MFJ	MFS	HoH	At least	But less than	Single	MFJ	MFS	HoH	At least	But less than	Single	MFJ	MFS	HoH
7,000	7,050	1,054	1,054	1,054	1,054	10,000	10,050	1,504	1,504	1,504	1,504	13,000	13,050	1,954	1,954	1,954	1,954
7,050	7,100	1,061	1,061	1,061	1,061	10,050	10,100	1,511	1,511	1,511	1,511	13,050	13,100	1,961	1,961	1,961	1,961
7,100	7,150	1,069	1,069	1,069	1,069	10,100	10,150	1,519	1,519	1,519	1,519	13,100	13,150	1,969	1,969	1,969	1,969
7,150	7,200	1,076	1,076	1,076	1,076	10,150	10,200	1,526	1,526	1,526	1,526	13,150	13,200	1,976	1,976	1,976	1,976
7,200	7,250	1,084	1,084	1,084	1,084	10,200	10,250	1,534	1,534	1,534	1,534	13,200	13,250	1,984	1,984	1,984	1,984
7,250	7,300	1,091	1,091	1,091	1,091	10,250	10,300	1,541	1,541	1,541	1,541	13,250	13,300	1,991	1,991	1,991	1,991
7,300	7,350	1,099	1,099	1,099	1,099	10,300	10,350	1,549	1,549	1,549	1,549	13,300	13,350	1,999	1,999	1,999	1,999
7,350	7,400	1,106	1,106	1,106	1,106	10,350	10,400	1,556	1,556	1,556	1,556	13,350	13,400	2,006	2,006	2,006	2,006
7,400	7,450	1,114	1,114	1,114	1,114	10,400	10,450	1,564	1,564	1,564	1,564	13,400	13,450	2,014	2,014	2,014	2,014
7,450	7,500	1,121	1,121	1,121	1,121	10,450	10,500	1,571	1,571	1,571	1,571	13,450	13,500	2,021	2,021	2,021	2,021
7,500	7,550	1,129	1,129	1,129	1,129	10,500	10,550	1,579	1,579	1,579	1,579	13,500	13,550	2,029	2,029	2,029	2,029
7,550	7,600	1,136	1,136	1,136	1,136	10,550	10,600	1,586	1,586	1,586	1,586	13,550	13,600	2,036	2,036	2,036	2,036
7,600	7,650	1,144	1,144	1,144	1,144	10,600	10,650	1,594	1,594	1,594	1,594	13,600	13,650	2,044	2,044	2,044	2,044
7,650	7,700	1,151	1,151	1,151	1,151	10,650	10,700	1,601	1,601	1,601	1,601	13,650	13,700	2,051	2,051	2,051	2,051
7,700	7,750	1,159	1,159	1,159	1,159	10,700	10,750	1,609	1,609	1,609	1,609	13,700	13,750	2,059	2,059	2,059	2,059
7,750	7,800	1,166	1,166	1,166	1,166	10,750	10,800	1,616	1,616	1,616	1,616	13,750	13,800	2,066	2,066	2,066	2,066
7,800	7,850	1,174	1,174	1,174	1,174	10,800	10,850	1,624	1,624	1,624	1,624	13,800	13,850	2,074	2,074	2,074	2,074
7,850	7,900	1,181	1,181	1,181	1,181	10,850	10,900	1,631	1,631	1,631	1,631	13,850	13,900	2,081	2,081	2,081	2,081
7,900	7,950	1,189	1,189	1,189	1,189	10,900	10,950	1,639	1,639	1,639	1,639	13,900	13,950	2,089	2,089	2,089	2,089
7,950	8,000	1,196	1,196	1,196	1,196	10,950	11,000	1,646	1,646	1,646	1,646	13,950	14,000	2,096	2,096	2,096	2,096

* This column must also be used by a qualifying widow(er).

Continued on next page

1996 Tax Table—Continued

If line 37 (taxable income) is—		And you are—			
At least	But less than	Single	Married filing jointly *	Married filing separately	Head of a household
		Your tax is—			

14,000

At least	But less than	Single	Married filing jointly	Married filing separately	Head of a household
14,000	14,050	2,104	2,104	2,104	2,104
14,050	14,100	2,111	2,111	2,111	2,111
14,100	14,150	2,119	2,119	2,119	2,119
14,150	14,200	2,126	2,126	2,126	2,126
14,200	14,250	2,134	2,134	2,134	2,134
14,250	14,300	2,141	2,141	2,141	2,141
14,300	14,350	2,149	2,149	2,149	2,149
14,350	14,400	2,156	2,156	2,156	2,156
14,400	14,450	2,164	2,164	2,164	2,164
14,450	14,500	2,171	2,171	2,171	2,171
14,500	14,550	2,179	2,179	2,179	2,179
14,550	14,600	2,186	2,186	2,186	2,186
14,600	14,650	2,194	2,194	2,194	2,194
14,650	14,700	2,201	2,201	2,201	2,201
14,700	14,750	2,209	2,209	2,209	2,209
14,750	14,800	2,216	2,216	2,216	2,216
14,800	14,850	2,224	2,224	2,224	2,224
14,850	14,900	2,231	2,231	2,231	2,231
14,900	14,950	2,239	2,239	2,239	2,239
14,950	15,000	2,246	2,246	2,246	2,246

15,000

At least	But less than	Single	Married filing jointly	Married filing separately	Head of a household
15,000	15,050	2,254	2,254	2,254	2,254
15,050	15,100	2,261	2,261	2,261	2,261
15,100	15,150	2,269	2,269	2,269	2,269
15,150	15,200	2,276	2,276	2,276	2,276
15,200	15,250	2,284	2,284	2,284	2,284
15,250	15,300	2,291	2,291	2,291	2,291
15,300	15,350	2,299	2,299	2,299	2,299
15,350	15,400	2,306	2,306	2,306	2,306
15,400	15,450	2,314	2,314	2,314	2,314
15,450	15,500	2,321	2,321	2,321	2,321
15,500	15,550	2,329	2,329	2,329	2,329
15,550	15,600	2,336	2,336	2,336	2,336
15,600	15,650	2,344	2,344	2,344	2,344
15,650	15,700	2,351	2,351	2,351	2,351
15,700	15,750	2,359	2,359	2,359	2,359
15,750	15,800	2,366	2,366	2,366	2,366
15,800	15,850	2,374	2,374	2,374	2,374
15,850	15,900	2,381	2,381	2,381	2,381
15,900	15,950	2,389	2,389	2,389	2,389
15,950	16,000	2,396	2,396	2,396	2,396

16,000

At least	But less than	Single	Married filing jointly	Married filing separately	Head of a household
16,000	16,050	2,404	2,404	2,404	2,404
16,050	16,100	2,411	2,411	2,411	2,411
16,100	16,150	2,419	2,419	2,419	2,419
16,150	16,200	2,426	2,426	2,426	2,426
16,200	16,250	2,434	2,434	2,434	2,434
16,250	16,300	2,441	2,441	2,441	2,441
16,300	16,350	2,449	2,449	2,449	2,449
16,350	16,400	2,456	2,456	2,456	2,456
16,400	16,450	2,464	2,464	2,464	2,464
16,450	16,500	2,471	2,471	2,471	2,471
16,500	16,550	2,479	2,479	2,479	2,479
16,550	16,600	2,486	2,486	2,486	2,486
16,600	16,650	2,494	2,494	2,494	2,494
16,650	16,700	2,501	2,501	2,501	2,501
16,700	16,750	2,509	2,509	2,509	2,509
16,750	16,800	2,516	2,516	2,516	2,516
16,800	16,850	2,524	2,524	2,524	2,524
16,850	16,900	2,531	2,531	2,531	2,531
16,900	16,950	2,539	2,539	2,539	2,539
16,950	17,000	2,546	2,546	2,546	2,546

17,000

At least	But less than	Single	Married filing jointly	Married filing separately	Head of a household
17,000	17,050	2,554	2,554	2,554	2,554
17,050	17,100	2,561	2,561	2,561	2,561
17,100	17,150	2,569	2,569	2,569	2,569
17,150	17,200	2,576	2,576	2,576	2,576
17,200	17,250	2,584	2,584	2,584	2,584
17,250	17,300	2,591	2,591	2,591	2,591
17,300	17,350	2,599	2,599	2,599	2,599
17,350	17,400	2,606	2,606	2,606	2,606
17,400	17,450	2,614	2,614	2,614	2,614
17,450	17,500	2,621	2,621	2,621	2,621
17,500	17,550	2,629	2,629	2,629	2,629
17,550	17,600	2,636	2,636	2,636	2,636
17,600	17,650	2,644	2,644	2,644	2,644
17,650	17,700	2,651	2,651	2,651	2,651
17,700	17,750	2,659	2,659	2,659	2,659
17,750	17,800	2,666	2,666	2,666	2,666
17,800	17,850	2,674	2,674	2,674	2,674
17,850	17,900	2,681	2,681	2,681	2,681
17,900	17,950	2,689	2,689	2,689	2,689
17,950	18,000	2,696	2,696	2,696	2,696

18,000

At least	But less than	Single	Married filing jointly	Married filing separately	Head of a household
18,000	18,050	2,704	2,704	2,704	2,704
18,050	18,100	2,711	2,711	2,711	2,711
18,100	18,150	2,719	2,719	2,719	2,719
18,150	18,200	2,726	2,726	2,726	2,726
18,200	18,250	2,734	2,734	2,734	2,734
18,250	18,300	2,741	2,741	2,741	2,741
18,300	18,350	2,749	2,749	2,749	2,749
18,350	18,400	2,756	2,756	2,756	2,756
18,400	18,450	2,764	2,764	2,764	2,764
18,450	18,500	2,771	2,771	2,771	2,771
18,500	18,550	2,779	2,779	2,779	2,779
18,550	18,600	2,786	2,786	2,786	2,786
18,600	18,650	2,794	2,794	2,794	2,794
18,650	18,700	2,801	2,801	2,801	2,801
18,700	18,750	2,809	2,809	2,809	2,809
18,750	18,800	2,816	2,816	2,816	2,816
18,800	18,850	2,824	2,824	2,824	2,824
18,850	18,900	2,831	2,831	2,831	2,831
18,900	18,950	2,839	2,839	2,839	2,839
18,950	19,000	2,846	2,846	2,846	2,846

19,000

At least	But less than	Single	Married filing jointly	Married filing separately	Head of a household
19,000	19,050	2,854	2,854	2,854	2,854
19,050	19,100	2,861	2,861	2,861	2,861
19,100	19,150	2,869	2,869	2,869	2,869
19,150	19,200	2,876	2,876	2,876	2,876
19,200	19,250	2,884	2,884	2,884	2,884
19,250	19,300	2,891	2,891	2,891	2,891
19,300	19,350	2,899	2,899	2,899	2,899
19,350	19,400	2,906	2,906	2,906	2,906
19,400	19,450	2,914	2,914	2,914	2,914
19,450	19,500	2,921	2,921	2,921	2,921
19,500	19,550	2,929	2,929	2,929	2,929
19,550	19,600	2,936	2,936	2,936	2,936
19,600	19,650	2,944	2,944	2,944	2,944
19,650	19,700	2,951	2,951	2,951	2,951
19,700	19,750	2,959	2,959	2,959	2,959
19,750	19,800	2,966	2,966	2,966	2,966
19,800	19,850	2,974	2,974	2,974	2,974
19,850	19,900	2,981	2,981	2,981	2,981
19,900	19,950	2,989	2,989	2,989	2,989
19,950	20,000	2,996	2,996	2,996	2,996

20,000

At least	But less than	Single	Married filing jointly	Married filing separately	Head of a household
20,000	20,050	3,004	3,004	3,004	3,004
20,050	20,100	3,011	3,011	3,015	3,011
20,100	20,150	3,019	3,019	3,029	3,019
20,150	20,200	3,026	3,026	3,043	3,026
20,200	20,250	3,034	3,034	3,057	3,034
20,250	20,300	3,041	3,041	3,071	3,041
20,300	20,350	3,049	3,049	3,085	3,049
20,350	20,400	3,056	3,056	3,099	3,056
20,400	20,450	3,064	3,064	3,113	3,064
20,450	20,500	3,071	3,071	3,127	3,071
20,500	20,550	3,079	3,079	3,141	3,079
20,550	20,600	3,086	3,086	3,155	3,086
20,600	20,650	3,094	3,094	3,169	3,094
20,650	20,700	3,101	3,101	3,183	3,101
20,700	20,750	3,109	3,109	3,197	3,109
20,750	20,800	3,116	3,116	3,211	3,116
20,800	20,850	3,124	3,124	3,225	3,124
20,850	20,900	3,131	3,131	3,239	3,131
20,900	20,950	3,139	3,139	3,253	3,139
20,950	21,000	3,146	3,146	3,267	3,146

21,000

At least	But less than	Single	Married filing jointly	Married filing separately	Head of a household
21,000	21,050	3,154	3,154	3,281	3,154
21,050	21,100	3,161	3,161	3,295	3,161
21,100	21,150	3,169	3,169	3,309	3,169
21,150	21,200	3,176	3,176	3,323	3,176
21,200	21,250	3,184	3,184	3,337	3,184
21,250	21,300	3,191	3,191	3,351	3,191
21,300	21,350	3,199	3,199	3,365	3,199
21,350	21,400	3,206	3,206	3,379	3,206
21,400	21,450	3,214	3,214	3,393	3,214
21,450	21,500	3,221	3,221	3,407	3,221
21,500	21,550	3,229	3,229	3,421	3,229
21,550	21,600	3,236	3,236	3,435	3,236
21,600	21,650	3,244	3,244	3,449	3,244
21,650	21,700	3,251	3,251	3,463	3,251
21,700	21,750	3,259	3,259	3,477	3,259
21,750	21,800	3,266	3,266	3,491	3,266
21,800	21,850	3,274	3,274	3,505	3,274
21,850	21,900	3,281	3,281	3,519	3,281
21,900	21,950	3,289	3,289	3,533	3,289
21,950	22,000	3,296	3,296	3,547	3,296

22,000

At least	But less than	Single	Married filing jointly	Married filing separately	Head of a household
22,000	22,050	3,304	3,304	3,561	3,304
22,050	22,100	3,311	3,311	3,575	3,311
22,100	22,150	3,319	3,319	3,589	3,319
22,150	22,200	3,326	3,326	3,603	3,326
22,200	22,250	3,334	3,334	3,617	3,334
22,250	22,300	3,341	3,341	3,631	3,341
22,300	22,350	3,349	3,349	3,645	3,349
22,350	22,400	3,356	3,356	3,659	3,356
22,400	22,450	3,364	3,364	3,673	3,364
22,450	22,500	3,371	3,371	3,687	3,371
22,500	22,550	3,379	3,379	3,701	3,379
22,550	22,600	3,386	3,386	3,715	3,386
22,600	22,650	3,394	3,394	3,729	3,394
22,650	22,700	3,401	3,401	3,743	3,401
22,700	22,750	3,409	3,409	3,757	3,409
22,750	22,800	3,416	3,416	3,771	3,416
22,800	22,850	3,424	3,424	3,785	3,424
22,850	22,900	3,431	3,431	3,799	3,431
22,900	22,950	3,439	3,439	3,813	3,439
22,950	23,000	3,446	3,446	3,827	3,446

* This column must also be used by a qualifying widow(er).

Continued on next page

1996 Tax Table—*Continued*

Column key for all tables — At least | But less than | Single | Married filing jointly* | Married filing separately | Head of a household. (*This column must also be used by a qualifying widow(er).)

23,000 / 24,000 / 25,000

At least	But less than	Single	Married filing jointly*	Married filing separately	Head of a household
23,000	23,050	3,454	3,454	3,841	3,454
23,050	23,100	3,461	3,461	3,855	3,461
23,100	23,150	3,469	3,469	3,869	3,469
23,150	23,200	3,476	3,476	3,883	3,476
23,200	23,250	3,484	3,484	3,897	3,484
23,250	23,300	3,491	3,491	3,911	3,491
23,300	23,350	3,499	3,499	3,925	3,499
23,350	23,400	3,506	3,506	3,939	3,506
23,400	23,450	3,514	3,514	3,953	3,514
23,450	23,500	3,521	3,521	3,967	3,521
23,500	23,550	3,529	3,529	3,981	3,529
23,550	23,600	3,536	3,536	3,995	3,536
23,600	23,650	3,544	3,544	4,009	3,544
23,650	23,700	3,551	3,551	4,023	3,551
23,700	23,750	3,559	3,559	4,037	3,559
23,750	23,800	3,566	3,566	4,051	3,566
23,800	23,850	3,574	3,574	4,065	3,574
23,850	23,900	3,581	3,581	4,079	3,581
23,900	23,950	3,589	3,589	4,093	3,589
23,950	24,000	3,596	3,596	4,107	3,596
24,000	24,050	3,607	3,604	4,121	3,604
24,050	24,100	3,621	3,611	4,135	3,611
24,100	24,150	3,635	3,619	4,149	3,619
24,150	24,200	3,649	3,626	4,163	3,626
24,200	24,250	3,663	3,634	4,177	3,634
24,250	24,300	3,677	3,641	4,191	3,641
24,300	24,350	3,691	3,649	4,205	3,649
24,350	24,400	3,705	3,656	4,219	3,656
24,400	24,450	3,719	3,664	4,233	3,664
24,450	24,500	3,733	3,671	4,247	3,671
24,500	24,550	3,747	3,679	4,261	3,679
24,550	24,600	3,761	3,686	4,275	3,686
24,600	24,650	3,775	3,694	4,289	3,694
24,650	24,700	3,789	3,701	4,303	3,701
24,700	24,750	3,803	3,709	4,317	3,709
24,750	24,800	3,817	3,716	4,331	3,716
24,800	24,850	3,831	3,724	4,345	3,724
24,850	24,900	3,845	3,731	4,359	3,731
24,900	24,950	3,859	3,739	4,373	3,739
24,950	25,000	3,873	3,746	4,387	3,746
25,000	25,050	3,887	3,754	4,401	3,754
25,050	25,100	3,901	3,761	4,415	3,761
25,100	25,150	3,915	3,769	4,429	3,769
25,150	25,200	3,929	3,776	4,443	3,776
25,200	25,250	3,943	3,784	4,457	3,784
25,250	25,300	3,957	3,791	4,471	3,791
25,300	25,350	3,971	3,799	4,485	3,799
25,350	25,400	3,985	3,806	4,499	3,806
25,400	25,450	3,999	3,814	4,513	3,814
25,450	25,500	4,013	3,821	4,527	3,821
25,500	25,550	4,027	3,829	4,541	3,829
25,550	25,600	4,041	3,836	4,555	3,836
25,600	25,650	4,055	3,844	4,569	3,844
25,650	25,700	4,069	3,851	4,583	3,851
25,700	25,750	4,083	3,859	4,597	3,859
25,750	25,800	4,097	3,866	4,611	3,866
25,800	25,850	4,111	3,874	4,625	3,874
25,850	25,900	4,125	3,881	4,639	3,881
25,900	25,950	4,139	3,889	4,653	3,889
25,950	26,000	4,153	3,896	4,667	3,896

26,000 / 27,000 / 28,000

At least	But less than	Single	Married filing jointly*	Married filing separately	Head of a household
26,000	26,050	4,167	3,904	4,681	3,904
26,050	26,100	4,181	3,911	4,695	3,911
26,100	26,150	4,195	3,919	4,709	3,919
26,150	26,200	4,209	3,926	4,723	3,926
26,200	26,250	4,223	3,934	4,737	3,934
26,250	26,300	4,237	3,941	4,751	3,941
26,300	26,350	4,251	3,949	4,765	3,949
26,350	26,400	4,265	3,956	4,779	3,956
26,400	26,450	4,279	3,964	4,793	3,964
26,450	26,500	4,293	3,971	4,807	3,971
26,500	26,550	4,307	3,979	4,821	3,979
26,550	26,600	4,321	3,986	4,835	3,986
26,600	26,650	4,335	3,994	4,849	3,994
26,650	26,700	4,349	4,001	4,863	4,001
26,700	26,750	4,363	4,009	4,877	4,009
26,750	26,800	4,377	4,016	4,891	4,016
26,800	26,850	4,391	4,024	4,905	4,024
26,850	26,900	4,405	4,031	4,919	4,031
26,900	26,950	4,419	4,039	4,933	4,039
26,950	27,000	4,433	4,046	4,947	4,046
27,000	27,050	4,447	4,054	4,961	4,054
27,050	27,100	4,461	4,061	4,975	4,061
27,100	27,150	4,475	4,069	4,989	4,069
27,150	27,200	4,489	4,076	5,003	4,076
27,200	27,250	4,503	4,084	5,017	4,084
27,250	27,300	4,517	4,091	5,031	4,091
27,300	27,350	4,531	4,099	5,045	4,099
27,350	27,400	4,545	4,106	5,059	4,106
27,400	27,450	4,559	4,114	5,073	4,114
27,450	27,500	4,573	4,121	5,087	4,121
27,500	27,550	4,587	4,129	5,101	4,129
27,550	27,600	4,601	4,136	5,115	4,136
27,600	27,650	4,615	4,144	5,129	4,144
27,650	27,700	4,629	4,151	5,143	4,151
27,700	27,750	4,643	4,159	5,157	4,159
27,750	27,800	4,657	4,166	5,171	4,166
27,800	27,850	4,671	4,174	5,185	4,174
27,850	27,900	4,685	4,181	5,199	4,181
27,900	27,950	4,699	4,189	5,213	4,189
27,950	28,000	4,713	4,196	5,227	4,196
28,000	28,050	4,727	4,204	5,241	4,204
28,050	28,100	4,741	4,211	5,255	4,211
28,100	28,150	4,755	4,219	5,269	4,219
28,150	28,200	4,769	4,226	5,283	4,226
28,200	28,250	4,783	4,234	5,297	4,234
28,250	28,300	4,797	4,241	5,311	4,241
28,300	28,350	4,811	4,249	5,325	4,249
28,350	28,400	4,825	4,256	5,339	4,256
28,400	28,450	4,839	4,264	5,353	4,264
28,450	28,500	4,853	4,271	5,367	4,271
28,500	28,550	4,867	4,279	5,381	4,279
28,550	28,600	4,881	4,286	5,395	4,286
28,600	28,650	4,895	4,294	5,409	4,294
28,650	28,700	4,909	4,301	5,423	4,301
28,700	28,750	4,923	4,309	5,437	4,309
28,750	28,800	4,937	4,316	5,451	4,316
28,800	28,850	4,951	4,324	5,465	4,324
28,850	28,900	4,965	4,331	5,479	4,331
28,900	28,950	4,979	4,339	5,493	4,339
28,950	29,000	4,993	4,346	5,507	4,346

29,000 / 30,000 / 31,000

At least	But less than	Single	Married filing jointly*	Married filing separately	Head of a household
29,000	29,050	5,007	4,354	5,521	4,354
29,050	29,100	5,021	4,361	5,535	4,361
29,100	29,150	5,035	4,369	5,549	4,369
29,150	29,200	5,049	4,376	5,563	4,376
29,200	29,250	5,063	4,384	5,577	4,384
29,250	29,300	5,077	4,391	5,591	4,391
29,300	29,350	5,091	4,399	5,605	4,399
29,350	29,400	5,105	4,406	5,619	4,406
29,400	29,450	5,119	4,414	5,633	4,414
29,450	29,500	5,133	4,421	5,647	4,421
29,500	29,550	5,147	4,429	5,661	4,429
29,550	29,600	5,161	4,436	5,675	4,436
29,600	29,650	5,175	4,444	5,689	4,444
29,650	29,700	5,189	4,451	5,703	4,451
29,700	29,750	5,203	4,459	5,717	4,459
29,750	29,800	5,217	4,466	5,731	4,466
29,800	29,850	5,231	4,474	5,745	4,474
29,850	29,900	5,245	4,481	5,759	4,481
29,900	29,950	5,259	4,489	5,773	4,489
29,950	30,000	5,273	4,496	5,787	4,496
30,000	30,050	5,287	4,504	5,801	4,504
30,050	30,100	5,301	4,511	5,815	4,511
30,100	30,150	5,315	4,519	5,829	4,519
30,150	30,200	5,329	4,526	5,843	4,526
30,200	30,250	5,343	4,534	5,857	4,534
30,250	30,300	5,357	4,541	5,871	4,541
30,300	30,350	5,371	4,549	5,885	4,549
30,350	30,400	5,385	4,556	5,899	4,556
30,400	30,450	5,399	4,564	5,913	4,564
30,450	30,500	5,413	4,571	5,927	4,571
30,500	30,550	5,427	4,579	5,941	4,579
30,550	30,600	5,441	4,586	5,955	4,586
30,600	30,650	5,455	4,594	5,969	4,594
30,650	30,700	5,469	4,601	5,983	4,601
30,700	30,750	5,483	4,609	5,997	4,609
30,750	30,800	5,497	4,616	6,011	4,616
30,800	30,850	5,511	4,624	6,025	4,624
30,850	30,900	5,525	4,631	6,039	4,631
30,900	30,950	5,539	4,639	6,053	4,639
30,950	31,000	5,553	4,646	6,067	4,646
31,000	31,050	5,567	4,654	6,081	4,654
31,050	31,100	5,581	4,661	6,095	4,661
31,100	31,150	5,595	4,669	6,109	4,669
31,150	31,200	5,609	4,676	6,123	4,676
31,200	31,250	5,623	4,684	6,137	4,684
31,250	31,300	5,637	4,691	6,151	4,691
31,300	31,350	5,651	4,699	6,165	4,699
31,350	31,400	5,665	4,706	6,179	4,706
31,400	31,450	5,679	4,714	6,193	4,714
31,450	31,500	5,693	4,721	6,207	4,721
31,500	31,550	5,707	4,729	6,221	4,729
31,550	31,600	5,721	4,736	6,235	4,736
31,600	31,650	5,735	4,744	6,249	4,744
31,650	31,700	5,749	4,751	6,263	4,751
31,700	31,750	5,763	4,759	6,277	4,759
31,750	31,800	5,777	4,766	6,291	4,766
31,800	31,850	5,791	4,774	6,305	4,774
31,850	31,900	5,805	4,781	6,319	4,781
31,900	31,950	5,819	4,789	6,333	4,789
31,950	32,000	5,833	4,796	6,347	4,796

* This column must also be used by a qualifying widow(er).

Continued on next page

1996 Tax Table—Continued

If line 37 (taxable income) is— At least	But less than	Single	Married filing jointly *	Married filing separately	Head of a household
32,000					
32,000	32,050	5,847	4,804	6,361	4,804
32,050	32,100	5,861	4,811	6,375	4,811
32,100	32,150	5,875	4,819	6,389	4,819
32,150	32,200	5,889	4,826	6,403	4,830
32,200	32,250	5,903	4,834	6,417	4,844
32,250	32,300	5,917	4,841	6,431	4,858
32,300	32,350	5,921	4,849	6,445	4,872
32,350	32,400	5,945	4,856	6,459	4,886
32,400	32,450	5,959	4,864	6,473	4,900
32,450	32,500	5,973	4,871	6,487	4,914
32,500	32,550	5,987	4,879	6,501	4,928
32,550	32,600	6,001	4,886	6,515	4,942
32,600	32,650	6,015	4,894	6,529	4,956
32,650	32,700	6,029	4,901	6,543	4,970
32,700	32,750	6,043	4,909	6,557	4,984
32,750	32,800	6,057	4,916	6,571	4,998
32,800	32,850	6,071	4,924	6,585	5,012
32,850	32,900	6,085	4,931	6,599	5,026
32,900	32,950	6,099	4,939	6,613	5,040
32,950	33,000	6,113	4,946	6,627	5,054
33,000					
33,000	33,050	6,127	4,954	6,641	5,068
33,050	33,100	6,141	4,961	6,655	5,082
33,100	33,150	6,155	4,969	6,669	5,096
33,150	33,200	6,169	4,976	6,683	5,110
33,200	33,250	6,183	4,984	6,697	5,124
33,250	33,300	6,197	4,991	6,711	5,138
33,300	33,350	6,211	4,999	6,725	5,152
33,350	33,400	6,225	5,006	6,739	5,166
33,400	33,450	6,239	5,014	6,753	5,180
33,450	33,500	6,253	5,021	6,767	5,194
33,500	33,550	6,267	5,029	6,781	5,208
33,550	33,600	6,281	5,036	6,795	5,222
33,600	33,650	6,295	5,044	6,809	5,236
33,650	33,700	6,309	5,051	6,823	5,250
33,700	33,750	6,323	5,059	6,837	5,264
33,750	33,800	6,337	5,066	6,851	5,278
33,800	33,850	6,351	5,074	6,865	5,292
33,850	33,900	6,365	5,081	6,879	5,306
33,900	33,950	6,379	5,089	6,893	5,320
33,950	34,000	6,393	5,096	6,907	5,334
34,000					
34,000	34,050	6,407	5,104	6,921	5,348
34,050	34,100	6,421	5,111	6,935	5,362
34,100	34,150	6,435	5,119	6,949	5,376
34,150	34,200	6,449	5,126	6,963	5,390
34,200	34,250	6,463	5,134	6,977	5,404
34,250	34,300	6,477	5,141	6,991	5,418
34,300	34,350	6,491	5,149	7,005	5,432
34,350	34,400	6,505	5,156	7,019	5,446
34,400	34,450	6,519	5,164	7,033	5,460
34,450	34,500	6,533	5,171	7,047	5,474
34,500	34,550	6,547	5,179	7,061	5,488
34,550	34,600	6,561	5,186	7,075	5,502
34,600	34,650	6,575	5,194	7,089	5,516
34,650	34,700	6,589	5,201	7,103	5,530
34,700	34,750	6,603	5,209	7,117	5,544
34,750	34,800	6,617	5,216	7,131	5,558
34,800	34,850	6,631	5,224	7,145	5,572
34,850	34,900	6,645	5,231	7,159	5,586
34,900	34,950	6,659	5,239	7,173	5,600
34,950	35,000	6,673	5,246	7,187	5,614

If line 37 (taxable income) is— At least	But less than	Single	Married filing jointly *	Married filing separately	Head of a household
35,000					
35,000	35,050	6,687	5,254	7,201	5,628
35,050	35,100	6,701	5,261	7,215	5,642
35,100	35,150	6,715	5,269	7,229	5,656
35,150	35,200	6,729	5,276	7,243	5,670
35,200	35,250	6,743	5,284	7,257	5,684
35,250	35,300	6,757	5,291	7,271	5,698
35,300	35,350	6,771	5,299	7,285	5,712
35,350	35,400	6,785	5,306	7,299	5,726
35,400	35,450	6,799	5,314	7,313	5,740
35,450	35,500	6,813	5,321	7,327	5,754
35,500	35,550	6,827	5,329	7,341	5,768
35,550	35,600	6,841	5,336	7,355	5,782
35,600	35,650	6,855	5,344	7,369	5,796
35,650	35,700	6,869	5,351	7,383	5,810
35,700	35,750	6,883	5,359	7,397	5,824
35,750	35,800	6,897	5,366	7,411	5,838
35,800	35,850	6,911	5,374	7,425	5,852
35,850	35,900	6,925	5,381	7,439	5,866
35,900	35,950	6,939	5,389	7,453	5,880
35,950	36,000	6,953	5,396	7,467	5,894
36,000					
36,000	36,050	6,967	5,404	7,481	5,908
36,050	36,100	6,981	5,411	7,495	5,922
36,100	36,150	6,995	5,419	7,509	5,936
36,150	36,200	7,009	5,426	7,523	5,950
36,200	36,250	7,023	5,434	7,537	5,964
36,250	36,300	7,037	5,441	7,551	5,978
36,300	36,350	7,051	5,449	7,565	5,992
36,350	36,400	7,065	5,456	7,579	6,006
36,400	36,450	7,079	5,464	7,593	6,020
36,450	36,500	7,093	5,471	7,607	6,034
36,500	36,550	7,107	5,479	7,621	6,048
36,550	36,600	7,121	5,486	7,635	6,062
36,600	36,650	7,135	5,494	7,649	6,076
36,650	36,700	7,149	5,501	7,663	6,090
36,700	36,750	7,163	5,509	7,677	6,104
36,750	36,800	7,177	5,516	7,691	6,118
36,800	36,850	7,191	5,524	7,705	6,132
36,850	36,900	7,205	5,531	7,719	6,146
36,900	36,950	7,219	5,539	7,733	6,160
36,950	37,000	7,233	5,546	7,747	6,174
37,000					
37,000	37,050	7,247	5,554	7,761	6,188
37,050	37,100	7,261	5,561	7,775	6,202
37,100	37,150	7,275	5,569	7,789	6,216
37,150	37,200	7,289	5,576	7,803	6,230
37,200	37,250	7,303	5,584	7,817	6,244
37,250	37,300	7,317	5,591	7,831	6,258
37,300	37,350	7,331	5,599	7,845	6,272
37,350	37,400	7,345	5,606	7,859	6,286
37,400	37,450	7,359	5,614	7,873	6,300
37,450	37,500	7,373	5,621	7,887	6,314
37,500	37,550	7,387	5,629	7,901	6,328
37,550	37,600	7,401	5,636	7,915	6,342
37,600	37,650	7,415	5,644	7,929	6,356
37,650	37,700	7,429	5,651	7,943	6,370
37,700	37,750	7,443	5,659	7,957	6,384
37,750	37,800	7,457	5,666	7,971	6,398
37,800	37,850	7,471	5,674	7,985	6,412
37,850	37,900	7,485	5,681	7,999	6,426
37,900	37,950	7,499	5,689	8,013	6,440
37,950	38,000	7,513	5,696	8,027	6,454

If line 37 (taxable income) is— At least	But less than	Single	Married filing jointly *	Married filing separately	Head of a household
38,000					
38,000	38,050	7,527	5,704	8,041	6,468
38,050	38,100	7,541	5,711	8,055	6,482
38,100	38,150	7,555	5,719	8,069	6,496
38,150	38,200	7,569	5,726	8,083	6,510
38,200	38,250	7,583	5,734	8,097	6,524
38,250	38,300	7,597	5,741	8,111	6,538
38,300	38,350	7,611	5,749	8,125	6,552
38,350	38,400	7,625	5,756	8,139	6,566
38,400	38,450	7,639	5,764	8,153	6,580
38,450	38,500	7,653	5,771	8,167	6,594
38,500	38,550	7,667	5,779	8,181	6,608
38,550	38,600	7,681	5,786	8,195	6,622
38,600	38,650	7,695	5,794	8,209	6,636
38,650	38,700	7,709	5,801	8,223	6,650
38,700	38,750	7,723	5,809	8,237	6,664
38,750	38,800	7,737	5,816	8,251	6,678
38,800	38,850	7,751	5,824	8,265	6,692
38,850	38,900	7,765	5,831	8,279	6,706
38,900	38,950	7,779	5,839	8,293	6,720
38,950	39,000	7,793	5,846	8,307	6,734
39,000					
39,000	39,050	7,807	5,854	8,321	6,748
39,050	39,100	7,821	5,861	8,335	6,762
39,100	39,150	7,835	5,869	8,349	6,776
39,150	39,200	7,849	5,876	8,363	6,790
39,200	39,250	7,863	5,884	8,377	6,804
39,250	39,300	7,877	5,891	8,391	6,818
39,300	39,350	7,891	5,899	8,405	6,832
39,350	39,400	7,905	5,906	8,419	6,846
39,400	39,450	7,919	5,914	8,433	6,860
39,450	39,500	7,933	5,921	8,447	6,874
39,500	39,550	7,947	5,929	8,461	6,888
39,550	39,600	7,961	5,936	8,475	6,902
39,600	39,650	7,975	5,944	8,489	6,916
39,650	39,700	7,989	5,951	8,503	6,930
39,700	39,750	8,003	5,959	8,517	6,944
39,750	39,800	8,017	5,966	8,531	6,958
39,800	39,850	8,031	5,974	8,545	6,972
39,850	39,900	8,045	5,981	8,559	6,986
39,900	39,950	8,059	5,989	8,573	7,000
39,950	40,000	8,073	5,996	8,587	7,014
40,000					
40,000	40,050	8,087	6,004	8,601	7,028
40,050	40,100	8,101	6,011	8,615	7,042
40,100	40,150	8,115	6,022	8,629	7,056
40,150	40,200	8,129	6,036	8,643	7,070
40,200	40,250	8,143	6,050	8,657	7,084
40,250	40,300	8,157	6,064	8,671	7,098
40,300	40,350	8,171	6,078	8,685	7,112
40,350	40,400	8,185	6,092	8,699	7,126
40,400	40,450	8,199	6,106	8,713	7,140
40,450	40,500	8,213	6,120	8,727	7,154
40,500	40,550	8,227	6,134	8,741	7,168
40,550	40,600	8,241	6,148	8,755	7,182
40,600	40,650	8,255	6,162	8,769	7,196
40,650	40,700	8,269	6,176	8,783	7,210
40,700	40,750	8,283	6,190	8,797	7,224
40,750	40,800	8,297	6,204	8,811	7,238
40,800	40,850	8,311	6,218	8,825	7,252
40,850	40,900	8,325	6,232	8,839	7,266
40,900	40,950	8,339	6,246	8,853	7,280
40,950	41,000	8,353	6,260	8,867	7,294

* This column must also be used by a qualifying widow(er).

Continued on next page

1996 Tax Table—Continued

If line 37 (taxable income) is— At least	But less than	Single	Married filing jointly *	Married filing separately	Head of a household
41,000					
41,000	41,050	8,367	6,274	8,881	7,308
41,050	41,100	8,381	6,288	8,895	7,322
41,100	41,150	8,395	6,302	8,909	7,336
41,150	41,200	8,409	6,316	8,923	7,350
41,200	41,250	8,423	6,330	8,937	7,364
41,250	41,300	8,437	6,344	8,951	7,378
41,300	41,350	8,451	6,358	8,965	7,392
41,350	41,400	8,465	6,372	8,979	7,406
41,400	41,450	8,479	6,386	8,993	7,420
41,450	41,500	8,493	6,400	9,007	7,434
41,500	41,550	8,507	6,414	9,021	7,448
41,550	41,600	8,521	6,428	9,035	7,462
41,600	41,650	8,535	6,442	9,049	7,476
41,650	41,700	8,549	6,456	9,063	7,490
41,700	41,750	8,563	6,470	9,077	7,504
41,750	41,800	8,577	6,484	9,091	7,518
41,800	41,850	8,591	6,498	9,105	7,532
41,850	41,900	8,605	6,512	9,119	7,546
41,900	41,950	8,619	6,526	9,133	7,560
41,950	42,000	8,633	6,540	9,147	7,574
42,000					
42,000	42,050	8,647	6,554	9,161	7,588
42,050	42,100	8,661	6,568	9,175	7,602
42,100	42,150	8,675	6,582	9,189	7,616
42,150	42,200	8,689	6,596	9,203	7,630
42,200	42,250	8,703	6,610	9,217	7,644
42,250	42,300	8,717	6,624	9,231	7,658
42,300	42,350	8,731	6,638	9,245	7,672
42,350	42,400	8,745	6,652	9,259	7,686
42,400	42,450	8,759	6,666	9,273	7,700
42,450	42,500	8,773	6,680	9,287	7,714
42,500	42,550	8,787	6,694	9,301	7,728
42,550	42,600	8,801	6,708	9,315	7,742
42,600	42,650	8,815	6,722	9,329	7,756
42,650	42,700	8,829	6,736	9,343	7,770
42,700	42,750	8,843	6,750	9,357	7,784
42,750	42,800	8,857	6,764	9,371	7,798
42,800	42,850	8,871	6,778	9,385	7,812
42,850	42,900	8,885	6,792	9,399	7,826
42,900	42,950	8,899	6,806	9,413	7,840
42,950	43,000	8,913	6,820	9,427	7,854
43,000					
43,000	43,050	8,927	6,834	9,441	7,868
43,050	43,100	8,941	6,848	9,455	7,882
43,100	43,150	8,955	6,862	9,469	7,896
43,150	43,200	8,969	6,876	9,483	7,910
43,200	43,250	8,983	6,890	9,497	7,924
43,250	43,300	8,997	6,904	9,511	7,938
43,300	43,350	9,011	6,918	9,525	7,952
43,350	43,400	9,025	6,932	9,539	7,966
43,400	43,450	9,039	6,946	9,553	7,980
43,450	43,500	9,053	6,960	9,567	7,994
43,500	43,550	9,067	6,974	9,581	8,008
43,550	43,600	9,081	6,988	9,595	8,022
43,600	43,650	9,095	7,002	9,609	8,036
43,650	43,700	9,109	7,016	9,623	8,050
43,700	43,750	9,123	7,030	9,637	8,064
43,750	43,800	9,137	7,044	9,651	8,078
43,800	43,850	9,151	7,058	9,665	8,092
43,850	43,900	9,165	7,072	9,679	8,106
43,900	43,950	9,179	7,086	9,693	8,120
43,950	44,000	9,193	7,100	9,707	8,134

If line 37 (taxable income) is— At least	But less than	Single	Married filing jointly *	Married filing separately	Head of a household
44,000					
44,000	44,050	9,207	7,114	9,721	8,148
44,050	44,100	9,221	7,128	9,735	8,162
44,100	44,150	9,235	7,142	9,749	8,176
44,150	44,200	9,249	7,156	9,763	8,190
44,200	44,250	9,263	7,170	9,777	8,204
44,250	44,300	9,277	7,184	9,791	8,218
44,300	44,350	9,291	7,198	9,805	8,232
44,350	44,400	9,305	7,212	9,819	8,246
44,400	44,450	9,319	7,226	9,833	8,260
44,450	44,500	9,333	7,240	9,847	8,274
44,500	44,550	9,347	7,254	9,861	8,288
44,550	44,600	9,361	7,268	9,875	8,302
44,600	44,650	9,375	7,282	9,889	8,316
44,650	44,700	9,389	7,296	9,903	8,330
44,700	44,750	9,403	7,310	9,917	8,344
44,750	44,800	9,417	7,324	9,931	8,358
44,800	44,850	9,431	7,338	9,945	8,372
44,850	44,900	9,445	7,352	9,959	8,386
44,900	44,950	9,459	7,366	9,973	8,400
44,950	45,000	9,473	7,380	9,987	8,414
45,000					
45,000	45,050	9,487	7,394	10,001	8,428
45,050	45,100	9,501	7,408	10,015	8,442
45,100	45,150	9,515	7,422	10,029	8,456
45,150	45,200	9,529	7,436	10,043	8,470
45,200	45,250	9,543	7,450	10,057	8,484
45,250	45,300	9,557	7,464	10,071	8,498
45,300	45,350	9,571	7,478	10,085	8,512
45,350	45,400	9,585	7,492	10,099	8,526
45,400	45,450	9,599	7,506	10,113	8,540
45,450	45,500	9,613	7,520	10,127	8,554
45,500	45,550	9,627	7,534	10,141	8,568
45,550	45,600	9,641	7,548	10,155	8,582
45,600	45,650	9,655	7,562	10,169	8,596
45,650	45,700	9,669	7,576	10,183	8,610
45,700	45,750	9,683	7,590	10,197	8,624
45,750	45,800	9,697	7,604	10,211	8,638
45,800	45,850	9,711	7,618	10,225	8,652
45,850	45,900	9,725	7,632	10,239	8,666
45,900	45,950	9,739	7,646	10,253	8,680
45,950	46,000	9,753	7,660	10,267	8,694
46,000					
46,000	46,050	9,767	7,674	10,281	8,708
46,050	46,100	9,781	7,688	10,295	8,722
46,100	46,150	9,795	7,702	10,309	8,736
46,150	46,200	9,809	7,716	10,323	8,750
46,200	46,250	9,823	7,730	10,337	8,764
46,250	46,300	9,837	7,744	10,351	8,778
46,300	46,350	9,851	7,758	10,365	8,792
46,350	46,400	9,865	7,772	10,379	8,806
46,400	46,450	9,879	7,786	10,393	8,820
46,450	46,500	9,893	7,800	10,407	8,834
46,500	46,550	9,907	7,814	10,421	8,848
46,550	46,600	9,921	7,828	10,435	8,862
46,600	46,650	9,935	7,842	10,449	8,876
46,650	46,700	9,949	7,856	10,463	8,890
46,700	46,750	9,963	7,870	10,477	8,904
46,750	46,800	9,977	7,884	10,491	8,918
46,800	46,850	9,991	7,898	10,505	8,932
46,850	46,900	10,005	7,912	10,519	8,946
46,900	46,950	10,019	7,926	10,533	8,960
46,950	47,000	10,033	7,940	10,547	8,974

If line 37 (taxable income) is— At least	But less than	Single	Married filing jointly *	Married filing separately	Head of a household
47,000					
47,000	47,050	10,047	7,954	10,561	8,988
47,050	47,100	10,061	7,968	10,575	9,002
47,100	47,150	10,075	7,982	10,589	9,016
47,150	47,200	10,089	7,996	10,603	9,030
47,200	47,250	10,103	8,010	10,617	9,044
47,250	47,300	10,117	8,024	10,631	9,058
47,300	47,350	10,131	8,038	10,645	9,072
47,350	47,400	10,145	8,052	10,659	9,086
47,400	47,450	10,159	8,066	10,673	9,100
47,450	47,500	10,173	8,080	10,687	9,114
47,500	47,550	10,187	8,094	10,701	9,128
47,550	47,600	10,201	8,108	10,715	9,142
47,600	47,650	10,215	8,122	10,729	9,156
47,650	47,700	10,229	8,136	10,743	9,170
47,700	47,750	10,243	8,150	10,757	9,184
47,750	47,800	10,257	8,164	10,771	9,198
47,800	47,850	10,271	8,178	10,785	9,212
47,850	47,900	10,285	8,192	10,799	9,226
47,900	47,950	10,299	8,206	10,813	9,240
47,950	48,000	10,313	8,220	10,827	9,254
48,000					
48,000	48,050	10,327	8,234	10,841	9,268
48,050	48,100	10,341	8,248	10,855	9,282
48,100	48,150	10,355	8,262	10,869	9,296
48,150	48,200	10,369	8,276	10,883	9,310
48,200	48,250	10,383	8,290	10,897	9,324
48,250	48,300	10,397	8,304	10,911	9,338
48,300	48,350	10,411	8,318	10,925	9,352
48,350	48,400	10,425	8,332	10,939	9,366
48,400	48,450	10,439	8,346	10,953	9,380
48,450	48,500	10,453	8,360	10,967	9,394
48,500	48,550	10,467	8,374	10,983	9,408
48,550	48,600	10,481	8,388	10,998	9,422
48,600	48,650	10,495	8,402	11,014	9,436
48,650	48,700	10,509	8,416	11,029	9,450
48,700	48,750	10,523	8,430	11,045	9,464
48,750	48,800	10,537	8,444	11,060	9,478
48,800	48,850	10,551	8,458	11,076	9,492
48,850	48,900	10,565	8,472	11,091	9,506
48,900	48,950	10,579	8,486	11,107	9,520
48,950	49,000	10,593	8,500	11,122	9,534
49,000					
49,000	49,050	10,607	8,514	11,138	9,548
49,050	49,100	10,621	8,528	11,153	9,562
49,100	49,150	10,635	8,542	11,169	9,576
49,150	49,200	10,649	8,556	11,184	9,590
49,200	49,250	10,663	8,570	11,200	9,604
49,250	49,300	10,677	8,584	11,215	9,618
49,300	49,350	10,691	8,598	11,231	9,632
49,350	49,400	10,705	8,612	11,246	9,646
49,400	49,450	10,719	8,626	11,262	9,660
49,450	49,500	10,733	8,640	11,277	9,674
49,500	49,550	10,747	8,654	11,293	9,688
49,550	49,600	10,761	8,668	11,308	9,702
49,600	49,650	10,775	8,682	11,324	9,716
49,650	49,700	10,789	8,696	11,339	9,730
49,700	49,750	10,803	8,710	11,355	9,744
49,750	49,800	10,817	8,724	11,370	9,758
49,800	49,850	10,831	8,738	11,386	9,772
49,850	49,900	10,845	8,752	11,401	9,786
49,900	49,950	10,859	8,766	11,417	9,800
49,950	50,000	10,873	8,780	11,432	9,814

* This column must also be used by a qualifying widow(er).

Continued on next page

1996 Tax Table—Continued

If line 37 (taxable income) is—		And you are—			
At least	But less than	Single	Married filing jointly *	Married filing separately	Head of a household
		Your tax is—			
50,000					
50,000	50,050	10,887	8,794	11,448	9,828
50,050	50,100	10,901	8,808	11,463	9,842
50,100	50,150	10,915	8,822	11,479	9,856
50,150	50,200	10,929	8,836	11,494	9,870
50,200	50,250	10,943	8,850	11,510	9,884
50,250	50,300	10,957	8,864	11,525	9,898
50,300	50,350	10,971	8,878	11,541	9,912
50,350	50,400	10,985	8,892	11,556	9,926
50,400	50,450	10,999	8,906	11,572	9,940
50,450	50,500	11,013	8,920	11,587	9,954
50,500	50,550	11,027	8,934	11,603	9,968
50,550	50,600	11,041	8,948	11,618	9,982
50,600	50,650	11,055	8,962	11,634	9,996
50,650	50,700	11,069	8,976	11,649	10,010
50,700	50,750	11,083	8,990	11,665	10,024
50,750	50,800	11,097	9,004	11,680	10,038
50,800	50,850	11,111	9,018	11,696	10,052
50,850	50,900	11,125	9,032	11,711	10,066
50,900	50,950	11,139	9,046	11,727	10,080
50,950	51,000	11,153	9,060	11,742	10,094
51,000					
51,000	51,050	11,167	9,074	11,758	10,108
51,050	51,100	11,181	9,088	11,773	10,122
51,100	51,150	11,195	9,102	11,789	10,136
51,150	51,200	11,209	9,116	11,804	10,150
51,200	51,250	11,223	9,130	11,820	10,164
51,250	51,300	11,237	9,144	11,835	10,178
51,300	51,350	11,251	9,158	11,851	10,192
51,350	51,400	11,265	9,172	11,866	10,206
51,400	51,450	11,279	9,186	11,882	10,220
51,450	51,500	11,293	9,200	11,897	10,234
51,500	51,550	11,307	9,214	11,913	10,248
51,550	51,600	11,321	9,228	11,928	10,262
51,600	51,650	11,335	9,242	11,944	10,276
51,650	51,700	11,349	9,256	11,959	10,290
51,700	51,750	11,363	9,270	11,975	10,304
51,750	51,800	11,377	9,284	11,990	10,318
51,800	51,850	11,391	9,298	12,006	10,332
51,850	51,900	11,405	9,312	12,021	10,346
51,900	51,950	11,419	9,326	12,037	10,360
51,950	52,000	11,433	9,340	12,052	10,374
52,000					
52,000	52,050	11,447	9,354	12,068	10,388
52,050	52,100	11,461	9,368	12,083	10,402
52,100	52,150	11,475	9,382	12,099	10,416
52,150	52,200	11,489	9,396	12,114	10,430
52,200	52,250	11,503	9,410	12,130	10,444
52,250	52,300	11,517	9,424	12,145	10,458
52,300	52,350	11,531	9,438	12,161	10,472
52,350	52,400	11,545	9,452	12,176	10,486
52,400	52,450	11,559	9,466	12,192	10,500
52,450	52,500	11,573	9,480	12,207	10,514
52,500	52,550	11,587	9,494	12,223	10,528
52,550	52,600	11,601	9,508	12,238	10,542
52,600	52,650	11,615	9,522	12,254	10,556
52,650	52,700	11,629	9,536	12,269	10,570
52,700	52,750	11,643	9,550	12,285	10,584
52,750	52,800	11,657	9,564	12,300	10,598
52,800	52,850	11,671	9,578	12,316	10,612
52,850	52,900	11,685	9,592	12,331	10,626
52,900	52,950	11,699	9,606	12,347	10,640
52,950	53,000	11,713	9,620	12,362	10,654

If line 37 (taxable income) is—		And you are—			
At least	But less than	Single	Married filing jointly *	Married filing separately	Head of a household
		Your tax is—			
53,000					
53,000	53,050	11,727	9,634	12,378	10,668
53,050	53,100	11,741	9,648	12,393	10,682
53,100	53,150	11,755	9,662	12,409	10,696
53,150	53,200	11,769	9,676	12,424	10,710
53,200	53,250	11,783	9,690	12,440	10,724
53,250	53,300	11,797	9,704	12,455	10,738
53,300	53,350	11,811	9,718	12,471	10,752
53,350	53,400	11,825	9,732	12,486	10,766
53,400	53,450	11,839	9,746	12,502	10,780
53,450	53,500	11,853	9,760	12,517	10,794
53,500	53,550	11,867	9,774	12,533	10,808
53,550	53,600	11,881	9,788	12,548	10,822
53,600	53,650	11,895	9,802	12,564	10,836
53,650	53,700	11,909	9,816	12,579	10,850
53,700	53,750	11,923	9,830	12,595	10,864
53,750	53,800	11,937	9,844	12,610	10,878
53,800	53,850	11,951	9,858	12,626	10,892
53,850	53,900	11,965	9,872	12,641	10,906
53,900	53,950	11,979	9,886	12,657	10,920
53,950	54,000	11,993	9,900	12,672	10,934
54,000					
54,000	54,050	12,007	9,914	12,688	10,948
54,050	54,100	12,021	9,928	12,703	10,962
54,100	54,150	12,035	9,942	12,719	10,976
54,150	54,200	12,049	9,956	12,734	10,990
54,200	54,250	12,063	9,970	12,750	11,004
54,250	54,300	12,077	9,984	12,765	11,018
54,300	54,350	12,091	9,998	12,781	11,032
54,350	54,400	12,105	10,012	12,796	11,046
54,400	54,450	12,119	10,026	12,812	11,060
54,450	54,500	12,133	10,040	12,827	11,074
54,500	54,550	12,147	10,054	12,843	11,088
54,550	54,600	12,161	10,068	12,858	11,102
54,600	54,650	12,175	10,082	12,874	11,116
54,650	54,700	12,189	10,096	12,889	11,130
54,700	54,750	12,203	10,110	12,905	11,144
54,750	54,800	12,217	10,124	12,920	11,158
54,800	54,850	12,231	10,138	12,936	11,172
54,850	54,900	12,245	10,152	12,951	11,186
54,900	54,950	12,259	10,166	12,967	11,200
54,950	55,000	12,273	10,180	12,982	11,214
55,000					
55,000	55,050	12,287	10,194	12,998	11,228
55,050	55,100	12,301	10,208	13,013	11,242
55,100	55,150	12,315	10,222	13,029	11,256
55,150	55,200	12,329	10,236	13,044	11,270
55,200	55,250	12,343	10,250	13,060	11,284
55,250	55,300	12,357	10,264	13,075	11,298
55,300	55,350	12,371	10,278	13,091	11,312
55,350	55,400	12,385	10,292	13,106	11,326
55,400	55,450	12,399	10,306	13,122	11,340
55,450	55,500	12,413	10,320	13,137	11,354
55,500	55,550	12,427	10,334	13,153	11,368
55,550	55,600	12,441	10,348	13,168	11,382
55,600	55,650	12,455	10,362	13,184	11,396
55,650	55,700	12,469	10,376	13,199	11,410
55,700	55,750	12,483	10,390	13,215	11,424
55,750	55,800	12,497	10,404	13,230	11,438
55,800	55,850	12,511	10,418	13,246	11,452
55,850	55,900	12,525	10,432	13,261	11,466
55,900	55,950	12,539	10,446	13,277	11,480
55,950	56,000	12,553	10,460	13,292	11,494

If line 37 (taxable income) is—		And you are—			
At least	But less than	Single	Married filing jointly *	Married filing separately	Head of a household
		Your tax is—			
56,000					
56,000	56,050	12,567	10,474	13,308	11,508
56,050	56,100	12,581	10,488	13,323	11,522
56,100	56,150	12,595	10,502	13,339	11,536
56,150	56,200	12,609	10,516	13,354	11,550
56,200	56,250	12,623	10,530	13,370	11,564
56,250	56,300	12,637	10,544	13,385	11,578
56,300	56,350	12,651	10,558	13,401	11,592
56,350	56,400	12,665	10,572	13,416	11,606
56,400	56,450	12,679	10,586	13,432	11,620
56,450	56,500	12,693	10,600	13,447	11,634
56,500	56,550	12,707	10,614	13,463	11,648
56,550	56,600	12,721	10,628	13,478	11,662
56,600	56,650	12,735	10,642	13,494	11,676
56,650	56,700	12,749	10,656	13,509	11,690
56,700	56,750	12,763	10,670	13,525	11,704
56,750	56,800	12,777	10,684	13,540	11,718
56,800	56,850	12,791	10,698	13,556	11,732
56,850	56,900	12,805	10,712	13,571	11,746
56,900	56,950	12,819	10,726	13,587	11,760
56,950	57,000	12,833	10,740	13,602	11,774
57,000					
57,000	57,050	12,847	10,754	13,618	11,788
57,050	57,100	12,861	10,768	13,633	11,802
57,100	57,150	12,875	10,782	13,649	11,816
57,150	57,200	12,889	10,796	13,664	11,830
57,200	57,250	12,903	10,810	13,680	11,844
57,250	57,300	12,917	10,824	13,695	11,858
57,300	57,350	12,931	10,838	13,711	11,872
57,350	57,400	12,945	10,852	13,726	11,886
57,400	57,450	12,959	10,866	13,742	11,900
57,450	57,500	12,973	10,880	13,757	11,914
57,500	57,550	12,987	10,894	13,773	11,928
57,550	57,600	13,001	10,908	13,788	11,942
57,600	57,650	13,015	10,922	13,804	11,956
57,650	57,700	13,029	10,936	13,819	11,970
57,700	57,750	13,043	10,950	13,835	11,984
57,750	57,800	13,057	10,964	13,850	11,998
57,800	57,850	13,071	10,978	13,866	12,012
57,850	57,900	13,085	10,992	13,881	12,026
57,900	57,950	13,099	11,006	13,897	12,040
57,950	58,000	13,113	11,020	13,912	12,054
58,000					
58,000	58,050	13,127	11,034	13,928	12,068
58,050	58,100	13,141	11,048	13,943	12,082
58,100	58,150	13,155	11,062	13,959	12,096
58,150	58,200	13,170	11,076	13,974	12,110
58,200	58,250	13,185	11,090	13,990	12,124
58,250	58,300	13,201	11,104	14,005	12,138
58,300	58,350	13,216	11,118	14,021	12,152
58,350	58,400	13,232	11,132	14,036	12,166
58,400	58,450	13,247	11,146	14,052	12,180
58,450	58,500	13,263	11,160	14,067	12,194
58,500	58,550	13,278	11,174	14,083	12,208
58,550	58,600	13,294	11,188	14,098	12,222
58,600	58,650	13,309	11,202	14,114	12,236
58,650	58,700	13,325	11,216	14,129	12,250
58,700	58,750	13,340	11,230	14,145	12,264
58,750	58,800	13,356	11,244	14,160	12,278
58,800	58,850	13,371	11,258	14,176	12,292
58,850	58,900	13,387	11,272	14,191	12,306
58,900	58,950	13,402	11,286	14,207	12,320
58,950	59,000	13,418	11,300	14,222	12,334

* This column must also be used by a qualifying widow(er).

Continued on next page

1996 Tax Table—_Continued_

Column group 1:

At least	But less than	Single	Married filing jointly *	Married filing separately	Head of a household
59,000					
59,000	59,050	13,433	11,314	14,238	12,348
59,050	59,100	13,449	11,328	14,253	12,362
59,100	59,150	13,464	11,342	14,269	12,376
59,150	59,200	13,480	11,356	14,284	12,390
59,200	59,250	13,495	11,370	14,300	12,404
59,250	59,300	13,511	11,384	14,315	12,418
59,300	59,350	13,526	11,398	14,331	12,432
59,350	59,400	13,542	11,412	14,346	12,446
59,400	59,450	13,557	11,426	14,362	12,460
59,450	59,500	13,573	11,440	14,377	12,474
59,500	59,550	13,588	11,454	14,393	12,488
59,550	59,600	13,604	11,468	14,408	12,502
59,600	59,650	13,619	11,482	14,424	12,516
59,650	59,700	13,635	11,496	14,439	12,530
59,700	59,750	13,650	11,510	14,455	12,544
59,750	59,800	13,666	11,524	14,470	12,558
59,800	59,850	13,681	11,538	14,486	12,572
59,850	59,900	13,697	11,552	14,501	12,586
59,900	59,950	13,712	11,566	14,517	12,600
59,950	60,000	13,728	11,580	14,532	12,614
60,000					
60,000	60,050	13,743	11,594	14,548	12,628
60,050	60,100	13,759	11,608	14,563	12,642
60,100	60,150	13,774	11,622	14,579	12,656
60,150	60,200	13,790	11,636	14,594	12,670
60,200	60,250	13,805	11,650	14,610	12,684
60,250	60,300	13,821	11,664	14,625	12,698
60,300	60,350	13,836	11,678	14,641	12,712
60,350	60,400	13,852	11,692	14,656	12,726
60,400	60,450	13,867	11,706	14,672	12,740
60,450	60,500	13,883	11,720	14,687	12,754
60,500	60,550	13,898	11,734	14,703	12,768
60,550	60,600	13,914	11,748	14,718	12,782
60,600	60,650	13,929	11,762	14,734	12,796
60,650	60,700	13,945	11,776	14,749	12,810
60,700	60,750	13,960	11,790	14,765	12,824
60,750	60,800	13,976	11,804	14,780	12,838
60,800	60,850	13,991	11,818	14,796	12,852
60,850	60,900	14,007	11,832	14,811	12,866
60,900	60,950	14,022	11,846	14,827	12,880
60,950	61,000	14,038	11,860	14,842	12,894
61,000					
61,000	61,050	14,053	11,874	14,858	12,908
61,050	61,100	14,069	11,888	14,873	12,922
61,100	61,150	14,084	11,902	14,889	12,936
61,150	61,200	14,100	11,916	14,904	12,950
61,200	61,250	14,115	11,930	14,920	12,964
61,250	61,300	14,131	11,944	14,935	12,978
61,300	61,350	14,146	11,958	14,951	12,992
61,350	61,400	14,162	11,972	14,966	13,006
61,400	61,450	14,177	11,986	14,982	13,020
61,450	61,500	14,193	12,000	14,997	13,034
61,500	61,550	14,208	12,014	15,013	13,048
61,550	61,600	14,224	12,028	15,028	13,062
61,600	61,650	14,239	12,042	15,044	13,076
61,650	61,700	14,255	12,056	15,059	13,090
61,700	61,750	14,270	12,070	15,075	13,104
61,750	61,800	14,286	12,084	15,090	13,118
61,800	61,850	14,301	12,098	15,106	13,132
61,850	61,900	14,317	12,112	15,121	13,146
61,900	61,950	14,332	12,126	15,137	13,160
61,950	62,000	14,348	12,140	15,152	13,174

Column group 2:

At least	But less than	Single	Married filing jointly *	Married filing separately	Head of a household
62,000					
62,000	62,050	14,363	12,154	15,168	13,188
62,050	62,100	14,379	12,168	15,183	13,202
62,100	62,150	14,394	12,182	15,199	13,216
62,150	62,200	14,410	12,196	15,214	13,230
62,200	62,250	14,425	12,210	15,230	13,244
62,250	62,300	14,441	12,224	15,245	13,258
62,300	62,350	14,456	12,238	15,261	13,272
62,350	62,400	14,472	12,252	15,276	13,286
62,400	62,450	14,487	12,266	15,292	13,300
62,450	62,500	14,503	12,280	15,307	13,314
62,500	62,550	14,518	12,294	15,323	13,328
62,550	62,600	14,534	12,308	15,338	13,342
62,600	62,650	14,549	12,322	15,354	13,356
62,650	62,700	14,565	12,336	15,369	13,370
62,700	62,750	14,580	12,350	15,385	13,384
62,750	62,800	14,596	12,364	15,400	13,398
62,800	62,850	14,611	12,378	15,416	13,412
62,850	62,900	14,627	12,392	15,431	13,426
62,900	62,950	14,642	12,406	15,447	13,440
62,950	63,000	14,658	12,420	15,462	13,454
63,000					
63,000	63,050	14,673	12,434	15,478	13,468
63,050	63,100	14,689	12,448	15,493	13,482
63,100	63,150	14,704	12,462	15,509	13,496
63,150	63,200	14,720	12,476	15,524	13,510
63,200	63,250	14,735	12,490	15,540	13,524
63,250	63,300	14,751	12,504	15,555	13,538
63,300	63,350	14,766	12,518	15,571	13,552
63,350	63,400	14,782	12,532	15,586	13,566
63,400	63,450	14,797	12,546	15,602	13,580
63,450	63,500	14,813	12,560	15,617	13,594
63,500	63,550	14,828	12,574	15,633	13,608
63,550	63,600	14,844	12,588	15,648	13,622
63,600	63,650	14,859	12,602	15,664	13,636
63,650	63,700	14,875	12,616	15,679	13,650
63,700	63,750	14,890	12,630	15,695	13,664
63,750	63,800	14,906	12,644	15,710	13,678
63,800	63,850	14,921	12,658	15,726	13,692
63,850	63,900	14,937	12,672	15,741	13,706
63,900	63,950	14,952	12,686	15,757	13,720
63,950	64,000	14,968	12,700	15,772	13,734
64,000					
64,000	64,050	14,983	12,714	15,788	13,748
64,050	64,100	14,999	12,728	15,803	13,762
64,100	64,150	15,014	12,742	15,819	13,776
64,150	64,200	15,030	12,756	15,834	13,790
64,200	64,250	15,045	12,770	15,850	13,804
64,250	64,300	15,061	12,784	15,865	13,818
64,300	64,350	15,076	12,798	15,881	13,832
64,350	64,400	15,092	12,812	15,896	13,846
64,400	64,450	15,107	12,826	15,912	13,860
64,450	64,500	15,123	12,840	15,927	13,874
64,500	64,550	15,138	12,854	15,943	13,888
64,550	64,600	15,154	12,868	15,958	13,902
64,600	64,650	15,169	12,882	15,974	13,916
64,650	64,700	15,185	12,896	15,989	13,930
64,700	64,750	15,200	12,910	16,005	13,944
64,750	64,800	15,216	12,924	16,020	13,958
64,800	64,850	15,231	12,938	16,036	13,972
64,850	64,900	15,247	12,952	16,051	13,986
64,900	64,950	15,262	12,966	16,067	14,000
64,950	65,000	15,278	12,980	16,082	14,014

Column group 3:

At least	But less than	Single	Married filing jointly *	Married filing separately	Head of a household
65,000					
65,000	65,050	15,293	12,994	16,098	14,028
65,050	65,100	15,309	13,008	16,113	14,042
65,100	65,150	15,324	13,022	16,129	14,056
65,150	65,200	15,340	13,036	16,144	14,070
65,200	65,250	15,355	13,050	16,160	14,084
65,250	65,300	15,371	13,064	16,175	14,098
65,300	65,350	15,386	13,078	16,191	14,112
65,350	65,400	15,402	13,092	16,206	14,126
65,400	65,450	15,417	13,106	16,222	14,140
65,450	65,500	15,433	13,120	16,237	14,154
65,500	65,550	15,448	13,134	16,253	14,168
65,550	65,600	15,464	13,148	16,268	14,182
65,600	65,650	15,479	13,162	16,284	14,196
65,650	65,700	15,495	13,176	16,299	14,210
65,700	65,750	15,510	13,190	16,315	14,224
65,750	65,800	15,526	13,204	16,330	14,238
65,800	65,850	15,541	13,218	16,346	14,252
65,850	65,900	15,557	13,232	16,361	14,266
65,900	65,950	15,572	13,246	16,377	14,280
65,950	66,000	15,588	13,260	16,392	14,294
66,000					
66,000	66,050	15,603	13,274	16,408	14,308
66,050	66,100	15,619	13,288	16,423	14,322
66,100	66,150	15,634	13,302	16,439	14,336
66,150	66,200	15,650	13,316	16,454	14,350
66,200	66,250	15,665	13,330	16,470	14,364
66,250	66,300	15,681	13,344	16,485	14,378
66,300	66,350	15,696	13,358	16,501	14,392
66,350	66,400	15,712	13,372	16,516	14,406
66,400	66,450	15,727	13,386	16,532	14,420
66,450	66,500	15,743	13,400	16,547	14,434
66,500	66,550	15,758	13,414	16,563	14,448
66,550	66,600	15,774	13,428	16,578	14,462
66,600	66,650	15,789	13,442	16,594	14,476
66,650	66,700	15,805	13,456	16,609	14,490
66,700	66,750	15,820	13,470	16,625	14,504
66,750	66,800	15,836	13,484	16,640	14,518
66,800	66,850	15,851	13,498	16,656	14,532
66,850	66,900	15,867	13,512	16,671	14,546
66,900	66,950	15,882	13,526	16,687	14,560
66,950	67,000	15,898	13,540	16,702	14,574
67,000					
67,000	67,050	15,913	13,554	16,718	14,588
67,050	67,100	15,929	13,568	16,733	14,602
67,100	67,150	15,944	13,582	16,749	14,616
67,150	67,200	15,960	13,596	16,764	14,630
67,200	67,250	15,975	13,610	16,780	14,644
67,250	67,300	15,991	13,624	16,795	14,658
67,300	67,350	16,006	13,638	16,811	14,672
67,350	67,400	16,022	13,652	16,826	14,686
67,400	67,450	16,037	13,666	16,842	14,700
67,450	67,500	16,053	13,680	16,857	14,714
67,500	67,550	16,068	13,694	16,873	14,728
67,550	67,600	16,084	13,708	16,888	14,742
67,600	67,650	16,099	13,722	16,904	14,756
67,650	67,700	16,115	13,736	16,919	14,770
67,700	67,750	16,130	13,750	16,935	14,784
67,750	67,800	16,146	13,764	16,950	14,798
67,800	67,850	16,161	13,778	16,966	14,812
67,850	67,900	16,177	13,792	16,981	14,826
67,900	67,950	16,192	13,806	16,997	14,840
67,950	68,000	16,208	13,820	17,012	14,854

* This column must also be used by a qualifying widow(er).

Continued on next page

1996 Tax Table—Continued

68,000

At least	But less than	Single	Married filing jointly *	Married filing separately	Head of a household
68,000	68,050	16,223	13,834	17,028	14,868
68,050	68,100	16,239	13,848	17,043	14,882
68,100	68,150	16,254	13,862	17,059	14,896
68,150	68,200	16,270	13,876	17,074	14,910
68,200	68,250	16,285	13,890	17,090	14,924
68,250	68,300	16,301	13,904	17,105	14,938
68,300	68,350	16,316	13,918	17,121	14,952
68,350	68,400	16,332	13,932	17,136	14,966
68,400	68,450	16,347	13,946	17,152	14,980
68,450	68,500	16,363	13,960	17,167	14,994
68,500	68,550	16,378	13,974	17,183	15,008
68,550	68,600	16,394	13,988	17,198	15,022
68,600	68,650	16,409	14,002	17,214	15,036
68,650	68,700	16,425	14,016	17,229	15,050
68,700	68,750	16,440	14,030	17,245	15,064
68,750	68,800	16,456	14,044	17,260	15,078
68,800	68,850	16,471	14,058	17,276	15,092
68,850	68,900	16,487	14,072	17,291	15,106
68,900	68,950	16,502	14,086	17,307	15,120
68,950	69,000	16,518	14,100	17,322	15,134

69,000

At least	But less than	Single	Married filing jointly *	Married filing separately	Head of a household
69,000	69,050	16,533	14,114	17,338	15,148
69,050	69,100	16,549	14,128	17,353	15,162
69,100	69,150	16,564	14,142	17,369	15,176
69,150	69,200	16,580	14,156	17,384	15,190
69,200	69,250	16,595	14,170	17,400	15,204
69,250	69,300	16,611	14,184	17,415	15,218
69,300	69,350	16,626	14,198	17,431	15,232
69,350	69,400	16,642	14,212	17,446	15,246
69,400	69,450	16,657	14,226	17,462	15,260
69,450	69,500	16,673	14,240	17,477	15,274
69,500	69,550	16,688	14,254	17,493	15,288
69,550	69,600	16,704	14,268	17,508	15,302
69,600	69,650	16,719	14,282	17,524	15,316
69,650	69,700	16,735	14,296	17,539	15,330
69,700	69,750	16,750	14,310	17,555	15,344
69,750	69,800	16,766	14,324	17,570	15,358
69,800	69,850	16,781	14,338	17,586	15,372
69,850	69,900	16,797	14,352	17,601	15,386
69,900	69,950	16,812	14,366	17,617	15,400
69,950	70,000	16,828	14,380	17,632	15,414

70,000

At least	But less than	Single	Married filing jointly *	Married filing separately	Head of a household
70,000	70,050	16,843	14,394	17,648	15,428
70,050	70,100	16,859	14,408	17,663	15,442
70,100	70,150	16,874	14,422	17,679	15,456
70,150	70,200	16,890	14,436	17,694	15,470
70,200	70,250	16,905	14,450	17,710	15,484
70,250	70,300	16,921	14,464	17,725	15,498
70,300	70,350	16,936	14,478	17,741	15,512
70,350	70,400	16,952	14,492	17,756	15,526
70,400	70,450	16,967	14,506	17,772	15,540
70,450	70,500	16,983	14,520	17,787	15,554
70,500	70,550	16,998	14,534	17,803	15,568
70,550	70,600	17,014	14,548	17,818	15,582
70,600	70,650	17,029	14,562	17,834	15,596
70,650	70,700	17,045	14,576	17,849	15,610
70,700	70,750	17,060	14,590	17,865	15,624
70,750	70,800	17,076	14,604	17,880	15,638
70,800	70,850	17,091	14,618	17,896	15,652
70,850	70,900	17,107	14,632	17,911	15,666
70,900	70,950	17,122	14,646	17,927	15,680
70,950	71,000	17,138	14,660	17,942	15,694

71,000

At least	But less than	Single	Married filing jointly *	Married filing separately	Head of a household
71,000	71,050	17,153	14,674	17,958	15,708
71,050	71,100	17,169	14,688	17,973	15,722
71,100	71,150	17,184	14,702	17,989	15,736
71,150	71,200	17,200	14,716	18,004	15,750
71,200	71,250	17,215	14,730	18,020	15,764
71,250	71,300	17,231	14,744	18,035	15,778
71,300	71,350	17,246	14,758	18,051	15,792
71,350	71,400	17,262	14,772	18,066	15,806
71,400	71,450	17,277	14,786	18,082	15,820
71,450	71,500	17,293	14,800	18,097	15,834
71,500	71,550	17,308	14,814	18,113	15,848
71,550	71,600	17,324	14,828	18,128	15,862
71,600	71,650	17,339	14,842	18,144	15,876
71,650	71,700	17,355	14,856	18,159	15,890
71,700	71,750	17,370	14,870	18,175	15,904
71,750	71,800	17,386	14,884	18,190	15,918
71,800	71,850	17,401	14,898	18,206	15,932
71,850	71,900	17,417	14,912	18,221	15,946
71,900	71,950	17,432	14,926	18,237	15,960
71,950	72,000	17,448	14,940	18,252	15,974

72,000

At least	But less than	Single	Married filing jointly *	Married filing separately	Head of a household
72,000	72,050	17,463	14,954	18,268	15,988
72,050	72,100	17,479	14,968	18,283	16,002
72,100	72,150	17,494	14,982	18,299	16,016
72,150	72,200	17,510	14,996	18,314	16,030
72,200	72,250	17,525	15,010	18,330	16,044
72,250	72,300	17,541	15,024	18,345	16,058
72,300	72,350	17,556	15,038	18,361	16,072
72,350	72,400	17,572	15,052	18,376	16,086
72,400	72,450	17,587	15,066	18,392	16,100
72,450	72,500	17,603	15,080	18,407	16,114
72,500	72,550	17,618	15,094	18,423	16,128
72,550	72,600	17,634	15,108	18,438	16,142
72,600	72,650	17,649	15,122	18,454	16,156
72,650	72,700	17,665	15,136	18,469	16,170
72,700	72,750	17,680	15,150	18,485	16,184
72,750	72,800	17,696	15,164	18,500	16,198
72,800	72,850	17,711	15,178	18,516	16,212
72,850	72,900	17,727	15,192	18,531	16,226
72,900	72,950	17,742	15,206	18,547	16,240
72,950	73,000	17,758	15,220	18,562	16,254

73,000

At least	But less than	Single	Married filing jointly *	Married filing separately	Head of a household
73,000	73,050	17,773	15,234	18,578	16,268
73,050	73,100	17,789	15,248	18,593	16,282
73,100	73,150	17,804	15,262	18,609	16,296
73,150	73,200	17,820	15,276	18,624	16,310
73,200	73,250	17,835	15,290	18,640	16,324
73,250	73,300	17,851	15,304	18,655	16,338
73,300	73,350	17,866	15,318	18,671	16,352
73,350	73,400	17,882	15,332	18,686	16,366
73,400	73,450	17,897	15,346	18,702	16,380
73,450	73,500	17,913	15,360	18,717	16,394
73,500	73,550	17,928	15,374	18,733	16,408
73,550	73,600	17,944	15,388	18,748	16,422
73,600	73,650	17,959	15,402	18,764	16,436
73,650	73,700	17,975	15,416	18,779	16,450
73,700	73,750	17,990	15,430	18,795	16,464
73,750	73,800	18,006	15,444	18,810	16,478
73,800	73,850	18,021	15,458	18,826	16,492
73,850	73,900	18,037	15,472	18,843	16,506
73,900	73,950	18,052	15,486	18,861	16,520
73,950	74,000	18,068	15,500	18,879	16,534

74,000

At least	But less than	Single	Married filing jointly *	Married filing separately	Head of a household
74,000	74,050	18,083	15,514	18,897	16,548
74,050	74,100	18,099	15,528	18,915	16,562
74,100	74,150	18,114	15,542	18,933	16,576
74,150	74,200	18,130	15,556	18,951	16,590
74,200	74,250	18,145	15,570	18,969	16,604
74,250	74,300	18,161	15,584	18,987	16,618
74,300	74,350	18,176	15,598	19,005	16,632
74,350	74,400	18,192	15,612	19,023	16,646
74,400	74,450	18,207	15,626	19,041	16,660
74,450	74,500	18,223	15,640	19,059	16,674
74,500	74,550	18,238	15,654	19,077	16,688
74,550	74,600	18,254	15,668	19,095	16,702
74,600	74,650	18,269	15,682	19,113	16,716
74,650	74,700	18,285	15,696	19,131	16,730
74,700	74,750	18,300	15,710	19,149	16,744
74,750	74,800	18,316	15,724	19,167	16,758
74,800	74,850	18,331	15,738	19,185	16,772
74,850	74,900	18,347	15,752	19,203	16,786
74,900	74,950	18,362	15,766	19,221	16,800
74,950	75,000	18,378	15,780	19,239	16,814

75,000

At least	But less than	Single	Married filing jointly *	Married filing separately	Head of a household
75,000	75,050	18,393	15,794	19,257	16,828
75,050	75,100	18,409	15,808	19,275	16,842
75,100	75,150	18,424	15,822	19,293	16,856
75,150	75,200	18,440	15,836	19,311	16,870
75,200	75,250	18,455	15,850	19,329	16,884
75,250	75,300	18,471	15,864	19,347	16,898
75,300	75,350	18,486	15,878	19,365	16,912
75,350	75,400	18,502	15,892	19,383	16,926
75,400	75,450	18,517	15,906	19,401	16,940
75,450	75,500	18,533	15,920	19,419	16,954
75,500	75,550	18,548	15,934	19,437	16,968
75,550	75,600	18,564	15,948	19,455	16,982
75,600	75,650	18,579	15,962	19,473	16,996
75,650	75,700	18,595	15,976	19,491	17,010
75,700	75,750	18,610	15,990	19,509	17,024
75,750	75,800	18,626	16,004	19,527	17,038
75,800	75,850	18,641	16,018	19,545	17,052
75,850	75,900	18,657	16,032	19,563	17,066
75,900	75,950	18,672	16,046	19,581	17,080
75,950	76,000	18,688	16,060	19,599	17,094

76,000

At least	But less than	Single	Married filing jointly *	Married filing separately	Head of a household
76,000	76,050	18,703	16,074	19,617	17,108
76,050	76,100	18,719	16,088	19,635	17,122
76,100	76,150	18,734	16,102	19,653	17,136
76,150	76,200	18,750	16,116	19,671	17,150
76,200	76,250	18,765	16,130	19,689	17,164
76,250	76,300	18,781	16,144	19,707	17,178
76,300	76,350	18,796	16,158	19,725	17,192
76,350	76,400	18,812	16,172	19,743	17,206
76,400	76,450	18,827	16,186	19,761	17,220
76,450	76,500	18,843	16,200	19,779	17,234
76,500	76,550	18,858	16,214	19,797	17,248
76,550	76,600	18,874	16,228	19,815	17,262
76,600	76,650	18,889	16,242	19,833	17,276
76,650	76,700	18,905	16,256	19,851	17,290
76,700	76,750	18,920	16,270	19,869	17,304
76,750	76,800	18,936	16,284	19,887	17,318
76,800	76,850	18,951	16,298	19,905	17,332
76,850	76,900	18,967	16,312	19,923	17,346
76,900	76,950	18,982	16,326	19,941	17,360
76,950	77,000	18,998	16,340	19,959	17,374

* This column must also be used by a qualifying widow(er).

Continued on next page

1996 Tax Table—*Continued*

If line 37 (taxable income) is—		And you are—				If line 37 (taxable income) is—		And you are—				If line 37 (taxable income) is—		And you are—			
At least	But less than	Single	Married filing jointly *	Married filing separately	Head of a household	At least	But less than	Single	Married filing jointly *	Married filing separately	Head of a household	At least	But less than	Single	Married filing jointly *	Married filing separately	Head of a household
		Your tax is—						Your tax is—						Your tax is—			
77,000						**80,000**						**83,000**					
77,000	77,050	19,013	16,354	19,977	17,388	80,000	80,050	19,943	17,194	21,057	18,228	83,000	83,050	20,873	18,034	22,137	19,068
77,050	77,100	19,029	16,368	19,995	17,402	80,050	80,100	19,959	17,208	21,075	18,242	83,050	83,100	20,889	18,048	22,155	19,082
77,100	77,150	19,044	16,382	20,013	17,416	80,100	80,150	19,974	17,222	21,093	18,256	83,100	83,150	20,904	18,062	22,173	19,098
77,150	77,200	19,060	16,396	20,031	17,430	80,150	80,200	19,990	17,236	21,111	18,270	83,150	83,200	20,920	18,076	22,191	19,113
77,200	77,250	19,075	16,410	20,049	17,444	80,200	80,250	20,005	17,250	21,129	18,284	83,200	83,250	20,935	18,090	22,209	19,129
77,250	77,300	19,091	16,424	20,067	17,458	80,250	80,300	20,021	17,264	21,147	18,298	83,250	83,300	20,951	18,104	22,227	19,144
77,300	77,350	19,106	16,438	20,085	17,472	80,300	80,350	20,036	17,278	21,165	18,312	83,300	83,350	20,966	18,118	22,245	19,160
77,350	77,400	19,122	16,452	20,103	17,486	80,350	80,400	20,052	17,292	21,183	18,326	83,350	83,400	20,982	18,132	22,263	19,175
77,400	77,450	19,137	16,466	20,121	17,500	80,400	80,450	20,067	17,306	21,201	18,340	83,400	83,450	20,997	18,146	22,281	19,191
77,450	77,500	19,153	16,480	20,139	17,514	80,450	80,500	20,083	17,320	21,219	18,354	83,450	83,500	21,013	18,160	22,299	19,206
77,500	77,550	19,168	16,494	20,157	17,528	80,500	80,550	20,098	17,334	21,237	18,368	83,500	83,550	21,028	18,174	22,317	19,222
77,550	77,600	19,184	16,508	20,175	17,542	80,550	80,600	20,114	17,348	21,255	18,382	83,550	83,600	21,044	18,188	22,335	19,237
77,600	77,650	19,199	16,522	20,193	17,556	80,600	80,650	20,129	17,362	21,273	18,396	83,600	83,650	21,059	18,202	22,353	19,253
77,650	77,700	19,215	16,536	20,211	17,570	80,650	80,700	20,145	17,376	21,291	18,410	83,650	83,700	21,075	18,216	22,371	19,268
77,700	77,750	19,230	16,550	20,229	17,584	80,700	80,750	20,160	17,390	21,309	18,424	83,700	83,750	21,090	18,230	22,389	19,284
77,750	77,800	19,246	16,564	20,247	17,598	80,750	80,800	20,176	17,404	21,327	18,438	83,750	83,800	21,106	18,244	22,407	19,299
77,800	77,850	19,261	16,578	20,265	17,612	80,800	80,850	20,191	17,418	21,345	18,452	83,800	83,850	21,121	18,258	22,425	19,315
77,850	77,900	19,277	16,592	20,283	17,626	80,850	80,900	20,207	17,432	21,363	18,466	83,850	83,900	21,137	18,272	22,443	19,330
77,900	77,950	19,292	16,606	20,301	17,640	80,900	80,950	20,222	17,446	21,381	18,480	83,900	83,950	21,152	18,286	22,461	19,346
77,950	78,000	19,308	16,620	20,319	17,654	80,950	81,000	20,238	17,460	21,399	18,494	83,950	84,000	21,168	18,300	22,479	19,361
78,000						**81,000**						**84,000**					
78,000	78,050	19,323	16,634	20,337	17,668	81,000	81,050	20,253	17,474	21,417	18,508	84,000	84,050	21,183	18,314	22,497	19,377
78,050	78,100	19,339	16,648	20,355	17,682	81,050	81,100	20,269	17,488	21,435	18,522	84,050	84,100	21,199	18,328	22,515	19,392
78,100	78,150	19,354	16,662	20,373	17,696	81,100	81,150	20,284	17,502	21,453	18,536	84,100	84,150	21,214	18,342	22,533	19,408
78,150	78,200	19,370	16,676	20,391	17,710	81,150	81,200	20,300	17,516	21,471	18,550	84,150	84,200	21,230	18,356	22,551	19,423
78,200	78,250	19,385	16,690	20,409	17,724	81,200	81,250	20,315	17,530	21,489	18,564	84,200	84,250	21,245	18,370	22,569	19,439
78,250	78,300	19,401	16,704	20,427	17,738	81,250	81,300	20,331	17,544	21,507	18,578	84,250	84,300	21,261	18,384	22,587	19,454
78,300	78,350	19,416	16,718	20,445	17,752	81,300	81,350	20,346	17,558	21,525	18,592	84,300	84,350	21,276	18,398	22,605	19,470
78,350	78,400	19,432	16,732	20,463	17,766	81,350	81,400	20,362	17,572	21,543	18,606	84,350	84,400	21,292	18,412	22,623	19,485
78,400	78,450	19,447	16,746	20,481	17,780	81,400	81,450	20,377	17,586	21,561	18,620	84,400	84,450	21,307	18,426	22,641	19,501
78,450	78,500	19,463	16,760	20,499	17,794	81,450	81,500	20,393	17,600	21,579	18,634	84,450	84,500	21,323	18,440	22,659	19,516
78,500	78,550	19,478	16,774	20,517	17,808	81,500	81,550	20,408	17,614	21,597	18,648	84,500	84,550	21,338	18,454	22,677	19,532
78,550	78,600	19,494	16,788	20,535	17,822	81,550	81,600	20,424	17,628	21,615	18,662	84,550	84,600	21,354	18,468	22,695	19,547
78,600	78,650	19,509	16,802	20,553	17,836	81,600	81,650	20,439	17,642	21,633	18,676	84,600	84,650	21,369	18,482	22,713	19,563
78,650	78,700	19,525	16,816	20,571	17,850	81,650	81,700	20,455	17,656	21,651	18,690	84,650	84,700	21,385	18,496	22,731	19,578
78,700	78,750	19,540	16,830	20,589	17,864	81,700	81,750	20,470	17,670	21,669	18,704	84,700	84,750	21,400	18,510	22,749	19,594
78,750	78,800	19,556	16,844	20,607	17,878	81,750	81,800	20,486	17,684	21,687	18,718	84,750	84,800	21,416	18,524	22,767	19,609
78,800	78,850	19,571	16,858	20,625	17,892	81,800	81,850	20,501	17,698	21,705	18,732	84,800	84,850	21,431	18,538	22,785	19,625
78,850	78,900	19,587	16,872	20,643	17,906	81,850	81,900	20,517	17,712	21,723	18,746	84,850	84,900	21,447	18,552	22,803	19,640
78,900	78,950	19,602	16,886	20,661	17,920	81,900	81,950	20,532	17,726	21,741	18,760	84,900	84,950	21,462	18,566	22,821	19,656
78,950	79,000	19,618	16,900	20,679	17,934	81,950	82,000	20,548	17,740	21,759	18,774	84,950	85,000	21,478	18,580	22,839	19,671
79,000						**82,000**						**85,000**					
79,000	79,050	19,633	16,914	20,697	17,948	82,000	82,050	20,563	17,754	21,777	18,788	85,000	85,050	21,493	18,594	22,857	19,687
79,050	79,100	19,649	16,928	20,715	17,962	82,050	82,100	20,579	17,768	21,795	18,802	85,050	85,100	21,509	18,608	22,875	19,702
79,100	79,150	19,664	16,942	20,733	17,976	82,100	82,150	20,594	17,782	21,813	18,816	85,100	85,150	21,524	18,622	22,893	19,718
79,150	79,200	19,680	16,956	20,751	17,990	82,150	82,200	20,610	17,796	21,831	18,830	85,150	85,200	21,540	18,636	22,911	19,733
79,200	79,250	19,695	16,970	20,769	18,004	82,200	82,250	20,625	17,810	21,849	18,844	85,200	85,250	21,555	18,650	22,929	19,749
79,250	79,300	19,711	16,984	20,787	18,018	82,250	82,300	20,641	17,824	21,867	18,858	85,250	85,300	21,571	18,664	22,947	19,764
79,300	79,350	19,726	16,998	20,805	18,032	82,300	82,350	20,656	17,838	21,885	18,872	85,300	85,350	21,586	18,678	22,965	19,780
79,350	79,400	19,742	17,012	20,823	18,046	82,350	82,400	20,672	17,852	21,903	18,886	85,350	85,400	21,602	18,692	22,983	19,795
79,400	79,450	19,757	17,026	20,841	18,060	82,400	82,450	20,687	17,866	21,921	18,900	85,400	85,450	21,617	18,706	23,001	19,811
79,450	79,500	19,773	17,040	20,859	18,074	82,450	82,500	20,703	17,880	21,939	18,914	85,450	85,500	21,633	18,720	23,019	19,826
79,500	79,550	19,788	17,054	20,877	18,088	82,500	82,550	20,718	17,894	21,957	18,928	85,500	85,550	21,648	18,734	23,037	19,842
79,550	79,600	19,804	17,068	20,895	18,102	82,550	82,600	20,734	17,908	21,975	18,942	85,550	85,600	21,664	18,748	23,055	19,857
79,600	79,650	19,819	17,082	20,913	18,116	82,600	82,650	20,749	17,922	21,993	18,956	85,600	85,650	21,679	18,762	23,073	19,873
79,650	79,700	19,835	17,096	20,931	18,130	82,650	82,700	20,765	17,936	22,011	18,970	85,650	85,700	21,695	18,776	23,091	19,888
79,700	79,750	19,850	17,110	20,949	18,144	82,700	82,750	20,780	17,950	22,029	18,984	85,700	85,750	21,710	18,790	23,109	19,904
79,750	79,800	19,866	17,124	20,967	18,158	82,750	82,800	20,796	17,964	22,047	18,998	85,750	85,800	21,726	18,804	23,127	19,919
79,800	79,850	19,881	17,138	20,985	18,172	82,800	82,850	20,811	17,978	22,065	19,012	85,800	85,850	21,741	18,818	23,145	19,935
79,850	79,900	19,897	17,152	21,003	18,186	82,850	82,900	20,827	17,992	22,083	19,026	85,850	85,900	21,757	18,832	23,163	19,950
79,900	79,950	19,912	17,166	21,021	18,200	82,900	82,950	20,842	18,006	22,101	19,040	85,900	85,950	21,772	18,846	23,181	19,966
79,950	80,000	19,928	17,180	21,039	18,214	82,950	83,000	20,858	18,020	22,119	19,054	85,950	86,000	21,788	18,860	23,199	19,981

* This column must also be used by a qualifying widow(er).

Continued on next page

1996 Tax Table—Continued

If line 37 (taxable income) is—		And you are—			
At least	But less than	Single	Married filing jointly *	Married filing separately *	Head of a house-hold
		Your tax is—			

86,000

At least	But less than	Single	Married filing jointly	Married filing separately	Head of a household
86,000	86,050	21,803	18,874	23,217	19,997
86,050	86,100	21,819	18,888	23,235	20,012
86,100	86,150	21,834	18,902	23,253	20,028
86,150	86,200	21,850	18,916	23,271	20,043
86,200	86,250	21,865	18,930	23,289	20,059
86,250	86,300	21,881	18,944	23,307	20,074
86,300	86,350	21,896	18,958	23,325	20,090
86,350	86,400	21,912	18,972	23,343	20,105
86,400	86,450	21,927	18,986	23,361	20,121
86,450	86,500	21,943	19,000	23,379	20,136
86,500	86,550	21,958	19,014	23,397	20,152
86,550	86,600	21,974	19,028	23,415	20,167
86,600	86,650	21,989	19,042	23,433	20,183
86,650	86,700	22,005	19,056	23,451	20,198
86,700	86,750	22,020	19,070	23,469	20,214
86,750	86,800	22,036	19,084	23,487	20,229
86,800	86,850	22,051	19,098	23,505	20,245
86,850	86,900	22,067	19,112	23,523	20,260
86,900	86,950	22,082	19,126	23,541	20,276
86,950	87,000	22,098	19,140	23,559	20,291

87,000

At least	But less than	Single	Married filing jointly	Married filing separately	Head of a household
87,000	87,050	22,113	19,154	23,577	20,307
87,050	87,100	22,129	19,168	23,595	20,322
87,100	87,150	22,144	19,182	23,613	20,338
87,150	87,200	22,160	19,196	23,631	20,353
87,200	87,250	22,175	19,210	23,649	20,369
87,250	87,300	22,191	19,224	23,667	20,384
87,300	87,350	22,206	19,238	23,685	20,400
87,350	87,400	22,222	19,252	23,703	20,415
87,400	87,450	22,237	19,266	23,721	20,431
87,450	87,500	22,253	19,280	23,739	20,446
87,500	87,550	22,268	19,294	23,757	20,462
87,550	87,600	22,284	19,308	23,775	20,477
87,600	87,650	22,299	19,322	23,793	20,493
87,650	87,700	22,315	19,336	23,811	20,508
87,700	87,750	22,330	19,350	23,829	20,524
87,750	87,800	22,346	19,364	23,847	20,539
87,800	87,850	22,361	19,378	23,865	20,555
87,850	87,900	22,377	19,392	23,883	20,570
87,900	87,950	22,392	19,406	23,901	20,586
87,950	88,000	22,408	19,420	23,919	20,601

88,000

At least	But less than	Single	Married filing jointly	Married filing separately	Head of a household
88,000	88,050	22,423	19,434	23,937	20,617
88,050	88,100	22,439	19,448	23,955	20,632
88,100	88,150	22,454	19,462	23,973	20,648
88,150	88,200	22,470	19,476	23,991	20,663
88,200	88,250	22,485	19,490	24,009	20,679
88,250	88,300	22,501	19,504	24,027	20,694
88,300	88,350	22,516	19,518	24,045	20,710
88,350	88,400	22,532	19,532	24,063	20,725
88,400	88,450	22,547	19,546	24,081	20,741
88,450	88,500	22,563	19,560	24,099	20,756
88,500	88,550	22,578	19,574	24,117	20,772
88,550	88,600	22,594	19,588	24,135	20,787
88,600	88,650	22,609	19,602	24,153	20,803
88,650	88,700	22,625	19,616	24,171	20,818
88,700	88,750	22,640	19,630	24,189	20,834
88,750	88,800	22,656	19,644	24,207	20,849
88,800	88,850	22,671	19,658	24,225	20,865
88,850	88,900	22,687	19,672	24,243	20,880
88,900	88,950	22,702	19,686	24,261	20,896
88,950	89,000	22,718	19,700	24,279	20,911

89,000

At least	But less than	Single	Married filing jointly	Married filing separately	Head of a household
89,000	89,050	22,733	19,714	24,297	20,927
89,050	89,100	22,749	19,728	24,315	20,942
89,100	89,150	22,764	19,742	24,333	20,958
89,150	89,200	22,780	19,756	24,351	20,973
89,200	89,250	22,795	19,770	24,369	20,989
89,250	89,300	22,811	19,784	24,387	21,004
89,300	89,350	22,826	19,798	24,405	21,020
89,350	89,400	22,842	19,812	24,423	21,035
89,400	89,450	22,857	19,826	24,441	21,051
89,450	89,500	22,873	19,840	24,459	21,066
89,500	89,550	22,888	19,854	24,477	21,082
89,550	89,600	22,904	19,868	24,495	21,097
89,600	89,650	22,919	19,882	24,513	21,113
89,650	89,700	22,935	19,896	24,531	21,128
89,700	89,750	22,950	19,910	24,549	21,144
89,750	89,800	22,966	19,924	24,567	21,159
89,800	89,850	22,981	19,938	24,585	21,175
89,850	89,900	22,997	19,952	24,603	21,190
89,900	89,950	23,012	19,966	24,621	21,206
89,950	90,000	23,028	19,980	24,639	21,221

90,000

At least	But less than	Single	Married filing jointly	Married filing separately	Head of a household
90,000	90,050	23,043	19,994	24,657	21,237
90,050	90,100	23,059	20,008	24,675	21,252
90,100	90,150	23,074	20,022	24,693	21,268
90,150	90,200	23,090	20,036	24,711	21,283
90,200	90,250	23,105	20,050	24,729	21,299
90,250	90,300	23,121	20,064	24,747	21,314
90,300	90,350	23,136	20,078	24,765	21,330
90,350	90,400	23,152	20,092	24,783	21,345
90,400	90,450	23,167	20,106	24,801	21,361
90,450	90,500	23,183	20,120	24,819	21,376
90,500	90,550	23,198	20,134	24,837	21,392
90,550	90,600	23,214	20,148	24,855	21,407
90,600	90,650	23,229	20,162	24,873	21,423
90,650	90,700	23,245	20,176	24,891	21,438
90,700	90,750	23,260	20,190	24,909	21,454
90,750	90,800	23,276	20,204	24,927	21,469
90,800	90,850	23,291	20,218	24,945	21,485
90,850	90,900	23,307	20,232	24,963	21,500
90,900	90,950	23,322	20,246	24,981	21,516
90,950	91,000	23,338	20,260	24,999	21,531

91,000

At least	But less than	Single	Married filing jointly	Married filing separately	Head of a household
91,000	91,050	23,353	20,274	25,017	21,547
91,050	91,100	23,369	20,288	25,035	21,562
91,100	91,150	23,384	20,302	25,053	21,578
91,150	91,200	23,400	20,316	25,071	21,593
91,200	91,250	23,415	20,330	25,089	21,609
91,250	91,300	23,431	20,344	25,107	21,624
91,300	91,350	23,446	20,358	25,125	21,640
91,350	91,400	23,462	20,372	25,143	21,655
91,400	91,450	23,477	20,386	25,161	21,671
91,450	91,500	23,493	20,400	25,179	21,686
91,500	91,550	23,508	20,414	25,197	21,702
91,550	91,600	23,524	20,428	25,215	21,717
91,600	91,650	23,539	20,442	25,233	21,733
91,650	91,700	23,555	20,456	25,251	21,748
91,700	91,750	23,570	20,470	25,269	21,764
91,750	91,800	23,586	20,484	25,287	21,779
91,800	91,850	23,601	20,498	25,305	21,795
91,850	91,900	23,617	20,512	25,323	21,810
91,900	91,950	23,632	20,526	25,341	21,826
91,950	92,000	23,648	20,540	25,359	21,841

92,000

At least	But less than	Single	Married filing jointly	Married filing separately	Head of a household
92,000	92,050	23,663	20,554	25,377	21,857
92,050	92,100	23,679	20,568	25,395	21,872
92,100	92,150	23,694	20,582	25,413	21,888
92,150	92,200	23,710	20,596	25,431	21,903
92,200	92,250	23,725	20,610	25,449	21,919
92,250	92,300	23,741	20,624	25,467	21,934
92,300	92,350	23,756	20,638	25,485	21,950
92,350	92,400	23,772	20,652	25,503	21,965
92,400	92,450	23,787	20,666	25,521	21,981
92,450	92,500	23,803	20,680	25,539	21,996
92,500	92,550	23,818	20,694	25,557	22,012
92,550	92,600	23,834	20,708	25,575	22,027
92,600	92,650	23,849	20,722	25,593	22,043
92,650	92,700	23,865	20,736	25,611	22,058
92,700	92,750	23,880	20,750	25,629	22,074
92,750	92,800	23,896	20,764	25,647	22,089
92,800	92,850	23,911	20,778	25,665	22,105
92,850	92,900	23,927	20,792	25,683	22,120
92,900	92,950	23,942	20,806	25,701	22,136
92,950	93,000	23,958	20,820	25,719	22,151

93,000

At least	But less than	Single	Married filing jointly	Married filing separately	Head of a household
93,000	93,050	23,973	20,834	25,737	22,167
93,050	93,100	23,989	20,848	25,755	22,182
93,100	93,150	24,004	20,862	25,773	22,198
93,150	93,200	24,020	20,876	25,791	22,213
93,200	93,250	24,035	20,890	25,809	22,229
93,250	93,300	24,051	20,904	25,827	22,244
93,300	93,350	24,066	20,918	25,845	22,260
93,350	93,400	24,082	20,932	25,863	22,275
93,400	93,450	24,097	20,946	25,881	22,291
93,450	93,500	24,113	20,960	25,899	22,306
93,500	93,550	24,128	20,974	25,917	22,322
93,550	93,600	24,144	20,988	25,935	22,337
93,600	93,650	24,159	21,002	25,953	22,353
93,650	93,700	24,175	21,016	25,971	22,368
93,700	93,750	24,190	21,030	25,989	22,384
93,750	93,800	24,206	21,044	26,007	22,399
93,800	93,850	24,221	21,058	26,025	22,415
93,850	93,900	24,237	21,072	26,043	22,430
93,900	93,950	24,252	21,086	26,061	22,446
93,950	94,000	24,268	21,100	26,079	22,461

94,000

At least	But less than	Single	Married filing jointly	Married filing separately	Head of a household
94,000	94,050	24,283	21,114	26,097	22,477
94,050	94,100	24,299	21,128	26,115	22,492
94,100	94,150	24,314	21,142	26,133	22,508
94,150	94,200	24,330	21,156	26,151	22,523
94,200	94,250	24,345	21,170	26,169	22,539
94,250	94,300	24,361	21,184	26,187	22,554
94,300	94,350	24,376	21,198	26,205	22,570
94,350	94,400	24,392	21,212	26,223	22,585
94,400	94,450	24,407	21,226	26,241	22,601
94,450	94,500	24,423	21,240	26,259	22,616
94,500	94,550	24,438	21,254	26,277	22,632
94,550	94,600	24,454	21,268	26,295	22,647
94,600	94,650	24,469	21,282	26,313	22,663
94,650	94,700	24,485	21,296	26,331	22,678
94,700	94,750	24,500	21,310	26,349	22,694
94,750	94,800	24,516	21,324	26,367	22,709
94,800	94,850	24,531	21,338	26,385	22,725
94,850	94,900	24,547	21,352	26,403	22,740
94,900	94,950	24,562	21,366	26,421	22,756
94,950	95,000	24,578	21,380	26,439	22,771

* This column must also be used by a qualifying widow(er).

Continued on next page

1996 Tax Table—*Continued*

If line 37 (taxable income) is—		And you are—				If line 37 (taxable income) is—		And you are—			
At least	But less than	Single	Married filing jointly *	Married filing separately	Head of a household	At least	But less than	Single	Married filing jointly *	Married filing separately	Head of a household
		Your tax is—						Your tax is—			
95,000						**98,000**					
95,000	95,050	24,593	21,394	26,457	22,787	98,000	98,050	25,523	22,268	27,537	23,717
95,050	95,100	24,609	21,408	26,475	22,802	98,050	98,100	25,539	22,283	27,555	23,732
95,100	95,150	24,624	21,422	26,493	22,818	98,100	98,150	25,554	22,299	27,573	23,748
95,150	95,200	24,640	21,436	26,511	22,833	98,150	98,200	25,570	22,314	27,591	23,763
95,200	95,250	24,655	21,450	26,529	22,849	98,200	98,250	25,585	22,330	27,609	23,779
95,250	95,300	24,671	21,464	26,547	22,864	98,250	98,300	25,601	22,345	27,627	23,794
95,300	95,350	24,686	21,478	26,565	22,880	98,300	98,350	25,616	22,361	27,645	23,810
95,350	95,400	24,702	21,492	26,583	22,895	98,350	98,400	25,632	22,376	27,663	23,825
95,400	95,450	24,717	21,506	26,601	22,911	98,400	98,450	25,647	22,392	27,681	23,841
95,450	95,500	24,733	21,520	26,619	22,926	98,450	98,500	25,663	22,407	27,699	23,856
95,500	95,550	24,748	21,534	26,637	22,942	98,500	98,550	25,678	22,423	27,717	23,872
95,550	95,600	24,764	21,548	26,655	22,957	98,550	98,600	25,694	22,438	27,735	23,887
95,600	95,650	24,779	21,562	26,673	22,973	98,600	98,650	25,709	22,454	27,753	23,903
95,650	95,700	24,795	21,576	26,691	22,988	98,650	98,700	25,725	22,469	27,771	23,918
95,700	95,750	24,810	21,590	26,709	23,004	98,700	98,750	25,740	22,485	27,789	23,934
95,750	95,800	24,826	21,604	26,727	23,019	98,750	98,800	25,756	22,500	27,807	23,949
95,800	95,850	24,841	21,618	26,745	23,035	98,800	98,850	25,771	22,516	27,825	23,965
95,850	95,900	24,857	21,632	26,763	23,050	98,850	98,900	25,787	22,531	27,843	23,980
95,900	95,950	24,872	21,646	26,781	23,066	98,900	98,950	25,802	22,547	27,861	23,996
95,950	96,000	24,888	21,660	26,799	23,081	98,950	99,000	25,818	22,562	27,879	24,011
96,000						**99,000**					
96,000	96,050	24,903	21,674	26,817	23,097	99,000	99,050	25,833	22,578	27,897	24,027
96,050	96,100	24,919	21,688	26,835	23,112	99,050	99,100	25,849	22,593	27,915	24,042
96,100	96,150	24,934	21,702	26,853	23,128	99,100	99,150	25,864	22,609	27,933	24,058
96,150	96,200	24,950	21,716	26,871	23,143	99,150	99,200	25,880	22,624	27,951	24,073
96,200	96,250	24,965	21,730	26,889	23,159	99,200	99,250	25,895	22,640	27,969	24,089
96,250	96,300	24,981	21,744	26,907	23,174	99,250	99,300	25,911	22,655	27,987	24,104
96,300	96,350	24,996	21,758	26,925	23,190	99,300	99,350	25,926	22,671	28,005	24,120
96,350	96,400	25,012	21,772	26,943	23,205	99,350	99,400	25,942	22,686	28,023	24,135
96,400	96,450	25,027	21,786	26,961	23,221	99,400	99,450	25,957	22,702	28,041	24,151
96,450	96,500	25,043	21,800	26,979	23,236	99,450	99,500	25,973	22,717	28,059	24,166
96,500	96,550	25,058	21,814	26,997	23,252	99,500	99,550	25,988	22,733	28,077	24,182
96,550	96,600	25,074	21,828	27,015	23,267	99,550	99,600	26,004	22,748	28,095	24,197
96,600	96,650	25,089	21,842	27,033	23,283	99,600	99,650	26,019	22,764	28,113	24,213
96,650	96,700	25,105	21,856	27,051	23,298	99,650	99,700	26,035	22,779	28,131	24,228
96,700	96,750	25,120	21,870	27,069	23,314	99,700	99,750	26,050	22,795	28,149	24,244
96,750	96,800	25,136	21,884	27,087	23,329	99,750	99,800	26,066	22,810	28,167	24,259
96,800	96,850	25,151	21,898	27,105	23,345	99,800	99,850	26,081	22,826	28,185	24,275
96,850	96,900	25,167	21,912	27,123	23,360	99,850	99,900	26,097	22,841	28,203	24,290
96,900	96,950	25,182	21,927	27,141	23,376	99,900	99,950	26,112	22,857	28,221	24,306
96,950	97,000	25,198	21,942	27,159	23,391	99,950	100,000	26,128	22,872	28,239	24,321
97,000											
97,000	97,050	25,213	21,958	27,177	23,407						
97,050	97,100	25,229	21,973	27,195	23,422						
97,100	97,150	25,244	21,989	27,213	23,438						
97,150	97,200	25,260	22,004	27,231	23,453						
97,200	97,250	25,275	22,020	27,249	23,469						
97,250	97,300	25,291	22,035	27,267	23,484						
97,300	97,350	25,306	22,051	27,285	23,500						
97,350	97,400	25,322	22,066	27,303	23,515						
97,400	97,450	25,337	22,082	27,321	23,531						
97,450	97,500	25,353	22,097	27,339	23,546						
97,500	97,550	25,368	22,113	27,357	23,562						
97,550	97,600	25,384	22,128	27,375	23,577						
97,600	97,650	25,399	22,144	27,393	23,593						
97,650	97,700	25,415	22,159	27,411	23,608						
97,700	97,750	25,430	22,175	27,429	23,624						
97,750	97,800	25,446	22,190	27,447	23,639						
97,800	97,850	25,461	22,206	27,465	23,655						
97,850	97,900	25,477	22,221	27,483	23,670						
97,900	97,950	25,492	22,237	27,501	23,686						
97,950	98,000	25,508	22,252	27,519	23,701						

$100,000 or over — use the Tax Rate Schedules on page 53

* This column must also be used by a qualifying widow(er).

1996 Tax Rate Schedules

Caution: *Use **only** if your taxable income (Form 1040, line 37) is $100,000 or more. If less, use the **Tax Table.** Even though you cannot use the Tax Rate Schedules below if your taxable income is less than $100,000, all levels of taxable income are shown so taxpayers can see the tax rate that applies to each level.*

Schedule X—Use if your filing status is Single

If the amount on Form 1040, line 37, is: Over—	But not over—	Enter on Form 1040, line 38	of the amount over—
$0	$24,000	.... 15%	$0
24,000	58,150	$3,600.00 + 28%	24,000
58,150	121,300	13,162.00 + 31%	58,150
121,300	263,750	32,738.50 + 36%	121,300
263,750	....	84,020.50 + 39.6%	263,750

Schedule Y-1—Use if your filing status is Married filing jointly or Qualifying widow(er)

If the amount on Form 1040, line 37, is: Over—	But not over—	Enter on Form 1040, line 38	of the amount over—
$0	$40,100	.... 15%	$0
40,100	96,900	$6,015.00 + 28%	40,100
96,900	147,700	21,919.00 + 31%	96,900
147,700	263,750	37,667.00 + 36%	147,700
263,750	....	79,445.00 + 39.6%	263,750

Schedule Y-2—Use if your filing status is Married filing separately

If the amount on Form 1040, line 37, is: Over—	But not over—	Enter on Form 1040, line 38	of the amount over—
$0	$20,050	.... 15%	$0
20,050	48,450	$3,007.50 + 28%	20,050
48,450	73,850	10,959.50 + 31%	48,450
73,850	131,875	18,833.50 + 36%	73,850
131,875	....	39,722.50 + 39.6%	131,875

Schedule Z—Use if your filing status is Head of household

If the amount on Form 1040, line 37, is: Over—	But not over—	Enter on Form 1040, line 38	of the amount over—
$0	$32,150	.... 15%	$0
32,150	83,050	$4,822.50 + 28%	32,150
83,050	134,500	19,074.50 + 31%	83,050
134,500	263,750	35,024.00 + 36%	134,500
263,750	....	81,554.00 + 39.6%	263,750

1996 Earned Income Credit (EIC) Table

Caution: *This is not a tax table.*

To find your credit: First, read down the "At least — But less than" columns and find the line that includes the amount you entered on line 6 or line 8 of the **Earned Income Credit Worksheet** on page 26. Next, read across to the column that includes the number of qualifying children you have. Then, enter the credit from that column on line 7 or line 9 of that worksheet, whichever applies.

If the amount on line 6 or line 8 of the worksheet on page 26 is— At least	But less than	No children	One child	Two children
$1	$50	$2	$9	$10
50	100	6	26	30
100	150	10	43	50
150	200	13	60	70
200	250	17	77	90
250	300	21	94	110
300	350	25	111	130
350	400	29	128	150
400	450	33	145	170
450	500	36	162	190
500	550	40	179	210
550	600	44	196	230
600	650	48	213	250
650	700	52	230	270
700	750	55	247	290
750	800	59	264	310
800	850	63	281	330
850	900	67	298	350
900	950	71	315	370
950	1,000	75	332	390
1,000	1,050	78	349	410
1,050	1,100	82	366	430
1,100	1,150	86	383	450
1,150	1,200	90	400	470
1,200	1,250	94	417	490
1,250	1,300	98	434	510
1,300	1,350	101	451	530
1,350	1,400	105	468	550
1,400	1,450	109	485	570
1,450	1,500	113	502	590
1,500	1,550	117	519	610
1,550	1,600	120	536	630
1,600	1,650	124	553	650
1,650	1,700	128	570	670
1,700	1,750	132	587	690
1,750	1,800	136	604	710
1,800	1,850	140	621	730
1,850	1,900	143	638	750
1,900	1,950	147	655	770
1,950	2,000	151	672	790
2,000	2,050	155	689	810
2,050	2,100	159	706	830
2,100	2,150	163	723	850
2,150	2,200	166	740	870
2,200	2,250	170	757	890
2,250	2,300	174	774	910
2,300	2,350	178	791	930
2,350	2,400	182	808	950
2,400	2,450	186	825	970
2,450	2,500	189	842	990
2,500	2,550	193	859	1,010
2,550	2,600	197	876	1,030
2,600	2,650	201	893	1,050
2,650	2,700	205	910	1,070
2,700	2,750	208	927	1,090
2,750	2,800	212	944	1,110
2,800	2,850	216	961	1,130
2,850	2,900	220	978	1,150
2,900	2,950	224	995	1,170
2,950	3,000	228	1,012	1,190
3,000	3,050	231	1,029	1,210
3,050	3,100	235	1,046	1,230
3,100	3,150	239	1,063	1,250
3,150	3,200	243	1,080	1,270

If the amount on line 6 or line 8 of the worksheet on page 26 is— At least	But less than	No children	One child	Two children
3,200	3,250	247	1,097	1,290
3,250	3,300	251	1,114	1,310
3,300	3,350	254	1,131	1,330
3,350	3,400	258	1,148	1,350
3,400	3,450	262	1,165	1,370
3,450	3,500	266	1,182	1,390
3,500	3,550	270	1,199	1,410
3,550	3,600	273	1,216	1,430
3,600	3,650	277	1,233	1,450
3,650	3,700	281	1,250	1,470
3,700	3,750	285	1,267	1,490
3,750	3,800	289	1,284	1,510
3,800	3,850	293	1,301	1,530
3,850	3,900	296	1,318	1,550
3,900	3,950	300	1,335	1,570
3,950	4,000	304	1,352	1,590
4,000	4,050	308	1,369	1,610
4,050	4,100	312	1,386	1,630
4,100	4,150	316	1,403	1,650
4,150	4,200	319	1,420	1,670
4,200	4,250	323	1,437	1,690
4,250	4,300	323	1,454	1,710
4,300	4,350	323	1,471	1,730
4,350	4,400	323	1,488	1,750
4,400	4,450	323	1,505	1,770
4,450	4,500	323	1,522	1,790
4,500	4,550	323	1,539	1,810
4,550	4,600	323	1,556	1,830
4,600	4,650	323	1,573	1,850
4,650	4,700	323	1,590	1,870
4,700	4,750	323	1,607	1,890
4,750	4,800	323	1,624	1,910
4,800	4,850	323	1,641	1,930
4,850	4,900	323	1,658	1,950
4,900	4,950	323	1,675	1,970
4,950	5,000	323	1,692	1,990
5,000	5,050	323	1,709	2,010
5,050	5,100	323	1,726	2,030
5,100	5,150	323	1,743	2,050
5,150	5,200	323	1,760	2,070
5,200	5,250	323	1,777	2,090
5,250	5,300	323	1,794	2,110
5,300	5,350	319	1,811	2,130
5,350	5,400	316	1,828	2,150
5,400	5,450	312	1,845	2,170
5,450	5,500	308	1,862	2,190
5,500	5,550	304	1,879	2,210
5,550	5,600	300	1,896	2,230
5,600	5,650	296	1,913	2,250
5,650	5,700	293	1,930	2,270
5,700	5,750	289	1,947	2,290
5,750	5,800	285	1,964	2,310
5,800	5,850	281	1,981	2,330
5,850	5,900	277	1,998	2,350
5,900	5,950	273	2,015	2,370
5,950	6,000	270	2,032	2,390
6,000	6,050	266	2,049	2,410
6,050	6,100	262	2,066	2,430
6,100	6,150	258	2,083	2,450
6,150	6,200	254	2,100	2,470
6,200	6,250	251	2,117	2,490
6,250	6,300	247	2,134	2,510
6,300	6,350	243	2,152	2,530
6,350	6,400	239	2,152	2,550

If the amount on line 6 or line 8 of the worksheet on page 26 is— At least	But less than	No children	One child	Two children
6,400	6,450	235	2,152	2,570
6,450	6,500	231	2,152	2,590
6,500	6,550	228	2,152	2,610
6,550	6,600	224	2,152	2,630
6,600	6,650	220	2,152	2,650
6,650	6,700	216	2,152	2,670
6,700	6,750	212	2,152	2,690
6,750	6,800	208	2,152	2,710
6,800	6,850	205	2,152	2,730
6,850	6,900	201	2,152	2,750
6,900	6,950	197	2,152	2,770
6,950	7,000	193	2,152	2,790
7,000	7,050	189	2,152	2,810
7,050	7,100	186	2,152	2,830
7,100	7,150	182	2,152	2,850
7,150	7,200	178	2,152	2,870
7,200	7,250	174	2,152	2,890
7,250	7,300	170	2,152	2,910
7,300	7,350	166	2,152	2,930
7,350	7,400	163	2,152	2,950
7,400	7,450	159	2,152	2,970
7,450	7,500	155	2,152	2,990
7,500	7,550	151	2,152	3,010
7,550	7,600	147	2,152	3,030
7,600	7,650	143	2,152	3,050
7,650	7,700	140	2,152	3,070
7,700	7,750	136	2,152	3,090
7,750	7,800	132	2,152	3,110
7,800	7,850	128	2,152	3,130
7,850	7,900	124	2,152	3,150
7,900	7,950	120	2,152	3,170
7,950	8,000	117	2,152	3,190
8,000	8,050	113	2,152	3,210
8,050	8,100	109	2,152	3,230
8,100	8,150	105	2,152	3,250
8,150	8,200	101	2,152	3,270
8,200	8,250	98	2,152	3,290
8,250	8,300	94	2,152	3,310
8,300	8,350	90	2,152	3,330
8,350	8,400	86	2,152	3,350
8,400	8,450	82	2,152	3,370
8,450	8,500	78	2,152	3,390
8,500	8,550	75	2,152	3,410
8,550	8,600	71	2,152	3,430
8,600	8,650	67	2,152	3,450
8,650	8,700	63	2,152	3,470
8,700	8,750	59	2,152	3,490
8,750	8,800	55	2,152	3,510
8,800	8,850	52	2,152	3,530
8,850	8,900	48	2,152	3,556
8,900	8,950	44	2,152	3,556
8,950	9,000	40	2,152	3,556
9,000	9,050	36	2,152	3,556
9,050	9,100	33	2,152	3,556
9,100	9,150	29	2,152	3,556
9,150	9,200	25	2,152	3,556
9,200	9,250	21	2,152	3,556
9,250	9,300	17	2,152	3,556
9,300	9,350	13	2,152	3,556
9,350	9,400	10	2,152	3,556
9,400	9,450	6	2,152	3,556
9,450	9,500	2	2,152	3,556
9,500	11,650	0	2,152	3,556
11,650	11,700	0	2,142	3,542

If the amount on line 6 or line 8 of the worksheet on page 26 is— At least	But less than	No children	One child	Two children
11,700	11,750	0	2,134	3,532
11,750	11,800	0	2,126	3,521
11,800	11,850	0	2,118	3,511
11,850	11,900	0	2,110	3,500
11,900	11,950	0	2,102	3,490
11,950	12,000	0	2,094	3,479
12,000	12,050	0	2,086	3,469
12,050	12,100	0	2,078	3,458
12,100	12,150	0	2,070	3,448
12,150	12,200	0	2,062	3,437
12,200	12,250	0	2,054	3,426
12,250	12,300	0	2,046	3,416
12,300	12,350	0	2,038	3,405
12,350	12,400	0	2,030	3,395
12,400	12,450	0	2,022	3,384
12,450	12,500	0	2,014	3,374
12,500	12,550	0	2,006	3,363
12,550	12,600	0	1,998	3,353
12,600	12,650	0	1,990	3,342
12,650	12,700	0	1,982	3,332
12,700	12,750	0	1,974	3,321
12,750	12,800	0	1,966	3,311
12,800	12,850	0	1,958	3,300
12,850	12,900	0	1,950	3,290
12,900	12,950	0	1,942	3,279
12,950	13,000	0	1,934	3,269
13,000	13,050	0	1,926	3,258
13,050	13,100	0	1,918	3,247
13,100	13,150	0	1,910	3,237
13,150	13,200	0	1,902	3,226
13,200	13,250	0	1,894	3,216
13,250	13,300	0	1,886	3,205
13,300	13,350	0	1,878	3,195
13,350	13,400	0	1,870	3,184
13,400	13,450	0	1,862	3,174
13,450	13,500	0	1,854	3,163
13,500	13,550	0	1,846	3,153
13,550	13,600	0	1,838	3,142
13,600	13,650	0	1,830	3,132
13,650	13,700	0	1,822	3,121
13,700	13,750	0	1,814	3,111
13,750	13,800	0	1,806	3,100
13,800	13,850	0	1,798	3,090
13,850	13,900	0	1,790	3,079
13,900	13,950	0	1,782	3,068
13,950	14,000	0	1,774	3,058
14,000	14,050	0	1,766	3,047
14,050	14,100	0	1,758	3,037
14,100	14,150	0	1,750	3,026
14,150	14,200	0	1,742	3,016
14,200	14,250	0	1,734	3,005
14,250	14,300	0	1,726	2,995
14,300	14,350	0	1,718	2,984
14,350	14,400	0	1,710	2,974
14,400	14,450	0	1,702	2,963
14,450	14,500	0	1,694	2,953
14,500	14,550	0	1,686	2,942
14,550	14,600	0	1,678	2,932
14,600	14,650	0	1,670	2,921
14,650	14,700	0	1,662	2,911
14,700	14,750	0	1,654	2,900
14,750	14,800	0	1,646	2,889
14,800	14,850	0	1,638	2,879
14,850	14,900	0	1,630	2,868

1996 Earned Income Credit (EIC) Table *Continued* (Not a tax table.)

If the amount on line 6 or line 8 of the worksheet on page 26 is—		And you have—		
At least	But less than	No children	One child	Two children
		Your credit is—		
14,900	14,950	0	1,622	2,858
14,950	15,000	0	1,614	2,847
15,000	15,050	0	1,606	2,837
15,050	15,100	0	1,598	2,826
15,100	15,150	0	1,591	2,816
15,150	15,200	0	1,583	2,805
15,200	15,250	0	1,575	2,795
15,250	15,300	0	1,567	2,784
15,300	15,350	0	1,559	2,774
15,350	15,400	0	1,551	2,763
15,400	15,450	0	1,543	2,753
15,450	15,500	0	1,535	2,742
15,500	15,550	0	1,527	2,732
15,550	15,600	0	1,519	2,721
15,600	15,650	0	1,511	2,710
15,650	15,700	0	1,503	2,700
15,700	15,750	0	1,495	2,689
15,750	15,800	0	1,487	2,679
15,800	15,850	0	1,479	2,668
15,850	15,900	0	1,471	2,658
15,900	15,950	0	1,463	2,647
15,950	16,000	0	1,455	2,637
16,000	16,050	0	1,447	2,626
16,050	16,100	0	1,439	2,616
16,100	16,150	0	1,431	2,605
16,150	16,200	0	1,423	2,595
16,200	16,250	0	1,415	2,584
16,250	16,300	0	1,407	2,574
16,300	16,350	0	1,399	2,563
16,350	16,400	0	1,391	2,552
16,400	16,450	0	1,383	2,542
16,450	16,500	0	1,375	2,531
16,500	16,550	0	1,367	2,521
16,550	16,600	0	1,359	2,510
16,600	16,650	0	1,351	2,500
16,650	16,700	0	1,343	2,489
16,700	16,750	0	1,335	2,479
16,750	16,800	0	1,327	2,468
16,800	16,850	0	1,319	2,458
16,850	16,900	0	1,311	2,447
16,900	16,950	0	1,303	2,437
16,950	17,000	0	1,295	2,426
17,000	17,050	0	1,287	2,416
17,050	17,100	0	1,279	2,405
17,100	17,150	0	1,271	2,395
17,150	17,200	0	1,263	2,384
17,200	17,250	0	1,255	2,373
17,250	17,300	0	1,247	2,363
17,300	17,350	0	1,239	2,352
17,350	17,400	0	1,231	2,342
17,400	17,450	0	1,223	2,331
17,450	17,500	0	1,215	2,321
17,500	17,550	0	1,207	2,310
17,550	17,600	0	1,199	2,300
17,600	17,650	0	1,191	2,289
17,650	17,700	0	1,183	2,279
17,700	17,750	0	1,175	2,268
17,750	17,800	0	1,167	2,258
17,800	17,850	0	1,159	2,247
17,850	17,900	0	1,151	2,237
17,900	17,950	0	1,143	2,226
17,950	18,000	0	1,135	2,216
18,000	18,050	0	1,127	2,205
18,050	18,100	0	1,119	2,194
18,100	18,150	0	1,111	2,184
18,150	18,200	0	1,103	2,173
18,200	18,250	0	1,095	2,163
18,250	18,300	0	1,087	2,152
18,300	18,350	0	1,079	2,142
18,350	18,400	0	1,071	2,131
18,400	18,450	0	1,063	2,121
18,450	18,500	0	1,055	2,110
18,500	18,550	0	1,047	2,100
18,550	18,600	0	1,039	2,089
18,600	18,650	0	1,031	2,079
18,650	18,700	0	1,023	2,068
18,700	18,750	0	1,015	2,058
18,750	18,800	0	1,007	2,047
18,800	18,850	0	999	2,037
18,850	18,900	0	991	2,026
18,900	18,950	0	983	2,015
18,950	19,000	0	975	2,005
19,000	19,050	0	967	1,994
19,050	19,100	0	959	1,984
19,100	19,150	0	951	1,973
19,150	19,200	0	943	1,963
19,200	19,250	0	935	1,952
19,250	19,300	0	927	1,942
19,300	19,350	0	919	1,931
19,350	19,400	0	911	1,921
19,400	19,450	0	903	1,910
19,450	19,500	0	895	1,900
19,500	19,550	0	887	1,889
19,550	19,600	0	879	1,879
19,600	19,650	0	871	1,868
19,650	19,700	0	863	1,858
19,700	19,750	0	855	1,847
19,750	19,800	0	847	1,836
19,800	19,850	0	839	1,826
19,850	19,900	0	831	1,815
19,900	19,950	0	823	1,805
19,950	20,000	0	815	1,794
20,000	20,050	0	807	1,784
20,050	20,100	0	799	1,773
20,100	20,150	0	792	1,763
20,150	20,200	0	784	1,752
20,200	20,250	0	776	1,742
20,250	20,300	0	768	1,731
20,300	20,350	0	760	1,721
20,350	20,400	0	752	1,710
20,400	20,450	0	744	1,700
20,450	20,500	0	736	1,689
20,500	20,550	0	728	1,679
20,550	20,600	0	720	1,668
20,600	20,650	0	712	1,657
20,650	20,700	0	704	1,647
20,700	20,750	0	696	1,636
20,750	20,800	0	688	1,626
20,800	20,850	0	680	1,615
20,850	20,900	0	672	1,605
20,900	20,950	0	664	1,594
20,950	21,000	0	656	1,584
21,000	21,050	0	648	1,573
21,050	21,100	0	640	1,563
21,100	21,150	0	632	1,552
21,150	21,200	0	624	1,542
21,200	21,250	0	616	1,531
21,250	21,300	0	608	1,521
21,300	21,350	0	600	1,510
21,350	21,400	0	592	1,499
21,400	21,450	0	584	1,489
21,450	21,500	0	576	1,478
21,500	21,550	0	568	1,468
21,550	21,600	0	560	1,457
21,600	21,650	0	552	1,447
21,650	21,700	0	544	1,436
21,700	21,750	0	536	1,426
21,750	21,800	0	528	1,415
21,800	21,850	0	520	1,405
21,850	21,900	0	512	1,394
21,900	21,950	0	504	1,384
21,950	22,000	0	496	1,373
22,000	22,050	0	488	1,363
22,050	22,100	0	480	1,352
22,100	22,150	0	472	1,342
22,150	22,200	0	464	1,331
22,200	22,250	0	456	1,320
22,250	22,300	0	448	1,310
22,300	22,350	0	440	1,299
22,350	22,400	0	432	1,289
22,400	22,450	0	424	1,278
22,450	22,500	0	416	1,268
22,500	22,550	0	408	1,257
22,550	22,600	0	400	1,247
22,600	22,650	0	392	1,236
22,650	22,700	0	384	1,226
22,700	22,750	0	376	1,215
22,750	22,800	0	368	1,205
22,800	22,850	0	360	1,194
22,850	22,900	0	352	1,184
22,900	22,950	0	344	1,173
22,950	23,000	0	336	1,163
23,000	23,050	0	328	1,152
23,050	23,100	0	320	1,141
23,100	23,150	0	312	1,131
23,150	23,200	0	304	1,120
23,200	23,250	0	296	1,110
23,250	23,300	0	288	1,099
23,300	23,350	0	280	1,089
23,350	23,400	0	272	1,078
23,400	23,450	0	264	1,068
23,450	23,500	0	256	1,057
23,500	23,550	0	248	1,047
23,550	23,600	0	240	1,036
23,600	23,650	0	232	1,026
23,650	23,700	0	224	1,015
23,700	23,750	0	216	1,005
23,750	23,800	0	208	994
23,800	23,850	0	200	984
23,850	23,900	0	192	973
23,900	23,950	0	184	962
23,950	24,000	0	176	952
24,000	24,050	0	168	941
24,050	24,100	0	160	931
24,100	24,150	0	152	920
24,150	24,200	0	144	910
24,200	24,250	0	136	899
24,250	24,300	0	128	889
24,300	24,350	0	120	878
24,350	24,400	0	112	868
24,400	24,450	0	104	857
24,450	24,500	0	96	847
24,500	24,550	0	88	836
24,550	24,600	0	80	826
24,600	24,650	0	72	815
24,650	24,700	0	64	805
24,700	24,750	0	56	794
24,750	24,800	0	48	783
24,800	24,850	0	40	773
24,850	24,900	0	32	762
24,900	24,950	0	24	752
24,950	25,000	0	16	741
25,000	25,050	0	8	731
25,050	25,100	0	*	720
25,100	25,150	0	0	710
25,150	25,200	0	0	699
25,200	25,250	0	0	689
25,250	25,300	0	0	678
25,300	25,350	0	0	668
25,350	25,400	0	0	657
25,400	25,450	0	0	647
25,450	25,500	0	0	636
25,500	25,550	0	0	626
25,550	25,600	0	0	615
25,600	25,650	0	0	604
25,650	25,700	0	0	594
25,700	25,750	0	0	583
25,750	25,800	0	0	573
25,800	25,850	0	0	562
25,850	25,900	0	0	552
25,900	25,950	0	0	541
25,950	26,000	0	0	531
26,000	26,050	0	0	520
26,050	26,100	0	0	510
26,100	26,150	0	0	499
26,150	26,200	0	0	489
26,200	26,250	0	0	478
26,250	26,300	0	0	468
26,300	26,350	0	0	457
26,350	26,400	0	0	446
26,400	26,450	0	0	436
26,450	26,500	0	0	425
26,500	26,550	0	0	415
26,550	26,600	0	0	404
26,600	26,650	0	0	394
26,650	26,700	0	0	383
26,700	26,750	0	0	373
26,750	26,800	0	0	362
26,800	26,850	0	0	352
26,850	26,900	0	0	341
26,900	26,950	0	0	331
26,950	27,000	0	0	320
27,000	27,050	0	0	310
27,050	27,100	0	0	299
27,100	27,150	0	0	289
27,150	27,200	0	0	278
27,200	27,250	0	0	267
27,250	27,300	0	0	257
27,300	27,350	0	0	246
27,350	27,400	0	0	236
27,400	27,450	0	0	225
27,450	27,500	0	0	215
27,500	27,550	0	0	204
27,550	27,600	0	0	194
27,600	27,650	0	0	183
27,650	27,700	0	0	173
27,700	27,750	0	0	162
27,750	27,800	0	0	152
27,800	27,850	0	0	141
27,850	27,900	0	0	131
27,900	27,950	0	0	120
27,950	28,000	0	0	110
28,000	28,050	0	0	99
28,050	28,100	0	0	88
28,100	28,150	0	0	78
28,150	28,200	0	0	67
28,200	28,250	0	0	57
28,250	28,300	0	0	46
28,300	28,350	0	0	36
28,350	28,400	0	0	25
28,400	28,450	0	0	15
28,450	28,495	0	0	5
28,495 or more		0	0	0

* If the amount on line 6 or line 8 of the worksheet is at least $25,050 **but less than** $25,078, your credit is $2. Otherwise, you **cannot** take the credit.

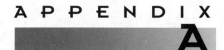

TAX RESEARCH WORKING PAPER FILE

George Dunn

Tax File

December 19XX

INDEX TO WORKING PAPERS

CARTER, PARKER, & ADAMS, CPAs
1011 Sunshine Blvd.
Tampa, Florida 33602

December 20, 19XX

Mr. George Dunn
15 Coral Court
Tampa, Florida 33611

We are pleased to report the results of our research concerning whether you will have to report any gain on the sale of your former residence. Before discussing our conclusions, I would like to restate briefly the facts that you related to me in our phone conversation of December 15. Please review these facts carefully because our conclusions depend upon an accurate understanding of all the relevant facts.

- - - (Summary of facts goes here.) - - -

Assuming that the preceding paragraphs constitute an accurate statement of all the relevant facts, we conclude that authority exists for viewing 105 Orange St. as your principal residence as of the date of sale. Accordingly, because the cost of your new residence exceeded the sales price (net of expenses) of your former residence, you may defer all of the gain. Deferral of the gain will reduce the basis of your new property. Whether a property constitutes your principal residence depends on all the facts and circumstances and your failure to occupy a house at the sale date does not automatically disqualify the house from being classified as your principal residence. We have a good faith belief that classification of 105 Orange St. as your principal residence on the sale date has a realistic possibility of being sustained administratively or judicially if challenged. However, if your return is audited, the Internal Revenue Service may argue that you are ineligible for deferral because, in their opinion, you had abandoned 105 Orange St. as your principal residence by the sale date. We will be happy to discuss this matter with you in more detail.

Thank you for consulting us. It is important that this letter be kept confidential. If you have any questions concerning our conclusions, please call.

Sincerely,

Patsy Partner

D-R-A-F-T

December 15, 19XX

MEMO TO FILE

FROM: Patsy Partner

SUBJECT: George Dunn-Tax Engagement

Today George Dunn called to inquire about the tax results of the sale of his former residence, 105 Orange St., Tampa, Florida. Basically, he wants to know whether he will have to report any gain on the sale.

Dunn purchased the house in 1963 for $75,000. He made no improvements to the house. In 1965 he married Linda Graves but continued to hold the house solely in his name. This is the first house that Dunn has owned. George and Linda occupied the house as their only residence until February 14, 19XX, when they decided to get a divorce. Mr. Dunn moved into an apartment on February 14, 19XX, and Mrs. Dunn continued to live in the house while she contemplated relocating to her hometown of Ponca City, Oklahoma. Dunn thought that if Mrs. Dunn did move back to Oklahoma, he would move back into the house after the divorce, provided Mrs. Dunn did not receive the house as part of her property settlement in connection with the divorce.

The divorce became final on September 13, 19XX, and Mrs. Dunn received stocks and bonds, but not the house, as her property settlement. She moved backed to Oklahoma on September 15, 19XX, and Mr. Dunn started making plans to move back into the house. Time pressures from business kept him too busy to move immediately. On September 25, 19XX, George decided to spend some of his free time touring model homes in a new development in Tampa. One of the homes, 15 Coral Court, turned out to be the house he had always dreamed of owning. He anticipated he could sell 105 Orange St. for almost as much as the asking price of 15 Coral Court.

Dunn thought about the new house for several days, and on October 4 he contracted to buy 15 Coral Court for $250,000. That same day he listed 105 Orange St. with the realtor who sold him his new house. On December 13, 19XX, Dunn sold his Orange St. house for $235,000 cash. There was no debt on his property. He incurred no fixing-up expenses, but his selling expenses totaled $15,000. Dunn will move to Coral Court by the end of this month. Subsequent to the move, he anticipates that this property will be his only residence.

Dunn hopes that his sale will be eligible for rollover of the gain under Sec. 1034. He is not 55 years old; consequently, he will not be eligible for the special rules affecting "older persons" who sell their homes.

We need to determine whether 105 Orange St. still qualifies as Dunn's principal residence, given that he did not live there for the period (approximately 10 months) between the date of the couple's decision to get a divorce and the sale date. I told Dunn we'd try to finish our research within a week. I have assigned Steve Staff the responsibility of researching this matter and drafting a client letter. Steve is to finish this assignment within 5 days. (He already has several other projects on which he is working.)

GEORGE DUNN

SUMMARY OF QUESTIONS AND CONCLUSIONS

Work
Paper
Reference

1. Does Dunn's sale qualify for a deferral of his realized gain?

Conclusion: It qualifies for deferral *provided* the house meets the principal residence test as of the sale date.

D-1

2. Did the house constitute Dunn's principal residence as of the sale date?

Conclusion: We have a good faith belief that classification of the house as his principal residence on the sale date, even though he did not occupy it on the date, is a position warranted in existing law. The IRS may, however, contend that he had abandoned this house as his principal residence. We should advise Dunn of the IRS's possible position and determine whether he wants us to file his return on the basis that he qualifies for deferral.

D-3

GEORGE DUNN

WORK PAPERS

1. Does Dunn's sale qualify for deferral of recognition of the gain?

Conclusion: Yes, provided 105 Orange St. meets the test of being Dunn's principal residence as of the sale date. Section 1034 is the controlling authority. It reads as follows:

SEC. 1034. ROLLOVER OF GAIN ON SALE OF PRINCIPAL RESIDENCE.

(a) **Nonrecognition of Gain.**—If property (in this section called "old residence") used by the taxpayer as his principal residence is sold by him, and, within a period beginning 2 years before the date of such sale and ending 2 years after such date, property (in this section called "new residence") is purchased and used by the taxpayer as his principal residence, gain (if any) from such sale shall be recognized only to the extent that the taxpayer's adjusted sales price (as defined in subsection (b)) of the old residence exceeds the taxpayer's cost of purchasing the new residence.

See ques. 2

See ques. 1(a)

(b) **Adjusted Sales Price Defined.**—

(1) **In general.**—For purposes of this section, the term "adjusted sales price" means the amount realized, reduced by the aggregate of the expenses for work performed on the old residence in order to assist in its sale.

See ques. 1(b)

(2) **Limitations.**

(c) **Rules for Application of Section.**

(d) **Limitation.**

Not Applicable

(e) **Basis of New Residence.**—Where the purchase of a new residence results, under subsection (a) or under section 112(n) of the Internal Revenue Code of 1939, in the nonrecognition of gain on the sale of an old residence, in determining the adjusted basis of the new residence as of any time following the sale of the old residence, the adjustments to basis shall include a reduction by an amount equal to the amount of the gain not so recognized on the sale of the old residence. For this purpose, the amount of the gain not so recognized on the sale of the old residence includes only so much of such gain as is not recognized by reason of the cost, up to such time, or purchasing the new residence.

If gain is deferred, the basis of the "new" house is affected.

(f) **Tenant-Stockholder in a Cooperative Housing Corporation.**

(g) **Husband and Wife.**

(h) **Members of Armed Forces.**

(i) **Special Rule for Condemnation.**

Not Applicable

(j) **Statute of Limitations.**—If the taxpayer during a taxable year sells at a gain property used by him as his principal residence, then–
(1) the statutory period for the assessment of any deficiency attributable to any part of such gain shall not expire before the expiration of 3 years from the date the Secretary is notified by the taxpayer (in such manner as the Secretary may be regulations prescribe) of–
(A) the taxpayer's cost of purchasing the new residence which the taxpayer claims results in nonrecognition of any part of such gain,
(B) the taxpayer's intention not to purchase a new residence within the period specified in subsection (a), or
(C) a failure to make such purchase within such period; and
(2) such deficiency may be assessed before the expiration of such 3-year period notwithstanding the provisions of any other law or rule of law which would otherwise prevent such assessment.

Cost will be reported on 19XX return.

(k) **Individual Whose Tax Home is Outside the United States.**

(l) **Cross Reference.**

Not Applicable

1 (a) What gain is recognized if 105 Orange St. constitutes his principal residence?

Conclusion: No gain is recognized *if* the old house is still Dunn's principal residence because the cost of the replacement residence exceeds the adjusted sales price of the old residence.

Adjusted sales price	$220,000	*See ques. 1(b)*
Minus: Cost of replacement residence	(250,000)	
Recognized gain (but not less than 0)	$ -0-	

1 (b) What is the adjusted sales price of the old residence?

Conclusion: The adjusted sales price is $220,000.

Amount realized	$220,000	*See ques. 1(c)*
Minus: Expenses for work performed to assist with sale	(-0-)	
Adjusted sales price	$220,000	

1 (c) What is the amount realized?

Conclusion: The amount realized is $220,000.

Section 1001(b) defines amount realized as follows:

(b) **Amount Realized.**—The amount realized from the sale or other disposition of property shall be the sum of any money received plus the fair market value of the property (other than money) received. In determining the amount realized—

(1) there shall not be taken into account any amount received as reimbursement for real property taxes which are treated under section 164(d) as imposed on the purchaser, and

(2) there shall be taken into account amounts representing real property taxes which are treated under section 164(d) as imposed on the taxpayer if such taxes are to be paid by the purchaser.

Money received ($235,000 − $15,000)	$220,000	*See ques. 1(d)*
Plus: FMV of other property received	-0-	
Amount realized	$220,000	

1 (d) How do the selling expenses affect the amount realized?

Conclusion: The selling expenses are subtracted from the sale price to compute the amount realized. Regulation Sec. 1.1034-1(b)(4) states that items that "are properly an offset against the considerations received upon the sale (such as commissions and expenses of advertising the property for sale, of preparing the deed, and of other legal services in connection with the sale)" are to be subtracted from the consideration received to arrive at the amount realized.

2 Did 105 Orange St. constitute Dunn's principal residence as of the date of disposition?

Conclusion: Reasonable authority exists to treat 105 Orange St. as his principal residence on the disposition date. However, because Dunn had not occupied the house for the approximate 10 month period immediately preceding its sale, the IRS may contend that he had abandoned the house as his principal residence.

2 (a) What is the definition of "principal residence"? Section 1034 does not define "principal residence," but Regulation Sec. 1.1034-1(c)(3) provides some guidance concerning the definition.

(3) **Property used by the taxpayer as his principal residence.** —(i) Whether or not property is used by the taxpayer as his residence, and whether or not property is used by the taxpayer as his principal residence (in the case of a taxpayer using more than one property as a residence), depends upon all the facts and circumstances in each case, including the good faith of the taxpayer. The mere fact that property is, or has been, rented is not determinative that such property is not used by the taxpayer as his principal residence. For example, if the taxpayer purchases his new residence before he sells his old residence, the fact that he temporarily rents out the new residence during the period before he vacates the old residence may not, in the light of all the facts and circumstances in the case, prevent the new residence from being considered as property used by the taxpayer as his principal residence. Property used by the taxpayer as his principal residence may include a houseboat, a house trailer, or stock held by a tenant-stockholder in a cooperative housing corporation (as those terms are defined in section 216(b)(1) and (2)), if the dwelling which the taxpayer is entitled to occupy as such stockholder is used by him as his principal residence (section 1034(f)). Property used by the taxpayer as his principal residence does not include personal property such as a piece of furniture, a radio, etc., which, in accordance with the applicable local law, is not a fixture.

Thus, whether a property constitutes one's principal residence is a factual issue, and property can be rented to another without its automatically being disqualified from principal residence status. The statement concerning renting property indicates that a property may still be a taxpayer's principal residence even though he does not live in such property as of the date of the sale.

According to the Committee Reports (H. Rept. No. 586, 82d Cong., 1st Sess., 109 (1951); S. Rept. No. 781 (Pt. 2), 82d Cong., 1st Sess., 32 (1951), accompanying the legislation that added the predecessor of Sec. 1034 to the Code, the word "residence" is used "in contradistinction to property used in trade or business and property held for the production of income." The Committee Reports also state that renting out either the old or the new residence will *not necessarily* prevent deferral of the gain.

Dunn did not hold 105 Orange St. for the production of income or use it in his trade or business. Thus, the argument can be made that treating 105 Orange St. as his principal residence is within the spirit of the legislation that authorized deferral of gain in certain situations.

2 (b) Do any judicial or administrative authorities address the availability of deferral under Sec. 1034 to taxpayers not occupying the property on the date of sale? If so, what result do such authorities reach?

Conclusion: There are numerous authorities, several of which are summarized below, that address the issue. The holdings differ, based upon the applicable facts. An analysis of such authorities leads to the conclusion that we have a good faith belief for adopting the position that the 105 Orange St. house was still his principal residence on the date of sale. Special emphasis is placed on *Clapham* and *Barry* (decided for the taxpayer) and *Young* (decided for the IRS).

Cases in Favor of Principal Residence Status:

Ralph L. Trisko, 29 T.C. 515 (1957), *acq.* 1959-1 C.B. 5. The taxpayer (T) leased his residence while working abroad. He intended to reoccupy the house upon his return but could not because of rent controls and a lease obligation. He later sold the house to generate funds to use for buying a replacement house. The court allowed deferral of the gain even though T had moved from the house several years earlier. The IRS stated it will follow *Trisko* only in cases which are "factually similar."

Robert W. Aagaard, 56 T.C. 191 (1971), *acq.* 1971-2 C.B. 1. Here the Tax Court held that Sec. 1034 was applicable, even though the taxpayer did not occupy the old residence at the time of sale *or intend to return* to the house.

Robert G. Clapham, 63 T.C. 505 (1975), *acq.* 1979-2 C.B. 1. Here the taxpayers (T) offered their old house for sale about 4 months prior to moving to rental property located in another city. T rented the old house (with an option to buy) for a year because of lack of offers. T leased it again for a short time and then let it stay vacant. T bought and moved into the new house about 9 months before finally selling the old one. T did not plan to return to the old house.

The Tax Court held that Sec. 1034 was available. It placed emphasis on the fact that T's *only desire* with respect to the old house *was to sell* it as soon as possible and that he accepted his first offer. The court stressed that T rented the old house because of "the *exigencies* of the real estate *market*."

Arthur R. Barry, 1971 PH T.C. Memo ¶ 71,179, 30 TCM 757. In this case taxpayer (T), a military officer, occupied a house in Maryland from August 1955 through July 1960. Then he was stationed in Germany and Colorado. At the time he moved from Maryland he planned to return to his home there upon his retirement from the military. He rented the home on a yearly basis until September 1965, when he listed it for sale because he had decided to live in Colorado after his retirement from the military in November 1965. He sold the Maryland house in August 1966 and in November 1966 occupied the house he had purchased in Colorado.

The Tax Court concluded that the Maryland house retained its status as T's principal residence until the sale date. It emphasized that T *at all times intended to occupy* this home and that he did not offer it for sale prior to his changing his principal residence to Colorado. It characterized the *change* in his principal residence in 1966 as resulting from "an *unexpected change of plans*." It added that he could not have adopted his temporary military quarters as "new" principal residence because his scheduled retirement time was in the near future.

Lee D. Andrews, 1981 PH T.C. Memo ¶ 81,247, 41 TCM 1533 (aff'd. by Fourth Circuit in unpublished opinion 7/6/82). In Andrews the taxpayers (T) lived in Washington D.C., during 1973 and the first half of 1974. In July 1974 they moved to North Carolina. In June 1974, in anticipation of their move, they listed their D.C. home for rent. In August 1974 they purchased a home in North Carolina. They sold their D.C. home in April 1975.

In allowing Sec. 1034 treatment, the Tax Court stressed that deferral is not automatically precluded just because the seller does not occupy the property on the date of the sale. In deciding that T had not abandoned the D.C. house as his principal residence, the Tax Court was influenced by the fact that when T moved to North Carolina, he was *uncertain whether he would stay* there or return to D.C. Because of the uncertainty of his plans, it was appropriate for him to keep the D.C. house.

Cases Denying Principal Residence Status:

William C. Stolk, 40 T.C. 345 (1963), *acq.* 1964-2 C.B. 7. In this case, Mr. Stolk (T) moved out of his old house located outside New York City in June 1953. Having no intention to return to the house, he had all of his furniture moved from it. T moved to an apartment in Manhattan. His old house stood vacant until its sale in July 1955. In September 1955 he purchased a house in Virginia. T then began spending his weekends in Virginia.

The Tax Court held that from about May 1953 until July 1955, at least, T's principal residence was his Manhattan apartment. It concluded that he had *abandoned* the old house as his principal residence. Although in *Trisko* the seller received deferral of gain with respect to a house he did not occupy at the time of sale, the court found *Stolk* to be distinguishable from *Trisko*. It stated that *Trisko* does not stand for the broad proposition that the taxpayer does not have to live in the property as of its sale date.

Richard T. Houlette, 48 T.C. 350 (1967). In *Houlette*, the taxpayer (T) was a Coast Guard Officer. In July 1955 he was transferred from Oregon to Alaska. For a few months prior to moving he tried to sell his house but could not do so without incurring a loss. Thus, he rented the property under a 2-year lease that he later extended for another year. Upon the expiration of the second lease, T again tried to sell. Having no success in selling, T rented the property again. In September, 1960, T purchased a new home. In the interim period he had lived in rental property. In May, 1961 T finally sold his old home.

The Tax Court denied Sec. 1034 treatment because it decided the old house no longer constituted T's principal residence. It recognized that actual occupancy on the sale date is not a universal requirement for qualifying for Sec. 1034. In its opinion, "however, the facts and circumstances must be exceptional and unusual to permit the conclusion that a principal residence is being used by the taxpayer at the time of sale if he is not in possession thereof and occupying same at that time." The court placed importance on the fact that T had *not occupied* the old house for almost *6 years*, that it was rented during the entire period, that T *persistently tried to sell it*, and that he had *no* intentions to reoccupy the house.

Claud R. Young, 1985 PH T.C. Memo ¶ 85,122, 49 TCM 981. Here Mr. Young (T) was divorced in October 1975. In the divorce proceedings he was awarded 25% interest in the house that he and his ex-wife had occupied. On the day of the divorce he moved into an apartment, and his ex-wife and child continued to live in the house. In November 1976 T and his ex-wife entered into an agreement whereby he conveyed to her his 25% interest in the house in exchange for being released from the obligation to pay alimony and the mortgage and other fees related to the house. In November 1977 T bought a new house.

The Tax Court declined to allow a deferral of the gain. It concluded that the old house ceased to be T's principal residence after he ceased to live there and the court awarded exclusive use to his ex-wife and child. It stated, "generally, cases in which taxpayers have been allowed the benefits of section 1034(a) even though they were not in possession of the old residence at the time of sale involve either the temporary rental of the property or . . . exceptional and unusual facts and circumstances over which the taxpayer had no control." It added that, "a divorce while often unpleasant and unwanted, is uniquely personal and is not the type of external objective circumstances that allows a taxpayer not in possession of a home to be deemed a resident therein for purposes of section 1034(a)."

} *See below*

Curtis B. Perry V. CIR, 78 AFTR 2d 96-5797, 96-2 USTC 50,405 (CA-9, 1996) also involved the sale of a home by a divorced taxpayer. Here, when his marriage broke up in June 1984, the taxpayer moved out of the house with no intention to return. The divorce was final in December 1985, and in accordance with the divorce settlement, the former wife and the child were given exclusive use of the home until the end of 1987, after which the house was to be sold as soon as possible and the sales proceeds divided equally between the two former spouses. The house was sold in March 1988, and the taxpayer treated the transaction as eligible for Sec. 1034. The court ruled that Sec. 1034 is not applicable in a situation such as here when the taxpayer leaves the home "permanently and with no intention to return, pursuant to a divorce settlement which gives the other spouse exclusive occupancy and which does not mandate that the house immediately be sold."

Application of the Cases to Dunn's Facts:

Dunn thought that he would move back to his old house unless his ex-wife received it as a property settlement. He did not place the home on the market until he had contracted to buy a new home. His purchase of a new home was a spur-of-the-moment decision. He sold his old home about 10 months after moving out of it and about 3 months after it was determined which spouse would receive the house in the property settlement. It was not possible, from an emotional standpoint, for him to occupy the house with his ex-wife after their final decision to seek a divorce.

A taxpayer is not unconditionally required to live in a property on the sale date in order for it to receive principal residence status. Whether a house is the taxpayer's principal residence depends on all the facts and circumstances. Dunn's move from his old house was a result of the "exigencies" (*Clapham*) of his pending divorce. Unlike *Stolk*, he never abandoned the old house; rather, like *Barry* his decision to sell resulted from an "unexpected change of plans." Dunn's facts meet the "exceptional and unusual circumstances" test described in *Houlette* as being a precondition to getting Sec. 1034 treatment for a property not occupied at the sale date.

If Dunn's return is audited, the IRS may argue that he had abandoned his old house. In fact, it may cite *Young* as holding that a divorce situation never meets the "exceptional and unusual" facts and circumstances test for qualifying a house that the taxpayer does not live in for nonrecognition under Sec. 1034. Our counterargument is that the language concerning divorce situations (page D-6) is not a holding to be applied across the board but, rather, is restricted to factual situations similar to those in *Young*. Unlike Dunn, Young knew when he moved from the house that he could not reoccupy it. His sale occurred 2 years after he moved in contrast with 10 months for Dunn's sale. Furthermore, Dunn sold his property about 2 months after his decision not to reoccupy it.

The recent case of *Perry* should not pose a problem because, unlike Mr. Perry, Dunn did not leave the house with no intention to return, and the ownership or use of the house was not addressed in Dunn's divorce.

We have a good faith belief for classifying 105 Orange St. as Dunn's principal residence on the sale date that is warranted in existing law. We should, however, advise Dunn of the position the IRS might take if it audits his return and inquire concerning what position he wants us to take.

APPENDIX B

TAX FORMS

SCHEDULE E
(Form 1040)

Department of the Treasury
Internal Revenue Service (99)

Supplemental Income and Loss

(From rental real estate, royalties, partnerships,
S corporations, estates, trusts, REMICs, etc.)

▶ Attach to Form 1040 or Form 1041. ▶ See Instructions for Schedule E (Form 1040).

OMB No. 1545-0074

1996

Attachment
Sequence No. **13**

Name(s) shown on return

Your social security number

Part I   **Income or Loss From Rental Real Estate and Royalties**   Note: Report income and expenses from your business of renting personal property on **Schedule C** or **C-EZ**. Report farm rental income or loss from **Form 4835** on page 2, line 39.

1 Show the kind and location of each **rental real estate property:**

A _____

B _____

C _____

2 For each rental real estate property listed on line 1, did you or your family use it for personal purposes for more than the greater of 14 days or 10% of the total days rented at fair rental value during the tax year? (See page E-1.)

	Yes	No
A		
B		
C		

Income:

			Properties			Totals
			A	B	C	(Add columns A, B, and C.)
3	Rents received	**3**				**3**
4	Royalties received	**4**				**4**

Expenses:

5	Advertising	**5**				
6	Auto and travel (see page E-2)	**6**				
7	Cleaning and maintenance	**7**				
8	Commissions	**8**				
9	Insurance	**9**				
10	Legal and other professional fees	**10**				
11	Management fees	**11**				
12	Mortgage interest paid to banks, etc. (see page E-2)	**12**				**12**
13	Other interest	**13**				
14	Repairs	**14**				
15	Supplies	**15**				
16	Taxes	**16**				
17	Utilities	**17**				
18	Other (list) ▶	**18**				
19	Add lines 5 through 18	**19**				**19**
20	Depreciation expense or depletion (see page E-2)	**20**				**20**
21	Total expenses. Add lines 19 and 20	**21**				
22	Income or (loss) from rental real estate or royalty properties. Subtract line 21 from line 3 (rents) or line 4 (royalties). If the result is a (loss), see page E-2 to find out if you must file **Form 6198**	**22**				
23	Deductible rental real estate loss. **Caution:** Your rental real estate loss on line 22 may be limited. See page E-3 to find out if you must file **Form 8582**. Real estate professionals must complete line 42 on page 2	**23**				
24	**Income.** Add positive amounts shown on line 22. **Do not** include any losses				**24**	
25	**Losses.** Add royalty losses from line 22 and rental real estate losses from line 23. Enter the total losses here				**25**	( )
26	Total rental real estate and royalty income or (loss). Combine lines 24 and 25. Enter the result here. If Parts II, III, IV, and line 39 on page 2 do not apply to you, also enter this amount on Form 1040, line 17. Otherwise, include this amount in the total on line 40 on page 2				**26**	

621491
12-20-96   LHA   **For Paperwork Reduction Act Notice, see Form 1040 instructions.**

Schedule E (Form 1040) 1996

Schedule E (Form 1040) 1996   Attachment Sequence No. **13**   Page **2**

Name(s) shown on return. Do not enter name and social security number if shown on Page 1.

Your social security number

Note: *If you report amounts from farming or fishing on Schedule E, you must enter your gross income from those activities on line 41 below. Real Estate professionals must complete line 42 below.*

Part II   Income or Loss From Partnerships and S Corporations

Note: *If you report a loss from an at-risk activity, you MUST check either column (e) or (f) of line 27 to describe your investment in the activity. If you check column (f) you must attach Form 6198.*

27	(a) Name	(b) Enter **P** for partnership; **S** for S corporation	(c) Check if foreign partnership	(d) Employer identification number	(e) All is at risk	(f) Some is not at risk
A						
B						
C						
D						
E						

	Passive Income and Loss		Nonpassive Income and Loss		
	(g) Passive loss allowed (attach **Form 8582** if required)	(h) Passive income from **Schedule K-1**	(i) Nonpassive loss from **Schedule K-1**	(j) Section 179 expense deduction from **Form 4562**	(k) Nonpassive income from **Schedule K-1**
A					
B					
C					
D					
E					

28a	Totals					
b	Totals					

29	Add columns (h) and (k) of line 28a	29	
30	Add columns (g), (i), and (j) of line 28b	30	( )
31	Total partnership and S corporation income or (loss). Combine lines 29 and 30. Enter the result here and include in the total on line 40 below	31	

Part III   Income or Loss From Estates and Trusts

32	(a) Name	(b) Employer identification number
A		
B		

	Passive Income and Loss		Nonpassive Income and Loss	
	(c) Passive deduction or loss allowed (attach **Form 8582** if required)	(d) Passive income from **Schedule K-1**	(e) Deduction or loss from **Schedule K-1**	(f) Other income from **Schedule K-1**
A				
B				

33a	Totals				
b	Totals				

34	Add columns (d) and (f) of line 33a	34	
35	Add columns (c) and (e) of line 33b	35	( )
36	Total estate and trust income or (loss). Combine lines 34 and 35. Enter the result here and include in the total on line 40 below	36	

Part IV   Income or Loss From Real Estate Mortgage Investment Conduits (REMICs) - Residual Holder

37	(a) Name	(b) Employer identification number	(c) Excess inclusion from **Schedules Q**, line 2c	(d) Taxable income (net loss) from **Schedules Q**, line 1b	(e) Income from **Schedules Q**, line 3b

38	Combine columns (d) and (e) only. Enter the result here and include in the total on line 40 below	38	

Part V   Summary

39	Net farm rental income or (loss) from **Form 4835**. Also, complete line 41 below	39	
40	TOTAL income or (loss). Combine lines 26, 31, 36, 38, and 39. Enter the result here and on Form 1040, line 17 ▶	40	
41	**Reconciliation of Farming and Fishing Income:** Enter your **gross** farming and fishing income reported on Form 4835, line 7; Schedule K-1 (Form 1065), line 15b; Schedule K-1 (Form 1120S), line 23; and Schedule K-1 (Form 1041), line 13 (see page E-4)	41	
42	**Reconciliation for Real Estate Professionals.** If you were a real estate professional enter the net income or (loss) you reported anywhere on Form 1040 from all rental real estate activities in which you materially participated under the passive activity loss rules	42	

621501
12-20-96

SCHEDULE F
(Form 1040)
Department of the Treasury
Internal Revenue Service (99)

Profit or Loss From Farming

▶ Attach to Form 1040, Form 1041, or Form 1065.
▶ See Instructions for Schedule F (Form 1040).

OMB No. 1545-0074

1996

Attachment
Sequence No. **14**

Name of proprietor

Social security number (SSN)

A Principal product. Describe in one or two words your principal crop or activity for the current tax year.

B Enter principal agricultural activity code
(from page 2) ▶

D Employer ID number (EIN), if any

C Accounting Method: **(1)** ☐ Cash **(2)** ☐ Accrual

E Did you "materially participate" in the operation of this business during 1996? If "No," see page F-2 for limit on passive losses. ☐ Yes ☐ No

Part I Farm Income - Cash Method. Complete Parts I and II (Accrual method taxpayers complete Parts II and III, and line 11 of Part I.)
Do not include sales of livestock held for draft, breeding, sport, or dairy purposes; report these sales on Form 4797.

1	Sales of livestock and other items you bought for resale			1		
2	Cost or other basis of livestock and other items reported on line 1			2		
3	Subtract line 2 from line 1				3	
4	Sales of livestock, produce, grains, and other products you raised				4	
5a	Total cooperative distributions (Form(s) 1099-PATR)	5a		5b Taxable amount	5b	
6a	Agricultural program payments	6a		6b Taxable amount	6b	
7	Commodity Credit Corporation (CCC) loans:					
a	CCC loans reported under election				7a	
b	CCC loans forfeited	7b		7c Taxable amount	7c	
8	Crop insurance proceeds and certain disaster payments:					
a	Amount received in 1996	8a		8b Taxable amount	8b	
c	If election to defer to 1997 is attached, check here ▶ ☐	8d Amount deferred from 1995			8d	
9	Custom hire (machine work) income				9	
10	Other income, including Federal and state gasoline or fuel tax credit or refund				10	
11	**Gross income.** Add amounts in the right column for lines 3 through 10. If accrual method taxpayer, enter the amount from page 2, line 51 ▶				11	

Part II Farm Expenses - Cash and Accrual Method. Do not include personal or living expenses such as taxes, insurance, repairs, etc., on your home.

12	Car and truck expenses (see page F-3 - also attach Form 4562)	12		25	Pension and profit-sharing plans	25	
13	Chemicals	13		26	Rent or lease (see page F-4):		
14	Conservation expenses (see page F-3)	14		a	Vehicles, machinery, and equipment	26a	
15	Custom hire (machine work)	15		b	Other (land, animals, etc.)	26b	
16	Depreciation and section 179 expense deduction not claimed elsewhere (see page F-4)	16		27	Repairs and maintenance	27	
				28	Seeds and plants purchased	28	
				29	Storage and warehousing	29	
17	Employee benefit programs other than on line 25	17		30	Supplies purchased	30	
18	Feed purchased	18		31	Taxes	31	
19	Fertilizers and lime	19		32	Utilities	32	
20	Freight and trucking	20		33	Veterinary, breeding, and medicine	33	
21	Gasoline, fuel, and oil	21		34	Other expenses (specify):		
22	Insurance (other than health)	22		a	_ _ _ _ _ _ _ _ _ _ _ _ _	34a	
23	Interest:			b	_ _ _ _ _ _ _ _ _ _ _ _ _	34b	
a	Mortgage (paid to banks, etc.)	23a		c	_ _ _ _ _ _ _ _ _ _ _ _ _	34c	
b	Other	23b		d	_ _ _ _ _ _ _ _ _ _ _ _ _	34d	
24	Labor hired (less employment credits)	24		e	_ _ _ _ _ _ _ _ _ _ _ _ _	34e	
				f		34f	

35	**Total expenses.** Add lines 12 through 34f ▶		35	
36	**Net farm profit or (loss).** Subtract line 35 from line 11. If a profit, enter on **Form 1040, line 18,** and ALSO on **Schedule SE, line 1.** If a loss, you MUST go on to line 37 (estates, trusts, and partnerships, see page F-5)		36	

37 If you have a loss, you MUST check the box that describes your investment in this activity (see page F-5). } 37a ☐ All investment is at risk.
If you checked 37a, enter the loss on **Form 1040, line 18,** and ALSO on **Schedule SE, line 1.** } 37b ☐ Some investment is not at risk.
If you checked 37b, you MUST attach **Form 6198.**

LHA **For Paperwork Reduction Act Notice, see Form 1040 Instructions.**

Schedule F (Form 1040) 1996

622001
12-20-96

Schedule F (Form 1040) 1996   Page **2**

Part III	**Farm Income – Accrual Method** (see page F-5)

Do not include sales of livestock held for draft, breeding, sport, or dairy purposes; report these sales on Form 4797 and do not include this livestock on line 46 below.

38	Sales of livestock, produce, grains, and other products during the year		**38**	
39a	Total cooperative distributions (Form(s) 1099-PATR)	**39a**	**39b** Taxable amount **39b**	
40a	Agricultural program payments	**40a**	**40b** Taxable amount **40b**	
41	Commodity Credit Corporation (CCC) loans:			
a	CCC loans reported under election		**41a**	
b	CCC loans forfeited	**41b**	**41c** Taxable amount **41c**	
42	Crop insurance proceeds		**42**	
43	Custom hire (machine work) income		**43**	
44	Other income, including Federal and state gasoline or fuel tax credit or refund		**44**	
45	Add amounts in the right column for lines 38 through 44		**45**	
46	Inventory of livestock, produce, grains, and other products at beginning of the year	**46**		
47	Cost of livestock, produce, grains, and other products purchased during the year	**47**		
48	Add lines 46 and 47	**48**		
49	Inventory of livestock, produce, grains, and other products at end of year	**49**		
50	Cost of livestock, produce, grains, and other products sold. Subtract line 49 from line 48*		**50**	
51	**Gross income.** Subtract line 50 from line 45. Enter the result here and on page 1, line 11 ▶		**51**	

* If you use the unit-livestock-price method or the farm-price method of valuing inventory and the amount on line 49 is larger than the amount on line 48, subtract line 48 from line 49. Enter the result on line 50. Add lines 45 and 50. Enter the total on line 51.

Part IV	**Principal Agricultural Activity Codes**

Caution: File **Schedule C** (Form 1040), Profit or Loss From Business or **Schedule C-EZ** (Form 1040), Net Profit From Business, instead of Schedule F if:

• Your principal source of income is from providing agricultural services such as soil preparation, veterinary, farm labor, horticultural, or management for a fee or on a contract basis, or

• You are engaged in the business of breeding, raising, and caring for dogs, cats, or other pet animals.

Select one of the following codes and write the 3-digit number on page 1, line B.

120   **Field crop,** including grains and nongrains such as cotton, peanuts, feed corn, wheat, tobacco, Irish potatoes, etc.

160   **Vegetables and melons,** garden-type vegetables and melons, such as sweet corn, tomatoes, squash, etc.

170   **Fruit and tree nuts,** including grapes, berries, olives, etc.

180   **Ornamental floriculture and nursery products**

185   **Food crops grown under cover,** including hydroponic crops

211   **Beefcattle feedlots**

212   **Beefcattle,** except feedlots

215   **Hogs, sheep, and goats**

240   **Dairy**

250   **Poultry and eggs,** including chickens, ducks, pigeons, quail, etc.

260   **General livestock,** not specializing in any one livestock category

270   **Animal specialty,** including bees, fur-bearing animals, horses, snakes, etc.

280   **Animal aquaculture,** including fish, shellfish, mollusks, frogs, etc., produced within confined space

290   **Forest products,** including forest nurseries and seed gathering, extraction of pine gum, and gathering of forest products

300   **Agricultural production,** not specified

622002
12-20-96

SCHEDULE EIC
(Form 1040A or 1040)

Department of the Treasury
Internal Revenue Service

Earned Income Credit
(Qualifying Child Information)
▶ Attach to Form 1040A or 1040.
▶ See Instructions for Schedule EIC.

OMB No. 1545-0074

1996

Attachment
Sequence No. **43**

Name(s) shown on return: First and initial(s) | Last | Your social security number

Before You Begin . . .

- See instructions for Form 1040A, line 29c, or Form 1040, line 54, to find out if you can take this credit.
- If you can take the credit, fill in the Earned Income Credit Worksheet in the Form 1040A or Form 1040 instructions to figure your credit. **But if you want the IRS to figure it for you, see instructions.**

Then, you **must** complete and attach Schedule EIC only if you have a qualifying child.

Information About Your Qualifying Child or Children

If you have more than two qualifying children, you only have to list two to get the maximum credit.

Caution: *If you do not attach Schedule EIC and fill in all the lines that apply, it will take us longer to process your return and issue your refund.*	**(a) Child 1**	**(b) Child 2**
1 Child's name		
2 Child's year of birth	19_____	19_____
3 If child was born **before 1978** AND ·		
a was **under age 24** at the end of 1996 **and** a student, check the "Yes" box, **OR**	☐ Yes	☐ Yes
b was permanently and totally disabled, check the "Yes" box	☐ Yes	☐ Yes
4 Enter the child's social security number. If born in December 1996, see instructions		
5 Child's relationship to you (for example, son, grandchild, etc.)		
6 Number of months child lived with you in the United States in 1996	_____ months	_____ months

Tip: Do you want the earned income credit added to your take-home pay in 1997? To see if you qualify, get **Form W-5** from your employer or by calling the IRS at 1-800-TAX-FORM (1-800-829-3676).

LHA **For Paperwork Reduction Act Notice, see Form 1040A or 1040 instructions.**

Schedule EIC (Form 1040A or 1040) 1996

621521
10-21-96

Instructions

Purpose of Schedule

If you can take the earned income credit and have a qualifying child, use Schedule EIC to give information about that child. To figure the amount of your credit, use the worksheet in the instructions for Form 1040A, line 29c, or Form 1040, line 54.

If you want the IRS to figure the credit for you, print "EIC" next to line 29c of Form 1040A or line 54 of Form 1040. Also, enter the amount and type of any nontaxable earned income in the spaces provided on Form 1040A, line 29c, or Form 1040, line 54, and attach Schedule EIC to your return.

Line 1

Enter each qualifying child's name.

Line 3a

If your child was born **before 1978** but was under age 24 at the end of 1996 and a student, put a checkmark in the "Yes" box.

Your child was a **student** if he or she—

● Was enrolled as a full-time student at a school during any 5 months of 1996, or

● Took a full-time, on-farm training course during any 5 months of 1996. The course had to be given by a school or a state, county, or local government agency.

A **school** includes technical, trade, and mechanical schools. It does not include on-the-job training courses or correspondence schools.

Line 3b

If your child was born **before 1978** and was permanently and totally disabled during any part of 1996, put a checkmark in the "Yes" box.

A person is **permanently and totally disabled** if **both** of the following apply.

1. He or she cannot engage in any substantial gainful activity because of a physical or mental condition.

2. A doctor determines the condition has lasted or can be expected to last continuously for at least a year or can lead to death.

Line 4

You must enter your child's social security number (SSN) on line 4 unless he or she was born in December 1996 or was born and died in 1996. If you do not enter the correct SSN, at the time we process your return, we may reduce or disallow your credit. If your child was born in December 1996 and does not have an SSN, enter "12/96" on line 4. If your child was born and died in 1996 and did not have an SSN, print "Died" on line 4.

If your child does not have an SSN, apply for one by filing **Form SS-5** with your local Social Security Administration (SSA) office. It usually takes about 2 weeks to get a number. If your child will not have an SSN by April 15, 1997, you can get an automatic 4-month extension by filing Form 4868 with the IRS by that date.

Line 6

Enter the number of months your child lived with you in your home in the United States during 1996. (If you were in the military on extended active duty outside the United States, your home is considered to be in the United States during that duty period.) Do not enter more than 12. Count temporary absences, such as for school, vacation, or medical care, as time lived in your home. If the child lived with you for more than half of 1996 but less than 7 months, enter "07" on this line.

Exception. If your child, including a foster child, was born or died in 1996 and your home was the child's home for the entire time he or she was alive during 1996, enter "12" on line 6.

Qualifying Child

A **qualifying child** is a child who:

is your:		was (at the end of 1996):		who:
son daughter adopted child grandchild stepchild or foster child	**AND**	under age 19 or under age 24 and a full-time student or any age and permanently and totally disabled	**AND**	lived with you in the U.S. for more than half of 1996* (or all of 1996 if a foster child*)

*If the child did not live with you for the required time (for example, was born in 1996), see the **Line 6** instructions above.

If the child was married or is also a qualifying child of another person (other than your spouse if filing a joint return), special rules apply. For details, see the instructions for Form 1040A, line 29c, or Form 1040, line 54. Also, the child must have an SSN (as defined in those instructions) unless he or she was born in December 1996 or was born and died in 1996.

SCHEDULE H (Form 1040)	Household Employment Taxes	OMB No. 1545-0074

SCHEDULE H (Form 1040)

Department of the Treasury
Internal Revenue Service   (99)

Household Employment Taxes
(For Social Security, Medicare, Withheld Income, and Federal Unemployment (FUTA) Taxes)
▶ **Attach to Form 1040, 1040A, 1040NR, 1040NR-EZ, 1-SS, or 1041.**
▶ **See separate instructions.**

OMB No. 1545-0074

1996

Attachment
Sequence No. **44**

Name of employer

Social security number

Employer identification number

A   Did you pay **any one** household employee cash wages of $1,000 or more in 1996? (If any household employee was your spouse, your child under age 21, your parent, or anyone under age 18, see the line A instructions on page 3 before you answer this question.)

☐ **Yes.**   Skip questions B and C and go to Part I.
☐ **No.**   Go to question B.

B   Did you withhold Federal income tax during 1996 for any household employee?

☐ **Yes.**   Skip question C and go to Part I.
☐ **No.**   Go to question C.

C   Did you pay **total** cash wages of $1,000 or more in **any** calendar **quarter** of 1995 or 1996 to household employees?
(**Do not** count cash wages paid in 1995 or 1996 to your spouse, your child under age 21, or your parent.)
☐ **No.**   **Stop.** Do not file this schedule.
☐ **Yes.**   Skip Part I and go to Part II on page 2.

Part I   **Social Security, Medicare, and Income Taxes**

1	Total cash wages subject to social security taxes	1	
2	Social security taxes. Multiply line 1 by 12.4% (.124)		2
3	Total cash wages subject to Medicare taxes	3	
4	Medicare taxes. Multiply line 3 by 2.9% (.029)		4
5	Federal income tax withheld, if any		5
6	Add lines 2, 4, and 5		6
7	Advance earned income credit (EIC) payments, if any		7
8	**Total social security, Medicare, and income taxes.** Subtract line 7 from line 6		8

9   Did you pay **total** cash wages of $1,000 or more in **any** calendar **quarter** of 1995 or 1996 to household employees?
(**Do not** count cash wages paid in 1995 or 1996 to your spouse, your child under age 21, or your parent.)

☐ **No.**   **Stop.** Enter the amount from line 8 above on Form 1040, line 50, or Form 1040A, line 27. If you are not required to file Form 1040 or 1040A, see the instructions.

☐ **Yes.**   Go to Part II on page 2.

LHA   **For Paperwork Reduction Act Notice, see Form 1040 instructions.**

Schedule H (Form 1040) 1996

610351
12-09-96

Schedule H (Form 1040) 1996   Page **2**

Part II   Federal Unemployment (FUTA) Tax

		Yes	No
10 Did you pay unemployment contributions to only one state?			
11 Did you pay all state unemployment contributions for 1996 by April 15, 1997?			
12 Were all wages that are taxable for FUTA tax also taxable for your state's unemployment tax?			

Next: If you answered **"Yes"** to **all** of the questions above, complete Section A.

If you answered **"No"** to **any** of the questions above, skip Section A and complete Section B.

Section A

13 Name of the state where you paid unemployment contributions .... ▶ _ _ _ _ _ _ _ _ _ _ _ _ _ _ _

14 State reporting number as shown on state unemployment tax return ...... ▶ _ _ _ _ _ _ _ _ _ _ _ _ _ _ _

15 Contributions paid to your state unemployment fund (see page 4) .... | **15** |

16 Total cash wages subject to FUTA tax (see page 4) .... | **16** |

17 **FUTA tax.** Multiply line 16 by .008. Enter the result here, skip Section B, and go to Part III .... | **17** |

Section B

18 Complete all columns below that apply

(a) Name of state	(b) State reporting number as shown on state unemployment tax return	(c) Taxable wages (as defined in state act)	(d) State experience rate period		(e) State experience rate	(f) Multiply col. (c) by .054	(g) Multiply col. (c) by col. (e)	(h) Subtract col. (g) from col. (f). If zero or less, enter -0-.	(i) Contributions paid to state unemployment fund
			From	To					

19 Totals .... | **19** |

20 Add columns (h) and (i) of line 19 .... | **20** |

21 Total cash wages subject to FUTA tax (see line 16 instructions on page 4) .... | **21** |

22 Multiply line 21 by 6.2% (.062) .... | **22** |

23 Multiply line 21 by 5.4% (.054) .... | **23** |

24 Enter the **smaller** of line 20 or line 23 .... | **24** |

25 **FUTA tax.** Subtract line 24 from line 22. Enter the result here and go to Part III .... | **25** |

Part III   Total Household Employment Taxes

26 Enter the amount from line 8 .... | **26** |

27 Add line 17 (or line 25) and line 26 .... | **27** |

28 Are you required to file Form 1040 or 1040A?

☐ **Yes. Stop.** Enter the amount from line 27 above on Form 1040, line 50, or Form 1040A, line 27. **Do not** complete Part IV below.

☐ **No.** You may have to complete Part IV. See instructions for details.

Part IV   Address and Signature - Complete this part **only** if required. See line 28 instructions on page 4.

Address (number and street) or P.O. box if mail is not delivered to street address	Apt., room, or suite no.

City, town or post office, state, and ZIP code

Under penalties of perjury, I declare that I have examined this schedule, including accompanying statements, and to the best of my knowledge and belief, it is true, correct, and complete. No part of any payment made to a state unemployment fund claimed as a credit was, or is to be, deducted from the payments to employees.

▶ _____   ▶ _____
  Employer's signature   Date

Schedule R
(Form 1040)

Department of the Treasury
Internal Revenue Service   (99)

Credit for the Elderly or the Disabled

▶ **Attach to Form 1040.**   ▶ **See separate instructions for Schedule R.**

OMB No. 1545-0074

1996

Attachment
Sequence No. **16**

Name(s) shown on Form 1040

Your social security number

You may be able to take this credit and reduce your tax if by the end of 1996:

- You were age 65 or older, **OR** • You were under age 65, you retired on **permanent and total** disability, and you received taxable disability income.

But you must also meet other tests. See the separate instructions for Schedule R.
Note: *In most cases, the IRS can figure the credit for you. See the instructions.*

Part I **Check the Box for Your Filing Status and Age**

If your filing status is:	And by the end of 1996:	Check only one box:

Single,
Head of household, or
Qualifying widow(er)
with dependent child

1 You were 65 or older .... 1 ☐

2 You were under 65 and you retired on permanent and total disability .... 2 ☐

Married filing a
joint return

3 Both spouses were 65 or older .... 3 ☐

4 Both spouses were under 65, but only one spouse retired on permanent and total disability .... 4 ☐

5 Both spouses were under 65, and both retired on permanent and total disability .... 5 ☐

6 One spouse was 65 or older, and the other spouse was under 65 and retired on permanent
and total disability .... 6 ☐

7 One spouse was 65 or older, and the other spouse was under 65 and **NOT** retired on
permanent and total disability .... 7 ☐

Married filing a
separate return

8 You were 65 or older and you lived apart from your spouse for all of 1996 .... 8 ☐

9 You were under 65, you retired on permanent and total disability, and you lived apart from your
spouse for all of 1996 .... 9 ☐

Did you check
box 1, 3, 7,
or 8? .

— **Yes** ——▶ Skip Part II and complete Part III on page 2.

— **No** ——▶ Complete Parts II and III.

Part II **Statement of Permanent and Total Disability** (Complete **only** if you checked box 2, 4, 5, 6, or 9 above.)

IF: **1** You filed a physician's statement for this disability for 1983 or an earlier year, or you filed a statement for tax years after 1983
and your physician signed line B on the statement, **AND**

2 Due to your continued disabled condition, you were unable to engage in any substantial gainful activity in 1996, check this box ...... ▶ ☐

- If you checked this box, you do not have to file another statement for 1996.
- If you **did not** check this box, have your physician complete the statement below.

Physician's Statement (See instructions at bottom of page 2.)

I certify that _____
Name of disabled person

was permanently and totally disabled on January 1, 1976, or January 1, 1977, **OR** was permanently and totally disabled on the date he or she

retired. If retired after 1976, enter the date retired. ▶ _____

Physician: Sign your name on **either** line A or B below.

A The disability has lasted or can be expected to
last continuously for at least a year .... _____

Physician's signature   Date

B There is no reasonable probability that the
disabled condition will ever improve .... _____

Physician's signature   Date

Physician's name

Physician's address

LHA   **For Paperwork Reduction Act Notice, see Form 1040 Instructions.**   **Schedule R (Form 1040) 1996**

624001
11-12-96

Schedule R (Form 1040) 1996   Page **2**

Part III Figure Your Credit

10 If you checked (in Part I):   **Enter:**

    Box 1, 2, 4, or 7 .... $5,000 ⎫

    Box 3, 5, or 6 .... $7,500 ⎬   **10**

    Box 8 or 9 .... $3,750 ⎭

Did you check box 2, 4, 5, 6, or 9 in Part I?	Yes ──────▶ You **must** complete line 11.
	No ──────▶ Enter the amount from line 10 on line 12 and go to line 13.

11 If you checked:

    ● Box 6 in Part I, add $5,000 to the taxable disability income of the spouse who was ⎫
      under age 65. Enter the total.

    ● Box 2, 4, or 9 in Part I, enter your taxable disability income. ⎬ **11**

    ● Box 5 in Part I, add your taxable disability income to your spouse's taxable disability
      income. Enter the total. ⎭

    TIP: For more details on what to include on line 11, see the instructions.

12 If you completed line 11, enter the **smaller** of line 10 or line 11; **all others,** enter the amount
from line 10 .... **12**

13 Enter the following pensions, annuities, or disability income that you (and
your spouse if filing a joint return) received in 1996:

    a Nontaxable part of social security benefits, and ⎫
    Nontaxable part of railroad retirement benefits treated as ⎬ **13a**
    social security. See instructions. ⎭

    b Nontaxable veterans' pensions, and ⎫
    Any other pension, annuity, or disability benefit that is ⎬ **13b**
    excluded from income under any other provision of law.
    See instructions. ⎭

    c Add lines 13a and 13b. (Even though these income items are not
    taxable, they **must** be included here to figure your credit.) If you did
    not receive any of the types of nontaxable income listed on line 13a
    or 13b, enter -0- on line 13c **13c**

14 Enter the amount from Form 1040, line 32 .... **14**

15 If you checked (in Part I):   **Enter:**

    Box 1 or 2 .... $7,500 ⎫

    Box 3, 4, 5, 6, or 7 .... $10,000 ⎬ **15**

    Box 8 or 9 .... $5,000 ⎭

16 Subtract line 15 from line 14. If zero or less,
enter -0- **16**

17 Enter one-half of line 16 .... **17**

18 Add lines 13c and 17 .... **18**

19 Subtract line 18 from line 12. If zero or less, **stop;** you **cannot** take the credit.
Otherwise, go to line 20 .... **19**

20 Multiply line 19 by 15% (.15). Enter the result here and on Form 1040, line 40. **Caution:** If you
file Schedule C, C-EZ, D, E, or F (Form 1040), your credit may be limited. See the instructions
for line 20 for the amount of credit you can claim **20**

Instructions for Physician's Statement

Taxpayer

If you retired after 1976, enter the date you retired in the space provided in Part II.

Physician

A person is permanently and totally disabled if **both** of the following apply:

  1. He or she cannot engage in any substantial gainful activity because of a physical or mental condition, and

2. A physician determines that the disability has lasted or can be expected to last continuously for at least a year or can lead to death.

624002
11-12-96

SCHEDULE SE
(Form 1040)

Department of the Treasury
Internal Revenue Service

Self-Employment Tax

▶ See Instructions for Schedule SE (Form 1040).
▶ Attach to Form 1040.

OMB No. 1545-0074

1996

Attachment
Sequence No. **17**

Name of person with **self-employment** income (as shown on Form 1040)

Social security number of
person with **self-employment**
income ▶

Who Must File Schedule SE

You must file Schedule SE if:

- You had net earnings from self-employment from **other than** church employee income (line 4 of Short Schedule SE or line 4c of Long Schedule SE) of $400 or more, **OR**
- You had church employee income of $108.28 or more. Income from services you performed as a minister or a member of a religious order **is not** church employee income. See page SE-1.

Note: Even if you have a loss or a small amount of income from self-employment, it may be to your benefit to file Schedule SE and use either "optional method" in Part II of Long Schedule SE. See page SE-3.

Exception. If your only self-employment income was from earnings as a minister, member of a religious order, or Christian Science practitioner, **and** you filed Form 4361 and received IRS approval not to be taxed on those earnings, **do not** file Schedule SE. Instead, write "Exempt-Form 4361" on Form 1040, line 45.

May I Use Short Schedule SE or MUST I Use Long Schedule SE?

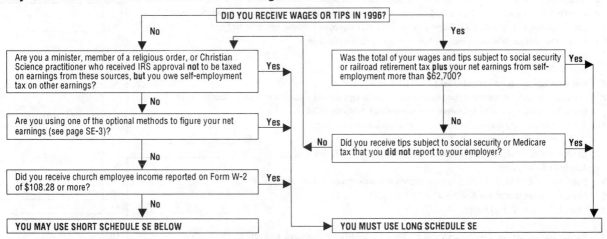

Section A - Short Schedule SE. Caution: *Read above to see if you can use Short Schedule SE.*

1 Net farm profit or (loss) from Schedule F, line 36, and farm partnerships, Schedule K-1 (Form 1065), line 15a	**1**	
2 Net profit or (loss) from Schedule C, line 31; Schedule C-EZ, line 3; and Schedule K-1 (Form 1065), line 15a (other than farming). Ministers and members of religious orders see page SE-1 for amounts to report on this line. See page SE-2 for other income to report	**2**	
3 Combine lines 1 and 2	**3**	
4 **Net earnings from self-employment.** Multiply line 3 by 92.35% (.9235). If less than $400, **do not** file this schedule; you **do not** owe self-employment tax ▶	**4**	
5 **Self-employment tax.** If the amount on line 4 is: • $62,700 or less, multiply line 4 by 15.3% (.153). Enter the result here and on **Form 1040, line 45.** • More than $62,700, multiply line 4 by 2.9% (.029). Then, add $7,774.80 to the result. Enter the total here and on **Form 1040, line 45.**	**5**	

6 **Deduction for one-half of self-employment tax.**
   Multiply line 5 by 50% (.5). Enter the result here and on **Form 1040, line 25** .... | **6** |

LHA   For Paperwork Reduction Act Notice, see Form 1040 Instructions.

Schedule SE (Form 1040) 1996

Schedule SE (Form 1040) 1996   Attachment Sequence No. **17**   Page **2**

Name of person with **self-employment** income (as shown on Form 1040)	Social security number of person with **self-employment** income ▶	

Section B - Long Schedule SE

Part I   Self-Employment Tax

Note: *If your only income subject to self-employment tax is* **church employee income,** *skip lines 1 through 4b. Enter -0- on line 4c and go to line 5a. Income from services you performed as a minister or a member of a religious order* **is not** *church employee income. See page SE-1.*

A   If you are a minister, member of a religious order, or Christian Science practitioner **and** you filed Form 4361, but you had $400 or more of **other** net earnings from self-employment, check here and continue with Part I .... ▶ ☐

1	Net farm profit or (loss) from Schedule F, line 36, and farm partnerships, Schedule K-1 (Form 1065), line 15a. **Note:** Skip this line if you use the farm optional method. See page SE-3	**1**	
2	Net profit or (loss) from Schedule C, line 31; Schedule C-EZ, line 3; and Schedule K-1 (Form 1065), line 15a (other than farming). Ministers and members of religious orders see page SE-1 for amounts to report on this line. See page SE-2 for other income to report. **Note:** Skip this line if you use the nonfarm optional method. See page SE-3	**2**	
3	Combine lines 1 and 2	**3**	
4 a	If line 3 is more than zero, multiply line 3 by 92.35% (.9235). Otherwise, enter amount from line 3	**4a**	
b	If you elected one or both of the optional methods, enter the total of lines 15 and 17 here	**4b**	
c	Combine lines 4a and 4b. If less than $400, **do not** file this schedule; you do not owe self-employment tax. **Exception.** If less than $400 and you had **church employee income,** enter -0- and continue. .... ▶	**4c**	
5 a	Enter your **church employee income** from Form W-2. **Caution:** *See page SE-1 for definition of church employee income* **5a**		
b	Multiply line 5a by 92.35% (.9235). If less than $100, enter -0-	**5b**	
6	**Net earnings from self-employment.** Add lines 4c and 5b	**6**	
7	Maximum amount of combined wages and self-employment earnings subject to social security tax or the 6.2% portion of the 7.65% railroad retirement (tier 1) tax for 1996	**7**	62,700.00
8 a	Total social security wages and tips (total of boxes 3 and 7 on Form(s) W-2) and railroad retirement (tier 1) compensation **8a**		
b	Unreported tips subject to social security tax (from Form 4137, line 9) **8b**		
c	Add lines 8a and 8b	**8c**	
9	Subtract line 8c from line 7. If zero or less, enter -0- here and on line 10 and go to line 11 .... ▶	**9**	
10	Multiply the **smaller** of line 6 or line 9 by 12.4% (.124)	**10**	
11	Multiply line 6 by 2.9% (.029)	**11**	
12	**Self-employment tax.** Add lines 10 and 11. Enter here and on **Form 1040, line 45**	**12**	
13	**Deduction for one-half of self-employment tax.** Multiply line 12 by 50% (.5). Enter the result here and on **Form 1040, line 25** **13**		

Part II   Optional Methods To Figure Net Earnings (See page SE-3.)

Farm Optional Method. You may use this method **only if:**
- Your gross farm income[1] was not more than $2,400 **or**
- Your gross farm income[1] was more than $2,400 and your net farm profits[2] were less than $1,733.

14	Maximum income for optional methods	**14**	1,600.00
15	Enter the **smaller** of: two-thirds (2/3) of gross farm income[1] (not less than zero) **or** $1,600. Also, include this amount on line 4b above	**15**	

Nonfarm Optional Method. You may use this method **only if:**
- Your net nonfarm profits[3] were less than $1,733 and also less than 72.189% of your gross nonfarm income,[4] **and**
- You had net earnings from self-employment of at least $400 in 2 of the prior 3 years.

Caution. *You may use this method no more than five times.*

16	Subtract line 15 from line 14	**16**	
17	Enter the **smaller** of: two-thirds (2/3) of gross nonfarm income[4] (not less than zero) **or** the amount on line 16. Also, include this amount on line 4b above	**17**	

[1] From Schedule F, line 11, and Schedule K-1 (Form 1065), line 15b.   [3] From Schedule C, line 31; Schedule C-EZ, line 3; and Schedule K-1 (Form 1065), line 15a.
[2] From Schedule F, line 36, and Schedule K-1 (Form 1065), line 15a.   [4] From Schedule C, line 7; Schedule C-EZ, line 1; and Schedule K-1 (Form 1065), line 15c.

LHA   **For Paperwork Reduction Act Notice, see Form 1040 Instructions.**

624502
10-21-96

Form
1040A

Department of the Treasury - Internal Revenue Service

U.S. Individual Income Tax Return **1996**

IRS Use Only - Do not write or staple in this space.

Label (See page 15.) **Use the IRS label.** Otherwise, please print or type.

OMB No. 1545-0085

L A B E L

H E R E

Your first name and initial	Last name
If a joint return, spouse's first name and initial	Last name
Home address (number and street). If you have a P.O. box, see page 15.	Apt. no.
City, town or post office, state, and ZIP code. If you have a foreign address, see page 15.	

Your social security number

Spouse's social security number

For Privacy Act and Paperwork Reduction Act Notice, see page 9.

Note: *Checking "Yes" will not change your tax or reduce your refund.*

Presidential Election Campaign Fund

	Yes	No
Do you want $3 to go to this fund?		
If a joint return, does your spouse want $3 to go to this fund?		

1 ☐ Single

2 ☐ Married filing joint return (even if only one had income)

3 ☐ Married filing separate return. Enter spouse's social security number above and full name here. ▶

4 ☐ Head of household (with qualifying person). If the qualifying person is a child but not your dependent, enter this child's name here. ▶

5 ☐ Qualifying widow(er) with dependent child (year spouse died ▶ 19   ).

6a ☐ **Yourself.** If your parent (or someone else) can claim you as a dependent on his or her tax return, **do not** check box 6a.

No. of boxes checked on lines 6a and 6b

b ☐ **Spouse**

No. of your children on line 6c who:
● lived with you

c **Dependents.** If more than six dependents, see page 17.

(1) First name Last Name	(2) Dependent's social security number. If born in Dec. 1996, see page 18.	(3) Dependent's relationship to you	(4) No. of months lived in your home in 1996

● did not live with you due to divorce or separation (see page 18)

Dependents on 6c not entered above

Add numbers entered in boxes above

d Total number of exemptions claimed .... ▶

7 Wages, salaries, tips, etc. This should be shown in box 1 of your W-2 form(s). Attach Form(s) W-2. **7** $

8a **Taxable** interest income. If over $400, attach Schedule 1. **8a** $

b **Tax-exempt** interest. DO NOT include on line 8a. **8b** $

9 Dividends. If over $400, attach Schedule 1. **9** $

10a Total IRA distributions. **10a** $ **10b** Taxable amount (see page 20). **10b** $

11a Total pensions and annuities. **11a** $ **11b** Taxable amount (see page 20). **11b** $

12 Unemployment compensation. **12** $

13a Social security benefits. **13a** $ **13b** Taxable amount (see page 22). **13b** $

14 Add lines 7 through 13b (far right column). This is your **total income.** ▶ **14** $

15a Your IRA deduction (see page 22). **15a** $

b Spouse's IRA deduction (see page 22). **15b** $

c Add lines 15a through 15b. These are your **total adjustments.** **15c** $

16 Subtract line 15c from line 14. This is your **adjusted gross income.** If under $28,495 (under $9,500 if a child did not live with you), see the instructions for line 29c on page 29. ▶ **16** $

Attach Copy B of W-2 and 1099-R here.

1996 Form 1040A page 1

LHA

610301
10-21-96

1996 Form 1040A page 2

17	Enter the amount from line 16.		17 $	

18a Check if: ☐ **You** were 65 or older ☐ Blind ☐ **Spouse** was 65 or older ☐ Blind   **Enter number of boxes checked** ▶ 18a ☐

b If you are married filing separately and your spouse itemizes deductions, see page 26 and check here .... ▶ 18b ☐

19 Enter the **standard deduction** for your filing status. **But** see page 26 if you checked any box on line 18a or b **OR** someone can claim you as a dependent.
- Single · $4,000
- Married filing jointly or Qualifying widow(er) · $6,700
- Head of household · $5,900
- Married filing separately · $3,350   19 $

20	Subtract line 19 from line 17. If line 19 is more than line 17, enter -0-.	20 $
21	Multiply $2,550 by the total number of exemptions claimed on line 6d.	21 $
22	Subtract line 21 from line 20. If line 21 is more than line 20, enter -0-. This is your **taxable income**. **If you want the IRS to figure your tax, see page 26.** ▶	22 $
23	Find the tax on the amount on line 22 (see page 26).	23 $
24a	Credit for child and dependent care expenses. Attach Schedule 2.	24a $
b	Credit for the elderly or the disabled. Attach Schedule 3.	24b $
c	Add lines 24a and 24b. These are your **total credits**.	24c $
25	Subtract line 24c from line 23. If line 24c is more than line 23, enter -0-.	25 $
26	Advance earned income credit payments from Form(s) W-2.	26 $
27	Household employment taxes. Attach Schedule H.	27 $
28	Add lines 25, 26 and 27. This is your **total tax**. ▶	28 $
29a	Total Federal income tax withheld from Forms W-2 and 1099.	29a $
b	1996 estimated tax payments and amount applied from 1995 return.	29b $
c	**Earned income credit.** Attach Schedule EIC if you have a qualifying child. Nontaxable earned income: amount ▶ and type ▶	29c $
d	Add lines 29a, 29b, and 29c (do not include nontaxable earned income). These are your **total payments.** ▶	29d $
30	If line 29d is more than line 28, subtract line 28 from line 29d. This is the amount you **overpaid**.	30 $
31a	Amount of line 30 you want **refunded to you.** If you want it sent directly to your bank account, see page 35 and fill in 31b, c, and d.	31a $

b Routing number _____   **c** Type: ☐ Checking ☐ Savings

d Account number _____

32	Amount of line 30 you want **applied to your 1997 estimated tax.**	32 $

33 If line 28 is more than line 29d, subtract line 29d from line 28. This is the **amount you owe.** For details on how to pay, including what to write on your payment, see page 36.   33 $

34 Estimated tax penalty (see page 36).   34 $

Sign here

Under penalties of perjury, I declare that I have examined this return and accompanying schedules and statements, and to the best of my knowledge and belief, they are true, correct, and accurately list all amounts and sources of income I received during the tax year. Declaration of preparer (other than the taxpayer) is based on all information of which the preparer has any knowledge.

Keep a copy of this return for your records.

Your signature ▶	Date	Your occupation
Spouse's signature. If joint return, BOTH must sign. ▶	Date	Spouse's occupation

Paid preparer's use only

Preparer's signature ▶	Date	Check if self-employed ☐	Preparer's SSN
Firm's name (or yours if self-employed) and address ▶		EIN	
		ZIP code	

1996 Form 1040A page 2

610302
11-06-96

Schedule 1
(Form 1040A)
(X)

Department of the Treasury—Internal Revenue Service

**Interest and Dividend Income
for Form 1040A Filers**

1996

OMB No. 1545-0085

Name(s) shown on Form 1040A: First and initial(s)	Last	Your social security number

Part I — Interest Income (See pages 19 and 50.)

Note: *If you received a Form 1099–INT, Form 1099–OID, or substitute statement from a brokerage firm, enter the firm's name and the total interest shown on that form.*

1 List name of payer. If any interest is from a seller-financed mortgage and the buyer used the property as a personal residence, see page 50 and list this interest first. Also, show that buyer's social security number and address.

Amount

1	$
	$
	$
	$
	$
	$
	$
	$
	$
	$

2 Add the amounts on line 1. **2** $

3 Excludable interest on series EE U.S. savings bonds issued after 1989 from Form 8815, line 14. You **must** attach Form 8815 to Form 1040A. **3** $

4 Subtract line 3 from line 2. Enter the result here and on Form 1040A, line 8a. **4** $

Part II — Dividend Income (See pages 20 and 50.)

Note: *If you received a Form 1099–DIV or substitute statement from a brokerage firm, enter the firm's name and the total dividends shown on that form.*

5 List name of payer

Amount

5	$
	$
	$
	$
	$
	$
	$
	$
	$
	$
	$
	$

6 Add the amounts on line 5. Enter the total here and on Form 1040A, line 9. **6** $

For Paperwork Reduction Act Notice, see Form 1040A instructions. Cat. No. 12075R **1996 Schedule 1 (Form 1040A)**

Schedule 2
(Form 1040A)
(X)

Department of the Treasury—Internal Revenue Service

**Child and Dependent Care
Expenses for Form 1040A Filers**

1996

OMB No. 1545-0085

Name(s) shown on Form 1040A: First and initial(s)	Last	Your social security number

You need to understand the following terms to complete this schedule: **Qualifying Person(s), Dependent Care Benefits, Qualified Expenses,** and **Earned Income.** See **Important Terms** on page 51.

Part I Persons or Organizations Who Provided the Care—You MUST complete this part.

1

(a) Care provider's name	(b) Address (number, street, apt. no., city, state, and ZIP code)	(c) Identifying number (SSN or EIN)	(d) Amount paid (see page 52)
			$
			$

(If you need more space, use the bottom of page 2.)

2 Add the amounts in column (d) of line 1.   **2** $

3 Enter the number of **qualifying persons** cared for in 1996 . . . . ▶

Did you receive **dependent care benefits?**	**No** ⟶ Complete only Part II below.
	Yes ⟶ Complete Part III on the back now.

Caution: *If the care was provided in your home, you may owe employment taxes. See the instructions for Form 1040A, line 27, on page 27.*

Part II Credit for Child and Dependent Care Expenses

4 Enter the amount of **qualified expenses** you incurred and paid in 1996. DO NOT enter more than 2,400 for one qualifying person or 4,800 for two or more persons. If you completed Part III, enter the amount from line 25.   **4** $

5 Enter YOUR **earned income.**   **5** $

6 If married filing a joint return, enter YOUR SPOUSE'S earned income (if student or disabled, see page 52); **all others,** enter the amount from line 5.   **6** $

7 Enter the **smallest** of line 4, 5, or 6.   **7** $

8 Enter the amount from Form 1040A, line 17.   **8** $

9 Enter on line 9 the decimal amount shown below that applies to the amount on line 8.

If line 8 is—		Decimal amount is	If line 8 is—		Decimal amount is
Over	But not over		Over	But not over	
$0	10,000	.30	$20,000	22,000	.24
10,000	12,000	.29	22,000	24,000	.23
12,000	14,000	.28	24,000	26,000	.22
14,000	16,000	.27	26,000	28,000	.21
16,000	18,000	.26	28,000	No limit	.20
18,000	20,000	.25			

9 × .

10 Multiply **line 7** by the decimal amount on line 9. Enter the result. Then, see page 53 for the amount of credit to enter on Form 1040A, line 24a.   **10** $

For Paperwork Reduction Act Notice, see Form 1040A instructions.   Cat. No. 107491   **1996 Schedule 2 (Form 1040A) page 1**

1996 Schedule 2 (Form 1040A) page 2

Part III **Dependent Care Benefits**—Complete this part **only** if you received these benefits.

11 Enter the total amount of **dependent care benefits** you received for 1996. This amount should be shown in box 10 of your W-2 form(s). DO NOT include amounts that were reported to you as wages in box 1 of Form(s) W-2. **11**$

12 Enter the amount forfeited, if any. See page 53. **12**$

13 Subtract line 12 from line 11. **13**$

14 Enter the total amount of **qualified expenses** incurred in 1996 for the care of the qualifying person(s). **14** $

15 Enter the **smaller** of line 13 or 14. **15** $

16 Enter YOUR **earned income.** **16** $

17 If married filing a joint return, enter YOUR SPOUSE'S earned income (if student or disabled, see the line 6 instructions); if married filing a separate return, see the instructions for the amount to enter; **all others,** enter the amount from line 16. **17** $

18 Enter the **smallest** of line 15, 16, or 17. **18** $

19 **Excluded benefits.** Enter here the **smaller** of the following:
● The amount from line 18, or
● 5,000 (2,500 if married filing a separate return **and** you were required to enter your spouse's earned income on line 17). **19**$

20 **Taxable benefits.** Subtract line 19 from line 13. Also, include this amount on Form 1040A, line 7. In the space to the left of line 7, print "DCB." **20**$

To claim the child and dependent care credit, complete lines 21–25 below, and lines 4–10 on the front of this schedule.

21 Enter the amount of qualified expenses you incurred and paid in 1996. DO NOT include on this line any excluded benefits shown on line 19. **21**$

22 Enter 2,400 (4,800 if two or more qualifying persons). **22** $

23 Enter the amount from line 19. **23** $

24 Subtract line 23 from line 22. If zero or less, **STOP.** You cannot take the credit. **Exception.** If you paid 1995 expenses in 1996, see the line 10 instructions. **24**$

25 Enter the **smaller** of line 21 or 24 here **and** on line 4 on the front of this schedule. **25**$

Form
1040EZ

Department of the Treasury - Internal Revenue Service
**Income Tax Return for Single and
Joint Filers With No Dependents**

1996 OMB No. 1545-0675

Use the IRS label here	Your first name and initial	Last name		**Your social security number**
	If a joint return, spouse's first name and initial	Last name		
	Home address (number and street). If you have a P.O. box, see instructions.		Apt. no.	**Spouse's social security number**
	City, town or post office, state and ZIP code. If you have a foreign address, see instructions.			

Presidential Election Campaign
(See page 7.)

Note: *Checking "Yes" will not change your tax or reduce your refund.*

Do you want $3 to go to this fund? ▶

If a joint return, does your spouse want $3 to go to this fund? ▶

Yes No
☐ ☐
☐ ☐

Income

Attach Copy B of Form(s) W-2 here. Enclose, but do not attach, any payment with your return.

Note: *You must check Yes or No.*

1 Total wages, salaries, and tips. This should be shown in box 1 of your W-2 form(s). Attach your W-2 form(s).   **1** _____

2 Taxable interest income of $400 or less. If the total is over $400, you cannot use Form 1040EZ.   **2** _____

3 Unemployment compensation.   **3** _____

4 Add lines 1, 2, and 3. This is your **adjusted gross income.** If under $9,500, see instructions to find out if you can claim the earned income credit on line 8.   **4** _____

5 Can your parents (or someone else) claim you on their return?

Yes. Enter amount from worksheet. ☐

No. If **single,** enter 6,550.00.
If **married,** enter 11,800.00.
See instructions for explanation. ☐

5 _____

6 Subtract line 5 from line 4. If line 5 is larger than line 4, enter 0. This is your **taxable income.** ▶ **6** _____

Payments and tax

7 Enter your Federal income tax withheld from box 2 of your W-2 form(s).   **7** _____

8 **Earned income credit** (see page 9). Enter type and amount of nontaxable earned income below.

Type _____ $ _____   **8** _____

9 Add lines 7 and 8 (do not include nontaxable earned income). These are your **total payments.**   **9** _____

10 **Tax.** Use the amount on **line 6** to find your tax in the tax table in the instruction booklet. Then, enter the tax from the table on this line.   **10** _____

Refund

Have it sent directly to your bank account! See instructions and fill in 11b, c, and d.

11a If line 9 is larger than line 10, subtract line 10 from line 9. This is your **refund.**   **11a** _____

b Routing number _____▶

c Type Checking ☐ Savings ☐

d Account number ▶ _____

Amount you owe

12 If line 10 is larger than line 9, subtract line 9 from line 10. This is the **amount you owe.** See page 13 for details on how to pay and what to write on your payment.   **12** _____

Sign here

Keep copy for your records.

I have read this return. Under penalties of perjury, I declare that to the best of my knowledge and belief, the return is true, correct, and accurately lists all amounts and sources of income I received during the tax year.

| Your signature | Spouse's signature if joint return |
| Date | Your occupation | Date | Spouse's occupation |

LHA   **For Privacy Act and Paperwork Reduction Act Notice, see page 5.**

Form 1040EZ (1996)

1996 Form 1040EZ page 2

Use this form if

- Your filing status is single or married filing jointly.
- You do not claim any dependents.

- You (and your spouse if married) were under 65 on January 1, 1997, and not blind at the end of 1996.
- Your taxable income (line 6) is less than $50,000.

- You had **only** wages, salaries, tips, taxable scholarship or fellowship grants, unemployment compensation, or Alaska Permanent Fund dividends, and your taxable interest income was $400 or less. **But** if you earned tips, including allocated tips, that are not included in box 5 and box 7 of your W-2, you may not be able to use Form 1040EZ. See page 8.

- You did not receive any advance earned income credit payments.

If you are not sure about your filing status, see page 7. If you have questions about dependents, use Tele-Tax topic 354 (see page 18). If you **can't use this form,** use Tele-Tax topic 352 (see page 18).

Filling in your return

For tips on how to avoid common mistakes, see page 3.

Because this form is read by a machine, please print your numbers inside the boxes like this:

9 8 7 6 5 4 3 2 1 0   Do not type your numbers. Do not use dollar signs.

If you received a scholarship or fellowship grant or tax-exempt interest income, such as on municipal bonds, see the booklet before filling in the form. Also, see the booklet if you received a Form 1099-INT showing income tax withheld or if tax was withheld from your Alaska Permanent Fund dividends.

Remember, you must report all wages, salaries, and tips even if you do not get a W-2 form from your employer. You must also report all your taxable interest income, including interest from banks, savings and loans, credit unions, etc., even if you do not get a Form 1099-INT.

Worksheet for dependents who checked "Yes" on line 5

Use this worksheet to figure the amount to enter on line 5 if someone can claim you (or your spouse if married) as a dependent, even if that person chooses not to do so. To find out if someone can claim you as a dependent, use Tele-Tax topic 354 (see page 18).

A. Enter the amount from line 1 on the front. A. _____

B. Minimum standard deduction. B. _____ 650.00

C. Enter the LARGER of line A or line B here. C. _____

D. Maximum standard deduction. If single, enter 4,000.00; if married, enter 6,700.00. D. _____

E. Enter the SMALLER of line C or line D here. This is your standard deduction. E. _____

F. Exemption amount.
  - If single, enter 0.
  - If married and both you and your spouse can be claimed as dependents, enter 0.
  - If married and only one of you can be claimed as a dependent, enter 2,550.00. F. _____

G. Add lines E and F. Enter the total here and on line 5 on the front. G. _____

If you checked "No" on line 5 because no one can claim you (or your spouse if married) as a dependent, enter on line 5 the amount shown below that applies to you.

- Single, enter 6,550.00. This is the total of your standard deduction (4,000.00) and personal exemption (2,550.00).

- Married, enter 11,800.00. This is the total of your standard deduction (6,700.00), exemption for yourself (2,550.00), and exemption for your spouse (2,550.00).

Mailing your return

Mail your return by **April 15, 1997.** Use the envelope that came with your booklet. If you do not have that envelope, see page 28 for the address to use.

Paid preparer's use only

See page 14.

Under penalties of perjury, I declare that I have examined this return, and to the best of my knowledge and belief, it is true, correct, and accurately lists all amounts and sources of income received during the tax year. This declaration is based on all information of which I have any knowledge.

Preparer's signature ▶	Date	Check if self-employed ☐	Preparer's SSN
Firm's name (or yours if self-employed) and address ▶		EIN	
		ZIP code	

Form **1040X**
(Rev. November 1996)

Department of the Treasury - Internal Revenue Service

Amended U.S. Individual Income Tax Return

OMB No. 1545-0091

This return is for calendar year ▶ 19____ , OR fiscal year ended ▶ _____ , 19____ .

Please Print or Type	Your first name and initial	Last name	Your social security number
	If a joint return, spouse's first name and initial	Last name	Spouse's social security number
	Home address (number and street). If you have a P.O. box, see instructions.	Apt. no.	Telephone number (optional)
	City, town or post office, state, and ZIP code. If you have a foreign address, see instructions.		For Paperwork Reduction Act Notice, see page 1 of separate instructions.

A If the name or address shown above is different from that shown on the original return, check here .... ▶ ☐

B Has the original return been changed or audited by the IRS or have you been notified that it will be? .... ☐ Yes ☐ No

C Filing status claimed. *Note: You cannot change from joint to separate returns after the due date has passed.*

On original return ▶ ☐ Single ☐ Married filing joint return ☐ Married filing separate return ☐ Head of household ☐ Qualifying widow(er)

On this return ▶ ☐ Single ☐ Married filing joint return ☐ Married filing separate return ☐ Head of household ☐ Qualifying widow(er)

Income and Deductions (see instructions) USE PART II ON PAGE 2 TO EXPLAIN ANY CHANGES		A. As originally reported or as previously adjusted	B. Net change - Increase or (Decrease) -explain on page 2	C. Correct amount
1 Adjusted gross income (see instructions)	1			
2 Itemized deductions or standard deduction	2			
3 Subtract line 2 from line 1	3			
4 Exemptions. If changing, fill in Parts I and II on page 2	4			
5 Taxable income. Subtract line 4 from line 3	5			
Tax Liability 6 Tax (see instructions). Method used in col. C _____	6			
7 Credits (see instructions)	7			
8 Subtract line 7 from line 6. Enter the result but not less than zero	8			
9 Other taxes (see instructions)	9			
10 Total tax. Add lines 8 and 9	10			
Payments 11 Federal income tax withheld and excess social security, Medicare, and RRTA taxes withheld. If changing, see instructions	11			
12 Estimated tax payments, including amount applied from prior year's return	12			
13 Earned income credit	13			
14 Credits for Federal tax paid on fuels, regulated investment company, etc	14			
15 Amount paid with Form 4868, 2688, or 2350 (application for extension of time to file)			15	
16 Amount of tax paid with original return plus additional tax paid after it was filed			16	
17 Total payments. Add lines 11 through 16 in column C			17	

Refund or Amount You Owe

18 Overpayment, if any, as shown on original return or as previously adjusted by the IRS	18	
19 Subtract line 18 from line 17	19	
20 **AMOUNT YOU OWE.** If line 10, column C, is more than line 19, enter the difference and see instructions	20	
21 If line 10, column C, is less than line 19, enter the difference	21	
22 Amount of line 21 you want **REFUNDED TO YOU**	22	
23 Amount of line 21 you want **APPLIED TO YOUR 19____ ESTIMATED TAX** 23		

Sign Here
Keep a copy of this return for your records.

Under penalties of perjury, I declare that I have filed an original return and that I have examined this amended return, including accompanying schedules and statements, and to the best of my knowledge and belief, this amended return is true, correct, and complete. Declaration of preparer (other than taxpayer) is based on all information of which the preparer has any knowledge.

▶ Your signature _____ Date _____

▶ Spouse's signature. If a joint return, BOTH must sign. _____ Date _____

Paid Preparer's Use Only

Preparer's signature ▶	Date	Check if self-employed ☐	Preparer's soc. sec. no.
Firm's name (or yours if self-employed) and address ▶		EIN	
		ZIP code	

LHA

Form **1040X** (Rev. 11-96)

Form 1040X (Rev. 11-96)   Page 2

Part I Exemptions

If you are **not changing your exemptions**, do not complete this part.
If claiming **more exemptions**, complete lines 24-30 and, if applicable, line 31.
If claiming **fewer exemptions**, complete lines 24-29.

		A. Number originally reported	B. Net change	C. Correct number

24 Yourself and spouse **24**

Caution: If your parents (or someone else) can claim you as a dependent (even if they chose not to), you cannot claim an exemption for yourself.

25 Your dependent children who lived with you **25**

26 Your dependent children who did not live with you due to divorce or separation **26**

27 Other dependents **27**

28 Total number of exemptions. Add lines 24 through 27 ...... **28**

29 Multiply the number of exemptions claimed on line 28 by the amount listed below for the tax year you are amending. Enter the result here and on line 4.

Tax Year	Exemption Amount	But see the instructions if the amount on line 1 is over:
1996	$2,550	$88,475
1995	2,500	86,025
1994	2,450	83,850
1993	2,350	81,350

29

30 Dependents (children and other) not claimed on original return:

Note: For tax years after 1994, **do not** complete column (b) below.

(a) First Name Last name	(b) Check if under age 1	(c) Dependent's social security number. If born in the tax year you are amending, see instructions	(d) Dependent's relationship to you	(e) No. of months lived in your home

No. of your children on line 30 who:
● lived with you .... ►
● **did not** live with you due to divorce or separation ...... ►
Dependents on line 30 not entered above ►

31 For tax years before 1996, if your child listed on line 30 did not live with you but is claimed as your dependent under a pre-1985 agreement, check here ... ►

Part II Explanation of Changes to Income, Deductions, and Credits

Enter the line number from page 1 for each item you are changing and give the reason for each change. Attach only the supporting forms and schedules for the items changed. If you do not attach the required information, your Form 1040X may be returned. Be sure to include your name and social security number on any attachments.

If the change relates to a net operating loss carryback or a general business credit carryback, attach the schedule or form that shows the year in which the loss or credit occurred. See instructions. Also, check here ...... ►

Part III Presidential Election Campaign Fund. Checking below will not increase your tax or reduce your refund.

If you did not previously want to have $3 go to the fund but now want to, check here ...... ►
If a joint return and your spouse did not previously want to have $3 go to the fund but now wants to, check here ...... ►

610702
11-16-96

Form 1065 Department of the Treasury Internal Revenue Service	**U.S. Partnership Return of Income** For calendar year 1996, or tax year beginning _____ , 1996, and ending _____ ,19 ____ .	OMB No. 1545-0099 **1996**

A Principal business activity	Use the IRS label. Other-wise, please print or type.	Name of partnership	D Employer identification number
B Principal product or service		Number, street, and room or suite no. (If a P.O. box, see page 10 of the instructions.)	E Date business started
C Business code number		City or town, state, and ZIP code	F Total assets $

G Check applicable boxes: **(1)** ☐ Initial return **(2)** ☐ Final return **(3)** ☐ Change in address **(4)** ☐ Amended return

H Check accounting method: **(1)** ☐ Cash **(2)** ☐ Accrual **(3)** ☐ Other (specify) ▶ _____

I Number of Schedules K-1. Attach one for each person who was a partner at any time during the tax year ▶ _____

Caution: Include **only** trade or business income and expenses on lines 1a through 22 below. See the instructions for more information.

Income

1 a	Gross receipts or sales	1a	
b	Less returns and allowances	1b	1c
2	Cost of goods sold (Schedule A, line 8)		2
3	Gross profit. Subtract line 2 from line 1c		3
4	Ordinary income (loss) from other partnerships, estates, and trusts (attach schedule)		4
5	Net farm profit (loss) (attach Schedule F (Form 1040))		5
6	Net gain (loss) from Form 4797, Part II, line 20		6
7	Other income (loss) (attach schedule)		7
8	**Total income (loss).** Combine lines 3 through 7		8

Deductions (see instructions for limitations)

9	Salaries and wages (other than to partners) (less employment credits)		9
10	Guaranteed payments to partners		10
11	Repairs and maintenance		11
12	Bad debts		12
13	Rent		13
14	Taxes and licenses		14
15	Interest		15
16 a	Depreciation	16a	
b	Less depreciation reported on Schedule A and elsewhere on return	16b	16c
17	Depletion **(Do not deduct oil and gas depletion.)**		17
18	Retirement plans, etc.		18
19	Employee benefit programs		19
20	Other deductions (attach schedule)		20
21	**Total deductions.** Add the amounts shown in the far right column for lines 9 through 20		21
22	**Ordinary income (loss)** from trade or business activities. Subtract line 21 from line 8		22

Please Sign Here

Under penalties of perjury, I declare that I have examined this return, including accompanying schedules and statements, and to the best of my knowledge and belief, it is true, correct, and complete. Declaration of preparer (other than general partner or limited liability company member) is based on all information of which preparer has any knowledge.

▶ _____ ▶ _____
Signature of general partner or limited liability company member | Date

Paid Preparer's Use Only

Preparer's signature ▶	Date	Check if self-employed ▶ ☐	Preparer's social security no.
Firm's name (or yours if self-employed) and address ▶		E.I. No. ▶	
		ZIP code ▶	

H761   **For Paperwork Reduction Act Notice, see page 1 of separate instructions.**   Form **1065** (1996)

611001
11-08-96

Form 1065 (1996)   Page **2**

Schedule A — Cost of Goods Sold

1	Inventory at beginning of year	1	
2	Purchases less cost of items withdrawn for personal use	2	
3	Cost of labor	3	
4	Additional section 263A costs *(attach schedule)*	4	
5	Other costs *(attach schedule)*	5	
6	**Total.** Add lines 1 through 5	6	
7	Inventory at end of year	7	
8	**Cost of goods sold.** Subtract line 7 from line 6. Enter here and on page 1, line 2	8	

9 a Check all methods used for valuing closing inventory:

    (i) ☐ Cost as described in Regulations section 1.471-3

    (ii) ☐ Lower of cost or market as described in Regulations section 1.471-4

    (iii) ☐ Other (specify method used and attach explanation) ▶ _____

  b Check this box if there was a writedown of "subnormal" goods as described in Regulations section 1.471-2(c) .... ▶ ☐

  c Check this box if the LIFO inventory method was adopted this tax year for any goods *(if checked, attach Form 970)* .... ▶ ☐

  d Do the rules of section 263A (for property produced or acquired for resale) apply to the partnership? .... ☐ Yes ☐ No

  e Was there any change in determining quantities, cost, or valuations between opening and closing inventory? .... ☐ Yes ☐ No

    If "Yes," attach explanation.

Schedule B — Other Information

		Yes	No
1	What type of entity is filing this return? Check the applicable box:		
	a ☐ General partnership **b** ☐ Limited partnership **c** ☐ Limited liability company		
	d ☐ Other ▶ _____		
2	Are any partners in this partnership also partnerships?		
3	Is this partnership a partner in another partnership?		
4	Is this partnership subject to the consolidated audit procedures of sections 6221 through 6233?		
	If "Yes," see **Designation of Tax Matters Partner** below		
5	Does this partnership meet **ALL THREE** of the following requirements?		
a	The partnership's total receipts for the tax year were less than $250,000;		
b	The partnership's total assets at the end of the tax year were less than $600,000: **AND**		
c	Schedules K-1 are filed with the return and furnished to the partners on or before the due date (including extensions) for the partnership return.		
	If "Yes," the partnership is not required to complete Schedules L, M-1, and M-2; Item F on page 1 of Form 1065;		
	or Item J on Schedule K-1		
6	Does this partnership have any foreign partners?		
7	Is this partnership a publicly traded partnership as defined in section 469(k)(2)?		
8	Has this partnership filed, or is it required to file, **Form 8264,** Application for Registration of a Tax Shelter?		
9	At any time during the calendar year 1996, did the partnership have an interest in or a signature or other authority over a financial account in		
	a foreign country (such as a bank account, securities account, or other financial account)?		
	(See the instructions for exceptions and filing requirements for Form TD F 90-22.1.)		
	If "Yes," enter the name of the foreign country. ▶ _____		
10	During the tax year, did the partnership receive a distribution from, or was it the grantor of, or transferor to, a foreign trust?		
	If "Yes," see page 14 of the instructions for other forms the partnership may have to file		
11	Was there a distribution of property or a transfer (e.g., by sale or death) of a partnership interest during the tax year?		
	If "Yes," you may elect to adjust the basis of the partnership's assets under section 754 by attaching the statement described		
	under **Elections Made By the Partnership**		

Designation of Tax Matters Partner

Enter below the general partner designated as the tax matters partner (TMP) for the tax year of this return:

Name of
designated TMP ▶ _____   Identifying
number of TMP ▶ _____

Address of
designated TMP ▶ _____

611011
11-08-96

Form 1065 (1996) Page 3

Schedule K Partners' Shares of Income, Credits, Deductions, etc.

	(a) Distributive share items			(b) Total amount
Income (Loss)	**1** Ordinary income (loss) from trade or business activities (page 1, line 22)		**1**	
	2 Net income (loss) from rental real estate activities (attach Form 8825)		**2**	
	3 a Gross income from other rental activities	**3a**		
	b Expenses from other rental activities (attach schedule)	**3b**		
	c Net income (loss) from other rental activities. Subtract line 3b from line 3a		**3c**	
	4 Portfolio income (loss): **a** Interest income		**4a**	
	b Dividend income		**4b**	
	c Royalty income		**4c**	
	d Net short-term capital gain (loss) (attach Schedule D (Form 1065))		**4d**	
	e Net long-term capital gain (loss) (attach Schedule D (Form 1065))		**4e**	
	f Other portfolio income (loss) (attach schedule)		**4f**	
	5 Guaranteed payments to partners		**5**	
	6 Net gain (loss) under section 1231 (other than due to casualty or theft) (attach Form 4797)		**6**	
	7 Other income (loss) (attach schedule)		**7**	
Deductions	**8** Charitable contributions (attach schedule)		**8**	
	9 Section 179 expense deduction (attach Form 4562)		**9**	
	10 Deductions related to portfolio income (itemize)		**10**	
	11 Other deductions (attach schedule)		**11**	
Invest-ment Interest	**12 a** Interest expense on investment debts		**12a**	
	b (1) Investment income included on lines 4a, 4b, 4c, and 4f above		**12b(1)**	
	(2) Investment expenses included on line 10 above		**12b(2)**	
Credits	**13 a** Low-income housing credit:			
	(1) From partnerships to which section 42(j)(5) applies for property placed in service before 1990		**13a(1)**	
	(2) Other than on line 13a(1) for property placed in service before 1990		**13a(2)**	
	(3) From partnerships to which section 42(j)(5) applies for property placed in service after 1989		**13a(3)**	
	(4) Other than on line 13a(3) for property placed in service after 1989		**13a(4)**	
	b Qualified rehabilitation expenditures related to rental real estate activities (attach Form 3468)		**13b**	
	c Credits (other than credits shown on lines 13a and 13b) related to rental real estate activities		**13c**	
	d Credits related to other rental activities		**13d**	
	14 Other credits		**14**	
Self-Employ-ment	**15 a** Net earnings (loss) from self-employment		**15a**	
	b Gross farming or fishing income		**15b**	
	c Gross nonfarm income		**15c**	
Adjustments and Tax Preference Items	**16 a** Depreciation adjustment on property placed in service after 1986		**16a**	
	b Adjusted gain or loss		**16b**	
	c Depletion (other than oil and gas)		**16c**	
	d (1) Gross income from oil, gas, and geothermal properties		**16d(1)**	
	(2) Deductions allocable to oil, gas, and geothermal properties		**16d(2)**	
	e Other adjustments and tax preference items (attach schedule)		**16e**	
Foreign Taxes	**17 a** Type of income ▶ _____ **b** Foreign country or U.S. possession ▶ _____			
	c Total gross income from sources outside the United States (attach schedule)		**17c**	
	d Total applicable deductions and losses (attach schedule)		**17d**	
	e Total foreign taxes (check one): ▶ ☐ Paid ☐ Accrued		**17e**	
	f Reduction in taxes available for credit (attach schedule)		**17f**	
	g Other foreign tax information (attach schedule)		**17g**	
Other	**18** Section 59(e)(2) expenditures: **a** Type ▶ _____ **b** Amount ▶		**18b**	
	19 Tax-exempt interest income		**19**	
	20 Other tax-exempt income		**20**	
	21 Nondeductible expenses		**21**	
	22 Distributions of money (cash and marketable securities)		**22**	
	23 Distributions of property other than money		**23**	
	24 Other items and amounts required to be reported separately to partners (attach schedule)			
Analysis	**25a** Income (loss). Combine lines 1 through 7 in column (b). From the result, subtract the sum of lines 8 through 12a, 17e, and 18b		**25a**	

b Analysis by type of partner	(a) Corporate	(b) Individual		(c) Partnership	(d) Exempt organization	(e) Nominee/Other
		i. Active	ii. Passive			
(1) General partners						
(2) Limited partners						

Form 1065 (1996)   Page **4**

Note: If Question 5 of Schedule B is answered "Yes," the partnership is not required to complete Schedules L, M-1, and M-2.

Schedule L   Balance Sheets per Books

Assets	Beginning of tax year		End of tax year	
	(a)	(b)	(c)	(d)
1 Cash				
2a Trade notes and accounts receivable				
b Less allowance for bad debts				
3 Inventories				
4 U.S. government obligations				
5 Tax-exempt securities				
6 Other current assets (attach schedule)				
7 Mortgage and real estate loans				
8 Other investments (attach schedule)				
9a Buildings and other depreciable assets				
b Less accumulated depreciation				
10a Depletable assets				
b Less accumulated depletion				
11 Land (net of any amortization)				
12a Intangible assets (amortizable only)				
b Less accumulated amortization				
13 Other assets (attach schedule)				
14 **Total** assets				
Liabilities and Capital				
15 Accounts payable				
16 Mortgages, notes, bonds payable in less than 1 year				
17 Other current liabilities (attach schedule)				
18 All nonrecourse loans				
19 Mortgages, notes, bonds payable in 1 year or more				
20 Other liabilities (attach schedule)				
21 Partners' capital accounts				
22 **Total** liabilities and capital				

Schedule M-1   Reconciliation of Income (Loss) per Books With Income (Loss) per Return

1 Net income (loss) per books		6 Income recorded on books this year not included on Schedule K, lines 1 through 7 (itemize):		
2 Income included on Schedule K, lines 1 through 4, 6, and 7, not recorded on books this year (itemize): _____		a Tax-exempt interest $ _____		
3 Guaranteed payments (other than health insurance)		7 Deductions included on Schedule K, lines 1 through 12a, 17e, and 18b, not charged against book income this year (itemize):		
4 Expenses recorded on books this year not included on Schedule K, lines 1 through 12a, 17e, and 18b (itemize):		a Depreciation $ _____		
a Depreciation $ _____				
b Travel and entertainment $ _____				
		8 Add lines 6 and 7		
5 Add lines 1 through 4		9 Income (loss) (Schedule K, line 25a). Subtract line 8 from line 5		

Schedule M-2   Analysis of Partners' Capital Accounts

1 Balance at beginning of year		6 Distributions: a Cash		
2 Capital contributed during year		b Property		
3 Net income (loss) per books		7 Other decreases (itemize): _____		
4 Other increases (itemize): _____				
		8 Add lines 6 and 7		
5 Add lines 1 through 4		9 Balance at end of year. Subtract line 8 from line 5		

611041
11-08-96

SCHEDULE D **(Form 1065)** Department of the Treasury Internal Revenue Service	**Capital Gains and Losses** ▶ Attach to Form 1065.	OMB No. 1545-0099 **1996**

Name of partnership	Employer identification number

Part I   Short-Term Capital Gains and Losses - Assets Held 1 Year or Less

(a) Description of property (e.g., 100 shares 7% preferred of "Z" Co.)	**(b)** Date acquired (mo., day, yr.)	**(c)** Date sold (mo., day, yr.)	**(d)** Sales price	**(e)** Cost or other basis	**(f)** Gain (loss) ((d) minus (e))
1					

2 Short-term capital gain from installment sales from Form 6252, line 26 or 37	2	
3 Short-term capital gain (loss) from like-kind exchanges from Form 8824	3	
4 Partnership's share of net short-term capital gain (loss), including specially allocated short-term capital gains (losses), from other partnerships, estates and trusts	4	
5 Net short-term capital gain (loss). Combine lines 1 through 4. Enter here and on Form 1065, Schedule K, line 4d or 7	5	

Part II   Long-Term Capital Gains and Losses - Assets Held More Than 1 Year

6					

7 Long-term capital gain from installment sales from Form 6252, line 26 or 37	7	
8 Long-term capital gain (loss) from like-kind exchanges from Form 8824	8	
9 Partnership's share of net long-term capital gain (loss), including specially allocated long-term capital gains (losses), from other partnerships, estates and trusts	9	
10 Capital gain distributions	10	
11 Net long-term capital gain (loss). Combine lines 6 through 10. Enter here and on Form 1065, Schedule K, line 4e or 7	11	

H761   **For Paperwork Reduction Act Notice, see the Instructions for Form 1065.**   **Schedule D (Form 1065) 1996**

SCHEDULE K-1
(Form 1065)
Department of the Treasury
Internal Revenue Service

Partner's Share of Income, Credits, Deductions, etc.
For calendar year 1996 or tax year
beginning   , 1996, and ending   , 19

OMB No. 1545-0099

1996

Partner's identifying number ▶
Partner's name, address, and ZIP code

Partnership's identifying number ▶
Partnership's name, address, and ZIP code

A This partner is a ☐ general partner ☐ limited partner
☐ limited liability company member

B What type of entity is this partner? ▶ _____

C Is this partner a ☐ domestic or a ☐ foreign partner?

D Enter partner's percentage of:

	(i) Before change or termination	(ii) End of year
Profit sharing	_____ %	_____ %
Loss sharing	_____ %	_____ %
Ownership of capital	_____ %	_____ %

E IRS Center where partnership filed return: _____

F Partner's share of liabilities:

Nonrecourse	$ _____
Qualified nonrecourse financing	$ _____
Other	$ _____

G Tax shelter registration number ▶ _____

H Check here if this partnership is a publicly traded partnership as defined in section 469(k)(2) .... ☐

I Check applicable boxes: **(1)** ☐ Final K-1 **(2)** ☐ Amended K-1

J Analysis of partner's capital account:

(a) Capital account at beginning of year	(b) Capital contributed during year	(c) Partner's share of lines 3, 4, and 7, Form 1065, Schedule M-2	(d) Withdrawals and distributions	(e) Capital account at end of year (combine columns (a) through (d))
			( )	

	(a) Distributive share item		(b) Amount	(c) 1040 filers enter the amount in column (b) on:
Income (Loss)	**1**	Ordinary income (loss) from trade or business activities	1	⎫ See Partner's Instructions for Schedule K-1 (Form 1065).
	2	Net income (loss) from rental real estate activities	2	
	3	Net income (loss) from other rental activities	3	⎭
	4	Portfolio income (loss):		
	a	Interest	4a	Sch. B, Part I, line 1
	b	Dividends	4b	Sch. B, Part II, line 5
	c	Royalties	4c	Sch. E, Part I, line 4
	d	Net short-term capital gain (loss)	4d	Sch. D, line 5, col. (f) or (g)
	e	Net long-term capital gain (loss)	4e	Sch. D, line 13, col. (f) or (g)
	f	Other portfolio income (loss) (attach schedule)	4f	Enter on applicable line of your return.
	5	Guaranteed payments to partner	5	⎱ See Partner's Instructions for Schedule K-1 (Form 1065).
	6	Net gain (loss) under section 1231 (other than due to casualty or theft)	6	
	7	Other income (loss) (attach schedule)	7	Enter on applicable line of your return.
Deductions	**8**	Charitable contributions (attach schedule)	8	Sch. A, line 15 or 16
	9	Section 179 expense deduction	9	⎫ See Partner's Instructions for Schedule K-1 (Form 1065).
	10	Deductions related to portfolio income (attach schedule)	10	
	11	Other deductions (attach schedule)	11	⎭
Investment Interest	**12 a**	Interest expense on investment debts	12a	Form 4952, line 1
	b	(1) Investment income included on lines 4a, 4b, 4c, and 4f above	b(1)	⎱ See Partner's Instructions for Schedule K-1 (Form 1065).
		(2) Investment expenses included on line 10 above	b(2)	
Credits	**13 a**	Low-income housing credit:		
		(1) From section 42(j)(5) partnerships for property placed in service before 1990	a(1)	⎫
		(2) Other than on line 13a(1) for property placed in service before 1990	a(2)	Form 8586, line 5
		(3) From section 42(j)(5) partnerships for property placed in service after 1989	a(3)	
		(4) Other than on line 13a(3) for property placed in service after 1989	a(4)	⎭
	b	Qualified rehabilitation expenditures related to rental real estate activities (see instructions)	13b	⎫
	c	Credits (other than credits shown on lines 13a and 13b) related to rental real estate activities	13c	See Partner's Instructions for Schedule K-1 (Form 1065).
	d	Credits related to other rental activities	13d	
	14	Other credits	14	⎭

H761 For Paperwork Reduction Act Notice, see Instructions for Form 1065.

Schedule K-1 (Form 1065) 1996

611151
11-06-96

Schedule K-1 (Form 1065) 1996   Page **2**

	(a) Distributive share item		(b) Amount	(c) 1040 filers enter the amount in column (b) on:
Self-employ-ment	15 a	Net earnings (loss) from self-employment	15a	Sch. SE, Section A or B
	b	Gross farming or fishing income	15b	See Partner's Instructions for Schedule K-1 (Form 1065).
	c	Gross nonfarm income	15c	
Adjustments and Tax Preference Items	16 a	Depreciation adjustment on property placed in service after 1986	16a	See Partner's Instructions for Schedule K-1 (Form 1065) and Instructions for Form 6251.
	b	Adjusted gain or loss	16b	
	c	Depletion (other than oil and gas)	16c	
	d	(1) Gross income from oil, gas, and geothermal properties	(d)1	
		(2) Deductions allocable to oil, gas, and geothermal properties	(d)2	
	e	Other adjustments and tax preference items (attach schedule)	16e	
Foreign Taxes	17 a	Type of income ▶		Form 1116, check boxes
	b	Name of foreign country or U.S. possession ▶		
	c	Total gross income from sources outside the United States (attach schedule)	17c	Form 1116, Part I
	d	Total applicable deductions and losses (attach schedule)	17d	
	e	Total foreign taxes (check one): ▶ ☐ Paid ☐ Accrued	17e	Form 1116, Part II
	f	Reduction in taxes available for credit (attach schedule)	17f	Form 1116, Part III
	g	Other foreign tax information (attach schedule)	17g	See Instructions for Form 1116.
Other	18	Section 59(e)(2) expenditures: a Type ▶		See page 9 of Partner's Instructions for Schedule K-1 (Form 1065).
	b	Amount	18b	
	19	Tax-exempt interest income	19	Form 1040, line 8b
	20	Other tax-exempt income	20	See Partner's Instructions for Schedule K-1 (Form 1065).
	21	Nondeductible expenses	21	
	22	Distributions of money (cash and marketable securities)	22	
	23	Distributions of property other than money	23	
	24	Recapture of low-income housing credit:		
	a	From section 42(j)(5) partnerships	24a	Form 8611, line 8
	b	Other than on line 24a	24b	

Supplemental Information	25	Supplemental information required to be reported separately to each partner (attach additional schedules if more space is needed):

_____
_____
_____
_____
_____
_____
_____
_____
_____
_____
_____
_____
_____
_____
_____
_____
_____
_____

OMB No. 1545-0121

Form **1116**

Department of the Treasury
Internal Revenue Service

Foreign Tax Credit

(Individual, Estate, Trust, or Nonresident Alien Individual)
▶ Attach to Form 1040, 1040NR, 1041, or 990-T.

1996

Attachment
Sequence No. **19**

Name | Identifying number as shown on page 1 of your tax return

Report all amounts in U.S. dollars except where specified in Part II. Use a separate Form 1116 for each category of income listed below. Check only **one** *box. Before you check a box, read* **Categories of Income** *on page 3 of the instructions. Complete this form for credit for taxes on:*

- a ☐ Passive income
- b ☐ High withholding tax interest
- c ☐ Financial services income
- d ☐ Shipping income
- e ☐ Dividends from a DISC or former DISC
- f ☐ Certain distributions from a foreign sales corporation (FSC) or former FSC
- g ☐ Lump-sum distributions (see Instructions before completing form)
- h ☐ General limitation income - all other income from sources outside the United States (including income from sources within U.S. possessions)

i Resident of (name of country) ▶

Note: *If you paid taxes to one foreign country or U.S. possession, use column A in Part I and line A in Part II. If you paid taxes to* **more than one** *foreign country or U.S. possession, use a separate column and line for each country or possession. However, see the exception under* **How To Complete Form 1116** *on page 1 of the instructions.*

Part I Figuring Taxable Income or Loss From Sources Outside the United States for Separate Category Checked Above

| | | Foreign Country or U.S. Possession | | | Total |
		A	B	C	(Add cols. A, B, and C)
j	Enter the name of the foreign country or U.S. possession .... ▶				
1	Gross income from sources within country shown above and of the type checked above: _____ _____ _____				**1**
	Deductions and losses:				
2	Expenses directly **definitely related** to the income on line 1 (attach statement)				
3	Pro rata share of other deductions **not definitely related:**				
a	Certain itemized deductions or standard deduction				
b	Other deductions (attach statement)				
c	Add lines 3a and 3b				
d	Gross foreign source income				
e	Gross income from all sources				
f	Divide line 3d by line 3e. Do not enter more than "1"				
g	Multiply line 3c by line 3f				
4	Pro rata share of interest expense:				
a	Home mortgage interest (Use worksheet on page 6 of the instructions)				
b	Other interest expense				
5	Losses from foreign sources				
6	Add lines 2, 3g, 4a, 4b, and 5				**6**
7	Subtract line 6 from line 1. Enter the result here and on line 14 ▶				**7**

Part II Foreign Taxes Paid or Accrued

Country	Credit is claimed for taxes (you must check one)	Foreign taxes paid or accrued									
		In foreign currency				In U.S. dollars					
	(k) ☐ Paid	Taxes withheld at source on:			(q) Other foreign taxes paid or accrued	Taxes withheld at source on:			(u) Other foreign taxes paid or accrued	(v) Total foreign taxes paid or accrued (add cols. (r) through (u))
	(l) ☐ Accrued									
	(m) Date paid or accrued	(n) Dividends	(o) Rents and royalties	(p) Interest		(r) Dividends	(s) Rents and royalties	(t) Interest		
A										
B										
C										
8	Add lines A through C, column (v). Enter the total here and on line 9 .... ▶								**8**	

LHA   For Paperwork Reduction Act Notice, see page 1 of separate Instructions.

Form **1116** (1996)

611501
10-11-96

Form 1116 (1996)   Page **2**

Part III	**Figuring the Credit**

9 Enter amount from line 8. These are your total foreign taxes paid or accrued
for the category of income checked above Part I **9**

10 Carryback or carryover (attach detailed computation) **10**

11 Add lines 9 and 10 .... **11**

12 Reduction in foreign taxes **12**

13 Subtract line 12 from line 11. This is the total amount of foreign taxes available for credit **13**

14 Enter amount from line 7. This is your taxable income or (loss) from sources outside the
United States (before adjustments) for the category of income checked above Part I. **14**

15 Adjustments to line 14 .... **15**

16 Combine the amounts on lines 14 and 15. This is your net foreign source taxable income.
(If the result is zero or less, you have no foreign tax credit for the category of income
you checked above Part I. Skip lines 17 through 21.) **16**

17 **Individuals:** Enter amount from Form 1040, line 35. If you are a nonresident alien,
enter amount from Form 1040NR, line 34. **Estates and trusts:** Enter your
taxable income without the deduction for your exemption **17**
Caution: *If you figured your tax using the maximum tax rate on capital gains, see instructions.*

18 Divide line 16 by line 17. If line 16 is more than line 17, enter the figure "1" **18**

19 **Individuals:** Enter amount from Form 1040, line 38, **less** any amounts on Form 1040, lines 39, 40, and any
mortgage interest credit (from Form 8396) on line 42. If you are a nonresident alien, enter amount from Form 1040NR,
line 37, less any amount on Form 1040NR, line 38 and any mortgage interest credit (from Form 8396) on line 40.
Estates and trusts: Enter amount from Form 1041, Schedule G, line 1c, or Form 990-T, lines 36 and 37 .... **19**

20 Multiply line 19 by line 18 (maximum amount of credit) **20**

21 Enter the amount from line 13 or line 20, whichever is **smaller.** If this is the only Form 1116 you are
completing, skip lines 22 through 29 and enter this amount on line 30. Otherwise,
complete the appropriate line in Part IV .... ▶ **21**

Part IV	**Summary of Credits From Separate Parts III**

22 Credit for taxes on passive income **22**

23 Credit for taxes on high withholding tax interest **23**

24 Credit for taxes on financial services income **24**

25 Credit for taxes on shipping income **25**

26 Credit for taxes on dividends from a DISC or former DISC **26**

27 Credit for taxes on certain distributions from a FSC or former FSC **27**

28 Credit for taxes on lump-sum distributions **28**

29 Credit for taxes on general limitation income (all other income from
sources outside the United States) **29**

30 Add lines 22 through 29 .... **30**

31 Reduction of credit for international boycott operations **31**

32 Subtract line 31 from line 30. This is your foreign tax credit. Enter here and on Form 1040, line 41;
Form 1040NR, line 39; Form 1041, Schedule G, line 2a; or Form 990-T, line 39a .... ▶ **32**

U.S. Corporation Income Tax Return

Form 1120
Department of the Treasury
Internal Revenue Service

For calendar year 1996 or tax year beginning _____, 19___, ending _____, 19___

▶ **Instructions are separate. See page 1 for Paperwork Reduction Act Notice.**

OMB No. 1545-0123

1996

A Check if a:		
1 Consolidated return (attach Form 851)	☐	Use IRS label. Otherwise, please print or type.
2 Personal holding co. (attach Sch. PH)	☐	
3 Personal service corp. (as defined in Temp. Regs. sec. 1.441-4T)	☐	

Name

Number, street, and room or suite no. (If a P.O. box, see page 6 of instructions.)

City or town, state, and ZIP code

B Employer identification number

C Date incorporated

D Total assets (see page 6 of Instructions)
$

E Check applicable boxes: (1) ☐ Initial return (2) ☐ Final return (3) ☐ Change of address

Income	1 a Gross receipts or sales	b Less returns and allowances	c Bal ▶	1c
	2 Cost of goods sold (Schedule A, line 8)			2
	3 Gross profit. Subtract line 2 from line 1c			3
	4 Dividends (Schedule C, line 19)			4
	5 Interest			5
	6 Gross rents			6
	7 Gross royalties			7
	8 Capital gain net income (attach Schedule D (Form 1120))			8
	9 Net gain or (loss) from Form 4797, Part II, line 20 (attach Form 4797)			9
	10 Other income (attach schedule)			10
	11 **Total income.** Add lines 3 through 10		▶	11
Deductions	12 Compensation of officers (Schedule E, line 4)			12
	13 Salaries and wages (less employment credits)			13
	14 Repairs and maintenance			14
	15 Bad debts			15
	16 Rents			16
	17 Taxes and licenses			17
	18 Interest			18
	19 Charitable contributions			19
	20 Depreciation (attach Form 4562)	20		
	21 Less depreciation claimed on Schedule A and elsewhere on return	21a		21b
	22 Depletion			22
	23 Advertising			23
	24 Pension, profit-sharing, etc., plans			24
	25 Employee benefit programs			25
	26 Other deductions (attach schedule)			26
	27 **Total deductions.** Add lines 12 through 26		▶	27
	28 Taxable income before net operating loss deduction and special deductions. Subtract line 27 from line 11			28
	29 **Less:** a Net operating loss deduction	29a		
	b Special deductions (Schedule C, line 20)	29b		29c
Tax and Payments	30 **Taxable income.** Subtract line 29c from line 28			30
	31 **Total tax** (Schedule J, line 10)			31
	32 **Payments:** a 1995 overpayment credited to 1996	32a		
	b 1996 estimated tax payments	32b		
	Less 1996 refund applied for c on Form 4466	32c ( )	d Bal ▶ 32d	
	e Tax deposited with Form 7004		32e	
	f Credit from regulated investment companies (attach Form 2439)		32f	
	g Credit for Federal tax on fuels (attach Form 4136)		32g	32h
	33 Estimated tax penalty. Check if Form 2220 is attached ▶ ☐			33
	34 **Tax due.** If line 32h is smaller than the total of lines 31 and 33, enter amount owed			34
	35 **Overpayment.** If line 32h is larger than the total of lines 31 and 33, enter amount overpaid			35
	36 Enter amount of line 35 you want: **Credited to 1997 estimated tax** ▶ Refunded ▶			36

Sign Here

Under penalties of perjury, I declare that I have examined this return, including accompanying schedules and statements, and to the best of my knowledge and belief, it is true, correct, and complete. Declaration of preparer (other than taxpayer) is based on all information of which preparer has any knowledge.

▶ _____ Signature of officer | Date | ▶ _____ Title

Paid Preparer's Use Only	Preparer's signature ▶	Date	Check if self-employed ☐	Preparer's social security number
	Firm's name (or yours if self-employed) and address ▶		E.I. No. ▶	
			ZIP code ▶	

611601
10-25-96   H761

Form 1120 (1996)   Page **2**

Schedule A | Cost of Goods Sold (See page 12 of instructions.)

1	Inventory at beginning of year	1	
2	Purchases	2	
3	Cost of labor	3	
4	Additional section 263A costs (attach schedule)	4	
5	Other costs (attach schedule)	5	
6	**Total**. Add lines 1 through 5	6	
7	Inventory at end of year	7	
8	**Cost of goods sold**. Subtract line 7 from line 6. Enter here and on page 1, line 2	8	

9 a Check all methods used for valuing closing inventory:

    (i) ☐ Cost as described in Regulations section 1.471-3

    (ii) ☐ Lower of cost or market as described in Regulations section 1.471-4

    (iii) ☐ Other (Specify method used and attach explanation.) ▶ _____

  b   Check if there was a writedown of subnormal goods as described in Regulations section 1.471-2(c) .... ▶ ☐

  c   Check if the LIFO inventory method was adopted this tax year for any goods (if checked, attach Form 970) ..... ▶ ☐

  d   If the LIFO inventory method was used for this tax year, enter percentage (or amounts) of

       closing inventory computed under LIFO .... | 9d |

  e   If property is produced or acquired for resale, do the rules of section 263A apply to the corporation? ...... ☐ Yes ☐ No

  f   Was there any change in determining quantities, cost, or valuations between opening and closing inventory?

      If "Yes," attach explanation .... ☐ Yes ☐ No

Schedule C | Dividends and Special Deductions

		(a) Dividends received	(b) %	(c) Special deductions (a) x (b)
1	Dividends from less-than-20%-owned domestic corporations that are subject to the 70% deduction (other than debt-financed stock)		70	
2	Dividends from 20%-or-more-owned domestic corporations that are subject to the 80% deduction (other than debt-financed stock)		80	
3	Dividends on debt-financed stock of domestic and foreign corporations (section 246A)		see instructions	
4	Dividends on certain preferred stock of less-than-20%-owned public utilities		42	
5	Dividends on certain preferred stock of 20%-or-more-owned public utilities		48	
6	Dividends from less-than-20%-owned foreign corporations and certain FSCs that are subject to the 70% deduction		70	
7	Dividends from 20%-or-more-owned foreign corporations and certain FSCs that are subject to the 80% deduction		80	
8	Dividends from wholly owned foreign subsidiaries subject to the 100% deduction (section 245(b))		100	
9	**Total**. Add lines 1 through 8			
10	Dividends from domestic corporations received by a small business investment company operating under the Small Business Investment Act of 1958		100	
11	Dividends from certain FSCs that are subject to the 100% deduction (section 245(c)(1))		100	
12	Dividends from affiliated group members subject to the 100% deduction (sec. 243(a)(3))		100	
13	Other dividends from foreign corporations not included on lines 3, 6, 7, 8, or 11			
14	Income from controlled foreign corporations under subpart F (attach Form(s) 5471)			
15	Foreign dividend gross-up (section 78)			
16	IC -DISC and former DISC dividends not included on lines 1, 2, or 3 (section 246(d))			
17	Other dividends			
18	Deduction for dividends paid on certain preferred stock of public utilities			
19	**Total dividends**. Add lines 1 through 17. Enter here and on line 4, page 1 ▶			

20 **Total special deductions**. Add lines 9, 10, 11, 12, and 18. Enter here and on line 29b, page 1 .... ▶

Schedule E | Compensation of Officers Complete Schedule E only if total receipts (line 1a plus lines 4 through 10 on page 1, Form 1120) are $500,000 or more.

(a) Name of officer	(b) Social security number	(c) Percent of time devoted to business	Percent of corporation stock owned		(f) Amount of compensation
			(d) Common	(e) Preferred	
1					

2	Total compensation of officers	
3	Compensation of officers claimed on Schedule A and elsewhere on return	
4	Subtract line 3 from line 2. Enter the result here and on line 12, page 1	

611611
10-25-96

Form 1120 (1996)   Page **3**

Schedule J Tax Computation (See page 13 of instructions.)

1 Check if the corporation is a member of a controlled group (see sections 1561 and 1563) .... ▶ ☐

Important: Members of a controlled group, see instructions on page 13.

2a If the box on line 1 is checked, enter the corporation's share of the $50,000, $25,000, and $9,925,000 taxable income brackets (in that order):

(1) $ _____   (2) $ _____   (3) $ _____

b Enter the corporation's share of:

(1) Additional 5% tax (not more than $11,750) $ _____

(2) Additional 3% tax (not more than $100,000) $ _____

3 Income tax. Check this box if the corporation is a qualified personal service corporation as defined in section 448(d)(2) | 3 |

(see instructions) .... ▶ ☐

4a Foreign tax credit (attach Form 1118)	4a	
b Possessions tax credit (attach Form 5735)	4b	
c Check: ☐ Nonconventional source fuel credit ☐ QEV credit (attach Form 8834)	4c	

d General business credit. Enter here and check which forms are attached:

☐ 3800 ☐ 3468 ☐ 5884 ☐ 6478 ☐ 6765 ☐ 8586 ☐ 8830

☐ 8826 ☐ 8835 ☐ 8844 ☐ 8845 ☐ 8846 ☐ 8820 ☐ 8847 | 4d |

e Credit for prior year minimum tax (attach Form 8827) .... | 4e |

5 **Total credits.** Add lines 4a through 4e	5	
6 Subtract line 5 from line 3	6	
7 Personal holding company tax (attach Schedule PH (Form 1120))	7	
8 Recapture taxes. Check if from: ☐ Form 4255 ☐ Form 8611	8	
9 Alternative minimum tax (attach Form 4626)	9	
10 **Total tax.** Add lines 6 through 9. Enter here and on line 31, page1	10	

Schedule K Other Information (See page 15 of instructions.)

		Yes	No			Yes	No

1 Check method of accounting: **a** ☐ Cash **b** ☐ Accrual

c ☐ Other (specify) ▶ _____

2 See page 17 of the instructions and state the principal:

a Business activity code no. ▶ _____

b Business activity ▶ _____

c Product or service ▶ _____

3 Did the corporation at the end of the tax year own, directly or indirectly, 50% or more of the voting stock of a domestic corporation? (For rules of attribution, see section 267(c).) ....

If "Yes," attach a schedule showing: (a) name and identifying number, (b) percentage owned, and (c) taxable income or (loss) before NOL and special deductions of such corporation for the tax year ending with or within your tax year.

4 Is the corporation a subsidiary in an affiliated group or a parent-subsidiary controlled group? ....

If "Yes," enter employer identification number and name of the parent corporation ▶ _____

_____

5 Did any individual, partnership, corporation, estate or trust at the end of the tax year own, directly or indirectly, 50% or more of the corporation's voting stock? (For rules of attribution, see section 267(c).) ....

If "Yes," attach a schedule showing name and identifying number. (Do not include any information already entered in 4 above.) Enter percentage owned ▶ _____

6 During this tax year, did the corporation pay dividends (other than stock dividends and distributions in exchange for stock) in excess of the corporation's current and accumulated earnings and profits? (See secs. 301 and 316.) ....

If "Yes," file Form 5452. If this is a consolidated return, answer here for the parent corporation and on **Form 851, Affiliations Schedule,** for each subsidiary.

7 Was the corporation a U.S. shareholder of any controlled foreign corporation? (See sections 951 and 957.) ....

If "Yes," attach Form 5471 for each such corporation. Enter number of Forms 5471 attached ▶ _____

8 At any time during the 1996 calendar year, did the corporation have an interest in or a signature or other authority over a financial account in a foreign country (such as a bank account, securities account, or other financial account) in a foreign country? ......

If "Yes," the corporation may have to file Form TD F 90-22.1.

If "Yes," enter name of foreign country ▶ _____

9 During the tax year, did the corporation receive a distribution from, or was it the grantor of, or transferor to, a foreign trust?

If "Yes," see page 16 of the instructions for other forms the corporation may have to file ....

10 Did one foreign person at any time during the tax year own, directly or indirectly, at least 25% of: **(a)** the total voting power of all classes of stock of the corporation entitled to vote, or **(b)** the total value of all classes of stock of the corporation? If "Yes,"

a Enter percentage owned ▶ _____

b Enter owner's country ▶ _____

c The corporation may have to file Form 5472. Enter number of Forms 5472 attached ▶ _____

11 Check this box if the corporation issued publicly offered debt instruments with original issue discount .... ▶ ☐

If so, the corporation may have to file Form 8281.

12 Enter the amount of tax-exempt interest received or accrued during the tax year ▶ $ _____

13 If there were 35 or fewer shareholders at the end of the tax year, enter the number ▶ _____

14 If the corporation has an NOL for the tax year and is electing to forego the carryback period, check here .... ▶ ☐

15 Enter the available NOL carryover from prior tax years (Do not reduce it by any deduction on line 29a.) ▶ $ _____

Form 1120 (1996) Page **4**

Schedule L	Balance Sheets per Books	Beginning of tax year		End of tax year	
	Assets	**(a)**	**(b)**	**(c)**	**(d)**
1	Cash				
2a	Trade notes and accounts receivable				
b	Less allowance for bad debts	( )		( )	
3	Inventories				
4	U.S. government obligations				
5	Tax-exempt securities				
6	Other current assets				
7	Loans to stockholders				
8	Mortgage and real estate loans				
9	Other investments				
10a	Buildings and other depreciable assets				
b	Less accumulated depreciation	( )		( )	
11a	Depletable assets				
b	Less accumulated depletion	( )		( )	
12	Land (net of any amortization)				
13a	Intangible assets (amortizable only)				
b	Less accumulated amortization	( )		( )	
14	Other assets				
15	Total assets				
	Liabilities and Stockholders' Equity				
16	Accounts payable				
17	Mortgages, notes, bonds payable in less than 1 year				
18	Other current liabilities				
19	Loans from stockholders				
20	Mortgages, notes, bonds payable in 1 year or more				
21	Other liabilities				
22	Capital stock: **a** Preferred stock				
	b Common stock				
23	Paid-in or capital surplus				
24	Retained earnings - Appropriated (attach schedule)				
25	Retained earnings - Unappropriated				
26	Less cost of treasury stock		( )		( )
27	Total liabilities and stockholders' equity				

Note: You are not required to complete Schedules M-1 and M-2 below if the total assets on line 15, column (d) of Schedule L are less than $25,000.

Schedule M–1	**Reconciliation of Income (Loss) per Books With Income per Return**

1 Net income (loss) per books
2 Federal income tax
3 Excess of capital losses over capital gains
4 Income subject to tax not recorded on books this year (itemize): _____

_____

5 Expenses recorded on books this year not deducted on this return (itemize):
  a Depreciation ...... $ _____
  b Contributions carryover .... $ _____
  c Travel and entertainment ... $ _____

_____

6 Add lines 1 through 5

7 Income recorded on books this year not included on this return (itemize):
  Tax-exempt interest $ _____

_____

_____

8 Deductions on this return not charged against book income this year (itemize):
  a Depreciation ...... $ _____
  b Contributions carryover .... $ _____

_____

9 Add lines 7 and 8
10 Income (line 28, page 1) - line 6 less line 9

Schedule M–2	**Analysis of Unappropriated Retained Earnings per Books (Line 25, Schedule L)**

1 Balance at beginning of year
2 Net income (loss) per books
3 Other increases (itemize): _____

_____

_____

_____

4 Add lines 1, 2, and 3

5 Distributions: **a** Cash
  b Stock
  c Property
6 Other decreases (itemize) : _____

_____

7 Add lines 5 and 6
8 Balance at end of year (line 4 less line 7)

611631
10-25-96

SCHEDULE D
(Form 1120)

Department of the Treasury
Internal Revenue Service

Capital Gains and Losses

To be filed with Forms 1120, 1120-A, 1120-IC-DISC, 1120-F,
1120-FSC, 1120-H, 1120-L, 1120-ND, 1120-PC, 1120-POL,
1120-REIT, 1120-RIC, 1120-SF, 990-C, and certain Forms 990-T

OMB No. 1545-0123

1996

Name | Employer identification number

Part I Short-Term Capital Gains and Losses - Assets Held One Year or Less

(a) Kind of property and description (Example, 100 shares of Z Co.)	(b) Date acquired (mo., day, yr.)	(c) Date sold (mo., day, yr.)	(d) Sales price (see instructions)	(e) Cost or other basis (see instructions)	(f) Gain or (loss) ((d) less (e))
1					

2 Short-term capital gain from installment sales from Form 6252, line 26 or 37	2	
3 Short-term gain or (loss) from like-kind exchanges from Form 8824	3	
4 Unused capital loss carryover (attach computation)	4	( )
5 Net short-term capital gain or (loss). Combine lines 1 through 4	5	

Part II Long-Term Capital Gains and Losses - Assets Held More Than One Year

6					

7 Enter gain from Form 4797, line 8 or 10	7	
8 Long-term capital gain from installment sales from Form 6252, line 26 or 37	8	
9 Long-term gain or (loss) from like-kind exchanges from Form 8824	9	
10 Net long-term capital gain or (loss). Combine lines 6 through 9	10	

Part III Summary of Parts I and II

11 Enter excess of net short-term capital gain (line 5) over net long-term capital loss (line 10)	11	
12 Net capital gain. Enter excess of net long-term capital gain (line 10) over net short-term capital loss (line 5)	12	
13 Add lines 11 and 12. Enter here and on Form 1120, page 1, line 8, or the proper line on other returns	13	

Note: If losses exceed gains, see **Capital losses** in the instructions.

H761   For Paperwork Reduction Act Notice, see page 1 of the Instructions for Forms 1120 and 1120-A.

Schedule D (Form 1120) 1996

Form **1120S**

Department of the Treasury
Internal Revenue Service

U.S. Income Tax Return for an S Corporation

▶ Do not file this form unless the corporation has timely filed
Form 2553 to elect to be an S corporation.

OMB No. 1545-0130

1996

For calendar year 1996, or tax year beginning _____ , and ending _____

A Date of election as an S corporation	Use IRS label. Otherwise, please print or type.
B Business code no. (see Specific Instructions)	

Name

Number, street, and room or suite no. (If a P.O. box, see page 9 of the instructions.)

City or town, state, and ZIP code

C Employer identification number

D Date incorporated

E Total assets (see Specific Instructions)
$

F Check applicable boxes: (1) ☐ Initial return (2) ☐ Final return (3) ☐ Change in address (4) ☐ Amended return

G Check this box if this S corporation is subject to the consolidated audit procedures of sections 6241 through 6245 (see instructions before checking this box) .... ▶ ☐

H Enter number of shareholders in the corporation at end of the tax year .... ▶

Caution: *Include only trade or business income and expenses on lines 1a through 21. See the instructions for more information.*

Income

1 a Gross receipts or sales _____ **b** Less returns and allowances _____ **c** Bal ▶	**1c**	
2 Cost of goods sold (Schedule A, line 8)	**2**	
3 Gross profit. Subtract line 2 from line 1c	**3**	
4 Net gain (loss) from Form 4797, Part II, line 20 *(attach Form 4797)*	**4**	
5 Other income (loss) *(attach schedule)*	**5**	
6 **Total income (loss).** Combine lines 3 through 5 ▶	**6**	

Deductions (See instructions for limitations)

7 Compensation of officers	**7**	
8 Salaries and wages (less employment credits)	**8**	
9 Repairs and maintenance	**9**	
10 Bad debts	**10**	
11 Rents	**11**	
12 Taxes and licenses	**12**	
13 Interest	**13**	
14 a Depreciation *(if required, attach Form 4562)* **14a**		
b Depreciation claimed on Schedule A and elsewhere on return **14b**		
c Subtract line 14b from line 14a	**14c**	
15 Depletion **(Do not deduct oil and gas depletion.)**	**15**	
16 Advertising	**16**	
17 Pension, profit-sharing, etc., plans	**17**	
18 Employee benefit programs	**18**	
19 Other deductions *(attach schedule)*	**19**	
20 **Total deductions.** Add the amounts shown in the far right column for lines 7 through 19 ▶	**20**	
21 Ordinary income (loss) from trade or business activities. Subtract line 20 from line 6	**21**	

Tax and Payments

22 **Tax: a** Excess net passive income tax *(attach schedule)* **22a**		
b Tax from Schedule D (Form 1120S) **22b**		
c Add lines 22a and 22b	**22c**	
23 **Payments: a** 1996 estimated tax payments and amount applied from 1995 return **23a**		
b Tax deposited with Form 7004 ..... **23b**		
c Credit for Federal tax paid on fuels *(attach Form 4136)* **23c**		
d Add lines 23a through 23c	**23d**	
24 Estimated tax penalty. Check if Form 2220 is attached ..... ▶ ☐	**24**	
25 **Tax due.** If the total of lines 22c and 24 is larger than line 23d, enter amount owed. See instructions for depositary method of payment ..... ▶	**25**	
26 **Overpayment.** If line 23d is larger than the total of lines 22c and 24, enter amount overpaid ..... ▶	**26**	
27 Enter amount of line 26 you want: **Credited to 1997 estimated tax** ▶ _____ **Refunded** ▶	**27**	

Please Sign Here

Under penalties of perjury, I declare that I have examined this return, including accompanying schedules and statements, and to the best of my knowledge and belief, it is true, correct, and complete. Declaration of preparer (other than taxpayer) is based on all information of which preparer has any knowledge.

▶ _____ Signature of officer _____ Date _____ ▶ _____ Title

Paid Preparer's Use Only

Preparer's signature ▶	Date	Check if self-employed ▶ ☐	Preparer's social security number
Firm's name (or yours if self-employed) and address ▶		E.I. No. ▶	
		ZIP code ▶	

611701
11-06-96   H761   **For Paperwork Reduction Act Notice, see page 1 of separate instructions.**

Form **1120S** (1996)

Form 1120S (1996) Page **2**

Schedule A — Cost of Goods Sold

1	Inventory at beginning of year	1	
2	Purchases	2	
3	Cost of labor	3	
4	Additional section 263A costs (attach schedule)	4	
5	Other costs (attach schedule)	5	
6	**Total.** Add lines 1 through 5	6	
7	Inventory at end of year	7	
8	**Cost of goods sold.** Subtract line 7 from line 6. Enter here and on page 1, line 2	8	

9 a Check all methods used for valuing closing inventory:

(i) ☐ Cost as described in Regulations section 1.471-3

(ii) ☐ Lower of cost or market as described in Regulations section 1.471-4

(iii) ☐ Other (specify method used and attach explanation) ▶ _____

b Check if there was a writedown of "subnormal" goods as described in Regulations section 1.471-2(c) ▶ ☐

c Check if the LIFO inventory method was adopted this tax year for any goods (if checked, attach Form 970) ▶ ☐

d If the LIFO inventory method was used for this tax year, enter percentage (or amounts) of closing inventory computed under LIFO ___ | 9d |

e Do the rules of section 263A (for property produced or acquired for resale) apply to the corporation? ☐ Yes ☐ No

f Was there any change in determining quantities, cost, or valuations between opening and closing inventory? ☐ Yes ☐ No
If "Yes," attach explanation.

Schedule B — Other Information

		Yes	No
1	Check method of accounting: **(a)** ☐ Cash **(b)** ☐ Accrual **(c)** ☐ Other (specify) ▶ _____		
2	Refer to the list on page 24 of the instructions and state the corporation's principal: **(a)** Business activity ▶ _____ **(b)** Product or service ▶ _____		
3	Did the corporation at the end of the tax year own, directly or indirectly, 50% or more of the voting stock of a domestic corporation? (For rules of attribution, see section 267(c).) If "Yes," attach a schedule showing: **(a)** name, address, and employer identification number and **(b)** percentage owned		
4	Was the corporation a member of a controlled group subject to the provisions of section 1561?		
5	At any time during calendar year 1996, did the corporation have an interest in or a signature or other authority over a financial account in a foreign country (such as a bank account, securities account, or other financial account)? (See page 14 of the instructions for exceptions and filing requirements for Form TD F 90-22.1.) If "Yes," enter the name of the foreign country ▶ _____		
6	During the tax year, did the corporation receive a distribution from, or was it the grantor of, or transferor to, a foreign trust? If "Yes," see page 14 of the instructions for other forms the corporation may have to file		
7	Check this box if the corporation has filed or is required to file **Form 8264,** Application for Registration of a Tax Shelter ▶ ☐		
8	Check this box if the corporation issued publicly offered debt instruments with original issue discount ▶ ☐ If so, the corporation may have to file **Form 8281,** Information Return for Publicly Offered Original Issue Discount Instruments.		
9	If the corporation: **(a)** filed its election to be an S corporation after 1986, **(b)** was a C corporation before it elected to be an S corporation **or** the corporation acquired an asset with a basis determined by reference to its basis (or the basis of any other property) in the hands of a C corporation, and **(c)** has net unrealized built-in gain (defined in section 1374(d)(1)) in excess of the net recognized built-in gain from prior years, enter the net unrealized built-in gain reduced by net recognized built-in gain from prior years ▶ $ _____		
10	Check this box if the corporation had subchapter C earnings and profits at the close of the tax year ▶ ☐		

Designation of Tax Matters Person

Enter below the shareholder designated as the tax matters person (TMP) for the tax year of this return:

Name of
designated TMP ▶ _____

Identifying
number of TMP ▶ _____

Address of
designated TMP ▶ _____

611711
11-06-96

Form 1120S (1996)   Page 3

Schedule K Shareholders' Shares of Income, Credits, Deductions, etc.

	(a) Pro rata share items			(b) Total amount
Income (Loss)	**1** Ordinary income (loss) from trade or business activities (page 1, line 21)		**1**	
	2 Net income (loss) from rental real estate activities (attach Form 8825)		**2**	
	3a Gross income from other rental activities	**3a**		
	b Expenses from other rental activities (attach schedule)	**3b**		
	c Net income (loss) from other rental activities. Subtract line 3b from line 3a		**3c**	
	4 Portfolio income (loss):			
	a Interest income		**4a**	
	b Dividend income		**4b**	
	c Royalty income		**4c**	
	d Net short-term capital gain (loss) (attach Schedule D (Form 1120S))		**4d**	
	e Net long-term capital gain (loss) (attach Schedule D (Form 1120S))		**4e**	
	f Other portfolio income (loss) (attach schedule)		**4f**	
	5 Net gain (loss) under section 1231 (other than due to casualty or theft) (attach Form 4797)		**5**	
	6 Other income (loss) (attach schedule)		**6**	
Deductions	**7** Charitable contributions (attach schedule)		**7**	
	8 Section 179 expense deduction (attach Form 4562)		**8**	
	9 Deductions related to portfolio income (loss) (itemize)		**9**	
	10 Other deductions (attach schedule)		**10**	
Investment Interest	**11a** Interest expense on investment debts		**11a**	
	b (1) Investment income included on lines 4a, 4b, 4c, and 4f above		**11b(1)**	
	(2) Investment expenses included on line 9 above		**11b(2)**	
Credits	**12a** Credit for alcohol used as a fuel (attach Form 6478)		**12a**	
	b Low-income housing credit:			
	(1) From partnerships to which section 42(j)(5) applies for property placed in service before 1990		**12b(1)**	
	(2) Other than on line 12b(1) for property placed in service before 1990		**12b(2)**	
	(3) From partnerships to which section 42(j)(5) applies for property placed in service after 1989		**12b(3)**	
	(4) Other than on line 12b(3) for property placed in service after 1989		**12b(4)**	
	c Qualified rehabilitation expenditures related to rental real estate activities (attach Form 3468)		**12c**	
	d Credits (other than credits shown on lines 12b and 12c) related to rental real estate activities		**12d**	
	e Credits related to other rental activities		**12e**	
	13 Other credits		**13**	
Adjustments and Tax Preference Items	**14a** Depreciation adjustment on property placed in service after 1986		**14a**	
	b Adjusted gain or loss		**14b**	
	c Depletion (other than oil and gas)		**14c**	
	d (1) Gross income from oil, gas, or geothermal properties		**14d(1)**	
	(2) Deductions allocable to oil, gas, or geothermal properties		**14d(2)**	
	e Other adjustments and tax preference items (attach schedule)		**14e**	
Foreign Taxes	**15a** Type of income ▶			
	b Name of foreign country or U.S. possession ▶			
	c Total gross income from sources outside the United States (attach schedule)		**15c**	
	d Total applicable deductions and losses (attach schedule)		**15d**	
	e Total foreign taxes (check one): ▶ ☐ Paid ☐ Accrued		**15e**	
	f Reduction in taxes available for credit (attach schedule)		**15f**	
	g Other foreign tax information (attach schedule)		**15g**	
Other	**16** Section 59(e)(2) expenditures: **a** Type ▶			
	b Amount		**16b**	
	17 Tax-exempt interest income		**17**	
	18 Other tax-exempt income		**18**	
	19 Nondeductible expenses		**19**	
	20 Total property distributions (including cash) other than dividends reported on line 22 below		**20**	
	21 Other items and amounts required to be reported separately to shareholders (attach schedule)			
	22 Total dividend distributions paid from accumulated earnings and profits		**22**	
	23 **Income (loss).** (Required only if Schedule M-1 must be completed.). Combine lines 1 through 6 in column (b). From the result, subtract the sum of lines 7 through 11a, 15e, and 16b		**23**	

611721
11-06-96

Form 1120S (1996)   Page 4

Schedule L — Balance Sheets

Assets	Beginning of tax year (a)	(b)	End of tax year (c)	(d)
1 Cash				
2 a Trade notes and accounts receivable				
b Less allowance for bad debts				
3 Inventories				
4 U.S. Government obligations				
5 Tax-exempt securities				
6 Other current assets				
7 Loans to shareholders				
8 Mortgage and real estate loans				
9 Other investments				
10 a Buildings and other depreciable assets				
b Less accumulated depreciation				
11 a Depletable assets				
b Less accumulated depletion				
12 Land (net of any amortization)				
13 a Intangible assets (amortizable only)				
b Less accumulated amortization				
14 Other assets				
15 Total assets				
Liabilities and Shareholders' Equity				
16 Accounts payable				
17 Mortgages, notes, bonds payable in less than 1 year				
18 Other current liabilities				
19 Loans from shareholders				
20 Mortgages, notes, bonds payable in 1 year or more				
21 Other liabilities				
22 Capital stock				
23 Paid-in or capital surplus				
24 Retained earnings				
25 Less cost of treasury stock	(	)	(	)
26 Total liabilities and shareholders' equity				

Schedule M-1 — Reconciliation of Income (Loss) per Books With Income (Loss) per Return

(You are not required to complete this schedule if the total assets on line 15, column (d), of Schedule L are less than $25,000.)

1 Net income (loss) per books		5 Income recorded on books this year not included on Schedule K, lines 1 through 6 (itemize):	
2 Income included on Schedule K, lines 1 through 6, not recorded on books this year (itemize): _____		a Tax-exempt interest $ _____	
3 Expenses recorded on books this year not included on Schedule K, lines 1 through 11a, 15e, and 16b (itemize):		6 Deductions included on Schedule K, lines 1 through 11a, 15e, and 16b, not charged against book income this year (itemize):	
a Depreciation $ _____		a Depreciation $ _____	
b Travel and entertainment $ _____			
		7 Add lines 5 and 6	
4 Add lines 1 through 3		8 Income (loss) (Schedule K, line 23). Line 4 less line 7	

Schedule M-2 — Analysis of Accumulated Adjustments Account, Other Adjustments Account, and Shareholders' Undistributed Taxable Income Previously Taxed

	(a) Accumulated adjustments account	(b) Other adjustments account	(c) Shareholders' undistributed taxable income previously taxed
1 Balance at beginning of tax year			
2 Ordinary income from page 1, line 21			
3 Other additions			
4 Loss from page 1, line 21	( )		
5 Other reductions	( )	( )	
6 Combine lines 1 through 5			
7 Distributions other than dividend distributions			
8 Balance at end of tax year. Subtract line 7 from line 6			

611731
11-06-96

SCHEDULE D
(Form 1120S)
Department of the Treasury
Internal Revenue Service

Capital Gains and Losses and Built-In Gains

▶ Attach to Form 1120S.

OMB No. 1545-0130

1996

Name	Employer identification number

Part I — Short-Term Capital Gains and Losses - Assets Held One Year or Less

(a) Kind of property and description (Example, 100 shares of "Z" Co.)	(b) Date acquired (mo., day, yr.)	(c) Date sold (mo., day, yr.)	(d) Sales price	(e) Cost or other basis (see instructions)	(f) Gain or (loss) ((d) less (e))
1					

2 Short-term capital gain from installment sales from Form 6252, line 26 or 37	2	
3 Short-term capital gain or (loss) from like-kind exchanges from Form 8824	3	
4 Combine lines 1 through 3 and enter here	4	
5 Tax on short-term capital gain included on line 31 below	5	
6 **Net short-term capital gain or (loss).** Subtract line 5 from line 4. Enter here and on Form 1120S, Schedule K, line 4d or line 6	6	

Part II — Long-Term Capital Gains and Losses - Assets Held More Than One Year

7					

8 Long-term capital gain from installment sales from Form 6252, line 26 or 37	8	
9 Long-term capital gain or (loss) from like-kind exchanges from Form 8824	9	
10 Combine lines 7 through 9 and enter here	10	
11 Tax on long-term capital gain included on lines 23 and 31 below	11	
12 **Net long-term capital gain or (loss).** Subtract line 11 from line 10. Enter here and on Form 1120S, Schedule K, line 4e or line 6	12	

Part III — Capital Gains Tax (See instructions **before** completing this part.)

13 Enter section 1231 gain from Form 4797, line 10	13	
14 Net long-term capital gain or (loss) - Combine lines 10 and 13	14	
Note: If the corporation is liable for the excess net passive income tax (Form 1120S, page 1, line 22a) or the built-in gains tax (Part IV below), see the line 15 instructions before completing line 15.		
15 Net capital gain. Enter excess of net long-term capital gain (line 14) over net short-term capital loss (line 4)	15	
16 Statutory minimum	16	$25,000
17 Subtract line 16 from line 15	17	
18 Enter 34% of line 17	18	
19 Taxable income (attach computation schedule)	19	
20 Enter tax on line 19 amount (attach computation schedule)	20	
21 Net capital gain from substituted basis property (attach computation schedule)	21	
22 Enter 35% of line 21	22	
23 **Tax.** Enter the smallest of line 18, 20, or 22 here and on Form 1120S, page 1, line 22b	23	

Part IV — Built-In Gains Tax (See instructions **before** completing this part.)

24 Excess of recognized built-in gains over recognized built-in losses (attach computation schedule)	24	
25 Taxable income (attach computation schedule)	25	
26 Net recognized built-in gain. Enter smaller of line 24, line 25, or line 9 of Schedule B	26	
27 Section 1374(b)(2) deduction	27	
28 Subtract line 27 from line 26. If zero or less, enter -0- here and on line 31.	28	
29 Enter 35% of line 28	29	
30 Business credit and minimum tax credit carryforwards under section 1374(b)(3) from C corporation years	30	
31 **Tax.** Subtract line 30 from line 29 (if zero or less, enter -0-). Enter here and on Form 1120S, page 1, line 22b	31	

H761   **For Paperwork Reduction Act Notice, see page 1 of Instructions for Form 1120S.**   Schedule D (Form 1120S) 1996

SCHEDULE K-1 (Form 1120S)	Shareholder's Share of Income, Credits, Deductions, etc.	OMB No. 1545-0130
Department of the Treasury Internal Revenue Service	▶ See separate instructions. For calendar year 1996 or tax year beginning _____ and ending _____	**1996**

Shareholder's identifying number ▶	Corporation's identifying number ▶
Shareholder's name, address, and ZIP code	Corporation's name, address, and ZIP code

A Shareholder's percentage of stock ownership for tax year (see Instructions for Schedule K-1) .... ▶ _____ %

B Internal Revenue Service Center where corporation filed its return ▶ _____

C Tax shelter registration number (see Instructions for Schedule K-1) .... ▶ _____

D Check applicable boxes: **(1)** ☐ Final K-1 **(2)** ☐ Amended K-1

		(a) Pro rata share items		(b) Amount	(c) Form 1040 filers enter the amount in column (b) on:
Income (Loss)	1	Ordinary income (loss) from trade or business activities	1		See pages 4 and 5 of the Shareholder's Instructions for Schedule K-1 (Form 1120S).
	2	Net income (loss) from rental real estate activities	2		
	3	Net income (loss) from other rental activities	3		
	4	Portfolio income (loss):			
		a Interest	4a		Sch. B, Part I, line 1
		b Dividends	4b		Sch. B, Part II, line 5
		c Royalties	4c		Sch. E, Part I, line 4
		d Net short-term capital gain (loss)	4d		Sch. D, line 5, col. (f) or (g)
		e Net long-term capital gain (loss)	4e		Sch. D, line 13, col. (f) or (g)
		f Other portfolio income (loss) (attach schedule)	4f		(Enter on applicable line of your return.)
	5	Net gain (loss) under section 1231 (other than due to casualty or theft)	5		See Shareholder's Instructions for Schedule K-1 (Form 1120S)
	6	Other income (loss) (attach schedule)	6		(Enter on applicable line of your return.)
Deductions	7	Charitable contributions (attach schedule)	7		Sch. A, line 15 or 16
	8	Section 179 expense deduction	8		See page 6 of the Shareholder's Instructions for Schedule K-1 (Form 1120S).
	9	Deductions related to portfolio income (loss) (attach schedule)	9		
	10	Other deductions (attach schedule)	10		
Investment Interest	11	a Interest expense on investment debts	11a		Form 4952, line 1
		b (1) Investment income included on lines 4a, 4b, 4c, and 4f above	b(1)		See Shareholder's Instructions for Schedule K-1 (Form 1120S).
		(2) Investment expenses included on line 9 above	b(2)		
Credits	12	a Credit for alcohol used as fuel	12a		Form 6478, line 10
		b Low-income housing credit:			
		(1) From section 42(j)(5) partnerships for property placed in service before 1990	b(1)		Form 8586, line 5
		(2) Other than on line 12b(1) for property placed in service before 1990	b(2)		
		(3) From section 42(j)(5) partnerships for property placed in service after 1989	b(3)		
		(4) Other than on line 12b(3) for property placed in service after 1989	b(4)		
		c Qualified rehabilitation expenditures related to rental real estate activities	12c		See page 7 of the Shareholder's Instructions for Schedule K-1 (Form 1120S).
		d Credits (other than credits shown on lines 12b and 12c) related to rental real estate activities	12d		
		e Credits related to other rental activities (see instructions)	12e		
	13	Other credits	13		
Adjustments and Tax Preference Items	14	a Depreciation adjustment on property placed in service after 1986	14a		See page 7 of the Shareholder's Instructions for Schedule K-1 (Form 1120S) and Instructions for Form 6251
		b Adjusted gain or loss	14b		
		c Depletion (other than oil and gas)	14c		
		d (1) Gross income from oil, gas, or geothermal properties	d(1)		
		(2) Deductions allocable to oil, gas, or geothermal properties	d(2)		
		e Other adjustments and tax preference items (attach schedule)	14e		

H761 **For Paperwork Reduction Act Notice, see page 1 of Instructions for Form 1120S.** **Schedule K-1 (Form 1120S) 1996**

	(a) Pro rata share items		(b) Amount	(c) Form 1040 filers enter the amount in column (b) on:
Foreign Taxes	**15 a** Type of income ▶ _____			Form 1116, Check boxes
	b Name of foreign country or U.S. possession ▶ _____			⎫
	c Total gross income from sources outside the United States (attach schedule) ...	**15c**		⎬ Form 1116, Part I
	d Total applicable deductions and losses (attach schedule)	**15d**		⎭
	e Total foreign taxes (check one): ▶ ☐ Paid ☐ Accrued	**15e**		Form 1116, Part II
	f Reduction in taxes available for credit (attach schedule)	**15f**		Form 1116, Part III
	g Other foreign tax information (attach schedule)	**15g**		See Instructions for Form 1116
Other	**16** Section 59(e)(2) expenditures: **a** Type ▶ _____			See Shareholder's Instructions for Schedule K-1 (Form 1120S).
	b Amount	**16b**		
	17 Tax-exempt interest income	**17**		Form 1040, line 8b
	18 Other tax-exempt income	**18**		⎫
	19 Nondeductible expenses	**19**		⎬ See page 7 of the Shareholder's Instructions for Schedule K-1 (Form 1120S).
	20 Property distributions (including cash) other than dividend distributions reported to you on Form 1099-DIV	**20**		⎭
	21 Amount of loan repayments for "Loans From Shareholders"	**21**		
	22 Recapture of low-income housing credit:			⎫
	a From section 42(j)(5) partnerships	**22a**		⎬ Form 8611, line 8
	b Other than on line 22a	**22b**		⎭

23 Supplemental information required to be reported separately to each shareholder (attach additional schedules if more space is needed):

Supplemental Information

Form **1120X**

(Rev. June 1995)
Department of the Treasury
Internal Revenue Service

Amended U.S. Corporation
Income Tax Return

OMB No. 1545-0132

For tax year ending in
▶ _____
(Enter month and year)

Please Type or Print

Name	Employer identification number
Number, street, and room or suite no. (If a P.O. box, see instructions.)	
City or town, state, and ZIP code	Telephone number (optional)

Enter name and address used on original return (If same as above, write "Same.")

Internal Revenue Service Center
where original return was filed ▶

Fill in Applicable Items and Use Part II To Explain Any Changes

Part I	Income and Deductions	(a) As originally reported or as previously adjusted	(b) Net change (increase or decrease- explain in Part II)	(c) Correct amount
1	Total income (Form 1120 or 1120-A, line 11)			
2	Total deductions (total of lines 27 and 29c, Form 1120, or lines 23 and 25c, Form 1120-A)			
3	Taxable income. Subtract line 2 from line 1			
4	Tax (Form 1120, line 31, or Form 1120-A, line 27)			

Payments and Credits

5a	Overpayment in prior year allowed as a credit			
b	Estimated tax payments			
c	Refund applied for on Form 4466			
d	Subtract line 5c from the sum of lines 5a and 5b			
e	Tax deposited with Form 7004			
f	Credit from regulated investment companies			
g	Credit for Federal tax on fuels			
6	Tax deposited or paid with (or after) the filing of the original return			
7	Add lines 5d through 6, column (c)			
8	Overpayment, if any, as shown on original return or as later adjusted			
9	Subtract line 8 from line 7			

Tax Due or Refund

10	**Tax due.** Subtract line 9 from line 4, column (c). Make check payable to "Internal Revenue Service" ▶	
11	**Refund.** Subtract line 4, column (c), from line 9 ▶	

Please Sign Here

Under penalties of perjury, I declare that I have filed an original return and that I have examined this amended return, including accompanying schedules and statements, and to the best of my knowledge and belief, this amended return is true, correct, and complete. Declaration of preparer (other than taxpayer) is based on all information of which preparer has any knowledge.

▶ _____ ▶ _____ ▶ _____
Signature of officer   Date   Title

Paid Preparer's Use Only

Preparer's signature ▶	Date	Check if self-employed ▶ ☐	Preparer's social security no.
Firm's name (or yours if self-employed) and address ▶		E.I. No. ▶	
		ZIP code ▶	

For Paperwork Reduction Act Notice, see instructions on page 3.

610711
12-09-96

Form **1120X** (Rev. 6-95)

Form 1120X (Rev. 6-95)   Page **2**

Part II **Explanation of Changes to Income, Deductions, Credits, etc. Enter the line number from page 1 for the items you are changing, and give the reason for each change. Show any computation in detail. Attach additional sheets if necessary.**

If the change is due to a net operating loss carryback, a capital loss carryback, or a general business credit carryback, see **Carryback Claims** on page 3, and check here .... ▶ ☐

Form **2210**

Department of the Treasury
Internal Revenue Service

Underpayment of
Estimated Tax by Individuals, Estates, and Trusts

▶ See separate instructions.
▶ Attach to Form 1040, 1040A, 1040NR, 1040NR-EZ, or 1041.

OMB No.1545-0140

1996

Attachment
Sequence No. **06**

Name(s) shown on tax return

Identifying number

Note: In most cases, you **do not** need to file Form 2210. The IRS will figure any penalty you owe and send you a bill. File Form 2210 **only** if one or more boxes in Part I apply to you. If you do not need to file Form 2210, you still may use it to figure your penalty. Enter the amount from line 20 or line 36 on the penalty line of your return, but do not attach Form 2210.

Part I	**Reasons for Filing -** If 1a, b, or c below applies to you, you may be able to lower or eliminate your penalty. But you MUST check the boxes that apply and file Form 2210 with your tax return. If 1d below applies to you, check that box and file Form 2210 with your tax return.

1 Check whichever boxes apply (if none apply, see the **Note** above):

a ☐ You request a **waiver**. In certain circumstances, the IRS will waive all or part of the penalty.
See **Waiver of Penalty** on page 2 of the instructions.

b ☐ You use the **annualized income installment method**. If your income varied during the year, this method may reduce the amount of one or more required installments. See page 4 of the instructions.

c ☐ You had Federal income tax withheld from wages and, for estimated tax purposes, you treat the withheld tax as paid on the dates it was actually withheld, instead of in equal amounts on the payments on the payment due dates. See the instructions for line 22 on page 3.

d ☐ Your required annual payment (line 13 below) is based on your 1995 tax and you filed or are filing a joint return for either 1995 or 1996 but not for both years.

Part II	**Required Annual Payment**		
2	Enter your 1996 tax after credits (see page 2 of the instructions)	**2**	
3	Other taxes (see page 2 of the instructions)	**3**	
4	Add lines 2 and 3	**4**	
5	Earned income credit ⟨**5**⟩		
6	Credit for Federal tax paid on fuels ⟨**6**⟩		
7	Add lines 5 and 6	**7**	
8	Current year tax. Subtract line 7 from line 4	**8**	
9	Multiply line 8 by 90% (.90) ⟨**9**⟩		
10	Withholding taxes. **Do not** include any estimated tax payments on this line (see page 2 of the instructions)	**10**	
11	Subtract line 10 from line 8. If less than $500, **stop here; do not** complete or file this form. You do not owe the penalty	**11**	
12	Enter the tax shown on your 1995 tax return (110% of that amount if the adjusted gross income shown on that return is more than $150,000, or if married filing separately for 1996, more than $75,000). **Caution:** See instructions.	**12**	
13	**Required annual payment.** Enter the **smaller** of line 9 or line 12	**13**	

Note: If line 10 is equal to or more than line 13, stop here; you do not owe the penalty. Do not file Form 2210 unless you checked box 1d above.

Part III	**Short Method (Caution:** See page 2 of the instructions to find out if you can use the short method. If you checked box **1b** or **c** in Part I, skip this part and go to Part IV.)		
14	Enter the amount, if any, from line 10 above ⟨**14**⟩		
15	Enter the total amount, if any, of estimated tax payments you made ⟨**15**⟩		
16	Add lines 14 and 15	**16**	
17	**Total underpayment for year.** Subtract line 16 from line 13. If zero or less, stop here; you do not owe the penalty. Do not file Form 2210 unless you checked box 1d above	**17**	
18	Multiply line 17 by .05914	**18**	
19	• If the amount on line 17 was paid **on or after** 4/15/97, enter -0-. • If the amount on line 17 was paid **before** 4/15/97, make the following computation to find the amount to enter on line 19. Amount on line 17 × Number of days paid before 4/15/97 × .00025	**19**	
20	**PENALTY.** Subtract line 19 from line 18. Enter the result here and on Form 1040, line 63; Form 1040A, line 34; Form 1040NR, line 63; Form 1040NR-EZ, line 26; or Form 1041, line 26 ▶	**20**	

LHA **For Paperwork Reduction Act Notice, see page 1 of separate instructions.**

Form **2210** (1996)

612501
11-16-96

Form 2210 (1996)   Page **2**

Part IV Regular Method

		Payment Due Dates			
Section A - Figure Your Underpayment		**(a)** 4/15/96	**(b)** 6/15/96	**(c)** 9/15/96	**(d)** 1/15/97
21	**Required installments.** If box 1b applies, enter the amounts from Schedule AI, line 26. Otherwise, enter 1/4 of line 13, Form 2210, in each column **21**				
22	**Estimated tax paid and tax withheld.** For column (a) only, also enter the amount from line 22 on line 26. If line 22 is equal to or more than line 21 for all payment periods, stop here; you do not owe the penalty. Do not file Form 2210 unless you checked a box in Part 1 .... **22**				
	Complete lines 23 through 29 of one column before going to the next column.				
23	Enter amount, if any, from line 29 of previous column ... **23**				
24	Add lines 22 and 23 .... **24**				
25	Add amounts on lines 27 and 28 of the previous column **25**				
26	Subtract line 25 from line 24. If zero or less, enter -0-. For column (a) only, enter the amount from line 22 **26**				
27	If the amount on line 26 is zero, subtract line 24 from line 25. Otherwise, enter -0- **27**				
28	**Underpayment.** If line 21 is equal to or more than line 26, subtract line 26 from line 21. Then go to line 23 of next column. Otherwise, go to line 29 ▶ **28**				
29	**Overpayment.** If line 26 is more than line 21, subtract line 21 from line 26. Then go to line 23 of next column ... **29**				

Section B - Figure the Penalty   (Complete lines 30 through 35 of one column before going to the next column.)

			(a)	(b)	(c)	(d)
Rate Period 1	**April 16, 1996 - June 30, 1996**		4/15/96	6/15/96		
	30	Number of days FROM the date shown above line 30 TO the date the amount on line 28 was paid **or** 6/30/96, whichever is earlier **30**	Days:	Days:		
	31	Underpayment on line 28 $\times$ $\dfrac{\text{Number of days on line 30}}{366}$ $\times$ .08 ▶ **31**	$	$		
Rate Period 2	**July 1, 1996 - December 31, 1996**		6/30/96	6/30/96	9/15/96	
	32	Number of days FROM the date shown above line 32 TO the date the amount on line 28 was paid **or** 12/31/96, whichever is earlier **32**	Days:	Days:	Days:	
	33	Underpayment on line 28 $\times$ $\dfrac{\text{Number of days on line 32}}{366}$ $\times$ .09 ▶ **33**	$	$	$	
Rate Period 3	**January 1, 1997 - April 15, 1997**		12/31/96	12/31/96	12/31/96	1/15/97
	34	Number of days FROM the date shown above line 34 TO the date the amount on line 28 was paid **or** 4/15/97, whichever is earlier **34**	Days:	Days:	Days:	Days:
	35	Underpayment on line 28 $\times$ $\dfrac{\text{Number of days on line 34}}{365}$ $\times$ .09 ▶ **35**	$	$	$	$

36 **PENALTY.** Add the amounts on lines 31, 33, and 35 in all columns. Enter the total here and on Form 1040, line 63; Form 1040A, line 34; Form 1040NR, line 63; Form 1040NR-EZ, line 26; or Form 1041, line 26 .... ▶ **36** $

Form 2210 (1996)   Page **3**

Schedule AI - Annualized Income Installment Method (see instructions)

Estates and trusts, **do not** use the period ending dates shown to the right. Instead, use the following: 2/29/96, 4/30/96, 7/31/96, and 11/30/96.		**(a)** 1/1/96 - 3/31/96	**(b)** 1/1/96 - 5/31/96	**(c)** 1/1/96 - 8/31/96	**(d)** 1/1/96 - 12/31/96

Part I Annualized Income Installments Caution: *Complete lines 20-26 of one column* **before** *going to the next column.*

			(a)	(b)	(c)	(d)
1	Enter your adjusted gross income for each period (see instructions). (Estates and trusts, enter your taxable income without your exemption for each period.)	1				
2	Annualization amounts. (Estates and trusts, see instructions.)	2	4	2.4	1.5	1
3	Annualized income. Multiply line 1 by line 2	3				
4	Enter your itemized deductions for the period shown in each column. If you do not itemize, enter -0- and skip to line 7. (Estates and trusts, enter -0-, skip to line 9, and enter the amount from line 3 on line 9.)	4				
5	Annualization amounts	5	4	2.4	1.5	1
6	Multiply line 4 by line 5 (see instructions if line 3 is more than $58,975)	6				
7	In each column, enter the full amount of your standard deduction from Form 1040, line 34; or Form 1040A, line 19 (Form 1040NR OR 1040NR-EZ filers, enter -0-. **Exception:** Indian students and business apprentices, enter standard deduction from Form 1040NR, line 33 or Form 1040NR-EZ, line 10.)	7				
8	Enter the **larger** of line 6 or line 7	8				
9	Subtract line 8 from line 3	9				
10	In each column, multiply $2,550 by the total number of exemptions claimed (see instructions if line 3 is more than line $88,475). (Estates and trusts and Form 1040NR or 1040NR-EZ filers, enter the exemption amount shown on your tax return.)	10				
11	Subtract line 10 from line 9	11				
12	Figure your tax on the amount on line 11 (see instructions)	12				
13	Form 1040 filers only, enter your self-employment tax from line 35 below	13				
14	Enter other taxes for each payment period (see instructions)	14				
15	Total tax. Add lines 12,13, and 14	15				
16	For each period, enter the same type of credits as allowed on Form 2210, lines 2, 5, and 6 (see instructions)	16				
17	Subtract line 16 from line 15. If zero or less, enter -0-	17				
18	Applicable percentage	18	22.5%	45%	67.5%	90%
19	Multiply line 17 by line 18	19				
20	Add the amounts in all preceding columns of line 26	20				
21	Subtract line 20 from line 19. If zero or less, enter -0-	21				
22	Enter ¼ of line 13 on page 1 of Form 2210 in each column	22				
23	Enter amount from line 25 of the preceding column of this schedule	23				
24	Add lines 22 and 23 and enter the total	24				
25	Subtract line 21 from line 24. If zero or less, enter -0-	25				
26	Enter the **smaller** of line 21 or line 24 here and on Form 2210, line 21 ▶	26				

Part II Annualized Self-Employment Tax

			(a)	(b)	(c)	(d)
27a	Net earnings from self-employment for the period (see instructions)	27a				
b	Annualization amounts	27b	4	2.4	1.5	1
c	Multiply line 27a by line 27b	27c				
28	Social security tax limit	28	$62,700	$62,700	$62,700	$62,700
29	Enter actual wages subject to social security tax or the 6.2% portion of the 7.65% railroad retirement (tier 1) tax	29				
30	Annualization amounts	30	4	2.4	1.5	1
31	Multiply line 29 by line 30	31				
32	Subtract line 31 from line 28. If zero or less, enter -0-	32				
33	Multiply the smaller of line 27c or line 32 by .124	33				
34	Multiply line 27c by .029	34				
35	Add lines 33 and 34. Enter the result here and on line 13 above ... ▶	35				

612551
11-16-96

Form **2220**	**Underpayment of Estimated Tax by Corporations**	OMB No. 1545-0142
Department of the Treasury Internal Revenue Service	▶ See separate instructions. ▶ Attach to the corporation's tax return.	**1996**

Name	Employer identification number

Note: In most cases, the corporation **does not** need to file Form 2220. The IRS will figure any penalty owed and bill the corporation. File Form 2220 **only** if any of the boxes or the **Note** in Part I applies to the corporation. If the corporation does not need to file Form 2220, it may still use it to figure the penalty. Enter the amount from line 36 on the penalty line of the corporation's income tax return, but do not attach Form 2220.

Part I   **Reasons For Filing -** Check the boxes below that apply to the corporation. If any box is checked or the **Note** below applies, the corporation must file Form 2220 with the corporation's tax return, even if it does not owe the penalty. If the box on line 1 or line 2 applies, the corporation may be able to lower or eliminate the penalty. See page 2 of the instructions.

1 ☐ The corporation is using the annualized income installment method.

2 ☐ The corporation is using the adjusted seasonal installment method.

3 ☐ The corporation is a "large corporation" figuring its first required installment based on the prior year's tax.

Note: The corporation must also file Form 2220 if it is claiming a waiver of the penalty. See **Waiver of penalty** on page 3 of the instructions.

Part II   **Figuring the Underpayment**

4	Total tax	**4**	
5a	Personal holding company tax included on line 4 (Schedule PH (Form 1120), line 26) **5a**		
b	Interest due under the look-back method of section 460(b)(2) for completed long-term contracts included on line 4 .... **5b**		
c	Credit for Federal tax paid on fuels **5c**		
d	**Total.** Add lines 5a through 5c	**5d**	
6	Subtract line 5d from line 4. If the result is less than $500, **do not** complete or file this form. The corporation does not owe the penalty	**6**	
7	Enter the tax shown on the corporation's 1995 income tax return. **(CAUTION: See page 2 of the instructions before completing this line.)**	**7**	
8	Enter the **smaller** of line 6 or line 7. If the corporation must skip line 7, enter the amount from line 6 on line 8	**8**	

			(a)	(b)	(c)	(d)
9	**Installment due dates.** Enter in columns (a) through (d) the 15th day of the 4th, 6th, 9th, and 12th months of the corporation's tax year .... ▶	**9**				
10	**Required installments.** If the box on line 1 or line 2 above is checked, enter the amounts from Schedule A, line 41. If the box on line 3 (but not 1 or 2) is checked, see page 2 of the instructions for the amounts to enter. If none of these boxes is checked, enter 25% of line 8 in each column	**10**				
11	Estimated tax paid or credited for each period (see page 2 of the instructions). For column (a) only, enter the amount from line 11 on line 15	**11**				
	Complete lines 12 through 18 of one column before going to the next column.					
12	Enter amount, if any, from line 18 of the preceding column	**12**				
13	Add lines 11 and 12	**13**				
14	Add amounts on lines 16 and 17 of the preceding column	**14**				
15	Subtract line 14 from line 13. If zero or less, enter -0-	**15**				
16	If the amount on line 15 is zero, subtract line 13 from line 14. Otherwise, enter -0-	**16**				
17	**Underpayment.** If line 15 is less than or equal to line 10, subtract line 15 from line 10. Then go to line 12 of the next column. Otherwise, go to line 18 (see page 3 of the instructions)	**17**				
18	**Overpayment.** If line 10 is less than line 15, subtract line 10 from line 15. Then go to line 12 of the next column	**18**				

Complete Part III on page 2 to figure the penalty. If there are no entries on line 17, no penalty is owed.

612801
12-31-96   H761   **For Paperwork Reduction Act Notice, see page 1 of the instructions.**   Form **2220** (1996)

Form 2220 (1996)   Page **2**

Part III   Figuring the Penalty

		(a)	(b)	(c)	(d)
19	Enter the date of payment or the 15th day of the 3rd month after the close of the tax year, whichever is earlier (see page 3 of the instructions). (Form 990-PF and Form 990-T filers: Use 5th month instead of 3rd month.) **19**				
20	Number of days from due date of installment on line 9 to the date shown on line 19 .... **20**				
21	Number of days on line 20 after 4/15/96 and before 7/1/96 ...... **21**				
22	Underpayment on line 17 x $\frac{\text{Number of days on line 21}}{366}$ x 8% **22**	$	$	$	$
23	Number of days on line 20 after 6/30/96 and before 1/1/97 ...... **23**				
24	Underpayment on line 17 x $\frac{\text{Number of days on line 23}}{366}$ x 9% **24**	$	$	$	$
25	Number of days on line 20 after 12/31/96 and before 4/1/97 ...... **25**				
26	Underpayment on line 17 x $\frac{\text{Number of days on line 25}}{365}$ x 9% **26**	$	$	$	$
27	Number of days on line 20 after 3/31/97 and before 7/1/97 ...... **27**				
28	Underpayment on line 17 x $\frac{\text{Number of days on line 27}}{365}$ x *% **28**	$	$	$	$
29	Number of days on line 20 after 6/30/97 and before 10/1/97 ...... **29**				
30	Underpayment on line 17 x $\frac{\text{Number of days on line 29}}{365}$ x *% **30**	$	$	$	$
31	Number of days on line 20 after 9/30/97 and before 1/1/98 ...... **31**				
32	Underpayment on line 17 x $\frac{\text{Number of days on line 31}}{365}$ x *% **32**	$	$	$	$
33	Number of days on line 20 after 12/31/97 and before 2/16/98 ...... **33**				
34	Underpayment on line 17 x $\frac{\text{Number of days on line 33}}{365}$ x *% **34**	$	$	$	$
35	Add lines 22, 24, 26, 28, 30, 32, and 34 .... **35**	$	$	$	$

36 **PENALTY.** Add columns (a) through (d), line 35. Enter the total here and on Form 1120; line 33, Form 1120-A; line 29; or comparable line for other income tax returns .... **36** $

* If the corporation's tax year ends after December 31, 1996, see **Lines 28, 30, 32,** and **34** on page 3 of the instructions.

612802
12-31-96

Form **2441**

Department of the Treasury
Internal Revenue Service

Child and Dependent Care Expenses

▶ **Attach to Form 1040.**
▶ **See separate instructions.**

OMB No. 1545-0068

1996

Attachment
Sequence No. **21**

Name(s) shown on Form 1040

Your social security number

You need to understand the following terms to complete this form:
**Qualifying Person(s), Dependent Care Benefits, Qualified
Expenses, and Earned Income.** See **Important Terms** on page 1
of the Form 2441 instructions.

PART I **Persons or Organizations Who Provided the Care** - You **must** complete this part.

1	**(a)** Care provider's name	**(b)** Address (number, street, apt. no., city, state, and ZIP code)	**(c)** Identifying number (SSN or EIN)	**(d)** Amount paid

2 Add the amounts in column (d) of line 1 .... | **2** |

3 Enter the number of **qualifying persons** cared for in 1996 .... ▶ [ ]

| Did you receive **dependent care benefits?** | **NO** ▶ Complete Part II below. |
| | **YES** ▶ Complete Part III on page 2. |

Caution: *If the care was provided in your home, you may owe employment taxes. See the instructions for Form 1040, line 50.*

PART II **Credit for Child and Dependent Care Expenses**

4 Enter the amount of **qualified expenses** you incurred and paid in 1996. DO NOT
enter more than $2,400 for one qualifying person or $4,800 for two or more persons.
If you completed Part III, enter the amount from line 25 .... | **4** |

5 Enter YOUR **earned income** .... | **5** |

6 If married filing a joint return, enter YOUR SPOUSE'S earned income (if student or
disabled, see instructions); **all others,** enter the amount from line 5 .... | **6** |

7 Enter the **smallest** of line 4, 5, or 6 .... | **7** |

8 Enter the amount from Form 1040, line 32 .... | **8** |

9 Enter on line 9 the decimal amount shown below that applies to the amount on line 8 ....

If line 8 is-		Decimal amount is	If line 8 is-		Decimal amount is		
Over	But not over		Over	But not over			
$0-10,000		.30	$20,000-22,000		.24	**9**	**X**
10,000-12,000		.29	22,000-24,000		.23		
12,000-14,000		.28	24,000-26,000		.22		
14,000-16,000		.27	26,000-28,000		.21		
16,000-18,000		.26	28,000-No limit		.20		
18,000-20,000		.25					

10 Multiply **line 7** by the decimal amount on line 9. Enter the result. Then, see the instructions for the amount
of credit to enter on Form 1040, line 39 .... | **10** |

Form 2441 (1996)   Page **2**

Part III **Dependent Care Benefits** - Complete this part **only** if you received these benefits.

11	Enter the total amount of **dependent care benefits** you received for 1996. This amount should be shown in box 10 of your W-2 form(s). DO NOT include amounts that were reported to you as wages in box 1 of Form(s) W-2	**11**
12	Enter the amount forfeited, if any. See the instructions	**12**
13	Subtract line 12 from line 11	**13**

14	Enter the total amount of **qualified expenses** incurred in 1996 for the care of the qualifying person(s)	**14**	
15	Enter the **smaller** of line 13 or 14	**15**	
16	Enter YOUR **earned income**	**16**	
17	If married filing a joint return, enter YOUR SPOUSE'S earned income (if student or disabled, see the line 6 instructions); if married filing a separate return, see the instructions for the amount to enter; **all others,** enter the amount from line 16	**17**	
18	Enter the **smallest** of line 15, 16, or 17	**18**	

19	**Excluded benefits.** Enter here the **smaller** of the following:
	• The amount from line 18, or
	• $5,000 ($2,500 if married filing a separate return **and** you were required to enter your spouse's earned income on line 17).

19

20	**Taxable benefits.** Subtract line 19 from line 13. Also, include this amount on Form 1040, line 7. On the dotted line next to line 7, write "DCB"	**20**

To claim the child and dependent care credit, complete
lines 21-25 below, and lines 4-10 on page 1 of this form.

21	Enter the amount of qualified expenses you incurred and paid in 1996. DO NOT include on this line any excluded benefits shown on line 19	**21**

22	Enter $2,400 ($4,800 if two or more qualifying persons)	**22**	
23	Enter the amount from line 19	**23**	

24	Subtract line 23 from line 22. If zero or less, **STOP.** You cannot take the credit. **Exception.** If you paid 1995 expenses in 1996, see the line 10 instructions	**24**
25	Enter the **smaller** of line 21 or 24 here **and** on line 4 on page 1 of this form	**25**

LHA

613752
10-22-96

Form **3903**	**Moving Expenses**	OMB No. 1545-0062

Form **3903**

Department of the Treasury
Internal Revenue Service

Moving Expenses

▶ **Attach to Form 1040.**

1996

Attachment
Sequence No. **62**

Name(s) shown on Form 1040 | Your social security number

Caution: If you are a member of the armed forces, see the instructions before completing this form.

1 Enter the number of miles from your **old home** to your **new workplace** .... | **1** | | miles |

2 Enter the number of miles from your **old home** to your **old workplace** .... | **2** | | miles |

3 Subtract line 2 from line 1. Enter the result but not less than zero .... | **3** | | miles |

Is line 3 at least 50 miles?

Yes ▶ Go to line 4. Also, see **Time Test** in the instructions.

No ▶ You **cannot** deduct your moving expenses. Do not complete the rest of this form.

4 Transportation and storage of household goods and personal effects .... | **4** | |

5 Travel and lodging expenses of moving from your old home to your new home. **Do not** include meals .... | **5** | |

6 Add lines 4 and 5 .... | **6** | |

7 Enter the total amount your employer paid for your move (including the value of services furnished in kind) that is **not** included in the wages box (box 1) of your W-2 form. This amount should be identified with code **P** in box 13 of your W-2 form .... | **7** | |

Is line 6 more than line 7?

Yes ▶ Go to line 8.

No ▶ You **cannot** deduct your moving expenses. If line 6 is less than line 7, subtract line 6 from line 7 and include the result in income on Form 1040, line 7.

8 Subtract line 7 from line 6. Enter the result here and on Form 1040, line 24. This is your **moving expense deduction** .... | **8** | |

LHA   **For Paperwork Reduction Act Notice, see separate Instructions.** | Form **3903** (1996)

Form **4626**	**Alternative Minimum Tax—Corporations**	OMB No. 1545-0175
Department of the Treasury Internal Revenue Service	▶ See separate instructions. ▶ Attach to the corporation's tax return.	19**96**

Name | Employer identification number

1 Taxable income or (loss) before net operating loss deduction. . . . . | **1**

2 Adjustments and preferences:

a Depreciation of post-1986 property . . . . | **2a**

b Amortization of certified pollution control facilities . . . . | **2b**

c Amortization of mining exploration and development costs . . . . | **2c**

d Amortization of circulation expenditures (personal holding companies only) . . | **2d**

e Adjusted gain or loss . . . . | **2e**

f Long-term contracts . . . . | **2f**

g Installment sales . . . . | **2g**

h Merchant marine capital construction funds . . . . | **2h**

i Section 833(b) deduction (Blue Cross, Blue Shield, and similar type organizations only) . . . . | **2i**

j Tax shelter farm activities (personal service corporations only) . . . . . . | **2j**

k Passive activities (closely held corporations and personal service corporations only) | **2k**

l Loss limitations . . . . | **2l**

m Depletion . . . . | **2m**

n Tax-exempt interest from specified private activity bonds . . . . | **2n**

o Charitable contributions . . . . | **2o**

p Intangible drilling costs . . . . | **2p**

q Accelerated depreciation of real property (pre-1987) . . . . | **2q**

r Accelerated depreciation of leased personal property (pre-1987) (personal holding companies only) . . . . | **2r**

s Other adjustments . . . . | **2s**

t Combine lines 2a through 2s . . . . | **2t**

3 Preadjustment alternative minimum taxable income (AMTI). Combine lines 1 and 2t . . . . . . | **3**

4 Adjusted current earnings (ACE) adjustment:

a Enter the corporation's ACE from line 10 of the worksheet on page 8 of the instructions | **4a**

b Subtract line 3 from line 4a. If line 3 exceeds line 4a, enter the difference as a negative amount (see examples beginning on page 4 of the instructions) . . | **4b**

c Multiply line 4b by 75% (.75). Enter the result as a positive amount . . . . | **4c**

d Enter the excess, if any, of the corporation's total increases in AMTI from prior year ACE adjustments over its total reductions in AMTI from prior year ACE adjustments (see page 5 of the instructions). **Note:** You **must** enter an amount on line 4d (even if line 4b is positive). . . . . | **4d**

e ACE adjustment:

● If you entered a positive number or zero on line 4b, enter the amount from line 4c here as a positive amount.

● If you entered a negative number on line 4b, enter the smaller of line 4c or line 4d here as a negative amount. | **4e**

5 Combine lines 3 and 4e. If zero or less, stop here; the corporation does not owe alternative minimum tax . . . . | **5**

6 Alternative tax net operating loss deduction (see page 5 of the instructions) . . . . | **6**

7 **Alternative minimum taxable income.** Subtract line 6 from line 5. . . . . | **7**

For Paperwork Reduction Act Notice, see separate instructions.   Cat. No. 12955I   Form **4626** (1996)

8   Enter the amount from line 7 (alternative minimum taxable income) . . . . | **8** |

9   **Exemption phase-out computation** (if line 8 is $310,000 or more, skip lines 9a and 9b and enter -0- on line 9c):

a   Subtract $150,000 from line 8 (if you are completing this line for a member of a controlled group, see page 5 of the instructions). If zero or less, enter -0- . . | **9a** |

b   Multiply line 9a by 25% (.25). . . . . | **9b** |

c   Exemption. Subtract line 9b from $40,000 (if you are completing this line for a member of a controlled group, see page 5 of the instructions). If zero or less, enter -0- . . . . | **9c** |

10 Subtract line 9c from line 8. If zero or less, enter -0- . . . . | **10** |

11 Multiply line 10 by 20% (.20). | **11** |

12 Alternative minimum tax foreign tax credit. See page 5 of the instructions for limitations. . . . . | **12** |

13 Tentative minimum tax. Subtract line 12 from line 11. . . . . | **13** |

14 Regular tax liability before all credits except the foreign tax credit and possessions tax credit . . . | **14** |

15 **Alternative minimum tax.** Subtract line 14 from line 13. Enter the result on the appropriate line of the corporation's income tax return (e.g., Form 1120, Schedule J, line 9). If zero or less, enter -0- . | **15** |

-- ▼ CUT HERE ▼ --

| Form **4868**
Department of the Treasury
Internal Revenue Service | **Application for Automatic Extension of Time
To File U.S. Individual Income Tax Return** | OMB No. 1545-0188
1996 |

1 Your name(s)		**2a Amount due-** Add lines 6c, d, and e ▶ $ _____
Address	**3** Your social security number	
City, town or post office, state, and ZIP code	**4** Spouse's social security no.	**b Amount you are paying** ▶ $

5 I request an automatic 4-month extension of time to August 15, 1997, to file my individual tax return for the calendar year
1996 or to _____ , 19 ____ , for the fiscal tax year ending _____ , 19 ____ .

6 Individual Income Tax Return

Gift or GST Tax Return(s)
Check here **ONLY** if filing a gift or GST tax return ... } Yourself ▶ ☐   Spouse ▶ ☐

   a Total income tax liability for 1996 ...... $ _____

   b Total payments for 1996 .... $ _____

   d Your gift/GST tax payment .... $ _____

   c Balance. Subtract 6b from 6a .... $ _____

   e Your spouse's gift/GST tax payment .... $ _____

LHA **For Paperwork Reduction Act Notice, see instructions.**

Form **4868** (1996)

Form **4952**	**Investment Interest Expense Deduction**	OMB No. 1545-0191
Department of the Treasury Internal Revenue Service	▶ **Attach to your tax return.**	**1996** Attachment Sequence No. **12A**

Name(s) shown on return	Identifying number

Part I — Total Investment Interest Expense

1	Investment interest expense paid or accrued in 1996.	**1**	
2	Disallowed investment interest expense from 1995 Form 4952, line 7	**2**	
3	**Total investment interest expense.** Add lines 1 and 2	**3**	

Part II — Net Investment Income

4a	Gross income from property held for investment (excluding any net gain from the disposition of property held for investment)		**4a**	
b	Net gain from the disposition of property held for investment	**4b**		
c	Net capital gain from the disposition of property held for investment	**4c**		
d	Subtract line 4c from line 4b. If zero or less, enter -0-		**4d**	
e	Enter all or part of the amount on line 4c that you elect to include in investment income. Do not enter more than the amount on line 4b ▶		**4e**	
f	Investment income. Add lines 4a, 4d, and 4e		**4f**	
5	Investment expenses		**5**	
6	**Net investment income.** Subtract line 5 from line 4f. If zero or less, enter -0-		**6**	

Part III — Investment Interest Expense Deduction

7	Disallowed investment interest expense to be carried forward to 1997. Subtract line 6 from line 3. If zero or less, enter -0-	**7**	
8	**Investment interest expense deduction.** Enter the smaller of line 3 or 6	**8**	

LHA **For Paperwork Reduction Act Notice, see separate instructions.**

Form **4952** (1996)

618901
10-07-96

Form **4972**

Department of the Treasury
Internal Revenue Service

Tax on Lump-Sum Distributions
From Qualified Retirement Plans

▶ Attach to Form 1040 or Form 1041.   ▶ See separate instructions.

OMB No. 1545-0193

1996

Attachment
Sequence No. **28**

Name of recipient of distribution

Identifying number

Part I Complete this part to see if you qualify to use Form 4972

		Yes	No
1	Was this a distribution of a plan participant's entire balance from all of an emplyer's qualified plans of one kind (pension, profit-sharing, or stock bonus)? If "No," do not use this form **1**		
2	Did you roll over any part of the distribution? If "Yes," do not use this form **2**		
3	Was this distribution paid to you as a beneficiary of a plan participant who died after reaching age 59 1/2 (or who had been born before 1936)? **3**		
4	Were you a plan partcipant who received this distribution after reaching age 59 1/2 **and** having been in the plan for at least 5 years before the year of the distribution? **4**		
	If you answered "No" to both questions 3 **and** 4, do not use this form.		
5a	Did you use Form 4972 after 1986 for a previous distribution from your own plan? If "Yes," do not use this form for a 1996 distribution from your own plan **5a**		
b	If you are receiving this distribution as a beneficiary of a plan participant who died, did you use Form 4972 for a previous distribution received for that plan participant after 1986? If "Yes," you may not use the form for this distribution **5b**		

Part II Complete this part to choose the 20% capital gain election. Do not complete this part unless the participant was born **before** 1936.

6	Capital gain part from box 3 of Form 1099-R	**6**	
7	Multiply line 6 by 20% (.20)	**7**	
	If you also choose to use Part III, go to line 8. Otherwise, include the amount from line 7 in the total on Form 1040, line 38, or Form 1041, Schedule G, line 1b, whichever applies.		

Part III Complete this part to choose the 5- or 10-year tax option

8	Ordinary income from Form 1099-R, box 2a minus box 3. If you did not complete Part II, enter the taxable amount from box 2a of Form 1099-R		**8**	
9	Death benefit exclusion for a beneficiary of a plan participant who died before August 21, 1996		**9**	
10	Total taxable amount. Subtract line 9 from line 8		**10**	
11	Current actuarial value of annuity (from Form 1099-R, box 8)		**11**	
12	Adjusted total taxable amount. Add lines 10 and 11. If this amount is $70,000 or more, **skip** lines 13 through 16, and enter this amount on line 17		**12**	
13	Multiply line 12 by 50% (.50), but **do not** enter more than $10,000	**13**		
14	Subtract $20,000 from line 12. If the result is less than zero, enter -0- **14**			
15	Multiply line 14 by 20% (.20)	**15**		
16	Minimum distribution allowance. Subtract line 15 from line 13		**16**	
17	Subtract line 16 from line 12		**17**	
18	Federal estate tax attributable to lump-sum distribution		**18**	
19	Subtract line 18 from line 17		**19**	
	If line 11 is blank, skip lines 20 through 22 and go to line 23.			
20	Divide line 11 by line 12 and enter the result as a decimal		**20**	
21	Multiply line 16 by the decimal on line 20		**21**	
22	Subtract line 21 from line 11		**22**	

LHA   **For Paperwork Reduction Act Notice, see separate instructions.**

Form **4972** (1996)

Part III 5- or 10-year tax option - CONTINUED

5-year tax option	23	Multiply line 19 by 20% (.20)	23
	24	Tax on amount on line 23. Use the Tax Rate Schedule for the 5-Year Tax Option in the instructions	24
	25	Multiply line 24 by five (5). If line 11 is blank, skip lines 26 through 28, and enter this amount on line 29	25
	26	Multiply line 22 by 20% (.20) 26	
	27	Tax on amount on line 26. Use the Tax Rate Schedule for the 5-Year Tax Option in the instructions 27	
	28	Multiply line 27 by five (5)	28
	29	Subtract line 28 from line 25. (Multiple recipients, see instructions.)	29
		Note: Complete lines 30 through 36 ONLY if the participant was born before 1936. Otherwise, enter the amount from line 29 on line 37.	
10-year tax option	30	Multiply line 19 by 10% (.10)	30
	31	Tax on amount on line 30. Use the Tax Rate Schedule for the 10-Year Tax Option in the instructions	31
	32	Multiply line 31 by ten (10). If line 11 is blank, skip lines 33 through 35, and enter this amount on line 36	32
	33	Multiply line 22 by 10% (.10) 33	
	34	Tax on amount on line 33. Use the Tax Rate Schedule for the 10-Year Tax Option in the instructions 34	
	35	Multiply line 34 by ten (10)	35
	36	Subtract line 35 from line 32. (Multiple recipients, see instructions.)	36
	37	Compare lines 29 and 36. Generally, you should enter the **smaller** amount here. .... ▶	37
	38	Tax on lump-sum distribution. Add lines 7 and 37. Also, include in the total on Form 1040, line 38, or Form 1041, Schedule G, line 1b, whichever applies .... ▶	38

Form **6251**

Department of the Treasury
Internal Revenue Service

Alternative Minimum Tax - Individuals

▶ Attach to Form 1040 or Form 1040NR.

OMB No. 1545-0227

1996

Attachment Sequence No. **32**

Name(s) shown on Form 1040

Your social security number

Part I Adjustments and Preferences

1	If you itemized deductions on Schedule A (Form 1040), go to line 2. Otherwise, enter your standard deduction from Form 1040, line 34, here and go to line 6	1
2	Medical and dental. Enter the smaller of Schedule A (Form 1040), line 4, **or** 2 1/2% of Form 1040, line 32	2
3	Taxes. Enter the amount from Schedule A (Form 1040), line 9	3
4	Certain interest on a home mortgage not used to buy, build, or improve your home	4
5	Miscellaneous itemized deductions. Enter the amount from Schedule A (Form 1040), line 26	5
6	Refund of taxes. Enter any tax refund from Form 1040, line 10 or 21	6
7	Investment interest. Enter difference between regular tax and AMT deduction	7
8	Post-1986 depreciation. Enter difference between regular tax and AMT depreciation	8
9	Adjusted gain or loss. Enter difference between AMT and regular tax gain or loss	9
10	Incentive stock options. Enter excess of AMT income over regular tax income	10
11	Passive activities. Enter difference between AMT and regular tax income or loss	11
12	Beneficiaries of estates and trusts. Enter the amount from Schedule K-1 (Form 1041), line 8	12
13	Tax-exempt interest from private activity bonds issued after 8/7/86	13

14 Other. Enter the amount, if any, for each item below and enter the total on line 14.

a Charitable contributions		**h** Loss limitations	
b Circulation expenditures		**i** Mining costs	
c Depletion		**j** Patron's adjustment	
d Depreciation (pre-1987)		**k** Pollution control facilities	
e Installment sales		**l** Research and experimental	
f Intangible drilling costs		**m** Tax shelter farm activities	
g Long-term contracts		**n** Related adjustments	14

15 **Total Adjustments and Preferences.** Combine lines 1 through 14 ▶ | 15 |

Part II Alternative Minimum Taxable Income

16	Enter the amount from **Form 1040, line 35.** If less than zero, enter as a (loss) ▶	16
17	Net operating loss deduction, if any, from Form 1040, line 21. Enter as a positive amount	17
18	If Form 1040, line 32, is over $117,950 (over $58,975 if married filing separately), and you itemized deductions, enter the amount, if any, from line 9 of the worksheet for Schedule A (Form 1040), line 28	18
19	Combine lines 15 through 18 ▶	19
20	Alternative tax net operating loss deduction.	20
21	**Alternative Minimum Taxable Income.** Subtract line 20 from line 19. (If married filing separately and line 21 is more than $165,000, see instructions.) ▶	21

Part III Exemption Amount and Alternative Minimum Tax

22 **Exemption Amount.** (If this form is for a child under age 14, see instructions.)

If your filing status is:	And line 21 is not over:	Enter on line 22:	
Single or head of household	$112,500	$33,750	
Married filing jointly or qualifying widow(er)	150,000	45,000	22
Married filing separately	75,000	22,500	

If line 21 is **over** the amount shown above for your filing status, see instructions.

23	Subtract line 22 from line 21. If zero or less, enter -0- here and on lines 26 and 28 ▶	23
24	If line 23 is $175,000 or less ($87,500 or less if married filing separately), multiply line 23 by 26% (.26). Otherwise, multiply line 23 by 28% (.28) and subtract $3,500 ($1,750 if married filing separately) from the result	24
25	Alternative minimum tax foreign tax credit.	25
26	Tentative minimum tax. Subtract line 25 from line 24 ▶	26
27	Enter your tax from Form 1040, line 38 (excluding any amount from Form 4972), minus any foreign tax credit from Form 1040, line 41	27
28	**Alternative Minimum Tax.** (If this form is for a child under age 14, see instructions.) Subtract line 27 from line 26. If zero or less, enter -0-. Enter here and on Form 1040, line 46 ▶	28

LHA **For Paperwork Reduction Act Notice, see separate instructions.**

Form **6251**(1996)

619481
11-08-96

Form **7004**

(Rev. June 1995)

Department of the Treasury
Internal Revenue Service

Application for Automatic Extension of Time
To File Corporation Income Tax Return

OMB No. 1545-0233

Name of corporation	Employer identification number

Number, street, and room or suite no. (if a P.O. box or outside the United States, see instructions)

City or town, state, and ZIP code

Check type of return to be filed:

☐ Form 1120	☐ Form 1120-FSC	☐ Form 1120-ND	☐ Form 1120-REIT	☐ Form 1120-SF
☐ Form 1120-A	☐ Form 1120-H	☐ Form 1120-PC	☐ Form 1120-RIC	☐ Form 990-C
☐ Form 1120-F	☐ Form 1120-L	☐ Form 1120-POL	☐ Form 1120S	☐ Form 990-T

Form 1120-F filers: Check here if you do not have an office or place of business in the United States .... ▶ ☐

1a   I request an automatic 6-month (or, for certain foreign corporations, 3-month) extension of time

until _____ , _____ , to file the income tax return of the corporation named above for   ▶ ☐ calendar

year 19 ____ or ▶ ☐ tax year beginning _____ , 19 ____ , and ending _____ , 19 ____ .

b   If this tax year is for less than 12 months, check reason:

☐ Initial return   ☐ Final return   ☐ Change in accounting period   ☐ Consolidated return to be filed

2   If this application also covers subsidiaries to be included in a consolidated return, complete the following:

Name and address of each member of the affiliated group	Employer identification number	Tax period

3	Tentative tax	**3**	
4	**Credits:**		
a	Overpayment credited from prior year **4a**		
b	Estimated tax payments for the tax year **4b**		
c	Less refund for the tax year applied for on Form 4466 .... **4c** ( ) Bal ▶ **4d**		
e	Credit from regulated investment companies **4e**		
f	Credit for Federal tax on fuels **4f**		
5	Total. Add lines 4d through 4f	**5**	
6	**Balance due.** Subtract line 5 from line 3. **Deposit this amount electronically or with a Federal Tax Deposit (FTD) Coupon**	**6**	

Signature. - Under penalties of perjury, I declare that I have been authorized by the above-named corporation to make this application, and to the best of my knowledge and belief, the statements made are true, correct, and complete.

_____   _____   _____
(Signature of officer or agent)   (Title)   (Date)

H761   **For Paperwork Reduction Act Notice, see instructions.**   Form **7004** (Rev. 6-95)

619741
11-20-96

Form 8283
(Rev. October 1995)
Department of the Treasury
Internal Revenue Service

Noncash Charitable Contributions

▶ **Attach to your tax return if you claimed a total deduction
of over $500 for all contributed property.**

OMB. No. 1545-0908

Attachment
Sequence No. **55**

Name(s) shown on your income tax return | Identifying number

NOTE: Figure the amount of your contribution deduction before completing this form. See your tax return instructions.

Section A - List in this section **only** items (or groups of similar items) for which you claimed a deduction of $5,000 or less. Also, list certain publicly traded securities even if the deduction is over $5,000.

Part I Information on Donated Property - If you need more space, attach a statement.

1	**(a)** Name and address of the donee organization	**(b)** Description of donated property
A		
B		
C		
D		
E		

Note: If the amount you claimed as a deduction for an item is $500 or less, you do not have to complete columns (d), (e), and (f).

	(c) Date of the contribution	**(d)** Date acquired by donor (mo., yr.)	**(e)** How acquired by donor	**(f)** Donor's cost or adjusted basis	**(g)** Fair market value	**(h)** Method used to determine the fair market value
A						
B						
C						
D						
E						

Part II Other Information - Complete line 2 if you gave less than an entire interest in property listed in Part I.
Complete line 3 if restrictions were attached to a contribution listed in Part I.

2 If, during the year, you contributed less than the entire interest in the property, complete lines a - e.

a   Enter the letter from Part I that identifies the property ▶ _____ . If Part II applies to more than one property, attach a separate statement.

b   Total amount claimed as a deduction for the property listed in Part I: **(1)** For this tax year ▶ _____
   (2) For any prior tax years ▶ _____ .

c   Name and address of each organization to which any such contribution was made in a prior year (complete only if different than the
   donee organization above): _____

   Name of charitable organization (donee)

   _____
   Address (number, street, and room or suite no.)

   _____
   City or town, state, and ZIP code

d   For tangible property, enter the place where the property is located or kept ▶ _____

e   Name of any person, other than the donee organization, having actual possession of the property ▶ _____

3 If conditions were attached to any contribution listed in Part I, answer questions a - c and attach the required statement.

		Yes	No
a	Is there a restriction, either temporary or permanent, on the donee's right to use or dispose of the donated property?		
b	Did you give to anyone (other than the donee organization or another organization participating with the donee organization in cooperative fundraising) the right to the income from the donated property or to the possession of the property, including the right to vote donated securities, to acquire the property by purchase or otherwise, or to designate the person having such income, possession, or right to acquire?		
c	Is there a restriction limiting the donated property for a particular use?		

LHA   For Paperwork Reduction Act Notice, see separate instructions.

Form **8283** (Rev. 10-95)

619931
09-10-96

Form 8283 (Rev. 10-95)   Page 2

Name(s) shown on your income tax return	Identifying number

Section B - **Appraisal Summary -** List in this section only items (or groups of similar items) for which you claimed a deduction of more than $5,000 per item or group. **Exception.** Report contributions of certain publicly traded securities only in Section A.

If you donated art, you may have to attach the complete appraisal. See the **Note** in Part I below.

Part I	Information on Donated Property - To be completed by the taxpayer and/or appraiser.

4   Check type of property:

☐ Art* (contribution of $20,000 or more)   ☐ Real Estate   ☐ Gems/Jewelry   ☐ Stamp Collections

☐ Art* (contribution of less than $20,000)   ☐ Coin Collections   ☐ Books   ☐ Other

*Art includes paintings, sculptures, watercolors, prints, drawings, ceramics, antique furniture, decorative arts, textiles, carpets, silver, rare manuscripts, historical memorabilia, and other similar objects.

Note: If your total art contribution deduction was $20,000 or more, you must attach a complete copy of the signed appraisal.

5	(a) Description of donated property (if you need more space, attach a separate statement)	(b) If tangible property was donated, give a brief summary of the overall physical condition at the time of the gift	(c) Appraised fair market value
A			
B			
C			
D			

(d) Date acquired by donor (mo., yr.)	(e) How acquired by donor	(f) Donor's cost or adjusted basis	(g) For bargain sales, enter amount received	See instructions	
				(h) Amount claimed as a deduction	(i) Average trading price of securities
A					
B					
C					
D					

Part II	Taxpayer (Donor) Statement - List each item included in Part I above that is separately identified in the appraisal as having a value of $500 or less.

I declare that the following item(s) included in Part I above has to the best of my knowledge and belief an appraised value of not more than $500 (per item). Enter identifying letter from Part I and describe the specific item. ▶ _____

Signature of taxpayer (donor) ▶ _____   Date ▶ _____

Part III	Declaration of Appraiser

I declare that I am not the donor, the donee, a party to the transaction in which the donor acquired the property, employed by, or related to any of the foregoing persons, or married to any person who is related to any of the foregoing persons. And, if regularly used by the donor, donee, or party to the transaction, I performed the majority of my appraisals during my tax year for other persons.

Also, I declare that I hold myself out to the public as an appraiser or perform appraisals on a regular basis; and that because of my qualifications as described in the appraisal, I am qualified to make appraisals of the type of property being valued. I certify that the appraisal fees were not based on a percentage of the appraised property value. Furthermore, I understand that a false or fraudulent overstatement of the property value as described in the qualified appraisal or this appraisal summary may subject me to the penalty under section 6701(a) (aiding and abetting the understatement of tax liability). I affirm that I have not been barred from presenting evidence or testimony by the Director of Practice.

Sign Here   Signature ▶ _____   Title ▶ _____   Date of appraisal ▶ _____

Business address (including room or suite no.)	Identifying number
City or town, state, and ZIP code	

Part IV	Donee Acknowledgment - To be completed by the charitable organization.

This charitable organization acknowledges that it is a qualified organization under section 170(c) and that it received the donated property as described in Section B, Part I, above on ▶ _____ .
                                                        (Date)

Furthermore, this organization affirms that in the event it sells, exchanges, or otherwise disposes of the property described in Section B, Part I (or any portion thereof) within 2 years after the date of receipt, it will file **Form 8282,** Donee Information Return, with the IRS and give the donor a copy of that form. This acknowledgment does not represent agreement with the claimed fair market value.

Name of charitable organization (donee)	Employer identification number
Address (number, street, and room or suite no.)	City or town, state, and ZIP code

Authorized signature	Title	Date

619932
09-10-96

Form **8332**

(Rev. June 1996)

Department of the Treasury
Internal Revenue Service

Release of Claim to Exemption
for Child of Divorced or Separated Parents

▶ **ATTACH** to noncustodial parent's return **EACH YEAR** exemption claimed.

OMB No. 1545-0915

Attachment
Sequence No. **51**

Name(s) of parent claiming exemption

Social security number

| **Part I** | Release of Claim to Exemption for Current Year |

I agree not to claim an exemption for _____

Name(s) of child (or children)

for the tax year 19 _____ .

Signature of parent releasing claim to exemption   Social security number   Date

If you choose not to claim an exemption for this child (or children) for future tax years, complete Part II.

| **Part II** | Release of Claim to Exemption for Future Years |

I agree not to claim an exemption for _____

Name(s) of child (or children)

for the tax year(s) _____

(Specify)

Signature of parent releasing claim to exemption   Social security number   Date

Paperwork Reduction Act Notice.-
We ask for the information on this form
to carry out the Internal Revenue laws
of the United States. You are required
to give us the information. We need it
to ensure that you are complying with
these laws and to allow us to figure and
collect the right amount of tax.

Form **8332** (Rev. 6-96)

Form **8582**

Department of the Treasury
Internal Revenue Service

Passive Activity Loss Limitations

▶ See separate Instructions.
▶ Attach to Form 1040 or Form 1041.

OMB No. 1545-1008

1996

Attachment
Sequence No. **88**

Name(s) shown on return

Identifying number

Part I   1996 Passive Activity Loss

Caution: See the instructions for Worksheets 1 and 2 on page 8 before completing Part I.

Rental Real Estate Activities With Active Participation (For the definition of active participation see **Active Participation in a Rental Real Estate Activity** in the instructions.)

1a Activities with net income (from Worksheet 1, column (a))	1a	
b Activities with net loss (from Worksheet 1, column (b))	1b	
c Prior year unallowed losses (from Worksheet 1, column (c))	1c	
d Combine lines 1a, 1b, and 1c	1d	

All Other Passive Activities

2a Activities with net income (from Worksheet 2, column (a))	2a	
b Activities with net loss (from Worksheet 2, column (b))	2b	
c Prior year unallowed losses (from Worksheet 2, column (c))	2c	
d Combine lines 2a, 2b, and 2c	2d	

3 Combine lines 1d and 2d. If the result is net income or zero, see the instructions for line 3. If this line and line 1d are losses, go to line 4. Otherwise, enter -0- on line 9 and go to line 10 .... **3**

Part II   Special Allowance for Rental Real Estate With Active Participation

Note: Enter all numbers in Part II as positive amounts. See page 9 of the instructions for examples.

4 Enter the **smaller** of the loss on line 1d or the loss on line 3	**4**	
5 Enter $150,000. If married filing separately, see the instructions	5	
6 Enter modified adjusted gross income, but not less than zero	6	

Note: If line 6 is equal to or greater than line 5, skip lines 7 and 8, enter -0-
on line 9, and then go to line 10. Otherwise, go to line 7.

7 Subtract line 6 from line 5	7	
8 Multiply line 7 by 50% (.5). **Do not** enter more than $25,000. If married filing separately, see instructions	**8**	
9 Enter the **smaller** of line 4 or line 8	**9**	

Part III   Total Losses Allowed

10 Add the income, if any, on lines 1a, and 2a and enter the total	**10**	
11 **Total losses allowed from all passive activities for 1996.** Add lines 9 and 10. See the instructions to find out how to report the losses on your tax return	**11**	

LHA   **For Paperwork Reduction Act Notice, see separate instructions.**

Form **8582** (1996)

619761
12-09-96

Form 8582-CR

Department of the Treasury
Internal Revenue Service

Passive Activity Credit Limitations

▶ See separate instructions.

▶ Attach to Form 1040 or 1041.

OMB No. 1545-1034

1996

Attachment
Sequence No. 88a

Name(s) shown on return | Identifying number

Part I — 1996 Passive Activity Credits

Caution: If you have credits from a publicly traded partnership, see **Publicly Traded Partnerships (PTPs)** on page 13 of the instructions.

Credits From Rental Real Estate Activities With Active Participation (Other Than Rehabilitation Credits and Low-Income Housing Credits) (See **Lines 1a through 1c** on page 8 of the instructions.)

1a	Credits from Worksheet 1, column (a)	1a	
b	Prior year unallowed credits from Worksheet 1, column (b)	1b	
c	Add lines 1a and 1b		1c

Rehabilitation Credits from Rental Real Estate Activities and Low-Income Housing Credits for Property Placed in Service Before 1990 (or From Pass-Through Interests Acquired Before 1990) (See **Lines 2a through 2c** on page 8 of the instructions.)

2a	Credits from Worksheet 2, column (a)	2a	
b	Prior year unallowed credits from Worksheet 2, column (b)	2b	
c	Add lines 2a and 2b		2c

Low-Income Housing Credits for Property Placed in Service After 1989 (See **Lines 3a through 3c** on page 8 of the instructions.)

3a	Credits from Worksheet 3, column (a)	3a	
b	Prior year unallowed credits from Worksheet 3, column (b)	3b	
c	Add lines 3a and 3b		3c

All Other Passive Activity Credits (See **Lines 4a through 4c** on page 8 of the instructions.)

4a	Credits from Worksheet 4, column (a)	4a	
b	Prior year unallowed credits from Worksheet 4, column (b)	4b	
c	Add lines 4a and 4b		4c
5	Add lines 1c, 2c, 3c, and 4c		5
6	Enter the tax attributable to net passive income (see instructions)		6
7	Subtract line 6 from line 5. If line 6 is more than or equal to line 5, enter -0- and see the instructions		7

Part II — Special Allowance for Rental Real Estate Activities With Active Participation

Note: Complete Part II if you have an amount on line 1c. Otherwise, go to Part III.

8	Enter the smaller of line 1c or line 7		8
9	Enter $150,000. If married filing separately, see instructions	9	
10	Enter modified adjusted gross income, but not less than zero (see instructions). If line 10 is equal to or greater than line 9, skip lines 11 through 15 and enter -0- on line 16	10	
11	Subtract line 10 from line 9	11	
12	Multiply line 11 by 50% (.50). Do not enter more than $25,000. If married filing separately, see instructions	12	
13	Enter the amount, if any, from line 9 of Form 8582	13	
14	Subtract line 13 from line 12	14	
15	Enter the tax attributable to the amount on line 14 (see page 9 of the instructions)		15
16	Enter the smaller of line 8 or line 15		16

LHA For Paperwork Reduction Act Notice, see separate instructions.

Cat. No. 64641R

Form **8582-CR** (1996)

619771
12-16-96

Form 8582-CR (1996)   Page **2**

Part III Special Allowance for Rehabilitation Credits From Rental Real Estate Activities and Low-Income Housing Credits for Property Placed in Service Before 1990 (or From Pass-Through Interests Acquired Before 1990)

Note: Complete Part III if you have an amount on line 2c. Otherwise, go to Part IV.

17	Enter the amount from line 7	**17**	
18	Enter the amount from line 16	**18**	
19	Subtract line 18 from line 17. If zero, enter -0- here and on lines 30 and 36, and then go to Part V	**19**	
20	Enter the smaller of line 2c or line 19	**20**	
21	Enter $250,000. If married filing separately, see instructions. (See instructions to see if you can skip lines 21 through 26.)	**21**	
22	Enter modified adjusted gross income, but not less than zero. (See instructions for Part II, line 10.) If line 22 is equal to or greater than line 21, skip lines 23 through 29, and enter -0- on line 30	**22**	
23	Subtract line 22 from line 21	**23**	
24	Multiply line 23 by 50% (.50). Do not enter more than $25,000. If married filing separately, see instructions	**24**	
25	Enter the amount, if any, from line 9 of Form 8582	**25**	
26	Subtract line 25 from line 24	**26**	
27	Enter the tax attributable to the amount on line 26 (see instructions)	**27**	
28	Enter the amount, if any, from line 18	**28**	
29	Subtract line 28 from line 27	**29**	
30	Enter the smaller of line 20 or line 29	**30**	

Part IV Special Allowance for Low-Income Housing Credits for Property Placed in Service After 1989

Note: Complete Part IV if you have an amount on line 3c. Otherwise, go to Part V.

31	If you completed Part III, enter the amount from line 19. Otherwise, subtract line 16 from line 7	**31**	
32	Enter the amount from line 30	**32**	
33	Subtract line 32 from line 31. If zero, enter -0- here and on line 36	**33**	
34	Enter the smaller of line 3c or line 33	**34**	
35	Tax attributable to the remaining special allowance (see instructions)	**35**	
36	Enter the smaller of line 34 or line 35	**36**	

Part V Passive Activity Credit Allowed

37	**Passive Activity Credit Allowed.** Add lines 6, 16, 30, and 36. See page 10 of the intrusctions to find out how to report the allowed credit on your tax return and how to allocate allowed and unallowed credits if you have more than one credit or credits from more than one activity. If have any credits from a publicly traded partnership, see **Publicly Traded Partnerships (PTPs)** on page 13 of the intructions	**37**	

Part VI Election to Increase Basis of Credit Property

38 If you disposed of your entire interest in a passive activity or former passive activity in a fully taxable transaction, and you elect to increase the basis of the credit property used in that activity by the unallowed credit that reduced the property's basis, check this box. See instructions .... ▶ ☐

39 Name of passive activity disposed of ▶ _____

40 Description of the credit property for which the election is being made ▶ _____

41 Amount of unallowed credit that reduced the property's basis .... ▶ $ _____

Form **8615**

Department of the Treasury
Internal Revenue Service

Tax for Children Under Age 14
Who Have Investment Income of More Than $1,300

▶ **Attach ONLY to the child's Form 1040, Form 1040A, Form 1040NR.**

OMB No. 1545-0998

1996

Attachment
Sequence No. **33**

Child's name shown on return | Child's social security number

A Parent's name (first, initial, and last). **Caution:** See instructions before completing. | **B** Parent's social security number

C Parent's filing status (check one):

☐ Single ☐ Married filing jointly ☐ Married filing separately ☐ Head of household ☐ Qualifying widow(er)

Step 1	Figure child's net investment income

1	Enter child's investment income, such as taxable interest and dividend income. If this amount is $1,300 or less, **stop;** do not file this form	1	
2	If the child DID NOT itemize deductions on Schedule A (Form 1040 or Form 1040NR), enter $1,300. If the child ITEMIZED deductions, see instructions	2	
3	Subtract line 2 from line 1. If the result is zero or less, **stop;** do not complete the rest of this form but ATTACH it to the child's return	3	
4	Enter the child's **taxable** income from Form 1040, line 37; Form 1040A, line 22; or Form 1040NR, line 36	4	
5	Enter the **smaller** of line 3 or line 4 ▶	5	

Step 2	Figure tentative tax based on the tax rate of the parent listed on line A

6	Enter parent's **taxable** income from Form 1040, line 37; Form 1040A, line 22; Form 1040EZ, line 6; TeleFile Tax Record, line J; Form 1040NR, line 36; or Form 1040NR-EZ, line 13. If the parent transferred property to a trust, see instructions	6	
7	Enter the total net investment income, if any, from Forms 8615, line 5, of ALL OTHER children of the parent identified above. **Do not** include the amount from line 5 above	7	
8	Add lines 5, 6, and 7	8	
9	Tax on line 8 based on the **parent's** filing status. If from Capital Gain Tax Worksheet, enter amount from line 4 of that worksheet here ▶	9	
10	Enter parent's tax from Form 1040, line 38; Form 1040A, line 23; Form 1040EZ, line 10; TeleFile Tax Record, line J; Form 1040NR, line 37; or Form 1040NR-EZ, line 14. If from **Capital Gain Tax Worksheet,** enter amount from line 4 of that worksheet here ▶	10	
11	Subtract line 10 from line 9. If line 7 is blank, enter on line 13 the amount from line 11; skip lines 12a and 12b	11	
12 a	Add lines 5 and 7	12a	
b	Divide line 5 by line 12a. Enter the result as a decimal (rounded to two places)	12b	X
13	Multiply line 11 by line 12b ▶	13	

Step 3	Figure child's tax - If lines 4 and 5 above are the same, enter -0- on line 15 and go to line 16.

14	Subtract line 5 from line 4	14	
15	Tax on line 14 based on the **child's** filing status. If from Capital Gain Tax Worksheet, enter amount from line 4 of that worksheet here ▶	15	
16	Add lines 13 and 15	16	
17	Tax on line 4 based on the **child's** filing status. If from Capital Gain Tax Worksheet, check here ▶ ☐	17	
18	Enter the **larger** of line 16 or 17 here and on Form 1040, line 38; Form 1040A, line 23; or Form 1040NR, line 37 ▶	18	

LHA For Paperwork Reduction Act Notice, see instructions.

Form **8615** (1996)

619821
01-12-97

Form **8829**

Department of the Treasury
Internal Revenue Service

Expenses for Business Use of Your Home

▶ File only with Schedule C (Form 1040). Use a separate Form 8829 for each
home you used for business during the year.

OMB No. 1545-1266

1996

Attachment
Sequence No. **66**

Name(s) of proprietor(s)

Your social security number

Part I — Part of Your Home Used for Business

1	Area used regularly and exclusively for business, regularly for day care, or for storage of inventory or product samples	1	
2	Total area of home	2	
3	Divide line 1 by line 2. Enter the result as a percentage	3	%

- **For day-care facilities not used exclusively for business, also complete lines 4-6.**
- **All others, skip lines 4-6 and enter the amount from line 3 on line 7.**

4	Multiply days used for day care during year by hours used per day	4		hr.
5	Total hours available for use during the year (366 days x 24 hours)	5		hr.
6	Divide line 4 by line 5. Enter the result as a decimal amount	6		
7	Business precentage. For day-care facilities not used exclusively for business, multiply line 6 by line 3 (enter the result as a percentage). All others, enter the amount from line 3 ▶	7		%

Part II — Figure Your Allowable Deduction

8	Enter the amount from Schedule C, line 29, **plus** any net gain or (loss) derived from the business use of your home and shown on Schedule D or Form 4797. If more than one place of business, see instructions			8	

See instructions for columns (a) and (b) before completing lines 9-20.

			(a) Direct expenses	(b) Indirect expenses		
9	Casualty losses	9				
10	Deductible mortgage interest	10				
11	Real estate taxes	11				
12	Add lines 9, 10, and 11	12				
13	Multiply line 12, column (b) by line 7		13			
14	Add line 12, column (a) and line 13				14	
15	Subtract line 14 from line 8. If zero or less, enter -0-				15	
16	Excess mortgage interest	16				
17	Insurance	17				
18	Repairs and maintenance	18				
19	Utilities	19				
20	Other expenses	20				
21	Add lines 16 through 20	21				
22	Multiply line 21, column (b) by line 7		22			
23	Carryover of operating expenses from 1995 Form 8829, line 41		23			
24	Add line 21 in column (a), line 22, and line 23				24	
25	Allowable operating expenses. Enter the **smaller** of line 15 or line 24				25	
26	Limit on excess casualty losses and depreciation. Subtract line 25 from line 15				26	
27	Excess casualty losses		27			
28	Depreciation of your home from Part III below		28			
29	Carryover of excess casualty losses and depreciation from 1995 Form 8829, line 42		29			
30	Add lines 27 through 29				30	
31	Allowable excess casualty losses and depreciation. Enter the **smaller** of line 26 or line 30				31	
32	Add lines 14, 25, and 31				32	
33	Casualty loss portion, if any, from lines 14 and 31. Carry amount to **Form 4684,** Section B				33	
34	Allowable expenses for business use of your home. Subtract line 33 from line 32. Enter here and on Schedule C, line 30. If your home was used for more than one business, see instructions ▶				34	

Part III — Depreciation of Your Home

35	Enter the **smaller** of your home's adjusted basis or its fair market value	35	
36	Value of land included on line 35	36	
37	Basis of building. Subtract line 36 from line 35	37	
38	Business basis of building. Multiply line 37 by line 7	38	
39	Depreciation percentage	39	%
40	Depreciation allowable. Multiply line 38 by line 39. Enter here and on line 28 above	40	

Part IV — Carryover of Unallowed Expenses to 1997

41	Operating expenses. Subtract line 25 from line 24. If less than zero, enter -0-	41	
42	Excess casualty losses and depreciation. Subtract line 31 from line 30. If less than zero, enter -0-	42	

620301/12-02-96

LHA For Paperwork Reduction Act Notice, see page 1 of separate instructions.

Form **8829** (1996)

MACRS AND ACRS TABLES

ACRS, MACRS and ADS Depreciation Methods Summary

System	Characteristics	Depreciation Method		Table No.[a]	
		MACRS	ADS	MACRS	ADS
MACRS & ADS	Personal Property:				
	1. Accounting Convention	Half-year or mid-quarter	Half-year or mid-quarter[b]		
	2. Life and Method				
	a. 3-year, 5-year, 7-year, 10-year	200% DB or elect straight-line	150% DB or elect straight-line	1, 2, 3, 4, 5, 8	9, 10[c]
	b. 15-year, 20-year	150% DB or elect straight-line	150% DB or elect straight-line[d]	1, 2, 3, 4, 5, 8	
	Real Property:				
	1. Accounting Convention	Mid-month	Mid-month		
	2. Life and Method				
	a. Residential rental property	27.5 years, straight-line	40 years straight-line	6	11
	b. Nonresidential real property	39 years, straight-line[e]	40 years straight-line	8	11

	Characteristics	ACRS	Table No.[a] ACRS
ACRS	Personal Property		
	1. Accounting Convention	Half-year	
	2. Life and Method		
	a. 3-year, 5-year, 10-year, 15-year	150% DB or elect straight-line[f]	12
	Real Property		
	1. Accounting Convention	First of month or Mid-month[g]	
	2. Life		
	a. 15-year property	Placed in service after 12/31/80 and before 3/16/84	16
	b. 18-year property	Placed in service after 3/15/84 and before 5/9/85	14, 15
	c. 19-year property	Placed in service after 5/8/85 and before 1/1/87	13
	3. Method		
	a. All but low-income housing	175% DB or elect straight-line	
	b. Low-income housing property	200% DB or elect straight-line	

		Table No.[a]
LUXURY AUTOMOBILE LIMITATIONS		17

[a] All depreciation tables in this appendix are based upon tables contained in Rev. Proc. 87-57.

[b] General and ADS tables are available for property lives from 2.5-50.0 years using the straight-line method. These tables are contained in Rev. Proc. 87-57 and are only partially reproduced here.

[c] The mid-quarter tables are available in Rev. Proc. 87-57, but are not reproduced here.

[d] Special recovery periods are assigned certain MACRS properties under the alternative depreciation system.

[e] A 31.5-year recovery period applied to nonresidential real property placed in service under the MACRS rules prior to May 13, 1993. (See Table 7)

[f] Special recovery periods are required or able to be elected for personalty and realty for which a straight-line ACRS election is made. These recovery periods can be as long as 45 years.

[g] The first-of-the-month convention is used with 15-year property and 18-year real property placed in service before June 23, 1984. The mid-month convention is used with 18-year real property placed in service after June 22, 1984 and 19-year real property.

▼ TABLE 1

General Depreciation System—MACRS
Personal Property Placed in Service after 12/31/86
Applicable Convention: Half-year
Applicable Depreciation Method: 200 or 150 Percent Declining Balance Switching to Straight Line

If the Recovery Year Is:	And the Recovery Period Is:					
	3-Year	5-Year	7-Year	10-Year	15-Year	20-Year
	The Depreciation Rate Is:					
1	33.33	20.00	14.29	10.00	5.00	3.750
2	44.45	32.00	24.49	18.00	9.50	7.219
3	14.81	19.20	17.49	14.40	8.55	6.677
4	7.41	11.52	12.49	11.52	7.70	6.177
5		11.52	8.93	9.22	6.93	5.713
6		5.76	8.92	7.37	6.23	5.285
7			8.93	6.55	5.90	4.888
8			4.46	6.55	5.90	4.522
9				6.56	5.91	4.462
10				6.55	5.90	4.461
11				3.28	5.91	4.462
12					5.90	4.461
13					5.91	4.462
14					5.90	4.461
15					5.91	4.462
16					2.95	4.461
17						4.462
18						4.461
19						4.462
20						4.461
21						2.231

▼ TABLE 2
General Depreciation System—MACRS
Personal Property Placed in Service after 12/31/86
Applicable Convention: Mid-quarter (Property Placed in Service in First Quarter)
Applicable Depreciation Method: 200 or 150 Percent Declining Balance Switching to Straight Line

If the Recovery Year Is:	And the Recovery Period Is:					
	3-Year	5-Year	7-Year	10-Year	15-Year	20-Year
	The Depreciation Rate Is:					
1	58.33	35.00	25.00	17.50	8.75	6.563
2	27.78	26.00	21.43	16.50	9.13	7.000
3	12.35	15.60	15.31	13.20	8.21	6.482
4	1.54	11.01	10.93	10.56	7.39	5.996
5		11.01	8.74	8.45	6.65	5.546
6		1.38	8.74	6.76	5.99	5.130
7			8.75	6.55	5.90	4.746
8			1.09	6.55	5.91	4.459
9				6.56	5.90	4.459
10				6.55	5.91	4.459
11				0.82	5.90	4.459
12					5.91	4.460
13					5.90	4.459
14					5.91	4.460
15					5.90	4.459
16					0.74	4.460
17						4.459
18						4.460
19						4.459
20						4.460
21						0.557

▼ TABLE 3

General Depreciation System—MACRS
Personal Property Placed in Service after 12/31/86
Applicable Convention: Mid-quarter (Property Placed in Service in Second Quarter)
Applicable Depreciation Method: 200 or 150 Percent Declining Balance Switching to Straight Line

If the Recovery Year Is:	And the Recovery Period Is:					
	3-Year	5-Year	7-Year	10-Year	15-Year	20-Year
	The Depreciation Rate Is:					
1	41.67	25.00	17.85	12.50	6.25	4.688
2	38.89	30.00	23.47	17.50	9.38	7.148
3	14.14	18.00	16.76	14.00	8.44	6.612
4	5.30	11.37	11.97	11.20	7.59	6.116
5		11.37	8.87	8.96	6.83	5.658
6		4.26	8.87	7.17	6.15	5.233
7			8.87	6.55	5.91	4.841
8			3.33	6.55	5.90	4.478
9				6.56	5.91	4.463
10				6.55	5.90	4.463
11				2.46	5.91	4.463
12					5.90	4.463
13					5.91	4.463
14					5.90	4.463
15					5.91	4.462
16					2.21	4.463
17						4.462
18						4.463
19						4.462
20						4.463
21						1.673

▼ TABLE 4

General Depreciation System—MACRS
Personal Property Placed in Service after 12/31/86
Applicable Convention: Mid-quarter (Property Placed in Service in Third Quarter)
Applicable Depreciation Method: 200 or 150 Percent Declining Balance Switching to Straight Line

If the Recovery Year Is:	And the Recovery Period Is:					
	3-Year	5-Year	7-Year	10-Year	15-Year	20-Year
	The Depreciation Rate Is:					
1	25.00	15.00	10.71	7.50	3.75	2.813
2	50.00	34.00	25.51	18.50	9.63	7.289
3	16.67	20.40	18.22	14.80	8.66	6.742
4	8.33	12.24	13.02	11.84	7.80	6.237
5		11.30	9.30	9.47	7.02	5.769
6		7.06	8.85	7.58	6.31	5.336
7			8.86	6.55	5.90	4.936
8			5.53	6.55	5.90	4.566
9				6.56	5.91	4.460
10				6.55	5.90	4.460
11				4.10	5.91	4.460
12					5.90	4.460
13					5.91	4.461
14					5.90	4.460
15					5.91	4.461
16					3.69	4.460
17						4.461
18						4.460
19						4.461
20						4.460
21						2.788

▼ TABLE 5

General Depreciation System—MACRS
Personal Property Placed in Service after 12/31/86
Applicable Convention: Mid-quarter (Property Placed in Service in Fourth Quarter)
Applicable Depreciation Method: 200 or 150 Percent Declining Balance Switching to Straight Line

If the Recovery Year Is:	And the Recovery Period Is:					
	3-Year	5-Year	7-Year	10-Year	15-Year	20-Year
	The Depreciation Rate Is:					
1	8.33	5.00	3.57	2.50	1.25	0.938
2	61.11	38.00	27.55	19.50	9.88	7.430
3	20.37	22.80	19.68	15.60	8.89	6.872
4	10.19	13.68	14.06	12.48	8.00	6.357
5		10.94	10.04	9.98	7.20	5.880
6		9.58	8.73	7.99	6.48	5.439
7			8.73	6.55	5.90	5.031
8			7.64	6.55	5.90	4.654
9				6.56	5.90	4.458
10				6.55	5.91	4.458
11				5.74	5.90	4.458
12					5.91	4.458
13					5.90	4.458
14					5.91	4.458
15					5.90	4.458
16					5.17	4.458
17						4.458
18						4.459
19						4.458
20						4.459
21						3.901

▼ **TABLE 6**

General Depreciation System—MACRS
Residential Rental Real Property Placed in Service after 12/31/86
Applicable Recovery Period: 27.5 Years
Applicable Convention: Mid-month
Applicable Depreciation Method: Straight Line

If the Recovery Year Is:	And the Month in the First Recovery Year the Property Is Placed in Service Is:											
	1	2	3	4	5	6	7	8	9	10	11	12
	The Depreciation Rate Is:											
1	3.485	3.182	2.879	2.576	2.273	1.970	1.667	1.364	1.061	0.758	0.455	0.152
2	3.636	3.636	3.636	3.636	3.636	3.636	3.636	3.636	3.636	3.636	3.636	3.636
3	3.636	3.636	3.636	3.636	3.636	3.636	3.636	3.636	3.636	3.636	3.636	3.636
4	3.636	3.636	3.636	3.636	3.636	3.636	3.636	3.636	3.636	3.636	3.636	3.636
5	3.636	3.636	3.636	3.636	3.636	3.636	3.636	3.636	3.636	3.636	3.636	3.636
6	3.636	3.636	3.636	3.636	3.636	3.636	3.636	3.636	3.636	3.636	3.636	3.636
7	3.636	3.636	3.636	3.636	3.636	3.636	3.636	3.636	3.636	3.636	3.636	3.636
8	3.636	3.636	3.636	3.636	3.636	3.636	3.636	3.636	3.636	3.636	3.636	3.636
9	3.636	3.636	3.636	3.636	3.636	3.636	3.636	3.636	3.636	3.636	3.636	3.636
10	3.637	3.637	3.637	3.637	3.637	3.637	3.636	3.636	3.636	3.636	3.636	3.636
11	3.636	3.636	3.636	3.636	3.636	3.636	3.637	3.637	3.637	3.637	3.637	3.637
12	3.637	3.637	3.637	3.637	3.637	3.637	3.636	3.636	3.636	3.636	3.636	3.636
13	3.636	3.636	3.636	3.636	3.636	3.636	3.637	3.637	3.637	3.637	3.637	3.637
14	3.637	3.637	3.637	3.637	3.637	3.637	3.636	3.636	3.636	3.636	3.636	3.636
15	3.636	3.636	3.636	3.636	3.636	3.636	3.637	3.637	3.637	3.637	3.637	3.637
16	3.637	3.637	3.637	3.637	3.637	3.637	3.636	3.636	3.636	3.636	3.636	3.636
17	3.636	3.636	3.636	3.636	3.636	3.636	3.637	3.637	3.637	3.637	3.637	3.637
18	3.637	3.637	3.637	3.637	3.637	3.637	3.636	3.636	3.636	3.636	3.636	3.636
19	3.636	3.636	3.636	3.636	3.636	3.636	3.637	3.637	3.637	3.637	3.637	3.637
20	3.637	3.637	3.637	3.637	3.637	3.637	3.636	3.636	3.636	3.636	3.636	3.636
21	3.636	3.636	3.636	3.636	3.636	3.636	3.637	3.637	3.637	3.637	3.637	3.637
22	3.637	3.637	3.637	3.637	3.637	3.637	3.636	3.636	3.636	3.636	3.636	3.636
23	3.636	3.636	3.636	3.636	3.636	3.636	3.637	3.637	3.637	3.637	3.637	3.637
24	3.637	3.637	3.637	3.637	3.637	3.637	3.636	3.636	3.636	3.636	3.636	3.636
25	3.636	3.636	3.636	3.636	3.636	3.636	3.637	3.637	3.637	3.637	3.637	3.637
26	3.637	3.637	3.637	3.637	3.637	3.637	3.636	3.636	3.636	3.636	3.636	3.636
27	3.636	3.636	3.636	3.636	3.636	3.636	3.637	3.637	3.637	3.637	3.637	3.637
28	1.970	2.273	2.576	2.879	3.182	3.485	3.636	3.636	3.636	3.636	3.636	3.636
29	0.000	0.000	0.000	0.000	0.000	0.000	0.152	0.455	0.758	1.061	1.364	1.667

▼ TABLE 7

General Depreciation System—MACRS
Nonresidential Rental Real Property Placed in Service after 12/31/86 and before 5/13/93
Applicable Recovery Period: 31.5 Years
Applicable Convention: Mid-month
Applicable Depreciation Method: Straight Line

If the Recovery Year Is:	And the Month in the First Recovery Year the Property Is Placed in Service Is:											
	1	2	3	4	5	6	7	8	9	10	11	12
	The Depreciation Rate Is:											
1	3.042	2.778	2.513	2.249	1.984	1.720	1.455	1.190	0.926	0.661	0.397	0.132
2	3.175	3.175	3.175	3.175	3.175	3.175	3.175	3.175	3.175	3.175	3.175	3.175
3	3.175	3.175	3.175	3.175	3.175	3.175	3.175	3.175	3.175	3.175	3.175	3.175
4	3.175	3.175	3.175	3.175	3.175	3.175	3.175	3.175	3.175	3.175	3.175	3.175
5	3.175	3.175	3.175	3.175	3.175	3.175	3.175	3.175	3.175	3.175	3.175	3.175
6	3.175	3.175	3.175	3.175	3.175	3.175	3.175	3.175	3.175	3.175	3.175	3.175
7	3.175	3.175	3.175	3.175	3.175	3.175	3.175	3.175	3.175	3.175	3.175	3.175
8	3.175	3.174	3.175	3.174	3.175	3.174	3.175	3.175	3.175	3.175	3.175	3.175
9	3.174	3.175	3.174	3.175	3.174	3.175	3.174	3.175	3.174	3.175	3.174	3.175
10	3.175	3.174	3.175	3.174	3.175	3.174	3.175	3.174	3.175	3.174	3.175	3.174
11	3.174	3.175	3.174	3.175	3.174	3.175	3.174	3.175	3.174	3.175	3.174	3.175
12	3.175	3.174	3.175	3.174	3.175	3.174	3.175	3.174	3.175	3.174	3.175	3.174
13	3.174	3.175	3.174	3.175	3.174	3.175	3.174	3.175	3.174	3.175	3.174	3.175
14	3.175	3.174	3.175	3.174	3.175	3.174	3.175	3.174	3.175	3.174	3.175	3.174
15	3.174	3.175	3.174	3.175	3.174	3.175	3.174	3.175	3.174	3.175	3.174	3.175
16	3.175	3.174	3.175	3.174	3.175	3.174	3.175	3.174	3.175	3.174	3.175	3.174
17	3.174	3.175	3.174	3.175	3.174	3.175	3.174	3.175	3.174	3.175	3.174	3.175
18	3.175	3.174	3.175	3.174	3.175	3.174	3.175	3.174	3.175	3.174	3.175	3.174
19	3.174	3.175	3.174	3.175	3.174	3.175	3.174	3.175	3.174	3.175	3.174	3.175
20	3.175	3.174	3.175	3.174	3.175	3.174	3.175	3.174	3.175	3.174	3.175	3.174
21	3.174	3.175	3.174	3.175	3.174	3.175	3.174	3.175	3.174	3.175	3.174	3.175
22	3.175	3.174	3.175	3.174	3.175	3.174	3.175	3.174	3.175	3.174	3.175	3.174
23	3.174	3.175	3.174	3.175	3.174	3.175	3.174	3.175	3.174	3.175	3.174	3.175
24	3.175	3.174	3.175	3.174	3.175	3.174	3.175	3.174	3.175	3.174	3.175	3.174
25	3.174	3.175	3.174	3.175	3.174	3.175	3.174	3.175	3.174	3.175	3.174	3.175
26	3.175	3.174	3.175	3.174	3.175	3.174	3.175	3.174	3.175	3.174	3.175	3.174
27	3.174	3.175	3.174	3.175	3.174	3.175	3.174	3.175	3.174	3.175	3.174	3.175
28	3.175	3.174	3.175	3.174	3.175	3.174	3.175	3.174	3.175	3.174	3.175	3.174
29	3.174	3.175	3.174	3.175	3.174	3.175	3.174	3.175	3.174	3.175	3.174	3.175
30	3.175	3.174	3.175	3.174	3.175	3.174	3.175	3.174	3.175	3.174	3.175	3.174
31	3.174	3.175	3.174	3.175	3.174	3.175	3.174	3.175	3.174	3.175	3.174	3.175
32	1.720	1.984	2.249	2.513	2.778	3.042	3.175	3.174	3.175	3.174	3.175	3.174
33	0.000	0.000	0.000	0.000	0.000	0.000	0.132	0.397	0.661	0.926	1.190	1.455

▼ TABLE 8

General Depreciation System—MACRS
Nonresidential Rental Real Property Placed in Service after 5/12/93
Applicable Recovery Period: 39 years
Applicable Depreciation Method: Straight Line

If the Recovery Year Is:	And the Month in the First Recovery Year the Property Is Placed in Service Is:											
	1	2	3	4	5	6	7	8	9	10	11	12
	The Depreciation Rate Is:											
1	2.461	2.247	2.033	1.819	1.605	1.391	1.177	0.963	0.749	0.535	0.321	0.107
2–39	2.564	2.564	2.564	2.564	2.564	2.564	2.564	2.564	2.564	2.564	2.564	2.564
40	0.107	0.321	0.535	0.749	0.963	1.177	1.391	1.605	1.819	2.033	2.247	2.461

▼ TABLE 9

Alternative Depreciation System—MACRS (Partial Table)
Property Placed in Service after 12/31/86
Applicable Convention: Half-year
Applicable Depreciation Method: 150 Percent Declining Balance Switching to Straight Line

If the Recovery Year Is:	And the Recovery Period Is:					
	3	4	5	7	10	12
	The Depreciation Rate Is:					
1	25.00	18.75	15.00	10.71	7.50	6.25
2	37.50	30.47	25.50	19.13	13.88	11.72
3	25.00	20.31	17.85	15.03	11.79	10.25
4	12.50	20.31	16.66	12.25	10.02	8.97
5		10.16	16.66	12.25	8.74	7.85
6			8.33	12.25	8.74	7.33
7				12.25	8.74	7.33
8				6.13	8.74	7.33
9					8.74	7.33
10					8.74	7.33
11					4.37	7.32
12						7.33
13						3.66

▼ TABLE 10

Alternative Depreciation System—MACRS (Partial Table)
Property Placed in Service after 12/31/86
Applicable Convention: Half-year
Applicable Depreciation Method: Straight Line

If the Recovery Year Is:	And the Recovery Period Is:					
	3	4	5	7	10	12
	The Depreciation Rate Is:					
1	16.67	12.50	10.00	7.14	5.00	4.17
2	33.33	25.00	20.00	14.29	10.00	8.33
3	33.33	25.00	20.00	14.29	10.00	8.33
4	16.67	25.00	20.00	14.28	10.00	8.33
5		12.50	20.00	14.29	10.00	8.33
6			10.00	14.28	10.00	8.33
7				14.29	10.00	8.34
8				7.14	10.00	8.33
9					10.00	8.34
10					10.00	8.33
11					5.00	8.34
12						8.33
13						4.17

▼ TABLE 11

Alternative Depreciation System—MACRS
Real Property Placed into Service after 12/31/86
Applicable Recovery Period: 40 years
Applicable Convention: Mid-month
Applicable Depreciation Method: Straight Line

If the Recovery Year Is:	And the Month in the First Recovery Year the Property Is Placed in Service Is:											
	1	2	3	4	5	6	7	8	9	10	11	12

The Depreciation Rate Is:

	1	2	3	4	5	6	7	8	9	10	11	12
1	2.396	2.188	1.979	1.771	1.563	1.354	1.146	0.938	0.729	0.521	0.313	0.104
2 to 40	2.500	2.500	2.500	2.500	2.500	2.500	2.500	2.500	2.500	2.500	2.500	2.500
41	0.104	0.312	0.521	0.729	0.937	1.146	1.354	1.562	1.771	1.979	2.187	2.396

▼ TABLE 12

Depreciation System—ACRS Cost-Recovery Rates for Tangible Personal Property
Property Placed in Service after 12/31/80 and before 1/1/87

Recovery Year	Recovery Classes[a]	
	3-Year	5-Year
1	25%	15%
2	38	22
3	37	21
4	—	21
5	—	21
Totals	100%	100%

[a] The percentages that are applicable to each year for 10-year property are year 1, 8%; year 2, 14%; year 3, 12%; years 4 through 6, 10%; and years 7 through 10, 9%. The percentages that apply to 15-year property are year 1, 5%; year 2, 10%; year 3, 9%; year 4, 8%; years 5 and 6, 7%; and years 7 through 15, 6%.

▼ TABLE 13

Depreciation System—ACRS
19-Year Real Property (19-Year 175% Declining Balance)
Mid-Month Convention
Property Placed in Service after 5/8/85 and before 1/1/87

If the Recovery Year Is:	And the Month in the First Recovery Year the Property Is Placed in Service Is:											
	1	2	3	4	5	6	7	8	9	10	11	12
	The Depreciation Rate Is:											
1	8.8	8.1	7.3	6.5	5.8	5.0	4.2	3.5	2.7	1.9	1.1	0.4
2	8.4	8.5	8.5	8.6	8.7	8.8	8.8	8.9	9.0	9.0	9.1	9.2
3	7.6	7.7	7.7	7.8	7.9	7.9	8.0	8.1	8.1	8.2	8.3	8.3
4	6.9	7.0	7.0	7.1	7.1	7.2	7.3	7.3	7.4	7.4	7.5	7.6
5	6.3	6.3	6.4	6.4	6.5	6.5	6.6	6.6	6.7	6.8	6.8	6.9
6	5.7	5.7	5.8	5.9	5.9	5.9	6.0	6.0	6.1	6.1	6.2	6.2
7	5.2	5.2	5.3	5.3	5.3	5.4	5.4	5.5	5.5	5.6	5.6	5.6
8	4.7	4.7	4.8	4.8	4.8	4.9	4.9	5.0	5.0	5.1	5.1	5.1
9	4.2	4.3	4.3	4.4	4.4	4.5	4.5	4.5	4.5	4.6	4.6	4.7
10	4.2	4.2	4.2	4.2	4.2	4.2	4.2	4.2	4.2	4.2	4.2	4.2
11	4.2	4.2	4.2	4.2	4.2	4.2	4.2	4.2	4.2	4.2	4.2	4.2
12	4.2	4.2	4.2	4.2	4.2	4.2	4.2	4.2	4.2	4.2	4.2	4.2
13	4.2	4.2	4.2	4.2	4.2	4.2	4.2	4.2	4.2	4.2	4.2	4.2
14	4.2	4.2	4.2	4.2	4.2	4.2	4.2	4.2	4.2	4.2	4.2	4.2
15	4.2	4.2	4.2	4.2	4.2	4.2	4.2	4.2	4.2	4.2	4.2	4.2
16	4.2	4.2	4.2	4.2	4.2	4.2	4.2	4.2	4.2	4.2	4.2	4.2
17	4.2	4.2	4.2	4.2	4.2	4.2	4.2	4.2	4.2	4.2	4.2	4.2
18	4.2	4.2	4.2	4.2	4.2	4.2	4.2	4.2	4.2	4.2	4.2	4.2
19	4.2	4.2	4.2	4.2	4.2	4.2	4.2	4.2	4.2	4.2	4.2	4.2
20	0.2	0.5	0.9	1.2	1.6	1.9	2.3	2.6	3.0	3.3	3.7	4.0

▼ TABLE 14

Depreciation System—ACRS
18-Year Real Property (18-Year 175% Declining Balance)
Mid-Month Convention
Property Placed in Service after 6/22/84 and before 5/9/85

If the Recovery Year Is:	And the Month in the First Recovery Year the Property Is Placed in Service Is:											
	1	2	3	4	5	6	7	8	9	10	11	12
	The Applicable Percentage Is:											
1	9	9	8	7	6	5	4	4	3	2	1	0.4
2	9	9	9	9	9	9	9	9	9	10	10	10.0
3	8	8	8	8	8	8	8	8	9	9	9	9.0
4	7	7	7	7	7	8	8	8	8	8	8	8.0
5	7	7	7	7	7	7	7	7	7	7	7	7.0
6	6	6	6	6	6	6	6	6	6	6	6	6.0
7	5	5	5	5	6	6	6	6	6	6	6	6.0
8	5	5	5	5	5	5	5	5	5	5	5	5.0
9	5	5	5	5	5	5	5	5	5	5	5	5.0
10	5	5	5	5	5	5	5	5	5	5	5	5.0
11	5	5	5	5	5	5	5	5	5	5	5	5.0
12	5	5	5	5	5	5	5	5	5	5	5	5.0
13	4	4	4	5	4	4	5	4	4	4	5	5.0
14	4	4	4	4	4	4	4	4	4	4	4	4.0
15	4	4	4	4	4	4	4	4	4	4	4	4.0
16	4	4	4	4	4	4	4	4	4	4	4	4.0
17	4	4	4	4	4	4	4	4	4	4	4	4.0
18	4	3	4	4	4	4	4	4	4	4	4	4.0
19		1	1	1	2	2	2	3	3	3	3	3.6

▼ TABLE 15

Depreciation System—ACRS
18-Year Real Property (18-Year 175% Declining Balance)
Full-Month Convention
Property Placed in Service after 3/15/84 and before 6/23/84

If the Recovery Year Is:	And the Month in the First Recovery Year the Property Is Placed in Service Is:											
	1	2	3	4	5	6	7	8	9	10	11	12
	The Applicable Percentage Is:											
1	10	9	8	7	6	6	5	4	3	2	2	1
2	9	9	9	9	9	9	9	9	9	10	10	10
3	8	8	8	8	8	8	8	8	9	9	9	9
4	7	7	7	7	7	7	8	8	8	8	8	8
5	6	7	7	7	7	7	7	7	7	7	7	7
6	6	6	6	6	6	6	6	6	6	6	6	6
7	5	5	5	5	6	6	6	6	6	6	6	6
8	5	5	5	5	5	5	5	5	5	5	5	5
9	5	5	5	5	5	5	5	5	5	5	5	5
10	5	5	5	5	5	5	5	5	5	5	5	5
11	5	5	5	5	5	5	5	5	5	5	5	5
12	5	5	5	5	5	5	5	5	5	5	5	5
13	4	4	4	5	5	4	4	5	4	4	4	4
14	4	4	4	4	4	4	4	4	4	4	4	4
15	4	4	4	4	4	4	4	4	4	4	4	4
16	4	4	4	4	4	4	4	4	4	4	4	4
17	4	4	4	4	4	4	4	4	4	4	4	4
18	4	4	4	4	4	4	4	4	4	4	4	4
19			1	1	1	2	2	2	3	3	3	4

▼ **TABLE 16**
Depreciation System—ACRS
Full Month Convention
1. All 15-Year Real Estate (Except Low-Income Housing)
Property Placed in Service after 12/31/80 and before 3/16/84

If the Recovery Year Is:	And the Month in the First Year the Property Is Placed in Service Is:											
	1	2	3	4	5	6	7	8	9	10	11	12
	The Applicable Percentage Is:											
1	12	11	10	9	8	7	6	5	4	3	2	1
2	10	10	11	11	11	11	11	11	11	11	11	12
3	9	9	9	9	10	10	10	10	10	10	10	10
4	8	8	8	8	8	8	9	9	9	9	9	9
5	7	7	7	7	7	7	8	8	8	8	8	8
6	6	6	6	6	7	7	7	7	7	7	7	7
7	6	6	6	6	6	6	6	6	6	6	6	6
8	6	6	6	6	6	6	5	6	6	6	6	6
9	6	6	6	6	5	6	5	5	5	6	6	6
10	5	6	5	6	5	5	5	5	5	5	6	5
11	5	5	5	5	5	5	5	5	5	5	5	5
12	5	5	5	5	5	5	5	5	5	5	5	5
13	5	5	5	5	5	5	5	5	5	5	5	5
14	5	5	5	5	5	5	5	5	5	5	5	5
15	5	5	5	5	5	5	5	5	5	5	5	5
16	—	—	1	1	2	2	3	3	4	4	4	5

2. Low-Income Housing
Property Placed in Service after 12/31/80 and before 5/9/85[a]

If the Recovery Year Is:	And the Month in the First Year the Property Is Placed in Service Is:											
	1	2	3	4	5	6	7	8	9	10	11	12
	The Applicable Percentage Is:											
1	13	12	11	10	9	8	7	6	4	3	2	1
2	12	12	12	12	12	12	12	13	13	13	13	13
3	10	10	10	10	11	11	11	11	11	11	11	11
4	9	9	9	9	9	9	9	9	10	10	10	10
5	8	8	8	8	8	8	8	8	8	8	8	8
6	7	7	7	7	7	7	7	7	7	7	7	7
7	6	6	6	6	6	6	6	6	6	6	6	6
8	5	5	5	5	5	5	5	5	5	5	6	6
9	5	5	5	5	5	5	5	5	5	5	5	5
10	5	5	5	5	5	5	5	5	5	5	5	5
11	4	5	5	5	5	5	5	5	5	5	5	5
12	4	4	4	5	4	5	5	5	5	5	5	5
13	4	4	4	4	4	4	5	4	5	5	5	5
14	4	4	4	4	4	4	4	4	4	5	4	4
15	4	4	4	4	4	4	4	4	4	4	4	4
16	—	—	1	1	2	2	2	3	3	3	4	4

[a]For the period after 5/8/85, see special IRS tables (not reproduced here).

▼ TABLE 17
Luxury Automobile Limitations

	Year Automobile is Placed in Service[a]:						
	1997	**1996**	**1995**	**1994**	**1993**	**1992**	**1991**
Year 1	3,160	3,060	3,060	2,960	2,860	2,760	2,660
Year 2	5,000	4,900	4,900	4,700	4,600	4,400	4,300
Year 3	3,050	2,950	2,950	2,850	2,750	2,650	2,550
Year 4 and Each Succeeding Year	1,775	1,775	1,775	1,675	1,675	1,575	1,575

[a]For years prior to 1991, see Revenue Procedure for appropriate year.

APPENDIX
D

GLOSSARY

Ability to pay A concept in taxation that holds that taxpayers be taxed according to their ability to pay such taxes, that is, taxpayers that have sufficient financial resources should pay the tax. This concept is an integral part of vertical equity.

Accelerated Cost Recovery System (ACRS) Established by ERTA in 1981, the ACRS provides an accelerated depreciation and shorter cost-recovery period for real and personal property. The Tax Reform Act of 1986 changed the previously allowed depreciation tables and assigned recovery periods that approach the asset's true economic life. The current depreciation system is referred to as MACRS.

Accounting method The method of determining the taxable year in which income and expenses are reported for tax purposes. Generally, the same method must be used for tax purposes as is used for keeping books and records. The accounting treatment used for any item of income or expense and of specific items (e.g., installment sales and contracts) is included in this term. See also each specific accounting method.

Accounting period The period of time, usually 12 months, used by taxpayers to compute their taxable income. Taxpayers who do not keep records must use a calendar year. Taxpayers who do keep books and records may choose between a calendar year or a fiscal year. The accounting period election is made on the taxpayer's first filed return and cannot be changed without IRS consent. The accounting period may be less than 12 months if it is the taxpayer's first or final return or if the taxpayer is changing accounting periods. Certain restrictions upon the use of a fiscal year apply to partnerships, S corporations, and personal service corporations.

Accountable plan A type of employee reimbursement plan that meets two tests, (1) substantiation, and (2) return of excess reimbursement. Under an accountable plan, reimbursements are excluded from the employee's gross income and the expenses are not deductible by the employee.

Accrual method of accounting Accounting method under which income is reported and expenses are deducted when (1) all events have occurred that fix the taxpayer's right to receive the income and (2) the amount of the item can be determined with reasonable accuracy. Taxpayers with inventories to report must use this method to report sales and purchases.

Accumulated earnings tax This penalty tax is intended to discourage companies from retaining excessive amounts of earnings if the funds are invested in earnings that are unrelated to the business's needs. The current tax rate is 39.6%.

Acquiescence policy IRS policy of announcing whether it agrees or disagrees with a regular Tax Court decision. Such statements are not issued for every case.

ACRS See Accelerated Cost Recovery System.

Active income Income that is produced by the taxpayer's involvement or participation—wages, salaries, and other business income—is considered active income. It is the opposite of passive income.

Additional depreciation The excess of the actual amount of accelerated depreciation (or cost-recovery deductions under ACRS) over the amount of depreciation that would be deductible under the straight-line method. Such depreciation applies to Section 1250 depreciable real property acquired prior to 1987.

Adjusted current earnings An AMT adjustment item for corporations used to compute the Alternative Minimum Tax. The term is a concept based on the traditional earnings and profits definition found in Sec. 312.

Adjusted gross income (AGI) A measure of taxable income that falls between gross income and taxable income. It is the income amount that is used as the basis for calculating the floor or the ceiling for numerous other tax computations.

Adjusted sales price The amount realized from the sale of a residence less any fixing-up expenses.

AGI See Adjusted gross income.

Alimony Payments made pursuant to divorce or separation or written agreement between spouses subject to conditions specified in the tax law. Alimony payments (as contrasted to property settlements) are deductible for AGI by the payor and are included in the gross income of the recipient.

All events test Rule holding that an accrual basis taxpayer must report an item of income (1) when all events have occurred that fix the taxpayer's right to receive the item of income and (2) when the amount of the item can be determined with reasonable accuracy. This test is not satisfied until economic performance has taken place.

Alternative minimum tax (AMT) Applies to individuals, corporations, and estates and trusts only if the tentative minimum tax (TMT) exceeds the taxpayer's regular tax liability. Most taxpayers are not subject to this tax.

Amount realized The amount realized equals the sum of money plus the fair market value of all other property received from the sale or other disposition of the property less any selling expenses (e.g., commissions, advertising, deed preparation costs, and legal expenses) incurred in connection with the sale.

AMT See Alternative Minimum Tax.

Annual accounting period See Accounting period.

Annuity A series of regular payments that will continue for either a fixed period of time or until the death of the recipient. Pensions are usually paid in this way.

Applicable federal rate The rate determined monthly by the federal government which is based on the rate paid by the government on borrowed funds. The rate varies with the term of the loan. Thus, short-term loans are for a period of under three years, mid-term loans are for over three years and under nine years, and long-term loans are for over nine years.

Asset depreciation range (ADR) system of depreciation Depreciation method allowed for property placed in service before January 1, 1981. This method prescribed useful lives for various classes of assets.

Average tax rate The taxpayer's total tax liability divided by the amount of his taxable income.

Backup withholding A modified withholding system intended to prevent abusive noncompliance situations.

Bad debt Bona fide debt that is uncollectible because it is worthless. Such debts are further characterized as "business bad debts," which give rise to an ordinary deduction, and "nonbusiness bad debts," which are treated as a short-term capital loss. A determination of whether a debt is worthless is made by reference to all the pertinent evidence (e.g., the debtor's general financial condition and whether the debt is secured by collateral). Such debts are deductible subject to certain requirements.

Bona fide debt A debt that (1) arises from a valid and enforceable obligation to pay a fixed or determinable sum of money and (2) results in a debtor-creditor relationship.

Boot Cash and nonlike-kind property given to complete an exchange of like-kind property where the property exchanged is not of equal vale. Gain on the exchange is limited to the amount of boot received.

Brother-sister controlled group This type of corporation exists if (1) five or fewer individuals, estates, or trusts own at least 80% of the stock of each corporation and (2) there is common ownership of at least 50% of the total value of all classes of the stock. Each shareholder must own an interest in each corporation.

Business bad debt See Bad debt.

Cafeteria plan Employer-financed plan that offers employees the option of choosing cash or statutory nontaxable fringe benefits (other than scholarships, fellowships, and Sec. 132 benefits such as discounts on merchandise). Such plans may not discriminate in favor of highly compensated individuals or their dependents or spouses.

Capital addition See Capital expenditure.

Capital asset This category of assets includes all assets except inventory, notes and accounts receivable, and depreciable property or land used in a trade or business (e.g., property, plant, and machinery).

Capital expenditure An expenditure that adds to the value of, substantially prolongs the useful life of, or adapts the property to a new or different use qualifies as a capital expenditure.

Capital gain Gain realized on the sale or exchange of a capital asset.

Capital gain dividend A distribution by a regulated investment company (i.e., a mutual fund) of capital gains realized from the sale of investments in the fund. Such dividends also include undistributed capital gains allocated to the shareholders.

Capital gain property Property that is contributed to a public charity upon which a long-term capital gain would be recognized if that property was sold at its fair market value.

Capital loss Loss realized on the sale or exchange of a capital asset.

Capital recovery A capital recovery amount is a deduction for depreciation or cost recovery. It is a factor in the determination of a property's adjusted basis.

Cash method of accounting Accounting method that requires the taxpayer to report income for the taxable year in which payments are actually or constructively received. Expenses are reported in the year they are paid. Most individuals and service businesses (i.e., businesses without inventories) use this method.

Cash receipts and disbursements method of accounting See Cash method of accounting.

Casualty loss Loss that arises from an identifiable event that was sudden, unexpected, or unusual (e.g., fire, storm, shipwreck, other casualty, or theft). Within certain limitations, individuals may deduct such losses from AGI. Business casualty losses are deductible for AGI.

C Corporation Form of business entity that is taxed as a separate tax-paying entity. Its income is subject to an initial tax at the corporate level. Its shareholders are subject to a second tax when dividends are paid from the corporation's earnings and profits. Under certain conditions, S corporation status may be elected for tax purposes. C corporations are sometimes referred to as "regular corporations."

CD See Certificate of deposit.

Charitable contribution deduction Contributions of money or property made to qualified organizations (i.e., public charities and private nonoperating foundations) may be deducted from AGI. The amount of the deduction depends upon (1) the type of charity receiving the contribution, (2) the type of property contributed, and (3) other limitations mandated by the tax law. See also Unrelated use property.

Closed-fact situation Situation or transaction that has already occurred.

Closely held C corporation For purposes of the at risk rules, a closely held C corporation is defined as a corporation where more than 50% of the stock is owned by five or fewer individuals at any time during the last half of the corporation's taxable year. These individuals may or may not be members of the same family.

Community income In any of the eight community property states, such income consists of the income from the personal efforts, investments, etc. of either spouse. Community income belongs equally to both spouses.

Compensation Payment for personal services. Salaries, wages, fees, commissions, tips, bonuses, and specialized forms of compensation such as director's fees and jury's fees fall into this category. However, certain fringe benefits and some foreign-earned income are not taxed.

Completed contract method of accounting Accounting method for long-term contracts undertaken by smaller companies. Income from the contract is reported in the taxable year in which the contract is completed. The completed contract method is limited to construction contracts undertaken by smaller companies.

Constant interest rate method Used to amortize the original issue discount ratably over the life of the bond, this method determines the amount of interest income by multiplying the interest yield to maturity by the adjusted issue price.

Constructive dividend Distribution that is intended to result in a deduction to the corporation. For example, excessive salary payments to shareholde-employees may be recharacterized as nondeductible dividends to the corporation to the extent that such amounts are not reasonable. The excess amount may be treated as dividend income to the shareholder-employees rather than as compensation provided that certain conditions are met.

Constructive receipt doctrine Rule holding that cash method taxpayers cannot turn their backs on the receipt of income if the funds are unqualifiedly made available.

Constructive stock ownership Shares that are indirectly or deemed to be owned by another shareholder due to related party situations.

Contributory pension plan A qualified pension plan to which employees make voluntary contributions.

Controlled group A controlled group is two or more separately incorporated businesses owned by the same individuals or entities. Such groups may consist of parent-subsidiary corporations, brother-sister corporations, or a combination of both (combined group).

Cost The amount paid for property in cash or the fair market value of the property given in exchange. The costs of acquiring the property and preparing it for use are included in the cost of the property.

Cost depletion method Calculation of the depletion of an asset (e.g., oil and gas properties) under which the asset's adjusted basis is divided by the estimated recoverable units to arrive at a per-unit depletion. This amount is then multiplied by the number of units sold to determine the cost depletion. This method may be alternated with the percentage depletion method as long as the calculation takes that into account.

Current year's exclusion The amount of the annuity payment that is excluded from gross income. This amount is determined by multiplying the exclusion ratio by the amount received during the year.

Customs duties A federal excise tax on imported goods.

Deductions for AGI Expenses one would see on an income statement prepared for financial accounting purposes, for example, compensation paid to employees, repairs to business property, and depreciation expenses. Certain nonbusiness deductions (e.g., alimony payments, moving expenses, and deductible payments to an individual retirement account (IRA) are also deductible for AGI.

Deductions from AGI Generally, deductions are allowed for certain personal expenses such as medical deductions and charitable contributions which are referred to as itemized deductions. Alternatively, individuals may deduct the standard deduction. Personal and dependency deductions are also deductions from AGI.

Deferred compensation Methods of compensating employees based upon their current service where the benefits are deferred until future periods (e.g., a pension plan).

Defined benefit pension plan Qualified pension plan which establishes a contribution formula based upon actuarial techniques that are intended to fund a fixed retirement benefit amount. Thus, the amount that will be available at the time of retirement is determined when the contributions are made.

Defined contribution pension plan Qualified pension plan under which a separate account is maintained for each participant and fixed amounts are contributed based upon a specific percentage-of-compensation formula. The retirement benefits are based on the value of the participant's account at the time of retirement. Defined contribution plans for self-employed individuals are referred to as *H.R. 10 plans.*

Dependent care assistance program Employer-financed programs that provide care for an employee's children or other dependents. An employee may exclude up to $5,000 from gross income although the ceiling amount (i.e., $2,400 or $4,800) on the child care credit is reduced by the amount of assistance that is excluded from gross income.

DIF See Discriminate Function System.

Discriminate Function System (DIF) System used by the IRS to select individual returns for audit. This system is intended to identify those tax returns which are most likely to contain errors.

Dividends-received deduction This deduction attempts to mitigate the triple taxation that would occur if one corporation paid dividends to a corporate shareholder who, in turn, distributed such amounts to its individual shareholders. Certain restrictions and limitations apply to this deduction.

E&P See Earnings and profits

Earnings and profits (E&P) A measure of the corporation's ability to pay a dividend from its current and accumulated earnings without an impairment of capital.

Economic performance test Economic performance occurs when the property or services to be provided are actually delivered.

Education expense Subject to certain limitations and restrictions, education expenses are deductible if they are incurred (1) to improve or maintain the individual's existing skills or (2) to meet requirements that are requisite to continued employment or meet the requirements of state law.

Effective tax rate The taxpayer's total tax liability divided by his total economic income.

Electronic Filing The method of filing a tax return with the IRS by electronic means instead of paper forms.

Employee achievement award Award given under circumstances that does not create a likelihood that it is really disguised compensation. It must be in the form of tangible personal property (other than cash) and be valued at no more than $400.

Employee stock ownership plan (ESOP) A qualified stock bonus plan or combined stock bonus plan and money purchase pension plan. ESOP's are funded by contributions of the employer's stock which are held for the employees' benefit.

Employment taxes Social security (FICA) and federal and state unemployment compensation taxes.

Entertainment expense Entertainment expenses (e.g., business meals) that are either directly related to or associated with the active conduct of a trade or business are deductible within certain limitations and restrictions. Directly related expenses are those that (1) derive a business benefit other than goodwill and (2) are incurred in a clear business setting. Expenses that are associated with the business are those that show a clear business purpose (e.g., obtaining new business) and occur on the same day the business is discussed.

ESOP See Employee stock ownership plan.

Estate tax Part of the federal unified transfer tax system, this tax is based upon the total property transfers an individual makes during his lifetime and at death.

Excess depreciation See Additional depreciation.

Exchange A transaction in which one receives a reciprocal transfer of property rather than cash and/or a cash equivalent.

Excise taxes Federal tax on alcohol, gasoline, telephone usage, oil and gas production, etc. State and local governments may impose similar taxes on goods and services.

Exclusion Any item of income that the tax law says is not taxable.

Exclusion ratio The portion of the annuity payment that is excluded from taxation. This amount equals the investment in the contract (its cost) divided by the expected return from the annuity.

Expected return The amount which a taxpayer can expect to receive from an annuity. It is determined by multiplying the amount of the annuity's annual payment by the expected return multiple.

Expected return multiple The number of years that the annuity is expected to continue. This amount may be a stated term or for the remainder of the taxpayer's life.

Fair market value (FMV) This amount is the price at which property would change hands between a willing buyer and a willing seller where neither party is under any compulsion to buy or sell.

Federal estate tax See estate tax.

Federal Insurance Contributions Act See FICA.

Federal Unemployment Tax Act See FUTA.

FICA Tax withheld through the payment of payroll taxes, FICA is intended to finance social security benefits for individuals who are not self-employed. Employees and employers contribute matching amounts until a federally-set annual earnings ceiling is reached. At that time, no further contributions need be made for that year. No ceiling exists for the hospital insurance (HI) portion of the tax. Self-employed individuals are subject to self-employment tax and currently receive a *for* AGI income tax deduction equal to 50% of their self-employment tax payments.

Field audit procedure Audit procedure generally used by the IRS for corporations or individuals engaged in a trade or business and conducted at either the taxpayer's place of business or his tax advisor's office. Generally, several items on the tax return are examined.

FIFO method of inventory valuation This flow of cost method assumes that the first goods purchased will be the first goods sold. Thus, the ending inventory consists of the last goods purchased.

Fiscal year An annual accounting period that ends on the last day of any month other than December. A fiscal year may be elected by taxpayers that keep books and records, such as businesses.

Fixing-up expenses Expenses incurred to assist in the sale of a residence (e.g., normal repairs and painting costs). Capital expenditures do not qualify as fixing-up expenses.

Flat tax See Proportional tax.

Foreign-earned income An individual's earnings from personal services rendered in a foreign country.

Foreign tax credit Tax credit given to mitigate the possibility of double taxation faced by U.S. taxpayers earning foreign income.

Former passive activity An activity that was formerly considered passive, but which is not considered to be passive with respect to the taxpayer for the current year.

Franchise tax State tax levy sometimes based upon a weighted average formula consisting of net worth, income, and sales.

Functional-use test A test used to determine whether property is considered similar or related in service or use for purposes of involuntary conversions of property under Sec. 1033. The functional-use test requires that the replacement property be functionally the same as the converted property.

FUTA Federal and state unemployment compensation tax.

GAAP See Generally accepted accounting principles.

Gain realized See Realized gain.

General business credit Special credit category consisting of tax credits commonly available to businesses. The more significant credit items are (1) the investment tax credit, (2) the targeted jobs credit, (3) the research credit, (4) the low-income housing credit, (5) the empowerment zone employment credit, (6) the disabled access credit.

Generally accepted accounting principles (GAAP) The accounting principles that govern the preparation of financial reports to shareholders. GAAP does not apply to the tax treatment unless the method clearly reflects income. It is used only when the regulations do not specify the treatment of an item or when the regulations provide more than one alternative accounting method.

Gift tax A tax that is imposed upon the donor for transfers that are not supported by full and adequate consideration. A $10,000 annual exclusion is allowed per donee.

Goodwill The excess of the purchase price of a business over the fair market value of all identifiable assets acquired.

Gross income All income received in cash, property, or services, from whatever source derived and from which the taxpayer derives a direct economic benefit.

Gross tax For income tax purposes, the amount determined by multiplying taxable income by the appropriate tax rate(s). The gross tax may also be found in the appropriate tax table for the taxpayer's filing status.

Half year convention An assumption with respect to depreciation that assumes that all asset acquisitions and dispositions are made at the midpoint of the tax year.

Holding period The length of time an asset is held before it is disposed of. This period is used to determine whether the gain or loss is long- or short-term.

Horizontal equity A concept in taxation that refers to the notion that similarly-situated taxpayers should be treated equally under the tax law.

H.R. 10 Plan Special retirement plan rules applicable to self-employed individuals. Such plans are often referred to as "Keogh plans."

Hybrid method of accounting Accounting method that combines the cash and accrual methods. Under this method, taxpayers can report sales and purchases under the accrual method and other income and expense items under the cash method. See also the cash method of accounting and the accrual method of accounting.

IDCs See Intangible drilling and development costs.

Incremental A concept in taxation that described how the tax law has been changed or modified over the years. Under incrementalism, the tax law is changed or an incremental basis rather than a complete revision basis.

Imputed interest rule This rule reallocates the payments received in an installment sale between interest (fully taxable) and principal (only gain is taxable). To avoid this, the stated interest rate must equal at least 100% of the applicable federal rate as determined monthly according to the rate paid by the government on borrowed funds.

Incentive stock option plan (ISO) Stock option plan that allows executives to receive a proprietary interest in the corporation. The option to participate in this type of plan must be exercised according to certain requirements and must follow certain procedures.

Income The economic concept of income measures the amount an individual can consume during a period and remain as well off at the end of the period as at the beginning. The accounting concept of income is a measure of the income that is realized in a transaction. The tax concept of income is close to the accounting concept. It includes both taxable and nontaxable income from any source. However, it does not include a return of capital.

Indeterminate market value If the market value of the property in question cannot be determined by the usual methods, the "open transaction" doctrine may be applied and the tax consequences may be deferred until the transaction is closed. Alternatively, the property may be valued by using the fair market value of the property that is given in the exchange (e.g., the value of the services rendered).

Individual retirement account (IRA) Contribution for AGI that is deductible if (1) neither the taxpayer nor his spouse are active participants in an employer-sponsored retirement plan or (2) certain income limitations are met. Taxpayers who do not meet these requirements may make nondeductible IRA contributions.

Information Release An administrative pronouncement concerning an issue the IRS thinks the general public will be interested in. Such releases are issued in lay terms.

Innocent spouse rule Rule that exempts a spouse from penalty of from liability for the tax if such spouse had no knowledge of nor reason to know about an item of community income.

Installment sale Any disposition of property which involves receiving at least one payment after the close of the taxable year in which the sale occurs.

Installment sale method of accounting Taxpayers may use this method of accounting to reduce the tax burden from gains on the sale of property paid for in installments. Under this method, payment of the tax is deferred until the sale proceeds are collected. This method is not applicable to sales of publicly traded property or to losses.

Intangible drilling and development costs (IDCs) Expenditures made by an operator for wages, fuel, repairs, hauling supplies, and so forth, incident to and necessary for the preparation and drilling of oil and gas wells.

Intangible property Property that does not have physical substance, such as goodwill, patents, stocks and bonds, etc.

Interest The cost charged by a lender for the use of money. For example, finance charges, loan discounts, premiums, loan origination fees, and points paid by a buyer to obtain a mortgage loan are all interest expenses. The deductibility of the expense depends upon the purpose for which the indebtedness was incurred.

Internal Revenue Code The primary legislative source and authority for tax research, planning, and compliance activities.

Internal Revenue Service (IRS) The branch of the Treasury Department that is responsible for administering the federal tax law.

Interpretative Regulations Treasury Regulations that serve to broadly interpret the provisions of the Internal Revenue Code.

Inter vivos gifts Gifts made during the donor's life-time.

Investment expenses All deductions other than interest that are directly connected with the production of investment income.

Investment income Gross income from property held for investment and any net gain attributable to the disposition of such property. See also Net investment income.

Investment interest Interest expense on indebtedness incurred to purchase or carry property held for investment (e.g., income from interest, dividends, annuities, and royalties). Interest expenses incurred from passive activities are not subject to the investment interest limitations and interest incurred to purchase or carry tax-exempt securities is not deductible. Interest incurred from passive activities is subject to the passive activity loss limitation rules.

Involuntary conversion Such a conversion occurs when property is compulsorily converted into money or other property due to theft, seizure, requisition, condemnation, or partial or complete destruction. For example, an involuntary conversion occurs when the government exercises its right of eminent domain.

IRA See Individual retirement account.

IRC See Internal Revenue Code.

IRR See Internal rate of return.

IRS See Internal Revenue Service.

ISO See Incentive stock option.

Itemized deductions Also known as "deductions from AGI," these personal expenditures are allowable for such items as medical expenses, state and local taxes, charitable contributions, unreimbursed employee business expenses, interest on a personal residence, and casualty and theft losses. There are specific requirements for and limitations on the deductibility of each of these items. In addition, only those taxpayers whose total itemized deductions exceed the standard deduction amount can itemize their deductions. In general, the total itemized deductions for an individual is reduced by 3% of AGI in excess of $114,700 ($57,350 for married individuals filing a separate return).

Joint income Income from jointly-held property.

Judicial decisions Decisions of a court of law.

Keogh plan Retirement plan for self-employed individuals. This type of plan is also known as an "H.R. 10 plan."

LCM See Lower of cost or market method of inventory valuation.

Legislative Regulations Treasury Regulations issued at the mandate of the Internal Revenue Code. Legislative regulations have a higher degree of authority than interpretative regulations.

Letter Ruling Letter rulings originate from the IRS at the taxpayer's request. They describe how the IRS will treat a proposed transaction. It is only binding on the person requesting the ruling providing the taxpayer completes the transaction as proposed in the ruling. Those of general interest are published as Revenue Rulings.

LIFO method of inventory valuation This method assumes a last-in, first out flow of cost. It results in the lowest taxable income during periods of inflation because it shows the lowest inventory value. Price indexes are used for the valuation. The information in these indexes is grouped into groups (pools) of similar items. See also Simplified LIFO method.

Like class Classes of assets defined by the Regulations that are considered to be property of a like kind for purposes of Sec. 1031. Like class property is tangible personal property that is in the same General Asset Class or the Same Product Class as other property.

Like-kind exchange A direct exchange of like-kind property. The transferred property and the received property must be held for productive use either (1) in a trade or business or (2) as an investment. Nonrecognition of gain or loss is mandatory. Certain like-kind exchanges between related parties are restricted if either party disposes of the property within two years of the exchange.

Like-kind property Property with a similar nature and character. This term does not refer to either the grade or quality of the property.

Limited liability company (LLC) A corporation that is generally taxed under the partnership rules. Although similar to an S corporation, there is no limit to (1) the number of shareholders, (2) the number of classes of stock, or (3) the types of investments in related entities.

Limited liability partnerships (LLP) LLPs are taxes as partnerships but enjoy limited liability under state partnership laws (i.e., individual partners are liable for their own acts and acts of persons under their direction and control but not for negligence or misconduct by other partners).

Liquidating distribution A distribution that liquidates a partner's entire partnership interest due to retirement, death, or other business reason. Such distributions result in a capital gain or loss to the partner whose interest is liquidated. In a corporate liquiddation, the liquidating corporation generally recognizes gains and losses on the distribution of the properties and its shareholders recognize capital gain or loss on the surrender of their stock.

Long-term capital gain (LTCG) Gain realized on the sale or exchange of a capital asset held longer than one year.

Long-term capital loss (LTCL) Loss realized on the sale or exchange of a capital asset held longer than one year.

Long-term contracts Building, manufacturing, installation, and construction contracts that are not completed in the same taxable year in which they are entered into. Service contracts do not qualify as long-term contracts. See also Completed contract method of accounting.

Look-back interest Interest that is assessed on any additional tax that would have been paid if the actual total cost of the contract was used to calculate the tax rather than the estimated cost. Thus, it is applicable to any contract of portion of a contract that is accounted for under either the hybrid or percentage of completion method of accounting.

Lower of cost or market method (LCM) of inventory valuation The valuation method is available to all taxpayers other than those using LIFO valuation. It is applied to each separate item in the inventory.

Marginal tax rate The tax that is applied to an incremental amount of taxable income that is added to the tax base. This rate can be used to measure the tax effect of a proposed transaction. Currently, the highest marginal tax rate for individuals is 39.6%.

Market value This term refers to replacement cost under the lower of cost or market inventory method. That is, it is the price at which the taxpayer can replace the goods in question. See also Fair market value.

Material participation The level of participation by a taxpayer in an activity that determines whether the activity is either passive or active. If a taxpayer does not meet the material participation requirements, the activity is treated as a passive activity.

Medical expense deduction Unreimbursed medical expenses incurred for medical procedures or treatments that are (1) legal in the locality in which they are performed and (2) incurred for the purpose of alleviating a physical or mental defect or illness that affects the body's structure or function are deductible from AGI. Out-of-pocket travel costs incurred while en route to a medical facility, certain capital expenditures affecting the sick person, premiums for medical insurance, and in-patient hospital care are also deductible. Certain restrictions and limitations apply to this deduction.

Memorandum decision Decision issued by the Tax Court. They deal with factual variations on matters which were decided in earlier cases.

Method of accounting See Accounting method.

Miscellaneous itemized deductions Certain unreimbursed employee expenses (e.g., required uniforms, travel, entertainment, and so on) fall into this category. Miscellaneous itemized deductions also include certain investment expenses, appraisal fees for charitable contributions and fees for tax return preparation. The nature of the deduction depends on whether the taxpayer is an employee or a self-employed individual.

Modified percentage of completion method A variation of the regular percentage of completion method where an election may be made to defer reporting profit from a long-term contract until at least 10% of the estimated total cost has been incurred.

Moving expense Expenses incurred in relation to employment-related job transfers.

Necessary expense Expense that is deductible because it is appropriate and helpful in the taxpayer's business. Such expenses must also qualify as ordinary.

Net investment income The excess of the taxpayer's investment income over his investment expenses. See also Investment income.

Net operating loss (NOL) A net operating loss occurs when business expenses exceed business income for any taxable year. Such losses may be carried back three years or carried forward 15 years to a year in which the taxpayer has taxable income. Loss must be carried back first and must be deducted from years in chronological order.

Net Present Value (NPV) Method used by investment analysts to determine the anticipated return on an investment. This method uses a fixed discount rate to compute the net present value of future cash flows.

NOL See Net operating loss.

Net unearned income The amount of unearned income of a child under age 14 that is taxed at the child's parent's top marginal tax rate.

Nonaccountable plan A type of employee reimbursement plan that does not meet either of the two tests for an accountable plan (see accountable plan). Under a nonaccountable plan, reimbursements are included in the employee's gross income and the expenses are deductible by the employee, subject to the 2% of AGI floor.

Nonbusiness bad debt See Bad debt.

Noncontributory pension plan Only the employer makes contributions to this type of pension plan.

Nonliquidating distribution Distribution that reduces but does not eliminate, a partner's partnership interest. Such distributions are generally treated as tax-free returns of capital.

Nonqualified deferred compensation plan Type of plan used by employer to provide incentives or supplementary retirement benefits for executives. Such plans are not subject to the nondiscrimination and vesting rules.

Nonqualified stock option Stock option that does not meet the requirements for an incentive stock option.

Nonrefundable credit Allowances, such as the dependent child care credit, that have been created for various social, economic, and political reasons. The tax credits in this category do not result from payments made to the government in advance. Thus, they can be deducted from the tax, but they are not payable to the taxpayer in situations where the credit exceeds the tax.

NPV See Net Present Value

Office audit procedure IRS audit of a specific item on an individual's tax return. An office audit takes place at the IRS branch office.

Open-fact situation A situation that has not yet occurred. That is, one for which the facts and events are still controllable and can be planned for.

Ordinary expense An expense that is deductible because it is reasonable in amount and bears a reasonable and proximate relationship to the income-producing activity or property.

Ordinary income property For purposes of the charitable contribution deduction, any property that would result in the recognition of ordinary income if the property were sold. Such property includes inventory, works of art or manuscripts created by the taxpayer, capital assets that have been held for one year or less, and Section 1231 property that results in ordinary income due to depreciation recapture.

Organizational expenditures The amortizable legal, accounting, filing, and other fees incidental to organizing a partnership or a corporation.

Parent-subsidiary controlled group To qualify, a common parent must own at least 80% of the stock of at least one subsidiary corporation and at least 80% of each other component member of the controlled group must be owned by other members of the controlled group.

Partnership Syndicate, group pool, joint venture, or other unincorporated organization which carries on a business or financial operation or venture.

Partnership interest The capital and/or profits interest in a partnership received in exchange for a contribution of properties or services (e.g., money or business equipment). The nature of a partnership interest is similar to that of corporate stock.

Passive activity To define what constitutes a passive activity for the purpose of applying the passive loss rules, it is necessary to (1) identify what constitutes an activity and (2) determine whether the taxpayer has materially participated in the activity. Temp. Reg. Sec. 1.469-4T contains detailed rules for making these determinations.

Passive income Income from an activity that does not require the taxpayer's material involvement or participation. Thus, income from tax shelters and rental activities fall into the category.

Passive loss Loss generated from a passive activity. Such losses are computed separately. They may be used to offset income from other passive activities, but may not be used to offset either active or portfolio income.

Percentage depletion method Depletion method for assets such as oil and gas that is equal to a specified percentage times the gross income from the property but which may not exceed 100% of the taxable income before depletion is deducted. Lease bonuses, advance royalties, and other amounts payable without regard to production may not be included in the calcualtion. This method is only available to small oil and gas producers and royalty owners and for certain mineral properties.

Percentage of completion method of accounting Accounting method generally used for long-term contracts under which income is reported in proportion to the amount of work that has been completed in a given year.

Personal exemption A deduction in an amount mandated by Congress. The amount for 1997 ($2,550 for 1996) is $2,650. For years after 1989 the amount is adjusted for increases in the cost of living. An additional exemption is allowed for each individual who is a dependent. Personal and dependency exemptions are phased out for high income taxpayers.

Personal holding company (PHC) A closely held corporation (1) that is owned by a five or fewer shareholders who own more than 50% of the corporation's outstanding stock at any time during the last half of its taxable year and (2) whose PHC income equals at least 60% of the corporation's adjusted gross income for the tax year. Certain corporations (e.g., S corporations) are exempt from this definition.

Personal holding company tax This tax is equal to 39.6% of the undistributed personal holding company income. It is intended to prevent closely held companies from converting an operating company into a nonoperating investment company.

Personal interest All interest other than active business interest, investment interest, interest incurred in a passive activity, qualified residence interest, and interest incurred when paying the estate tax on an installment basis. Personal interest is currently treated as a nondeductible personal expenditure. See also Interest.

Personal property Property that is other than real property, such as equipment.

Personal service corporation (PSC) A regular C corporation whose principal activity is the performance of personal services that are substantially performed by owner-employees who own more than 10% of the value of the corporation's stock.

PHC See Personal holding company.

Portfolio income Dividends, interest, annuities, and royalties not derived in the ordinary course of business. Gains and losses on property that produces portfolio income are included in such income.

Primary cite The highest level official reporter which reports a particular case is called the primary cite.

Principal partner A partner owning 5% or more of the partnership profits and capital interests.

Principal residence The residence that the taxpayer occupies most of the time.

Private activity bond Obligation issued by a state of local government to finance nongovernmental activities (e.g., a sports arena).

Private Letter Ruling See Letter Ruling

Production of income An activity of the taxpayer that is generally related to investment activities or matters connected with the determination of any tax. Deductions related to production of income activities are usually *from AGI*, although is some instances they may be *for AGI*, such as expenses connected with rental property.

Profit-sharing plan A qualified defined benefit plan which may be established in lieu of or in addition to a qualified pension plan. Contributions to a profit-sharing plan are usually based upon profits. Incidental benefits may or may not be included. In addition, the plan must meet certain requirements concerning determination of the amount and timing of the employer's contribution, how the employee wants to receive the employer's contribution, vesting, and forfeitures.

Progressive rate Tax that increases as the taxpayer's taxable income increases. The U.S. income tax is an example of a progressive tax.

Property settlement The division of property between spouses upon their separation or divorce.

Property tax Federal, state, or local tax levied on real and/or personal property (e.g., securities, a personal automobile).

Proportional tax A method of taxation under which the tax rate is the same for all taxpayers regardless of their income. State and local sales taxes are examples of this form of tax.

Proposed Regulations Issued following changes in the tax law. May or may not be amended after hearings are conducted and comments received. Proposed regulations are not binding on taxpayers.

PSC See Personal service corporation.

Qualified pension plan Pension plan that includes (1) systematic and definite payments made to a pension trust based upon actuarial methods and (2) usually provides for incidental benefits such as disability, or medical insurance benefits.

Qualified plan award Employee achievement awards given under a written plan or program that does not discriminate in favor of highly compensated employees. Such awards must be in the form of tangible personal property other than cash and be worth no more than $1,600.

Qualified residence interest Interest on an indebtedness which is secured by the taxpayer's qualified residence when it is paid or accrued. A taxpayer may have two qualified residences: a principal residence and a residence that he has personally used more than the greater of 14 days or 10% of the rental days during the year.

Readily ascertainable fair market value The fair market value of nonqualified stock options can be readily ascertained where the option is traded on an established options exchange.

Real property Property that is land or any structure permanently attached to the land, such as buildings.

Realized gain or loss The gain or loss computed by taking the amount realized from a sale of property and subtracting the property's adjusted basis.

Recapture provision A provision requiring recapture of earlier alimony payments as ordinary income by the payor if the payments decline sharply in either the second or third year.

Recovery of basis doctrine Rule that allows taxpayers to recover the basis of an asset without being taxed. Such amounts are considered a return of capital.

Refundable credit See Tax credit.

Regressive tax A form of taxation under which the tax rate decreases as the tax base (e.g., income) increases.

Regular corporation See C corporation.

Regular decision Tax Court decision that is issued on a particular issue for the first time.

Regulation See Treasury Regulation

Replacement property Property that is acquired to replace converted property in order to retain nonrecognition of gain status. Such property must generally be functionally the same as the converted property. For example, a business machine must be replaced with a similar business machine. There are exceptions to this rule: The taxpayer-use test applies to the involuntary conversion of rental property owned by an investor; condemnations of real property held for business or investment use may be replaced by like-kind property.

Residential rental property Property from which at least 80% of the gross rental income is rental from dwelling units. Residential units include manufactured homes that are used for rental purposes, but not hotels, motels, or other establishments for transient use.

Restricted property plan Such plans are used to attract and retain key executives by giving them an ownership interest in the corporation. The income recognition rules contained in Sec. 83 govern this type of plan.

Revenue Amounts received by the taxpayer from any source. It includes both taxable and nontaxable amounts and items that are a return of capital. Although closely related to income or gross income, differences between these items do exist.

Revenue Procedure Issued by the national office of the IRS, Revenue Procedures reflect the IRS' position on compliance relating to tax preparation issues. Revenue Procedures, which are published in the Cumulative Bulletin, have less weight than Treasury Regulations.

Revenue Ruling Issued by the national office of the IRS, Revenue Rulings reflect the IRS's interpretation of a narrow tax issue. Revenue Rulings, which are published in the Cumulative Bulletin, have less weight than the Treasury Regulations.

Royalties Ordinary income arising from amounts paid for the right to use property that belongs to another and is transferred for valuable consideration (e.g., a patent right where substantially all rights are transferred).

Sale A transaction where one receives cash and/or the equivalent of cash, including the assumption of debt, in exchange for an asset.

Sales tax State or local tax on purchases. Generally, food items and medicines are exempt from such tax.

S corporation Small business corporations may elect S corporation status if they meet the 35-shareholer limitation, the type of shareholder restrictions, and the one class of stock restriction. Taxation of such corporations parallels the tax rules that apply to partnerships.

Secondary cite Citation to secondary source (i.e., unofficial reporter).

Section 401(k) plan Type of plan that is often used to supplement a company's regular qualified pension and profit-sharing plan. Such plans, which generally contain a salary reduction feature, permit the employer to receive either cash or an equivalent contribution to the company's profit-sharing plan. The amount of the contribution is limited.

Section 1231 property Real or depreciable property that is (1) held for more than one year and (2) used in a trade or business. Certain property, such as inventory, U.S. government publications, copyrights, literary, musical, or artistic compositions, and letters, are excluded from this definition.

Section 1245 property Certain property subject to depreciation and, in some cases, amortization. Depreciable personal property such as equipment is Section 1245 property. However, most real property is not.

Section 1250 property Any real property that (1) is not Section 1245 property and (2) is subject to a depreciation allowance.

Security A long-term debt obligation. Long-term is generally defined as 10 years or more.

Separate property All property that is owned before marriage and any gifts or inheritances acquired after marriage are separate property. This distinction depends on the state of residence. However, it is possible even in community property states.

Severance damages Compensation for a decline in the value of the property remaining after part of the taxpayer's property is condemned. The IRS considers such damages analogous to the proceeds from property insurance.

Shifting income The process of transferring income from one family member to another. Methods for shifting income include gifts of stock or bonds to family members who are in lower tax brackets.

Short sale An investment activity where an investor sells a security at its current price and purchases the same security at a future date. A short sale is generally used when the price of a security is expected to decline.

Short-term capital gain (STCG) Gain realized on the sale or exchange of a capital asset held for one year or less.

Short-term capital loss (STCL) Loss realized on the sale or exchange of a capital asset held for one year or less.

Simplified LIFO method This method of inventory valuation allows taxpayers to use a single LIFO pool rather than multiple pools. See also LIFO method.

Small cases procedure When $10,000 or less is in question for a particular year, the taxpayer may opt to have the case heard by a special commissioner rather than the regular Tax Court. The decision of the commissioner cannot be appealed.

Social security benefits These benefits include (1) the basic monthly retirement and disability benefits paid under social security and (2) tier-one railroad retirement benefits.

Sole proprietorship Form of business entity owned by an individual who reports all items of income, expense, on his individual return on Schedule C.

Specific write-off method of accounting Method of accounting used for bad debts. Under this method, the taxpayer deducts each bad debt individually as it becomes worthless. This is the only allowable accounting method for bad debts arising after 1986.

Splitting income The process of creating additional taxable entities, especially corporations, in order to reduce an individual's effective tax rate.

Standard deduction A floor amount set by Congress to simplify the tax computation. It is used by taxpayers who do not have enough deductions to itemize. The amount of the deduction varies according to the taxpayer's filing status, age, and vision. Taxpayers who use this standard deduction are not required to keep records.

State corporate income tax See Franchise tax.

Statements on Responsibilities in Tax Practice (SRTP) Ethical guidelines of the AICPA-Federal Tax Division for CPAs to promote high standards of tax practice.

Statute of Limitations A period of time as provided by law in which a taxpayer's return may not be changed either by the IRS or the taxpayer. The Statute of Limitations is generally three years from the later of the date the tax return is filed or its due date. There is no Statute of Limitations for a fraudulent return.

Stock bonus plan A special type of defined benefit plan under which the employer's stock is contributed to a trust. The stock is then allocated and distributed to the participants. See also Employee stock ownership plan.

Stock dividend A dividend paid in the form of stock in the corporation issuing the dividend.

Stock option plan This category includes incentive stock options and nonqualified

Stock option arrangements. Such plans are used to attract and retain key employees.

Substance-over-form doctrine Judicial weighing of a transaction's economic substance more heavily than its legal form.

Surviving spouse A special filing status available to widows and widowers who file a joint return for the year his or her spouse dies and for the following two years. The surviving spouse may not have remarried, must be a U.S. citizen or resident, have qualified to file a joint return for the year, and must have at least one dependent child living at home during the year.

Syndication fees The nonamortizable fees (e.g., brokerage and registration fees) incurred to promote and market partnership interests. Such fees are generally associated with tax-sheltered limited partnership interests.

Tangible property Property that has physical substance, such as land, buildings, natural resources, equipment, etc.

Tax A mandatory assessment levied under the authority of a political entity for the purpose of raising revenue to be used for public or governmental purposes. Such taxes may be levied by the federal, state, or local government.

Taxable income For individuals, taxable income is adjusted gross income reduced by deductions from adjusted gross income.

Tax base The amount to which the tax rate is applied to determine the tax due. For income tax purposes, the tax base is taxable income.

Tax benefit rule Recovery of an amount in a subsequent year that produced a tax benefit in a prior year and is thus taxable to the recipient.

Tax credit Amount that can be deducted from the gross tax to arrive at the net tax due or refund due. Prepaid amounts, that is, amounts paid to the government during the year, are tax credits. Such prepaid amounts are often referred to as "refundable credits."

Tax Deferred Bonds Bonds on which the interest is not subject to current taxation but is deferred to a future period of time, such as Series EE U.S. Savings Bonds.

Tax Exempt Bonds Bonds on which the interest is completely exempt from federal income taxation, such as state and municipal bonds.

Tax law The tax law is comprised of the Internal Revenue Code, administrative and judicial interpretations, and the committee reports issued by the Congressional committees involved in the legislative process.

Taxpayer Compliance Measurement Program (TCMP) A stratified random sample used to select tax returns for audit. The program is intended to test the extent to which taxpayers are in compliance with the law.

Taxpayer-use test A test used to determine whether property is considered similar or related in service or use for purposes of involuntary conversions of property. This test is used by owner-investors (as opposed to owner-users) of property.

Tax research Search for the best possible solution to a problem involving either a proposed or completed transaction.

Tax shelter Passive activity which may lack economic substance other than creating tax deductions and credits that enable taxpayers to reduce or eliminate the income tax liability from their regular business activities. Section 469 restricts the current use of deductions and credits arising from passive activities.

Tax year See Accounting period.

TCMP See Taxpayer Compliance Measurement Program.

Technical Advice Memorandum Such memoranda are administrative interpretations issued in the form of letter ruling. Taxpayers may request them if they need guidance about the tax treatment of complicated technical matters which are being audited.

Temporary Regulations Temporary Regulations are Treasury Regulations that are issued to provide guidance for taxpayers pending the issuance of the final regulations. They are binding upon taxpayers. Temporary Regulations are also required to be issued as proposed regulations and must expire within three years.

Testamentary gift Transfer of property made at the death of the donor (i.e., bequests, devises, and inheritances).

Theft loss Loss of business, investment, or personal-use property due to crimes such as, but not limited to, larceny, embezzlement, robbery, extortion, blackmail, or kidnapping for ransom. Such losses are deductible from AGI, subject to certain limitations.

Total economic income The amount of the taxpayer's income, including exclusions and deductions from the tax base (e.g., tax-exempt bonds), is categorized as total economic income.

Trade or business A business activity of the taxpayer in which deductions are allowed as *for AGI* deductions.

Transportation expense The deductibility of this type of expense depends upon whether it is trade- or business-related,

whether it is related to the production of income, whether the expense is employment related and therefore subject to the 2% nondeductible floor for miscellaneous itemized deductions. Commuting expenses are nondeductible. See also Travel expense.

Travel expense Such expenses include transportation, meals, and lodging incurred in the pursuit of a trade, business, or employment-related activity. There are limitations and restrictions on the deductibility of these expenses. See also Transportation expense.

Treasury bill Short-term (i.e., 90-day) obligation that is issued by the government at a discount from the maturity amount. The difference between the issue price and the maturity amount represents the interest income.

Treasury Regulation The principal administrative source of the federal tax law, these Regulations reflect the Treasury and the IRS's interpretation of the Internal Revenue Code. They may be either legislative or interpretative and they may be issued in either proposed, temporary, or final form.

Unfunded deferred compensation plan This type of plan is used for highly-compensated employees who wish to defer the recognition of income until future periods. Funding is generally accomplished through an escrow account for the employee's benefit.

Uniform Capitalization rules (UNICAP) The requirements under the tax law for determining inventory cost. Under UNICAP certain indirect overhead costs are required to be included in inventory for tax purposes which are generally not included for financial accounting.

Unrelated use property Capital gain property which is also tangible personal property and which is contributed to a public charity for a use that is unrelated to the charity's function. The contribution deduction (from AGI) for such property is equal to the property's fair market value minus the capital gain that would be recognized if the property was sold at that value.

Unreported decision District Court decisions that are not officially reported in the Federal Supplement. Such decisions may be reported in secondary reporters that report only tax-related cases.

U.S. Treasury Bill See Treasury bill.

Vertical equity A concept in taxation that provides that the incidence of taxation should be borne by taxpayers who have the ability to pay the tax. Taxpayers who are not similarly-situated should be treated differently under the tax law.

Wash sale A wash sale results when the taxpayer (1) sells stock or securities and (2) purchases substantially identical stock or securities within the 61-day period extending from 30 days before the date of sale to 30 days after the date of sale.

Wealth transfer tax A tax imposed upon the value of property transferred during one's lifetime (i.e., a gift tax) or upon the death of the transferor (i.e., an esate tax). The tax is imposed upon the transferor of property or upon the estate.

Writ of certiorari A petition to the U.S. Supreme court to request that the Court agree to hear a case. A writ of certiorari is requested by the party (IRS or taxpayer) that lost at the Court of Appeals level.

Zero coupon bond Bond that is issued at a cost that is substantially less than the current market rate because no interest payments are made. The original issue discount (OID) must be amortized over the term of the bond by investors using the constant rate method. Such bonds offer cash-flow advantages to corporate issuers since no cash outlay for interest is required until the bonds mature.

AICPA STATEMENTS ON RESPONSIBILITIES IN TAX PRACTICE NOS. 1–8 (1991 REVISION)

STATEMENT NO. 1
TAX RETURN POSITIONS

INTRODUCTION

.01 This statement sets forth the standards a CPA should follow in recommending tax return positions and in preparing or signing tax returns including claims for refunds. For this purpose, a "tax return position" is (1) a position reflected on the tax return as to which the client has been specifically advised by the CPA or (2) a position as to which the CPA has knowledge of all material facts and, on the basis of those facts, has concluded that the position is appropriate.

STATEMENT

.02 With respect to tax return positions, a CPA should comply with the following standards:
  a. A CPA should not recommend to a client that a position be taken with respect to the tax treatment of any item on a return unless the CPA has a good faith belief that the position has a realistic possibility of being sustained administratively or judicially on its merits if challenged.
  b. A CPA should not prepare or sign a return as an income tax return preparer if the CPA knows that the return takes a position that the CPA could not recommend under the standard expressed in paragraph .02a.
  c. Notwithstanding paragraphs .02a and .02b, a CPA may recommend a position that the CPA concludes is not frivolous so long as the position is adequately disclosed on the return or claim for refund.
  d. In recommending certain tax return positions and in signing a return on which a tax return position is taken, a CPA should, where relevant, advise the client as to the potential penalty consequences of the recommended tax return position and the opportunity, if any, to avoid such penalties through disclosure.

.03 The CPA should not recommend a tax return position that—
  a. Exploits the Internal Revenue Service (IRS) audit selection process; or
  b. Serves as a mere "arguing" position advanced solely to obtain leverage in the bargaining process of settlement negotiation with the Internal Revenue Service.

.04 A CPA has both the right and responsibility to be an advocate for the client with respect to any positions satisfying the aforementioned standards.

EXPLANATION

.05 Our self-assessment tax system can only function effectively if taxpayers report their income on a tax return that is true, correct, and complete. A tax return is primarily a taxpayer's representation of facts, and the taxpayer has the final responsibility for positions taken on the return.

.06 CPAs have a duty to the tax system as well as to their clients. However, it is well-established that the taxpayer has no obligation to pay more taxes than are legally owed, and the CPA has a duty to the client to assist in achieving that result. The aforementioned standards will guide the CPA in meeting responsibilities to the tax system and to clients.

.07 The standards suggested herein require that a CPA in good faith believe that the position is warranted in existing law or can be supported by a good faith argument for an extension, modification, or reversal of existing law. For example, the CPA may reach such a conclusion on the basis of well-reasoned articles, treatises, IRS General Counsel Memoranda, a General Explanation of a Revenue Act prepared by the staff of the Joint Committee on Taxation and Internal Revenue Service written determinations (for example, private letter rulings), whether or not such sources are treated as "authority" under section 6661. A position would meet these standards even though, for example, it is later abandoned due to practical or procedural aspects of an IRS administrative hearing or in the litigation process.

.08 Where the CPA has a good faith belief that more than one position meets the standards suggested herein, the CPA's advice concerning alternative acceptable positions may include a discussion of the likelihood that each such position might or might not cause the client's tax return to be examined and whether the position would be challenged in an examination.

.09 In some cases, a CPA may conclude that a position is not warranted under the standard set forth in the preceding paragraph, .02a. A client may, however, still wish to take such a tax return position. Under such circumstances, the client should have the opportunity to make such an assertion, and the CPA should be able to prepare and sign the return provided the the position is adequately disclosed on the return or claim for refund and the position is not frivolous. A "frivolous" position is one which is knowingly advanced in bad faith and is patently improper.

.10 The CPA's determination of whether information is adequately disclosed by the client is based on the facts and circumstances of the particular case. No detailed rules have been formulated, for purposes of this statement, to prescribe the manner in which information should be disclosed.

.11 Where the particular facts and circumstances lead the CPA to believe that a taxpayer penalty might be asserted, the CPA should so advise the client and should discuss with the client issues related to disclosure on the tax return. Although disclosure is not required if the position meets the standard in paragraph .02a, the CPA may nevertheless recommend that a client disclose a position. Disclosure should be considered when the CPA believes it would mitigate the likelihood of claims of taxpayer penalties under the Internal Revenue Code or would avoid the possible application of the six-year statutory period for assessment under section 6501(e). Although the CPA should advise the client with respect to disclosure, it is the client's responsibility to decide whether and how to disclose.

TAX RETURN POSITIONS: TAX PRACTICE INTERPRETATION OF STATEMENT NO. 1

1. REALISTIC POSSIBILITY STANDARD BACKGROUND

.01 The AICPA Tax Division issues Statements on Responsibilities in Tax Practice (SRTPs). The primary purpose of these advisory statements on appropriate standards of tax practice is educational. This interpretation does not have the force of authority, in contrast, for example, to the regulations contained in Treasury Department Circular 230 or the preparer penalty provisions of the Internal Revenue Code.

.02 SRTP No. 1, *Tax Return Positions*, contains the standards a CPA should follow in recommending tax return positions and in preparing or signing tax returns and claims for refunds. In general, a CPA should have "a good-faith belief that the [tax return] position [being recommended] has a realistic possibility of being sustained administratively or judicially on its merits if challenged" (see SRTP No. 1, paragraph .02a). This is referred to here as the "realistic possibility standard." If a CPA concludes that a tax return position does not meet the realistic possibility standard, the CPA may still recommend the position to the client or, if the position is not frivolous and is adequately disclosed on the tax return or claim for refund, the CPA may prepare and sign a return containing the position.

.03 A "frivolous" position is one which is knowingly advanced in bad faith and is patently improper (see SRTP No. 1, paragraph .09). The CPA's determination of whether information is adequately disclosed on the client's tax return or claim for refund is based on the facts and circumstances of the particular case (see SRTP No. 1, paragraph .10).

.04 If the CPA believes there is a possibility that a tax return position might result in penalties being asserted against the client, the CPA should so advise the client and should discuss with the client the opportunity, if any, of avoiding such penalties through disclosure (see SRTP No. 1, paragraph .11).

GENERAL INTERPRETATION

.05 To meet the realistic possibility standard, a CPA should have a good-faith belief that the position is warranted in existing law or can be supported by a good faith argument for an extension, modification, or reversal of existing law through the administrative or judicial process. The CPA should have an honest belief that the position meets the realistic possibility standard. Such a belief must be based on sound interpretations of the tax law. A CPA should not take into account the likelihood of audit or detection in determining whether this standard is met (see SRTP No. 1, paragraph .03a).

.06 The realistic possibility standard cannot be expressed in terms of percentage odds. The realistic possibility standard is less stringent than the "substantial authority" and the "more likely than not" standards that apply under the Internal Revenue Code to substantial understatements of liability by taxpayers. It is more strict than the "reasonable basis" standard under regulations issued prior to the Revenue Reconciliation Act of 1989.

.07 In determining whether a tax return position meets the realistic possibility standard, a CPA may rely on authorities in addition to those evaluated when determining whether substantial authority exists. Accordingly, CPAs may rely on well-reasoned treatises, articles in recognized professional tax publications, and other reference tools and sources of tax analysis commonly used by tax advisors and preparers of returns.

.08 In determining whether a realistic possibility exists, the CPA should do all of the following.[1]

1. Establish relevant background facts.
2. Distill the appropriate questions from those facts.
3. Search for authoritative answers to those questions.
4. Resolve the questions by weighing the authorities uncovered by that search.
5. Arrive at a conclusion supported by the authorities.

.09 The CPA should consider the weight of each authority in order to conclude whether a position meets the realistic possibility standard. In determining the weight of an authority, the CPA should consider its persuasiveness, relevance, and source. Thus, the type of authority is a significant factor. Other important factors include whether the facts stated by the authority are distinguishable from those of the client and whether the authority contains an analysis of the issue or merely states a conclusion.

.10 The realistic possibility standard may be met despite the absence of certain types of authority. For example, a CPA may conclude that the realistic possibility standard is met when the position is supported only by a well-reasoned construction of the applicable statutory provision.

.11 In determining whether the realistic possibility standard has been met, the extent of research required is left to the judgment of the CPA with respect to all the facts and circumstances known to the CPA. The CPA may conclude that more than one position meets the realistic possibility standard.

SPECIFIC ILLUSTRATIONS

.12 The following illustrations deal with general fact patterns. Accordingly, the application of the guidance discussed above to variances in such general facts or to particular facts or circumstances may lead to different conclusions. In each illustration there is no authority other than that indicated.

Illustration 1. The CPA's client has engaged in a transaction that is adversely affected by a new statutory provision. Prior law supports a position favorable to the client. The client believes, and the CPA concurs, that the new statute is inequitable as applied to the client's situation. The statute is clearly drafted and unambiguous. The committee reports discussing the new statute contain general comments that do not specifically address the client's situation.

The CPA should recommend the return position supported by the new statute. A position contrary to a clear, unambiguous statute would ordinarily be considered a frivolous position.

Illustration 2. The facts are the same as in illustration 1 except that the committee reports discussing the new statute specifically address the client's situation and take a position favorable to the client.

In a case where the statute is clearly and unambiguously against the taxpayer's position but a contrary position exists based on committee reports specifically addressing the client's situation, a return position based on either the statutory language or the legislative history satisfies the realistic possibility standard.

Illustration 3. The facts are the same as in illustration 1 except that the committee reports can be interpreted to provide some evidence or authority in support of the taxpayer's position; however, the legislative history does not specifically address the situation.

In a case where the statute is clear and unambiguous, a contrary position based on an interpretation of committee reports that do not explicitly address the client's situation does not meet the realistic possibility standard. However, since the committee reports provide some support or evidence for the taxpayer's position, such a return position is not frivolous. The CPA may recommend the position to the client if it is adequately disclosed on the tax return.

Illustration 4. A client is faced with an issue involving the interpretation of a new statute. Following its passage, the statute was widely recognized to contain a drafting error, and a technical correction proposal has been introduced. The IRS issues an announcement indicating how it will administer the provision. The IRS pronouncement interprets the statute in accordance with the proposed technical correction.

Return positions based on either the existing statutory language or the IRS pronouncement satisfy the realistic possibility standard.

Illustration 5. The facts are the same as in illustration 4 except that no IRS pronouncement has been issued.

In the absence of an IRS pronouncement interpreting the statute in accordance with the technical correction, only a return position based on the existing statutory language will meet the realistic possibility standard. A return position based on the proposed technical correction may be recommended if it is adequately disclosed, since it is not frivolous.

Illustration 6. A client is seeking advice from a CPA regarding a recently amended Internal Revenue Code (Code) section. The CPA has reviewed the Code section, committee reports that specifically address the issue, and a recently published IRS

---

[1] See Ray M. Sommerfeld, et al., *Tax Research Techniques*, 3d rev. ed. (New York: AICPA, 1989), for a discussion of this process.

Notice. The CPA has concluded in good faith that, based on the Code section and the committee reports, the IRS's position as stated in the Notice does not reflect congressional intent.

The CPA may recommend the position supported by the Internal Revenue Code section and the committee reports since it meets the realistic possibility standard.

Illustration 7. The facts are the same as in illustration 6 except that the IRS pronouncement is a temporary regulation.

In determining whether the position meets the realistic possibility standard, the CPA should determine the weight to be given the regulation by analyzing factors such as whether the regulation is legislative, interpretative, or inconsistent with the statute. If the CPA concludes the position does not meet the realistic possibility standard, the position may nevertheless be recommended if it is adequately disclosed, since it is not frivolous.

Illustration 8. A tax form published by the IRS is incorrect, but completion of the form as published provides a benefit to the client. The CPA knows that the IRS has published an announcement acknowledging the error.

In these circumstances, a return position in accordance with the published form is a frivolous position.

Illustration 9. The client wants to take a position that the CPA has concluded is frivolous. The client maintains that even if the return is examined by the IRS, the issue will not be raised.

The CPA should not consider the likelihood of audit or detection when determining whether the realistic possibility standard has been met. The CPA should not prepare or sign a return that contains a frivolous position even if it is disclosed.

Illustration 10. Congress passes a statute requiring the capitalization of certain expenditures. The client believes, and the CPA concurs, that in order to comply fully, the client will need to acquire new computer hardware and software and implement a number of new accounting procedures. The client and the CPA agree that the costs of full compliance will be significantly greater than the resulting increase in tax due under the new provision. Because of these cost considerations, the client makes no effort to comply. The client wants the CPA to prepare and sign a return on which the new requirement is simply ignored.

The return position desired by the client is frivolous, and the CPA should neither prepare nor sign the return.

Illustration 11. The facts are the same as in illustration 10 except that the client has made a good-faith effort to comply with the law by calculating an estimate of expenditures to be capitalized under the new provision.

In this situation, the realistic possibility standard has been met. When using estimates in the preparation of a return, the CPA should refer to SRTP No. 4, *Use of Estimates.*

Illustration 12. On a given issue, the CPA has located and weighed two authorities. The IRS has published its clearly enunciated position in a Revenue Ruling. A court opinion is favorable to the client. The CPA has considered the source of both authorities and has concluded that both are persuasive and relevant.

The realistic possibility standard is met by either position.

Illustration 13. A tax statute is silent on the treatment of an item under the statute. However, the committee reports explaining the statute direct the IRS to issue regulations that will require specified treatment of this item. No regulations have been issued at the time the CPA must recommend a position on the tax treatment of the item.

The CPA may recommend the position supported by the committee reports, since it meets the realistic possibility standard.

Illustration 14. The client wants to take a position that the CPA concludes meets the realistic possibility standard based on an assumption regarding an underlying nontax legal issue. The CPA recommends that the client seek advice from its legal counsel, and the client's attorney gives an opinion on the nontax legal issue.

A legal opinion on a nontax legal issue may, in general, be relied upon by a CPA. The CPA must, however, use professional judgment when relying on a legal opinion. If, on its face, the opinion of the client's attorney appears to be unreasonable, unsubstantiated, or unwarranted, the CPA should consult his or her attorney before relying on the opinion.

Illustration 15. The client has obtained from its attorney an opinion on the tax treatment of an item and requests that the CPA rely on the opinion.

The authorities on which a CPA may rely include well-reasoned sources of tax analysis. If the CPA is satisfied as to the source, relevance, and persuasiveness of the legal opinion, the CPA may rely on that opinion when determining whether the realistic possibility standard has been met.

STATEMENT NO. 2 ANSWERS TO QUESTIONS ON RETURNS

INTRODUCTION

.01 This statement considers whether a CPA may sign the preparer's declaration on a tax return where one or more questions on the return have not been answered. The term "questions" includes requests for information on the return, in the instructions, or in the regulations, whether or not stated in the form of a question.

STATEMENT

.02 A CPA should make a reasonable effort to obtain from the client, and provide, appropriate answers to all questions on a tax return before signing as pre-parer.

EXPLANATION

.03 It is recognized that the questions on tax returns are not of uniform importance, and often they are not applicable to the particular taxpayer. Nevertheless, aside from administrative convenience to the Internal Revenue Service, there are at least two considerations which dictate that a CPA should be satisfied that a reasonable effort has been made to provide appropriate answers to the questions on the return which are applicable to the taxpayer:

  a. A question may be of importance in determining taxable income or loss, or the tax liability shown on the return, in which circumstance the omission tends to detract from the quality of the return.

  b. The CPA must sign the preparer's declaration stating that the return is true, correct, and complete.

.04 While an effort should be made to provide an answer to each question on the return that is applicable to the taxpayer, reasonable grounds may exist for omitting an answer. For example, reasonable grounds may include the following:

  a. The information is not readily available and the answer is not significant in terms of taxable income or loss, or the tax liability shown on the return.

  b. Genuine uncertainty exists regarding the meaning of the question in relation to the particular return.

  c. The answer to the question is voluminous; in such cases, assurance should be given on the return that the data will be supplied upon examination.

.05 The fact that an answer to a question might prove disadvantageous to the client does not justify omitting an answer.

.06 Where reasonable grounds exist for omission of an answer to an applicable question, a CPA is not required to provide on the return an explanation of the reason for the omission. In this connection, the CPA should consider whether the omission of an answer to a question may cause the return to be deemed incomplete.

STATEMENT NO. 3
CERTAIN PROCEDURAL
ASPECTS OF PREPARING
RETURNS

INTRODUCTION

.01 This statement considers the responsibility of the CPA to examine or verify certain supporting data or to consider information related to another client when preparing a client's tax return.

STATEMENT

.02 In preparing or signing a return, the CPA may in good faith rely without verification upon information furnished by the client or by third parties. However, the CPA should not ignore the implications of information furnished and should make reasonable inquiries if the information furnished appears to be incorrect, incomplete, or inconsistent either on its face or on the basis of other facts known to the CPA. In this connection, the CPA should refer to the client's returns for prior years whenever feasible.

.03 Where the Internal Revenue Code or income tax regulations impose a condition to deductibility or other tax treatment of an item (such as taxpayer maintenance of books and records or substantiating documentation to support the reported deduction or tax treatment), the CPA should make appropriate inquiries to determine to his or her satisfaction whether such condition has been met.

.04 The individual CPA who is required to sign the return should consider information actually known to that CPA from the tax return of another client when preparing a tax return if the information is relevant to that tax return, its consideration is necessary to properly prepare that tax return, and use of such information does not violate any law or rule relating to confidentiality.

EXPLANATION

.05 The preparer's declaration on the income tax return states that the information contained therein is true, correct, and complete to the best of the preparer's knowledge and belief "based on all information of which preparer has any knowledge." This reference should be understood to relate to information furnished by the client or by third parties to the CPA in connection with the preparation of the return.

.06 The preparer's declaration does not require the CPA to examine or verify supporting data. However, a distinction should be made between (1) the need to either determine by inquiry that a specifically required condition (such as maintaining books and records or substantiating documentation) has been satisfied, or to obtain information when the material furnished appears to be incorrect or incomplete, and (2) the need for the CPA to examine underlying information. In fulfilling his or her obligation to exercise due diligence in preparing a return, the CPA ordinarily may rely on information furnished by the client unless it appears to be incorrect, incomplete, or inconsistent. Although the CPA has certain responsibilities in exercising due diligence in preparing a return, the client has ultimate responsibility for the contents of the return. Thus, where the client presents unsupported data in the form of lists of tax information, such as dividends and interest received, charitable contributions, and medical expenses, such information may be used in the preparation of a tax return without verification unless it appears to be incorrect, incomplete, or inconsistent either on its face or on the basis of other facts known to the CPA.

.07 Even though there is no requirement to examine underlying documentation, the CPA should encourage the client to provide supporting data where appropriate. For example, the CPA should encourage the client to submit underlying documents for use in tax return preparation to permit full consider-ation of income and deductions arising from security transactions and from pass-through entities such as estates, trusts, partnerships, and S corporations. This should reduce the possibility of misunderstanding, inadvertent errors, and administrative problems in the examination of returns by the Internal Revenue Service.

.08 The source of information provided to the CPA by a client for use in preparing the return is often a pass-through entity, such as a limited partnership, in which the client has an interest but is not involved in management. In some instances, it may be appropriate for the CPA to advise the client to ascertain the nature and amount of possible exposures to tax deficiencies, interest, and penalties, by contact with management of the pass-through entity. However, the CPA need not require the client to do so and may accept the information provided by the pass-through entity without further inquiry, unless there is reason to believe it is incorrect, incomplete, or inconsistent either on its face or on the basis of other facts known to the CPA.

.09 The CPA should make use of the client's prior years' returns in preparing the current return whenever feasible. Reference to prior returns and discussion with the client of prior year tax determinations should provide information as to the client's general tax status, avoid the omission or duplication of items, and afford a basis for the treatment of similar or related transactions. As with the examination of information supplied for the current year's return, the extent of comparison of the details of income and deduction between years depends upon the particular circumstances.

STATEMENT NO. 4
USE OF ESTIMATES

INTRODUCTION

.01 This statement considers the CPA's responsibility in connection with the CPA's use of the taxpayer's estimates in the preparation of a tax return. The CPA may advise on estimates used in the preparation of a tax return, but responsibility for estimated data is that of the client, who should provide the estimated data. Appraisals or valuations are not considered estimates for purposes of this statement.

STATEMENT

.02 A CPA may prepare tax returns involving the use of the taxpayer's estimates if it is impracticable to obtain exact data and the estimated amounts are reasonable under the facts and circumstances known to the CPA. When the taxpayer's estimates are used, they should be presented in such a manner as to avoid the implication of greater accuracy than exists.

EXPLANATION

.03 Accounting requires the exercise of judgment and in many instances the use of approximations based on judgment. The application of such accounting judgments, as long as not in conflict with methods set forth in the Internal Revenue Code, is acceptable and expected. These judgments are not estimates within the purview of this statement. For example, the income tax regulations provide that if all other conditions for accrual are met, the exact amount of income or expense need not be known or ascertained at year end if the amount can be determined with reasonable accuracy.

.04 In the case of transactions involving small expenditures, accuracy in recording some data may be difficult to achieve. Therefore, the use of estimates by the taxpayer in determining the amount to be deducted for such items may be appropriate.

.05 In other cases where all of the facts relating to a transaction are not accurately known, either because records are missing or because precise information is not available at the time the return must be filed, estimates of the missing data may be made by the taxpayer.

.06 Estimated amounts should not be presented in a manner which provides a misleading impression as to the degree of factual accuracy.

.07 Although specific disclosure that an estimate is used for an item in the return is not required in most instances, there are unusual circumstances where such disclosure is needed to avoid misleading the Internal Revenue Service regarding the degree of accuracy of the return. Some examples of unusual circumstances include the following:

a. The taxpayer has died or is ill at the time the return must be filed.

b. The taxpayer has not received a K-1 for a flow-through entity at the time the tax return is to be filed.

c. There is litigation pending (for example, a bankruptcy proceeding) which bears on the return.

d. Fire or computer failure destroyed the relevant records.

STATEMENT NO. 5 DEPARTURE FROM A POSITION PREVIOUSLY CONCLUDED IN AN ADMINISTRATIVE PROCEEDING OR COURT DECISION

INTRODUCTION

.01 This statement discusses whether a CPA may recommend a tax return position that departs from the treatment of an item as concluded in an administrative proceeding or a court decision with respect to a prior return of the taxpayer. For this purpose, a "tax return position" is (1) a position reflected on the tax return as to which the client has been specifically advised by the CPA, or (2) a position about which the CPA has knowledge of all material facts and, on the basis of those facts, has concluded that the position is appropriate.

.02 For purposes of this statement, "administrative proceeding" includes an examination by the Internal Revenue Service or an appeals conference relating to a return or a claim for refund.

.03 For purposes of this statement, "court decision" means a decision by any federal court having jurisdiction over tax matters.

STATEMENT

.04 The recommendation of a position to be taken concerning the tax treatment of an item in the preparation or signing of a tax return should be based upon the facts and the law as they are evaluated at the time the return is prepared or signed by the CPA. Unless the taxpayer is bound to a specified treatment in the later year, such as by a formal closing agreement, the treatment of an item as part of concluding an administrative proceeding or as part of a court decision does not restrict the CPA from recommending a different tax treatment in a later year's return. Therefore, if the CPA follows the standards in SRTP No. 1, the CPA may recommend a tax return position, prepare, or sign a tax return that departs from the treatment of an item as concluded in an administrative proceeding or a court decision with respect to a prior return of the taxpayer.

EXPLANATION

.05 A CPA usually will recommend a position with respect to the tax treatment of an item that is the same as was consented to by the taxpayer for a similar item as a result of an administrative proceeding or that was subject to a court decision concerning a prior year's return of the taxpayer. The question is whether the CPA is required to do so. Considerations include the following:

a. The Internal Revenue Service tends to act consistently with the manner in which an item was disposed of in a prior administrative proceeding, but is not bound to do so. Similarly, a taxpayer is not bound to follow the tax treatment of an item as consented to in an earlier administrative proceeding.

b. An unfavorable court decision does not prevent a taxpayer from taking a position contrary to the earlier court decision in a subsequent year.

c. The consent in an earlier administrative proceeding and the existence of an unfavorable court decision are factors that the CPA should consider in evaluating whether the standards in SRTP No. 1 are met.

d. The taxpayer's consent to the treatment in the administrative proceeding or the court's decision may have been caused by a lack of documentation, whereas supporting data for the later year is adequate.

e. The taxpayer may have yielded in the administrative proceeding for settlement purposes or not appealed the court decision even though the position met the standards in SRTP No. 1.

f. Court decisions, rulings, or other authorities that are more favorable to the taxpayer's current position may have developed since the prior administrative proceeding was concluded or the prior court decision was rendered.

STATEMENT NO. 6 KNOWLEDGE OF ERROR: RETURN PREPARATION

INTRODUCTION

.01 This statement considers the responsibility of a CPA who becomes aware of an error in a client's previously filed tax return or of the client's failure to file a required tax return. As used herein, the term "error" includes any position, omission, or method of accounting that, at the time the return is filed, fails to meet the standards set out in SRTP No. 1. The term "error" also includes a position taken on a prior year's return that no longer meets these standards due to legislation, judicial decisions, or administrative pronouncements having retroactive effect. However, an error does not include an item that has an insignificant effect on the client's tax liability.

.02 This statement applies whether or not the CPA prepared or signed the return that contains the error.

STATEMENT

.03 The CPA should inform the client promptly upon becoming aware of an error in a previously filed return or upon becoming aware of a client's failure to file a required return. The CPA should recommend the measures to be taken. Such recommendation may be given orally. The CPA is not obligated to inform the Internal Revenue Service, and the CPA may not do so without the client's permission, except where required by law.

.04 If the CPA is requested to prepare the current year's return and the client has not taken appropriate action to correct an error in a prior year's return, the CPA should consider whether to withdraw from preparing the return and whether to continue a professional relationship with the client. If the CPA does prepare such current year's return, the CPA should take reasonable steps to ensure that the error is not repeated.

EXPLANATION

.05 While performing services for a client, a CPA may become aware of an error in a previously filed return or may become aware that the client failed to file a required return. The CPA should advise the client of the error (as required by Treasury Department Circular 230) and the measures to be taken. It is the client's responsibility to decide whether to correct the error. In appropriate cases, particularly where it appears that the Internal Revenue Service might assert the charge of fraud or other criminal misconduct, the client should be advised to consult legal counsel before taking any action. In the event that the client does not correct an error, or agree to take the necessary steps to change from an erroneous method of accounting, the CPA should consider whether to continue a professional relationship with the client.[2]

.06 If the CPA decides to continue a professional relationship with the client and is requested to prepare a tax return for a year subsequent to that in which the error occurred, then the CPA should take reasonable steps to ensure that the error is not repeated. If a CPA learns the client is using an erroneous method of accounting, when it is past the due date to request IRS permission to change to a method meeting the standards of SRTP No. 1, the CPA may sign a return for the current year, providing the return includes appropriate disclosure of the use of the erroneous method.

.07 Whether an error has no more than an insignificant effect on the client's tax liability is left to the judgment of the individual CPA based on all the facts and circumstances known to the CPA. In judging whether an erroneous method of accounting has more than an insignificant effect, the CPA should consider the method's cumulative effect and its effect on the current year's return.

.08 Where the CPA becomes aware of the error during an engagement which does not involve tax return preparation, the responsibility of the CPA is to advise the client of the existence of the error and to recommend that the error be discussed with the client's tax return preparer.

STATEMENT NO. 7 KNOWLEDGE OF ERROR: ADMINISTRATIVE PROCEEDINGS

INTRODUCTION

.01 This statement considers the responsibility of a CPA who becomes aware of an error in a return that is the subject of an administrative proceeding, such as an examination by the IRS or an appeals conference relating to a return or a claim for refund. As used herein, the term "error" includes any position, omission, or method of accounting, which, at the time the return is filed, fails to meet the standards set out in SRTP No. 1. The term "error" also includes a position taken on a prior year's return that no longer meets these standards due to legislation, judicial decisions, or administrative pronouncements having retroactive effect. However, an error does not include an item that has an insignificant effect on the client's tax liability.

.02 This statement applies whether or not the CPA prepared or signed the return that contains the error; it does not apply where a CPA has been engaged by legal counsel to provide assistance in a matter relating to the counsel's client.

STATEMENT

.03 When the CPA is representing a client in an administrative proceeding with respect to a return which contains an error of which the CPA is aware, the CPA should inform the client promptly upon becoming aware of the error. The CPA should recommend the measures to be taken. Such recommendation may be given orally. The CPA is neither obligated to inform the Internal Revenue Service nor may the CPA do so without the client's permission, except where required by law.

---

[2] The CPA should consider consulting his or her own legal counsel before deciding upon recommendations to the client and whether to continue a professional relationship with the client. The potential for violating AICPA Rule of Conduct 301 (relating to the CPA's confidential client relationship), the Internal Revenue Code and income tax regulations, or state laws on privileged communications and other considerations may create a conflict between the CPA's interests and those of the client.

.04 The CPA should request the client's agreement to disclose the error to the Internal Revenue Service. Lacking such agreement, the CPA should consider whether to withdraw from representing the client in the administrative proceeding and whether to continue a professional relationship with the client.

EXPLANATION

.05 When the CPA is engaged to represent the client before the Internal Revenue Service in an administrative proceeding with respect to a return containing an error of which the CPA is aware, the CPA should advise the client to disclose the error to the Internal Revenue Service. It is the client's responsibility to decide whether to disclose the error. In appropriate cases, particularly where it appears that the Internal Revenue Service might assert the charge of fraud or other criminal misconduct, the client should be advised to consult legal counsel before taking any action. If the client refuses to disclose or permit disclosure of an error, the CPA should consider whether to withdraw from representing the client in the administrative proceeding and whether to continue a professional relationship with the client.[3]

.06 Once disclosure is agreed upon, it should not be delayed to such a degree that the client or CPA might be considered to have failed to act in good faith or to have, in effect, provided misleading information. In any event, disclosure should be made before the conclusion of the administrative proceeding.

.07 Whether an error has an insignificant effect on the client's tax liability should be left to the judgment of the individual CPA based on all the facts and circumstances known to the CPA. In judging whether an erroneous method of accounting has more than an insignificant effect, the CPA should consider the method's cumulative effect and its effect on the return which is the subject of the administrative proceeding.

STATEMENT NO. 8
FORM AND CONTENT OF
ADVICE TO CLIENTS

INTRODUCTION

.01 This statement discusses certain aspects of providing tax advice to a client and considers the circumstances in which the CPA has a responsibility to communicate with the client when subsequent developments affect advice previously provided. The statement does not, however, cover the CPA's responsibili-

ties when it is expected that the advice rendered is likely to be relied upon by parties other than the CPA's client.[4]

STATEMENT

.02 In providing tax advice to a client, the CPA should use judgment to ensure that the advice given reflects professional competence and appropriately serves the client's needs. The CPA is not required to follow a standard format or guidelines in communicating written or oral advice to a client.

.03 In advising or consulting with a client on tax matters, the CPA should assume that the advice will affect the manner in which the matters or transactions considered ultimately will be reported on the client's tax returns. Thus, for all tax advice the CPA gives to a client, the CPA should follow the standards in SRTP No. 1 relating to tax return positions.

.04 The CPA may choose to communicate with a client when subsequent developments affect advice previously provided with respect to significant matters. However, the CPA cannot be expected to have assumed responsibility for initiating such communication except while assisting a client in implementing procedures or plans associated with the advice provided or when the CPA undertakes this obligation by specific agreement with the client.

EXPLANATION

.05 Tax advice is recognized as a valuable service provided by CPAs. The form of advice may be oral or written and the subject matter may range from routine to complex. Because the range of advice is so extensive and because advice should meet specific needs of a client, neither standard format nor guidelines for communicating advice to the client can be established to cover all situations.

.06 Although oral advice may serve a client's needs appropriately in routine matters or in well-defined areas, written communications are recommended in important, unusual, or complicated transactions. In the judgment of the CPA, oral advice may be followed by a written confirmation to the client.

.07 In deciding on the form of advice provided to a client, the CPA should exercise professional judgment and should consider such factors as the following:

a. The importance of the transaction and amounts involved

b. The specific or general nature of the client's inquiry

c. The time available for development and submission of the advice

d. The technical complications presented

---

[3] The CPA should consider consulting his or her own legal counsel before deciding upon recommendations to the client and whether to continue a professional relationship with the client. The potential of violating Rule of Conduct 301 (relating to the CPA's confidential client relationship), the Internal Revenue Code and income tax regulations, or state laws on privileged communications and other considerations may create a conflict between the CPA's interests and those of the client.

[4] The CPA's responsibilities when providing advice that will be relied upon by third parties will be addressed in a future statement.

e. The existence of authorities and precedents

f. The tax sophistication of the client and the client's staff

g. The need to seek legal advice

.08 The CPA may assist a client in implementing procedures or plans associated with the advice offered. During this active participation, the CPA continues to advise and should review and revise such advice as warranted by new developments and factors affecting the transaction.

.09 Sometimes the CPA is requested to provide tax advice but does not assist in implementing the plans adopted. While developments such as legislative or administrative changes or further judicial interpretations may affect the advice previously provided, the CPA cannot be expected to communicate later developments that affect such advice unless the CPA undertakes this obligation by specific agreement with the client. Thus, the communication of significant developments affecting previous advice should be considered an additional service rather than an implied obligation in the normal CPA-client relationship.

.10 The client should be informed that advice reflects professional judgment based on an existing situation and that subsequent developments could affect previous professional advice. CPAs should use precautionary language to the effect that their advice is based on facts as stated and authorities that are subject to change.

APPENDIX F

INDEX OF CODE SECTIONS

INDEX OF TREASURY REGULATIONS

INDEX OF GOVERNMENT PROMULGATIONS

INDEX OF COURT CASES

APPENDIX J

SUBJECT INDEX

1997
TAX RATE SCHEDULES

ESTATES AND TRUSTS

If Taxable Income Is:		The Tax Is:	
Over—	But Not Over—		Of the Amount Over—
$0	$1,650	15%	$0
1,650	3,900	$247.50 + 28%	1,650
3,900	5,950	877.50 + 31%	3,900
5,950	8,100	1,513.00 + 36%	5,950
8,100		2,287.00 + 39.6%	8,100

CORPORATIONS

If Taxable Income Is:		The Tax Is:	
Over—	But Not Over—		Of the Amount Over—
$ 0	$ 50,000	15%	$ 0
50,000	75,000	$ 7,500 + 25%	50,000
75,000	100,000	13,750 + 34%	75,000
100,000	335,000	22,250 + 39%	100,000
335,000	10,000,000	113,900 + 34%	335,000
10,000,000	15,000,000	3,400,000 + 35%	10,000,000
15,000,000	18,333,333	5,150,000 + 38%	15,000,000
18,333,333		6,416,667 + 35%	18,333,333

UNIFIED CREDIT AMOUNT FOR ESTATE AND GIFT TAX

Year of Gift/ Year of Death	Amount of Credit	Exemption Equivalent
January through June, 1977	$ 6,000	$ 30,000
July through December, 1977	30,000	120,666
1978	34,000	134,000
1979	38,000	147,333
1980	42,500	161,563
1981	47,000	175,625
1982	62,800	225,000
1983	79,300	275,000
1984	96,300	325,000
1985	121,800	400,000
1986	155,800	500,000
1987 and later years	192,800	600,000